NATIONAL TRAIL COMPANION

PUBLISHER:
TIM STILWELL

EDITOR:
MARTIN DOWLING

D0317276

STILWELL
Publishing

Distributed in Great Britain, Europe & the Commonwealth by Orca Book Services, Stanley House, 3 Fleets Lane, Poole, Dorset BH15 3AJ (Tel: 01202 665432) and available from all good bookshops. Distributed in North America by Seven Hills Book Distributors, 49 Central Ave, Cincinatti, OH 45202, USA (Tel: 513 381 3881).

ISBN 1-900861-25-9.

Published by Stilwell Publishing, ¡
59 Charlotte Road, Shoreditch, London, EC2A 3QW.
Tel: 020 7739 7179. Fax: 020 7739 7191. E-mail: info@stilwell.co.uk

© Stilwell Publishing Ltd, April 2001 (unless otherwise stated).
Mapping for walks in the Republic of Ireland based on Ordnance Survey Ireland by permission of the Government, permit no. 6822, © Government of Ireland. Mapping for the Ulster Way based on OSNI material with the permission of the Controller of HMSO, © Crown Copyright, permit no. 1263.

Publisher: Tim Stilwell
Editor: Martin Dowling
Design and Maps: Nigel Simpson

Printed in the Channel Islands by the Guernsey Press Company, Guernsey, Channel Islands.

Contents

Introduction

The story behind this book is simple. My wife and I set out to walk the North Downs Way over several weekends in the summer of 1991. Neither of us are born to camping, nor could we afford to stay in expensive hotels. We decided on B&Bs and found a problem straightaway. One could not find good value bed and breakfast accommodation along the route without going to a lot of trouble. Local libraries, directory enquiries, six different Tourist Information Centres and a large pile of brochures yielded nothing but a hotchpotch of B&B addresses, most of them miles out of our way. We abandoned the research and did the walk in one-day stretches, high-tailing it back to our London home each evening on the train.

The point is that we didn't really want to take the train back, especially when the time spent in waiting and travelling matched the time spent walking. A good weekend's walk would have been ideal, but we didn't know where to stay. The Law of Sod dictates that wherever you choose to finish your day's walk, there is either nothing in sight or a large country house hotel charging £100 for a one night stay. The train proved the logical option.

We did the South Downs Way like this, too, in 1992. In 1993 we set out to spend a week walking the first half of Offa's Dyke and realised that we were hooked. Once you have walked one trail, you tend to want to walk another one fairly soon. Is there a collective noun for these poor obsessives? Anyway, as most trails are not a short train journey from home, the accommodation problem now loomed much larger. We eventually found out about the Offa's Dyke Association's excellent accommodation pamphlet. Planning walks along other paths, I soon realised that a path has an accommodation list only if it has a strong Association behind it or proper commitment from a local County Council, and that even then, publishing standards vary. Many of you will know that when a path crosses a county boundary the standard and quality of signposting can change dramatically. This is true of all support services for a path and accommodation lists are no exception.

So we set out to create a directory that, for the price of the average compass, publishes accommodation details for all the National Trails in the order that they appear along the path. Why? Well, when I consider walking a long distance path, I wish to seize the moment, to book my room now. 'Next weekend, please', is the cry that goes up in this household. This book helps the armchair walker to achieve his or her desire in precisely that respect. No more accommodation research, no more long distance telephone calls to tourist information centres, no more sending off cheques for £1.85 for leaflets that arrive a week later. Moreover, the reader is now more at leisure to think of a path as a series of weekend walks rather than as a 10-day procession. Itineraries are easier to work out, any pressure to complete a walk inside an allotted time begins to fade and paths previously thought difficult become a distinct possibility.

One issue should be set straight before anything else. This book is not intended as a map guide. It is no substitute for one at all. Aurum Press, Constable, Cicerone and several small publishers have brought out guides dedicated to describing routes on foot (details of which can be found in the chapter introduction for each path). These guides provide invaluable information regarding mileage, history, sights and navigation; they also include maps of a scale most suited to a walker's needs. Nevertheless, such books should be used with proper maps such as the Ordnance Survey's Landranger or Pathfinder series - or the specialist path maps published by Footprint of Stirling. In general, a guidebook does not include accommodation details, because the edition is intended to last several years and such details will change radically over such a period. The National Trail Companion is intended to be used alongside the guides - hence the title.

All the National Trails as set out by the Countryside Commission and Scottish Heritage are represented in this book, plus some of the more famous long distance footpaths, many of which are up for recognition as National Trails. The information published in these pages has been collected over one year and provided by the owners themselves. The vast majority offer bed and breakfast at well under £25 per person per night, which we consider near the limit a walker would wish to pay. The pink highlight boxes are advertisements. Once again, we should make it clear that inclusion in these pages does not imply personal recommendation - we have not visited them all, merely written to them or phoned them. A simple glance over the salient details on any page, however, and the reader will be his or her own guide.

Owners were asked to provide their lowest rates per person per night for the year in question. The rates are thus forecasts and are in any case always subject to fluctuation in demand. Of course, some information may already be out of date. Grades may go up or down, or be removed altogether. British Telecom may alter exchange numbers. Proprietors may decide on a whim to move out of the business altogether. That is why the National Trail Companion has to be a yearbook; in general, though, the information published here will be accurate, pertinent and useful for many a year.

One of the most important considerations for any walker planning a night's rest at a hostel or B&B is 'how far off the path is it?' Our concern has been, of course, to research Youth Hostels and B&Bs that are at least close to a given path; the reader can gauge at a glance how far one village is from the path compared with another. At the beginning of each entry, the reader will also see a figure in brackets, showing how many miles the premises are from the path. Where it says 'On path', this means that the premises are either directly on the path or within 100 yards of it. Some also show a car sign, indicating a valuable service indeed. The owners will pick you up by car from the path and drop you off again in the morning. I should stress that this service is provided within reason - i.e., from the closest possible point with vehicle access. It is also subject to such mundane matters as afternoon shopping trips, school collections and even flat tyres, so please have some understanding for the owner's needs.

The accommodation lists are published in the order in which they appear along the path. We have numbered the locations to make cross-referencing easier. We have also included pubs and inns that serve food in the evenings. For many walkers, the promise of an evening meal will be of prime importance in deciding where to stay. The direction in which the locations are listed is determined by popular choice and not by personal preference. If you wish to walk Offa's Dyke from North to South or the Thames Path from Kemble to London, then you will simply have to flick backwards through the chapter's pages rather than forwards. As far as mapping is concerned, I have omitted giving Landranger map numbers, except in the introduction to each path. The Ordnance Survey's national grid references are more important; to this end we have indicated grid labels and lines at the edge of each map.

Throughout the book you will find boxes offering advice to walkers staying at B&Bs. Some of you may think these a waste of time. Their pompous tone made one reviewer feel tempted to tread mud into carpets at the first opportunity and to order impossible sandwiches at the very last minute. I apologise for this. In fact, these boxes are a publishing trick. They fill space and tidy the page up. But we really have heard horror stories about walkers from B&B owners, mainly concerning disregard for other people's property. Much of this is done through thoughtlessness and not by intent. If a few words can remind someone of his or her obligations, then these boxes, however self-important, will have done the trick.

Some readers will be disappointed - the path that they wished to walk is not included. I can offer some consolation here. We have the technology to provide accommodation lists immediately for most paths in the UK and probably in Ireland too (provided we have such accommodation in our databases) - even paths that walkers devise for themselves, long or short. The presentation may not be as professional and we would make a small charge, depending on the nature of the task. If anyone wishes to make use of this facility, please contact us at the address at the front of the book. Lastly, we still wish to improve the scope and coverage with each edition. If any readers have criticisms or wish to make suggestions regarding forthcoming editions, please write in to us - again, at the address published at the front of the book. Happy walking!

Tim Stilwell
Stoke Newington, April 2001.

Path Locations

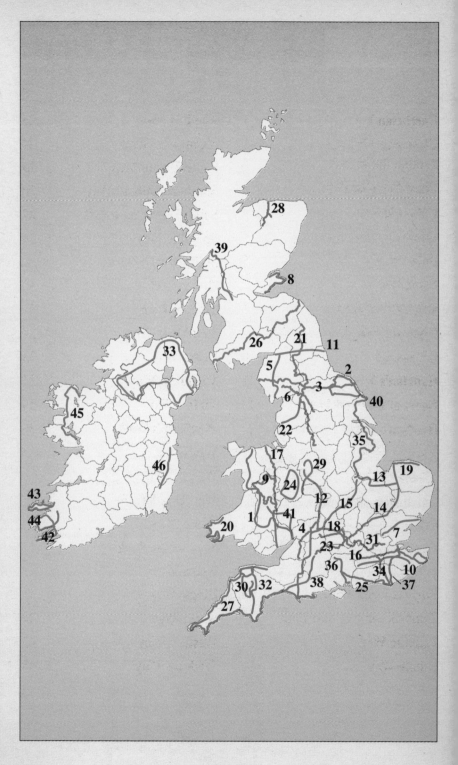

Cleveland Way & Tabular Hills Link

The **Cleveland Way** is a waymarked National Trail, consisting of 100 miles of heather moorland and coastal path, starting at the little Yorkshire market town of Helmsley, skirting the western and northern edges of the North York Moors National Park (where it coincides for a few miles with the **Coast to Coast Path**), before leaving to head south-east on a magnificent and famous stretch of North Sea coastline with superb, towering cliffs, passing Whitby, Scarborough and ending in Filey. There is also a link called the **Tabular Hills Link** which connects Scarborough with Helmsley, along the southern side of the National Park, turning a linear path into a 148-mile circular route. This one can be wet; you are well-advised therefore to dress accordingly.

Maps: 1:50000 Ordnance Survey Landranger Series: 93, 94, 99, 100 and 101.
The Cleveland Way (4-colour linear route map), ISBN 1 8711490 9 6, published by Footprint, Unit 87, Stirling Enterprise Park, Stirling, FK7 7RP, tel. 01786 479866, price £3.50 (+ 40p p&p)

Guides (all available from good map shops unless stated):

Cleveland Way by Ian Sampson (ISBN 1 85410 021 1), published by Aurum Press in association with the Countryside Commission and Ordnance Survey, price £10.99

Walking the Cleveland Way and the Missing Link by Malcolm Boyes (ISBN 1 8528401 4 5), published by Cicerone Press, 2 Police Square, Milnthorpe, Cumbria, LA7 7PY, (tel. 01539 562069), price £5.99 (+ 75p p&p)

Cleveland Way Companion by Paul Hannon (ISBN 1 8701411 7 2), published by Hillside Publications, 12 Broadlands, Keighley, W. Yorks, BD20 6HX, tel. 01535 681505, price £5.99 (+60p p&p)

The Link through the Tabular Hills Walk, (ISBN 0 907480 44 6), published by the North York Moors National Park Authority and available only by post: write to The Old Vicarage, Bondgate, Helmsley, York, YO6 5BP, (tel. 01439 770657), price £3.95 (+50p p&p)

Cleveland Way Plus the Tabular Hills Link by M Collins (ISBN 1 855681 13 7), published by Dalesman Pulishing Ltd, Clapham, Lancaster, LA2 8EB, (tel. 015242 51225), price £6.99 (+£1 p&p)

Comments on the path to: **Malcolm Hodgson**, Cleveland Way Project, North York Moors National Park, The Old Vicarage, Bondgate, Helmsley, N. Yorks, YO6 5BP (tel. 01439 770657).

Helmsley 1

National Grid Ref: SE6184

⋈ ⛺ White Rose, Feathers, Black Swan, Crown, Tudor Rose, Hawnby Hotel, Royal Oak, Hare

(▲ **On path**) **Helmsley Youth Hostel,** Carlton Lane, Helmsley, York, North Yorkshire, YO62 5HB.
Tel: **01439 770433**
Under 18: £6.50 **Adults:** £9.25
Self-catering facilities, Showers, Laundry facilities, Lounge, Dining room, Drying room, Cycle store, Evening meal at 7.00pm, No smoking, Kitchen facilities, Breakfast available, Credit cards accepted
The hostel is in the centre of the market town of Helmsley, a short distance from both the market square and the castle. It is a great base for walkers, starting the Cleveland Way.

(0.5m) *4 Ashdale Road, Helmsley, York, YO62 5DD.*
Quiet private house 5 minutes from Market Square and shops.
Tel: **01439 770375** Mrs Barton.
D: £15.00-£16.00 **S:** £16.00.
Open: All Year (not Xmas)
Beds: 1D 1T
Baths: 1 Sh
🅿 (2) ⌿ ☐ ⌁ ♨ Ⓥ ∮

(0.5m 🚌) *14 Elmslac Road, Helmsley, York, YO62 5AP.*
Actual grid ref: SE612841
Quiet house 4 mins' walk from market square. Pleasant situation.
Tel: **01439 770287**
Mrs Holding.
D: £13.50-£14.50 **S:** £14.00.
Open: All Year
Beds: 1D
Baths: 1 Pr
🛏 (12) ⌿

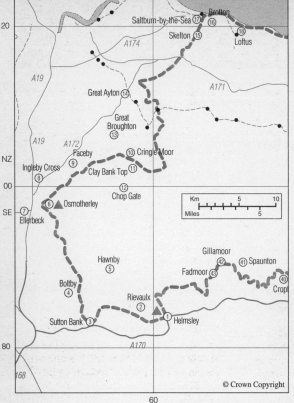

20

Saltburn-by-the-Sea ⑰ ⑯ Brotton

Skelton ⑮

Loftus ⑱

A174

A19

A171

Great Ayton ⑭

Great Broughton ⑬

A19 A172

NZ

Faceby ⑨ ⑩ Cringle Moor

Ingleby Cross ⑧

Clay Bank Top ⑪

00

⑫

Chop Gate

SE

Ellerbeck ⑦

⑥ Osmotherley

Km 5 10

Miles 5

Hawnby ⑤

Gillamoor

Fadmoor ㊸ ㊷ Spaunton ㊶

Boltby ④

Rievaulx ②

Crop ㊵

Sutton Bank ③

Helmsley ①

80

A170

168

60

© Crown Copyright

D = Price range per person sharing in a double room

(0.25m 🚌) *High House Farm,* Sutton Bank, Thirsk, N. Yorks, YO7 2HA.
Actual grid ref: SE523830
Family-run dairy farm set in open countryside in a tranquil part of W Yorks.
Tel: **01845 597557** Mrs Hope.
D: £20.00-£25.00 **S:** £22.00-£26.00.
Open: Easter to Nov
Beds: 1F 1D **Baths:** 1 Sh

Boltby 4

National Grid Ref: SE4986

Carpenters' Arms, Whitstoncliffe Hotel, Hambleton Inn

(1.5m 🚌) *Willow Tree Cottage,* Boltby, Thirsk, N. Yorkshire, YO7 2DY.
Actual grid ref: SE492865
Large luxurious room with kitchenette. Quiet hillside village, spectacular views.
Tel: **01845 537406** Townsend.
Fax no: 01845 537073
D: £22.00-£30.00 **S:** £30.00-£38.00.
Open: All Year (not Xmas)
Beds: 1F **Baths:** 1 En

(0.25m) *Low Paradise Farm,* Boltby, Thirsk, N. Yorks, YO7 2HS.
Actual grid ref: SE502882
Warm welcome. Hill walking, cycling and Herriot Museum nearby.
Tel: **01845 537253** Mrs Todd.
D: £17.00-£18.00 **S:** £20.00-£20.00.
Open: March to Nov
Beds: 1D 2T
Baths: 1 Sh

(1m 🚌) *Town Pasture Farm,* Boltby, Thirsk, N. Yorks, YO7 2DY.
Actual grid ref: SE494866
Comfortable farmhouse in beautiful village, central for Yorkshire Dales.
Grades: ETC 3 Diamond
Tel: **01845 537298** Mrs Fountain.
D: £17.50-£19.50 **S:** £18.50-£20.00.
Open: All Year (not Xmas)
Beds: 1F 1T **Baths:** 2 En

(On path) *Stilworth House,* 1 Church Street, Helmsley, York, YO62 5AD.
Elegant rooms, beautiful location overlooking castle, hearty breakfast, warm welcome.
Grades: ETC 4 Diamond
Tel: **01439 771072** Mrs Swift.
D: £17.50-£27.50 **S:** £30.00-£40.00.
Open: All Year (not Xmas)
Beds: 1F 2D 1T **Baths:** 3 Pr 1 Sh

(0.5m) *Buckingham House,* 33 Bridge St, Helmsley, York, YO62 5DX.
Actual grid ref: SE616836
Comfortable Georgian town house. Warm welcome and good food.
Tel: **01439 770613** Mrs Wood.
D: £18.00-£23.00 **S:** £18.00-£27.00.
Open: All Year (not Xmas)
Beds: 1D 1T 1S **Baths:** 1 En 1 Sh

Pay B&Bs by cash or cheque and be prepared to pay up front.

Rievaulx 2

National Grid Ref: SE5785

Hare, Swan

(On path) *Barn Close Farm,* Rievaulx, Helmsley, York, YO62 5LH.
Barn close. Hill farm in valley of Rievaulx. Recommended in Telegraph.
Tel: **01439 798321** Mrs Milburn.
D: £20.00-£25.00.
Open: All Year
Beds: 1F 1D **Baths:** 1 En 1 Pr

Sutton Bank 3

National Grid Ref: SE5182

Hambleton Inn, Hare Inn

(On path) *Cote Faw, Hambleton Cottages, Sutton Bank, Thirsk, N. Yorks, YO7 2EZ.*
Actual grid ref: SE522830
Comfortable cottage in National Park, central for visiting North Yorkshire.
Tel: **01845 597363** Mrs Jeffray.
D: £16.00-£17.00 **S:** £16.00-£17.00.
Open: All Year (not Xmas)
Beds: 1F 1D 1S **Baths:** 1 Sh

All paths are popular: you are well-advised to book ahead

Hawnby 5

National Grid Ref: SE5489

⏣ Hawnby Hotel, Hare Inn

**(3m 🚗) *Laskill Farm,* Hawnby,
Helmsley, York,** *YO62 5NB.*
Actual grid ref: SE564908
Laskill Farm is built on a medieval
site once belonging to Rievaulx
Abbey.
Grades: ETC 4 Diamond,
AA 4 Diamond
Tel: 01439 798268 Mrs Smith.
Fax no: 01439 798498
D: £27.50 **S:** £27.50.
Open: All Year
Beds: 3D 2T 1S
Baths: 5 En 1 Pr
🛏 🅿 (20) ⛾ 🍴 ✕ 👶 🎢 🔥 👩 Ⓥ 🎒 ⚡

Osmotherley 6

National Grid Ref: SE4597

**(▲ On path) *Osmotherley Youth
Hostel,* Cote Ghyll, Osmotherley,
Northallerton, North Yorkshire,**
DL6 3AH.
Actual grid ref: SE461981
Tel: 01609 883575
Under 18: £6.90 **Adults:** £10.00
Self-catering facilities, Television,
Showers, Laundry facilities, Wet
weather shelter, Lounge, Games
room, Drying room, Cycle store,
Parking, Evening meal at 7.00pm,
No smoking, WC, Kitchen
facilities, Breakfast available,
Credit cards accepted
*Surrounded by woodland, the youth
hostel is fully modernised with
excellent facilities, right on the
edge of the North York Moors
National Park.*

Ellerbeck 7

National Grid Ref: SE4397

⏣ Golden Lion, Kings Head

(1m 🚗) *Old Mill House,*
*Ellerbeck, Osmotherley,
Northallerton, N. Yorks,* *DL6 2RY.*
Delightful C17th mill set central
for walking touring North
Yorkshire.
Tel: 01609 883466 Mrs Shepherd.
D: £20.00-£25.00 **S:** £20.00-£25.00.
Open: Easter to November
Beds: 1T 2D
Baths: 1 En 1Shared
🅿 (4) ✓ ⛾ 🐾

**Taking your dog?
Book** *in advance*
**ONLY with owners
who accept dogs (🐾)**

**Please take muddy
boots off before
entering premises**

Ingleby Cross 8

National Grid Ref: NZ4500

⏣ Black Horse, Blue Bell

**(0.25m 🚗) *North York Moors
Adventure Ctr,* Park House,
Ingleby Cross, Northallerton,
N. Yorks,** *DL6 3PE.*
Actual grid ref: SE453995
Park House, traditional sandstone
farmhouse set in The National
Park.
Tel: 01609 882571 (also fax no)
Mr Bennett.
D: £15.00 **S:** £15.00.
Open: Easter to Oct
Beds: 3F 1D 3T **Baths:** 2 Sh
🛏 (1) 🅿 (20) ⛾ 🍴 ✕ 👶 🎢 Ⓥ 🎒 ⚡

**(1m 🚗) *Blue Bell Inn,* Ingleby
Cross, Northallerton, N. Yorks,**
DL6 3NF.
Family run, real ales, coal fire,
quiet annexed accommodation.
Tel: 01609 882272 Mrs Kinsella.
D: £20.00-£20.00 **S:** £20.00-£20.00.
Open: All Year
Beds: 4F 1D 4T
Baths: 5 En
🛏 🅿 (20) ⛾ ✕ 👶 🎢 Ⓥ 🎒 ⚡

Faceby 9

National Grid Ref: NZ4903

**(1.25m 🚗) *Four Wynds,* Whorl
Hill, Faceby, Middlesbrough,**
TS9 7BZ.
Actual grid ref: NZ487033
Small holding in beautiful
countryside. Located off A172
between Swainby/ Faceby.
Grades: ETC 3 Diamond
Tel: 01642 701315 Mr Barnfather.
D: £18.00-£20.00 **S:** £18.00-£20.00.
Open: All Year
Beds: 1F 1D 1T
Baths: 1 En 1 Sh
🛏 🅿 (8) ⛾ 🍴 ✕ 👶 🎢 Ⓥ 🎒 ⚡

Cringle Moor 10

National Grid Ref: NZ5503

⏣ Buck Inn

**(0.5m 🚗) *Beakhills Farm,* Cold
Moor, Cringle Moor, Chop Gate,
Stokesley, Middlesbrough,** *TS9 7JJ.*
Actual grid ref: NZ545024
Cosy farmhouse on working farm.
Tel: 01642 778371 Mrs Cook.
D: £16.00 **S:** £16.00.
Open: All Year
Beds: 1F 1T 1D
🛏 🅿 ⛾ 🐾 ✕ 🎒 ⚡

Clay Bank Top 11

National Grid Ref: NZ5701

**(1m 🚗) *Maltkiln House,* Clay Bank
Top, Bilsdale, Middlesbrough,**
TS9 7HZ.
Actual grid ref: NZ571017
Stone farmhouse in secluded
moorland location with
magnificent views. Licensed.
Tel: 01642 778216 (also fax no)
Mr & Mrs Broad.
D: £17.00-£18.50 **S:** £17.00-£18.50.
Open: All Year
Beds: 1D 2T
Baths: 1 En 1 Sh
🛏 (8) 🅿 (3) ✓ ⛾ ✕ 👶 🎢 Ⓥ 🎒 ⚡

Chop Gate 12

National Grid Ref: SE5599

⏣ Buck

**(1.75m 🚗) *Hill End Farm,* Chop
Gate, Bilsdale, Stokesley North
Yorkshire,** *TS9 7JR.*
Actual grid ref: NZ576978
Grades: ETC 3 Diamond
Tel: 01439 798278 Mrs Johnson.
D: £21.00-£21.00 **S:** £25.00-£25.00.
Open: Easter to Nov
Beds: 1F 1T
Baths: 2 Ensuite
🛏 (5) 🅿 (3) ✓ ⛾ 🐾 ✕ 👶 🎢 Ⓥ 🎒
Recommended by Which? Good
Bed and Breakfast Guide. Hill End
farm beautiful views down the
valley of Bilsdale which is midway
between the market towns of
Helmsley and Stokesley. Near to
Herriot, Heartbeat and Captain
Cook Country

**(2m 🚗) *Buck Inn Hotel,* Chop
Gate, Stokesley, Middlesbrough,**
TS9 7JL.
Actual grid ref: SE559994
Friendly inn with restaurant;
splendid views of Bilsdale Valley.
Tel: 01642 778334 Mrs Stewart.
D: £21.00-£24.00 **S:** £28.00-£32.00.
Open: All Year (not Xmas)
Beds: 1F 1D 4T
Baths: 6 Pr
🛏 🅿 ⛾ ✕ 👶 🎢 Ⓥ 🎒 ⚡

Great Broughton 13

National Grid Ref: NZ5406

⏣ Bay Horse, Black Horse, Jet Miners,
Wainstones Hotel

**(2m 🚗) *Ingle Hill,* Ingleby Road,
Great Broughton, North Yorks,** *TS9
7ER.*
Actual grid ref: NZ548063
Spectacular views North York
Moors, warm welcome, transport to
walks.
Tel: 01642 712449 Mrs Sutcliffe.
D: £17.50-£17.50 **S:** £18.50-£18.50.
Open: All Year (not Xmas)
Beds: 1F 1D 2T
Baths: 2 En 2 Sh
🛏 🅿 (4) ✓ ⛾ 🐾 👶 🎢 👩 Ⓥ 🎒 ⚡

Great Ayton 14

National Grid Ref: NZ5611

⊪ ⌸ Royal Oak, Buck Hotel

(1.5m 🚍) *The Wheelhouse,*
Langbaurgh Grange, Great Ayton,
Middlesbrough, Cleveland, TS9 6QQ.
Actual grid ref: NZ555116
Tel: **01642 724523**
D: £17.00-£17.00 **S:** £19.00-£19.00.
Open: All Year
Beds: 1F 1D
Baths: 2 Pr
🛏 🅿 (3) 🖵 🛏 🎍 🛒 ⅏ 🎥 🛢 ✦
Converted barn/mill in half acre
gardens with open views to
Cleveland Hills. Close to coast and
several historic sites. e.g. Mount
Grace Priory and Captain Cook
attractions. Coast to Coast,
Cleveland Way long distance
walks - 1 mile. Lifts available.

(1.5m 🚍) *The Granary,*
Langbaurgh Grange, Great Ayton,
Middlesbrough, TS9 6QQ.
Attractive converted barn near
Captain Cook village with beautiful
garden and lovely views.
Tel: **01642 723357** Ms Jones.
D: £17.00-£17.00 **S:** £17.00-£17.00.
Open: Mar to Dec
Beds: 1D 1T **Baths:** 1 Pr
🛏 (3) 🅿 (2) 🖵 🛒 ⅏ 🎥 ✦

(1.5m 🚍) *Eskdale Cottage,*
31 Newton Road, Great Ayton,
Middlesbrough, TS9 6DT.
Actual grid ref: NZ564115
Lovely Victorian cottage near
North Yorkshire Moors, all amen-
ities in bedrooms.
Tel: **01642 724306** Mrs Houghton.
D: £14.00-£19.00 **S:** £16.00-£20.00.
Open: All Year (not Xmas)
Beds: 2T
Baths: 1 Sh
🛏 (2) 🅿 (2) 🖵 🗙 🎍 🛒 ⅏ 🎥 🛢 ✦

Skelton (Saltburn) 15

National Grid Ref: NZ6518

⊪ ⌸ Holly Bush Blacksmiths Arms, Ship,
Lingdale Tavern

(On path 🚍) *Westerlands Guest*
House, 27 East Parade, Skelton,
Saltburn-by-the-Sea, N. Yorks,
TS12 2BJ.
Large modern detached house,
beautiful views sea-countryside,
alongside Cleveland Way long
distance path.
Tel: **01287 650690** Mr Bull.
D: £15.00-£15.00 **S:** £15.00-£15.00.
Open: Mar to Oct
Beds: 6F 3D 3S
Baths: 3 Pr
🛏 🅿 (5) 🖵 🛏 🗙 🎍 🛒 ⅏ 🎥 🛢 ✦

S = Price range for a single
person in a room

D = Price range per person
sharing in a double room

Brotton 16

National Grid Ref: NZ6820

(2m) *The Arches Hotel, Birkbeck*
Low Farm, Brotton, Saltburn-by-
the- Sea, TS12 2QX.
Tel: **01287 677512**
Fax no: 01287 677150
D: £20.00-£30.00 **S:** £30.00-£35.00.
Open: All Year
Beds: 11F 5T 6D
Baths: Pr
🅿 (20) 🖵 🛒 ⅏ 🎥 ✦
Beautiful coastal and golf course
views, with the warmest welcome
assured. Special terms for long
stays - log fires - visit Whitby.
Staithes, North York's steam rail-
way.

Saltburn-by-the-Sea 17

National Grid Ref: NZ6722

⊪ ⌸ Holly Bush, Blacksmiths Arms, Ship,
Lingdale

(0.5m 🚍) *Runswick Bay Hotel,*
Runswick Bay, Saltburn-by-the-Sea,
Cleveland, TS13 5HR.
In well-known village of Runswick
Bay and within North York Moors
National Park.
Tel: **01947 840997**
D: £22.50-£25.00 **S:** £25.00-£28.00.
Open: All Year (not Xmas/
New Year)
Beds: 1F 1T 4D
Baths: 6 En
🛏 🅿 🛒 🛏 🗙 🎍 🛒 ⅏ 🎥 🛢 ✦

(0.5m 🚍) *The Spa Hotel, Saltbank,*
Saltburn-by-the-Sea, Cleveland,
TS12 1HH.
Our reputation is built on tradition-
al quality accommodation and food.
Tel: **01287 622544** Mr Devnay.
Fax no: 01287 625870
D: £25.00-£25.00 **S:** £35.00-£35.00.
Open: All Year
Beds: 4F 20D 7T
Baths: 31 En
🛏 🅿 (40) 🖵 🛏 🗙 🎍 🛒 ⅏ 🛗 🎥 🛢 ✦

Loftus 18

National Grid Ref: NZ7118

(1m) *White Horse Inn, 73 High*
Street, Loftus, Saltburn-by- the- Sea,
TS13 4HG.
Friendly village pub near to
Yorkshire moors and seaside.
Tel: **01287 640758** Rowe.
D: £15.00-£18.00 **S:** £15.00-£18.00.
Open: All Year (not Xmas)
Beds: 2F 1T
Baths: 1 En 1 Sh
🛏 🅿 (5) 🖵 🛏 🗙 🎍 🛒 ⅏ 🎥 🛢 ✦

Staithes 19

National Grid Ref: NZ7718

⊪ ⌸ Fox & Hounds, Royal George

(0.25m) *Brooklyn, Brown's*
Terrace, Staithes, Saltburn-by-the-
Sea, TS13 5BG.
Actual grid ref: NZ782187
Sea-captain's house, central, but
quiet, in picturesque fishing village.
Tel: **01947 841396** Ms Heald.
D: £18.50-£18.50 **S:** £18.50-£18.50.
Open: All Year (not Xmas)
Beds: 1T 2D
Baths: 2 Sh
🛏 🖵 🛏 🎍 🛒 🎥

(0.5m) *Springfields, 42 Staithes*
Lane, Staithes, Saltburn-by-the-
Sea, N Yorks, TS13 5AD.
Actual grid ref: NZ779180
Victorian house with countryside
views. Lounge available. In
National Park.
Grades: ETC 3 Diamond
Tel: **01947 841011** Mrs Verrill.
D: £15.00-£15.00 **S:** £15.00-£15.00.
Open: All Year
Beds: 1D 1S
Baths: 1 En 1 Sh
🅿 (1) 🖵 🛒 ⅏ 🎥

(On path 🚍) *Black Lion Hotel,*
High Street, Staithes, Saltburn-by-
the-Sea, N Yorks, TS13 5BQ.
Georgian coaching inn. Short
breaks. Open fires. Picturesque
fishing village.
Tel: **01947 841132** Mr Stead.
D: £22.50-£25.00 **S:** £22.50-£30.00.
Open: All Year
Beds: 4F 4D 1S
Baths: 9 En
🛏 🅿 🖵 🛏 🗙 🎍 🎥 🛢 ✦

Runswick Bay 20

National Grid Ref: NZ8016

⊪ ⌸ Royal Hotel

(On path) *Cockpit House, The Old*
Village, Runswick Bay, Saltburn-
by-the-Sea, N Yorks, TS13 5HU.
Actual grid ref: NZ810161
Seafront position, near pub, beach,
cafe, all sea views.
Grades: ETC 2 Diamond
Tel: **01947 840504**
Mrs Smith.
D: £17.00 .
Open: All Year
Beds: 1D 2T
Baths: 1 Sh
🛏 (5) 🖵 🛏 🎍 🛒 ⅏ 🎥 ✦

Bringing children with
you? Always ask for
any special rates.

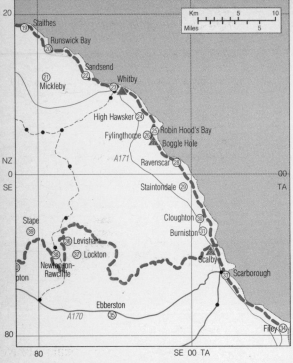

(▲ 0.5m) *Harbour Grange*
Bunkhouse, Spital Bridge, Whitby,
North Yorkshire, YO22 4EG.
Actual grid ref: NZ901104
Tel: 01947 600817
Adults: £7.00

(0.5m) *Kirklands Hotel, 17 Abbey*
Terrace, Whitby, North Yorkshire,
YO21 3HQ.
Tel: 01947 603868 (also fax no)
Mr Halton.
D: £24.00-£24.00
S: £35.00-£35.00.
Open: Feb to Nov
Beds: 6F 3D 2T 1S
Baths: 6 En 3 Pr 3 Sh
🛇 🏠 🛏 ✕ ⚓ 🖤 Ⓥ 🖃
The Kirklands is privately run,
close to all amenities, comfortable
rooms (en suite) some with private
bathrooms, TVs, coffee and tea
faculties, an excellent breakfast.
Pets and schools welcome, easy
access to the North York Moors
and villages and other major tourist
attractions.

(0.5m) *Arches Guest House,*
8 Havelock Place, Hudson Street,
Whitby, YO21 3ER.
Tel: 01947 601880 Mr Brew.
D: £20.00-£22.00 **S:** £25.00-£32.00.
Open: All Year
Beds: 3F 2T 6D
Baths: 8 En 1 Pr 2 Sh
🛇 ⚡✕🖵 🛏 ⚓ 🖤 ⚓ Ⓥ 🖃
Friendly, family run guesthouse,
where a warm welcome and a large
breakfast is always assured. The
ideal base for experiencing the old
world charms of this historic
seaside town, exploring the
beautiful North Yorkshire Moors or
walking the Cleveland Way.

(0.5m) *Rosslyn Guest House,*
11 Abbey Terrace, Whitby,
YO21 3HQ.
Quality accommodation at afford-
able prices, close to harbourside
and moorlands.
Tel: 01947 604086 (also fax no)
Briers.
D: £16.50-£18.50 **S:** £20.00-£20.00.
Open: All Year (not Xmas)
Beds: 2F 2D 1T 1S
Baths: 5 En 1 Pr
🛇 🏠 (2)🖵✕ 🖤 Ⓥ 🖃 ✍

(0.5m) *Seaview Guest House,*
5 East Crescent, Whitby, N Yorks,
YO21 3HD.
Grades: ETC 3 Diamond
Tel: 01947 604462 Boettger.
D: £19.00-£22.00 **S:** £19.00-£21.00.
Open: All Year (not Xmas/New
Year)
Beds: 1F 5D 2S
Baths: 6 En 1 Sh
🛇 🖵 🛏 ⚓ 🖤 Ⓥ
Family run guest house with high
standard of cleanliness. Close to
beach and town. Breakfast freshly
cooked form menu. Beautiful
views of sea and abbey.

Mickleby   21

National Grid Ref: NZ8012

🍴 🍺 Ellerby Hotel

(5m) *Northfield Farm, Mickleby,*
Saltburn-by-the-Sea, N Yorks,
TS13 5NE.
Actual grid ref: NZ808142
Quiet, friendly, comfortable farm-
house. Open views, ideal situation
for walking.
Tel: 01947 840343 Mrs Prudom.
D: £15.00-£20.00 **S:** £18.00-£18.00.
Open: Easter to Oct
Beds: 1F 1D 1T
Baths: 1 En 1 Sh
🛇 🖵 ✕🖵 🛏 ⚓ 🖤 Ⓥ ✍

Sandsend   22

National Grid Ref: NZ8612

🍴 🍺 Hart Inn, White Horse, Griffin

(On path) *Estbek House,*
Sandsend, Whitby, N. Yorks,
YO21 3SU.
Fully equipped designer bedrooms.
Fresh food, licensed restaurant.
Grades: ETC 3 Diamond
Tel: 01947 893424 (also fax no)
Mr Cooper.
D: £29.50-£29.50 **S:** £27.50-£39.50.
Open: All Year
Beds: 1F 2D 2T **Baths:** 4 En 1 Pr
🛇 🖵 ✕🖵 ✕ ⚓ 🖤 Ⓥ 🖃 ✍

Whitby   23

National Grid Ref: NZ8910

🍴 🍺 Plough, Granby, Shepherd's Purse, White
House, Dolphin

(▲ On path) *Whitby Youth Hostel,*
East Cliff, Whitby, North
Yorkshire, YO22 4JT.
Actual grid ref: NZ902111
Tel: 01947 602878
Under 18: £6.90 **Adults:** £10.00
Self-catering facilities, Showers,
Lounge, Dining room, Drying
room, Security lockers, Cycle
store, Evening meal at 7.00pm, No
smoking, Kitchen facilities,
Breakfast available, Credit cards
accepted
Converted stable range near
abbey, at top of 199 steps above the
harbour of this ancient fishing
town.

All paths are
popular: you are
well-advised to
book ahead

(0.5m) *Falcon Guest House,*
29 Falcon Terrace, Whitby, N.
Yorks, YO21 1EH.
Quiet private house near centre.
Sunny breakfast room, organic
produce.
Tel: **01947 603507** Mr Lyth.
D: £18.00-£18.00 **S:** £20.00-£20.00.
Open: All Year
Beds: 2F **Baths:** 1 Sh
ॐ ⅍ ⬜ ⬛ ⚙ ∅

(0.5m) *Havelock Guest House,*
30 Hudson Street, Whitby, YO21 3ED.
Conveniently situated for the spa,
beach, harbour and shops. Sauna
available.
Tel: **01947 602295** (also fax no)
Ryder.
D: £17.00-£19.50 **S:** £17.00-£17.00.
Open: All Year (not Xmas)
Beds: 2F 5D 1T 5S
Baths: 7 En 0 Pr 2 Sh
ॐ ⬜ ⊁ ⬛ ⚙ ∅

(0.5m) *Haven Guest House,*
4 East Crescent, Whitby, N. Yorks,
YO21 3HD.
Comfortable friendly guest house
with sea views. Comprehensive
breakfast menu.
Tel: **01947 603842** Mrs Smith.
D: £18.00-£24.00 **S:** £21.00-£23.00.
Open: Easter to Oct
Beds: 1F 5D 2S **Baths:** 5 En 1 Sh
ॐ (5) ⬜ ⬛ ⚙ ∅

(0.5m 🚲) *Arundel House Hotel,*
Bagdale, Whitby, North Yorkshire,
YO21 1QJ.
Manor house near town centre, pri-
vate parking, restaurant & bar.
Tel: **01947 603645** (also fax no)
D: £20.00-£25.00 **S:** £25.00-£35.00.
Open: All Year
Beds: 3F 5D 2T 1S
Baths: 11 En
ॐ ℗ (7) ⬜ ⊁ ✕ ⬛ ⚙ ∅

High Hawsker 24

National Grid Ref: NZ9207

🍴 🍺 Hare & Hounds

(0.5m) *Old Blacksmiths Arms,*
High Hawsker, Whitby, N. Yorks,
YO21 4LH.
Actual grid ref: NZ927075
Originally first pub in village.
Large garden with pond.
Tel: **01947 880800** Mrs Stubbs.
D: £18.00-£19.00 **S:** £21.00-£24.00.
Open: Easter to Oct
Beds: 1T 2D
Baths: 2 Sh
ॐ (12) ℗ (3) ⬜ ⊁ ⬛ ⚙ ∅

Planning a longer
stay? Always ask for
any special rates.

Please take muddy
boots off before
entering premises

Robin Hood's Bay 25

National Grid Ref: NZ9504

🍴 🍺 Bay Hotel, Dolphin, Flyingdale Inn,
Grosvenor, Victoria

(0.25m) *Glen-lyn, Station Road,*
Robin Hood's Bay, Whitby,
N Yorks, YO22 4RA.
Tel: **01947 880391** Mrs Price.
D: £20.00-£20.00 .
Open: All Year
Beds: 1T 1D
Baths: 2 En
℗ ⊁ ⬜ ⬛ ⚙ ∅
Come and sample the delights of
Robin Hoods Bay and stay in a
tastefully decorated, well appointed
detached bungalow. You can relax
in the large, well maintained,
mature gardens with seating area
around a pond with water feature.

(0.25m) *Clarence Dene, Station*
Road, Robin Hood's Bay, Whitby,
North Yorks, YO22 4RH.
Tel: **01947 880272** Mrs Howard.
D: £20.00-£20.00 .
Open: All Year
Beds: 1F 1T 3D **Baths:** 5 En
ॐ ℗ ⊁ ⬜ ⬛ ⚙ ∅
Situated above this historic village.
Clarence Dene retains many
original Art Nouveau features. the
spacious bedrooms have been
sympathetically decorated and
furnished, all are clean. comfortable
and well appointed with ensuite
facilities.

(On path) *The White Owl, Station*
Road, Robin Hood's Bay, Whitby,
N. Yorks, YO22 4RL.
Interesting house and garden.
Centre of village near cliff edge.
Tel: **01947 880879**
Mr & Mrs Higgins.
D: £20.00-£20.00 **S:** £20.00-£20.00.
Open: All Year
Beds: 1F 1D 1T 1S
Baths: 4 En
ॐ ℗ (3) ⬜ ⬛ ⚙ ∅

(On path) *Meadowfield, Mount*
Pleasant North, Robin Hood's Bay,
Whitby, N. Yorks, YO22 4RE.
Refurbished Victorian house.
Friendly, comfortable, plenty of
food. Non-smoking.
Tel: **01947 880564**
Mrs Luker.
D: £17.00-£19.50 **S:** £20.00-£24.00.
Open: All Year (not Xmas)
Beds: 2D 1T 2S
Baths: 1 En 1 Sh
⊁ ⬜ ⬛ ⚙ ∅

(On path) *Rosegarth, Thorpe Lane,*
Robin Hood's Bay, Whitby,
N. Yorks, YO22 4RN.
Friendly comfortable
accommodation. Ideal centre
touring and walking.
Tel: **01947 880578** Mrs Stubbs.
D: £16.50-£17.00 **S:** £17.00.
Open: Easter to Nov
Beds: 1D 1T 1S
Baths: 1 Sh
ॐ (9) ℗ (4) ⬜ ⬛ ⚙ ∅

(0.25m) *Flask Inn, Robin Hood's*
Bay, Fylingdales, Whitby, YO22 4QH.
Friendly family-run coaching inn.
Excellent food served lunchtimes
and evenings.
Tel: **01947 880305** Allison.
Fax no: 01947 880592
D: £22.00-£22.00 **S:** £28.00.
Open: All year
Beds: 3F 4D 4T 1S
Baths: 12 En
ॐ ℗ ⬜ ✕ ⬛ ⚙ ∅

Fylingthorpe 26

National Grid Ref: NZ9404

🍴 🍺 Fylingdales, Victoria

(1m) *Red House, Thorpe Lane,*
Fylingthorpe, Whitby, North
Yorkshire, YO22 4TH.
Large Victorian house and garden.
Panelled staircase and gallery.
Beautiful views.
Tel: **01947 880079** Mrs Collinson.
D: £18.00-£22.50 **S:** £20.00-£25.00.
Open: Easter to Oct
Beds: 1T 2D
Baths: 1 En 1 Sh
℗ (3) ⬜ ⊁ ⬛ ⚙ ∅

(1m) *South View, Sledgates,*
Fylingthorpe, Robin Hood's Bay,
Whitby, N. Yorks, YO22 4TZ.
Comfortable detached house. Sea
& country views. Touring area.
Bed time drink.
Tel: **01947 880025**
Mrs Reynolds.
D: £16.00-£18.00 .
Open: Easter to Oct
Beds: 2D
Baths: 1 Sh
ॐ (5) ℗ (2) ⬜ ⊁

(1m 🚲) *Low Farm, Fylingthorpe,*
Whitby, N Yorks, YO22 4QF.
Actual grid ref: NZ941040
Tel: **01947 880366** (also fax no)
Mrs Hodgson.
D: £18.00-£21.00 .
Open: May to Nov
Beds: 1F
Baths: 1 En
℗ (1) ⊁ ⬜ ⬛ ⚙ ∅
Imposing Georgian farmhouse built
from local stone, set in beautiful
countryside on our working farm,
1.5 miles from the picturesque
village of Robin Hood's Bay. Safe
off road parking. Superb views over
garden and beyond. Large
breakfasts. Genuine Yorkshire
welcome.

(1m) *Croft Farm, Fylingthorpe, Whitby, N. Yorks, YO22 4PW.*
All rooms have extensive views over the sea, moors and country-side.
Grades: ETC 4 Diamond
Tel: 01947 880231 (also fax no)
Mrs Featherstone.
D: £22.00-£24.00 **S:** £22.00-£27.00.
Open: Easter to Oct
Beds: 2D 1S **Baths:** 2 En 1 Pr
ॐ (5) ☐ (4) ⊬☐ ♨ ▥ Ⅵ ⓐ ✦

Boggle Hole   27

National Grid Ref: NZ9504

(▲ On path) *Boggle Hole Youth Hostel, Mill Beck, Boggle Hole, Robin Hood's Bay, Whitby, North Yorkshire, YO22 4UQ.*
Actual grid ref: NZ954040
Tel: 01947 880352
Under 18: £6.75 **Adults:** £10.00
Self-catering facilities, Television, Showers, Licensed bar, Lounge, Dining room, Cycle store, Parking, Evening meal at 6.00 to 7.00pm, WC, Drying facilities, Kitchen facilities, Breakfast available, Credit cards accepted
A former mill in a wooded ravine, Boggle Hole has the North Sea tide coming up to the doorstep and the North York Moors behind.

Ravenscar   28

National Grid Ref: NZ9801

⊯ ⌕ Bryherstones Inn, Falcon

(On path 🚌) *Bide A While Guest House, 3 Loring Road, Ravenscar, Scarborough, N. Yorks, YO13 0LY.*
Grades: ETC 3 Diamond
Tel: 01723 870643
Mr & Mrs Leach.
Fax no: 01723 871577
D: £16.50-£21.50 **S:** £20.00-£20.00.
Open: All Year
Beds: 1F 2D 1T
Baths: 3 En 1Private
ॐ ☐ ☐ ✕ ♨ ▥ Ⅵ ⓐ ✦
Small family guest house offering home comforts, home cooking a speciality. Situated on the edge of North York Moors, ideal for touring or walking the Yorkshire Dales. 1 hours scenic drive to York 11 miles from Scarborough and Whitby 500 metres from the sea.

(1m) *Smugglers Rock Country Guest House, Ravenscar, Scarborough, N. Yorks, YO13 0ER.*
Former smuggling inn twixt Whitby and Scarborough, refurbished and restored.
Grades: ETC 3 Diamond, AA 3 Diamond
Tel: 01723 870044
Mr & Mrs Gregson.
D: £23.00-£25.00 **S:** £26.00-£28.00.
Open: All Year (not Xmas)
Beds: 1F 4D 2T 1S
Baths: 8 En
ॐ ☐ (12) ⊬☐ ♨ ✕ ♨ ▥ Ⅵ ⓐ ✦

(On path 🚌) *Dunelm, Raven Hall Road, Ravenscar, Scarborough, N. Yorks, YO13 0NA.*
Actual grid ref: NZ980014
Friendly, flexible B&B. Splendid view. Walkers especially welcome!
Tel: 01723 870430 Jenny Bartlet.
D: £16.00-£18.00 **S:** £16.00-£18.00.
Open: All Year (not Xmas)
Beds: 1D 1T 1S
Baths: 2 Sh
ॐ ☐ ☐ ⊬☐ ♨ ✕ ♨ ▥ Ⅵ ⓐ ✦

Staintondale   29

National Grid Ref: SE9998

⊯ ⌕ Falcon

(1m 🚌) *Island House, Island Farm, Staintondale, Scarborough, N Yorks, YO13 0EB.*
Space, tranquillity, relaxation, tennis, snooker, on organic farm. Beautiful countryside.
Grades: ETC 4 Diamond
Tel: 01723 870249 Clarke.
D: £20.00-£25.00 **S:** £25.00-£27.00.
Open: Easter to Nov
Beds: 1T 2D
Baths: 3 En
ॐ ☐ (6) ⊬☐ ♨ ▥ Ⅵ ✦

(1m) *Tofta Farm, Staintondale, Scarborough, N. Yorks, YO13 0EB.*
Actual grid ref: SE982985
Beautiful modernised farmhouse in 1.5 acres landscaped gardens.
Tel: 01723 870298 Mrs Dobson.
D: £16.00-£22.00 **S:** £20.00-£20.00.
Open: All Year (not Xmas/New Year)
Beds: 1F 3D
Baths: 1 En 1 Sh
ॐ ☐ ☐ ✕ ♨ ▥ Ⅵ

Cloughton   30

National Grid Ref: TA0094

(1.5m 🚌) *Gowland Farm, Gowland Lane, Cloughton, Scarborough, N. Yorks, YO13 0DU.*
Actual grid ref: SE991960
Warm, friendly, peaceful, beautiful views, quiet, convenient Whitby/Scarborough/coast.
Tel: 01723 870924 Mr Martin.
D: £16.50-£18.00 **S:** £16.50-£18.00.
Open: Easter to Sep
Beds: 1D 1T 1S **Baths:** 1 Sh
ॐ (3) ☐ (6) ☐ ✕ ▥ ✦

🚌 **sign means that,** *given due notice,* **owners will pick you up from the path and drop you off** *within reason.*

Burniston   31

National Grid Ref: TA0192

⊯ ⌕ Three Jolly Sailors, Oakwheel

(1m 🚌) *Harmony Country Lodge, Limestone Road, Burniston, Scarborough, N Yorks, YO13 0DG.*
Octagonal peaceful retreat with superb sea views and 360° panorama.
Grades: ETC 4 Diamond
Tel: 0800 2985840
Mr & Mrs Hewitt.
D: £22.50-£25.50 **S:** £20.50-£30.00.
Open: All Year
Beds: 5D 1T 1S **Baths:** 4 En 3 Sh
ॐ (7) ☐ (10) ⊬☐ ♨ ✕ ♨ ▥ Ⅵ ⓐ ✦

Scalby   32

National Grid Ref: TA0190

(▲ 0.5m) *Scarborough Youth Hostel, The White House, Burniston Road, Scalby, Scarborough, North Yorkshire, YO13 0DA.*
Actual grid ref: TA026907
Tel: 01723 361176
Under 18: £6.90 **Adults:** £10.00
Self-catering facilities, Showers, Laundry facilities, Lounge, Drying room, Cycle store, Parking, Evening meal at 7.00pm, No smoking, WC, Kitchen facilities, Breakfast available, Credit cards accepted
A converted water mill by a bridge on the Sea Cut, just outside Scarborough, 10 minutes' walk from the Cleveland Way.

Scarborough   33

National Grid Ref: TA0388

⊯ ⌕ Cask, Copper Horse, Crescent, Highlander, Ivanhoe, Little Jack's Bar, Newlands Park, Oakwheel, Poacher's Pocket, Rosette Inn, Scalby Manor, Scarborough Arms, Three Jolly Sailors

(0.5m) *Howdale Hotel, 121 Queens Parade, Scarborough, N. Yorks, YO12 7HU.*
Comfortable hotel, panoramic sea views, memorable breakfasts, ten minutes town.
Tel: 01723 372696 (also fax no)
Mr & Mrs Abbott.
D: £17.00-£22.00 **S:** £25.00-£26.50.
Open: Easter to Oct
Beds: 1F 11D 2T 1S
Baths: 13 En 2 Sh
ॐ (9) ☐ ♨ ♨ ▥ Ⅵ ⓐ ✦

(0.5m) *Ryndle Court Hotel, 47 Northstead Manor Drive, Scarborough, N. Yorks, YO12 6AF.*
Actual grid ref: TA033893
Looking for high standards at reasonable rates? Call us now!
Grades: ETC 2 Star, RAC 2 Star
Tel: 01723 375188 (also fax no)
Mr & Mrs Davies.
D: £28.00-£30.00 **S:** £28.00-£38.00.
Open: Feb to Nov
Beds: 1F 6D 5T 2S **Baths:** 14 En
ॐ ☐ (10) ☐ ✕ ♨ ▥ Ⅵ ⓐ ✦

All rates are subject to alteration at the owners' discretion.

(0.25m) *Richmond Private Hotel,* 135 Columbus Ravine, Scarborough, N. Yorks, YO12 7QZ. Small, comfortable, family-run hotel. Friendly atmosphere, good home cooking.
Tel: **01723 362934**
Mr & Mrs Shaw.
D: £15.00-£18.00 **S:** £15.00-£18.00.
Open: All Year
Beds: 2F 4D 1T 1S
Baths: 3 En 1 Sh
⌂🏠🛇🐾✕🏧🏛️Ⅴ🅿

(0.5m) *Wheatcroft Lodge,* 156 Filey Road, Scarborough, N. Yorks, YO11 3AA. High standards at reasonable rates. R.A.C. Sparkling Diamond Award.
Grades: RAC 3 Diamond
Tel: **01723 374613** Mrs Batty.
D: £21.50-£21.50 **S:** £21.50-£21.50.
Open: All Year (not Xmas)
Beds: 4D 2T 1S **Baths:** 7 En
🅿 (10)🛇⌂🏛️Ⅴ

(0.5m) *Red Lea Hotel,* Prince Of Wales Terrace, Scarborough, N. Yorks, YO11 2AJ. Traditional hotel with good facilities and expansive sea views.
Grades: ETC 2 Star Hotel, RAC 2 Star
Tel: **01723 362431** Mr & Mrs Lee.
Fax no: 01723 371230
D: £27.00-£36.00 **S:** £27.00-£36.00.
Open: All Year
Beds: 7F 16D 23T 22S
Baths: 68 En
⌂⌂✕🏛️Ⅴ🅿

(0.5m) *Russell Hotel,* 22 Ryndleside, Scarborough, N Yorks, YO12 6AD.
Tel: **01723 365453**
Stanley & Glen Martin.
D: £17.00-£20.00 **S:** £18.00-£21.00.
Open: All Year
Beds: 4F 2D 2T 2S **Baths:** 7 En
⌂🅿(10)⌂🏠🐾✕🏧🏛️&Ⅴ🅿⚡
Detached 10 bedroom hotel, licensed, overlooking Peasholm Glen. Convenient for all North Bay attractions, all bedrooms on 2 floors, 7 ensuite large bedrooms with TV and tea/coffee making facilities, private car parking.

Taking your dog? Book *in advance* ONLY with owners who accept dogs (🐾)

(0.5m) *Leeway Hotel,* 71 Queens Parade, Scarborough, YO12 7HT. A family run licensed hotel overlooking The North Bay and Castle.
Tel: **01723 374371** Mr Saville.
D: £17.00-£20.00 **S:** £17.00-£18.00.
Open: Easter to Nov
Beds: 2F 5D 2S
Baths: 6 En
⌂🅿(6)🛇⌂✕🏧🏛️Ⅴ

(0.5m) *Fixton,* Scarborough, N Yorks, YO11 3UD. Rural location near coast, Moors, Wolds, warm welcome, secure parking.
Tel: **01723 890272** (also fax no) Mrs Wheater.
D: £18.00-£20.00 **S:** £18.00-£18.00.
Open: All Year (not Xmas)
Beds: 2F 2D 1S
Baths: 2 En 1 Sh

(0.5m) *Casablanca Hotel,* 20 Ryndleside, Scarborough, N. Yorks, YO12 6AD. Overlooking Peasholm Park. Comfortable accommodation.
Tel: **01723 362288** (also fax no) Mrs Akel.
D: £21.00-£23.00 **S:** £23.00-£25.00.
Open: All Year
Beds: 5F 6D 1T 1S
Baths: 13 En
⌂🅿(12)⌂🏠🐾✕🏧🏛️Ⅴ

(0.5m) *Wharncliffe Hotel,* 26 Blenheim Terrace, Scarborough, N Yorks, YO12 7HD. Overlooking beautiful North Bay. Central, licensed bar. Clean and comfortable.
Grades: ETC 4 Diamond
Tel: **01723 374635**
Mr & Mrs Clarke-Irons.
D: £22.00-£24.00 **S:** £26.00-£28.00.
Open: Easter to Oct
Beds: 2F 7D 3T
Baths: 12 En
⌂(2)🅿(1)⌂✕🏧🏛️Ⅴ

(0.5m) *Interludes,* 32 Princess Street, Scarborough, N. Yorks, YO11 1QR. Warm friendly hotel. Close to all Scarborough attractions. No children.
Grades: AA 4 Diamond
Tel: **01723 360513** Mr Grundy.
Fax no: 01723 368597
D: £21.00-£28.00 **S:** £23.00-£33.00.
Open: All Year (not Xmas/New Year)
Beds: 3D 2T **Baths:** 4 En 1 Sh
🛇⌂✕🏧🏛️Ⅴ

(0.5m) *Northcote Quality Serviced Holiday Suites,* 114 Columbus Ravine, Scarborough, N. Yorks, YO12 7QZ. Well established modern semi-detached hotel.
Tel: **01723 367758** Thompson.
D: £7.50-£25.00 .
Open: March to Nov
Beds: 4F/D **Baths:** 9 Pr
⌂🅿(5)🛇🏠🐾✕🏧🏛️Ⅴ

Pay B&Bs by cash or cheque and be prepared to pay up front.

(0.5m) *The Terrace Hotel,* 69 Westborough, Scarborough, N. Yorks, YO11 1TS. Close Railway station, town centre and all Scarborough's many attractions.
Tel: **01723 374937** Mr & Mrs Kirk.
D: £16.00-£21.00 **S:** £16.00-£21.00.
Open: All Year (not Xmas/New Year)
Beds: 3F 3D 1S
Baths: 2 En 2Shared
⌂🅿(4)⌂✕🏛️Ⅴ

(0.5m) *Derwent House Hotel,* 6 Rutland Terrace, Queens Parade, Scarborough, N. Yorks, YO12 7JB. Located near Castle, town, theatres and all major attractions.
Tel: **01723 373880**
Mr & Mrs Greenhough.
D: £17.00-£24.00 **S:** £20.00-£30.00.
Open: All Year
Beds: 4F 12D 4T 2S
Baths: 6 En 3 Sh
⌂(5)🅿⌂✕🏧🏛️Ⅴ🅿

(0.5m) *Villa Marina Hotel,* 59 Northstead Manor Drive, Scarborough, N. Yorks, YO12 6AF. Detached, quiet location overlooking Peasholm Park, close to north side attractions.
Grades: ETC 4 Diamond
Tel: **01723 361088**
Mr & Mrs Pearson.
D: £22.00-£28.00 .
Open: Easter to Oct
Beds: 2F 6D 2T
Baths: 10 En
⌂(5)🅿(9)🛇⌂✕🏧🏛️Ⅴ

(0.25m 🐾) *The Girvan Hotel,* 61 Northstead Manor Drive, Scarborough, N. Yorks, YO12 6AF. Modern detached hotel close to Peasholm Park and North Bay.
Tel: **01723 364518** (also fax no) Mrs Hurrell.
D: £15.00-£24.00
S: £20.00-£29.00.
Open: All Year
Beds: 4F 2D 4T 2S
Baths: 12 En
⌂🅿(10)⌂🏠🐾✕🏧🏛️&Ⅴ🅿⚡

(0.5m 🐾) *Hotel Fantasia,* 157 North Marine Road, Scarborough, N Yorks, YO12 7HU. Family-run friendly hotel, licensed bar, close to sea front.
Tel: **01723 368357**
Mr & Mrs Torr.
D: £15.00-£17.00 .
Open: All Year
Beds: 1F
Baths: 3 En 1 Sh
⌂(0)🛇⌂🏧🏛️Ⅴ🅿

(0.5m) *The Duke Of York Guest House,* 1-2 Merchants Row, Eastborough, Scarborough, N. Yorks, YO11 1NQ.
Georgian guesthouse overlooking Scarborough's seafront. Home cooking. Warm welcome.
Tel: **01723 373875** Mr Addis.
D: £15.00-£17.50 **S:** £15.00-£17.50.
Open: All Year
Beds: 2F 6D 2T 2S **Baths:** 12 En
🛏 🅿 (7) ✔ 🛏 ✕ 🛎 📖 ♥

(0.5m) *Anatolia Hotel,* 21 West Street, Scarborough, N Yorks, YO11 2QR.
Select Victorian house of charm and character, good home cooking.
Grades: ETC 3 Diamond
Tel: **01723 360864**
Mr & Mrs Simpson.
D: £18.00-£20.00 **S:** £18.00-£20.00.
Open: May to Oct
Beds: 2F 3D 2T 2S
Baths: 9 En 1 Pr
🛏 (5) 🅿 ✔ 🛏 ✕ 🛎 📖 ♥

(0.25m) *Glenderry Non-Smoking Guest House,* 26 The Dene, Scarborough, N. Yorks, YO12 7NJ.
Actual grid ref: TA035891
Small, select, family-run guest house, quiet residential area, ideally situated for Peasholm Park.
Tel: **01723 362546** Mrs Dugdale.
D: £15.00-£18.50 **S:** £15.00-£22.00.
Open: All Year (not Xmas)
Beds: 3F 1D 1S
Baths: 2 En 1 Sh
🛏 (4) ✔ 🛏 ✕ 🛎 📖 ♥ 🅿 ♿

(0.25m) *Meadow Court Hotel,* Queens Terrace, Scarborough, N. Yorks, YO12 7HJ.
Family-run licensed hotel.
Tel: **01723 360839** Mr Buckle.
D: £13.00-£14.00 **S:** £13.00-£14.00.
Open: All Year
Beds: 2F 4D 2T 2S
Baths: 2 Sh
🛏 🐾 ✕ 🛎 📖 ♥ 🅿

(On path) *Brincliffe Edge Hotel,* 105 Queens Parade, Scarborough, N. Yorks, YO12 7HY.
Comfortable family-run hotel overlooking North Bay.
Tel: **01723 364834**
Mr & Mrs Sutcliffe.
D: £18.25-£22.00 **S:** £18.25-£22.00.
Open: Easter to Oct
Beds: 1F 8D 1T 1S
Baths: 9 En 2 Sh
🛏 (2) 🅿 (7) 🛏 ✕ 🛎 📖 ♥ 🅿

(1m) *Stewart Hotel,* St Nicholas Cliff, Scarborough, N. Yorks, YO11 2ES.
Overlooking the south bay, Georgian Grade II Listed hotel; good breakfast.
Tel: **01723 361095** Mr Pummell.
D: £20.00-£25.00 **S:** £20.00-£25.00.
Open: All Year
Beds: 3F 9D 2T
Baths: 14 En
🛏 🛏 🛎 📖 ♥ 🅿

(0.5m 🐾) *Roslen Guest House,* 110 North Marine Road, Scarborough, N. Yorks, YO12 7JA.
Licensed Victorian-style guest house close North Bay amenities and walking distance town centre.
Tel: **01723 363492**
Mr & Mrs Walker.
Fax no: 01723 507318
D: £13.00-£15.00 **S:** £13.00-£15.00.
Open: All Year (not Xmas)
Beds: 5F 3S **Baths:** 2 Sh
🛏 (3) 🛏 ✕ 🛎 📖 ♥ 🅿

(0.5m) *Gordon Hotel,* 24 Ryndleside, Scarborough, N. Yorks, YO12 6AD.
North Bay overlooking Peasholm Park. Comfortable licensed family-run hotel.
Tel: **01723 362177** Mr Strickland.
D: £17.00-£22.00 **S:** £17.00-£22.00.
Open: All Year (not Xmas)
Beds: 3F 1T 5D 1S
Baths: 8 En 2 Pr
🛏 🅿 (7) 🛏 🐾 ✕ 🛎 📖 ♥

(0.25m) *Philamon,* 108 North Marine Road, Scarborough, N. Yorks, YO12 7JA.
Friendly guest house overlooking cricket ground. Convenient for golf and theatres.
Tel: **01723 373107** Mrs Hunter.
D: £14.50-£18.00 **S:** £14.50-£18.00.
Open: All Year
Beds: 1F 3D 2T 2S
Baths: 3 En 1 Sh
🛏 (2) 🛏 ✕ 🛎 📖 ♥ 🅿 ♿

Filey 34

National Grid Ref: TA1180

(0.5m) *The Gables,* 2a Rutland Street, Filey, N Yorks, YO14 9JB.
Grades: ETC 3 Diamond
Tel: **01723 514750** Broome.
D: £19.00-£23.00 **S:** £21.00-£28.00.
Open: All Year
Beds: 1F 2T 2D **Baths:** 5 En
🛏 🛏 🐾 ✕ 🛎 📖 ♥ 🅿
Characteristic Edwardian guest house offering friendly accommodation, comfortable ensuite rooms, colour television, hospitality tray. Central to all amenities. Reductions for 3 people or more nights.

(0.5m) *The Forge,* 23 Rutland Street, Filey, N. Yorks, YO14 9JA.
Edwardian townhouse. Small, friendly, non-smoking, good food.
Tel: **01723 512379** Appleyard.
D: £17.50-£19.00 **S:** £22.50-£24.00.
Open: All Year (not Xmas/New Year)
Beds: 1F 1T 2D **Baths:** 4 En 1 Pr
🛏 (3) 🅿 🛏 🐾 ✕ 🛎 📖 ♿ ♥ 🅿 ♿

S = Price range for a single person in a room

For those wishing to walk back to Helmsley, this is the Tabular Hills Walk.

Ebberston 35

National Grid Ref: SE8982

🍴🛏 Grapes, Foxholme Hotel

(3m) *Foxholm Hotel,* Ebberston, Scarborough, N. Yorks, YO13 9NJ.
Actual grid ref: SE900825
Peaceful, licensed ground floor rooms country inn in quiet picturesque village.
Grades: ETC 3 Diamond
Tel: **01723 859550** (also fax no)
Mrs Clyde.
D: £25.50-£28.50 **S:** £30.50-£33.50.
Open: All Year (not Xmas)
Beds: 2D 2T
Baths: 4 En
🛏 🅿 (20) ✔ 🛏 🐾 ✕ 🛎 📖 ♥ 🅿

(3m) *Studley House,* 67 Main Street, Ebberston, Scarborough, N. Yorks, YO13 9NR.
Hearty rooms, hearty breakfast. Picturesque village. Central for all attractions.
Grades: ETC 3 Diamond
Tel: **01723 859285** (also fax no)
Mrs Hodgson.
D: £20.00-£25.00 **S:** £25.00-£30.00.
Open: All Year (not Xmas/New Year)
Beds: 1D 1T 1S
Baths: 3 En
🛏 (10) 🅿 (3) ✔ 🛏 🛎 📖 ♥ 🅿

Levisham 36

National Grid Ref: SE8390

(0.5m 🐾) *Rectory Farmhouse,* Levisham, Pickering, N. Yorks, YO18 7NL.
Actual grid ref: SE833905
Grades: ETC 4 Diamond
Tel: **01751 460304**
Mrs Holt.
D: £20.00-£25.00 **S:** £24.00-£24.00.
Open: All Year
Beds: 2D 1T
Baths: 3 En
🛏 🅿 (8) ✔ 🛏 🐾 ✕ 🛎 📖 ♥ 🅿 ♿
Picturesque village surrounded by beautiful scenery; excellent walking, horse riding or just relaxing. Central location for coast, city of York, quaint market towns, historic and stately homes. Comfortable and welcoming. Afternoon teas/home baking. Riding holiday with own horse.

Please take muddy boots off before entering premises

Lockton 37

National Grid Ref: SE8489

(▲ 0.5m) *Lockton Youth Hostel,*
The Old School, Lockton,
Pickering, North Yorkshire,
YO18 7PY.
Actual grid ref: SE844900
Tel: 01751 460376
Under 18: £5.20 **Adults:** £7.50
Self-catering facilities, Showers,
Cycle store, Parking, No smoking,
WC, Kitchen facilities, Credit cards
accepted
Former village school in rural
hamlet just off main Pickering-
Whitby road. Enjoy walks in
Cropton and Dalby Forests.

Newton-on-Rawcliffe 38

National Grid Ref: SE8190

Horseshoe, White Swan

(0.25m ☎) *Rawcliffe House*
Farm, Newton-on-Rawcliffe,
Pickering, N. Yorks, YO18 8JA.
Actual grid ref: SE798917
Charming ensuite ground floor
rooms with every convenience.
A warm welcome and excellent
accommodation.
Grades: ETC 4 Diamond
Tel: 01751 473292 Mrs Ducat.
Fax no: 01751 473766
D: £25.50-£28.50 **S:** £30.50-£33.50.
Open: Easter to Oct
Beds: 2D 1T
Baths: 3 En

(On path ☎) *Swan Cottage,*
Newton-on-Rawcliffe, Pickering,
N. Yorks, YO18 8QA.
Actual grid ref: SE813906
Picturesque tranquil Village, Quiet
pub next door. Wide breakfast
choice.
Grades: ETC 3 Diamond
Tel: 01751 472502 Mrs Heaton.
D: £15.50-£16.50 **S:** £15.50-£16.50.
Open: All Year
Beds: 1D 1T 1S **Baths:** 1 Sh

Stape 39

National Grid Ref: SE7993

Horseshoe Inn

(On path) *Seavy Slack Farm,*
Stape, Pickering, N. Yorks,
YO18 8HZ.
Actual grid ref: SE799922
Comfortable farmhouse on a work-
ing farm serving good food.
Grades: ETC 3 Diamond
Tel: 01751 473131 Mrs Barrett.
D: £20.00-£25.00 **S:** £25.00-£25.00.
Open: All Year (not Xmas)
Beds: 1T 2D **Baths:** 3 En

Cropton 40

National Grid Ref: SE7589

New Inn

(0.25m) *Burr Bank Cottage,*
Cropton, Pickering, N. Yorks,
YO18 8HL.
Actual grid ref: SE759898
Grades: ETC 5 Diamond, Gold
Tel: 01751 417777 Ms Richardson.
Fax no: 01751 417789
D: £27.00-£27.00 **S:** £27.00-£27.00.
Open: All Year
Beds: 1D 1T
Baths: 2 En
Peace and quiet in 80 acres. Walks,
rides and drives to coast, moors,
dales, Wolds and York all less than
45 minutes away. Ensuite accom-
modation. Winner for Yorkshire
'Guesthouse Accommodation of the
Year' 2000. Ground floor.

(On path) *High Farm, Cropton,*
Pickering, N. Yorks, YO18 8HL.
Actual grid ref: SE758950
Lovely Victorian house, beautiful
garden overlooking National
Parkland, home baking.
Tel: 01751 417461 Mrs Feaster.
Fax no: 01751 473250
D: £20.00-£20.00 .
Open: All Year
Beds: 3D **Baths:** 3 En

Spaunton 41

National Grid Ref: SE7289

Blacksmiths Arms

(On path ☎) *Holywell House,*
Spaunton Bank Foot, Spaunton,
Appleton Le Moors, York, YO62 6TR.
Actual grid ref: SE723904
C18th beamed cottage with large
garden.
Grades: ETC 4 Diamond
Tel: 01751 417624
Mrs Makepeace.
D: £36.00-£36.00 **S:** £18.00-£18.00.
Open: All Year (not Xmas/
New Year)
Beds: 1D 1T 1S

Gillamoor 42

National Grid Ref: SE6889

Royal Oak

(On path) *The Manor Farm,*
Gillamoor, Kirkbymoorside, York,
YO62 7HX.
Actual grid ref: SE685900
Warm welcome family farm central
location for walking cycling
touring.
Tel: 01751 432695 (also fax no)
Mrs Gibson.
D: £17.00-£18.00 **S:** £20.00.
Open: All Year
Beds: 1F 2D 1T **Baths:** 2 En 1 Pr

Fadmoor 43

National Grid Ref: SE6789

(0.5m) *Mount Pleasant, Rudland,*
Fadmoor, York, YO62 7JJ.
Actual grid ref: SE655720
Friendly welcome. Ideal for walk-
ing, touring from moors. Brochure
available.
Grades: ETC 3 Diamond
Tel: 01751 431579 Clarke.
D: £15.00-£16.00 **S:** £15.00-£16.00.
Open: All Year (not Xmas)
Beds: 1F 1T **Baths:** 1 Sh

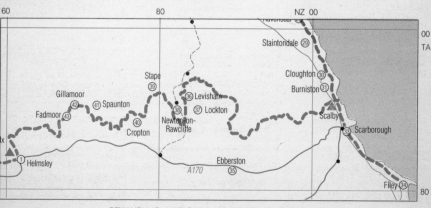

Coast to Coast

Passing through three National Parks - the Lake District, the Yorkshire Dales and the North York Moors - the Coast to Coast Path was the special creation of Alfred Wainwright, the man whose sketches and guidebooks mean so much to fellwalkers old and young. Featured on the television, the radio and in countless books, the Coast to Coast is now probably as famous as the Pennine Way itself. Running from the Cumbrian Coast to the North Sea, it is the most popular long distance path as yet unrecognised by the **Countryside Commission**. Despite this fame, there are still some debatable stretches which do not follow rights of way as defined at present. Please therefore take care in these areas and pay attention to diversion signs where they appear - local goodwill depends on walkers' behaviour. With regard to accommodation, although there is plenty of it, you are well advised to book ahead - don't just expect to turn up and find a place waiting for you.

The **Youth Hostels Association** run a useful **Accommodation Booking Bureau** for the **Coast to Coast Path**, based on their hostels and local B&Bs along the path. Ring 01629 825850 and ask for the Coast to Coast Booking Bureau Pack form and they can sort out your entire itinerary without further ado. There are also a couple of passenger minibus or taxi services handling luggage delivery, safe car-parking and back-up; **White Knight** (flexible backup service - tel 01903 766475 and **Coast to Coast Packhorse** (fixed bus service - tel 01768 371680). Both provide a useful fallback for weary or injured walkers or just those who do not wish to carry a large pack (most of us, probably).

Maps: 1:50000 Ordnance Survey Landranger Series: 89, 90, 91, 92, 93, 94, 98, 99. *Coast to Coast, Part One - West,* ISBN 1 871149 11 8 and *Coast to Coast, Part Two - East,* ISBN 1 871149 12 6, both 4-colour linear route maps, published by Footprint and available from all good map shops or directly from their offices (Unit 87, Stirling Enterprise Park, Stirling, FK7 7RP), £3.50 (+ 40p p&p)

Guides: *The Coast to Coast Walk* by Paul Hannon (ISBN 1 870141 18 0), published by Hillside Publications and available from all good map shops or directly from the publishers (12 Broadlands, Keighley, W. Yorks, BD20 6HX, tel. 01535 681505), £7.99 (+60p p&p)

A Coast to Coast Walk by A. Wainwright is still available, but readers should be reminded that significant changes have taken place since the path's creator put down his pen. You can obtain an updated version (published by Michael Joseph, ISBN 0 718140 72 9) from the Rambler's Association National Office (1/5 Wandsworth Road, London, SW8 2XX, tel. 020 7339 8500), price £11.99 (+ £1 p&p)

D = Price range per person sharing in a double room

St Bees 1

National Grid Ref: NX9711

⚭ ⚭ Queens Head, Manor House, Oddfellows

(0.25m) *Tomlin Guest House, 1 Tomlin House, St Bees, Cumbria, CA27 0EN.*
Actual grid ref: NX963118
Comfortable Victorian house convenient to beach and St Bees Head.
Tel: **01946 822284** Mrs Whitehead.
Fax no: 01946 824243
D: £15.00-£18.00 **S:** £18.00-£18.00.
Open: All Year (not Xmas)
Beds: 1F 2D 1T 0S **Baths:** 2 En 2 Sh
🛇 🅿 (2) ⌀ 🛏 🔭 🍴 Ⅲ Ⅴ ⚓ ⚡

(0.5m 🚐) *Stonehouse Farm, Main Street, St Bees, Cumbria, CA27 0DE.*
Actual grid ref: NX972119
Modern Georgian farmhouse in centre of village, next to railway station.
Grades: ETC 3 Diamond
Tel: **01946 822224** Mrs Smith.
D: £16.00-£20.00 **S:** £20.00-£20.00.
Open: All Year (not Xmas)
Beds: 1F 2D 2T 1S
Baths: 4 En 1 Sh
🛇 🅿 (20) ⌀ 🛏 🔭 🍴 Ⅲ Ⅴ ⚓ ⚡

(0.5m) *Fairladies Barn Guest House, Main Street, St Bees, CA27 0AD.*
Large converted barn located in centre of seaside village.
Tel: **01946 822718** Mrs Carr.
D: £16.00-£16.00 **S:** £16.00-£16.00.
Open: All Year
Beds: 6D 2T 1S **Baths:** 3 En 2 Sh
🛇 🅿 (10) ⌀ 🔭 Ⅲ Ⅴ ⚓

(0.75m 🚌) *Outrigg House,*
St Bees, Cumbria, CA27 0AN.
Georgian guest house of unique
character located in village centre.
Tel: **01956 822348** (also fax no)
Mrs Moffat.
D: £16.00-£16.00 **S:** £16.00-£16.00.
Open: All Year (not Xmas)
Beds: 1F 1T 1S **Baths:** 1 Sh
🛏 🅿 (2) ⊬ ⏁ 🕮 ⅙ ∦

Sandwith 2

National Grid Ref: NX9614

🍴 ⅙ Lowther Arms

(▲ 0.25m) *Tarn Flatt Camping
Barn,* Tarnflat Hall, Sandwith,
Whitehaven, Cumbria, CA28 9UX.
Actual grid ref: NX947146
Tel: **017687 72645**
Adults: £3.35
*Situated on St Bees Head overlook-
ing Scottish coastline and the Isle
of Man. RSPB seabird reserve and
lighthouse nearby. ADVANCE
BOOKING ESSENTIAL.*

(On path 🚌) *The Old Granary,*
Spout Howse, Sandwith,
Whitehaven, Cumbria, CA28 9UG.
Actual grid ref: NX964147
Tastefully converted barn on C2C
route and Coast to Coast path.
Tel: **01946 692097** Mrs Buchanan.
D: £17.00 **S:** £16.00.
Open: All Year
Beds: 1F 1D 1T **Baths:** 2 En
🛏 🅿 (2) ⏁ 🖈 ⚓ Ⅴ ∦ ∦

Ennerdale Bridge 3

National Grid Ref: NY0715

🍴 ⅙ Shepherds Arms

(On path) *The Shepherds Arms
Hotel,* Ennerdale Bridge, Cleator,
Cumbria, CA23 3AR.
Small friendly hotel in the Lake
District National Park which has
been completely refurbished.
Grades: ETC 2 Star
Tel: **01946 861249** (also fax no)
Mr Stanfield.
D: £28.00-£28.00 **S:** £30.00-£35.00.
Open: All Year
Beds: 1F 3D 3T 1S **Baths:** 6 En 2 Pr
🛏 🅿 (6) ⏁ 🖈 ⚓ 🕮 Ⅴ ∦ ∦

Ennerdale 4

National Grid Ref: NY0815

🍴 ⅙ Fox & Hounds, Shepherds Arms

(On path 🚌) *The Old Vicarage,*
Ennerdale Bridge, Cleator,
Cumbria, CA23 3AG.
Actual grid ref: NY065156
Charming old former vicarage with
spectacular views of Ennerdale
Fells.
Tel: **01946 861107** Mrs Lake.
-£18.00 -£18.00.
Open: All Year (not Xmas)
Beds: 1F 2D 1T 1S **Baths:** 3 Sh
🛏 🅿 (6) ⏁ 🖈 ⚓ 🕮 Ⅴ ∦ ∦

Gillerthwaite 5

National Grid Ref: NY1314

(▲ On path) *Ennerdale Youth
Hostel,* Cat Crag, Gillerthwaite,
Ennerdale, Cleator, Cumbria,
CA23 2AX.
Actual grid ref: NY142141
Tel: **01946 861237**
Under 18: £6.50 **Adults:** £9.25
Shop, Lounge, Drying room,
Parking limited, Evening meal at
7.00pm, No smoking, WC, Kitchen
facilities, Breakfast available,
Credit cards accepted
*Two converted forest cottages, with
real log fires and no electricity,
dramatically situated in peaceful
valley, 1 mile east of Ennerdale
Water.*

Black Sail 6

National Grid Ref: NY1912

(▲ On path) *Black Sail Youth
Hostel,* Black Sail Hut, Black Sail,
Ennerdale, Cleator, Cumbria,
CA23 3AY.
Actual grid ref: NY194124
Tel: **07711 108450**
Under 18: £6.50 **Adults:** £9.25
Self-catering facilities, Showers,
Lounge, Evening meal at 7.00pm,
No smoking, WC, Kitchen
facilities, Breakfast available,
Credit cards accepted
*A former shepherd's bothy, this is
the most isolated, excitingly situat-
ed hostel in England!*

Honister Pass 7

National Grid Ref: NY2213

(▲ On path) *Honister Pass Youth
Hostel,* Honister House, Honister
Pass, Seatoller, Keswick, Cumbria,
CA12 5XN.
Actual grid ref: NY224133
Tel: **017687 77267**
Under 18: £6.50 **Adults:** £9.25
Self-catering facilities, Showers,
Wet weather shelter, Lounge, Drying
room, Parking Limited, Evening
meal at 7.00pm, No smoking, WC,
Kitchen facilities, Breakfast
available, Credit cards accepted
*A purpose-built youth hostel
dramatically situated at the summit
of Honister Pass, with superb views
of Honister Crag. Hearty and
substantial food.*

Longthwaite 8

National Grid Ref: NY2514

(▲ On path) *Borrowdale Youth
Hostel,* Longthwaite, Borrowdale,
Keswick, Cumbria, CA12 5XE.
Actual grid ref: NY254142
Tel: **017687 77257**
Under 18: £7.75 **Adults:** £11.00
Self-catering facilities, Showers,
Shop, Laundry facilities, Lounge,
Dining room, Drying room, Cycle
store, Parking, Evening meal at
7.00pm, No smoking, Kitchen
facilities, Breakfast available,
Credit cards accepted
*Purpose-built hostel constructed
from Canadian Red cedar wood in
extensive riverside grounds in the
beautiful Borrowdale valley.*

Rosthwaite (Borrowdale) 9

🍴 ⅙ Langstrath Inn, Royal Oak, Scafell Hotel,
Riverside Bar

(▲ 0.5m) *Dinah Hoggus
Camping Barn,* Hazel Bank,
Rosthwaite, Keswick, Cumbria,
CA12 5XB.
Actual grid ref: NY259151
Tel: **017687 72645**
Adults: £3.35
*Traditional Lakeland field barn or
Hogg-house. ADVANCE BOOK-
ING ESSENTIAL.*

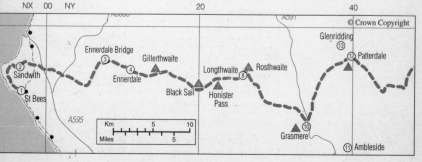

(On path) *Royal Oak Hotel,* Rosthwaite, Keswick, Cumbria, *CA12 5XB.*
Actual grid ref: NY259148
Grades: ETC 1 Star
Tel: **017687 77214** (also fax no)
Mr Dowie.
D: £26.00 **S:** £25.00.
Open: All Year
Beds: 6F 5D 2T 2S **Baths:** 12 En 3 Sh
🛏 🄿 (15) 🖵 🍴 ⊁ 🛋 🎞 Ⅴ 🎁 ✦
A traditional family-run walkers' hotel in the heart of beautiful Borrowdale. Come and enjoy our friendly service, cosy bar, open fire and good home cooking. Brochure, tariffs and special breaks available.

(On path) *The How,* Rosthwaite, Keswick, Cumbria, *CA12 5BX.*
Tel: **017687 77692**
D: £19.00-£20.50 **S:** £22.00-£23.00.
Open: Mar to Nov
Beds: 1T 2D **Baths:** 2 Sh
🄿 (4) 🖵 🍴 ⊁ 🛋 🎞 Ⅴ ✦
Rosthwaite is in the beautiful Borrowdale Valley about six miles from Keswick. Fell and riverside walking. Country house in well kept garden. Comfortable lounge with television, log fire when required. Breakfast room. Superb views.

(On path) *Yew Craggs,* Rosthwaite, Keswick, Cumbria, *CA12 5XB.*
Central Borrowdale, spectacular views, car park, riverside location (by the bridge).
Tel: **017687 77260** Mr & Mrs Crofts
D: £17.00-£21.00 **S:** £25.00.
Open: Mar to Nov
Beds: 2F 3D **Baths:** 1 Sh
🛏 (6) 🄿 (6) ⊁ 🎁 ✦

(On path) *Chapel House Farm Campsite,* Borrowdale, Keswick, Cumbria, *CA12 5XG.*
Actual grid ref: NY257142
Comfortable, homely, clean and good views.
Tel: **017687 77602** Mrs Dunkerly.
D: £18.00-£18.00 **S:** £18.00-£18.00.
Open: Feb to Nov **Beds:** 2D 2T 1S
🄿 (5) ⊁ 🛋 🎁 ✦

Grasmere 10

National Grid Ref: NY3307

🍴 🍺 Traveller's Rest, Rowan Tree, Red Lion, Tweedies Bistro

(🔺 On path) *Grasmere (Thorney How) Youth Hostel,* Thorney How, Grasmere, Ambleside, Cumbria, LA22 9QW.
Actual grid ref: NY332084
Tel: **015394 35591**
Under 18: £6.90 **Adults:** £10.00
Self-catering facilities, Showers, Lounge, Dining room, Drying room, Parking, Evening meal at 7.00pm, No smoking, Kitchen facilities
An old Lakeland farmhouse, full of character, open as a hostel since 1932 - 1m from centre of Grasmere, and very popular with walkers.

(🔺 On path) *Grasmere (Butterlip How) Youth Hostel,* Butterlip How, Grasmere, Ambleside, Cumbria, LA22 9QG.
Actual grid ref: NY336077
Tel: **015394 35316**
Under 18: £8.50 **Adults:** £12.50
Self-catering facilities, Television, Showers, Licensed bar, Laundry facilities, Lounge, Dining room, Games room, Drying room, Cycle store, Parking, Evening meal at 6.45-7.30pm, Kitchen facilities, Breakfast available, Credit cards accepted
Victorian Lakeland stone house in large grounds with rhododendrons & azaleas. Impressive views of the surrounding fells.

(On path) *Oak Lodge,* Easedale Road, Grasmere, Ambleside, Cumbria, LA22 9QJ.
Actual grid ref: NY331081
Quiet location with open views of the Easedale Valley.
Tel: **015394 35527**
Mrs Dixon.
D: £22.00-£26.00 **S:** £30.00.
Open: Feb to Dec
Beds: 2D 1T
Baths: 3 En
🛏 (10) 🄿 (3) ⊁ 🖵 🛋 🎞 Ⅴ 🎁 ✦

(On path) *Titteringdales,* Pye Lane, Grasmere, Ambleside, Cumbria, LA22 9RQ.
Quietly situated guest house with character, in the village of Grasmere.
Tel: **015394 35439** (also fax no)
Mr Scott.
D: £18.50-£25.00 .
Open: All Year (not Xmas/New Year)
Beds: 6D 1T 7F
Baths: 6 En 1 Pr
🛏 (12) 🄿 (7) ⊁ 🖵 🛋 🎞 Ⅴ ✦

Ambleside 11

National Grid Ref: NY3704

🍴 🍺 White Lion, The Unicorn, Queen's Head, Drunken Duck Inn, Outgate Inn, Lucy's, Traveller's Rest

(3m) *The Old Vicarage,* Vicarage Road, Ambleside, Cumbria, LA22 9DH.
Grades: ETC 4 Diamond
Tel: **015394 33364**
Mrs Burt.
Fax no: 015394 34734
D: £25.00-£30.00
S: £30.00-£40.00.
Open: All Year
Beds: 2F 6D 2T
Baths: 10 En
🛏 🄿 (15) ⊁ 🖵 🍴 ⊁ 🛋 🎞 & Ⅴ ✦
Quality bed & breakfast accommodation in a peaceful location in central Ambleside. Large car park. Pets welcome. All bedrooms are well-appointed and have multi-channel TV, hairdryers, radio alarm, mini fridge, kettle, private bath/shower and WC.

(3m) *Rothay House,* Rothay Road, Ambleside, Cumbria, LA22 2EE.
Quality establishment, professional care, first class breakfast. Private car park.
Tel: **015394 32434**
D: £21.00-£26.00 **S:** £30.00-£35.00.
Open: Feb to Dec
Beds: 1F 1T 4D
Baths: 6 En
🛏 (2) 🄿 (9) 🖵 🛋 🎞 Ⅴ ✦

(3m 🚐) *How Head Barn,* Fairview Road, Ambleside, Cumbria, LA22 9ED.
Spectacular views over Lakeland fells, with easy access to Ambleside. Available from July 2001.
Tel: **015394 32948** Mrs Walker.
D: £15.00-£15.00 **S:** £16.50-£16.50.
Open: All Year
Beds: 1D 2S
🛏 (1) ⊁ 🖵 ✕ 🛋 🎞 Ⅴ 🎁 ✦

(3m 🚐) *Fisherbeck Cottage,* Lake Road, Low Fold, Ambleside, Cumbria, LA22 0DN.
Lovely stone-built cottage, own gardens. Quiet location near village.
Tel: **015394 33353** Mrs Dawson.
D: £15.00-£16.00 **S:** £15.00-£16.00.
Open: All Year
Beds: 2D 1T 1S
Baths: 1 Sh
🄿 🖵 🍴 ⊁ 🛋 🎞 Ⅴ ✦

(3m) *Fern Cottage,* 6 Waterhead Terrace, Ambleside, Cumbria, LA22 0HA.
Homely Lakeland stone terraced cottage, two minutes from Lake Windermere.
Grades: ETC 3 Diamond
Tel: **015394 33007** Rushby.
D: £15.00-£17.00 **S:** £18.00-£20.00.
Open: All Year (not Xmas)
Beds: 2D 1T
Baths: 1 Sh
🛏 (4) ⊁ 🖵 🍴 ⊁ 🛋 🎞 Ⅴ 🎁 ✦

(3m) *Cowrie Creek,* 5 Stockghyll Brow, Ambleside, Cumbria, LA22 0QZ.
Small B&B, quiet location, 5 mins centre, 2 mins waterfalls.
Tel: **015394 33732**
D: £20.00-£28.00 **S:** £25.00-£40.00.
Open: May to Oct
Beds: 2D 1T
Baths: 2 En 1 Pr
🄿 (3) ⊁ 🖵 🛋 🎞 Ⅴ ✦

(3m) *Rowanfield Country House,* Kirkstone Road, Ambleside, Cumbria, LA22 9ET.
Idyllic, quiet location. Central Lakeland. Breathtaking views, beautiful house.
Grades: ETC 5 Diamond, AA 5 Diamond, RAC 5 Diamond
Tel: **015394 33686** Mrs Butcher.
Fax no: 015394 31569
D: £31.00-£45.00 **S:** £52.00-£65.00.
Open: Mar to Dec
Beds: 1F 5D 1T **Baths:** 8 En
🛏 (8) 🄿 (9) ⊁ 🖵 ✕ 🛋 🎞 & Ⅴ 🎁 ✦

(3m) *Norwood House,* Church
Street, Ambleside, Cumbria,
LA22 0BT.
Local knowledge and experienced
fell walking advice a speciality.
Tel: **015394 33349**
D: £17.00-£22.50 -£22.50.
Open: All Year (not Xmas)
Beds: 2F 1T 3D 2S
Baths: 8 En
🛇 ⅏ ▢ 🛌 ▥ Ⓥ ⌁

(3m) *3 Cambridge Villas,* Church
Street, Ambleside, Cumbria,
LA22 9DL.
Actual grid ref: NY375043
Substantial English or vegetarian
breakfast, good facilities, attractive
decor.
Tel: **015394 32307**
Mr & Mrs Richardson.
D: £16.00-£20.00 S: £16.00-£20.00.
Open: Feb to Nov
Beds: 4D 2T 2S
Baths: 4 En 1 Pr 2 Sh
🛇 (3) ⅏ ▢ 🛌 ▥ Ⓥ ⌶

(3m) *The Gables,* Church Walk,
Ambleside, Cumbria, *LA22 9DJ.*
Central situation. All ensuite.
Tel: **015394 33272** Mr Burt.
Fax no: 015394 34734
D: £23.00 S: £23.00.
Open: All Year
Beds: 5F 5D 3S
Baths: 13 En
🛇 🅿 (10) ⅏ ▢ 🛏 ✕ 🛌 ▥ Ⓥ ⌁ ⌶

(3m) *Cross Parrock,* 5 Waterhead
Terrace, Ambleside, Cumbria,
LA22 0HA.
Comfortable Victorian terrace
house. No smoking, all home
cooked food.
Tel: **015394 32372**
Mrs Siddall.
D: £15.00-£18.00 S: £20.00-£25.00.
Open: Feb to Nov
Beds: 2D 1T
Baths: 1 Sh
⅏ 🛏 ✕ 🛌 ▥ Ⓥ ⌶

(3m) *Lyndhurst Hotel,* Wansfell
Road, Ambleside, Cumbria,
LA22 0EG.
Traditional Victorian Lakeland
stone house.
Tel: **015394 32421** (also fax no)
Mrs Green.
D: £18.50-£27.50 .
Open: All Year
Beds: 4D 2T
Baths: 6 Pr
🅿 (8) ▢ ✕ 🛌 Ⓥ

(3m) *Hillsdale Hotel,* Church
Street, Ambleside, Cumbria,
LA22 0BT.
Friendly comfortable with gener-
ous breakfast; centrally situated for
all attractions.
Tel: **015394 33174** Mr Staley.
D: £16.00-£25.00 S: £17.00-£25.00.
Open: All Year (not Xmas)
Beds: 2F 6D 1T 1S
Baths: 4 En 2 Sh
🛇 ⅏ ▢ 🛌 ▥ Ⓥ ⌶

(3m) *Thorneyfield,* Compston
Road, Ambleside, Cumbria,
LA22 9DJ.
Thorneyfield guest house is a one
hundred year old Victorian
property.
Tel: **015394 32464** Mrs Doano.
Fax no: 0870 063 7262
D: £15.00-£25.00 S: £15.00.
Open: All Year
Beds: 2F 3D 1T **Baths:** 6 En
🛇 (4) 🅿 (3) ▢ 🛌 ▥ Ⓥ

Patterdale 12

National Grid Ref: NY3915

(▲ On path) *Patterdale Youth
Hostel,* Goldrill House, Patterdale,
Penrith, Cumbria, CA11 0NW.
Actual grid ref: NY399156
Tel: **017684 82394**
Under 18: £7.75 **Adults:** £11.00
Self-catering facilities, Showers,
Laundry facilities, Lounge, Dining
room, Drying room, Cycle store,
Parking, Evening meal at 7.00pm,
Kitchen facilities, Breakfast avail-
able, Credit cards accepted
*Purpose-built hostel open all day,
to the south of Ullswater. On the
Coast to Coast Path, and a good
base for those who want to climb
Helvellyn.*

(0.5m 🚲) *Greenbank Farm,*
Patterdale, Penrith, Cumbria,
CA11 0NR.
C16th converted comfortable
farmhouse.
Tel: **017684 82292** Mrs Iredale.
D: £14.00 S: £14.00.
Open: All Year (not Xmas)
Beds: 1F 1T **Baths:** 1 Sh
🛇 (1) 🅿 (4) ⅏ ▢ ✕ 🛌 ▥ Ⓥ ⌶ ⌁

Glenridding 13

National Grid Ref: NY3816

🍴 🍺 Traveller's Rest, White Lion

(▲ 2.5m) *Helvellyn Youth Hostel,*
Greenside, Glenridding, Penrith,
Cumbria, CA11 0QR.
Actual grid ref: NY366173
Tel: **017684 82269**
Under 18: £6.90 **Adults:** £10.00
Self-catering facilities, Showers,
Lounge, Dining room, Games
room, Drying room, Cycle store,
Parking, Evening meal at 7.00pm,
No smoking, WC, Kitchen
facilities, Breakfast available,
Credit cards accepted
*Isolated, peaceful hostel 900 ft
above sea level beneath the tower-
ing mass of the Helvellyn range.
Steam boat trips on Ullswater.*

S = Price range for a single

person in a single room

(▲ 3m) *Swirral Camping Barn,*
Greenside, Glenridding, Penrith,
Cumbria, CA11 0PL.
Actual grid ref: NY364174
Tel: **017687 72645 Adults:** £3.35
*One of group of nine buildings at
1,000 ft on the flank of the
Helvellyn range. ADVANCE
BOOKING ESSENTIAL.*

(▲ 3m) *Striding Edge Hostel,*
Greenside, Glenridding, Penrith,
Cumbria, CA11 0PL.
Actual grid ref: NY364174
Tel: **017687 72803 Adults:** £6.00
Self-catering facilities, Showers,
Wet weather shelter, Lounge,
Drying room, Drying room, No
smoking
*Located on the slopes of Helvellyn.
Ideal walking/cycling base.*

(On path) *Grisedale Lodge,*
Grisedale Bridge, Patterdale,
Penrith, Cumbria, CA11 0PJ.
Actual grid ref: NY391162
Quietly situated, comfortable
accommodation.
Tel: **017684 82084**
Mrs Martin.
Fax no: 017684 82327
D: £17.00-£25.00 S: £21.00-£25.00.
Open: All Year (not Xmas/
New Year)
Beds: 1D 2T
Baths: 2 Sh
🛇 (11) 🅿 (3) ⅏ ▢ 🛏 🛌 ▥ Ⓥ ⌶ ⌁

Shap 14

National Grid Ref: NY5615

🍴 🍺 Bulls Head, The Greyhound, The Crown

(▲ 0.25m) *Rest Easy Bunkhouse,*
2 Central Buildings, Shap, Penrith,
Cumbria, CA10 3NG.
Actual grid ref: NY563153
Tel: **01931 716538**
Adults: £8.00

(On path 🚲) *Fell House,* Shap,
Penrith, Cumbria, CA10 3NY.
Spacious Victorian house
convenient for Lakes and Dales.
Tel: **01931 716343**
Mr & Mrs Smith.
D: £16.50-£20.00
S: £18.50-£24.00.
Open: All Year
Beds: 3F 1D 1T **Baths:** 1 En 2 Sh
🛇 🅿 ⅏ ▢ 🛏 🛌 ▥ Ⓥ ⌶ ⌁

(0.5m) *Brookfield,* Shap, Penrith,
Cumbria, CA10 3PZ.
Renowned for good food,
comfort and personal attention.
Ensuite, licensed.
Grades: AA 4 Diamond
Tel: **01931 716397** (also fax no)
Mrs Brunskill.
D: £19.00-£23.00 S: £19.00-£25.00.
Open: All Year (not Xmas/
New Year)
Beds: 3F 5D 3T 1S
Baths: 4 En 4 Pr 1 Sh
🛇 🅿 (20) ⅏ ▢ ✕ 🛌 ▥ Ⓥ ⌶ ⌁

(On path) *1 The Rockery, Shap, Penrith, Cumbria, CA10 3LY.*
Actual grid ref: NY564157
C18th coaching inn.
Tel: **01931 716340** Mrs Hicks.
D: £18.00 **S:** £18.00.
Open: All Year (not Xmas)
Beds: 1F 1D 1T **Baths:** 2 Sh
⅓ P (4) ✔ ☐ ✖ ⛹ ▥ Ⓥ

Newbiggin-on-Lune 15

National Grid Ref: NY7005

⍟ ▧ Kings Head

(⛺ 0.5m) *Bents Camping Barn, Bents Farm, Newbiggin-on-Lune, Kirkby Stephen, Cumbria, CA17 4NX.*
Actual grid ref: NY708065
Tel: **017687 72645 / 015396 23681**
Adults: £3.35
Converted farm building close to the Howgill Fells. ADVANCE BOOKING ESSENTIAL.

(0.5m ⇆) *Tranna Hill, Newbiggin-on-Lune, Kirkby Stephen, Cumbria, CA17 4NY.*
Actual grid ref: NY705053
Fantastic views, good food, warm welcome, excellent for walking.
Tel: **015396 23227** Mrs Boustead.
D: £17.00-£18.00 **S:** £20.00-£20.00.
Open: Easter to Oct
Beds: 1D 1T **Baths:** 1 En 1 Pr
⅓ P (4) ✔ ☐ ✖ ⛹ ▥ Ⓥ ⛴ ✦

Ravenstonedale 16

National Grid Ref: NY7203

⍟ ▧ Black Swan, Kings Head

(2m ⇆) *Bowber Head, Ravenstonedale, Kirkby Stephen, Cumbria, CA17 4NL.*
Actual grid ref: NY741032
C17th farmhouse, open views, centre for classic coach tours.
Tel: **015396 23254** (also fax no)
Mr Hamer.
D: £20.00-£22.00 **S:** £20.00-£22.00.
Open: All Year
Beds: 1F 2D 2T **Baths:** 1 En 2 Pr
⅓ P (6) ✔ ☐ ✖ ⛹ ▥ ⅙ Ⓥ ⛴ ✦

Kirkby Stephen 17

National Grid Ref: NY7708

⍟ ▧ King's Arms, Old Forge, Pennine Hotel

(⛺ On path) *Kirkby Stephen Youth Hostel, Fletcher Hill, Market Street, Kirkby Stephen, Cumbria, CA17 7QQ.*
Actual grid ref: NY774085
Tel: **017683 71793**
Under 18: £6.90 **Adults:** £10.00
Self-catering facilities, Showers, Laundry facilities, Lounge, Dining room, Drying room, Cycle store, Parking, Evening meal at 7.00pm, No smoking, WC, Kitchen facilities, Breakfast available, Luggage store, Credit cards accepted
Attractive converted chapel, just south of the town square in this interesting old market town in the Upper Eden Valley.

(On path) *The Old Coach House, Faraday Road, Kirkby Stephen, Cumbria, CA17 4QL.*
Quiet comfortable C18th coach house close to town centre.
Tel: **017683 71582** Mrs rome.
D: £17.00-£19.00 **S:** £17.00-£22.00.
Open: All Year
Beds: 1D 1T 1S
Baths: 1 En 1 Sh
⅓ P (5) ✔ ☐ ⛹ ▥ Ⓥ ⛴ ✦

(0.25m ⇆) *Cold Keld Guided Walking Holidays, Fell End, Kirkby Stephen, Cumbria, CA17 4LN.*
Actual grid ref: SD729998
Guided walking holidays.
Delectable dining. Suit all abilities.
Singles welcome.
Tel: **015396 23273** (also fax no)
Mr & Mrs Trimmer.
D: £20.00-£30.00
S: £20.00-£30.00.
Open: All Year (not Xmas/New Year)
Beds: 1F 3D 1T 2S
Baths: 7 En
⅓ P (12) ✔ ☐ ✖ ⛹ ▥ Ⓥ ⛴ ✦

(On path ⇆) *Lyndhurst, 46 South Road, Kirkby Stephen, Cumbria, CA17 4SN.*
Actual grid ref: NY772078
A warm welcome to a delightful Victorian home. Lovely breakfast.
Tel: **017683 71448**
Mrs Bell.
D: £16.00-£20.00 **S:** £20.00-£22.50.
Open: All Year (not Xmas/New Year)
Beds: 1D 2T
Baths: 1 Pr 1 Sh
⅓ P (3) ✔ ☐ ✖ ⛹ ⛴ ▥ Ⓥ ⅙ ✦

(On path) *Lockholme, 48 South Road, Kirkby Stephen, Cumbria, CA17 4SN.*
Friendly Victorian home with antique furnishings and king sized beds.
Tel: **017683 71321**
Mrs Graham.
D: £16.00-£18.00 **S:** £16.00-£22.00.
Open: All Year (not Xmas)
Beds: 1F 1T 1D 1S
Baths: 2 En 1 Sh
⅓ P (4) ✔ ☐ ✖ ⛹ ▥ Ⓥ ⅙ ✦

Keld 18

National Grid Ref: NY8901

⍟ ▧ Farmers' Arms

(⛺ 1m) *Keld Youth Hostel, Keld Lodge, Keld, Upper Swaledale, Richmond, N. Yorks, DL11 6LL.*
Tel: **01748 886259**
Under 18: £6.50
Adults: £9.25
Self-catering facilities, Television, Showers, Lounge, Dining room, Drying room, Cycle store, Evening meal at 7.00pm, No smoking, Kitchen facilities, Breakfast available, Credit cards accepted
Close to both the Pennine and the Coast-to-Coast long distance paths, this onetime shooting lodge is ideal for walkers. Swaledale has moorland, waterfalls, and abundant wildlife.

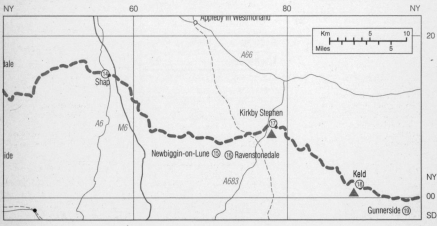

(0.75m) *Greenlands, Keld,*
Richmond, DL11 6DY.
Actual grid ref: NY889000
Refurbished farmhouse amidst the
peace and beauty of Upper
Swaledale.
Tel: **01748 886576**
Mrs Thompson.
D: £19.50-£19.50 .
Open: All Year
Beds: 2D
Baths: 2 En
P (2) ⊬ ❏ ≜ 🖿 Ⅵ ▮ ⚡

Gunnerside 19

National Grid Ref: SD9598

⚑ Oxnop Hall

(1m) *Oxnop Hall, Low Oxnop,*
Gunnerside, Richmond, N. Yorks,
DL11 6JJ.
Oxnop Hall is in an environment-
ally sensitive area. Stone walls and
barns.
Tel: **01748 886253** Mrs Porter.
D: £24.00-£31.00 **S:** £24.00-£34.00.
Open: All Year (not Xmas)
Beds: 1F 3D 1T 1S
Baths: 6 Pr
❤ (7) P (6) ⊬ ❏ ✕ ≜ 🖿 Ⅵ ▮ ⚡

Arkengarthdale 20

National Grid Ref: NZ0002

⚑ Buck Hotel, Great Britain

(2.5m) *The White House, Arkle*
Town, Arkengarthdale, Richmond,
N. Yorks, DL11 6RB.
Actual grid ref: NZ005020
A 200-year-old former farmhouse
offering ensuite accommodation,
fine home cooking and off-road
parking.
Tel: **01748 884088**
Mrs Whitworth.
Fax no: 01748 884203
D: £18.50-£21.00 **S:** £26.00-£30.00.
Open: Mar to Oct
Beds: 2D 1T
Baths: 2 Pr 1 Sh
❤ (10) P (5) ⊬ ❏ ✕ ≜ 🖿 Ⅵ ▮ ⚡

Reeth 21

National Grid Ref: SE0399

⚑ Kings Arms Hotel, Bridge Inn, Black Bull,
Buck Hotel

(On path) *Elder Peak,*
Arkengarthdale Road, Reeth,
Richmond, N Yorks, DL11 6QX.
Actual grid ref: SE036999
Friendly welcome. Good food.
Peaceful, beautiful views. Ideal
walking, touring.
Grades: ETC 3 Diamond
Tel: **01748 884770**
Mrs Peacock.
D: £17.00-£17.00
S: £17.00-£17.00.
Open: Easter to Oct
Beds: 1D 1T
Baths: 1 Sh
❤ (5) P (2) ❏ ≜ 🖿 Ⅵ ▮ ⚡

(On path) *Arkle House, Mill Lane,*
Reeth, Richmond, North Yorks,
DL11 6SJ.
Old Georgian house full of charac-
ter located alongside Arkle Beck.
Grades: ETC 4 Diamond
Tel: **01748 884815**
D: £20.00-£25.00 **S:** £25.00-£27.50.
Open: All Year
Beds: 1F 1D **Baths:** 2 En
❤ P (2) ⊬ ❏ ≜ 🖿 Ⅵ ▮

(On path) *2 Bridge Terrace, Reeth,*
Richmond, N. Yorks, DL11 6TP.
Actual grid ref: SD041991
Dry-cured Gloucester Old Spot
bacon, local bread, fresh fruit,
yoghurt.
Grades: ETC 1 Diamond
Tel: **01748 884572** Mrs Davies.
D: £16.50-£17.50 **S:** £20.00-£22.00.
Open: Easter to Nov
Beds: 1D 1T **Baths:** 1 Sh
❤ ⊬ 🖿 ▮ ⚡

(On path) *The Black Bull, Reeth,*
Richmond, N. Yorks, DL11 6SZ.
In Yorkshire Dales National Park.
On Inn Way.
Grades: ETC 3 Diamond
Tel: **01748 884213** (also fax no)
Mrs Sykes.
D: £20.00-£25.00 **S:** £20.00-£37.50.
Open: All Year **Beds:** 1F 1T 7D
Baths: 6 En 1 Pr 2 Sh
❤ ❏ 🐾 ✕ ≜ 🖿 Ⅵ ▮ ⚡

Grinton 22

National Grid Ref: SE0498

(▲1.25m) *Grinton Lodge Youth*
Hostel, Grinton Lodge, Grinton,
Richmond, N. Yorks, DL11 6HS.
Tel: **01748 884206**
Under 18: £6.90 **Adults:** £10.00
Self-catering facilities, Television,
Showers, Laundry facilities,
Lounge, Games room, Drying
room, Cycle store, Evening meal at
7pm, WC, Breakfast available,
Credit cards accepted
A useful stopover for the Coast to
Coast path and the Yorkshire Dales
Cycleway. Harkerside Moor has tra-
ditional drystone walling and field
barns. The hostel itself was once a
shooting lodge and retains its log
fires among other original features.

Richmond 23

National Grid Ref: NZ1701

⚑ Angel, Buck Hotel, Black Lion, Shoulder Of
Mutton, Holly Hill, Turf Hotel

(▲0.5m) *The Bunkhouse,*
Richmond Equestrian Centre, Brough
Park, Richmond, N. Yorks, DL10 7PL.
Tel: **01748 811629**
Under 18: £12.50 **Adults:** £12.50
Self-catering facilities, Television,
Showers, Licensed bar, Laundry
facilities, Lounge, Dining room,
Drying room, Parking, Facilities for
disabled people, No smoking
Riding school, overlooking the
Dales and North Yorkshire Moors.

(0.25m) *Pottergate Guest House,*
4 Pottergate, Richmond, N Yorks,
DL10 4AB.
Comfortable guest house, friendly
service, excellent value for money.
Grades: ETC 2 Diamond,
AA 2 Diamond
Tel: **01748 823826** Mrs Firby.
D: £19.00-£19.00 **S:** £20.00-£20.00.
Open: All Year
Beds: 1F 3D 1T 2S
Baths: 3 Sh
❤ P (3) ⊬ ❏ ✕ ≜ 🖿 Ⅵ ▮ ⚡

(0.25m) *66 Frenchgate, Richmond,*
DL10 7AG.
Actual grid ref: NZ173013
Comfortable rooms in beautiful old
house. Stunning views of
Richmond.
Tel: **01748 823421**
Mrs Woodward.
D: £20.00-£21.00 **S:** £25.00-£26.00.
Open: All Year (not Xmas)
Beds: 2D 1T
Baths: 2 En 1 Pr
❤ ❏ 🐾 ≜ 🖿 Ⅵ ▮ ⚡

(0.5m) *Caldwell Lodge, Gilling*
West, Richmond, N. Yorks, DL10 5JB.
Friendly welcome. Pretty village.
1 mile Scotch Corner.
Tel: **01748 825468** Mrs Bolton.
D: £18.00-£20.00 **S:** £20.00-£22.00.
Open: Easter to Oct
Beds: 1F 1D
Baths: 1 Sh
❤ P (4) ❏ ≜ 🖿 Ⅵ ▮ ⚡

(On path) *West Cottage, Victoria*
Road, Richmond, N. Yorks, DL10 4AS.
Large Georgian town house. Easy
walk into Richmond market place.
Tel: **01748 824046** Mrs Gibson.
D: £22.00-£25.00 **S:** £30.00-£40.00.
Open: Easter to Oct
Beds: 1D 1T
Baths: 2 Pr
❤ (5) P (2) ⊬ ❏ ≜ 🖿 Ⅵ ▮ ⚡

(On path) *Channel House,*
8 Frenchgate, Richmond,
N. Yorks, DL10 4JG.
Georgian town house near castle,
shops, restaurants. Warm friendly
welcome.
Tel: **01748 823844** (also fax no)
Mrs Gould.
D: £17.00-£19.00 **S:** £20.00-£25.00.
Open: All Year
Beds: 1F 1D
Baths: 1 En 1 Sh
❤ (3) ⊬ ❏ 🐾 ≜ 🖿 Ⅵ

(0.5m) *Westwood House,*
5 Newbiggin, Richmond,
N. Yorks, DL10 4DR.
Comfortable Georgian town house
situated just off Richmond market
square.
Tel: **01748 823453**
Mr Walker.
D: £17.00-£17.00 **S:** £17.00-£17.00.
Open: All Year
Beds: 1F 1D 1T
Baths: 1 Sh
❤ (7) ⊬ ❏ ≜ 🖿 Ⅵ ▮ ⚡

(0.5m 🚍) *Windsor House,* 9 Castle
Hill, Richmond, N. Yorks, DL10 4QP.
Grade II Listed Georgian house
with large rooms and washing
facilities.
Tel: **01748 823285** (also fax no)
Mrs Adams.
D: £17.00-£20.00 **S:** £17.00-£20.00.
Open: All Year
Beds: 2F 5D 2T 1S
Baths: 2 Sh
🛇 ⌷ 🛏 ✕ 🍴 🔥 Ⅲ Ⅴ 🗎 ∕

(On path) *The Castle Tavern,*
Market Place, Richmond, N. Yorks,
DL10 4HU.
Actual grid ref: NZ173013
Grade II Listed building of great
character.
Tel: **01748 823187** Mrs Chaplin.
D: £16.00-£22.00 **S:** £22.00-£22.00.
Open: All Year
Beds: 1F 1D 2T **Baths:** 2 Sh
🛇 ⌷ 🛏 ✕ 🍴 Ⅴ 🗎

(0.5m) *The Buck Inn,*
27 Newbiggin, Richmond,
N. Yorks, DL10 4DX.
All rooms maintained to the highest
standard of cleanliness and a sub-
stantial breakfast.
Tel: **01748 822259** Mrs Fluen.
D: £19.00-£22.00 **S:** £25.00-£25.00.
Open: All Year
Beds: 2F 1D 1T 1S **Baths:** 6 En
🛇 ⌷ 🛏 🍴 Ⅲ Ⅴ

(0.5m) *Victoria House,* 49 Maison
Dieu, Richmond, N Yorks, DL10 7AU.
Gateway to beautiful Yorkshire
Dales, countryside with scenic
walks, many places of historic
interest.
Tel: **01748 824830** Mr & Mrs Tate.
D: £18.00-£20.00 **S:** £18.00-£20.00.
Open: All Year (not Xmas)
Beds: 2D 1T
Baths: 3 En
🛇 ∕ ⌷ 🛏 🍴 Ⅲ Ⅴ

High season,
bank holidays and
special events mean
low availability
everywhere.

S = Price range for a single
person in a single room

Catterick 24

National Grid Ref: SE2497

🍴 🍺 Fathers Arms

(0.75m) *Rose Cottage Guest
House,* 26 High Street, Catterick,
Richmond, N. Yorks, DL10 7LJ.
Small cosy stone-built guest house,
midway London-Edinburgh.
Grades: ETC 3 Diamond,
AA 3 Diamond
Tel: **01748 811164**
Mrs Archer.
D: £18.50-£21.00 **S:** £22.00-£27.00.
Open: All Year (not Xmas)
Beds: 1D 2T 1S
Baths: 2 En 1 Sh
🛇 ⌷ (4) ⌷ 🛏 ✕ 🍴 Ⅲ Ⅴ

Bolton-on-Swale 25

National Grid Ref: SE2599

🍴 🍺 Farmers Arms

(On path) *School House,* Bolton-
on-Swale, Richmond, N. Yorks,
DL10 6AQ.
Actual grid ref: SE252993
Early C18th converted school
house in delightful rural setting.
Tel: **01748 818532**
Mrs Robinson.
D: £20.00-£20.00
S: £20.00-£20.00.
Open: Apr to Oct
Beds: 2T
Baths: 1 Sh
∕ ⌷ 🛏 🍴 Ⅲ Ⅴ 🗎

Lovesome Hill 26

National Grid Ref: SE3599

(▲ 0.25m) *Lovesome Hill
Camping Barn,* Lovesome Hill
Farm, (off A167), Northallerton,
N Yorks, DL6 2PB
Tel: **01609 772311**
Adults: £3.50
Showers, Running water, WC,
Meals available, Kitchen facilities,
Breakfast available

Northallerton 27

National Grid Ref: SE3794

🍴 🍺 Bassetts, Black Swan, Golden Lion, Pepper
Mill, New Inn

(3m) *Porch House,* 68 High Street,
Northallerton, N. Yorks, DL7 8EG.
Built 1584 original fireplaces and
beams between Yorkshire Dales
and Moors.
Grades: ETC 4 Diamond, Silver,
AA 4 Diamond
Tel: **01609 779831** Barrow.
Fax no: 01609 778603
D: £24.50-£26.00 **S:** £33.00-£35.00.
Open: All year (not Xmas)
Beds: 4D 2T **Baths:** 6 En
🛇 (12) ⌷ (6) ∕ ⌷ 🍴 Ⅲ Ⅴ

(3m) *Honeypots,* 4 Pennine View,
Northallerton, DL7 8HP.
Well-recommended guest house
(visitors love it!) decorated to
extremely high standard.
Tel: **01609 777264**
D: £18.00-£20.00 **S:** £18.00-£20.00.
Open: All Year (not Xmas/New Year)
Beds: 1T **Baths:** 1P
🛇 (12) ⌷ (1) ∕ ⌷ ✕ 🍴 Ⅲ Ⅴ 🗎

(3m 🚍) *Alverton Guest House,*
26 South Parade, Northallerton,
N. Yorks, DL7 8SG.
Actual grid ref: SE367934
Modernised Victorian town house
convenient for all the county town
facilities.
Tel: **01609 776207** (also fax no)
Mr Longley.
D: £18.00-£19.50 **S:** £17.50-£24.00.
Open: All Year (not Xmas)
Beds: 1F 1D 1T 2S **Baths:** 3 En 1 Sh
🛇 ⌷ (4) ⌷ 🍴 Ⅲ Ⅴ 🗎 ∕

Ingleby Cross 28

National Grid Ref: NZ4500

🍴 🍺 Black Horse, Blue Bell

(On path 🚍) *North York Moors
Adventure Ctr,* Park House,
Ingleby Cross, Northallerton,
N. Yorks, DL6 3PE.
Actual grid ref: SE453995
Park House, traditional sandstone
farmhouse set in The National Park.
Tel: **01609 882571** (also fax no)
Mr Bennett. **D:** £15.00 **S:** £15.00.
Open: Easter to Oct
Beds: 3F 1D 3T **Baths:** 2 Sh
🛇 (1) ⌷ (20) ⌷ 🛏 ✕ 🍴 Ⅲ Ⅴ 🗎 ∕

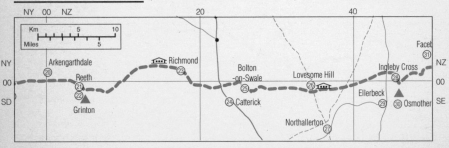

(On path 🚍) *Blue Bell Inn,*
Ingleby Cross, Northallerton,
N. Yorks, DL6 3NF.
Family run, real ales, coal fire,
quiet annexed accommodation.
Tel: **01609 882272** Mrs Kinsella.
D: £20.00-£20.00 **S:** £20.00-£20.00.
Open: All Year
Beds: 4F 1D 4T **Baths:** 5 En
🛏 🅿 (20) 🗖 🗙 🎩 🛏 🔟 Ⅴ ♦ ∦

Ellerbeck 29

National Grid Ref: SE4397

🍴 🍺 Golden Lion, Kings Head

(2m 🚍) *Old Mill House, Ellerbeck,*
Osmotherley, Northallerton,
N. Yorks, DL6 2RY.
Delightful C17th mill set central for
walking touring North Yorkshire.
Tel: **01609 883466** Mrs Shepherd.
D: £20.00-£25.00 **S:** £20.00-£25.00.
Open: Easter to November
Beds: 1T 2D **Baths:** 1 En 1Shared
🅿 (4) ⊁ 🗖 🛏

Osmotherley 30

National Grid Ref: SE4597

(🔺 1m) *Osmotherley Youth*
Hostel, Cote Ghyll, Osmotherley,
Northallerton, North Yorkshire,
DL6 3AH.
Actual grid ref: SE461981
Tel: **01609 883575**
Under 18: £6.90 **Adults:** £10.00
Self-catering facilities, Television,
Showers, Laundry facilities, Wet
weather shelter, Lounge, Games
room, Drying room, Cycle store,
Parking, Evening meal at 7.00pm,
No smoking, WC, Kitchen
facilities, Breakfast available,
Credit cards accepted
Surrounded by woodland, the youth
hostel is fully modernised with
excellent facilities, right on the
edge of the North York Moors
National Park.

D = Price range per person
sharing in a double room

Faceby 31

National Grid Ref: NZ4903

(1m 🚍) *Four Wynds, Whorl Hill,*
Faceby, Middlesbrough, TS9 7BZ.
Actual grid ref: NZ487033
Small holding in beautiful country-
side. Located off A172 between
Swainby/ Faceby.
Grades: ETC 3 Diamond
Tel: **01642 701315**
Mr Barnfather.
D: £18.00-£20.00 **S:** £18.00-£20.00.
Open: All Year
Beds: 1F 1D 1T
Baths: 1 En 1 Sh
🛏 🅿 (8) 🗖 🛏 🗙 🎩 🛏 🔟 Ⅴ ♦ ∦

Cringle Moor 32

National Grid Ref: NZ5503

🍴 🍺 Buck Inn

(0.5m 🚍) *Beakhills Farm, Cold*
Moor, Cringle Moor, Chop Gate,
Stokesley, Middlesbrough, TS9 7JJ.
Actual grid ref: NZ545024
Cosy farmhouse on working farm.
Tel: **01642 778371**
Mrs Cook.
D: £16.00 **S:** £16.00.
Open: All Year
Beds: 1F 1T 1D
🛏 🅿 🗖 🛏 🗙 ♦ ∦

Great Broughton 33

National Grid Ref: NZ5406

🍴 🍺 Bay Horse, Black Horse, Jet Miners,
Wainstones Hotel

(2m 🚍) *Ingle Hill, Ingleby Road,*
Great Broughton, North Yorks,
TS9 7ER.
Actual grid ref: NZ548063
Spectacular views North York
Moors, warm welcome, transport to
walks.
Tel: **01642 712449**
Mrs Sutcliffe.
D: £17.50-£17.50 **S:** £18.50-£18.50.
Open: All Year (not Xmas)
Beds: 1F 1D 2T
Baths: 2 En 2 Sh
🛏 🅿 (4) ⊁ 🗖 🛏 🎩 🛏 🔟 Ⅴ ♦ ∦

Chop Gate 34

National Grid Ref: SE5599

🍴 🍺 Buck

(2m 🚍) *Hill End Farm, Chop*
Gate, Bilsdale, Stokesley North
Yorkshire, TS9 7JR.
Actual grid ref: NZ576978
Grades: ETC 3 Diamond
Tel: **01439 798278** Mrs Johnson.
D: £21.00-£21.00 **S:** £25.00-£25.00.
Open: Easter to Nov
Beds: 1F 1T
Baths: 2 Ensuite
🛏 (5) 🅿 (3) ⊁ 🗖 🛏 🗙 🎩 🛏 🔟 Ⅴ
Recommended by Which? Good
Bed and Breakfast Guide. Hill End
farm beautiful views down the
valley of Bilsdale which is midway
between the market towns of
Helmsley and Stokesley. Near to
Herriot, Heartbeat and Captain
Cook Country

(2m 🚍) *Buck Inn Hotel, Chop*
Gate, Stokesley, Middlesbrough,
TS9 7JL.
Actual grid ref: SE559994
Friendly inn with restaurant;
splendid views of Bilsdale Valley.
Tel: **01642 778334** Mrs Stewart.
D: £21.00-£24.00 **S:** £28.00-£32.00.
Open: All Year (not Xmas)
Beds: 1F 1D 4T
Baths: 6 Pr
🛏 🅿 🗖 🗙 🎩 🛏 🔟 Ⅴ ♦ ∦

Clay Bank Top 35

National Grid Ref: NZ5701

(1m) *Maltkiln House, Clay Bank*
Top, Bilsdale, Middlesbrough,
TS9 7HZ.
Actual grid ref: NZ571017
Stone farmhouse in secluded
moorland location with magnificent
views. Licensed.
Tel: **01642 778216** (also fax no)
Mr & Mrs Broad.
D: £17.00-£18.50
S: £17.00-£18.50.
Open: All Year
Beds: 1D 2T
Baths: 1 En 1 Sh
🛏 (8) 🅿 (3) ⊁ 🗖 🗙 🎩 🛏 ♦ ∦

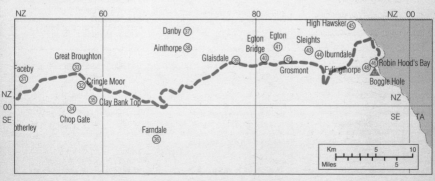

Farndale 36

National Grid Ref: SE6697

⊯ ⬩ Royal Oak, Crown, Plough

(2m 🚌) *Keysbeck Farm, Farndale, Kirkbymoorside, York, YO62 6UZ.*
Old oak-beamed farmhouse.
Tel: **01751 433221** Mrs Featherstone
D: £14.00 **S:** £14.00.
Open: All Year
Beds: 1D 1T 1S **Baths:** 1 Sh
🛇 🅿 🛏 ✕ 🟊

(2m) *Olive House Farm, Farndale, Kirkbymoorside, York, YO60 7JY.*
Homely accommodation, working farm, Heartbeat country, abbey ruins & stately homes.
Tel: **01751 433207** Mrs Blacklock.
D: £12.50-£12.50 **S:** £14.00-£14.00.
Open: Easter to Oct **Beds:** 2F
🛇 🅿 (4) 🛏 🟊

Danby 37

National Grid Ref: NZ7008

⊯ ⬩ Fox & Hounds, Duke Of Wellington, Moorlands Hotel, Shepherds' Hall

(2.5m 🚌) *Holly Lodge Farm, Danby Head, Danby, Whitby, N Yorks, YO21 2NW.*
Actual grid ref: NZ686064
Tel: **01287 660469** Mrs Shirley.
D: £18.00-£19.00 **S:** £18.00-£20.00.
Open: Easter to Oct
Beds: 1D 1T 1S
Baths: 1 Pr
🛇 🅿 (4) ⅍ ⬚ ✕ ⬚ 🍴 ⬚ 📺 🎇 ⚿ ✿
Farmhouse with beautiful views over Danby Dale near to Heartbeat and Herriot country, Whitby, York and North Yorks Steam Railway, offering high class accommodation, lounge, separate dining room, bathroom with bath and good food, comfortable beds and shower.

(2.5m 🚌) *Sycamore House, Danby, Whitby, N. Yorks, YO21 2NW.*
Actual grid ref: NZ688058
C17th farmhouse with stunning views. Ideal area for walking/touring.
Grades: ETC 3 Diamond
Tel: **01287 660125** Mr Lowson.
Fax no: 01287 669122
D: £20.00 **S:** £20.00.
Open: All Year (not Xmas)
Beds: 1F 1D 1T 1S
Baths: 1 En 1 Sh
🛇 🅿 (6) ⅍ ⬚ 🛏 ✕ ⬚ 🍴 📺 🎇 ⚿ ✿

(2.5m) *Botton Grove Farm, Danby Head, Danby, Whitby, N. Yorks, YO21 2NH.*
Large stone built farmhouse; excellent views of Danby Dale; warm welcome.
Grades: ETC 3 Diamond
Tel: **01287 660284** Mrs Tait.
D: £18.00-£18.00 **S:** £18.00-£25.00.
Open: May to March
Beds: 1D 1T 2S **Baths:** 1 Sh
🛇 🅿 (3) ⬚ 🛏 ⬚ 🍴 🎇 ⚿ ✿

Ainthorpe 38

⊯ ⬩ Fox & Hounds

(2.5m 🚌) *Rowantree Farm, Ainthorpe, Danby, Whitby, N. Yorks, YO21 2LE.*
Situated in the heart of the North Yorkshire Moors, with panoramic moorland views.
Grades: ETC 3 Diamond
Tel: **01287 660396** Mrs Tindall.
D: £17.00-£18.00 **S:** £17.00-£18.00.
Open: All Year (not Xmas/New Year)
Beds: 1F 1T
Baths: 2 Sh
🛇 🅿 (4) ⬚ 🛏 ✕ ⬚ 🍴 🎇 ⚿ ✿

Glaisdale 39

National Grid Ref: NZ7603

⊯ ⬩ Angler's Rest, Moon & Sixpence, Wheatsheaf

(On path) *Arncliffe Arms Hotel, Glaisdale, Whitby, N. Yorks, YO21 2QL.*
Actual grid ref: NZ782055
Tel: **01947 897209** (also fax no)
Mr Westwood.
D: £15.00-£15.00 **S:** £15.00-£15.00.
Open: All Year
Beds: 2D 2T 1S
Baths: 1 Sh
🛇 🅿 ⬚ 🛏 ✕ ⬚ 🍴 🎇 ⚿ ✿
Very friendly & comfortable accommodation. A must for curry lovers, romantic area along River Esk, close Beggars Bridge. 1 min from railway station. Entertainment if required. Car park, Coast to Coast drop off/pick up point.

(0.25m) *Postgate Farm, Glaisdale, Whitby, N Yorks, YO21 2PZ.*
Actual grid ref: NZ758044
Grades: ETC 4 Diamond
Tel: **01947 897353** (also fax no)
Mrs Thompson.
D: £16.00-£21.00 **S:** £20.00-£30.00.
Open: All Year (not Xmas)
Beds: 2D 1T
Baths: 3 En
🅿 (4) ⬚ ⬚ 🍴 📺 🎇 ⚿ ✿
C17th Listed farmhouse in beautiful Esk Valley, a walkers' paradise. Whitby - 10 miles. Steam railway and 'Heartbeat Country' - 5 miles. Guest kitchen, fridge and microwave. Games room, laundry, drying facilities. All ensuite with TV, courtesy tray, hairdryer, clock-radio. Also studio flat self catering.

(0.25m) *Hollins Farm, Glaisdale, Whitby, N. Yorks, YO21 2PZ.*
Comfortable C16th farmhouse near moors, 8 miles coast, wonderful scenery.
Grades: ETC 3 Diamond
Tel: **01947 897516** Mrs Mortimer.
D: £15.00 .
Open: All Year (not Xmas)
Beds: 3F 1D 2T
Baths: 2 Sh
🛇 🅿 (6) ⬚ 🛏 ⬚ 🍴 📺 🎇 ⚿ ✿

(0.25m 🚌) *Egton Banks Farm, Glaisdale, Whitby, N. Yorks, YO21 2QP.*
Lovely old farmhouse in secluded valley, pretty decor. Warm welcome.
Grades: ETC 4 Diamond
Tel: **01947 897289** Richardson.
D: £16.00-£18.00 **S:** £17.00-£18.00.
Open: All Year (not Xmas/New Year)
Beds: 1F 1T 1D **Baths:** 1 En 1 Sh
🛇 🅿 ⅍ ⬚ ✕ ⬚ 🍴 📺 🎇 ⚿ ✿

(On path) *Red House Farm, Glaisdale, Whitby, N. Yorks, YO21 2PZ.*
Actual grid ref: NZ772049
Listed Georgian farmhouse, refurbished, but retaining original features.
Tel: **01947 897242** (also fax no)
Mr Spashett.
D: £22.50-£22.50 **S:** £22.50-£30.00.
Open: All Year
Beds: 2D **Baths:** 1 En 1 Sh
🛇 🅿 (6) ⅍ ⬚ ⬚ 🍴 📺 🎇 ⚿ ✿

Egton Bridge 40

National Grid Ref: NZ8005

(On path 🚌) *Broom House, Broom House Lane, Egton Bridge, Whitby, N Yorks, YO21 1XD.*
Broom House - an excellent place to stay. We provide comfortable ensuite rooms.
Tel: **01947 895279** Mrs White.
Fax no: 01947 895657
D: £19.50-£19.50 **S:** £25.00.
Open: All Year (not Xmas)
Beds: 2F 2D 1T **Baths:** 5 En
🛇 🅿 (7) ⅍ ⬚ ✕ ⬚ 🍴 📺 🎇 ⚿ ✿

Egton 41

National Grid Ref: NZ8006

⊯ ⬩ Horseshoe, Wheatsheaf

(0.5m) *Flushing Meadow, Egton, Whitby, N Yorks, YO21 1UA.*
Superb moorland views. Ideal base for Esk Valley and steam railway.
Grades: ETC 3 Diamond
Tel: **01947 895395** Mrs Johnson.
D: £15.00-£19.50 **S:** £15.00-£17.00.
Open: All Year
Beds: 1D 1T 1S **Baths:** 1 En 1 Sh
🅿 (3) ⅍ ⬚ ⬚ 🍴 📺 🎇 ⚿ ✿

Grosmont 42

National Grid Ref: NZ8205

⊯ ⬩ Post Gate

(On path) *Eskdale, Grosmont, Whitby, N. Yorks, YO22 5PT.*
Actual grid ref: NZ825054
Detached Georgian house overlooking Esk Valley, North York Moors NP.
Tel: **01947 895385** (also fax no)
Mrs Counsell.
D: £17.00-£17.50 **S:** £17.00-£17.50.
Open: Easter to Nov
Beds: 2D 2S **Baths:** 1 Sh
🛇 🅿 (3) ⬚ 🛏 ⬚ 🍴 📺 🎇 ⚿ ✿

Sleights 43

National Grid Ref: NZ8607

¶ol ⌐ Plough

(0.5m) *Ryedale House, 154-8
Coach Road, Sleights, Whitby,
N. Yorks, YO22 5EQ.*
National Park country 3.5 miles
Whitby. Magnificent
moor/dale/coastal scenery.
Grades: ETC 4 Diamond
Tel: **01947 810534** (also fax no)
Mrs Beale.
D: £19.50-£21.00 **S:** £17.00-£22.00.
Open: April to Oct
Beds: 2D 2S **Baths:** 2 En 1 Pr
🄿 (3) ⅏ ⌂ ⚲ ▥ ⓥ 🖢 ∥

Iburndale 44

National Grid Ref: NZ8707

¶ol ⌐ Plough

(1.25m 🚍) *8 Mill Lane, Iburndale,
Sleights, Whitby, N. Yorks,
YO22 5DU.*
Actual grid ref: NZ873071
Ideal for North York Moors, coast,
North Yorkshire steam trains.
Tel: **01947 810009** (also fax no)
Mrs Hebdon.
D: £18.00-£23.00. **S:** £20.00-£23.00.
Open: All Year (not Xmas)
Beds: 2D **Baths:** 1 En 1 Sh
🆑 🄿 (4) ⅏ ⚲ ▥ ⓥ 🖢 ∥

High Hawsker 45

National Grid Ref: NZ9207

¶ol ⌐ Hare & Hounds

(0.5m) *Old Blacksmiths Arms,
High Hawsker, Whitby, N. Yorks,
YO22 4LH.*
Actual grid ref: NZ927075
Originally first pub in village.
Large garden with pond.
Tel: **01947 880800** Mrs Stubbs.
D: £18.00-£19.00 **S:** £21.00-£24.00.
Open: Easter to Oct
Beds: 1T 2D **Baths:** 2 Sh
🆑 (12) 🄿 (3) ⅏ ⅊ ⚲ ▥ ⅌ ⓥ 🖢 ∥

Robin Hood's Bay 46

National Grid Ref: NZ9504

¶ol ⌐ Bay Hotel, Dolphin, Flyingdale Inn,
Grosvenor, Victoria

(0.25m) *Glen-lyn, Station Road,
Robin Hood's Bay, Whitby,
N Yorks, YO22 4RA.*
Tel: **01947 880391** Mrs Price.
D: £20.00-£20.00 .
Open: All Year
Beds: 1T 1D **Baths:** 2 En
🄿 ⅏ ⅊ ▥ ⅌ 🖢 ∥
Come and sample the delights of
Robin Hoods Bay and stay in a
tastefully decorated, well appointed
detached bungalow. You can relax
in the large, well maintained,
mature gardens with seating area
around a pond with water feature.

(0.25m) *Clarence Dene, Station
Road, Robin Hood's Bay, Whitby,
North Yorks, YO22 4RH.*
Tel: **01947 880272** Mrs Howard.
D: £20.00-£20.00 .
Open: All Year
Beds: 1F 1T 3D
Baths: 5 En
🆑 🄿 ⅏ ⅊ ⚲ ▥ ⓥ 🖢 ∥
Situated above this historic village.
Clarence Dene retains many
original Art Nouveau features. the
spacious bedrooms have been
sympathetically decorated and
furnished, all are clean.
comfortable and well appointed
with ensuite facilities.

(On path) *The White Owl, Station
Road, Robin Hood's Bay, Whitby,
N. Yorks, YO22 4RL.*
Interesting house and garden.
Centre of village near cliff edge.
Tel: **01947 880879**
Mr & Mrs Higgins.
D: £20.00-£20.00 **S:** £20.00-£20.00.
Open: All Year
Beds: 1F 1D 1T 1S
Baths: 4 En
🆑 🄿 (3) ⅊ ⚲ ▥ ⓥ ∥

(On path) *Meadowfield, Mount
Pleasant North, Robin Hood's Bay,
Whitby, N. Yorks, YO22 4RE.*
Refurbished Victorian house.
Friendly, comfortable, plenty of
food. Non-smoking.
Tel: **01947 880564** Mrs Luker.
D: £17.00-£19.50 **S:** £20.00-£24.00.
Open: All Year (not Xmas)
Beds: 2D 1T 2S
Baths: 1 En 1 Sh
⅌ ⅏ ⚲ ▥ ⓥ 🖢 ∥

(On path) *Rosegarth, Thorpe Lane,
Robin Hood's Bay, Whitby,
N. Yorks, YO22 4RN.*
Friendly comfortable
accommodation. Ideal centre
touring and walking.
Tel: **01947 880578** Mrs Stubbs.
D: £16.50-£17.00 **S:** £17.00.
Open: Easter to Nov
Beds: 1D 1T 1S
Baths: 1 Sh
🆑 (9) 🄿 (4) ⅏ ⚲ ▥ ⓥ ∥

(0.25m) *Flask Inn, Robin Hood's
Bay, Fylingdales, Whitby, YO22 4QH.*
Friendly family-run coaching inn.
Excellent food served lunchtimes
and evenings.
Tel: **01947 880305** Allison.
Fax no: 01947 880592
D: £22.00-£22.00 **S:** £28.00.
Open: All year
Beds: 3F 4D 4T 1S
Baths: 12 En
🆑 🄿 ⅏ ✕ ⚲ ▥ ⓥ 🖢 ∥

Boggle Hole 47

(▲ On path) *Boggle Hole Youth
Hostel, Mill Beck, Boggle Hole,
Robin Hood's Bay, Whitby, North
Yorkshire, YO22 4UQ.*

Actual grid ref: NZ954040
Tel: **01947 880352**
Under 18: £6.75 **Adults:** £10.00.
Self-catering facilities, Television,
Showers, Licensed bar, Lounge,
Dining room, Cycle store, Parking,
Evening meal at 6.00 to 7.00pm,
WC, Drying facilities, Kitchen
facilities, Breakfast available,
Credit cards accepted
*A former mill in a wooded ravine,
Boggle Hole has the North Sea tide
coming up to the doorstep and the
North York Moors behind.*

Fylingthorpe 48

National Grid Ref: NZ9404

¶ol ⌐ Fylingdales, Victoria

(1m) *Red House, Thorpe Lane,
Fylingthorpe, Whitby, North
Yorkshire, YO22 4TH.*
Large Victorian house and garden.
Panelled staircase and gallery.
Beautiful views.
Tel: **01947 880079**
Mrs Collinson.
D: £18.00-£22.50
S: £20.00-£25.00.
Open: Easter to Oct
Beds: 1T 2D
Baths: 1 En 1 Sh
🄿 (3) ⅏ ⅊ ⚲ ▥ ⓥ 🖢 ∥

(1m) *South View, Sledgates,
Fylingthorpe, Robin Hood's Bay,
Whitby, N. Yorks, YO22 4TZ.*
Comfortable detached house. Sea
& country views. Touring area.
Bed time drink. **Tel:** **01947 880025**
Mrs Reynolds. **D:** £16.00-£18.00 .
Open: Easter to Oct
Beds: 2D **Baths:** 1 Sh
🆑 (5) 🄿 (2) ⅏ ⅊

(1m 🚍) *Low Farm, Fylingthorpe,
Whitby, N Yorks, YO22 4QF.*
Actual grid ref: NZ941040
Tel: **01947 880366** (also fax no)
Mrs Hodgson.**D:** £18.00-£21.00 .
Open: May to Nov
Beds: 1F **Baths:** 1 En
🄿 (1) ⅌ ⅏ ⚲ ▥ ⓥ ∥
Imposing Georgian farmhouse built
from local stone, set in beautiful
countryside on our working farm,
1.5 miles from the picturesque village of Robin Hood's Bay. Safe off
road parking. Superb views over
garden and beyond. Large breakfasts. Genuine Yorkshire welcome.

(0.5m) *Croft Farm, Fylingthorpe,
Whitby, N. Yorks, YO22 4PW.*
All rooms have extensive views over
the sea, moors and countryside.
Grades: ETC 4 Diamond
Tel: **01947 880231** (also fax no)
Mrs Featherstone.
D: £22.00-£24.00 **S:** £22.00-£27.00.
Open: Easter to Oct
Beds: 2D 1S **Baths:** 2 En 1 Pr
🆑 (5) 🄿 (4) ⅌ ⅏ ⚲ ▥ ⓥ 🖢 ∥

Cotswold Way

Officially 97 miles, the **Cotswold Way** leads south west along the Cotswold escarpment from Chipping Campden in North Gloucestershire to glorious Bath in North East Somerset. The steepness of the scarp gives the impression of a coastal rather than an inland path, with wide views over the Severn Vale. The Cotswolds are rightly famous for their English beauty; this route takes in many pretty little villages and interesting historic sites, so be prepared to take detours. Although the **Cotswold Way** is some way off from becoming a National Trail, the voluntary wardens who look after the Cotswold Area of Outstanding Natural Beauty have made sure that the path is well way-marked. Much of the path is across cultivated land, so the usual care must be taken with dogs and gates. This also means that it can be very muddy in wet weather.

Guides (all available from good map shops unless stated):
A Guide to the Cotswold Way by Richard Sale

(ISBN 1 861262 75 2), published by Crowood Press £12.99 (26 April 1999)
The Cotswold Way by Anthony Burton (ISBN 1 85410 3172), published by Aurum Press in association with *Ordnance Survey,* £10.99
The Cotswold Way by Mark Richards (ISBN 1 873877 10 2), published by Reardon Publishing, £3.95

Cotswold Way Handbook by RA Glos Area (ISBN 1 901184 18 8), published by Reardon Pulishing and available only by post from the Rambler's Association National Office (1/5 Wandsworth Road, London, SW8 2XX, tel. 020 7339 8500), £2.00 (+70p p&p)

Comments on the path to: **Cotswold AONB Service,** Environment Dept, Shire Hall Gloucester GL1 2TH

Maps: 1:50000 Ordnance Survey Landranger Series: 150, 151, 162, 163, 172, 173

Chipping Campden   1
National Grid Ref: SP1539

¶| ♨ Bakers' Arms, Volunteer Inn, King's Arms, Butchers' Arms, Three Ways, Ebrington Arms, Wheatsheaf Inn

(On path) *The Guest House, Lower High Street, Chipping Campden, Glos, GL55 6DZ.*
Period Cotswold stone cottage, easy walking to local beauty spots and shops.
Tel: **01386 840163**
Mrs Benfield.
D: £19.00-£22.00
S: £25.00.
Open: Easter to Nov
Beds: 1D 1T
Baths: 2 En
🖵 🛏 🕭 🎟 Ⅴ 🖉 ✦

(On path 🚗) *Weston Park Farm, Dovers Hill, Chipping Campden, Glos, GL55 6UW.*
Penod farmhouse in magnificent setting, adjacent NT, on small farm.
Tel: **01386 840835**
Mr Whitehouse.
D: £25.00-£25.00
S: £25.00-£25.00.
Open: All Year
Beds: 1F 1D
Baths: 1 En
🐂 🄿 🖵 🕭 🎟 Ⅴ 🆔 ✦

(On path) *Catbrook House, Catbrook, Chipping Campden, Glos, GL55 6DE.*
Quietly situated with lovely views over fields & meadows, only 10 mins walk town centre.
Tel: **01386 841499**
Mrs Klein.
D: £20.50-£24.50 S: £35.00-£44.00.
Open: All Year (not Xmas)
Beds: 2D 1T
Baths: 1 En 2 Pr
🐂 (9) 🄿 (3) ⊁ 🕭 🎟 Ⅴ

Broad Campden   2
National Grid Ref: SP1537

¶| ♨ Bakers Arms

(0.25m) *Marnic House, Broad Campden, Chipping Campden, Glos, GL55 6UR.*
Actual grid ref: SP159378
Comfortable, friendly and well furnished family home. Peacefully situated, scenic views.
Grades: ETC 4 Diamond, Gold, AA 4 Diamond
Tel: **01386 840014** Mrs Rawlings.
Fax no: 01386 840441
D: £22.00-£25.00 S: £38.00-£40.00.
Open: All Year (not Xmas/New Year)
Beds: 2D 1T
Baths: 2 En 1 Pr
🐂 (10) 🄿 (4) 🖵 🕭 🎟 Ⅴ ✦

(1m) *Wyldlands, Broad Campden, Chipping Campden, Glos, GL55 6UR.*
Actual grid ref: SP156381
Cotswold stone house with open views over countryside in conservation village.
Tel: **01386 840478**
Mrs Wadey.
Fax no: 01386 849031
D: £22.00-£22.00 S: £28.00-£28.00.
Open: All Year (not Xmas)
Beds: 1D 1T 1S
Baths: 2 En 1 Pr
🐂 🄿 (4) ⊁ 🖵 🕭 🎟 Ⅴ ✦

Ebrington 3

National Grid Ref: SP1840

◨◧ ◖ Ebrington Arms

(2m ⊟) *Holly House, Ebrington, Chipping Campden, Glos, GL55 6NL.*
Actual grid ref: SP190400
Situated in centre of picturesque Cotswold village, 2 miles Chipping Campden.
Grades: AA 4 Diamond
Tel: **01386 593213** Mrs Hutsby.
Fax no: 01386 593181
D: £21.00-£24.00 **S:** £30.00-£40.00.
Open: All Year (not Xmas)
Beds: 3F/D/T
Baths: 3 En
⌂ 🅿 (5) ⅋ 🖵 🖩 Ⅴ ⅋

Aston Magna 4

National Grid Ref: SP1935

(3.5m ⊟) *Bran Mill Cottage, Aston Magna, Moreton in Marsh, Glos, GL56 9QP.*
Actual grid ref: SP193370
Small traditional B&B in peaceful Cotswold cottage. Friendly, welcoming, homely.
Grades: ETC 3 Diamond
Tel: **01386 593517**
D: £16.00-£18.00 **S:** £19.00-£25.00.
Open: All Year (not Xmas)
Beds: 1D 1T 1S
Baths: 1 Pr 1 Sh
⌂ (14) 🅿 (3) ⅋ 🖵 🖩 Ⅴ ⅋

Pay B&Bs by cash or cheque and be prepared to pay up front.

S = Price range for a single person in a single room

Broadway 5

National Grid Ref: SP0937

◨◧ ◖ Crown & Trumpet, Horse & Hounds, Sandy Arms, Fox & Trumpet, Childswickham Arms, Pheasant, Swan Hotel, Bell Inn, Fleece, Olivers

(On path) *Crown & Trumpet Inn, Church Street, Broadway, Worcs, WR12 7AE.*
Grades: ETC 3 Diamond
Tel: **01386 853202** Mr Scott.
Fax no: 01386 834650
D: £24.00 .
Open: All Year
Beds: 3D 1T **Baths:** 4 En
⌂ 🅿 (6) ⽧ ✕ ⊟ 🖩 Ⅴ
C17th Cotswold inn in picturesque village (also on the Cotswold Way). With log fires and oak beams, the Inn specialises in homemade local & seasonal dishes. Ideal base for touring & walking.
http://www.cotswoldholidays.co.uk

(0.25m ⊟) *Southwold House, Station Road, Broadway, Worcs, WR12 7DE.*
Actual grid ref: SP092377
Grades: ETC 4 Diamond, AA 4 Diamond
Tel: **01386 853681** Mrs Smiles.
Fax no: 01386 854610
D: £24.00-£25.00 **S:** £25.00-£27.00.
Open: All Year
Beds: 1F 4D 2T 1S **Baths:** 7 En
⌂ 🅿 (8) ⅋ 🖵 ⽧ ☖ 🖩 Ⅴ ⅋
We invite you to our spacious and tastefully decorated Edwardian house situated in one of the Cotswolds most picturesque villages. We are 4 minutes walk from pubs, restaurants and Cotswold Way. Stately houses and gardens abound. Stratford-upon-Avon 22 minutes.

(On path) *Brook House, Station Road, Broadway, Worcs, WR12 7DE.*
Tel: **01386 852313** Mrs Thomas.
D: £20.00-£26.00 **S:** £20.00-£40.00.
Open: All Year (not Xmas)
Beds: 2F 2D 1S
Baths: 3 En 1 Pr 1 Sh
⌂ 🅿 (6) 🖵 ⽧ ☖ 🖩 Ⅴ ⅋
Traditional Victorian house with large rooms, overlooking fields, hills and gardens. Five minutes walk from the village centre. Brookhouse is an ideal centre for exploring Cotswold villages gardens, wildlife centres. With golf courses, fishing river trips and horseriding nearby. Reductions for three or more nights.

(0.5m) *Whiteacres Guest House, Station Road, Broadway, Worcs, WR12 7DE.*
Actual grid ref: SP090380
Tastefully decorated Victorian house, two rooms having four poster beds.
Grades: ETC 4 Diamond, AA 4 Diamond
Tel: **01386 852320** Mr Allen.
D: £25.00-£27.50 .
Open: All Year (not Xmas)
Beds: 4D 1T **Baths:** 5 En
🅿 (8) ⅋ 🖵 🖩 Ⅴ ⅋

(0.25m) *Quantocks, Evesham Road, Broadway, Worcs, WR12 7PA.*
Large detached house in 3 acres with superb views of Cleeve/Bredon/Malvern hills.
Tel: **01386 853378**
Mr & Mrs Stephens.
D: £22.50-£25.00 **S:** £30.00-£35.00.
Open: March to November
Beds: 1F 1T **Baths:** 2 En
⌂ 🅿 ⅋ 🖵 ☖ 🖩 ⅋ Ⅴ

D = Price range per person sharing in a double room

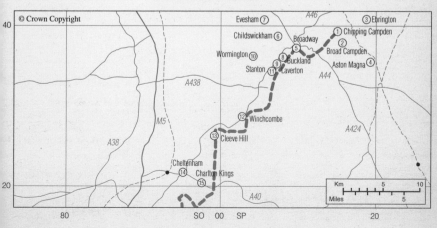

© Crown Copyright

(On path 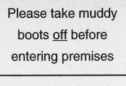) *Windrush House,*
Station Rd, Broadway, Worcs, WR12
7DE.
Elegant Edwardian detached house
located near Broadway village
green.
Grades: ETC 4 Diamond,
AA 4 Diamond, RAC 4 Diamond
Tel: **01386 853577** Pinder.
Fax no: 01386 853790
D: £25.00-£30.00 **S:** £25.00-£40.00.
Open: All Year
Beds: 3D 2T **Baths:** 5 En
🛇 🅿 (6) ⊬ ⟷ ≯ ✕ ♨ ⛁ Ⓥ 🛈 ⅏

Bringing children with
you? Always ask for
any special rates.

**Please take muddy
boots off before
entering premises**

(2.5m) *The Driffold Guest House,*
Murcot Turn, A44, Broadway,
Worcs, WR12 7HT.
Actual grid ref: SP075405
Country house, large rear garden,
near Broadway. Friendly, welcom-
ing atmosphere.
Tel: **01386 830825** (also fax no)
Mr Reohorn and Mrs B Byrne.
D: £20.00-£30.00 **S:** £20.00-£20.00.
Open: All Year
Beds: 1F 1D 1T 3S
Baths: 2 En 1 Sh
🛇 (3) 🅿 (10) ⊬ ⟷ ≯ ♨ ⛁ Ⓥ ⅏

(On path) *Olive Branch Guest*
House, 78 High Street, Broadway,
Worcs, WR12 7AJ.
Actual grid ref: SP102375
Family-run C16th Grade II Listed
guest house on Cotswold Way.
Tel: **01386 853440** Mr Talboys.
Fax no: 01386 859070
D: £23.50-£30.00 **S:** £35.00-£50.00.
Open: All Year
Beds: 2F 3D 2T 1S
Baths: 7 En 1 Pr
🛇 🅿 (8) ⊬ ⟷ ♨ ⛁ Ⓥ

(On path) *Pathlow House, 82 High*
Street, Broadway, Worcs, WR12 7AJ.
Actual grid ref: SP101375
Beautiful Cotswold stone house,
with separate small cottage built in
1720s.
Tel: **01386 853444** (also fax no)
Mr Green.
D: £17.50-£25.00 **S:** £25.00-£45.00.
Open: All Year
Beds: 2F 5D 1T
Baths: 6 En 2 Sh
🛇 🅿 (8) ⊬ ⟷ ≯ ✕ ⅙ 🛈 ⅏

Childswickham 6

National Grid Ref: SP0738

(2.5m) *Mount Pleasant Farm,*
Childswickham, Broadway, Worcs,
WR12 7HZ.
Working farm three miles from
Broadway. Very quiet
accommodation, excellent views.
Grades: ETC 4 Diamond,
AA 4 Diamond, RAC 4 Diamond
Tel: **01386 853424** Mrs Perry.
D: £23.00-£25.00 **S:** £30.00.
Open: All Year
Beds: 2D 1T 1S
Baths: 4 Pr
🛇 (5) 🅿 (10) ⊬ ⟷ ♨ ⛁ Ⓥ

Evesham 7

National Grid Ref: SP0343

🍴 🍺 Bell, Anchor, Royal Oak, Crown,
Strawberry Fields, Fish & Anchor, Witherspoons

(5m 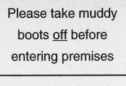) *Anglers View, 90 Albert*
Road, Evesham, Worcs, WR11 4LA.
5 minutes from town/bus stations
and River Avon.
Tel: **01386 442141** Tomkotwicz.
D: £17.50-£30.00 **S:** £20.00-£35.00.
Open: All Year
Beds: 1F 3T
Baths: 1 Pr 2 Sh
🛇 🅿 (2) ⊬ ⟷ ≯ ✕ ♨ ⛁ Ⓥ 🛈

(5m 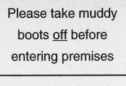) *Park View Hotel,*
Waterside, Evesham, Worcs,
WR11 6BS.
Friendly family-run riverside hotel
tour the Cotswolds and
Shakespeare country.
Tel: **01386 442639**
Mr & Mrs Spires.
D: £19.00-£21.00 **S:** £21.00-£24.00.
Open: All Year (not Xmas)
Beds: 6D 10T 10S
Baths: 7 Sh
🛇 🅿 (30) ⟷ ≯ ✕ 🛈 ⅏

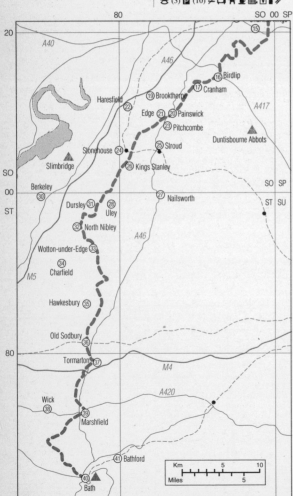

Buckland 8

National Grid Ref: SP0736

|❍| ⌸ Snowshill Arms

(0.25m 🚗) *Garretts Farm,
Buckland, Broadway, Worcs,
WR12 7LY.*
Friendly welcome awaits in peaceful village, near all Cotswolds attractions.
Tel: **01386 852091** (also fax no)
Mrs Smith.
D: £20.00-£30.00 **S:** £22.00-£40.00.
Open: All Year (not Xmas)
Beds: 1T
Baths: 1 Pr
🛆 🅿 (2) 🛆🛇 🖤 🛏 🎿 ▥ ▣ ♦

Laverton 9

National Grid Ref: SP0735

|❍| ⌸ Mount Inn

(0.5m) *Gunners Orchard,
Laverton, Broadway, Glos,
WR12 7NA.*
Comfortable private house in quiet and beautiful setting personal attention.
Tel: **01386 584213**
Mrs Stephenson.
D: £18.00-£20.00 **S:** £25.00-£30.00.
Open: All Year (not Xmas/New Year)
Beds: 1D 1T
Baths: 1 Sh
🛆 (10) 🅿 (6) ⌇🛆 🛏 🎿 ▥ ♦

Wormington 10

National Grid Ref: SP0336

|❍| ⌸ Pheasant Inn

(3m) *Manor Farm, Wormington,
Broadway, Worcs, WR12 7NL.*
C16th listed Tudor farmhouse in quiet village near church.
Tel: **01386 584302** Mrs Russell.
D: £20.00-£22.00 **S:** £20.00-£30.00.
Open: All Year
Beds: 2D 1T
Baths: 2 En 1 Pr
🛆 (5) 🅿 (4) ⌇🛆 🛏 🎿 ▥ ▣

Stanton 11

National Grid Ref: SP0634

|❍| ⌸ The Mount Inn

(On path 🚗) *Shenberrow Hill,
Stanton, Broadway, Worcs,
WR12 7NE.*
Actual grid ref: SP073343
Charming house and cottage accommodation in beautiful unspoilt village. Unforgettable.
Grades: ETC 4 Diamond
Tel: **01386 584468** (also fax no)
Mrs Neilan.
D: £25.00-£27.50 **S:** £30.00.
Open: All Year (not Xmas)
Beds: 1F 1D 1T
Baths: 2 En 1 Pr
🛆 (5) 🅿 (5) 🛆🛏🗙 🎿 ▥ ▣ ♦

Winchcombe 12

National Grid Ref: SP0228

|❍| ⌸ Plaisterers Arms, Harvest Home, Hobnails, Pheasant, Royal Oak, White Hart, Corner Cupboards

(1m) *Ireley Grounds, Barnhouse,
Broadway Road, Winchcombe,
Cheltenham, Glos, GL54 5NY.*
Grades: ETC 4 Diamond
Tel: **01242 603736** Mr Wright.
D: £22.50-£32.50 **S:** £22.50-£32.50.
Open: All Year (not Xmas)
Beds: 1F 3D **Baths:** 4 En
🛆 🅿 (20) ⌇🛆 🛏 🎿 ▥ ▣
IRELEY GROUNDS is a stunning Cotswold house in 6 acres of attractive gardens with magnificent views of the countryside and Great Western Railway. Relax in the lounge with its sofas and log fires. A function suite is available for up to 100 people.

(1m) *The Homestead, Smithy
Lane, Greet, Winchcombe,
Cheltenham, Glos, GL54 5BP.*
C16th country house in beautiful Cotswold countryside, local pub nearby.
Tel: **01242 603808** Mrs Bloom.
D: £20.00-£22.50 **S:** £20.00-£30.00.
Open: FEV to Nov
Beds: 2F 2D **Baths:** 3 En 2 Pr 1 Sh
🛆 (6) 🅿 (4) 🛆 🛏 🎿 ▥ ▣

(0.5m 🚗) *Ireley Farm, Ireley
Road, Winchcombe, Cheltenham,
Glos, GL54 5PA.*
Actual grid ref: SP037304
C18th Cotswold stone character farmhouse. Relaxed excellent breakfasts.
Tel: **01242 602445** Mrs Warmington
D: £20.00-£25.00 **S:** £20.00-£25.00.
Open: Jan to Nov
Beds: 1F 1D 1T **Baths:** 2 En 1 Pr
🛆 🅿🛆🗙 🎿 ▥ ▣ ♦

(1m 🚗) *Manor Farm, Winchcombe,
Cheltenham, Glos, GL54 5BJ*
Cotswold manor on family farm. S/c cottages, camping and caravan space on farm.
Grades: ETC 4 Diamond
Tel: **01242 602423** (also fax no)
Mr & Mrs Day.
D: £25.00-£30.00 **S:** £30.00.
Open: All Year (not Xmas)
Beds: 2D 1T **Baths:** 3 En
🛆 🅿 (20) 🛆 🛏 ▥ ▣ ♦

(1m) *Blair House, 41 Gretton
Road, Winchcombe, Cheltenham,
Glos, GL54 5EG.*
Actual grid ref: SP023287
Georgian house in historic town. Warm friendly welcome, excellent breakfasts.
Grades: ETC 3 Diamond
Tel: **01242 603626** Mrs Chisholm.
Fax no: 01242 604214
D: £20.00-£21.00 **S:** £22.00-£25.00.
Open: All Year
Beds: 1D 1T 2S **Baths:** 1 En 1 Sh
🛆 🅿 (1) ⌇🛆 🛏 🎿 ▥ ▣ ♦

(1m) *Sudeley Hill Farm,
Winchcombe, Cheltenham, Glos,
GL54 5JB.*
Actual grid ref: SP0427
Comfortably furnished C15th farmhouse.
Grades: ETC 4 Diamond,
AA 4 Diamond
Tel: **01242 602344** (also fax no)
Mrs Scudamore.
D: £22.00-£25.00 **S:** £30.00-£32.00.
Open: All Year (not Xmas)
Beds: 1F 1D 1T
Baths: 3 En
🛆 🅿 (10) 🛆 🛏 🎿 ▥ ♦

(On path) *Gower House, 16 North
Street, Winchcombe, Cheltenham,
Glos, GL54 5LH.*
C18th town house near shops.
Tel: **01242 602616** Mrs Simmonds.
D: £20.00-£22.50 **S:** £30.00-£40.00.
Open: All Year (not Xmas)
Beds: 1D 2T
Baths: 3 En
🛆 🅿 (3) 🛆 🛏 🎿 ▥ ▣ ♦

(1m 🚗) *Elms Farm, Gretton,
Winchcombe, Cheltenham, Glos,
GL54 5HQ.*
Farmhouse set in peaceful location, close to places of interest.
Grades: ETC 4 Diamond
Tel: **01242 620150** (also fax no)
Quilter.
D: £25.00-£30.00 **S:** £30.00-£35.00.
Open: All Year (not Xmas)
Beds: 1F 1T
Baths: 2 En
🛆 🅿 (4) ⌇🛆 🛏 🎿 ▥ ▣

(0.5m 🚗) *Postlip Hall Farm,
Winchcombe, Cheltenham, Glos,
GL54 5AQ.*
Actual grid ref: SO998268
Highly commended, superb location. Quiet, scenic, lovely farmhouse. Great base Cotswold attractions.
Tel: **01242 603351** Mrs Albutt.
D: £21.00-£23.00 **S:** £25.00-£35.00.
Open: All Year (not Xmas)
Beds: 2D 1T
Baths: 2 En 1 Pr
🛆 (5) 🅿 (6) ⌇🛆 🛏 🎿 ▥ ▣ ♦

Cleeve Hill 13

National Grid Ref: SO9826

|❍| ⌸ Apple Tree, Plough, High Roost, Royal Oak, Kings Arms, Rising Sun

(0.25m) *Heron Haye, Cleeve Hill,
Cheltenham, Glos, GL52 3PW.*
Actual grid ref: SO987273
Quiet location, 3 miles Cheltenham Racecourse. Comfortable home. Full English breakfast. Superb views.
Tel: **01242 672516**
Mr Saunders.
D: £22.50-£30.00 **S:** £25.00-£30.00.
Open: All Year
Beds: 2D 1S
Baths: 1 Sh
🅿 (4) ⌇🛆 🗙 🛏 ▥ ▣

(1m 🚌) *Cleyne Hage, Southam Lane, Cleeve Hill, Cheltenham, Glos, GL52 3NY.*
Actual grid ref: SO968256
Views of Malverns, Cleeve Hill, Racecourse. 3 miles Cheltenham. Ideally situated walking, touring.
Tel: **01242 518569** Mrs Blankenspoor.
Fax no: 01242 238068
D: £18.00 **S:** £20.00.
Open: All Year
Beds: 1F 1D 1T 1S
Baths: 2 En 1 Pr 1 Sh
🛏 🄿 (8) ⅍ 🗆 🛉 🛒 🏬 ⅊ 🅥 🛡 ⅋

Cheltenham   14

National Grid Ref: SO9422

🍴 🍺 Apple Tree, Bell, Plough, High Roost, Royal Oak, Kings Arms, Rising Sun, Hewlett Arms, Flynns, Sherborne Inn, Bentley's

(3m) *Parkview, 4 Pittville Crescent, Cheltenham, Glos, GL52 2QZ.*
Actual grid ref: SO955237
Regency house in Cheltenham - nicest area. Cotswolds, Sudeley Castle, Stratford are nearby.
Grades: ETC 3 Diamond
Tel: **01242 575567** Mrs Sparrey.
D: £20.00-£25.00 **S:** £20.00-£25.00.
Open: All Year
Beds: 1F 1T 1S **Baths:** 2 En 2 Sh
🛏 🗆 🛉 🛒 🏬 🅥 🛡

(3m) *Central Hotel, 7-9 Portland Street, Cheltenham, Glos, GL52 2NZ.*
Grade II Listed building in town centre, one block from shops and Regent Arcade.
Grades: ETC 3 Diamond
Tel: **01242 582172** Mr Rouse.
D: £22.00-£28.50 **S:** £27.00-£37.00.
Open: All Year
Beds: 2F 3D 5T 4S
Baths: 6 En 2 Sh
🛏 🄿 (8) ⅍ 🗆 ✕ 🛒 🅥 ⅋

(3m) *Beaumont House Hotel, Shurdington Road, Cheltenham, Glos, GL53 0JE.*
Relaxed, friendly, peaceful, comfortable, totally non smoking. Four poster rooms. Garden.
Grades: ETC 4 Diamond, Sliver, AA 4 Diamond, RAC 4 Diamond
Tel: **01242 245986**
Fax no: 01242 520044
D: £30.00-£40.00 **S:** £42.00-£56.00.
Open: All Year (not Xmas/ New Year)
Beds: 1F 3T 10D 2S
Baths: 16 En
🛏 (10) 🄿 (16) ⅍ 🛒 🏬 🅥 ⅋

(3m) *Clun House, 4 The Oaks, Up Hatherley, Cheltenham, Glos, GL51 5TS.*
Spacious, modern, quiet house; lounge available, easy access M5.
Tel: **01242 523255** Mrs Hyde.
D: £16.00-£18.00 **S:** £16.00-£18.00.
Open: All Year (not Xmas)
Beds: 1D 2S
Baths: 1 Pr 1 Sh
🛏 (10) 🄿 (5) ⅍ 🗆 🛒 🏬 🅥

(1m) *Crossways Guest House, Oriel Place, 57 Bath Road, Cheltenham, Glos, GL53 7LH.*
Fine Regency house in the centre of Cheltenham.
Grades: ETC 3 Diamond
Tel: **01242 527683** Mr Lynch .
Fax no: 01242 577226
D: £22.00-£25.00 .
Open: All Year
Beds: 3F 1T 1D 1S
Baths: 3 En 1 Sh
🛏 ⅍ 🗆 🛉 🛒 🏬 🅥 🛡 ⅋

(3m) *Lonsdale House, Montpellier Drive, Cheltenham, Glos, GL50 1TX.*
Comfortable rooms in Regency house; easy walk into town centre.
Tel: **01242 232379** (also fax no)
Mr Mallinson.
D: £20.00-£24.00 **S:** £20.00-£30.00.
Open: All Year
Beds: 3F 2D 1T 4S
Baths: 3 En 2 Pr 2 Sh
🛏 🄿 (6) 🗆 🛉 🏬 🅥

(3m) *St Michaels Guest House, 4 Montpellier Drive, Cheltenham, Glos, GL50 1TX.*
Five minutes' walk from centre. Non smoking, parking, highly commended.
Tel: **01242 513587** (also fax no)
Mrs Perkin.
D: £20.00-£25.00 **S:** £27.00-£45.00.
Open: All Year
Beds: 1F 2D 1T
Baths: 3 En 1 Pr
🛏 🄿 (4) ⅍ 🗆 🛒 🏬 🅥 ⅋

(3m) *Strayleaves, 282 Gloucester Road, Cheltenham, Glos, GL51 7AG.*
Conveniently situated for the railway station and the town centre.
Tel: **01242 572303** (also fax no)
Mr Andrews.
D: £19.00-£22.50 **S:** £26.00-£30.00.
Open: All Year
Beds: 1F 1D 1T 1S
Baths: 4 En
🛏 🄿 🗆 🛉 ✕ 🛒 🏬 🛡

Charlton Kings   15

National Grid Ref: SO9620

🍴 🍺 Ryeworth Inn, Reservoir Inn

(On path 🚌) *Langett, London Road, Cheltenham, Glos, GL54 4HG.*
Actual grid ref: SO986198
On Cotswold Way, adjoining large woodland, super walks, large bungalow.
Tel: **01242 820192** (also fax no)
Mr Cox.
D: £18.00-£20.00 **S:** £20.00-£23.00.
Open: All Year (not Xmas)
Beds: 1D 1T **Baths:** 1 Sh
🛏 (5) 🄿 (10) 🗆 🛒 🏬 🅥 ⅋

D = Price range per person sharing in a double room

Birdlip   16

National Grid Ref: SO9214

🍴 🍺 Air Balloon

(0.25m) *Beechmount, Birdlip, Gloucester, GL4 8JH.*
Grades: ETC 3 Diamond
Tel: **01452 862262** (also fax no)
Mrs Carter.
D: £16.00-£21.00 **S:** £16.00-£32.00.
Open: All Year
Beds: 2F 2D 2T **Baths:** 2 En 2 Sh
🛏 (7) ⅍ 🗆 🛉 ✕ 🛒 🏬 🅥 ⅋
Warm welcome in family-run guest house. Personal attention. Ideal centre for walking, touring.

Cranham   17

National Grid Ref: SO8913

🍴 🍺 Black Horse Inn

(1m 🚌) *Pound Cottage, Cranham, Gloucester, GL4 8HP.*
Actual grid ref: SO897130
Cotswold cottage in quiet village surrounded by countryside and woodlands.
Tel: **01452 812581** Ms Dann.
Fax no: 01452 814380
D: £20.00-£20.00 **S:** £25.00-£25.00.
Open: All Year (not Xmas)
Beds: 1D 1T **Baths:** 1 Sh
🛏 (2) 🄿 (1) ⅍ 🛉 🛒 🏬 🅥 🛡 ⅋

Duntisbourne Abbots   18

National Grid Ref: SO9608

🍴 🍺 Five Mile House, Highwayman

(4.25m 🚌) *Dixs Barn, Duntisbourne Abbots, Cirencester, Glos, GL7 7JN.*
Actual grid ref: SO979080
Converted barn on family run farm on edge of village with magnificent views.
Tel: **01285 821249** Mrs Wilcox.
D: £20.00-£25.00 **S:** £25.00-£30.00.
Open: All Year
Beds: 1D 1T **Baths:** 1 En 1 Pr
🛏 (8) ⅍ 🗆 🛉 ✕ 🛒 🏬 🅥 🛡 ⅋

Brookthorpe   19

National Grid Ref: SO8312

🍴 🍺 Four Mile House

(2m) *Brookthorpe Lodge, Stroud Rd, Brookthorpe, Gloucester, GL4 0UQ.*
Actual grid ref: SO834128
Grades: ETC 3 Diamond
Tel: **01452 812645** Mr Bailey.
D: £20.00-£27.50 **S:** £31.00-£33.00.
Open: All Year **Beds:** 2F 2D 2T 3S
Baths: 6 En 2 Pr 1 Sh
🛏 🄿 (15) 🗆 🛉 ✕ 🛒 🏬 ⅊ 🅥 ⅋
Licensed family-run three storey Georgian house in lovely countryside at foot of Cotswold escarpment, 4 miles from Gloucester. Close to ski slope, horse riding and golfing. Good walking country - ideal base for Cotswolds, Gloucester docks and cathedral. Separate smoking area.

Painswick 20

National Grid Ref: SO8609

¶ᛏ Black Horse, Royal Oak, Gither Bar, Falcon Inn, Edgemoor Inn

(On path) *Thorne, Friday Street, Painswick, Stroud, Glos,* GL6 6QJ.
Tudor merchants house with market hall pillars 'in situ' on Cotswolds Way.
Tel: **01452 812476** Mrs Blatchley.
D: £23.00-£25.00 **S:** £25.00-£25.00.
Open: Easter to Nov
Beds: 2T
Baths: 2 Pr
🅿 ☐ 🛋 Ⅲ V ∥

(On path 🚍) *Castle Lodge, The Beacon, Painswick, Stroud, Glos,* GL6 6TU.
Actual grid ref: SO877127
Set high in woodland, adjacent golf. Trout fishing, riding nearby.
Grades: ETC 4 Diamond, Silver
Tel: **01452 813603** (also fax no)
Mrs Cooke.
D: £26.00-£30.00 **S:** £30.00-£30.00.
Open: All Year
Beds: 1F 1D 1T
Baths: All En
🏵 🅿 ⅍ ☐ ⁙ ☐ 🛋 Ⅲ V ∥

(0.25m) *Wheatleys, Cotswold Mead, Painswick, Stroud, Glos,* GL6 6XB.
Actual grid ref: SO862092
Grades: ETC 5 Diamond, Gold
Tel: **01452 812167** Mrs Burgess.
Fax no: 01452 814270
D: £25.00 **S:** £35.00.
Open: All Year (not Xmas)
Beds: 1D 1T **Baths:** 2 En
🏵 (10) 🅿 (4) ⅍ ☐ 🛋 Ⅲ V
Set in a beautiful Cotswold village, Wheatley's offers a relaxing base to unwind. A particularly well-appointed suite with connecting sitting room. Guests have full use of the pleasant secluded garden (with croquet), and breakfast can be served on the terrace.

(0.25m 🚍) *Upper Doreys Mill, Edge, Painswick, Stroud, Glos,* GL6 6NF.
C18th cloth mill by stream. Old beams and log fires.
Tel: **01452 812459** Mrs Marden.
D: £22.00-£25.00 .
Open: All Year
Beds: 2D 1T **Baths:** 3 En
🏵 🅿 (4) ⅍ ☐ 🛋 V ∥

All rooms full and nowhere else to stay? Ask the owner if there's anywhere nearby

Edge 21

National Grid Ref: SO8509

¶ᛏ Edgemoor Inn

(0.5m 🚍) *Wild Acre, Back Edge Lane, Edge, Stroud, Glos,* GL6 6PE.
Actual grid ref: SO849099
Rural location overlooking Painswick. Ideal base for touring the Cotswolds.
Grades: ETC 3 Diamond
Tel: **01452 813077** Mrs Sanders.
D: £18.00-£20.00 **S:** £20.00-£22.00.
Open: Easter to Oct
Beds: 1D 1T **Baths:** 1 En 1 Sh
🏵 (3) 🅿 (3) ⅍ ☐ ⁙ 🛋 Ⅲ & V ∥

Haresfield 22

National Grid Ref: SO8110

¶ᛏ Beacon Hotel

(1m 🚍) *Lower Green Farmhouse, Haresfield, Stonehouse, Glos,* GL10 3DS.
Actual grid ref: SO811097
C18th Listed Cotswold stone farmhouse with countryside views.
Tel: **01452 728264** (also fax no)
Mrs Reed.
D: £18.50-£18.50 **S:** £20.00-£20.00.
Open: All Year (not Xmas/New Year)
Beds: 1F 1T **Baths:** 2 Sh
🏵 🅿 (6) ☐ ⁙ 🛋 Ⅲ ∥

Pitchcombe 23

National Grid Ref: SO8508

¶ᛏ Edgemoor Inn

(1m 🚍) *Gable End, Pitchcombe, Stroud, Glos,* GL6 6LN.
C16th-17th house commands an elevated position overlooking Painswick Valley.
Grades: ETC 3 Diamond
Tel: **01452 812166** Mrs Partridge.
Fax no: 01452 812719
D: £22.50-£22.50 **S:** £30.00-£30.00.
Open: All Year (not Xmas/New Year)
Beds: 2D **Baths:** 2 En
🏵 (5) 🅿 (4) 🛋 Ⅲ V ∥

Stonehouse 24

National Grid Ref: SO8005

¶ᛏ Beacon Hotel, Ryford Lodge

(0.5m 🚍) *Tiled House Farm, Oxlynch, Stonehouse, Glos,* GL10 3DF
Grades: ETC 4 Diamond
Tel: **01453 822363** Mrs Jeffrey.
D: £19.00-£21.00 **S:** £18.00-£20.00.
Open: All Year (not Xmas)
Beds: 1D 1T 1S **Baths:** 1 Pr 1 Sh
🏵 (10) 🅿 (2) ⅍ ☐ 🛋 Ⅲ V ∥
C16th black and white half-timbered farmhouse, with oak beams and Inglewood fireplace. Large garden. This a working Dairy Farm with pedigree Friesian cattle, situated at the edge of Cotswolds and towards Severn vale. close to Slimbridge, Painswick, Berkeley Castle.

(On path 🚍) *Merton Lodge, 8 Ebley Road, Stonehouse, Glos,* GL10 2LQ.
Off road, large beautiful house and garden, lovely views, parking.
Grades: ETC 2 Diamond
Tel: **01453 822018** Mrs Hodge.
D: £19.00-£21.00 **S:** £19.00-£21.00.
Open: All Year (not Xmas/New Year)
Beds: 3D
Baths: 1 En 1 Sh
🏵 🅿 ⅍ ☐ ⁙ 🛋 Ⅲ ∥

Stroud 25

National Grid Ref: SO8405

¶ᛏ Tipputs Inn, Imperial Hotel, Downfield Hotel, Clothiers' Arms, Vine Tree, British Oak

(2m 🚍) *The Downfield Hotel, Cainscross Road, Stroud, Glos,* GL5 4HN.
Stunning views of the hills and valleys. An unforgettable holiday.
Grades: ETC 3 Diamond,
AA 3 Diamond, RAC 3 Diamond
Tel: **01453 764496**
Fax no: 01453 753150
D: £20.00-£27.00 **S:** £30.00-£45.00.
Open: All Year
Beds: 2F 9D 6T 4S
Baths: 11 En 10 Sh
🏵 🅿 (25) ⅍ ☐ ⁙ ✕ 🛋 Ⅲ V ∥

(3m 🚍) *Clothiers Arms, Bath Road, Stroud, Glos,* GL5 3JJ.
Grades: ETC 3 Diamond
Tel: **01453 763801** Mrs Close.
Fax no: 01453 757161
D: £20.00-£33.00 **S:** £23.00-£35.00.
Open: All Year
Beds: 7F 3D 2T
Baths: 6 En 1 Pr
🏵 🅿 (50) ⅍ ☐ ⁙ ✕ 🛋 Ⅲ V ∥
The Clothiers Arms is within walking distance of Stroud town centre, trains and bus station. Ideal location for Bath, Cheltenham, Cirencester. We have large beer garden, children's play area, 50 seater restaurant and ample car parking facilities.

(4m) *Cairngall Guest House, 65 Bisley Old Road, Stroud, Glos,* GL5 1NF.
Large elegant Victorian Listed house, elevated position with superb views.
Tel: **01453 766689**
Mr & Mrs Fabb.
D: £23.00-£25.00 **S:** £23.00-£25.00.
Open: All Year (not Xmas)
Beds: 2D 1T 1S
Baths: 2 Sh
🏵 (10) 🅿 (6) ⅍ ☐ 🛋 Ⅲ V

D = Price range per person sharing in a double room

(0.5m 🚐) *Court Farm, Randwick,
Stroud, Glos, GL6 6HH.*
Actual grid ref: SO8307
C17th beamed Cotswold farm-
house, large garden, abundant
wildlife, good views.
Tel: **01453 764210** Mr Taylor.
D: £19.00-£20.00 **S:** £19.00-£20.00.
Open: All Year (not Xmas)
Beds: 2F 1T **Baths:** 2 En 1 Sh
🛏 �P (6) ⊬⏢🛏✗🐾🖿💷🗤🛇♦

Kings Stanley   26

National Grid Ref: SO8103

🍴 ⬛ Kings Head

(0.25m 🚐) *Old Chapel House,
Broad Street, Kings Stanley,
Stonehouse, Glos, GL10 3PN.*
Actual grid ref: SO813033
Converted chapel on Cotswold
Way overlooking escarpment.
Tel: **01453 826289**
Mrs Richards Hanna.
D: £21.50-£21.50 **S:** £20.00-£20.00.
Open: All Year (not Xmas)
Beds: 1F 1D 2T 1S
Baths: 2 En 1 Sh
🛏 (5) �P (4) ⏢✗🐾🖿💷🗤♦

(0.25m) *Nurashell, Bath Road,
Kings Stanley, Stonehouse, Glos,
GL10 3JG.*
Actual grid ref: SO811034
Victorian house. Village centre.
Shops and pubs close. Station 2
miles. Bus route.
Tel: **01453 823642** Mrs Rollins.
D: £18.00 **S:** £18.00.
Open: All Year
Beds: 1D 1T
Baths: 1 Sh
🛏 �P ⊬⏢🛏🐾🖿💷🗤♦

Nailsworth   27

National Grid Ref: ST8499

🍴 ⬛ Rose & Crown, Egypt Mill, The George

(2m) *The Vicarage, Nailsworth,
Stroud, Glos, GL6 0BS.*
Large, comfortable, quiet Victorian
vicarage. Beautiful garden. Good
breakfast.
Tel: **01453 832181** Mrs Strong.
D: £23.00-£23.00 **S:** £22.00.
Open: All Year
Beds: 1T 3S
Baths: 1 Pr 1 Sh
🛏 (2) �P (4) ⊬⏢🛏🐾🖿💷🗤♦

(2m 🚐) *Aaron Farm, Nympsfield
Road, Nailsworth, Stroud, Glos,
GL6 0ET.*
Actual grid ref: SO837001
Warm and friendly, central for
walking and touring Cotswolds and
Gloucestershire.
Tel: **01453 833598** (also fax no)
Mrs Mulligan.
D: £20.00-£21.00 **S:** £28.00-£30.00.
Open: All Year
Beds: 1D 2T **Baths:** 3 En
🛏 �P (5) ⊬⏢🛏🐾✗🖿💷🗤🛇♦

Uley   28

National Grid Ref: ST7898

🍴 ⬛ Old Crown, Rose & Crown

(0.25m 🚐) *Hill House, Crawley
Hill, Uley, Dursley, Glos, GL11 5BH.*
Very warm welcome. Cotswold
stone house, beautiful views, quiet
location.
Tel: **01453 860267**
Mr & Mrs Kent.
D: £18.50-£22.00 **S:** £17.00-£30.00.
Open: All Year (not Xmas)
Beds: 1F 1D 1T 1S
Baths: 2 En 1 Sh
🛏 �P (5) ⊬⏢✗🖿💷🗤🛇♦

Slimbridge   29

National Grid Ref: SO7303

(▲ 4m) *Slimbridge Youth Hostel,
Shepherd's Patch, Slimbridge,
Gloucester, GL2 7BP.*
Actual grid ref: ST730043
Tel: **01453 890275**
Under 18: £6.90 **Adults:** £10.00
Self-catering facilities, Showers,
Shop, Laundry facilities, Lounge,
Games room, Drying room, Cycle
store, Parking, Evening meal at
7.00pm, No smoking, Kitchen
facilities, Breakfast available,
Credit cards accepted
*Purpose-built youth hostel, with its
own pond & wildfowl collection,
next to the Sharpness Canal and
Sir Peter Scott's famous wildfowl
reserve.*

Berkeley   30

National Grid Ref: ST6899

🍴 ⬛ Black Horse North Nibley, Stage Coach

(3.5m 🚐) *Pickwick Farm,
Berkeley, Glos, GL13 9EU.*
Ensuite annexe room overlooks
large garden, views to Cotswolds,
golf nearby.
Grades: ETC 3 Diamond
Tel: **01453 810241** Mrs Jordan.
D: £18.00-£20.00 **S:** £18.00-£19.00.
Open: All Year (not Xmas)
Beds: 1F 1D 1T
Baths: 1 En 1 Sh
🛏 (2) �P (4) ⊬⏢🛏🖿💷🗤♦

🚐 **sign means that,**
given due notice,
owners will pick you
up from the path
and drop you off *with-*
in reason.

Dursley   31

National Grid Ref: ST7698

🍴 ⬛ Old Bell

(0.25m) *Drakestone House,
Stinchcombe, Dursley, Glos,
GL11 6AS.*
Tel: **01453 542140** (also fax no)
Mr & Mrs St John Mildmay.
D: £31.50-£36.50 **S:** £36.50-£36.50.
Open: Feb to Nov
Beds: 1D 2T
Baths: 1 Pr 1 Sh
🛏 �P (4) ⊬⏢🛏🐾🖿💷🗤🛇♦
Drakestone is charming. An Arts
and Crafts building with a large
garden from the same period.
Romantic and restful, the house sits
on a wooded hillside with
magnificent views. Nearby is
Berkeley Castle, Slimbridge, Bath,
Bristol and Cheltenham.

(0.25m) *Stanthill House, Uley
Road, Dursley, Glos, GL11 4PF.*
Actual grid ref: ST759979
Lovely Georgian town house;
spacious rooms, comfortable beds,
good food.
Tel: **01453 549037** Liz Gresko.
D: £21.00-£23.50 **S:** £21.00-£23.50.
Open: All Year
Beds: 2D 1T
Baths: 2 En 1 Pr
🛏 �P ⊬⏢🛏🐾🖿🗤♦

North Nibley   32

National Grid Ref: ST7395

🍴 ⬛ Black Horse

(On path) *Nibley House, North
Nibley, Dursley, Glos, GL11 6DL.*
Actual grid ref: ST736958
Magnificent Georgian manor
house, centrepiece of 200-acre
farm.
Tel: **01453 543108**
Mrs Eley.
D: £22.00-£25.00 **S:** £22.00-£25.00.
Open: All Year (not Xmas)
Beds: 1F 1D 1T
Baths: 2 En 1 Pr
🛏 �P (12) ⊬⏢🛏✗🖿💷🗤🛇♦

Wotton-under-Edge   33

National Grid Ref: ST7692

🍴 ⬛ Royal Oak

(On path) *Wotton Guest House,
31a Long Street, Wotton-under-
Edge, Glos, GL12 7BX.*
C17th Manor house, superb food
in adjoining coffee shop.
Tel: **01453 843158**
Mrs Nixon.
Fax no: 01453 842410
D: £24.00-£24.00
S: £30.00-£30.00.
Open: All Year
Beds: 1F 2D 2T 2S
Baths: 7 En
🛏 �P (12) ⊬⏢🛏🐾🖿💷🗤🛇♦

(0.25m) *The Ridings, Wotton-under-Edge, Glos, GL12 7PT.*
Situated on edge of Cotswolds, panoramic views, golf courses opposite.
Tel: **01453 842128** (also fax no)
Ms Poole.
D: £18.00-£18.00
S: £18.00-£18.00.
Open: All Year (not Xmas)
Beds: 3D
Baths: 2 Pr

(0.25m 🚗) *Bridge Farm, Kilcott, Wotton-under-Edge, Gloucestershire, GL12 7RL.*
Actual grid ref: ST787891
Listed C17th streamside farmhouse set in secluded Cotswold Valley.
Tel: **01454 238254**
Mr & Mrs Watchman.
D: £20.00-£22.00
S: £22.00-£25.00.
Open: All Year (not Xmas)
Beds: 2D 1T 1S
Baths: 1 Pr 1 Sh
🅿 (6) ⅍ 🖵 🕇 🗶 🛓 🛏 🎟 🛡 ⌀

Charfield   34

National Grid Ref: ST7191

🍴 🍺 Pear Tree, Railway Tavern

(2m 🚗) *Falcon Cottage, 15 Station Road, Charfield, Wotton-under-Edge, Glos, GL12 8SY.*
Convenient for M5, Bath, Bristol, Cheltenham, Cotswolds, Cotswold Way.
Grades: ETC 4 Diamond
Tel: **01453 843528** Mrs Haddrell.
D: £20.00-£20.00 **S:** £20.00-£20.00.
Open: All Year (not Xmas)
Beds: 2T
Baths: 1 Sh
🐾 🅿 (2) ⅍ 🖵 🛓 🛏 🎟 🛡 ⌀

Hawkesbury   35

National Grid Ref: ST7686

(0.25m 🚗) *Ivy Cottage, Inglestone Common, Hawkesbury, Badminton, GL9 1BX.*
Comfortable cottage surrounded by ancient woodland on edge of Cotswolds.
Tel: **01454 294237** Mrs Canner.
D: £19.00-£20.00 **S:** £22.00-£25.00.
Open: All Year (not Xmas/New Year)
Beds: 1F 1D 1T 1S
Baths: 2 Sh
🐾 🅿 (3) ⅍ 🖵 🕇 🗶 🛓 🛏 ⅊ 🛡 ⌀

Old Sodbury   36

National Grid Ref: ST7581

🍴 🍺 Dog Inn, The Bell, Old Home

(On path) *Dornden Guest House, Church Lane, Old Sodbury, Bristol, BS37 6NB.*
Actual grid ref: ST756818
Former vicarage, quietly situated, views to Welsh hills.
Grades: ETC 4 Diamond
Tel: **01454 313325** Mrs Paz.
Fax no: 01454 312263
D: £27.00-£30.00 **S:** £25.00-£40.00.
Open: All Year (not Xmas)
Beds: 5F 2T 2S
Baths: 6 En 2 Sh
🐾 🅿 (15) ⅍ 🖵 🕇 🗶 🛓 🛏 🎟 🛡 ⌀

(On path 🚗) *1 The Green, Old Sodbury, Bristol, BS37 6LY.*
Actual grid ref: ST753816
Close M4 M5 ideal location for Cotswold Way, Bath and Bristol.
Tel: **01454 314688**
Mr & Mrs Rees.
D: £22.00-£26.00 **S:** £22.00-£26.00.
Open: All Year (not Xmas)
Beds: 2D 1T 3S **Baths:** 1 En 2 Sh
🅿 (4) ⅍ 🖵 🛓 🛏 🎟 🛡 ⌀

Tormarton   37

National Grid Ref: ST7678

🍴 🍺 The Portcullis

(0.25m) *Chestnut Farm, Tormarton, Badminton, GL9 1HS.*
Small Georgian farmhouse.
Tel: **01454 218563** (also fax no)
Ms Cadei.
D: £30.00-£40.00 **S:** £30.00-£40.00.
Open: All Year
Beds: 1F 4D 2T
Baths: 7 Pr
🐾 🅿 (8) 🖵 🕇 🗶 🛓 🛏 🎟 🛡 ⌀

(On path) *The Portcullis, Tormarton, Badminton, GL9 1HZ.*
Traditional ivy-clad inn and restaurant in pretty Cotswold village.
Tel: **01454 218263**
Fax no: 01454 218094
D: £20.00-£25.00 **S:** £28.00-£30.00.
Open: All Year (not Xmas)
Beds: 1F 2D 4T **Baths:** 7 En
🐾 🅿 (6) 🖵 🗶 🛓 🛏 🎟 🛡 ⌀

Wick   38

National Grid Ref: ST7072

🍴 🍺 Rose & Crown

(1m) *Toghill House Farm, Toghill, Wick, Bristol, BS15 5RT.*
Actual grid ref: ST725730
Warm cosy farmhouse, formally resting house for monks (4 miles Bath).
Tel: **01225 891261** Mrs Bishop.
D: £23.00-£25.00 **S:** £29.00-£37.00.
Open: All Year
Beds: 2F 6D 3T **Baths:** 8 Pr
🐾 🅿 (20) ⅍ 🖵 🕇 🛓 🛏 ⅊ 🛡 ⌀

Marshfield   39

National Grid Ref: ST7773

🍴 🍺 Catherine Wheel

(3m 🚗) *Knowle Hill Farm, Beeks Lane, Marshfield, Chippenham, Wilts, SN14 8BB.*
Actual grid ref: ST777735
Farmhouse in beautiful, peaceful surroundings. 8 miles Bath, 5 miles M4 (J18).
Tel: **01225 891503** Mrs Bond.
D: £18.00-£20.00 **S:** £18.00-£20.00.
Open: All Year (not Xmas)
Beds: 1F 1D 1T
Baths: 1 En 1 Sh
🐾 🅿 (3) 🖵 🕇 🗶 🛓 🛏 🎟 🛡 ⌀

Bath   40

National Grid Ref: ST7464

🍴 🍺 Royal Oak, Dolphin, Wheelwrights Arms, Old Crown, Huntsman, George, Devonshire Arms, Sportsman, Waldergrave Arms, Bear, Park Tavern, Rose & Crown, Weston Walk, Boathouse, Lambridge Harvester, Green Park Station, Saracen's Head, Hop Pole

(🔺 On path) *Bath Youth Hostel, Bathwick Hill, Bath, Somerset, BA2 6JZ.*
Actual grid ref: ST766644
Tel: **01225 465674**
Under 18: £7.75 **Adults:** £11.00
Self-catering facilities, Television, Showers, Shop, Laundry facilities, Lounge, Drying room, Security lockers, Cycle store, Evening meal at 6.00 to 8.00pm, Kitchen facilities, Breakfast available, Credit cards accepted
Handsome Italianate mansion, set in beautiful, secluded gardens, with views of historic city and surrounding hills.

(0.5m) *Bailbrook Lodge, 35-37 London Road West, Bath, BA1 7HZ.*
Grades: ETC 3 Diamond, AA 3 Diamond
Tel: **01225 859090** Mrs Sexton.
Fax no: 01225 852299
D: £30.00-£40.00 **S:** £39.00-£50.00.
Open: All Year
Beds: 4F 4D 4T
Baths: 12 En
🐾 🅿 (14) ⅍ 🖵 🗶 🛓 🛏 🎟 🛡 ⌀
A warm welcome is assured at Bailbrook Lodge, an imposing Georgian House set it its own gardens. The elegant period bedrooms (some four posters) offer ensuite facilities, TV and hospitality trays. Private parking. 1.5 miles from Bath centre. Close to M4.

Pay B&Bs by cash or cheque and be prepared to pay up front.

All paths are popular: you are well-advised to book ahead

(0.5m 🚗) *Sarnia, 19 Combe Park, Weston, Bath, BA1 3NR.*
Actual grid ref: ST730656
Grades: AA 4 Diamond
Tel: **01225 424159**
Mr & Mrs Fradley.
Fax no: 01225 337689
D: £25.00-£32.50 **S:** £30.00-£40.00.
Open: All Year (not Xmas/New Year)
Beds: 1F 1D 1T
Baths: 2 En 1 Pr
🛇 🅿 (3) ⊬ ☐ 🐾 🖿 Ⅶ 🛇 ⚡
Superb bed & breakfast in large Victorian home, easy reach of town centre. Spacious bedrooms, private facilities, newly decorated, attractively furnished. Breakfast in sunny dining room, English, Continental and vegetarian menus, home made jams, marmalades, comfortable lounge, secluded garden, private parking & children welcome.

(0.5m) *Dene Villa, 5 Newbridge Hill, Bath, BA1 3PW.*
Victorian family-run guest house, a warm welcome is assured.
Tel: **01225 427676**
Mrs Surry.
Fax no: 01225 482684
D: £20.00-£22.50 **S:** £19.00-£22.00.
Open: All Year
Beds: 1F 1D 1T 1S
Baths: 3 En
🛇 (3) 🅿 (4) ☐ 🐾 🖿 Ⅶ ⚡

(1.25m 🚗) *Koryu B&B, 7 Pulteney Gardens, Bath, Somerset, BA2 4HG.*
Tel: **01225 337642** (also fax no)
Mrs Shimizu.
D: £22.00-£25.00 **S:** £22.00-£25.00.
Open: All Year
Beds: 1F 2D 2T 2S
Baths: 5 En 2 Sh
🛇 🅿 (2) ⊬ ☐ ✕ 🐾 🖿 Ⅶ
Completely renovated Victorian home run by a young Japanese lady, extremely clean, delicious breakfasts with wide menu, beautiful linens; a bright, cheerful and welcoming house. Abbey and Roman baths 5 mins, gorgeous Kennet and Avon canal 2 mins.

(0.25m 🚗) *Wentworth House Hotel, 106 Bloomfield Road, Bath, BA2 2AP.*
Grades: AA 2 Star,
RAC 4 Diamond Sparkling
Tel: **01225 339193**
Mrs Boyle.
Fax no: 01225 310460
D: £25.00-£47.50 **S:** £40.00-£60.00.
Open: All Year
Beds: 2F 12D 2T 2S
Baths: 17 En 1 Pr
🛇 (5) 🅿 (20) ☐ 🐾 ✕ 🐾 🖿 Ⅶ 🛇 ⚡
A Victorian mansion 15 minutes' walk from the city. Quiet location with large garden and car park. Heated swimming pool, licensed restaurant and cocktail bar. Golf and walks nearby. Lovely rooms, some with four-poster beds and conservatories.

(0.5m 🚗) *Marlborough House, 1 Marlborough Lane, Bath, BA1 2NQ.*
Grades: ETC 4 Diamond, AA 4 Diamond
Tel: **01225 318175** Dunlop.
Fax no: 01225 466127
D: £32.50-£47.50 **S:** £45.00-£75.00.
Open: All Year
Beds: 2F 1T 3D 1S
Baths: 7 En
🛇 🅿 ⊬ ☐ 🐾 ✕ 🐾 🖿 Ⅶ 🛇 ⚡
An enchanting Victorian small hotel in the heart of Georgian Bath, exquisitely furnished, but run in a friendly and informal style. Specialising in organic vegetarian world cuisine. Our central location, gorgeous rooms, and unique menu make Marlborough House truly special.

(0.5m) *3 Thomas Street, Walcot, Bath, Somerset, BA1 5NW.*
Charming Georgian house convenient to all city amenities and shops.
Grades: ETC 3 Diamond
Tel: **01225 789540** Ms Saunders.
D: £20.00-£22.50 **S:** £20.00-£22.50.
Open: All Year (not Xmas)
Beds: 2T
Baths: 1 En 1 Sh
⊬ ☐ 🐾 🖿 Ⅶ

(0.5m) *Cranleigh, 159 Newbridge Hill, Bath, N E Somerset, BA1 3PX.*
Grades: AA 4 Diamonds
Tel: **01225 310197** Mr Poole.
Fax no: 01225 423143
D: £33.00-£40.00 **S:** £45.00-£55.00.
Open: All Year (not Xmas)
Beds: 3F 2T 4D
Baths: 8 En
🛇 (5) 🅿 (5) ⊬ ☐ 🐾 🖿 Ⅶ ⚡
Charming Victorian house a short distance from the city centre. Spacious bedrooms, most with country views, offer comfort and quality. Imaginative breakfasts served in elegant dining room include fresh fruit salad and scrambled eggs with smoked salmon.

(0.5m) *Blairgowrie House, 55 Wellsway, Bath, BA2 4RT.*
Fine late Victorian Residence operating as a privately owned family-run guest house.
Grades: AA 4 Diamond
Tel: **01225 332266** Mr Roberts.
Fax no: 01225 484535
D: £27.50-£30.00 .
Open: All Year
Beds: 1T 2D
Baths: 2 En 1 Pr
🛇 🅿 ⊬ ☐ 🐾 🖿 Ⅶ ⚡

Please take muddy boots off before entering premises

(0.5m) *The Old Red House, 37 Newbridge Road, Bath, BA1 3HE.*
A romantic Victorian gingerbread house with stained glass windows, comfortable bedrooms, superbly cooked breakfasts.
Grades: AA 3 Diamond
Tel: **01225 330464**
Fax no: 01225 331661
D: £22.00-£33.00
S: £30.00-£45.00.
Open: Mar to Dec
Beds: 1F 4D 1T 1S
Baths: 3 En 1 Pr 1 Sh
🛇 (4) 🅿 (4) ⊬ ☐ 🐾 🖿 Ⅶ

(1m) *The Albany Guest House, 24 Crescent Gardens, Bath, BA1 2NB.*
Grades: ETC 4 Diamond, Silver
Tel: **01225 313339**
Mrs Wotley.
D: £17.00-£25.00
S: £22.00-£25.00
Open: All Year (not Xmas/New Year)
Beds: 2D 1T 2S
Baths: 1 En 1 Sh
🛇 (5) 🅿 (3) ⊬ ☐ 🐾 🖿 Ⅶ
Jan & Bryan assure you of a warm welcome to their Victorian home. Only five minutes walk to the city centre - Roman Baths, Abbey, Royal Crescent etc. Delicious English or vegetarian breakfast. Imaginatively decorated rooms and first class service.

(0.5m 🚗) *Wellsway Guest House, 51 Wellsway, Bath, BA2 4RS.*
Edwardian house near Alexandra Park. Easy walks to city centre.
Grades: ETC 2 Diamond
Tel: **01225 423434**
Mrs Strong.
D: £18.00-£20.00 **S:** £20.00-£20.00.
Open: All Year
Beds: 1F 1D 1T 1S
Baths: 4 Sh
🛇 🅿 (4) ☐ 🐾 🖿 ⚡

(0.75m) *Flaxley Villa, 9 Newbridge Hill, Bath, BA1 3PW.*
Comfortable Victorian house near Royal Crescent. 15 minute walk to centre.
Grades: ETC 3 Diamond
Tel: **01225 313237**
Mrs Cooper.
D: £20.00-£25.00 **S:** £18.00-£36.00.
Open: All Year
Beds: 3D 1T 1S **Baths:** 3 En
🛇 🅿 (5) ☐ 🐾 🖿 Ⅶ

(On path) *14 Raby Place, Bathwick Hill, Bath, Somerset, BA2 4EH.*
Charming Georgian terraced house with beautiful interior rooms.
Grades: ETC 4 Diamond
Tel: **01225 465120**
Mrs Guy.
Fax no: 01225 465283
D: £22.50-£25.00 **S:** £25.00-£35.00.
Open: All Year
Beds: 1F 2D 1T 1S
Baths: 3 En 2 Pr
🛇 ⊬ ☐ 🐾 🖿 Ⅶ ⚡

(0.5m 🐾) *Forres House, 172 Newbridge Road, Bath, BA1 3LE.*
A warm welcome, comfortable bed and big breakfast awaits you.
Grades: ETC 3 Diamond
Tel: 01225 427698 Jones.
D: £20.00-£25.00 **S:** £30.00-£35.00.
Open: All Year
Beds: 2F 1T 2D
Baths: 5 En
🛇 🅿 (5) ⊬ 🗆 🏃 🏠 Ⅲ. Ⅵ

(0.5m) *Cherry Tree Villa, 7 Newbridge Hill, Bath, Somerset, BA1 3PW.*
Small friendly Victorian home 1 mile from city centre.
Grades: ETC 3 Diamond
Tel: 01225 331671 Ms Goddard.
D: £18.00-£24.00 **S:** £20.00-£30.00.
Open: All Year (not Xmas/New Year)
Beds: 1F 1D 1S
Baths: 1 Sh
🛇 (4) 🅿 🗆 🏃 Ⅲ. Ⅵ ✦

(On path) *No 2 Crescent Gardens, Upper Bristol Road, Bath, BA1 2NA.*
Beautiful B&B in the heart of Bath. Warm welcome.
Grades: ETC 4 Diamond
Tel: 01225 331186 Mr Bez.
D: £19.00-£25.00 **S:** £19.00-£25.00.
Open: All Year (not Xmas/New Year)
Beds: 1F 3T 3D
Baths: 3 En 1 Sh
⊬ 🗆 🏃 Ⅲ. Ⅵ

(0.5m) *Grove Lodge, 11 Lambridge , Bath, BA1 6BJ.*
Elegant, Georgian villa, large rooms with views.
Tel: 01225 310860 Miles.
Fax no: 01225 429630
D: £25.00-£30.00 **S:** £30.00-£35.00.
Open: All Year (not Xmas/New Year)
Beds: 1F 1T 2D 1S
Baths: 3 Pr
🛇 (6) ⊬ 🗆 🏃 Ⅲ. Ⅵ ▮

(0.25m) *Ashley House, 8 Pulteney Gardens, Bath, BA2 4HG.*
Actual grid ref: ST757646
Comfortable Victorian house level walk to attractions/ stations.
Grades: ETC 3 Diamond
Tel: 01225 425027 Mrs Pharo.
D: £23.00-£33.00 **S:** £25.00-£30.00.
Open: All Year
Beds: 1F 4D 1T 1S
Baths: 5 Pr 2 Sh
🛇 ⊬ 🗆 🏃 Ⅲ. Ⅵ ▮

(0.5m 🐾) *Westerlea, 87 Greenway Lane, Bath, BA2 4LN.*
Georgian style house, large gardens, friendly, ensuite accommodation, cars garaged.
Grades: ETC 4 Diamond
Tel: 01225 311543 (also fax no)
D: £27.50-£37.50 **S:** £45.00-£65.00.
Open: All Year (not Xmas)
Beds: 2D
Baths: 2 En
🛇 (12) 🅿 (2) ⊬ 🗆 🏠 🏃 Ⅲ. Ⅵ ✦

(0.5m) *Georgian Guest House, 34 Henrietta Street, Bath, BA2 6LR.*
Situated just 2 mins' walk to city centre in a peaceful location.
Grades: ETC 3 Diamond
Tel: 01225 424103 Mr Kingwell.
Fax no: 01225 425279
D: £30.00-£35.00 **S:** £30.00-£50.00.
Open: All Year (not Xmas)
Beds: 7D 2T 2S
Baths: 7 En 1 Sh
🛇 ⊬ 🗆 🏃 Ⅲ. Ⅵ

(0.25m) *The Terrace Guest House, 3 Pulteney Terrace, Bath, BA2 4HJ.*
Mid-terrace house, 7 minutes from city centre and railway station.
Tel: 01225 316578
Mrs Gould.
D: £16.00-£17.50 **S:** £18.00-£20.00.
Open: All Year (not Xmas)
Beds: 1D 1T
Baths: 1 Sh
🛇 (6) 🗆 🏃 Ⅲ. Ⅵ ✦

(0.5m) *Joanna House, 5 Pulteney Avenue, Bath, BA2 4HH.*
City centre Victorian house near railway, Kennet and Avon canal.
Tel: 01225 335246 Mr House.
D: £16.00-£19.00 **S:** £15.00-£18.00.
Open: All Year
Beds: 1F 1D 1T 1S
🛇 ⊬ 🗆 🏃 Ⅲ. Ⅵ

(0.5m 🐾) *Brinsley Sheridan Guest House, 95 Wellsway, Bearflat, Bath, BA2 4RU.*
Lovely friendly guest house only short walk from city centre.
Tel: 01225 429562
Fax no: 01225 429616
D: £17.50-£25.00
S: £17.50-£30.00.
Open: All Year
Beds: 1F 2D 1T
Baths: 1 En 1 Pr 2 Sh
🛇 ⊬ 🗆 🏃 Ⅲ. Ⅵ

(0.75m 🐾) *Kinlet Guest House, 99 Wellsway, Bath, BA2 4RA.*
Actual grid ref: ST745636
Home from home. Friendly, comfortable, easy walk into the city.
Tel: 01225 420268 (also fax no)
Mrs Bennett.
D: £19.00-£20.00
S: £22.00-£27.00.
Open: All Year
Beds: 1F 1D 1S
Baths: 1 Sh
🛇 ⊬ 🗆 🏃 Ⅲ. Ⅵ ▮ ✦

(0.5m 🐾) *Cairngorm, 3 Gloucester Road, Lower Swainswick, Bath, BA1 7BH.*
Charming detached home with beautiful views over city and countryside.
Tel: 01225 429004
Mrs Biggs.
D: £16.50-£20.00
S: £18.00.
Open: All Year (not Xmas)
Beds: 2D 1T
Baths: 3 En
🛇 (2) 🅿 (3) ⊬ 🗆 🏃 Ⅲ. 🅰 Ⅵ ✦

(0.5m) *Glan y Dwr, 14 Newbridge Hill, Bath, BA1 3PU.*
Personal attention to ensure you have a comfortable stay in Bath.
Tel: 01225 317521
Mr Kones.
D: £16.00-£24.00
S: £18.00-£35.00.
Open: All Year
Beds: 2D 1T 3S
Baths: 1 En 1 Pr 1 Sh
🛇 (11) 🅿 (3) ⊬ 🏠 🏃 Ⅲ. 🅰 Ⅵ ✦

(0.5m) *Cedar Lodge, 13 Lambridge London Road, Bath, BA1 6BJ.*
Come, stay, enjoy. Welcoming, comfortable lovely, well-placed period house.
Tel: 01225 423468
Mr & Mrs Beckett.
D: £25.00
S: £30.00.
Open: All Year
Beds: 1T 2D
Baths: 2 En 1 Pr
🛇 (10) 🅿 (6) ⊬ 🗆 🏃 Ⅲ. Ⅵ ✦

Bathford 41

National Grid Ref: ST7966

🍴 🍺 The Crown

(3m) *Bridge Cottage, Northfield End, Ashley Road, Bathford, Bath, BA1 7TT.*
Pretty cottage with lovely gardens. Village location near Bath city.
Tel: 01225 852399
Mrs Bright.
D: £20.00-£27.50 **S:** £25.00-£40.00.
Open: All Year (not Xmas)
Beds: 2D 1T
Baths: 2 Pr
🛇 🅿 ⊬ 🗆 🏠 🏃 Ⅲ. 🅰 Ⅵ

(3m 🐾) *Garston Cottage, Ashley Road, Bathford, Bath, N E Somerset, BA1 7TT .*
Country cottage, 2 miles from Bath, courtyard garden with jacuzzi.
Tel: 01225 852510
Ms Smart.
Fax no: 01225 852793
D: £20.00-£25.00 **S:** £25.00-£30.00.
Open: All Year
Beds: 1F 1D 1T
Baths: 3 En
🛇 🅿 (2) ⊬ 🗆 🏠 🏃 Ⅲ. Ⅵ ✦

Cumbria Way

The **Cumbria Way** provides a great introduction to Lakeland walking for the first-time visitor. So many people first see the Lakes from a car window - this path is the ideal alternative. Most of the path lies in the valleys rather than over the mountains, so the walker is sheltered from the worst of bad weather; and at 70 miles it's one that can be done inside a week. There is a link with the **Coast to Coast Path** as they cross in the Borrowdale Fells.

From the old textile centre of Ulverston, close to the shores of Morecambe Bay, the path meanders northwards, skirting the west side of Coniston Water. At Great Langdale you stroll among the moraines before reaching the craggy slopes that lead to Stake Pass. You come down by Langstrath Beck through the Borrowdale villages to Derwent Water and then Keswick, before crossing to Skiddaw Forest, curving around its eastern base. At this point two alternative routes can be taken, either north westerly to Orthwaite or north easterly up to the Caldbeck Fells and descending to Caldbeck. The concluding walk to historic Carlisle is pleasantly relaxed.

Maps: 1:50000 Ordnance Survey Landranger Series: 85, 90, 97

Guides: *The Cumbria Way* by John Trevelyan (ISBN 1 85568 000 9), published by Dalesman Publishing Co Ltd, Clapham, Lancaster, LA2 8EB (tel. 015242 51225), price £4.95 (+ 70p p&p)

Ulverston 1

National Grid Ref: SD2878

⊮ ⊪ Rose & Crown, Pier Castle, Farmers Arms

(0.5m 🚍) *Sefton House , Queen St, Ulverston, Cumbria, LA12 7AF.*
Georgian town house in the busy market town of Ulverston.
Tel: **01229 582190** Mrs Glaister.
Fax no: 01229 581773
D: £20.00-£22.50 **S:** £27.50-£30.00.
Open: All Year (not Xmas)
Beds: 1F 1D 1S 1T **Baths:** 4 En
🛇 🅿 (15) 🖵 🕮 ⅏ ⅋

(0.5m) *Rock House, 1 Alexander Rd, Ulverston, Cumbria, LA12 0DE.*
Actual grid ref: SD287779
Large family rooms. Convenient to railway/bus station/town centre.
Grades: ETC 4 Diamond
Tel: **01229 586879** Mr Ramsay.
D: £20.00-£20.00 **S:** £20.00-£20.00.
Open: March to October
Beds: 3F 1S **Baths:** 1 Sh
🛇 ⅏ 🖵 ✗ 🕮 ⅏ ⅋

Lowick 2

National Grid Ref: SD2986

⊮ ⊪ Red Lion

(1m 🚍) *Garth Row, Lowick Green, Lowick, Ulverston, Cumbria, LA12 8EB.*
Actual grid ref: SD328855
Traditional Lakeland house; warm welcome; super, peaceful setting; quality accommodation.
Grades: ETC 3 Diamond
Tel: **01229 885633** Mrs Wickens.
D: £18.00-£20.00 **S:** £23.00-£25.00.
Open: All Year (not Xmas/New Year)
Beds: 1F 1D **Baths:** 1 Sh
🛇 ⅏ (4) ⅏ 🖵 🕮 ⅏ ⅋

Torver 3

National Grid Ref: SD2894

⊮ ⊪ Church House Inn

(0.5m) *The Coach House, Torver, Coniston, Cumbria, LA21 8AY.*
Actual grid ref: SD286945
Tranquil country house in beautiful surroundings at the foot of Coniston Old Man.
Tel: **01594 41592** Mrs Newport.
Fax no: 015394 41092
D: £20.00-£22.00 .
Open: Mar to Nov
Beds: 2D 1T **Baths:** 3 En
🛇 (8) 🅿 (4) ⅏ 🖵 🕮 ⅏ ⅋

D = Price range per person sharing in a double room

Little Arrow 4

National Grid Ref: SD2895

⊮ ⊪ Church House Inn, Wilson Arms,

(0.5m 🚍) *Browside, Little Arrow, Coniston, Cumbria, LA21 8AU.*
Actual grid ref: SD290950
Panoramic views across Coniston Water to Brantwood, Grisdale Forest and Ambleside Fells.
Grades: AA 4 Diamond
Tel: **015394 41162**
Mrs Dugdale.
D: £18.00-£22.00 **S:** £20.00-£25.00.
Open: Feb to Nov
Beds: 1T 1D
Baths: 2 En
🛇 🅿 ⅏ 🖵 🕮 ⅏ ⅋

(0.5m 🚍) *Wheelgate Country Guest House, Little Arrow, Coniston, Cumbria, LA21 8AU.*
Former farmhouse, beautifully converted with high quality furnishings throughout.
Tel: **015394 41418**
Mr & Mrs Lupton.
Fax no: 015394 41114
D: £23.00-£30.00 **S:** £28.00-£30.00.
Open: Mar to Nov
Beds: 1F 1D 1T 2S **Baths:** 5 En
🛇 🅿 (8) ⅏ 🖵 🕮 ⅏ ⅋

(0.5m) *Arrowfield, Little Arrow, Coniston, Cumbria, LA21 8AU.*
Elegant house with lovely views. Homemade produce and friendly welcome.
Tel: **015394 41741** Mrs Walton.
D: £21.00-£24.00 **S:** £21.00-£24.00.
Open: Mar to Nov
Beds: 3D 1T 1S **Baths:** 4 En 1 Pr
🛇 (3) 🅿 (6) ⅏ 🖵 🕮 ⅏

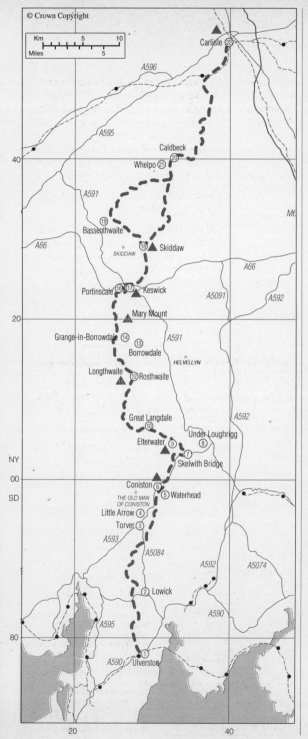

© Crown Copyright

Waterhead 5

National Grid Ref: NY3803

(▲ *3m*) ***Ambleside Youth Hostel***, *Waterhead, Ambleside, Cumbria, LA22 0EU.*
Actual grid ref: NY377031
Tel: **015394 32304**
Under 18: £9.50 **Adults:** £13.50
Self-catering facilities, Television, Showers, Licensed bar, Laundry facilities, Lounge, Games room, Drying room, Cycle store, Parking, Evening meal at 5.30-7.30pm, Kitchen facilities, Breakfast available, Luggage store, Credit cards accepted
Former hotel refurbished to a high standard of comfort with many small rooms and lake views. Hostel has its own waterfront and jetty.

Coniston 6

National Grid Ref: SD3097

⊖ ⚐ Sun, Crown, Wilson Arms, Church House Inn, Yewdale, Swan, Ship Inn

(▲ *0.25m*) ***Coniston (Holly How) Youth Hostel***, *Holly How, Far End, Coniston, Cumbria, LA21 8DD.*
Actual grid ref: SD302980
Tel: **015394 41323**
Under 18: £6.90 **Adults:** £10.00
Self-catering facilities, Television, Showers, Laundry facilities, Lounge, Games room, Drying room, Cycle store, Parking, Evening meal at 7.00pm, No smoking, WC, Kitchen facilities, Breakfast available, Credit cards accepted
Traditional Lakeland slate building in its own attractive gardens, dominated in the distance by the 'Old Man of Coniston'.

(▲ *1m*) ***Coniston Coppermines Youth Hostel***, *Coppermine House, Coniston, Cumbria, LA21 8HP.*
Actual grid ref: SD289986
Tel: **015394 41261**
Under 18: £6.50 **Adults:** £9.25
Self-catering facilities, Lounge, Drying room, Parking, Evening meal at 7.00pm, No smoking, WC, Kitchen facilities, Breakfast available, Credit cards accepted
Small hostel close to Coniston yet distant enough to feel isolated, surrounded by Coniston Fells, and once the home of the manager of the old copper mines.

Please respect
a B&B's wishes
regarding children,
animals & smoking.

(On path) *Kirkbeck House*, *Lake Road, Coniston, Cumbria, LA21 8EW.*
Actual grid ref: SD303979
Tel: **015394 41358** Mrs Potter.
D: £16.00-£16.00 **S:** £18.00-£18.00.
Open: All Year
Beds: 1F 1D 1T
⌷ ⌷ (3) ⌷ ⌷ ⌷ ⌷ ⌷ ⌷
Long Established family run bed and breakfast offering a warm friendly atmosphere. Comfortable bedrooms with pleasant views, good food, attractive garden and private parking. Situated in the quiet area of Coniston Village. Within walking distance of all amenities.

(0.25m) *Thwaite Cottage*, *Waterhead, Coniston, Cumbria, LA21 8AJ.*
Actual grid ref: SD311977
Beautiful C17th cottage. Peaceful location near head of Coniston Water.
Grades: ETC 3 Diamond
Tel: **015394 41367** Mrs Aldridge.
D: £21.00-£24.00 .
Open: All Year (not Xmas)
Beds: 2D 1T **Baths:** 1 En 2 Pr
⌷ ⌷ (3) ⌷ ⌷ ⌷ ⌷ ⌷ ⌷

(On path ⌷) *Crown Hotel*, *Coniston, Cumbria, LA21 8EA.*
Situated in the picturesque village of Coniston within easy reach of the famous lake.
Grades: ETC 2 Diamond, RAC 2 Diamond
Tel: **015394 41243** Mr Tiidus.
Fax no: 015394 41804
D: £25.00-£35.00 **S:** £30.00-£40.00.
Open: All Year (not Xmas)
Beds: 8D 6T
Baths: 12 En
⌷ ⌷ (20) ⌷ ⌷ ✕ ⌷ ⌷ ⌷ ⌷ ⌷

(On path ⌷) *Oaklands*, *Yewdale Road, Coniston, Cumbria, LA21 8DX.*
Beautiful spacious lakeland house, near village centre, private parking.
Tel: **015394 41245** (also fax no)
Mrs Myers.
D: £20.00-£25.00 **S:** £20.00-£25.00.
Open: All Year (not Xmas/New Year)
Beds: 1T 2D **Baths:** 1 En 1 Sh
⌷ (4) ⌷ ⌷ ⌷ ⌷ ⌷ ⌷

(On path ⌷) *Waverley*, *Lake Road, Coniston, Cumbria, LA21 8EW.*
Actual grid ref: SD302974
Clean and friendly, excellent value. Large Victorian house.
Tel: **015394 41127** (also fax no)
Mrs Graham.
D: £16.00 **S:** £16.00.
Open: All Year (not Xmas)
Beds: 1F 1D 1T **Baths:** 1 Pr 2 Sh
⌷ ⌷ (3) ⌷ ⌷ ⌷ ⌷ ⌷ ⌷ ⌷

S = Price range for a single person in a single room

Order your packed lunches the *evening before* you need them.
Not at breakfast!

(On path ⌷) *Lakeland House*, *Tilberthwaite Avenue, Coniston, Cumbria, LA21 8ED.*
Actual grid ref: SD303976
Friendly, family-run, village centre, lounge/log fire, groups welcome.
Grades: ETC 3 Diamond
Tel: **015394 41303** Mrs Holland.
D: £16.00-£35.00 **S:** £16.00-£35.00.
Open: All Year (not Xmas)
Beds: 5F 2D 1T 1S
Baths: 3 En 3 Sh
⌷ ⌷ ⌷ ⌷ ⌷ ⌷ ⌷

(2m ⌷) *Knipe Ground Farm*, *(East of Lake), Coniston, Cumbria, LA21 8AE.*
Actual grid ref: SD321976
Comfortable, peaceful C16th farmhouse in fields overlooking woodland, lake, mountains.
Tel: **015394 41221** Mrs Dutton.
D: £16.00-£20.00 **S:** £16.00-£18.00.
Open: All Year (not Xmas)
Beds: 2D 2S
Baths: 1 Sh
⌷ (8) ⌷ (2) ⌷ ⌷ ⌷ ⌷

(On path ⌷) *Sunny Brae Cottage*, *Hawes Bank, Coniston, Cumbria, LA21 8AP.*
Quality B&B in traditional whitewashed cottage on outskirts of village.
Tel: **015394 41654** Mr Beacock.
Fax no: 015394 41532
D: £18.00-£30.00 **S:** £18.00-£30.00.
Open: All Year
Beds: 2D 2T 1S
Baths: 4 En 1 Pr
⌷ ⌷ (4) ⌷ ⌷ ⌷ ⌷ ⌷ ⌷ ⌷ ⌷

Skelwith Bridge 7

National Grid Ref: NY3403

⌷ ⌷ The Talbot

(On path) *Greenbank*, *Skelwith Bridge, Ambleside, Cumbria, LA22 9NW.*
Actual grid ref: NY345033
Comfortable, friendly B & B in superb central lakes location.
Grades: ETC 4 Diamond, Silver
Tel: **015394 33236**
Mr Green.
D: £22.00-£25.00 **S:** £32.00-£35.00.
Open: Feb to Nov
Beds: 2D 1T
Baths: 3 En
⌷ (8) ⌷ (5) ⌷ ⌷ ⌷ ⌷ ⌷ ⌷

Under Loughrigg 8

National Grid Ref: NY3404

⌷ ⌷ White Lion

(▲ 1m) *Langdale (High Close) Youth Hostel*, *High Close, Under Loughrigg, Ambleside, Cumbria, LA22 9HJ.*
Actual grid ref: NY338052
Tel: **015394 32304**
Under 18: £6.90 **Adults:** £10.00
Self-catering facilities, Self-catering facilities, Television, Showers, Wet weather shelter, Lounge, Dining room, Games room, Drying room, Cycle store, Parking, Evening meal at 6.30pm, WC, Kitchen facilities, Credit cards accepted, Credit cards accepted
Victorian mansion set in extensive grounds between Elterwater and Grasmere, owned by National Trust. Close to Langdale Pikes.

(1m) *Foxghyll*, *Lake Road, Under Loughrigg, Ambleside, Cumbria, LA22 9LL.*
Large country house. 2 acre garden, 4 poster bed, spa bath, parking.
Grades: ETC 4 Diamond
Tel: **015394 33292** Mrs Mann.
D: £23.50-£27.00 **S:** £23.50-£27.00.
Open: All Year
Beds: 1D 2T **Baths:** 3 En
⌷ (5) ⌷ (7) ⌷ ⌷ ⌷ ⌷ ⌷ ⌷

Elterwater 9

National Grid Ref: NY3204

⌷ ⌷ Britannia Inn

(▲ 1m) *Elterwater (Langdale) Youth Hostel*, *Elterwater, Ambleside, Cumbria, LA22 9HX.*
Actual grid ref: NY327046
Tel: **015394 37245**
Under 18: £6.50 **Adults:** £9.25
Showers, Lounge, Drying room, Cycle store, Evening meal at 7.00pm, No smoking, WC, Kitchen facilities, Breakfast available, Credit cards accepted
Converted farmhouse and barn on the edge of the hamlet of Elterwater. Close to the fells at the head of Langdale, at the heart of classic Lakeland scenery - a favourite with walkers and climbers.

(On path) *Britannia Inn*, *Elterwater, Langdale, Ambleside, Cumbria, LA22 9HP.*
Actual grid ref: NY331048
Traditional Lakeland inn overlooking village green. Cosy bars with log fires.
Grades: ETC 1 Star
Tel: **015394 37210** Fry.
Fax no: 015394 37311
D: £24.00-£39.00 **S:** £24.00-£30.00.
Open: All Year (not Xmas)
Beds: 9D 3T **Baths:** 9 En 3 Sh
⌷ ⌷ (10) ⌷ ⌷ ✕ ⌷ ⌷ ⌷ ⌷ ⌷

Great Langdale   10

National Grid Ref: NY3006

🍴 ◀ New Dungeon

(0.5m) *The New Dungeon Ghyll Hotel, Great Langdale, Ambleside, Cumbria, LA22 9JY.*
Amidst Lakeland's dramatic fells at the head of the famed Langdale Valley.
Tel: **015394 37213**
D: £30.00-£36.00.
S: £40.00-£46.00.
Open: All Year
Beds: 13D 7T
Baths: 20 En
🛇 🅿 🖵 🗙 ⚡ 🖭 Ⓥ ▮ ✦

Longthwaite   11

National Grid Ref: NY2514

(▲ 0.5m) *Borrowdale Youth Hostel, Longthwaite, Borrowdale, Keswick, Cumbria, CA12 5XE.*
Actual grid ref: NY254142
Tel: **017687 77257**
Under 18: £7.75
Adults: £11.00
Self-catering facilities, Showers, Shop, Laundry facilities, Lounge, Dining room, Drying room, Cycle store, Parking, Evening meal at 7.00pm, No smoking, Kitchen facilities, Breakfast available, Credit cards accepted
Purpose-built hostel constructed from Canadian Red cedar wood in extensive riverside grounds in the beautiful Borrowdale valley.

Rosthwaite (Borrowdale) 12

🍴 ◀ Langstrath Inn, Royal Oak, Scafell Hotel, Riverside Bar

(▲ 0.5m) *Dinah Hoggus Camping Barn, Hazel Bank, Rosthwaite, Keswick, Cumbria, CA12 5XB.*
Actual grid ref: NY259151
Tel: **017687 72645**
Adults: £3.35
Traditional Lakeland field barn or Hogg-house. ADVANCE BOOKING ESSENTIAL.

(On path) *Royal Oak Hotel, Rosthwaite, Keswick, Cumbria, CA12 5XB.*
Actual grid ref: NY259148
Grades: ETC 1 Star
Tel: **017687 77214** (also fax no)
Mr Dowie.
D: £26.00 S: £25.00.
Open: All Year
Beds: 6F 5D 2T 2S
Baths: 12 En 3 Sh
🛇 🅿 (15) 🖵 🗙 ⚡ 🖭 Ⓥ ▮ ✦
A traditional family-run walkers' hotel in the heart of beautiful Borrowdale. Come and enjoy our friendly service, cosy bar, open fire and good home cooking. Brochure, tariffs and special breaks available.

(On path) *The How, Rosthwaite, Keswick, Cumbria, CA12 5BX.*
Tel: **017687 77692**
D: £19.00-£20.50 S: £22.00-£23.00.
Open: Mar to Nov
Beds: 1T 2D
Baths: 2 Sh
🅿 (4) 🖵 ⚡ 🖭 Ⓥ ✦
Rosthwaite is in the beautiful Borrowdale Valley about six miles from Keswick. Fell and riverside walking. Country house in well kept garden. Comfortable lounge with television, log fire when required. Breakfast room. Superb views.

(On path) *Yew Craggs, Rosthwaite, Keswick, Cumbria, CA12 5XB.*
Central Borrowdale, spectacular views, car park, riverside location (by the bridge).
Tel: **017687 77260**
Mr & Mrs Crofts.
D: £17.00-£21.00 S: £25.00.
Open: Mar to Nov
Beds: 2F 3D
Baths: 1 Sh
🛇 (6) 🅿 (6) ✦ ▮ ✦

(On path) *Chapel House Farm Campsite, Borrowdale, Keswick, Cumbria, CA12 5XG.*
Comfortable, homely, clean and good views.
Tel: **017687 77602** Mrs Dunkerly.
D: £18.00-£18.00 S: £18.00-£18.00.
Open: Feb to Nov
Beds: 2D 2T 1S
🅿 (5) ✦ 🖭 ▮ ✦

Borrowdale   13

National Grid Ref: NY2417

🍴 ◀ Black Lion, Langstrath, Dog & Gun, Riverside

(3m) *Greenbank Country House Hotel, Borrowdale, Keswick, Cumbria, CA12 5UY.*
Grades: ETC 4 Diamond, Silver, AA 4 Diamond, RAC 4 Diamond, Sparkling
Tel: **017687 77215** Mrs Wood.
D: £28.00-£34.00 S: £30.00-£42.00.
Open: Feb to Xmas Eve & New Year
Beds: 1F 2T 7D
Baths: 10 En
🛇 (2) 🅿 (15) 🖵 🗙 ⚡ 🖭 Ⓥ ▮ ✦
Greenbank is quietly situated in the heart of Borrowdale. Superb walking area and lovely views. 10 ensuite bedrooms with tea & coffee-making facilities etc. Two lounges with log fires. Excellent cuisine and warm welcome.

Pay B&Bs by cash or
cheque and be prepared
to pay up front.

(3m) *Ashness Cottage, Borrowdale, Keswick, Cumbria, CA12 5UN.*
Actual grid ref: NY270194
Cosy cottage, in pleasant grounds, near Ashness Bridge, overlooking Derwent Water.
Tel: **017687 77244**
Mrs Hamilton-Wright.
D: £15.00-£16.00 S: £16.00.
Open: All Year (not Xmas)
Beds: 1D 1T
Baths: 1 Sh
🛇 (10) 🅿 (2) ✦ 🖵 ⚡ 🖭 Ⓥ

(0.25m) *Mary Mount, Country House Hotel, Borrowdale, Keswick, Cumbria, CA12 5UU.*
Country house in gardens and woodlands on shores of Derwent Water.
Grades: ETC 2 Star
Tel: **017687 77223** Mrs Mawdsley.
D: £27.00-£32.00 S: £27.00-£32.00.
Open: All Year
Beds: 3F 6T 4D 1S
Baths: 14 En
🛇 🅿 (25) 🖵 🗙 ⚡ 🖭 ⚘ Ⓥ ▮ ✦

(0.5m) *Hollows Farm, Grange-in-Borrowdale, Keswick, Cumbria, CA12 5UQ.*
Comfortably furnished C17th farmhouse, working farm in beautiful location.
Tel: **017687 77298** Mr Fearon.
D: £17.00-£21.00 .
Open: Feb to Dec
Beds: 3D
Baths: 2 En 1 Pr
🛇 🅿 (3) ✦ 🖵 ⚡ 🖭 Ⓥ ▮ ✦

(3m) *Derwent House, Borrowdale, Keswick, Cumbria, CA12 5UY.*
Family-run guest house with beautiful Fell views from bedrooms.
Tel: **017687 77658** Lopez.
Fax no: 017687 77217
D: £19.00-£25.00 S: £23.00-£25.00.
Open: Feb to Dec
Beds: 1F 5D 3T 1S
Baths: 6 En 1 Sh
🛇 (5) 🅿 (15) ✦ 🖵 🗙 ⚡ 🖭 Ⓥ ▮ ✦

Grange-in-Borrowdale 14

National Grid Ref: NY2517

🍴 ◀ Swinside Inn, Riverside Inn, Mary Mount

(0.25m) *Grayrigg, Grange-in-Borrowdale, Keswick, Cumbria, CA12 5UY.*
Tel: **017687 77607**
Mrs Figg.
D: £19.00-£22.00 S: £19.00-£30.00.
Open: All Year (not Xmas)
Beds: 1F 1D 1T
Baths: 2 En 1 Pr
🛇 🅿 (4) ✦ 🖵 🔥 ⚡ 🖭 Ⓥ ▮ ✦
Situated just below Peace How at a quiet location on the outskirts of Grange Village. Grayrigg is a comfortable and friendly house, often described as being 'home from home'. A warm welcome awaits you.

Mary Mount 15

National Grid Ref: NY2619

(▲ 1m) *Derwentwater Youth Hostel, Barrow House, Mary Mount, Borrowdale, Keswick, Cumbria, CA12 5UR.*
Actual grid ref: NY268200
Tel: **017687 77246**
Under 18: £7.75 **Adults:** £11.00
Television, Showers, Licensed bar, Laundry facilities, Lounge, Games room, Drying room, Parking, Evening meal at 7.00pm, WC, Kitchen facilities, Breakfast available, Credit cards accepted
Magnificent 200-year-old mansion overlooking beautiful Derwent Water in lovely Borrowdale.

Portinscale 16

National Grid Ref: NY2523

⊮◫ Farmers Arms, Swinside Inn

(On path) *Skiddaw Croft, Portinscale, Keswick, Cumbria, CA12 5RD.*
Actual grid ref: NY251235
Tel: **017687 72321** (also fax no) Downer.
D: £20.00-£25.00
S: £20.00-£25.00.
Open: All Year
Beds: 1F 1T 2D 2S
Baths: 4 En 1 Sh
⌘ P (6) ⊬ ◻ ⊶ ⊀ ⋢ ⊞ Ⅴ ⋔ ⊘
Comfortable & friendly B&B in charming village. Easy walk to Keswick (15 mins) Splendid lake & mountain views. Health & hearty breakfasts. Vegetarians welcome. Good base for hill & water sports (marina 5 mins).

(0.5m 🚗) *Rickerby Grange, Portinscale, Keswick, Cumbria, CA12 5RH.*
Set within own garden, private parking. In the pretty village of Portinscale.
Grades: ETC 4 Diamond, AA 4 Diamond, RAC 4 Diamond, Sparkling
Tel: **017687 72344** Mrs Bradley.
D: £28.00-£30.00 **S:** £28.00-£30.00.
Open: All Year
Beds: 3F 9D 2S
Baths: 14 En
⌘ (5) P (14) ⊬ ◻ ⊶ ⊀ ⋢ ⊞ Ⅴ ⋔ ⊘

(0.5m) *Thirnbeck Guest House, Portinscale, Keswick, Cumbria, CA12 5RD.*
Comfortable Georgian guest house with fine views over Derwent Water.
Grades: AA 3 Diamond
Tel: **017687 72869** Savage.
D: £23.00-£23.00
S: £23.00-£23.00.
Open: All Year (not Xmas)
Beds: 4D 1T 1S
Baths: 5 En 1 Pr
⌘ (4) P (4) ⊬ ◻ ⊶ ⋢ ⊞ Ⅴ ⋔ ⊘

Keswick 17

National Grid Ref: NY2623

⊮◫ Packhouse, Packhouse Covet, Sun Inn, Four In Hand, Twa Dogs, Chaucer House, George Hotel, Kitchin's Cellar Bar, Skiddaw Hotel, Dog & Gun, Golden Lion, Farmers Arms, Pheasant, Bank, Wild Strawberry

(▲ 0.25m) *Keswick Youth Hostel, Station Road, Keswick, Cumbria, CA12 5LH.*
Actual grid ref: NY267235
Tel: **017687 72484**
Under 18: £7.75 **Adults:** £11.00
Self-catering facilities, Television, Showers, Laundry facilities, Lounge, Dining room, Drying room, Cycle store, Evening meal at 7.00pm, Kitchen facilities, Breakfast available, Credit cards accepted
Standing above the River Greta, this hostel is ideally placed in Keswick - the northern hub of the Lake District - for superb views across the park to Skiddaw.

(0.5m 🚗) *Spooney Green, Spooney Green Lane, Keswick, Cumbria, CA12 4PJ.*
Tel: **017687 72601** Ms Wallace.
D: £20.00-£25.00 **S:** £25.00-£40.00.
Open: All Year
Beds: 1T 1D
Baths: 1 En 1Private
⌘ P (5) ⊬ ◻ ⊀ ⋢ ⊞ Ⅴ ⋔ ⊘
Only 15 minutes' walk into Keswick yet on the foothills of Skiddaw, Spooney Green provides a relaxing country retreat. All rooms have extensive views of the western fells. The large wildlife garden includes woodland wetland and flower meadow.

(0.5m) *Chaucer House Hotel, Derwentwater Place, Keswick, Cumbria, CA12 4DR.*
Grades: RAC 2 Star
Tel: **017687 72318**
Mr Pechartscheck.
Fax no: 017687 75551
D: £30.00-£40.00 **S:** £30.00-£40.00.
Open: Feb to Dec
Beds: 4F 9D 12T 8S
Baths: 29 En 4 Pr
⌘ P ◻ ⊶ ⊀ ⋢ ⊞ ♿ Ⅴ ⋔ ⊘
Lakeland hospitality at its best. Quiet setting, surrounded by spectacular mountains. Close to Theatre, Market place and Lake. Renowned for a relaxed informal atmosphere and excellent freshly prepared food. Friendly, professional staff always available to help you enjoy your stay, plan tours and walks.

D = Price range per person sharing in a double room

Please respect a B&B's wishes regarding children, animals & smoking.

(0.5m) *Sunnyside Guest House, 25 Southey Street, Keswick, Cumbria, CA12 4EF.*
Grades: ETC 4 Diamond, AA 4 Diamond, RAC 4 Diamond
Tel: **017687 72446**
Mr & Mrs Newton.
Fax no: 017687 74447
D: £19.00 **S:** £24.00.
Open: All Year (not Xmas)
Beds: 1F 4D 1T 1S
Baths: 5 En 2 Sh
⌘ P (7) ⊬ ◻ ⊶ ⋢ ⊞ Ⅴ ⋔ ⊘
This recently refurbished Victorian building is situated just five minutes walk from the town centre and ten minutes walk from the lake, yet provides quiet and comfortable accommodation throughout. Relaxing guest lounge with views of Skiddaw.

(0.5m) *Badgers Wood Guest House, 30 Stanger Street, Keswick, Cumbria, CA12 5JU.*
All rooms have mountain views in this outstanding guest house.
Grades: ETC 4 Diamond, AA 4 Diamond
Tel: **017687 72621** Ms Godfrey.
D: £18.00-£22.00 **S:** £18.00.
Open: All Year (not Xmas)
Beds: 3D 1T 2S
Baths: 4 En 1 Sh
⊬ ◻ ⋢ ⊞ Ⅴ ⊘

(0.5m) *Brookfield, Penrith Road, Keswick, Cumbria, CA12 4LJ.*
Tel: **017687 72867** Mr Gregory.
D: £16.00-£20.00 **S:** £16.00-£20.00.
Open: All Year
Beds: 2F 2D
Baths: 4 En
⌘ P (4) ⊬ ◻ ⊶ ⊀ ⋢ ⊞ Ⅴ ⋔ ⊘
A warm welcome awaits you at this family run Victorian guest house. Walking distance to the historic stone circle. Ample street parking. Some rooms with a view of Latrigg. Local information books and videos. Walking boots welcome. Family discounts.

(0.25m 🚗) *The Paddock Guest House, Wordsworth Street, Keswick, Cumbria, CA12 4HU.*
Delightful 1800's residence. Close to town, lake, parks and Fells.
Grades: ETC 4 Diamond
Tel: **017687 72510**
D: £19.00-£21.00 **S:** £25.00-£40.00.
Open: All Year (not Xmas)
Beds: 1F 1T 4D
Baths: All En
⌘ P (5) ⊬ ◻ ⊶ ⋢ ⊞ Ⅴ ⋔ ⊘

(0.5m) *Watendlath, 15 Acorn Street, Keswick, Cumbria, CA12 4EA.*
Grades: ETC 3 Diamond
Tel: 017687 74165
D: £17.00-£20.00 .
Open: All Year
Beds: 2F 2D **Baths:** 3 En 1 Sh
♿ ❑ ♨ Ⅲ.Ⅴ ∥
Just a few mins from Keswick town centre, Watendlath is a quiet and relaxed retreat, small, tasteful and renowned for its superb traditional English breakfasts. The attractive rooms have everything to make your holiday a home-from-home experience.

(0.5m) *Lairbeck Hotel, Vicarage Hill, Keswick, Cumbria, CA12 5QB.*
Secluded setting, superb mountain views. Spacious parking. No single supplements.
Grades: ETC 2 Star, Silver, AA 2 Star, RAC 2 Star
Tel: 017687 73373 Mr Coy.
Fax no: 017687 73144
D: £30.00-£38.00 **S:** £30.00-£38.00.
Open: Mar to Jan
Beds: 1F 8D 1T 4S
Baths: 14 En
♿ (5) ❑ (16) ❑ ✕ ♨ Ⅲ.Ⅴ ∥ ∥

(0.5m) *Berkeley Guest House, The Heads, Keswick, Cumbria, CA12 5ER.*
Grades: ETC 4 Diamond
Tel: 017687 74222 Mrs Crompton.
D: £17.00-£24.00 **S:** £20.00-£20.00.
Open: Jan to Dec
Beds: 1F 2D 1T 1S
Baths: 3 En 2 Sh
♿ (3) ❑ ♨ Ⅲ.Ⅴ ∥ ∥
Friendly relaxed guest house with superb mountain views from each comfortable room. Situated on a quiet road on the edge of town, close to the lake, an ideal base for walking or water sports. Delicious breakfast choice and warm welcome assured.

(0.5m) *Tamara Guest House, 10 Stanger Street, Keswick, Cumbria, CA12 5JU.*
Cosy house, minute walk from town centre with private parking.
Tel: 017687 72913 Miss Dussoye.
D: £16.00-£18.00 **S:** £16.00-£18.00.
Open: All Year
Beds: 1T 3D **Baths:** 1 Sh
♿ ❑ (4) ❑ ✕ ♨ Ⅲ.Ⅴ ∥

(0.5m) *Claremont House, Chestnut Hill, Keswick, Cumbria, CA12 4LT.*
Grades: AA 4 Diamond
Tel: 017687 72089 Werfel.
D: £21.00-£25.00 .
Open: Easter to Nov
Beds: 3D 1T
Baths: 4 En
♿ (12) ❑ (5) ❑ ♨ Ⅲ.Ⅴ ∥ ∥
Claremont House, built about 150 years ago as a lodge house to the Fieldside estate, stands elevated about one mile from Keswick centre. Fine accommodation in pleasant surroundings, all tastes catered for with our substantial breakfasts.

(0.25m) *Lynwood House, 35 Helvellyn Street, Keswick, Cumbria, CA12 4EP.*
Victorian-style with modern comforts. Traditional or home-made organic breakfasts.
Grades: ETC 4 Diamond, Silver
Tel: 017687 72398
Mr Picken.
D: £17.00-£20.50 **S:** £18.50-£23.00.
Open: All Year
Beds: 1F 2D 1S **Baths:** 1 En
♿ (3) ∥ ❑ ♨ Ⅲ.Ⅴ ∥

(0.5m) *Clarence House, 14 Eskin Street, Keswick, Cumbria, CA12 4DQ.*
Lovely detached Victorian house, excellent ensuite accommodation. Cleanliness guaranteed. No smoking.
Tel: 017687 73186
Mr & Mrs Robertson.
Fax no: 017687 72317
D: £20.00-£28.00 **S:** £20.00-£28.00.
Open: All Year (not Xmas)
Beds: 1F 4D 3T 1S
Baths: 8 Pr
♿ (5) ∥ ❑ ♨ Ⅲ.Ⅴ

(0.5m) *Glendale Guest House, 7 Eskin Street, Keswick, Cumbria, CA12 4DH.*
Victorian House, Mountain views, Close to the town and lake.
Tel: 017687 73562 Mr Lankester.
D: £16.00-£20.00 **S:** £16.00-£20.00.
Open: All Year
Beds: 1F 2T 2D 1S
Baths: 3 En 2 Sh
♿ ∥ ❑ ♨ Ⅲ.Ⅴ

(0.5m) *Hawcliffe House, 30 Eskin Street, Keswick, Cumbria, CA12 4DG.*
Warm welcome assured. Short walk to lake and town centre.
Tel: 017687 73250 McConnell.
D: £16.00-£18.00 **S:** £16.00-£18.00.
Open: All Year
Beds: 1T 2D 2S
Baths: 2 Sh
∥ ❑ ♨ Ⅲ.Ⅴ ∥

(0.5m) *High Hill Farm, High Hill, Keswick, Cumbria, CA12 5NY.*
Modernised former farmhouse, special breaks, available all year, lovely views.
Tel: 017687 74793
Ms Davies.
D: £18.00-£19.00 .
Open: All Year
Beds: 2D 1T
Baths: 3 En
❑ (3) ∥ ❑ ♨ Ⅲ.Ⅴ ∥

(0.5m) 🚍 *The Queens Hotel, Main Street, Keswick, Cumbria, CA12 5JF.*
Comfortable, traditional Lake District hotel.
Grades: ETC 3 Star, RAC 3 Star
Tel: 017687 73333
Fax no: 017687 71144
D: £30.00-£44.00 **S:** £30.00-£44.00.
Open: All Year (not Xmas)
Beds: 1F 20D 5S
Baths: 35 En
♿ ❑ ❑ ✕ ♨ Ⅲ.Ⅴ ∥ ∥

(0.25m) *Dalkeith House, 1 Leonards Street, Keswick, Cumbria, CA12 4EJ.*
Clean, comfortable and friendly accommodation. Quiet area close to town.
Tel: 017687 72696 (also fax no)
Mr & Mrs Marsden.
D: £18.00-£22.00 **S:** £18.00-£22.00.
Open: All Year (not Xmas/New Year)
Beds: 4D 1T 1S 1F
Baths: 4 En 3 Sh
♿ ∥ ❑ ✕ ♨ Ⅲ.Ⅴ ∥ ∥

(0.5m) *Century House, 17 Church Street, Keswick, Cumbria, CA12 4DT.*
Warm, friendly guesthouse - The house of many returns.
Tel: 017687 72843 (also fax no)
North.
D: £17.50-£19.50 **S:** £17.50-£19.50.
Open: All Year (not Xmas/New Year)
Beds: 1F 1T 3D
Baths: 4 En 1 Pr
♿ ∥ ❑ ♨ Ⅲ.Ⅴ ∥ ∥

(0.25m) *Derwentdale Guest Hotel, 8 Blencathra Street, Keswick, Cumbria, CA12 4HP.*
Friendly, family-run guest house close to lake and parks.
Grades: ETC 3 Diamond
Tel: 017687 74187 (also fax no)
Mrs Riding.
D: £17.50-£21.00 **S:** £17.50-£18.00.
Open: All Year
Beds: 3D 1T 2S
Baths: 2 En 3 Pr
♿ ∥ ❑ ✕ ♨ Ⅲ.Ⅴ ∥

(0.5m 🚍) *Greenside, 48 St John Street, Keswick, Cumbria, CA12 5AG.*
Listed building in conservation area. Views, vegetarian and snack making facilities.
Tel: 017687 74491 Mrs Dalkins.
D: £15.00-£17.00 **S:** £25.00-£30.00.
Open: All Year
Beds: 1D 1T
Baths: 2 En
♿ (12) ❑ (2) ∥ ❑ ♨ Ⅲ.Ⅴ ∥ ∥

(0.5m) *Sandon Guest House, 13 Southey Street, Keswick, Cumbria, CA12 4EG.*
Victorian guest house conveniently situated close to lake and theatre.
Grades: ETC 3 diamond
Tel: 017687 73648
D: £18.00-£21.00 **S:** £18.00-£21.00.
Open: All Year (not Xmas)
Beds: 2T 2D 2S
Baths: 4 En 1 Sh
♿ ∥ ❑ ✕ ♨ Ⅲ.Ⅴ ∥ ∥

Pay B&Bs by
cash or cheque and
be prepared to
pay up front.

(0.5m) *Cumbria House,*
1 Derwentwater Place, Ambleside
Road, Keswick, Cumbria, *CA12 4DR.*
Ideal base for a Lakeland holiday -
quiet, 3 minutes from centre of
Keswick.
Tel: **017687 73171** (also fax no)
Mr Colam.
D: £18.00-£23.50 **S:** £18.00-£23.50.
Open: Feb to Nov
Beds: 1F 3D 2T 3S
Baths: 4 En 2 Sh
⛄ ⬇ (7) 🍴 📠 ⊁ ✕ 🎔 Ⅲ. Ⅴ ♦

(0.5m) *Portland House,*
19 Leonard Street, Keswick,
Cumbria, *CA12 4EL.*
Comfortable and quiet Edwardian
house, short walk from town
centre.
Tel: **017687 74230**
D: £20.00-£20.00 **S:** £20.00-£20.00.
Open: All Year (not Xmas)
Beds: 1F 2D 1T 1S **Baths:** 5 En
⛄ (3) 🅿 (3) ⊁ 📠 🎔 🐾 🎔 Ⅲ.& Ⅴ ■

(0.5m) *Avondale,* *20 Southey*
Street, Keswick, Cumbria, *CA12 4EF.*
Actual grid ref: NY268233
Quality accommodation; great
breakfasts & close to all amenities.
Tel: **Freephone 0800 0286831**
Mr Williams.
Fax no: 017687 75431
D: £19.75-£21.50 **S:** £19.75-£21.50.
Open: All Year (not Xmas)
Beds: 4D 1T 1S **Baths:** 6 En
⛄ (12) ⊁ 📠 🐾 Ⅲ. Ⅴ ■

(0.5m) *Beckside,* *5 Wordsworth*
Street, Keswick, Cumbria, *CA12 4HU.*
Quality ensuite accommodation.
Hearty breakfasts. Close to all
amenities.
Tel: **017687 73093**
Mr & Mrs Helling.
D: £15.00-£19.50 **S:** £22.00.
Open: All Year (not Xmas)
Beds: 1F 2D 1T
Baths: 4 En
⛄ ⊁ 📠 ✕ 🐾 Ⅲ. Ⅴ ■ ♦

(0.5m) *Glaramara Guest House,*
9 Acorn Street, Keswick,
Cumbria, *CA12 4EA.*
Actual grid ref: NY269232
Cosy family B&B. Good food, cen-
tral, bike hire, C2C storage/holiday
stabling.
Tel: **017687 73216** (also fax no)
Mrs Harbage (BHSII).
D: £17.00-£22.00 **S:** £17.00-£25.00.
Open: All Year
Beds: 1F 1D 1T 1S
Baths: 2 Pr 2 Sh
⛄ 🅿 (3) ⊁ 📠 🐾 🎔 Ⅲ. Ⅴ ■

(0.75m) 🚌 *Daresfield,* *Chestnut*
Hill, Keswick, Cumbria, *CA12 4LS.*
Actual grid ref: NY279236
Homely accommodation - good
views.
Tel: **017687 72531** Mrs Spencer.
D: £16.00-£18.00 **S:** £16.00-£18.00.
Open: All Year (not Xmas)
Beds: 1F 1D 1S **Baths:** 1 Sh
⛄ 🅿 (3) ⊁ 📠 🐾 🎔 Ⅲ. Ⅴ ■

(0.75m) *Foye House,* *23 Eskin*
Street, Keswick, Cumbria, *CA12 4DQ.*
Foye house is a well-appointed,
small, friendly Victorian guest
house.
Tel: **017687 73288**
Mr & Mrs Sharpe.
D: £19.00-£21.00 **S:** £16.00-£17.00.
Open: All Year
Beds: 1F 2D 1T 2S
Baths: 4 Pr 2 Sh
⛄ (5) ⊁ 📠 ⬇ 🎔 Ⅲ. Ⅴ ♦

(0.5m) *Hall Garth,* *37 Blencathra*
Street, Keswick, Cumbria, *CA12 4HX.*
Select family-run and non-smoking
guest house in quiet, yet convenient
location.
Tel: **017687 72627** Mrs Baker.
D: £18.00-£22.00 **S:** £17.00.
Open: All Year
Beds: 1F 3D 1T
Baths: 2 En 1 Pr 2 Sh
⛄ ⊁ 📠 🐾 ⬇ Ⅲ. Ⅴ ■ ♦

(1m) *Hunters Way,* *4 Eskin Street,*
Keswick, Cumbria, *CA12 4DH.*
Spacious comfortable ensuite
rooms, close to Keswick Centre
and countryside.
Tel: **017687 72324**
D: £20.00-£23.00 **S:** £17.00-£20.00.
Open: All Year (not Xmas)
Beds: 3D 1T 2S
Baths: 4 En 1 Sh
⛄ (6) ⊁ 📠 ✕ ⬇ 🎔 Ⅲ. Ⅴ ■ ♦

(0.5m) *Melbreak House,*
29 Church Street, Keswick,
Cumbria, *CA12 4DX.*
Close to town centre. Arrive a
guest - leave as a friend.
Tel: **017687 73398** Ms Hardman.
D: £18.75-£21.50 .
Open: All Year
Beds: 4F 6D
Baths: 10 En
⛄ ⊁ 📠 🐾 ✕ ⬇ Ⅲ. Ⅴ ♦

(On path 🚌) *Greystoke House,*
9 Leonard Street, Keswick,
Cumbria, *CA12 4EL.*
Traditional Lakeland town house.
Two minutes walk from the heart
of the town.
Tel: **017687 72603** Mrs Harbage.
D: £19.00-£20.00 **S:** £16.00-£17.00.
Open: All Year
Beds: 4D 2S
Baths: 4 En 2 Sh
⛄ ⊁ 📠 🐾 🎔 Ⅲ. Ⅴ ♦

🚌 **sign means that,**
given due notice,
owners will pick you
up from the path
and drop you off
within reason.

National Grid Ref: NY2629

(🔺 On path) *Skiddaw House*
Youth Hostel, Skiddaw,
Bassenthwaite, Keswick, Cumbria,
CA12 4QX.
Actual grid ref: NY288291
Tel: **016974 78325**
Under 18: £5.25 **Adults:** £7.50
Self-catering facilities, Showers,
Games room, Drying room, Cycle
store, No smoking, WC, Kitchen
facilities, Breakfast available
At 1550 ft this is one of the highest,
most remote and isolated hostels in
the UK, with no sign of civilisation
in any direction, beneath the summit
of Skiddaw. A torch is a necessity.

National Grid Ref: NY2332

🍴 🍺 Sun Inn

(2.5m 🚌) *Parkergate,*
Bassenthwaite, Keswick, Cumbria,
CA12 4QG.
Actual grid ref: NY234303
Wonderful views of mountains and
lake. Cosy. Tranquil and relaxing.
Tel: **017687 76376**
Mr & Mrs Phillips.
Fax no: 017687 76911
D: £18.00-£25.00 **S:** £25.00-£30.00.
Open: All year (not Xmas)
Beds: 1F 2D 1T **Baths:** 3 En 1 Pr
⛄ (5) 🅿 (4) ⊁ 📠 🐾 ✕ ⬇ Ⅲ. Ⅴ ♦

(2m) *Bassenthwaite Hall Farm,*
Bassenthwaite, Keswick, Cumbria,
CA12 4QP.
Charming, olde worlde, farmhouse
- excellent accommodation. By a
stream with ducks!
Tel: **017687 76393** (also fax no)
Mrs Trafford.
D: £16.00-£20.00 **S:** £25.00-£30.00.
Open: All Year
Beds: 1D 1T **Baths:** 2 Sh
⛄ (10) 🅿 (4) ⊁ 📠 ⬇ Ⅲ. Ⅴ ♦

(1m 🚌) *Chapel Farm,*
Bassenthwaite Lake,
Bassenthwaite, Keswick, Cumbria,
CA12 4QH.
Working family farm, friendly
accommodation, good home
cooking.
Tel: **017687 76495** Mrs Fell.
D: £15.00-£17.00 **S:** £15.00-£17.00.
Open: All Year
Beds: 1T 1D **Baths:** 1 Sh
⛄ 🅿 (3) 📠 🐾 ✕ ■ ♦

(0.25m 🚌) *Mirkholme Farm,*
Bassenthwaite, Keswick, Cumbria,
CA12 4QX.
Near the Cumbrian Way on the
back 'o' Skiddaw. Friendly.
Tel: **016973 71333** Mrs Todd.
D: £16.00-£17.00 **S:** £16.00-£17.00.
Open: All Year
Beds: 1F 1D **Baths:** 1 Sh
⛄ 🅿 📠 🐾 ✕ ⬇ Ⅴ ■ ♦

(1.25m) *Willow Cottage,*
Bassenthwaite, Keswick, Cumbria,
CA12 4QP.
Peaceful village location, log fires,
stencilling, patchwork, beams,
flagged floors.
Tel: **017687 76440** Mrs Beaty.
D: £20.00-£22.50 S: £25.00-£30.00.
Open: All Year (not Xmas)
Beds: 1D 1T
Baths: 2 En
🅿 (2) ⅍ 🗇 🎄 ⅏ 📖 Ⅴ 🛆 ⚡

Caldbeck   20

National Grid Ref: NY3239

🍽 🍺 Oddfellow Arm

(On path) *The Briars, Friar Row,*
Caldbeck, Wigton, Cumbria,
CA7 8DS.
Actual grid ref: NY3339
In Caldbeck village, right on
Cumbria Way. 2 mins' walk pub.
Grades: ETC 3 Diamond
Tel: **016974 78633** Mrs Coulthard.
D: £18.50-£20.00 S: £18.50-£20.00.
Open: All Year (not Xmas)
Beds: 1D 1T 1S **Baths:** 1 En 1 Sh
🅿 (4) ⅍ 🗇 🎄 ⅏ 📖 Ⅴ ⚡

Whelpo   21

National Grid Ref: NY3039

(0.5m 🚗) *Swaledale Watch,*
Whelpo, Caldbeck, Wigton,
Cumbria, CA7 8HQ.
Actual grid ref: NY309397
Enjoy great comfort, excellent
home cooking, warm friendly
farmhouse welcome.
Tel: **016974 78409** (also fax no)
Mrs Savage.
D: £17.50-£20.50 S: £18.50-£25.00.
Open: All Year (not Xmas)
Beds: 2F 2D 1T
Baths: 4 En 1 Pr
🐾 🅿 (10) ⅍ 🗇 🗙 ⅏ 📖 Ⅴ 🛆 ⚡

Carlisle   22

National Grid Ref: NY3955

🍽 🍺 Metal Bridge Inn, The Beehive, Mary's
Pantry, Crown & Thistle, Coach & Horses,
Golden Fleece, Black Lion

(▲ 0.25m) *Carlisle Youth Hostel,*
University of Northumbria, The
Old Brewery Residences, Bridge
Lane, Caldewgate, Carlisle,
Cumbria, CA2 5SR.
Actual grid ref: NY394560
Tel: **01228 597352**
Under 18: £8.75 **Adults:** £13.00
Self-catering facilities, Showers,
Cycle store, Parking, Facilities for
disabled people, No smoking, WC,
Kitchen facilities
University accommodation in an
award-winning conversion of the
former Theakston's brewery. Single
study bedrooms with shared
kitchen and bathroom in flats for
up to 7 people.

(0.25m) *Howard Lodge, 90*
Warwick Road, Carlisle, Cumbria,
CA1 1JU.
Actual grid ref: NY407558
Grades: ETC 4 Diamond,
AA 3 Diamond
Tel: **01228 529842** Mr Hendrie.
D: £15.00-£25.00 S: £20.00-£30.00.
Open: All Year
Beds: 2F 1D 2T 1S
Baths: 6 En 1 Sh
🐾 🅿 (6) 🗇 🎄 🗙 ⅏ 📖 Ⅴ 🛆
Friendly family-run guest house in
comfortable Victorian town house
in conservation area. Spacious
rooms all fully ensuite with satel-
lite TV, welcome tray, hairdryer
and clock radio. Large breakfasts.
5 minutes' walk from station and
city centre. Evening meals by prior
arrangement. Private car park.

(0.25m) *Craighead, 6 Hartington*
Place, Carlisle, Cumbria, CA1 1HL.
Actual grid ref: NY405559
Grades: ETC 3 Diamond
Tel: **01228 596767** Mrs Smith.
D: £17.00 S: £16.00.
Open: All Year (not Xmas)
Beds: 1F 2D 1T 1S
Baths: 1 En 2 Sh
🐾 🗇 🎄 ⅏ 📖 Ⅴ ⚡
You will receive a warm welcome
at Craighead, a Grade II Listed
spacious Victorian town house with
comfortable rooms and original
features. CTV, tea/coffee tray in all
rooms. Minutes' walk to city centre
bus and rail stations and all
amenities. Friendly personal
service.

(0.5m 🚗) *Cherry Grove,*
87 Petteril Street, Carlisle,
Cumbria, CA1 2AW.
Lovely red brick building close to
golf club and town.
Grades: AA 3 Diamond
Tel: **01228 541942**
Mr & Mrs Houghton.
D: £17.50-£20.00 S: £20.00-£30.00.
Open: All Year
Beds: 3F 2D
Baths: 5 En
🐾 🅿 (3) ⅍ 🗇 🎄 ⅏ 📖 Ⅴ 🛆 ⚡

(0.5m) *Angus Hotel & Almonds*
Bistro, 14 Scotland Road, Stanwix,
Carlisle, Cumbria, CA3 9DG.
Actual grid ref: NY400571
Grades: AA 4 Diamond
Tel: **01228 523546** Mr Webster.
Fax no: 01228 531895
D: £20.00-£27.00 S: £26.00-£42.00.
Open: All Year
Beds: 4F 3D 4T 3S
Baths: 11 En 3 Sh
🐾 🅿 (6) 🗇 🎄 🗙 ⅏ 📖 Ⅴ 🛆 ⚡
Victorian town house, foundations
on Hadrian's Wall. Excellent food,
Les Routiers Awards, local
cheeses, home baked bread.
Genuine warm welcome from own-
ers. Licensed, draught beer, lounge,
meeting room, internet cafe, direct
dial telephones, secure garaging.
Group rates for cyclists available.

(0.5m) *Avondale, 3 St Aidans*
Road, Carlisle, Cumbria, CA1 1LT.
Attractive comfortable Edwardian
house. Quiet central position con-
venient M6 J43.
Grades: ETC 4 Diamond
Tel: **01228 523012** (also fax no)
Mr & Mrs Hayes.
D: £20.00-£20.00 S: £20.00-£40.00.
Open: All Year (not Xmas)
Beds: 1D 2T
Baths: 1 En 1 Pr
🐾 🅿 (3) ⅍ 🗇 🗙 ⅏ 📖 Ⅴ 🛆 ⚡

(0.5m 🚗) *Dalroc, 411 Warwick*
Road, Carlisle, Cumbria, CA1 2RZ.
Small friendly house. Midway city
centre and M6 motorway.
Tel: **01228 542805** Mrs Irving.
D: £16.00-£16.00 S: £16.00-£16.00.
Open: All Year (not Xmas/
New Year)
Beds: 1T 1D 1S
🐾 (7) 🅿 🗇 🗙 ⅏ 📖 Ⅴ 🛆 ⚡

(0.5m 🚗) *Kingstown Hotel, 246*
Kingstown Road, Carlisle, CA3 0DE.
Grades: AA 3 Diamond
Tel: **01228 515292** (also fax no)
Mrs Marshall.
D: £23.50 S: £35.00-£40.00.
Open: All Year
Beds: 1F 4D 2T
Baths: 7 En
🐾 🅿 (14) 🗇 🎄 🗙 ⅏ 📖 🛢 Ⅴ ⚡
Just off the M6 (Jct. 44) we are a
licensed hotel providing high-qual-
ity accommodation. You will find a
friendly and relaxed atmosphere,
freshly-prepared cuisine and fine
wine at reasonable prices. A good
base to explore Cumbria,
Northumbria, Lake District,
Scotland

(1m) *Chatsworth Guest House,*
22 Chatsworth Square, Carlisle,
Cumbria, CA1 1HF.
City centre Grade II Listed
building, close to all amenities.
Grades: ETC 3 Diamond
Tel: **01228 524023** (also fax no)
Mrs Mackin.
D: £19.00-£22.00 S: £25.00-£25.00.
Open: All Year (not Xmas)
Beds: 1F 1D 2T 1S
Baths: 5 En
🐾 🅿 (2) ⅍ 🗇 🛢 ⅏ 📖 Ⅴ

(0.5m) *Corner House Hotel &*
Bar, 4 Grey St, Carlisle, CA1 2JP.
Grades: ETC 3 Diamond
Tel: **01228 533239** Mrs Anderson.
Fax no: 01228 546628
D: £17.50-£22.00 S: £20.00-£30.00.
Open: All Year
Beds: 3F 4D 4T 3S
Baths: All En
🐾 🗇 🎄 🗙 ⅏ 📖 🛢 Ⅴ ⚡
Refurbished family run hotel. All
rooms ensuite., colour TV, phones,
tea/coffee, radio, toiletries etc.
Cosy bar, sky TV lounge, games
room, easy access city centre,
bus/train. Base for golf, walking,
cycling, touring the Lakes, Roman
Wall, Carlisle/ Settle line etc.

(0.5m) *Ashleigh House, 46 Victoria Place, Carlisle, Cumbria, CA1 1EX.*
Beautifully decorated town house. Two minutes from city centre.
Grades: ETC 4 Diamond
Tel: **01228 521631**
Mr Davies.
D: £19.00-£22.50 **S:** £25.00-£30.00.
Open: All Year (not Xmas/ New Year)
Beds: 3F 1T 2D 1S
Baths: 7 En
♿ (5) ⛶ ♨ 🏛 Ⅴ

(0.25m 🚐) *Cornerways Guest House, 107 Warwick Road, Carlisle, Cumbria, CA1 1EA.*
Large Victorian town house.
Grades: ETC 4 Diamond
Tel: **01228 521733**
Mrs Fisher.
D: £14.00-£18.00 **S:** £16.00-£18.00.
Open: All Year (not Xmas)
Beds: 2F 1D 4T 3S
Baths: 3 En 2 Sh
♿ 🅿 (4) ⛶ ✿ ✕ ♨ 🏛 Ⅴ ▮

(0.5m 🚐) *Courtfield Guest House, 169 Warwick Road, Carlisle, Cumbria, CA1 1LP.*
Short walk to historic city centre. Close to M6, J43.
Grades: ETC 4 Diamond
Tel: **01228 522767** Mrs Dawes.
D: £18.00-£22.00 **S:** £25.00.
Open: All Year (not Xmas)
Beds: 1F 2D 2T **Baths:** 5 En
♿ 🅿 (4) ⛶ ♨ 🏛 Ⅴ

(0.25m 🚐) *East View Guest House, 110 Warwick Road, Carlisle, Cumbria, CA1 1JU.*
Actual grid ref: NY407560
10 minutes' walking distance from city centre, railway station and restaurants.
Grades: ETC 3 Diamond, AA 3 Diamond, RAC 3 Diamond
Tel: **01228 522112** (also fax no)
Mrs Glease.
D: £18.00-£20.00 **S:** £20.00-£25.00.
Open: All Year (not Xmas)
Beds: 3F 2D 1T 1S **Baths:** 7 En
♿ 🅿 (4) ⛶ ♨ 🏛 Ⅴ ✿

(0.5m) *Cambro House, 173 Warwick Road, Carlisle, Cumbria, CA1 1LP.*
Grades: AA 3 Diamond
Tel: **01228 543094** (also fax no)
Mr & Mrs Mawson.
D: £17.00-£20.00 **S:** £20.00-£25.00.
Open: All Year
Beds: 2D 1T **Baths:** 3 En
🅿 (2) ⛶ ♨ 🏛 Ⅴ ▮ ✿
Guests can expect warm hospitality and friendly service at this attractively decorated and well-maintained guest house. Each ensuite bedroom includes TV, clock, radio, hairdryer and welcome tray. Private off-road parking available, non-smoking, close to golf course.

Planning a longer stay? Always ask for any special rates.

BRITAIN: BED & BREAKFAST

The essential guide to B&Bs in England, Scotland & Wales

The Bed & Breakfast is one of the great British institutions. Like Fish & Chips, it's known by people around the world. But you don't have to be a tourist to enjoy this traditional accommodation. Whether you're travelling, on holiday, away on business or just escaping from it all, the B&B is a great value alternative to expensive hotels and a world away from camping and caravanning.

Stilwell's Britain: Bed & Breakfast 2001 is the most comprehensive guide of its kind, containing over 7,750 entries listed by country, county and location, in England, Scotland and Wales. Each entry includes room rates, facilities, Tourist Board grades and a brief description of the B&B and its location and surroundings.

Stilwell's Britain: Bed & Breakfast 2001: The indispensable guide to great value accommodation:

Private houses, country halls, farms, cottages, inns, small hotels and guest houses

Over 7,750 entries
Average price £19 per person per night
All official grades shown
Local maps
Pubs serving hot evening meals shown
Tourist Information Centres listed
Handy size for easy packing

£9.95 from all good bookstores (ISBN 1-900861-22-4) or £11.95 (inc p&p) from Stilwell Publishing, 59 Charlotte Road, London EC2A 3QW (020 7739 7179)

Dales Way

The 84-mile **Dales Way** is another good one for walkers to cut their teeth on, especially those new to walking in Northern England. The path splits naturally into two halves - the slow ascent to Ribblehead to cross the Pennines and the gradual descent from Newby Head. The route links the **Yorkshire Dales** and the **Lake District National Parks** in almost a straight line from Ilkley Moor to Lake Windermere through Wharfedale and Dentdale and the views over the fells and dales are spectacular. It is relatively short, with good transport links at Ilkley, Ribblehead, Kendal and Windermere and thus a good candidate for doing in stages over a couple of long weekends.

Guides (available from all good map shops):
Dales Way Companion by Paul Hannon (ISBN 1 870141 09 1), published by Hillside Publications and available from all good map shops or directly from the publishers (12 Broadlands, Keighley, W. Yorks, BD20 6HX, tel. 01535 681505), £5.99 (+60p p&p)

The Dales Way (Ilkley-Windermere) by Colin Speakman (ISBN 1 855680 72 6), published by Dalesman Publishing Ltd and available from the Rambler's Association National Office

(1/5 Wandsworth Road, London, SW8 2XX, tel. 020 7339 8500), £4.95 (+70p p&p)

The Dales Way by Anthony Burton (ISBN 1 85410 3148), published by Aurum Press in association with Ordnance Survey and available from all major bookshops, £12.99

The Dales Way by Terry Marsh, (ISBN 1 85284 102 8) published by Cicerone Press and available from all good map shops or directly from the publishers (2 Police Square, Milnthorpe, Cumbria, LA7 7PY, 01539 562069), £6.99 (+75p p&p)

Dales Way Route Guide by Arthur Gemmell & Colin Speakman (ISBN 0 906886 72 4), published by Stile Publications and available from by post from the RA National Office or from the publishers (24 Lisker Drive, Otley, W. Yorks, LS21 1DQ, tel. 01943 466326), £4.00 (+50p p&p)

Maps: 1:50000 Ordnance Survey Landranger Series: 97, 98, 104.

The Dales Way (4-colour linear route map), ISBN 1 871149 05 3, published by Footprint and available in all good map shops or by post from their offices (Unit 87, Stirling Enterprise Park, Stirling, FK7 7RP), £3.50 (+ 40p p&p)

Ilkley   1

National Grid Ref: SE1147

◄ Riverside, Rose & Crown, Wharfedale Gate, Sailor, Crescent

(0.5m) *63 Skipton Road,* Ilkley, W. Yorks, LS29 9BH.
Imposing stone detached house, gardens and ground-floor ensuite bedrooms.
Grades: ETC 2 Diamond
Tel: **01943 817542** Mrs Roberts.
D: £18.00-£20.00 S: £25.00-£25.00.
Open: All Year
Beds: 2D 1T **Baths:** 2 En 1 Sh

(On path) *Archway Cottage,* 24 Skipton Rd, Ilkley, W. Yorks, LS29 9EP
Beautiful Victorian cottage in central Ilkley with outstanding moorland views.
Grades: ETC 3 Diamond
Tel: **01943 603399** Mrs Green.
D: £17.50-£20.00 S: £20.00-£25.00.
Open: All Year
Beds: 1F 2D 1T **Baths:** 1 En 2 Sh

(0.5m) *The Grove Hotel,* 66 The Grove, Ilkley, W. Yorks, LS29 9PA.
Delightful Victorian hotel in lovely surroundings, personally run by owners.
Tel: **01943 600298**
Mr & Mrs Thompson.
Fax no: 01943 817426
D: £29.50-£32.00 S: £42.00-£45.00.
Open: All Year (not Xmas)
Beds: 2F 2D 2T
Baths: 6 En 1 Sh
⊗ (5) 🅿 (5) ⌷ 🛏 📶 Ⓥ

Ben Rhydding   2

National Grid Ref: SE1347

(1m) *1 Tivoli Place,* Ben Rhydding, Ilkley, West Yorkshire, LS29 8SU.
Conveniently situated in the lovely town of Ilkley. Easy walking distance to station, moor.
Tel: **01934 609483**
Fax no: 01943 600320
D: £25.00-£25.00 S: £30.00-£30.00.
Open: All Year
Beds: 1F 2D 1T
Baths: 3 En 1 Pr

Many rates vary according to season - the lowest only are shown here

Barden (Skipton) 3

National Grid Ref: SE0557

(1m 🚌) *Little Gate Farm,*
Drebley, Barden, Skipton, N Yorks,
BD23 6AU.
Tel: **01756 720200**
D: £19.00-£19.00 **S:** £19.00-£19.00.
Open: Easter to Nov
Beds: 1F 1D 1T
Baths: 1 Pr 1 Sh
🛇 🅿 ⅍ ▢ 🗮 🖳 Ⅶ 🏦
Beautiful Grade I Listed C15th
Dales farmhouse; all rooms look
down the valley to the River
Wharfe. We are a working sheep-
rearing farm, breeding our own col-
lies.

(0.5m) *Howgill Lodge, Barden,*
Skipton, N. Yorks, BD23 6DJ.
Actual grid ref: SE065593
Uninterrupted views over beautiful
Wharfedale. Once experienced,
you will return.
Tel: **01756 720655** Mrs Foster.
D: £27.00-£30.00 **S:** £32.00-£35.00.
Open: All Year (not Xmas)
Beds: 1F 2D 1T
Baths: 4 En
🛇 🅿 (10) ▢ ✕ 🗮 🖳 Ⅶ 🏦 ⅍

Burnsall 4

National Grid Ref: SE0361

🍴 🍺 Fountain

(On path) *Burnsall Manor House*
Hotel, Burnsall, Skipton, N. Yorks,
BD23 6BW.
Comfortable, friendly, relaxed.
Good food, ideal base for walking.
Tel: **01756 720231** (also fax no)
Mr Lodge.
D: £24.50-£28.50 **S:** £24.50-£28.50.
Open: All Year
Beds: 5D 3T **Baths:** 5 En 1 Pr 2 Sh
🛇 🅿 (9) ⅍ ▢ 🐾 ✕ 🗮 🖳 Ⅶ 🏦

(On path 🚌) *Holly Tree Farm,*
Thorpe, Burnsall, Skipton, N.
Yorks, BD23 6BJ.
Actual grid ref: SE014617
Quiet, homely Dales sheep farm.
Tel: **01756 720604** Mrs Hall.
D: £18.00-£20.00 **S:** £18.00-£20.00.
Open: All Year (not Xmas)
Beds: 1D 1S **Baths:** 1 Sh
🛇 (5) 🅿 (2) ⅍ ▢ Ⅶ ⅍

Hebden 5

National Grid Ref: SE0263

🍴 🍺 Clarendon

(2m) *Court Croft, Church Lane,*
Hebden, Skipton, BD23 5DX.
Grades: ETC 2 Diamond
Tel: **01756 753406** Mrs Kitching.
D: £17.50 **S:** £17.50-£20.00.
Open: All Year
Beds: 2T **Baths:** 1 Sh
🛇 🅿 ▢ 🖳 🏦 ⅍
Family farmhouse in quiet village
close to the Dales Way.

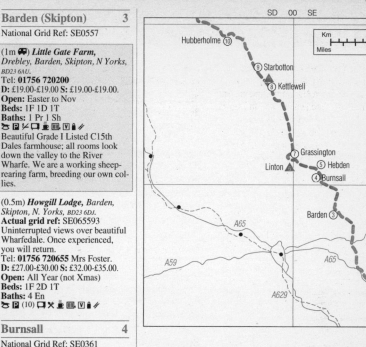

SD   00   SE

Hubberholme ⑩

⑨ Starbotton

⑧ Kettlewell

⑦ Grassington
Linton 🔺 ⑤ Hebden
④ Burnsall

Barden ③

A65   A59

A59   A65

A629   Ilkley ①②
Ben Rhydding

Linton 6

National Grid Ref: SD9962

(🔺 0.25m) *Linton Youth Hostel,*
The Old Rectory, Linton, Skipton,
North Yorkshire, BD23 5HH.
Actual grid ref: SD998627
Tel: **01756 752400**
Under 18: £6.90 **Adults:** £10.00
Self-catering facilities, Wet weath-
er shelter, Dining room, Drying
room, Cycle store, Parking,
Evening meal at 7.00pm, No smok-
ing, WC, Kitchen facilities
C17th former rectory in own
grounds, across the stream from
the village green, in one of
Wharfedale's most picturesque and
unspoilt villages.

Grassington 7

National Grid Ref: SE0064

🍴 🍺 Black Horse, Devonshire, Old Hall,
Foresters' Arms

(On path 🚌) *Mayfield Bed &*
Breakfast, Low Mill Lane,
Grassington, Skipton, N. Yorks,
BD23 5BX.
Actual grid ref: SE000635
Beautiful Dales longhouse. Guest
rooms overlook fells and river.
Tel: **01756 753052**
Mr & Mrs Trewartha.
D: £22.00-£25.00 **S:** £25.00-£25.00.
Open: All Year
Beds: 1F 1D 1T **Baths:** 1 En 1 Sh
🛇 🅿 (5) ⅍ 🐾 🗮 🖳 Ⅶ 🏦 ⅍

(0.5m) *Town Head Guest House,*
1 Low Lane, Grassington, Skipton,
N. Yorks, BD23 5AU.
Actual grid ref: SE040799
Friendly guest house at the head of
the village between cobbled streets
and moors.
Tel: **01756 752811** Mrs Lister.
D: £25.00-£25.00 **S:** £30.00-£30.00.
Open: All Year (not Xmas)
Beds: 3D 1T
Baths: 4 En
🅿 (3) ⅍ ▢ 🗮 🖳 Ⅶ

(0.25m) *Lythe End, Wood Lane,*
Grassington, Skipton, N. Yorks,
BD23 5DF.
Actual grid ref: SE000647
Modern stone detached house,
stunning views, quiet village
location.
Tel: **01756 753196** Mrs Colley.
D: £22.00-£25.00 **S:** £30.00-£30.00.
Open: All Year (not Xmas)
Beds: 1F 1D
Baths: 1 En 1 Pr
🛇 (12) 🅿 (2) ⅍ 🗮 🖳 Ⅶ 🏦 ⅍

(0.5m) *Craiglands, 1 Brooklyn,*
Threshfield, Grassington, Skipton,
BD23 5ER.
Elegant Edwardian house offering
quality accommodation and superb
breakfasts.
Grades: ETC 4 Diamond
Tel: **01756 752093** Mrs Wallace.
D: £21.00-£26.00 **S:** £20.00-£28.00.
Open: All Year (not Xmas)
Beds: 2D 1T 1S **Baths:** 3 En 1 Pr
🅿 (3) ⅍ ▢ 🗮 🖳 Ⅶ ⅍

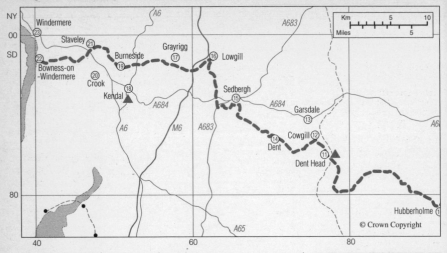

© Crown Copyright

(On path) *Kirkfield, Hebden Road, Grassington, Skipton, N. Yorks, BD23 5LJ.*
Large house in own gardens. Panoramic views of Wharfe Valley.
Tel: **01756 752385** Mr Lockyer.
D: £18.00-£25.00 **S:** £20.00-£20.00.
Open: All Year
Beds: 3F 1T 1S
Baths: 2 En 1 Pr 1 Sh
🛇 🅿 (8) 🗲 ⬜ 🏇 ✕ ⊞ 🛆 ♦

(0.25m) *Burtree Cottage, Hebden Road, Grassington, Skipton, N. Yorks, BD23 5LH.*
Old cottage, comfortable rooms, lovely garden. Ideal walking/touring centre.
Tel: **01756 752442** Mrs Marsden.
D: £17.50-£17.50 .
Open: Mar to Oct
Beds: 1D 1T **Baths:** 1 Sh
🛇 (10) 🅿 (2) 🗲 ⬜ ⊞ 🛆 ♦

(On path) *Springroyd House, 8a Station Road, Grassington, Skipton, N. Yorks, BD23 5NQ.*
Actual grid ref: SD980631
Conveniently situated, friendly family home.
Tel: **01756 752473**
Mrs Robertshaw.
D: £18.00-£20.00 **S:** £20.00-£22.00.
Open: All Year
Beds: 1D 2T
Baths: 1 En 2 Sh
🛇 🅿 (3) 🗲 ⬜ 🏇 ⊞ ⊞ ⒱ 🛆 ♦

(On path) *New Laithe House, Wood Lane, Grassington, Skipton, N. Yorks, BD23 5LU.*
A converted barn situated in the picturesque village of Grassington.
Tel: **01756 752764** Mrs Chaney.
D: £21.00-£24.00 **S:** £25.00-£40.00.
Open: All year (not Xmas)
Beds: 1F 4D 2T
Baths: 4 En 1 Pr
🛇 🅿 (7) ⬜ ⊞ ⊞ & ⒱

Kettlewell 8

National Grid Ref: SD9772

🍴 🍺 Queen's Head, Race Horses, King's Head, The Bluebell

(▲ On path) *Kettlewell Youth Hostel, Whernside House, Kettlewell, Skipton, North Yorkshire, BD23 5QU.*
Actual grid ref: SD970724
Tel: **01756 760232**
Under 18: £6.90 **Adults:** £10.00
Self-catering facilities, Television, Showers, Lounge, Drying room, Cycle store, Parking Lomoted, Evening meal at 7.00pm, No smoking, Kitchen facilities, Breakfast available, Luggage store, Credit cards accepted
Large house right in the middle of pretty Wharfedale village of Kettlewell, ideal for families and small groups.

(On path) *Lynburn, Kettlewell, Skipton, N. Yorks, BD23 5RF.*
Well preserved property with well tended grounds. Peaceful surroundings.
Grades: ETC 3 Diamond
Tel: **01756 760803**
Mrs Thornborrow.
D: £19.00-£20.00 **S:** £25.00-£25.00.
Open: Mar to Oct
Beds: 1D 1T **Baths:** 1 Sh
🛇 (12) 🅿 (2) ⬜ ⊞ ⊞ ⒱ 🛆 ♦

Taking your dog?
Book *in advance*
ONLY with owners
who accept dogs (🏇)

🚐 sign means that, *given due notice*, owners will pick you up from the path and drop you off *within reason.*

(On path) *Langcliffe Country House, Kettlewell, Skipton, N. Yorks, BD23 5RJ.*
Grades: AA 4 Diamond, RAC 4 Diamond
Tel: **01756 760243** Mr Elliott.
D: £45.00-£50.00 **S:** £65.00-£70.00.
Open: All Year (not Xmas)
Beds: 1F 2T 2D
Baths: 5 Pr 1 En
🛇 🅿 🗲 ⬜ 🏇 ✕ ⊞ ⊞ & ⒱ 🛆 ♦
Kettlewell in Upper Wharfedale. Traditional stone house with beautiful gardens. Ensuite bedrooms. Elegant lounge with log fire. Conservatory restaurant serving superb food in a panoramic setting.

Starbotton 9

National Grid Ref: SD9574

🍴 🍺 Fox

(0.25m) *Fox & Hounds Inn, Starbotton, Skipton, N. Yorks, BD23 5HY.*
Traditional cosy Dales inn.
Tel: **01756 760269**
Mr & Mrs McFadyen.
Fax no: 01756 760862
D: £27.50-£27.50 **S:** £35.00-£35.00.
Open: Mar to Dec
Beds: 1D 1T
🅿 (12) 🗲 ⬜ 🏇 ✕ ⊞ ⊞ ⒱ 🛆

Hubberholme 10

National Grid Ref: SD9278

🍴 🍺 George Inn

(On path 🚍) *Church Farm,*
Hubberholme, Skipton, N. Yorks,
BD23 5JE.
Actual grid ref: SD935773
Traditional C16th Dales farmhouse
on working hill farm. Ideal for
walking/touring.
Grades: ETC 4 Diamond
Tel: **01756 760240** Mrs Huck.
D: £20.00-£20.00 **S:** £20.00-£20.00.
Open: All Year
Beds: 2D 2T **Baths:** 1 En 1 Pr
🛇 🅿 🍴 ☐ 📺 📖 Ⅴ 🎍 ⬩

Dent Head 11

National Grid Ref: SD7587

(🔺 On path) *Dentdale Youth*
Hostel, Dent Head, Cowgill,
Sedbergh, Cumbria, LA10 5RN.
Actual grid ref: SD773850
Tel: **015396 25251**
Under 18: £6.50 **Adults:** £9.25
Showers, Lounge, Dining room,
Drying room, Cycle store, Parking,
Evening meal at 7.00pm, No smok-
ing, WC, Kitchen facilities,
Breakfast available, Credit cards
accepted
A listed former shooting lodge,
beside the River Dee in the upper
reaches of magnificent Dentdale.

Cowgill 12

🍴 🍺 Sportsman Inn, George & Dragon

(On path 🚍) *The Sportsman's Inn,*
Cowgill, Dent, Sedbergh, Cumbria,
LA10 5RG.
Family owned freehouse 1670,
scenic location, rooms overlooking
River Dee.
Tel: **015396 25282**
Mr & Mrs Martin.
D: £17.50-£23.50 **S:** £17.50-£23.50.
Open: All Year
Beds: 1F 2D 3T **Baths:** 3 Sh
🛇 🅿 (10) 🍴 📺 📖 Ⅴ 🎍 ⬩

(On path 🚍) *Scow Cottage,*
Cowgill, Dent, Sedbergh, Cumbria,
LA10 5RN.
Actual grid ref: SD774853
Attractive and comfortable 250-
year-old Dales farmhouse, set in
beautiful countryside.
Tel: **015396 25445** Mrs Ferguson.
D: £16.00-£17.00 **S:** £19.00-£25.00.
Open: All Year
Beds: 1D 1T **Baths:** 1 Sh
🛇 (12) 🅿 (4) 🍴 📺 📖 🎍 ⬩

Garsdale 13

National Grid Ref: SD7389

🍴 🍺 Dalesman, Red Lion, Bull Hotel

(1m 🚍) *Farfield Country Guest*
House, Garsdale Road, Garsdale,
Sedbergh, Cumbria, LA10 5JN.
Actual grid ref: SD677919
Quietly located amongst some of
the finest walking country in the
Yorkshire Dales.
Tel: **015396 20537**
Mr & Mrs Wilson.
D: £19.00-£24.00 **S:** £20.00-£21.00.
Open: All Year
Beds: 1F 4D 1T 1S
Baths: 4 En 1 Pr 2 Sh
🛇 🅿 (12) 📺 📖 Ⅴ 🎍 ⬩

Dent 14

National Grid Ref: SD7086

🍴 🍺 George & Dragon, Sun Inn, Sportsmans Inn

(🔺 0.25m) *Whernside Manor,*
Dent, Sedbergh, Cumbria, LA10 5RE.
Actual grid ref: SD725858
Tel: **015396 25213**
Under 18: £5.00 **Adults:** £5.00
Self-catering facilities, Television,
Showers, Grounds available for
games, Drying room, Cycle store,
Parking
Set in the grounds of a historic
house - excellent situation.

(On path 🚍) *Rash House, Dent*
Foot, Dent, Sedbergh, Cumbria,
LA10 5SU.
Actual grid ref: SD6690
Charming C18th farmhouse situat-
ed in picturesque Dentdale.
Tel: **015396 20113** (also fax no)
Mrs Hunter.
D: £16.00-£18.00 **S:** £18.00-£20.00.
Open: All Year (not Xmas)
Beds: 1F 1D
Baths: 1 Sh
🛇 🅿 (2) ☐ 📺 📖 Ⅴ 🎍 ⬩

(0.25m 🚍) *Garda View Guest*
House, Dent, Sedbergh, Cumbria,
LA10 5QL.
Village centre, friendly family
house. Hearty breakfasts, walking
information available.
Tel: **015396 25209** Mrs Smith.
D: £17.00-£17.00 **S:** £17.00-£17.00.
Open: All Year (not Xmas)
Beds: 2D 1T 1S
Baths: 1 Sh
🛇 🅿 (2) ☐ 📺 Ⅴ 🎍 ⬩

(0.25m 🚍) *Stone Close Tea Shop,*
Main Street, Dent, Sedbergh,
Cumbria, LA10 5QL.
Actual grid ref: SD705868
C17th oak beamed tea shop with
log fires.
Tel: **015396 25231** Mr Rushton.
D: £17.00-£25.00 **S:** £19.50-£49.00.
Open: Feb to Dec
Beds: 1F 2D 1S
Baths: 1 En 1 Sh
🛇 🅿 (4) 📺 📖 🎍 ⬩

(On path 🚍) *Smithy Fold,*
Whernside Manor, Dent, Sedbergh,
Cumbria, LA10 5RE.
Actual grid ref: SD725859
Small C18th country house.
Tel: **015396 25368** Mrs Cheetham.
D: £17.50-£17.50 **S:** £17.50-£17.50.
Open: All Year (not Xmas)
Beds: 1F 1D 1T
Baths: 1 Sh
🛇 (4) 🅿 (6) ☐ 🍴 📺 📖 Ⅴ 🎍 ⬩

(0.25m) *Little Oak, Helmside*
View, Dent, Sedbergh, Cumbria,
LA10 5QY.
Oak-beamed studio for two, warm
welcome, pretty, unspoilt village.
Tel: **015396 25330**
Mr & Mrs Priestley.
D: £18.00-£18.00 **S:** £18.00.
Open: All Year (not Xmas)
Beds: 1D
📖 ☐ 📺 Ⅴ

(0.25m) *Syke Fold, Dent,*
Sedbergh, Cumbria, LA10 5RE.
Actual grid ref: SD726859
Peaceful country hose with stun-
ning views. Quiet location 1.5
miles east of cobbled Dent.
Tel: **015396 25486** Mrs Newsham.
D: £21.50-£23.00 **S:** £21.50-£23.00.
Open: Feb to Nov
Beds: 1F 1D
Baths: 2 En
🛇 🅿 (2) ☐ 🍴 🎍 ⬩

(0.25m) *The White House, Dent,*
Sedbergh, Cumbria, LA10 5QR.
House in picturesque Dales village.
Quiet location, garden, superb
walking.
Tel: **015396 25041** Mrs Allen.
D: £17.00-£18.00 **S:** £17.00-£18.00.
Open: Easter to Oct
Beds: 1D 1T 1S **Baths:** 2 Sh
🅿 (2) 📖 📺 Ⅴ ⬩

Sedbergh 15

National Grid Ref: SD6592

🍴 🍺 Dalesman Inn, Cross Keys, Red Lion, Bull
Hotel

(On path) *Stable Antiques, 15 Back*
Lane, Sedbergh, Cumbria, LA10 5AQ.
Actual grid ref: SD659921
C18th wheelwright's cottage with
wonderful views of Howgill Fells.
Grades: ETC 2 Diamond
Tel: **015396 20251** Miss Thurlby.
D: £18.00-£19.00 **S:** £18.00-£19.00.
Open: All Year
Beds: 1D 1T **Baths:** 1 Sh
🛇 (10) ☐ 📺 📖 Ⅴ 🎍 ⬩

(0.5m 🚐) *Holmecroft, Station Rd,*
Sedbergh, Cumbria, LA10 5DW.
Actual grid ref: SD650919
Recommended by 'Which' Good
Bed and Breakfast Guide.
Grades: ETC 3 Diamond
Tel: **015396 20754** (also fax no)
Mrs Sharrocks.
D: £19.00-£19.00 **S:** £19.00-£19.00.
Open: All Year (not Xmas)
Beds: 1D 1T 1S **Baths:** 1 Sh
🛏 🅿 (6) ⚲ ❑ 👜 🛋 Ⅲ. Ⅴ 🔒 ✦

(0.5m) *Sun Lea, Joss Lane,*
Sedbergh, Cumbria, LA10 5AS.
Large Victorian family house near
town centre run by walkers.
Tel: **015396 20828**
Mr & Mrs Ramsden.
D: £18.00-£20.00 **S:** £18.00-£20.00.
Open: All Year (not Xmas/
New Year)
Beds: 2D 1T **Baths:** 2 En 1 Sh
🛏 🅿 (3) ⚲ ❑ 👜 🛋 Ⅲ. Ⅴ 🔒 ✦

(0.75m 🚐) *Marshall House, Main*
Street, Sedbergh, Cumbria, LA10 5BL.
Which? recommended Dales town
house situated under the magnifi-
cent Howgill Fells.
Tel: **015396 21053** Mrs Kerry.
D: £22.00-£27.00 **S:** £35.00-£45.00.
Open: All Year (not Xmas)
Beds: 1D 2T **Baths:** 2 En 1 Pr
🛏 (12) 🅿 (5) ❑ 👜 Ⅲ. & Ⅴ 🔒 ✦

Lowgill 16

National Grid Ref: SD6297

(🔺 1m) *Cowperthwaite Barn,*
Cowperthwaite Farm, Lowgill,
Kendal, Cumbria, LA8 9BZ.
Tel: 01539 824240
Adults: £8.00
Showers, Running water, WC,
Drying facilities, Washing
facilities, Kitchen facilities,
Breakfast available

Grayrigg 17

National Grid Ref: SD5797

(0.5m) *Punchbowl House,*
Grayrigg, Kendal, Cumbria,
LA8 9BU.
Actual grid ref: SD580972
Spacious and comfortable former
Victorian farmhouse in the centre
of the village.
Grades: ETC 4 Diamond, Silver
Tel: **01539 824345** (also fax no)
Mrs Johnson.
D: £20.00-£25.00 **S:** £20.00-£40.00.
Open: Mar to Dec
Beds: 2D 1T **Baths:** 1 En 1 Sh
🅿 (4) ⚲ ❑ ✕ 👜 Ⅲ. Ⅴ 🔒 ✦

Bringing children with
you? Always ask for
any special rates.

(1m) *Grayrigg Hall Farm,*
Grayrigg, Kendal, Cumbria,
LA8 9BU.
An C18th farmhouse in beautiful
open countryside. Working farm.
Convenient M6 (J38).
Tel: **01539 824689**
Mrs Bindloss.
D: £16.00-£17.00 **S:** £17.00-£18.00.
Open: Easter to Nov
Beds: 1F 1D 1S
Baths: 1 Sh
🛏 🅿 (2) ❑ 👜 ✕ 👜 Ⅲ. Ⅴ 🔒 ✦

Kendal 18

National Grid Ref: SD5192

🍴 🍺 Blue Bell, Gilpin Bridge, Hare & Hounds,
Stricklands Arms, Kendal Arms, Station, Castle,
Plough, Union, Ye Olde Fleece, Wheatsheaf,
Castle Inn, Punch Bowl, Moon, Watermill,
Brown Horse, Gateway Hotel

(🔺 On path) *Kendal Youth Hostel,*
118 Highgate, Kendal, Cumbria,
LA9 4HE.
Actual grid ref: SD515924
Tel: **015397 24066**
Under 18: £10.00 **Adults:** £13.00
Television, Showers, Lounge,
Dining room 2, Drying room,
Cycle store, Evening meal at
pre-booked, Kitchen facilities
Converted Georgian town house,
adjoining Brewery Arts Centre in
the centre of Kendal.

(2m 🚐) *Sonata, 19 Burnside Road,*
Kendal, Cumbria, LA9 4RL.
Actual grid ref: SD513933
Grades: ETC 3 Diamond
Tel: **015397 32290** Mr Wilkinson.
D: £22.00-£22.00 **S:** £30.00-£30.00.
Open: All Year
Beds: 1F 2D 1T
Baths: 4 En
🛏 ❑ 👜 ✕ 👜 Ⅲ. Ⅴ 🔒 ✦
Friendly, family-run, Georgian,
terraced guest house with
comfortable, ensuite bedrooms
containing radio, alarm, colour TV,
complimentary beverage facilities,
hairdryer and independently
controlled central heating.
Shopping centres 3 mins walk,
Windermere 10 mins drive.

(4m 🚐) *Bridge House, 65 Castle*
Street, Kendal, Cumbria, LA9 4RL.
Actual grid ref: SD522929
Grades: ETC 4 Diamond
Tel: **015397 22041** Mrs Brindley.
D: £18.00-£25.00 **S:** £20.00-£30.00.
Open: All Year
Beds: 1D 1T
Baths: 1 En 1 Sh
🛏 ⚲ ❑ 👜 Ⅲ. Ⅴ 🔒 ✦
Beautiful Georgian Listed building
a short walk from Kendal castle
and the River Kent. Home made
bread and preserves a speciality.
Complimentary Kendal mint cake
for our visitors. A lovely private
garden for guests' use. A warm and
friendly welcome.

(0.5m 🚐) *Sundial House,*
51 Milnthorpe Road, Kendal,
Cumbria, LA9 5QG.
Actual grid ref: SD515916
Quality guest house comfortable
rooms car park excellent breakfast.
Tel: **01539 724468**
Mr & Mrs Richardson.
Fax no: 01539 736900
D: £17.50-£25.00 **S:** £18.50-£22.50.
Open: All Year (not Xmas)
Beds: 1F 1D 1T 1S
Baths: 1 En 2 Sh
🛏 🅿 (8) ❑ 👜 👜 Ⅲ. Ⅴ 🔒 ✦

(2m 🚐) *Birslack Grange, Hutton*
Lane, Levens, Kendal, Cumbria,
LA8 8PA.
Actual grid ref: SD486866
Converted farm buildings in rural
setting overlooking the scenic Lyth
Valley.
Tel: **015395 60989**
Mrs Carrington-Birch.
D: £18.00-£20.00 **S:** £20.00-£25.00.
Open: All Year (not Xmas)
Beds: 1F 1D 2T 2S
Baths: 4 En 2 Sh
🛏 (3) 🅿 (6) ⚲ ❑ 👜 ✕ 👜 Ⅲ. & Ⅴ ✦

(1m) *Hillside Guest House,*
4 Beast Banks, Kendal, Cumbria,
LA9 4JW.
Large Victorian guest house, town
centre. Ideal for Lake District and
Yorkshire Dales.
Grades: ETC 3 Diamond
Tel: **015397 22836** Mrs Denison.
D: £18.00-£21.00 **S:** £18.00-£22.00.
Open: Mar to Nov
Beds: 3D 1T 3S
Baths: 5 En 4 Pr 1 Sh
🛏 (4) 🅿 (4) ❑ 👜 Ⅲ. Ⅴ ✦

(0.5m) *Fairways, 102 Windermere*
Road, Kendal, Cumbria, LA9 5EZ.
Victorian guest house, ensuite rooms.
TV, tea/coffee. Lovely views.
Grades: ETC 3 Diamond
Tel: **015397 25564** Mrs Paylor.
D: £18.00-£20.00 **S:** £20.00-£25.00.
Open: All Year
Beds: 1F 2D 1S **Baths:** 3 En 1 Pr
🛏 (2) 🅿 (4) ⚲ ❑ 👜 Ⅲ. Ⅴ 🔒 ✦

(2m) *Highgate Hotel, 128*
Highgate, Kendal, Cumbria, LA9 4HE
Grade II* Listed town centre B&B.
Private car park. Built 1769.
Tel: **01539 724229** (also fax no)
Mr Dawson.
D: £21.50-£23.50 **S:** £27.00-£29.00.
Open: All Year (not Xmas/New
Year)
Beds: 1F 4D 2T 3S
Baths: 10 En
🛏 🅿 (10) ⚲ ❑ 👜 Ⅲ. Ⅴ 🔒 ✦

Planning a longer
stay? Always ask for
any special rates.

(2m 🚗) *Airethwaite House,*
1 Airethwaite, Horncop Lane,
Kendal, Cumbria, LA9 4SP.
Unspoilt Victorian guesthouse with
spacious rooms, many original
features and antique furniture.
Tel: **01539 730435** Mrs Dean.
D: £20.00-£22.00 **S:** £25.00-£25.00.
Open: All Year
Beds: 3D/T
Baths: 3 En
🛇 🅿 (3) ⊬ ⬜ 🏠 ⭍ Ⅲ. Ⅴ ∥ ✦

(2m) *Magic Hills House,*
123 Appleby Road, Kendal,
Cumbria, LA9 6HF.
Tel: **01539 736248** Moseley.
D: £18.50-£22.50 **S:** £21.00-£27.00.
Open: All Year (not Xmas)
Beds: 2D 1T
Baths: 1 En 1 Pr 1 Sh
🛇 (12) ⊬ ⬜ 🏠 ⭍ Ⅲ. Ⅴ ⓘ ∥ ✦
Late Victorian family house,
comfortably furnished and
tastefully decorated. 10 minutes
walk to centre. Convenient for
Lakes, Yorkshire Dales and Dales
Way. Conservatory for relaxing.
Generous home-cooked breakfast.
Rural views. Personally run by
Christine and Richard Moseley.

(2m 🚗) *Mitchelland House, Off*
Crook Road, Kendal, Cumbria,
LA8 8LL.
Delightful country location, only
5 minutes Lake Windermere and
all attractions.
Grades: ETC 4 Diamond
Tel: **015394 48589**
D: £18.00-£24.00 **S:** £21.00-£26.00.
Open: All Year (not Xmas)
Beds: 1F 1D 1T
Baths: 1 En 1 Sh
🛇 🅿 (10) ⬜ 🏠 ⭍ Ⅲ. Ⅴ ⓘ ✦

(2m 🚗) *Meadow Croft Country*
Hotel, Ings, Staveley, Kendal,
Cumbria, LA8 9PY.
Superior ensuite accommodation in
village hotel, 2 miles from
Windermere.
Tel: **01539 821171** Mr Cross.
D: £24.00-£28.00 **S:** £30.00-£38.00.
Open: Easter to Dec
Beds: 3F 3D 2T **Baths:** 7 En 1 Pr
🛇 🅿 (10) ⬜ ✕ ⭍ Ⅲ. Ⅴ ⓘ ✦

(2m) *Winlea, 88 Windermere*
Road, Kendal, Cumbria, LA9 5EZ.
Friendly Victorian guest house
lovely views 10 minutes walk town
centre.
Tel: **015397 23177** Mrs Ellison.
D: £18.00-£20.00 .
Open: All Year (not Xmas)
Beds: 1F 2D 1T **Baths:** 2 En
🛇 (8) 🅿 (4) ⊬ ⬜ 🏠 ⭍ Ⅲ. Ⅴ

**Pay B&Bs by cash or
cheque and be prepared
to pay up front.**

(2m) *7 Thorny Hills, Kendal,*
Cumbria, LA9 7AL.
Listed building in a peaceful
location near the town centre.
Grades: ETC 3 Diamond
Tel: **015397 20207** Mrs Jowett.
D: £21.00-£21.00 **S:** £24.00-£24.00.
Open: Jan to Nov
Beds: 2D 1T
Baths: 2 En 1 Pr
🛇 ⊬ ⬜ ✕ ⭍ Ⅲ. Ⅴ ⓘ

(0.5m) *Garnette House Farm,*
Burneside, Kendal, Cumbria,
LA9 5SF.
Actual grid ref: SD500959
C15th farmhouse on edge of
Burneside Village & 10 mins from
Windermere.
Tel: **015397 24542** (also fax no)
Mrs Beaty.
D: £16.00-£21.00 .
Open: All Year (not Xmas)
Beds: 2F 3D 1T
Baths: 4 En 2 Sh
🛇 🅿 (6) ⬜ ⭍ Ⅲ. Ⅴ

(2m) *The Glen, Oxenholme,*
Kendal, Cumbria, LA9 7RF.
Actual grid ref: SD534900
Quiet location under 'The Helm'
(local walk and viewpoint
Lakeland fells).
Tel: **015397 26386** Mrs Green.
D: £18.00-£25.00 **S:** £25.00-£30.00.
Open: All Year (not Xmas)
Beds: 1F 2D
Baths: 3 En
🛇 (8) 🅿 (10) ⊬ ⬜ ✕ ⭍ Ⅲ. Ⅴ ⓘ ✦

(2m) *Glenholme Guest House,*
43 Milnthorpe Road, Kendal,
Cumbria, LA9 5QG.
Well-established family guest
house situated in historical Kendal
market town.
Tel: **015397 21489**
D: £16.00-£25.00 **S:** £16.00-£22.00.
Open: All Year
Beds: 1F 1D 2T 2S
Baths: 4 En 2 Sh
🛇 ⬜ 🏠 ✕ ⭍ Ⅲ. Ⅴ ⓘ ✦

(2m) *The Headlands Hotel,*
53 Milnthorpe Road, Kendal,
Cumbria, LA9 5QG.
Private hotel, bar, TV lounge,
secure car park, ensuite facilities.
Tel: **015397 32464**
Mr & Mrs Kellington.
D: £18.00-£22.00 **S:** £18.00-£30.00.
Open: All Year
Beds: 1F 3D 2T **Baths:** 5 En 1 Pr
🛇 🅿 ⊬ ⬜ ✕ ⭍ Ⅲ. Ⅴ ⓘ ✦

(2m 🚗) *West Mount,*
39 Milnthorpe Road, Kendal,
Cumbria, LA9 5QG.
Well-appointed Victorian house on
southern outskirts of popular
market town.
Tel: **015397 24621** Mr Keep.
Fax no: 01539 725282
D: £20.00-£23.00 **S:** £23.00-£23.00.
Open: All Year
Beds: 1F 2D **Baths:** 3 En
🛇 (3) 🅿 (3) ⊬ ⬜ ✕ ⭍ Ⅲ. Ⅴ ∥ ✦

Burneside 19

National Grid Ref: SD5095

(1m) *Gateside House Farm,*
Windermere Road, Burneside,
Kendal, Cumbria, LA9 5SE.
Gateside farm is a working dairy
and sheep farm.
Grades: ETC 3 Diamond
Tel: **015397 22036** (also fax no)
Mrs Ellis.
D: £18.00-£23.00 **S:** £18.00-£23.00.
Open: All Year
Beds: 1F 3D 1T
Baths: 3 En 2 Sh
🛇 🅿 (5) ⬜ 🏠 ✕ ⭍ Ⅲ. Ⅴ ✦

Crook 20

National Grid Ref: SD4695

🍴 🍺 Brown Horse Inn

(2m) *Mitchelland Farm*
Bungalow, Crook, Kendal,
Cumbria, LA8 8LL.
Wheelchair accessible spacious
working farm bungalow.
Wonderful views near
Windermere.
Tel: **015394 47421** Mr Higham.
D: £22.00-£26.00 **S:** £25.00-£30.00.
Open: All Year
Beds: 1T 1D
Baths: 1 En 1 Pr
🛇 🅿 (5) ⊬ ⬜ 🏠 ⭍ Ⅲ. ♿ Ⅴ

Staveley 21

National Grid Ref: SD4698

🍴 🍺 Railway Inn, Duke William, Eagle & Child

(On path) *Stock Bridge Farm,*
Staveley, Kendal, Cumbria, LA8 9LP.
Actual grid ref: SD473978
Modernised comfortable C17th
farmhouse in picturesque village
close to Lakes.
Tel: **01539 821580** Mrs Fishwick.
D: £16.50-£17.50 **S:** £16.50-£17.50.
Open: Mar to Oct
Beds: 1F 4D 1T 1S
Baths: 1 Sh
🛇 🅿 (6) ⬜ 🏠 Ⅲ. ⓘ ∥ ✦

(0.5m) *Heywood, Kentmere Road,*
Staveley, Kendal, Cumbria, LA8 9JF.
Peaceful spacious bungalow in
hamlet with views of Kentmere
Valley.
Tel: **01539 821198**
D: £18.00-£20.00 **S:** £20.00-£20.00.
Open: Feb to Nov
Beds: 1D
Baths: 1 En
🅿 (1) ⊬ ⭍ Ⅲ. Ⅴ ⓘ ∥ ✦

**All paths are popular:
you are well-advised to
book ahead**

(0.5m 🚌) *The Old Vicarage*, *Brow Lane, Staveley, Kendal, Cumbria, LA8 9PH.*
Actual grid ref: SD466984
Peaceful retreat with panoramic views in national park.
Overlooking village. Midway Kendal/Windermere.
Tel: **01539 822432**
Mrs Ellwood.
Fax no: 01539 822375
D: £17.00-£20.00 **S:** £20.00-£25.00.
Open: All Year
Beds: 1F 2D 1T
Baths: 1 En 2 Pr
🅿 (4) ⊬ 🗆 🛏 🎩 🖳 Ⅴ ✦

Bowness-on-Windermere22

National Grid Ref: SD4097

🍴 🍺 Royal Oak, Hole In T'wall, Brown Horse, Sun Inn, Jacksons, The Mariners , Village Inn

(On path) *The Fairfield*, *Brantfell Road, Bowness-on-Windermere, Windermere, Cumbria, LA23 3AE.*
Actual grid ref: SD404967
Grades: ETC 4 Diamond,
AA 4 Diamond, RAC 4 Diamond
Tel: **015394 46565** (also fax no)
Mr & Mrs Hood.
D: £25.00 **S:** £34.00.
Open: Feb to Oct
Beds: 2F 5D 1T 1S
Baths: 8 En 1 Pr
🛌 🅿 (12) ⊬ 🗆 🛏 🎩 🖳 Ⅴ 🛈 ✦
Small friendly family-run hotel in Bowness at the end of the Dales Way. Ensuite rooms with colour TVs. Leisure facilities. Ideal venue to end your walk. Private car park. Genuine hospitality in a homely atmosphere.

(0.25m) *Lingwood*, *Birkett Hill, Bowness-on-Windermere, Windermere, Cumbria, LA23 3EZ.*
Actual grid ref: SD402964
Friendly, comfortable, family guest house within 400 yards of lake.
Grades: ETC 3 Diamond
Tel: **015394 44680**
Mr & Mrs Atkinson.
D: £19.00-£30.00 **S:** £19.00-£30.00.
Open: All Year
Beds: 2F 3D 1T
Baths: 4 En 2 Pr
🛌 🅿 (6) 🗆 🎩 🖳 Ⅴ ✦

(On path) *Virginia Cottage*, *Kendal Road, Bowness-on-Windermere, Windermere, Cumbria, LA23 3EJ.*
C19th house set in heart of village.
Friendly welcome assured.
Grades: ETC 3 Diamond,
AA 3 Diamond
Tel: **015394 44891**
Mr Tyler.
Fax no: 015394 44855
D: £18.00-£36.00
S: £20.00-£30.00.
Open: All Year
Beds: 1F 1T 8D 1S
Baths: 9 En 2 Pr
🛌 🅿 (9) ⊬ 🗆 🛏 🎩 🖳 Ⅴ 🛈 ✦

(1m 🚌) *Elim House*, *Bisky Howe Road, Bowness-on-Windermere, Windermere, Cumbria, LA23 2JP.*
Warm, friendly and peaceful family-run guest house with award winning garden.
Grades: AA 3 Diamond
Tel: **015394 42021**
D: £16.00-£50.00 **S:** £20.00-£50.00.
Open: All Year
Beds: 2F 11D 2T **Baths:** 7 En 2 Sh
🛌 (7) 🅿 (6) 🗆 🛏 🎩 🖳 Ⅴ 🛈 ✦

(1m) *Rosemount*, *Lake Road, Bowness-on-Windermere, Windermere, Cumbria, LA23 2EQ.*
Grades: ETC 3 Diamond,
AA 3 Diamond
Tel: **015394 43739** Mr Thomas.
Fax no: 015394 48978
D: £20.00-£30.00 **S:** £20.00-£30.00.
Open: All Year
Beds: 3F 10D 1T 3S
Baths: 15 En 2 Pr
🛌 🅿 (12) ⊬ 🗆 🎩 🖳 Ⅴ
Firm comfortable beds and breakfasts worth getting up for at this impressive Victorian guest house with elegant public rooms. Between Windermere and Bowness, yet seconds from a wood where the loudest thing you'll hear is a stream seeking the lake.

(0.5m) *Annisgarth House*, *2 Annisgarth, Bowness-on-Windermere, Windermere, Cumbria, LA23 2HF.*
Views of lake and mountains.
Private parking. Quiet location.
Tel: **015394 48049** (also fax no)
Mrs Erwig.
D: £16.00-£22.00 **S:** £21.00-£27.00.
Open: Mar to Dec
Beds: 1T 1D
Baths: 1 En 1 Sh
🛌 🅿 (3) 🗆 🛏 🎩 🖳 Ⅴ ✦

(1m) *Langthwaite*, *Crook Road, Ferry View, Bowness-on-Windermere, Windermere, Cumbria, LA23 3JB.*
Beautiful bungalow. Luxurious, quiet accommodation, breakfast in conservatory, warm welcome.
Grades: AA 4 Diamond
Tel: **015394 43329** Mr Newham.
D: £20.00-£26.00 **S:** £30.00-£40.00.
Open: Feb to Nov
Beds: 2D 1T **Baths:** 3 En
🅿 (4) ⊬ 🗆 🎩 🖳 Ⅴ 🛈

(0.5m 🚌) *Thornleigh*, *Thornbarrow Road, Bowness-on-Windermere, Windermere, Cumbria, LA23 2EW.*
Friendly licensed guest house.
Excellent home cooking and a warm welcome.
Grades: ETC 3 Diamond
Tel: **015394 44203** Mrs Grant.
D: £16.00-£26.00 **S:** £16.00-£26.00.
Open: All Year (not Xmas/New Year)
Beds: 1T 3D 1F 1S
Baths: 4 En 2 Sh
🛌 🅿 (3) ⊬ 🗆 🛏 🎩 🖳 Ⅴ 🛈

(0.5m) *Bay House Lake View*, *Guest House, Fallbarrow Road, Bowness-on-Windermere, Windermere, Cumbria, LA23 3DJ.*
Informal, fun & friendly. Close to all amenities. Vegetarians catered for.
Tel: **015394 43383**
Mrs Large.
D: £17.50-£35.00.
S: £22.50-£30.00.
Open: All Year
Beds: 5D 1T
Baths: 2 Sh
🛌 🅿 (4) 🗆 🛏 🎩 🖳 Ⅴ 🛈 ✦

(1m) *Langdale View Guest House*, *114 Craig Walk, Helm Road, Bowness-on-Windermere, Windermere, Cumbria, LA23 3AX.*
Enjoy this quiet location, warm welcome good food, private parking.
Tel: **015394 44076**
D: £17.00-£25.00
S: £20.00-£25.00.
Open: All Year (not Xmas)
Beds: 1F 2D 1T 1S
Baths: 3 En 2 Pr
🛌 (2) 🅿 (5) ⊬ 🗆 🗙 🎩 🖳 Ⅴ 🛈 ✦

(1m 🚌) *Lowfell*, *Ferney Green, Bowness-on-Windermere, Windermere, Cumbria, LA23 3ES.*
Close Lake Windermere, in heart of English Lake District.
Tel: **015394 45612**
Broughton.
Fax no: 015394 48411
D: £25.00-£25.00 .
Open: All Year (not Xmas)
Beds: 1F 1T 1D
Baths: 3 En
🛌 🅿 (6) ⊬ 🗆 🎩 🖳 Ⅴ 🛈 ✦

(1m 🚌) *Elim Lodge*, *Bisky Howe Road, Bowness-on-Windermere, Windermere, Cumbria, LA23 2JP.*
Comfortable family-run guest house with a lovely garden and private parking.
Tel: **015394 47299**
Mrs Mickelfield.
D: £16.00-£28.00
S: £16.00-£28.00.
Open: All Year
Beds: 2F 2D 1T 1S
Baths: 3 En 2 Sh
🛌 🅿 (6) 🗆 🛏 🗙 🎩 🖳 Ⅴ 🛈

🚌 sign means that, *given due notice*, owners will pick you up from the path and drop you off *within reason.*

Windermere 23

National Grid Ref: SD4198

⚑ ⬥ Brown Horse, The Lamplighter, Grey Walls Inn, Elleray Hotel, Queen's, Village Inn, Chase, Waverley

(0.5m 🚗) **Kenilworth Guest House,** Holly Road, Windermere, Cumbria, LA23 2AF.
Actual grid ref: SD413982
Tel: **015394 44004** Mr Roberts.
Fax no: 015394 46554
D: £16.00 **S:** £16.00.
Open: All Year
Beds: 1F 2T 2D 1S
Baths: 3 En 3 Sh
🛪 🅿 (3) ⮸ ☐ ★ ♋ ≞ Ⅲ. Ⅵ ﹟ ✦
Comfortable Victorian house, two minutes centre Windermere. Convenient centre for exploring all Lakeland's beautiful scenery. Memorable breakfast. Helpful friendly hosts. Free transport to/from station.

(1m) **Braemount House,** Sunny Bank Road, Windermere, Cumbria, LA23 2EN.
Grades: ETC 4 Diamond
Tel: **015394 45967** (also fax no)
D: £23.00-£27.00 **S:** £23.00-£27.00.
Open: All Year (not Xmas)
Beds: 3F 2D 1T **Baths:** 6 En
🛪 🅿 (6) ⮸ ☐ ★ ♋ ≞ Ⅲ. Ⅵ ﹟ ✦
Our guest book reads 'immaculate accommodation and lots of extras not normally available', 'excellent, especially breakfast in bed', 'great once again', 'wonderful', 'lovely room, brilliant hospitality, yummy breakfast', 'we will be back' and many more. Why not come and read it?

(1m 🚗) **Westbury House,** 27 Broad Street, Windermere, Cumbria, LA23 2AB.
Victorian house, centre of Windermere. Near lake, shops, trains. Lovely food.
Grades: ETC 3 Diamond
Tel: **015394 46839** Mrs Baker.
Fax no: 015394 42784
D: £14.00-£23.00 **S:** £16.00-£30.00.
Open: All Year
Beds: 2F 3D 1T **Baths:** 4 En 1 Sh
🛪 (2) 🅿 (5) ☐ ≞ Ⅲ. Ⅵ ﹟ ✦

(1m) **Heatherbank,** 13 Birch Street, Windermere, Cumbria, LA23 1EG.
Grades: ETC 3 Diamond
Tel: **015394 46503** (also fax no)
Mrs Houghton.
D: £19.00-£27.00 **S:** £20.00-£30.00.
Open: All Year (not Xmas)
Beds: 3D 2T **Baths:** 5 En
🅿 (4) ⮸ ☐ ≞ Ⅲ. Ⅵ
Heatherbank is a quiet, comfortable, non-smoking, Lakeland stone guest house. Situated in the centre of Windermere village, it is within 5 mins walk of the rail/bus station. Heatherbank is noted for its superb English breakfast.

(1m) **Villa Lodge,** Cross Street, Windermere, Cumbria, LA23 1AE.
Grades: ETC 4 Diamond,
AA 4 Diamond
Tel: **015394 43318** (also fax no)
Mr Rooney.
D: £22.00-£35.00 **S:** £22.00-£30.00.
Open: All Year
Beds: 5D 1T 2S
Baths: 8 En
🛪 🅿 (8) ⮸ ☐ ★ ✗ ♋ ≞ Ⅲ. Ⅵ ﹟ ✦
Warm welcome, extremely comfortable and traditional accommodation in peaceful area overlooking Windermere village, yet two minutes from bus/ rail stations. All bedrooms are ensuite. English breakfast a speciality in delightful dining room. An excellent base for exploring the Lake District.

(1m) **Meadfoot,** New Road, Windermere, Cumbria, LA23 2LA.
Detached house, large garden, patio and summerhouse. Warm welcome assured.
Grades: ETC 4 Diamond
Tel: **015394 42610** Shaw.
Fax no: 015394 45280
D: £20.00-£27.00 **S:** £22.50-£27.00.
Open: All Year
Beds: 1F 3D 2T 1S
Baths: 7 En
🛪 🅿 (7) ⮸ ☐ ★ ♋ ≞ Ⅲ. Ⅵ ✦

(1m) **Firgarth,** Ambleside Road, Windermere, Cumbria, LA23 1EU.
Actual grid ref: SD407993
Comfortable Victorian country house, fine views, opposite riding stables.
Grades: ETC 3 Diamond,
AA 3 Diamond
Tel: **015394 46974**
Mr & Mrs Lucking.
Fax no: 015394 42384
D: £17.50-£21.00 **S:** £17.50-£24.00.
Open: All Year
Beds: 1F 3D 3T 1S
Baths: 8 Pr
🛪 🅿 (9) ☐ ★ ≞ Ⅲ. Ⅵ ﹟ ✦

(1.5m 🚗) **Holly Lodge Guest House,** 6 College Road, Windermere, Cumbria, LA23 1BX.
Actual grid ref: SD412984
Family-run centrally situated traditional Lakeland guest house. Good English breakfasts.
Grades: ETC 3 Diamond,
AA 3 Diamond
Tel: **015394 43873** (also fax no)
Mr Priestley.
D: £18.00-£27.00 **S:** £18.00-£27.00.
Open: All Year (not Xmas)
Beds: 2F 5D 3T 1S
Baths: 6 En 2 Sh
🛪 🅿 (7) ☐ ★ ≞ Ⅲ. Ⅵ ﹟ ✦

S = Price range for a single person in a single room

(1m) **Ivy Bank,** Holly Road, Windermere, Cumbria, LA23 2AF.
Pretty Victorian stone built home offering comfortable and attractive accommodation.
Grades: ETC 4 Diamond
Tel: **015394 42601** Mr Clothier.
D: £18.00-£25.00 .
Open: All Year (not Xmas/ New Year)
Beds: 1F 1T 3D
Baths: 5 En
🛪 🅿 (6) ⮸ ☐ ★ ♋ ≞ Ⅲ. Ⅵ ✦

(1m) **The Buzzards,** off Thornbarrow Road, Windermere, Cumbria, LA23 2DF.
Bungalow with mountain views. Ideal centre for cycling, walking, sailing.
Tel: **015394 42271** Whelan.
D: £14.50-£19.50 **S:** £14.50-£19.50.
Open: All Year (not Xmas)
Beds: 1D 1S
Baths: 1 Sh
🅿 (6) ⮸ ☐ ≞ Ⅲ. Ⅵ ✦

(1m) **Autumn Leaves Guest House,** 29 Broad Street, Windermere, Cumbria, LA23 2AB.
Victorian house, five minutes from station, one minute from centre.
Grades: ETC 3 Diamond
Tel: **015394 48410**
D: £14.00-£24.00 **S:** £14.00-£20.00.
Open: All Year
Beds: 1F 1T 3D 1S
Baths: 3 En 1 Sh
🛪 ⮸ ☐ ★ ✗ ≞ Ⅲ. Ⅵ ✦

(1m) **Aspen Cottage,** 6 Havelock Road, Windermere, Cumbria, LA23 1EH.
Stone built cottage. Ten minute walk to lake Windermere.
Tel: **015394 43946** Mrs Walsh.
D: £15.00-£17.00 **S:** £16.00-£18.00.
Open: All Year
Beds: 1F 2D **Baths:** 2 Sh
🛪 🅿 (2) ☐ ★ ≞ Ⅲ. Ⅵ

(0.25m) **Westbourne,** Biskey Howe Road, Windermere, Cumbria, LA23 2JR.
Situated below picturesque Biskley Howe view point. 2 minutes off the Dales Way.
Grades: ETC 4 Diamond
Tel: **015394 43625** (also fax no)
Mr Wright.
D: £20.00-£50.00 **S:** £28.00-£38.00.
Open: All Year (not Xmas)
Beds: 2F 7D 2T 1S **Baths:** 9 En
🛪 🅿 (11) ⮸ ☐ ★ ♋ ≞ Ⅲ. Ⅵ ﹟ ✦

(1m 🚗) **Chestnuts Cottage,** Princes Road, Windermere, Cumbria, LA23 2DD.
Chestnuts offers hotel accommodation at guest house prices.
Grades: ETC 4 Diamond
Tel: **015394 46999**
Mr Reed.
D: £22.50-£45.00 .
Open: All Year
Beds: 6D **Baths:** 4 Pr 1 Sh
🛪 🅿 (6) ⮸ ☐ ★ ≞ Ⅲ. ♋ Ⅵ

(1m) *Broadlands Guest House,*
19 Broad Street, Windermere,
Cumbria, LA23 2AB.
Small family run guest house near
village centre. ideal touring base.
Grades: AA 3 Diamond
Tel: **015394 46532** Mrs Pearson.
Fax no: 015394 48474
D: £19.00-£25.00 .
Open: All Year (not Xmas)
Beds: 1F 1T 2D **Baths:** 4 En
⌂⅏✗⬚⊁⇘🏫.Ⅵⓘ

(1m) *Lingmoor, 7 High Street,*
Windermere, Cumbria, LA23 1AF.
Excellent value. Small family-run
guest house, very close to all local
amenities.
Tel: **015394 44947** Mr Hill.
D: £12.00-£20.00 **S:** £12.00-£20.00.
Open: All Year
Beds: 1F 4D 2T 1S
Baths: 2 En 2 Sh
⌂⅏✗⬚⊁⇘.Ⅵⓘ✦

(1m) *Cambridge House, 9 Oak St,*
Windermere, Cumbria, LA23 1EN.
Actual grid ref: SD413996
A traditional Lakeland stone guest
house situated in Windermere vil-
lage centre.
Tel: **015394 43846** Mr Fear.
D: £16.00-£20.00 .
Open: All Year (not Xmas)
Beds: 1F 5D **Baths:** 6 En
⌂(5)⊁⬚⇘.Ⅵⓘ✦

All paths are
popular: you are
well-advised to
book ahead

(1m 🚐) *Rockside, Ambleside Rd,*
Windermere, Cumbria, LA23 1AQ.
Superb accommodation in
Windermere Village 150 yards
from train and bus station.
Tel: **015394 45343** (also fax no)
Mrs Coleman.
D: £19.50-£28.00 **S:** £19.50-£28.00.
Open: All Year
Beds: 13F 1D 3T **Baths:** 10 En 5 Sh
⌂🅿(10)⬚⇘.Ⅵ

(1m) *Kays Cottage, 7 Broad Street,*
Windermere, Cumbria, LA23 2AB.
Actual grid ref: SD412983
Small guest house, comfortable
ensuite rooms, conveniently
situated, generous breakfast.
Tel: **015394 44146** Ms Richardson.
D: £15.00-£22.00 **S:** £22.00-£30.00.
Open: Feb to Nov
Beds: 1F 3D **Baths:** 4 En
⌂(4)⬚⇘.Ⅵ

(1m) *Upper Oakmere Guest*
House, 3 Upper Oak Street,
Windermere, Cumbria, LA23 2LB.
Ideal location. Friendly atmos-
phere, home cooking, 100 yards
Main Street.
Tel: **015394 45649**
D: £12.00-£18.00 **S:** £12.00-£18.00.
Open: All Year
Beds: 1F 3D 2T **Baths:** 2 En 1 Sh
⌂🅿(2)⬚⇘✗⇘.Ⅵⓘ

(1m 🚐) *Glencree Private Hotel,*
Lake Road, Windermere, Cumbria,
LA23 2EQ.
A very warm welcome awaits you
at this recently refurbished tradi-
tional Lakeland house.
Tel: **015394 45822** Mrs Butterworth
D: £20.00-£30.00 **S:** £25.00-£40.00.
Open: All Year
Beds: 1F 5D **Baths:** 6 En
⌂(5)🅿(5)⊁⬚⇘✗⇘.Ⅵⓘ✦

(0.75m) *Clifton House,*
28 Ellerthwaite Road, Windermere,
Cumbria, LA23 2AH.
Actual grid ref: SD413981
Friendly guest house. All ensuite
with TV. Non-smoking.
Tel: **015394 44968**
D: £15.00-£25.00 **S:** £15.00-£30.00.
Open: All Year
Beds: 1F 2D 1T 1S **Baths:** 5 En
⌂(6)⊁⬚⇘.Ⅵ✦

(0.25m 🚐) *Eastbourne Hotel,*
Biskey Howe Road, Windermere,
Cumbria, LA23 2JR.
Located below Biskey Howe
Viewpoint and close to Lake and
all amenities.
Tel: **015394 43525** Mr Whitfield.
Fax no: 015394 43338
D: £19.00-£30.00 **S:** £27.00-£35.00.
Open: Feb to Dec
Beds: 1F 5D 1T 1S **Baths:** 7 En 1 Pr
⌂(5)🅿(6)⊁⬚⇘.Ⅵ✦

(1m 🚐) *Gillthwaite Rigg,*
Heathwaite Manor, Lickbarrow
Road, Windermere, Cumbria,
LA23 2NQ.
Actual grid ref: SD419969
Peaceful manor house close to lake,
fells, golf course, restaurants.
Tel: **015394 46212** Mrs Graham.
D: £23.00-£25.00 **S:** £25.00-£25.00.
Open: All Year (not Xmas)
Beds: 1D 1T **Baths:** 2 En
⌂🅿(3)⊁⬚⇘.Ⅵ✦

Please take muddy
boots off before
entering premises

IRELAND: BED & BREAKFAST 2001

The essential guide to B&Bs in the Republic of Ireland and Northen Ireland

Think of Ireland and you think of that famous Irish hospitality. The warmth of the welcome is as much a part of this great island as the wild and beautiful landscapes, the traditional folk music and the Guiness. Wherever you go, town or country, North or South, you can't escape it.

There are few better ways of experiencing this renowned hospitality, when traveling through Ireland, than by staying at one of the country's many Bed & Breakfasts. They offer a great value alternative to expensive hotels, each has its own individual charm and you get a home cooked breakfast to help you start your day.

Stilwell's Ireland: Bed & Breakfast 2001 is the most comprehensive guide of its kind, with over 1,400 entries listed by county and location, in both Northern Ireland and the Republic of Ireland. Each entry includes room rates, facilities, Tourist Board grades, local maps and a brief description of the B&B, its location and surroundings.

Treat yourself to some Irish hospitality with **Stilwell Ireland: Bed & Breakfast 2001.**

Private Houses, Country Halls, Farms, Cottages, Inns, Small Hotels and Guest Houses

Over 1,400 entries
Average price £18 per person per night ($32 per person per night)
All official grades shown
Local maps
Pubs serving hot evening meals shown
Tourist Information Offices listed
Handy size for easy packing!

£6.95 from all good bookstores (ISBN 1-900861-24-0) or £7.95 (inc p&p) from Stilwell Publishing, 59 Charlotte Road, London EC2A 3QW (020 7739 7179)

Essex Way

Covering a distance of 81 miles, the **Essex Way** stretches from Epping in the south-west to Harwich, the busy sea port, in the northeast. The path is perfect for Londoners who want easy access to a good, waymarked long-distance footpath. It is well-placed for public transport, which is accessible at all points of the path. You get to see a rural Essex unheard of outside the county boundaries - ancient woodland, open farmland, the tree-flanked River Colne, leafy valleys, green country lanes and saltmarshes. A good spring-time or autumn walk - the terrain is very easy going, but can be muddy after rain.

Guides: *The Essex Way* by Essex County Council (ISBN 1 852810 87 4), published by Essex County Council and available directly from their offices (Ways Through Essex, TOPS Dept, County Hall, Chelmsford, Essex, CM1 1LF, tel. 01245 437649), £3.00

Maps: 1:50000 Ordnance Survey Landranger Series: 167, 168, 169

Margaret Roding 1	High Easter 2	Braintree 3
National Grid Ref: TL5912	National Grid Ref: TL6214	National Grid Ref: TL7623

Margaret Roding 1

National Grid Ref: TL5912

(1m 🚍) *Greys, Ongar Road, Margaret Roding, Great Dunmow, Essex, CM6 1QR.*
Actual grid ref: TL605112
Old beamed cottage, pleasantly situated amidst our farmland tiny village.
Grades: ETC 3 Diamond, AA 3 Diamond
Tel: 01245 231509 Mrs Matthews.
D: £22.00 **S:** £23.00.
Open: All Year (not Xmas)
Beds: 2D 1T **Baths:** 1 Sh
🛏 (10) 🅿 (3) ⅍ ⬚ 🕮 ⅍

High Easter 2

National Grid Ref: TL6214

(On path) *The Cock & Bell, The Street, High Easter, Chelmsford, Essex, CM1 4QW.*
14th Century former Coaching Inn - operating as charming Guest House.
Tel: 01245 231296 Steel.
D: £19.50-£24.50 **S:** £22.50-£27.50.
Open: All Year (not Xmas/ New Year)
Beds: 2D 1F 1S
Baths: 2 En 1 Sh
🅿 ⬚ ✕ 🍴 🕮 Ⓥ ⅃

Braintree 3

National Grid Ref: TL7623

(2m 🚍) *The Old House Guesthouse, 11 Bradford Street, Braintree, Essex, CM7 9AS.*
Actual grid ref: TL760238
Family-run, C16th guest house within walking distance town centre.
Tel: 01376 550457 Mrs Hughes.
Fax no: 01376 343863
D: £19.00-£30.00 **S:** £23.00-£30.00.
Open: All Year
Beds: 2F 5D 1T
Baths: 6 Pr 2 Sh
🛏 🅿 (10) ⅍ ⬚ ✕ 🍴 🕮 Ⓥ ⅃ ⅍

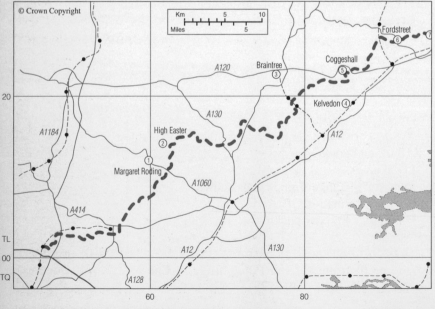
© Crown Copyright

Kelvedon 4

National Grid Ref: TL8518

🍴 🍺 Sun Inn

(2m 🚐) *Highfields Farm,*
Kelvedon, Colchester, Essex,
CO5 9BJ.
Farmhouse in quiet countryside
location, convenient for A12 and
London.
Grades: ETC 3 Diamond
Tel: **01376 570334** (also fax no)
Mrs Bunting.
D: £22.00-£22.00 **S:** £22.00-£24.00.
Open: All Year
Beds: 1D 2T **Baths:** 2 En 1 Pr
🛏 🅿 (4) 🍴 🖵 🐾 🎇 🛏 📺 🔌 🖗

Coggeshall 5

National Grid Ref: TL8522

🍴 🍺 Woolpack Inn

(0.25m) *White Heather Guest*
House, 19 Colchester Road,
Coggeshall, Colchester, Essex,
CO6 1RP.
Actual grid ref: TL859228
Modern, family-run guest house,
overlooking farmland.
Tel: **01376 563004** Mrs Shaw.
D: £22.00-£22.50 **S:** £22.00-£25.00.
Open: All Year (not Xmas)
Beds: 2D 2S **Baths:** 2 En 1 Sh
🅿 (8) 🍴 🖵 🛏 📺 🔌 📺

🚐 sign means that,
given due notice,
owners will pick you
up from the path
and drop you off *with-*
in reason.

All rates are subject
to alteration at the
owners' discretion.

Fordstreet 6

National Grid Ref: TL9226

🍴 🍺 Coopers Arms, Queen's Head, Shoulder of
Mutton

(On path) *Old House,* Fordstreet,
Aldham, Colchester, Essex, CO6 3PH.
Actual grid ref: TL920270
Fascinating Grade II Listed C14th
hall house - oak beams, log fires,
large garden.
Grades: ETC 3 Diamond
Tel: **01206 240456** (also fax no)
Mrs Mitchell.
D: £20.00-£25.00 **S:** £27.50.
Open: All Year
Beds: 1F 1T 1S
Baths: 1 En 2 Pr
🛏 🅿 (6) 🖵 🛏 📺 📺 🔌

West Bergholt 7

National Grid Ref: TL9627

🍴 🍺 Queens Head, White Hart, Treble Tile

(On path) *The Old Post House,*
10 Colchester Road, West
Bergholt, Colchester, Essex,
CO6 3JG.
Actual grid ref: TL9527
Large Victorian private house,
warm welcome, quiet secluded
garden.
Grades: ETC 3 Diamond
Tel: **01206 240379** Mrs Brown.
Fax no: 01206 243301
D: £20.00-£25.00 **S:** £20.00.
Open: All Year
Beds: 1F 1D 1T
Baths: 1 En 1 Sh
🛏 (1) 🅿 (3) 🖵 🛏 📺 🔌 🖗

Nayland 8

National Grid Ref: TL9734

🍴 🍺 The Lion, White Hart

(0.5m 🚐) *Gladwins Farm,*
Harpers Hill, Nayland, Colchester,
Essex, CO6 4NU.
Actual grid ref: TL961347
Grades: ETC 4 Diamond
Tel: **01206 262261** Mrs Dossor.
Fax no: 01206 263001
D: £28.00-£30.00 **S:** £25.00-£30.00.
Open: All Year (not Xmas)
Beds: 2D 1S
Baths: 2 En 1 Pr
🛏 (8) 🅿 (14) 🍴 🖵 🗶 🐾 🎇 📺 🔌 🖗
Traditional Suffolk farmhouse
B&B with ensuite rooms, in 22
acres of beautiful rolling Constable
country, or choose a self-catering
cottage. Heated indoor pool, sauna,
aromatherapy suite, hard tennis
court, fishing lake, children's
playground. Pets welcome. Colour
brochure from resident owners.

(0.5m 🚐) *Hill House, Gravel Hill,*
Nayland, Colchester, Essex,
CO6 4JB.
Actual grid ref: TL975345
C16th beamed hall house on edge
of historic Constable village.
Tel: **01206 262782** Mrs Heigham.
D: £20.00-£26.00 **S:** £22.00-£25.00.
Open: All Year (not Xmas)
Beds: 1D 1T 1S
Baths: 1 En 2 Pr
🛏 (8) 🅿 (6) 🍴 🖵 🛏 📺 🔌 🖗

Many rates vary
according to season -
the lowest only are
shown here

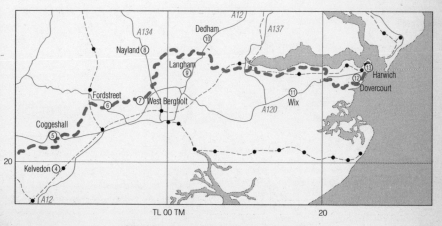

Langham 9

National Grid Ref: TM0233

⚞⚟ Shepherd & Dog

(1m ⚌) *Oak Apple Farm,*
Greyhound Hill, Langham,
Colchester, Essex, CO4 5QF.
Actual grid ref: TM023320
Comfortable farmhouse tastefully
decorated with large attractive garden
Grades: ETC 4 Diamond
Tel: **01206 272234** Mrs Helliwell.
D: £22.00 **S:** £22.00.
Open: All Year (not Xmas)
Beds: 2T 1S **Baths:** 1 Sh
⚞ ⊞ (6) ▢ ⚐ ▥ ▥ ⓥ ⓐ ✦

Dedham 10

National Grid Ref: TM0533

⚞⚟ Marlborough Head

(0.5m) *Mays Barn Farm, Mays*
Lane, Dedham, Colchester, Essex,
CO7 6EW.
Actual grid ref: TM0531
A Comfortable well-furnished old
house with wonderful views of
Dedham Vale.
Grades: ETC 4 Diamond
Tel: **01206 323191** Mrs Freeman.
D: £20.00-£22.00 **S:** £25.00-£30.00.
Open: All Year
Beds: 1D 1T **Baths:** 1 En 1 Pr
⚞ (12) ⊞ (3) ✄ ▢ ⚐ ▥ ⓥ

Wix 11

National Grid Ref: TM1628

⚞⚟ Village Maid

(1.5m ⚌) *Dairy House Farm,*
Bradfield Road, Wix, Manningtree,
Essex, CO11 2SR.
Spacious quality, rural
accommodation. A really relaxing
place to stay.
Grades: ETC 4 Diamond, Gold
Tel: **01255 870322**
Mrs Whitworth.
Fax no: 01255 870186
D: £18.50-£20.00
S: £26.00-£26.00.
Open: All Year (not Xmas)
Beds: 1D 2T
Baths: 2 En 1 Pr
⚞ (12) ⊞ (4) ▢ ⚐ ▥ ⓥ ⓐ ✦

Pay B&Bs by

cash or cheque and

be prepared to

pay up front.

Dovercourt 12

National Grid Ref: TM2531

⚞⚟ Royal Oak Inn

(0.25m) *Dudley Guest House,*
34 Cliff Road, Dovercourt,
Harwich, Essex, CO12 3PP.
Family-run Victorian house.
Railway/buses short walk. Pubs,
restaurants, shops, banks close by.
Grades: ETC 2 Diamond
Tel: **01255 504927** Mr Rackham.
D: £14.00-£18.00 **S:** £18.00-£22.00.
Open: All Year
Beds: 1F 1D 1T 1S
Baths: 1 En 2 Sh
⚞ ⊞ (4) ✄ ▢ ⚐ ▥ ⓥ

Harwich 13

National Grid Ref: TM2431

⚞⚟ The Royal Oak

(1m ⚌) *Tudor Rose, 124 Fronks*
Road, Dovercourt, Harwich,
CO12 4EQ.
Harwich international port.
Seafront, Railway 5 minutes.
London 1 hour.
Tel: **01255 552398**
D: £17.50-£17.50 **S:** £20.00-£30.00.
Open: May to Aug
⚞ ⊞ (2) ✄ ▢ ⚐ ▥ ⓥ ✦

STILWELL'S BRITAIN CYCLEWAY COMPANION

23 Long Distance Cycleways * Where to Stay * Where to Eat

County Cycleways – Sustrans Routes

The first guide of its kind, **Stilwell's Britain Cycleway Companion** makes planning accommodation for your cycling trip easy. It lists B&Bs, hostels, campsites and pubs– in the order they appear along the selected cycleways – allowing the cyclist to book ahead. No more hunting for a room, a hot meal or a cold drink after a long day in the saddle. Stilwell's gives descriptions of the featured routes and includes such relevant information as maps, grid references and distance from route; Tourist Board ratings; and the availability of drying facilities and packed lunches. No matter which route – or part of a route – you decide to ride, let the **Cycleway Companion** show you where to sleep and eat.

As essential as your tyre pump – the perfect cycling companion: **Stilwell's Britain Cycleway Companion**.

Cycleways Sustrans
Carlisle to Inverness – Clyde to Forth - Devon Coast to Coast - Hull to Harwich – Kingfisher Cycle Trail - Lon Las Cymru – Sea to Sea (C2C) – Severn and Thames - West Country Way – White Rose Cycle Route

County
Round Berkshire Cycle Route – Cheshire Cycleway – Cumbria Cycleway – Essex Cycle Route – Icknield Way - Lancashire Cycleway – Leicestershire County Cycleway – Oxfordshire Cycleway – Reivers Cycle Route – South Downs Way - Surrey Cycleway – Wiltshire Cycleway – Yorkshire Dales Cycleway

£9.95 from all good bookstores (ISBN 1-900861-26-7) or £10.95 (inc p&p) from Stilwell Publishing, 59 Charlotte Road, London EC2A 3QW (020 7739 7179)

Greensand Way

This is a lovely part of the country, kept secret by natives of Surrey and Kent. Between the great chalk ridges of the North and South Downs there runs a sandstone strip that stands out peculiarly from the ordinary clay vales of the Sussex Weald. There is sand underfoot - in dry weather it can be like walking on a beach.

The full 110-mile **Greensand Way** was opened in 1989, beginning at Haslemere in Surrey and finishing at Hamstreet in Kent. The Surrey section has the more extensive Lower Greensand hills (including the two highest points, Leith Hill and Gibbet Hill); towards Dorking the path crosses farmland and cuts through villages; the North Downs are ever present. On the Kent side, much of the Greensand ridge's mature oaks and beeches

were devastated by the great storm of 1987. So now the woodland floor is covered with young silver birch. The path is prone to mud at times, but much of the walk is over freely draining sand, providing firm walking ground most of the year.

Guide: *Along and Around the Greensand Way* by Bea Cowan (ISBN 1 873010 91 5), published jointly by Kent and Surrey County Councils and available from bookshops or directly from Kent CC, tel. 01622 22152 or Surrey CC, tel. 020 8541 9463, price £7.95

Map: 1:50000 Ordnance Survey Landranger Series: 186, 187, 188, 189

Hindhead 1

National Grid Ref: SU8836

(▲ 1m) *Hindhead Youth Hostel, Highcoombe Bottom, Bowlhead Green, Hindhead, Godalming, Surrey, GU7 6NS.*
Actual grid ref: SU892368
Tel: **01428 604285**
Under 18: £5.25 **Adults:** £7.50
Self-catering facilities, Lounge, No smoking, Kitchen facilities
A superbly simple hostel, set in the peaceful haven of the Devil's Punchbowl, converted from three National Trust cottages and refurbished to a high standard.

Thursley 2

National Grid Ref: SU9039

|●| ◀ Three Horseshoes, The Star, White Hart, Pride of the Valley

(0.5m 🚐) *Hindhead Hill Farm, Portsmouth Road, Thursley, Godalming, Surrey, GU8 6NN.*
Actual grid ref: SU906387
Small Christian family farm. Our own free-range eggs for breakfast.
Tel: **01428 684727** Mrs Roe.
Fax no: 01428 685004
D: £19.00-£19.00 **S:** £20.00-£20.00.
Open: All Year (not Xmas)
Beds: 1F 1T **Baths:** 1 En 1 Pr
🛉 (5) ▣ (4) ⅍☐✗🕭▥ Ⓥ 🛏

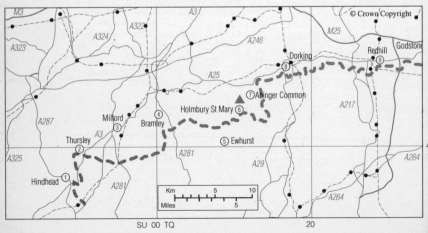

Always telephone to get directions to the B&B - you will save time!

(On path) *Little Cowdray Farm,*
Thursley, Godalming, Surrey,
GU8 6QJ.
Quiet peaceful situation, good
walking area, edge of Devils Punch
Bowl.
Tel: **01428 605016** Mrs Goble.
D: £31.00-£31.00 **S:** £18.00-£18.00.
Open: All Year (not Xmas/
New Year)
Beds: 1T **Baths:** 1 Sh
🅿🗌🏠✕🌂🛏🎱Ⓥ🛆⚲

Milford   3
National Grid Ref: SU9442

🍴🍺 The Star, Red Lion

(2m 🚌) *Coturnix House, Rake*
Lane, Milford, Godalming, Surrey,
GU8 5AB.
Modern house, family atmosphere,
countryside position, easy access
road/rail.
Tel: **01483 416897** Mr Bell.
D: £20.00-£20.00 **S:** £20.00-£20.00.
Open: All Year
Beds: 1D 1T 1S **Baths:** 1 Pr 1 Sh
🐾(1)🅿(6)🌂🗌🏠🛏🎱Ⓥ

D = Price range per

person sharing in a

double room

Bramley   4
National Grid Ref: TQ0044

🍴🍺 Jolly Farmer, Grantley Arms

(1.75m) *Beevers Farm, Chinthurst*
Lane, Bramley, Guildford, Surrey,
GU5 0DR.
Peaceful surroundings, friendly
atmosphere, own preserves, honey,
eggs, nearby villages.
Grades: ETC 3 Diamond
Tel: **01483 898764** (also fax no)
Mr Cook.
D: £18.00-£25.00 **S:** £30.00.
Open: Easter to Nov
Beds: 1F 2T **Baths:** 1 Pr 1 Sh
🐾🅿(10)🌂🗌🛏🎱Ⓥ🛆⚲

Ewhurst   5
National Grid Ref: TQ0940

🍴🍺 The Windmill, Scarlett Arms, Bull's Head

(1.5m) *High Edser, Shere Road,*
Ewhurst, Cranleigh, Surrey,
GU6 7PQ.
Grades: ETC 3 Diamond
Tel: **01483 278214**
Mrs Franklin-Adams.
Fax no: 01483 278200
D: £27.50-£27.50 **S:** £30.00-£35.00.
Open: All Year (not Xmas)
Beds: 2D 1T **Baths:** 1 Sh
🐾🅿(6)🌂🗌🏠🛏🎱Ⓥ⚲
C16th farmhouse in Area of
Outstanding Natural Beauty, a
beautiful setting for a restful break.
We are close to many National
Trust Properties and within easy
reach of London. Gatwick/London
airports are 30/45 minutes drive.

S = Price range for a single

person in a single room

(1m 🚌) *Malricks, The Street,*
Ewhurst, Cranleigh, Surrey,
GU6 7RH.
Actual grid ref: TQ093401
Modern detached house, village
location. Large attractive garden
overlooking fields.
Tel: **01483 277575** Mrs Budgen.
D: £19.00-£19.00 **S:** £19.00-£19.00.
Open: All Year
Beds: 1F 1T
Baths: 1 En 1 Sh
🐾🅿(3)🌂🗌🏠🎱⚲

(1.5m) *Yard Farm, North Breache*
Road, Ewhurst, Cranleigh, Surrey,
GU6 7SN.
Traditional C16th farmhouse in
Surrey countryside surrounded by
farmland.
Tel: **01483 276649** (also fax no)
Mrs Nutting.
D: £22.50-£22.50 **S:** £22.50-£25.00.
Open: All Year (not Xmas)
Beds: 1D 2T 1S
Baths: 2 En 1 Pr
🐾(12)🅿(6)🗌🏠🛏🎱Ⓥ🛆⚲

Holmbury St Mary   6
National Grid Ref: TQ1144

🍴🍺 Royal Oak, Parrot Inn, The Volunteer,
King's Head

(▲ 1m) *Holmbury St Mary Youth*
Hostel, Radnor Lane, Holmbury St
Mary, Dorking, Surrey, RH5 6NW.
Actual grid ref: TQ104450
Tel: **01306 730777**
Under 18: £6.90 **Adults:** £10.00
Self-catering facilities, Showers,
Wet weather shelter, Lounge,
Drying room, Cycle store, Evening
meal at 7.00pm, No smoking,
Kitchen facilities, Breakfast
available, Credit cards accepted
Set in its own 5,000 acres of
woodland grounds, this purpose-
built hostel offers tranquil beauty
among the Surrey Hills.

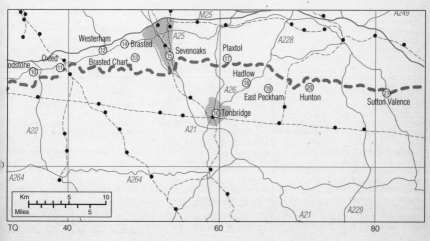

D = Price range per person
sharing in a double room

(On path) *Bulmer Farm,*
Holmbury St Mary, Dorking,
Surrey, RH5 6LG.
Actual grid ref: TQ114441
Quiet modernised C17th farm-
house/barn, large garden, pic-
turesque village, self-catering.
Grades: ETC 4 Diamond
Tel: **01306 730210** Mrs Hill.
D: £22.00-£24.00 **S:** £22.00-£35.00.
Open: All Year
Beds: 3D 5T **Baths:** 5 En 2 Sh
🛏 (12) 🅿 (12) ⊬ ⛌ �🛏 🖤 🛆 🔲 ⋔

Abinger Common 7

National Grid Ref: TQ1145

🍴 ⊠ Plough Inn

(0.5m) *Park House Farm,* Leith
Hill Road, Abinger Common,
Dorking, Surrey, RH5 6LW.
Tel: **01306 730101** Mr & Mrs
Wallis.
Fax no: 01306 730643
D: £20.00-£30.00 **S:** £30.00-£50.00.
Open: All Year (not Xmas/
New Year)
Beds: 1T 2D
Baths: 3 En
🛏 (12) 🅿 (10) ⊬ ⛌ 🛏 🖤 🔲
Set in 25 acres in an Area of
Outstanding Natural Beauty, you
are welcome to join us in a large
spacious home which provides
bright, tastefully decorated rooms,
all with excellent views. Easy
access to Gatwick and Heathrow.

Dorking 8

National Grid Ref: TQ1649

🍴 ⊠ King's Arms, Old School House, King
William, The Bush, Inn on the Green

(2m) *The Waltons,* 5 *Rose Hill,*
Dorking, Surrey, RH4 2EG.
Listed house in conservation area.
Beautiful views and friendly
atmosphere.
Tel: **01306 883127** (also fax no)
Mrs Walton.
D: £17.50-£20.00 **S:** £20.00-£32.50.
Open: All Year
Beds: 1F 1D 1T 1S
Baths: 3 Sh
🛏 🅿 (3) ⊬ ⛌ 🛏 ⛌ 🖤 🔲 ⋔

(0.75m) *Shrub Hill,* 3 *Calvert*
Road, Dorking, Surrey, RH4 1LT.
Actual grid ref: TQ167504
Quiet comfortable family home
with excellent views.
Tel: **01306 885229** Mrs Scott Kerr.
D: £25.00-£26.00 **S:** £35.00.
Open: All Year (not Xmas)
Beds: 1T 1S 1D
Baths: 1 Sh 1 En
🛏 (8) 🅿 (2) ⊬ ⛌ 🛏 ⛌ 🖤 🔲 ⋔

(0.25m) 🚍 *Torridon Guest House,*
Longfield Road, Dorking, Surrey,
RH4 3DF.
Large chalet bungalow - quiet loca-
tion.
Grades: ETC 3 Diamond
Tel: **01306 883724** Mrs Short.
Fax no: 01306 880759
D: £23.00-£24.00 **S:** £26.00-£28.00.
Open: All Year
Beds: 1D 1T 1S **Baths:** 1 Sh
🛏 🅿 (4) ⊬ ⛌ 🛏 ⛌ 🖤 🛆 🔲 ⋔

Redhill 9

National Grid Ref: TQ2750

🍴 ⊠ The Sun

(0.75m) *Lynwood Guest House,*
50 *London Road, Redhill, Surrey,*
RH1 1LN.
Actual grid ref: TQ280511
Adjacent to a lovely park, within
6 minutes walking from railway
station, town centre.
Grades: AA 3 Diamond
Tel: **01737 766894** Mrs Trozado.
Fax no: 01737 778253
D: £25.00-£28.00 **S:** £32.00-£35.00.
Open: All Year
Beds: 4F 2D 1T 2S
Baths: 3 En 6 Pr 1 Sh
🛏 🅿 (8) 🔲 🛏 🖤 🔲 ⋔

Godstone 10

National Grid Ref: TQ3551

🍴 ⊠ Coach House

(1m) *Godstone Hotel, The Green,*
Godstone, Surrey, RH9 8DT.
Tel: **01883 742461** (also fax no)
Mr Howe.
D: £27.50 **S:** £39.00.
Open: All Year
Beds: 6D 2T **Baths:** 8 Pr
🛏 🅿 🔲 🛏 ⛌ ⛌ 🖤 🔲 ⋔
C16th coaching house, original features, inglenook fireplaces. Our
restaurant 'The Coach House' is
renowned in the vicinity for superb
cuisine at sensible prices - well
worth a visit. Pre-booking is highly
recommended. Our friendly staff
look forward to welcoming you.

Oxted 11

National Grid Ref: TQ3852

🍴 ⊠ The Oxted, Old Bell, The Crown, The
George, The Gurkha, Royal Oak

(0.5m) *Pinehurst Grange Guest*
House, East Hill (Part of A25),
Oxted, Surrey, RH9 9AE.
Actual grid ref: TQ393525
Comfortable Victorian ex-farm-
house with traditional service and
relaxed friendly atmosphere.
Tel: **01883 716413** Mr Rodgers.
D: £21.00-£21.00 **S:** £26.00-£26.00.
Open: All Year (not Xmas/
New Year)
Beds: 1D 1T 1S **Baths:** 1 Sh
🛏 (5) 🅿 (3) ⊬ ⛌ 🛏 ⛌ 🖤 🔲 ⋔

(0.5m) 🚍 *Meads,* 23 *Granville*
Road, Oxted, Surrey, RH8 0BX.
Tudor style house on Kent/Surrey
border station to London.
Grades: ETC 4 Diamond
Tel: **01883 730115** Mrs Holgate.
D: £25.00-£28.00 **S:** £28.00-£30.00.
Open: All Year
Beds: 1T 1D
Baths: 1 En 1 Pr
🛏 🅿 ⊬ ⛌ 🛏 ⛌ 🖤 🔲 ⋔

(0.5m) 🚍 *Old Forge House, Merle*
Common, Oxted, Surrey, RH8 0JB.
Actual grid ref: TQ416493
Welcoming family home in rural
surroundings. Ten minutes from
M25.
Tel: **01883 715969** Mrs Mills.
D: £18.00-£20.00 **S:** £18.00-£20.00.
Open: All Year (not Xmas)
Beds: 1D 1T 1S
Baths: 1 Sh
🛏 🅿 (4) 🔲 🛏 ⛌ ⋔

Westerham 12

National Grid Ref: TQ4454

🍴 ⊠ The Bull, White Hart

(On path) *Corner Cottage, Toys*
Hill, Westerham, Kent, TN16 1PY.
Attractive self contained accommo-
dation in Laura Ashley fabrics.
Spectacular panoramic views.
Grades: ETC 4 Diamond, Silver
Tel: **01732 750362**
Mrs Olszowska.
Fax no: 01959 561911
D: £45.00-£50.00
S: £30.00-£35.00.
Open: All Year
Beds: 1F
🛏 🅿 (1) ⊬ ⛌ 🛏 ⛌ 🖤 🔲 ⋔

Brasted Chart 13

National Grid Ref: TQ4653

🍴 ⊠ The Bull, White Hart

(1m 🚍) *The Orchard House,*
Brasted Chart, Westerham, Kent,
TN16 1LR.
Actual grid ref: TQ469537
Family home, quiet, rural
surroundings, near Chartwell,
Hever, Knole, Gatwick.
Grades: ETC 3 Diamond
Tel: **01959 563702**
Mrs Godsal.
D: £21.00 **S:** £22.00.
Open: All Year (not Xmas)
Beds: 2T 1S
Baths: 2 Sh
🛏 🅿 (4) ⊬ ⛌ 🖤 🛆 ⋔

All rates are subject
to alteration at the
owners' discretion.

Brasted   14

National Grid Ref: TQ4755

🍴 🍺 The Bull

(1.25m 🚌) *Holmesdale House,*
High Street, Brasted, Westerham,
Kent, TN16 1HS.
Actual grid ref: TQ469550
Delightful Victorian house (part
C17th). Chartwell, Hever, Knole
and Mainline Station.
Tel: **01959 564834** (also fax no)
Mr Jinks.
D: £20.00-£27.50 **S:** £30.00-£30.00.
Open: All Year
Beds: 1F 3D 1T
Baths: 3 En 1 Sh
🛏 🅿 (7) 🔌 🛋 🚿 🖥 🛁 ♿ 🎸 ♿ ✓

(1.25m) *Lodge House,* High Street,
Brasted, Westerham, Kent, TN16 1HS.
Character property, a short walk
from popular village pubs.
Tel: **01959 562195**
Mr & Mrs Marshall.
D: £20.00-£25.00 **S:** £25.00-£30.00.
Open: All Year
Beds: 1F 2D
Baths: 1 En 1 Sh
🛏 🅿 (3) 🔌 🛋 🚿 🖥 🛁 Ⓥ

Sevenoaks   15

National Grid Ref: TQ5255

🍴 🍺 White Hart, The Chequers, Rose & Crown,
The Bull

(2m 🚌) *40 Robyns Way,*
Sevenoaks, Kent, TN13 3EB.
Quiet location, station 10 minutes
walk. French spoken, self catering
available.
Tel: **01732 452401**
Mrs Ingram.
D: £25.00-£28.00 **S:** £27.00-£30.00.
Open: All Year
Beds: 1F 1D 1T
Baths: 2 En 1 Sh
🛏 🅿 (3) 🔌 🛋 🚿 🖥 🛁 ♿ Ⓥ

(2m) *Green Tiles, 46 The Rise,*
Sevenoaks, Kent, TN13 1RJ.
Quiet annexe in lovely garden, own
entrance, for 1-5 guests.
Tel: **01732 451522** (also fax no)
Mrs Knoops.
D: £20.00-£22.00 **S:** £30.00.
Open: All Year
Beds: 1F
Baths: 1 En
🛏 🅿 (2) 🔌 🛋 🚿 🖥 🛁 Ⓥ

(2m) *56 The Drive, Sevenoaks,*
Kent, TN13 3AF.
Lovely Edwardian house and
garden close to station and town.
Peaceful.
Grades: ETC 3 Diamond
Tel: **01732 453236**
Mrs Lloyd.
D: £19.00-£24.50 **S:** £22.00-£28.00.
Open: All Year (not Xmas)
Beds: 2T 2S
Baths: 2 Sh
🅿 (4) 🛋 🛁 Ⓥ ✓

(2m) *Sevenoaks Star House,* Star
Hill, Sevenoaks, Kent, TN14 6HA.
Country house, large garden, stun-
ning views. Near Sevenoaks and
M25.
Grades: ETC 3 Diamond
Tel: **01959 533109**
D: £18.00-£20.50
S: £20.00-£22.50.
Open: All Year (not Xmas)
Beds: 2T 1D
Baths: 2 Pr
🛏 🅿 🔌 🛋 🚿 🖥 🛁 Ⓥ ✓

**Many rates vary
according to season -
the lowest only are
shown here**

(2m) *Burley Lodge, Rockdale*
Road , Sevenoaks, Kent, TN13 1JT.
Beautiful Edwardian house situated
in conservation area in a cul-de-sac
off the High Street.
Tel: **01732 455761** Ms Latter.
Fax no: 01732 458178
D: £20.00-£20.00 **S:** £27.00-£27.00.
Open: All Year
Beds: 1F
Baths: 1 En
🛏 🅿 🔌 🛋 🍴 ✗ 🛁 🖥 🛁 Ⓥ 🎸 ✓

Tonbridge   16

National Grid Ref: TQ5946

🍴 🍺 Kentish Rifleman, Chaser Inn

(1.25m) *Starvecrow Place,*
Starvecrow Hill, Shipbourne Road,
Tonbridge, Kent, TN11 9NL.
Relaxed luxury accommodation set
in delightful woodlands. Heated
outdoor swimming pool.
Tel: **01732 356863**
Mrs Batson.
D: £19.00-£22.00 **S:** £30.00-£30.00.
Open: All Year (not Xmas)
Beds: 2D 1T
Baths: 2 En 1 Pr
🛏 (13) 🅿 (6) 🔌 🛋 🚿 🖥 🛁 Ⓥ ✓

Plaxtol   17

National Grid Ref: TQ6053

🍴 🍺 Kentish Rifleman

(0.5m) *Periwick Place, The Street,*
Plaxtol, Sevenoaks, Kent, TN15 0QF.
Early Victorian village house sur-
rounded by mature pretty garden
(visitors welcome to use this).
Tel: **01732 811024** Mrs Golding.
D: £27.00-£27.00 **S:** £27.50-£27.50.
Open: All Year (not Xmas)
Beds: 1D 1T
Baths: 1 Sh
🛏 (10) 🅿 (4) 🔌 🛋 🚿 🖥 🛁 Ⓥ ✓

**All rooms full and
nowhere else to stay?
Ask the owner if
there's anywhere
nearby**

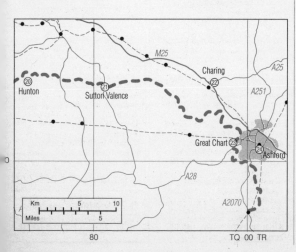

Hadlow 18

National Grid Ref: TQ6350

¶ ◑ Carpenters' Arms

(1.5m) *Dunsmore, Hadlow Park, Hadlow, Tonbridge, Kent, TN11 0HX.*
Private park, quiet, own entrance to ground floor accommodation.
Tel: **01732 850611** (also fax no)
Mrs Tubbs.
D: £18.00-£20.00 **S:** £20.00-£25.00.
Open: All Year (not Xmas)
Beds: 1T **Baths:** 1 Pr
🛏 🅿 🖃 🚽 🌆 🎹 Ⓥ

East Peckham 19

National Grid Ref: TQ6648

¶ ◑ The Bush, Blackbird & Thrush

(On path) *Roydon Hall, off Seven Mile Lane, East Peckham, Tonbridge, Kent, TN12 5NH.*
Actual grid ref: TQ665517
Grades: ETC 3 Diamond
Tel: **01622 812121** Mrs Bence.
Fax no: 01622 813959
D: £17.50-£22.50 **S:** £21.00-£55.00.
Open: All Year (not Xmas/New Year)
Beds: 4F 2D 6T 2S
Baths: 7 En 1 Pr 5 Sh
🛏 🅿 ⅍ 🖃 ✗ 🚽 🌆 Ⓥ ⌀
Very attractive 16th century manor in 10 acres of woodlands and gardens. Peaceful atmosphere, magnificent views. Comfortable rooms. Organic meals available. Less than one hour from central London, Dover and south coast. Perfect for exploring historic towns and beautiful houses and gardens of Kent and Sussex.

Hunton 20

National Grid Ref: TQ7149

¶ ◑ The Bull, Walnut Tree

(0.75m) *The Woolhouse, Grove Lane, Hunton, Maidstone, Kent, ME15 0SE.*
Actual grid ref: TQ715495
C17th Listed beamed converted barn, peaceful lovely atmosphere, antique furniture.
Tel: **01622 820778** Mrs Wetton.
Fax no: 01622 820645
D: £25.00-£25.00 **S:** £25.00-£25.00.
Open: All Year (not Xmas)
Beds: 4F 1D 2T 1S **Baths:** 3 En 1 Pr
🅿 (10) 🖃 🐾 🚽 🌆 Ⓥ

Taking your dog?
Book *in advance*
ONLY with owners
who accept dogs (🐾)

S = Price range for
a single person
in a room

(0.75m) *Wealden Hall House, East Street, Hunton, Maidstone, Kent, ME15 0RB.*
Get away from it all
- stay at Wealden Hall.
Tel: **01622 820246** Mrs Horrocks.
D: £20.00-£23.00 **S:** £30.00-£30.00.
Open: Mar to Dec
Beds: 3D
Baths: 2 En 1 Pr
🛏 (12) 🅿 (4) ⅍ 🖃 🚽 🌆 Ⓥ ⌀

Sutton Valence 21

National Grid Ref: TQ8149

(0.25m) *The Queens Head, High Street, Sutton Valence, Maidstone, Kent, ME17 3AG.*
Tel: **01622 843225** Pilcher.
Fax no: 01622 842651
D: £22.50-£25.00 **S:** £22.50-£25.00.
Open: All Year
Beds: 2F 1T 1D
Baths: 1 Sh
🛏 🅿 ⅍ 🖃 🚽 🌆 Ⓥ ℹ
Spectacular countryside views of Weald of Kent, built 1460 and features Oak Beams, Inglenook fireplace and low ceilings. Excellent home cooked food in countryside style. Award winning viewpoint Garden. Historical village over 1000 years old with Castle Ruins.

Charing 22

National Grid Ref: TQ9549

¶ ◑ Rose & Crown, Royal Oak, Munday Bois

(3m) *23 The Moat, Charing, Ashford, Kent, TN27 0JH.*
Actual grid ref: TQ955492
On North Downs Way. Shops, buses, trains, London, Canterbury, Eurostar.
Tel: **01233 713141**
Mrs Micklewright.
D: £20.00-£20.00 **S:** £25.00-£25.00.
Open: Apr to Sep
Beds: 1T **Baths:** 1 En
🛏 🅿 (1) ⅍ 🖃 🚽 🌆 Ⓥ

(2.5m) 🐾 *Barnfield, Charing, Ashford, Kent, TN27 0BN.*
Actual grid ref: TQ923484
Charming C15th farmhouse in superb location, overlooking lake and garden.
Grades: ETC 3 Diamond
Tel: **01233 712421** (also fax no)
Mrs Pym.
D: £22.00-£24.00 **S:** £24.00-£28.00.
Open: All Year (not Xmas)
Beds: 2D 1T 3S **Baths:** 1 Sh
🛏 🅿 (99) ⅍ 🖃 🚽 🌆 Ⓥ ⌀

Pay B&Bs by
cash or cheque and
be prepared to
pay up front.

Great Chart 23

National Grid Ref: TQ9842

(0.5m 🐾) *Goldwell Manor, Great Chart, Ashford, Kent, TN23 3BY.*
Actual grid ref: TQ968425
Historic C11th manor, quiet, secluded and comfortable with country views.
Tel: **01233 631495** (also fax no)
Mr Wynn-Green.
D: £23.00-£28.00 **S:** £25.00-£35.00.
Open: All Year (not Xmas)
Beds: 1F 2D 1T 1S
Baths: 1 En 1 Pr 1 Sh
🛏 (1) 🅿 (10) 🖃 🐾 ✗ 🚽 🌆 Ⓥ ⌀

Ashford 24

National Grid Ref: TR0042

¶ ◑ Hare & Hounds, Pilgrims' Rest, Harvesters, Wetherspoons, Downtown Diner

(1m) *Warren Cottage Hotel, 136 The Street, Willesborough, Ashford, Kent, TN24 0NB.*
Grades: ETC 3 Diamond
Tel: **01233 621905** Mrs Jones.
Fax no: 01233 623400
D: £25.00-£35.00 **S:** £20.00-£39.90.
Open: All Year
Beds: 1F 3D 1T 1S **Baths:** 6 En
🛏 🅿 (20) ⅍ 🖃 🐾 ✗ 🚽 🌆 Ⓥ ℹ
17th Century hotel set in 2.5 acres. M20, Junction 10. All rooms ensuite. Carpark CCTV security. Minutes to Ashford International Station and Channel Tunnel Ports.

(1m) *Heather House, 40 Burton Road, Kennington, Ashford, Kent, TN24 9DS.*
Grades: ETC 3 Diamond
Tel: **01233 661826** Mrs Blackwell.
Fax no: 01233 635183
D: £20.00 **S:** £20.00.
Open: All Year (not Xmas/New Year)
Beds: 1T 1D 1S **Baths:** 2 Sh
🅿 🅿 🖃 Ⓥ
Heather House offers a warm, friendly welcome in quiet residential area. Near Eurostar.

D = Price range per person
sharing in a double room

(1m) *Quantock House, Quantock Drive, Ashford, Kent, TN24 8QH.*
Quiet residential area. Easy walk to town centre. Comfortable and welcoming.
Grades: ETC 3 Diamond
Tel: **01233 638921**
Mr & Mrs Tucker.
D: £19.00-£22.00 **S:** £20.00-£22.00.
Open: All Year (not Xmas)
Beds: 1F 1D 1T 1S
Baths: 3 En
☼ (7) ₱ (3) ⌿ ⌷ ♨ 🏭 Ⓥ

(1m) *Mayflower House,*
61 Magazine Road, Ashford,
Kent, TN24 8NH.
Friendly atmosphere, large garden. Close to town centre, international station.
Grades: ETC 3 Diamond
Tel: **01233 621959** (also fax no)
Mrs Simmons.
D: £16.50-£17.50 **S:** £18.00-£20.00.
Open: All Year (not Xmas)
Beds: 1D 2S **Baths:** 1 Sh
☼ ₱ ✕ ♨ 🏭 Ⓥ 🛈 ⌿

(1m 🐾) *Glenmoor, Maidstone Road, Ashford, Kent, TN25 4NP.*
Victorian gamekeepers cottage close to international station and motorway.
Grades: ETC 3 Diamond
Tel: **01233 634767** Mrs Rowlands.
D: £17.00-£17.00 **S:** £20.00-£20.00.
Open: All Year (not Xmas/New Year)
Beds: 2D 1T **Baths:** 1 Sh
☼ (5) ₱ (3) ⌿ ₱ ♨ 🏭 Ⓥ 🛈 ⌿

(1m) *Ashford Guest House,*
15 Canterbury Road, Ashford,
Kent, TN24 8LE.
Elegant Victorian building, spacious rooms, private parking, near town centre.
Grades: ETC 4 Diamond
Tel: **01233 640460** Mrs Noel.
Fax no: 01233 626504
D: £20.00-£20.00 **S:** £25.00-£25.00.
Open: All Year (not Xmas)
Beds: 2F 2D 2T
Baths: 6 En
₱ (6) ⌿ ₱ ♨ 🏭 Ⓥ ⌿

(1m) *Vickys Guest House, 38 Park Road North, Ashford, Kent, TN24 8LY.*
Town centre, close to international station, Canterbury, Folkestone and Dover nearby.
Grades: AA 2 Diamond
Tel: **01233 631061** Mrs Ford.
Fax no: 01233 640420
D: £18.00-£21.00 **S:** £18.00-£21.00.
Open: All Year
Beds: 1F 1D 1S
Baths: 2 Pr 1 Sh
☼ ₱ ₱ ♜ ✕ ♨ 🏭 Ⓥ 🛈 ⌿

(1m) *2-4 Canterbury Road,*
Ashford, Kent, TN24 8JX.
Victorian semi-detached. 10 mins Eurostar station, 4 mins walk London coach stop.
Tel: **01233 623030** (also fax no)
Mr & Mrs Lavender.
D: £19.00-£20.00 **S:** £20.00-£21.00.
Open: All Year (not Xmas/New Year)
Beds: 2T 2S
Baths: 1 Sh
☼ (5) ₱ (4) ⌿ ₱ 🏭

Hadrian's Wall

From Wallsend to Bowness-on-Solway, Mark Richards' route runs for 83 miles - another one to do in under a week or over a couple of long weekends. **Hadrian's Wall** is still the most impressive monument to the Romans' presence in Britain; indeed, it stands alongside the Pyramids and the Parthenon as a World Heritage Site. Its scale and presence is quite breathtaking, despite its approaching 1,900 years. As with **Offa's Dyke**, to walk along the wall is to sense an atavistic purpose in your stride; on these bleak hills, as the wall's long line leads the way ahead, you truly march in step with shadows. There is a proposed National Trail for the Wall, but the plans are controversial and the final go-ahead could be years away. This route thus has no official sanction, although one part of it coincides with the **Pennine Way**. There are no special waymarks, so for the time being you will have to rely on Mark Richards' excellent guide. Carry suitable clothing, for the northern winds still possess a cold edge even in summer. Weatherproofs and good strong boots are essential.

Guides: *Hadrian's Wall: The Wall Walk* (Vol.1) by Mark Richards (ISBN 1 85284 128 1), published by Cicerone Press and available from all good map shops or directly from the publishers (2 Police Square, Milnthorpe, Cumbria, LA7 7PY, 01539 562069), £7.99

Maps: 1:50000 Ordnance Survey Landranger Series: 85, 86, 87 and 88.

Comments on the proposed Hadrian's Wall National Trail to: **David McGlade**, Countryside Commission, 4th Floor, Warwick House, Grantham Road, Newcastle upon Tyne, NE2 1QF, Tel. 0191 232 8252.

Newcastle-upon-Tyne 1

National Grid Ref: NZ2564

(▲ On path) *Newcastle-upon-Tyne Youth Hostel, 107 Jesmond Rd, Newcastle-upon-Tyne, NE2 1NJ.*
Actual grid ref: NZ257656
Tel: **0191 281 2570**
Under 18: £7.75 **Adults:** £11.00
Self-catering facilities, Television, Showers, Lounge, Dining room, Cycle store, Parking, Evening meal at 7.00pm, Kitchen facilities, Breakfast available, Credit cards accepted
A large town house conveniently located for the centre of this vibrant city, the regional capital of the North East.

(On path) *Chirton House Hotel, 46 Clifton Road, Newcastle-upon-Tyne, NE4 6SH.*
Victorian-style house, conveniently situated for city, airport, Northumberland and Durham.
Tel: **0191 273 0407** (also fax no)
Mrs Turnbull.
D: £18.00-£23.00 **S:** £26.00-£36.00.
Open: All Year
Beds: 3F 2D 3T 3S
Baths: 6 En 5 Sh
⛺ 🅿 🏠 ⛄ 🛁 🛏 Ⓥ ✦

S = Price range for a single person in a single room

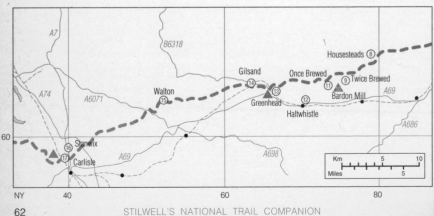

Wylam 2

National Grid Ref: NZ1164

(3m 🚐) *Wormald House, Main Street, Wylam, Northd, NE41 8DN.*
Very welcoming, pleasant country home in attractive Tyne Valley village.
Grades: ETC 4 Diamond
Tel: 01661 852529 (also fax no)
Mr & Mrs Craven.
D: £19.50-£21.00 **S:** £19.50-£21.00.
Open: All Year (not Xmas)
Beds: 1D 1T
Baths: 2 En
🛏 🅿 (3) ⅟ 🗆 🕳 🎍 📖 ⓥ ⅋

Newton 3

National Grid Ref: NZ0364

🍴 🍺 Robin Hood

(2m 🚐) *Crookhill Farm, Newton, Stocksfield, Northd, NE43 7UX.*
Actual grid ref: NZ056652
Comfortable welcoming farmhouse ideal for exploring Hadrian's Wall.
Grades: ETC 3 Diamond
Tel: 01661 843117 Mrs Leech.
Fax no: 01661 844702
D: £20.00-£20.00 **S:** £20.00-£20.00.
Open: All Year
Beds: 1F 1T 1S
Baths: 1 Sh
🛏 🅿 (4) ⅟ 🗆 ✕ 🎍 📖 ⓥ ⅃ ⅋

Corbridge 4

National Grid Ref: NY9964

🍴 🍺 Black Bull, The Angel, The Wheatsheaf

(2.5m) *The Hayes Guest House, Newcastle Road, Corbridge, Northd, NE45 5LP.*
Large house in historic village with views over valley.
Tel: 01434 632010
Mrs Matthews.
D: £20.00-£25.00 **S:** £20.00-£25.00.
Open: All Year (not Xmas/New Year)
Beds: 2F 1D 1T 1S
Baths: 2 En 1 Sh
🛏 🅿 (12) 🗆 🕳 🎍 📖 ⓥ ⅋

(0.5m) *Priorfield, Hippingstones Lane, Corbridge, Northd, NE45 5JP.*
Elegantly furnished family house. Peaceful location. Whirlpool bath in double room.
Grades: ETC 4 Diamond, AA 4 Diamond
Tel: 01434 633179 (also fax no)
Mrs Steenberg.
D: £18.00-£25.00 **S:** £25.00-£32.00.
Open: All Year
Beds: 1D 1T **Baths:** 2 En
🛏 (5) 🅿 (2) ⅟ 🗆 🎍 📖 ⓥ ⅋

Hexham 5

National Grid Ref: NY9364

🍴 🍺 Dipton Mill, Boatside Inn, Heart Of All England, Rose & Crown, Angel

(0.5m 🚐) *Burncrest Guest House, Burnland Terrace, Hexham, Northd, NE46 3JT.*
Spacious terraced house, home from home, private car park.
Tel: 01434 605163 (also fax no)
Mr Ellery.
D: £20.00-£25.00 **S:** £20.00-£25.00.
Open: All Year
Beds: 3D
Baths: 2 Sh
🛏 🅿 (3) ⅟ 🗆 🎍 📖 ⓥ ⅃ ⅋

(0.5m) *Old Red House Farm, Dipton Mill, Hexham, NE46 1XY.*
Superbly appointed C19th private stone cottage in lovely rural location.
Grades: ETC 4 Diamond
Tel: 01434 604463 Mrs Bradley.
D: £23.00-£25.00 **S:** £30.00-£30.00.
Open: Feb to Oct
Beds: 1T
Baths: 1 Pr
🅿 (2) ⅟ 🗆 🕳 🎍 📖 ⓥ ⅋

Planning a longer stay? Always ask for any special rates.

High season, bank holidays and special events mean low availability *everywhere.*

(0.5m) *East Peterel Field Farm, Yarridge Road, Hexham, NE46 2JT.*
Beautiful award winning manor house in rolling countryside.
Tel: 01434 607209
Mrs Carr.
Fax no: 01434 601753
D: £25.00-£30.00
S: £35.00.
Open: All Year
Baths: 2 En 1 Pr
🛏 (10) 🗆 🕳 ✕ 🎍 📖 ⓥ ⅃ ⅋

(0.5m) *Kitty Frisk House, Corbridge Road, Hexham, Northumberland, NE46 1UN.*
Elegant Edwardian country house in Hexham. Good base for touring.
Grades: ETC 4 Diamond
Tel: 01434 601533 (also fax no)
Humphrey.
D: £24.00-£25.00
S: £32.00-£50.00.
Open: All Year
Beds: 1D 2T
Baths: 2 En 1 Pr
🛏 🅿 (6) ⅟ 🗆 🎍 📖 ⓥ

(0.5m 🚐) *Dukeslea, 32 Shaws Park, Hexham, Northd, NE46 3BJ.*
Actual grid ref: NY924645
Comfortable, modern, detached family home, overlooking golf course. Quiet location.
Tel: 01434 602947 (also fax no)
Mrs Theobald.
D: £18.00-£20.00
S: £20.00-£26.00.
Open: All Year (not Xmas)
Beds: 2D
Baths: 2 En
🛏 (1) 🅿 (4) ⅟ 🗆 🎍 📖 ⓥ ⅋

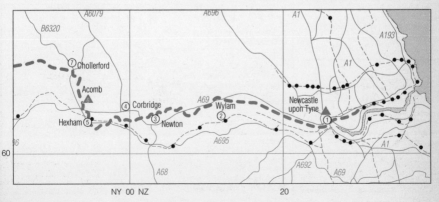

(0.5m) *West Close House, Hextol Terrace, Hexham, Northd, NE46 2AD.*
Actual grid ref: NY930636
Charming, secluded detached 1920s villa. Immaculately maintained.
Tel: **01434 603307**
Patricia Graham-Tomlinson.
D: £20.00-£26.00 **S:** £18.00-£21.00.
Open: All Year
Beds: 2D 2S
Baths: 2 En 1 Sh
🛏 (12) 🅿 (4) ⌇⌷ 🕮 🖳 Ⅴ ⌁

(3m) *Topsy Turvy, 9 Leazes Lane, Hexham, Northd, NE46 3BA.*
As my guests say, 'Comfortable, colourful, friendly and peaceful'.
Tel: **01434 603152**
Ms McCormick.
D: £19.00-£20.00 **S:** £25.00-£25.00.
Open: All Year
Beds: 2D
Baths: 2 En
🛏 🅿 (4) ⌇⌷ 🕮 🖳 Ⅴ ⌁

(0.5m 🚐) *Laburnum House, 23 Leazes Crescent, Hexham, Northumberland, NE46 3JZ.*
Actual grid ref: NY928644
An especially warm welcome awaits you in our lovely, spacious family home.
Tel: **01434 601828**
Mr Place.
D: £17.50-£19.50
S: £17.50-£19.50.
Open: All Year (not Xmas)
Beds: 1D 1T 2S
Baths: 1 Sh
🛏 ⌇⌷ ✕ 🕮 🖳 Ⅴ ⌁

Acomb   6

National Grid Ref: NY9366

(▲0.25m) *Acomb Youth Hostel, Main Street, Acomb, Hexham, Northumberland, NE46 4PL.*
Actual grid ref: NY934666
Tel: **01434 602864**
Under 18: £4.75
Adults: £6.75
Self-catering facilities, Showers, Lounge, Drying room, Cycle store, No smoking, WC, Kitchen facilities, Credit cards accepted
A simple youth hostel, converted from stable buildings in a small village in the valley of the River Tyne.

🚐 sign means that, *given due notice*, owners will pick you up from the path and drop you off *within reason.*

S = Price range for a single person in a single room

(0.25m) *Mariner's Cottage Hotel, Fallowfield Dene Road, Acomb, Hexham, Northd, NE46 4RP.*
Tel: **01434 603666** Mrs Darling.
D: £18.00-£20.00 **S:** £18.00-£20.00.
Open: All Year
Beds: 1F 1D 1T 2S
Baths: 3 Pr 2 Sh
🛏 (5) 🅿 (60) 🕮 ⌇ ✕ 🕮 🖳 Ⅴ ⌁
Hotel set in country, 3 miles from market town of Hexham & within easy reach of Hadrian's Wall, Kielder Water, Beamish Museum, Metro Shopping Centre.

Chollerford   7

National Grid Ref: NY9170

🍴 🍺 Hadrian Hotel, Crown Inn

(On path 🚐) *Brunton Water Mill, Chollerford, Hexham, Northd, NE46 4EL.*
Beautifully converted water mill on the doorstep of Brunton Turrett.
Grades: ETC 4 Diamond
Tel: **01434 681002** Mrs Pesarra.
D: £24.00-£26.00 **S:** £40.00-£40.00.
Open: All Year
Beds: 1D 1T
Baths: 2 En 1 Sh
🛏 (12) 🅿 (8) ⌇⌷ 🕮 🖳 Ⅴ ⌁

Housesteads   8

National Grid Ref: NY7868

🍴 🍺 Milecastle Inn

(On path 🚐) *Crindledykes Farm, Housesteads, Bardon Mill, Hexham, Northd, NE47 7AF.*
Actual grid ref: NY782672
Well-maintained C17th farmhouse, good food and a warm welcome.
Grades: ETC 4 Diamond
Tel: **01434 344316** Mrs Davidson.
D: £17.00-£20.00 **S:** £20.00.
Open: Easter to Nov
Beds: 1D 1T **Baths:** 1 Sh
🛏 🅿 ⌇⌷ ✕ 🕮 🖳 Ⅴ ⌁

Twice Brewed   9

National Grid Ref: NY7567

(1m 🚐) *Saughy Rigg Farm, Twice Brewed, Haltwhistle, Northumberland, NE49 9PT.*
Actual grid ref: NY740685
Near Hadrian's Wall, delicious food, comfortable accommodation, children & pets welcome.
Grades: ETC 3 Diamond
Tel: **01434 344746** Ms McNulty.
D: £15.00-£15.00 **S:** £15.00-£15.00.
Open: All Year
Beds: 1F 1T **Baths:** 1 En 1 Pr
🛏 🅿 🕮 ✕ 🕮 🖳 Ⅴ ⌁

Bardon Mill   10

National Grid Ref: NY7865

(0.5m) *Carrsgate East, Bardon Mill, Hexham, Northumberland, NE47 7EX.*
Relaxing, comfortable C17th home. Great views, good exploration base.
Grades: ETC 4 Diamond
Tel: **01434 344376** Mrs Armstrong.
Fax no: 01434 344011
D: £23.00-£27.00 **S:** £25.00-£27.00.
Open: Feb to Nov
Beds: 2D **Baths:** 2 En
🅿 (6) ⌇⌷ 🕮 🖳 Ⅴ ⌁

Once Brewed   11

National Grid Ref: NY7566

(▲0.5m) *Once Brewed Youth Hostel, Military Road, Once Brewed, Bardon Mill, Hexham, Northumberland, NE47 7AN.*
Actual grid ref: NY752668
Tel: **01434 344360**
Under 18: £7.75 **Adults:** £11.00
Self-catering facilities, Showers, Laundry facilities, Lounge, Dining room, Games room, Drying room, Cycle store, Parking, Evening meal at 6.00-7.00pm, No smoking, WC, Kitchen facilities, Breakfast available
Excellent residential accommodation with small bedrooms and superb range of facilities. Close to Hadrian's Wall and the Roman Forts.

Haltwhistle   12

National Grid Ref: NY7064

🍴 🍺 Spotted Cow, Manor House, Centre Of Britain Hotel, Milecastle Inn

(2m) *Manor House Hotel, Main Street, Haltwhistle, Northd, NE49 0BS.*
Tel: **01434 322588** Nicholson.
D: £15.00-£22.00 **S:** £20.00-£25.00.
Open: All Year
Beds: 1F 1D 4T
Baths: 3 En 3 Sh
🛏 🅿 (4) 🕮 ✕ 🕮 🖳 Ⅴ ⌁
Small hotel with busy public bar serving good selection of real ales wines & spirits. Very popular for meals at an affordable price. Separate dining area available away from bar. Hotel centrally situated 2 miles from Hadrian's Wall. Warm welcome from Kathleen and Raymond Nicholson.

Bringing children with you? Always ask for any special rates.

Taking your dog?

Book *in advance*

ONLY with owners

who accept dogs (🐕)

(1.5m 🚌) *The Old School House,* Fair Hill, Haltwhistle, Northumberland, *NE49 9EE.*
Actual grid ref: NY712642
Friendly welcome. Brilliant breakfast - no need for lunch! Hadrian's Wall on doorstep.
Grades: ETC 4 Diamond
Tel: **01434 322595** (also fax no)
Mrs O'Hagan.
D: £18.00-£20.00 **S:** £25.00-£30.00.
Open: All Year (not Xmas)
Beds: 2D 1T
Baths: 3 Pr
🅿 (6) ⌿ 🖵 🖳 Ⅲ Ⅴ ⚡

(1.5m) *Hall Meadows,* Main Street, Haltwhistle, Northd, *NE49 0AZ.*
Large comfortable C19th private house, central for Hadrian's Wall.
Grades: ETC 3 Diamond
Tel: **01434 321021** Mrs Humes.
D: £17.00-£17.00 **S:** £18.00-£18.00.
Open: All Year (not Xmas)
Beds: 1D 1T 1S
Baths: 1 Sh
🕭 🅿 (3) 🖵 🖳 Ⅲ Ⅴ ⚡

(1m) *Ald White Craig Farm,* Hadrian's Wall, Shield Hill, Haltwhistle, Northd, *NE49 9NW.*
Actual grid ref: NY714650
Snug old rambling single storey farmhouse.
Tel: **01434 320565** (also fax no)
Ms Laidlow.
D: £21.00-£25.00
S: £28.00-£32.00.
Open: Easter to Oct
Beds: 1D 1T
Baths: 2 En
🅿 (2) ⌿ 🖵 🖳 Ⅲ ♿ Ⅴ ⚡

Greenhead 13

National Grid Ref: NY6665

🍴 ◪ Holmhead Bar

(▲ 0.5m) *Greenhead Youth Hostel,* Greenhead, Carlisle, Cumbria, CA6 7HG.
Actual grid ref: NY659655
Tel: **016977 47401**
Under 18: £6.50 **Adults:** £9.25
Self-catering facilities, Showers, Shop, Lounge, Drying room, Cycle store, Evening meal at 7.00pm, No smoking, WC, Kitchen facilities, Breakfast available, Credit cards accepted
This traditional Methodist chapel with its thick stone walls is curiously cosy. Useful for a rest for walkers of the Pennine Way, this is also a popular haunt for cyclists.

(▲ On path) *Holmhead Stone Tent, Thirlwall Castle Farm,* Greenhead, Brampton, CA8 7HY
Tel: **016977 47402**
Under 18: £3.50 **Adults:** £3.50
Wet weather shelter, Cycle store, No smoking
Stone building. Outside toilet, gas lamp, camping gas, cold water tap. Hadrian's Wall path.

(0.5m) *Holmhead Licensed Guest House,* Thirlwall Castle Farm, Hadrian's Wall, Greenhead, Brampton, Cumbria, CA8 7HY.
Actual grid ref: NY661659
Enjoy fine food and hospitality with a personal touch.
Grades: ETC 4 Diamond
Tel: **016977 47402** (also fax no)
Mr & Mrs Staff.
D: £28.00-£29.00
S: £37.00-£38.00.
Open: All Year (not Xmas)
Beds: 1F 1D 2T **Baths:** 4 En
🕭 🅿 (4) ⌿ 🖵 ✕ 🖳 Ⅲ Ⅴ ⚡

D = Price range per person

sharing in a double room

Gilsland 14

National Grid Ref: NY6366

🍴 ◪ Samson Inn

(On path 🚌) *The Hill on the Wall,* Gilsland, Brampton, Cumbria, CA8 7DA.
Fascinating Listed C16th 'fortified farmhouse' overlooking Hadrian's Wall.
Grades: ETC 4 Diamond
Tel: **016977 47214** (also fax no)
Mr Swan.
D: £20.00-£22.00
S: £25.00-£27.00.
Open: All Year
Beds: 2D 1T
Baths: 3 En
🕭 🅿 ⌿ 🖵 🐕 ✕ 🖳 Ⅲ Ⅴ 🛈 ⚡

(1m) *Howard House Farm,* Gilsland, Carlisle, Cumbria, CA6 7AN.
Actual grid ref: NY633670
Comfortable farmhouse on Roman wall.
Tel: **016977 47285**
Mrs Woodmass.
D: £19.00-£22.00
S: £19.00-£22.00.
Open: All Year
Beds: 1F 1D 1T
Baths: 1 En 1 Sh
🕭 (5) 🅿 (4) 🖵 🐕 ✕ 🖳 Ⅲ Ⅴ 🛈 ⚡

Walton 15

National Grid Ref: NY5264

🍴 ◪ Stag, Centurion, Lane End Inn

(On path 🚌) *High Rigg Farm,* Walton, Brampton, Cumbria, CA8 2AZ.
Grades: ETC 3 Diamond
Tel: **016977 2117**
Mrs Mounsey.
D: £16.00-£18.00
S: £18.00.
Open: All Year (not Xmas)
Beds: 2F
Baths: 1 Pr 1 Sh
🕭 🅿 (4) ⌿ 🖵 ✕ 🖳 Ⅲ Ⅴ 🛈 ⚡
A warm welcome to our Listed beautiful Georgian farmhouse with breath taking views of the Pennines & Lake District hills. Comfortable spacious accommodation, excellent food, much home produced. A working dairy sheep farm. Good parking. Central for visits to Roman Wall/Lakes.

All rooms full and

nowhere else to stay?

Ask the owner if

there's anywhere

nearby

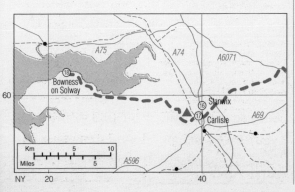

(0.5m) ***Low Rigg Farm,*** *Walton, Brampton, Cumbria, CA8 2DX.*
Actual grid ref: NY522651
Comfortable accommodation on a working farm in beautiful Hadrian's Wall country. Excellent home cooking.
Tel: **016977 3233**
Mrs Thompson.
D: £15.00-£18.00
S: £18.00-£20.00.
Open: All Year (not Xmas)
Beds: 1F
Baths: 1 Sh
(6)

Stanwix 16

National Grid Ref: NY3957

Cumbria Park Hotel

(1m) ***No. 1,*** *1 Etterby Street, Stanwix, Carlisle, Cumbria, CA3 9JB.*
Homely accommodation in easy reach of Hadrians Wall & Scotland lakes.
Grades: ETC 3 Diamond
Tel: **01228 547285**
Ms Nixon.
D: £17.00-£20.00 **S:** £17.00-£20.00.
Open: All Year (not Xmas/ New Year)
Beds: 1D 2S
(4) (1)

Carlisle 17

National Grid Ref: NY3955

Metal Bridge Inn, The Beehive, Mary's Pantry, Crown & Thistle, Coach & Horses, Golden Fleece, Black Lion

(0.75m) ***Carlisle Youth Hostel,*** *University of Northumbria, The Old Brewery Residences, Bridge Lane, Caldewgate, Carlisle, Cumbria, CA2 5SR.*
Actual grid ref: NY394560
Tel: **01228 597352**
Under 18: £8.75
Adults: £13.00
Self-catering facilities, Showers, Cycle store, Parking, Facilities for disabled people, No smoking, WC, Kitchen facilities
University accommodation in an award-winning conversion of the former Theakston's brewery. Single study bedrooms with shared kitchen and bathroom in flats for up to 7 people.

(1m) ***Cherry Grove,*** *87 Petteril Street, Carlisle, Cumbria, CA1 2AW.*
Lovely red brick building close to golf club and town.
Grades: AA 3 Diamond
Tel: **01228 541942**
Mr & Mrs Houghton.
D: £17.50-£20.00
S: £20.00-£30.00.
Open: All Year
Beds: 3F 2D
Baths: 5 En
(3)

(0.75m) ***Howard Lodge,*** *90 Warwick Road, Carlisle, Cumbria, CA1 1JU.*
Actual grid ref: NY407558
Grades: ETC 4 Diamond, AA 3 Diamond
Tel: **01228 529842** Mr Hendrie.
D: £15.00-£25.00 **S:** £20.00-£30.00.
Open: All Year
Beds: 2F 1D 2T 1S
Baths: 6 En 1 Sh
(6)
Friendly family-run guest house in comfortable Victorian town house in conservation area. Spacious rooms all fully ensuite with satellite TV, welcome tray, hairdryer and clock radio. Large breakfasts. 5 minutes' walk from station and city centre. Evening meals by prior arrangement. Private car park.

(0.25m) ***Craighead,*** *6 Hartington Place, Carlisle, Cumbria, CA1 1HL.*
Actual grid ref: NY405559
Grades: ETC 3 Diamond
Tel: **01228 596767** Mrs Smith.
D: £17.00 **S:** £16.00.
Open: All Year (not Xmas)
Beds: 1F 2D 1T 1S
Baths: 1 En 2 Sh
You will receive a warm welcome at Craighead, a Grade II Listed spacious Victorian town house with comfortable rooms and original features. CTV, tea/coffee tray in all rooms. Minutes' walk to city centre bus and rail stations and all amenities. Friendly personal service.

(On path) ***Angus Hotel & Almonds Bistro,*** *14 Scotland Road, Stanwix, Carlisle, Cumbria, CA3 9DG.*
Actual grid ref: NY400571
Grades: AA 4 Diamond
Tel: **01228 523546**
Mr Webster.
Fax no: 01228 531895
D: £20.00-£27.00 **S:** £26.00-£42.00.
Open: All Year
Beds: 4F 3D 4T 3S
Baths: 11 En 3 Sh
(6)
Victorian town house, foundations on Hadrian's Wall. Excellent food, Les Routiers Awards, local cheeses, home baked bread. Genuine warm welcome from owners. Licensed, draught beer, lounge, meeting room, internet cafe, direct dial telephones, secure garaging. Group rates for cyclists available.

Bringing children with you? Always ask for any special rates.

(0.5m) ***Avondale,*** *3 St Aidans Road, Carlisle, Cumbria, CA1 1LT.*
Attractive comfortable Edwardian house. Quiet central position convenient M6 J43.
Grades: ETC 4 Diamond
Tel: **01228 523012** (also fax no)
Mr & Mrs Hayes.
D: £20.00-£20.00 **S:** £20.00-£40.00.
Open: All Year (not Xmas)
Beds: 1D 2T
Baths: 1 En 1 Pr
(3)

(1m) ***Dalroc,*** *411 Warwick Road, Carlisle, Cumbria, CA1 2RZ.*
Small friendly house. Midway city centre and M6 motorway.
Tel: **01228 542805** Mrs Irving.
D: £16.00-£16.00 **S:** £16.00-£16.00.
Open: All Year (not Xmas/ New Year)
Beds: 1T 1D 1S
(7)

(1m) ***Chatsworth Guest House,*** *22 Chatsworth Square, Carlisle, Cumbria, CA1 1HF.*
City centre Grade II Listed building, close to all amenities.
Grades: ETC 3 Diamond
Tel: **01228 524023** (also fax no)
Mrs Mackin.
D: £19.00-£22.00 **S:** £25.00-£25.00.
Open: All Year (not Xmas)
Beds: 1F 1D 2T 1S
Baths: 5 En
(2)

(1m) ***Kingstown Hotel,*** *246 Kingstown Road, Carlisle, CA3 0DE.*
Grades: AA 3 Diamond
Tel: **01228 515292** (also fax no)
Mrs Marshall.
D: £23.50 **S:** £35.00-£40.00.
Open: All Year
Beds: 1F 4D 2T **Baths:** 7 En
(14)
Just off the M6 (Jct. 44) we are a licensed hotel providing high-quality accommodation. You will find a friendly and relaxed atmosphere, freshly-prepared cuisine and fine wine at reasonable prices. A good base to explore Cumbria, Northumbria, Lake District, Scotland

(1m) ***Corner House Hotel & Bar,*** *4 Grey Street, Carlisle, CA1 2JP.*
Grades: ETC 3 Diamond
Tel: **01228 533239** Mrs Anderson.
Fax no: 01228 546628
D: £17.50-£22.00 **S:** £20.00-£30.00.
Open: All Year
Beds: 3F 4D 4T 3S
Baths: All En
Refurbished family run hotel. All rooms ensuite, colour TV, phones, tea/coffee, radio, toiletries etc. Cosy bar, sky TV lounge, games room, easy access city centre, bus/train. Base for golf, walking, cycling, touring the Lakes, Roman Wall, Carlisle/ Settle line etc.

(1m) *Ashleigh House, 46 Victoria Place, Carlisle, Cumbria, CA1 1EX.*
Beautifully decorated town house. Two minutes from city centre.
Grades: ETC 4 Diamond
Tel: **01228 521631** Mr Davies.
D: £19.00-£22.50 **S:** £25.00-£30.00.
Open: All Year (not Xmas/ New Year)
Beds: 3F 1T 2D 1S
Baths: 7 En
⌂ (5) ⌷ ⏚ ▥ Ⓥ

(1m 🚗) *Cornerways Guest House, 107 Warwick Road, Carlisle, Cumbria, CA1 1EA.*
Large Victorian town house.
Grades: ETC 4 Diamond
Tel: **01228 521733** Mrs Fisher.
D: £14.00-£18.00 **S:** £16.00-£18.00.
Open: All Year (not Xmas)
Beds: 2F 1D 4T 3S
Baths: 3 En 2 Sh
⌂ �P (4) ⌷ ⋔ ✕ ⏚ ▥ Ⓥ ⓐ

(0.75m 🚗) *Courtfield Guest House, 169 Warwick Road, Carlisle, Cumbria, CA1 1LP.*
Short walk to historic city centre. Close to M6, J43.
Grades: ETC 4 Diamond
Tel: **01228 522767** Mrs Dawes.
D: £18.00-£22.00 **S:** £25.00.
Open: All Year (not Xmas)
Beds: 1F 2D 2T
Baths: 5 En
⌂ P (4) ⍭ ⌷ ⏚ ▥ Ⓥ

(1m 🚗) *East View Guest House, 110 Warwick Road, Carlisle, Cumbria, CA1 1JU.*
Actual grid ref: NY407560
10 minutes' walking distance from city centre, railway station and restaurants.
Grades: ETC 3 Diamond, AA 3 Diamond, RAC 3 Diamond
Tel: **01228 522112** (also fax no) Mrs Glease.
D: £18.00-£20.00 **S:** £20.00-£25.00.
Open: All Year (not Xmas)
Beds: 3F 2D 1T 1S
Baths: 7 En
⌂ P (4) ⍭ ⌷ ⏚ ▥ Ⓥ ⌀

(1m) *Cambro House, 173 Warwick Road, Carlisle, Cumbria, CA1 1LP.*
Grades: AA 3 Diamond
Tel: **01228 543094** (also fax no) Mr & Mrs Mawson.
D: £17.00-£20.00
S: £20.00-£25.00.
Open: All Year
Beds: 2D 1T
Baths: 3 En
P (2) ⍭ ⌷ ⏚ ▥ Ⓥ ⓐ ⌀
Guests can expect warm hospitality and friendly service at this attractively decorated and well-maintained guest house. Each ensuite bedroom includes TV, clock, radio, hairdryer and welcome tray. Private off-road parking available, non-smoking, close to golf course.

Bowness-on-Solway   18

National Grid Ref: NY2262
🏨 🍺 Kings Arms

(On path) *Maia Lodge, Bowness-on-Solway, Wigton, Cumbria, CA7 5BH.*
Actual grid ref: NY225627
Panoramic views of Solway Firth and Scottish Borders. End of Hadrian's Wall.
Grades: ETC 3 Diamond
Tel: **016973 51955** Mrs Chettle.
D: £17.00-£20.00 **S:** £20.00-£20.00.
Open: All Year (not Xmas)
Beds: 1F 1D 1T **Baths:** 2 Sh
⌂ (5) P (4) ⍭ ✕ ⏚ ▥ Ⓥ ⓐ

(On path) *The Old Rectory, Bowness-on-Solway, Carlisle, Cumbria, CA75AF.*
Actual grid ref: NY224626
Fully ensuite old rectory at end of Hadrian's Wall. www.wallsend.net.
Grades: ETC 4 Diamond
Tel: **016973 51055**
Mr & Mrs Knowles Wallsand.
D: £20.00-£25.00 **S:** £20.00-£25.00.
Open: All Year (not Xmas)
Beds: 1F 2D 1S **Baths:** 4 En
⌂ (5) P (6) ⍭ ⌷ ⋔ ✕ ⏚ ▥ Ⓥ ⌀

D = Price range per person sharing in a double room

Heart of England Way

This is a good find in the Midlands - like the North Downs Way, never far away from busy city life, but somehow keeping it at a healthy distance - a good mixture of the rural and the urban. The 100-mile **Heart of England** Way is waymarked and has easy access to public transport at most points along the route. From the Cannock Chase heathland the path heads off to Lichfield, the Tame Valley, Arden and the Avon Valley and then on to Bourton-on-the-Water in the Cotswolds. The path also usefully connects the **Staffordshire Way** with the **Cotswold Way** and the **Oxfordshire Way**. This makes it possible to walk, if you really wish, from the Cheshire border right down to Bath or London along waymarked footpaths.

Guides: *The Heart of England Way* by John Roberts (ISBN 0 947708 40 5), published by Walkways and available from good map shops or directly from the publishers (67 Cliffe Way, Warwick, CV34 5JG, tel: 01926 776363), who also offer a free amendments service, £6.95

Maps: 1:50000 Ordnance Survey Landranger Series: 127, 128, 139, 140, 150, 151, 163

Comments about the path to: **Heart of England Way Association**, 50 George Road, Water Orton, Birmingham B46 1PE (membership £3.00).

S = Price range for a single person in a single room

Stafford 1

National Grid Ref: SJ9223

꿷 ◁█ Red Lion, Picture House, Sun Inn, Crown Inn, The Shropshire, The Radford, Bank Inn, Barley Mow

(0.5m) *Bailey Hotel, 63 Lichfield Rd, Stafford, Staffordshire, ST17 4LL.*
Grades: ETC 3 Diamond
Tel: **01785 214133**
Mr & Mrs Ayres.
Fax no: 01785 227920
D: £18.00-£23.00 **S:** £21.50-£30.00.
Open: All Year (not Xmas)
Beds: 1F 5D 3T 2S
Baths: 4 En 2 Sh
☎ ℗ (11) ❑ ⊁ ≟ Ⅲ. Ⅵ
Modern detached hotel, comfortably furnished, parking in own grounds.

D = Price range per person sharing in a double room

(0.5m) *Cedarwood, 46 Weeping Cross, Stafford, Staffordshire, ST17 0DS.*
Grades: ETC 4 Diamond, Silver
Tel: **01785 662981** Mrs Welsby.
D: £15.00-£18.00 **S:** £15.00-£18.00.
Open: All Year (not Xmas)
Beds: 1D 1T 1S **Baths:** 2 Sh
☎ (9) ℗ (3) ⊬ ❑ ≟ Ⅲ. Ⅵ
Unusual detached bungalow in own grounds, excellent accommodation and hospitality.

(0.5m) *Leonards Croft Hotel, 80 Lichfield Road, Stafford, Staffordshire, ST17 4LP.*
Victorian house in award winning garden walking distance town centre.
Grades: AA 4 Diamond, RAC 4 Diamond
Tel: **01785 223676** Mrs Johnson.
D: £25.00-£30.00 **S:** £30.00-£35.00.
Open: All Year (not Xmas/New Year)
Beds: 4F 3D 2T **Baths:** 4 En 4 Sh
☎ ℗ (10) ❑ ⊁ ⊁ ≟ Ⅲ. Ⅵ

(0.5m) *Vine Hotel, Salter Street, Stafford, Staffordshire, ST16 2JU.*
This haven of your imagination is the Vine Hotel.
Grades: AA 2 Stars
Tel: **01785 244112** Mr Austin.
Fax no: 01785 246612
D: £25.00-£26.00 **S:** £30.00-£40.00.
Open: All Year
Beds: 1F 10D 3T 10S
Baths: 24 Pr 1 En
☎ ℗ (20) ❑ ⊁ ≟ Ⅲ. Ⅵ ⏃

Farewell 2

National Grid Ref: SK0811

꿷 ◁█ The Nelson

(1.5m) *Little Pipe Farm, Little Pipe Lane, Farewell, Lichfield, Staffs, WS13 8BS.*
Actual grid ref: SK080105
Arable and beef working farm.
C19th farmhouse superb views.
Tel: **01543 683066** Mrs Clewley.
D: £16.00-£20.00 **S:** £18.00-£20.00.
Open: All Year
Beds: 1F 1D 1T **Baths:** 1 Sh
☎ ℗ (10) ❑ ⊁ ≟ Ⅲ. Ⅵ ⏃ ⊬

Chorley 3

National Grid Ref: SK0710

꿷 ◁█ The Windmill, Red Lion, Nelson

(0.25m) *'Stone House' Farm, Farewell, Chorley, Lichfield, Staffs, WS13 8DS.*
Actual grid ref: SK076115
17th Century stone cottage surrounded by beautiful countryside.
Peaceful hamlet.
Grades: AA 4 Diamond
Tel: **01543 682575** (also fax no)
Mrs Cowell.
D: £17.00-£22.00 **S:** £17.00-£24.00.
Open: All Year
Beds: 3D 1S **Baths:** 1 En 2 Sh
☎ (5) ℗ ⊬ ❑ ⊁ ≟ Ⅲ. ⏃ Ⅵ ⏃ ⊬

Bringing children with you? Always ask for any special rates.

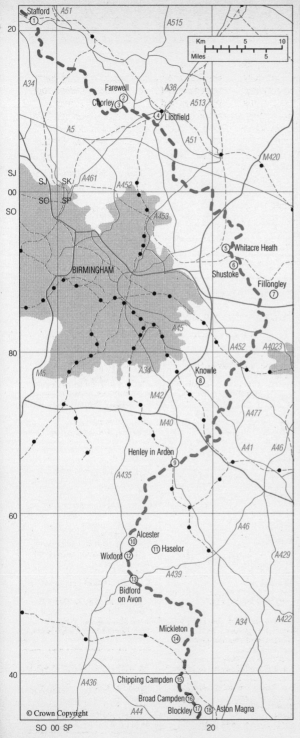

Lichfield 4

National Grid Ref: SK1109

🍽 🍺 The Boat, Three Tuns, The Greyhound, Little Barrow, Shoulder of Mutton, Pig & Truffle

(0.25m) *Netherstowe House North, Netherstowe Lane, Eastern Avenue, Lichfield, Staffs, WS13 6AY.* Grade II Listed Georgian building 3/4 mile from Lichfield city centre. **Grades:** ETC 2 Diamond Tel: **01543 254631** Mrs Marshall. **D:** £19.00-£21.00 **S:** £21.00-£22.00. **Open:** All Year **Beds:** 1F 1T **Baths:** 1 Pr 1 Sh
🛏 (1) 🅿 (6) ✕ ☐ 🎱 🏛 Ⅴ

(0.5m) *Altair House, 21 Shakespeare Avenue, Lichfield, Staffs, WS14 9BE.* House, near town, bus & rail stations. Approx 15 miles NEC Birmingham. Tel: **01543 252900** Mrs Hattersley. **D:** £18.00-£25.00 **S:** £20.00. **Open:** All Year (not Xmas) **Beds:** 2T 1S **Baths:** 2 Sh
🛏 (5) 🅿 (4) ✕ ☐ 🎱 🏛 Ⅴ 🔒 ⚡

(0.5m) *8 The Close, Lichfield, Staffs, WS13 7LD.* A C19th Grade II Listed Victorian town house situated in the historic Cathedral Close. Tel: **01543 418483** (also fax no) Mrs Jones. **D:** £21.00-£25.00 **S:** £22.00-£26.00. **Open:** All Year (not Xmas) **Beds:** 2D 1T 1S **Baths:** 1 Sh
🛏 (1) 🅿 ✕ ☐ ✗ 🎱 🏛 Ⅴ 🔒 ⚡

Whitacre Heath 5

National Grid Ref: SP2192

🍽 🍺 Swan

(1m) *Heathland Farm, Birmingham Road, Whitacre Heath, Coleshill, W Mids, B46 2ER.* **Actual grid ref:** SP213928 Comfortable quiet secluded farmhouse, outskirts of village, courtyard parking. **Grades:** ETC 3 Diamond Tel: **01675 462129** Mr Barnes. **D:** £21.00-£22.00 **S:** £25.00-£28.00. **Open:** All Year (not Xmas) **Beds:** 3T 2S **Baths:** 5 En 1 Pr
🅿 (10) ☐ 🎱 🏛 Ⅴ 🔒 ⚡

Pay B&Bs by cash or cheque and be prepared to pay up front.

Shustoke 6

National Grid Ref: SP2290

🍴 🍺 The Plough

(0.25m) *The Old Vicarage,
Shustoke, Coleshill, Birmingham,
Warks, B46 2LA.*
Actual grid ref: SP243909
Business at the NEC Birmingham,
airport, walking the Heart of
England Way.
Tel: **01675 481331** (also fax no)
Mrs Hawkins.
D: £20.00-£20.00 **S:** £20.00-£22.00.
Open: All Year (not Xmas)
Beds: 3D
Baths: 2 Sh
🛌 🅿 (6) 🖵 🗙 👱 🛏 ▥ Ⓥ 🔒 ✦

Fillongley 7

National Grid Ref: SP2887

🍴 🍺 Manor House, Saracen's Head, Cottage Inn,
Horse & Jockey, Weavers' Arms

(1m) *Bourne Brooke Lodge, Mill
Lane, Fillongley, Coventry,
W Mids, CV7 8EE.*
Peace and tranquillity, high stan-
dards of comfort and cleanliness,
no smoking
Grades: ETC 4 Diamond
Tel: **01676 541898** (also fax no)
Mrs Chamberlain.
D: £20.00-£25.00 **S:** £20.00-£30.00.
Open: All Year
Beds: 1D 2T 1S
Baths: 3 En
🅿 (6) 🖌 🖵 👱 🛏 ▥ Ⓥ

Knowle 8

National Grid Ref: SP1876

🍴 🍺 Black Boy, Heron's Nest, Wilson Arms

(On path) *Ivy House, Warwick
Road, Knowle, Solihull, W Mids,
B93 0EB.*
Large rural country house.
Grades: ETC 3 Diamond,
AA 3 Diamond
Tel: **01564 770247**
Mr & Mrs Townsend.
Fax no: 01564 778063
D: £22.50-£30.00
S: £30.00-£45.00.
Open: All Year
Beds: 1F 2D 3T 2S
Baths: 8 En
🛌 🅿 (20) 🖌 🖵 🏹 👱 🛏 ▥ & Ⓥ ✦

(2m) *Achill House, 35 Hampton
Road, Knowle, Solihull, W. Mids,
B93 0NR.*
Located in the historic village of
Knowle 100 metres from the High
Street.
Tel: **01564 774090** (also fax no)
Mrs Liszewski.
D: £17.50-£25.00 **S:** £20.00-£28.00.
Open: All Year
Beds: 1F 2T 1D 1S
Baths: 3 En 2 Sh
🛌 🅿 (6) 🖵 👱 🛏 ▥ Ⓥ ✦

Henley-in-Arden 9

National Grid Ref: SP1566

🍴 🍺 Black Swan

(0.25m) *Holland Park Farm,
Buckley Green, Henley-in-Arden,
Solihull, W Mids, B95 5QF.*
Actual grid ref: SP158669
Tel: **01564 792625** (also fax no)
Mrs Connolly.
D: £22.00-£25.00 **S:** £25.00-£30.00.
Open: All Year
Beds: 2F **Baths:** 2 En
🛌 🅿 (4) 🖵 🏹 👱 🛏 ▥ Ⓥ ✦
A Georgian style house set in cen-
tre of peaceful farmland including
the historic grounds of the Mount
and other interesting walks ideally
situated in Shakespeare's country
convenient to airport NEC NAC
and Cotswolds closed on Christmas
day H of E 3 stars.

Alcester 10

National Grid Ref: SP0857

(0.25m) *Roebuck Inn, Birmingham
Road, Alcester, Warks, B49 5QA.*
Traditional country inn, non-smok-
ing, restaurants, excellent food,
beer, beds.
Tel: **01789 762410**
Fax no: 01789 765794
D: £22.50-£30.00 **S:** £35.00-£45.00.
Open: All Year
Beds: 1F 6D 4T **Baths:** 11 En
🛌 🅿 🖌 🖵 🏹 🗙 👱 🛏 & Ⓥ ✦

Haselor 11

National Grid Ref: SP1257

🍴 🍺 King's Head

(2m) *Walcote Farm, Walcote,
Haselor, Alcester, Warks, B49 6LY.*
Actual grid ref: SP126582
Easy to find, our beautiful C16th
listed oak-beamed farmhouse with
inglenook firelaces.
Tel: **01789 488264** (also fax no)
Mr & Mrs Finnemore..
D: £20.00-£23.00 **S:** £25.00-£30.00.
Open: All Year (not Xmas)
Beds: 2D 1T
Baths: 3 En
🛌 🅿 (6) 🖌 🖵 👱 🛏 ▥ ✦

Wixford 12

National Grid Ref: SP0854

🍴 🍺 The Fish

(On path) *Orchard Lawns,
Wixford, Alcester, Warks, B49 6DA.*
Actual grid ref: SP087547
Delightful house and grounds in
small village, ideal touring centre.
Grades: ETC 4 Diamond, Silver
Tel: **01789 772668** Mrs Kember.
D: £20.00-£22.00 **S:** £20.00-£22.00.
Open: All Year (not Xmas)
Beds: 1D 1T 1S **Baths:** 1 En 1 Sh
🛌 (5) 🅿 (6) 🖌 🖵 🏹 🛏 ✦

Bidford-on-Avon 13

National Grid Ref: SP0952

🍴 🍺 Frog & Bullrush, Bull's Head

(0.25m) *Fosbroke House, 4 High
Street, Bidford-on-Avon, Alcester,
Warks, B50 4BU.*
Welcoming period house close to
riverside walks and country pubs.
Grades: ETC 4 Diamond
Tel: **01789 772327**
Mr & Mrs Newbury.
D: £20.00-£25.00 **S:** £25.00-£30.00.
Open: Feb to Dec
Beds: 1F 2D 1T 1S
Baths: 5 En
🛌 🅿 (8) 🖵 🏹 👱 🛏 ▥ Ⓥ 🔒 ✦

Mickleton 14

National Grid Ref: SP1643

🍴 🍺 Bakers' Arms, Volunteer Inn, King's Arms,
Butchers' Arms, Three Ways

(0.25m 🚐) *The Bank House,
Mickleton, Chipping Campden,
Glos, GL55 6RX.*
Actual grid ref: SP161435
Period house with tranquil old
world garden in heart of historic
village.
Tel: **01386 438302**
Mrs Billington.
D: £21.00-£22.50 **S:** £30.00-£32.00.
Open: All Year (not Xmas)
Beds: 1F 1D 2T
Baths: 1 En 2 Pr
🛌 🅿 (3) 🖌 🖵 👱 🛏 ▥ Ⓥ ✦

Chipping Campden 15

National Grid Ref: SP1539

🍴 🍺 Bakers' Arms, Volunteer Inn, King's Arms,
Butchers' Arms, Three Ways, Ebrington Arms,
Wheatsheaf Inn

(On path) *The Guest House, Lower
High Street, Chipping Campden,
Glos, GL55 6DZ.*
Period Cotswold stone cottage,
easy walking to local beauty spots
and shops.
Tel: **01386 840163**
Mrs Benfield.
D: £19.00-£22.00 **S:** £25.00.
Open: Easter to Nov
Beds: 1D 1T
Baths: 2 En
🖵 🏹 👱 🛏 ▥ Ⓥ 🔒 ✦

(On path 🚐) *Weston Park Farm,
Dovers Hill, Chipping Campden,
Glos, GL55 6UW.*
Penod farmhouse in magnificent
setting, adjacent NT, on small
farm.
Tel: **01386 840835**
Mr Whitehouse.
D: £25.00-£25.00
S: £25.00-£25.00.
Open: All Year
Beds: 1F 1D
Baths: 1 En
🛌 🅿 🖵 👱 🛏 ▥ Ⓥ 🔒 ✦

(On path) *Catbrook House,*
Catbrook, Chipping Campden,
Glos, GL55 6DE.
Quietly situated with lovely views
over fields & meadows, only 10
mins walk town centre.
Tel: **01386 841499** Mrs Klein.
D: £20.50-£24.50 **S:** £35.00-£44.00.
Open: All Year (not Xmas)
Beds: 2D 1T **Baths:** 1 En 2 Pr
🛇 (9) 🅿 (3) ⚡🖵 🎍 💷 Ⓥ

Broad Campden 16

National Grid Ref: SP1537

🍴 🍺 Bakers Arms

(1m) *Marnic House, Broad*
Campden, Chipping Campden,
Glos, GL55 6UR.
Actual grid ref: SP159378
Comfortable, friendly and well
furnished family home. Peacefully
situated, scenic views.
Grades: ETC 4 Diamond, Gold,
AA 4 Diamond
Tel: **01386 840014** Mrs Rawlings.
Fax no: 01386 840441
D: £22.00-£25.00 **S:** £38.00-£40.00.
Open: All Year (not Xmas/
New Year)
Beds: 2D 1T **Baths:** 2 En 1 Pr
🛇 (10) 🅿 (4) 🖵 🎍 💷 Ⓥ ⚡

(On path) *Wyldlands, Broad*
Campden, Chipping Campden,
Glos, GL55 6UR.
Actual grid ref: SP156381
Cotswold stone house with open
views over countryside in conser-
vation village.
Tel: **01386 840478** Mrs Wadey.
Fax no: 01386 840441
D: £22.00-£22.00 **S:** £28.00-£28.00.
Open: All Year (not Xmas)
Beds: 1D 1T 1S
Baths: 2 En 1 Pr
🛇 🅿 (4) ⚡🖵 🎍 💷 Ⓥ ⚡

Pay B&Bs by cash or
cheque and be prepared
to pay up front.

Blockley 17

National Grid Ref: SP1634

🍴 🍺 Great Western Inn, Crown Hotel

(On path 🚃) *Tudor House, High*
Street, Blockley, Moreton in Marsh,
Glos, GL56 9EX.
Excellent walking, gardens to visit.
Tel: **01386 700356** Mrs Thompson.
D: £25.00-£30.00 **S:** £25.00-£30.00.
Open: All Year (not Xmas)
Beds: 1D 1T **Baths:** 1 Sh
🛇 (10) 🅿 (2) ⚡🖵 🎍 💷 Ⓥ

(On path 🚃) *Arreton Guest*
House, Station Road, Blockley,
Moreton-in-Marsh, Glos, GL56 6DT.
Grades: ETC 4 Diamond,
AA 4 Diamond
Tel: **01386 701077** (also fax no)
D: £20.00-£22.00 **S:** £28.00-£30.00.
Open: All Year
Beds: 1F 1D 1T **Baths:** 3 En
🛇 ⚡🖵 🎍 💷 Ⓥ 🛈 ⚡
Arreton is situated in the north
Cotswold in the village of
Blockley. Once famous in the
1700's for its silk trade, Arreton
dates from 1600 being built of
Mellow Cotswold stone.

(On path 🚃) *Park Farm, Blockley,*
Moreton in Marsh, Glos, GL56 9TA.
Beautiful old farmhouse; idyllic
location, easy walk village. Warm
welcome.
Tel: **01386 700266** Mr & Mrs Dee.
D: £17.00 **S:** £17.00.
Open: All Year
Beds: 1D 1T 2S
Baths: 1 Sh
🛇 🅿 (6) ⚡🖵 🎍 💷 Ⓥ 🛈 ⚡

(On path) *The Malins, 21 Station*
Road, Blockley, Moreton In Marsh,
Glos, GL56 9ED.
Attractive Cotswold stone house,
many facilities, friendly hosts.
Grades: ETC 3 Diamond
Tel: **01386 700402** (also fax no)
Mrs Malin.
D: £18.00 **S:** £25.00.
Open: All Year
Beds: 1D 2T
Baths: 3 Pr
🛇 🅿 (5) ⚡🖵 🎍 💷 Ⓥ 🛈

Aston Magna 18

National Grid Ref: SP1935

🍴 🍺 Ebrington Arms

(3m 🚃) *Bran Mill Cottage, Aston*
Magna, Moreton in Marsh, Glos,
GL56 9QP.
Small traditional B&B in peaceful
Cotswold cottage. Friendly,
welcoming, homely.
Grades: ETC 3 Diamond
Tel: **01386 593517**
D: £16.00-£18.00
S: £19.00-£25.00.
Open: All Year (not Xmas)
Beds: 1D 1T 1S
Baths: 1 Pr 1 Sh
🛇 (14) 🅿 (3) ⚡🖵 🎍 💷 Ⓥ ⚡

Lower Swell 19

National Grid Ref: SP1725

🍴 🍺 Golden Ball

(On path) *Golden Ball Inn, Lower*
Swell, Stow-on-the-Wold, Glos,
GL54 1LF.
Actual grid ref: SP175254
Delightful C17th village inn,
genuine home-cooked food,
friendly atmosphere, pets welcome.
Grades: ETC 2 Diamond
Tel: **01451 830247** Knowles.
D: £22.50-£27.50 **S:** £30.00-£35.00.
Open: All Year
Beds: 3D 1T
Baths: 4 En
🛇 🅿 (15) 🖵 🍴 ✕ 🎍 💷 Ⓥ 🛈 ⚡

Lower Slaughter 20

National Grid Ref: SP1623

🍴 🍺 Coach & Horses, Plough Inn

(1m 🚃) *Seymour House Farm,*
Fosseway, Lower Slaughter,
Bourton-on-the-Water,
Cheltenham, Glos, GL54 2HW.
Traditional Cotswold house on
working small holding. Excellent
touring centre.
Tel: **01451 820132** (also fax no)
Mr & Mrs Hedges.
D: £17.50-£20.00 .
Open: All Year
Beds: 1F 1D
🛇 🅿 (6) ⚡🖵 🍴 🎍 💷 Ⓥ ⚡

(0.75m) *Lakeside, Fosseway,*
Lower Slaughter, Cheltenham,
Glos, GL54 2EY.
Actual grid ref: SP175227
Comfortable home on edge of
unspoilt village. One mile north of
Bourton-on-the-Water on A429.
Tel: **01451 821206**
Mrs Goss.
D: £16.00-£20.00
S: £20.00-£20.00.
Open: All Year (not Xmas)
Beds: 1F 1D
Baths: 1 En 1 Pr
🛇 (4) 🅿 (5) ⚡🖵 🎍 💷 Ⓥ 🛈 ⚡

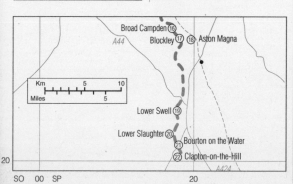

Bourton-on-the-Water 21

National Grid Ref: SP1620

¶ ⌂ Plough, Kingsbridge Inn, Mouse Trap Inn, Coach & Horses, Duke of Wellington

(On path) *Lansdowne House, Lansdowne, Bourton-on-the-Water, Cheltenham, Glos, GL54 2AT.*
Actual grid ref: SP160210
Tastefully furnished ensuite accommodation. Combination of old and antique furniture.
Grades: ETC 4 Diamond
Tel: 01451 820812 Mrs Garwood.
Fax no: 01451 822484
D: £17.50-£20.00 **S:** £30.00-£35.00.
Open: All Year (not Xmas)
Beds: 1F 2D **Baths:** 3 En
📷 🅿 (4) 🗗 🛄 ⅷ ✦

(On path) *6 Moore Road, Bourton-on-the-Water, Cheltenham, Glos, GL54 2AZ.*
Cotswold stone house, quiet road, yards to village, peaceful garden.
Tel: 01451 820767 Mrs Mustoe.
D: £19.00-£21.00 **S:** £20.00-£25.00.
Open: Feb to Dec
Beds: 1D 1T
Baths: 1 En 1 Pr
📷 (5) 🅿 (3) ✄🗗🐾🛄ⅷ✦

(0.25m 🚌) *Holly House, Station Road, Bourton-on-the-Water, Cheltenham, Glos, GL54 2ER.*
Actual grid ref: SP168212
Spacious Cotswold style house. Breakfast in conservatory overlooking delightful gardens.
Grades: ETC 4 Diamond
Tel: 01451 821302
Mr Stanfield.
D: £20.00-£25.00
S: £28.00-£32.00.
Open: Feb to Oct
Beds: 2D 1T 1S
Baths: 4 En
📷 🅿 (6) ✄🗗✕🛄ⅷ⌀✦

(On path 🚌) *Lansdowne Villa Guest House, Bourton-on-the-Water, Cheltenham, Glos, GL54 2AR.*
This large, detached Cotswold stone house stands at the end of this beautiful village.
Tel: 01451 820673
Mr & Mrs Harris.
Fax no: 01451 822099
D: £24.00
S: £32.00.
Open: Feb to Dec
Beds: 8D 2T 2S
Baths: 12 En
📷 🅿 (14) ✄🗗✕🛄ⅷ⌀✦

Clapton-on-the-Hill 22

National Grid Ref: SP1617

¶ ⌂ Plough, Kingsbridge Inn, Mouse Trap Inn, Coach & Horses

(On path) *Farncombe, Clapton-on-the-Hill, Bourton-on-the-Water, Cheltenham, Glos, GL54 2LG.*
Come and share our peace and tranquillity with superb views.
Grades: ETC 4 Diamond
Tel: 01451 820120 (also fax no)
Mrs Wright.
D: £20.00-£23.00 **S:** £25.00-£30.00.
Open: All Year (not Xmas)
Beds: 2D 1T **Baths:** 1 En 2 Sh
📷 🅿 (4) ✄🗗🛄ⅷ⌀✦

(On path) *Upper Farm, Clapton-on-the-Hill, Bourton-on-the-Water, Cheltenham, Glos, GL54 2LG.*
Period farmhouse, spectacular views warm welcome, superior accommodation, village location.
Grades: ETC 5 Diamond
Tel: 01451 820453 Mrs Adams.
Fax no: 01451 810185
D: £20.00-£22.50 **S:** £25.00-£30.00.
Open: Feb to Dec
Beds: 1F 2D 1T **Baths:** 3 En 1 Sh
📷 (6) 🅿 (6) ✄🗗🛄&ⅷ

BRITAIN: BED & BREAKFAST

The essential guide to B&Bs in England, Scotland & Wales

The Bed & Breakfast is one of the great British institutions. Like Fish & Chips, it's known by people around the world. But you don't have to be a tourist to enjoy this traditional accommodation. Whether you're travelling, on holiday, away on business or just escaping from it all, the B&B is a great value alternative to expensive hotels and a world away from camping and caravanning.

Stilwell's Britain: Bed & Breakfast 2001 is the most comprehensive guide of its kind, containing over 7,750 entries listed by country, county and location, in England, Scotland and Wales. Each entry includes room rates, facilities, Tourist Board grades and a brief description of the B&B and its location and surroundings.

Stilwell's Britain: Bed & Breakfast 2001: The indispensable guide to great value accommodation:

Private houses, country halls, farms, cottages, inns, small hotels and guest houses

Over 7,750 entries
Average price £19 per person per night
All official grades shown
Local maps
Pubs serving hot evening meals shown
Tourist Information Centres listed
Handy size for easy packing

£9.95 from all good bookstores (ISBN 1-900861-22-4) or £11.95 (inc p&p) from Stilwell Publishing, 59 Charlotte Road, London EC2A 3QW (020 7739 7179)

Hereward Way

Here is a curious path - it runs for most of its length below sea-level. The **Hereward Way** is the waymarked 'path across the fens', named after the English hero **Hereward the Wake**, who eluded the Normans in this area for so long, until finally besieged and defeated on the Isle of Ely. Its flatness clearly makes for easy walking. Starting at Oakham near Rutland Water, it heads off through the Fens to Ely with its lovely cathedral (built by the Normans to commemorate the defeat of Hereward), before heading off to Brandon and the Brecklands of West Norfolk.

The mountaineers among you will be bored; the naturalists and historians will be fascinated. The path links up with the **Viking Way** and the **Peddars Way** and, via the latter, the **Icknield Way**.
Guide: *Hereward Way* (ISBN 0 900613 57 2) by Trevor Noyes, published by the Ramblers Association and available from their National office (1/5 Wandsworth Road, London, SW8 2XX, tel. 020 7339 8500), £1.50 (+50p p&p).
Maps: 1:50000 Ordnance Survey Landranger Series: 141, 142, 143, 144

All paths are popular: you are well-advised to book ahead

Pay B&Bs by cash or cheque and be prepared to pay up front.

Oakham   1

National Grid Ref: SK8508

⊯ ⊲ Admiral Hornblower, Nicks, White Lion, Odd House, Whippen Inn

(On path) *Angel House, 20 Northgate, Oakham, Rutland, LE15 6QS.*
Unique Victorian house. Converted outbuildings. Secluded courtyard. Lounge, patio, fridge/freezer, microwave.
Tel: **01572 756153**
Mrs Weight.
D: £11.00-£17.00 **S:** £22.00-£34.00.
Open: All Year
Beds: 1D 2T
Baths: 3 En
🛇 🅿 ☐ 🖢 ☑ ⓘ ⊘

Empingham   2

National Grid Ref: SK9508

⊯ ⊲ White Horse

(On path) *Little Hoo, Nook Lane, Empingham, Oakham, Rutland, LE15 8PT.*
Actual grid ref: SK947085
C16th luxury cottage, 2 minutes from Rutland Water. Barn for drying clothes.
Tel: **01780 460293** Mr Coxhead.
D: £22.50-£22.50 **S:** £26.00-£26.00.
Open: All Year
Beds: 1F 3T 1S **Baths:** 2 Pr
🛇 (2) 🅿 (10) ⊬ ☐ 🖈 ✗ 🖢 ▦ ☑ ⓘ ⊘

Taking your dog?
Book *in advance*
ONLY with owners
who accept dogs (🖈)

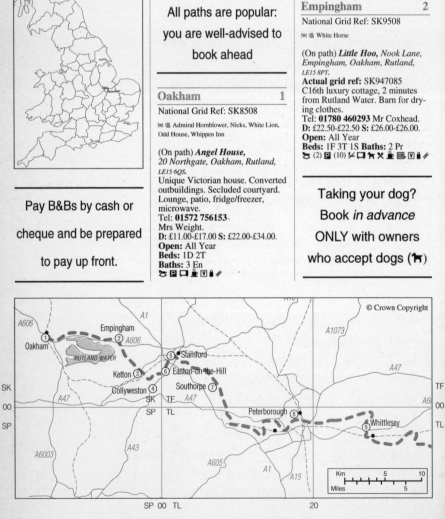

© Crown Copyright

Ketton 3

National Grid Ref: SK9704

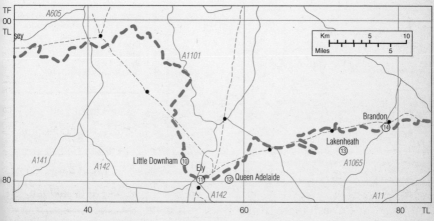 Northwick Arms

(On path) *16 Northwick Road, Ketton, Stamford, PE9 3SB.*
Actual grid ref: SK978043
Split-level stone bungalow. Warm welcome. Between Rutland Water and Stamford.
Tel: **01780 721411** Coyne.
D: £16.50-£16.50 **S:** £16.50-£16.50.
Open: Feb to Nov
Beds: 1T 1S
Baths: 1 Sh
▣ (1) ⊬ ▢ ▥

Collyweston 4

National Grid Ref: SK9902

(0.5m) *Highfields, 31 Main Road, Collyweston, Stamford, Lincs, PE9 3PF.*
Detached black & white chalet house surrounded by fields.
Tel: **01780 444339** Mrs Hindley.
D: £20.00-£21.00
S: £20.00-£21.00.
Open: All Year
Beds: 1D 1T 1S **Baths:** 1 En 1 Sh
⛺ (4) ▣ (4) ▢ ⊀ ✕ ▣ ▥ ᵫ ▼ ⬧ ⚡

Stamford 5

National Grid Ref: TF0207

⊫ St Mary's Vaults, Hole in the Wall, The Bull, The Swan, The Dolphin, George Hotel, St Peters Inn, Green Man, Golden Pheasant

(0.5m) *Birch House, 4 Lonsdale Road, Stamford, Stamford, Lincs, PE9 2RW.*
Established well-presented family-run suburban house one mile from Stamford.
Tel: **01780 754876** Mrs Headland.
D: £18.50-£25.00 **S:** £18.50-£25.00.
Open: All Year (not Xmas)
Beds: 2D 2S **Baths:** 1 Sh
⛺ (5) ▣ (3) ⊬ ▢ ᵫ ▥ ▼

Pay B&Bs by cash or cheque and be prepared to pay up front.

(0.5m) *The Lincolnshire Poacher, Broad Street, Stamford, Lincs, PE9 1PX.*
Historic converted brewery in the centre of Stamford.
Tel: **01780 764239** Martin.
D: £18.00 **S:** £18.00.
Open: All Year
Beds: 1F 2T 1S
Baths: 1 Sh
⛺ (1) ⊬ ▢ ⊀ ᵫ ▥ ▼

(0.5m) *5 Rock Terrace, Scotgate, Stamford, Lincs., PE9 2YJ.*
Early Victorian terraced house on edge of town centre, bedrooms are well furnished.
Tel: **01780 755475** Mrs Averdieck.
D: £20.00-£27.50 .
Open: All Year
Beds: 1D 1T **Baths:** 2 Pr
⊬ ▢ ᵫ ▥

Easton-on-the-Hill 6

National Grid Ref: TF0004

⊫ Oak

(On path) *Hillcroft House, 25 High Street, Easton-on-the-Hill, Stamford, Lincs, PE9 3LN.*
Converted stone farmhouse, spacious grounds, quiet position in conservation village.
Tel: **01780 755598** Mrs McCallum.
D: £17.50-£20.00 **S:** £20.00-£22.50.
Open: All Year (not Xmas)
Beds: 1D 2T
Baths: 1 Pr 1 Sh
⛺ ▣ (4) ⊬ ▢ ⊀ ᵫ ▥ ▼

Southorpe 7

National Grid Ref: SK8995

⊫ Millstone Inn

(0.5m) *Midstone Farm House, Midstone House, Southorpe, Stamford, Lincs, PE9 3BX.*
Beautiful stone Georgian house in quiet location. Meet George the pot bellied pig.
Grades: ETC 4 Diamond
Tel: **01780 740136**
Mrs Harrison Smith.
Fax no: 01780 749294
D: £25.00-£30.00
S: £25.00-£30.00.
Open: All Year
Beds: 1D 1T
Baths: 1 En 1 Pr
⛺ ▣ ⊬ ▢ ⊀ ✕ ᵫ ▥ ▼ ᵫ ⚡

Peterborough 8

National Grid Ref: TL1999

⊫ Cherry Tree, Exeter Arms, Barnyards, Botolph Arms, Fitzwilliam Arms

(▲ 0.5m) *Peterborough Youth Hostel, Thorpe Meadows, Peterborough, PE3 6GA.*
Tel: **01629 592707**
Under 18: £7.75 **Adults:** £11.00
Lounge, Parking, Evening meal at 7.00pm, WC, Breakfast available
Due to open in 2001. It is within the sculpture Park.

All rooms full and nowhere else to stay? Ask the owner if there's anywhere nearby

---

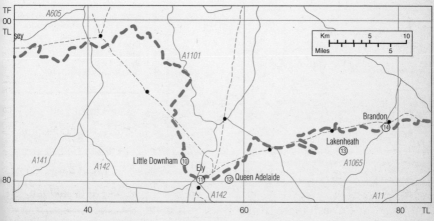

(0.5m) *Aragon House, 75/77 London Road, Peterborough, Cambs, PE2 9BS.*
Actual grid ref: TL192969
Comfortable, friendly, easy parking and close to city centre.
Grades: ETC 3 Diamond
Tel: 01733 563718 (also fax no)
Mr & Mrs Spence.
D: £19.00-£22.00 **S:** £20.00-£30.00.
Open: All Year (not Xmas)
Beds: 1F 3D 2T 6S
Baths: 3 En 2 Sh
🛇 🅿 (8) ⅊ 🗇 🛏 🖢 🎟 Ⓥ ♦ ⫽

(0.5m 🚗) *Montana, 15 Fletton Ave, Peterborough, Cambs, PE2 8AX.*
Clean, friendly, family-run. Close city centre. Traditional breakfasts.
Grades: ETC 3 Diamond
Tel: 01733 567917 (also fax no)
Mr & Mrs Atkins.
D: £17.00-£20.00 **S:** £19.00-£25.00.
Open: All Year (not Xmas)
Beds: 1D 2T 4S **Baths:** 2 Sh
🅿 (6) ⅊ 🗇 🛏 🖢 🎟 Ⓥ ♦ ⫽

(0.5m) *Rose-Marie, 14 Eastfield Rd, Peterborough, Cambs, PE1 4AN.*
The Rose Marie is a family-run guest house close to city centre.
Tel: 01733 557548 Mr Doyle.
Fax no: 01733 764801
D: £15.00-£18.00 **S:** £18.00-£20.00.
Open: All Year
Beds: 1F 2D 1T 2S **Baths:** 1 Sh
🛇 🗇 🛏 🖢 🎟 Ⓥ ♦ ⫽

Whittlesey   9

National Grid Ref: TL2797

🍴 🍺 Mortons Fork

(On path 🚗) *Cobwebs Guest House, 21 The Delph, Whittlesey, Peterborough, Cambs, PE7 1QH.*
Close to diving centre, fishing, lakes East of England showground.
Tel: 01733 350960 Mrs Ekins.
D: £15.00-£20.00 **S:** £15.00-£20.00.
Open: All Year (not Xmas)
Beds: 1F 5T **Baths:** 1 Pr 2 Sh
🅿 (4) 🗇 🛏 ✗ 🖢 🎟 ⚕ Ⓥ ♦ ⫽

Little Downham   10

National Grid Ref: TL5283

🍴 🍺 Plough, Anchor

(On path) *Bury House, 11 Main Street, Little Downham, Ely, Cambs, CB6 2ST.*
Actual grid ref: TL526841
Grade 2 Listed ex-farmhouse large comfortable bedrooms in friendly home.
Tel: **01353 698766**
Mrs Ambrose.
D: £18.00-£18.00 **S:** £18.00.
Open: All Year (not Xmas)
Beds: 1F 2T
Baths: 2 Sh
🛇 🅿 (2) ⅊ 🗇 🛏 🖢 🎟 Ⓥ ♦ ⫽

Ely   11

National Grid Ref: TL5480

🍴 🍺 The Crown, Red Lion, High Flyer, Old Boathouse, Cutter Inn, Stagecoach, Maids Head

(0.5m) *82 Broad Street, Ely, Cambs, CB7 4BE.*
Comfortable rooms, central Ely. Near station, cathedral & river.
Tel: **01353 667609**
Mr & Mrs Hull.
Fax no: 01353 667005
D: £15.00-£18.00 **S:** £20.00.
Open: All Year (not Xmas)
Beds: 1F 1T 1S
Baths: 1 En 1 Pr 1 Sh
🛇 🅿 🗇 🛏 🖢 🎟 Ⓥ ♦ ⫽

High season,
bank holidays and
special events mean
low availability
everywhere.

(0.5m) *Cathedral House, 17 St Mary's Street, Ely, Cambs, CB7 4ER.*
Grade II Listed house, in shadow of cathedral, close to museums, restaurants, shops
Grades: ETC 4 Diamond, Silver
Tel: 01353 662124 (also fax no)
Mr & Mrs Farndale.
D: £25.00-£30.00 **S:** £35.00-£45.00.
Open: All Year (not Xmas)
Beds: 1F 1D 1T
Baths: 3 En
🛇 🅿 (4) ⅊ 🗇 🛏 🖢 🎟 Ⓥ

(0.5m 🚗) *84 Broad Street, Ely, Cambs, CB7 4BE.*
Renovated cottage, court yard garden. Near river, cathedral and station.
Tel: **01353 666862** Mrs Collins.
D: £16.00-£16.00 **S:** £18.00-£18.00.
Open: All Year
Beds: 1F 1D
Baths: 1 Sh
🛇 ⅊ 🗇 🛏 🖢 🎟 Ⓥ ♦ ⫽

(On path 🚗) *The Nyton Hotel, 7 Barton Road, Ely, Cambs, CB7 4HZ.*
Residential family hotel; lovely situation, close city centre and cathedral.
Tel: 01353 662459 Mr Setchell.
Fax no: 01353 666217
D: £25.00-£30.00 **S:** £35.00-£40.00.
Open: All Year
Beds: 3F 3D 2T 2S **Baths:** 10 En
🛇 🅿 (26) ⅊ 🗇 🛏 ✗ 🖢 🎟 ♿ Ⓥ ♦ ⫽

(0.5m) *Annesdale Lodge, 8 Annesdale, Ely, Cambs, CB7 4BN.*
Riverside home from home accommodation near railway station. Great views.
Tel: 01353 667533 Mr Drage.
Fax no: 01353 667005
D: £16.00-£22.50 **S:** £25.00-£35.00.
Open: All Year
Beds: 1D 1T **Baths:** 2 Pr
🛇 🅿 (1) ⅊ 🗇 🛏 🖢 Ⓥ ♦ ⫽

(0.5m) *Sycamore House, 91 Cambridge Road, Ely, Cambs, CB7 4HX.*
Newly renovated Edwardian family home set in acre of mature gardens.
Tel: 01353 662139 Mrs Webster.
D: £22.00-£25.00 **S:** £28.00-£30.00.
Open: All Year (not Xmas)
Beds: 2D 2T
Baths: 3 En 1 Pr
🅿 (8) ⅊ 🗇 🛏 🖢 🎟 Ⓥ

Order your
packed lunches the
evening before you
need them.
Not at breakfast!

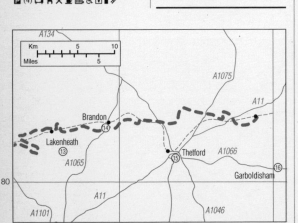

Queen Adelaide 12

National Grid Ref: TL5580

⊮ꢀ Highflyer

(2m ⊟) *Greenways, Prickwillow Road, Queen Adelaide, Ely, Cambs, CB7 4TZ.*
Comfortable ground floor accommodation, 1 mile cathedral city of Ely.
Tel: **01353 666706**
Mr Dunlop-Hill.
D: £21.00-£26.00 **S:** £26.00.
Open: All Year
Beds: 1F 1D 1T 1S **Baths:** 4 En
ॐ ◪ (6) ⊡ ⊁ ♨ ▥ ⅋ ⱽ ⊬

Lakenheath 13

National Grid Ref: TL7182

⊮ꢀ Bell Inn

(3m ⊟) *Bell Inn, 20 High St, Lakenheath, Brandon, Suffolk, IP27 9DS.*
Old coaching house.
Tel: **01842 860308** (also fax no)
Guy.
D: £20.00-£45.00 **S:** £20.00-£30.00.
Open: All Year
Beds: 2F 1T 2D 1S **Baths:** 6 En
ॐ ◪ (20) ⊡ ⊁ ✕ ♨ ▥ ⱽ ⊹ ⅋

Brandon 14

National Grid Ref: TL7886

(On path) *Riverside Lodge, 78 High Street, Brandon, Suffolk, IP27 0AU.*
Home comforts abound. Charming Listed house with attractive riverside setting. Licensed bar.
Tel: **01842 811236** Mrs Arnold.
D: £15.00-£22.50 **S:** £17.50-£30.00.
Open: All Year
Beds: 3F 4D 3T **Baths:** 7 En 3 Sh
ॐ ◪ (15) ⊡ ⊁ ✕ ♨ ▥ ⱽ ⊹ ⅋

Thetford 15

National Grid Ref: TL8783

⊮ꢀ Black Horse, Anchor Hotel

(5.5m) *43 Magdalen Street, Thetford, Norfolk, IP24 2BP.*
House built in 1575 close to town centre.
Tel: **01842 764564** Mrs Findlay.
D: £36.00-£36.00 **S:** £18.00-£18.00.
Open: All Year (not Xmas/ New Year)
Beds: 2T 1S
Baths: 1 Sh
ॐ ◪ (1) ⊡ ♨ ▥ ⱽ ⊹ ⅋

Garboldisham 16

National Grid Ref: TM0081

⊮ꢀ The Fox, White Horse

(3.5m ⊟) *Ingleneuk Lodge, Hopton Road, Garboldisham, Diss, Norfolk, IP22 2RQ.*
Actual grid ref: TM002801
Pretty rural location with all rooms overlooking partly wooded grounds.
Tel: **01953 681541**
Mr & Mrs Stone.
Fax no: 01953 681638
D: £27.50-£27.50 **S:** £33.00-£33.00.
Open: All Year
Beds: 3D 3T 1S 1F
Baths: 8 En
ॐ ◪ (15) ⊡ ⊁ ♨ ▥ ⅋ ⱽ ⊹

Please don't camp on *anyone's* land without first obtaining their permission.

Icknield Way

The **Icknield Way** proper is a series of prehistoric pathways, ancient even when the Romans came, following the great chalk ridges of southern England. The **Icknield Way** long distance footpath covers only part of this long road, but it links the **Ridgeway** and the **Peddars Way** National Trails, which between them cover the rest of the old way. This is a good path for restless Londoners, with easy access back to the capital. From the Ivinghoe Beacon, the route passes through rural Hertfordshire and up into South Cambridgeshire, before heading off to the open heath of the Breckland in West Norfolk.

Guides: *The Icknield Way - A Walker's Guide* by Alan Jenyon (ISBN 0 9521819 0 8), published by the Icknield Way Association and available from the Rambler's Association National Office (1/5 Wandsworth Road, London, SW8 2XX, tel. 020 7339 8500), £4.50 (+ 70p p&p)

Maps: 1:50000 Ordnance Survey Landranger Series: 144, 153, 154, 155, 165, 166

Ivinghoe   1

National Grid Ref: SP9416

(▲ 1m) *Ivinghoe Youth Hostel, The Old Brewery House, High Street, Ivinghoe, Leighton Buzzard, LU7 9EP.*
Actual grid ref: SP945161
Tel: 01296 668251
Under 18: £6.90 **Adults:** £10.00
Self-catering facilities, Television, Showers, Lounge, Drying room, Cycle store, Parking, Evening meal at 7.00pm, Kitchen facilities, Breakfast available
Georgian mansion, once home of a local brewer, next to village church in Chilterns' Area of Outstanding Natural Beauty.

S = Price range for a single person in a room

D = Price range per person sharing in a double room

Edlesborough   2

National Grid Ref: SP9719

¶ ⌘ The Golden Rule

(1m 🚌) *Ridgeway End, 5 Ivinghoe Way, Edlesborough, Dunstable, Beds, LU6 2EL.*
Actual grid ref: SP975183
Pretty bungalow in private road, surrounded by fields and views of the Chiltern Hills.
Tel: 01525 220405 (also fax no)
Mrs Lloyd.
D: £20.00-£22.00 **S:** £22.00-£24.00.
Open: All Year (not Xmas)
Beds: 1D 1T **Baths:** 1 En
🛇 (2) 🅿 (3) ✕ ☐ 🍽 🛋 🎮 Ⓥ 🅰 ✔

Totternhoe   3

National Grid Ref: SP9821

¶ ⌘ Old Farm Inn, Cross Keys

(0.5m) *Country Cottage, 5 Brightwell Avenue, Totternhoe, Dunstable, Beds, LU6 1QT.*
Actual grid ref: SP994210
Quiet village house in countryside with views of Dunstable Downs.
Tel: 01582 601287 (also fax no)
Mrs Mardell.
D: £25.00-£25.00 **S:** £25.00-£25.00.
Open: All Year (not Xmas)
Beds: 1T 1D 1S **Baths:** 2 En 1Sh
🛇 🅿 (3) ✕ ☐ 🛋 🎮 Ⓥ 🅰 ✔

All rates are subject to alteration at the owners' discretion.

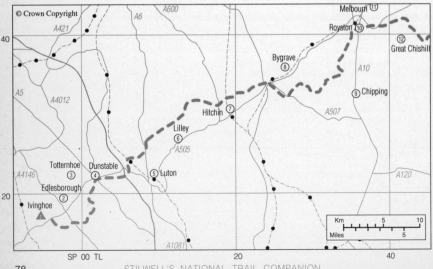

© Crown Copyright

Dunstable 4

National Grid Ref: TL0121

⚑ ◫ Sugar Loaf

(1m) *Regent House Guest House,*
79a High Street North, Dunstable,
Beds, LU6 1JF.
Dunstable town centre, close to MI.
Tel: **01582 660196**
Mr Woodhouse.
D: £17.00-£17.00
S: £20.00-£20.00.
Open: All Year
Beds: 5T 5S 1F
Baths: 4 En
⛄ ₽ (6) ◻ ↑ ≞ ▥ Ⅵ ▮ ∥

High season,
bank holidays and
special events mean
low availability
everywhere.

Luton 5

National Grid Ref: TL0921

⚑ ◫ Wigmore Arms, O'Shea's

(1.25m) *Stockwood Hotel,*
41-43 Stockwood Crescent, Luton,
Beds, LU1 3SS.
Actual grid ref: TL090206
Tudor-style town centre premises,
near M1, airport, golf course.
Tel: **01582 721000** Mr Blanchard.
D: £20.00 **S:** £25.00.
Open: All Year (not Xmas)
Beds: 1F 2D 6T 9S
Baths: 4 Pr 3 Sh
⛄ ₽ (14) ◻ ✗ ▥

(1.25m) *Belzayne, 70 Lalleford*
Road, Luton, Beds, LU2 9JH.
Modern semi, close to London bus
stop. Old fashioned hospitality.
Tel: **01582 736591** (also fax no)
Mrs Bell.
D: £12.00-£14.00 **S:** £18.00.
Open: All Year (not Xmas)
Beds: 1F 2T
Baths: 2 Sh
⛄ (7) ₽ (5) ≞ ▥ Ⅵ

Lilley 6

National Grid Ref: TL1126

⚑ ◫ Lilley Arms

(1m) *Lilley Arms, West Street,*
Lilley, Luton, Beds, LU2 8LN.
Early C18th coaching inn.
Tel: **01462 768371** Mrs Brown.
D: £20.00-£30.00 .
Open: All Year
Beds: 1F 1D 3T **Baths:** 3En 1 Sh
⛄ ₽ ⚡ ◻ ↑ ✗ ≞ ▥ Ⅵ ▮ ∥

Hitchin 7

National Grid Ref: TL1828

(1m) *Firs Hotel, 83 Bedford Road,*
Hitchin, Herts, SG5 2TY.
Comfortable hotel with relaxed
informal atmosphere. Excellent
rail/road links and car parking.
Grades: RAC Star
Tel: **01462 422322** Girgenti.
Fax no: 01462 432051
D: £26.00-£30.00 **S:** £37.50-£50.00.
Open: All Year
Beds: 3F 3D 8T 16S **Baths:** 30 En
⛄ ₽ (30) ⚡ ◻ ↑ ✗ ≞ ▥ Ⅵ ▮

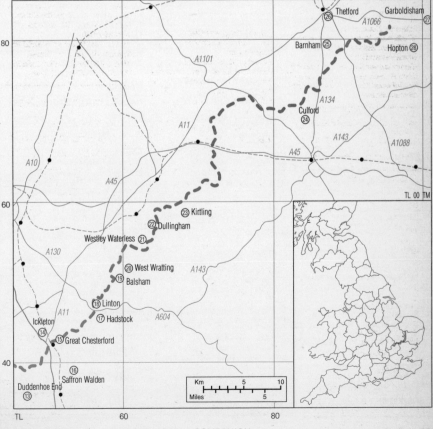

Bygrave 8

National Grid Ref: TL2636

|O| ▦ Bushel & Strike, Rose & Crown, Engine

(0.5m) *Bygrave B&B, 59 Ashwell Road, Bygrave, Baldock, Hertfordshire, SG7 5DY.*
Friendly family home, rural location. Guests' room, use of garden.
Tel: **01462 894749** Mrs Spaul.
D: £22.00-£25.00 **S:** £22.00-£25.00.
Open: All Year (not Xmas)
Beds: 2D 2T 1S
Baths: 2 En 1 Sh
ॐ **P** (5) ⊬ ☐ ఉ ▥ Ⓥ

Chipping 9

National Grid Ref: TL3532

|O| ▦ Countryman Inn

(2m 🚍) *Ashford Cottage, Chipping, Buntingford, Herts, SG9 0PG.*
Elizabethan thatched cottage, acre of gardens, heavily timbered.
Tel: **01763 274163**
Mr & Mrs Kenyon.
Fax no: 01763 271655
D: £22.50-£22.50 **S:** £22.50-£22.50.
Open: All Year
Beds: 1D 2S **Baths:** 1 Sh
ॐ **P** (6) ⊬ ☐ ✕ ఉ ▥ Ⓥ ⋔ ⋇

Royston 10

National Grid Ref: TL3541

|O| ▦ Jockey Inn, White Bear Lodge, Green Man

(0.25m) *Jockey Inn, 31-33 Baldock Street, Royston, Herts, SG8 5BD.*
Traditional public house, real ales. Comfortable rooms - ensuite/cable TV. Hearty breakfast.
Tel: **01763 243377**
D: £26.50-£28.50 **S:** £29.95-£34.00.
Open: All Year
Beds: 3T 1F **Baths:** 5 En
ॐ (8) **P** (5) ☐ ✕ ఉ ▥ Ⓥ ⋇

Melbourn 11

National Grid Ref: TL3844

|O| ▦ The Star, Black Horse, The Chequers

(3m 🚍) *The Carlings, Melbourn, Royston, SG8 6DX.*
Luxurious rooms in delightful secluded setting. Separate entrance, conservatory gardens.
Tel: **01763 260686** Mrs Howard.
Fax no: 01763 261988
D: £22.00-£22.00 **S:** £30.00-£35.00.
Open: All Year (not Xmas)
Beds: 1D 1T **Baths:** 2 En
ॐ **P** (3) ⊬ ☐ ⋔ ▥ ఉ Ⓥ ⋇

D = Price range per person sharing in a double room

Great Chishill 12

National Grid Ref: TL4238

|O| ▦ The Pleasant

(1m) *Hall Farm, Great Chishill, Royston, Cambridgeshire, SG8 8SH.*
Grades: ETC 4 Diamond
Tel: **01763 838263** (also fax no)
Mrs Wiseman.
D: £20.00-£30.00 **S:** £30.00-£35.00.
Open: All Year
Beds: 1F 1T 1D **Baths:** 1 En 1 Sh
ॐ **P** (4) ⊬ ☐ ⋔ ఉ Ⓥ �
Beautiful Manor house in secluded gardens on the edge of this pretty hilltop village 11 miles south of Cambridge, wonderful views and footpaths. Duxford Air Museum 4 miles. Good local food. Working Arable farm. Comfortable new beds.

Duddenhoe End 13

National Grid Ref: TL4636

|O| ▦ Axe and Compass

(2m) *Rockells Farm, Duddenhoe End, Saffron Walden, Essex, CB11 4UY.*
Georgian farmhouse with lake view.
Grades: ETC 4 Diamond
Tel: **01763 838053**
Mrs Westerhuis.
D: £20.00-£25.00 **S:** £20.00-£25.00.
Open: All Year (not Xmas/New Year)
Beds: 1F 1T 1S **Baths:** 3 En
ॐ **P** (4) ☐ ✕ ఉ ▥ ఉ Ⓥ ᠠ ⋇

Ickleton 14

National Grid Ref: TL4843

|O| ▦ Red Lion

(1m) *New Inn House, 10 Brookhampton Street, Ickleton, Duxford, Cambs, CB10 1SP.*
Tel: **01799 530463** Mrs Fletcher.
Fax no: 01799 531499
D: £15.00-£19.00 **S:** £25.00-£30.00.
Open: All Year (not Xmas)
Beds: 1D 1T
Baths: 1 Sh
ॐ (5) **P** (6) ⊬ ☐ ఉ ▥ Ⓥ
Traditional beamed property combining comfortable modern facilities with historic charm. Luxury guest shower room. Good breakfasts. Small rural village, 3 miles Duxford Imperial War Museum. Handy for Cambridge and Saffron Walden. 2 miles M11.

Great Chesterford 15

National Grid Ref: TL5042

|O| ▦ The Plough

(0.5m) *White Gates, School Street, Great Chesterford, Saffron Walden, Essex, CB10 1PH.*
C18th timber framed cottage in heart of historic village.
Grades: ETC 4 Diamond
Tel: **01799 530249** Mrs Mortimer.
D: £19.00-£25.00 **S:** £23.00-£25.00.
Open: All Year
Beds: 1F 1T 1S **Baths:** 1 En 1 Sh
ॐ **P** (3) ⊬ ☐ ఉ ▥ Ⓥ

Saffron Walden 16

National Grid Ref: TL5438

|O| ▦ Crown, Eight Bells, Rose & Crown, White Hart

(2m) *Rowley Hill Lodge, Little Walden Road, Saffron Walden, Essex, CB10 1UZ.*
Actual grid ref: TL542407
C19th farm lodge thoughtfully enlarged. Both bedrooms with baths & power showers.
Grades: ETC 4 Diamond
Tel: **01799 525975**
Mr & Mrs Haslam.
Fax no: 01799 516622
D: £24.00 **S:** £28.00.
Open: All Year (not Xmas)
Beds: 1D 1T
Baths: 2 Pr
ॐ **P** (4) ☐ ఉ ▥ Ⓥ ⋇

Hadstock 17

National Grid Ref: TL5544

|O| ▦ Kings Head

(0.5m) *Yardleys, Orchard Pightle, Hadstock, Cambridge, CB1 6PQ.*
Grades: ETC 4 Diamond
Tel: **01223 891822** (also fax no)
Mrs Ludgate.
D: £22.00-£25.00 **S:** £25.00-£32.00.
Open: All Year (not Xmas/New Year)
Beds: 2T 1D **Baths:** 1 En 2 Pr
ॐ **P** (5) ⊬ ☐ ✕ ఉ ▥ Ⓥ
Peace and quiet in pretty village only 20 minutes Cambridge, 10 minutes Saffron Walden. Warm welcome and excellent breakfasts in comfortable home with guest lounge, garden and conservatory. Convenient for M11, Duxford, Newmarket, Stansted and Harwich. E.M by arrangement or good local restaurants.

Linton 18

National Grid Ref: TL5646

🍴 🍺 Crown, Dog & Duck

(0.5m) *Cantilena, 4 Harefield Rise, Linton, Cambridge, CB1 6LS.*
Spacious bungalow, quiet cul-de-sac, edge of historic village.
Cambridge, 9 miles.
Tel: **01223 892988** (also fax no)
Mr & Mrs Clarkson.
D: £18.00-£20.00 **S:** £18.00-£25.00.
Open: All Year
Beds: 1F 1D 1T
Baths: 1 Sh
🛇 🅿 (3) 🔄 🖵 🔥 🛍 &. Ⓥ ∦

(0.5m) *Linton Heights,
36 Wheatsheaf Way, Linton,
Cambridge, Cambs, CB1 6XB.*
Actual grid ref: TL573475
Comfortable, friendly home,
sharing lounge, convenient
Duxford, Cambridge, Newmarket,
Saffron Walden, Bury.
Tel: **01223 892516**
Mr & Mrs Peake.
D: £17.00-£20.00 **S:** £17.00-£20.00.
Open: All Year (not Xmas)
Beds: 1T 1S **Baths:** 1 Sh
🛇 (6) 🅿 (2) 🔄 🖵 🔥 🛍 Ⓥ 🛆 ∦

Balsham 19

National Grid Ref: TL5849

(0.5m �)) *The Garden End,
10 West Wratting Road, Balsham,
Cambridge, CB1 6DX.*
Actual grid ref: TL587506
Self-contained ground floor suite -
children / pets welcome all year.
Tel: **01223 894021** (also fax no)
Mrs Greenaway.
D: £18.00-£18.00 **S:** £20.00.
Open: All Year
Beds: 1F
Baths: 1 En 1 Pr
🛇 🅿 (2) 🔄 🖵 🔥 🗙 🛍 🔥 🛆 ∦ 🛆

West Wratting 20

National Grid Ref: TL5951

🍴 🍺 The Chesnut

(0.5m) *The Old Bakery, West
Wratting, Cambridge, CB1 5LU.*
Period cottage situated in quiet vil-
lage with nice garden.
Tel: **01223 290492**
Mr & Mrs Denny.
Fax no: 01223 290845
-£22.50 -£22.50.
Open: All Year
Beds: 2T 3D **Baths:** 1 En 1 Pr
🛇 🅿 (2) 🖵 🔥 🛍 Ⓥ 🛆

Pay B&Bs by cash or
cheque and be prepared
to pay up front.

Westley Waterless 21

National Grid Ref: TL6256

🍴 🍺 Kings Head

(0.75m) *Westley House, Westley
Waterless, Newmarket, Suffolk,
CB8 0RQ.*
C18th Georgian country home in
quiet rural area 5 miles from
Newmarket.
Tel: **01638 508112**
Mrs Galpin.
Fax no: 01638 508113
D: £22.50-£24.00 **S:** £24.00-£25.00.
Open: All Year
Beds: 2T 2S
Baths: 2 Sh
🛇 (4) 🅿 (6) 🖵 🔥 🗙 🛍 🛆 ∦

Dullingham 22

National Grid Ref: TL6257

(0.5m) *The Old School,
Dullingham, Newmarket, Suffolk,
CB8 9XF.*
Attractive conversion, spacious
rooms, delightful village, nearby
pub serves food.
Tel: **01638 507813**
Mrs Andrews.
Fax no: 01638 507022
D: £23.00-£25.00 .
Open: All Year
Beds: 1D
Baths: 1 En
🛇 🅿 (2) 🔄 🔥 🛍 Ⓥ ∦

Kirtling 23

National Grid Ref: TL6858

🍴 🍺 Rain Deer

(2.75m 🚍) *Hill Farm Guest
House, Kirtling, Newmarket,
Suffolk, CB8 9HQ.*
Grades: ETC 3 Diamond,
AA 3 Diamond
Tel: **01638 730253** (also fax no)
Mrs Benley.
D: £25.00-£50.00 **S:** £25.00-£25.00.
Open: All Year
Beds: 1D 1T 1S
Baths: 2 En 1 Pr
🅿 (5) 🔄 🔥 🗙 🛍 Ⓥ 🛆 ∦
Delightful farm house in rural
setting.

Culford 24

National Grid Ref: TL8369

🍴 🍺 Woolpack, Linden Tree

(2m) *47 Benyon Gardens, Culford,
Bury St Edmunds, Suffolk, IP28 6EA.*
A modern bungalow overlooking
fields and quietly situated.
Tel: **01284 728763**
Mrs Townsend.
D: £16.00-£32.00 **S:** £18.00-£18.00.
Open: All Year (not Xmas/
New Year)
🅿 (4) 🔄 🖵 🛍.

Barnham 25

National Grid Ref: TL8779

🍴 🍺 Grafton Arms, Dolphin

(2m 🚍) *East Farm, Barnham,
Thetford, Norfolk, IP24 2PB.*
Come & stay in large welcoming
farmhouse and enjoy the farm
countryside.
Grades: ETC 4 Diamond
Tel: **01842 890231** Mrs Heading.
D: £20.00-£22.50 **S:** £23.00-£25.00.
Open: All Year (not Xmas)
Beds: 1D 1T
Baths: 2 En
🛇 🅿 (6) 🔄 🔥 🛍 Ⓥ 🛆 ∦

Thetford 26

National Grid Ref: TL8783

🍴 🍺 Black Horse, Anchor Hotel

(4m) *43 Magdalen Street,
Thetford, Thetford, Norfolk,
IP24 2BP.*
House built in 1575 close to town
centre.
Tel: **01842 764564** Mrs Findlay.
D: £36.00-£36.00 **S:** £18.00-£18.00.
Open: All Year (not Xmas/
New Year)
Beds: 2T 1S
Baths: 1 Sh
🛇 🅿 (1) 🔄 🔥 🛍 Ⓥ 🛆 ∦

Garboldisham 27

National Grid Ref: TM0081

🍴 🍺 The Fox, White Horse

(3.5m 🚍) *Ingleneuk Lodge,
Hopton Road, Garboldisham, Diss,
Norfolk, IP22 2RQ.*
Actual grid ref: TM002801
Pretty rural location with all rooms
overlooking partly wooded
grounds.
Tel: **01953 681541**
Mr & Mrs Stone.
Fax no: 01953 681638
D: £27.50-£27.50 **S:** £33.00-£33.00.
Open: All Year
Beds: 3D 3T 1S 1F
Baths: 8 En
🛇 🅿 (15) 🖵 🔥 🛍 🔥 &. Ⓥ 🛆

Hopton 28

National Grid Ref: TL9978

🍴 🍺 The Fox

(3m 🚍) *Holly Bank, High Street,
Hopton, Diss, IP22 2QX.*
Converted 1960s public house,
guests' lounge, comfortable bed-
rooms. Sauna available at extra
cost.
Tel: **01953 688147** (also fax no)
Mr & Mrs Tomlinson.
D: £17.50-£17.50 **S:** £20.00-£20.00.
Open: All Year
Beds: 2D 1T
Baths: 1 Sh
🛇 🅿 (8) 🔄 🔥 🛍 Ⓥ 🛆 ∦

Macmillan Way

The **Macmillan Way** is a recently developed trail running 235 miles south west through English limestone country from Oakham in Rutland, England's recently re-established smallest county, to the coast just south of Abbotsbury in Dorset. Together with the **Wolds Way** and the **Viking Way**, which it meets at Oakham, the path follows the whole course of the oolitic limestone belt: you will encounter throughout villages and towns built in the same distinctive honey-coloured stone, for which the Cotswold section of the way is most renowned. From Oakham wend your way through the gentle hills of southern Rutland and cross the Welland into Northamptonshire, where the path passes close to several stately homes, including Cottesbrooke Hall, Holdenby House and Canons Ashby. The Warwickshire section climbs the limestone scarp of Edge Hill, site of the first major confrontation of the English Civil War; in Gloucestershire you'll reach Stow-on-the-Wold, where the last was fought (stop for refreshment at the Royalist Hotel, the oldest inn in England). The long trek through the beautiful Cotswolds leads through Wiltshire to Castle Combe, widely regarded as one of the most picturesque villages in England. Up the Frome Valley and through Somerset you arrive at Sherborne in Dorset, important since the days of the old Saxon kingdom of Wessex. The final stage takes you through Hardy country to Abbotsbury and beyond the village St Catherine's Chapel: from here it's a swift descent to the sea. The path is named after Douglas Macmillan, who was born and grew up in Castle Cary, Somerset, a small town on the route, and connected with the **Macmillan Cancer Relief** fund, which he founded. The **Macmillan Way Association**, which administers the trail, runs a sponsorship scheme which awards certificates and badges to walkers of the whole or part of the way: proceeds from this and sales of their guide book go to the fund. As well as the **Viking Way**, at Oakham the path also links up with the **Hereward Way**; in Gloucestershire at Lower Slaughter you cross the path of the **Heart of England Way** (which connects to the start of the **Cotswold Way** at Chipping Campden) and you are about a mile from Bourton-on-the-Water, start of the **Oxfordshire Way**, and at Tarlton about a mile and a half from Thames Head, source of the **Thames** and its **Path**; Maiden Newton in Dorset sees a crossover with the **Wessex Ridgeway** path and at Abbotsbury you can join the **South West Coast Path**.

Guide: *The Macmillan Way* by Peter Titchmarsh (ISBN 0 952685 10 8), published by the Macmillan Way Association and available from them (see below), price £6.50 (inc p&p)

Maps: 1:50000 Ordnance Survey Landranger Series: 141, 151, 152, 162, 163, 173, 183, 194

To make any comments on the path and for further information, contact the **Macmillan Way Association** at St Mary's Barn, Pillerton Priors, Warwick CV35 0PG, tel. 01789 740852

All rates are subject to alteration at the owners' discretion.

D = Price range per person sharing in a double room

Oakham 1

National Grid Ref: SK8508

|●| ◁ Admiral Hornblower, Nicks, White Lion, Odd House, Whippen Inn

(On path) *Angel House,*
20 Northgate, Oakham,
Rutland, LE15 6QS.
Unique Victorian house. Converted outbuildings. Secluded courtyard. Lounge, patio, fridge/freezer, microwave.
Tel: **01572 756153** Mrs Weight.
D: £11.00-£17.00 **S:** £22.00-£34.00.
Open: All Year
Beds: 1D 2T **Baths:** 3 En
🛏 🄿 🖵 ≒ Ⅴ 🖥 ∥

Brooke 2

National Grid Ref: SK8505

|●| ◁ Plough and Blue Ball

(On path) *The Old Rectory,*
Brooke, Oakham, Rutland, LE15 8DE.
Stone thatch cottage in quiet hamlet. Large garden, good walking area.
Tel: **01572 770558** (also fax no)
Mrs Clemence.
D: £20.00-£25.00 **S:** £20.00-£25.00.
Open: All Year
Beds: 1F 1T 1S
Baths: 3 En
🛏 🄿 (6) ⊱ ≒ ≒ ▥ Ⅴ 🖥 ∥

S = Price range for a single person in a single room

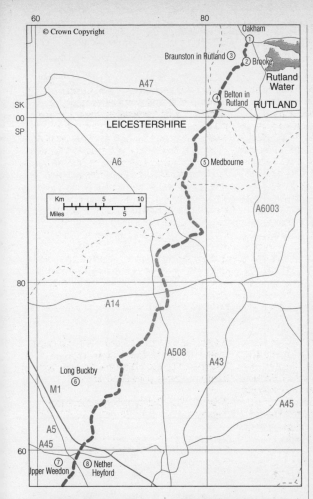

© Crown Copyright

60 · 80 · Oakham ①

Braunston in Rutland ③ ② Brooke

Rutland Water

A47

Belton in ④ Rutland · RUTLAND

SK 00

SP

LEICESTERSHIRE

A6 · ⑤ Medbourne

Km 5 10 / Miles 5

A6003

80

A14

A508 · A43

Long Buckby ⑥

M1 · A45

A5 · A45

60

⑦ Upper Weedon · ⑧ Nether Heyford

(1m) **College Farm,** *College Farm Road, Belton in Rutland, Oakham, Rutland, LE15 9AF.*
Set in idyllic Rutland countryside.
Ramblers and bird watchers paradise. 1 mile A47.
Tel: **01572 717440**
Mrs Brown.
D: £20.00-£20.00 **S:** £20.00-£20.00.
Open: All Year
Beds: 1T
Baths: 1 Pr

Medbourne 5

National Grid Ref: SP7993

Nevill Arms

(3m) **Medbourne Grange,** *Nevill Holt, Medbourne, Market Harborough, Leics, LE16 8EF.*
Actual grid ref: SP816946
Comfortable farmhouse with breathtaking views; quiet location & heated pool.
Tel: **01858 565249**
Mrs Beaty.
Fax no: 01858 565257
D: £19.00-£22.00 **S:** £19.00-£25.00.
Open: All Year (not Xmas)
Beds: 2D 1T
Baths: 1 Sh 2 En

Long Buckby 6

National Grid Ref: SP6267

Stag's Head

(4m) **Murcott Mill,** *Murcott, Long Buckby, Northampton, NN6 7QR.*
Beautifully situated Georgian Mill house, ideal for Althorp House & stopovers.
Tel: **01327 842236**
Mrs Hart.
Fax no: 01327 844524
D: £20.00-£21.00
S: £20.00-£25.00.
Open: All Year
Beds: 1F 1D 2T
Baths: 3 En

Upper Weedon 7

National Grid Ref: SP6258

Globe Hotel, Cross Roads Hotel

(1m) **Mullions,** *9 Oak Street, Upper Weedon, Northampton, NN7 4RQ.*
Actual grid ref: SP625589
C17th stone cottage, quiet location.
Fields view from back garden.
Grades: ETC 4 Diamond
Tel: **01327 341439** (also fax no)
Mrs Piercey.
D: £19.00-£19.00 **S:** £19.00-£19.00.
Open: All Year (not Xmas)
Beds: 1D
Baths: 1 Pr

Braunston in Rutland 3

National Grid Ref: SK8306

Old Plough

(1m) **Rutland Cottages,** *5 Cedar Street, Braunston in Rutland, Oakham, Rutland, LE15 8QS.*
B&B with a difference! Guests have freedom of a cottage.
Tel: **01572 722049**
John & Connie Beadman.
Fax no: 01572 770928
D: £20.00-£25.00 **S:** £25.00-£30.00.
Open: All Year
Beds: 2D 2S **Baths:** 2 Pr

Bringing children with you? Always ask for any special rates.

Belton in Rutland 4

National Grid Ref: SK8101

Bewicke Arms, Fox Inn, Vaults, Sun Inn, Blue Ball, Noel's Arms, Salisbury Arms, Cuckoo

(On path) **The Old Rectory,** *4 New Road, Belton in Rutland, Oakham, Rutland, LE15 9LE.*
Actual grid ref: SK814010
Grades: RAC 3 Diamond
Tel: **01572 717279** Mr Peach.
Fax no: 01572 717343
D: £16.00-£23.00 **S:** £16.00-£30.00.
Open: All Year
Beds: 2F 2D 3T 1S
Baths: 5 En 1 Sh
Large country house & guest annexe in conservation village overlooking Eyebrook valley & rolling Rutland countryside. Comfortable/ varied selection of rooms, mostly ensuite, direct outside access. Real farmhouse or continental breakfast. Public house 100 yds. 10 minutes Rutland Water.

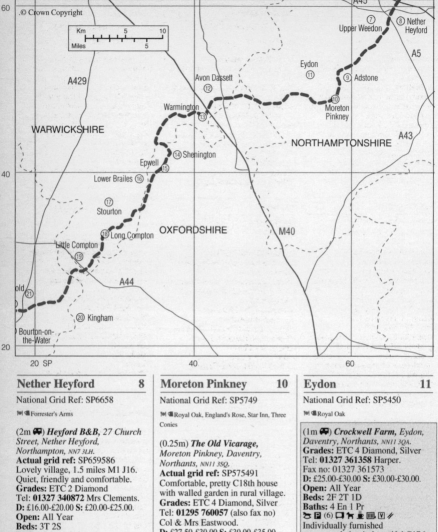

60

WARWICKSHIRE

A429

A45

⑦ Upper Weedon

⑧ Nether Heyford

A5

Eydon
⑪

⑨ Adstone

⑩
Moreton
Pinkney

Avon Dassett
⑫

Warmington
⑬

NORTHAMPTONSHIRE

A43

⑭ Shenington

Epwell
⑮

40

Lower Brailes ⑯

OXFORDSHIRE

M40

⑰
Stourton

⑱ Long Compton

Little Compton
⑲

A44

...old
㉑

⑳ Kingham

Bourton-on-
the-Water

20

20 SP   40   60

Nether Heyford   8

National Grid Ref: SP6658

⚫ Forrester's Arms

(2m) **Heyford B&B,** *27 Church Street, Nether Heyford, Northampton, NN7 3LH.*
Actual grid ref: SP659586
Lovely village, 1.5 miles M1 J16. Quiet, friendly and comfortable.
Grades: ETC 2 Diamond
Tel: **01327 340872** Mrs Clements.
D: £16.00-£20.00 **S:** £20.00-£25.00.
Open: All Year
Beds: 3T 2S
Baths: 2 En 1 Sh
🛇 🅿 (8) 🖵 🛏 🎜 💷 Ⅵ 🛈 ✠

Adstone   9

National Grid Ref: SP5951

⚫ Royal Oak

(0.5m) **Manor Farm,** *Adstone, Towcester, Northants, NN12 8DT.*
Actual grid ref: SP595512
C17th stone farmhouse, tiny quiet village; ideal location for relaxation or exploring.
Tel: **01327 860284** Mrs Paton.
Fax no: 01327 860685
D: £20.00-£25.00 **S:** £20.00-£25.00.
Open: All Year
Beds: 1F 1D 1S **Baths:** 2 En 1 Pr
🛇 🅿 ✂ 🖵 🛏 🎜 💷 Ⅵ 🛈 ✠

Moreton Pinkney   10

National Grid Ref: SP5749

⚫ Royal Oak, England's Rose, Star Inn, Three Conies

(0.25m) **The Old Vicarage,** *Moreton Pinkney, Daventry, Northants, NN11 3SQ.*
Actual grid ref: SP575491
Comfortable, pretty C18th house with walled garden in rural village.
Grades: ETC 4 Diamond, Silver
Tel: **01295 760057** (also fax no)
Col & Mrs Eastwood.
D: £27.50-£30.00 **S:** £30.00-£35.00.
Open: All Year (not Xmas)
Beds: 1D 1T
Baths: 1 En 1 Pr
🛇 (7) 🅿 (3) ✂ 🖵 🛏 🎜 🗙 🎜 💷 🛈 ✠

(0.25m) **England's Rose,** *Upper Green, Moreton Pinkney, Daventry, Northants, NN11 3SG.*
C17th coaching inn. Open fires, a la carte restaurant, four poster bedroom.
Grades: ETC 3 Diamond,
AA 3 Diamond
Tel: **01295 760353** (also fax no)
D: £25.00-£50.00 **S:** £25.00-£50.00.
Open: All Year
Beds: 2F 3T 4D 1S
Baths: 10 En
🛇 🅿 ✂ 🖵 🛏 🗙 🎜 💷 ♿ Ⅵ 🛈

Eydon   11

National Grid Ref: SP5450

⚫ Royal Oak

(1m) **Crockwell Farm,** *Eydon, Daventry, Northants, NN11 3QA.*
Grades: ETC 4 Diamond, Silver
Tel: **01327 361358** Harper.
Fax no: 01327 361573
D: £25.00-£30.00 **S:** £30.00-£30.00.
Open: All Year
Beds: 2F 2T 1D
Baths: 4 En 1 Pr
🛇 🅿 (6) 🖵 🛏 🎜 💷 Ⅵ ✠
Individually furnished accommodation in beautiful C17th barns. All bedrooms have south facing views over open countryside. Accommodation benefits from excellent kitchen and sitting room facilities. Fantastic food served at our own village pub. Events catered for in vaulted hall.

Pay B&Bs by
cash or cheque and
be prepared to
pay up front.

Avon Dassett 12

National Grid Ref: SP4150

IOI ⊄ Butchers' Arms, The Avon

(1m ♠) *Crandon House, Avon Dassett, Leamington Spa, Warks, CV33 0AA.*
Actual grid ref: SP418506
Luxury farmhouse accommodation, quiet location, superb views, extensive breakfast menu.
Grades: ETC 5 Diamond, Silver
Tel: 01295 770652 Miss Lea.
Fax no: 01295 770632
D: £20.00-£25.00 **S:** £30.00.
Open: All Year (not Xmas)
Beds: 3D 2T **Baths:** 4 En 1 Pr
� (8) P (8) ⌷ ⍾ ⍾ ⍾ ⍾ V ⍾ ⍾

Warmington 13

National Grid Ref: SP4147

IOI ⊄ The Plough

(On path) *The Old Rectory, Warmington, Banbury, Oxfordshire, OX17 1BU.*
Tel: 01295 690531 Mrs Cockcroft.
Fax no: 01295 690526
D: £25.00-£30.00 **S:** £35.00.
Open: All Year (not Xmas)
Beds: 2T 1D **Baths:** 3 En
P (3) ⍾ ⌷ ⍾ ⍾ V
Beautiful C18th house with lovely garden on the green in idyllic peaceful village. Ideal for visiting Stratford-upon-Avon, Oxford, Warwick Castle, Blenheim Palace, the Cotswolds, Upton House and many gardens open to the public, among them Brook Cottage.

(On path ♠) *Pond Cottage, The Green, Warmington, Banbury, Oxon, OX17 1BU.*
Picturesque Grade II Listed cottage, overlooking duckpond. 6 miles from M40 (J11/12).
Tel: 01295 690682 Mrs Viljoen.
D: £20.00-£20.00 **S:** £21.00-£30.00.
Open: Feb to Nov
Beds: 1D 1S **Baths:** 1 Sh
P (2) ⍾ ⌷ ⍾ ⍾ V ⍾

(On path) *The Glebe House, Warmington, Banbury, Oxon, OX17 1BT.*
Farmhouse style offering a warm welcome, comfort and peace.
Tel: 01295 690642 (also fax no)
Mrs Thornton.
D: £20.00-£24.00 **S:** £20.00-£24.00.
Open: Easter to Nov
Beds: 2D 1T **Baths:** 2 En 1 Pr
ఠ (5) P (6) ⍾ ⌷ ⍾ ⍾ ⍾ V ⍾

All paths are popular:
you are well-advised to
book ahead

Shenington 14

National Grid Ref: SP3742

IOI ⊄ The Bell Inn

(1m) *Top Farm House, Shenington, Banbury, Oxfordshire, OX15 6LZ.*
C18th Horton stone farmhouse set on the edge of village green.
Grades: ETC 3 Diamond
Tel: 01295 670226
Fax no: 01295 678170
D: £20.00-£25.00 **S:** £25.00-£30.00.
Open: All Year (not Xmas/New Year)
Beds: 1T 2D
Baths: 1 Ensuite 1 Shared
ఠ P (4) ⍾ ⌷ ⍾ ⍾ V ⍾

Epwell 15

National Grid Ref: SP3441

IOI ⊄ The Bell

(1m ♠) *Yarnhill Farm, Shenington Road, Epwell, Banbury, Oxon, OX15 6JA.*
Peaceful farmhouse; ideally situated for Cotswolds, Stratford upon Avon, Oxford.
Grades: ETC 3 Diamond
Tel: 01295 780250
D: £18.00-£25.00 **S:** £18.00-£25.00.
Open: All Year (not Xmas)
Beds: 1D 1T 1S
Baths: 1 Pr 1 Sh
ఠ (8) P (6) ⍾ ⌷ ⍾ ⍾ V ⍾

Lower Brailes 16

National Grid Ref: SP3139

IOI ⊄ George Hotel, Gate Inn, Peacock

(2m) *The George Hotel, High Street, Lower Brailes, Banbury, Oxon, OX15 5NU.*
Tel: 01608 685223
Fax no: 01608 685916
D: £25.00-£60.00 **S:** £25.00-£60.00.
Open: All Year
Beds: 1F 8T 1D 1S
Baths: 1 En 9 Pr 1 Sh
ఠ (1) P (80) ⍾ ⌷ ⍾ ⍾ ⍾ ⍾ V ⍾ ⍾ ⍾
A C12th inn, good, friendly public bar, large gardens with 'undercover' outside eating area. On Cotswolds near Stratford-upon-Avon (14 miles). Well-kept local, off-road foot ways. Good centre to visit entire Cotswold area.

(3m) *New House Farm, Lower Brailes, Banbury, Oxon, OX15 5BD.*
New House farm is set between two villages in outstanding area of beauty.
Grades: AA 4 Diamond
Tel: 01608 686239
Ms Taylor.
Fax no: 01608 686455
D: £18.00-£20.00 **S:** £20.00-£25.00.
Open: All Year (not Xmas)
Beds: 2D 1T **Baths:** 2 En 1 Pr
ఠ P (10) ⌷ ⍾ ⍾ ⍾ ⍾ V ⍾ ⍾

Stourton 17

National Grid Ref: SP2937

IOI ⊄ Cherrington Arms

(2m) *Brook House, Stourton, Shipston-on-Stour, Warwickshire, CV36 5HQ.*
Lovely old house, edge pretty Cotswold village. Ideal touring Stratford, Oxford, Cotswolds.
Tel: 01608 686281 Mrs McDonald.
D: £22.00-£23.00 **S:** £27.00-£30.00.
Open: All Year (not Xmas/New Year)
Beds: 1F 1D
Baths: 1 En 1 Pr
ఠ (7) P (4) ⌷ ⍾ ⍾ ⍾ V ⍾

Long Compton 18

National Grid Ref: SP2832

IOI ⊄ Red Lion

(1m) *Tallet Barn, Yerdley Farm, Long Compton, Shipston-on-Stour, Warks, CV36 5LH.*
Comfortable annexed rooms, a warm welcome and a quiet village location.
Grades: ETC 4 Diamond
Tel: 01608 684248
Mrs Richardson.
Fax no: 01068 684248
D: £20.00-£21.00 **S:** £25.00-£25.00.
Open: All Year
Beds: 1D 1T
Baths: 2 En
ఠ (6) P (2) ⍾ ⌷ ⍾ ⍾ V ⍾

Little Compton 19

National Grid Ref: SP2630

(1m ♠) *Rigside, Little Compton, Moreton-in-Marsh, Glos, GL56 0RR.*
Lovely landscaped gardens backing onto farmland.
Grades: AA 4 Diamond
Tel: 01608 674128 (also fax no)
Ms Cox.
D: £22.00-£23.00 **S:** £20.00-£22.00.
Open: All Year
Beds: 2D 1S 1T
Baths: 2 En 1 Sh
ఠ (9) P (6) ⌷ ⍾ ⍾ ⍾ V ⍾ ⍾

Kingham 20

National Grid Ref: SP2524

IOI ⊄ Kings Head

(2m ♠) *The Old Stores, Foscot, Kingham, Chipping Norton, Oxon, OX7 6RH.*
Actual grid ref: SP2522
Charming Cotswold stone cottage in lovely rural location, 1.5 miles from Kingham.
Tel: 01608 659844 (also fax no)
D: £18.00-£20.00 **S:** £22.00-£23.00.
Open: Mar to Nov
Beds: 1D
Baths: 1 Pr
P (2) ⍾ ⌷ ⍾ ⍾ ⍾ V ⍾

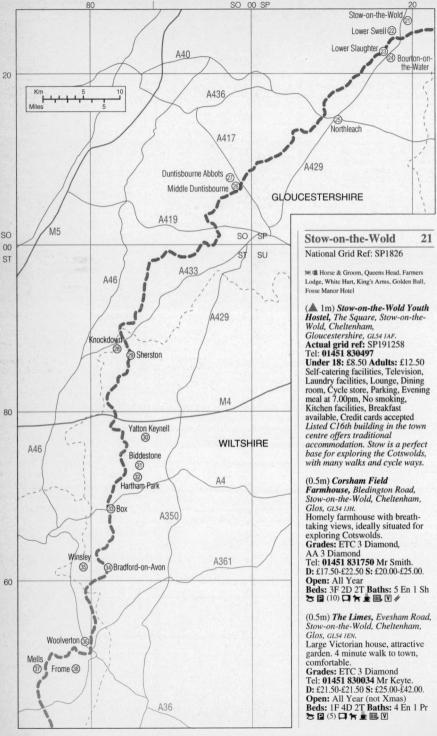

Stow-on-the-Wold ㉑
Lower Swell ㉒
Lower Slaughter ㉓
㉔ Bourton-the-Water

A40

A436

A417

㉕ Northleach

A429

Duntisbourne Abbots ㉗
Middle Duntisbourne ㉖

GLOUCESTERSHIRE

A419

SO SP
ST SU

M5

A46

A433

A429

M4

Knockdown ㉘
㉙ Sherston

Yatton Keynell ㉚

WILTSHIRE

A46

Biddestone ㉛
Hartham Park ㉜

㉝ Box

A4

A350

Winsley ㉟
㉞ Bradford-on-Avon

A361

Woolverton ㊱

Mells ㊲ ㊳ Frome

A36

Stow-on-the-Wold   21

National Grid Ref: SP1826

🍴 🍺 Horse & Groom, Queens Head, Farmers Lodge, White Hart, King's Arms, Golden Ball, Fosse Manor Hotel

(▲ 1m) *Stow-on-the-Wold Youth Hostel, The Square, Stow-on-the-Wold, Cheltenham, Gloucestershire, GL54 1AF.*
Actual grid ref: SP191258
Tel: **01451 830497**
Under 18: £8.50 **Adults:** £12.50
Self-catering facilities, Television, Laundry facilities, Lounge, Dining room, Cycle store, Parking, Evening meal at 7.00pm, No smoking, Kitchen facilities, Breakfast available, Credit cards accepted *Listed C16th building in the town centre offers traditional accommodation. Stow is a perfect base for exploring the Cotswolds, with many walks and cycle ways.*

(0.5m) *Corsham Field Farmhouse, Bledington Road, Stow-on-the-Wold, Cheltenham, Glos, GL54 1JH.*
Homely farmhouse with breath-taking views, ideally situated for exploring Cotswolds.
Grades: ETC 3 Diamond, AA 3 Diamond
Tel: **01451 831750** Mr Smith.
D: £17.50-£22.50 **S:** £20.00-£25.00.
Open: All Year
Beds: 3F 2D 2T **Baths:** 5 En 1 Sh
🛏 🅿 (10) 🛌 🍴 ♨ 🏠 Ⓥ ✐

(0.5m) *The Limes, Evesham Road, Stow-on-the-Wold, Cheltenham, Glos, GL54 1EN.*
Large Victorian house, attractive garden. 4 minute walk to town, comfortable.
Grades: ETC 3 Diamond
Tel: **01451 830034** Mr Keyte.
D: £21.50-£21.50 **S:** £25.00-£42.00.
Open: All Year (not Xmas)
Beds: 1F 4D 2T **Baths:** 4 En 1 Pr
🛏 🅿 (5) 🛌 🍴 ♨ 🏠 Ⓥ

(0.5m 🚌) *Fifield Cottage, Fosse Lane, Stow-on-the-Wold, Cheltenham, Glos, GL54 1EH.*
Cottage: private road, peaceful situation. Close to town. Attractive garden.
Tel: **01451 831056** Mrs Keyte.
D: £19.00-£22.00 **S:** £23.00.
Open: All Year (not Xmas)
Beds: 1F 1D 1T **Baths:** 2 En 1 Pr
🛏 🅿 (4) 🗀 🛉 🖾 🎢 ⅏ 🗓 ✦

(0.5m) *South Hill Farmhouse, Fosseway, Stow-on-the-Wold, Cheltenham, Glos, GL54 1JU.*
Listed Cotswold farmhouse. On-site parking, ideal for walkers.
Grades: ETC 3 Diamond
Tel: **01451 831888**
Mr & Mrs Cassie.
Fax no: 01451 832255
D: £24.00 **S:** £35.00.
Open: All Year
Beds: 1F 2D 2T 1S
Baths: 1 Pr 5 En
🛏 🅿 (10) ⅏ 🗀 ⅏ 🎢 ⅏ 🗓 🛆

(0.5m 🚌) *The Gate Lodge, Stow Hill, Stow-on-the-Wold, Cheltenham, Glos, GL54 1JZ.*
Grade 2 Listed building; formerly gate lodge to Netherswell Manor.
Grades: ETC 4 Diamond
Tel: **01451 832103**
Mr & Mrs Feasey.
D: £18.00-£20.00 **S:** £20.00-£25.00.
Open: All Year (not Xmas)
Beds: 2D **Baths:** 2 En
🛏 🅿 (4) ⅏ 🗀 ⅏ 🎢 ⅏ 🗓 ✦

(0.5m) *Pear Tree Cottage, High Street, Stow-on-the-Wold, Cheltenham, Glos, GL54 1DL.*
Period cottage with very relaxed atmosphere, convenient to town square.
Grades: ETC 3 Diamond
Tel: **01451 831210** Mr Henderson.
D: £20.00-£25.00 **S:** £30.00-£35.00.
Open: All Year
Beds: 2D
Baths: 2 En
🛏 (1) 🅿 (2) 🗀 🎢 ⅏ 🎢 ⅏ 🗓 ✦

(0.5m) *Old Farmhouse Hotel, Lower Swell, Stow-on-the-Wold, Cheltenham, Glos, GL54 1LF.*
C16th converted manor farm in quiet hamlet, 1 mile west of Stow.
Tel: **Freephone 0800 0561150**
Mr Burger.
Fax no: 01451 870962
D: £20.00-£57.50 **S:** £30.00-£67.50.
Open: All Year
Beds: 3F 6D 3T
Baths: 10 En 2 Sh
🛏 🅿 (25) 🗀 🎢 ⅏ 🎢 ⅏ 🗓 🛆 ✦

Please take muddy boots off before entering premises

Lower Swell 22

National Grid Ref: SP1725

🍴 🍺 Golden Ball

(1m) *Golden Ball Inn, Lower Swell, Stow-on-the-Wold, Glos, GL54 1LF.*
Actual grid ref: SP175254
Delightful C17th village inn, genuine home-cooked food, friendly atmosphere, pets welcome.
Grades: ETC 2 Diamond
Tel: **01451 830247** Knowles.
D: £22.50-£27.50 **S:** £30.00-£35.00.
Open: All Year
Beds: 3D 1T
Baths: 4 En
🛏 🅿 (15) 🗀 🎢 ✕ ⅏ 🎢 ⅏ 🗓 ✦

Lower Slaughter 23

National Grid Ref: SP1623

🍴 🍺 Coach & Horses, Plough Inn

(1m 🚌) *Seymour House Farm, Fosseway, Lower Slaughter, Bourton-on-the-Water, Cheltenham, Glos, GL54 2HW.*
Traditional Cotswold house on working small holding. Excellent touring centre.
Tel: **01451 820132** (also fax no)
Mr & Mrs Hedges.
D: £17.50-£20.00 .
Open: All Year
Beds: 1F 1D
🛏 🅿 (6) ⅏ 🗀 🎢 ⅏ 🎢 ⅏ 🗓 ✦

(0.75m) *Lakeside, Fosseway, Lower Slaughter, Cheltenham, Glos, GL54 2EY.*
Actual grid ref: SP175227
Comfortable home on edge of unspoilt village. One mile north of Bourton-on-the-Water on A429.
Tel: **01451 821206** Mrs Goss.
D: £16.00-£20.00 **S:** £20.00-£20.00.
Open: All Year (not Xmas)
Beds: 1F 1D
Baths: 1 En 1 Pr
🛏 (4) 🅿 (5) ⅏ 🗀 ⅏ 🎢 ⅏ 🗓 🛆 ✦

Bourton-on-the-Water 24

National Grid Ref: SP1620

🍴 🍺 Plough, Kingsbridge Inn, Mouse Trap Inn, Coach & Horses, Duke of Wellington

(1m) *Lansdowne House, Lansdowne, Bourton-on-the-Water, Cheltenham, Glos, GL54 2AT.*
Actual grid ref: SP164210
Tastefully furnished ensuite accommodation. Combination of old and antique furniture.
Grades: ETC 4 Diamond
Tel: **01451 820812**
Mrs Garwood.
Fax no: 01451 822484
D: £17.50-£20.00 **S:** £30.00-£35.00.
Open: All Year (not Xmas)
Beds: 1F 2D
Baths: 3 En
🛏 🅿 (4) 🗀 🎢 ⅏ 🗓 ✦

(1m) *6 Moore Road, Bourton-on-the-Water, Cheltenham, Glos, GL54 2AZ.*
Cotswold stone house, quiet road, yards to village, peaceful garden.
Tel: **01451 820767** Mrs Mustoe.
D: £19.00-£21.00 **S:** £20.00-£25.00.
Open: Feb to Dec
Beds: 1D 1T
Baths: 1 En 1 Pr
🛏 (5) 🅿 (3) ⅏ 🗀 🎢 ⅏ 🎢 ⅏ 🗓 ✦

(1m 🚌) *Holly House, Station Road, Bourton-on-the-Water, Cheltenham, Glos, GL54 2ER.*
Actual grid ref: SP168212
Spacious Cotswold style house. Breakfast in conservatory overlooking delightful gardens.
Grades: ETC 4 Diamond
Tel: **01451 821302** Mr Stanfield.
D: £20.00-£25.00 **S:** £28.00-£32.00.
Open: Feb to Oct
Beds: 2D 1T 1S
Baths: 4 En
🛏 🅿 (6) ⅏ 🗀 ✕ ⅏ 🎢 ⅏ 🗓 🛆 ✦

(1m 🚌) *Lansdowne Villa Guest House, Bourton-on-the-Water, Cheltenham, Glos, GL54 2AR.*
This large, detached Cotswold stone house stands at the end of this beautiful village.
Tel: **01451 820673**
Mr & Mrs Harris.
Fax no: 01451 822099
D: £24.00 **S:** £32.00.
Open: Feb to Dec
Beds: 8D 2T 2S
Baths: 12 En
🛏 🅿 (14) ⅏ 🗀 ✕ ⅏ 🎢 ⅏ 🗓 🛆 ✦

Northleach 25

National Grid Ref: SP1114

🍴 🍺 Plough Inn

(1m) *Market House, The Square, Northleach, Cheltenham, Glos, GL54 3EJ.*
400-year-old house in the heart of the Cotswolds.
Tel: **01451 860557** Mr Eastman.
D: £19.00 **S:** £22.00.
Open: Mar to Oct
Beds: 1D 1T 2S **Baths:** 1 Pr 1 Sh
🛏 (12) ⅏ 🗀 ⅏ 🎢 ⅏ 🗓 🛆

Middle Duntisbourne 26

National Grid Ref: SO9806

🍴 🍺 Five Mile, The Bell

(1m) *Manor Farm, Middle Duntisbourne, Cirencester, Glos, GL7 7AR.*
Farmhouse set in beautiful Duntisbourne.
Grades: ETC 3 Diamond
Tel: **01285 658145** Mrs Barton.
Fax no: 01285 641504
D: £20.00-£25.00 **S:** £40.00-£45.00.
Open: All Year (not Xmas/New Year)
Beds: 1D 1T **Baths:** 1 En 1 Pr
🛏 🅿 (8) ⅏ 🗀 🎢 ⅏ 🎢 ⅏ 🗓

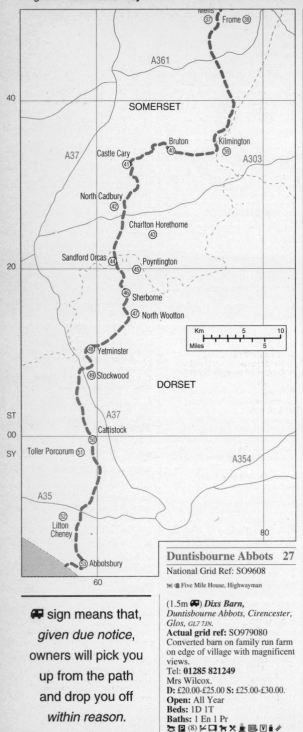

🚐 sign means that, *given due notice,* **owners will pick you up from the path and drop you off** *within reason.*

Knockdown 28

National Grid Ref: ST8388

⊯ ⊈ Holford Arms

(0.25m 🚐) *Avenue Farm,*
Knockdown, Tetbury, Glos, GL8 8QY.
300-year-old farmhouse in farm
adjoining Westonbirt Arboretum.
Bath, Bristol & Gloucester within
easy reach.
Grades: ETC 3 Diamond
Tel: 01454 238207 Mrs King.
Fax no: 01454 238033
D: £20.00-£25.00 **S:** £25.00-£25.00.
Open: All Year
Beds: 1F 1D 2T
Baths: 2 En 1 Sh
🖙 🅿 (6) ⊬ 🖵 🍽 🎄 🛒 Ⓥ 🛡 ⊀

Sherston 29

National Grid Ref: ST8586

⊯ ⊈ Rattlebone Inn, Carpenters Arms

(0.5m 🚐) *Widleys Farm, Sherston,*
Malmesbury, Wilts, SN16 0PY.
200-year-old farmhouse. Peaceful
and quiet. Log fires in season.
Working farm.
Grades: ETC 3 Diamond
Tel: 01666 840213 Mrs Hibbard.
Fax no: 01666 840156
D: £20.00-£25.00 **S:** £20.00-£25.00.
Open: All Year (not Xmas)
Beds: 1F 1D 1T
Baths: 1 En 1 Sh
🖙 🅿 (6) 🖵 🎄 🛒 Ⓥ 🛡 ⊀

Yatton Keynell 30

National Grid Ref: ST8676

⊯ ⊈ Bell Inn, Salutation Inn

(2m) *Oakfield Farm, Easton*
Piercy Lane, Yatton Keynell,
Chippenham, Wilts, SN14 6JU.
Cotswold stone farmhouse in open
countryside. Ideal for Cotswolds,
Bath, Stonehenge.
Tel: 01249 782355 Mrs Read.
Fax no: 01249 783458
D: £20.00-£22.50 **S:** £25.00-£30.00.
Open: Mar to Oct
Beds: 2D 1T
Baths: 1 En 1 Sh
🖙 🅿 (8) ⊬ 🖵 🎄 🛒 Ⓥ ⊀

Duntisbourne Abbots 27

National Grid Ref: SO9608

⊯ ⊈ Five Mile House, Highwayman

(1.5m 🚐) *Dixs Barn,*
Duntisbourne Abbots, Cirencester,
Glos, GL7 7JN.
Actual grid ref: SO979080
Converted barn on family run farm
on edge of village with magnificent
views.
Tel: 01285 821249
Mrs Wilcox.
D: £20.00-£25.00 **S:** £25.00-£30.00.
Open: All Year
Beds: 1D 1T
Baths: 1 En 1 Pr
🖙 🅿 (8) ⊬ 🖵 🐾 ✕ 🎄 🛒 Ⓥ 🛡 ⊀

Biddestone 31

National Grid Ref: ST8673

⊯ ⊈ White Horse

(1.5m 🚐) *Home Place,*
Biddestone, Chippenham,
Wiltshire, SN14 7DG.
End of farmhouse, on Village
Green. Opposite Duck Pond.
Grades: ETC 2 Diamond
Tel: 01249 712928 Ms Hall.
D: £15.00-£17.50 **S:** £15.00-£17.50.
Open: All Year
Beds: 1F 1T 1S
Baths: 1 Sh
🖙 🅿 (2) ⊬ 🖵 🎄 🛒 Ⓥ 🛡

(1.5m) *Home Farm*, Biddestone, Chippenham, Wilts, SN14 7DQ.
Listed C17th farmhouse working farm, picturesque village. Stroll to pubs.
Tel: **01249 714475**
Mr & Mrs Smith.
Fax no: 01249 701488
D: £20.00-£22.50 **S:** £25.00-£30.00.
Open: All Year (not Xmas)
Beds: 2F 1D **Baths:** 2 En 1 Pr
🛏 🅿 (4) ⅍ 🗆 👗 🛍 Ⅴ ⬤ ✦

Hartham Park 32

National Grid Ref: ST8672

(1m) *Church Farm*, Hartham Park, Corsham, Wiltshire, SN13 0PU.
Actual grid ref: ST861715
Cotswold farmhouse in rural location, stunning views, quiet and peaceful.
Grades: ETC 4 Diamond,
AA 4 Diamond
Tel: **01249 715180** Mrs Jones.
Fax no: 01249 715572
D: £20.00-£25.00 **S:** £20.00-£22.00.
Open: All Year (not Xmas/
New Year)
Beds: 1F 1D 1S **Baths:** 2 En 1 Pr
🛏 (1) 🅿 (6) ⅍ 🗆 👗 🛍 Ⅴ ⬤ ✦

Box 33

National Grid Ref: ST8268

🍽 🍺 Swan

(0.5m) *Owl House*, Lower Kingsdown Road, Kingsdown, Box, Corsham, Wilts, SN13 8BB.
Actual grid ref: ST812672
Situated 4 miles from Bath, offering spectacular views over the Avon Valley.
Grades: AA 5 Diamond
Tel: **01225 743883** Venus.
Fax no: 01225 744450
D: £25.00-£32.50 **S:** £25.00-£35.00.
Open: All Year
Beds: 1F 1D 1T 1S
Baths: 3 En 1 Pr
🛏 (8) 🅿 (4) ⅍ 🗆 👗 🛍 Ⅴ

Bradford-on-Avon 34

National Grid Ref: ST8261

🍽 🍺 Barge, Bear, Beehive, Cross Guns, Hop Pole, King's Arms, New Inn, Plough, Seven Stars, Three Horseshoes

(0.25m) *Chard's Barn*, Leigh Grove, Bradford-on-Avon, Wilts, BA15 2RF.
Tel: **01225 863461**
Mr & Mrs Stickney.
D: £20.00-£23.00 **S:** £20.00-£20.00.
Open: All Year (not Xmas)
Beds: 1D 1T 1S **Baths:** 2 En 1 Pr
🛏 🅿 (4) ⅍ 🗆 🏇 👗 🛍 🔥 Ⅴ
Quiet C17th barn in unspoilt countryside with lovely gardens, view and walks. All ground floor, individually styled bedrooms, choice of breakfasts. Historic town and golf course, one mile. Close - Bath, Castle Combe, Longleat. Easy for Salisbury Plain and Stonehenge.

(0.25m 🚲) *The Locks*, 265 Trowbridge Road, Bradford-on-Avon, Wilts, BA15 1UA.
Adjoining canal tow path. Ideal walking/cycling 7/8 mile town centre.
Tel: **01225 863358** Mrs Benjamin.
D: £17.50-£20.00 **S:** £20.00-£30.00.
Open: All Year
Beds: 1F 2T
Baths: 1 En 1 Pr 1 Sh
🛏 (3) 🅿 (6) ⅍ 🗆 👗 🛍 Ⅴ ⬤ ✦

(0.25m) *Great Ashley Farm*, Ashley Lane, Bradford-on-Avon, Wilts, BA15 2PP.
Actual grid ref: ST813619
Delightful rooms. Great hospitality. Delicious breakfast. Colour brochure. Sliver award.
Grades: ETC 4 Diamond
Tel: **01225 864563** (also fax no)
Mrs Rawlings.
D: £20.00-£24.00 **S:** £25.00-£45.00.
Open: All Year (not Xmas)
Beds: 1F 2D
Baths: 3 En
🛏 🅿 ⅍ 🗆 👗 🛍 Ⅴ ✦

(0.25m) *Springfields*, 182a Great Ashley, Bradford on Avon, Wilts, BA15 2PP.
Unique ground-level ensuite double room with adjoining dining-room/lounge. Peaceful countryside setting.
Grades: ETC 3 Diamond
Tel: **01225 866125** Ms Rawlings.
D: £20.00-£22.50 **S:** £30.00-£35.00.
Open: All Year
Beds: 1D
Baths: 1En
⅍ 🗆 ✗ 👗 Ⅴ

(0.25m) *Avonvilla*, Avoncliff, Bradford-on-Avon, Wilts, BA15 2HD.
Superb canal and riverside setting. Free parking and fishing. Excellent walking.
Tel: **01225 863867**
Mrs Mumford.
D: £17.00-£17.00
 S: £20.00-£20.00.
Open: All Year
Beds: 1D 1T 1S
🛏 (5) 🅿 ⅍ 👗 🛍 Ⅴ

Winsley 35

National Grid Ref: ST7961

🍽 🍺 Seven Stars

(1m 🚲) *Conifers*, 4 King Alfred Way, Winsley, Bradford-on-Avon, Wilts, BA15 2NG.
Quiet area, pleasant outlook, friendly atmosphere, convenient Bath, lovely walks.
Grades: ETC 2 Diamond
Tel: **01225 722482**
Mrs Kettley.
D: £17.00-£18.00
 S: £18.00-£20.00.
Open: All Year
Beds: 1T 1D
Baths: 1 Sh
🛏 🅿 ⅍ 🗆 👗 🛍 Ⅴ ✦

(0.5m) *3 Corners*, Cottles Lane, Winsley, Bradford-on-Avon, Wilts, BA15 2HJ.
House in quiet village edge location, attractive rooms and gardens.
Tel: **01225 865380** Mrs Cole.
D: £22.50-£25.00 **S:** £26.00-£30.00.
Open: All Year (not Xmas)
Beds: 1F 1D **Baths:** 1 En 1 Pr
🛏 🅿 (4) ⅍ 🗆 👗 🛍 Ⅴ ✦

(1m 🚲) *Serendipity*, 19 Bradford Road, Winsley, Bradford-on-Avon, Wilts, BA15 2HW.
Bungalow with beautiful gardens, badgers feeding nightly, ground floor room available.
Grades: ETC 4 Diamond
Tel: **01225 722380** Mrs Shepherd.
Fax no: 01225 723451
D: £21.00-£22.50 **S:** £30.00-£40.00.
Open: All Year
Beds: 1F 1D 1S **Baths:** 3 En
🛏 🅿 (5) ⅍ 🗆 👗 🛍 🔥 Ⅴ ⬤ ✦

Woolverton 36

National Grid Ref: ST7854

🍽 🍺 Red Lion

(1m) *The Old School House*, Woolverton, Bath, Somerset, BA3 6RH.
Homely accommodation. Converted Victorian school, 10 minutes south of Bath.
Tel: **01373 830200** (also fax no)
Thornton.
D: £20.00-£25.00 **S:** £25.00-£30.00.
Open: All Year (not Xmas/New Year)
Beds: 1F 1T 2D **Baths:** Sh
🛏 🅿 ⅍ 👗 🛍 Ⅴ

Mells 37

National Grid Ref: ST7249

🍽 🍺 Talbot Inn

(0.5m) *Wadbury House*, Mells, Frome, Somerset, BA11 3PA.
An historic country house with galleried hall, surrounded by gardens and parkland.
Grades: ETC 3 Diamond
Tel: **01373 812359** Mrs Brinkmann
D: £25.00-£36.00 **S:** £28.00-£40.00.
Open: All Year
Beds: 1F 2T 1D **Baths:** 3 En 1 Pr
🛏 🅿 (10) 🗆 🏇 ✗ 👗 🛍 Ⅴ ⬤ ✦

Frome 38

National Grid Ref: ST7747

🍽 🍺 Royal Oak, Sun, Masons' Arms, Talbot

(2m) *Kensington Lodge Hotel*, The Butts, Frome, Somerset, BA11 4AA.
Comfortable hotel fitness and leisure facilities near Bath, Longleat, Cheddar Caves.
Grades: AA 2 Diamond
Tel: **01373 463935** Mr Aryan.
Fax no: 01373 303570
D: £25.00-£25.00 **S:** £30.00-£40.00.
Open: All Year
Beds: 1F 2D 3T 1S **Baths:** 6 En
🛏 🅿 (40) 🗆 👗 🛍 Ⅴ

(2m 🚐) *Higher West Barn Farm,*
Witham Friary, Frome, BA11 5HH.
Attractive barn conversion, friendly
atmosphere, excellent home cook-
ing, countryside location.
Grades: ETC 4 Diamond, Silver
Tel: **01749 850819** Mrs Harrison.
D: £25.00-£27.50 **S:** £30.00-£35.00.
Open: All Year
Beds: 2D 1T
Baths: 1 En 2 Pr
🅿 (6) ⅏ ◻ ✕ 🖢 ⅲ ⅙ Ⓥ 🛉

Kilmington 39

National Grid Ref: ST7736

⊫ ◨ Spread Eagle

(1m 🚐) *The Red Lion Inn,*
On B3092 (Mere to Frome road),
Kilmington, Warminster, Wilts,
BA12 6RP.
Actual grid ref: ST786354
Unspoilt 15th century traditional
inn. Stourhead 1 mile. Comfortable
beds, good breakfasts.
Tel: **01985 844263** Mr Gibbs.
D: £17.50-£17.50 **S:** £25.00-£25.00.
Open: All Year (not Xmas/
New Year)
Beds: 1D 1T **Baths:** 1 Sh
🐾 (4) 🅿 (25) ⅏ ⅓ 🖢 ⅲ Ⓥ ⅙

Bruton 40

National Grid Ref: ST6834

⊫ ◨ Royal Oak

(On path 🚐) *The Old Forge,* 89
High Street, Bruton, Somerset, BA10
0AL.
High-quality accommodation in
Saxon town. Surrounded by beauti-
ful countryside.
Tel: **01749 812585** (also fax no)
Mr Dunn.
D: £17.50-£20.00 **S:** £20.00-£25.00.
Open: All Year (not Xmas)
Beds: 1D 1T
Baths: 1 En 1 Sh
🐾 🅿 (2) ⅏ ◻ 🖢 ⅲ Ⓥ ⅙

Castle Cary 41

National Grid Ref: ST6332

⊫ ◨ George Hotel, Pilgrims Rest

(1m) *Orchard Farm, Castle Cary,*
Somerset, BA7 7NY.
Comfortable farmhouse in large
gardens and quiet countryside.
Grades: ETC 3 Diamond
Tel: **01963 350418** (also fax no)
Mr & Mrs Boyer.
D: £18.00-£24.00 **S:** £18.00-£24.00.
Open: All Year
Beds: 1F 1D **Baths:** 2 Pr
🐾 🅿 (4) ◻ ⅓ ✕ 🖢 ⅲ Ⓥ

D = Price range per person

sharing in a double room

North Cadbury 42

National Grid Ref: ST6327

(On path 🚐) *Ashlea House,* High
Street, North Cadbury, Yeovil,
Somerset, *BA22 7DP.*
1 km A303, centre village, highly
commended service, accommoda-
tion, home cooking.
Grades: ETC 4 Diamond
Tel: **01963 440891**
Mr & Mrs Wade.
D: £22.00-£25.00
S: £25.00-£27.00.
Open: All Year (not Xmas/
New Year)
Beds: 1T 1D
Baths: 1 En 1 Pr
🅿 (2) ⅏ ◻ ✕ 🖢 ⅲ Ⓥ 🛉 ⅙

Charlton Horethorne 43

National Grid Ref: ST6623

⊫ ◨ Mitre Inn, Britannia Inn, Kings Arms, Old
Inn, Half Moon, Queens Arms

(3m 🚐) *Ashclose Farm, Charlton*
Horethorne, Sherborne, Dorset,
DT9 4PG.
Comfortable farmhouse, peaceful
countryside, friendly welcome and
relaxed atmosphere.
Grades: ETC 3 Diamond
Tel: **01963 220360**
Mr & Mrs Gooding.
D: £18.00-£22.00
S: £18.00-£22.00.
Open: All Year (not Xmas)
Beds: 1D 1T 1S
Baths: 1 En 1 Sh
🐾 🅿 (5) ◻ ⅓ 🖢 ⅲ Ⓥ ⅙

(3m 🚐) *Beech Farm, Sigwells,*
Charlton Horethorne, Sherborne,
Dorset, DT9 4LN.
Comfortable, spacious farmhouse
with relaxed atmosphere on dairy
farm with horses.
Tel: **01963 220524** Mrs Stretton.
D: £16.00-£16.00 **S:** £16.00-£16.00.
Open: All Year (not Xmas)
Beds: 1F 1D 1T
Baths: 1 En 1 Sh
🐾 🅿 (6) ◻ ⅓ ✕ 🖢 ⅲ Ⓥ 🛉 ⅙

Sandford Orcas 44

National Grid Ref: ST6220

⊫ ◨ Mitre Inn

(On path) *The Alders, Sandford*
Orcas, Sherborne, Dorset, DT9 4SB.
Actual grid ref: ST622209
Situated in unspoilt picturesque
conservation village; sitting room
with log fire in inglenook fireplace.
Tel: **01963 220666**
Fax no: 01963 220106
D: £22.50-£25.00
S: £35.00-£38.00.
Open: All Year
Beds: 1D 1T
Baths: 2 Pr
🐾 🅿 (4) ⅏ ◻ 🖢 ⅲ Ⓥ ⅙

Poyntington 45

National Grid Ref: ST6420

⊫ ◨ Crown Inn

(1m) *Welgoer, Poyntington,*
Sherborne, Dorset, DT9 4LF.
Comfortable accommodation in
quiet village near Sherborne. Ideal
touring base.
Grades: ETC 3 Diamond
Tel: **01963 220737** Mrs Neville.
D: £20.00-£25.00 **S:** £20.00-£25.00.
Open: All Year
Beds: 1T 1D
Baths: 1 En 1 Pr
🐾 (5) 🅿 (2) ⅏ ◻ 🖢 ⅲ Ⓥ

Sherborne 46

National Grid Ref: ST6316

⊫ ◨ Queen's Arms, Mitre Inn, Crown Hotel,
Half Moon, Britannia Inn, Kings Arms, Old Inn

(0.25m) *Britannia Inn, Sherborne,*
Dorset, DT9 3EH.
Listed building, town centre, 300
years old.
Grades: ETC 2 Diamond
Tel: **01935 813300** Mr Blackmore.
D: £20.00-£35.00 **S:** £20.00-£35.00.
Open: All Year
Beds: 2F 1D 2T 2S
Baths: 1 En 3 Sh
🐾 🅿 (6) ⅏ ◻ ⅓ ✕ 🖢 ⅲ Ⓥ 🛉 ⅙

(0.25m) *Bridleways, Oborne Road,*
Sherborne, Dorset, DT9 3RX.
Grades: ETC 3 Diamond
Tel: **01935 814716** (also fax no)
Mr & Mrs Dimond.
D: £18.00-£22.00 **S:** £20.00-£22.00.
Open: All Year (not Xmas)
Beds: 1D 2T **Baths:** 1 En 1 Pr
🐾 🅿 (5) ◻ ⅓ 🖢 ⅲ Ⓥ ⅙
Comfortable house overlooking
castle, 10 mins walk to historic
town centre, station, with plenty of
eating places, off road parking for
5 cars. Holiday cottages and horse
riding available on premises.
Situated 1/4 mile off A30.

(0.25m 🚐) *Clatcombe Grange,*
Bristol Road, Sherborne, Dorset,
DT9 4RH.
Charming Listed converted barn.
elevated views, spacious house/gar-
den, ample parking, peaceful and
friendly.
Grades: AA 4 Diamond
Tel: **01935 814355**
D: £25.00-£25.00 **S:** £30.00-£36.00.
Open: All Year
Beds: 1T 1D 1S **Baths:** 2 En 1 Pr
🐾 🅿 ⅏ ◻ ✕ 🖢 ⅲ Ⓥ 🛉 ⅙

Bringing children with

you? Always ask for

any special rates.

North Wootton 47

National Grid Ref: ST6514

|●| ⊌ Three Elms

(1m) *Stoneleigh Barn, North Wootton, Sherborne, Dorset, DT9 5JW.*
Beautiful stone barn close to Sherborne. A special place.
Grades: ETC 4 Diamond, Silver
Tel: 01935 815964 Mrs Chant.
D: £23.00-£25.00 **S:** £30.00-£37.50.
Open: All Year (not Xmas/New Year)
Beds: 1F 1D **Baths:** 1 En 1 Pr
ঠ (6) �**P** (4) ⌇⍁ ⊟ ⚲ ▥, Ⅴ

Yetminster 48

National Grid Ref: ST5910

(On path 🚌) *Manor Farm House, High Street, Yetminster, Sherborne, Dorset, DT9 6LF.*
Tel: 01935 872247 (also fax no)
Mr & Mrs Partridge.
D: £30.00-£35.00 -£35.00.
Open: All Year (not Xmas)
Beds: 2T 1D 1S
Baths: 4 En
P (20) ⌇⍁ ⊟ ✕ ⚲ ▥, Ⅴ ⓐ ⌁
Interesting manor farmhouse rebuilt in C17th, with many architectural features.

Stockwood 49

National Grid Ref: ST5806

|●| ⊌ Chetnole Inn

(1m) *Church Farm, Stockwood, Dorchester, Dorset, DT2 0NG.*
Actual grid ref: ST590069
Spoil yourself and stay on a traditional working dairy farm.
Tel: 01935 83221 Mrs House.
Fax no: 01935 83771
D: £20.00-£25.00 **S:** £20.00-£35.00.
Open: All Year
Beds: 2D 1T
Baths: 3 En
ঠ **P** (3) ⌇⍁ ⊟ ⚲ ▥, Ⅴ ⌁

Cattistock 50

National Grid Ref: SY5999

(0.5m 🚌) *Sandhills Cottage, Sandhills, Cattistock, Dorchester, DT2 0HQ.*
Grades: ETC 4 Diamond
Tel: 01300 321146
Mr & Mrs Roca.
Fax no: 01300 321 146
D: £22.00-£24.00 **S:** £25.00-£28.00.
Open: All Year
Beds: 2T 1D
Baths: 3 En
ঠ (12) **P** (8) ⌇⍁ ⊟ ⚲ ▥, Ⅴ ⓐ ⌁
Sandhills cottage lies in a rural hamlet within ten minutes walk the village of Cattistock has a shop/P.O., pub and a beautiful church. Sandhills offers superb scenery and good walking, some of Dorset's finest beaches are within easy driving distance.

Toller Porcorum 51

National Grid Ref: SY5698

|●| ⊌ Marquis of Lorne, Three Horseshoes, The Spyway, Askers Well

(2m) *Colesmoor Farm, Toller Porcorum, Dorchester, Dorset, DT2 0DU.*
Actual grid ref: SY556971
Small family farm in quiet setting with excellent views.
Grades: ETC 4 Diamond
Tel: 01300 320812 Mrs Geddes.
Fax no: 01300 321402
D: £20.00-£20.00 **S:** £25.00-£25.00.
Open: May to Feb
Beds: 1D 1T **Baths:** 2 En
ঠ **P** (4) ⌇⍁ ⊟ ⚲ ▥, & Ⅴ ⌁

Please take muddy

boots <u>off</u> before

entering premises

(2m) *The Kingcombe Centre, Toller Porcorum, Dorchester, Dorset, DT2 0EQ.*
Actual grid ref: SY554991
Study centre beside the River Hooke surrounded by nature reserve.
Grades: ETC 2 Diamond
Tel: 01300 320684 Mr Spring.
Fax no: 01300 021409
D: £15.00-£20.00 **S:** £15.00-£20.00.
Open: All Year
Beds: 3F 3T 2D 3S
Baths: 11 Sh
ঠ **P** (20) ⌇⍁ ⊟ ⊨ ✕ ⚲ ▥, & Ⅴ ⓐ ⌁

Litton Cheney 52

National Grid Ref: SY5590

(▲ 2m) *Litton Cheney Youth Hostel, Litton Cheney, Dorchester, Dorset, DT2 9AT.*
Actual grid ref: SY548900
Tel: 01308 482340
Under 18: £6.90 **Adults:** £10.00
Self-catering facilities, Showers, Lounge, Drying room, Cycle store, Parking Limited, No smoking, Kitchen facilities, Credit cards accepted
Traditional Dutch barn in the Bride Valley, once a cheese factory. This is an Area of Outstanding Natural Beauty.

Abbotsbury 53

National Grid Ref: SY5785

|●| ⊌ Kings Arms, Swan Inn

(0.25m) *Swan Lodge, Abbotsbury, Weymouth, Dorset, DT3 4JL.*
Comfortable modern rooms with tea and coffee facilities and colour TVs.
Grades: ETC 3 Diamond
Tel: 01305 871249 (also fax no)
Mr Roper.
D: £22.00-£28.00 **S:** £30.00-£45.00.
Open: All Year
Beds: 3D
Baths: 3 En
ঠ **P** ⊟ ⊨ ✕ ⚲ ▥, Ⅴ ⓐ ⌁

North Downs Way

For 141 miles you walk through the woodland and downland of Surrey and Kent, along the northern chalk escarpment up to the Medway and then right down to Dover. Much of the route coincides with the old **Pilgrim's Way** from Winchester and there is a loop link that will take you via the historic cathedral city of Canterbury, should you so wish. For a path that cuts right through the South East commuter belt, only a few hedges away from the motorway, it's remarkably rural and peaceful, a glorious breath of fresh air. In fact, the proximity of the roads and railway makes this a great one for Londoners seeking a trail they can do at weekends - every stretch of the walk has a railway line bisecting it or running alongside it. The terrain is easy, the main gradients occurring as you come onto the escarpment itself and off again. Parts of the walk can be muddy in winter, while on some stretches in summer the nettles are tall, the brambles thick and the hedgerows overgrown: so dress accordingly.

Guides: *A Guide to the Pilgrims Way & North Downs Way* by C J Wright (ISBN 0 094722 30 7), published by Constable & Co Ltd and available from all good map shops, £10.95

North Downs Way by Neil Curtis (ISBN 1 85410 187 0), published by Aurum Press in association with the Countryside Commission and Ordnance Survey and available from all major bookshops, £10.99.

Maps: 1:50000 Ordnance Survey Landranger Series: 177, 178, 179, 186, 187, 188, 189

Comments on the path to: North Downs Way Project Officer, c/o Planning Dept, Kent County Council, Springfield, Maidstone, Kent ME14 2LX

Farnham 1

National Grid Ref: SU8446

⬤ ◀ Bat & Ball, The Cricketers, Hare & Hound, Cherry Tree, Prince Of Wales, The Anchor, Spotted Cow, Hen & Chicken, Jolly Farmer, Wellington's

(0.25m) *Heath Lodge,*
91a Shortheath Road, Farnham,
Surrey, GU9 8SF.
Period house, quiet situation, Surrey/Hants border & Waterloo Station close by.
Tel: **01252 722918** Mrs Jones.
D: £22.50 **S:** £28.00.
Open: All Year
Beds: 2T
Baths: 1 Sh
☕ 🅿 (4) ⌁ 🗆 ✕ 🏊 🛏 Ⅵ 🅰 ✦

(2m) *Orchard House,*
13 Applelands Close, Farnham,
Surrey, GU10 4TL.
Actual grid ref: SU835438
Visitors warmly welcomed at our quietly located home overlooking countryside.
Tel: **01252 793813** Mrs Warburton.
D: £18.00-£20.00 **S:** £18.00-£20.00.
Open: All Year (not Xmas)
Beds: 1T 1S
Baths: 1 Sh
☕ 🅿 (3) ⌁ 🗆 🏊 🛏 Ⅵ

D = Price range per person sharing in a double room

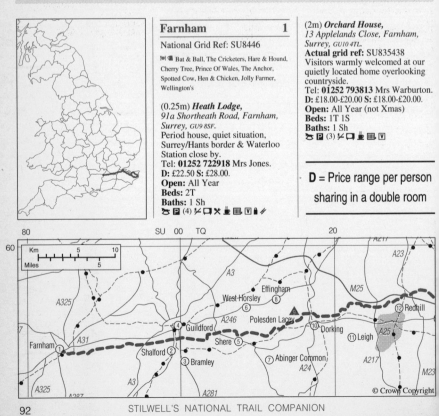
© Crown Copyright

(1.5m) *Hawkridge, 20 Upper Old Park Lane, Farnham, Surrey,*
GU9 0AT.
Actual grid ref: SU831485
Large house with lovely gardens in
beautiful countryside.
Tel: **01252 722068**
Mr & Mrs Ackland.
D: £20.00-£25.00 **S:** £20.00-£25.00.
Open: All Year
Beds: 1D 1T 1S **Baths:** 1 Sh
🛏 (10) 🅿 (6) ⊬ ❑ ✕ 🌺 Ⅷ, Ⅵ 🛉

Shalford 2

National Grid Ref: TQ0046

🍴 🍺 Sea Horse Pub

(1m) *The Laurels, 23 Dagden Road, Shalford, Guildford, Surrey,*
GU4 8DD.
Quiet detached house. Direct
access to footpaths. Near Guildford
centre.
Tel: **01483 565753** Mrs Deeks.
D: £20.00-£23.00 **S:** £22.00-£22.00.
Open: All Year **Beds:** 1T 1D
🛏 (6) 🅿 (5) ⊬ ❑ ★ 🌺 Ⅷ, Ⅵ 🛉 ∥

Bramley 3

National Grid Ref: TQ0044

🍴 🍺 Jolly Farmer, Grantley Arms

(1.5m) *Beevers Farm, Chinthurst Lane, Bramley, Guildford, Surrey,*
GU5 0DR.
Peaceful surroundings, friendly
atmosphere, own preserves, honey,
eggs, nearby villages.
Grades: ETC 3 Diamond
Tel: **01483 898764** (also fax no)
Mr Cook.
D: £18.00-£25.00 **S:** £30.00.
Open: Easter to Nov
Beds: 1F 2T **Baths:** 1 Pr 1 Sh
🛏 🅿 (10) ⊬ ❑ 🌺 Ⅷ, Ⅵ 🛉 ∥

S = Price range for a single
person in a single room

Guildford 4

National Grid Ref: SU9949

🍴 🍺 King's Head, Jolly Farmer, Hare & Hounds,
The Fox, White House, George Abbot, Grantley
Arms

(1m) *Weybrook House, 113 Stoke Road, Guildford, Surrey, GU1 1ET.*
Actual grid ref: SU998504
Quiet family B&B. A320 Near
town centre/stations. Delicious
breakfast.
Tel: **01483 302394**
Mr & Mrs Bourne.
D: £20.00-£22.00 **S:** £28.00-£28.00.
Open: All Year (not Xmas)
Beds: 1F 1D 1S **Baths:** 2 Sh
🛏 ❑ ★ 🌺 Ⅷ, Ⅵ 🛉 ∥

(1m) *Atkinsons Guest House, 129 Stoke Road, Guildford, Surrey, GU1 1ET.*
Small comfortable family-run guest
house close to town centre & all
local amenities.
Tel: **01483 538260** Mrs Atkinson.
D: £20.00-£22.50 **S:** £28.00-£45.00.
Open: All Year
Beds: 1D 1T 2S **Baths:** 2 En 1 Sh
🛏 (6) 🅿 (2) ❑ 🌺 Ⅷ, Ⅵ ∥

(1m 🚗) *Westbury Cottage, Waterden Road, Guildford, Surrey, GU1 2AN.*
Cottage-style house in large seclud-
ed garden, 5 mins town centre,
2 mins station.
Tel: **01483 822602** (also fax no)
Mrs Smythe.
D: £25.00-£25.00 **S:** £30.00-£30.00.
Open: All Year (not Xmas)
Beds: 1D 2T **Baths:** 1 Sh
🛏 (6) 🅿 (3) ⊬ ❑ 🌺 Ⅷ, Ⅵ ∥

(1m) *25 The Chase, Guildford, Surrey, GU2 5UA.*
10 minutes to town and station.
Easy access to A3.
Tel: **01483 569782** Mrs Ellis.
S: £16.00-£16.00.
Open: All Year (not Xmas/
New Year)
Beds: 2S
⊬ ❑ Ⅷ,

(1m) *2 Wodeland Avenue, Guildford, GU2 4JX.*
Centrally located rooms with
panorama. Friendly and mod-
ernised family home.
Tel: **01483 451142** Mrs Hay.
Fax no: 01483 572980
D: £20.00-£22.00 **S:** £20.00-£25.00.
Open: All Year (not Xmas)
Beds: 1D 1T
Baths: 1 Pr 1 Sh
🛏 (3) 🅿 (3) ⊬ ❑ 🌺 Ⅷ, 🅰 Ⅵ ∥

(1m 🚗) *Quietways, 29 Liddington Hall Drive, Guildford, Surrey, GU3 3AE.*
Off A323, quiet cottage, end of
cul-de-sac. Lounge, conservatory,
pleasant garden.
Tel: **01483 232347** Mr White.
D: £19.00 **S:** £25.00.
Open: Jan to Nov
Beds: 1D 1T
Baths: 1 En 1 Pr
🅿 (2) ⊬ ❑ 🌺 Ⅷ, 🅰 Ⅵ ∥

(1m 🚗) *Field Villa, Liddington New Road, Guildford, Surrey, GU3 3AH.*
Small private B&B in a quiet
private road. Friendly welcome
awaits.
Tel: **01483 233961** Mrs Townsend.
Fax no: 01483 234045
D: £19.00-£20.00 **S:** £19.00-£20.00.
Open: All Year (not Xmas)
Beds: 1D 1T 2S
Baths: 1 Pr 1 Sh
🛏 🅿 (5) ⊬ ❑ ✕ 🌺 Ⅷ, Ⅵ

Shere 5

National Grid Ref: TQ0747

🍴 🍺 White Horse, Prince of Wales

(0.5m) *Manor Cottage, Shere, Guildford, Surrey, GU5 9JE.*
C16th cottage with old world gar-
den, in centre of beautiful village.
Tel: **01483 202979** Mrs James.
D: £20.00-£20.00 **S:** £20.00-£20.00.
Open: May to Sep
Beds: 1D 1S
Baths: 1 Sh
🛏 (5) 🅿 ⊬ 🌺 Ⅵ ∥

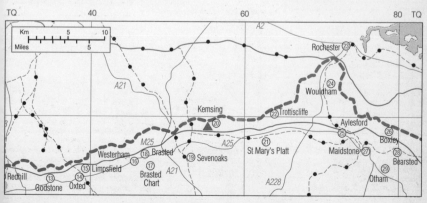

(0.75m) *Cherry Trees*, Gomshall, Shere, Guildford, Surrey, GU5 9HE.
Actual grid ref: TQ072487
Quiet comfortable house, lovely garden, village foot of North Downs.
Tel: **01483 202288** Mrs Warren.
D: £25.00 **S:** £25.00-£30.00.
Open: All Year (not Xmas/New Year)
Beds: 2D 3F 1S **Baths:** 2 En 1 Sh
ॐ 🅿 (4) ⊬ ⌂ 🔟 🖥 🕹 🛇 🔧

West Horsley   6

National Grid Ref: TQ0752

⚓ ⊿ King William IV

(3m 🚅) *Brinford*, Off Shere Road, West Horsley, Leatherhead, KT24 6EJ.
Comfortable modern house in peaceful rural location with panoramic views.
Tel: **01483 283636** Mrs Wiltshire.
D: £20.00-£25.00 **S:** £25.00.
Open: All Year
Beds: 1D 1T 1S
Baths: 1 En 1 Sh
🅿 (4) ⊬ ⌂ 🖥 🔟 🛇

Abinger Common   7

National Grid Ref: TQ1145

⚓ ⊿ Plough Inn

(2m) *Park House Farm*, Leith Hill Road, Abinger Common, Dorking, Surrey, RH5 6LW.
Tel: **01306 730101**
Mr & Mrs Wallis.
Fax no: 01306 730643
D: £20.00-£30.00 **S:** £30.00-£50.00.
Open: All Year (not Xmas/New Year)
Beds: 1T 2D
Baths: 3 En
ॐ (12) 🅿 (10) ⊬ ⌂ 🖥 🔟 🛇
Set in 25 acres in an Area of Outstanding Natural Beauty, you are welcome to join us in a large spacious home which provides bright, tastefully decorated rooms, all with excellent views. Easy access to Gatwick and Heathrow.

Effingham   8

National Grid Ref: TQ1153

⚓ ⊿ Douglas Haig

(3m 🚅) *Chalklands*, Beech Avenue, Effingham, Surrey, KT24 5PJ.
Actual grid ref: TQ117523
Large detached house overlooking golf course. Good pub food nearby.
Grades: ETC 3 Diamond
Tel: **01372 454936** Mrs Reilly.
Fax no: 01372 459569
D: £22.00-£23.00 **S:** £30.00-£35.00.
Open: All Year (not Xmas)
Beds: 1F 1D 1T
Baths: 2 En 1 Pr
ॐ 🅿 (8) ⊬ ⌂ 🕹 ✗ 🖥 🔟 🛇 🔧

Polesden Lacey   9

National Grid Ref: TQ1352

(▲ 0.25m) *Tanners Hatch Youth Hostel*, Polesden Lacey, Ranmore Road, Dorking, Surrey, RH5 6BE.
Actual grid ref: TQ140515
Tel: **01306 877964**
Under 18: £5.75 **Adults:** £8.50
Self-catering facilities, Showers, Lounge, Cycle store, No smoking, WC, Kitchen facilities, Credit cards accepted
A renovated black and white cottage in the Surrey Hills Area of Outstanding Natural Beauty. Facilities are basic, and taking a torch is recommended. The lounge has an open fire.

Dorking   10

National Grid Ref: TQ1649

⚓ ⊿ King's Arms, Old School House, King William, The Bush, Inn on the Green

(2m) *The Waltons*, 5 Rose Hill, Dorking, Surrey, RH4 2EG.
Listed house in conservation area. Beautiful views and friendly atmosphere.
Tel: **01306 883127** (also fax no)
Mrs Walton.
D: £17.50-£20.00 **S:** £20.00-£32.50.
Open: All Year
Beds: 1F 1D 1T 1S
Baths: 3 Sh
ॐ 🅿 (3) ⊬ ⌂ 🕹 ✗ 🖥 🔟 🛇

(0.5m) *Shrub Hill*, 3 Calvert Road, Dorking, Surrey, RH4 1LT.
Actual grid ref: TQ167504
Quiet comfortable family home with excellent views.
Tel: **01306 885229** Mrs Scott Kerr.
D: £25.00-£26.00 **S:** £35.00.
Open: All Year (not Xmas)
Beds: 1T 1S 1D
Baths: 1 Sh 1 En
ॐ (8) 🅿 (2) ⊬ ⌂ 🕹 🖥 🔟 🛇 🔧

(0.5m 🚅) *Torridon Guest House*, Longfield Road, Dorking, Surrey, RH4 3DF.
Large chalet bungalow - quiet location.
Grades: ETC 3 Diamond
Tel: **01306 883724** Mrs Short.
Fax no: 01306 880759
D: £23.00-£24.00 **S:** £26.00-£28.00.
Open: All Year
Beds: 1D 1T 1S
Baths: 1 Sh
ॐ 🅿 (4) ⊬ ⌂ 🕹 ✗ 🖥 🔟 🛇 🔧

Bringing children with you? Always ask for any special rates.

Order your packed lunches the *evening before* you need them.
Not at breakfast!

Leigh   11

National Grid Ref: TQ2246

⚓ ⊿ The Plough

(3m 🚅) *Barn Cottage*, Church Road, Leigh, Reigate, Surrey, RH2 8RF.
Converted C17th barn, gardens with swimming pool, 100 yards from pub, 0.25 hr Gatwick.
Tel: **01306 611347** Mrs Comer.
D: £25.00-£30.00 **S:** £35.00-£35.00.
Open: All Year
Beds: 1D 1T
Baths: 1 Sh
ॐ 🅿 (3) ⊬ ⌂ 🕹 ✗ 🖥 🔟 🛇 🔧

Redhill   12

National Grid Ref: TQ2750

⚓ ⊿ The Sun

(0.5m) *Lynwood Guest House*, 50 London Road, Redhill, Surrey, RH1 1LN.
Actual grid ref: TQ280511
Adjacent to a lovely park, within 6 minutes walking from railway station, town centre.
Grades: AA 3 Diamond
Tel: **01737 766894** Mrs Trozado.
Fax no: 01737 778253
D: £25.00-£28.00 **S:** £32.00-£35.00.
Open: All Year
Beds: 4F 2D 1T 2S
Baths: 3 En 6 Pr 1 Sh
ॐ 🅿 (8) ⌂ 🖥 🔟 🛇 🔧

Godstone   13

National Grid Ref: TQ3551

⚓ ⊿ Coach House

(1.5m) *Godstone Hotel*, The Green, Godstone, Surrey, RH9 8DT.
Tel: **01883 742461** (also fax no)
Mr Howe.
D: £27.50 **S:** £39.00.
Open: All Year
Beds: 6D 2T
Baths: 8 Pr
ॐ 🅿 ⌂ 🕹 ✗ 🖥 🔟 🛇 🖥 🔧
C16th coaching house, original features, inglenook fireplaces. Our restaurant 'The Coach House' is renowned in the vicinity for superb cuisine at sensible prices - well worth a visit. Pre-booking is highly recommended. Our friendly staff look forward to welcoming you.

Oxted 14

National Grid Ref: TQ3852

⊯ ⊲ The Oxted, Old Bell, The Crown, The George, The Gurkha, Royal Oak

(1m) *Pinehurst Grange Guest House, East Hill (Part of A25), Oxted, Surrey, RH8 9AE.*
Actual grid ref: TQ393525
Comfortable Victorian ex-farm-house with traditional service and relaxed friendly atmosphere.
Tel: **01883 716413** Mr Rodgers.
D: £21.00-£21.00 **S:** £26.00-£28.00.
Open: All Year (not Xmas/ New Year)
Beds: 1D 1T 1S
Baths: 1 Sh
ॐ (5) ❑ (3) ⊬❑♨ Ⅲ.Ⅵ♠⊬

(1m) *Meads, 23 Granville Road, Oxted, Surrey, RH8 0BX.*
Tudor style house on Kent/Surrey border; station to London.
Grades: ETC 4 Diamond
Tel: **01883 730115** Mrs Holgate.
D: £25.00-£28.00 **S:** £28.00-£30.00.
Open: All Year
Beds: 1T 1D
Baths: 1 En 1 Pr
ॐ❑⊬❑♨Ⅲ.Ⅵ⊬

(3m) *Old Forge House, Merle Common, Oxted, Surrey, RH8 0JB.*
Actual grid ref: TQ416493
Welcoming family home in rural surroundings. Ten minutes from M25.
Tel: **01883 715969** Mrs Mills.
D: £18.00-£20.00 **S:** £18.00-£20.00.
Open: All Year (not Xmas)
Beds: 1D 1T 1S
Baths: 1 Sh
ॐ❑(4)❑♞Ⅲ.⊬

Limpsfield 15

National Grid Ref: TQ4052

⊯ ⊲ The George, The Crown, The Gurkha

(1.75m) *Arawa, 58 Granville Road, Limpsfield, Oxted, Surrey, RH8 0BZ.*
Actual grid ref: TQ402532
Friendly, comfortable, welcoming. Lovely garden, excellent breakfast, good London trains.
Grades: ETC 3 Diamond
Tel: **01883 714104** (also fax no) Gibbs.
D: £18.00-£30.00 **S:** £18.00-£30.00.
Open: All Year
Beds: 1F 2T
Baths: 1 En 1 Sh
ॐ❑(3)⊬❑♞Ⅲ.⊲Ⅵ♠⊬

Pay B&Bs by cash or cheque and be prepared to pay up front.

Westerham 16

National Grid Ref: TQ4454

⊯ ⊲ The Bull, White Hart

(1.5m) *Corner Cottage, Toys Hill, Westerham, Kent, TN16 1PY.*
Attractive self contained accommo-dation in Laura Ashley fabrics. Spectacular panoramic views.
Grades: ETC 4 Diamond, Silver
Tel: **01732 750362**
Mrs Olszowska.
Fax no: 01959 561911
D: £45.00-£50.00.
S: £30.00-£35.00.
Open: All Year
Beds: 1F
ॐ❑(1)⊬❑♨Ⅲ.Ⅵ♠⊬

Brasted Chart 17

National Grid Ref: TQ4653

⊯ ⊲ The Bull, White Hart

(2.5m) *The Orchard House, Brasted Chart, Westerham, Kent, TN16 1LR.*
Actual grid ref: TQ469537
Family home, quiet, rural surround-ings, near Chartwell, Hever, Knole, Gatwick.
Grades: ETC 3 Diamond
Tel: **01959 563702**
Mrs Godsal.
D: £21.00 **S:** £22.00.
Open: All Year (not Xmas)
Beds: 2T 1S
Baths: 2 Sh
ॐ❑(4)⊬❑Ⅲ.⊲♠⊬

Brasted 18

National Grid Ref: TQ4755

⊯ ⊲ The Bull

(1.25m) *Holmesdale House, High Street, Brasted, Westerham, Kent, TN16 1HS.*
Actual grid ref: TQ469550
Delightful Victorian house (part C17th). Chartwell, Hever, Knole and Mainline Station.
Tel: **01959 564834** (also fax no) Mr Jinks.
D: £20.00-£27.50
S: £30.00-£30.00.
Open: All Year
Beds: 1F 3D 1T
Baths: 3 En 1 Sh
ॐ❑(7)❑♨Ⅲ.⊲♠⊬

(1.25m) *Lodge House, High Street, Brasted, Westerham, Kent, TN16 1HS.*
Character property, a short walk from popular village pubs.
Tel: **01959 562195**
Mr & Mrs Marshall.
D: £20.00-£25.00
S: £25.00-£30.00.
Open: All Year
Beds: 1F 2D
Baths: 1 En 1 Sh
ॐ❑(3)⊬❑♨Ⅲ.Ⅵ

Sevenoaks 19

National Grid Ref: TQ5255

⊯ ⊲ White Hart, The Chequers, Rose & Crown, The Bull

(1.5m) *40 Robyns Way, Sevenoaks, Kent, TN13 3EB.*
Quiet location, station 10 minutes walk. French spoken, self catering available.
Tel: **01732 452401** Mrs Ingram.
D: £25.00-£28.00 **S:** £27.00-£30.00.
Open: All Year
Beds: 1F 1D 1T
Baths: 2 En 1 Sh
ॐ❑(3)⊬❑♨Ⅲ.⊲Ⅵ

(2m) *Green Tiles, 46 The Rise, Sevenoaks, Kent, TN13 1RJ.*
Quiet annexe in lovely garden, own entrance, for 1-5 guests.
Tel: **01732 451522** (also fax no)
Mrs Knoops.
D: £20.00-£22.00 **S:** £30.00.
Open: All Year
Beds: 1F
Baths: 1 En
ॐ❑(2)⊬❑♨Ⅲ.Ⅵ

(2m) *56 The Drive, Sevenoaks, Kent, TN13 3AF.*
Lovely Edwardian house and garden close to station and town. Peaceful.
Grades: ETC 3 Diamond
Tel: **01732 453236** Mrs Lloyd.
D: £19.00-£24.50 **S:** £22.00-£28.00.
Open: All Year (not Xmas)
Beds: 2T 2S
Baths: 2 Sh
❑(4)❑♨Ⅵ⊬

(2m) *Sevenoaks Star House, Star Hill, Sevenoaks, Kent, TN14 6HA.*
Country house, large garden, stun-ning views. Near Sevenoaks and M25.
Grades: ETC 3 Diamond
Tel: **01959 533109**
D: £18.00-£20.50 **S:** £20.00-£22.50.
Open: All Year (not Xmas)
Beds: 2T 1D
Baths: 2 Pr
ॐ❑⊬❑♨Ⅲ.Ⅵ⊬

(2m) *Burley Lodge, Rockdale Road, Sevenoaks, Kent, TN13 1JT.*
Beautiful Edwardian house situated in conservation area in a cul-de-sac off the High Street.
Tel: **01732 455761** Ms Latter.
Fax no: 01732 458178
D: £20.00-£20.00 **S:** £27.00-£27.00.
Open: All Year
Beds: 1F **Baths:** 1 En
ॐ❑❑♞✗♨Ⅲ.Ⅵ♠⊬

All paths are popular: you are well-advised to book ahead

Kemsing 20

National Grid Ref: TQ5558

(▲ On path) *Kemsing Youth Hostel*, Church Lane, Kemsing, Sevenoaks, Kent, TN15 6LU.
Actual grid ref: TQ555588
Tel: **01732 761341**
Under 18: £6.90
Adults: £10.00
Self-catering facilities, Television, Showers, Lounge, Dining room, Drying room, Cycle store, Evening meal at 7.00pm, Kitchen facilities, Breakfast available, Credit cards accepted
Imposing Victorian vicarage in its own grounds at the foot of the North Downs.

St Mary's Platt 21

National Grid Ref: TQ6057

⊯ ◁ Brickmakers' Arms

(1m 🚗) *Stone Cottage*, Maidstone Road, St Mary's Platt, Borough Green, Sevenoaks, Kent, TN15 8JH.
Convenient M20/M25 and Brands Hatch. 40 minutes to London.
Tel: **01732 883098**
Mrs Record.
D: £20.00-£20.00 **S:** £20.00-£20.00.
Open: All Year (not Xmas)
Beds: 1F 1D
Baths: 1 Sh
🛏 (3) 🅿 (10) ⊬ 🖵 🖭 🖳 Ⅴ ⱷ ♦

Trottiscliffe 22

National Grid Ref: TQ6460

⊯ ◁ The Plough

(0.75m) *Bramble Park*, Church Lane, Trottiscliffe, West Malling, Kent, ME19 5EB.
Actual grid ref: TQ644563
Secluded tranquil Victorian rectory in beautiful private parkland. Spacious comfortable.
Tel: **01732 822397** Mrs Towler.
D: £20.00-£20.00 **S:** £20.00-£20.00.
Open: All Year
Beds: 1F 1D 1S
Baths: 1 Pr 2 Sh
🛏 🅿 (6) 🖵 🖭 ⱷ

Rochester 23

National Grid Ref: TQ7468

⊯ ◁ Royal Oak, King's Head, Waterman's Arms, Queen Charlotte, White Horse

(2m 🚗) *255 High Street*, Rochester, Kent, ME1 1HQ.
Actual grid ref: TQ748681
Victorian family house near station. Antique four poster bed.
Tel: **01634 842737** Mrs Thomas.
D: £14.00-£16.00 **S:** £16.00-£25.00.
Open: All Year (not Xmas)
Beds: 1F 1D 1T
Baths: 1 Pr 1 Sh
🛏 🖵 🖳 Ⅴ ♦

(2m) *St Ouen*, 98 Borstal Road, Rochester, Kent, ME1 3BD.
Actual grid ref: TQ735675
Victorian house with comfortable rooms overlooking River Medway. Amenities close-by.
Tel: **01634 843528** Mrs Beggs.
D: £16.00-£20.00 **S:** £18.00-£20.00.
Open: All Year (not Xmas)
Beds: 1D 1T 1S
Baths: 1 Sh
🛏 ⊬ 🖵 🛏 🖳 🖭 Ⅴ ⱷ ♦

(2m) *St Martin*, 104 Borstal Road, Rochester, Kent, ME1 3BD.
Actual grid ref: TQ737674
Comfortable Victorian home overlooking river, easy walk to city centre.
Tel: **01634 848192** Mrs Colvin.
D: £16.00-£18.00 **S:** £16.00-£18.00.
Open: All Year (not Xmas)
Beds: 1D 2T
Baths: 2 Sh
🛏 🖵 🛏 🗙 🛏 🖭 Ⅴ ⱷ ♦

(2m) *52 Borstal Street*, Rochester, Kent, ME1 3HL.
Comfortable Victorian Terraced house. Suitable for cat lovers. Smokers welcome.
Tel: **01634 812347** Ms Walker.
D: £12.50 **S:** £20.00.
Open: All Year
Beds: 1D
Baths: 1Shared
🅿 🖵 🛏 🖭 Ⅴ ⱷ

(2m 🚗) *11 Ethelbert Road*, Rochester, Kent, ME1 3EU.
Large family home 10 minutes walk from historic city centre.
Tel: **01634 403740**
Mrs Jenkinson.
D: £18.00-£20.00 **S:** £20.00-£20.00.
Open: All Year (not Xmas)
Beds: 1D 1T
⊬ 🖵 🛏 🖭 Ⅴ

(2m) *19 Roebuck Road*, Rochester, Kent, ME1 1UE.
Modern, comfortable, in a Victorian house, quiet street near centre.
Tel: **01634 827153**
Mrs Smithwhite.
D: £18.00-£21.00 **S:** £17.00.
Open: All Year
Beds: 1D 1T
Baths: 1 Sh
🛏 (1) 🖵 🛏 🛏 🖭 Ⅴ ⱷ

(0.5m) *Walnut Tree House*, 21 Mount Road, Rochester, Kent, ME1 3NQ.
Actual grid ref: TQ739665
Comfortable family home in quiet area of Rochester.
Tel: **01634 849355**
Mrs Hext.
Fax no: 01634 402730
D: £17.00-£18.00 **S:** £18.00-£19.00.
Open: All Year (not Xmas)
Beds: 1D 1T
Baths: 2 Sh
🛏 ⊬ 🖵 🛏 🖭 Ⅴ ⱷ

Wouldham 24

National Grid Ref: TQ7164

⊯ ◁ Watermans

(0.5m 🚗) *Wouldham Court Farmhouse*, 246 High Street, Wouldham, Rochester, Kent, ME1 3TY.
Actual grid ref: TQ714643
Beamed Grade II Listed farmhouse, inglenook fireplace, overlooking River Medway.
Grades: ETC 3 Diamond
Tel: **01634 683271** (also fax no)
Ms Parnell.
D: £22.00-£22.00 **S:** £18.00-£22.00.
Open: All Year (not Xmas)
Beds: 1F 1D 1S **Baths:** 2 Sh
🛏 🅿 (1) ⊬ 🖵 🛏 🗙 🛏 🖭 Ⅴ ⱷ ♦

Aylesford 25

National Grid Ref: TQ7258

⊯ ◁ Chequers

(2m) *Wickham Lodge, The Quay*, High Street, Aylesford, Kent, ME20 7AY.
Grades: ETC 4 Diamond, AA 4 Diamond, RAC 4 Diamond
Tel: **01622 717267** Mrs Kelsey Bourne.
Fax no: 01622 792855
D: £25.00-£27.50 -£27.50.
Open: All Year
Beds: 1F 1D 1S
Baths: 2 En 1 Pr
🛏 🅿 (4) ⊬ 🖵 🛏 🛏 🖭 Ⅴ ♦
Fine Georgian house on the banks of the River Medway near the historic Aylesford Bridge. Lawns to river at the front with an old English walled garden to the rear. Recent refurbishment throughout the house.

(2m 🚗) *The Guest House*, The Friars, Aylesford Priory, Aylesford, Kent, ME20 7BX.
Tel: **01622 717272** Larcombe.
Fax no: 01622 715575
D: £19.00-£24.00 **S:** £19.00-£24.00.
Open: All Year (not Xmas/New Year)
Beds: 2F 1D **Baths:** 2 Pr
🛏 🅿 (50) ⊬ 🖵 🗙 🖭 ⱷ ♦
Picturesque priory home to a community of Carmelite Friars, founded in 1242. Come and enjoy the peaceful setting, the gardens, shops, pottery. The shrine and chapels house some wonderful modern works of art. Situated between Rochester and Maidstone, close to motorway.

Please take muddy boots off before entering premises

(2m ⊞) *Court Farm, High Street, Aylesford, Maidstone, Kent,*
ME20 7AZ.
Beams, four poster, spa, antiques, drawing room. Sorry, no children.
Tel: **01622 717293** (also fax no)
Mrs Tucker.
D: £25.00 **S:** £25.00.
Open: All Year
Beds: 2D 1T 1S **Baths:** 3 En 1 Pr
🅿 (6) ⊬⟶🛏🗙 🕳 📟 Ⅴ ⏳

Boxley 26

National Grid Ref: TQ7757

⊯ ⊲ Kings Arms, The Bull

(1m) *Barn Cottage, Harbourland, Boxley, Maidstone, Kent, ME14 3DN.*
Converted C16th barn convenient for motorways and Channel Tunnel.
Tel: **01622 675891** Mrs Munson.
D: £15.00-£20.00 **S:** £15.00-£20.00.
Open: All Year (not Xmas)
Beds: 1D 1T **Baths:** 2 En
⏳ (5) 🅿 ⊬⟶🗙 🕳 📟 Ⅴ ⏳ ⚡

Maidstone 27

National Grid Ref: TQ7655

⊯ ⊲ The Chequers, The Plough, White House, Grangemoor Hotel, Muggleton's, Chiltern Hundreds, The Fountain, Fox & Goose, Crown & Horseshoes, Ten Bells

(3m) *Grove House, Grove Green Road, Weavering, Maidstone, Kent, ME14 5JT.*
Attractive front garden for guests to enjoy quiet peaceful surroundings.
Grades: ETC 4 Diamond, AA 4 Diamond
Tel: **01622 738441** Costella.
D: £22.50-£25.00 **S:** £25.00-£35.00.
Open: All Year
Beds: 1T 2D **Baths:** 1 En 1 Sh
🅿 (6) ⊬⟶ 🕳 📟 Ⅴ ⏳

(3m ⊞) *Wits End Guest House, 78 Bower Mount Road, Maidstone, Kent, ME16 8AT.*
Quiet Edwardian Licensed guest house, close to town centre.
Grades: ETC 3 Diamond
Tel: **01622 752684** Mrs King.
Fax no: 01622 688943
D: £22.00-£30.00 **S:** £23.00-£30.00.
Open: All Year
Beds: 2F 1D 2T 2S
Baths: 4 En 2 Sh
⏳ 🅿 (8) ⟶🛏 🕳 📟 Ⅴ

(3m ⊞) *Fairlawn, Whiterock Place, Terrace Road, Maidstone, Kent, ME16 8HX.*
Bungalow in secluded garden. Ten minute walk town centre. Rail/bus links nearby.
Grades: ETC 2 Diamond, AA 2 Diamond, RAC 2 Diamond
Tel: **01622 763642** (also fax no)
Mrs Outlaw.
D: £15.00-£17.00 **S:** £18.00-£24.00.
Open: All Year (not Xmas/New Year)
Beds: 1D 1T 1S
🅿 (13) ⊬⟶🛏 🕳 📟 ⎈ Ⅴ

(3m ⊞) *Emmaus, 622 Loose Road, Maidstone, Kent, ME15 9UW.*
Original post office, detached house, above Loose Valley. Guest lounge.
Tel: **01622 745745** Mrs Hodgson.
D: £36.00-£40.00 **S:** £18.00-£20.00.
Open: All Year
Beds: 1T 2S **Baths:** 2 Sh
⏳ (5) ⊬⟶ 🕳 📟 Ⅴ ⚡

(3m ⊞) *10 Fant Lane, Maidstone, Kent, ME16 8NL.*
Character cottage; colour TV, tea/coffee facilities. Close to railway station, M20, M2.
Tel: **01622 729883** Mrs Layton.
D: £15.00-£20.00 **S:** £15.00-£25.00.
Open: All Year
Beds: 1F 1T 1S **Baths:** 1 Sh
⏳ 🅿 (2) ⊬⟶🗙 🕳 📟 Ⅴ ⏳

(3m) *51 Bower Mount Road, Maidstone, Kent, ME16 8AX.*
Actual grid ref: TQ748555
Large, comfortable Edwardian. Semi-easy access town centre and motorway.
Tel: **01622 762948** Mrs Haddow.
D: £17.00-£18.00 **S:** £16.00-£18.00.
Open: All Year (not Xmas)
Beds: 1F 1T 1S
Baths: 1 Sh
⏳ (9) ⊬⟶ 🕳 📟 Ⅴ ⏳

(3m) *54 Mote Avenue, Maidstone, Kent, ME15 7ST.*
Spacious home by Mote Park, convenient for town and countryside.
Tel: **01622 754016** Mrs Seager.
D: £16.00-£17.00 **S:** £17.00-£18.00.
Open: All Year
Beds: 1D 1T
Baths: 1 Sh
⏳ (12) 🅿 (2) ⊬⟶ 🕳 📟 Ⅴ

Bearsted 28

National Grid Ref: TQ7955

⊯ ⊲ White Horse

(2m ⊞) *The Hazels, 13 Yeoman Way, Bearsted, Maidstone, Kent, ME15 8PQ.*
Actual grid ref: TQ795548
Large, comfortable family home in quiet location, easy access M20 and A20.
Grades: ETC 4 Diamond
Tel: **01622 737943**
Mr & Mrs Buse.
D: £20.00-£25.00 **S:** £22.00-£25.00.
Open: All Year
Beds: 1T
Baths: 1 En
⏳ (2) 🅿 (2) ⊬⟶ 🕳 📟 Ⅴ ⏳ ⚡

**All rates are subject
to alteration at the
owners' discretion.**

Otham 29

National Grid Ref: TQ7953

⊯ ⊲ The Plough

(3m) *Valley View Guest House, Valley View, Greenhill, Otham, Maidstone, Kent, ME15 8RR.*
A large detached property, charmingly converted from a single storey barn and stable block.
Tel: **01622 862279** (also fax no)
Mr Crouch.
D: £20.00-£24.00 **S:** £25.00-£32.00.
Open: All Year
Beds: 2F 2D 2T 2S
Baths: 6 En 2 Pr
⏳ 🅿 (10) ⊬⟶ 🕳 📟 ⎈ Ⅴ ⏳

Hollingbourne 30

National Grid Ref: TQ8455

⊯ ⊲ Windmill, Sugar Loaves, Dirty Habit

(1m ⊞) *The Limes, 53 Eyhorne Street, Hollingbourne, Maidstone, Kent, ME17 1TS.*
Actual grid ref: TQ835545
Peaceful C18th home, large walled garden and conservatory; nearby village pubs, Leeds Castle, M20.
Grades: ETC 4 Diamond
Tel: **01622 880554** Mrs Reed.
Fax no: 01622 880063
D: £20.00-£22.50 **S:** £25.00-£30.00.
Open: Feb to Dec
Beds: 1D 2S
Baths: 1 Pr 1 Sh
⏳ (10) 🅿 (5) ⊬⟶ 🕳 📟 Ⅴ ⏳ ⚡

(0.75m ⊞) *Woodhouses, 49 Eyhorne Street, Hollingbourne, Maidstone, Kent, ME17 1TR.*
Actual grid ref: TQ833546
C17th interconnected cottages close to village pubs and Leeds Castle.
Grades: ETC 4 Diamond
Tel: **01622 880594** (also fax no)
Mr & Mrs Woodhouse.
D: £20.00-£20.00
S: £22.00-£25.00.
Open: All Year
Beds: 3T
Baths: 3 En
⏳ (10) 🅿 (3) ⊬⟶ 🕳 📟 Ⅴ ⏳ ⚡

Harrietsham 31

National Grid Ref: TQ8752

⊯ ⊲ Dog & Bear

(1m) *Homestay, 14 Chippendayle Drive, Harrietsham, Maidstone, Kent, ME17 1AD.*
Close to Leeds castle and ideally situated for exploring Kent.
Grades: ETC 3 Diamond
Tel: **01622 858698** (also fax no)
Ms Beveridge.
D: £18.00-£20.00
S: £23.00-£24.00.
Open: All Year (not Xmas/New Year)
Beds: 2 T
⊬⟶🗙 🕳 📟 Ⅴ ⚡

Charing 32

National Grid Ref: TQ9549

⑩ ◫ Rose & Crown, Royal Oak, Munday Bois

(0.25m) *23 The Moat, Charing, Ashford, Kent, TN27 0JH.*
Actual grid ref: TQ955492
On North Downs Way. Shops, buses, trains, London, Canterbury, Eurostar.
Tel: 01233 713141
Mrs Micklewright.
D: £20.00-£20.00 **S:** £25.00-£25.00.
Open: Apr to Sep
Beds: 1T
Baths: 1 En
ᗺ 🅿 (1) ⊬ �djᵢ ⚑ ▥ 🕎

(2.5m 🚗) *Barnfield, Charing, Ashford, Kent, TN27 0BN.*
Actual grid ref: TQ923484
Charming C15th farmhouse in superb location, overlooking lake and garden.
Grades: ETC 3 Diamond
Tel: 01233 712421 (also fax no)
Mrs Pym.
D: £22.00-£24.00
S: £24.00-£28.00.
Open: All Year (not Xmas)
Beds: 2D 1T 3S
Baths: 1 Sh
ᗺ 🅿 (99) ⊬ ⊡ ⚑ ▥ 🕎 ⊬

Westwell 33

National Grid Ref: TQ9847

⑩ ◫ Royal Oak

(0.5m) *Dean Court Farm, Challock Lane, Westwell, Ashford, Kent, TN25 4NH.*
Actual grid ref: TQ989488
Period rural farmhouse, central for channel ports and touring Kent.
Tel: 01233 712924 Mrs Lister.
D: £20.00-£25.00 **S:** £20.00-£25.00.
Open: All Year (not Xmas)
Beds: 1D 2T
Baths: 1 Sh
ᗺ 🅿 (3) ⊡ ⚑ ▥ 🕎 ⊬

Ashford 34

National Grid Ref: TR0042

⑩ ◫ Hare & Hounds, Pilgrims' Rest, Harvesters, Wetherspoons, Downtown Diner

(4m) *Warren Cottage Hotel, 136 The Street, Willesborough, Ashford, Kent, TN24 0NB.*
Grades: ETC 3 Diamond
Tel: 01233 621905 Mrs Jones.
Fax no: 01233 623400
D: £25.00-£35.00 **S:** £20.00-£39.90.
Open: All Year
Beds: 1F 3D 1T 1S
Baths: 6 En
ᗺ 🅿 (20) ⊬ ⊡ ⼊ ✕ ⚑ ▥ 🕎 ⓐ
17th Century hotel set in 2.5 acres. M20, Junction 10. All rooms ensuite. Carpark CCTV security. Minutes to Ashford International Station and Channel Tunnel Ports.

D = Price range per person sharing in a double room

(4m) *Heather House, 40 Burton Road, Kennington, Ashford, Kent, TN24 9DS.*
Grades: ETC 3 Diamond
Tel: 01233 661826 Mrs Blackwell.
Fax no: 01233 635183
D: £20.00 **S:** £20.00.
Open: All Year (not Xmas/ New Year)
Beds: 1T 1D 1S
Baths: 2 Sh 🅿 ⊡ 🕎
Heather House offers a warm, friendly welcome in quiet residential area. Near Eurostar.

(4m) *Quantock House, Quantock Drive, Ashford, Kent, TN24 8QH.*
Quiet residential area. Easy walk to town centre. Comfortable and welcoming.
Grades: ETC 3 Diamond
Tel: 01233 638921
Mr & Mrs Tucker.
D: £19.00-£22.00 **S:** £20.00-£22.00.
Open: All Year (not Xmas)
Beds: 1F 1D 1T 1S **Baths:** 3 En
ᗺ (7) 🅿 (3) ⊬ ⊡ ⚑ ▥ 🕎

(4m) *Mayflower House, 61 Magazine Road, Ashford, Kent, TN24 8NH.*
Friendly atmosphere, large garden. Close to town centre, international station.
Grades: ETC 3 Diamond
Tel: 01233 621959 (also fax no)
Mrs Simmons.
D: £16.50-£17.50 **S:** £18.00-£20.00.
Open: All Year (not Xmas)
Beds: 1D 2S **Baths:** 1 Sh
ᗺ ⊡ ✕ ⚑ ▥ 🕎 ⓐ ⊬

(4m 🚗) *Glenmoor, Maidstone Road, Ashford, Kent, TN25 4NP.*
Victorian gamekeepers cottage close to international station and motorway.
Grades: ETC 3 Diamond
Tel: 01233 634767
Mrs Rowlands.
D: £17.00-£17.00 **S:** £20.00-£20.00.
Open: All Year (not Xmas/ New Year)
Beds: 2D 1T
Baths: 1 Sh
ᗺ (5) 🅿 (3) ⊬ ⊡ ⚑ ▥ 🕎 ⓐ ⊬

(4m) *Ashford Guest House, 15 Canterbury Road, Ashford, Kent, TN24 8LE.*
Elegant Victorian building, spacious rooms, private parking, near town centre.
Grades: ETC 4 Diamond
Tel: 01233 640460 Mrs Noel.
Fax no: 01233 626504
D: £20.00-£20.00 **S:** £25.00-£25.00.
Open: All Year (not Xmas)
Beds: 2F 2D 2T **Baths:** 6 En
🅿 (6) ⊬ ⊡ ⚑ ▥ 🕎 ⊬

(4m) *Vickys Guest House, 38 Park Rd North, Ashford, Kent, TN24 8LY.*
Town centre, close to international station, Canterbury, Folkestone and Dover nearby.
Grades: AA 2 Diamond
Tel: 01233 631061 Mrs Ford.
Fax no: 01233 640420
D: £18.00-£21.00 **S:** £18.00-£21.00.
Open: All Year
Beds: 1F 1D 1S
Baths: 2 Pr 1 Sh
ᗺ 🅿 ⊡ ⼊ ✕ ⚑ ▥ 🕎 ⊬

(4m) *2-4 Canterbury Road, Ashford, Kent, TN24 8JX.*
Victorian semi-detached. 10 mins Eurostar station, 4 mins walk London coach stop.
Tel: 01233 623030 (also fax no)
Mr & Mrs Lavender.
D: £19.00-£20.00
S: £20.00-£21.00.
Open: All Year (not Xmas/ New Year)
Beds: 2T 2S
Baths: 1 Sh
ᗺ (5) 🅿 (4) ⊬ ⊡ ⚑

Bilting 35

National Grid Ref: TR0449

⑩ ◫ Tickled Trout

(On path) *The Old Farm House, Soakham Farm, White Hill, Bilting, Ashford, Kent, TN25 4HB.*
Actual grid ref: TR041488
Tel: 01233 813509
Mrs Feakins.
D: £16.00-£19.00 **S:** £18.00-£25.00.
Open: All Year (not Xmas)
Beds: 1F 1D 1T
ᗺ 🅿 ⊬ ⊡ ⚑ ▥ 🕎
Set in beautiful rolling countryside on the North Downs Way, Soakham is a working farm and its location is ideal for walking or visiting many places in the South East. You are assured of a friendly welcome.

For the Canterbury Loop see nos. 47-51.

Wye 36

National Grid Ref: TR0546

⑩ ◫ The Hawksenbury, Shant Hotel, New Flying Horse

(On path) *Selsfield, 46 Oxenturn Road, Wye, Ashford, Kent, TN25 5AZ.*
Ideal stop Channel Tunnel/ferries, North Downs Way- Pilgrim's Way Sustrans.
Tel: 01233 812133 (also fax no)
Morris.
D: £20.00 **S:** £25.00.
Open: All Year
Beds: 2T
🅿 ⊬ ⊡ ⚑ ▥ 🕎 ⊬

(On path) **Mistral**, *3 Oxenturn Road, Wye, Ashford, Kent, TN25 5BH.*
Grades: ETC 3 Diamond
Tel: **01233 813011**
Mr & Mrs Chapman.
Fax no: 01233813011
D: £25.00-£25.00 **S:** £25.00-£25.00.
Open: Jan to Dec
Beds: 1T 1S **Baths:** 1 Sh
⛺ 🅿 (2) ⌇ 🕯 📺 Ⅴ 🛄 ✦
Comfortable and well appointed house, mature garden, secluded but readily accessible to Wye village. Convenient for Ashford International Station, Canterbury, Dover, Leeds Castle, Sissinghurst, Stour Festival and Wye Downs.

Farthing Common   37

National Grid Ref: TR1340

📶 🍴 New Inn

(0.5m 🚐) **Southfields**, *Farthing Common, Lyminge, Folkestone, Kent, CT18 8DH.*
Actual grid ref: TR138404
Southfields is a family home on the North Downs, with panoramic views.
Tel: **01303 862391** Ms Wadie.
D: £20.00 **S:** £20.00.
Open: Mar to Oct
Beds: 1F 1T **Baths:** 1 Sh
⛺ 🅿 (6) ⌇ 🕯 ✕ 📺 Ⅴ ✦

Hythe   38

National Grid Ref: TR1634

📶 🍴 White Hart

(4m 🚐) **Maccassil**, *50 Marine Parade, Hythe, Kent, CT21 6AW.*
A warm and friendly B&B in an idyllic peaceful location.
Tel: **01303 261867**
D: £18.00-£21.00 **S:** £20.00-£25.00.
Open: All Year
Beds: 1F 1D 1T **Baths:** 2 En 1 Sh
⛺ 🅿 (3) ⌇ 🕯 📺 ♿ Ⅴ

(4m) **Hill View**, *4south Road, Hythe, Kent, CT21 6AR.*
Late Victorian house close to sea swimming pool and town.
Tel: **01303 269783** Mrs Warbuton.
D: £16.00-£18.00 **S:** £18.00-£20.00.
Open: All Year (not Xmas)
Beds: 1F 1T **Baths:** 1 Sh
⛺ (5) 🕯 📺 Ⅴ ✦

Densole   39

National Grid Ref: TR2141

(3m 🚐) **Garden Lodge**,
324 Canterbury Road, Densole, Folkestone, Kent, CT18 7BB.
Attractive family-run guest house, heated swimming pool, cream teas.
Tel: **01303 893147** (also fax no)
Mrs Cooper, MCFA.
D: £25.00-£30.00 **S:** £25.00-£30.00.
Open: All Year
Beds: 1F 1D 1T 3S **Baths:** 4 En
⛺ 🅿 (12) ⌇ 🕯 ✕ 🕯 📺 ♿ Ⅴ 🛄 ✦

Folkestone   40

National Grid Ref: TR2136

📶 🍴 Ship Inn, Carpenters, New Inn, Castle Inn, Wetherspoons, Cat & Custard Pot

(1.5m) **Wycliffe Hotel**, *63 Bouverie Rd West, Folkestone, Kent, CT20 2RN.*
Clean, comfortable, affordable accommodation near shuttle, Seacat, 15 minutes Dover Port.
Tel: **01303 252186** (also fax no)
Mr & Mrs Shorland.
D: £18.00-£21.00 **S:** £18.00-£21.00.
Open: All Year
Beds: 2F 5D 4T 1S
Baths: 1 Pr 2 Sh
⛺ 🅿 (8) ⌇ 🕯 ✕ 📺 Ⅴ ✦

(1.5m) **Seacliffe**, *3 Wear Bay Road, Folkestone, Kent, CT19 6AT.*
Homely comfortable family run very convenient for beach, port, tunnel.
Tel: **01303 254592** Ms Foot.
D: £16.00-£18.00 **S:** £16.00-£20.00.
Open: All Year (not Xmas)
Beds: 1F 1D 1T **Baths:** 1 Sh
⛺ ⌇ 🕯 📺 Ⅴ ✦

(1.5m) **Rosa Villa Guest House**,
237 Dover Road, Folkestone, Kent, CT19 6NH.
Friendly, family welcome. Good base for exploring Kent, excellent walking. Smoke free.
Tel: **01303 251415** Mr Elcombe.
D: £15.00-£20.00 **S:** £18.00-£24.00.
Open: All Year (not Xmas)
Beds: 2F 2D 1T
Baths: 1 Sh
⛺ ⌇ 🕯 📺 Ⅴ

(2m) **Normandie Guest House**,
39 Cheriton Road, Folkestone, Kent, CT20 1DD.
Small family run guest house near town centre.
Tel: **01303 256233** Mrs Watts.
D: £16.00-£17.50 **S:** £16.00-£17.50.
Open: All Year (not Xmas/ New Year)
Beds: 2F 1D 2T 1S **Baths:** 1 Sh
⛺ (4) 🕯 📺 Ⅴ 🛄

(1m) **Sunny Lodge Guest House**,
85 Cheriton Road, Folkestone, Kent, CT20 2QL.
Noted for its high standards, situated 5 minutes' drive to Shuttle & Seacat terminals.
Tel: **01303 251498** Mrs Dowsett.
Fax no: 01303 258267
D: £17.50-£19.00 **S:** £17.50-£19.00.
Open: All Year
Beds: 2F 3D 1T 2S
Baths: 4 En 1 Sh
⛺ 🅿 (5) 🕯 📺 Ⅴ 🛄 ✦

Planning a longer stay? Always ask for any special rates.

Bringing children with you? Always ask for any special rates.

(1.5m) **Abbey House Hotel**,
5-6 Westbourne Gardens, off Sandgate Road, Folkestone, Kent, CT20 2JA.
Licensed hotel, close to beautiful Lees Promenade and Country Park.
Tel: **01303 255514** Mr Donoghue.
Fax no: 01303 245098
D: £18.00-£25.00 **S:** £20.00-£30.00.
Open: All Year
Beds: 4F 3D 5T 2S
Baths: 4 En 4 Pr 4 Sh
⛺ ⌇ 🕯 📺 Ⅴ

(1.5m) **Horseshoe Hotel**, *29 Westbourne Gardens, Folkestone, Kent, CT20 2HY.*
Victorian house, close to famous Leas Promenade, sea, shuttle and town.
Tel: **01303 258643**
Max & Jackie Dunlop.
Fax no: 01303 243433
D: £19.00-£23.00 **S:** £19.00-£25.00.
Open: All Year
Beds: 2F 4D 2T 2S
Baths: 4 En 1 Pr 1 Sh
⛺ 🅿 (2) 🕯 ✕ 📺 Ⅴ ✦

Alkham   41

National Grid Ref: TR2542

📶 🍴 Marquis Of Granby

(3m) **Owler Lodge**, *Alkham Valley Rd, Alkham, Dover, Kent, CT15 7DF.*
Lovely house in beautiful village for touring East Kent.
Grades: ETC 4 Diamond, Silver
Tel: **01304 826375** Mrs Owler.
Fax no: 01304 829372
D: £21.00-£24.00 **S:** £35.00-£38.00.
Open: All Year (not Xmas)
Beds: 1F 1D 1T **Baths:** 3 En
⛺ (5) 🅿 (3) ⌇ 🕯 ✕ 🕯 📺 Ⅴ 🛄

Chilham   42

National Grid Ref: TR0653

📶 🍴 White Horse, The George

(0.25m) **Stour Valley House**,
Pilgrims Lane, Chilham, Canterbury, Kent, CT1 3RS.
Bedrooms with scenic views, all ensuite, hearty breakfast, evening meals.
Tel: **01227 738991** (also fax no)
Mrs Ely.
D: £25.00-£30.00 **S:** £20.00-£60.00.
Open: All Year (not Xmas)
Beds: 1F 1D 1T
Baths: 1 Sh
⛺ 🅿 ⌇ 🕯 ✕ 🕯 📺 ♿ Ⅴ 🛄 ✦

Petham 43

National Grid Ref: TR1351

🍴 🍺 The Compasses, The Chequers

(4m) *South Wootton House, Capel Lane, Petham, Canterbury, Kent, CT4 5RG.*
A beautiful farmhouse with conservatory set in extensive gardens, surrounded by fields and woodland.
Tel: **01227 700643** Mount.
Fax no: 01227 700613
D: £40.00-£45.00 **S:** £25.00-£30.00.
Open: All Year (not Xmas/New Year)
Beds: 1F 1T
Baths: 1 Pr
🛏 🅿 �🍴 🗋 🛆 🎹 Ⅵ 🎱 ✦

(4m) *Upper Ansdore, Duckpit Lane, Petham, Canterbury, Kent, CT4 5QB.*
Tudor farmhouse overlooking nature reserve; quiet, rural, Canterbury 15 mins.
Tel: **01227 700672** (also fax no)
Mr & Mrs Linch.
D: £21.00-£21.00 **S:** £30.00-£35.00.
Open: All Year
Beds: 3F 1D 1T 1S
Baths: 3 Pr
🛏 (5) 🅿 (5) ⏀ 🍵 🎹 Ⅵ ✦

🚐 **sign means that, *given due notice,* owners will pick you up from the path and drop you off *within reason.***

For Dover listings see pp100-101.

Canterbury 44

National Grid Ref: TR151560

🍴 🍺 King's Head, Bat & Ball, Thomas A Becket, Westgate Inn, Bishop's Finger, Old City, White Hart, Three Tuns, The Unicorn, The George, The Gravnille, White Horse, Wetherspoons

(▲ 0.5m) *Canterbury Youth Hostel, Ellerslie, 54 New Dover Road, Canterbury, Kent, CT1 3DT.*
Actual grid ref: TR157570
Tel: **01227 462911**
Under 18: £7.75 **Adults:** £11.00
Self-catering facilities, Television, Showers, Laundry facilities, Lounge, Cycle store, Parking, Evening meal at 6.00pm to 7.30pm, Kitchen facilities, Breakfast available, Credit cards accepted
A Victorian villa close to centre of principal cathedral city of England.

(▲ 0.5m) *Kipps Independent Hostel, 40 Nunnery Fields, Canterbury, Kent, CT1 3JH.*
Tel: **01227 786121 Adults:** £11.00
Self-catering facilities, Television, Showers, Central heating, Shop, Laundry facilities, Lounge, Dining room, Cycle store, Parking, No smoking
100-year-old town house. Cathedral 10 minutes' walk away.

(0.5m) *Tudor House, 6 Best Lane, Canterbury, Kent, CT1 2JB.*
Comfortable family guest house city centre, near cathedral and shops. Tel: **01227 765650**
D: £18.00-£23.00 **S:** £20.00-£35.00.
Open: All Year
Beds: 1F 4D 2T 1S
Baths: 3 En 5 Sh
🛏 🅿 (2) 🗋 🛆 🎹 Ⅵ

(0.5m) *Castle Court Guest House, 8 Castle Street, Canterbury, Kent, CT1 2QF.*
Grades: ETC 2 Diamond
Tel: **01227 463441** (also fax no)
Mr Turner.
D: £21.00-£26.00 **S:** £21.00-£24.00.
Open: All Year
Beds: 3F 2D 3T 1S
Baths: 4 En 3 Sh
🛏 🅿 (3) 🗋 🛏 🛆 🎹 Ⅵ 🎱 ✦
One of eight guesthouses within the city wall, dated 1836. A Listed Georgian building, close to cathedral. Colour TV all rooms, some ensuite. Friendly family house offering comfortable and clean accommodation. Just 2 minutes walk to shops, buses & trains.

(0.5m) *London Guest House, 14 London Rd, Canterbury, Kent, CT2 8LR.*
Recommended by Let's Go and Which? Good B&B guides.
Grades: ETC 2 Diamond
Tel: **01227 765860** Mrs Cabrini.
Fax no: 01227 456721
D: £18.00-£22.00 **S:** £18.00.
Open: All Year
Beds: 1F 1D 2T 2S **Baths:** 2 Sh
🛏 🗋 🛆 🎹 Ⅵ 🎱

(0.5m) *Chaucer Lodge, 62 New Dover Rd, Canterbury, Kent, CT1 3DT*
Grades: ETC 4 Diamond, AA 4 Diamond
Tel: **01227 459141** (also fax no)
Mr Wilson. **D:** £20.00 **S:** £24.00.
Open: All Year
Beds: 2F 2T 3D 2S **Baths:** 9 En
🛏 🅿 (10) ⏀ 🗋 🗶 🛆 🎹 Ⅵ 🎱
Family-run friendly guest house close to City Centre. Cathedral, Cricket Club and Hospitals. Colour TV, fridges, mini-bars and tea/coffee-making facilities in all rooms. Breakfast menu. High standard of cleanliness and service provided in a relaxed atmosphere. Secure off-road parking.

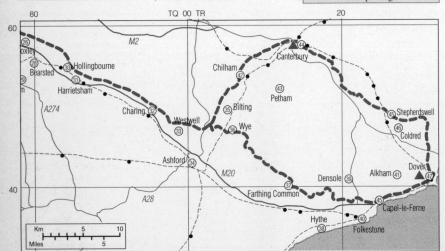

(0.25m) *Clare Ellen Guest House*, 9 Victoria Road, Canterbury, Kent, CT1 3SG.
Actual grid ref: TR144574
Grades: ETC 4 Diamond, Silver, AA 4 Diamond, 2 Eggcups
Tel: **01227 760205** Mrs Williams.
Fax no: 01227 784482
D: £24.00-£26.00 **S:** £26.00-£28.00.
Open: All Year
Beds: 1F 2D 2T 1S
Baths: 6 En
⌂ **P** (8) ⌷ ⌷ ⤵ ⌷ **V** ⌷ ✦
Large elegant ensuite rooms with TV, hairdryer, clock/radio and tea/coffee facilities. Full English breakfast. Vegetarian and special diets catered for on request. Six minutes' walk to town centre, bus and train station. Parking/garage available. Credit cards accepted.

(On path) *Oriel Lodge*, 3 Queens Avenue, Canterbury, Kent, CT2 8AY.
Actual grid ref: TR143580
Near city centre, private parking, lounge, log fire, afternoon tea.
Grades: ETC 4 Diamond, Silver, AA 4 Diamond
Tel: **01227 462845** (also fax no)
Mr & Mrs Rishworth.
D: £22.00-£33.00 **S:** £26.00-£32.00.
Open: All Year
Beds: 1F 3D 1T 1S
Baths: 2 En 2 Sh
⌂ (6) **P** (6) ⌷ ⤵ ⌷ **V**

(2m) *Abberley House*, 115 Whitstable Road, Canterbury, Kent, CT2 8EF.
Comfortable B&B in residential area close to centre. Warm welcome. **Grades:** ETC 3 Diamond
Tel: **01227 450265** Mr Allcorn.
Fax no: 01227 478626
D: £20.00-£23.50 **S:** £25.00-£25.00.
Open: All Year (not Xmas)
Beds: 2D 1T **Baths:** 1 En 1 Sh
P (3) ✄ ⌷ ⌷ ⤵ ⌷ **V**

(3m 🐾) *Abbey Lodge Guest House*, 8 New Dover Road, Canterbury, Kent, CT1 3AP.
Actual grid ref: TR155573
Cathedral city centre 10 mins walk, Dover 20 mins ride.
Tel: **01227 462878** Mrs Gardner.
D: £17.00-£20.00 **S:** £20.00-£25.00.
Open: All Year
Beds: 1F 1T 1S **Baths:** 2 En 1 Sh
⌂ **P** (16) ✄ ⌷ ⤵ ⌷.

(0.5m 🐾) *Little Courtney Guest House*, 5 Whitstable Road, St Dunstans, Canterbury, Kent, CT2 8DG.
Tel: **01227 454207** Mrs Mercer.
D: £17.50-£20.00 **S:** £20.00-£25.00.
Open: All Year
Beds: 2T 1S **Baths:** 1 Sh
P (1) ✄ ⌷ ⌷ ⤵ ⌷ **V** ✦
A warm welcome awaits you at our small family run guest house, we are close to the town centre of Canterbury, University and Railway station. Ideal for destinations with the coast only a short drive away.

(0.5m) *Cathedral Gate Hotel*, 36 Burgate, Canterbury, Kent, CT1 2HA.
Family-run medieval hotel next to Canterbury Cathedral. Warm welcome.
Grades: ETC 3 Diamond, AA 3 Diamond
Tel: **01227 464381**
Mrs Jubber.
Fax no: 01227 462800
D: £22.00-£40.50 **S:** £23.00-£54.00.
Open: All Year
Beds: 5F 9D 7T 6S
Baths: 12 En 3 Sh
⌂ ⌷ ⌷ ⌷ ✕ ⤵ ⌷ **V** ⌷ ✦

(0.5m) *Milton House*, 9 South Canterbury Road, Canterbury, Kent, CT1 3LH.
Railway cricket ground cathedral 15 minutes walk. Dover 15 miles.
Tel: **01227 765531** Mrs Wright.
D: £15.00-£18.00 **S:** £20.00-£20.00.
Open: All Year (not Xmas/New Year)
Beds: 1D 1T **Baths:** 1 Sh
P ⌷ ⌷ ⤵ ⌷ **V**

(0.5m 🐾) *Kingsmead House*, 68 St Stephen's Road, Canterbury, Kent, CT2 7JF.
Comfortable C17th home, quiet yet close to city centre.
Grades: ETC 3 Diamond
Tel: **01227 760132** Clark.
D: £22.00-£25.00 .
Open: All Year (not Xmas)
Beds: 2D 1T
Baths: 3 En
⌂ (8) **P** (3) ⌷ ⌷ ⤵ ⌷ **V** ✦

(0.5m) *Corner House*, 1 13 Whitstable Road, Canterbury, Kent, CT2 8DA.
Pilgrim's first view of the cathedral! 2 minutes from the Corner House.
Tel: **01227 761352** Prof McDonnell.
Fax no: 01227 761065
D: £19.00-£22.50 **S:** £25.00-£35.00.
Open: All Year (not Xmas)
Beds: 1F 1T 1S
Baths: 2 En 1 Sh
⌂ (10) **P** (4) ⌷ ⌷ ⤵ ⌷ **V**

(0.5m) *Acacia Lodge*, 39 London Road, Canterbury, Kent, CT2 8LF.
Beautiful period house near centre, cathedral, station. Very friendly and clean.
Tel: **01227 769955** Mrs Cain.
Fax no: 01227 478960
D: £17.00-£22.00 **S:** £20.00-£30.00.
Open: All Year
Beds: 2D 1T
Baths: 3 Pr
⌂ **P** (3) ✄ ⌷ ⌷ ⤵ ⌷ **V**

S = Price range for a single person in a single room

(0.5m) *Tanglewood Cottage*, 40 London Road, Canterbury, Kent, CT2 8LF.
Actual grid ref: TR140582
Converted farmworker's cottage close to A2/M2 slip road, convenient university and rail stations.
Tel: **01227 786806**
D: £17.00-£21.00 **S:** £25.00.
Open: All Year (not Xmas)
Beds: 2D 1T
Baths: 2 En 1 Pr
P (4) ✄ ⌷ ⤵ ⌷ **V**

(0.5m) *The Plantation*, Iffin Lane, Canterbury, Kent, CT4 7BD.
Actual grid ref: 14305670
Quiet, modern house in 5 acres, beautiful gardens, overlooking cathedral.
Tel: **01227 472104** (also fax no)
D: £19.00-£24.00 **S:** £25.00-£25.00.
Open: All Year (not Xmas)
Beds: 1D 1T
Baths: 2 En
⌂ (5) **P** (4) ✄ ⌷ ⌷ ⤵ ⌷ **V** ⌷ ✦

Shepherdswell   45

National Grid Ref: TR2547

🍴 🍺 Crown Inn, The Bell

(On path 🐾) *Sunshine Cottage*, The Green, Mill Lane, Shepherdswell or Sibertswold, Dover, Kent, CT15 7LQ.
Actual grid ref: TR262478
C17th cottage on village green, beautifully restored. Pretty garden/courtyard.
Grades: ETC 4 Diamond, Silver
Tel: **01304 831359**
Mrs Popple.
D: £22.00-£25.00 **S:** £30.00-£35.00.
Open: All Year
Beds: 6F 5D 1T
Baths: 4 En 2 Pr 4 Sh
⌂ **P** (6) ✄ ⌷ ✕ ⤵ ⌷. ⌷ **V** ✦

Coldred   46

National Grid Ref: TR2746

🍴 🍺 The Lydden Bell

(0.25m 🐾) *Colret House*, The Green, Coldred, Dover, Kent, CT15 5AP.
Grades: ETC 4 Diamond
Tel: **01304 830388**
Mrs White.
Fax no: 01304 830348
D: £25.00-£30.00
S: £25.00-£30.00.
Open: All Year
Beds: 2F
Baths: 2 En
⌂ **P** ✄ ⌷ ⌷ ✕ ⤵ ⌷. ⌷ ⌷ **V** ⌷ ✦
Garden rooms in grounds of detached Edwardian property facing the village green of Coldred - twice recently voted the best kept village in Kent. Easy access from A2 - Canterbury/Sandwich/Dover all within 15 minutes drive. Ideal overnight stop for ferries/shuttle.

Dover 47

National Grid Ref: TR3141

▶◀ ◖ Chequers Inn, Red Lion, Park Inn, Eight
Bells, White Horse, Marquis of Granby,
Lighthouse, The Britannia, The Plough,
The Swingate

(▲ 0.5m) *Dover Youth Hostel,*
306 London Road, Dover, Kent,
CT17 0SY.
Actual grid ref: TR311421
Tel: 01304 201314
Under 18: £7.75 **Adults:** £11.00
Self-catering facilities, Television,
Showers, Lounge, Games room,
Evening meal at 6.30pm to 7.30pm,
Kitchen facilities, Breakfast
available
There are two buildings for hostel
accommodation in historic Dover,
both recently refurbished.

(0.5m) *Hubert House, 9 Castle*
Hill Road, Dover, Kent, CT16 1QW.
Comfortable Georgian house with
parking; ideally situated for local
attractions and ferries.
Grades: ETC 3 Diamond
Tel: 01304 202253 Mr Hoynes.
D: £20.00-£25.00 **S:** £28.00-£30.00.
Open: Nov to Sep
Beds: 2F 2D 2T 1S
Baths: 7 En
ੴ 🄿 (6) ❑ 🛏 Ⅲ. Ⓥ

(0.5m) *Valjoy Guest House,*
237 Folkestone Rd, Dover,
Kent, CT17 9SL.
Victorian family house situated
near rail, ferry and tunnel
terminals.
Tel: 01304 212160 Mr Bowes.
D: £15.00-£20.00 **S:** £15.00-£20.00.
Open: All Year (not Xmas)
Beds: 3F 1S **Baths:** 1 Sh
ੴ 🄿 (5) ❑ ✕ 🛏 Ⅲ. Ⓥ ♿ ✦

(0.5m) *Bleriot's, Belper House,*
47 Park Avenue, Dover, Kent,
CT16 1HE.
A Victorian residence with ensuite
rooms and off-road parking.
Grades: ETC 2 Diamond
Tel: 01304 211394 Mrs Casey.
D: £18.00-£23.00 **S:** £20.00-£46.00.
Open: All Year (not Xmas)
Beds: 2F 3D 2T 1S
Baths: 6 En 2 Sh
ੴ 🄿 (8) ❑ 🛏 Ⅲ. Ⓥ

(0.5m) *Beulah House,*
94 Crabble Hill, Dover, Kent,
CT17 0SA.
Welcome to this imposing award-
winning guest house in 1 acre of
magnificent topiaried gardens.
Grades: AA 4 Diamond
Tel: 01304 824615 Mrs Owen.
Fax no: 01304 828850
D: £22.00-£25.00 **S:** £30.00-£35.00.
Open: All Year
Beds: 2F 4D 3T **Baths:** 9 En
ੴ 🄿 ✂ ❑ 🛏 Ⅲ. Ⓥ ♿

(0.5m) *Number One Guest House,*
1 Castle Street, Dover, Kent,
CT16 1QH.
Georgian town house. All rooms
ensuite. GARAGE PARKING.
Port nearby
Grades: AA 4 Diamond,
RAC 4 Diamond Sparkling Award
Tel: 01304 202007 Ms Reidy.
Fax no: 01304 214078
D: £20.00-£25.00 **S:** £25.00-£30.00.
Open: All Year
Beds: 1F 2D 2T **Baths:** All Ensuite
ੴ 🄿 (4) ❑ 🛏 Ⅲ. Ⓥ

D = Price range per person

sharing in a double room

(0.5m) *Dover Blakes Of Dover, 52*
Castle Street, Dover, Kent, CT16 1PJ.
Blakes of Dover, restaurants, local
fish, real ales, 52 whiskeys.
Grades: ETC 3 Star
Tel: 01304 202194 (also fax no)
Toomey.
D: £27.50-£40.00 **S:** £27.50-£40.00.
Open: All Year (not Xmas)
Beds: 2F 3D 2T **Baths:** 6 En
ੴ ❑ ✕ 🛏 Ⅲ. Ⓥ ♿

(0.5m 🐾) *Talavera House, 275*
Folkestone Rd, Dover, Kent, CT17 9LL.
Spacious late Victorian house close
to stations, ferries, town centre.
Grades: ETC 3 Diamond
Tel: 01304 206794 Hilton.
Fax no: 01304 207067
D: £15.00-£22.00 **S:** £18.00-£25.00.
Open: All Year
Beds: 1F 1T 1D 1S **Baths:** 1 En 1 Sh
ੴ 🄿 (3) ❑ 🛏 ✕ 🛏 Ⅲ. Ⓥ ✦

(0.5m) *Dover's Restover Bed &*
Breakfast, 69 Folkestone Road,
Dover, Kent, CT17 9RZ.
Highly recommended, beautifully
refurbished ensuite rooms, central-
ly situated for all amenities.
Tel: 01304 206031 Mrs Adams.
D: £15.00-£25.00 **S:** £18.00-£27.00.
Open: All Year
Beds: 1F 4D 1T **Baths:** 3 En 1 Sh
ੴ 🄿 (3) ❑ 🛏 Ⅲ. Ⓥ

(0.5m 🐾) *Whitmore Guest House,*
261 Folkestone Road, Dover, Kent,
CT17 9LL.
Warm welcome at a highly
recommended family-run Victorian
guest house.
Tel: 01304 203080 Mrs Brunt.
Fax no: 01304 240110
D: £15.00-£22.00 **S:** £17.00-£25.00.
Open: All Year (not Xmas)
Beds: 2F 1D 1T **Baths:** 2 En 1 Sh
ੴ 🄿 (6) ✂ ❑ 🛏 Ⅲ. Ⓥ ♿ ✦

IRELAND: BED & BREAKFAST 2001

The essential guide to B&Bs in the Republic of Ireland and Northen Ireland

Think of Ireland and you think of that famous Irish hospitality. The warmth of the welcome is as much a part of this great island as the wild and beautiful landscapes, the traditional folk music and the Guiness. Wherever you go, town or country, North or South, you can't escape it.

There are few better ways of experiencing this renowned hospitality, when traveling through Ireland, than by staying at one of the country's many Bed & Breakfasts. They offer a great value alternative to expensive hotels, each has its own individual charm and you get a home cooked breakfast to help you start your day.

Stilwell's Ireland: Bed & Breakfast 2001 is the most comprehensive guide of its kind, with over 1,400 entries listed by county and location, in both Northern Ireland and the Republic of Ireland. Each entry includes room rates, facilities, Tourist Board grades, local maps and a brief description of the B&B, its location and surroundings.

Treat yourself to some Irish hospitality with **Stilwell Ireland: Bed & Breakfast 2001.**

Private Houses, Country Halls, Farms, Cottages, Inns, Small Hotels and Guest Houses

Over 1,400 entries
Average price £18 per person per night ($32 per person per night)
All official grades shown
Local maps
Pubs serving hot evening meals shown
Tourist Information Offices listed
Handy size for easy packing!

£6.95 from all good bookstores (ISBN 1-900861-24-0) or £7.95 (inc p&p) from Stilwell Publishing, 59 Charlotte Road, London EC2A 3QW (020 7739 7179)

Oxfordshire Way

The **Oxfordshire Way** is only 65 miles long but takes the walker through the best bits of Oxfordshire from the Cotswolds down to the Chilterns. You start in beautiful Bourton-on-the-Water (actually in Gloucestershire) and head off through the pretty 'Wychwoods', near Blenheim Palace to the deserted villages of Otmoor, before heading south-east to chalk hills, beech woods and noble Henley-on-Thames on the banks of the river. The county looks after its paths well - the **Oxfordshire Way** is very well waymarked and in our opinion, the walking literature that comes from Oxfordshire County Council is the best in the country. This path links up with the

Cotswold Way (via the **Heart of England** extension - q.v.) and the **Thames Footpath**. The start is also about 1 mile from the **Macmillan Way** through the Gloucestershire 'Slaughters'.
Guides: *The Oxfordshire Way* by K Wheal (ISBN 0 7509 0356 2), published by Oxfordshire County Council in association with Alan Sutton Publishing Ltd and available directly from their offices (Countryside Services, Dept for Leisure & Arts, Library HQ, Holton, Oxford, OX32 1QQ, tel. 01865 810226). £5.99 + 50p p&p.
Maps: 1:50000 Ordnance Survey Landranger Series: 163, 164, 165, 175

Bourton-on-the-Water   1

National Grid Ref: SP1620

|ᛃ| ⬛ Plough, Kingsbridge Inn, Mouse Trap Inn, Coach & Horses, Duke of Wellington

(On path) *Lansdowne House, Lansdowne, Bourton-on-the-Water, Cheltenham, Glos, GL54 2AT.*
Actual grid ref: SP164210
Tastefully furnished ensuite accommodation. Combination of old and antique furniture.
Grades: ETC 4 Diamond
Tel: 01451 820812 Mrs Garwood.
Fax no: 01451 822484
D: £17.50-£20.00 **S:** £30.00-£35.00.
Open: All Year (not Xmas)
Beds: 1F 2D
Baths: 3 En
🛇 🅿 (4) ⊡ 🛏 ▥ Ⓥ ⚕

(On path) *6 Moore Road, Bourton-on-the-Water, Cheltenham, Glos, GL54 2AZ.*
Cotswold stone house, quiet road, yards to village, peaceful garden.
Tel: 01451 820767
Mrs Mustoe.
D: £19.00-£21.00 **S:** £20.00-£25.00.
Open: Feb to Dec
Beds: 1D 1T
Baths: 1 En 1 Pr
🛇 (5) 🅿 (3) ⊬⊡ 🛏 🛏 ▥ Ⓥ ⚕

(0.25m 🚐) *Holly House, Station Road, Bourton-on-the-Water, Cheltenham, Glos, GL54 2ER.*
Actual grid ref: SP168212
Spacious Cotswold style house. Breakfast in conservatory overlooking delightful gardens.
Grades: ETC 4 Diamond
Tel: 01451 821302
Mr Stanfield.
D: £20.00-£25.00 **S:** £28.00-£32.00.
Open: Feb to Oct
Beds: 2D 1T 1S
Baths: 4 En
🛇 🅿 (6) ⊬⊡✗ 🛏 ▥ Ⓥ ⚕ ⚕

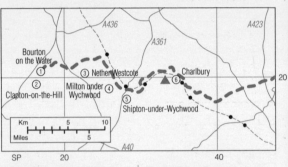

(0.25m 🚐) *Lansdowne Villa Guest House, Bourton-on-the-Water, Cheltenham, Glos, GL54 2AR.*
This large, detached Cotswold stone house stands at the end of this beautiful village.
Tel: 01451 820673
Mr & Mrs Harris.
Fax no: 01451 822099
D: £24.00 **S:** £32.00.
Open: Feb to Dec
Beds: 8D 2T 2S
Baths: 12 En
🛇 🅿 (14) ⊬⊡✗ 🛏 ▥ Ⓥ ⚕ ⚕

Clapton-on-the-Hill   2

National Grid Ref: SP1617

|ᛃ| ⬛ Plough, Kingsbridge Inn, Mouse Trap Inn, Coach & Horses

(2m) *Farncombe, Clapton-on-the-Hill, Bourton-on-the-Water, Cheltenham, Glos, GL54 2LG.*
Come and share our peace and tranquillity with superb views.
Grades: ETC 4 Diamond
Tel: 01451 820120 (also fax no)
Mrs Wright.
D: £20.00-£23.00 **S:** £25.00-£30.00.
Open: All Year (not Xmas)
Beds: 2D 1T **Baths:** 1 En 2 Sh
🛇 🅿 (4) ⊬⊡ 🛏 ▥ Ⓥ ⚕ ⚕

(0.25m) *Upper Farm, Clapton-on-the-Hill, Bourton-on-the-Water, Cheltenham, Glos, GL54 2LG.*
Period farmhouse, spectacular views warm welcome, superior accommodation, village location.
Grades: ETC 5 Daimond
Tel: 01451 820453
Mrs Adams.
Fax no: 01451 810185
D: £20.00-£22.50
S: £25.00-£30.00.
Open: Feb to Dec
Beds: 1F 2D 1T
Baths: 3 En 1 Sh
🛇 (6) 🅿 (6) ⊬⊡ 🛏 ▥ & Ⓥ

🚐 sign means that, *given due notice*, owners will pick you up from the path and drop you off *within reason.*

Nether Westcote   3

National Grid Ref: SP2220

᛫᛫᛫ ⊞ Merrymouth Inn

(0.5m) *Cotswold View Guest House*, *Nether Westcote, Chipping Norton, Oxon, OX7 6SD.*
Actual grid ref: SP225203
Grades: ETC 3 Diamond
Tel: 01993 830699 Mr Gibson.
D: £20.00-£25.00 **S:** £25.00-£30.00.
Open: All Year (not Xmas/
New Year)
Beds: 2D 2T 1S 2F
Baths: 5 En 2 Pr
🛏 🅿 (8) ⊬ 🗔 🐾 ✕ 🏋 🔟 Ⓥ 🔌 ⊬
We welcome you to Cotswold view guesthouse, which we have built on the site of my family's farmyard. In the unspoilt and quiet village of Nether Westcote. We offer luxury accomodation and a hearty English breakfast.

All rooms full and nowhere else to stay? Ask the owner if there's anywhere nearby

---

Milton-under-Wychwood   4

National Grid Ref: SP2618

᛫᛫᛫ ⊞ Quart Pot, Lamb Inn

(0.25m) *Sunset House, Jubilee Lane, Milton-under-Wychwood, Chipping Norton, Oxfordshire, OX7 6EW.*
Period Cotswold house, charming bedrooms with ensuite private facilities.
Tel: 01993 830581 Mrs Durston.
D: £23.50-£25.00 **S:** £27.50-£30.00.
Open: All Year
Beds: 2D 1T **Baths:** 2 En 1 Pr
🛏 (5) 🅿 (3) ⊬ 🗔 🏋 🔟 Ⓥ

Shipton-under-Wychwood   5

National Grid Ref: SP2717

᛫᛫᛫ ⊞ Red Horse, Lamb Inn, Crown Hotel

(0.25m 🚍) *Garden Cottage, Fiddlers Hill, Shipton-under-Wychwood, Chipping Norton, Oxon, OX7 6DR.*
Attractive stone cottage, country views, quiet, ideal for exploring Cotswolds.
Grades: ETC 3 Diamond
Tel: 01993 830640 Worker.
D: £15.00-£25.00 **S:** £25.00-£35.00.
Open: All Year (not Xmas)
Beds: 1D 1T **Baths:** 2 En
🛏 (8) 🅿 (2) ⊬ 🗔 🏋 🔟 Ⓥ 🔌 ⊬

(0.25m 🚍) *6 Courtlands Road, Shipton-under-Wychwood, Chipping Norton, Oxon, OX7 6DF.*
Friendly, quiet, comfortable house/garden.
Tel: 01993 830551
Mr & Mrs Fletcher.
D: £17.50-£22.50 **S:** £20.00-£25.00.
Open: All Year
Beds: 2D 1T **Baths:** 2 En 1 Pr
🅿 (3) ⊬ 🗔 🏋 🔟 Ⓥ 🔌 ⊬

Charlbury   6

National Grid Ref: SP3619

᛫᛫᛫ ⊞ Bull Inn

(▲ On path) *Charlbury Youth Hostel, The Laurels, The Slade, Charlbury, Chipping Norton, Oxfordshire, OX7 3SJ.*
Actual grid ref: SP361198
Tel: 01608 810202
Under 18: £6.90 **Adults:** £10.00
Cycle store, Facilities for disabled people, No smoking, WC, Breakfast available
Old glove factory, recently refurbished. 2 bedrooms sleep up to 8.

S = Price range for a single person in a single room

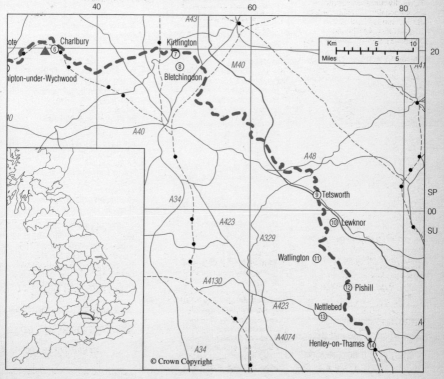

© Crown Copyright

(1m) *Cotswold View Caravan & Camping Site,* *Banbury Hill Farm, Enstone Road, Charlbury, Chipping Norton, Oxon, OX7 3JH.*
Actual grid ref: SP363209
Situated on eastern edge of Cotswolds, overlooking the Evenlode Valley.
Grades: ETC 4 Diamond
Tel: 01608 810314 Mrs Widdows.
Fax no: 01608 811891
D: £18.00-£25.00 **S:** £20.00-£35.00.
Open: All Year (not Xmas)
Beds: 7F 2D 3T 1S
Baths: 11 En 1 Sh
🛇 🅿 (10) 🗲 ❏ 🕮 ᵭ ♿ Ⓥ

Kirtlington 7

National Grid Ref: SP4919

🅂🄴 Oxford Arms

(0.25m) *Two Turnpike Cottages,* *Kirtlington, Oxford, OX5 3HB.*
Cotswold stone cottage with pretty gardens in village setting.
Tel: 01869 350706 Mrs Jones.
D: £21.00-£24.00 **S:** £25.00-£25.00.
Open: All Year
Beds: 2D **Baths:** 1 Sh
🛇 🅿 (2) 🗲 ❏ 🕇 ᵭ 🕮 Ⓥ

Bletchingdon 8

National Grid Ref: SP5018

(1.75m) *Stonehouse Farm,* *Weston Road, Bletchingdon, Kidlington, Oxon, OX5 3EA.*
C17th farmhouse set in 560 acres 15 mins from Oxford.
Tel: 01869 350585 Mrs Hedges.
D: £18.00-£22.00 **S:** £20.00-£24.00.
Open: All Year (not Xmas/ New Year)
Beds: 1F 1D 1T 1S **Baths:** 2 Sh
🛇 (12) 🅿 (6) 🗲 ❏ ᵭ 🕮 Ⓥ

Tetsworth 9

National Grid Ref: SP6802

🅂🄴 Lion On The Green

(On path 🚲) *The Lion on the Green,* *40 High Street, Tetsworth, Thame, Oxon, OX9 7AS.*
Tel: 01844 281274 Mr Hodgkinson.
D: £16.50-£20.00 **S:** £25.00-£30.00.
Open: All Year
Beds: 1F 2T
Baths: 1 Sh
🛇 🅿 (20) ❏ 🕇 🕆 ᵭ 🕮 Ⓥ
Privately owned country inn & restaurant right on the Oxfordshire Way. We specialise in top quality home-cooked food at affordable prices. Your pleasure is our business!

D = Price range per person sharing in a double room

Always telephone to get directions to the B&B - you will save time!

(On path 🚲) *Little Acre,* *4 High Street, Tetsworth, Thame, Oxon, OX9 7AT.*
Actual grid ref: SP682022
Tel: 01844 281423 (also fax no) Ms Tanner.
D: £18.00-£22.50 **S:** £25.00-£35.00.
Open: All Year
Beds: 1F 2D 2T
Baths: 3 En 2 Sh
🛇 🅿 (5) ❏ 🕇 ᵭ 🕮 ᵭ Ⓥ
We offer a warm welcome, hearty breakfasts, comfy beds and beautiful gardens and fields to stroll in, with the dreaming spires of oxford and the Cotswolds on the doorstep, you'll never be short of activities to give your holiday a special touch.

Lewknor 10

National Grid Ref: SU7197

🅂🄴 Leathern Bottle

(1m 🚲) *Moorcourt Cottage,* *Weston Road, Lewknor, Watlington, Oxfordshire, OX9 5RU.*
Beautiful C15th cottage, open views, very quiet, friendly and comfortable.
Tel: 01844 351419 (also fax no) Mrs Hodgson.
D: £22.50-£22.50 **S:** £30.00-£30.00.
Open: All Year
Beds: 1T 1D
Baths: 1 En 1 Pr
🅿 (4) ❏ ᵭ 🕮 Ⓥ

Watlington 11

National Grid Ref: SU6894

(0.5m 🚲) *Woodgate Orchard Cottage, Howe Road, Watlington, Oxon, OX9 5EL.*
Actual grid ref: SU691937
Tel: 01491 612675 (also fax no) Roberts.
D: £25.00-£35.00 **S:** £30.00-£30.00.
Open: All Year
Beds: 1F 1T 1D
Baths: 1 En 1 Pr
🛇 🅿 (8) 🗲 ❏ 🕆 ᵭ 🕮 Ⓥ ᵭ
Warm welcome, countryside location, comfortable rooms, home-cooking, restful gardens, red kites gliding above. 500m off Ridgeway, convenient for Oxfordshire Way and Cycle Path, Chiltern Way, Thames Path and towns of Oxford, Henley, Reading, Windsor, Heathrow. Oxford Tube bus stop 2 miles away Lewknor - transport arrangements.

Pishill 12

National Grid Ref: SU7289

🅂🄴 The Crown

(On path 🚲) *Bank Farm,* *Pishill, Henley-on-Thames, Oxon, RG9 6HJ.*
Actual grid ref: SU724898
Quiet comfortable farmhouse, beautiful countryside. Convenient Oxford, London, Windsor.
Grades: ETC 2 Diamond
Tel: 01491 638601 Mrs Lakey.
D: £23.00-£23.00 **S:** £20.00-£23.00.
Open: All Year (not Xmas)
Beds: 1F 1S
Baths: 1 En 1 Sh
🛇 🅿 (5) 🗲 ❏ 🕇 ᵭ 🕮 Ⓥ ᵭ ᵭ

(1m) *Orchard House, Pishill, Henley-on-Thames, Oxfordshire, RG9 6HJ.*
Property in area outstanding natural Beauty surrounded by ancient Woodlands.
Tel: 01491 638351 (also fax no) Mrs Connolly.
D: £25.00-£25.00 **S:** £25.00-£25.00.
Open: All Year
Beds: 2F 1D 1T
Baths: 3 En 1 Pr
🛇 🅿 Ⓥ 🗲 ❏ 🕇 ✕ ᵭ 🕮 Ⓥ ᵭ

Nettlebed 13

National Grid Ref: SU6986

🅂🄴 Crown Inn

(1.75m 🚲) *Park Corner Farm House, Nettlebed, Henley-on-Thames, Oxon, RG9 6DX.*
Queen Anne farmhouse in AONB between Henley-on-Thames and Oxford.
Tel: 01491 641450 Mrs Rutter.
D: £22.50 **S:** £22.50
Open: All Year (not Xmas/ New Year)
Beds: 2T 1S **Baths:** 1 Sh 1 Pr
🛇 🅿 (6) 🗲 🕇 ᵭ 🕮 Ⓥ ᵭ ᵭ

Henley-on-Thames 14

National Grid Ref: SU7682

🅂🄴 Anchor, Bottle & Glass, Golden Ball, Rose & Crown

(0.25m 🚲) *Ledard, Rotherfield Road, Henley-on-Thames, Oxon, RG9 INN.*
Actual grid ref: SU761814
Elegant Victorian house and garden within easy reach of Henley.
Tel: 01491 575611 Mrs Howard.
D: £20.00-£20.00 **S:** £20.00-£20.00.
Open: All Year (not Xmas)
Beds: 1F 1D 1T **Baths:** 2 Pr
🛇 🅿 (4) 🗲 ❏ ᵭ 🕮 Ⓥ ᵭ ᵭ

S = Price range for a single person in a single room

(1m) *Alftrudis, 8 Norman Avenue, Henley-on-Thames, Oxon, RG9 1SG.*
Victorian home, quiet cul-de-sac two minutes town centre station, river.
Grades: ETC 4 Diamond
Tel: 01491 573099 Mrs Lambert.
Fax no: 01491 411747
D: £25.00-£30.00 **S:** £40.00-£50.00.
Open: All Year
Beds: 2D 1T
Baths: 2 En 1 Pr
🛏 (8) 🅿 (2) ⅍ 🗆 🍴 🎟 🔲

Order your packed lunches the *evening before* you need them. Not at breakfast!

(0.75m) *4 Coldharbour Close, Henley-on-Thames, Oxon, RG9 1QP.*
Large sunny bungalow in quiet location; secluded garden with patio.
Grades: ETC 3 Diamond
Tel: 01491 575297 (also fax no)
Mrs Bower.
D: £24.00-£28.00 **S:** £27.00-£30.00.
Open: Easter to Nov
Beds: 1D 1T
Baths: 1 Pr 1 En
🛏 🅿 (3) ⅍ 🗆 ✕ 🍴 🎟 🔲 ⅙ ⅌

(0.5m 🚌) *Lenwade, 3 Western Road, Henley-on-Thames, Oxon, RG9 1JL.*
Beautiful Victorian family home, convenient river, restaurants, public transport.
Tel: 01491 573468 (also fax no)
Mrs Williams.
D: £25.00-£27.50 **S:** £25.00-£27.50.
Open: All Year (not Xmas)
Beds: 2D 1T
Baths: 2 En 1 Pr
🛏 🅿 (2) ⅍ 🗆 🍴 🎟 🔲 ⅙ ⅌

(0.5m 🚌) *New Lodge, Henley Park, Henley-on-Thames, Oxon, RG9 6HU.*
Actual grid ref: SU758847
Victorian cottage, Area of Outstanding Natural Beauty. Minimum stay two nights.
Tel: 01491 576340 (also fax no)
Mrs Warner.
D: £19.00-£21.00 **S:** £24.00-£27.00.
Open: All Year
Beds: 2D
Baths: 1 En 1 Pr
🛏 🅿 (5) ⅍ 🗆 🍴 🎟 ⅙ 🔲

Please don't camp on *anyone's* land without first obtaining their permission.

Peddars Way and Norfolk Coast Path

Two paths - one ancient and the other brand new - provide an easy-going 98-mile walk through flat but very different landscapes. The **Peddars Way** is a flinty old Roman road, running straight as a die through the heaths, forest and military training grounds of Breckland in West Norfolk up to the sea. At Hunstanton it joins the **Norfolk Coast Path**, which leads among the famous dunes, salt marshes, creeks and shingle ridges of North Norfolk, rich in birds and wildlife. A good path to cut your teeth on over a couple of long weekends or on a week's break in winter or summer. There is also a path association - membership details from the **Peddars Way Association**, 150 Armes Street, Norwich, NR2 4EG.

Guide (available from all good map shops):
Peddars Way & Norfolk Coast Path by Bruce Robinson (ISBN 1 85410 408 X), published by Aurum Press in association with the Countryside Commission and Ordnance Survey, £10.99

Maps: 1:50000 Ordnance Survey Landranger Series: 132, 133 and 134

Comments on the path to the association and to: Peddar's Way Officer, Norfolk Coast Project, 6 Station Road, Wells-next-the-Sea, Norfolk, NR23 1AE.

Thetford 1

National Grid Ref: TL8783

⚋ ⚐ Black Horse, Anchor Hotel

(5.5m) 43 Magdalen Street, *Thetford, Thetford, Norfolk, IP24 2BP.*
House built in 1575 close to town centre.
Tel: **01842 764564**
Mrs Findlay.
D: £36.00-£36.00 **S:** £18.00-£18.00.
Open: All Year (not Xmas/ New Year)
Beds: 2T 1S
Baths: 1 Sh
⊗ ₱ (1) ⌷ ⚐ ⛒ ⓥ ⓐ ⚋

Great Hockham 2

National Grid Ref: TL9492

(2m) Manor Farm, *Vicarage Road, Great Hockham, Thetford, Norfolk, IP24 1PE.*
Actual grid ref: TL951926
Escape to Manor Farm. Relax and unwind at this C16th refurbished farmhouse.
Tel: **01953 498204**
Mrs Thomas.
D: £18.00-£24.00 **S:** £18.00-£21.00.
Open: All Year (not Xmas)
Beds: 1D 1T 1S
Baths: 1 En 1 Sh
₱ (4) ⚿⌷✗⚐⛒ⓥⓐ⚋

Please don't camp on anyone's land without first obtaining their permission.

Thompson 3

National Grid Ref: TL9196

⚋ ⚐ Chequers

(2m) College Farm, *Thompson, Thetford, Norfolk, IP24 1QG.*
Actual grid ref: TL933966
Converted C14th college of priests; 3 acre garden, wonderful breakfasts.
Tel: **01953 483318** (also fax no)
Mrs Garnier.
D: £20.00-£20.00 **S:** £20.00-£20.00.
Open: All Year
Beds: 2D 1T
Baths: 1 Pr 1 Sh 2 En
⊗ (7) ₱ (10) ⌷ ⛒ ⓐ ⚋

All paths are popular: you are well-advised to book ahead

(1.5m 🚌) The Thatched House, *Pockthorpe Corner, Thompson, Thetford, Norfolk, IP24 1PJ.*
16th Century, delightful village on the edge of the Brecklands.
Tel: **01953 483577** Mrs Mills.
D: £20.00 **S:** £25.00.
Open: All Year
Beds: 1D 2T **Baths:** 2 Sh 1 Pr
⊗ (6) ₱ (4) ⚿⌷⚑✗⚐⛒⚿ⓥⓐ⚋

Little Cressingham 4

National Grid Ref: TF8700

⚋ ⚐ White Horse

(On path) Sycamore House, *Little Cressingham, Thetford, Norfolk, IP25 6NE.*
Large country home, tranquil village, luxurious jacuzzi bathroom, numerous attractions.
Tel: **01953 881887** (also fax no)
Mr Wittridge.
D: £22.00-£22.00 **S:** £22.00-£22.00.
Open: All Year
Beds: 2D 1T 1S **Baths:** 1 En 1 Sh
⊗ ₱ (10) ⌷ ⚐ ⛒ ⓥ ⓐ ⚋

D = Price range per person sharing in a double room

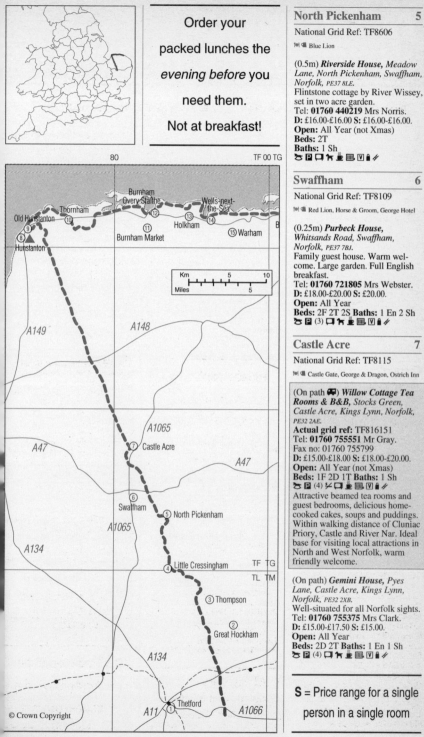

Order your

packed lunches the

evening before you

need them.

Not at breakfast!

80   TF 00 TG

© Crown Copyright

North Pickenham 5

National Grid Ref: TF8606

🍴 🍺 Blue Lion

(0.5m) *Riverside House, Meadow Lane, North Pickenham, Swaffham, Norfolk, PE37 8LE.*
Flintstone cottage by River Wissey, set in two acre garden.
Tel: **01760 440219** Mrs Norris.
D: £16.00-£16.00 **S:** £16.00-£16.00.
Open: All Year (not Xmas)
Beds: 2T
Baths: 1 Sh
🛇 🅿 🖵 🕇 🖢 🎟 Ⅵ ⬥ ∦

Swaffham 6

National Grid Ref: TF8109

🍴 🍺 Red Lion, Horse & Groom, George Hotel

(0.25m) *Purbeck House, Whitsands Road, Swaffham, Norfolk, PE37 7BJ.*
Family guest house. Warm welcome. Large garden. Full English breakfast.
Tel: **01760 721805** Mrs Webster.
D: £18.00-£20.00 **S:** £20.00.
Open: All Year
Beds: 2F 2T 2S **Baths:** 1 En 2 Sh
🛇 🅿 (3) 🖵 🕇 🖢 🎟 Ⅵ ⬥ ∦

Castle Acre 7

National Grid Ref: TF8115

🍴 🍺 Castle Gate, George & Dragon, Ostrich Inn

(On path 🚐) *Willow Cottage Tea Rooms & B&B, Stocks Green, Castle Acre, Kings Lynn, Norfolk, PE32 2AE.*
Actual grid ref: TF816151
Tel: **01760 755551** Mr Gray.
Fax no: 01760 755799
D: £15.00-£18.00 **S:** £18.00-£20.00.
Open: All Year (not Xmas)
Beds: 1F 2D 1T **Baths:** 1 Sh
🛇 🅿 (4) ⬥ 🖵 🖢 🎟 Ⅵ ⬥ ∦
Attractive beamed tea rooms and guest bedrooms, delicious home-cooked cakes, soups and puddings. Within walking distance of Cluniac Priory, Castle and River Nar. Ideal base for visiting local attractions in North and West Norfolk, warm friendly welcome.

(On path) *Gemini House, Pyes Lane, Castle Acre, Kings Lynn, Norfolk, PE32 2XB.*
Well-situated for all Norfolk sights.
Tel: **01760 755375** Mrs Clark.
D: £15.00-£17.50 **S:** £15.00.
Open: All Year
Beds: 2D 2T **Baths:** 1 En 1 Sh
🛇 🅿 (4) 🖵 🕇 🖢 🎟 Ⅵ ⬥ ∦

S = Price range for a single person in a single room

(1m) *Lodge Farm, Castle Acre, Kings Lynn, Norfolk, PE32 2BS.*
Large comfortable farmhouse, gardens and paddocks, near Peddars Way.
Grades: ETC 4 Diamond, AA 4 Diamond
Tel: **01760 755506**
Mrs Coghill.
D: £23.00-£25.00 **S:** £23.00-£25.00.
Open: All Year (not Xmas)
Beds: 3T
Baths: 1 Pr 1 Sh
😃 (5) 🅿 (6) ⵕ⦁🗶 🏠 📖 Ⓥ ⦁ ✦

Hunstanton   8

National Grid Ref: TF6740

🍴 🍺 Golden Lion, Marine Bar, Le Strange Arms, Ancient Mariner, Platters

(▲ 1m) *Hunstanton Youth Hostel, 15 Avenue Road, Hunstanton, Norfolk, PE36 5BW.*
Actual grid ref: TF674406
Tel: **01485 532061**
Under 18: £6.90
Adults: £10.00
Self-catering facilities, Television, Showers, Wet weather shelter, Lounge, Dining room, Drying room, Cycle store, Evening meal at 7.00pm, Kitchen facilities, Luggage store, Credit cards accepted
Large Victorian house in seaside resort with Blue Flag beach, famous for bird and seal watching and ecology studies.

(1.5m) *Kiama Cottage, 23 Austin Street, Hunstanton, Norfolk, PE36 6AN.*
Grades: ETC 3 Diamond
Tel: **01485 533615**
Mr & Mrs Gardiner.
D: £18.00-£25.00
S: £20.00-£25.00.
Open: All year (not Xmas)
Beds: 2F 2D
Baths: 3 En 1 Pr
😃 ⵕ⦁🗶 🏠 📖 Ⓥ ⦁ ✦
A warm welcome awaits you at our Victorian-style cottage located in a quiet residential area and ideally situated for visiting Hunstanton attractions and West Norfolk generally. Hosts Neville & Beverley are well travelled and are sensitive to your needs.

🚐 sign means that, *given due notice,* owners will pick you up from the path and drop you off *within reason.*

All paths are popular: you are well-advised to book ahead

(2m 🚐) *Peacock House, 28 Park Road, Hunstanton, Norfolk, PE36 5BY.*
A large warm and comfortable Victorian house serving memorable breakfasts.
Grades: ETC 3 Diamond
Tel: **01485 534551**
Mrs Sandercock.
D: £17.50-£24.50 **S:** £24.00-£30.00.
Open: All Year
Beds: 1F 1T 1D
Baths: 3 En
😃 (5) ⵕ⦁🗶 🏠 📖 Ⓥ ⦁ ✦

(2m) *The Gables, 28 Austin Street, Hunstanton, PE36 6AW.*
Recently refurbished attractive Edwardian home retaining many original features.
Grades: ETC 4 Diamond, AA 4 Diamond
Tel: **01485 532514** Mrs Bamfield.
D: £17.00-£23.00 .
Open: All Year
Beds: 5F 1D 1T
Baths: 5 En
😃 ⵕ⦁🗶 🗶 🏠 📖 Ⓥ ⦁ ✦

(1m) *Rosamaly Guest House, 14 Glebe Avenue, Hunstanton, Norfolk, PE36 6BS.*
Warm, friendly atmosphere. Hearty breakfasts, tasty evening meals. Comfy ensuite bedrooms, quiet, convenient location.
Grades: ETC 3 Diamond
Tel: **01485 534187** Mrs Duff Dick.
D: £18.00-£23.00 **S:** £20.00-£25.00.
Open: All Year (not Xmas)
Beds: 1F 3D 1T 1S **Baths:** 5 En
😃 🅿 🗶 🗶 🏠 📖 Ⓥ ✦

(2m) *Burleigh Hotel, 7 Cliff Terrace, Hunstanton, Norfolk, PE36 6DY.*
Victorian family-run hotel, close to sea front and gardens.
Grades: ETC 4 Diamond
Tel: **01485 533080**
Mr & Mrs Abos.
D: £21.00-£25.00 **S:** £23.00-£25.00.
Open: All Year
Beds: 4F 4D 2T 1S
Baths: 9 En 2 Pr
😃 (5) 🅿 (7) 🗶 🗶 🏠 📖 Ⓥ ⦁ ✦

(2m) *Sutton House Hotel, 24 Northgate, Hunstanton, Norfolk, PE36 6AP.*
Edwardian house near town/sea.
Tel: **01485 532552** (also fax no)
Mr Emsdon.
D: £20.00-£27.00 **S:** £25.00-£25.00.
Open: All Year
Beds: 2F 2D 3T 1S **Baths:** 8 En
😃 (1) 🅿 (5) 🗶 🗶 🗶 🏠 📖 Ⓥ ⦁ ✦

(2m) *Ellinbrook Guest House, 37 Avenue Road, Hunstanton, Norfolk, PE36 5HW.*
Friendly family establishment situated 5 minutes from seafront and shops.
Tel: **01485 532022**
Mr & Mrs Vass.
D: £15.00-£21.00
S: £15.00-£21.00.
Open: All Year (not Xmas)
Beds: 2F 2D 1T 1S
Baths: 1 Sh
😃 🅿 (5) ⵕ⦁🗶 🗶 🏠 📖 Ⓥ ⦁

Old Hunstanton   9

National Grid Ref: TF6842

🍴 🍺 Mariners Inn

(1m) *Cobbler's Cottage, 3 Wodehouse Road, Old Hunstanton, Hunstanton, Norfolk, PE36 6JD.*
Quietly situated 500 yards from sandy natural beach. Birdwatching at Titchwell, Snettisham Holme.
Tel: **01485 534036**
Ms Poore.
D: £20.00-£27.00
S: £27.00-£32.00.
Open: Feb to Nov
Beds: 1D 2T
Baths: 3 En
🅿 (8) 🗶 🗶 🏠 📖 Ⓥ ✦

Thornham   10

National Grid Ref: TF7343

🍴 🍺 King's Head, The Lifeboat, Titchwell Manor

(On path 🚐) *Orchard House, Thornham, Hunstanton, Norfolk, PE36 6LY.*
Tucked away in large garden, centre of conservation village.
Grades: ETC 4 Diamond
Tel: **01485 512259**
Mrs Rutland.
D: £22.50-£30.00
S: £35.00-£45.00.
Open: All Year (not Xmas Day)
Beds: 2T 2D
Baths: 3 En 1 Pr
😃 (8) 🅿 (6) ⵕ⦁🗶 🏠 📖 Ⓥ ⦁ ✦

Burnham Market   11

National Grid Ref: TF8342

🍴 🍺 Host Arms

(1m 🚐) *Wood Lodge, Millwood, Herrings Lane, Burnham Market, King's Lynn, Norfolk, PE31 8DP.*
Peaceful, luxurious coastal lodge.
Grades: ETC 4 Daimond
Tel: **01328 730152**
Mrs Leftley.
Fax no: 01328 730158
D: £27.50-£30.00
S: £35.00-£45.00.
Open: All Year (not Xmas)
Beds: 1D 1T
😃 (8) 🅿 ⵕ⦁🗶 🗶 🏠 📖 Ⓥ

Burnham Overy Staithe 12

National Grid Ref: TF8444

|●| ◁| The Hero

(0.25m) *Domville Guest House,*
Glebe Lane, Burnham Overy
Staithe, Kings Lynn, Norfolk,
PE31 8JQ.
Quietly situated family-run guest
house. Home cooking a speciality.
Grades: ETC 3 Diamond
Tel: **01328 738298** (also fax no)
Mrs Smith.
D: £18.00-£23.00 **S:** £20.00-£25.00.
Open: All Year (not Xmas)
Beds: 2T 3S 2D **Baths:** 4 En
ᗡ (6) ☑ (10) ⅍☐✗⚲ₓ Ⅵ⌂⚡

Holkham 13

National Grid Ref: TF8943

|●| ◁| The Nelson

(1m ☏) *Peterstone Cutting,*
Peterstone, Holkham, Wells-next-
the-Sea, Norfolk, NR23 1RR.
Peterstone Cutting nestles in the
old railway cutting, adjacent to
Holkham Hall Parkland.
Tel: **01328 730171** (also fax no)
Mr & Mrs Platt.
D: £18.00-£24.00 **S:** £30.00-£40.00.
Open: All Year (not Xmas)
Beds: 4D 1T **Baths:** 1 En 1 Pr 1 Sh
ᗡ ☑ (4) ⅍✗⚲ₓ⛬Ⅵ⌂⚡

Wells-next-the-Sea 14

National Grid Ref: TF9143

|●| ◁| Crown Hotel, The Edinburgh, Ark Royal,
Lifeboat Inn, Three Horseshoes

(0.5m ☏) *Greengates, Stiffkey*
Road, Wells-next-the-Sea, Norfolk,
NR23 1QB.
Actual grid ref: TF9243
C18th cottage with views over salt
marsh to sea.
Tel: **01328 711040** Mrs Jarvis.
D: £19.00-£23.00 **S:** £20.00-£25.00.
Open: All Year (not Xmas)
Beds: 1D 1T **Baths:** 1 En 1 Pr 1 Sh
☑ (2) ⅍☐⚲ₓ₍ₘₗ₎Ⅵ

(On path ☏) *East House, East*
Quay, Wells-next-the-Sea, Norfolk,
NR23 1LE.
Actual grid ref: TF921437
Old house overlooking marsh,
creeks and boats to distant sea.
Tel: **01328 710408** Mrs Scott.
D: £22.50-£22.50 **S:** £26.00-£26.00.
Open: All Year (not Xmas)
Beds: 2T **Baths:** 2 En
ᗡ (7) ☑ (2) ☐⚲ₓₘₗ⚡

All rates are subject
to alteration at the
owners' discretion.

Planning a longer
stay? Always ask for
any special rates.

(0.25m ☏) *St Heliers Guest*
House, Station Road, Wells-next-
the-Sea, Norfolk, NR25 1EA.
Actual grid ref: TF917436
Central Georgian family house in
secluded gardens with excellent
breakfasts.
Tel: **01328 710361** (also fax no)
Mrs Kerr.
D: £16.00-£25.00 **S:** £18.00-£30.00.
Open: 10 months
Beds: 1D 1T 1S **Baths:** 2 Sh 1 En
☑ (4) ⅍☐⚲ₓₘₗ Ⅵ⌂⚡

(On path) *Mill House, Northfield*
Lane, Wells-next-the-Sea, Norfolk,
NR23 1JZ.
Mill House: a former mill-owner's
house in secluded gardens.
Tel: **01328 710739** Mr Downey.
D: £17.00 **S:** £17.50.
Open: All Year
Beds: 1F 3D 3T 2S
Baths: 1F En 2 Pr
ᗡ (8) ☑ (10) ☐⚲ₓₘₗ⛬Ⅵ⌂

(0.5m) *The Warren, Warham*
Road, Wells-next-the-Sea, Norfolk,
NR23 1NE.
Actual grid ref: TF922430
Ideally situated for ornithologists,
walkers, cyclists, beach lovers and
historians.
Tel: **01328 710273** Mrs Wickens.
D: £20.00-£20.00 **S:** £22.00-£25.00.
Open: All Year (not Xmas)
Beds: 1D 1T **Baths:** 1 En 1 Pr
☑ (2) ⅍☐⚲ₘₗ Ⅵ

(0.5m) *Brooklands, 31 Burnt*
Street, Wells-next-the-Sea, Norfolk,
NR23 1HP.
Charming beamed 250-year-old
house. Delightful cottage garden.
Tel: **01328 710768** Mrs Wykes.
D: £16.00-£16.00 **S:** £20.00.
Open: Apr to Oct
Beds: 1F 1D **Baths:** 1 Sh
ᗡ (7) ☑ (2) ⅍☐⚲⛬ₘₗⅤ

Warham 15

National Grid Ref: TF9441

|●| ◁| Three Horseshoes

(1m ☏) *The Three Horseshoes /*
The Old Post Office, 69 Bridge
Street, Warham, Wells-next-the-
Sea, Norfolk, NR21 1NL.
Dream country cottage adjoining
award-winning village pub.
Tel: **01328 710547** Mr Salmon.
D: £24.00-£26.00 **S:** £24.00-£24.00.
Open: All Year (not Xmas)
Beds: 3D 1S **Baths:** 1 En 1 Sh
ᗡ (14) ☑ (10) ⅍☐⚲✗⚲ₓₘₗ⌂

Blakeney 16

National Grid Ref: TG0243

|●| ◁| Kings Arms, White Horse

(On path ☏) *White Barn,*
Back Lane, Blakeney, Norfolk,
NR25 7NP.
Delightful ensuite annexe with
individual access near Blakeney
Quay.
Tel: **01263 741359** (also fax no)
Mr & Mrs Millard.
D: £20.00-£20.00 **S:** £25.00-£35.00.
Open: All Year (not Xmas)
Beds: 1D 1T **Baths:** 2 En
☑ (5) ⅍☐⚲ₘₗ Ⅵ⌂⚡

(On path) *Dallinga, 71 Morston Rd,*
Blakeney, Holt, Norfolk, NR25 7BD.
Tel: **01263 740943**
Mr & Mrs Ward.
D: £18.75-£21.25 .
Open: All Year
Beds: 1D 1T **Baths:** 2 En
ᗡ (12) ☑ (6) ☐⚲ₘₗ Ⅵ⌂
4-5 minutes walk to Blakeney
Quay. Excellent breakfast menu
from local produce and fish.

Cley-next-the-Sea 17

National Grid Ref: TG0443

|●| ◁| George & Dragon, Three Swallows

(On path) *Cley Windmill, Cley-*
next-the-Sea, Holt, Norfolk,
NR25 7NN.
Actual grid ref: TG045441
Historic windmill overlooking
beautiful unspoilt Norfolk coastal
marshes. Wonderfully atmospheric.
Tel: **01263 740209** (also fax no)
Mr Bolam.
D: £35.00-£49.00 **S:** £70.00-£70.00.
Open: All Year
Beds: 4D 3T
Baths: 7 Pr
ᗡ ☑ (12) ☐⚲✗⚲ₘₗ⛬Ⅵ

(On path ☏) *Marshlands, High*
Street, Cley-next-the-Sea, Holt,
Norfolk, NR25 7RB.
Actual grid ref: TG045438
Victorian old town hall house, with
warm and friendly atmosphere.
Tel: **01263 740284**
Mr & Mrs Kinsella.
D: £16.00 **S:** £28.00.
Open: All Year (not Xmas/
New Year)
Beds: 1D 2T
Baths: 2 En 1 Pr
ᗡ (12) ⅍☐⚲✗⚲ₘₗ Ⅵ⌂⚡

Bringing children with
you? Always ask for
any special rates.

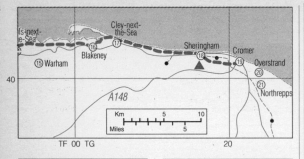

Sheringham 18

National Grid Ref: TG1543

🏨 🍴 Two Lifeboats, Crown, Wyndham Arms, Sherry & Ham, Lobster, Crown, Marmalade, Red Lion

(▲ 0.25m) *Sheringham Youth Hostel, 1 Cremer's Drift, Sheringham, Norfolk, NR26 8BJ.*
Actual grid ref: TG159428
Tel: **01263 823215**
Under 18: £7.75 **Adults:** £11.00
Self-catering facilities, Self-catering facilities, Television, Lounge, Dining room, Drying room, Cycle store, Parking, Evening meal at 6.00 to 7.00pm, Facilities for disabled people, Facilities for disabled people, Kitchen facilities, Breakfast available, Credit cards accepted
Victorian building with modern annexe & facilities for disabled. Wide sandy beaches, good birdwatching & a seal colony on this coast.

(0.25m) *Sheringham Lodge, 50 Cromer Road, Sheringham, Norfolk, NR26 8RS.*
Grades: ETC 3 Diamond
Tel: **01263 821954**
Mr & Mrs Hare.
D: £18.00-£21.00
S: £18.00-£21.00.
Open: All Year
Beds: 5F 1T 3D 1S
Baths: 1 En 3 Pr 1 Sh
🛇 (5) 🅿 ⊠ (6) ⍝ 🗆 🛆 📺 ♥
Attractive guest house run by Gordon and Jean Hare with ensuite facilities to most rooms. Residents lounge with TV and video. Very close to town centre, railway station and bus stop. Discounts for senior citizens.

High season, bank holidays and special events mean low availability *everywhere*.

Always telephone to get directions to the B&B - you will save time!

(0.25m) *The Melrose, 9 Holway Road, Sheringham, Norfolk, NR26 8HN.*
Grades: ETC 3 Diamond
Tel: **01263 823299** Parsonage.
D: £20.00-£22.00 **S:** £20.00-£27.00.
Open: All Year
Beds: 1F 2T 2D 1S
Baths: 6 En
🛇 🅿 🗆 🛆 ✗ 🛆 📺 ♥ ⋔
We are in walking distance of rail and bus stations, town centre and beach. Dine by firelight in winter - we have a licensed bar.

(0.25m) *Whelk Coppers, Westcliff, Sheringham, Norfolk, NR26 8LD.*
Tel: **01263 825771** Foster.
D: £17.00-£20.00 **S:** £17.00-£20.00.
Open: All Year (not Xmas/New Year)
Beds: 1F 1D
Baths: 1 En 1 Pr
🛇 🗆 📺 ♥
Traditional English tea-rooms panelled in Indian teak from old sailing ship, views over sea front & golf course. All that can be heard are the sounds of the sea yet only 2 minutes walk from a wealth of pubs, restaurants and interesting shops.

(0.25m) *The Bay-Leaf Guest House, 10 St Peters Road, Sheringham, Norfolk, NR26 8QY.*
Charming Victorian licensed guest house, nestled between steam railway and sea.
Grades: ETC 3 Diamond, AA 3 Diamond
Tel: **01263 823779**
Mr Pigott.
D: £18.00-£22.00 **S:** £20.00-£25.00.
Open: All Year
Beds: 2F 3D 2T
Baths: 7 En
🛇 🅿 (4) 🗆 🛆 📺 🛆 ♥ ⋔

(0.25m) *The Birches, 27 Holway Road, Sheringham, Norfolk, NR26 8HW.*
Grades: AA 4 Diamond
Tel: **01263 823550** Ms Pearce.
D: £20.00-£25.00 **S:** £25.00-£25.00.
Open: April to Oct
Beds: 1D 1T
Baths: 2 En
🛇 (12) 🅿 (2) ⍝ 🗆 ✗ 🛆 📺 🛆 ♥ ⋔
Small guest house conveniently situated for town and sea front. Ideal centre for touring North Norfolk. Attractions include The North Norfolk Railway, National Trust Properties, some of England's best bird watching areas and award winning beaches.

(0.25m) *Canton House, 14 Cliff Road, Sheringham, Norfolk, NR26 8BJ.*
Warm welcome. Comfortable surroundings. Excellent breakfast. Home made bread.
Tel: **01263 824861** Ms Rayment.
D: £20.50-£21.00 **S:** £20.50-£21.00.
Open: All Year (not Xmas/New Year)
Beds: 1F 1T 1D
Baths: 2 En 2 Sh
🛇 (1) 🗆 🛆 ✗ 🛆 📺 ♥

(0.25m ⊕) *The Old Vicarage, Sheringham, Norfolk, NR26 8NH.*
Excellent accommodation, comfortable, well-furnished bedsitting rooms. Superb breakfasts. Quiet location.
Tel: **01263 822627** Mrs Lees.
D: £25.00-£27.00 **S:** £28.00-£40.00.
Open: Mar to Nov
Beds: 1D 1T **Baths:** 3 En
🛇 (12) 🅿 (6) 🗆 🛆 ✗ 🛆 📺 🛆 ♥ ⋔

(0.25m) *Sans Souci, 19 Waterbank Rd, Sheringham, Norfolk, NR26 8RB.*
A charming Victorian guest house, 3 minutes from all amenities.
Tel: **01263 824436** Mrs Majewski.
D: £17.00-£20.00 **S:** £17.00-£20.00.
Open: Easter to Oct
Beds: 1D 1T 1S **Baths:** 1 Sh
🛇 🅿 (3) ⍝ 🗆 🛆 🛆 📺 ♥ ⋔

(0.25m ⊕) *Holly Cottage, 14a The Rise, Sheringham, Norfolk, NR26 8QB.*
Beamed cottage, quiet area, ground floor ensuite. Special winter breaks.
Tel: **01263 822807** Mrs Perkins.
D: £13.33-£25.00 **S:** £18.00-£34.00.
Open: All Year (not Xmas)
Beds: 1D 1T
Baths: 2 En 1 Pr
🛇 🅿 (2) ⍝ 🗆 🛆 📺 🛆 ♥ ⋔

All paths are popular: you are well-advised to book ahead

(0.25m) *Montague Lodge,*
1 Montague Road, Sheringham,
Norfolk, NR26 8LN.
Large house in quiet road.
Tel: **01263 822267** Mrs Childs.
D: £16.50-£22.50 **S:** £16.50.
Open: All Year (not Xmas)
Beds: 4F 2D 2T 1S
Baths: 5 En 5 Pr 1 Sh
⛺ (10) ▯ ▢ ★ ✕ ♨ Ⅲ, ♿ Ⅴ ▮

Cromer   19

National Grid Ref: TG2142

🍴 🍺 Red Lion

(0.25m) *Cambridge House, Sea*
Front, East Cliff, Cromer, Norfolk,
NR27 9HD.
Superb uninterrupted sea views
above the promenade and beach.
Good touring base.
Grades: ETC 3 Diamond
Tel: **01263 512085** Mrs Wass.
D: £18.00-£25.00 **S:** £18.00-£25.00.
Open: All Year (not Xmas/
New Year)
Beds: 3F 1D 1S
Baths: 3 En 1 Pr 1 Sh
⛺ ▯ (5) ⅍ ▢ ★ ✕ ♨ Ⅲ, Ⅴ ▮ ✦

(1m 🚐) *Crowmere Guest House, 4*
Vicarage Road, Cromer, Norfolk,
NR27 9DQ.
Charming Victorian house. Situated
conveniently for beach and town.
Quiet location.
Grades: AA 3 Diamond
Tel: **01263 513056** Ms Marriott.
D: £17.00-£20.00 **S:** £20.00-£40.00.
Open: Easter to Oct
Beds: 1F 2D 1T **Baths:** 4 En
⛺ ▯ (4) ⅍ ▢ ♨ Ⅲ, Ⅴ ✦

Overstrand   20

National Grid Ref: TG2440

🍴 🍺 White Horse

(0.5m) *Danum House, 22 Pauls*
Lane, Overstrand, Cromer,
Norfolk, NR27 0PE.
Built in 1818 in the popular
Poppyland Coastal Area of North
Norfolk.
Tel: **01263 579327** (also fax no)
Mr Sim.
D: £16.00-£19.00 **S:** £16.00-£19.00.
Open: All Year
Beds: 2F 2D 2T **Baths:** 5 En
⛺ ▯ (4) ▢ ★ ♨ Ⅲ, Ⅴ

Northrepps   21

National Grid Ref: TG2439

(4m) *Shrublands Farm,*
Northrepps, Cromer, Norfolk,
NR27 0AA.
Shrublands is a 300 acre family
arable farm 2 miles south-east of
Cromer.
Tel: **01263 579297** (also fax no)
Mrs Youngman.
D: £21.00-£23.00 **S:** £25.00-£27.00.
Open: All Year (not Xmas)
Beds: 1D 2T
⛺ ▯ (4) ⅍ ▢ ✕ ♨ Ⅲ, Ⅴ ✦

Taking your dog?

Book *in advance*

ONLY with owners

who accept dogs (🐕)

Pennine Way

This is the great-grandfather of all the National Trails in Britain, running for 256 miles along Britain's backbone, the great upland mass of hills and dales that divides the East and West of the country. Officially opened in 1965, the path has actually been developing since the 1930s: it runs from Edale in Derbyshire right the way up to Kirk Yetholm, just inside the Scottish border. It is still probably the toughest trail of the lot and should be attempted only by fit, experienced fell-walkers, fully equipped for rough weather, boggy conditions and mist. There are stretches, especially towards the North, where accommodation is very sparse and well off the beaten track. Take care therefore with the logistics of your route-planning - this is not a path to be under-estimated; many set out only to have their resolve broken by the testing conditions after a couple of days! This said, the walking is superb, passing bare moors, bogs, industrial landscape, limestone country, dales and meadowland, rugged valleys with racing rivers, Hadrian's Wall, conifer forest and the bleak, dramatic Border ridge of the Cheviot massif. To get an idea of the first-class walking country in the North of England, it can't be beaten. Why attempt the path all in one go? Spend a summer doing it bit by bit. There are stretches that make ideal weekend walks, which test the stamina less and make the walk more memorable. That's part of the reason for this book - to show that you don't have to yomp the whole trail at once.

The Youth Hostels Association run a useful Accommodation Booking Bureau for the **Pennine Way**, based on their hostels and local B&Bs along the path. Ring 01629 825850 and ask for the Pennine Way Booking Bureau Pack and they can sort out your entire itinerary without further ado.

Guides (available from all major bookshops unless stated):
Pennine Way South: Edale to Bowes (ISBN 1 85410 3210) and *Pennine Way North: Bowes to Kirk Yetholm* (ISBN 1 85410 0181), both by Tony Hopkins and published by Aurum Press in association with the Countryside Commission and Ordnance Survey, £10.99

A Guide to the Pennine Way by C J Wright (ISBN 09 470640 9), published by Constable & Co Ltd, £10.95

Maps: 1:50000 Ordnance Survey Landranger Series: 74, 80, 86, 87, 91, 92, 98, 103, 109 and 110.
The Pennine Way, Part One - South, ISBN 1 871149 01 0 (4-colour linear route map) and *The Pennine Way, Part Two - North*, ISBN 1 871149 02 9 (4-colour linear route map), both published by Footprint and available from all good map shops or directly from their offices (Unit 87, Stirling Enterprise Park, Stirling, FK7 7RP), £3.50 (+ 40p p&p) each.

All comments on the path to: **Tony Philpin**, Pennine Way Coordinator, Area Countryside Office, Clegg Nook, Cragg Road, Mytholmroyd, W. Yorks, HX7 5EB.

Castleton	1

National Grid Ref: SK1582

🍴 🍺 George Hotel, Castle Hotel

(▲ 4m) *Castleton Youth Hostel*, Castleton Hall, Castleton, Hope Valley, *S33 8WG*.
Actual grid ref: SK150828
Tel: **01433 620235**
Under 18: £7.75 **Adults:** £11.00
Self-catering facilities, Television, Showers, Licensed bar, Lounge, Games room, Drying room, Cycle store, Evening meal at 6.00-7.00pm, Kitchen facilities, Breakfast available, Luggage store, Credit cards accepted
Comprising an C18th hall and C19th vicarage, this centrally-placed hostel is ideal for families and perfect for exploring the Peak District National Park.

(4m 🚌) *Bray Cottage*, Market Place, Castleton, Hope Valley, *S33 8WQ*.
Actual grid ref: SK150827
Charming C18th cottage, excellent accommodation, hearty breakfast, very friendly atmosphere.
Tel: **01433 621532** Mrs Heard.
D: £21.00-£21.00 **S:** £23.00-£23.00.
Open: All Year (not Xmas)
Beds: 2D
Baths: 1 En 1 Pr
♿ 🅿 (1) ⚡ 🗙 🍴 ⚓ 🎦 Ⅲ Ⓥ ♟ ✦

Please take muddy boots <u>off</u> before entering premises

S = Price range for a single person in a room

Edale 2

National Grid Ref: SK1285

🍴 🍺 Nags Head, Rambler Inn, Cheshire Cheese, Poachers' Arms

(▲ 1.5m) *Edale Youth Hostel,*
Rowland Cote, Nether Booth,
Edale, Hope Valley, Derbyshire,
S33 7ZH.
Actual grid ref: SJ139865
Tel: **01433 670302**
Under 18: £7.75 **Adults:** £11.00
Showers, Licensed bar, Laundry
facilities, Lounge, Games room,
Grounds available for games,
Drying room, Parking, Evening
meal at 5.30-7.15pm, Kitchen
facilities, Breakfast available,
Credit cards accepted
*Large former private house set in
extensive grounds on hillside below
Kinder Scout Plateau.*

D = Price range per person sharing in a double room

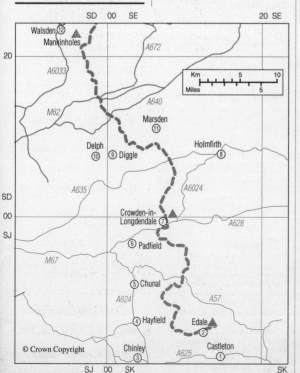
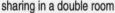
© Crown Copyright

(On path) *The Old Parsonage,*
Grindsbrook, Edale, Hope Valley,
S33 7ZD.
Actual grid ref: SK123861
Secluded C17th house & garden.
Walk straight into the hills.
Tel: **01433 670232** Mrs Beney.
D: £15.00-£15.50 **S:** £15.00-£15.50.
Open: Mar to Oct
Beds: 1D 1T 1S
Baths: 1 Sh
🛇 🅿 (1) 💢 🗭 🍲 🖳 Ⅴ 🛡 ≉

(On path) *Mam Tor House,*
Grindsbrook, Edale, Hope Valley,
Derbyshire, S33 7ZA.
Edwardian family home, 2 minutes
from start of Pennine way.
Tel: **01433 670253** Mrs Jackson.
D: £17.50-£17.50 **S:** £17.50-£17.50.
Open: All Year
Beds: 1F 2T
🛇 🅿 (4) 🗭 🗡 🗭 🍲 🖳 🕭 Ⅴ 🛡 ≉

(0.5m) *Brookfield, Edale, Hope*
Valley, S33 7ZL.
Actual grid ref: SK113847
Peaceful, high-quality accommoda-
tion, outstanding views, excellent
food and beds.
Grades: ETC 2 Diamond
Tel: **01433 670227** Mrs Chapman.
D: £18.00 **S:** £20.00.
Open: Easter to Oct
Beds: 1D 1T
Baths: 1 Sh
🅿 (3) 💢 🗭 🍲 🖳 Ⅴ 🛡 ≉

(On path) *Stonecroft, Grindsbrook,*
Edale, Hope Valley, S33 7ZA.
Luxury country house accommoda-
tion in spectacular situation
amongst Derbyshire Hills.
Grades: ETC 4 Diamond, Silver
Tel: **01433 670262** (also fax no)
Mrs Reid.
D: £26.00-£29.00 **S:** £36.00-£39.00.
Open: All Year (not Xmas)
Beds: 2D
Baths: 1 En 1 Pr
🛇 (12) 🅿 (2) 💢 🗭 🗡 🍲 🖳 Ⅴ 🛡 ≉

Chinley 3

National Grid Ref: SK0482

🍴 🍺 Crown & Mitre, Squirrels Hotel, Cross Keys Inn

(2.5m 🚍) *Craigside, 4 Buxton*
Road, Chinley, High Peak, SK23 6DJ.
Warm welcome, small, clean, com-
fortable. Good walking and cycling
location.
Tel: **01663 750604** Mrs Cameron.
D: £16.00-£20.00 **S:** £16.00-£20.00.
Open: All Year (not Xmas)
Beds: 1D 1T 1S
Baths: 1 Sh
🛇 🅿 (2) 🗭 🗡 🍲 🖳 Ⅴ ≉

(2m) *Mosley House Farm,*
Maynestone Road, Chinley, High
Peak, SK23 6AH.
Actual grid ref: SK0482
Family farm in Peak District, offer-
ing comfort and hospitality.
Ensuite facilities.
Grades: ETC 3 Diamond
Tel: **01663 750240** (also fax no)
Mrs Goddard.
D: £19.00-£20.00 **S:** £20.00-£22.00.
Open: All Year (not Xmas/
New Year)
Beds: 1F 2D **Baths:** 1 En 1 Pr
🛇 🅿 (4) 🗭 🍲 🖳 Ⅴ 🛡

Hayfield 4

National Grid Ref: SK0386

🍴 🍺 Lantern Pike, The Grouse, Pack Horse

(3.25m) *Shudehill, Hayfield, High*
Peak, SK22 2EP.
Actual grid ref: SK035872
Private suite, C1700 farmhouse,
charming village, great pubs,
wonderful walks.
Tel: **01663 742784** Sadleir.
Fax no: 07971 046755
D: £25.00-£25.00 **S:** £27.00-£27.00.
Open: All Year (not Xmas)
Beds: 1T
Baths: 1 Pr
🅿 (1) 💢 🗭 🍲 🖳 Ⅴ ≉

All rates are subject to alteration at the owners' discretion.

🚌 sign means that, *given due notice*, owners will pick you up from the path and drop you off *within reason*.

Chunal 5

National Grid Ref: SK0491

🍴 🍺 Grouse Inn

(5m) *Stanley Farm, Chunal, Glossop, Derbyshire, SK13 9JY.*
Actual grid ref: SK035915
Beautiful country house in wonderful location offers friendly welcome.
Tel: **01457 863727**
Mrs Brown.
D: £20.00-£20.00
S: £20.00-£25.00.
Open: All Year
Beds: 1F 1D 1T
Baths: 1 En 1 Sh
🛇 **P** (20) ⅋ ☐ ✕ 🌲 🎍 Ⅲ. Ⅴ 🛢 ⌗

Padfield 6

National Grid Ref: SK0296

(3m) *The Peels Arms, Temple Street, Padfield, Hyde, Cheshire, SK14 7ET.*
Country inn, oak beams, log fires, real ale, fine foods.
Manchester/Sheffield 40 minutes.
Grades: ETC 3 Diamond
Tel: **01457 852719** Mrs Murray.
Fax no: 01457 850536
D: £20.00-£25.00 **S:** £25.00-£25.00.
Open: All Year
Beds: 3D 2T
Baths: 3 En 1 Sh
🛇 **P** (20) ☐ 🎍 ✕ 🌲 🎍 Ⅲ. Ⅴ 🛢 ⌗

Crowden 7

National Grid Ref: SK0799

(▲ On path) *Crowden Youth Hostel, Crowden, Glossop, Derbyshire, SK14 7HZ.*
Actual grid ref: SJ073995
Tel: **01457 852135**
Under 18: £6.50
Adults: £9.25
Self-catering facilities, Showers, Lounge, Dining room, Drying room, Cycle store, Evening meal at 7.30pm, No smoking, WC, Kitchen facilities, Breakfast available, Credit cards accepted
Formerly a row of railwaymen's cottages, right on the Pennine Way in a remote part of Longdendale.

Holmfirth 8

National Grid Ref: SE1408

🍴 🍺 Victoria Inn, Royal Oak, Old Bridge

(1m 🚌) *Holme Castle Country Hotel, Holme Village, Holmfirth, Huddersfield, W. Yorks, HD7 1QG.*
Actual grid ref: SE110017
Grades: AA 4 Diamond
Tel: **01484 680680** Ms Hayfield.
Fax no: 01484 686764
D: £27.50-£37.50 **S:** £35.00-£55.00.
Open: All Year
Beds: 1F 2T 4D 1S
Baths: 5 Pr 1 Sh
🛇 **P** (12) ⅋ ☐ ✕ 🌲 🎍 Ⅲ. Ⅴ 🛢 ⌗
Unusual mill house in Peak Park. 8 unique bedrooms, splendid views. Oak panelling, antiques, open fires. Hospitality, delicious fresh food, world wines. 'Room with a view' gallery cafe. Meetings, celebrations, midweek offers. Established 1983. A6024 2.5 miles SW Holmfirth.

(5m 🚌) *Springfield House, 95 Huddersfield Road, Holmfirth, Huddersfield, W. Yorks, HD7 1JA.*
Victorian house on bus route in 'Last of the Summer Wine' town.
Grades: ETC 3 Diamond
Tel: **01484 683031** (also fax no)
Mr Brook.
D: £16.00-£18.50 **S:** £21.00-£24.00.
Open: All Year
Beds: 2F1D 1T
Baths: 2 En 1 Sh
🛇 **P** (2) ⅋ ☐ 🎍 🌲 🎍 Ⅲ. Ⅴ 🛢 ⌗

(3.5m 🚌) *Valley Guest House, 97 Huddersfield Road, Holmfirth, Huddersfield, W. Yorks, HD7 1JA.*
Comfortable warm spacious Georgian residence, near M1 and M62 network.
Tel: **01484 681361**
Mr & Mrs Kilner.
D: £17.00-£19.00
S: £23.00-£26.00.
Open: All Year
Beds: 1F 1D 1T
Baths: 2 En 1 Sh
🛇 (3) **P** (3) ⅋ ☐ 🎍 🌲 🎍 Ⅲ. Ⅴ 🛢 ⌗

Diggle 9

National Grid Ref: SE0008

🍴 🍺 Diggle Hotel, Floating Light, Church Inn, Navigation Inn

(0.5m 🚌) *New Barn, Harrop Green Farm, Diggle, Oldham, Lancs, OL3 5LW.*
Working farm, lovely views over Saddleworth villages. Close to Standedge Canal Tunnel.
Tel: **01457 873937**
Mr Rhodes.
D: £16.00-£17.00
S: £16.00-£18.00.
Open: All Year (not Xmas)
Beds: 1F 1D 1T 1S
Baths: 1 Pr 1 Sh
🛇 **P** (10) ☐ 🎍 🌲 🎍 Ⅲ. Ⅴ 🛢 ⌗

(1.5m 🚌) *Sunfield, Diglea, Diggle, Saddleworth, Oldham, Lancs, OL3 5LA.*
Actual grid ref: SE00908
Scenic Saddleworth Canal towpaths, walking, cycling, horse riding, its all here.
Tel: **01457 874030**
Mr & Mrs Francis.
Fax no: 01457 810488
D: £15.00-£18.00 **S:** £20.00-£25.00.
Open: All Year
Beds: 1F 3D 2T 1S **Baths:** 7 En
🛇 **P** (8) ⅋ ☐ 🎍 🌲 🎍 Ⅲ. & Ⅴ 🛢 ⌗

Delph 10

National Grid Ref: SD9807

🍴 🍺 Old Bell

(1.75m 🚌) *Old Bell Inn Hotel, Delph, Oldham, Lancs, OL3 5EG.*
Actual grid ref: SD988075
C18th coaching inn. Delightful bedrooms. Fine food and ales.
Tel: **01457 870130** Mr Grew.
Fax no: 01457 876597
D: £25.00-£35.00 **S:** £30.00-£35.00.
Open: All Year
Beds: 6D 1T 3S **Baths:** 9 En 1 Pr
🛇 **P** (25) ☐ 🎍 ✕ 🌲 🎍 Ⅲ. Ⅴ 🛢 ⌗

(0.25m) *Globe Farm Guest House, Huddersfield Road, Standedge, Delph, Oldham, Lancashire, OL3 5LU.*
Actual grid ref: SE012097
Former coaching house converted into comfortable ensuite bed & breakfast.
Tel: **01457 873040** (also fax no)
D: £19.75 **S:** £25.00.
Open: All Year (not Xmas)
Beds: 1F 5D 4T 4S **Baths:** 14 En
🛇 **P** (30) ☐ ✕ 🌲 🎍 Ⅴ 🛢 ⌗

Marsden 11

National Grid Ref: SE0411

🍴 🍺 White House, Olive Branch, Coach & Horses, Carriage House

(0.25m 🚌) *Throstle Nest Cottage, 3 Old Mount Road, Marsden, Huddersfield, West Yorkshire, HD7 6DU.*
Olde Worlde C17th country cottage in beautiful Colne Valley. Close to all amenities.
Grades: ETC 3 Diamond
Tel: **01484 846371** (also fax no)
Ms Hayes.
D: £15.00-£20.00 **S:** £18.00-£20.00.
Open: All Year (not Xmas)
Beds: 1F 1T **Baths:** 1 Sh
🛇 (2) **P** (3) ☐ 🎍 🌲 🎍 Ⅲ. Ⅴ ⌗

Planning a longer stay? Always ask for any special rates.

D = Price range per person sharing in a double room

(3.5m) *Forest Farm,* Mount Road, Marsden, Huddersfield, W. Yorks, *HD7 6NN.*
Come as a guest, leave as a friend.
Tel: **01484 842687** (also fax no)
Mr & Mrs Fussey.
D: £16.00-£18.00 **S:** £16.00-£18.00.
Open: All Year (not Xmas)
Beds: 1F 1D 1T
Baths: 2 Sh
⚄ �P (6) 🛏 🕇 ✕ ⚖ 🎱 Ⅵ 🏕 ⚡

(3.5m 🚗) *Marche Dean House,* 1 Binn Road, Marsden, Huddersfield, W. Yorks, *HD7 6HF.*
Remarkable landscapes breath-taking scenery steeped in local history and folklore.
Tel: **01484 846763** Miss Ellis.
D: £15.00-£15.00 **S:** £20.00-£20.00.
Open: All Year
Beds: 1F 1D 2T
Baths: 2 Sh
⚄ �P (2) 🛏 ✕ ⚖ 🎱 Ⅵ 🏕 ⚡

Walsden   12

National Grid Ref: SD9322

🍴 ⚐ Bird I'th Hand

(1.5m) *Highstones Guest House,* Lane Bottom, Walsden, Todmorden, West Yorkshire, *OL14 6TY.*
Actual grid ref: SD939209
Large house set in half an acre with lovely views over open countryside.
Grades: ETC 2 Diamond
Tel: **01706 816534** Mrs Pegg.
D: £17.00-£17.00 **S:** £17.00-£17.00.
Open: All Year
Beds: 2D 1S
Baths: 2 Sh
⚄ �P (3) ⚡ 🛏 🕇 ✕ 🎱 🏕 ⚡

Mankinholes   13

National Grid Ref: SD9623

🍴 ⚐ Top Brink

(▲ 0.5m) *Mankinholes Youth Hostel,* Mankinholes, Todmorden, West Yorkshire, OL14 6HR.
Actual grid ref: SD960235
Tel: **01706 812340**
Under 18: £6.90 **Adults:** £10.00
Self-catering facilities, Showers, Laundry facilities, Dining room, Parking, Evening meal at 7.00pm, Facilities for disabled people, No smoking, WC, Kitchen facilities, Luggage store, Credit cards accepted
Listed ancient manor house in a conservation village with typical South Pennine architecture, surrounded by moorland.

(0.5m) *Cross Farm,* Mankinholes, Todmorden, West Yorkshire, *OL14 7JQ.*
400 year old stone Pennine farmhouse and barn with hillside views.
Grades: ETC 4 Diamond
Tel: **01706 813481** Mrs Hancock.
D: £19.50-£19.50 **S:** £19.50-£19.50.
Open: All Year
Beds: 2T 2D **Baths:** 3 Pr
⚄ ⚐ (4) ⚡ ⚐ ✕ ⚖ 🎱 Ⅵ 🏕 ⚡

Todmorden   14

National Grid Ref: SD9424

🍴 ⚐ Rose & Crown

(1.5m) *The Berghof Hotel,* Cross Stone Road, Todmorden, W. Yorks, *OL14 8RQ.*
Authentic Austrian hotel and restaurant, function suite and conference facilities.
Tel: **01706 812966** (also fax no)
Mrs Brandstatter.
D: £27.50-£35.00 **S:** £42.50-£55.00.
Open: All Year
Beds: 5D 2T
Baths: 7 En
⚄ ⚐ (40) ⚐ 🕇 ✕ ⚖ 🎱 Ⅵ 🏕 ⚡

(1.5m 🚗) *Cherry Tree Cottage,* Woodhouse Road, Todmorden, W. Yorks, *OL14 5RJ.*
Actual grid ref: SD955244
C17th detached country cottage nestling amidst lovely Pennine countryside.
Grades: ETC 4 Diamond
Tel: **01706 817492**
Mrs Butterworth.
D: £16.00-£24.50 **S:** £16.00.
Open: All Year (not Xmas)
Beds: 1F 1D 1T 1S
Baths: 3 En 1 Pr 1 Sh
⚄ ⚐ ⚐ 🕇 ✕ ⚖ 🎱 Ⅵ 🏕 ⚡

Mytholmroyd   15

National Grid Ref: SE0126

🍴 ⚐ Shoulder Of Mutton

(2.75m) *Reedacres,* Mytholmroyd, Hebden Bridge, W. Yorks, *HX7 5DQ.*
Homely, modern detached house with large garden, adjacent to Rochdale Canal.
Tel: **01422 884423**
Mr & Mrs Boggis.
D: £18.00-£20.00 **S:** £20.00-£25.00.
Open: All Year (not Xmas)
Beds: 2D **Baths:** 1 En 1 Sh
⚄ ⚐ (4) ⚐ 🎱 ⚡

(3m) *Southfield,* Burnley Road, Mytholmroyd, Hebden Bridge, *HX7 5PD.*
Large Victorian family home set amidst large gardens overlooking the River Calder.
Tel: **01422 883007** (also fax no)
D: £25.00-£25.00 **S:** £35.00-£35.00.
Open: All Year (not Xmas)
Beds: 2D **Baths:** 2 En
⚄ ⚐ (14) ⚐ ✕ ⚖ 🎱 Ⅵ 🏕 ⚡

Blackshaw Head   16

National Grid Ref: SD9527

🍴 ⚐ Shoulder Of Mutton, Sportsman, New Delight

(On path) *Badger Fields Farm,* Badger Lane, Blackshaw Head, Hebden Bridge, W. Yorks, *HX7 7JX.*
Actual grid ref: SD968277
Amidst beautiful gardens, spectacular views, 2 miles from Hebden Bridge.
Grades: ETC 3 Diamond
Tel: **01422 845161**
Mrs Whitaker.
D: £19.00-£20.00 **S:** £20.00-£22.00.
Open: All Year
Beds: 1F 1D
Baths: 1 Sh
⚄ ⚐ (3) ⚡ ⚐ 🕇 ⚖ 🎱 & Ⅵ 🏕 ⚡

(1m 🚗) *Higher Earnshaw,* Blackshaw Head, Hebden Bridge, W. Yorks, *HX7 7JB.*
Family smallholding, comfortable old farmhouse in lovely country-side. Warm welcome.
Tel: **01422 844117**
Mr & Mrs Redmond.
D: £20.00-£20.00
S: £21.00-£21.00.
Open: All Year (not Xmas/ New Year)
Beds: 1F 1D 1S
Baths: 1 Sh
⚄ ⚐ (4) ⚡ ⚐ 🕇 ⚖ 🎱 🏕 ⚡

Hebden Bridge   17

National Grid Ref: SD9927

🍴 ⚐ Stubbing Wharf, White Lion, White Swan, Hinchliffe Arms, Shoulder Of Mutton, Sportsman

(1m 🚗) *Myrtle Grove,* Old Les Road, Hebden Bridge, West Yorkshire, *HX7 8HL.*
Tel: **01422 846078**
Mrs Audsley.
D: £20.00-£30.00
S: £25.00-£35.00.
Open: All Year
Beds: 1F 1D
Baths: 1 En 1 Sh
⚄ ⚐ (1) ⚡ ⚐ 🕇 ⚖ 🎱 Ⅵ 🏕 ⚡
Homely stone cottage overlooking Hebden Bridge with scenic views of the Calder Valley. Self contained, ensuite comfortable double room. CH, TV, tea coffee facilities, non smoking. Vegetarian food a speciality. Perfect location for walking and relaxing.

All rooms full and nowhere else to stay? Ask the owner if there's anywhere nearby

Always telephone to get directions to the B&B - you will save time!

(2m) *8 Birchcliffe (off Sandy Gate)*, *Hebden Bridge, West Yorkshire, HX7 8JA.*
Actual grid ref: SD997176
Stone cottage, close town centre, overlooking Calderdale valley. Continental breakfast.
Grades: ETC 3 Diamond
Tel: **01422 844777**
Ms Handley.
D: £15.00 .
Open: All Year
Beds: 1D
Baths: 1 En
🅿 (1) 🖵 🍽 🛏 🚽 &, ☒ ✦

(1m) *1 Primrose Terrace*, *Hebden Bridge, W. Yorks, HX7 6HN.*
Actual grid ref: SD990271
Pleasant Canal side location. In easy reach of town centre.
Grades: ETC 2 Diamond
Tel: **01422 844747**
Ms McNamee.
-£32.00 -£16.00.
Open: All Year
Beds: 1D 1S
Baths: 1 Sh
🅿 (1) 🖵 🛏 🚽 ☒ ✦

(1m) *Hebden Lodge Hotel*, *6-10 New Road, Hebden Bridge, West Yorkshire, HX7 8AD.*
In the centre of Hebden Bridge overlooking the marina.
Tel: **01422 845272**
D: £25.00-£35.00 **S:** £25.00-£45.00.
Open: All Year
Beds: 1F 7D 4T 2S
Baths: 14 En
🖑 ✂ 🖵 🍽 ✗ 🚽 ☒ ☒ 🛡

(1m 🐾) *Hinchliffe Arms*, *Cragg Vale, Hebden Bridge, HX7 5TA.*
Warm welcome in the idyllic valley of Cragg Vale.
Tel: **01422 883256** (also fax no)
D: £20.00-£27.00 **S:** £30.00-£36.00.
Open: All Year
Beds: 3D
Baths: 3 En
🅿 (30) ✂ 🖵 ✗ 🚽 ☒ 🛡

High season, bank holidays and special events mean low availability *everywhere*.

Heptonstall   18

National Grid Ref: SD9728

(0.5m) *Poppyfields House*, *29 Slack Top, Heptonstall, Hebden Bridge, West Yorkshire, HX7 7HA.*
Actual grid ref: SD978287
Grades: ETC 3 Diamond
Tel: **01422 843636** Mrs Simpson.
Fax no: 01422 845621
D: £19.00-£22.00 **S:** £22.00-£25.00.
Open: All Year
Beds: 1F 1D
Baths: 2 En
🖑 🅿 (4) ✂ 🖵 🍽 🛏 ✗ 🚽 ☒ ☒ ✦
Pennine House set amidst the dramatic hills of Calderdale. Wooded valley's, tumbling streams and Pennine Calderdale Way's close by. First class warm hospitality, friendly atmosphere, high standard of comfort, hearty breakfasts. Easy access by bus-rail-car-foot.

Stanbury   19

National Grid Ref: SE0137

🍽 🍺 Old Silent Inn, Friendly Inn, Wuthering Heights Inn

(0.25m) *Wuthering Heights Inn*, *26 Main Street, Stanbury, Keighley, W. Yorks, BD22 0HB.*
Warm & friendly country pub, excellent food and traditional ales.
Tel: **01535 643332** Mrs Mitchell.
D: £17.00-£17.00 **S:** £17.00-£17.00.
Open: All Year
Beds: 1F 1D 1T 1S
Baths: 2 Sh
🖑 🅿 (20) ✂ 🖵 🍽 ✗ 🚽 ☒ ☒ ✦

(On path) *Ponden House*, *Stanbury, Haworth, Keighley, W. Yorks, BD22 0HR.*
Actual grid ref: SD991371
Bronte country, relax in tranquil historic setting, enjoy panoramic views of moors and reservoir.
Tel: **01535 644154** Mrs Taylor.
D: £22.00-£22.00 **S:** £22.00-£30.00.
Open: All Year (not Xmas)
Beds: 1F 1D 1T 1S
Baths: 1 En 2 Pr 2 Sh
🖑 🅿 🍽 ✗ 🚽 ☒ 🛡 ✦

Oxenhope   20

National Grid Ref: SE0335

🍽 🍺 Three Sisters

(3m 🐾) *Springfield Guest House*, *Shaw Lane, Oxenhope, Keighley, W. Yorks, BD22 9QL.*
Large Victorian Residence set in large well kept grounds.
Tel: **01535 643951** Mrs Hargreaves.
Fax no: 01535 644672
D: £20.00-£20.00 **S:** £22.50-£25.00.
Open: All Year
Beds: 1F 3D 1T 3S
Baths: 2 En 2 Sh
🖑 🅿 (6) 🖵 🍽 ✗ 🚽 ☒ ☒ 🛡 ✦

Haworth   21

National Grid Ref: SE0337

🍽 🍺 Silent Inn

(▲ 4m) *Haworth Youth Hostel*, *Longlands Hall, Longlands Drive, Lees Lane, Haworth, Keighly, West Yorkshire, BD22 8RT.*
Actual grid ref: SE038378
Tel: **01535 642234**
Under 18: £6.90 **Adults:** £10.00
Self-catering facilities, Showers, Laundry facilities, Lounge, Games room, Drying room, Cycle store, Parking, Evening meal at 6.30pm, No smoking, WC, Kitchen facilities, Breakfast available, Credit cards accepted
Victorian mill owner's mansion with interesting architectural features, set in extensive grounds just outside the Bronte village. Good home-cooked meals.

(2m) *The Old Registry*, *4 Main Street, Haworth, Keighley, West Yorkshire, BD22 8DA.*
Victorian guesthouse, where courtesy and charm extend, four poster beds, ensuite rooms.
Tel: **01535 646503** Mrs Herdman.
D: £18.00-£25.00 **S:** £18.00-£30.00.
Open: All Year
Beds: 1F 3T 5D 1S
Baths: 9 En 1 Pr
🅿 ✂ 🖵 ✗ 🚽 ☒ 🛡 ✦

(2m) *Kershaw House*, *90 West Lane, Haworth, Keighley, West Yorkshire, BD22 8EN.*
Situated on the edge of the moors, in the heart of Bronte country.
Grades: ETC 4 Diamond
Tel: **01535 642074**
D: £20.00-£20.00 **S:** £25.00-£25.00.
Open: All Year (not Xmas)
Beds: 1T 2D 1S
Baths: 3 En 1 Pr
🅿 (4) ✂ 🖵 🚽 ☒ 🛡 ✦

Sutton-in-Craven   22

National Grid Ref: SE0043

(3.5m 🐾) *Ravenshill*, *Holme Lane, Sutton-in-Craven, Keighley, W. Yorks, BD20 7LN.*
Attached house opposite village park. Warm welcome in family home.
Tel: **01535 633276** (also fax no)
Mrs Barwick-Nicholson.
D: £18.00-£20.00 **S:** £18.00-£20.00.
Open: All Year (not Xmas)
Beds: 1D 1T 1S
Baths: 1 Sh
🖑 (12) 🅿 (2) ✂ 🖵 ✗ 🚽 ☒ 🛡 ✦

S = Price range for a single person in a single room

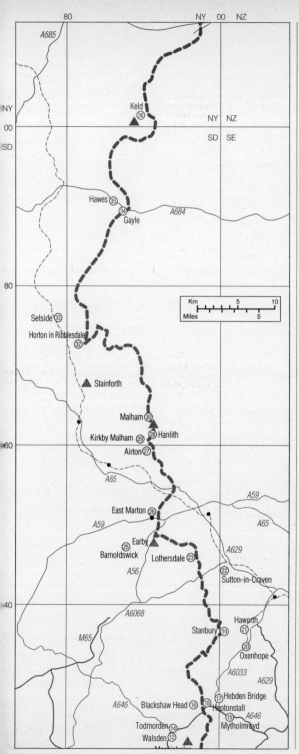

Lothersdale 23

National Grid Ref: SD9645

🍴 🍺 Hare & Hounds

(On path) **Lynmouth**, *Dale End,
Lothersdale, Skipton, N Yorks,
BD20 8EH.*
Actual grid ref: SD958460
On path, pretty bungalow set in
lovely grounds.
Tel: **01535 632744** (also fax no)
Mrs Foster.
D: £17.50-£17.50 **S:** £17.50-£17.50.
Open: All Year (not Xmas)
Beds: 1F 1D 1T **Baths:** 3 En
🛏 🅿 (4) ✂ 🖵 🕯 🎱 🛁 🕎 🔥 ✦

Earby 24

National Grid Ref: SD9046

(▲ 1m) **Earby Youth Hostel**, *Glen
Cottage, Birch Hall Lane, Earby,
Colne, Lancashire, BB8 6JX.*
Actual grid ref: SD915468
Tel: **01282 842349**
Under 18: £6.50 **Adults:** £9.25
Self-catering facilities, Showers,
Lounge 2, Dining room, Drying
room, Cycle store, Parking, No
smoking, WC, Kitchen facilities,
Credit cards accepted
*Attractive cottage with own pic-
turesque garden and waterfall, on
NE outskirts of Earby. Convenient
for Pendle.*

Barnoldswick 25

National Grid Ref: SD8746

🍴 🍺 Fosters Arms, Fanny Grey, Milano's

(On path 🐕) **Foster's House**,
*203 Gisburn Road, Barnoldswick,
Lancs, BB18 5JU.*
A warm welcome awaits at our
beautiful home from home.
Grades: ETC 2 Diamond
Tel: **01282 850718**
Mr & Mrs Edwards.
D: £20.00-£20.00 **S:** £20.00-£20.00.
Open: All Year
Beds: 2D 2T **Baths:** 3 En 1 Sh
🛏 🅿 (4) 🖵 🐾 🕯 🎱 🛁 🕎 🔥 ✦

East Marton 26

National Grid Ref: SD9050

|◎| ⊕ Cross Keys

(0.25m 🚌) *Drumlins, Heber Drive, East Marton, Skipton, North Yorkshire, BD23 3LS.*
Grades: ETC 4 Diamond
Tel: 01282 843521
Ms Moran.
D: £22.00-£22.00
S: £26.00-£26.00.
Open: All Year
Beds: 1F 1T 1D
Baths: 3 En
🛏 🅿 ⊁ 🗆 ✗ 🛋 🎹 🔥 🔽 ▮ ⚡
Drumlins is situated in a Quiet cul-de-sac off the A59 open views and easy access to the Dales, Pennine way, and the market town of Skipton, ensuite facilities with welcome tray, separate lounge and dining room ample parking private garden.

(On path) *Sawley House, East Marton, Skipton, N. Yorks, BD23 3LP.*
C12th farmhouse - farm & stables by canal on Pennine Way.
Tel: 01282 843207
Mrs Pilling.
D: £20.00-£22.00
S: £22.00.
Open: All Year (not Xmas)
Beds: 3T
Baths: 2 Sh
🅿 (12) 🗆 🕇 🛋 🔽 ⚡

Airton 27

National Grid Ref: SD9059

(▲ 0.25m) *Airton Quaker Hostel, Airton, Skipton, North Yorkshire, BD23 4AE.*
Actual grid ref: SD904592
Tel: 01729 830263
Under 18: £3.00
Adults: £5.00
Self-catering facilities, Showers, Dining room, No smoking
Attached to C17th meeting house in quiet Dales village close to Pennine Way.

All rooms full and nowhere else to stay? Ask the owner if there's anywhere nearby

Hanlith 28

National Grid Ref: SD9061

|◎| ⊕ Buck

(On path) *Coachmans Cottage, Hanlith, Malham, Skipton, N. Yorks, BD23 4BP.*
17th Century cottage with beautiful view. Every comfort.
Tel: 01729 830538
Mrs Jenkins.
D: £23.00-£23.00 .
Open: Easter to Dec
Beds: 2D **Baths:** 2 En
🛏 (10) 🅿 (3) ⊁ 🗆 🛋 🔽 ▮ ⚡

Kirkby Malham 29

National Grid Ref: SD8961

|◎| ⊕ Victoria

(0.5m) *Yeoman's Barn, Kirkby Malham, Skipton, North Yorks, BD23 4BL.*
Tel: 01729 830639 Mrs Turner.
D: £20.00-£25.00 **S:** £25.00-£25.00.
Open: All Year (not Xmas/ New Year)
Beds: 2D **Baths:** 2 En
🛏 (5) 🅿 🛋 🎹 🔽 ⚡
Converted C17th barn, large oak beams, newly decorated bedrooms. Warm welcome, tea tray on arrival, open fire. Market towns of Skipton, Settle and Hawes all nearby. Malham Cove, Janets Foss and Gordale Scar - all suitable for the weekend walker.

Malham 30

National Grid Ref: SD9062

|◎| ⊕ Listers, Buck Inn

(▲ On path) *Malham Youth Hostel, John Dower Memorial Hostel, Malham, Skipton, North Yorkshire, BD23 4DE.*
Actual grid ref: SD901629
Tel: 01729 830321
Under 18: £7.75
Adults: £11.00
Self-catering facilities, Television, Showers, Shop, Laundry facilities, Drying room, Security lockers, Cycle store, Parking, Evening meal at 7.00pm, WC, Kitchen facilities, Breakfast available, Credit cards accepted
Superbly located purpose-built hostel close to centre of picturesque Malham village, in the middle of caving, walking and cycling district.

(On path) *Eastwood Guest House, Malham, Skipton, North Yorkshire, BD23 4DA.*
High quality bed and breakfast in central village location.
Tel: 01729 830409
Mrs McIntyre.
D: £20.00-£25.00
S: £18.00-£30.00.
Open: All Year
Beds: 1F 1T 1D
Baths: 3 En
🛏 ⊁ 🗆 🛋 🎹 🔽 ▮ ⚡

Stainforth 31

National Grid Ref: SD8267

(▲ 4m) *Stainforth Youth Hostel, Taitlands, Stainforth, Settle, North Yorkshire, BD24 9PA.*
Actual grid ref: SD821668
Tel: 01729 823577
Under 18: £7.75
Adults: £11.00
Self-catering facilities, Showers, Lounge, Dining room, Drying room, Cycle store, Parking, Evening meal at 7.00pm, Facilities for disabled people, No smoking, Kitchen facilities, Breakfast available, Credit cards accepted
Georgian listed building with fine interior, set in extensive grounds with grazing paddock, a short walk from the village. Central for many walks, including the Pennine and Ribble Ways, and the Yorkshire Dales Cycleway.

Horton-in-Ribblesdale 32

National Grid Ref: SD8072

|◎| ⊕ Crown, Golden Lion

(On path) *The Willows, Horton-in-Ribblesdale, Settle, N. Yorks, BD24 0HT.*
Large detached house, luxurious bedrooms in lovely Yorkshire Dales.
Tel: 01729 860373 (also fax no)
Mrs Barker.
D: £20.00-£24.00
S: £20.00-£25.00.
Open: Easter to Sep
Beds: 1F 1D 1T
Baths: 1 En 1 Pr 1 Sh
🛏 🅿 (5) 🗆 🕇 ✗ 🛋 🎹 🔽 ▮ ⚡

The Grid Reference beneath the location heading is for the village or town - *not* for individual houses, which are shown (where supplied) in each entry itself.

🚌 sign means that, *given due notice*, owners will pick you up from the path and drop you off *within reason.*

S = Price range for a single

person in a room

(0.25m) *The Rowe House,* Horton-in-Ribblesdale, Settle, N. Yorks, *BD24 0HT.*
Actual grid ref: SD804728
Distinctive Georgian country house in half-acre grounds TV lounge.
Tel: **01729 860212**
Mr & Mrs Lane.
D: £18.00-£22.00 **S:** £22.00-£26.00.
Open: Mar to Oct
Beds: 2D 3T **Baths:** 3 En 2 Sh
🛇 (12) 🅿 (6) ⌨ 🌐 🛁 🎦 🔟 👜 ✂

Selside   33

National Grid Ref: SD7875

▣ Crown

(3m 🚌**)** *South House Farm,* Selside, Settle, N. Yorks, *BD24 0HU.*
Comfortable farmhouse accommodation set in the centre of the Peaks.
Tel: **01729 860271** Ms Kenyon.
D: £20.00-£20.00 **S:** £20.00-£20.00.
Open: Easter to Oct
Beds: 1F 2D 1T **Baths:** 1 En
🛇 (1) 🅿 (6) ✂ ⌨ 🌐 🛁 🎦 🔟 👜 ✂

Gayle   34

National Grid Ref: SD8789

▣ Board, Fountain, Crown, White Hart

(0.5m) *Blackburn Farm/Trout Fishery,* Gayle, Hawes, N Yorks, *DL8 3NX.*
Idyllic location. Quiet, rural but within walking distance of Hawes.
Grades: ETC 3 Diamond
Tel: **01969 667524** Ms Moore.
D: £17.00-£18.00 .
Open: Easter to Oct
Beds: 2D
Baths: 1 En 1 Pr
🅿 (4) ✂ ⌨ 🖈 🛁 🎦 🔟 ✂

(0.25m) *East House,* Gayle, Hawes, N. Yorks, *DL8 3RZ.*
Actual grid ref: SD871892
Delightful house. Superb views, ideal centre for touring the dales.
Grades: ETC 4 Diamond
Tel: **01969 667405** Mrs Ward.
D: £18.00-£21.00 **S:** £18.00-£18.00.
Open: Feb to Nov
Beds: 1T 1D 1S **Baths:** 1 En 1 Sh
🛇 🅿 ✂ ⌨ 🛁 🎦 🔟 👜 ✂

Please take muddy boots off before entering premises

(On path) *Gayle Laithe,* Gayle, Hawes, N. Yorks, *DL8 3RR.*
Modern, comfortable, converted barn. Ideal for touring, cycling and walking.
Tel: **01969 667397** Mrs McGregor.
D: £16.00-£17.00 **S:** £16.00-£17.00.
Open: Easter to Nov
Beds: 1D 1T 1S
Baths: 1 Sh
🛇 🅿 (2) ⌨ 🛁 🎦 🔟 👜 ✂

Hawes   35

▣ White Hart, Herriot's Hotel, Board Hotel, Fountain, Stone House, Wensleydale Pantry

(▲ 0.25m) *Hawes Youth Hostel,* Lancaster Terrace, Hawes, N Yorks, *DL8 3LQ.*
Actual grid ref: SD867897
Tel: **01969 667368**
Under 18: £6.90 **Adults:** £10.00
Self-catering facilities, Television, Laundry facilities, Lounge, Games room, Drying room, Cycle store, Evening meal at 7.00pm, No smoking, Kitchen facilities, Breakfast available, Credit cards accepted
Friendly and attractively refurbished purpose-built hostel overlooking Hawes and Wensleydale.

(0.5m) *The Bungalow,* Springbank, Hawes, N. Yorks, *DL8 3NW.*
Large bungalow, excellent views, quiet, off road parking.
Grades: ETC 2 Diamond
Tel: **01969 667209**
Mrs Garnett.
D: £18.00-£20.00 .
Open: Easter to Oct
Beds: 2D 1T
Baths: 2 En 1 Sh
🛇 (4) 🅿 ⌨ 🖈 🛁 🎦 🔟 👜

(On path) *Ebor House,* Burtersett Road, Hawes, N. Yorks, *DL8 3NT.*
Actual grid ref: SD876897
Family-run friendly and central. Off road parking and cycle store.
Grades: ETC 3 Diamond
Tel: **01969 667337** (also fax no)
Mrs Clark.
D: £17.00-£20.00
S: £19.00-£25.00.
Open: All Year (not Xmas)
Beds: 2D 1T
Baths: 1 En 1 Sh
🛇 🅿 (5) ✂ ⌨ 🖈 🛁 🎦 🔟 👜 ✂

(On path) *The Green Dragon Inn,* Hardraw, Hawes, N. Yorks, *DL8 3LZ.*
A 100' waterfall in spectacular back garden.
Tel: **01969 667392**
Mr Stead.
D: £23.50-£27.50
S: £24.50-£28.50.
Open: All Year (not Xmas)
Beds: 2F 8D 2T 4S
Baths: 16 Pr
🛇 🅿 (30) ⌨ 🖈 ✕ 🛁 🎦 🔟 👜 ✂

(0.5m) *Overdales View,* Simonstone, Hawes, N Yorks, *DL8 3LY.*
Friendly welcome. Lovely views, peaceful surroundings, comfortable beds good food.
Tel: **01969 667186** Mrs Sunter.
D: £16.00-£18.00 **S:** £18.00-£20.00.
Open: Easter to Oct
Beds: 1F/T 1D 1S
Baths: 1 Sh
🛇 🅿 (5) ✂ ⌨ 🛁 🎦 🔟 ✂

(1m) *Tarney Fors,* Hawes, N. Yorks, *DL8 3LS.*
Grade II Listed ex-farmhouse, now a comfortable guest house, in beautiful setting.
Tel: **01969 667475** Mrs Harpley.
D: £25.00-£28.00 **S:** £40.00-£45.00.
Open: Easter to Nov
Beds: 3D
Baths: 2 En 1 Pr
🛇 (7) 🅿 (8) ✂ ⌨ 🛁 🎦 🔟 👜 ✂

(0.25m 🚌**)** *Steppe Haugh Guest House,* Townhead, Hawes, N. Yorks, *DL8 3RH.*
Actual grid ref: SD869898
C17th house offering a wealth of character and atmosphere.
Tel: **01969 667645** Mrs Grattan.
D: £18.00-£26.00 **S:** £20.00-£23.00.
Open: All Year (not Xmas)
Beds: 3D 1T 1S
Baths: 5 En
🛇 (7) 🅿 (6) ✂ ⌨ 🖈 🛁 🎦 🔟 👜 ✂

Keld   36

National Grid Ref: NY8901

▣ Farmers' Arms

(▲ 1m) *Keld Youth Hostel,* Keld Lodge, Keld, Upper Swaledale, Richmond, N. Yorks, *DL11 6LL.*
Tel: **01748 886259**
Under 18: £6.50
Adults: £9.25
Self-catering facilities, Television, Showers, Lounge, Dining room, Drying room, Cycle store, Evening meal at 7.00pm, No smoking, Kitchen facilities, Breakfast available, Credit cards accepted
Close to both the Pennine and the Coast-to-Coast long distance paths, this onetime shooting lodge is ideal for walkers. Swaledale has moorland, waterfalls, and abundant wildlife.

(0.75m) *Greenlands,* Keld, Richmond, *DL11 6DY.*
Actual grid ref: NY889000
Refurbished farmhouse amidst the peace and beauty of Upper Swaledale.
Tel: **01748 886576**
Mrs Thompson.
D: £19.50-£19.50 .
Open: All Year
Beds: 2D
Baths: 2 En
🅿 (2) ✂ ⌨ 🛁 🎦 🔟 👜 ✂

All details shown are as supplied by B&B owners in Autumn 2001.

Blackton   37

National Grid Ref: NY9317

(▲ 0.25m) *Baldersdale Youth Hostel, Blackton, Baldersdale, Barnard Castle, County Durham, DL12 9UP.*
Actual grid ref: NY931179
Tel: **01833 650629**
Under 18: £6.50 **Adults:** £9.25
Self-catering facilities, Television, Showers, Shop, Dining room, Games room, Drying room, Cycle store, Evening meal at 7.00pm, No smoking, WC, Kitchen facilities, Breakfast available, Credit cards accepted
Fully modernised farmhouse at mid-point of the Pennine Way.

Lunedale   38

National Grid Ref: NY9221

(1m 🚍) *Wemmergill Hall Farm, Lunedale, Middleton in Teesdale, Barnard Castle, County Durham, DL12 0PA.*
Traditional farmhouse, views over Moorland and Reservoir. walkers/birdwatchers paradise!
Grades: ETC 3 Diamond
Tel: **01833 640379** (also fax no)
Mrs Stoddart.
D: £18.00-£20.00 **S:** £20.00-£25.00.
Open: Jan to Nov
Beds: 1F 1D
⛄ (4) 🅿 (2) ⌿✕ 🏧 ▦ Ⓥ ⋔ ≉

D = Price range per person sharing in a double room

Middleton in Teesdale   39

National Grid Ref: NY9425

🍴🍺 Kings Head, Talbot Hotel, Teesdale Hotel, Bridge Inn, Chatterbox,

(▲ 0.5m) *Kingsway Adventure Centre, .*
Tel: **Adults:** £9.00
Showers, Running water, WC, Drying facilities, Meals available, Washing facilities, Kitchen facilities, Breakfast available

(0.25m) *Brunswick House, 55 Market Place, Middleton in Teesdale, Barnard Castle, Co Durham, DL12 0QH.*
Charming C18th guest house, excellent food. Many beautiful walks.
Grades: ETC 4 Diamond,
AA 4 Diamond
Tel: **01833 640393** (also fax no)
Mr & Mrs Milnes.
D: £20.00-£24.00 **S:** £22.50-£30.00.
Open: All Year
Beds: 3D 2T **Baths:** 5 En
⛄ 🅿 (5) ⌿⌗✕ 🏧 ▦ Ⓥ ⋔ ≉

All rooms full and nowhere else to stay? Ask the owner if there's anywhere nearby

(0.5m) *Bluebell House, Market Place, Middleton in Teesdale, Barnard Castle, Co Durham, DL12 0GG.*
Former inn, beautiful walks, good food, friendly family atmosphere guaranteed.
Grades: ETC 3 Diamond
Tel: **01833 640584** Ms Northey.
D: £16.00-£17.00 **S:** £21.00-£25.00.
Open: All Year (not Xmas)
Beds: 2D 2T
Baths: 3 En 1 Pr
⛄ 🅿 (2) ⌿⌗🏐 🏧 ▦ ⚘ Ⓥ ≉

(0.25m 🚍) *Kingsway Adventure Centre, Alston Road, Middleton in Teesdale, Barnard Castle, Co Durham, DL12 0UU.*
A warm friendly family run outdoor activity centre.
Tel: **01833 640881** Mr Hearn.
Fax no: 01833 640155
D: £13.00 **S:** £13.00.
Open: All Year (not Xmas/ New Year)
Beds: 3F 2T
Baths: 2 En 2 Sh
⛄ 🅿 (10) ⌿✕ 🏧 ▦ ⚘ Ⓥ ⋔ ≉

(0.25m) *Lonton South, Middleton in Teesdale, Barnard Castle, Co Durham, DL12 0PL.*
Beautiful view. Farmhouse. Comfortable beds, good breakfast. Overlook garden.
Grades: ETC 3 Diamond
Tel: **01833 640409** Mrs Watson.
D: £18.00-£20.00 **S:** £20.00-£24.00.
Open: Mar to Oct
Beds: 1D 1S
Baths: 1 Sh
⛄ (9) 🅿 (6) ⌿⌗🏐 🏧 ▦ Ⓥ ⋔ ≉

(On path) *25 Bridge Street, Middleton in Teesdale, Barnard Castle, Co Durham, DL12 0QB.*
Victorian private house.
Tel: **01833 640549** Mrs Sowerby.
D: £20.00-£20.00 **S:** £20.00-£20.00.
Open: All Year
Beds: 1D 4T 1S **Baths:** 1 Sh
⛄ (12) 🅿 ⌿⌗🏐 🏐 ▦ Ⓥ ⋔ ≉

(0.5m) *Belvedere House, 54 Market Place, Middleton-in-Teesdale, Barnard Castle, Co Durham, DL12 0QA.*
Actual grid ref: NY947255
Recently renovated C18th stone house situated in Dales village.
Tel: **01833 640884** (also fax no)
Mrs Finn.
D: £15.00-£16.00 **S:** £17.00-£17.00.
Open: All Year (not Xmas)
Beds: 3D 1T **Baths:** 3 En 1 Pr
⛄ 🅿 (3) ⌿⌗🏐 🏧 ▦ Ⓥ ≉

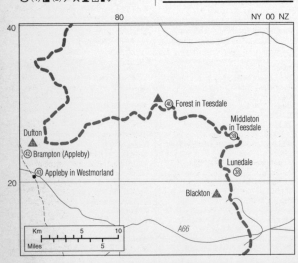

Bringing children with you? Always ask for any special rates.

Please respect

a B&B's wishes

regarding children,

animals & smoking.

Forest in Teesdale 40

National Grid Ref: NY8629

(▲ On path) *Langdon Beck Youth Hostel, Forest in Teesdale, Barnard Castle, County Durham, DL12 0XN.*
Actual grid ref: NY860304
Tel: **01833 622228**
Under 18: £6.90
Adults: £10.00
Self-catering facilities, Showers, Laundry facilities, Wet weather shelter, Lounge, Drying room, Cycle store, Parking, Evening meal at 7.00pm, No smoking, Kitchen facilities, Breakfast available, Credit cards accepted
Purpose-built hostel in Upper Teesdale with an excellent standard of accommodation.

Dufton 41

National Grid Ref: NY6825

⛵ ⬥ Stag Inn

(▲ On path) *Dufton Youth Hostel, Redstones, Dufton, Appleby-in-Westmorland, Cumbria, CA16 6DB.*
Actual grid ref: NY688251
Tel: **017683 51236**
Under 18: £6.50
Adults: £9.25
Showers, Shop, Lounge, Dining room 2, Drying room, Parking, Evening meal at 7.00pm, No smoking, Kitchen facilities, Breakfast available, Luggage store, Credit cards accepted
Large stone-built house with log fire in attractive C18th village surrounded by fine scenery of the Eden Valley.

(On path) *Sycamore House, Dufton, Appleby-in-Westmorland, Cumbria, CA16 6DB.*
Actual grid ref: NY689253
Listed cottage, cosy living room, close to pub and shop.
Tel: **017683 51296**
Mrs O'Halloran.
D: £18.00-£20.00
S: £17.00-£20.00.
Open: Easter to Dec
Beds: 1D 1T 2S
Baths: 1 En 1 Sh
⛵ 🅿 (2) 🛏 🐾 🖾 📺 🛈 🌿

Brampton (Appleby) 42

National Grid Ref: NY6723

⛵ ⬥ New Inn, Drove Inn, White Lion

(1.5m) *Sunray, Brampton (Appleby), Appleby-in-Westmorland, Cumbria, CA16 6JS.*
Modern bungalow. Guest rooms overlook Pennines, comfortable, welcoming, good breakfast.
Tel: **017683 52905** Mrs Tinkler.
D: £15.00-£20.00 **S:** £18.00-£20.00.
Open: Easter to Oct
Beds: 2D
Baths: 1 En
⛵ 🅿 (10) 🌿 🖾 🛏 🐾 ✗ 🖾 📺 🛈 🌿

Appleby-in-Westmorland 43

National Grid Ref: NY6820

⛵ ⬥ Royal Oak, Crown & Cushion

(2.5m) *Limnerslease, Bongate, Appleby-in-Westmorland, Cumbria, CA16 6UE.*
Family-run guest house 10 mins town centre. Lovely golf course & many walks.
Tel: **017683 51578** Mrs Coward.
D: £17.00-£17.00 .
Open: All Year (not Xmas)
Beds: 2D 1T
Baths: 1 Pr 1 Sh
⛵ (13) 🅿 (3) 🖾 🛏 🖾 📺 🛈 🌿

(2.5m 🚗) *Wemyss House, 48 Boroughgate, Appleby-in-Westmorland, Cumbria, CA16 6XG.*
Actual grid ref: NY684203
Georgian house in small country town.
Tel: **017683 51494** Mrs Hirst.
D: £17.00-£17.00 **S:** £17.00-£17.00.
Open: Easter to Oct
Beds: 1D 1T 1S
Baths: 2 Sh
⛵ 🅿 (2) 🖾 🖾 📺 🌿

(2m) *Church View, Bongate, Appleby-in-Westmorland, Cumbria, CA16 6UN.*
C18th character house, near old coaching inn and town facilities.
Tel: **017683 51792** (also fax no)
Mrs Kemp.
D: £16.00-£18.00 **S:** £18.00-£20.00.
Open: All Year (not Xmas)
Beds: 1F 1D 1S
Baths: 1 Sh
⛵ (5) 🅿 (4) 🌿 🖾 🖾 🌿

(2.5m 🚗) *Bongate House, Appleby-in-Westmorland, Cumbria, CA16 6UE.*
Actual grid ref: NY687202
This large Georgian guest house is in an acre of secluded gardens.
Tel: **017683 51245** Mrs Dayson.
Fax no: 017683 51423
D: £18.50-£21.00 **S:** £18.50-£28.00.
Open: Mar to Nov
Beds: 1F 3D 3T 1S
Baths: 5 En
⛵ (5) 🅿 (8) 🖾 🛏 ✗ 🖾 📺 🛈 🌿

Garrigill 44

National Grid Ref: NY7441

⛵ ⬥ George & Dragon

(On path) *Ivy House, Garrigill, Alston, Cumbria, CA9 3DU.*
Actual grid ref: NY744414
C17th converted farmhouse. Comfortable, friendly atmosphere. Picturesque North Pennines village.
Tel: **01434 382501**
Mrs Humble.
Fax no: 01434 382660
D: £17.00-£19.50
S: £26.00-£29.00.
Open: All Year
Beds: 2F 1T
Baths: 3 En
⛵ 🅿 (10) 🌿 🖾 🐾 ✗ 🖾 📺 🛈 🌿

Nenthead 45

National Grid Ref: NY7843

⛵ ⬥ Miners Arms

(2m) *The Miners Arms, Nenthead, Alston, Cumbria, CA9 3PF.*
Friendly family pub. Real ales, real food, real fires.
Tel: **01434 381427**
Miss Clark.
D: £15.00-£15.00
S: £15.00-£15.00.
Open: All Year
Beds: 2F 2D 2T 2S
⛵ 🅿 🌿 🖾 🐾 ✗ 🖾 📺 🛈 🌿

(2m) *Mill Cottage Bunkhouse, Nenthead, Alston, Cumbria, CA9 3PD.*
Tel: **01434 382771**
D: £12.00-£12.00 **S:** £12.00-£12.00.
Open: All Year
Beds: 2F
⛵ 🅿 (4) 🌿 🖾 🖾 📺 🛈 🌿
Bunkhouse in spectacular landscape, part of Nenthead Mines heritage site.

Alston 46

National Grid Ref: NY7146

⛵ ⬥ Blue Bell Inn, Angel Inn, Turks Head, Crown

(▲ On path) *Alston Youth Hostel, The Firs, Alston, Cumbria, CA9 3RW.*
Actual grid ref: NY717461
Tel: **01434 381509**
Under 18: £6.50
Adults: £9.25
Self-catering facilities, Showers, Lounge, Dining room, Drying room, Cycle store, Parking, Evening meal at 7.00pm, No smoking, WC, Kitchen facilities, Breakfast available, Credit cards accepted
Purpose-built hostel overlooking River South Tyne, on outskirts of Alston, the highest market town in England.

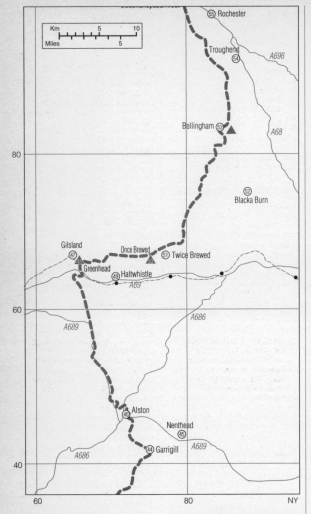

Km 5 10
Miles 5

55 Rochester

Trougheng 54 *A696*

Bellingham 53 *A68*

52 Blacka Burn

80

Gilsland
47
Once Brewed
51 Twice Brewed
Greenhead
49 Haltwhistle
A69
A686

60

A689
A686

Alston
46
Nenthead
45
44 Garrigill
A689

40

60 80 NY

(0.25m 🚌) *Nentholme, The Butts,
Alston, Cumbria,* CA9 3JQ.
Actual grid ref: NY719467
Quiet location, 1 min walk to town
C2C and walkers welcome.
Tel: **01434 381523** (also fax no)
Mrs Thompson.
D: £17.00-£20.00 **S:** £22.00-£25.00.
Open: All Year
Beds: 2F 3D 3T 1S
Baths: 2 En 1 Sh
🛏 🅿 (6) ⅍ ☐ ┢ ✕ 🔋 🛒 Ⅴ 🛉 ⅍

**Bringing children with
you? Always ask for
any special rates.**

D = Price range per person
sharing in a double room

(1m) *Greycroft, Middle Park,
The Raise, Alston, Cumbria,*
CA9 3AR.
Actual grid ref: NY747408
In North Pennines with open views
south to Crossfell. 1 mile historic
town Alston.
Tel: **01434 381383** (also fax no)
Mrs Dent.
D: £18.00-£22.00
S: £20.00-£24.00.
Open: All Year (not Xmas)
Beds: 1D 1T
Baths: 2 En
🛏 🅿 (2) ⅍ ☐ ✕ 🔋 🛒 ⅍ Ⅴ 🛉 ⅍

Gilsland 47

National Grid Ref: NY6366

🍴 🍺 Samson Inn

(1.5m 🚌) *The Hill on the Wall,
Gilsland, Brampton, Cumbria,*
CA8 7DA.
Fascinating Listed C16th 'fortified
farmhouse' overlooking Hadrian's
Wall.
Grades: ETC 4 Diamond
Tel: **016977 47214** (also fax no)
Mr Swan.
D: £20.00-£22.00 **S:** £25.00-£27.00.
Open: All Year
Beds: 2D 1T **Baths:** 3 En
🛏 🅿 ⅍ ☐ ┢ ✕ 🔋 🛒 Ⅴ 🛉 ⅍

(1m) *Howard House Farm,
Gilsland, Carlisle, Cumbria,*
CA6 7AN.
Actual grid ref: NY633670
Comfortable farmhouse on Roman
wall.
Tel: **016977 47285** Mrs Woodmass.
D: £19.00-£22.00 **S:** £19.00-£22.00.
Open: All Year
Beds: 1F 1D 1T **Baths:** 1 En 1 Sh
🛏 (5) 🅿 (4) ☐ ┢ ✕ 🔋 🛒 Ⅴ 🛉 ⅍

Greenhead 48

National Grid Ref: NY6665

🍴 🍺 Holmhead Bar

(▲ On path) *Greenhead Youth
Hostel, Greenhead, Carlisle,
Cumbria, CA6 7HG.*
Actual grid ref: NY659655
Tel: **016977 47401**
Under 18: £6.50 **Adults:** £9.25
Self-catering facilities, Showers,
Shop, Lounge, Drying room, Cycle
store, Evening meal at 7.00pm, No
smoking, WC, Kitchen facilities,
Breakfast available, Credit cards
accepted
*This traditional Methodist chapel
with its thick stone walls is curious-
ly cosy. Useful for a rest for walk-
ers of the Pennine Way, this is also
a popular haunt for cyclists.*

(▲ 0.5m) *Holmhead Stone Tent,
Thirlwall Castle Farm, Greenhead,
Brampton, CA8 7HY.*
Tel: **016977 47402**
Under 18: £3.50 **Adults:** £3.50
Wet weather shelter, Cycle store,
No smoking
*Stone building. Outside toilet, gas
lamp, camping gas, cold water tap.
Hadrian's Wall path.*

**High season,
bank holidays and
special events mean
low availability
*everywhere.***

**Always telephone
to get directions to
the B&B - you will
save time!**

(On path) *Holmhead Licensed
Guest House,* Thirlwall Castle
Farm, Hadrian's Wall, Greenhead,
Brampton, Cumbria, *CA8 7HY.*
Actual grid ref: NY661659
Enjoy fine food and hospitality
with a personal touch.
Grades: ETC 4 Diamond
Tel: **016977 47402** (also fax no)
Mr & Mrs Staff.
D: £28.00-£29.00 **S:** £37.00-£38.00.
Open: All Year (not Xmas)
Beds: 1F 1D 2T **Baths:** 4 En
🛇 🅿 (4) ✂ 🗖 ✕ 🚿 🏬 Ⅴ 🛉 ⌁

Haltwhistle 49

National Grid Ref: NY7064

🍴 🍺 Spotted Cow, Manor House, Centre Of
Britain Hotel, Milecastle Inn

(2m) *Manor House Hotel,* Main
Street, Haltwhistle, Northd,
NE49 0BS.
Tel: **01434 322588** Nicholson.
D: £15.00-£22.00 **S:** £20.00-£25.00.
Open: All Year
Beds: 1F 1D 4T
Baths: 3 En 3 Sh
🛇 🅿 (4) 🗖 ✕ 🚿 🏬 Ⅴ 🛉 ⌁
Small hotel with busy public bar
serving good selection of real ales
wines & spirits. Very popular for
meals at an affordable price.
Separate dining area available
away from bar. Hotel centrally
situated 2 miles from Hadrian's
Wall. Warm welcome from
Kathleen and Raymond Nicholson.

(1.5m 🚗) *The Old School House,*
Fair Hill, Haltwhistle,
Northumberland, *NE49 9EE.*
Actual grid ref: NY712642
Friendly welcome. Brilliant break-
fast - no need for lunch! Hadrian's
Wall on doorstep.
Grades: ETC 4 Diamond
Tel: **01434 322595** (also fax no)
Mrs O'Hagan.
D: £18.00-£20.00 **S:** £25.00-£30.00.
Open: All Year (not Xmas)
Beds: 2D 1T
Baths: 3 Pr
🅿 (6) ✂ 🗖 🚿 🏬 Ⅴ ⌁

**Bringing children with
you? Always ask for
any special rates.**

(1.5m) *Hall Meadows,* Main
Street, Haltwhistle, Northd,
NE49 0AZ.
Large comfortable C19th private
house, central for Hadrian's Wall.
Grades: ETC 3 Diamond
Tel: **01434 321021**
Mrs Humes.
D: £17.00-£17.00.
S: £18.00-£18.00.
Open: All Year (not Xmas)
Beds: 1D 1T 1S
Baths: 1 Sh
🛇 🅿 (3) 🗖 🚿 🏬 Ⅴ 🛉 ⌁

(1m) *Ald White Craig Farm,*
Hadrian's Wall, Shield Hill,
Haltwhistle, Northd, *NE49 9NW.*
Actual grid ref: NY714650
Snug old rambling single storey
farmhouse.
Tel: **01434 320565** (also fax no)
Ms Laidlow.
D: £21.00-£25.00
S: £28.00-£32.00.
Open: Easter to Oct
Beds: 1D 1T
Baths: 2 En
🅿 (2) ✂ 🗖 🚿 🏬 Ⅴ 🛉 ⌁

Once Brewed 50

National Grid Ref: NY7566

(⛰ 0.5m) *Once Brewed Youth
Hostel,* Military Road, Once
Brewed, Bardon Mill, Hexham,
Northumberland, *NE47 7AN.*
Actual grid ref: NY752668
Tel: **01434 344360**
Under 18: £7.75
Adults: £11.00
Self-catering facilities, Showers,
Laundry facilities, Lounge, Dining
room, Games room, Drying room,
Cycle store, Parking, Evening meal
at 6.00-7.00pm, No smoking, WC,
Kitchen facilities, Breakfast
available
*Excellent residential accommoda-
tion with small bedrooms and
superb range of facilities. Close to
Hadrian's Wall and the Roman
Forts.*

Twice Brewed 51

National Grid Ref: NY7567

(1m 🚗) *Saughy Rigg Farm,* Twice
Brewed, Haltwhistle,
Northumberland, *NE49 9PT.*
Actual grid ref: NY740685
Near Hadrian's Wall, delicious
food, comfortable accommodation,
children & pets welcome.
Grades: ETC 3 Diamond
Tel: **01434 344746**
Ms McNulty.
D: £15.00-£15.00
S: £15.00-£15.00.
Open: All Year
Beds: 1F 1T
Baths: 1 En 1 Pr
🛇 🅿 🗖 ✕ 🚿 🏬 Ⅴ 🛉 ⌁

Blacka Burn 52

National Grid Ref: NY8278

🍴 🍺 Battlesteads Hotel

(0.5m 🚗) *Hetherington Farm,*
Blacka Burn, Wark, Hexham,
Northd, *NE48 3DR.*
Actual grid ref: NY824782
Traditional farmhouse in lovely
countryside. Ideal walking, touring,
warm welcome.
Tel: **01434 230260** Mrs Nichol.
D: £18.00-£25.00 **S:** £18.00-£25.00.
Open: Easter to Nov
Beds: 4F 1D 1S
Baths: 1 En 1 Pr 1 Sh
🛇 (10) 🅿 (4) 🚿 🏬 Ⅴ 🛉 ⌁

Bellingham 53

National Grid Ref: NY8383

🍴 🍺 Rose & Crown, Cheviot Hotel

(⛰ On path) *Bellingham Youth
Hostel,* Woodburn Road,
Bellingham, Hexham,
Northumberland, NE48 2ED.
Actual grid ref: NY843834
Tel: **01434 220313**
Under 18: £5.75
Adults: £8.50
Self-catering facilities, Showers,
Lounge, Cycle store, No smoking,
WC, Kitchen facilities
*Hostel built of red cedarwood on
the Pennine Way, high above the
small Borders town of Bellingham.
Near Kielder Water (with forest
trails and watersports) and
Hadrian's Wall.*

(On path 🚗) *Lyndale Guest
House,* Bellingham, Hexham,
Northd, *NE48 2AW.*
Grades: ETC 4 Diamond
Tel: **01434 220361** (also fax no)
Mrs Gaskin.
D: £23.50-£25.00 **S:** £23.50.
Open: All Year (not Xmas)
Beds: 1F 2D 1T 1S
Baths: 2 En 1 Pr 1 Sh
🛇 🅿 (5) ✂ 🗖 ✕ 🚿 🏬 ♿ Ⅴ 🛉 ⌁
Tour the Borders, good walking,
Hadrian's Wall, Pennine Way,
Kielder Water or cycle the Reivers'
Route. Enjoy a welcome break.
Relax in our walled garden.
Sunlounge with panoramic views.
Excellent dinners, choice of
breakfasts, quality ground floor
ensuites. Special discounts.

**High season,
bank holidays and
special events mean
low availability
*everywhere.***

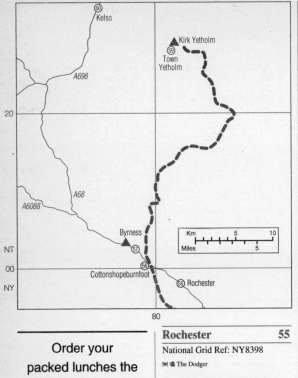

Kelso

Kirk Yetholm

Town Yetholm

A698

20

A68

A6088

Byrness

NT

00

Cottonshopeburnfoot

NY

Rochester

| Km | 5 | 10 |
| Miles | | 5 |

80

Order your packed lunches the *evening before* you need them. Not at breakfast!

Troughend 54

National Grid Ref: NY8692

⋈ 🍺 Bay Horse

(3m 🚐) *Brown Rigg Cottage,* Troughend, Otterburn, Newcastle-upon-Tyne, *NE19 1LG.*
Actual grid ref: NY854938
Wind and solar powered stone cottage. Peacefully situated. Open countryside.
Tel: **01830 520541** Mrs Boon.
D: £18.00-£20.00 **S:** £20.00-£20.00.
Open: All Year
Beds: 1F 1D **Baths:** 1 Pr
🅿 (6) ⊁ 🛏 🛏 ✕ 🏊 ⅲ 🛚 🔒 ✓

Bringing children with you? Always ask for any special rates.

Rochester 55

National Grid Ref: NY8398

⋈ 🍺 The Dodger

(3m) *Redesdale Arms Hotel,* Rochester, Otterburn, Newcastle-upon-Tyne, *NE19 1TA.*
Family-run 600-year-old coaching inn. Superb home cooking.
Tel: **01830 520668**
Mrs Wright.
Fax no: 01830 520063
D: £28.00-£33.00
S: £36.00.
Open: All Year (not Xmas)
Beds: 3F 3D 4T
Baths: 10 En
🛏 🅿 (20) 🖵 🛏 ✕ 🏊 ⅲ 🛚 🔒 ✓

Cottonshopeburnfoot 56

National Grid Ref: NT7801

⋈ 🍺 Byrness Hotel, Redesdale Arms

(On path 🚐) *Border Forest Caravan Park,* Cottonshopeburnfoot, Otterburn, Newcastle-upon-Tyne, *NE19 1TF.*
Actual grid ref: NT779014
Attractive motel, chalet rooms situated in picturesque Kielder Forest Park.
Tel: **01830 520259**
Mr & Mrs Bell.
D: £19.00-£19.00
S: £21.00.
Open: All Year (not Xmas)
Beds: 2F
Baths: 2 En
🛏 (1) 🅿 (10) ⊁ 🖵 🛏 🏊 ⅲ 🛚 🔒 ✓

Byrness 57

National Grid Ref: NT7602

⋈ 🍺 Byrness Hotel, The Redesdale

(▲ 0.25m) *Byrness Youth Hostel,* 7 Otterburn Green, Byrness, Newcastle upon Tyne, *NE19 1TS.*
Actual grid ref: NT764027
Tel: **01830 520425**
Under 18: £4.75
Adults: £6.75
Self-catering facilities, Showers, Shop, Lounge, Dining room, Games room, Drying room, Cycle store, Parking, No smoking, WC, Kitchen facilities, Credit cards accepted
Formerly two adjoining Forestry Commission houses in peaceful village, in foothills of Cheviot Hills, close to the Scottish border.

(1m 🚐) *Low Byrness Farm,* Byrness, Otterburn, Newcastle-upon-Tyne, Northumberland, *NE19 1TF.*
150 year old house in the Northumberland National Park.
Grades: ETC 4 Diamond
Tel: **01830 520648**
Mrs Cranston.
Fax no: 01830 520733
D: £9.00-£10.00
S: £22.00-£28.00.
Open: All Year (not Xmas/New Year)
Beds: 1F 3D
Baths: 2 En 1 Sh
🛏 (12) 🅿 (8) ⊁ 🖵 🛏 ✕ 🏊 ⅲ 🛚 🔒 ✓

Kirk Yetholm 58

National Grid Ref: NT8228

⋈ 🍺 Border Hotel, Cobbles Inn, Plough Hotel

(▲ On path) *Kirk Yetholm Youth Hostel,* Kirk Yetholm, Kelso, Roxburghshire, TD5 8PG.
Actual grid ref: NT826282
Tel: **01573 420631**
Under 18: £7.00
Adults: £8.25
Self-catering facilities, Shop nearby, Lounge, Parking Limited, No smoking, WC, Kitchen facilities
Kirk Yetholm is at the north end of the Pennine Way and mid-point on St Cuthbert's Way. Many abbeys and castles to visit. Good cycling, including the Tweed Cycle Way.

(0.5m 🚐) *Valleydene,* High Street, Kirk Yetholm, Kelso, Roxburghshire, TD5 8PH.
Traditional Scottish welcome. Log fire. Comfortable rooms with excellent views.
Tel: **01573 420286** Mrs Campbell.
D: £22.00-£22.00 **S:** £25.00-£30.00.
Open: All Year
Beds: 2T 1D
Baths: 2 En 1 Pr
🛏 (12) 🅿 (4) 🛏 ✕ 🏊 ⅲ 🛚 🔒 ✓

(2m) *Spring Valley, The Green, Kirk Yetholm, Roxburghshire, TD5 8PQ.*
C18th house with superb views, situated in conservation village.
Grades: ETC 3 Star
Tel: **01573 420253** Mrs Ogilvie.
D: £20.00-£22.00 **S:** £27.00-£27.00.
Open: All Year (not Xmas)
Beds: 1D 1T **Baths:** 2 Pr
ざ (1) 🅿 (3) 🗲🖵🏠🕯🖳💻Ⅴ🛇✦

Town Yetholm 59

National Grid Ref: NT8127

🍴🍺 Border Hotel, Cobbles Inn, Plough Hotel

(2m) *Lochside, Town Yetholm, Kelso, Roxburghshire, TD5 8PD.*
Victorian country house. Peaceful, spacious, ensuite bedrooms. Beautiful countryside.
Grades: ETC 3 Star B&B
Tel: **01573 420349** Mrs Hurst.
D: £20.00-£22.50 **S:** £22.50-£22.50.
Open: Apr to Oct
Beds: 1D 1T **Baths:** 2 En
ざ (2) 🅿 (2) 🗲🖵🏠🕯🖳💻Ⅴ✦

D = Price range per person sharing in a double room

(0.25m 🚍) *Blunty's Mill, Kirk Yetholm, Kelso, Roxburghshire, TD5 6PG.*
Fabulous rural location set in 6 acres. Friendly welcome guaranteed.
Grades: ETC 2 Star
Tel: **01573 420288** Mrs Brooker.
D: £22.00-£30.00 .
Open: All Year
Beds: 2T **Baths:** 1 Sh
ざ 🅿 (10) 🖵🏠✕🕯🛇Ⅴ🛇✦

Planning a longer stay? Always ask for any special rates.

Kelso 60

National Grid Ref: NT7234

🍴🍺 Black Swan, Border Hotel, Cobbles Inn, Plough Hotel, Queen's Head, Wagon & Horses

(7m) *Craignethan House, Jedburgh Road, Kelso, Roxburghshire, TD5 8AZ.*
Grades: ETC 3 Star
Tel: **01573 224818** Mrs McDonald.
D: £18.50-£18.50 **S:** £18.50-£18.50.
Open: All Year
Beds: 2D 1T
Baths: 1 Pr 1 Sh
ざ 🅿 (6) 🖵🏠🕯🖳💻🛇Ⅴ🛇✦
Comfortable welcoming family home with relaxed informal atmosphere. Breakfast to suit all tastes and times. Afternoon tea, tea/coffee in evening, home baking, attractive garden, breathtaking panoramic views of Kelso/Tweed Valley to Floors Castle from all bedrooms. Scottish Border Abbeys, Floors Castle, Tweed Valley, Walter Scott country.

Ribble Way

This is a first class river walk leading through excellent Lancashire walking country up into the Yorkshire Dales, past caves and potholes, to the source of the Ribble (should you so wish). It runs for 70 miles from the sea marshes west of Preston, past lovely Ribchester and Giggleswick right up to Ribblehead in the Pennines. All along the route the river is ever present, changing character the further upstream you move, from the broad river plain to rushing gills and waterfalls. The **Ribble Way** is a good one to do over a couple of long weekends and it meets up with the **Dales Way** and the **Pennine Way** for good measure. The path is well waymarked in Lancashire, although it loses out to other waymarks once into Yorkshire.

Guides:
The Ribble Way by Gladys Sellers (ISBN 1 85284 107 9), published by Cicerone Press and available from all good map shops or directly from the publishers (2 Police Square, Milnthorpe, Cumbria, LA7 7PY, 01539 562069), £5.99 (+ 75p p&p)

Maps:
1:50000 Ordnance Survey Landranger Series: 98, 102, 103

Longton   1
National Grid Ref: SD4726

๏๏ ⌂ Rose & Crown, Midge Hall

(0.25m ☎) *Moorside Villa,*
Drumacre Lane West, Longton,
Preston, Lancs, PR4 4SB.
Actual grid ref: SD490247
Comfortable and homely accommodation close to M6 and M62, M65 access.
Grades: ETC 4 Diamond
Tel: **01772 616612**
D: £22.00-£27.50 **S:** £25.00-£30.00.
Open: All Year (not Xmas)
Beds: 2D 1T **Baths:** 2 En
🅿 (6) ⊬ ⛱ ⛛ ⊞ Ⅴ ▮ ✠

Preston   2
National Grid Ref: SD5329

๏๏ ⌂ Welcome Tavern

(0.25m ☎) *Stanley Guest House,*
7 Stanley Terrace, Preston, PR1 8JE.
Five minutes' walk to town centre, overlooking quiet bowling area.
Tel: **01772 253366**
Fax no: 01772 252802
D: £16.00-£18.00.
S: £20.00-£25.00.
Open: All Year
Beds: 3F 2D 2S
Baths: 2 En 1 Sh
🛏 🅿 (5) ⛱ ⊬ ✕ ⛛ ⊞ Ⅴ ▮

(0.25m ☎) *Willow Cottage,*
Longton Bypass, Longton, Preston,
Lancs, PR4 4RA.
Old cottage set in beautiful gardens and countryside with its own horse stud farm.
Tel: **01772 617570**
Mrs Caunce.
D: £22.00-£25.00 **S:** £22.00-£25.00.
Open: All Year
Beds: 3D
Baths: 1 En 1 Pr 2 Sh
🛏 🅿 (10) ⛱ ✕ ⛛ ⊞ Ⅴ ✠

Ribchester   3
National Grid Ref: SD6435

๏๏ ⌂ Hall's Arms, Punch Bowl, Black Bull, White Bull

(0.5m ☎) *New House Farm,*
Preston Road, Ribchester, Preston,
Lancs, PR3 3XL.
Actual grid ref: SD648354
Old renovated farmhouse, rare breeds.
Tel: **01254 878954** Bamber.
D: £18.00-£22.00 **S:** £22.00-£25.00.
Open: All Year
Beds: 1F 1D 1T **Baths:** 3 En
🛏 (4) 🅿 (8) ⊬ ⛱ ⛛ ⊞ Ⅴ ✠

(1.5m ☎) *Smithy Farm,*
Huntingdon Hall Lane, Dutton,
Ribchester, Preston, Lancs, PR3 2ZT.
Unspoilt countryside 15 mins M6.
Friendly hospitality, children half price.
Tel: **01254 878250** Jackson.
D: £12.50-£12.50 **S:** £18.00-£18.00.
Open: Mar to Nov
Beds: 1F 1D 1T **Baths:** 1 Sh
🛏 🅿 ⛱ ⋔ ✕ ⛛ Ⅴ ▮ ✠

Planning a longer stay? Always ask for any special rates.

Hurst Green 4

National Grid Ref: SD6838

|🍴 🍺 The Shireburn

(3m) *Shireburn Arms Hotel,*
Whalley Road, Hurst Green,
Clitheroe, Lancs, BB6 9QJ.
A warm friendly welcome,
excellent inn and restaurant,
unrivalled views.
Grades: ETC 2 Star, AA 2 Star
Tel: **01254 826518**
Alcock.
Fax no: 01254 826208
D: £32.50-£42.50
S: £45.00-£65.00.
Open: All Year
Beds: 1S 2F 12D 3T
Baths: 18 En
🛏 🅿 (50) 🖊 🗋 🛏 ✗ 🔔 🛏 ♿ Ⅵ 🅰 ⚡

Great Mitton 5

National Grid Ref: SD7138

(0.25m) *Aspinall Arms Hotel,*
Great Mitton, Clitheroe, Lancs,
BB7 9PQ.
Actual grid ref: SD718388
Originally the ferryman's house,
the Aspinall Arms dates back to
coach and horses times.
Tel: **01254 826223**
Mr Morrell.
D: £22.50-£22.50 **S:** £30.00-£30.00.
Open: All Year
Beds: 2D 1S
Baths: 3 En
🅿 (50) 🗋 🔔 🛏 Ⅵ 🅰 ⚡

Clitheroe 6

National Grid Ref: SD7441

🍴 🍺 Swan With Two Necks, Edisford Bridge
Inn, Edisford Inn, Old Post House

(0.25m 🚐) *Selborne House, Back*
Commons, Clitheroe, Lancs,
BB7 2DX.
Detached house on quiet lane
giving peace and tranquillity.
Excellent for walking, bird-
watching, fishing.
Grades: ETC 3 Diamond
Tel: **01200 423571** (also fax no)
Barnes.
D: £18.50-£20.00 **S:** £21.00-£22.50.
Open: All Year
Beds: 1F 2D 1T **Baths:** 4 En
🛏 (1) 🅿 (4) 🗋 🛏 ✗ 🔔 🛏 Ⅵ 🅰 ⚡

(0.75m 🚐) *Brooklands, 9 Pendle*
Road, Clitheroe, Lancs, BB7 1JQ.
Actual grid ref: SD750414
A warm welcome. Detached com-
fortable Victorian home. Town
centre nearby.
Grades: ETC 3 Diamond
Tel: **01200 422797** (also fax no)
Lord.
D: £16.00-£19.50 **S:** £17.00-£22.00.
Open: All Year
Beds: 1D 2T **Baths:** 1 En 1 Sh
🛏 🅿 (5) 🗋 🔔 🛏 Ⅵ 🅰 ⚡

🚐 sign means that,
given due notice,
owners will pick you
up from the path
and drop you off
within reason.

All rates are subject to alteration at the owners' discretion.

Waddington 7

National Grid Ref: SD7243

🍴 🍺 Moorcock Inn, Duke of York

(2m) *Moorcock Inn, Slaidburn*
Road, Waddington, Clitheroe,
Lancs, BB7 3AA.
A warm welcome awaits at this
friendly country inn.
Grades: ETC 2 Star
Tel: **01200 422333** Fillary.
D: £30.00-£35.00 **S:** £38.00-£42.00.
Open: All Year
Beds: 3D 8T
Baths: 11 Pr
🛏 🅿 (150) 🗋 🛏 ✗ 🔔 🛏 Ⅵ 🅰 ⚡

(1m) *Waddington Arms, Clitheroe*
Road, Waddington, Clitheroe,
Lancs, BB7 3HP.
Traditional country inn, real beer,
real food, real bedrooms.
Tel: **01200 423262**
Warburton.
D: £25.00-£35.00 **S:** £35.00-£45.00.
Open: All Year
Beds: 4D 2T
Baths: 6 En
🛏 🅿 (50) 🖊 🗋 🛏 ✗ 🔔 🛏 ♿ Ⅵ 🅰 ⚡

Planning a longer stay? Always ask for any special rates.

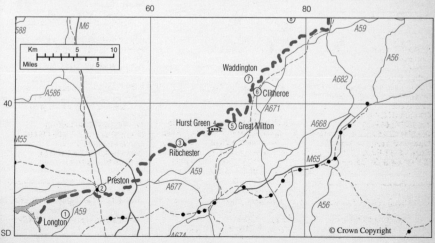

Bolton by Bowland   8

National Grid Ref: SD7849

(0.5m) *Middle Flass Lodge, Settle Road, Bolton by Bowland, Clitheroe, Yorkshire, BB7 4NY.*
Idyllic countryside location. Chef prepared cuisine. Cosy rooms. Friendly welcome.
Grades: ETC 4 Diamond,
AA 4 Diamond
Tel: **01200 447259** Mrs Simpson.
Fax no: 01200 447300
D: £22.00-£30.00 **S:** £27.00-£35.00.
Open: All Year
Beds: 1F 2D 2T
Baths: 5 En suite
🛆 🅿 (24) ✍ ⌷ ✕ ♨ ▥ Ⓥ 🛉 ⁄

Long Preston   9

National Grid Ref: SD8358

🍴 🍺 Maypole Inn

(0.5m) *Inglenook, 22 Main Street, Long Preston, Skipton, BD23 4PH.*
Traditional Mullion windowed cottage, village setting, ideal for Dales exploration.
Tel: **01729 840511** Mrs Parton.
D: £18.00-£20.00 **S:** £25.00-£30.00.
Open: All Year
Beds: 1F **Baths:** 1 Pr
🅿 (4) ⌷ 🛏 ♨ ▥ Ⓥ 🛉 ⁄

D = Price range per person sharing in a double room

The Grid Reference beneath the location heading is for the village or town - *not* for individual houses, which are shown (where supplied) in each entry itself.

Giggleswick   10

National Grid Ref: SD8164

🍴 🍺 Black Horse, Hart's Head

(0.25m 🚪) *Yorkshire Dales Field Centre, Holme Beck, Raines Road, Giggleswick, Settle, N. Yorks, BD24 0AQ.*
Actual grid ref: SD813641
Excellent cooking - comfortable well-appointed converted barn.
Tel: **01729 824180** (also fax no)
Mrs Barbour.
D: £10.50-£10.50
S: £10.50-£10.50.
Open: All Year
Beds: 6F 2S
Baths: 5 Sh
🛆 🅿 (7) ✍ ⌷ 🛏 ✕ ♨ ▥ Ⓥ 🛉 ⁄

Settle   11

National Grid Ref: SD8163

🍴 🍺 Golden Lion, Crown, Royal Oak

(0.5m) *Liverpool House, Chapel Square, Settle, N. Yorks, BD24 9HR.*
Actual grid ref: SD822635
Situated in quiet area yet within 3 mins' walk town square.
Grades: AA 3 Diamond
Tel: **01729 822247**
Mr & Mrs Duerden.
D: £19.00-£23.00
S: £19.00-£20.00.
Open: All Year
Beds: 4D 1T 2S
Baths: 2 En 2 Sh
🛆 🅿 (8) ✍ ⌷ 🛏 ▥ Ⓥ 🛉 ⁄

(0.5m) *The Yorkshire Rose Guest House, Duke Street, Settle, North Yorkshire, BD24 9AW.*
Comfortable family run establishment close to town centre/station. Relax.
Grades: ETC 3 Diamond,
AA 3 Diamond
Tel: **01729 822032**
D: £15.00-£23.50
S: £15.00-£23.50.
Open: All Year
Beds: 1F 1T 2D 1S
Baths: 2 En 1 Sh
🛆 🅿 (6) ✍ ⌷ 🛏 ▥ Ⓥ 🛉 ⁄

(0.5m 🚪) *The Oast Guest House, 5 Penyghent View, Church Street, Settle, N. Yorks, BD24 9JJ.*
High standards with a Yorkshire welcome await you.
Tel: **01729 822989** (also fax no)
Mr & Mrs King.
D: £18.50-£23.00
S: £15.50-£17.50.
Open: All Year
Beds: 1F 2D 2T 1S
Baths: 3 En 3 Sh
🛆 🅿 (4) ✍ ⌷ ✕ ♨ ▥ Ⓥ 🛉 ⁄

Stainforth   12

National Grid Ref: SD8267

(▲ 0.25m) *Stainforth Youth Hostel, Taitlands, Stainforth, Settle, North Yorkshire, BD24 9PA.*
Actual grid ref: SD821668
Tel: **01729 823577**
Under 18: £7.75
Adults: £11.00
Self-catering facilities, Showers, Lounge, Dining room, Drying room, Cycle store, Parking, Evening meal at 7.00pm, Facilities for disabled people, No smoking, Kitchen facilities, Breakfast available, Credit cards accepted
Georgian listed building with fine interior, set in extensive grounds with grazing paddock, a short walk from the village. Central for many walks, including the Pennine and Ribble Ways, and the Yorkshire Dales Cycleway.

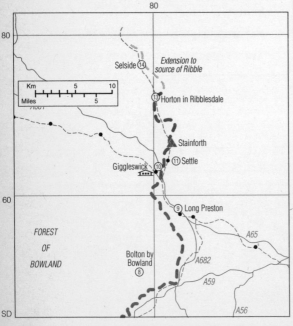

S = Price range for a single person in a single room

Horton-in-Ribblesdale 13

National Grid Ref: SD8072

(0.25m) *The Willows, Horton-in-Ribblesdale, Settle, N. Yorks, BD24 0HT* Large detached house, luxurious bedrooms in lovely Yorkshire Dales.
Tel: **01729 860373** (also fax no)
Mrs Barker.
D: £20.00-£24.00
S: £20.00-£25.00.
Open: Easter to Sep
Beds: 1F 1D 1T
Baths: 1 En 1 Pr 1 Sh
🛏 🅿 (5) 🗐 🍴 🗙 🕯 🛏 Ⅴ ⓘ ∕

(0.25m) *The Rowe House, Horton-in-Ribblesdale, Settle, N. Yorks, BD24 0HT.*
Actual grid ref: SD804728
Distinctive Georgian country house in half-acre grounds TV lounge.
Tel: **01729 860212**
Mr & Mrs Lane.
D: £18.00-£22.00
S: £22.00-£26.00.
Open: Mar to Oct
Beds: 2D 3T
Baths: 3 En 2 Sh
🛏 (12) 🅿 (6) 🗐 🕯 🛏 Ⅴ ⓘ ∕

All paths are popular: you are well-advised to book ahead

Planning a longer stay? Always ask for any special rates.

Selside 14

National Grid Ref: SD7875

🍴 🍺 Crown

(1m 🚌) *South House Farm, Selside, Settle, N. Yorks, BD24 0HU.*
Comfortable farmhouse accommodation set in the centre of the Peaks.
Tel: **01729 860271** Ms Kenyon.
D: £20.00-£20.00 **S:** £20.00-£20.00.
Open: Easter to Oct
Beds: 1F 2D 1T **Baths:** 1 En
🛏 (1) 🅿 (6) ⅙ 🗐 🍴 🗙 🕯 🛏 Ⅴ ⓘ ∕

The Ridgeway

The Ridgeway is the name for a series of ancient pathways following the line of a chalk escarpment that extends for 85 miles from Avebury in Wiltshire, with its famous stone circle, up to the Ivinghoe Beacon in Buckinghamshire. You head over the beacons to Goring, where the River Thames bisects the path and then you turn east to cross the Thames Valley to the Chilterns. The western part is all open downland, following the ancient track on the ridge, while the eastern part is largely through leafy woods. In the height of a hot summer the hard, broken chalk track of the western section will test the ankles; and after rain the surface becomes awkward, so look after your feet. There are links with four other paths featured in this book: the **Wessex Ridgeway**, the **Thames Path,** the **Oxfordshire Way** and the **Icknield Way**. An excellent series of information leaflets can be had from the Ridgeway Officer at the **Oxfordshire County Council** address given below.

Guides (available from all good book-shops, unless stated):
The Ridgeway by Neil Curtis (ISBN 1 854104 90 X), published by Aurum Press in association with the Countryside Commission and Ordnance Survey, £10.99

Discovering the Ridgeway by Vera Burden (ISBN 0-7478026-7-X), published by Shire Publications and available by post from the publishers (Cromwell House, Church Street, Princes Risborough, Bucks, HP27 9AA, tel. 01844 344301), £3.95 (+ £1 p&p)

Maps: 1:50000 Ordnance Survey Landranger Series: 165, 173, 174 and 175.
Also *The Ridgeway*, ISBN 1 871149 03 7 (4-colour linear route map), published by Footprint and available directly from their offices (Unit 87, Stirling Enterprise Park, Stirling, FK7 7RP), £3.50 (+ 40p p&p)

All comments on the path to: Ridgeway Officer, O.C.C. Countryside Service, Library HQ, Holton, Oxford, OX33 1QQ

Avebury   1

National Grid Ref: SU1069

⚑ Waggon & Horses, Red Lion

(1.25m 🚌) *6 Beckhampton Road,* Avebury, Marlborough, Wilts, *SN8 1QT.*
Nearby Avebury Stone Circle, Ridgeway Walk, Silbury Hill, bus route.
Tel: **01672 539588** Mrs Dixon.
D: £16.00-£20.00 **S:** £25.00-£30.00.
Open: All Year (not Xmas)
Beds: 1D 1T
Baths: 1 Sh
🛏🅿 (6) 🖵 🕯 🛋 Ⅴ 🖺 ⁄

Lockeridge   2

National Grid Ref: SU1467

⚑ Who'd A Thought It

(3m 🚌) *The Taffrail,* Back Lane, Lockeridge, Marlborough, Wilts, *SN8 4ED*
Actual grid ref: SU150675
Great welcome, comfort, tranquillity. Delightful modern home and lovely garden.
Tel: **01672 861266** (also fax no)
Mrs Spencer.
D: £17.50-£17.50 **S:** £20.00-£20.00.
Open: Jan to Nov
Beds: 1D 1T 1S **Baths:** 1 Sh
🛏 (8) 🅿 (3) ⁄ 🖵 🛋 ⁄

Chiseldon   3

National Grid Ref: SU1879

⚑ Patriots' Arms, Calley Arms

(1m 🚌) *Courtleigh House,* 40 Draycott Road, Chiseldon, Swindon, Wilts, *SN4 0LS.*
Actual grid ref: SU184791
Large well-appointed country home; large garden with downland views. **Grades:** ETC 3 Diamond
Tel: **01793 740246** Ms Hibberd.
D: £18.50-£21.00 **S:** £22.00-£25.00.
Open: All Year (not Xmas)
Beds: 2T 1S **Baths:** 1 En 1 Sh
🛏 🅿 (3) ⁄ 🖵 🛋 🖾 Ⅴ 🖺 ⁄

D = Price range per person sharing in a double room

(1m 🚌) *Norton House,* 46 Draycott Road, Chiseldon, Swindon, Wilts, *SN4 0LT.*
Actual grid ref: SU185789
Executive countryside house, peaceful surroundings, easy access Bath, Oxford, Cotswolds.
Tel: **01793 741210** Mrs Dixon.
D: £21.00-£23.00 **S:** £20.00-£20.00.
Open: All Year (not Xmas)
Beds: 1F 1D 1T 1S **Baths:** 2 En
🛏 (5) 🅿 (5) ⁄ 🖵 🛋 🖾 Ⅴ ⁄

🚌 sign means that, *given due notice*, owners will pick you up from the path and drop you off *within reason.*

Manton 4

National Grid Ref: SU1768

⊯ ⬧ Oddfellows Arms

(3m) *Sunrise Farm, Manton, Marlborough, Wilts, SN8 4HL.*
Actual grid ref: SU168682
Peacefully located approximately 1 mile from Marlborough. Friendly, comfortable, relaxing atmosphere.
Grades: ETC 3 Diamond
Tel: **01672 512878** (also fax no)
Mrs Couzens.
D: £19.00-£20.00 **S:** £19.00-£25.00.
Open: March to Oct
Beds: 1D 2T **Baths:** 2 Pr
⤳ (14) ℙ (3) ⚡◻♨ ⬙ ⅏ V ⬥

Marlborough 5

National Grid Ref: SU1869

⊯ ⬧ Bear, Roebuck, Sun, Oddfellows Arms

(3.5m) *Beam End, 67 George Lane, Marlborough, Wilts, SN8 4BY.*
Peaceful detached house, every comfort, good centre for touring Wiltshire.
Grades: ETC 3 Diamond
Tel: **01672 515048** (also fax no)
Mrs Drew.
D: £20.00-£27.50 **S:** £20.00-£30.00.
Open: All Year (not Xmas)
Beds: 1T 2S
Baths: 1 En 1 Sh
ℙ (3) ⚡◻♨ ⬙ ⅏ V ⬥

**All details shown
are as supplied
by B&B owners in
Autumn 2001.**

(3.5m 🚌) *Cartref, 63 George Lane, Marlborough, Wilts, SN8 4BY.*
Actual grid ref: SU1969
Family home near town centre. Ideal for Avebury, Savernake, Wiltshire Downs.
Tel: **01672 512771** Mrs Harrison.
D: £18.00-£18.00 **S:** £20.00-£20.00.
Open: All Year (not Xmas)
Beds: 1F 1D 1T
Baths: 1 Sh
⤳ (6) ℙ (2) 🐾 ⬙ ⬦ ⬥

Ogbourne St George 6

National Grid Ref: SU1974

⊯ ⬧ Old Crown

(0.5m 🚌) *The Old Crown, Marlborough Road, Ogbourne St George, Marlborough, Wilts, SN8 1SQ.*
Actual grid ref: SU202743
Close to historic Marlborough. Covered well in restaurant.
Tel: **01672 841445**
Mr & Mrs Shaw.
Fax no: 01672 841056
D: £20.00-£30.00 **S:** £35.00-£45.00.
Open: All Year (not Xmas/New Year)
Beds: 2T **Baths:** 2 Pr
⤳ ℙ (15) ⚡◻🐾✕ ⬙ ⅏ V ⬥ ⬦

Lower Wanborough 7

National Grid Ref: SU2083

(2m 🚌) *Iris Cottage, Bury Croft, Lower Wanborough, Swindon, Wilts, SN4 0AP.*
Very comfortable village cottage. Swindon 4 miles. Near Ridgeway Path.
Tel: **01793 790591** Mrs Rosier.
D: £19.00-£19.00 **S:** £20.00-£20.00.
Open: All Year (not Xmas)
Beds: 2S
Baths: 1 Sh
ℙ (2) ⚡◻ ⬙ ⬦ ⬥

Bishopstone (Swindon) 8

National Grid Ref: SU2483

⊯ ⬧ Royal Oak

(1m 🚌) *Prebendal Farm, Bishopstone, Swindon, Wilts, SN6 8PT.*
Actual grid ref: SU244836
Farmhouse serving local organic produce, short walk to excellent pubs.
Tel: **01793 790485** Mrs Selbourne.
D: £25.00-£30.00 **S:** £25.00-£30.00.
Open: All Year (not Xmas)
Beds: 2D 1T 1S **Baths:** 2 Sh
⤳ ℙ (12) ◻🐾✕ ⬙ ⅏ V ⬥ ⬦

Woolstone 9

National Grid Ref: SU2988

⊯ ⬧ White Horse

(0.5m 🚌) *Hickory House, Woolstone, Faringdon, Oxon, SN7 7QL.*
Actual grid ref: SU294877
Tel: **01367 820303**
Mr & Mrs Grist.
Fax no: 01367 820958
D: £19.00-£25.00 **S:** £21.00-£25.00.
Open: All Year (not Xmas)
Beds: 2T **Baths:** 2 En
⤳ (12) ℙ (2) ⚡◻ ⬙ ⅏ V ⬥
Situated in a delightful picturesque village beneath the White Horse Hill near the Ridgeway, Hickory House offers comfortable accommodation in a recently built self-contained extension. Pub serving food is a minutes walk. Oxford, Bath and the Cotswolds are within easy driving distance.

S = Price range for a single
person in a single room

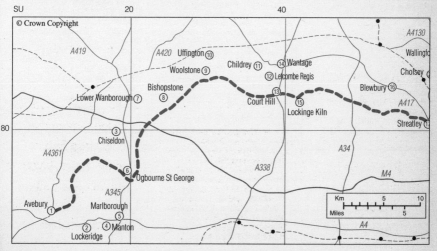

Uffington 10

National Grid Ref: SU3089

🍴 🍺 Fox & Hounds

(1.5m 🚐) *Norton House,*
Broad Street, Uffington,
Faringdon, Oxon, SN7 7RA.
Actual grid ref: SU305895
Friendly C18th family home in
centre of quiet, pretty village.
Tel: **01367 820230** (also fax no)
Mrs Oberman.
D: £20.00-£21.00 **S:** £23.00-£26.00.
Open: All Year (not Xmas)
Beds: 1F 1D 1S **Baths:** 2 Pr
🛇 🅿 (3) ⌁⌂ 🐾 🗓 📺 Ⓥ 🛆 ⚡

(1.25m) *The Craven, Uffington,*
Faringdon, Oxon, SN7 7RD.
C17th thatched, beamed farm-
house/hotel.
Tel: **01367 820449** Mrs Wadsworth
D: £20.00 **S:** £25.00.
Open: All Year
Beds: 1F 3D 2T 2S
Baths: 2 Pr 2 Sh
🛇 🅿 (9) ⌂ 🐾 ✕ 🗓 🛆 ⚡

Childrey 11

National Grid Ref: SU3587

🍴 🍺 The Hatchett

(1.75m 🚐) *Ridgeway House, West*
Street, Childrey, Wantage, Oxon,
OX12 9UL.
Actual grid ref: SU335873
Luxury, countryside home in quiet
Downland village near the
Ridgeway.
Tel: **01235 751538** (also fax no)
Mrs Roberts.
D: £20.00-£22.50 **S:** £23.00-£29.00.
Open: All Year
Beds: 1F 1T 1S **Baths:** 2 En
🛇 🅿 (5) ⌁⌂ 🗓 📺 Ⓥ 🛆 ⚡

Letcombe Regis 12

National Grid Ref: SU3886

🍴 🍺 Greyhound, Lamb

(0.5m 🚐) *Quince Cottage,*
Letcombe Regis, Wantage, Oxon,
OX12 9JP.
Large thatched cottage, exposed
beams, near Ridgeway, warm fami-
ly atmosphere.
Tel: **01235 763652** Mrs Boden.
D: £21.00-£25.00 **S:** £25.00-£25.00.
Open: All Year
Beds: 1T 1S **Baths:** 1 Pr
🛇 (1) 🅿 (2) ⌁⌂ 🗓 📺 Ⓥ 🛆 ⚡

> **Pay B&Bs by**
> **cash or cheque and**
> **be prepared to**
> **pay up front.**

🚐 sign means that,
given due notice,
owners will pick you
up from the path
and drop you off
within reason.

(0.5m 🚐) *Old Vicarage, Letcombe*
Regis, Wantage, Oxon, OX12 9JP.
Delightful Victorian home, elegant
accommodation, near pub, pretty
downland village.
Tel: **01235 765827**
Mrs Barton.
Fax no: 020 8743 8740
D: £22.00-£25.00
S: £22.00-£30.00.
Open: All Year (not Xmas)
Beds: 1D 1T 1S
Baths: 1 En 1 Sh
🛇 🅿 (2) ⌁⌂ 🗓 🛆 ⚡

Court Hill 13

National Grid Ref: SU3885

(🔺 0.5m) *Ridgeway Youth Hostel,*
Courth Hill Ridgeway Centre,
Court Hill, Wantage, Oxfordshire,
OX12 9NE.
Actual grid ref: SU393851
Tel: **01235 760253**
Under 18: £6.90
Adults: £10.00
Self-catering facilities, Television,
Showers, Showers, Laundry
facilities, Lounge, Dining room,
Drying room, Cycle store, Parking,
Evening meal at 7.00pm, No
smoking, WC, Kitchen facilities,
Breakfast available, Luggage store,
Credit cards accepted
Modern hostel, beautifully
reconstructed from five barns,
with beechwood grounds,
panoramic views and stabling for
four horses.

Wantage 14

National Grid Ref: SU4087

(3m) *The Bell Inn, 38 Market*
Place, Wantage, Oxon, OX12 8AH.
C16th market town inn. Good beer
and home-cooked food in warm
friendly atmosphere.
Tel: **01235 763718** (also fax no)
Mrs Williams.
D: £22.50-£27.50
S: £20.00-£35.00.
Open: All Year
Beds: 2F 5D 4T 7S
Baths: 11 En 2 Sh
🛇 ⌂ 🐾 ✕ 🗓 📺 Ⓥ 🛆

Lockinge Kiln 15

National Grid Ref: SU4283

(0.5m) *Lockinge Kiln Farm,*
The Ridgeway, Lockinge Kiln,
Wantage, Oxon, OX12 8PA.
Actual grid ref: SU424834
Quiet comfortable farmhouse
working farm ideal walking riding
cycling country.
Tel: **01235 763308** (also fax no)
Mrs Cowan.
D: £19.00-£19.00
S: £22.00-£22.00.
Open: All Year (not Xmas)
Beds: 1D 1T 1S
Baths: 3 Sh
🛇 (10) 🅿 (3) ⌁⌂ ✕ 🗓 📺 Ⓥ ⚡

Blewbury 16

National Grid Ref: SU5385

🍴 🍺 Barley Mow

(2m) *Barley Mow, London Road,*
Blewbury, Oxfordshire, OX11 9NU.
Local pub with separate
accommodation, lovely walks and
picturesque village.
Tel: **01235 850296**
F Cox & M Hughes.
D: £30.00-£30.00
S: £40.00-£40.00.
Open: All Year
Beds: 2T 1S
Baths: 3 En
🅿 (4) ⌁⌂ ✕ 🗓 📺 Ⓥ

Streatley 17

National Grid Ref: SU5980

🍴 🍺 The Bull, Catherine Wheel

(🔺 0.5m) *Streatley-on-Thames*
Youth Hostel, Hill House, Reading
Road, Streatley, Reading, Berks,
RG8 9JJ.
Actual grid ref: SU591806
Tel: **01491 872278**
Under 18: £7.75
Adults: £11.00
Self-catering facilities, Television,
Showers, Dining room, Drying
room, Cycle store, Parking
Limited, Evening meal at 7.00pm,
No smoking, WC, Kitchen
facilities, Breakfast available,
Credit cards accepted
Homely Victorian family house,
completely refurbished, in a
beautiful riverside village.

> **High season,**
> **bank holidays and**
> **special events mean**
> **low availability**
> *everywhere.*

(0.5m 🚌) *Pennyfield,*
The Coombe, Streatley, Reading,
Berkshire, RG8 9QT.
Pretty village house with attractive
terraced garden. Friendly welcoming hosts.
Grades: ETC 4 Diamond
Tel: 01491 872048 (also fax no)
D: £22.50-£25.00
S: £22.50-£25.00.
Open: All Year (not Xmas/
New Year)
Beds: 1T 2D
Baths: 2 En 1 Sh
🅿 (4) ⊁❑🐾🔥📷 Ⓥ🔒↯

Goring 18

National Grid Ref: SU6081

🍴🍺 Catherine Wheel, John Barleycorn, Miller
Of Mansfield, Bull Inn, Perch & Pike

(0.25m) *The Catherine Wheel,*
Station Road, Goring, Reading,
Berks, RG8 9HB.
Accommodation in a Victorian
cottage in riverside village.
Tel: 01491 872379
Mrs Kerr.
D: £20.00
S: £25.00.
Open: All Year
Beds: 2D 1T
Baths: 2 Sh
🛏⊁❑🐾🔥📷 Ⓥ

North Stoke 19

National Grid Ref: SU6186

(On path) *Footpath Cottage,*
The Street, North Stoke,
Wallingford, Oxon, OX10 6BJ.
Lovely old cottage, peaceful river
village. Warm welcome, excellent
food.
Tel: 01491 839763 Mrs Tanner.
D: £19.00-£20.00 **S:** £20.00-£20.00.
Open: All Year
Beds: 2D 1S **Baths:** 1 En 1 Sh
🛏❑🐾✕🔥📷 Ⓥ🔒↯

Wallingford 20

National Grid Ref: SU6089

🍴🍺 Shepherd's Hut, Six Bells, Bell, The Queens
Head

(0.5m) *Little Gables,*
166 Crowmarsh Hill, Wallingford,
Oxford, OX10 8BG.
Actual grid ref: SU623889
Delightfully large private house
where a warm welcome awaits you.
Grades: ETC 3 Diamond
Tel: 01491 837834 Mrs Reeves.
Fax no: 01491 834426
D: £25.00-£35.00 **S:** £30.00-£35.00.
Open: All Year
Beds: 2F 2D 3T 1S
Baths: 2 En 1 Pr
🛏🅿⊁❑🔥📷♿Ⓥ🔒↯

(1m 🚌) *Munts Mill, Castle Lane,*
Wallingford, Oxfordshire, OX10 0BN.
Actual grid ref: SU609895
Near town centre on edge of
Chilterns - advance booking only.
Tel: **01491 836654**
Mrs Broster.
S: £20.00-£25.00.
Open: All Year (not Xmas)
Beds: 2S
⊁❑🔥📷 Ⓥ↯

(2.5m 🚌) *North Farm,*
Shillingford Hill, Wallingford,
Oxon, OX10 8NB.
Actual grid ref: SU586924
Quiet comfortable farmhouse on
working farm, close to River
Thames.
Tel: **01865 858406**
Mrs Warburton.
Fax no: 01865 858519
D: £24.00-£28.00 **S:** £28.00-£38.00.
Open: All Year (not Xmas)
Beds: 2D 1T
Baths: 1 En 2 Pr
🛏 (8) 🅿 (6) ⊁❑🔥📷 Ⓥ🔒↯

Pay B&Bs by cash or
cheque and be prepared
to pay up front.

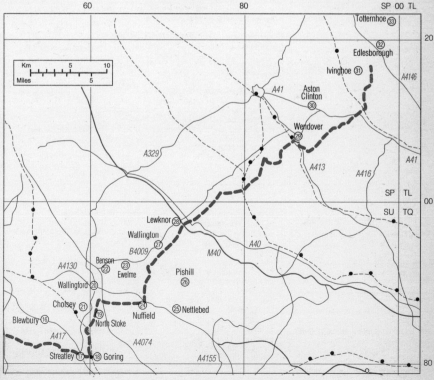

Cholsey 21

National Grid Ref: SU5886

The Beatle and Wedge

(2m) ***The Well Cottage,*** *Caps Lane, Cholsey, Wallingford, Oxon, OX10 9HQ.*
Delightful cottage with ensuite bedrooms in secluded garden flat.
Tel: **01491 651959** Alexander.
Fax no: 01491 651675
D: £15.00-£25.00 **S:** £20.00-£30.00.
Open: All Year
Beds: 2T 1D **Baths:** 2 En 1 Pr

Benson 22

National Grid Ref: SU6191

Three Horseshoes, Crown

(2m) ***Fyfield Manor,*** *Brook Street, Benson, Wallingford, Oxon, OX10 6HA.*
Medieval dining room. Beautiful water gardens. Essentially a family house.
Tel: **01491 835184** Mrs Brown.
Fax no: 01491 825635
D: £25.00-£25.00 **S:** £30.00-£30.00.
Open: All Year (not Xmas/ New Year)
Beds: 1D 1T **Baths:** 2 En 1 Pr
(10) (6)

Ewelme 23

National Grid Ref: SU6491

Crown, Shepherds Hut

(2m) ***Fords Farm,*** *Ewelme, Wallingford, Oxon, OX10 6HU.*
Picturesque setting in historic village. Warm, friendly atmosphere. Good views.
Grades: ETC 4 Diamond
Tel: **01491 839272** Miss Edwards.
D: £24.00-£25.00 **S:** £30.00-£35.00.
Open: All Year
Beds: 1D 2T
Baths: 1 Pr 1 Sh
(8)

(1m) ***May's Farm,*** *Turner's Court, Ewelme, Wallingford, Oxon, OX10 6QF.*
Working stock farm. Fabulous views, quiet location, good walking.
Tel: **01491 641294** Mrs Passmore.
Fax no: 01491 641697
D: £19.00-£22.00 **S:** £25.00-£30.00.
Open: All Year
Beds: 1F 1T 1S
Baths: 1 En 1 Sh
(4)

All paths are popular: you are well-advised to book ahead

Nuffield 24

National Grid Ref: SU6687

The Crown

(On path) ***The Rectory,*** *Nuffield, Henley-on-Thames, Oxon, RG9 5SN.*
Actual grid ref: SU667875
Working Rectory on the Ridgeway Path at 700 feet; Aga breakfasts
Tel: **01491 641305** (also fax no) Mr Shearer.
D: £15.00-£18.00
S: £18.00-£20.00.
Open: All Year
Beds: 1D 1T 1S
Baths: 1 Private
(4)

Nettlebed 25

National Grid Ref: SU6986

Crown Inn

(0.5m) ***Park Corner Farm House,*** *Nettlebed, Henley-on-Thames, Oxon, RG9 6DX.*
Queen Anne farmhouse in AONB between Henley-on-Thames and Oxford.
Tel: **01491 641450**
Mrs Rutter.
-£22.50 -£25.00.
Open: All Year (not Xmas/New Year)
Beds: 2T 1S
Baths: 1 Sh 1 Pr
(6)

Pishill 26

National Grid Ref: SU7289

The Crown

(2m) ***Bank Farm,*** *Pishill, Henley-on-Thames, Oxon, RG9 6HJ.*
Actual grid ref: SU724898
Quiet comfortable farmhouse, beautiful countryside. Convenient Oxford, London, Windsor.
Grades: ETC 2 Diamond
Tel: **01491 638601**
Mrs Lakey.
D: £23.00-£23.00
S: £20.00-£23.00.
Open: All Year (not Xmas)
Beds: 1F 1S
Baths: 1 En 1 Sh
(5)

(2m) ***Orchard House,*** *Pishill, Henley-on-Thames, Oxfordshire, RG9 6HJ.*
Property in area outstanding natural Beauty surrounded by ancient Woodlands.
Tel: **01491 638351** (also fax no) Mrs Connolly.
D: £25.00-£25.00
S: £25.00-£25.00.
Open: All Year
Beds: 2F 1D 1T
Baths: 3 En 1 Pr

Watlington 27

National Grid Ref: SU6894

(0.25m) ***Woodgate Orchard Cottage,*** *Howe Road, Watlington, Oxon, OX9 5EL.*
Actual grid ref: SU691937
Tel: **01491 612675** (also fax no) Roberts.
D: £25.00-£35.00 **S:** £30.00-£30.00.
Open: All Year
Beds: 1F 1T 1D
Baths: 1 En 1 Pr
(8)
Warm welcome, countryside location, comfortable rooms, home-cooking, restful gardens, red kites gliding above. 500m off Ridgeway, convenient for Oxfordshire Way and Cycle Path, Chiltern Way, Thames Path and towns of Oxford, Henley, Reading, Windsor, Heathrow. Oxford Tube bus stop 2 miles away Lewknor - transport arrangements.

Lewknor 28

National Grid Ref: SU7197

Leathern Bottle

(1m) ***Moorcourt Cottage,*** *Weston Road, Lewknor, Watlington, Oxfordshire, OX9 5RU.*
Beautiful C15th cottage, open views, very quiet, friendly and comfortable.
Tel: **01844 351419** (also fax no) Mrs Hodgson.
D: £22.50-£22.50 **S:** £30.00-£30.00.
Open: All Year
Beds: 1T 1D **Baths:** 1 En 1 Pr
(4)

Wendover 29

National Grid Ref: SP8608

Red Lion

(0.5m) ***46 Lionel Avenue,*** *Wendover, Aylesbury, Bucks, HP22 6LP.*
Actual grid ref: SP863087
Family home. Lounge, conservatory, garden. English/vegetarian breakfasts. Tea/coffee always available.
Grades: ETC 3 Diamond
Tel: **01296 623426**
Mr & Mrs MacDonald.
D: £22.00-£22.00 **S:** £24.00-£24.00.
Open: All Year (not Xmas/ New Year)
Beds: 1T 2S **Baths:** 1 Sh
(3)

Please take muddy boots off before entering premises

D = Price range per person sharing in a double room

Aston Clinton 30

National Grid Ref: SP8712

⬥⬥ Rising Sun

(2.5m) **B&B at 103,** *103 London Road, Aston Clinton, Aylesbury, Bucks, HP22 5LD.*
Actual grid ref: SP895115
Superior, comfortable B&B, centrally located for business/tourists. French & German spoken.
Tel: **01296 631313**
Mr & Mrs Taylor.
Fax no: 01296 631616
D: £20.00-£24.00 **S:** £30.00-£35.00.
Open: All Year
Beds: 1D 2T
Baths: 2 En 1 Sh
⬥ (8) ⬤ (6) ⬥⬥⬥⬥⬥⬥⬥⬥

All rates are subject to alteration at the owners' discretion.

Ivinghoe 31

National Grid Ref: SP9416

(▲ 1m) *Ivinghoe Youth Hostel, The Old Brewery House, High Street, Ivinghoe, Leighton Buzzard, LU7 9EP.*
Actual grid ref: SP945161
Tel: **01296 668251**
Under 18: £6.90 **Adults:** £10.00
Self-catering facilities, Television, Showers, Lounge, Drying room, Cycle store, Parking, Evening meal at 7.00pm, Kitchen facilities, Breakfast available
Georgian mansion, once home of a local brewer, next to village church in Chilterns' Area of Outstanding Natural Beauty.

Edlesborough 32

National Grid Ref: SP9719

⬥⬥ The Golden Rule

(1m 🚐) *Ridgeway End, 5 Ivinghoe Way, Edlesborough, Dunstable, Beds, LU6 2EL.*
Actual grid ref: SP975183
Pretty bungalow in private road, surrounded by fields and views of the Chiltern Hills.
Tel: **01525 220405** (also fax no)
Mrs Lloyd.
D: £20.00-£22.00 **S:** £22.00-£24.00.
Open: All Year (not Xmas)
Beds: 1D 1T **Baths:** 1 En
⬥ (2) ⬤ (3) ⬥⬥⬥⬥⬥⬥

S = Price range for a single person in a single room

Totternhoe 33

National Grid Ref: SP9821

⬥⬥ Old Farm Inn, Cross Keys

(5m) *Country Cottage, 5 Brightwell Avenue, Totternhoe, Dunstable, Beds, LU6 1QT.*
Actual grid ref: SP994210
Quiet village house in countryside with views of Dunstable Downs.
Tel: **01582 601287** (also fax no)
Mrs Mardell.
D: £25.00-£25.00 **S:** £25.00-£25.00.
Open: All Year (not Xmas)
Beds: 1T 1D 1S
Baths: 2 En 1Shared
⬥ ⬤ (3) ⬥⬥⬥⬥⬥⬥⬥

🚐 sign means that, *given due notice*, owners will pick you up from the path and drop you off *within reason.*

Shropshire Way

The **Shropshire Way** is a 140-mile way-marked circular walk starting in Shrewsbury and is well worth coming a long way for. Shropshire is an extraordinary county. Its strange hills - the Stiperstones, the Long Mynd, Wenlock Edge and the Wrekin; the classic English market town of Ludlow; those little villages near the Welsh Border that begin with 'Clun'- the 'quietest places under the sun'; the relics of the Industrial Revolution at Ironbridge - all make for a walk which you will remember for a long time. The local **Rambler's Association** have done an excellent job on this path together with their county council. Buy the book and walk it now!

Guides: *Rambler's Guide to the Shropshire Way* by the Shropshire Area RA (ISBN 0 94667 94 44), published by Management Update and available from Powney's Bookshop (4-5 St Alkmund's Place, Shrewsbury, SY1 1UJ, tel. 01743 369165), £5.99 (+£1 p&p)

Maps: 1:50000 Ordnance Survey Landranger Series: 117, 126, 127, 137, 138

Shrewsbury   1

National Grid Ref: SJ4912

🍴 🍺 Talbot Inn, Boathouse Inn, Armory, Abbey Hotel, Dun Cow Inn, Lea Cross Inn, Bull, Three Fishes, Crown, New Inn, Cornhouse, Red Lion, Red Barn, Traitors' Gate, Old Bell, Severn Apprentice

(▲ On path) *Shrewsbury Youth Hostel, The Woodlands, Abbey Foregate, Shrewsbury, Shropshire, SY2 6LZ.*
Actual grid ref: SJ505120
Tel: 01743 360179
Under 18: £6.50 **Adults:** £9.25
Self-catering facilities, Television, Laundry facilities, Lounge, Cycle store, Parking, Evening meal at 7.00pm, Kitchen facilities, Breakfast available, Luggage store, Credit cards accepted
Former Victorian ironmaster's house built in red sandstone. The hostel is on the outskirts of the town, but only about a mile from the Abbey and town centre.

(0.25m) *The Bancroft , 17 Coton Crescent, Shrewsbury, Shropshire, SY1 2NY.*
Actual grid ref: SJ490134
Within easy walking distance of town centre and railway station.
Grades: ETC 3 Diamond
Tel: 01743 231746 (also fax no)
Mrs Oldham-Malcolm.
D: £16.00-£19.00 **S:** £18.00-£22.00.
Open: All Year (not Xmas)
Beds: 1D 1T 2S
Baths: 2 Sh
🛏 🅿 (4) ⊬ 🗀 🛉 🏚 🎱 Ⓥ 🖤 ⚡

(0.5m 🚗) *2 Lythwood Hall, Bayston Hill, Shrewsbury, Shropshire, SY3 0AD.*
Actual grid ref: SJ470085
Quality accommodation in a comfortable spacious Georgian house.
Grades: ETC 3 Diamond, AA 3 Diamond
Tel: 07074 874747
Mr & Mrs Bottomley.
Fax no: 07074 874747
D: £20.00-£20.00 **S:** £20.00-£20.00.
Open: All Year
Beds: 1D 1T **Baths:** 1 Pr 1 Sh
🛏 🅿 (2) ⊬ 🗀 🛏 ✕ 🛉 🏚 Ⓥ 🖤 ⚡

(0.5m) *Castlecote Guest House, 77 Monkmoor Road, Shrewsbury, Shropshire, SY2 5AT.*
Actual grid ref: SJ503127
Family-run, comfortable Victorian house, close to all amenities.
Grades: ETC 3 Diamond
Tel: 01743 245473 Mrs Tench.
D: £17.50-£22.00 **S:** £17.50-£22.00.
Open: All Year (not Xmas)
Beds: 2F 4D 2T 0S
Baths: 1 En 2 Sh
🛏 🅿 (4) 🗀 🛏 🛉 🏚 Ⓥ

D = Price range per person sharing in a double room

(0.5m) *The Stiperstones, 18 Coton Crescent, Coton Hill, Shrewsbury, SY1 2NZ.*
Very comfortable, quality accommodation. High standard of cleanliness. Extensive facilities.
Grades: ETC 3 Diamond, AA 3 Diamond
Tel: 01743 246720
Mrs MacLeod.
Fax no: 01743 350303
D: £18.50-£20.00 **S:** £22.50-£22.50.
Open: All Year
Beds: 1F 2D 2T 1S
Baths: 4 Sh
🛏 🅿 (6) ⊬ 🗀 🛉 🏚 🎱 Ⓥ 🖤 ⚡

(0.5m 🚗) *Avonlea, 33 Coton Crescent, Coton Hill, Shrewsbury, Shropshire, SY1 2NZ.*
Actual grid ref: SJ4813
Tel: 01743 359398
Mrs O'Keefe.
D: £17.00-£19.00
S: £18.00-£20.00.
Open: Jan to Mid Dec
Beds: 2T 1S
Baths: 1 En 1 Sh
🛏 🅿 (11) 🗀 🛉 🏚 🎱 Ⓥ 🖤 ⚡
Comfortable, attractive Edwardian town house. Ten minute walk from town centre, Railway, Bus stations, records and research library. Shrewsbury Castle, 'Brother Cadfael' trail. Town centre attractions of historical Shrewsbury. Quarry park, Dingle Agric show ground. Venue for flower show.

(0.5m) *Meole Brace Hall, Meole Brace , Shrewsbury, Shropshire, SY3 9HF.*
Beautiful house set in 3 acres yet close to town.
Grades: ETC 5 Diamond, Silver
Tel: **01743 235566** Mrs Hathaway.
Fax no: 01743 236886
D: £24.50-£28.00 **S:** £39.00-£46.00.
Open: All Year (not Xmas/
New Year)
Beds: 1T 2D
Baths: 2 En 1Private
⌂ (12) 🅿 (12) ✠☐🐾✕🎣▥Ⅴ🛈✦

All paths are popular:
you are well-advised to
book ahead

Many rates vary
according to season -
the lowest only are
shown here

(0.5m) *Trevellion House,
1 Bradford Street, Shrewsbury,
Shropshire, SY2 5DP.*
Comfortable Victorian family-run guest house, Shrewsbury's attractions within easy walking distance.
Grades: ETC 3 Diamond
Tel: **01743 249582** Ms Taplin.
Fax no: 01743 232096
D: £17.00-£20.00 **S:** £17.00-£20.00.
Open: All Year
Beds: 2T 1D **Baths:** 1 Pr 1 Sh
⌂☐🐾🎣▥Ⅴ🛈✦

(0.5m) 🚌 *Glynndene Park Terrace, Abbey Foregate, Shrewsbury, Shropshire, SY2 6BL.*
A beautiful Victorian house opposite abbey and walking distance of town.
Tel: **01743 352488** (also fax no)
Mrs Arnold.
D: £18.00-£20.00 .
Open: All Year
Beds: 1D 2T
Baths: 1 Sh
⌂ (9) ✠☐🎣▥Ⅴ

Please take muddy
boots <u>off</u> before
entering premises

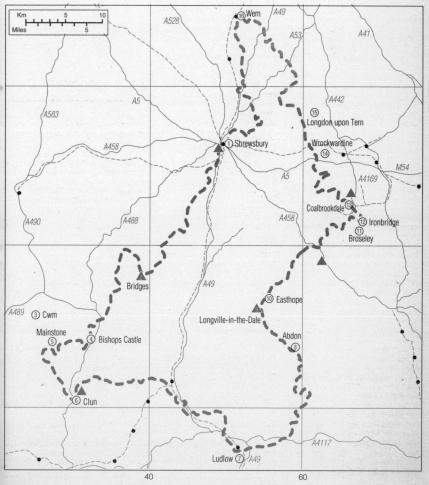

(0.5m) *Berwyn House,*
14 Holywell Street, Abbey
Foregate, Shrewsbury, Shropshire,
SY2 5DB.
Victorian townhouse sited on origi-
nal C11th abbey courtyard, 8 mins'
walk Shrewsbury centre.
Grades: AA 2 Diamond
Tel: 01743 354858
Mrs Simpson.
Fax no: 07970 502321
D: £20.00-£26.00 **S:** £20.00-£28.00.
Open: All Year (not Xmas)
Beds: 1F 1D 1T 1S
Baths: 1 Sh
🛏 (1) 🅿 (1) ⌿ 🗇 🏃 ⚕ Ⅲ, ⓥ

(0.5m) *Anton House, 1 Canon*
Street, Monkmoor, Shrewsbury,
SY2 5HG.
Luxurious comfortable Victorian
house, 10 minute stroll from town
centre.
Grades: ETC 4 Diamond
Tel: 01743 359275
Mrs Herbert.
Fax no: 01743 270168
D: £20.00-£20.00 **S:** £25.00-£25.00.
Open: All Year (not Xmas)
Beds: 1F 1D 1T
Baths: 2 Sh
🛏 (5) 🅿 (3) ⌿ 🗇 ⚕ Ⅲ, ⓥ

(0.5m) *Abbey Court House,*
134 Abbey Foregate, Shrewsbury,
Shropshire, SY2 6AU.
Abbey Court house situated close
to many places of historical inter-
est.
Grades: ETC 3 Diamond
Tel: 01743 364416 Mrs Turnock.
Fax no: 01743 358559
D: £19.00-£23.00 **S:** £20.00-£30.00.
Open: All Year (not Xmas/
New Year)
Beds: 1F 3D 4T 2S
Baths: 4 En 2 Sh
🛏 (10) 🅿 (10) 🗇 ⚕ Ⅲ, ⓥ ⚲

(0.5m) *Merevale House,*
66 Ellesmere Road, Shrewsbury,
SY1 2QP.
Actual grid ref: SJ493139
Lovely Victorian house, 10 min-
utes' walk to Shrewsbury railway
and bus stations.
Tel: 01743 243677
Mrs Spooner.
D: £17.00-£17.00 **S:** £16.00.
Open: All Year (not Xmas)
Beds: 3D
Baths: 1 Sh
🛏 🅿 (3) 🗇 ⚕ Ⅲ, ⓥ

(0.5m) *Restawhile, 36 Coton*
Crescent, Shrewsbury, SY1 2NZ.
A warm welcome awaits you. Cosy
rooms & good food.
Tel: 01743 240969
Mr & Mrs Cox.
Fax no: 01743 231841
D: £18.00-£21.00
S: £25.00-£30.00.
Open: All Year
Beds: 2D 1T
Baths: 3 En
🅿 (5) 🗇 ⚕ Ⅲ, ⓥ ⚲

Bridges 2

National Grid Ref: SO3996

(🔺 On path) *Bridges Long Mynd*
Youth Hostel, Bridges,
Ratlinghope, Shrewsbury, SY5 0SP.
Actual grid ref: SO395965
Tel: 01588 650656
Under 18: £5.75 **Adults:** £8.50
Self-catering facilities, Wet weath-
er shelter, Lounge, Drying room,
Cycle store, Evening meal at
7.00pm, No smoking, WC,
Washing facilities, Kitchen facili-
ties, Breakfast available
Former village school offering
basic accommodation in beautiful
countryside between Long Mynd
and Stiperstones in the Shropshire
Hills. Ideal place for walking and
birdwatching.

Cwm 3

National Grid Ref: SO2590
🍴 ⬛ Dragon Hotel, Castle Hotel

(3m 🐾) *The Drewin Farm, Cwm,*
Church Stoke, Montgomery,
Powys, SY15 6TW.
Actual grid ref: SO261905
C17th farmhouse with panoramic
views. Offa's Dyke footpath on
doorstep.
Tel: 01588 620325 (also fax no)
Mrs Richards.
D: £20.00-£21.00 **S:** £22.00-£22.00.
Open: Easter to Oct
Beds: 1F 1T **Baths:** 2 En
🛏 🅿 (6) ⌿ 🗇 🏃 ✕ ⚕ Ⅲ, ⓥ ⚲

Bishop's Castle 4

National Grid Ref: SO3288
🍴 ⬛ Castle Hotel, Boar's Head, Six Bells, Three
Tuns

(🔺 1m) *Broughton Bunkhouse,*
Lower Broughton Farm, Bishop's
Castle, Shropshire, SY15 6SZ.
Actual grid ref: SO313906
Tel: 01588 638393
Under 18: £7.50 **Adults:** £10.00
Self-catering facilities, Television,
Showers, Central heating, Laundry
facilities, Wet weather shelter,
Lounge, Dining room, Grounds
available for games, Drying room,
Cycle store, Parking, No smoking
Comfortable accommodation in
C17th barn in Shropshire's walking
country.

(1m 🐾) *Lower Broughton Farm,*
Bishop's Castle, Shropshire,
SY15 6SZ.
Actual grid ref: S0313906
Originally a medieval hall house,
now a spacious and comfortable
farmhouse.
Tel: 01588 638393
Mr & Mrs Bason.
D: £17.00-£20.00 **S:** £20.00-£25.00.
Open: Feb to Dec
Beds: 2D 1T **Baths:** 1 En 1 Sh
🛏 🅿 (6) ⌿ 🗇 🏃 ⚕ Ⅲ, ⓥ ⚲

Mainstone 5

National Grid Ref: SO2787
🍴 ⬛ Sun Inn, White Horse, Castle Hotel, Three
Tuns, Bishop's Castle

(1m 🐾) *New House Farm,*
Mainstone, Clun, Craven Arms,
Shropshire, SY7 8NJ.
Actual grid ref: SO275863
Peaceful, isolated C18th farm-
house, set high in Clun Hills near
Welsh border.
Tel: 01588 638314 Mrs Ellison.
D: £24.00-£25.00 **S:** £25.00-£28.00.
Open: Easter to Oct
Beds: 1F 1T **Baths:** 1 En 1 Pr
🅿 (6) ⌿ 🗇 🏃 ⚕ Ⅲ, ⓥ ⓐ ⚲

Clun 6

National Grid Ref: SO3080
🍴 ⬛ Sun Inn, White Horse, Castle Hotel, Three
Tuns, Bishop's Castle

(🔺 On path) *Clun Mill Youth*
Hostel, The Mill, Clun, Craven
Arms, Shropshire, SY7 8NY.
Actual grid ref: SO303812
Tel: 01588 640582
Under 18: £6.50 **Adults:** £9.25
Self-catering facilities, Showers,
Lounge, Cycle store, Parking, No
smoking, WC, Kitchen facilities,
Credit cards accepted
Former watermill (workings still
visible) upgraded yet unspoilt by
modern development, set in stone-
built town (C16th humpbacked
bridge) and Norman castle.

(On path 🐾) *The Old Stables And*
Saddlery, Crown House, Church
Street, Clun, Craven Arms,
Shropshire, SY7 8JW.
Actual grid ref: SO305805
Superb self-contained Georgian
stable conversion in lovely
courtyard garden.
Grades: ETC 4 Diamond
Tel: 01588 640780
Mrs Bailey & Mr R Maund.
D: £20.00-£22.50 **S:** £22.00-£25.00.
Open: All Year (not Xmas)
Beds: 1D 1T 1S
Baths: 1 En 1 Pr 1 Sh
🛏 (8) 🅿 (2) ⌿ 🗇 🏃 ⚕ Ⅲ, ⓥ ⓐ ⚲

**The Grid Reference
beneath the location
heading is for the
village or town -** *not*
**for individual houses,
which are shown
(where supplied) in
each entry itself.**

(0.5m) *Llanhedric Farm, Clun, Craven Arms, Shropshire, SY7 8NG.*
Actual grid ref: SO283842
Tranquil country retreat - rooms overlooking beautiful views of Clun Valley.
Tel: **01588 640203** (also fax no)
Mrs Jones.
D: £18.00-£20.00 **S:** £18.00-£21.00.
Open: Easter to Nov
Beds: 1F 1D 1T **Baths:** 1 En 1 Sh
🛏 🅿 (5) 🚫 🗙 🔅 🛏 🔟 ▥ 🛢 ⚡

(0.25m 🚗) *Clun Farm, High Street, Clun, Craven Arms, Shropshire, SY7 8JB.*
Actual grid ref: SO302808
C16th double cruck character farmhouse in the heart of the village.
Tel: **01588 640432**
Mr & Mrs Whitfield.
D: £18.00-£20.00 **S:** £18.00.
Open: All Year (not Xmas)
Beds: 1F 1T 2S
Baths: 1 En 1 Sh
🛏 🅿 (6) 🔟 🛢 ⚡

Ludlow 7

National Grid Ref: SO5174

🍴 🍺 Unicorn Inn, Charlton Arms, The Cookhouse, Church Inn

(0.25m) *Henwick House, Gravel Hill, Ludlow, Shropshire, SY8 1QU.*
Grades: ETC 3 Diamond
Tel: **01584 873338**
Mrs Cecil-Jones.
D: £20.00-£20.00 **S:** £18.00-£18.00.
Open: Apr to Dec
Beds: 1D 2T 1S
Baths: 2 En
🛏 🅿 (3) 🚫 🗙 🔅 🛏 🔟 ▥ 🛢 ⚡
Warm, comfortable Georgian coach house. Friendly, informal atmosphere, good traditional English breakfast. En suite Bedrooms, comfortable beds, TV, tea/coffee facilities and much more. Easy walking distances from town centre and local inns.

(0.25m 🚗) *Bull Hotel, Bull Ring, Ludlow, Shropshire, SY8 1AD.*
Centrally located inn with private parking, very comfortable guest rooms.
Grades: ETC 3 Diamond
Tel: **01584 873611**
Mr & Mrs Maile.
Fax no: 01584 873666
D: £22.50-£22.50 **S:** £30.00-£30.00.
Open: All Year
Beds: 1F 2D 1T
Baths: 4 En
🛏 🅿 (6) 🔟 🗙 🛏 🔟 ▥ 🛢

> **All rates are subject
> to alteration at the
> owners' discretion.**

(1m) *Hen & Chickens Guest House, 103 Old Street, Ludlow, Shropshire, SY8 1NU.*
Characterful building, convenient location, near castle, interesting shops, excellent restaurants.
Grades: ETC 3 Diamond
Tel: **01584 874318** Mrs Ross.
D: £20.00-£25.00 **S:** £20.00-£30.00.
Open: All Year (not Xmas)
Beds: 2D 1T 2S
Baths: 2 Sh 1 En
🛏 🅿 (6) 🚫 🔅 🛏 🔟 ▥ 🛢

(0.25m) *Arran House, 42 Gravel Hill, Ludlow, Shropshire, SY8 1QR.*
Comfortable Victorian house, 5 mins to town and railway station.
Tel: **01584 873764** Mrs Bowen.
D: £17.00. **S:** £18.00.
Open: All Year
Beds: 1D 1T 2S **Baths:** 1 Sh
🛏 (5) 🅿 (5) 🔟 🗙 🔅 🛏 🔟 ▥ 🛢 ⚡

(1m 🚗) *Hucks Barn Farm, Overton Road, Ludlow, Shropshire, SY8 4AA.*
Actual grid ref: SO508730
Family farmhouse home, quiet, accessible, beautiful rural views, non-smokers only.
Tel: **01584 873950** (also fax no)
Mr & Mrs Davies.
D: £19.00-£20.00 **S:** £30.00-£30.00.
Open: Easter to Nov
Beds: 1F 1D 1T **Baths:** 2 Sh
🛏 (9) 🅿 (6) 🔅 🔟 ⚡

Abdon 8

National Grid Ref: SO5786

🍴 🍺 Boyne Arms

(0.25m) *Earnstrey Hill House, Abdon, Craven Arms, Shropshire, SY7 9HU.*
Actual grid ref: SO587873
Grades: ETC 4 Diamond
Tel: **01746 712579** Mrs Scurfield.
Fax no: 01746 712631
D: £25.00-£25.00 **S:** £25.00.
Open: All Year (not Xmas)
Beds: 1D 2T **Baths:** 1 En 2 Sh
🛏 🅿 🔟 🗙 🔅 🛏 🔟 ▥ 🛢 ⚡
Comfortable, warm, spacious family house 1200 ft up Brown Clee Hill. Superb views westwards towards Long Mynd and Wales. We keep horses, sheep, dogs, free-range hens on our 11 acres. Wonderful walking and riding. Experienced walking hosts will help plan/guide.

(0.1m 🚗) *Spring Cottage, Cockshutford Road, Abdon, Craven Arms, Shropshire, SY9 9HU.*
Actual grid ref: SO584863
Magnificent hillside location, stunning views, relaxing friendly atmosphere, near Shropshire Way.
Tel: **01746 712551** Mrs Langham.
Fax no: 01746 712001
D: £20.00-£27.50 **S:** £23.00-£30.00.
Open: All Year (not Xmas)
Beds: 1D 1T 1S **Baths:** 2 En 1 Pr
🛏 (8) 🅿 (6) 🚫 🔅 🛏 🗙 🔟 ▥ 🛢 ⚡

Longville-in-the-Dale 9

National Grid Ref: SO5393

(🔺 On path) *Wilderhope Manor Youth Hostel, The John Cadury Memorial Hostel, Longville-in-the-Dale, Easthope, Much Wenlock, Shropshire, TF13 6EG.*
Actual grid ref: SO544928
Tel: **01694 771363**
Under 18: £7.75 **Adults:** £11.00
Self-catering facilities, Showers, Lounge, Games room, Drying room, Parking, Evening meal at 7.00pm, No smoking, WC, Kitchen facilities, Breakfast available, Credit cards accepted
Exquisite Elizabethan manor house owned by the National Trust, with lots of original features, idyllically situated atop Wenlock Edge.

Easthope 10

National Grid Ref: SO5695

🍴 🍺 Wenlock Edge Inn, Longvine Arms

(0.25m) *Madam's Hill, Hill Top, Easthope, Much Wenlock, Shropshire, TF13 6DJ.*
Once two weavers' cottages, Madams Hill nestles into Wenlock Edge, a designated AONB.
Tel: **01746 785269** (also fax no)
Mr & Mrs Bushell.
D: £19.00-£20.00 **S:** £20.00-£22.00.
Open: All Year (not Xmas)
Beds: 1D 1T **Baths:** 1 Sh
🛏 🅿 (2) 🚫 🔅 🛏 🔟 ▥ ⚡

Broseley 11

National Grid Ref: SJ6701

🍴 🍺 The Lion, The Pheasant, Brewery Inn

(1m) *Lord Hill Guest House, Duke St, Broseley, Shropshire, TF12 5LU.*
Former public house, easy access to Ironbridge, Telford and museums.
Tel: **01952 884270** Mr McNally.
D: £16.00-£20.00 **S:** £16.00-£20.00.
Open: All Year
Beds: 7F 1D 1T 2S
Baths: 1 En 3 Pr 3 Sh
🛏 (6) 🅿 (9) 🔅 🛏 🔟 ♿

Ironbridge 12

National Grid Ref: SJ6703

🍴 🍺 Malthouse, Meadow Inn, Horse & Jockey, Old Vaults, Moat House

(On path) *Post Office House, 6 The Square, Ironbridge, Telford, Shropshire, TF8 7AQ.*
Comfortable C18th house overlooking Iron Bridge. Central for museums.
Grades: ETC 3 Diamond
Tel: **01952 433201** Mrs Jones.
Fax no: 01952 433582
D: £19.00-£22.00 **S:** £29.00-£34.00.
Open: All Year
Beds: 1F/T 2D **Baths:** 1 En 1 Sh
🛏 🅿 (2) 🔅 🛏 🔟 ▥ 🛢

(On path 🚲) *The Library House,*
11 Severn Bank, Ironbridge,
Telford, Shropshire, TF8 7AN.
Grade II Listed building situated in
a quiet and pretty backwater.
Tel: **01952 432299** Mr Maddocks.
Fax no: 01952 433967
D: £25.00-£27.50 **S:** £45.00-£45.00.
Open: All Year (not Xmas)
Beds: 1F 3D 1T 4S
Baths: 3 En
🛏 (10) 🅿 ⊁ ☐ 🛌 🧺 🏠 Ⅲ Ⅵ ⓘ ⊬

Coalbrookdale   13

National Grid Ref: SJ6604

(🔺 0.25m) *Ironbridge Gorge*
Youth Hostel (2), Paradise,
Coalbrookdale, Telford, Shropshire
TF8 7HT.
Actual grid ref: SJ671043
Tel: **01952 588755**
Under 18: £7.75 **Adults:** £11.00
Television, Showers, Lounge,
Games room, Drying room,
Evening meal at 6.00-7.00pm, WC,
Breakfast available
The hostel is sited in C19th
Literary and Scientific Institute, a
stone's throw from the original
Iron Bridge, the birthplace of the
Industrial Revolution, now a World
Heritage Site. This hostel is paired
with the one in Coalbrookdale, 3
miles away.

Pay B&Bs by cash or
cheque and be prepared
to pay up front.

Wrockwardine   14

National Grid Ref: SJ6211

🍴 🍺 The Plough

(0.5m 🚲) *Church Farm,*
Wrockwardine, Wellington,
Telford, Shropshire, TF6 5DG.
Actual grid ref: SJ624120
Down a lime-tree avenue lies our
superb situated C18th village farm-
house.
Tel: **01952 244917** (also fax no)
Mrs Savage.
D: £20.00-£26.00 **S:** £25.00-£36.00.
Open: All Year
Beds: 3D 3T **Baths:** 3 Pr 1 Sh
🛏 (5) 🅿 (20) ☐ 🛌 🗙 🧺 Ⅲ Ⅵ ⊬

Longdon upon Tern   15

National Grid Ref: SJ6215

🍴 🍺 Bucks Head

(1m 🚲) *Red House Farm,*
Longdon upon Tern, Wellington,
Telford, Shropshire, TF6 6LE.
Tel: **01952 770245**
Mrs Jones.
D: £18.00-£25.00 **S:** £20.00-£25.00.
Open: All Year
Beds: 1F 1T 1D 1S
Baths: 2 En 1 Sh
🛏 🅿 (4) ☐ 🛌 🧺 Ⅵ ⓘ ⊬
Red House Farm is a late Victorian
farmhouse with comfortable well
furnished rooms. TV and drinks
tray. Excellent breakfasts.
Longdon-on-Tern is central for
Shrewsbury, Telford, Ironbridge.
Ideal for business or pleasure.
Families welcome, 'home comforts
with personal attention'.

Wem   16

National Grid Ref: SJ5129

🍴 🍺 Raven, Bull & Dog, Old Post Office,
Dicken Arms

(0.25m 🚲) *Forncet, Soulton Road,*
Wem, Shrewsbury, Shropshire,
SY4 5HR.
Actual grid ref: SJ521292
Grades: ETC 2 Diamond
Tel: **01939 232996**
Mr & Mrs James.
D: £17.50-£17.50 **S:** £17.50-£17.50.
Open: All Year (not Xmas)
Beds: 1F 1T 1S **Baths:** 2 Sh
🛏 🅿 (6) ⊁ ☐ 🗙 🧺 Ⅲ Ⅵ ⓘ ⊬
Forncet is a spacious Victorian
house with attractively furnished
rooms and a large well maintained
garden. Enjoy good home cooking,
the billiard room provides enter-
tainment for the evenings and a
large selection of videos and board
games is also available.

(0.75m) *Lowe Hall Farm, The*
Lowe, Wem, Shrewsbury,
Shropshire, SY4 5UE.
Actual grid ref: SJ501306
Historically famous C16th farm-
house. Antique furnishings.
Highest standard of accommoda-
tion gauranteed.
Tel: **01939 232236** Mrs Jones.
D: £20.00-£20.00 **S:** £22.00-£22.00.
Open: All Year
Beds: 1F 1D 1T **Baths:** 2 En 1 Pr
🛏 🅿 (6) ⊁ ☐ 🧺 Ⅲ Ⅵ ⊬

D = Price range per person
sharing in a double room

STILWELL'S BRITAIN CYCLEWAY COMPANION

23 Long Distance Cycleways * Where to Stay * Where to Eat

County Cycleways – Sustrans Routes

The first guide of its kind, **Stilwell's Britain Cycleway Companion** makes planning accommodation for your cycling trip easy. It lists B&Bs, hostels, campsites and pubs– in the order they appear along the selected cycleways – allowing the cyclist to book ahead. No more hunting for a room, a hot meal or a cold drink after a long day in the saddle. Stilwell's gives descriptions of the featured routes and includes such relevant information as maps, grid references and distance from route; Tourist Board ratings; and the availability of drying facilities and packed lunches. No matter which route – or part of a route – you decide to ride, let the **Cycleway Companion** show you where to sleep and eat.

As essential as your tyre pump – the perfect cycling companion: **Stilwell's Britain Cycleway Companion**.

Cycleways Sustrans
Carlisle to Inverness – Clyde to Forth - Devon Coast to Coast -
Hull to Harwich – Kingfisher Cycle Trail - Lon Las Cymru –
Sea to Sea (C2C) – Severn and Thames - West Country Way –
White Rose Cycle Route

County
Round Berkshire Cycle Route – Cheshire Cycleway –
Cumbria Cycleway – Essex Cycle Route – Icknield Way -
Lancashire Cycleway – Leicestershire County Cycleway –
Oxfordshire Cycleway – Reivers Cycle Route – South Downs Way
- Surrey Cycleway – Wiltshire Cycleway –
Yorkshire Dales Cycleway

£9.95 from all good bookstores (ISBN 1-900861-26-7) or £10.95 (inc p&p) from Stilwell Publishing, 59 Charlotte Road, London EC2A 3QW (020 7739 7179)

South Downs Way

The **South Downs Way** runs for 96 miles from Eastbourne to Winchester along the line of famous chalk hills that dominates the Sussex skyline. The Way is a bridleway, too, and is thus open to horse-riders and cyclists, although only walkers may take the Seven Sisters alternative out of Eastbourne. The downlands are very popular; from Eastbourne to Buriton you will rarely be alone. On hot days you will see hang-gliders, balloonists and para-gliders; the forests and the hilltops are favourite spots for picknickers. And there are many walkers, too. The path itself makes up for any lack of solitude, though. On an early summer day, with larks rising and with views far out to sea and across the Sussex Weald, the walk defies superlatives. The terrain is principally chalk path which, wet or dry, will test the ankles. The path is well way-marked up until the Hampshire border, at which point your map-reading skills will be tested, for this last section of the Way has only recently been approved. An excellent feature of the **South Downs Way** is its accessibility by rail. Eastbourne, Brighton, Worthing, Chichester, Portsmouth and Winchester are all termini for lines that bisect the Downs. This is therefore another good path to walk in weekend stretches.

Guides (all available from good bookshops unless stated):

South Downs Way by Paul Millmore (ISBN 1 854 10 40 71), published by Aurum Press in association with the Countryside Commission and Ordnance Survey, £10.99

Along the South Downs Way to Winchester by Harry Comber (ISBN 0 907168 08 6), published by the Society of Sussex Downsmen and available from the RA's National Office (1/5 Wandsworth Road, London, SW8 2XX, tel. 020 7339 8500), £5.00 (+ £1.00 p&p)

A Guide to the South Downs Way by Miles Jebb (ISBN 0 094711 70 4), published by Constable & Co Ltd, £10.95

South Downs Way & the Downs Link by Kev Reynolds (ISBN 1 85284 023 4), published by Cicerone Press and also available from the publishers (2 Police Square, Milnthorpe, Cumbria, LA7 7PY, 01539 562069), £5.99 (+75p p&p)

Maps: 1:50000 Ordnance Survey Landranger Series: 185, 197, 198 and 199

Comments on the path to: **Russell Robson**, South Downs Way Officer, Sussex Downs Conservation Board, Chanctonbury House, Church St, Storrington, W. Sussex, RH20 4LT

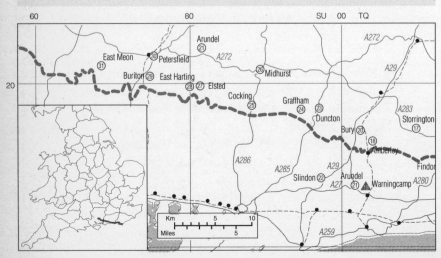

Eastbourne 1

National Grid Ref: TQ5900

🍴 🍺 The Marine, Town House, Castle Inn, Lamb Inn, The Beach, The Waterfront, The Pilot, The Alexander

(▲ On path) *Eastbourne Youth Hostel, East Dean Road, Eastbourne, East Sussex, BN20 8ES.*
Actual grid ref: TV588990
Tel: **01323 721081**
Under 18: £6.90
Adults: £10.00
Self-catering facilities, Showers, Lounge, Dining room, Drying room, Cycle store, Parking Limited, No smoking, WC, Kitchen facilities, Credit cards accepted
Former golf clubhouse on South Downs, 450 ft above sea level with sweeping views across Eastbourne & Pevensey Bay.

(1m) *Heatherdene Hotel, 26-28 Elms Avenue, Eastbourne, E. Sussex, BN21 3DN.*
Grades: ETC 3 Diamond
Tel: **01323 723598** (also fax no)
Mrs Mockford.
D: £17.00-£45.00
S: £16.00-£25.00.
Open: All Year
Beds: 1F 4D 8T 3S
Baths: 6 En 3 Sh
🛇 🗓 🛏 ✕ 🟥 🎱 🖳 🔥 ᐸ 🖤
You will find good food and comfortable rooms at the Heatherdene. This family-run licensed hotel, set in a pleasant avenue, is close to the sea front and town centre. Train and coach stations are nearby, as are the theatres.

S = Price range for a single
person in a single room

(1m) *Innisfree House, 130a Royal Parade, Eastbourne, East Sussex, BN22 7JY.*
Tel: **01323 646777** (also fax no)
Mrs Petrie.
D: £19.00-£20.00 **S:** £25.00-£30.00.
Open: All Year (not Xmas)
Beds: 1F 1D 1T **Baths:** 3 En
🛇 ✕ 🗓 🖳 🖤 ☑
Small family-run B&B on seafront, close to amenities, refurbished to high standards. Exclusive location with sea views, easy parking on road outside. Motorcycle storage. Stay a day or stay a week, your comfort & praise we aim to seek.

(1m) *Sheldon Hotel, 9-11 Burlington Place, Eastbourne, East Sussex, BN21 4AS.*
Situated within a few minutes walk of sea front, theatres. Licensed.
Tel: **01323 724120**
Fax no: 01323 430406
D: £24.00-£27.00 **S:** £24.00-£27.00.
Open: All Year
Beds: 4F 8D 6S **Baths:** 24 En
🛇 🗓 🖤 🛏 ✕ 🟥 🖳 🖳 🖤 🔥

(0.75m) *Ambleside Private Hotel, 24 Elms Avenue, Eastbourne, E. Sussex, BN21 3DN.*
Tel: **01323 724991** Mr Pattenden.
D: £18.00-£18.00 **S:** £18.00-£25.00.
Open: All Year
Beds: 4D 4T 2S **Baths:** 2 Sh 2 En
🗓 🛏 ✕ 🟥 🖳 🖤 🔥
Situated on quiet avenue adjacent to seafront, pier, town centre, theatres, convenient for railway and coach stations. Short distance from South Downs Way, Wealdway. Colour TV in bedrooms. Compliant with environmental and fire regulations.

D = Price range per person
sharing in a double room

(1m) *Camberley Hotel, 27-29 Elms Avenue, Eastbourne, E. Sussex, BN21 3DN.*
Tel: **01323 723789**
D: £18.00-£21.00
S: £18.00-£21.00.
Open: Mar to Oct
Beds: 4F 3D 3T 2S
Baths: 7 En 2 Sh
🛇 🗓 (3) 🗓 🖳 🖤 🖤
Situated in a pleasant avenue close to town centre, sea front and all amenities. Licensed, ensuite, tea-making, colour TV in bedrooms. English breakfast.

(0.5m) *Cherry Tree Hotel, 15 Silverdale Road, Eastbourne, E. Sussex, BN20 7AJ.*
Actual grid ref: TV612982
Award-winning family-run hotel, close to sea front, downlands and theatres.
Grades: ETC 4 Diamond, Silver
Tel: **01323 722406**
Mr Henley.
Fax no: 01323 648838
D: £26.00-£33.00
S: £26.00-£33.00.
Open: All Year
Beds: 1F 3D 4T 2S
Baths: 10 En
🛇 (7) ✕ 🗓 ✕ 🛏 🖳 🖤 🖤

(1m) *The Manse, 7 Dittons Road, Eastbourne, East Sussex, BN21 1DW.*
Tel: **01323 737851**
Mrs Walker.
D: £15.00-£20.00
S: £20.00-£25.00.
Open: All Year (not Xmas)
Beds: 1F 2T
Baths: 2 En 1 Pr
🛇 (8) 🗓 (1) 🗓 🛏 🖳 🖤 🖤 🔥
Originally a Presbyterian manse, this character house is located in a quiet area yet within 5 minutes' walk of the town centre with its shops, restaurants and theatres. Seafront, South Downs, castles and Downland villages nearby.

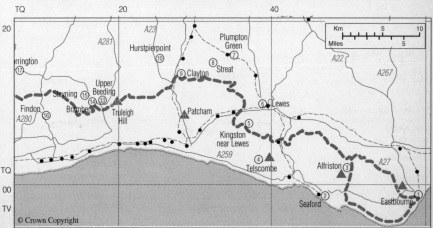

© Crown Copyright

(0.75m) *Southcroft Hotel, 15 South Cliff Avenue, Eastbourne, E. Sussex, BN20 7AH.*
Actual grid ref: TV609979
Friendly, family-run, non-smoking hotel. Close to Downs, sea and theatre.
Grades: ETC 4 Diamond
Tel: 01323 729071 Mrs Skriczka.
D: £25.00-£28.00 **S:** £25.00-£28.00.
Open: All Year
Beds: 3D 2T 1S **Baths:** 6 En
🗶☐🗶🛏🖫🎹Ⓥ🎿

(1m) *Edelweiss Hotel, 10-12 Elms Ave, Eastbourne, E. Sussex, BN21 3DN*
Central family-run Hotel just off sea front. Comfortable and welcoming.
Grades: ETC 3 Diamond
Tel: 01323 732071 (also fax no)
Mr & Mrs Butler.
D: £16.00-£20.00 **S:** £16.00-£25.00.
Open: All Year
Beds: 1F 6D 5T 2S
Baths: 3 En 4 Sh
🗶☐🗶🛏🖫🎹Ⓥ🎿

(1m) *Cromwell Private Hotel, 23 Cavendish Place, Eastbourne, E. Sussex, BN21 3EJ.*
Family run hotel in Victorian Town House (1851). Centrally located.
Grades: ETC 4 Diamond
Tel: 01323 725288 (also fax no)
Mr & Mrs Millar.
D: £19.00-£24.00 **S:** £19.00-£23.00.
Open: Easter to Nov
Beds: 2F 3D 3T 3S **Baths:** 5 Pr 2 Sh
🗶☐🗶🛏🖫🎹Ⓥ

(1m) *Courtlands Hotel, 68 Royal Parade, Eastbourne, E. Sussex, BN22 7AQ.*
Seafront position, business/touring base.
Tel: 01323 721068
D: £20.00-£25.00 **S:** £20.00-£25.00.
Open: All Year
Beds: 3F 2D 1T 2S **Baths:** 3 En 1 Pr
🗶🅿(2)☐🗶🛏🖫🎿

(1m) *La Mer Guest House, 7 Marine Road, Eastbourne, E. Sussex, BN22 7AU.*
Just 50 yards from Eastbourne's beautiful seafront and beach, easy access to South Downs
Tel: 01323 724926 Mrs Byrne.
D: £18.00-£24.00 **S:** £18.00-£24.00.
Open: May to Sep
Beds: 2D 2T 2S **Baths:** 2 En
🗶(14)🅿☐🗶🛏🖫🎹🎿

(1m) *Channel View Hotel, 57 Royal Parade, Eastbourne, E. Sussex, BN22 7AQ.*
A friendly family-run seafront hotel situated opposite the Redoubt Gardens.
Tel: 01323 736730
Fax no: 01323 644299
D: £17.00-£21.00 **S:** £22.00-£32.00.
Open: All Year (not Xmas)
Beds: 1F 2D 3T 2S
Baths: 4 En 1 Sh
🗶☐🛏🗶🛏🖫🎹Ⓥ

(1m) 🚲 *Beachy Rise, 20 Beachy Head Road, Eastbourne, E. Sussex, BN20 7QN.*
In Meads village near Beachy Head and sea and university. Ensuite bedrooms.
Tel: **01323 639171**
D: £22.00-£28.00 **S:** £25.00-£29.00.
Open: All Year
Beds: 1F 4D 1T
Baths: 6 En
🗶(1)☐🛏🖫🎹Ⓥ🎿

(1m) *Downland Hotel, 37 Lewes Road, Eastbourne, East Sussex, BN21 2BU.*
Charming small hotel, ideally located for all main amenities and commercial centre.
Tel: **01323 732689**
Fax no: 01323 720321
D: £25.00-£37.50 **S:** £30.00-£40.00.
Open: All Year
Beds: 2F 7D 2T 1S
Baths: 12 En
🅿(9)🗶☐🗶🛏🖫🎹Ⓥ🎿

Seaford 2

National Grid Ref: TV4898

🍴🍺 White Lion

(2m) 🚲 *Holmes Lodge, 72 Claremont Road, Seaford, East Sussex, BN25 2BJ.*
Grades: ETC 3 Diamond
Tel: 01323 898331 Parr.
Fax no: 01323 491346
D: £19.00-£25.00 **S:** £20.00-£30.00.
Open: All Year
Beds: 3F 2D 1T 6S
Baths: 1 Pr 2 Sh
🗶🅿(10)🗶☐🛏🖫🎹Ⓥ🎿
Sherlock Holmes theme. Convenient for Downs, walks/cycling, Cuckmere Haven, 7 Sisters, Beachy Head, Newhaven Ferry. Beach/town/trains 300 metres, bus-stop outside, singles/groups welcome all year. Bar/restaurant adjacent. Free tea/coffee room into conservatory, large garden, sea views.

(2m) *Silverdale, 21 Sutton Park Road, Seaford, E. Sussex, BN25 1RH.*
Family run town centre house hotel excellent value for money.
Grades: AA 4 Diamond,
RAC 4 Diamond
Tel: 01323 491849 Mr Cowdrey.
Fax no: 01323 891131
D: £13.00-£28.00 **S:** £25.00-£45.00.
Open: All Year
Beds: 2F 6D
Baths: 6 En 2 Sh
🗶🅿(5)☐🛏🗶🛏🖫🎹♿Ⓥ🎿

> Pay B&Bs by cash or cheque and be prepared to pay up front.

Alfriston 3

National Grid Ref: TQ5103

🍴🍺 Wingrove Inn, Ye Olde Smuggler's Inn, The George

(▲ 2.5m) *Alfriston Youth Hostel, Frog Firle, Alfriston, Polegate, East Sussex, BN26 5TT.*
Actual grid ref: TQ518019
Tel: **01323 870423**
Under 18: £6.90 **Adults:** £10.00
Self-catering facilities, Showers, Wet weather shelter, Lounge, Drying room, Parking, Evening meal at 6.30pm, WC, Kitchen facilities, Breakfast available, Credit cards accepted
A comfortable Sussex country house dating from 1530, set in Cuckmere Valley with views over river and Litlington.

(0.5m) 🚲 *Meadowbank, Sloe Lane, Alfriston, East Sussex, BN26 5UR.*
Tel: **01323 870742**
Mrs Petch.
D: £20.00-£25.00 **S:** £30.00-£35.00.
Open: All Year (not Xmas/ New Year)
Beds: 1T 2D
Baths: 1 En 2 Sh
🅿(4)🗶☐🛏🖫🎹♿Ⓥ🎿
The beautiful private dwelling in tranquil setting, offers views of Cuckmere Valley and South Downs. only 3 minutes walk village centre. Ideal for walkers/cyclists. Private car park. Lovely gardens and conservatory in which to relax. Delicious English breakfast.

(0.5m) *Dacres, Alfriston, Polegate, East Sussex, BN26 5TP.*
Country cottage. Beautiful gardens. Near South Downs Way Glyndebourne, Seven Sisters.
Tel: **01323 870447** Mrs Embry.
D: £25.00-£25.00 **S:** £40.00.
Open: All Year
Beds: 1T
Baths: 1 Pr
🅿(1)🗶☐🛏🖫♿Ⓥ

Telscombe 4

National Grid Ref: TQ4003

(▲ 1.5m) *Telscombe Youth Hostel, Bank Cottages, Telscombe, Lewes, East Sussex, BN7 3HZ.*
Actual grid ref: TQ405033
Tel: **01273 301357**
Under 18: £6.50
Adults: £9.25
Self-catering facilities, Showers, Lounge, Drying room, Cycle store, Parking By arrangement, No smoking, WC, Kitchen facilities
Three 200-year-old cottages combined into one hostel, next to the Norman church in a small unspoilt village in Sussex Downs Area of Outstanding Natural Beauty.

Kingston near Lewes 5

National Grid Ref: TQ3908

⚍ ◫ The Juggs

(0.5m) *Settlands, Wellgreen Lane, Kingston near Lewes, Lewes, E Sussex, BN7 3NP.*
Actual grid ref: TQ398082
Grades: ETC 4 Diamond
Tel: **01273 472295** (also fax no)
Mrs Arlett.
D: £20.00-£25.00 **S:** £25.00-£27.50.
Open: All Year (not Xmas)
Beds: 1D 1T
Baths: 2 Sh
♿ ℗ (3) ⌁ ☐ 🖭 ▥ 📖 Ⅵ ▮ ⚡
Swedish timber-framed house in picturesque down land village. Excellent walking, coast 6 miles. Friendly atmosphere, comfortable accommodation. Historic Lewes, Glyndebourne, ferries nearby.

Lewes 6

National Grid Ref: TQ4110

⚍ ◫ Royal Oak, Pelham Arms, Cock Inn, Steward's Enquiry, King's Head

(3m) *Sussex Country Accommodation, Crink House, Barcombe Mills, Lewes, E. Sussex, BN8 5BJ.*
Grades: ETC 4 Diamond, Silver
Tel: **01273 400625** Mrs Gaydon.
D: £25.00-£30.00 **S:** £30.00-£40.00.
Open: All Year (not Xmas)
Beds: 2D 1T
Baths: 3 En
♿ ℗ (10) ⌁ ☐ 🖭 ▥ 📖 Ⅵ
Victorian farmhouse with panoramic views. Welcoming rural family home, ideal base for exploring Sussex with its wealth of walks and attractions, castles, country houses, gardens, museums. Within reach Brighton, Eastbourne, Glyndebourne - self catering also available.

(1.5m) *Castle Banks Cottage, 4 Castle Banks, Lewes, E. Sussex, BN7 1UZ.*
Beamed cottage, pretty garden, quiet lane, close to castle, shops, restaurants.
Tel: **01273 476291** (also fax no)
Mrs Wigglesworth.
D: £22.50-£22.50 **S:** £22.50-£30.00.
Open: All Year (not Xmas)
Beds: 1T 1S
Baths: 1 Sh
♿ ⌁ ☐ 🖭 ▥ 📖 Ⅵ ⚡

(3m) *Phoenix House, 23 Gundreda Road, Lewes, E Sussex, BN7 1PT.*
Comfortable family home - quiet road - 5 minutes to town centre.
Tel: **01273 473250** Mrs Greene.
D: £17.50-£22.50 **S:** £25.00-£25.00.
Open: All Year (not Xmas/ New Year)
Beds: 1T 1D 1S
Baths: 1 Pr 1 Sh
♿ ℗ (2) ⌁ ☐ 🖭 ▥ 📖 Ⅵ ▮ ⚡

(3m) *Normandy, 37 Houndean Rise, Lewes, East Sussex, BN7 1EQ.*
Comfortable room in large detached family house, additional bed available, overlooking South Downs.
Tel: **01273 473853** (also fax no)
Mrs Kemp.
D: £22.00-£25.00 **S:** £30.00-£35.00.
Open: All Year (not Xmas)
Beds: 1D
Baths: 1 Pr
♿ ⌁ ☐ 🖭 ▥ 📖 Ⅵ

Plumpton Green 7

National Grid Ref: TQ3616

⚍ ◫ Winning Post

(3m 🚌**)** *Farthings, Station Road, Plumpton Green, Lewes, E. Sussex, BN7 3BY.*
Actual grid ref: TQ365172
Relaxed, friendly atmosphere in village setting under South Downs.
Tel: **01273 890415**
Mrs Baker.
D: £20.00-£25.00
S: £22.00-£30.00.
Open: All Year (not Xmas)
Beds: 2D 1T
Baths: 1 En 1 Sh
♿ ℗ (11) ℗ (4) ⌁ ☐ 🖭 ✕ ▥ 📖 Ⅵ ▮ ⚡

Streat 8

National Grid Ref: TQ3515

⚍ ◫ The Bull

(1.5m 🚌**)** *North Acres, Streat, Hassocks, E. Sussex, BN6 8RX.*
Unique Victorian country house in tiny Hamlet near South Downs.
Tel: **01273 890278** (also fax no)
Eastwood.
D: £20.00-£20.00 **S:** £20.00-£25.00.
Open: All Year (not Xmas)
Beds: 2F 2T 1S
Baths: 3 Sh
♿ ℗ (20) ⌁ ☐ 🖭 ▥ 📖 Ⅵ ▮ ⚡

Clayton 9

National Grid Ref: TQ3014

⚍ ◫ Jack & Jill

(0.25m) *Dower Cottage, Underhill Lane, Clayton, Hassocks, W. Sussex, BN6 9PL.*
Actual grid ref: TQ309136
Tel: **01273 843363** Mrs Bailey.
Fax no: 01273 846503
D: £22.50-£30.00 **S:** £30.00-£50.00.
Open: All Year (not Xmas)
Beds: 2F 2D 1T 1S **Baths:** 2 En 1 Sh
♿ ℗ (8) ⌁ ☐ 🖭 ▥ ▮ ⚡
Large country house in beautiful location overlooking the Sussex Weald. Ideal for walking, cycling, riding the South Downs yet only 15 mins from Brighton for nightlife. Library for guest use & colour TVs in all rooms. Peace & quiet away from city stress!

Hurstpierpoint 10

National Grid Ref: TQ2816

⚍ ◫ The Pilgrim, The Goose

(2.5m 🚌**)** *Wickham Place, Wickham Drive, Hurstpierpoint, Hassocks, W. Sussex, BN6 9AP.*
Large house in a lovely village just off the A23.
Tel: **01273 832172**
Mrs Moore.
D: £22.50-£25.00 **S:** £30.00-£30.00.
Open: All Year (not Xmas)
Beds: 1D 2T
Baths: 1 Sh
♿ ℗ (5) ⌁ ☐ 🐾 ▥ 📖 Ⅵ

Patcham 11

National Grid Ref: TQ3008

(▲ 3.5m) *Brighton Youth Hostel, Patcham Place, London Road, Patcham, Brighton, East Sussex, BN1 8YD.*
Actual grid ref: TQ300088
Tel: **01273 556196**
Under 18: £6.90 **Adults:** £10.00
Self-catering facilities, Television, Showers, Laundry facilities, Lounge, Games room, Security lockers, Cycle store, Evening meal at 6.30 to 7.30, Kitchen facilities, Breakfast available, Credit cards accepted
Splendid country house with Queen Anne front, on the edge of Brighton and the South Downs.

Truleigh Hill 12

National Grid Ref: TQ2210

(▲ On path) *Truleigh Hill Youth Hostel, Tottington Barn, Truleigh Hill, Shoreham-by-Sea, West Sussex, BN43 5FB.*
Actual grid ref: TQ220105
Tel: **01903 813419**
Under 18: £6.90
Adults: £10.00
Television, Showers, Showers, Lounge, Dining room, Cycle store, Parking, Evening meal at 7.00pm, No smoking, WC, Credit cards accepted
Modern hostel in the Sussex Downs Area of Outstanding Natural Beauty with conservation project and old dew pond in grounds.

Taking your dog?

Book *in advance*

ONLY with owners

who accept dogs (🐾)

Upper Beeding 13

National Grid Ref: TQ1910

(0.25m) *The Rising Sun, Upper Beeding, Steyning, W. Sussex, BN44 3TQ.*
Actual grid ref: TQ197097
Tel: **01903 814424**
Mr & Mrs Taylor-Mason.
D: £17.00-£17.00 **S:** £20.00-£20.00.
Open: All Year (not Xmas)
Beds: 2D 1T 2S
Baths: 1 Sh
🅿 (20) 🛏 🕭 ✕ 🏃 🌲 🎹 🔞 ⍾
A delightful Georgian country inn, set amidst the South Downs. Tony & Sue offer a warm welcome, fine selection of real ales and traditional home-cooked food lunchtime and evenings. Comfortable rooms, all with wash basin. Renowned full English breakfast.

Bramber 14

National Grid Ref: TQ1810

(1m) *Castle Hotel, The Street, Bramber, Steyning, W. Sussex, BN44 3WE.*
Actual grid ref: TQ189106
Pretty village, spacious characterful romantic friendly inn.
Tel: **01903 812102**
Mr & Mrs Mitchell.
Fax no: 01903 816711
D: £22.00-£30.00 **S:** £35.00-£40.00.
Open: All Year
Beds: 1F 6D 3T
Baths: 10 En
🛏 🅿 (15) ⍾ 🛏 ✕ 🏃 🌲 🎹 🔞 ⍾

Steyning 15

National Grid Ref: TQ1711

⍾ Star Inn, The Fountain, The Chequers

(1m) *Wappingthorn Farmhouse, Horsham Road, Steyning, West Sussex, BN44 3AA.*
Grades: ETC 4 Diamond
Tel: **01903 813236** Mr Shapland.
D: £20.00-£25.00 **S:** £27.50-£35.00.
Open: All Year
Beds: 1F 1T 1D 1S
Baths: 4 En
🛏 🅿 (8) ⍾ 🛏 🎹
Traditional farmhouse, recently refurbished, set in 2 acres of gardens. Located within our family operated, 300 acre dairy farm. All rooms overlook fields and the South Downs. Includes breakfast. 10 miles Brighton. 8 miles Worthing. Steyning Village 1 mile.

(0.75m ⍾) *5 Coxham Lane, Steyning, W. Sussex, BN44 3LG.*
Comfortable house in quiet lane.
Tel: **01903 812286** Mrs Morrow.
D: £16.00-£16.00 **S:** £16.00-£16.00.
Open: All Year
Beds: 2T 1S
Baths: 1 Sh
🅿 (3) 🏃 🌲 🎹 🔞 ⍾

(1.5m) *Sheppenstrete House, Sheep Pen Lane, Steyning, W. Sussex, BN44 3GP.*
Charming, comfortable period house, hidden just off High Street.
Tel: **01903 813179** Mrs Wood.
Fax no: 01903 814400
D: £25.00-£30.00 **S:** £25.00-£40.00.
Open: All Year (not Xmas)
Beds: 1T 1S
🅿 (1) ⍾ 🛏 ✕ 🏃 🌲 🎹 🔞 ⍾

Findon 16

National Grid Ref: TQ1208

⍾⍾ The Gun, Findon Manor, Black Horse

(2m) *The Coach House, 41 High Street, Findon, Worthing, West Sussex, BN14 0SU.*
Actual grid ref: TQ123084
Village location in South Downs. Excellent walks/cycling. Close to coast.
Tel: **01903 873924** Goble.
D: £19.50-£22.00 **S:** £25.00-£27.50.
Open: All Year
Beds: 1F 1T 1D **Baths:** 3 En
🛏 🅿 (3) 🛏 🃏 🃏 🎹 🔞

(2m ⍾) *Findon Tower, Cross Lane, Findon, Worthing, W Sussex, BN14 0UG.*
Actual grid ref: TQ123083
Elegant Edwardian country house, walking distance excellent village pubs/restaurants.
Tel: **01903 873870**
Mr & Mrs Smith.
D: £25.00-£30.00 **S:** £30.00-£40.00.
Open: All Year (not Xmas)
Beds: 2D 1T 1S **Baths:** 3 En
🛏 🅿 (10) ⍾ 🏃 🌲 🎹 🔞 ⍾

Storrington 17

National Grid Ref: TQ0814

⍾⍾ Anchor Inn, Old Forge, New Moon

(1.5m ⍾) *Willow Tree Cottage, Washington Road, Storrington, Pulborough, W. Sussex, RH20 4AF.*
Actual grid ref: TQ104134
Welcoming, friendly, quiet. All rooms ensuite. Colour TV, tea-making facilities.
Tel: **01903 740835** Mrs Smith.
D: £20.00-£22.50 **S:** £25.00-£30.00.
Open: All Year (not Xmas)
Beds: 2D 1T **Baths:** 3 Pr
🛏 🅿 (10) ⍾ 🛏 🃏 🏃 🌲 🎹 🔞 ⍾

(1.75m ⍾) *No 1, Lime Chase (off Fryern Road), Storrington, Pulborough, W. Sussex, RH20 4LX.*
Actual grid ref: TQ089147
Award winning luxury accommodation in secluded village setting. Restaurants close by.
Grades: ETC 5 Diamnd, Gold
Tel: **01903 740437** (also fax no)
Mrs Warton.
D: £32.50-£40.00 **S:** £45.00-£55.00.
Open: All Year
Beds: 1T 1D **Baths:** 1 En 1 Pr
🛏 🅿 (10) 🅿 (5) ⍾ 🛏 🃏 🏃 🌲 🎹 🔞 ⍾

(1.5m ⍾) *Hampers End, Rock Road, Storrington, Pulborough, W Sussex, RH20 3AF.*
Mike and Lorna Cheeseman welcome you to their lovely mellowed country house.
Tel: **01903 742777**
Fax no: 01903 742776
D: £22.50-£27.50 .
Open: All Year (not Xmas)
Beds: 1F 2D 1T
Baths: 3 En 1 Pr
🛏 🅿 (10) 🅿 (6) 🛏 🏃 🌲 🎹 🔞 ⍾

Amberley 18

National Grid Ref: TQ0313

⍾⍾ The Sportsman, Black Horse

(1m) *Bacons, Amberley, Arundel, W. Sussex, BN18 9NJ.*
Pretty old cottage in the heart of the village.
Tel: **01798 831234** Mrs Jollands.
D: £18.00 **S:** £18.00.
Open: All Year (not Xmas)
Beds: 2T **Baths:** 1 Sh
🛏 🃏 🎹 ⍾

(0.75m ⍾) *Woodybanks, Crossgates, Amberley, Arundel, W. Sussex, BN18 9NR.*
Actual grid ref: TQ041136
Magnificent elevated views across the beautiful Wildbrooks, situated in picturesque historic Amberley.
Tel: **01798 831295**
Mr & Mrs Hardy.
D: £18.00-£18.00 **S:** £20.00-£25.00.
Open: All Year
Beds: 1D 1T **Baths:** 1 Sh
🛏 🅿 (2) ⍾ 🛏 🏃 🌲 🎹 🔞 ⍾

Warningcamp 19

National Grid Ref: TQ0306

(🔺 3.5m) *Arundel Youth Hostel, Warningcamp, Arundel, West Sussex, BN18 9QY.*
Actual grid ref: TQ032076
Tel: **01903 882204**
Under 18: £7.75 **Adults:** £11.00
Self-catering facilities, Television, Showers, Showers, Wet weather shelter, Lounge, Dining room, Games room, Drying room, Cycle store, Parking, Evening meal at 7.00pm, WC, WC, Breakfast available, Breakfast available, Credit cards accepted
Georgian building 1.5 miles from ancient town of Arundel, dominated by its castle & the South Downs.

Please take muddy boots off before entering premises

Bury 20

National Grid Ref: TQ0113

🏷 🍺 George & Dragon, The Swan

(0.75m 🚪) *Tanglewood, Houghton Lane, Bury, Pulborough, W Sussex, RH20 1PD.*
Warm welcome in our comfortable home, with beautiful views of South Downs.
Tel: **01798 831606** (also fax no)
Mrs House.
D: £22.00-£25.00 **S:** £18.00-£20.00.
Open: All Year
Beds: 1D 1S **Baths:** 1 Sh
🅿 (3) 🛏 🕮 💷 🕮 🔍

(0.75m) *Pulborough Eedes Cottage, Bignor Park Road, Bury Gate, Bury, Pulborough, W Sussex, RH20 1EZ.*
Actual grid ref: TQ003161
Quiet country house surrounded by farmland, very warm personal welcome.
Grades: ETC 4 Diamond
Tel: **01798 831438**
Fax no: 01798 831942
D: £22.50-£25.00 **S:** £25.00-£30.00.
Open: All Year (not Xmas)
Beds: 1D 2T **Baths:** 1 En 1 Sh
🛏 🅿 (10) 🛏 🕬 💷 🕮 🔍

(0.75m) *Harkaway, 8 Houghton Lane, Bury, Pulborough, W. Sussex, RH20 1PD.*
Actual grid ref: TQ012130
Quiet location beneath South Downs. Full English and vegetarian breakfast.
Tel: **01798 831843** Mrs Clark.
D: £17.00-£19.00 **S:** £17.00-£19.00.
Open: All Year
Beds: 1D 2T
Baths: 1 En 1 Sh
🛏 (6) 🅿 (3) 🔍 🛏 🕮 💷 🕮 🔍

Arundel 21

National Grid Ref: TQ0106

🏷 🍺 George & Dragon, Six Bells, The Spur, White Hart

(3m) *Portreeves Acre, The Causeway, Arundel, W. Sussex, BN18 9JL.*
Actual grid ref: TQ0207
3 minute from station, castle and town centre.
Tel: **01903 883277** Mr Rogers.
D: £21.00-£23.00 **S:** £30.00-£35.00.
Open: All Year (not Xmas/New Year)
Beds: 1F 1D 1T **Baths:** 2 En 1 Pr
🛏 (12) 🅿 (6) 🔍 🛏 🕮 💷 🕮 🔍

Bringing children with

you? Always ask for

any special rates.

Slindon 22

National Grid Ref: SU9608

🏷 🍺 Newburgh Arms

(2.75m 🚪) *Mill Lane House, Mill Lane, Slindon, Arundel, W. Sussex, BN18 0RP.*
Actual grid ref: SU964084
In peaceful village on South Downs, views to coast.
Grades: ETC 3 Diamond
Tel: **01243 814440** Mrs Fuente.
Fax no: 01243 814436
D: £22.50-£22.50 **S:** £28.50-£28.50.
Open: All Year
Beds: 2D 1T **Baths:** 3 En
🛏 🅿 (7) 🛏 🕬 🗡 🕮 💷 🔍

Duncton 23

National Grid Ref: SU9517

🏷 🍺 Cricketers

(1.5m) *Drifters, Duncton, Petworth, W. Sussex, GU28 0JZ.*
Quiet comfortable country house - TV - tea & coffee making facilities in rooms.
Grades: ETC 3 Diamond
Tel: **01798 342706** Mrs Folkes.
D: £20.00-£25.00 **S:** £25.00.
Open: All Year (not Xmas)
Beds: 1D 2T 1S **Baths:** 1 En 1 Sh
🅿 (3) 🔍 🗡 🛏 🕮 💷 🔍

Graffham 24

National Grid Ref: SU9217

🏷 🍺 The Foresters, White Horse

(1m 🚪) *Brook Barn, Selham Road, Graffham, Petworth, W Sussex, GU28 0PU.*
Actual grid ref: 19831023
Grades: ETC 4 Diamond, Silver
Tel: **01798 867356** Mr & Mrs Jollands
D: £25.00-£25.00 **S:** £30.00-£30.00.
Open: All Year (not Xmas)
Beds: 1D **Baths:** 1 En
🛏 🅿 (2) 🔍 🛏 🕮 💷 🔍
Large double bedroom with ensuite bathroom, leads directly to own conservatory and secluded 2-acre garden. Close to South Downs Way, excellent pubs within walking distance, in quiet rural village in beautiful area of Sussex, ideal for a relaxing break.

Cocking 25

National Grid Ref: SU8717

🏷 🍺 Bell Inn

(0.25m) *Moonlight Cottage Tea Rooms, Chichester Road, Cocking, Midhurst, W. Sussex, GU29 0HN.*
Warm welcome, pretty tea rooms/ garden. comfortable bed, excellent breakfast.
Grades: ETC 3 Diamond
Tel: **01730 813336** Mrs Longland.
D: £20.00-£23.00 **S:** £20.00-£23.00.
Open: All Year
Beds: 2D 1T **Baths:** 1 Sh
🛏 🅿 (5) 🛏 🕮 💷 🔍

Midhurst 26

National Grid Ref: SU8821

🏷 🍺 The Wheatsheaf, Half Moon, Bricklayers Arms, The Swan, The Elsted

(3m 🚪) *Oakhurst Cottage, Carron Lane, Midhurst, W. Sussex, GU29 9LF.*
Beautiful cottage in lovely surroundings within easy reach of Midhurst amenities.
Grades: ETC 3 Diamond
Tel: **01730 813523**
Mrs Whitmore Jones.
D: £25.00-£30.00 **S:** £25.00-£30.00.
Open: All Year
Beds: 1D 1T 1S
Baths: 1 En 1 Sh
🛏 (4) 🅿 (2) 🔍 🛏 🕮 🔍

(3m) *The Crown Inn, Edinburgh Square, Midhurst, W. Sussex, GU29 9NL.*
Actual grid ref: SU887215
C16th character inn, real ales, log fires, home-cooked food.
Tel: **01730 813462** Mr Stevens.
D: £17.50-£20.00 **S:** £20.00-£25.00.
Open: All Year
Beds: 1D 1T 1S
Baths: 1 Sh
🔍 🛏 🗡 🛏 🕮 💷 🔍

(3m 🚪) *Carrondune, Carron Lane, Midhurst, W Sussex, GU29 9LD.*
Comfortable old family country house, quiet location, 5 mins town centre.
Tel: **01730 813558**
Mrs Beck.
D: £20.00-£25.00
S: £25.00-£30.00.
Open: Feb to Nov
Beds: 1D 1T
Baths: 1 Sh
🛏 (5) 🅿 (4) 🛏 🕮 💷 🔍

Elsted 27

National Grid Ref: SU8119

🏷 🍺 The Wheatsheaf, Half Moon, Bricklayers Arms, The Swan, The Elsted, Three Horseshoes

(3m) *Three, Elsted, Midhurst, W Sussex, GU29 0JY.*
Oldest house in village (1520). Pub, cricket ground, church nearby. Warm welcome.
Tel: **01730 825065** Mrs Hill.
Fax no: 01730 825496
D: £25.00 **S:** £22.50.
Open: Mar to Nov
Beds: 1D 1T 1S
Baths: 1 Pr 1 Sh

All paths are popular:

you are well-advised to

book ahead

East Harting 28

National Grid Ref: SU7919

The Ship, Three Horseshoes, White Hart

(0.5m) ***Oakwood,*** *Eastfield Lane, East Harting, Petersfield, Hampshire, GU31 5NF.*
Actual grid ref: SU802193
Foot of South Downs, beautiful countryside, Chichester, Portsmouth easy reach.
Tel: **01730 825245** Mrs Brightwell.
D: £20.00-£22.50 **S:** £20.00-£25.00.
Open: All Year
Beds: 2T
Baths: 2 Pr

Buriton 29

National Grid Ref: SU7320

(1m) ***Nursted Farm,*** *Buriton, Petersfield, Hants, GU31 5RW.*
Relax in the atmosphere of our 300 year old farmhouse.
Tel: **01730 264278** Mrs Bray.
D: £18.00-£18.00 **S:** £18.00-£18.00.
Open: May to Feb
Beds: 3T
Baths: 1 Pr 1 Sh

Petersfield 30

National Grid Ref: SU7423

Harrow Inn, Half Moon, Good Intent, Five Bells

(4m) ***Heath Farmhouse,*** *Sussex Road, Petersfield, Hants, GU31 4HU.*
Actual grid ref: SU7522
Georgian farmhouse, lovely views, large garden, quiet surroundings, near town.
Grades: ETC 3 Diamond
Tel: **01730 264709**
Mrs Scurfield.
D: £18.00-£20.00 **S:** £20.00-£25.00.
Open: All Year
Beds: 1F 1D 1T
Baths: 1 En 1 Sh
(5)

(4m) ***Heathside,*** *36 Heath Road East, Petersfield, Hants, GU31 4HR.*
Petersfield pretty market square and shops. 15 minutes walk across heath. **Grades:** ETC 3 Diamond
Tel: **01730 262337** Mrs Cafferata.
D: £20.00-£25.00 **S:** £22.00-£25.00.
Open: All Year (not Xmas)
Beds: 1T 2S **Baths:** 1 En 1 Pr 1 Sh
(3)

(4m) ***Ridgefield,*** *Station Road, Petersfield, Hants, GU32 3DE.*
Actual grid ref: SU743237
Friendly family atmosphere, near town & station; Portsmouth ferries: 20 mins drive.
Grades: ETC 2 Diamond
Tel: **01730 261402** Mrs West.
D: £20.00-£20.00 **S:** £25.00-£30.00.
Open: All Year (not Xmas)
Beds: 1D 2T **Baths:** 2 Sh
(4)

(4m) ***Beaumont,*** *22 Stafford Road, Petersfield, Hampshire, GU32 2JG.*
Warm welcome, comfortable beds, excellent breakfasts with home-made preserves.
Grades: ETC 3 Diamond
Tel: **01730 264744** (also fax no)
Mrs Bewes.
D: £20.00-£20.00 **S:** £20.00-£25.00.
Open: All Year (not Xmas)
Beds: 2T 1S **Baths:** 1 Sh
(12) (2)

East Meon 31

National Grid Ref: SU6822

Old George Inn, The Thomas Lord

(0.75m) ***Drayton Cottage,*** *East Meon, Petersfield, Hants, GU32 1PW.*
Actual grid ref: SU669232
Luxury country cottage; antiques and oak beams, overlooking glorious countryside.
Tel: **01730 823472** Mrs Rockett.
D: £20.00-£23.00 **S:** £25.00-£25.00.
Open: All Year
Beds: 1D 1T **Baths:** 1 En 1 Pr
(3)

(On path) ***Coombe Cross House & Stables,*** *Coombe Road, East Meon, Petersfield, Hants, GU32 1HQ.*
Actual grid ref: SU667210
Early Georgian House on South Downs, beautiful views, tranquil setting.
Tel: **01730 823298** Mrs Bulmer.
Fax no: 01730 823515
D: £25.00 **S:** £30.00.
Open: All Year (not Xmas)
Beds: 1D 2T 1S
Baths: 2 Pr 1 Sh
(12) (10)

Cheriton 32

National Grid Ref: SU5828

Flower Pots

(2m) ***The Garden House,*** *Cheriton, Alresford, Hampshire, SO24 0QQ.*
Edge of pretty village. Tennis court. Near Cheriton Battle Field. Personal tour by arrangement
Tel: **01962 771352** Mrs Verney.
Fax no: 01962 771667
D: £20.00-£24.00 **S:** £20.00-£24.00.
Open: All Year
Beds: 2T 1D
Baths: 1 Pr 1 Sh
(4)

Owslebury 33

National Grid Ref: SU5123

Ship Inn

(1.5m) ***Mays Farmhouse,*** *Longwood Dean, Owslebury, Winchester, Hants, SO21 1JS.*
Actual grid ref: SU547241
Lovely C16th farmhouse, beautiful countryside; peaceful with good walks.
Tel: **01962 777486** Mrs Ashby.
Fax no: 01962 777747
D: £22.50-£25.00 **S:** £25.00-£30.00.
Open: All Year
Beds: 1F 1D 1T **Baths:** 3 Pr
(7) (5)

Winchester 34

National Grid Ref: SU4829

Roebuck Inn, Queen Inn, Bell Inn, Wykeham Arms, White Horse, Stanmore Hotel, Cart Horse, Plough

(On path) ***Winchester Youth Hostel,*** *The City Mill, 1 Water Lane, Winchester, Hampshire, SO23 8EJ.*
Actual grid ref: SU486293
Tel: **01962 853723**
Under 18: £6.50 **Adults:** £9.25
Showers, Lounge, Cycle store, No smoking, Kitchen facilities, Breakfast available 7.00pm, Credit cards accepted
Charming C18th watermill (NT) straddling the River Itchen at East End of King Alfred's capital, a half mile from the cathedral

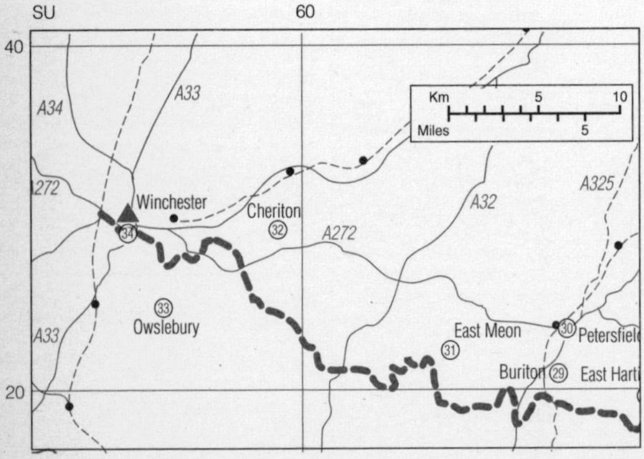

(1m) *The Farrells, 5 Ranelagh Road, Winchester, Hants, SO23 9TA.*
Actual grid ref: SU476287
Grades: ETC 3 Diamond
Tel: **01962 869555** (also fax no)
Mr Farrell.
D: £20.00-£25.00 **S:** £22.00-£22.00.
Open: All Year (not Xmas)
Beds: 1F 1D 1T 1S
Baths: 1 En 1 Pr 2 Sh
🛏 (5) 🍴 ⬛ 🌳 🎤 📺 ♿
Turn of the century Victorian villa, furnished in that style. We are close to the Cathedral and like to share our love of Winchester with our guests.

(1.5m) 🚗 *8 Salters Acres, Winchester, Hants, SO22 5JW.*
Detached family home in large gardens. Breakfast in conservatory, easy access to city centre.
Tel: **01962 856112**
Mr & Mrs Cater.
D: £19.00-£22.50 **S:** £25.00-£30.00.
Open: All Year (not Xmas/New Year)
Beds: 1T 1D 1S **Baths:** 1 Pr 1 Sh
🛏 (8) ⬛ (8) 🍴 ⬛ 🌳 🎤 📺 ♿

(1.5m) *Sycamores, 4 Bereweeke Close, Winchester, Hants, SO22 6AR.*
Actual grid ref: SU472304
Convenient but peaceful location about 2 km north-west of city centre. **Grades:** ETC 3 Diamond
Tel: **01962 867242** Mrs Edwards.
Fax no: 01962 620300
D: £20.00-£20.00 .
Open: All Year
Beds: 2D 1T **Baths:** 3 Pr
⬛ (3) 🍴 ⬛ 🌳 🎤 📺

(1m) *85 Christchurch Road, Winchester, Hants, SO23 9QY.*
Actual grid ref: SU473282
Comfortable detached Victorian family house, convenient base for Hampshire sightseeing.
Grades: ETC 4 Diamond
Tel: **01962 868661** (also fax no)
Mrs Fetherston-Dilke.
D: £25.00-£26.00 **S:** £25.00-£30.00.
Open: All Year
Beds: 1D 1T 1S **Baths:** 2 En 1 Sh
🛏 ⬛ (3) 🍴 ⬛ 🌳 🎤 📺 ♿

(1.5m) *St Margaret's, 3 St Michael's Road, Winchester, Hampshire, SO23 9JE.*
Comfortable rooms in Victorian house, close to cathedral and colleges.
Grades: ETC 2 Diamond .
Tel: **01962 861450** Mrs Brett.
D: £20.00-£21.00 **S:** £22.00-£22.00.
Open: All Year (not Xmas)
Beds: 1D 1T 2S
Baths: 2 Sh
🛏 (4) ⬛ (1) 🍴 ⬛ 🌳 🎤 📺

(1.5m) *Rocquaine, 19 Downside Road, Winchester, SO22 5LT.*
Spacious welcoming detached family home in quiet residential area.
Tel: **01962 861426**
Mrs Quick.
D: £18.00-£19.00 **S:** £20.00-£25.00.
Open: All Year (not Xmas)
Beds: 1D 1T 1S
Baths: 1 Sh
🛏 (8) ⬛ (4) 🍴 ⬛ 🌳 🎤 📺 ♿

(1m) *32 Hyde Street, Winchester, Hants, SO23 7DX.*
Actual grid ref: SU481301
Attractive C18th town house, close to city centre.
Tel: **01962 851621**
Mrs Tisdall.
D: £17.00-£18.00
S: £26.00-£26.00.
Open: All Year (not Xmas/New Year)
Beds: 1F 1D
Baths: 1 Sh
🛏 🍴 ⬛ 🌳 🎤 📺

(1.5m) 🚗 *Portland House Hotel, 63 Tower Street, Winchester, Hants, SO23 8TA.*
Quiet city centre location a few minutes from major sites.
Grades: ETC 3 Diamond
Tel: **01962 865195**
Mr & Mrs Knight.
D: £22.50-£55.00
S: £48.00-£48.00.
Open: All Year (not Xmas/New Year)
Beds: 1F 1T 2D
Baths: 4 En
🛏 (5) ⬛ (5) ⬛ 🌳 🎤 📺

(3m) 🚗 *The Lilacs, 1 Harestock Close, off Andover Road North, Winchester, Hants, SO22 6NP.*
Attractive, Georgian-style family home. Comfortable, clean and excellent cuisine.
Tel: **01962 884122**
Mrs Pell.
D: £17.50-£18.00 **S:** £22.00-£25.00.
Open: All Year (not Xmas)
Beds: 1D 1T
Baths: 1 Sh
🛏 (3) 🍴 ⬛ 🌳 🎤 📺 🎵 ♿

(1.5m) *Giffard House Hotel, 50 Christchurch Road, St Cross, Winchester, Hants, SO23 9SU.*
Comfortable Victorian house within ten minutes' walk of the city centre.
Tel: **01962 852628**
Fax no: 01962 856722
D: £25.00-£35.00
S: £35.00-£45.00.
Open: All Year
Beds: 1F 6D 2T 5S
Baths: 14 En
🛏 ⬛ (14) ⬛ 🌳 🎤 📺

(1.5m) *Shawlands, 46 Kilham Lane, Winchester, Hants, SO22 5QD.*
Actual grid ref: SU456289
Attractive house on edge of Winchester in quiet lane overlooking fields.
Tel: **01962 861166** (also fax no)
Mrs Pollock.
D: £19.00-£22.50
S: £27.00-£30.00.
Open: All Year
Beds: 2F 1D 2T
Baths: 1 Pr 2 Sh
🛏 (5) ⬛ (4) 🍴 ⬛ 🎤 🌳 🎤 📺 ♿ 📺 ♿

All paths are popular: you are well-advised to book ahead

South West Coast Path

The coast of Britain's South Western peninsula is rightly famous for its scenery, which ranks among the best in Europe. Spectacular cliffs, lonely beaches, wide river estuaries, buzzing resorts and tranquil coves - all are bounded by the Atlantic as its pushes up the English Channel on the South and into the Irish Sea and the Bristol Channel to the North. In the summer the coast is crowded with holiday-makers and the path is popular, but there are still long stretches where you will keep your own company.

The **South West Coast Path** is by far and away the longest of Britain's National Trails. It combines the **Somerset & North Devon, Cornwall, South Devon** and **Dorset Coastal Paths**, running up a total of some 613 miles. Not many walkers will complete the path in one go. In fact, it's a natural candidate for walking in sections. Take the prevailing wind (a south-westerly) into consideration when planning your walk, for this path is certainly exposed. Do you wish to walk into the wind or to have it at your back?

Squalls and gales can blow up unexpectedly and cliff-walking can be become quite dangerous in these conditions, so take care to listen to the right forecasts.

One of the most enjoyable features of the **South West Coast Path** is the number of estuaries one must cross. While some are fordable, it is strongly recommended that ferries are used wherever possible, as river conditions may prove unpredictable, if not perilous. If there is no ferry, allowances for a detour must be made. Details of ferries can be had locally, but to plan the route properly, there is an excellent book published by the **South West Way Association**. Called simply *The South West Way*, it publishes both tide and ferry timetables, public transport details and suggested itineraries. Ring 01803 873061 for more details.

Comments on the path to: **David Venner**, South West Coast Path Project, Luscombe House, County Hall, Exeter, EX2 4QW

Somerset & North Devon

This section of the **South West Coast Path** runs for only a short way in Somerset from Minehead, then past the North Devon resorts of Ilfracombe and Woolacombe and the major towns of Barnstaple and Bideford, to the border with Cornwall.

Guides: *South West Way: Vol I (Minehead to Penzance)* by Martin Collins (ISBN 1 85284 025 0), published by Cicerone Press and also available from the publishers (2 Police Square, Milnthorpe, Cumbria, LA7 7PY, 01539 562069), £8.99

South West Way: Minehead to Padstow by Roland Tarr (ISBN 1 85410 4152), published by Aurum Press in association with the Countryside Commission and Ordnance Survey, £10.99

There is also invaluable local information in *The South West Way 2001* by the South West Way Association, available directly from them at 25 Clobells, South Brent, Devon, TQ10 9JW, tel. 01364 73859, £7.00 (inc. p&p)

Maps: Ordnance Survey 1:50,000 Landranger series: 180, 181 and 190

Alcombe Combe 1

National Grid Ref: SS9745

(⚠ 2m) *Minehead Youth Hostel, Alcombe Combe, Minehead, Somerset, TA24 6EW.*
Actual grid ref: SS973442
Tel: 01643 702595
Under 18: £6.90
Adults: £10.00
Self-catering facilities, Showers, Lounge, Dining room, Drying room, Parking Limited, Evening meal at 7.00pm, No smoking, WC, Breakfast available, Credit cards accepted
In a secluded position up a wooded combe on the edge of Exmoor

Minehead 2

National Grid Ref: SS9646

🍴 🍺 Queen's Head, Beach Hotel, York House

(0.75m) *Rectory House Hotel, Northfield Road, Minehead, TA24 5QH.*
Former rectory, magnificent hill and sea views. Putting green.
Grades: RAC 2 Star
Tel: **01643 702611**
Mr Wilson.
D: £30.00-£30.00 **S:** £30.00-£30.00.
Open: All Year
Beds: 3F 2D 2T
Baths: 7 En
🛏 🅿 (8) 🛏 🍴 ✗ 🐾 🖳 🎥 ✦

(0.75m) *1 Glenmore Road, Minehead, Somerset, TA24 5BQ.*
Tel: **01643 706225**
Mrs Sanders.
D: £16.50-£18.50
S: £16.50-£16.50.
Open: All Year
Beds: 1F 1D 1T 1S
Baths: 2 En 1 Sh
🛏 🅿 (6) 🌿 ✗ 🖳 🎥
A superior Victorian family-run guest house offering a friendly welcome and relaxing atmosphere, an excellent range of breakfasts including vegetarian. Number one is perfectly situated just back from the promenade with only a short level walk to local amenities.

(On path) *Beaconwood Hotel,*
Church Road, North Hill,
Minehead, Somerset, TA24 5SB.
Grades: ETC 2 Star
Tel: **01643 702032** (also fax no)
Mr Roberts.
D: £30.00-£35.00 **S:** £33.00-£40.00.
Open: All Year
Beds: 2F 6D 6T **Baths:** 14 En
🌣 🅿 (25) ⬜ ⑂ ✕ ⚊ 🕮 Ⅵ ⋔ ⫽
Edwardian country house hotel, set
in 2 acres of terraced gardens with
panoramic views of Exmoor area.
With heated outdoor swimming
pool & grass tennis court. 200
yards from South West Coast Path.

(0.75m) *The Parks Guest House,*
26 The Parks, Minehead, Somerset,
TA24 8BT.
Comfortable family run B&B,
lounge bar, close to Exmoor coast
and town centre.
Tel: **01643 703547**
Mr & Mrs Gibson.
Fax no: 01643 708088
D: £16.50-£19.00 **S:** £19.00-£22.00.
Open: All Year (not Xmas)
Beds: 4F 1D 1T
Baths: 4 En 1 Sh
🌣 🅿 (8) ⬜ ✕ ⚊ 🕮 Ⅵ ⋔ ⫽

Porlock 3

National Grid Ref: SS8846

Royal Oak, Ship Inn, Castle Hotel, Culbone
Inn, Overstream Hotel

(1m 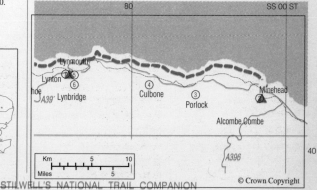) *Overstream Hotel,*
Parsons Street, Porlock, Minehead,
Somerset, TA24 8QJ.
Situated in the centre of Porlock,
between Exmoor and the sea.
Tel: **01643 862421** (also fax no)
D: £21.00-£30.00 **S:** £30.00-£30.00.
Open: Easter to November
Beds: 1F 2T 4D 2S **Baths:** 9 En
🌣 🅿 ⫽ ⬜ ✕ ⚊ 🕮 Ⅵ ⋔ ⫽

(1m) *Leys, The Ridge,*
Bossington Lane, Porlock,
Minehead, Somerset, TA24 8HA.
Actual grid ref: SS892469
Beautiful family home, delightful
garden, with magnificent views.
Tel: **01643 862477** (also fax no)
Mrs Stiles-Cox.
D: £19.00-£19.00 **S:** £19.00-£19.00.
Open: All Year (not Xmas)
Beds: 1D/T 2S **Baths:** 1 Sh
🌣 🅿 (4) ⫽ ⬜ ⑂ ⚊ 🕮 Ⅵ ⋔ ⫽

(0.25m) *Hurlstone, Sparkhayes*
Lane, Porlock, Minehead,
Somerset, TA24 8NE.
Actual grid ref: SS887469
Quiet house near village centre sea
and moorland views.
Tel: **01643 862650** Mrs Coombs.
D: £18.00-£18.00 **S:** £18.00-£18.00.
Open: All Year (not Xmas)
Beds: 1D 1T
Baths: 1 Sh
🌣 🅿 ⑂ ⚊ Ⅵ ⋔ ⫽

(On path) *West Porlock House,*
Country House Hotel, West
Porlock, Porlock, Minehead,
Somerset, TA24 8NX.
Actual grid ref: SS870470
Superbly set in beautiful woodland
garden with magnificent sea views.
Grades: ETC 4 Diamond
Tel: **01643 862880** Mrs Dyer.
D: £25.50-£27.50 **S:** £30.00.
Open: Feb to Nov
Beds: 1F 2D 2T
Baths: 2 En 3 Pr
🌣 (6) 🅿 (8) ⫽ ⬜ ⚊ 🕮 Ⅵ ⋔ ⫽

(1m) *Lorna Doone Hotel, High*
Street, Porlock, Minehead,
Somerset, TA24 8PS.
Actual grid ref: SS888468
Village centre Victorian Hotel with
extensive dinner menu.
Tel: **01643 862404** Mr Thornton.
Fax no: 01643 863018
D: £22.00-£27.50 **S:** £24.00-£26.00.
Open: All Year (not Xmas)
Beds: 5D 6T 4S
Baths: 15 En
🅿 (7) ⬜ ⑂ ✕ ⚊ 🕮 Ⅵ ⫽

(On path) *Sea View Cottage,*
Porlock Weir, Porlock, Minehead,
Somerset, TA24 8PE.
Actual grid ref: SS864478
Comfortable cottage near harbour
ideally situated for exploring
Exmoor.
Tel: **01643 862523**
Mrs Starr.
D: £18.00-£22.00 **S:** £20.00-£22.00.
Open: All Year (not Xmas)
Beds: 1D 1T
Baths: 1 En 1 Sh
🌣 🅿 (2) ⬜ ⑂ ⚊ 🕮 Ⅵ ⋔

Culbone 4

National Grid Ref: SS8448

Culbone Inn

(On path) *Silcombe Farm,*
Culbone, Porlock, Minehead,
Somerset, TA24 8JN.
Actual grid ref: SS833482
Comfortable secluded Exmoor
farmhouse overlooking sea in
beautiful walking country.
Tel: **01643 862248**
Mrs Richards.
D: £18.00-£20.00 **S:** £20.00-£20.00.
Open: All Year (not Xmas)
Beds: 1D 2T 1S
Baths: 1 En 1 Sh
🌣 (4) 🅿 (6) ⬜ ⑂ ✕ ⚊ 🕮 Ⅵ ⋔ ⫽

Lynmouth 5

National Grid Ref: SS7249

Riverside Cottages, Village Inn

(0.25m) *Glenville House, 2 Tors*
Road, Lynmouth, Devon, EX35 6ET.
Grades: AA 4 Diamond
Tel: **01598 752202**
Mr & Mrs Francis.
D: £22.00-£26.00
S: £22.00-£30.00.
Open: Feb to Nov
Beds: 4D 1T 1S
Baths: 3 En 1 Pr 2 Sh
🌣 (12) ⫽ ⬜ ⚊ 🕮 Ⅵ ⋔ ⫽
Idyllic riverside setting. Delightful
Victorian house full of character
and charm. Licensed. Tastefully
decorated bedrooms. Picturesque
harbour, village and unique Cliff
Railway nestled amidst wooded
valley. Magnificent Exmoor
scenery, spectacular coastline and
beautiful walks. Peaceful, tranquil,
romantic - a very special place.

© Crown Copyright

(0.25m) *Tregonwell Riverside Guest House, 1 Tors Road, Lynmouth, Devon, EX35 6ET.*
Actual grid ref: SS725493
Grades: ETC 3 Diamond,
AA 3 Diamond
Tel: **01598 753369** Mrs Parker.
D: £22.00-£27.00 **S:** £22.00-£25.00.
Open: All Year (not Xmas)
Beds: 2F 5D 1T 1S
Baths: 5 En 1 Pr 3 Sh
♿ **P** (7) ⊬ ☐ ✠ ☀ Ⅲ Ⅴ ⓐ ⅋
Award-winning, romantic, elegant riverside (former sea captain's) stone-built house, snuggled amidst waterfalls, cascades, wooded valleys, soaring cliff tops, lonely beaches, enchanting harbourside 'Olde Worlde' smugglers' village. Shelley, Wordsworth, Coleridge stayed here. 'England's Switzerland'. Pretty bedrooms, dramatic views. Garaged parkings.

Lynbridge 6

National Grid Ref: SS7248

(1m) *Lynton Youth Hostel, Lynbridge, Lynton, Devon, EX35 6BE.*
Actual grid ref: SS720487
Tel: **01598 753237**
Under 18: £6.90 **Adults:** £10.00
Self-catering facilities, Showers, Shop, Laundry facilities, Lounge, Dining room, Drying room, Cycle store, Parking Limited, Evening meal at 7.00pm, No smoking, WC, Kitchen facilities, Breakfast available, Credit cards accepted
Victorian house in the steep wooded gorge of the West Lyn River, where Exmoor reaches the sea, with opportunities to explore the National Park, the sea shore and the river valley.

All paths are popular: you are well-advised to book ahead

Lynton 7

National Grid Ref: SS7149

Rising Sun Inn, Staghunters Inn, Ye Olde Cottage Inn, Royal Castle, Sandrock

(0.5m) *The Turret, 33 Lee Road, Lynton, Devon, EX35 6BS.*
Grades: ETC 3 Diamond
Tel: **01598 753284** (also fax no)
Mrs Wayman.
D: £18.00-£23.00 **S:** £25.00.
Open: All Year
Beds: 5D 1T **Baths:** 4 En
♿ (12) ☐ ✠ ☀ Ⅲ Ⅴ ⅋
Step back in time and experience old world hospitality. Built in 1898, the charm of our hotel will relax and welcome you. Beautiful ensuite bedrooms, enhanced with all the modern facilities. Evening meals served in cosy dining room. Vegetarian and special dietary needs catered for.

(0.25m) *Victoria Lodge, Lee Road, Lynton, Devon, EX35 6BP.*
Awarded B&B of the Year for S.W. England by South West Tourism.
Grades: AA 5 Diamond
Tel: **01598 753203** (also fax no)
Mr & Mrs Bennett.
D: £26.00-£36.00 **S:** £35.00-£54.00.
Open: Feb to Nov
Beds: 1F 7D 1T **Baths:** 9 En
♿ **P** (7) ⊬ ☐ ✠ ☀ Ⅲ Ⅴ

(0.5m 🚍) *The Denes Guest House, Longmead, Lynton, Devon, EX35 6DQ.*
Grades: ETC 3 Diamond
Tel: **01598 753573** Mr McGowan.
D: £16.00-£22.50 **S:** £16.00-£22.50.
Open: All Year
Beds: 3F 2D
Baths: 2 En 1 Pr 2 Sh
♿ **P** (5) ⊬ ☐ ✠ ☀ Ⅲ ⓐ ⅋
A warm friendly greeting awaits you at The Denes, with its Edwardian charm. Comfortable accommodation and home cooked food, evening meals served in our licensed dining room. Ideal base to explore Exmoor on the South West Coastal Path. An Exmoor paths partner.

(0.25m 🚍) *Lynhurst Hotel, Lynton, Devon, EX35 6AX.*
Character Victorian residence situated in gardens/woodland overlooking Lynmouth Bay.
Grades: AA 4 Diamond
Tel: **01598 752241** (also fax no)
Mr Townsend.
D: £22.00-£30.00
S: £25.00-£28.00.
Open: All Year
Beds: 2F 5D 1T 1S
Baths: 7 En
♿ (1) **P** (2) ☐ ✠ ☀ Ⅲ Ⅴ ⅋

(0.5m) *Gable Lodge, Lee Road, Lynton, Devon, EX35 6BS.*
Actual grid ref: SS718495
Large Victorian house with views along the East Lyn valley.
Tel: **01598 752367** (also fax no)
Mr & Mrs Bowman.
D: £18.50-£19.50
S: £18.50-£19.50.
Open: Easter to Oct
Beds: 1F 5D
Baths: 5 En 1 Sh
♿ **P** (8) ⊬ ☐ ✠ ☀ Ⅲ Ⅴ

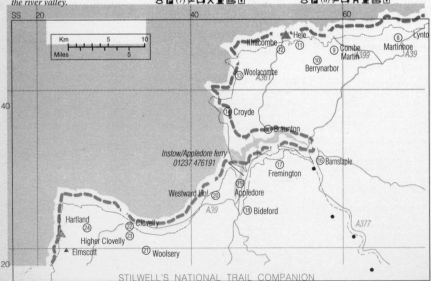

(0.5m) *Croft House Hotel, Lydiate Lane, Lynton, Devon, EX35 6HE.*
Croft house nestling in the village, built 1828 for a sea captain.
Tel: **01598 752391** (also fax no)
Mrs Johnson.
D: £17.00-£27.00 **S:** £20.00-£30.00.
Open: All Year (not Xmas)
Beds: 5D 2T
Baths: 6 En 1 Pr
⊬□↑✕♨🖤Ⅶ🛇∥

Martinhoe 8

National Grid Ref: SS6648

Hunters Inn, Fox & Goose

(0.25m) *Mannacott Farm, Martinhoe, Parracombe, Barnstaple, Devon, EX31 4QS.*
Actual grid ref: SS662481
In area of outstanding natural scenery. Ideal for walkers, bird watchers. Near coast.
Tel: **01598 763227** Mrs Dallyn.
D: £15.00-£16.00 **S:** £16.00-£17.00.
Open: Apr to mid-Oct
Beds: 1D 1T 1S **Baths:** 1 Sh
🅿(2)⊬□🖤∥

Combe Martin 9

National Grid Ref: SS5846

Dolphin Inn, Focsle Inn, Royal Marine

(On path) *Royal Marine, Seaside, Combe Martin, Ilfracombe, EX34 0AW.*
Award winning pub with five superbly appointed licensee.
Ensuite rooms, cooked food, sea views.
Tel: **01271 882470** Mr Lethaby.
Fax no: 01271 889080
D: £20.00-£25.00 **S:** £20.00-£25.00.
Open: All Year
Beds: 5F
Baths: 5 En
🅿□🖤∥

(On path) *Crimond, King Street, Combe Martin, Ilfracombe, EX34 0BS.*
Friendly comfortable Victorian house. Hearty English breakfast. Close to sea.
Tel: **01271 882348** (also fax no) Mr Parkes.
D: £17.00 **S:** £17.00.
Open: All Year (not Xmas)
Beds: 1F 1D 1T 1S
Baths: 1 Sh 4 En
🅿⊬□↑♨🖤Ⅶ

(On path) *Hillview Guest House, Woodlands, Combe Martin, Ilfracombe, Devon, EX34 0AT.*
Actual grid ref: SS575469
Beautifully situated Edwardian house. Quiet position offering comfort and cleanliness.
Tel: **01271 882331** Mrs Bosley.
D: £16.00-£18.50 **S:** £18.00-£20.50.
Open: Easter to Oct
Beds: 2D 1T
Baths: 2 En 1 Pr
🅿(6)⊬□♨🖤Ⅶ🛇∥

(On path 🚐) *Glendower, King Street, Combe Martin, Ilfracombe, Devon, EX34 0AL.*
Close to South West Coastal Path and seaside.
Tel: **01271 883449**
Mr & Mrs Barry.
D: £13.00-£14.00 **S:** £16.00-£18.00.
Open: Easter to Nov
Beds: 2D 1S **Baths:** 2 En 1 Sh
🚐(1)□🖤↑♨🖤Ⅶ🛇∥

Berrynarbor 10

National Grid Ref: SS5646

Old Goose, Globe Inn, Miss Muffits

(0.25m) *Tower Cottage, Berrynarbor, Ilfracombe, Devon, EX34 9SE.*
Charming Cottage with beautiful garden in 'Best kept village Berrynarbor'.
Tel: **01271 883408**
D: £18.00-£22.00 **S:** £25.00-£25.00.
Open: All Year (not Xmas/New Year)
Beds: 1F 1D **Baths:** 2 En
🚐🅿⊬□♨🖤Ⅶ∥

(0.25m 🚐) *Langleigh House, Berrynarbor, Ilfracombe, Devon, EX34 9SG.*
Set in delightful North Devon. Lovely gardens with stream, barbecue area.
Tel: **01271 883410**
Mr & Mrs Pierpoint.
Fax no: 01271 882396
D: £17.50-£24.50 **S:** £23.50-£24.50.
Open: All Year (not Xmas)
Beds: 1F 3D 1T **Baths:** 5 En 2 Pr
🚐🅿(6)⊬□↑♨🖤Ⅶ

(0.25m 🚐) *Sloley Farm, Castle Hill, Berrynarbor, Ilfracombe, Devon, EX34 9SX.*
Actual grid ref: SS564466
Enjoy the peace of Berrynarbor, a quintessential English village, from our superb ensuite rooms.
Tel: **01271 883032** Mrs Mountain & Mr & Mrs J Boxall.
Fax no: 01271 882675
D: £18.00-£25.00 **S:** £18.00-£25.00.
Open: All Year (not Xmas)
Beds: 2D 1T **Baths:** 3 En
🅿(10)⊬□✕♨🖤🛇Ⅶ∥

Hele (Ilfracombe) 11

National Grid Ref: SS5347

Hele Bay hotel, Ye Olde Globe

(1m) *Moles Farmhouse, Old Berrynarbor Road, Hele, Ilfracombe, Devon, EX34 9RB.*
Actual grid ref: SSS34474
Beautifully restored former farmhouse, situated in picturesque Hele Valley, near Ilfracombe.
Tel: **01271 862099** (also fax no) Ms Grindlay.
D: £17.00-£20.00 .**Open:** All Year
Beds: 1F 1T 1D **Baths:** 2 En 1 Sh

Ilfracombe 12

National Grid Ref: SS5147

Williams Arms, Agricultural Inn, Cider Apple, Crown, Sherbourne Lodge, Hele Bay, Ye Old Globe

(On path) *Ilfracombe Youth Hostel, Ashmour House, 1 Hillsborough Terrace, Ilfracombe, Devon, EX34 9NR.*
Actual grid ref: SS524476
Tel: **01271 865337**
Under 18: £6.90 **Adults:** £10.00
Self-catering facilities, Showers, Licensed bar, Drying room, Cycle store, Evening meal at 7.00pm, No smoking, Kitchen facilities, Breakfast available, Credit cards accepted
End house on a fine Georgian terrace, overlooking the picturesque harbour and the Bristol Channel.

(0.5m 🚐) *Cairn House Hotel, 43 St Brannocks Road, Ilfracombe, Devon, EX34 8EH.*
Grades: ETC 1 StarRAC 1 Star
Tel: **01271 863911** (also fax no)
Mrs Tupper.
D: £18.00-£21.50 **S:** £18.00-£21.50.
Open: All Year (not Xmas/New Year)
Beds: 3F 6D 1S
Baths: 10 En
🅿□↑✕♨🖤Ⅶ🛇
The Cairn House Hotel is a beautiful Victorian hotel delightfully situated in its own grounds with extensive views over town, sea and surrounding countryside. There is a comfortable lounge/bar to relax in before or after your evening meal.

(0.5m) *Beechwood Hotel, Torrs Park, Ilfracombe, Devon, EX34 8AZ.*
Grades: ETC 2 Star
Tel: **01271 863800** (also fax no)
Burridge.
D: £22.00-£25.00 **S:** £22.00-£25.00.
Open: Mar to Oct
Beds: 2T 5D
Baths: 7 En
🅿(8)⊬□♨🖤Ⅶ
Peacefully situated non-smoking Victorian mansion, own woods bordering spectacular National Trust lands and coast path. Superb views over town and countryside to sea. Just 10 minutes walk to harbour and town. Spacious well appointed guest rooms, good food. Licensed. Parking.

Pay B&Bs by
cash or cheque and
be prepared to
pay up front.

(0.5m) *Lyncott Guest House,*
56 St Brannock's Road, Ilfracombe,
Devon, EX34 8EQ.
Actual grid ref: SS517463
Grades: ETC 4 Diamond
Tel: 01271 862425 (also fax no)
Mr & Mrs Holdsworth.
D: £18.00-£21.00 **S:** £18.00.
Open: All Year
Beds: 2F 3D 1S
Baths: 6 En
⌂ 🅿 (5) ⏰ ⬚ ✕ ₤ ▥ ✓
Join David and Marianna in their
charming, lovingly refurbished
Victorian house pleasantly situated
near lovely Bicclescombe Park.
Relax in elegant, smoke-free
surroundings. Enjoy delightful,
spacious, individually designed
ensuite bedrooms and sample their
scrumptious home-made fare.

(0.25m) *Strathmore Hotel,*
57 St Brannock's Road, Ilfracombe,
Devon, EX34 8EQ.
Grades: ETC 4 Diamond,
AA 4 Diamond, RAC 4 Diamond
Tel: 01271 862248
Mr Smith.
Fax no: 01271 862243
D: £20.00-£28.00
S: £25.00-£33.00.
Open: All Year
Beds: 1F 5D 1T 1S
Baths: 8 Pr
⌂ 🅿 (7) ⥥ ⬚ ⏰ ✕ ₤ ▥ ▣ ✓
Delightful Victorian Hotel near to
Ilfracombe town centre,
Bicclescombe Park, Cairn Nature
Reserve and glorious beaches. All
rooms are ensuite with colour TV
and hospitality trays. We offer
varied and delicious menus. All
meals are freshly prepared on the
premises.

(0.25m) *Combe Lodge Hotel,*
Chambercombe Park, Ilfracombe,
Devon, EX34 9QW.
Actual grid ref: SS530473
Quiet position, overlooking har-
bour, ideal for walking, cycling,
golf holidays.
Tel: 01271 864518
Mr & Mrs Wileman.
D: £16.50-£18.50
S: £20.50-£22.50.
Open: All Year (not Xmas)
Beds: 2F 4D 2S
Baths: 4 En 1 Pr 1 Sh
⌂ (1) 🅿 (8) ⥥ ⬚ ⏰ ✕ ₤ ▥ ▣ ✓

🚐 sign means that,
given due notice,
owners will pick you
up from the path
and drop you off *with-*
in reason.

**S = Price range for a single
person in a room**

(0.25m) *Varley House,*
Chambercombe Park, Ilfracombe,
Devon, EX34 9QW.
Period house with attractive ensuite
accommodation, close to coastal
walks. **Tel: 01271 863927**
Mrs S O'Sullivan & Mr D Small.
Fax no: 01271 879299
D: £24.00-£25.00 **S:** £23.00-£24.00.
Open: Easter to Oct
Beds: 2F 4D 1T 1S
Baths: 7 En 1 Pr
⌂ (5) 🅿 (7) ⬚ ⏰ ₤ ▥ ▣

(0.25m) *Westwell Hall, Torrs Park,*
Ilfracombe, Devon, EX34 8AZ.
Elegant Victorian gentleman's
residence in own grounds - superb
views.
Tel: 01271 862792 (also fax no)
Mr & Mrs Lomas.
D: £22.00-£24.00 **S:** £22.00-£24.00.
Open: All Year
Beds: 7D 2T 1S **Baths:** 10 En
⌂ 🅿 ⬚ ⏰ ✕ ₤ ▥ ▣

(0.5m) *Harcourt Hotel, Fore*
Street, Ilfracombe, Devon, EX34 9DS.
Friendly licensed hotel ensuite
rooms TV tea coffee, sea views.
Tel: 01271 862931 Mr Doorbar.
D: £17.00-£24.00 **S:** £17.00-£24.00.
Open: All Year
Beds: 3F 4D 1T 2S **Baths:** 8 En 2 Sh
⌂ 🅿 (4) ⬚ ⏰ ✕ ▥ ▣ ✓

(0.5m) *Sherborne Lodge Hotel,*
Torrs Park, Ilfracombe, Devon,
EX34 8AY.
Friendly, fully-licensed family
hotel providing good food, wine,
comfortable accommodation.
Tel: 01271 862297
Mr & Mrs Millington.
Fax no: 01271 865520
D: £15.50-£21.50 **S:** £15.50-£21.50.
Open: All Year
Beds: 1F 8D 2T 1S
⌂ 🅿 (10) ⬚ ⏰ ✕ ₤ ▥ ▣ ✓ ✓

Woolacombe 13

National Grid Ref: SS4543

Jubilee Inn, Chichester Arms, Red Barn,
Stables, Golden Hind, The Mill

(0.5m) *Camberley, Beach Road,*
Woolacombe, Devon, EX34 7AA.
Actual grid ref: SS465437
Large Victorian house with views
to sea and NT land. Use of indoor
pool.
Grades: ETC 3 Diamond
Tel: 01271 870231
Mr & Mrs Riley.
D: £20.00-£25.00 **S:** £19.00-£24.00.
Open: All Year (not Xmas)
Beds: 3F 3D 1T **Baths:** 6 En 1 Pr
⌂ 🅿 (10) ⬚ ⏰ ▥ ▣ ✓

(0.5m 🚐) *Ossaborough House,*
Woolacombe, Devon, EX34 7HJ.
Grades: ETC 3 Diamond
Tel: 01271 870297 Mr & Mrs Day.
D: £21.00-£25.00 **S:** £21.00-£25.00.
Open: All Year
Beds: 2F 2T 2D
Baths: 5 En 1 Pr
⌂ 🅿 (8) ⥥ ⏰ ✕ ₤ ▥ ▣ ✓
Escape to our lovely C17th country
house originating in the days of
Saxon England - rustic beams.
Thick stone walls, inglenook
fireplaces, candlelit dinners. All
rooms sympathetically restored.
Explore rolling hills, rugged cliffs,
picturesque villages, stunning
golden beaches and secluded coves.

(0.25m 🚐) *Barton Lea, Beach*
Road, Woolacombe, Devon,
EX34 7BT.
Warm welcome, sea views, big
breakfast menu, close to Coastal
Foot Path.
Tel: 01271 870928 Mrs Vickery.
D: £15.50-£20.00 **S:** £20.00-£25.00.
Open: Easter to Oct
Beds: 1F 1D 1T
Baths: 3 En
⌂ 🅿 (7) ⥥ ⏰ ₤ ▥ ▣ ✓

(0.5m) *Sunny Nook, Beach Road,*
Woolacombe, Devon, EX34 7AA.
Actual grid ref: SS466438
Delightful home in lovely situation,
wonderful views and excellent
breakfasts. No smoking throughout.
Tel: 01271 870964 Mr Fenn.
D: £18.00-£23.00 **S:** £25.00-£30.00.
Open: All Year (not Xmas)
Beds: 1F 1D 1T
Baths: 2 En 1 Pr
⌂ (8) 🅿 (5) ⥥ ⬚ ✕ ₤ ▥ ▣ ✓

(On path) *Clyst House, Rockfield*
Road, Woolacombe, Devon,
EX34 7DH.
Friendly, comfortable guest house
close blue flag beach. Delicious
English breakfast. Beautiful
walking area.
Tel: 01271 870220
Mrs Braund.
D: £20.00-£22.00 **S:** £20.00-£22.00.
Open: Mar to Nov
Beds: 1F 1D 1T
Baths: 1 Sh
⌂ (7) 🅿 ⥥ ⬚ ✕ ₤ ▥ ▣ ✓

Croyde 14

National Grid Ref: SS4439

Manor, Thatched Barn Inn

(0.5m 🚐) *Oamaru, Down End,*
Croyde, Braunton, Devon, EX33 1QE.
400m from top surfing beach and
village. Relaxed friendly
atmosphere.
Tel: 01271 890765
Mr & Mrs Jenkins.
D: £17.50-£25.00 **S:** £17.50-£25.00.
Open: All Year
Beds: 1F 1D
Baths: 1 En 1 Pr
⌂ 🅿 (6) ⥥ ⬚ ₤ ▥ ▣ ▣ ✓

Please take muddy

boots <u>off</u> before

entering premises

(On path 🚗) *Moorsands, Moor Lane, Croyde Bay, Braunton, Devon, EX33 1NP.*
Grades: ETC 3 Diamond
Tel: **01271 890781**
Mr & Mrs Davis.
D: £20.00-£26.00
S: £20.00-£26.00.
Open: All Year
Beds: 1F 1T 2D 1S
Baths: 5 En
🛁 🅿 (6) 🍴 🗗 🏕 � 💻 🖤 ✦
Originally a large Victorian coast guard station with stunning views, Moorsands offers short walks to beach, village and local facilities. Come and surf, ride, cycle etc. or simply relax with our comfortable ensuite rooms, guest lounge, beautiful surroundings and superb breakfasts.

(On path) *West Winds Guest House, Moor Lane, Croyde Bay, Croyde, Braunton, Devon, EX33 1PA.*
Actual grid ref: SS433396
Stunning waters' edge location with views over Croyde Beach.
Grades: ETC 4 Diamond,
AA 4 Diamond
Tel: **01271 890489** (also fax no)
Mr & Mrs Gedling.
D: £26.00-£31.00
S: £26.00-£31.00.
Open: Mar to Nov
Beds: 3D 2T
Baths: 3 Pr 2 Sh
🛁 🅿 (6) 🍴 🗗 🏕 ✗ 🌄 💻 🖤 🖰

(On path) *Chapel Farm, Hobbs Hill, Croyde, Braunton, Devon, EX33 1NE.*
Actual grid ref: SS444390
C16th thatched farmhouse, 10 minutes to beach.
Tel: **01271 890429**
Mrs Windsor.
D: £18.00-£26.00
S: £18.00-£30.00.
Open: Easter to Nov
Beds: 1F 2D
Baths: 3 En
🛁 🅿 (6) 🍴 🗗 🌄 💻 🖤 🖰 ✦

Many rates vary

according to season -

the lowest only are

shown here

Braunton 15

National Grid Ref: SS4936

🍴 🍺 Agricultural Inn

(0.75m 🚗) *St Merryn, Higher Park Road, Braunton, Devon, EX33 2LG.*
Tel: **01271 813805** Mrs Bradford.
Fax no: 01271 812097
D: £20.00-£22.00 **S:** £20.00-£22.00.
Open: Jan to Dec
Beds: 1F 1T 1D
Baths: 1 En 2 Pr
🛁 🅿 (5) 🍴 🗗 🏕 ✗ 🌄 💻 🖤 🖰 ✦
Beautiful 1930's home set in delightful large garden. Tranquil setting with excellent parking and within easy walking distance of village. Excellent beaches and golf courses within a short drive.

(0.25m) *Pixie Dell, 1 Willand Rd, Braunton, N. Devon, EX33 1AX.*
Large chalet bungalow and garden. Warm welcome assured.
Tel: **01271 812233** Mrs Dale.
D: £18.00-£18.00 **S:** £18.00-£20.00.
Open: All Year (not Xmas)
Beds: 1D 2T 1S
Baths: 2 Sh
🛁 🅿 (4) 🍴 🗗 🐾 🌄 💻 🖤 & 🖤 ✦

Barnstaple 16

National Grid Ref: SS5633

🍴 🍺 Windsor Arms, Williams Arms, Rolle Quay Inn, North Country Inn, Pyne Arms, Ring O'Bells, Chichester Arms

(0.25m) *Crossways, Braunton Road, Barnstaple, Devon, EX31 1JY.*
Detached house - town & Tarka Trail 150 yards, bicycle hire.
Tel: **01271 379120** Mr & Mrs Tysn
D: £15.00 **S:** £17.00.
Open: All Year
Beds: 1F 1D 1T **Baths:** 2 Pr 1 Sh
🛁 🅿 (6) 🍴 🗗 🌄 💻 🖤 🖰 ✦

(1.5m) *Mount Sandford, Landkey Road, Barnstaple, Devon, EX32 0HL.*
Georgian house in 1.5 acres gardens. 2 double, 1 twin, all ensuite.
Tel: **01271 342354** Mrs White.
D: £18.00-£22.00 **S:** £20.00.
Open: All Year (not Xmas)
Beds: 1F 1D 1T
Baths: 3 En
🛁 (3) 🅿 (3) 🍴 🗗 🌄 💻 🖤 ✦

Order your

packed lunch the

evening before you

need them.

Not at breakfast!

D = Price range per person sharing in a double room

Fremington 17

National Grid Ref: SS5132

🍴 🍺 New Inn, Boat House

(0.5m 🚗) *Lower Yelland Farm, Yelland Road, Fremington, Barnstaple, Devon, EX31 3EN.*
Tel: **01271 860101** (also fax no)
Mr Day.
D: £20.00-£20.00 **S:** £20.00-£20.00.
Open: All Year (not Xmas/ New Year)
Beds: 1T 2D
Baths: 3 En
🛁 🅿 (6) 🗗 🐾 🌄 💻 🖤 🖰 ✦
North Devon Coast beautifully situated period house on Taw Estuary. Ideal touring centre, Instow beach/marina approximately 1 mile, Bideford, Barnstaple 4.5 miles. Several golf courses in the vicinity. Adjacent to bird sanctuary. Private off road parking.

Bideford 18

National Grid Ref: SS4526

🍴 🍺 Tanton's Hotel, Farmers Arms, Crab & Ale, Royal Hotel, Swan Inn, Joiners' Arms, Hunters' Inn, Sunset Hotel

(0.5m 🚗) *The Mount Hotel, Northdown Road, Bideford, Devon, EX39 3LP.*
Actual grid ref: SS449269
Grades: AA 4 Diamond
Tel: **01237 473748**
Mr & Mrs Laugharne.
D: £23.00-£25.00 **S:** £25.00-£33.00.
Open: Jan to Dec
Beds: 1F 3D 1T 2S **Baths:** 7 En
🛁 🅿 (4) 🍴 🗗 🌄 💻 & 🖤 ✦
Charming Georgian licensed guest house only 5 minutes' walk to town centre, private lounge for guests' use, all rooms ensuite, attractive garden, car parking for guests. Convenient for touring N Devon coastline, Clovelly, Lundy, Exmoor and Dartmoor. No smoking.

Appledore (Bideford) 19

National Grid Ref: SS4630

🍴 🍺 Seagate Hotel

(On path) *The Seagate Hotel, The Quay, Appledore, Bideford, Devon, EX39 1QS.*
C17th riverside inn. Quaint fishing village on Torridge Estuary.
Tel: **01237 472589** (also fax no)
Mr & Mrs Gent.
D: £25.00-£35.00 **S:** £29.00-£35.00.
Open: All Year
Beds: 1F 5D 1T **Baths:** 7 Pr
🛁 🅿 (10) 🗗 🐾 ✗ 🌄 💻 🖤

Westward Ho! 20

National Grid Ref: SS4329

🍴 ☕The Waterfront, The Elizabethan, Pig On The Hill, Village Inn, Country Cousins

(On path) *Eversley, 1 Youngaton Road, Westward Ho!, Bideford, Devon, EX39 1HU.*
Victorian gentleman's residence. Superb accommodation. Sea views, beach 2 mins.
Grades: ETC 4 Diamond
Tel: 01237 471603
Mr Sharratt.
D: £18.00-£20.00
S: £24.00-£29.00.
Open: All Year
Beds: 1F 1D 1T
Baths: 1 En 1 Sh
ॐ 🅿 (3) 🗫 🖬 🏃 🏠 🖳 Ⅴ ⚡

(On path 🚐) *Brockenhurst, 11 Atlantic Way, Westward Ho!, Bideford, Devon, EX39 1HX.*
Actual grid ref: SS432290
Comfortable, detached house. Views of Lundy Island and vast beach.
Grades: ETC 3 Diamond
Tel: 01237 423346 (also fax no)
Mrs Snowball.
D: £22.50-£25.00
S: £27.00-£30.00.
Open: All Year (not Xmas)
Beds: 2D 1T
Baths: 3 En
🅿 (4) 🗫 🖬 🏃 🏠 🖳 Ⅴ ⚡

(0.25m) *Mayfield, Avon Lane, Westward Ho!, Bideford, Devon, EX39 1LR.*
Victorian house close to beach. Sea views, full English breakfast.
Tel: 01237 477128 Mrs Clegg.
D: £14.00 **S:** £14.00
Open: All Year (not Xmas/New Year)
Beds: 2D 1T 1S
Baths: 2 Sh
ॐ 🅿 (1) ⚭ 🗫 🖬 🖳 Ⅴ ⚡

(0.5m 🚐) *Four Winds, Cornborough Road, Westward Ho!, Bideford, Devon, EX39 1AA.*
Beautiful Edwardian house 0.75 mile from beach and coastal footpath.
Tel: 01237 421741 Mr Evers.
D: £18.00-£20.00 **S:** £18.00-£20.00.
Open: All Year
Beds: 1F 2T
Baths: 3 Pr
ॐ 🅿 ⚭ 🗫 🖬 🏃 🏠 🖳 & Ⅴ ⚡

Please don't camp on *anyone's* land without first obtaining their permission.

Planning a longer stay? Always ask for any special rates.

Woolsery (Woolfardisworthy) 21

National Grid Ref: SS3321

🍴 ☕Farmers Arms, Hart Inn, Manor Inn

(4m) *Stroxworthy Farm, Woolsery, Bideford, Devon, EX39 5QB.*
Delightful farmhouse, working dairy farm 4 miles from Clovelly.
Tel: 01237 431333 Mrs Beck.
D: £20.00-£20.00 **S:** £20.00-£20.00.
Open: Easter to Oct
Beds: 1F 2D 1S
Baths: 3 En 1 Pr
ॐ 🅿 (10) 🗫 🖳 Ⅴ

Clovelly 22

National Grid Ref: SS3225

🍴 ☕New Inn, Farmers Arms, Red Lion

(0.50m) *The Old Smithy, Slerra Hill, Clovelly, Bideford, Devon, EX39 5ST.*
Actual grid ref: SS3124
Cottage - converted C17th blacksmith's forge. Large rooms, warm welcome.
Tel: 01237 431202 Mrs Vanstone.
D: £16.50-£20.50 .
Open: All Year (not Xmas)
Beds: 2F 1D
Baths: 1 En 1 Pr 1 Sh
ॐ 🅿 (4) ⚭ 🗫 🖳 🖳 Ⅴ ⚡

(0.25m) *Boat House Cottage, 148 Slerra Hill, Clovelly, Bideford, Devon, EX39 5ST.*
Delightful C17th cottage. Sea views. Comfortable rooms, warm welcome
Tel: 01237 431209
Mrs May.
D: £15.00-£16.00 **S:** £17.00-£18.00.
Open: Jan to Dec
Beds: 1F 1D 1T
Baths: 1 En 1 Sh
ॐ (3) 🅿 (3) ⚭ 🗫 🖬 🏃 🏠 🖳 Ⅴ ⚡

(0.25m) *New Inn Hotel, Clovelly, Bideford, Devon, EX39 4TQ.*
Beautifully restored inn. Heart of peaceful heritage village. Sea views.
Grades: AA 2 Star
Tel: 01237 431303
Mr Murphy.
Fax no: 01237 431636
D: £34.25-£42.25 **S:** £34.25-£57.25.
Open: All Year
Beds: 7D 1S
Baths: 8 En
ॐ 🅿 (200) 🗫 🖬 🏃 🖳 🖳 Ⅴ

Higher Clovelly 23

National Grid Ref: SS3124

🍴 ☕Farmers Arms, Hart Inn, New Inn, Red Lion

(0.25m) *Dyke Green Farm, Higher Clovelly, Bideford, Devon, EX39 5RU.*
Actual grid ref: SS311237
Beautiful converted barn, every comfort.
Tel: 01237 431699 (also fax no)
Mrs Johns.
D: £15.50 **S:** £18.50.
Open: All Year (not Xmas)
Beds: 2D 1T
Baths: 2 Pr 1 Sh
ॐ 🅿 (6) ⚭ 🗫 🖬 🏃 🏠 🖳 Ⅴ ⚡

(0.5m 🚐) *Fuchsia Cottage, Burscott Lane, Higher Clovelly, Bideford, Devon, EX39 5RR.*
Situated in a quiet lane, beautiful coastal and countryside views.
Grades: ETC 3 Diamond, AA 3 Diamond
Tel: 01237 431398
Mrs Curtis.
D: £18.50-£18.50 **S:** £16.00.
Open: All Year (not Xmas/New Year)
Beds: 1F 1D 1S
Baths: 2 En 1 Sh
ॐ 🅿 (3) ⚭ 🗫 🖬 🏃 🏠 🖳 & Ⅴ ⚡

Hartland 24

National Grid Ref: SS2624

🍴 ☕Hartland Quay Hotel, Manor Inn

(0.25m 🚐) *West Titchberry Farm, Hartland, Bideford, Devon, EX39 6AU.*
Actual grid ref: SS242271
Typical Devon long house on traditional family run coastal stock farm.
Tel: 01237 441287 (also fax no)
Mrs Heard.
D: £17.00-£18.00
S: £17.00-£18.00.
Open: All Year (not Xmas)
Beds: 1F 1D 1T
Baths: 2 Sh
ॐ 🅿 ⚭ ✕ 🖳 🖳 Ⅴ ⚡

Elmscott 25

National Grid Ref: SS2321

(▲0.5m) *Elmscott Youth Hostel, Elmscott, Hartland, Bideford, Devon, EX39 6ES.*
Actual grid ref: SS231217
Tel: 01237 441367
Under 18: £6.90
Adults: £10.00
Self-catering facilities, Showers, Wet weather shelter, Lounge, Dining room, Cycle store, No smoking, WC, Credit cards accepted
Former Victorian schoolhouse and enclosed garden in a remote Area of Outstanding Natural Beauty with views of Lundy island.

BRITAIN: BED & BREAKFAST

The essential guide to B&Bs in England, Scotland & Wales

The Bed & Breakfast is one of the great British institutions. Like Fish & Chips, it's known by people around the world. But you don't have to be a tourist to enjoy this traditional accommodation. Whether you're travelling, on holiday, away on business or just escaping from it all, the B&B is a great value alternative to expensive hotels and a world away from camping and caravanning.

Stilwell's Britain: Bed & Breakfast 2001 is the most comprehensive guide of its kind, containing over 7,750 entries listed by country, county and location, in England, Scotland and Wales. Each entry includes room rates, facilities, Tourist Board grades and a brief description of the B&B and its location and surroundings.

Stilwell's Britain: Bed & Breakfast 2001: The indispensable guide to great value accommodation:

Private houses, country halls, farms, cottages, inns, small hotels and guest houses

Over 7,750 entries
Average price £19 per person per night
All official grades shown
Local maps
Pubs serving hot evening meals shown
Tourist Information Centres listed
Handy size for easy packing

£9.95 from all good bookstores (ISBN 1-900861-22-4) or £11.95 (inc p&p) from Stilwell Publishing, 59 Charlotte Road, London EC2A 3QW (020 7739 7179)

Cornwall

This section of the **South West Coast Path** covers the entire Cornish coast, from the exposed and rugged cliffs of the North, past Land's End and the Lizard to the quieter creeks and bold promontories of the South (see beginning of chapter for more **South West Coast Path** details).

Guides: *South West Way: Vol I* (Minehead to Penzance), ISBN 1 85284 025 0, and *South West Way: Vol II* (Penzance to Poole), ISBN 1 85284 026 9, both by Martin Collins and published by Cicerone Press and available from the publishers (2 Police Square, Milnthorpe, Cumbria, LA7 7PY, 01539 562069), £8.99 (+75p p&p) each

South West Way: Minehead to Padstow by Roland Tarr (ISBN 1 854104 15 2), published by Aurum Press in association with the countryside commision and Ordnance Survey, £10.99

South West Way: Padstow to Falmouth by John Macadam (ISBN 1 85410 3873), published by Aurum Press in association with the Countryside Commission and Ordnance Survey, £10.99

South West Way: Falmouth to Exmouth by Brian Le Messurier (ISBN 1 85410 3881), published by Aurum Press in association with the Countryside Commission and Ordnance Survey, £10.99

There is also invaluable local information in *The South West Way 2001* by the **South West Way Association**, available directly from them at 25 Clobells, South Brent, Devon, TQ10 9JW, tel. 01364 73859 £7.00 (inc. p&p)

Maps: Ordnance Survey 1:50,000 Landranger series: 190, 200, 201, 203 and 204

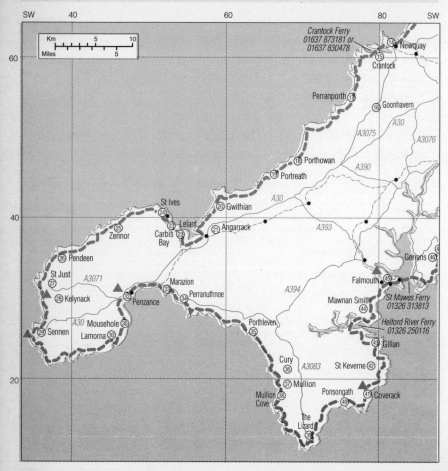

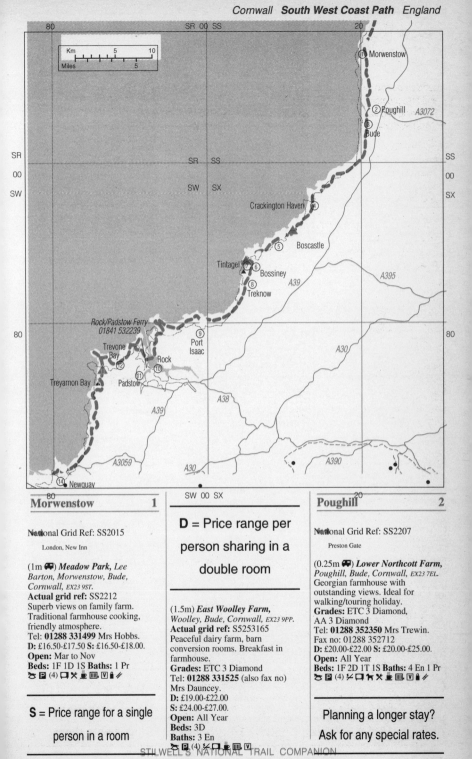

Km 5 10
Miles 5

SR 00 SS 20

SR 00 SW

SR SS
SW SX
00

① Morwenstow

② Poughill *A3072*
③ Bude

Crackington Haven ④

⑤ Boscastle

Tintagel ⑦⑥ Bossiney
⑧ Treknow *A39* *A395*

Rock/Padstow Ferry
01841 532239

Trevone Bay ⑫ ⑨ Port Isaac

Rock ⑩
Treyarnon Bay ⑪ Padstow

A39 *A38* *A30*

A3059 *A30* *A390*

⑭ Newquay

---

80 SW 00 SX 20

Morwenstow   1

National Grid Ref: SS2015

London, New Inn

(1m 🚌) *Meadow Park, Lee Barton, Morwenstow, Bude, Cornwall, EX23 9ST.*
Actual grid ref: SS2212
Superb views on family farm. Traditional farmhouse cooking, friendly atmosphere.
Tel: **01288 331499** Mrs Hobbs.
D: £16.50-£17.50 **S:** £16.50-£18.00.
Open: Mar to Nov
Beds: 1F 1D 1S **Baths:** 1 Pr
🛏 🅿 (4) 🗖 ✕ 🛋 🛒 Ⅴ 🎫 🌿

D = Price range per person sharing in a double room

(1.5m) *East Woolley Farm, Woolley, Bude, Cornwall, EX23 9PP.*
Actual grid ref: S5253165
Peaceful dairy farm, barn conversion rooms. Breakfast in farmhouse.
Grades: ETC 3 Diamond
Tel: **01288 331525** (also fax no) Mrs Dauncey.
D: £19.00-£22.00
S: £24.00-£27.00.
Open: All Year
Beds: 3D
Baths: 3 En
🛏 🅿 (4) ⚡ 🗖 🛋 🛒 Ⅴ

S = Price range for a single person in a room

Poughill   2

National Grid Ref: SS2207

Preston Gate

(0.25m 🚌) *Lower Northcott Farm, Poughill, Bude, Cornwall, EX23 7EL.*
Georgian farmhouse with outstanding views. Ideal for walking/touring holiday.
Grades: ETC 3 Diamond, AA 3 Diamond
Tel: **01288 352350** Mrs Trewin.
Fax no: 01288 352712
D: £20.00-£22.00 **S:** £20.00-£25.00.
Open: All Year
Beds: 1F 2D 1T 1S **Baths:** 4 En 1 Pr
🛏 🅿 (4) ⚡ 🗖 🐾 ✕ 🛋 🛒 Ⅴ 🎫 🌿

Planning a longer stay?
Ask for any special rates.

Bude 3

National Grid Ref: SS2106

Crooklets, Sportsman, Preston Gate, Bencoolen Inn, Inn On The Green, Falcon Inn, Kings Arms

(0.5m) **Sunrise Guest House,** 6 Burn View, Bude, Cornwall, EX23 8BY.
Grades: ETC 4 Diamond
Tel: **01288 353214**
Mr Masters.
D: £18.00-£23.00 **S:** £18.00-£25.00.
Open: Feb to Nov
Beds: 1F 3D 1T 1S
Baths: 6 En
⌂ (3) ▣ (2) ⊬ ☐ ♨ ⅏ ⅃ & Ⅵ ♦ ⚡
'The general standards are high and many of the features are delightful. The hospitality of the owners and the cleanliness experienced count for a lot.' (English Tourist Board Assessment) Come see for yourselves! Centrally located. All rooms ensuite.

(0.5m) **St Merryn,** Coastview, Bude, Cornwall, EX23 8AG.
Tel: **01288 352058** Miss Abbot.
Fax no: 01288 359050
D: £14.00-£16.00 **S:** £20.00-£25.00.
Open: All Year
Beds: 1F 1D 1T 1S
Baths: 2 Sh
⌂ ▣ (4) ⊬ ☐ ♖ ♨ ⅏ & Ⅵ ⚡
A large dormer bungalow with good sized ground floor bedrooms each having vanity unit with hot/cold water, colour TV with remote and tea/coffee making facilities situated on A3072 approximately 500 yards from A39 Atlantic highway, off-road parking.

(0.5m) **Link's Side Guest House,** Burn View, Bude, Cornwall, EX23 8BY.
Victoria house town centre, beaches, path, overlooking golf course.
Grades: ETC 4 Diamond
Tel: **01288 352410** Mr & Mrs Dockrill.
D: £16.00-£21.00 **S:** £16.00-£21.00.
Open: All Year
Beds: 1F 4D 1T 1S
Baths: 5 En 1 Sh
⌂ ⊬ ☐ ♖ ♨ ⅏ & Ⅵ ♦ ⚡

(0.5m) **Laundry Cottage,** Higher Wharf, Bude, Cornwall, EX23 8LW.
Tel: **01288 353560**
Mrs Noakes.
D: £17.00-£21.00 **S:** £17.00-£21.00.
Open: All Year (not Xmas)
Beds: 1D 1T
Baths: 1 Sh 1 Pr
⌂ (10) ▣ (2) ☐ ♨ ⅏ Ⅵ ♦ ⚡
Grade II Listed cottage in two acres of garden on historic Bude canal. Secluded yet only a few minutes' walk from town centre, restaurants, coastal path, beach, cycle routes etc. Rooms overlook garden and canal. Quiet, many extras, private parking.

Always telephone to get directions to the B&B - you will save time!

(1.5m 🚌) **Marhamrise Guest House,** 50 Kings Hill, Bude, Cornwall, EX23 8QH.
Beautiful views. Gardens. Ground floor bedrooms. Plenty good home cooking.
Tel: **01288 354713** Mrs Thornton.
D: £15.00-£17.00 **S:** £15.00-£18.00.
Open: May to Sept
Beds: 1F 2D 1S
Baths: 1 En 2 Sh
⌂ (3) ▣ (5) ☐ ♖ ♨ ⅏ & Ⅵ ♦ ⚡

(0.5m 🚌) **Meadow View,** Kings Hill Close, Bude, Cornwall, EX23 8RR.
A large house 400 yds from canal. Room overlooks garden and fields.
Tel: **01288 355095** Mrs Shepherd.
D: £15.00-£16.00 **S:** £15.00-£16.00.
Open: All Year
Beds: 1D
Baths: 1 Pr
⊬ ☐ ♨ ⅏ Ⅵ ⚡

(0.5m 🚌) **Raetor,** Stratton Road, Bude, Cornwall, EX23 8AQ.
Modern detached house situated on the main road. Bude one mile.
Tel: **01288 354128** Barnard.
D: £15.00-£15.00 **S:** £15.00-£15.00.
Open: All Year
Beds: 1D 1T 1S
Baths: 1 Sh
▣ (2) ☐ ♨ ⅏ Ⅵ

(On path 🚌) **Kisauni,** 4 Downs View, Bude, Cornwall, EX23 8RF.
Bright, airy Victorian house. 2 minutes beach. Romantic four poster bed. Home cooking.
Tel: **01288 352653**
Mrs Kimpton.
D: £14.00-£16.00
S: £14.00-£16.00.
Open: All Year (not Xmas)
Beds: 2F 1D 1T 1S
Baths: 3 En 3 Sh
⌂ ▣ (5) ☐ ♖ ✗ ♨ & Ⅵ ♦ ⚡

(0.5m) **Pencarrol Guest House,** 21 Downs View, Bude, Cornwall, EX23 8RF.
Pencarrol overlooks Bude's 18-hole golf course and offers comfortable B&B accommodation.
Tel: **01288 352478**
Mr & Mrs Payne.
D: £17.00-£19.00
S: £15.00-£22.00.
Open: All Year (not Xmas)
Beds: 1F 3D 1T 2S
Baths: 3 En 1 Pr 3 Sh
⊬ ☐ ♨ ⅏ Ⅵ ♦ ⚡

Crackington Haven 4

National Grid Ref: SX1496

Coombe Barton Inn

(0.75m 🚌) **Venn Park Farm,** Crackington Haven, Bude, Cornwall, EX23 0LB.
Tel: **01840 230159** (also fax no)
Ms Wilson.
D: £18.00-£20.00 **S:** £20.00-£22.00.
Open: All Year
Beds: 1F 2D
Baths: 2 En 1 Pr
⌂ ▣ ⊬ ☐ ♖ ✗ ♨ ⅏ Ⅵ ♦ ⚡
Relaxation opportunity. Modernised farmhouse with extensive sea, countryside views. Ensuite, family bedrooms, colour TV. Coastal/ Moorland walks, fishing, golfing & cycling easily accessible. Participation farm/ natural environmental tasks arrangeable. Close picturesque Boscastle/Crackington Beach. Traditionally cooked food, Vegetarian option.

(0.75m 🚌) **Hallagather,** Crackington Haven, Bude, Cornwall, EX23 0LA.
Actual grid ref: SX146956
Ancient farmhouse, warm, welcoming. Substantial buffet style breakfast. Spectacular scenery.
Grades: ETC 4 Diamond, AA 4 Diamond
Tel: **01840 230 276** Mrs Anthony.
Fax no: 01840 230 449
D: £17.50-£24.00 **S:** £18.00-£26.00.
Open: Feb to Nov
Beds: 1F 1D 1S
Baths: 4 En
⌂ (11) ▣ (6) ⊬ ☐ ♖ ♨ ⅏ Ⅵ ♦ ⚡

Boscastle 5

National Grid Ref: SX1090

Napoleon Inn, Cobweb Inn, Wellington Hotel, Olde Manor House, Tolcarne House

(On path) **Boscastle Harbour Youth Hostel,** Palace Stables, Boscastle, Cornwall, PL35 0HD.
Actual grid ref: SX096915
Tel: **01840 250287**
Under 18: £6.90 **Adults:** £10.00
Self-catering facilities, Showers, Lounge, Drying room, Cycle store, Evening meal at 7.00pm, No smoking, WC, Kitchen facilities, Credit cards accepted
In superb position right on harbour edge where River Valency enters NT fishing harbour.

D = Price range per person sharing in a double room

(0.5m) *The Old Coach House,*
Tintagel Road, Boscastle,
Cornwall, PL35 0AS.
Actual grid ref: SX096906
Grades: ETC 4 Diamond,
AA 4 Diamond
Tel: 01840 250398
Mrs & Mrs Parsons.
Fax no: 01840 250346
D: £19.00-£22.00 **S:** £25.00-£36.00.
Open: All Year
Beds: 3F 4D 1T
Baths: 8 En
⛺ �P (9) ⅋ ⬜ ⊀ ⛎ ⚲ ⬛ ⓥ 🛏 ⚡
300-year-old coach house which
guarantees a warm, helpful and
friendly welcome. In an Area of
Outstanding Natural Beauty. A
centre for coastal and woodland
walks. Close to unspoilt National
Trust harbour. All rooms ensuite.
Parking.

(0.5m 🐾) *Pencarmol, The*
Harbour, Boscastle, Cornwall,
PL35 0HA.
Tel: 01840 250435 Mrs Murphy.
D: £20.00-£22.50 **S:** £25.00-£30.00.
Open: Feb to Oct
Beds: 1F 2D
Baths: 3 En
P (3) ⅋ ⬜ 🛏 ⚲ ⬛ ⓥ 🛏 ⚡
Pencarmol is a 300-year-old Listed
house dramatically situated
overlooking Boscastle Harbour.
Comfortable bedrooms, all
enjoying harbour views. Beautiful
cliff garden adjacent coastal path.
Full English or vegetarian
breakfast. A warm welcome is
assured from congenial hosts.

(0.25m) *Tolcarne House Hotel &*
Restaurant, Tintagel Road,
Boscastle, Cornwall, PL35 0AS.
Actual grid ref: SX098905
Victorian character house with
spectacular views and large
grounds.
Grades: ETC 4 Diamond
Tel: 01840 250654 (also fax no)
Mr & Mrs Crown.
D: £25.00-£32.00 **S:** £30.00-£32.00.
Open: Mar to Nov
Beds: 1F 2T 4D 2S **Baths:** 9 En
⛺ (10) P (12) ⬜ 🛏 ⊀ ⛎ ⚲ ⬛ ⓥ 🛏 ⚡

(0.5m 🐾) *Bottreaux House Hotel,*
Boscastle, Cornwall, PL35 0BG.
High quality Silver Award B&B
accommodation. Free video of
hotel.
Grades: ETC 2 Star, Silver
Tel: 01840 250231 Mr Mee.
Fax no: 01840 250170
D: £16.00-£30.00 **S:** £20.00-£30.00.
Open: All Year
Beds: 5D 2T **Baths:** 7 En
⛺ (10) P (9) ⅋ ⬜ 🛏 ⊀ ⛎ ⚲ ⬛ ⓥ 🛏 ⚡

S = Price range for a single
person in a single room

(0.25m 🐾) *The Wellington Hotel,*
The Harbour, Boscastle, Cornwall,
PL35 0AQ.
Actual grid ref: SX009913
Historic C16th Anglo/French
restaurant & freehouse pub. Log
fires and beams.
Tel: 01840 250202 Mrs Tobutt.
D: £29.00-£38.00 **S:** £32.00-£44.00.
Open: All Year
Beds: 11D 2T 4S **Baths:** 16 En 1 Pr
⛺ (7) P (20) ⬜ 🛏 ⊀ ⛎ ⚲ ⬛ ⓥ 🛏 ⚡

(0.5m 🐾) *Myrtle Cottage, Fore*
Street, Boscastle, Cornwall,
PL35 0AX.
Old village cottage. Extensive gar-
den to river, homely atmosphere.
Tel: 01840 250245 Ms Webber.
D: £14.50-£17.50 **S:** £14.50-£17.50.
Open: All Year
Beds: 1F 1D 1T **Baths:** 2 Sh
⛺ P (1) ⬜ 🛏 ⛎ ⚲ ⬛ ⓥ 🛏 ⚡

Bossiney 6

National Grid Ref: SX0688

Tintagel Arms, Cornishman, Mill House,
Willapark Manor Hotel

(0.25m 🐾) *The Old Borough*
House, Bossiney, Tintagel,
Cornwall, PL34 0AY.
Actual grid ref: SX066888
Traditional C16th Cornish house
close to coastal path, luxury
bedrooms.
Tel: 01840 770475 (also fax no)
Mrs Bryant.
D: £25.00-£30.00 **S:** £35.00-£35.00.
Open: All Year (not Xmas)
Beds: 3D 1T **Baths:** 3 En 1 Pr
⛺ (12) P (10) ⅋ ⬜ ⊀ ⚲ 🛏 ⚡

Tintagel 7

National Grid Ref: SX0588

Tintagel Arms, The Cornishman, Mill House

(On path) *Tintagel Youth*
Hostel, Dunderhole Point,
Tintagel, Cornwall, PL34 0DW.
Actual grid ref: SX047881
Tel: 01840 770334
Under 18: £6.90 **Adults:** £10.00
Self-catering, Showers,
Lounge, Cycle store, Parking Limited,
No smoking, Kitchen facilities
150-year-old slate quarry cottage
now owned by NT, in spectacular
clifftop setting, with extensive
views across Port Isaac Bay.

(0.25m) *Tintagel Arms Hotel, Fore*
Street, Tintagel, Cornwall, PL34 0DB.
Actual grid ref: SX057883
Grades: AA 4 Diamond
Tel: 01840 770780 Mr Hunter.
D: £20.00-£25.00 **S:** £25.00-£30.00.
Open: All Year
Beds: 1F 4D 2T **Baths:** 7 En
⛺ P (8) ⬜ ⊀ ⛎ ⚲ 🛏 ⚡
200 year old stone building built on
site of Chapel of St Dennis (1400
AD).

(0.5m) *Bosayne Guest House,*
Atlantic Road, Tintagel, Cornwall,
PL34 0DE.
Warm, friendly family-run guest
house with sea views, serving a
great breakfast.
Grades: ETC 3 Diamond
Tel: 01840 770514 Mr Clark.
D: £16.00-£20.00 **S:** £16.00-£18.00.
Open: All Year
Beds: 2F 3D 1T 3S
Baths: 4 En 3 Sh
⛺ ⅋ ⬜ 🛏 ⊀ ⛎ ⚲ & ⓥ ⚡

(0.5m) *Pendrin House, Atlantic*
Road, Tintagel, Cornwall, PL34 0DE.
Beautiful Victorian house close to
many amenities, castle and
beaches.
Grades: ETC 3 Diamond
Tel: 01840 770560 (also fax no)
Mrs Howe.
D: £16.00-£19.00 **S:** £16.00-£16.00.
Open: March to Nov
Beds: 2F 2T 4D 1S
Baths: 3 En 3 Sh
⛺ P (5) ⅋ ⬜ 🛏 ⊀ ⛎ ⚲ & ⓥ 🛏 ⚡

(On path) *Grange Cottage,*
Tintagel, Cornwall, PL34 0AX.
Actual grid ref: SX885065
Peaceful traditional stone cottage.
Close Tintagel Castle, cliff walks,
beach.
Tel: 01840 770487 Mrs Jones.
D: £18.00-£25.00 **S:** £18.00-£18.00.
Open: Easter to Nov
Beds: 1T 1D 1S
Baths: 1 En 1 Sh
⛺ (4) P (4) ⅋ ⬜ ⛎ ⚲ ⬛ ⓥ 🛏 ⚡

(0.5m) *Bossiney Cottage, Tintagel,*
Cornwall, PL34 0AY.
Character cottage, carefully
restored. Good touring base, close
coastal footpath.
Tel: 01840 770327
D: £16.00-£16.00 **S:** £16.00-£20.00.
Open: All Year (not Xmas)
Beds: 1F 2D
Baths: 1 Sh
⛺ (3) P (4) ⅋ ⬜ ⊀ ⚲ 🛏 ⚡

(0.5m) *The Cornishman Inn, Fore*
Street, Tintagel, Cornwall, PL34 0DB.
C14th olde worlde inn set in the
heart of King Arthur country.
Tel: 01840 770238 Mr Knight.
Fax no: 01840 770078
D: £22.50-£27.50 **S:** £25.00-£27.50.
Open: All Year
Beds: 2F 4D 4T
Baths: 10 En
⛺ P (40) ⬜ ⊀ ⛎ ⚲ ⓥ 🛏

Taking your dog?
Book *in advance*
ONLY with owners
who accept dogs (🐾)

Treknow 8

National Grid Ref: SX0586

Millhouse Inn, Port William

(0.5m) *Challoch Guest House,*
Treknow, Tintagel, Cornwall,
PL34 0EN.
Small friendly guest house, superb
views, near beautiful surfing beach.
Tel: **01840 770273** Mrs May.
D: £17.00-£19.00 **S:** £19.00-£20.00.
Open: Easter to Oct
Beds: 2D 1T
⛄ 🅿 🛋 🍴 🗙 🏃 🖳 V 🛗 ✦

(0.5m) *Hillscroft,* Treknow,
Tintagel, Cornwall, PL34 0EN.
Scenic views across Trebarwith
Valley. Use of garden and summer
house.
Tel: **01840 770551** Mrs Nutt.
D: £16.00-£20.00 **S:** £16.00-£20.00.
Open: All Year (not Xmas/
New Year)
Beds: 1T 2D **Baths:** 2 En 1 Sh
⛄ (8) 🅿 (6) 🛋 🍴 🏃 🖳 V ✦

(0.5m) *Atlantic View Hotel,*
Treknow, Tintagel, Cornwall,
PL34 0EJ.
Victorian house, glorious position,
set 300 yards from cliff top.
Grades: ETC 2 Star
Tel: **01840 770221**
Fax no: 01840 770995
D: £28.00-£32.00 **S:** £32.00-£32.00.
Open: Feb to Dec.
Beds: 2F 1T 6D **Baths:** 9 En
⛄ 🅿 (10) 🛋 🍴 🗙 🏃 🖳 V 🛗 ✦

Port Isaac 9

National Grid Ref: SW9980

Port Gaverne Hotel

(On path 🚌) *Bay Hotel, 1 The*
Terrace, Port Isaac, Cornwall,
PL29 3SG.
Actual grid ref: SW998809
Small, friendly Victorian hotel
overlooking bay with wonderful
views. Tel: **01208 880380**
Mr Hawkes & J Burns.
D: £22.00-£29.50 **S:** £20.00-£28.00.
Open: All Year
Beds: 9F 2T 1D 6 S
Baths: 8 En 1 Pr 1 Sh
⛄ 🅿 (9) 🛋 🍴 🏃 🖳 V 🛗

(0.25m) *Fairholme, 30 Trewetha*
Lane, Port Isaac, Cornwall,
PL29 3RW.
Actual grid ref: SX001805
Beautiful house in historic
picturesque fishing village, near
coastal paths.
Tel: **01208 880397**
Mrs Von-Lintzgy.
Fax no: 01208 880198
D: £17.00-£20.00 **S:** £20.00-£25.00.
Open: All Year (not Xmas/New Year)
Beds: 2F 3D 1T **Baths:** 2 Pr 2 Sh
⛄ 🅿 (6) 🛋 🍴 🗙 🏃 🖳 V 🛗 ✦

Rock 10

National Grid Ref: SW9476

Roskarnon House

(On path) *Silvermead, Rock,*
Wadebridge, Cornwall, PL27 6LB.
Actual grid ref: SW937758
Grades: ETC 3 Diamond,
AA 3 Diamond
Tel: **01208 862425**
Mrs Martin.
Fax no: 01208 862919
D: £20.00-£26.00 **S:** £20.00-£45.00.
Open: All Year
Beds: 2F 3D 2T 2S
Baths: 6 En 1 Sh
⛄ 🅿 (9) 🛋 🍴 🗙 🏃 🖳 V ✦
Ten-bedroom family-run guest
house overlooking Camel Estuary,
adjoining St Enodoc golf courses. 2
minutes' walk to beach, sailing
club. Most rooms ensuite.
Licensed.

(0.5m) *Roskarnon House Hotel,*
Rock, Wadebridge, Cornwall,
PL27 6LD.
Edwardian hotel, overlooking
estuary, 100 metres from ferry to
Padstow.
Grades: ETC 3 Diamond,
AA 3 Diamond, RAC 3 Diamond
Tel: **01208 862785** Mr Veall.
D: £25.00-£35.00 **S:** £30.00-£40.00.
Open: Mar to Oct
Beds: 2F 4D 4T 2S
Baths: 10 En 1 Sh
⛄ (5) 🅿 (14) ⅟ 🛋 🍴 🗙 🏃 🖳 V
🛗 ✦

(0.5m) *Tzitzikama Lodge, Rock*
Road, Rock, Wadebridge,
Cornwall, PL27 6NP.
Stylish accommodation near the
Camel Estuary and the North
Cornish coast.
Tel: **01208 862839**
Mr Cox & Alison Jones.
D: £22.00-£27.00
S: £32.00-£37.00.
Open: All Year (not Xmas)
Beds: 1F 1D 1T
Baths: 3 En
⛄ 🅿 ⅟ 🛋 🍴 🏃 🖳 V

Padstow 11

National Grid Ref: SW9175

Golden Lion, Old Customs House, London
Inn, Ring of Bells

(0.5m 🚌) *Hemingford House, 21*
Grenville Road, Padstow,
Cornwall, PL28 8EX.
Comfortable relaxed style. Hearty
breakfast. 10 minutes walk to
harbour. Welcome.
Tel: **01841 532806** (also fax no)
Mr Tamblin.
D: £22.50-£27.50
S: £25.00-£30.00.
Open: All Year
Beds: 1T 2D
Baths: 1 En 1 Pr 1 Sh
⛄ (12) 🅿 (1) ⅟ 🛋 🏃 🖳 V ✦

(0.5m) *Mother Ivey Cottage,*
Trevose Head, Padstow, Cornwall,
PL28 8SL.
Actual grid ref: SW859763
Tel: **01841 520329** (also fax no)
Mrs Woosnam Mills.
D: £22.50 **S:** £25.00.
Open: Easter to Oct
Beds: 2T
Baths: 2 En
⛄ (6) 🅿 🛋 🍴 🏃 🏊 🖳 V 🛗 ✦
Traditionally-built Cornish clifftop
house with stunning sea views,
overlooking Trevose Head with a
beach below. The area is renowned
for swimming, fishing, surfing and
walking. A championship golf
course - Trevose - is nearby. The
Cornwall Coastal Path is adjacent.

(1m) *Khandalla, Sarahs Lane,*
Padstow, Cornwall, PL28 8EL.
Traditional bed and breakfast in
elegant surroundings with estuary
views.
Tel: **01841 532961** Mrs Hair.
D: £20.00-£25.00 **S:** £20.00-£40.00.
Open: All Year
Beds: 1D 1S
Baths: 2 En 1 Sh
⛄ 🅿 (3) ⅟ 🛋 🏃 🖳 V 🛗 ✦

(0.5m) *Althea Library B&B, 27*
High Street, Padstow, Cornwall,
PL28 8BB.
Converted library, short walk from
harbour, old part of town.
Grades: ETC 4 Diamond, Silver
Tel: **01841 532717**
D: £24.00-£30.00 **S:** £27.00-£60.00.
Open: All Year (not Xmas)
Beds: 2D 1T
Baths: 3 En
🅿 (3) ⅟ 🛋 🏃 🖳 V

Trevone Bay 12

National Grid Ref: SW8876

Well Parc Hotel

(0.25m 🚌) *Well Parc Hotel,*
Trevone Bay, Padstow, Cornwall,
PL28 8QN.
Family run hotel and inn very close
to beaches, two miles from
Padstow.
Tel: **01841 520318** Mrs Mills.
D: £20.00-£28.00 **S:** £20.00-£28.00.
Open: All Year (not Xmas)
Beds: 4F 4D 1T 1S
Baths: 7 En 3 Sh
⛄ 🅿 🛋 🗙 🏃 🖳 V 🛗

🚌 sign means that,
given due notice,
owners will pick you
up from the path
and drop you off
within reason.

Treyarnon Bay 13

National Grid Ref: SW8674

(▲ On path) ***Treyarnon Bay Youth Hostel,*** *Tregonnan, Treyarnon, Padstow, Cornwall, PL28 8JR.*
Actual grid ref: SW859741
Tel: **01841 520322**
Under 18: £6.90 **Adults:** £10.00
Self-catering facilities, Showers, Lounge, Drying room, Cycle store, Parking, Evening meal at 7.00pm, No smoking, WC, Kitchen facilities, Breakfast available, Credit cards accepted
Overlooking sandy cove in designated Area of Outstanding Natural Beauty.

Newquay 14

National Grid Ref: SW8161

⚭ The Fort, Godolphin Arms, Red Lion, Olde Dolphin, Chy An Mor Inn, Great Western

(0.25m) ***Chichester Guest House,*** *14 Bay View Terrace, Newquay, Cornwall, TR7 2LR.*
Actual grid ref: SW814613
Good coffee, we provide walking, mineral collecting and archaeology weeks.
Grades: ETC 3 Diamond
Tel: **01637 874216** Miss Harper.
D: £16.50-£16.50 **S:** £16.50-£16.50.
Open: Mar to Nov
Beds: 2F 2D 2T 1S **Baths:** 2 Sh
⌂ (2) P (6) ⬜ ✕ 🖥 ⬛ �📺 ♦ ✦

(0.25m) ***The Croft Hotel,*** *37 Mount Wise, Newquay, Cornwall, TR7 2BL.*
Ideally situated close to beaches, pubs and clubs, coach and rail stations.
Tel: **01637 871520** Duffin.
D: £14.00-£25.00 **S:** £20.00-£40.00.
Open: All Year (not Xmas)
Beds: 4F 2T 2D
Baths: 4 En 2 Pr 1 Sh
⌂ P ✦ ✕ 🖥 ⬛ 📺 ♦ ✦

(0.25m) ***Alicia,*** *136 Henver Road, Newquay, Cornwall, TR7 3EQ.*
Guaranteed to take your breath away. Soaring Cliffs, sheltered Coves.
Tel: **01637 874328** Mrs Limer.
D: £15.00-£25.00 **S:** £20.00-£27.50.
Open: All Year
Beds: 2F 2D 1T 1S
Baths: 2 En 3 Sh
⌂ P (6) ✦ ⬜ ✕ 🖥 ⬛ 📺

Many rates vary according to season - the lowest only are shown here

All details shown are as supplied by B&B owners in Autumn 2001.

(0.25m) ***Pengilley,*** *12 Trebarwith Crescent, Newquay, Cornwall, TR7 1DX.*
Tel: **01637 872039**
D: £15.00-£23.00 **S:** £15.00-£25.00.
Open: All Year
Beds: 2F 2D 1T 1S
Baths: 4 En 2 Sh
⌂ (5) ⬜ 🛏 ✕ 🖥 ⬛ 📺 ✦
A friendly atmosphere awaits you at Pengilley, one minute from town, beach, close to shops and Newquay's famous nightlife and restaurants. For those wishing to try surfing, an introduction to Newquay's coolest surf school - West Coast Surfari.

(0.25m) ***Cotehele Lodge,*** *84 Tower Road, Newquay, Cornwall, TR7 1LY.*
Close to all beaches. Also town centre. Car park. Ensuite rooms.
Tel: **01637 873421** Mrs Drysdale.
D: £16.00-£22.00 **S:** £25.00-£35.00.
Open: All Year (not Xmas)
Beds: 2F 4D
Baths: 4 En 2 Sh
⌂ P (4) ✦ ⬜ ✕ 🖥 ⬛ 📺 ♦

(0.25m) ***Stratford House,*** *31 Berry Road, Newquay, Cornwall, TR7 1AS.*
Actual grid ref: SW816614
Large Victorian private house close to all amenities.
Tel: **01637 875603** Mrs Clark.
D: £12.00-£17.00 **S:** £12.00-£17.00.
Open: All Year
Beds: 1F 3D 1T 1S
Baths: 5 En 1 Sh
P (2) ⬜ ✕ 🖥 📺

Crantock 15

National Grid Ref: SW7960

⚭ Albion, Bowgie

(0.5m 🚗) ***Carden Cottage,*** *Halwyn Hill, Crantock, Newquay, Cornwall, TR8 5RR.*
Tel: **01637 830806** Mr Clark.
D: £20.00 **S:** £20.00.
Open: All Year (not Xmas/New Year)
Beds: 1T 2D
Baths: 3 En
⌂ (10) P (4) ✦ ⬜ 🖥 ⬛ 📺 ♦
A beautiful place with king-size beds, tea & coffee, soap and towels and a full English breakfast, situated in the heart of the village, with two pubs, a church and a few minutes walks from a lovely sandy beach.

Goonhavern 16

National Grid Ref: SW7853

⚭ Smugglers Dew Inn

(3m 🚗) ***September Lodge,*** *Wheal Hope, Goonhavern, Truro, Cornwall, TR4 9QJ.*
Modern house with countryside views. Ideally situated for touring Cornwall.
Grades: ETC 3 Diamond
Tel: **01872 571435** (also fax no)
Mr Philipps.
D: £20.00-£20.00 **S:** £25.00-£28.00.
Open: All Year (not Xmas/New Year)
Beds: 1F 1D **Baths:** 2 En
⌂ P (10) ✦ ⬜ 🛏 🖥 ⬛ 📺 ✦

Perranporth 17

National Grid Ref: SW7554

⚭ Bolingey Inn, Seinner's Arms, Waterfront Bar, Tywarnhayle Inn

(▲ On path) ***Perranporth Youth Hostel,*** *Droskyn Point, Perranporth, Cornwall, TR6 0DS.*
Actual grid ref: SW752544
Tel: **01872 573812**
Under 18: £6.50 **Adults:** £9.25
Self-catering facilities, Showers, Lounge, Drying room, Cycle store, No smoking, WC, Kitchen facilities, Credit cards accepted
Single-storey hostel high up on the cliffs, with spectacular views along 3 miles of surf beach, looking across to Ligger Point. The hostel has a surfboard store, and the drying room is wetsuit friendly.

(0.25m) ***Tremore,*** *Liskey Hill Crescent, Perranporth, Cornwall, TR6 0HP.*
Tel: **01872 573537** (also fax no)
Ms Crofts.
D: £19.00-£22.00 **S:** £20.00-£25.00.
Open: All Year (not Xmas)
Beds: 3D 1T 1S
Baths: 3 En 2 Sh
⌂ (11) P (6) ✦ ⬜ 🖥 ⬛ 📺 ✦
A warm welcome awaits in our well-established and highly recommended guest house. Totally non-smoking. Special diets catered for. Off-road parking. Ideal for touring. Excellent value. Try us, you won't be disappointed.

(On path) ***Chy an Kerensa,*** *Cliff Road, Perranporth, Cornwall, TR6 0DR.*
Panoramic coastal views from lounge, bar/dining room and ensuite bedrooms. 200 metres beach.
Grades: ETC 3 Diamond
Tel: **01872 572470** Mrs Woodcock.
D: £17.00-£24.00 **S:** £17.00-£24.00.
Open: All Year
Beds: 3F 2D 2T 2S
Baths: 6 En 2 Sh
⌂ P (4) ⬜ 🛏 🖥 ⬛ 📺 ✦

Porthtowan 18

National Grid Ref: SW6847

¶⊲ Commodore Inn

(0.25m ⊷) *Buzby View, Forthvean Road, Porthtowan, Truro, Cornwall, TR4 8AY.*
Actual grid ref: SW691473
Large, modern, detached, dormer bungalow set in beautiful secluded gardens.
Tel: **01209 891178** (also fax no)
Mrs Parkinson.
D: £18.00 **S:** £18.00.
Open: Easter to Oct
Beds: 2D 1T 1S **Baths:** 1 Sh
⌂ (12) **P** (6) ⊬ ⌷ 📖 ♟ ✿

Portreath 19

National Grid Ref: SW6545

¶⊲ Bassett Arms, Waterfront Inn, Portreath Arms

(0.25m ⊷) *Fountain Springs, Glenfeadon House, Portreath, Redruth, Cornwall, TR16 4JU.*
Listed Georgian house. Peaceful valley. Gardens, aviary, wooded/cliff walks.
Tel: **01209 842650** (also fax no)
Keast.
D: £18.50-£20.00 **S:** £20.00-£25.00.
Open: Feb to Dec
Beds: 3F 1D 2T 1S
Baths: 5 En 1 Sh
⌂ **P** (12) ⊬ ⌷ ⍏ ♟ 📖 & Ⅴ ♟ ✿

(On path) *Cliff House, The Square, Portreath, Redruth, Cornwall, TR16 4LB.*
Actual grid ref: SW656455
200-year-old whitewashed cottage; clean and comfortable.
Tel: **01209 842008** Mrs Healan.
D: £17.50-£20.00 **S:** £20.00-£25.00.
Open: All Year (not Xmas)
Beds: 1D 1T 2S
Baths: 2 En 2 Pr
⌂ (7) **P** (4) ⌷ ♟ 📖 Ⅴ ♟ ✿

(On path ⊷) *Bensons, 1 The Hillside, Portreath, Redruth, Cornwall, TR16 4LL.*
Actual grid ref: SW658453
Beautiful accommodation - panoramic sea views - quiet, warm, friendly and comfortable.
Grades: AA 4 Diamond
Tel: **01209 842534**
Mr & Mrs Smythe.
Fax no: 01209 843578
D: £20.00-£20.00 **S:** £25.00-£25.00.
Open: Easter to Sept
Beds: 2D 2S
Baths: 4 En
⌂ **P** (6) ⊬ ⌷ ♟ 📖 Ⅴ ♟

S = Price range for a single person in a single room

Gwithian 20

National Grid Ref: SW5841

¶⊲ Pendarves Arms

(1.5m ⊷) *Nanterrow Farm, Gwithian, Hayle, Cornwall, TR27 5BP*
Actual grid ref: SW599412
Tel: **01209 712282** Mrs Davies.
D: £16.00-£18.00 **S:** £16.00-£20.00.
Open: All Year (not Xmas)
Beds: 1F 1D 1S **Baths:** 2 Sh
⌂ **P** (4) ⌷ ⍏ ♟ Ⅴ ♟ ✿
Come and enjoy a relaxing stay on our traditional working farm situated in a quiet traffic-free valley 1.5 miles from St Ives Bay. 3 miles of sandy beaches; good area for coastal walks; many other local attractions. Good farmhouse fare.

(0.75m) *Calize Country House, Prosper Hill, Gwithian, Hayle, Cornwall, TR27 5BW.*
Actual grid ref: SW588409
Country house overlooking sea. Rural location near beautiful beaches/countryside.
Grades: AA 3 Diamond
Tel: **01736 753268** (also fax no)
Mrs Bailey.
D: £16.00-£19.00 **S:** £15.50-£19.00.
Open: All Year
Beds: 3D 2T **Baths:** 3 En 1 Sh
⌂ (10) **P** (5) ⊬ ⌷ ⍏ ♟ 📖 Ⅴ ♟ ✿

Angarrack 21

National Grid Ref: SW5838

¶⊲ Angarrack Inn

(2m ⊷) *Byways, 22 Steamers Hill, Angarrack, Hayle, Cornwall, TR27 5JB*
Actual grid ref: SW586383
Informal family-run guest house in pretty village. Beach 2 miles.
Tel: **01736 753463** Mrs Pooley.
D: £13.00-£16.00 **S:** £13.00-£25.00.
Open: Mar to Oct
Beds: 2D 1T **Baths:** 3 En
P (3) ⊬ ⌷ ✕ ♟ 📖 Ⅴ

Lelant 22

National Grid Ref: SW5437

¶⊲ Badger Inn

(0.5m) *Hindon Hall, Lelant, St Ives, Cornwall, TR26 3EN.*
Actual grid ref: SW543369
Tel: **01736 753046** (also fax no)
Ms O'Sullivan.
D: £23.00-£30.00 **S:** £34.00-£38.00.
Open: All Year (not Xmas/New Year)
Beds: 4D **Baths:** 4 En
P (10) ⊬ ⌷ ♟ 📖 Ⅴ ♟ ✿
A delightful setting in a conservation area village. Lovely Edwardian house overlooking RSPB, has luxurious double rooms with lots of extras, super breakfasts and small bar. Nearby beaches, cycle hire, golf, gardens, galleries. Ideal base for touring West Cornwall.

Carbis Bay 23

National Grid Ref: SW5238

¶⊲ Cornish Arms, Badger Inn

(0.25m) *Chy-An-Gwedhen, St Ives Road, Carbis Bay, St Ives, Cornwall, TR26 3JW.*
'Haven for non-smokers'. Chy-An-Gwedhen offers a warm and relaxed atmosphere.
Tel: **01736 798684** Hart.
D: £20.00-£25.00 **S:** £25.00-£28.00.
Open: All Year (not Xmas)
Beds: 4D 1T
Baths: 5 En
P (7) ⊬ ⌷ ✕ ♟ 📖 Ⅴ ♟ ✿

St Ives 24

National Grid Ref: SW5140

¶⊲ Sheaf of Wheat, Stennack, Sloop Inn, Castle, Golden Lion, Queen's Arms, Croft, Cornish Arms, Union Inn

(0.25m) *Rivendell, 7 Porthminster Terrace, St Ives, Cornwall, TR26 2DQ.*
Tel: **01736 794923** Ms Walker.
D: £16.00-£25.00 **S:** £16.00-£21.00.
Open: All Year
Beds: 1F 4D 1T 1S
Baths: 3 En 1 Sh
⌂ **P** (6) ⊬ ⌷ ✕ ♟ 📖 Ⅴ ♟
Highly recommended family-run guest house. Superb sea views from many rooms. Close to town, beaches, bus and rail stations. Friendly hospitality, excellent food. As featured in the TV drama 'Wycliffe'.

(0.25m ⊷) *Whitewaves, 4 Sea View, St Ives, Cornwall, TR26 2DH.*
Small, warm, friendly, family-run non-smoking guest house in quiet private road.
Tel: **01736 796595** (also fax no)
Mrs Webb.
D: £14.00-£20.00 **S:** £14.00-£20.00.
Open: All Year (not Xmas)
Beds: 1F 3D 1T 2S
Baths: 3 Sh
⌂ **P** ⊬ ⌷ ♟ 📖 Ⅴ ♟ ✿

(0.25m) *Carlill, 9 Porthminster Terrace, St Ives, Cornwall, TR26 2DQ.*
Friendly, comfortable, licensed, family-run guest house. Good food. Highly recommended.
Tel: **01736 796738** Mrs Bowden.
D: £16.00-£23.00 **S:** £18.00-£22.00.
Open: 27/12/99 to 23/12/00
Beds: 2F 2D 2T 1S
Baths: 1 En 2 Pr 2 Sh
⌂ (5) **P** (6) ⊬ ⌷ ⍏ ✕ ♟ 📖 Ⅴ ♟

Please respect
a B&B's wishes
regarding children,
animals & smoking.

(0.5m 🚍) *Chy-An-Creet Hotel,*
The Stennack, St Ives, Cornwall,
TR26 2HA.
Actual grid ref: SW507399
Warm welcome, relaxing home
comfort, excellent touring and
walking base.
Grades: ETC 3 Diamond,
AA 3 Diamond
Tel: 01736 796559 (also fax no)
Mr & Mrs Tremelling.
D: £20.00-£27.00 **S:** £20.00-£27.00.
Open: Jan to Nov
Beds: 2F 4D 2T 1S
Baths: 9 En
🛇 🅿 (10) ❑ ➤ ✗ 🏊 ⅙ 🎟 Ⅵ ♦

(0.5m) *Downlong Cottage Guest*
House, 95 Back Road East, St Ives,
Cornwall, TR26 1PF.
Tel: 01736 798107
D: £15.00-£21.00 **S:** £16.00-£20.00.
Open: All Year (not Xmas)
Beds: 1F 4D 1T
Baths: 4 En 1 Sh
🛇 (11) ❑ 🏊 🎟 Ⅵ
Ideally situated in the heart of
Downlong, the old fishing quarter
of picturesque St Ives, Downlong
Cottage is only minutes away from
the harbour and beaches. St Ives is
famous for its artists and galleries
including the Tate.

(0.5m) *The Anchorage, 5 Bunkers*
Hill, St Ives, Cornwall, TR26 1LJ.
Harbour location, cobbled street, 1
minute walk to Tate Gallery.
Grades: ETC 4 Diamond
Tel: 01736 797135 (also fax no)
Mrs Brown.
D: £20.00-£25.00
S: £20.00-£25.00.
Open: All Year
Beds: 1F 1T 3D 1S
Baths: 4 En 1 Sh
🛇 (1) ⅙ ❑ 🏊 🎟 Ⅵ

(0.5m) *Making Waves Vegan*
Guest House, 3 Richmond Place,
St Ives, Cornwall, TR26 1JN.
Eco-renovated Victorian house.
100% animal-free, organic.
Relaxed, friendly, sea views.
Tel: 01736 793895
Money.
D: £18.50-£25.00
S: £22.00-£22.00.
Open: Easter to Oct
Beds: 1F 1T 1D
Baths: 2 Sh
🛇 🅿 (1) ⅙ ❑ ✗ 🏊 🎟 Ⅵ ♦

(On path) *Kynance, The Warren, St*
Ives, Cornwall, TR26 2EA.
Former Tin- miners cottage. Beach/
harbour location. Railway/bus sta-
tions 100 yards.
Grades: AA 4 Diamond
Tel: 01736 796636
Mr & Mrs Norris.
D: £21.00-£25.00
S: £20.00.
Open: Mar to Nov
Beds: 4D 1T 1F
Baths: 5 En 1 Pr
🛇 (7) 🅿 (4) ⅙ ❑ 🏊 🎟 Ⅵ

(0.25m) *Chy-Roma Guest House,*
2 Sea View Terrace, St Ives,
Cornwall, TR26 2DH.
Family run guest house with superb
sea views overlooking town
harbour.
Tel: **01736 797539** Mrs Marks.
D: £15.00-£25.00 **S:** £15.00-£20.00.
Open: All Year
Beds: 2F 3D 1T 2S
Baths: 2 En 2 Sh
🛇 (5) 🅿 (5) ❑ ➤ ✗ 🏊 🎟 Ⅵ

(0.5m) *Bay View, 5 Pednolver*
Terrace, St Ives, Cornwall, TR26 2EL.
Delightfully situated overlooking
harbour and St Ives Bay.
Tel: **01736 796765** Mrs Simmons.
D: £18.00-£24.00 **S:** £18.00-£24.00.
Open: Easter to Nov
Beds: 2F 2D 1T
Baths: 4 Pr 1 Sh
🛇 (5) 🅿 (5) ❑ 🏊 Ⅵ

(0.25m 🚍) *The Old Vicarage*
Hotel, Parc-An-Creet, St Ives,
Cornwall, TR26.
Actual grid ref: SW515404
Large Victorian vicarage,
beautifully converted, peaceful
location, wooded grounds.
Tel: **01736 796124**
Mr & Mrs Sykes.
D: £19.00-£25.00 **S:** £22.00-£26.00.
Open: Easter to Oct
Beds: 3F 4D 1T
Baths: 4 Pr 2 Sh
🛇 🅿 (12) ❑ ➤ 🏊 🛈 ♦

Zennor   25

National Grid Ref: SW4538

🍴 ⅏ Tinners' Arms, Gurnard's Head

(🔺 0.5m) *The Old Chapel*
Backpackers, Zennor, St. Ives,
Cornwall, TR26 3PY.
Tel: **01736 798307**
Under 18: £10.00 **Adults:** £10.00
Television, Showers, Licensed bar,
Central heating, Shop, Laundry
facilities, Dining room, Grounds
available for games, Drying room,
Parking, Evening meal available,
No smoking
Converted chapel with clear views
over sea and Moorlands.

(0.5m) *Boswednack Manor,*
Zennor, St Ives, Cornwall, TR26 3DD.
Actual grid ref: SW442378
Peaceful, vegetarian, non-smoking.
Organic gardens, superb views, sea
sunsets.
Tel: **01736 794183** Mrs Gynn.
D: £17.00-£22.00 **S:** £18.00-£23.00.
Open: Easter to Oct
Beds: 1F 2D 1T 1S
Baths: 2 En 1 Sh
🛇 🅿 (6) ⅙ 🏊 Ⅵ ♦

D = Price range per person
sharing in a double room

(0.5m) *Rosmorva, Boswednack,*
Zennor, St Ives, Cornwall, TR26 3DD.
Actual grid ref: SW443378
Lovely views from garden. Superb
walking on cliffs and moorland.
Tel: **01736 796722** Ms Hamlett.
D: £16.50-£17.50 **S:** £16.50-£17.50.
Open: All Year
Beds: 1F 1D 1S
Baths: 1 Sh, 1 En
🛇 (4) 🅿 (3) ⅙ 🏊 🎟 Ⅵ ♦

(0.5m) *Trewey Farm, Zennor,*
St Ives, Cornwall, TR26 3DA.
Actual grid ref: SW454384
Working farm. Peaceful attractive
surroundings. Warm welcome,
excellent food.
Tel: **01736 796936** Mrs Mann.
D: £18.00-£21.00 **S:** £19.00-£21.00.
Open: Feb to Nov
Beds: 2F 2D 1T 1S
Baths: 1 Sh
🛇 🅿 (6) ❑ ➤ 🏊 Ⅵ ♦

Pendeen   26

National Grid Ref: SW3834

🍴 ⅏ North Inn

(0.5m) *The Old Count House,*
Boscaswell Downs, Pendeen,
Penzance, Cornwall, TR19 7ED.
Actual grid ref: SW383344
Old granite house in quiet village,
on the dramatic North Coast.
Tel: **01736 788058** Mrs Dymond.
D: £16.00-£18.00 **S:** £16.00-£18.00.
Open: Easter to Oct
Beds: 2D **Baths:** 1 Sh
🛇 (2) 🅿 (4) ❑ 🏊 🎟 Ⅵ ♦

(1m 🚍) *Quiddles, Boscaswell*
Downs, Pendeen, Penzance,
Cornwall, TR19 7DW.
Actual grid ref: SW383344
Beautiful 200-year-old granite
house, 1 mile from North Coast
Path.
Tel: **01736 787278** Ms Bailey.
D: £12.00-£19.00 **S:** £12.00-£19.00.
Open: All year (not Xmas)
Beds: 1F 1D 1T
Baths: 1 En 1 Sh
🛇 🅿 (6) ❑ ✗ 🏊 Ⅵ ♦

(1m) *Manor Farm, Pendeen,*
Penzance, Cornwall, TR19 7ED.
A rare opportunity to visit a beauti-
ful Grade I Listed building on
Granite Coast.
Tel: **01736 788753** (also fax no)
Ms Davey.
D: £18.00-£20.00 .
Open: All Year
Beds: 1F 3D 1T
Baths: 1 En 1 Pr 1 Sh
🛇 🅿 ❑ ➤ 🏊 🎟 Ⅵ ♦

St Just-in-Penwith 27

National Grid Ref: SW3631

l⊲ The Wellington

(▲ On path) *Land's End Youth Hostel, Letcha Vean, St Just, Penzance, Cornwall, TR19 7NT.*
Actual grid ref: SW364305
Tel: **01736 788437**
Under 18: £6.90
Adults: £10.00
Self-catering facilities, Showers, Lounge, Cycle store, Evening meal at 7.00pm, No smoking, WC, Kitchen facilities, Breakfast available, Credit cards accepted
House with sea views in the peaceful Cot Valley, with a path leading to the cove.

(0.25m **⊞**) *Boscean Country Hotel, St Just-in-Penwith, Penzance, Cornwall, TR19 7QP.*
Grades: ETC 3 Diamond
Tel: **01736 788748** (also fax no)
Mr & Mrs Wilson.
D: £22.00-£22.00.
S: £27.00-£27.00.
Open: All Year (not Xmas)
Beds: 3F 4D 5T
Baths: 12 En
⛄ **P** (15) □ ✗ 🛌 ▥ ▣ ♦ ✦
A warm & hospitable welcome awaits you at Boscean - a magnificent country house in three acres of private walled garden, set amidst some the most dramatic scenery in West Cornwall. Home cooking, using fresh local and home-grown produce.

(0.5m **⊞**) *Bosavern House, St Just-in-Penwith, Penzance, Cornwall, TR19 7RD.*
Actual grid ref: SW374300
Pleasant C17th Cornish manor house. Delightful grounds. Warm welcome awaits.
Grades: ETC 3 Diamond
Tel: **01736 788301** (also fax no)
Mr & Mrs Lilley.
D: £19.00-£26.00
S: £19.00-£26.00.
Open: All Year (not Xmas)
Beds: 3F 2D 2T 1S
Baths: 7 En 1 Pr
⛄ **P** (15) ✂ □ ➤ 🛌 ▥ & ▣ ♦ ✦

(0.5m) *Boswedden House Hotel, Cape Cornwall, St Just-in-Penwith, Penzance, Cornwall, TR19 7NJ.*
Spacious Georgian mansion. Quiet country setting. Large garden, warm welcome.
Grades: ETC 3 Diamond
Tel: **01736 788733** (also fax no)
Miss Griffiths.
D: £20.00-£25.00.
S: £20.00-£30.00.
Open: All Year
Beds: 1F 2D 3T 2S
Baths: 8 En
⛄ **P** ✂ □ ➤ 🛌 ▥ ▣ ♦ ✦

Kelynack 28

National Grid Ref: SW3630

(▲ 1m) *Kelynack Caravan & Camping Park Hostel, Kelynack, St Just, Penzance, Cornwall, TR19 7RE.*
Actual grid ref: SW373301
Tel: **01736 787633**
Under 18: £4.00 **Adults:** £7.00
Self-catering facilities, Showers, Shop, Laundry facilities, Wet weather shelter, Grounds available for games, Drying room, Cycle store, Parking, No smoking
In beautiful valley near coast. Ideal for exploring West Cornwall.

Sennen 29

National Grid Ref: SW3525

l⊲ Sunny Bank

(▲ 0.5m) *Land's End Backpackers' Hostel, Whitesands Lodge, Sennen, Penzance, Cornwall, TR19 7AR.*
Actual grid ref: SW366264
Tel: **01736 871776**
Under 18: £10.00 **Adults:** £10.00
Self-catering facilities, Television, Showers, Licensed bar, Laundry facilities, Lounge, Dining room, Games room, Grounds available for games, Drying room, Cycle store, Parking, No smoking
Colourful, friendly hostel close to stunning coast, great beaches and much more.

(0.5m) *Sunny Bank Hotel, Seaview Hill, Sennen, Lands End, Penzance, Cornwall, TR19 7AR.*
Actual grid ref: SW365263
Comfortable detached hotel, close beaches, Minack Theatre, good food, licensed.
Tel: **01736 871278**
Mr & Mrs Comber.
D: £15.00-£20.00.
S: £15.00-£25.00.
Open: Jan to Nov
Beds: 2F 5D 2T 2S
Baths: 2 Sh
⛄ **P** (15) □ ✗ 🛌 ▥ ▣ ♦ ✦

Lamorna 30

National Grid Ref: SW4425

l⊲ Lamorna Hotel

(0.25m **⊞**) *Tremeneth Hotel, Lamorna, Penzance, Cornwall, TR19 6XL.*
Set in the heart of a wooded valley.
Tel: **01736 731367** (also fax no)
Rowley.
D: £22.00-£26.00
S: £18.00-£20.00.
Open: Easter to Oct
Beds: 3D 1T 1S 1F
Baths: 5 En 1 Sh
⛄ (2) ⊠ (8) □ ➤ ✗ 🛌 ▥ ▣ ♦ ✦

Please take muddy boots off before entering premises

Mousehole 31

National Grid Ref: SW4626

(On path **⊞**) *Carn Du Hotel, Mousehole, Penzance, Cornwall, TR19 6SS.*
Actual grid ref: SW468258
Peaceful comfortable hotel. Superb views, food, accommodation overlooking Mounts Bay.
Tel: **01736 731233** (also fax no)
Mr Field.
D: £25.00-£35.00 **S:** £35.00-£45.00.
Open: All Year
Beds: 4D 3T
Baths: 6 En 1 Pr
⛄ **P** (12) □ ✗ 🛌 ▥ ▣ ♦ ✦

Penzance 32

National Grid Ref: SW467299

l⊲ Bosun's Locker, Turk's Head, The Coalstreamer, Dolphin & Neptune, The Lugger, Union Hotel, White Hart, Admiral Benbow, Mounts Bay, Olde Bath Inn, Tarbert Hotel, Long Boat, Yacht Inn

(▲ 0.5m) *Penzance Youth Hostel, Castle Horneck, Alverton, Penzance, Cornwall, TR20 8TF.*
Actual grid ref: SW457302
Tel: **01736 362666**
Under 18: £7.75 **Adults:** £11.00
Self-catering facilities, Television, Showers, Laundry facilities, Lounge, Drying room, Security lockers, Security lockers, Cycle store, Parking, Evening meal at 5.30pm to 7.45pm, Breakfast available, Credit cards accepted
Early Georgian manor house in landscaped gardens, with extensive views of Mount's Bay and the Lizard Peninsula.

(▲ 0.25m) *Penzance Backpackers - The Blue Dolphin, The Blue Dolphin, Alexandra Road, Penzance, Cornwall, TR18 4LZ.*
Tel: **01736 363836 Adults:** £9.00
Self-catering facilities, Television, Showers, Central heating, Shop, Laundry facilities, Lounge, Dining room, Cycle store, No smoking
Victorian house near town centre and close to sea front.

All rates are subject to alteration at the owners' discretion.

(On path) *Lynwood Guest House,*
41 Morrab Road, Penzance,
Cornwall, TR18 4EX.
Grades: RAC 3 Diamond
Tel: **01736 365871** (also fax no)
Mrs Stacey.
D: £13.50-£17.50 **S:** £12.50-£16.50.
Open: All Year
Beds: 6F 2D 2T 2S
Baths: 4 En 2 Pr 2 Sh
🛇 ⛚ 🛏 🖙 🌲 🎹 Ⓥ ✓
Family-run Victorian guest house.
Internationally recommended for
good food, cleanliness. Close to all
amenities. Ideally situated for visit-
ing Land's End and St Michael's
Mount.

(0.25m) *Glencree Private Hotel,* 2
Mennaye Road, Penzance,
Cornwall, TR18 4NG.
Grades: ETC 3 Diamond
Tel: **01736 362026** (also fax no)
Mr Hodgetts.
D: £16.00-£20.00 **S:** £19.00-£22.00.
Open: Mar to Oct
Beds: 2F 4D 1T 2S
Baths: 7 En 2 Sh
🛇 (5) ⛚ 🛏 🗙 🌲 🎹 Ⓥ ✓
A charming Victorian house in a
quiet road 100 yards off seafront.
Spacious rooms, some with sea
views and some with four poster
beds. Highly recommended for its
comfort, cleanliness, excellent food
& friendly personal service. Town
centre 10 minutes walk.

(0.25m) *Chy an Gof Guest House,*
10 Regent Terrace, Penzance,
Cornwall, TR18 4DW.
Listed Regency house overlooking
Penzance promenade and the
lovely Mount's Bay
Tel: **01736 332361** (also fax no)
Mr & Mrs Schofield.
D: £22.00-£22.00 **S:** £22.00-£22.00.
Open: All Year
Beds: 2T 2S
Baths: 4 En
⛚ (4) 🖙 🌲 🎹 Ⓥ ✓

(On path) *Carnson House Private*
Hotel, East Terrace, Market Jew
St, Penzance, Cornwall, TR18 2TD.
Centrally located, friendly, small
hotel near station and harbour.
Tel: **01736 365589**
Mr & Mrs Smyth.
Fax no: 01736 365594
D: £18.00-£24.50 **S:** £20.00.
Open: All Year
Beds: 3D 2T 2S
Baths: 2 Pr 1 Sh
🛇 (12) 🖙 🖙 🌲 🎹 Ⓥ 🅰

(0.25m) *Mount Royal Hotel,*
Chyandour Cliff, Penzance,
Cornwall, TR18 3LQ.
Small family-run hotel facing the
sea & overlooking the entrance of
Penzance harbour.
Grades: AA 3 Diamond, RAC 3
Diamond
Tel: **01736 362233** (also fax no)
Mr Cox.
D: £22.50-£27.50 **S:** £25.00-£27.50.
Open: March-Oct
Beds: 3F 3D 2T
Baths: 5 En 2 Sh
🛇 (1) ⛚ (10) 🖙 🖙 🌲 🎹 Ⓥ ✓

(0.25m) *Pendennis Hotel,*
Alexandra Road, Penzance,
Cornwall, TR18.
Victorian licensed hotel built in
1830 in a quiet tree lined residen-
tial area.
Grades: AA 3 Diamond
Tel: **01736 363823** (also fax no)
Mrs Cook.
D: £15.00-£22.00 **S:** £15.00-£22.00.
Open: All Year
Beds: 5F 2D
Baths: 7 En 1 Sh
🛇 🖙 🖙 🗙 🌲 🎹 Ⓥ ✓

(0.25m) *Woodstock Guest House,*
29 Morrab Road, Penzance,
Cornwall, TR18 4EZ.
Actual grid ref: SW472299
Central Penzance. Ideal for touring
and visiting the Lands End
Peninsula.
Grades: ETC 3 Diamond
RAC 3 Diamond
Tel: **01736 369049** (also fax no)
Mr & Mrs Hopkins.
D: £14.00-£20.00 **S:** £14.00-£20.00.
Open: All Year
Beds: 1F 2T 3D 2S
Baths: 4 En 1 Pr 1 Sh
🛇 ⛚ 🖙 🖙 🛏 🌲 🎹 & Ⓥ 🅰

(0.25m) *Trewella Guest House,*
18 Mennaye Road, Penzance,
Cornwall, TR18 4NG.
Actual grid ref: SW473299
Large Victorian house.
Recommended for good food. Ideal
touring centre.
Tel: **01736 363818**
Mr & Mrs Glenn.
D: £18.00-£19.00 **S:** £16.00-£23.00.
Open: Mar to Oct
Beds: 2F 4D 2S
Baths: 6 En 1 Sh
🛇 (5) 🖙 🗙 🌲 🎹 Ⓥ

(0.25m) *Kimberley House,* 10
Morrab Road, Penzance, Cornwall,
TR18 4EZ.
Convenient bus and railway
station. Minutes walk town and
seafront.
Grades: AA 3 Diamond
Tel: **01736 362727**
Mr & Mrs Bashford.
D: £15.00-£21.00 **S:** £15.00-£18.00.
Open: Feb to Dec
Beds: 2F 2D 3T 1S
Baths: 3 En 2 Pr 3 Sh
🛇 (5) ⛚ (3) 🖙 🖙 🌲 🎹 Ⓥ

(0.25m) *Penalva Guest House,*
Alexandra Road, Penzance,
Cornwall, TR18 4LZ.
Victorian guest house walking dis-
tance from sea front and town centre.
Grades: AA 3 Diamond
Tel: **01736 369060** (also fax no)
Mrs Buswell.
D: £15.00-£22.00 **S:** £15.00-£22.00.
Open: All Year
Beds: 1F 2D 1T 1S
Baths: 4 En 1 Pr
🛇 (5) 🖙 🖙 🌲 🎹 Ⓥ ✓

(0.25m) *Tarbert Hotel,* Clarence
St, Penzance, Cornwall, TR18 2NU.
Georgian house with an atmos-
phere of quality, character and
charm.
Grades: AA 2 Star, RAC 2 Star
Tel: **01736 363758** Mrs Evans.
Fax no: 01736 331336
D: £26.00-£38.00 **S:** £30.00-£38.00.
Open: Feb to Dec
Beds: 2F 7D 1T 2S
🛇 ⛚ (4) 🖙 🗙 🌲 🎹 Ⓥ 🅰 ✓

(0.25m) *Boscreeg Guest House,*
10 Mennaye Road, Penzance,
Cornwall, TR18 4NG.
Family run guest house, good food,
warm welcome, friendly atmos-
phere.
Tel: **01736 364067** Mrs Davies.
D: £16.00-£20.00 **S:** £18.00-£22.00.
Open: All Year
Beds: 1F 1T 1S 2D
🛇 🖙 🖙 🛏 🗙 🌲 Ⓥ 🅰

(0.25m) *Ocean View, Chayndour*
Cliffe, Penzance, Cornwall,
TR18 3LQ.
Actual grid ref: SW478308
Charming, comfortable seafront
guest house.
Tel: **01736 351770** Mr Mayes.
D: £13.00-£18.00 **S:** £18.00.
Open: All Year (not Xmas)
Beds: 2D 1T **Baths:** 2 Sh
🛇 ⛚ (3) 🖙 🌲 🎹 & Ⓥ 🅰

(On path 🚗) *Keigwin Hotel,*
Alexandra Road, Penzance,
Cornwall, TR18 4LZ.
Eat and sleep smoke-free.
Comfortable family-run guest
house, ensuite and standard rooms
available.
Tel: **01736 363930**
Mr & Mrs Flint.
D: £15.00-£23.00 **S:** £15.00-£19.00.
Open: All Year
Beds: 2F 2D 2T 2S
Baths: 5 En 3 Sh
🛇 🖙 🖙 🗙 🌲 🎹 Ⓥ 🅰 ✓

**Many rates vary
according to season -
the lowest only are
shown here**

**Please don't camp
on *anyone's* land
without first obtaining
their permission.**

(0.25m) *Trevelyan Hotel, 16 Chapel Street, Penzance, Cornwall, TR18 4AN.*
Popular hotel, comfortable and friendly, centrally situated, good English breakfast.
Tel: **01736 362494** Mr Fitzgerald.
D: £15.00-£18.00 **S:** £16.00-£25.00.
Open: All Year (not Xmas)
Beds: 3F 2D 2T 2S
Baths: 5 En 1 Pr 2 Sh
ॐ ♿ (6) ▢ ♨ ▥ Ⅴ ♣

(0.25m) *Con Amore Guest House, 38 Morrab Road, Penzance, Cornwall, TR18 4EX.*
Retired Victorian gentleman's residence, ideally situated between the sea front and town centre.
Tel: **01736 363423** (also fax no)
Mr & Mrs Richards.
D: £13.00-£19.00 **S:** £13.00-£19.00.
Open: All Year
Beds: 2F 2D 2T 2S
Baths: 3 En 3 Sh
ॐ ♔ ♫ ▥ ♣

(0.25m) *Seaforth Guest House, 20 Mennaye Road, Penzance, Cornwall, TR18 4NG.*
Seaforth is a lovely Victorian house which is quietly situated, offering comfortable accommodation.
Tel: **01736 331682**
D: £15.00-£20.00 .
Open: All Year
Beds: 4D 2T **Baths:** 2 En 1 Sh
⧖ ▢ ♨ ▥ Ⅴ ♣

(0.25m) *The Dock Inn, 17 Quay Street, Penzance, Cornwall, TR18 4BD.*
Quayside friendly character inn, very much a local in the true sense.
Tel: **01736 362833**
D: £20.00-£25.00 **S:** £30.00-£40.00.
Open: All Year (not Xmas)
Beds: 2D 1T **Baths:** 3 En
ॐ ▢ ♙ ♨ ▥ Ⅴ

Marazion 33

National Grid Ref: SW5130

(0.25m ♠) *Chymorvah Private Hotel, Marazion, Cornwall, TR17 0DQ.*
Cheerful, coastal Victorian family house. Comfortable ensuite rooms, good breakfasts.
Tel: **01736 710497** Mrs Bull.
Fax no: 01736 710508
D: £26.00-£30.50 **S:** £26.00-£30.50.
Open: All Year (not Xmas)
Beds: 9F 5D 3T 1S
Baths: 9 En 1 Sh
ॐ ▣ (12) ▢ ♔ ♫ × ♨ ▥ Ⅴ ♣ ♣

**All paths are popular:
you are well-advised to
book ahead**

Perranuthnoe 34

National Grid Ref: SW5329

♥⦿ ♿ Victoria Inn

(On path) *Ednovean House, Perranuthnoe, Penzance, Cornwall, TR20 9LZ.*
Grades: AA 3 Diamond
Tel: **01736 711071**
Mr & Mrs Whittington.
D: £20.00-£27.00 **S:** £24.00-£25.00.
Open: All Year (not Xmas/New Year)
Beds: 2T 4D 2S
Baths: 6 En 2 Sh
ॐ (7) ▣ (10) ▢ ♔ × ♨ ♨ ▥ Ⅴ ♣ ♣
Beautiful 180 year old country house standing above Perranuthnoe village in one acre of lovely gardens. Surrounded by farmland. Stunning views across Mounts Bay, overlooking St. Michael's Mount and beyond to Penzance, Newlyn and Mousehole. Putting green and licensed bar.

Porthleven 35

National Grid Ref: SW6225

♥⦿ ♿ Atlantic Inn, Ship Inn, Harbour Inn

(On path ♠) *Seefar, Peverell Terrace, Porthleven, Helston, Cornwall, TR13 9DZ.*
Traditional Cornish Victorian mine captain's house, overlooking sea.
Grades: ETC 3 Diamond
Tel: **01326 573778**
Mr & Mrs Hallam.
D: £16.00-£21.00 **S:** £15.00-£16.00.
Open: Mar to Nov
Beds: 2D 1T 1S
Baths: 2 En 1 Pr 1 Sh
ॐ ▣ (1) ♔ ▢ ♔ ♫ ♨ ▥ Ⅴ ♣ ♣

(On path ♠) *Greystones, 40 West End, Porthleven, Helston, Cornwall, TR13 9JL.*
Overlooking sea. Close, harbour/beach/shops/restaurants/pubs. Dogs welcome.
Tel: **01326 565583** (also fax no)
Mrs Woodward.
D: £15.00-£20.00
S: £20.00-£25.00.
Open: All Year (not Xmas)
Beds: 1F 1D 1S
Baths: 1 Sh
ॐ ▢ ♫ ♨ ▥ ♣

(On path ♠) *Pentre House, Peverell Terrace, Porthleven, Helston, Cornwall, TR13 9DZ.*
Actual grid ref: SW630255
Spectacular sea views, delightful village, home-baked bread. Highly recommended.
Tel: **01326 574493**
Mrs Cookson.
D: £16.50-£17.50 .
Open: Easter to Oct
Beds: 1D 1T 2S
Baths: 1 Sh
ॐ ▢ ♔ ♫ ♨ ▥ Ⅴ ♣ ♣

Cury 36

National Grid Ref: SW6721

♥⦿ ♿ Old Mill Wheel Inn, Black Swan, Hazlephron Inn

(3m ♠) *Tregaddra Farmhouse, Cury, Helston, Cornwall, TR12 7BB.*
Farmhouse B&B quiet, peaceful, set in Area of Outstanding Natural Beauty.
Grades: ETC 4 Diamond
Tel: **01326 240235** (also fax no)
Mrs Lugg.
D: £20.00-£25.00 **S:** £20.00-£25.00.
Open: All Year (not Xmas)
Beds: 2F 4D 1T
Baths: 6 En 1 Pr
ॐ ▣ (10) ♔ ▢ × ♨ ▥ Ⅴ ♣ ♣

Mullion 37

National Grid Ref: SW6719

♥⦿ ♿ Old Inn, Mounts Bay Inn, Black Swan, Hazlephron Inn

(0.5m ♠) *Meaver Farm, Mullion, Helston, Cornwall, TR12 7DN.*
Grades: ETC 4 Diamond, Silver
Tel: **01326 240128** Stanland.
Fax no: 01326 240011
D: £22.50-£25.00 **S:** £25.00-£30.00.
Open: All Year
Beds: 1T 2D
Baths: 3 En
▣ (3) ♔ ▢ ♔ ♨ ▥ Ⅴ ♣
300 year old former farmhouse in quiet valley on beautiful Lizard Peninsula. Spectacular coastline and romantic Helford River nearby. Exposed beams, log fire, luxury bathrooms, Aga breakfasts. A warm welcome awaits you. Come and unwind - let Cornwall work its magic - wonderful any time of year.

(0.5m ♠) *Campden House, The Commons, Mullion, Helston, Cornwall, TR12 7HZ.*
Actual grid ref: SW673195
One acre of gardens. Home-grown vegetables when in season.
Tel: **01326 240365**
Mr & Mrs Hyde.
D: £15.50-£16.50 **S:** £15.50-£16.50.
Open: All Year (not Xmas)
Beds: 2F 5D 1T 2S
Baths: 2 Sh
ॐ ▣ (9) ▢ ♔ × ♨ Ⅴ ♣ ♣

(0.25m) *Trenance Farmhouse, Mullion, Helston, Cornwall, TR12 7HB.*
Actual grid ref: SW673184
Victorian farmhouse: breakfast in garden room; summer pool; 0.5 mile beach.
Tel: **01326 240639** (also fax no)
Mr & Mrs Tyler-Street.
D: £18.50-£23.00
S: £18.50-£23.00.
Open: Easter to Sep
Beds: 3D 1T
Baths: 4 En
ॐ (8) ▣ (7) ▢ ♔ ♨ ♨ ▥ Ⅴ ♣ ♣

(On path) *Mullion Cove Hotel, Mullion Cove, Mullion, Helston, Cornwall, TR12 7EP.*
Actual grid ref: SW666180
Stunning coastal views, superb food and a relaxed friendly atmosphere.
Tel: **01326 240328** Mrs Davis.
Fax no: 01326 240998
D: £28.00-£69.00 **S:** £28.00-£99.00.
Open: All Year
Beds: 5F 15D 6T 2S
Baths: 25 En 3 Pr
🛇 🅿 (35) 🗆 🏠 ✕ 🔥 🎟 Ⓥ 🖪 ✦

Mullion Cove   38

National Grid Ref: SW6617

🍴 🍺 Ridgeback Hotel

(On path 🚍) *Criggan Mill, Mullion Cove, Helston, Cornwall, TR12 7EU.*
Actual grid ref: SW667180
Timber Lodges 200 yards from fishing harbour and coastal footpath.
Tel: **01326 240496** Mr Bolton.
Fax no: 0870 1640549
D: £17.00-£22.00 **S:** £20.00-£25.00.
Open: Easter to Oct
Beds: 5F 6D 4T **Baths:** 3 En
🛇 (1) 🅿 🗆 🏠 ✕ 🔥 Ⓥ ✦

The Lizard   39

National Grid Ref: SW7012

🍴 🍺 Top House

(0.5m) *Parc Brawse House, Penmenner Road, The Lizard, Helston, Cornwall, TR12 7NR.*
Old Cornish house with extensive sea views and secluded garden.
Tel: **01326 290466** (also fax no)
Mrs Brookes.
D: £16.50-£23.00 **S:** £16.50-£29.00.
Open: All Year
Beds: 1F 1T 4D 1S
Baths: 4 Pr 2 Sh
🛇 🅿 (7) 🗆 🏠 ✕ 🔥 🎟 ♿ Ⓥ 🖪 ✦

(On path 🚍) *The Most Southerly House, Lizard Point, The Lizard, Helston, Cornwall, TR12 7NU.*
Actual grid ref: SW702115
England's most southerly house. Magnificent location on coastal path.
Tel: **01326 290300** (also fax no)
Mrs Sowden.
D: £18.00-£20.00 **S:** £20.00-£20.00.
Open: All Year (not Xmas/New Year)
Beds: 1T 1D 1S
Baths: 1 Sh
🛇 (7) 🅿 (4) ✦ 🗆 🔥 🎟 🖪 ✦

Ponsongath   40

National Grid Ref: SW7517

(0.75m 🚍) *Wych Elm, Ponsongath, Helston, Cornwall, TR12 6SQ.*
Actual grid ref: SW756179
Idyllic quiet setting close secluded Lankidden Cove. Backwoodsmen's bliss!
Tel: **01326 280576** Mrs Whitaker.
D: £18.00-£18.00 **S:** £20.00-£20.00.
Open: All Year (not Xmas)
Beds: 1T
Baths: 1 En
🛇 (8) 🅿 (2) ✦ 🗆 🏠 ✕ 🎟

Coverack   41

National Grid Ref: SW7818

🍴 🍺 Paris Hotel

(▲ 0.25m) *Coverack Youth Hostel, Parc Behan, School Hill, Coverack, Helston, Cornwall, TR12 6SA.*
Actual grid ref: SW782184
Tel: **01326 280687**
Under 18: £6.90 **Adults:** £10.00
Self-catering facilities, Showers, Lounge, Dining room, Games room, Parking, Evening meal at 7.00pm, WC, Kitchen facilities, Breakfast available
Large country house situated above old fishing village and smugglers' haunt, with views of bay and coastline.

(On path 🚍) *Boak House, Coverack, Helston, Cornwall, TR12 6SH.*
Seaside guest house.
Tel: **01326 280608**
Mrs Watters.
D: £18.00-£22.00 **S:** £18.00-£22.00.
Open: All Year (not Xmas)
Beds: 3D 1T 1S
🛇 🗆 🏠 ✕ 🔥 Ⓥ ✦

St Keverne   42

National Grid Ref: SW7921

🍴 🍺 White Hart, Three Tuns

(1m 🚍) *Trevinock, St Keverne, Helston, Cornwall, TR12 6QP.*
Actual grid ref: SW802216
Tel: **01326 280498**
Mrs Kelly.
D: £18.00-£22.00 **S:** £18.00-£22.00.
Open: Easter to Oct
Beds: 2D 2S
Baths: 1 En 1 Sh
🛇 🅿 (5) ✦ 🗆 🏠 ✕ 🔥 Ⓥ 🖪 ✦
Excellent food and accommodation. Ideally situated in a very lovely and unspoilt part of Cornwall. Near to Helford River, beaches and places of interest. All rooms of high standard, overlooking colourful gardens. Ample off road parking. Ensuite available. Near coastal footpath.

(1m) *Tregoning Lea, Laddenvean, St Keverne, Heltson, Cornwall, TR12 6QE.*
New bungalow in quiet valley setting close to village amenities.
Tel: **01326 280947** (also fax no)
Mr & Mrs Perry.
D: £17.00-£19.00 **S:** £18.00-£25.00.
Open: All Year (not Xmas/New Year)
Beds: 1T 1D 2T
Baths: 1 En 1 Pr
🛇 (10) 🅿 (6) ✦ 🗆 🎟 🖪

Gillan   43

National Grid Ref: SW7824

🍴 🍺 New Inn

(On path 🚍) *Porthvean, Gillan, Manaccan, Helston, Cornwall, TR12 6HL.*
Actual grid ref: SW783251
Specially suitable for walkers on SW Coastal Path, view of Gillan Creek and Helford.
Tel: **01326 231204** Mrs Whale.
D: £15.00-£15.00 **S:** £15.00-£15.00.
Open: All Year (not Xmas)
Beds: 1T **Baths:** 1 Pr
🅿 (3) ✦ 🏠 🔥 🎟 Ⓥ ✦

Mawnan Smith   44

National Grid Ref: SW7728

🍴 🍺 Red Lion Inn, Ferry Boat Inn

(0.75m) *Carwinion Vean, Grove Hill, Mawnan Smith, Falmouth, Cornwall, TR11 5ER.*
Lovely country house near beautiful Helford River, gardens, coastal footpaths and beaches.
Tel: **01326 250513** Mrs Spike.
D: £20.00-£23.00 **S:** £20.00-£25.00.
Open: All Year (not Xmas)
Beds: 1F 3D 2T
Baths: 2 En 2 Sh
🛇 (5) 🅿 (6) 🗆 🏠 🔥 🎟 Ⓥ 🖪 ✦

(1m 🚍) *The White House, 28 Castle View Park, Mawnan Smith, Falmouth, Cornwall, TR11 5HB.*
Actual grid ref: SW779289
Friendly family guest house near village centre and easy access from coast.
Tel: **01326 250768** Mrs Grant.
D: £18.00-£20.00 **S:** £20.00-£25.00.
Open: All Year
Beds: 1F 1D 1T 1S
Baths: 1 En 1 Sh
🛇 🅿 (2) 🗆 ✕ 🔥 🎟 Ⓥ 🖪 ✦

Falmouth 45

National Grid Ref: SW8032

🍴 🍺 Seaview Inn, Quayside Inn, Cross Keys, Falmouth Hotel, Chain Locker, Norway Inn, Pandora Inn, Bosanneth Hotel, Warehouse Bistro, Laughing Pirate

(▲ 0.5m) *Pendennis Castle Youth Hostel, Falmouth, Cornwall, TR11 4LP.*
Actual grid ref: SW823319
Tel: 01326 311435
Under 18: £6.20 **Adults:** £9.15
Evening meal at 7.00pm
Victorian barracks building, flood-lit at night, in grounds of a C16th castle on the promontory beyond Falmouth town.

(0.5m) *Trevu House Hotel, 45 Melvill Road, Falmouth, Cornwall, TR11 4DG.*
Tel: 01326 312852 Mrs Eustice.
Fax no: 01326 318631
D: £17.50-£21.50 **S:** £17.50-£21.50.
Open: All year (not Xmas)
Beds: 1F 2D 3T 3S
Baths: 9 En
🛏 (5) 🅿 ⅍ 🍴 ✕ 🍽 🌰 Ⅲ Ⅴ 🔥 ⚡
Small select, non-smoking hotel. Superb for town, Princess Pavilion and beautiful gardens. Sandy beaches, coastal walks and some the finest scenery in Cornwall. All en-suite rooms some with 6' wide beds. Ground-floor bedroom.

(0.25m) *Melvill House Hotel, 52 Melvill Road, Falmouth, Cornwall, TR11 4DQ.*
Grades: AA 4 Diamond
Tel: 01326 316645
Mr & Mrs Crawford.
Fax no: 01326 211608
D: £19.00-£24.50
S: £19.00-£25.00.
Open: All Year (not Xmas)
Beds: 2F 3D 2T
Baths: 7 En
🛏 🅿 (9) ⅍ ✕ 🍽 🌰 Ⅲ Ⅴ 🔥
Friendly hotel run by Franco-Scottish couple. It has spacious, comfortable and attractive rooms with views of the sea and harbour. Excellent home cooking, table licence, special diets catered for. Lots of ideas for trips and visits for all ages.

(0.5m) *Beachwalk House, 39 Castle Drive, Falmouth, Cornwall, TR11 4NF.*
Actual grid ref: SW826317
Fabulous views, seafront position, overlooks Falmouth Bay, beaches and castle.
Tel: 01326 319841
Mr & Mrs Clarke.
D: £18.00-£20.00
S: £20.00-£25.00.
Open: All Year (not Xmas)
Beds: 3D 1T
Baths: 4 En
🛏 🅿 (4) 🍴 🔥 🌰 Ⅲ Ⅴ 🔥 ⚡

(0.5m) *20 Dracaena Avenue, Falmouth, Cornwall, TR11 2EQ.*
Friendly, comfortable, homely Victorian house.
Tel: 01326 211784 Mr Blowers.
D: £16.00 **S:** £18.00.
Open: Easter to Oct
Beds: 1D 2T
🛏 🅿 (3) 🍴 🔥 🌰 Ⅲ Ⅴ

(0.5m) *Rosemullion Hotel, Gyllyngvase Hill, Falmouth, Cornwall, TR11 4DF.*
Imposing Tudor-style building with balcony rooms, sea view, king-size beds and town centre.
Grades: AA 4 Diamond
Tel: 01326 314690
Mrs Jones.
Fax no: 01326 210098
D: £21.50-£26.00 **S:** £24.50-£26.00.
Open: All Year
Beds: 3T 9D 1S
Baths: 1 En 2 Pr
🅿 ⅍ 🍴 🌰 Ⅲ Ⅴ

(0.25m 🚗) *Ambleside Guest House, 9 Marlborough Road, Falmouth, Cornwall, TR11 3LP.*
Actual grid ref: SW807327
Victorian guest house. Relaxed & friendly.
Tel: 01326 319630
Mr Walker.
D: £18.00 **S:** £18.00.
Open: All Year
Beds: 1F 2D 1T 1S
Baths: 1 Sh
🛏 🅿 🍴 🔥 🌰 Ⅲ Ⅴ 🔥

(0.25m) *Dolvean Hotel, 50 Melvill Road, Falmouth, Cornwall, TR11 4DQ.*
Grades: AA 4 Diamond
Tel: 01326 313658
Mrs Crocker.
Fax no: 01326 313995
D: £23.00-£27.00 **S:** £25.00-£30.00.
Open: All Year (not Xmas)
Beds: 1F 6D 3T 2S
Baths: 12 En
🛏 (12) 🅿 (12) ⅍ 🔥 🌰 Ⅲ Ⅴ 🔥 ⚡
The Dolvean is a traditional Victorian hotel with old fashioned standards of care and courtesy. However, whilst retaining the charm and dignity of yesterday, The Dolvean offers you a warm welcome, today's modern amenities, and just a touch of luxury.

(0.5m) *Castleton Guest House, 68 Killigrew Street, Falmouth, Cornwall, TR11 3PR.*
Convenient to town centre and all local attractions.
Tel: 01326 311072
Mr & Mrs Davies.
Fax no: 01326 317613
D: £16.00-£20.00
S: £20.00-£20.00.
Open: All Year (not Xmas/New Year)
Beds: 2D 3T
Baths: 4 En
🛏 (4) 🍴 🔥 🌰 Ⅲ Ⅴ

(On path 🚗) *The Grove Hotel, Grove Place, Falmouth, Cornwall, TR11 4AU.*
Actual grid ref: SW812324
Harbourside Georgian hotel, friendly atmosphere. Central for all local amenities.
Tel: 01326 319577 Mrs Cumins.
D: £22.00-£24.00 **S:** £22.00-£24.00.
Open: All Year (not Xmas)
Beds: 2F 2D 6T 2S
Baths: 13 En 2 Sh
🛏 🍴 ✕ 🔥 🌰 Ⅲ Ⅴ 🔥 ⚡

(0.5m) *Bosanneth Hotel, Gyllyngvase Hill, Falmouth, Cornwall, TR11 4DW.*
A warm welcome, delightful garden and sea views over Falmouth Bay.
Tel: 01326 314649 (also fax no)
Mrs McGonagle.
D: £24.00-£26.00 **S:** £24.50-£26.00.
Open: Mar to Oct
Beds: 1F 5D 1T 1S
Baths: 8 En
🅿 (7) 🍴 ✕ 🔥 🌰 Ⅲ Ⅴ

(0.5m) *The Seaview Inn, Wodehouse Terrace, Falmouth, Cornwall, TR11 3EP.*
Cornish pub with an excellent range of beers with panoramic views.
Tel: 01326 311359 Mrs Hughes.
Fax no: 01326 210008
D: £17.50-£22.50 **S:** £18.50-£18.50.
Open: All Year (not Xmas)
Beds: 2D 2T 1S
Baths: 1 En 1 Sh
🛏 🍴 ✕ 🔥 🌰 Ⅲ Ⅴ 🔥

(0.5m) *The Clearwater, 59 Melvill Road, Falmouth, Cornwall, TR11 4DF.*
Enjoy modern comfortable quality accommodation close to sandy beaches.
Tel: 01326 311344 Mr Carruthers.
D: £17.00-£22.00 **S:** £17.00-£22.00.
Open: All Year (not Xmas)
Beds: 1F 5D 4T 2S **Baths:** 6 En
🛏 🅿 (10) 🍴 🔥 🌰 Ⅲ Ⅴ 🔥 ⚡

(0.5m) *Ivanhoe, 7 Melvill Road, Falmouth, Cornwall, TR11 4AZ.*
A warm and comfortable guest house with well-equipped, ensuite rooms.
Tel: 01326 319083 (also fax no)
D: £20.00-£25.00 **S:** £20.00-£25.00.
Open: All Year
Beds: 1F 3D 1T 2S
Baths: 4 En 1 Sh
🅿 (4) 🍴 🔥 🌰 Ⅲ Ⅴ

> **Please don't camp on *anyone's* land without first obtaining their permission.**

Gerrans 46

National Grid Ref: SW8735

⚍ ⬤ Royal Standard, Plume of Feathers

(0.5m ⌂) **Harberton House,**
Churchtown Road, Gerrans,
Portscatho, Truro, Cornwall,
TR2 5DZ.
Large traditionally-built family
home with excellent views.
Tel: **01872 580598**
Mr & Mrs Davis.
Fax no: 01872 580789
D: £19.00-£19.00 **S:** £19.00-£19.00.
Open: Easter to Oct
Beds: 1D 1T
Baths: 2 Sh
⛵ ⯅ (6) ⅍ ⌂ ⬥ ▥ Ⓥ ⓘ ⌁

Portscatho 47

⚍ ⬤ Plume of Feathers, The Boat House

(0.25m ⌂) **Hillside House,** 8 The
Square, Portscatho, Truro,
Cornwall, *TR2 5HW.*
Actual grid ref: SW877353
Tel: **01872 580526** Mrs Hart.
Fax no: 01872 580527
D: £17.50-£20.00 **S:** £17.50-£20.00.
Open: All Year
Beds: 1F 2D 1T
Baths: 1 Pr 2 Sh
⛵ ⯅ (2) ⌂ ⬥ ▥ Ⓥ ⓘ ⌁
Charming Georgian house in centre
of unspoilt picturesque fishing vil-
lage. Beaches, harbour, coastal
path only yards away. Comfortable
bedrooms, loads of hot water,
excellent Aga cooking. Children,
dogs and walkers welcome. Those
choosing to visit will find a special
place.

Ruan High Lanes 48

National Grid Ref: SW9039

⚍ ⬤ Kings Arms, New Inn

(0.75m ⌂) **Trenona Farm,** Ruan
High Lanes, Truro, Cornwall,
TR2 5JS.
Victorian farmhouse on mixed
working farm. Enjoy our Cornish
hospitality.
Tel: **01872 501339** (also fax no)
Mrs Carbis.
D: £15.00-£20.00 **S:** £15.00-£20.00.
Open: March to Oct
Beds: 4F
Baths: 2 En 2 Sh
⛵ ⯅ (6) ⅍ ⌂ ⯓ ⬥ Ⓥ ⓘ

(0.75m ⌂) **Trenestall Farm,** Ruan
High Lanes, Truro, Cornwall,
TR2 5LX.
Family-run farm on central
Roseland Peninsula close to sea.
Tel: **01872 501259** Mrs Palmer.
D: £16.00-£18.00 **S:** £15.00.
Open: Feb to Nov
Beds: 1D 2T
Baths: 2 Sh
⛵ ⯅ (6) ⅍ ⌂ ⯓ ✕ ▥ ⬥ ⓘ ⌁

Veryan 49

National Grid Ref: SW9139

⚍ ⬤ New Inn

(1m) **The New Inn,** Veryan, Truro,
Cornwall, *TR2 5QA.*
Tel: **01872 501362** Mr Gayton.
Fax no: 01872 501078
D: £22.50-£22.50 **S:** £22.50-£32.50.
Open: All Year (not Xmas)
Beds: 1D 1T 1S
Baths: 2 En 1 Sh
⌂ ✕ ⬥ ▥ Ⓥ ⅍
The inn is based on a pair of C16th
cottages. The single bar is welcom-
ing and unspoilt. Situated in a
beautiful village close by safe
bathing beaches. Renowned locally
for a high standard of catering.

Portloe 50

National Grid Ref: SW9339

(On path) **Pine Cottage,** Portloe,
Truro, Cornwall, *TR2 5QU.*
Actual grid ref: SW935395
Friendly welcome, peaceful fishing
village, award-winning home cook-
ing.
Tel: **01872 501385** Mrs
Holdsworth.
D: £30.00-£35.00 **S:** £35.00-£40.00.
Open: Easter to Oct
Beds: 1D 1T
Baths: 1 En 1 Private
⛵ ⅍ ⯓ ✕ ⓘ ⌁

Boswinger 51

National Grid Ref: SW9840

(⬆ 0.25m) **Boswinger Youth
Hostel,** Boswinger, Gorran, St
Austell, Cornwall, PL26 6LL.
Actual grid ref: SW991411
Tel: **01726 843234**
Under 18: £6.90 **Adults:** £10.00
Self-catering facilities, Laundry
facilities, Lounge, Dining room,
Drying room, Cycle store, Parking,
Evening meal at 7.00pm, No smok-
ing, WC, Kitchen facilities,
Breakfast available, Credit cards
accepted
Stone-built cottages and a convert-
ed barn in area with outstanding
coastal scenery. Sandy bathing
beaches nearby.

(1m ⌂) **The Granary,** Boswinger,
Gorran, St Austell, Cornwall,
PL26 6LL.
Actual grid ref: SW991410
Comfortable bedrooms.
Scrumptious breakfasts/suppers.
Spectacular sea views. Warm
welcome.
Tel: **01726 844381** Chubb.
D: £16.00-£19.00 **S:** £18.00-£22.00.
Open: All Year (not Xmas/New
Year)
Beds: 2D 1T
Baths: 2 Pr 1 Sh
⛵ ⯅ (3) ⌂ ✕ ⬥ ▥ Ⓥ ⓘ ⌁

Gorran Haven 52

National Grid Ref: SX0041

⚍ ⬤ Barleysheaf, Llawnroc Inn

(0.25m) **Homestead,** 34 Chute
Lane, Gorran Haven, St Austell,
Cornwall, *PL26 6NU.*
Cottage/ beach 100m/ overlooking
garden/ parking/ easy reach
Heligon/ Eden.
Tel: **01726 842567**
Mr & Mrs Smith.
D: £25.00-£25.00 **S:** £50.00-£50.00.
Open: All Year
Beds: 1T 1D
Baths: 2 Pr
⯅ ⅍ ▥

(On path) **Piggys Pantry,** The
Willows, Gorran Haven, St Austell,
Cornwall, *PL26 6JG.*
Detached family bungalow with
large garden, near safe, sandy
beach.
Tel: **01726 843545** Mrs Mott.
D: £20.00-£20.00 **S:** £20.00-£20.00.
Open: All Year (not Xmas)
Beds: 1D 1T
Baths: 2 Sh
⛵ ⯅ (5) ⅍ ⌂ ⯓ ✕ ⬥ ▥ Ⓥ ⓘ ⌁

(0.25m) **Wosteweth,** Wansford
Meadow, Gorran Haven, St Austell,
Cornwall, *PL26 6HU.*
Dormer bungalow close to sandy
beaches and Heligan Gardens.
Tel: **01726 843934** Mr Howe.
D: £18.00-£18.00 **S:** £20.00-£20.00.
Open: All Year (not Xmas)
Beds: 2D 1T
Baths: 1 En 2 Pr
⯅ (5) ⅍ ⌂ ⬥ ⓘ ⌁

Mevagissey 53

National Grid Ref: SX0145

(0.25m) **Mevagissey House,**
Vicarage Hill, Mevagissey, St
Austell, *PL26 6SZ.*
Peaceful Georgian house in three
acres, close to Eden Project.
Tel: **01726 842427**
Mrs Dodds.
Fax no: 01726 844327
D: £20.00-£25.00 **S:** £30.00-£35.00.
Open: March to October
Beds: 1F 1T 1D
Baths: 3 En
⛵ ⯅ (8) ⌂ ⯓ ⬥ ▥ Ⓥ ⌁

(0.25m) **Kerryanna,** Valley Road,
Mevagissey, St Austell, Cornwall,
PL26 6RZ.
Stunning position overlooking vil-
lage close to Heligan and Eden.
Grades: ETC 4 Diamond,
AA 4 Diamond
Tel: **01726 843558** (also fax no)
Mr Hennah.
D: £24.00-£27.00 .
Open: Easter to Oct
Beds: 1F 1T 4D
Baths: 6 En
⛵ (5) ⯅ (6) ⌂ ✕ ⬥ ▥ Ⓥ

Pentewan 54

National Grid Ref: SX0147

⚑ Ship Inn

(0.25m) *Piskey Cove, The Square, Pentewan, St Austell, Cornwall, PL26 6DA.*
Tel: **01726 843781** (also fax no)
Ms Avery.
D: £22.50-£35.00 **S:** £22.50-£30.00.
Open: All Year (not Xmas/New Year)
Beds: 1F 2T 3D **Baths:** 3 En 1 Pr
🛏 🅿 (1) 🖵 🦮 ✕ ♨ Ⓥ 🛉 ⬥
Close to 'The Eden Project' and Heligan Gardens. Family run and situated in peaceful, pretty coastal village. Ideal base for cosy winter, refreshing spring, British summer and beautiful autumn breaks, to visit Cornwall's sites. Complimentary and sports therapy in house.

(0.25m) *Willow Brook, North Rd, Pentewan, Cornwall, PL26 6DG.*
Lovely riverside house, main bedroom overlooks garden to water's edge.
Tel: **01726 844292** Mrs Mersy.
D: £17.50-£20.00 **S:** £20.00-£25.00.
Open: All Year
Beds: 2D **Baths:** 1 Pr
🅿 (2) ⊬ 🖵 ♨ 🎞 Ⓥ ⬥

**Taking your dog?
Book *in advance*
ONLY with owners
who accept dogs (🦮)**

**D = Price range per
person sharing in a
double room**

St Austell 55

National Grid Ref: SX0252

⚑ Britannia Inn, Polgooth Inn, Western Inn

(1m) *Crossways, 6 Cromwell Road, St Austell, Cornwall, PL25 4PS.*
Beaches, golf, Heligan, Eden Project, coastal walks nearby. Contractor welcome.
Tel: **01726 77436**
Mrs Nancarrow.
Fax no: 01726 66877
D: £16.00-£25.00
S: £22.00-£26.00.
Open: All Year
Beds: 2F 2D 1T 1S
Baths: 1 En 1 Sh
🅿 ⊬ 🖵 🦮 ♨ 🎞 Ⓥ 🛉

(1m) *Cornerways Guest House, Penwinnick Road, St Austell, Cornwall, PL25 5DS.*
Cornerways stands in its own grounds surrounded by garden/large car park.
Tel: **01726 61579**
Edwards.
Fax no: 01726 66871
D: £16.50-£19.00
S: £16.50-£22.50.
Open: All Year
Beds: 1F 1T 1S
Baths: 2 En 1Shared
🅿 (10) 🖵 🦮 ♨ 🎞 Ⓥ ⬥

(3m) *Poltarrow Farm, St Mewan, St Austell, Cornwall, PL26 7DR.*
Tel: **01726 67111** (also fax no)
Mrs Nancarrow.
D: £23.00-£25.00 **S:** £28.00-£30.00.
Open: All Year (not Xmas/New Year)
Beds: 1F 3D 1T
Baths: 4 En 1 Pr
🛏 🅿 (10) 🖵 ♨ 🎞 Ⓥ
The charming farmhouse at Poltarrow, with pretty ensuite rooms, delicious breakfast and all year indoor swimming pool. Can be the perfect place to stay any time of year. Secluded, yet central for beaches, gardens and the exciting Eden Project.

Par 56

National Grid Ref: SX0753

(0.25m) *Hidden Valley Gardens, Treesmill, Par, Cornwall, PL24 2TU.*
Secluded location. Near Eden Project and Fowey, in own grounds.
Tel: **01208 873225**
D: £20.00-£22.00
S: £22.00-£24.00.
Open: Easter to Oct
Beds: 2D
Baths: 2 En
🅿 (7) ⊬ ♨ 🎞 Ⓥ

**All paths are
popular: you are
well-advised to
book ahead**

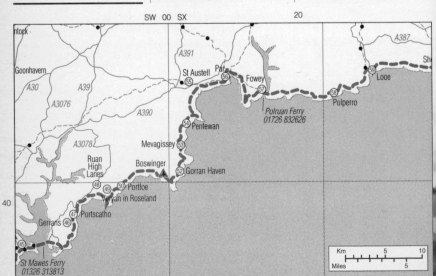

All rooms full and nowhere else to stay? Ask the owner if there's anywhere nearby

---

Fowey 57

National Grid Ref: SX1251

|○| ◀ Fowey Galleon, Polruan Galleon, Old Ferry Inn, The Ship, Safe Harbour

(0.5m) *Safe Harbour Hotel,*
Lostwithiel Road, Fowey,
Cornwall, PL23 1BD.
Friendly inn, river views, car parking, quiet lounge bar, full menu available.
Tel: **01726 833379**
D: £21.00-£25.00
S: £25.00-£25.00.
Open: All Year
Beds: 2F 2D 1T
Baths: 5 En
⛺ 🅿 (8) ⊬ 🖵 🕇 🗶 ♨ 🎔 Ⅵ ⓐ ⚡

(0.5m) *St Keverne, 4 Daglands Road, Fowey, Cornwall, PL23 1JL.*
Comfortable Edwardian house close to town centre, with river views
Tel: **01726 833164**
Mrs Eardley.
D: £20.00-£20.00
S: £20.00-£20.00.
Open: All Year (not Xmas/ New Year)
Beds: 2D
Baths: 2 En
🅿 (1) ⊬ 🖵 🕇 ♨ Ⅵ ⓐ ⚡

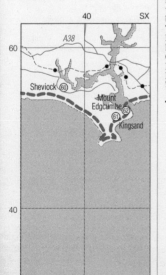

(On path 🚐) *Coombe Farm,*
Coombe, Fowey, Cornwall,
PL23 1HW.
Charming farmhouse overlooking walled garden, serving cream teas. Sea views.
Tel: **01726 833123** Mrs Paull.
D: £15.50-£22.50 S: £17.50-£25.00.
Open: All Year
Beds: 1D 1T **Baths:** 1 En
⛺ 🅿 🕇 ♨ ⓐ ⚡

(0.5m 🚐) *Carnethic House,*
Lambs Barn, Fowey, Cornwall,
PL23 1HQ.
Regency house, 2 acres mature gardens. Parking. Family run.
Grades: ETC 4 Diamond,
AA 4 Diamond
Tel: **01726 833336** Mr Hogg.
Fax no: 01726 833296
D: £25.00-£35.00 S: £40.00-£50.00.
Open: Feb to Nov
Beds: 1F 5D 2T **Baths:** 7 En 1 Sh
⛺ 🅿 🖵 🕇 🗶 ♨ ▥ Ⅵ ⚡

Polperro 58

National Grid Ref: SX2050

|○| ◀ Old Mill House, Three Pilchards, Penryn House, Crumplehorn Inn

(0.5m) *Crumplehorn Inn,*
Polperro, Cornwall, PL13 2RJ.
Actual grid ref: SX206515
Inn & watermill in quaint Cornish fishing village. B&B, S/C, 2-8.
Tel: **01503 272348**
Andrew & Joanne Taylor.
D: £22.50-£32.50 S: £27.50-£60.00.
Open: All Year
Beds: 4F 3T 3D **Baths:** 10 Pr
⛺ 🅿 🕇 🗶 ♨ ▥ Ⅵ ⓐ ⚡

(0.5m) *Little Tregue, Langreek Road, Polperro, Cornwall, PL13 2PR.*
Pretty country cottage near sea and village, tranquil surroundings, great breakfasts.
Tel: **01503 272758** (also fax no)
Ms Kellaway.
D: £15.00-£20.00 S: £15.00-£30.00.
Open: All Year (not Xmas/ New Year)
Beds: 1F 1T **Baths:** 2 En 1 Sh
⛺ 🅿 (30) 🖵 🕇 ♨ Ⅵ ⓐ ⚡

The Grid Reference beneath the location heading is for the village or town - *not* for individual houses, which are shown (where supplied) in each entry itself.

🚐 sign means that, *given due notice,* owners will pick you up from the path and drop you off *within reason.*

(0.25m) *Penryn House Hotel, The Coombes, Polperro, Looe, Cornwall, PL13 2RQ.*
Charming Victorian hotel in village centre close to path and harbour.
Tel: **01503 272157** Ms Kay.
Fax no: 01503 273055
D: £24.00-£30.00 S: £32.00-£38.00.
Open: All Year
Beds: 9D 1T **Baths:** 10 En
⛺ 🅿 (16) 🖵 🕇 ♨ ▥ Ⅵ ⓐ ⚡

(0.25m) *Chyavallon, Landaviddy Lane, Polperro, Looe, Cornwall, PL13 2RT.*
Situated in central village with views towards the harbour and sea.
Tel: **01503 272788**
D: £17.00-£19.50 S: £20.00-£30.00.
Open: All Year (not Xmas)
Beds: 2D 1T **Baths:** 3 En
⛺ 🅿 (3) 🖵 🕇 ♨ ▥ Ⅵ ⓐ ⚡

Looe 59

National Grid Ref: SX2553

|○| ◀ Harbour Moon, Salutation Arms, Jolly Sailors, Harbour Moon, The Ship, Ye Olde Salvation Inne, Killarney Hotel, Tom Sawyers Inn, Dagger

(On path) *The Beach House, Marine Drive, Looe, Cornwall, PL13 2DH.*
Tel: **01503 262598**
Fax no: 01503 262298
D: £20.00-£28.00 S: £25.00-£38.00.
Open: All Year
Beds: 2T 3D **Baths:** 4 En 1 Pr
⛺ (12) 🅿 (5) ⊬ 🖵 ♨ ▥ Ⅵ ⓐ ⚡
On the sea front / SW coastal path, we enjoy uninterrupted views of Looe Bay. Ideally placed for boating, fishing, diving, rambling or bird watching, we aim to offer quality, comfort, stunning sea views, delicious breakfasts and a very special welcome.

(On path) *Marwinthy Guest House, East Cliff, Looe, Cornwall, PL13 1DE.*
Actual grid ref: SX256533
Small friendly guest house, on coastal footpath overlooking beach. In Which? Guide.
Tel: **01503 264382** Mawby.
D: £17.00 S: £17.00.
Open: All Year
Beds: 2F 2D 1T **Baths:** 2 Pr 1 Sh
⛺ (4) 🖵 🕇 ♨ Ⅵ ⓐ ⚡

(0.25m) *Tidal Court, 3 Church
Street, Looe, Cornwall, PL13 2EX.*
Tel: **01503 263695** Mrs Hocking.
D: £16.00-£21.00 **S:** £16.00-£25.00.
Open: All Year (not Xmas)
Beds: 3F 1D 1T 1S
Baths: 5 En 1 Pr
⛱ 🅿 (3) 🗗 ♁ ⬚ 🎞 Ⅴ ✦
Tidal court is situated in floral
award-winning street just 50 yards
from harbour central for coast and
woodland walks. Various boating
activities and shoreline safaris.

(On path) *Schooner Point Guest
House, 1 Trelawney Terrace,
Polperro Road, Looe, Cornwall,
PL13 2AG.*
Actual grid ref: SX252537
Family guest house, river views,
close to centre and beach.
Tel: **01503 262670**
Mr & Mrs Neaves.
D: £14.00-£20.00 **S:** £14.00-£17.00.
Open: Jan to Nov
Beds: 1F 3D 2S **Baths:** 2 En 1 Sh
⛱ 🅿 (2) 🗗 ♁ 🎞 Ⅴ ▮

(0.25m) *Sea Haze, Polperro Road,
Looe, PL13 2JS.*
Country/ sea views friendly family,
award winning garden, good food.
Tel: **01503 262708** (also fax no)
Mr & Mrs Dearsley.
D: £17.00-£20.00 **S:** £17.00-£20.00.
Open: All Year (not Xmas)
Beds: 1F 4D 1T **Baths:** 1 En 2 Sh
⛱ (2) 🅿 (7) ⊬ 🗗 ♁ 🎞 & Ⅴ

(On path) *Sea Breeze Guest
House, Lower Chapel Street, Looe,
Cornwall, PL13 1AT.*
In Old Looe, close to beach, har-
bour, restaurants and shops.
Tel: **01503 263131** Mr Jenkin.
Fax no: 01503 263131
D: £16.00-£21.00 **S:** £16.00-£20.00.
Open: All Year
Beds: 4D 1T **Baths:** 3 Pr 1 Sh
⛱ 🅿 (2) 🗗 ♁ ⬚ 🎞 Ⅴ ▮ ✦

(0.25m) *Westcliff Hotel,
Hannafore Road, Looe, Cornwall,
PL13 2DE.*
A family run hotel where a friendly
welcome awaits you.
Tel: **01503 262500**
Mr & Mrs Petrie.
D: £15.00-£17.00 **S:** £15.00-£17.00.
Open: March to Nov
Beds: 4F 2D 4T 2S
Baths: 4 Sh
⛱ 🅿 (6) ⊬ 🗗 ♁ 🗙 ⬚ 🎞 Ⅴ ▮

(On path) *Kantara Guest House, 7
Trelawny Terrace, Looe,
Cornwall, PL13 2AG.*
Comfortable family-run guest
house convenient for harbour,
beach and town.
Tel: **01503 262093**
Mr & Mrs Storer.
D: £14.00-£16.00 **S:** £14.00-£16.00.
Open: All Year
Beds: 3F 4D 2T 3S
Baths: 4 Sh
⛱ 🅿 (1) 🗗 ♁ 🗙 ⬚ 🎞 ▮ ✦

(0.75m) *Bucklawren Farm, St
Martin, Looe, Cornwall, PL13 1NZ.*
Beautiful farmhouse in the country-
side beside the sea.
Grades: ETC 4 Diamond, Silver
Tel: **01503 240738** Mrs Henly.
Fax no: 01503 240481
D: £22.00-£25.00 **S:** £27.00-£30.00.
Open: Mar to Oct
Beds: 2F 2T 2D
Baths: 6 En
⛱ (5) 🅿 (6) 🗗 ♁ 🗙 ⬚ 🎞 & Ⅴ ✦

(On path) *Trevanion Hotel,
Hannafore Road, Looe, Cornwall,
PL13 2DE.*
Turn of century residence, over-
looking river, beach, harbour. 20 m
headland.
Grades: ETC 3 Diamond
Tel: **01503 262003** Mr Fildes.
Fax no: 01503 265408
D: £17.66-£26.50 **S:** £19.66-£28.50.
Open: All Year
Beds: 2F 6D 2S **Baths:** 10 En
⛱ 🅿 (5) 🗗 ♁ 🗙 ⬚ 🎞 Ⅴ ▮ ✦

(0.5m) *Killarney Hotel, Shutta
Road, Looe, Cornwall, PL13 1HW.*
Charming licensed Victorian hotel
overlooking harbour. Stunning
views, intimate bar.
Tel: **01503 262307** Mr Charnock.
D: £17.50-£21.00 **S:** £17.50-£21.00.
Open: All Year (not Xmas)
Beds: 2F 6D 1T 1S
Baths: 6 En 1 Sh
⛱ (7) 🅿 (3) 🗗 ♁ 🗙 ⬚ 🎞 Ⅴ

(0.25m) *Grasmere Guest House, St
Martins Road, East Looe, Looe,
Cornwall, PL13 1LP.*
Actual grid ref: 5X255542
Clean, comfortable, friendly, guest
house with splendid river views.
Tel: **01503 262556** Mr Eveleigh.
D: £15.00-£16.00 **S:** £15.00-£20.00.
Open: All Year (not Xmas)
Beds: 2F 3D **Baths:** 1 Sh
⛱ (3) 🅿 (5) 🗗 🗙 ⬚ 🎞 Ⅴ ▮

(0.25m) *Driftwood, Portuan Road,
Hannafore, Looe, Cornwall,
PL13 2DN.*
Lovely house, superb sea and
island views, quiet area, parking.
Tel: **01503 262990** (also fax no)
Mr Pickering.
D: £17.00-£24.00 **S:** £17.00-£24.00.
Open: All Year (not Xmas)
Beds: 2F 1D
Baths: 2 En 1 Sh
⛱ ⊬ 🗗 ♁ ⬚ 🎞 Ⅴ ✦

Sheviock   60

National Grid Ref: SX3755

🍴 🍺 Finnygook Inn

(1m 🚍) *Sheviock Barton,
Sheviock, Torpoint, Cornwall, PL11
3EH.*
Beautifully restored 300-year-old
farmhouse. Guests' sitting room.
Tel: **01503 230793** (also fax no)
Mr Johnson.
D: £20.00-£20.00 **S:** £25.00-£25.00.
Open: all year (not Xmas)
Beds: 1F 2D
Baths: 2 En 1 Pr
⛱ 🅿 (10) ⊬ 🗗 ♁ ⬚ 🎞 Ⅴ ✦

Kingsand   61

National Grid Ref: SX4350

🍴 🍺 Halfway House, Rising Sun

(0.25m 🚍) *Cliff House, Devon
Port Hill, Kingsand, Torpoint,
Cornwall, PL10 1NT.*
Listed comfortable house. Sea and
country views. Great wholefood
cookery.
Tel: **01752 823110**
Mrs Heasman.
Fax no: 01752 822595
D: £21.00-£25.00 **S:** £25.00-£35.00.
Open: All Year
Beds: 3F 3T 2D
Baths: 3 En 3 Pr
⛱ 🅿 (3) ⊬ 🗗 ♁ ⬚ 🎞 Ⅴ ▮ ✦

(On path) *Clarendon, Garrett
Street, Cawsand, Kingsand,
Torpoint, Cornwall, PL10 1PD.*
Cornish fishing village. Close to
Mount Edgecombe Park. Resident
chef.
Tel: **01752 823460**
Mrs Goodwright.
D: £16.00-£18.00 .
Open: All Year (not Xmas/New
Year)
Beds: 1D 1T 1S
Baths: 1 Sh
⛱ (5) 🎞 ▮

(0.25m 🚐) *Algoma, The Green, Kingsand, Cawsand Bay, Cornwall, PL10 1NH.*
Actual grid ref: SX434506
Family run guest house in picturesque, unspoilt village overlooking Plymouth Sound.
Tel: **01752 822706**
Mr Ogilvie.
D: £20.00-£20.00
S: £20.00-£40.00.
Open: All Year (not Xmas/ New Year)
Beds: 1F 1D
Baths: 2 En
🛇 🖵 ⚽ 🖳 Ⓥ 🛇 ⚡

Mount Edgcumbe   62
National Grid Ref: SX4552

(On path) *Friary Manor Hotel, Maker Heights, Mount Edgcumbe, Millbrook, Torpoint, Cornwall, PL10 1JB.*
Actual grid ref: SX435517
C17th former Vicarage. Close to sea and smugglers villages.
Tel: **01752 822112** Mrs Bartlett.
Fax no: 01752 822804
D: £22.50-£29.00 **S:** £35.00-£41.50.
Open: All Year
Beds: 3F 3D 3T 2S **Baths:** 6 En 1 Pr
🛇 🅿 (25) 🖵 🛏 ✕ ⚽ 🖳 Ⓥ 🛇 ⚡

High season,

bank holidays

and

special events mean

low availability

everywhere.

South Devon

This section of the **South West Coast Path** runs from the great sprawl of Plymouth, past numerous river estuaries and inlets to the border with Dorset, just before Lyme Regis (see beginning of chapter for more **South West Coast Path** details).

Guides: *South West Way: Vol II* (Penzance to Poole) by Martin Collins (ISBN 1 85284 026 9), published by Cicerone Press and available from the publishers (2 Police Square, Milnthorpe, Cumbria, LA7 7PY, 01539 562069), £8.99
South West Way: Falmouth to Exmouth by Brian Le Messurier (ISBN 1 85410 3881), published by Aurum Press in association with the Countryside Commission and Ordnance Survey, £10.99
South West Way: Exmouth to Poole by Roland Tarr (ISBN 1 85410 389X), published by Aurum Press in association with the Countryside Commission and Ordnance Survey, £10.99. There is also invaluable local information in *The South West Way 2001* by the **South West Way Association**, available directly from them at 25 Clobells, South Brent, Devon, TQ10 9JW, tel. 01364 73859, £7.00 (inc. p&p)

Maps: Ordnance Survey 1:50,000 Landranger series: 192, 193, 201 and 202

Plymouth 1

National Grid Ref: SX4756

|o| ⬛ West Hoe, Brown Bear, Odd Wheel, Eddystone Inn, The Walrus, Sippers, The Yardarm, Frog & Frigate, Waterfront, Notte Inn

(▲ 0.5m) *Plymouth Youth Hostel,* Belmont House, Devonport Road, Stoke, Plymouth, Devon, PL3 4DW.
Actual grid ref: SX461555
Tel: **01752 562189**
Under 18: £7.75
Adults: £11.00
Self-catering facilities, Television, Showers, Wet weather shelter, Lounge, Games room, Drying room, Cycle store, Parking, Evening meal at 7.00pm, Kitchen facilities, Breakfast available, Luggage store, Credit cards accepted
Classical Greek-style house built in 1820 for a wealthy banker, set in own grounds, within easy walking distance of the city centre.

(▲ 0.5m) *Plymouth Backpackers' Hostel,* 172 Citadel Road, The Hoe, Plymouth, Devon, PL1 3DB.
Actual grid ref: SX483537
Tel: **01752 225158**
Adults: £7.50

(0.5m) *Mountbatten Hotel,* 52 Exmouth Road, Stoke, Plymouth, Devon, PL1 4QH.
Grades: ETC 3 Diamond
Tel: **01752 563843** Mr Hendy.
Fax no: 01752 606014
D: £23.00-£25.00 **S:** £20.00-£27.00.
Open: All Year
Beds: 3F 6D 2T 4S
Baths: 7 En 2 Sh
⛅ 🅿 (4) 🗙 ⌨ ⊁ 🍴 📺 🖥 📶
Small licensed Victorian hotel over-looking parkland with river views. Quiet cul de sac. Close city centre/ferryport. Good access Cornwall. Walking distance Naval base, Royal Fleet Club, FE College. Secure parking. Well appointed rooms. Tea/coffee, CTVs, telephones. Credit cards accepted.

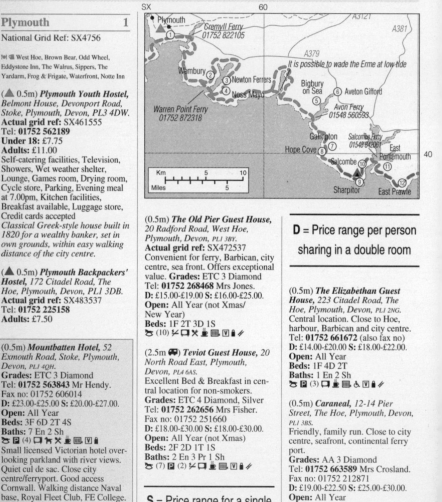

It is possible to wade the Erme at low tide

Gremyll Ferry 01752 822105
Warren Point Ferry 01752 872318
Avon Ferry 01548 560593
Salcombe Ferry 01548 842061

Wembury · Newton Ferrers · Noss Mayo · Bigbury on Sea · Aveton Gifford · Galmpton · Hope Cove · Salcombe · East Portlemouth · Sharpitor · East Prawle

(0.5m) *The Old Pier Guest House,* 20 Radford Road, West Hoe, Plymouth, Devon, PL1 3BY.
Actual grid ref: SX472537
Convenient for ferry, Barbican, city centre, sea front. Offers exceptional value. **Grades:** ETC 3 Diamond
Tel: **01752 268468** Mrs Jones.
D: £15.00-£19.00 **S:** £16.00-£25.00.
Open: All Year (not Xmas/New Year)
Beds: 1F 2T 3D 1S
⛅ (10) ⊁ ⌨ 🗙 🍴 📶 📺

(2.5m 🚗) *Teviot Guest House,* 20 North Road East, Plymouth, Devon, PL4 6AS.
Excellent Bed & Breakfast in central location for non-smokers.
Grades: ETC 4 Diamond, Silver
Tel: **01752 262656** Mrs Fisher.
Fax no: 01752 251660
D: £18.00-£30.00 **S:** £18.00-£30.00.
Open: All Year (not Xmas)
Beds: 2F 2D 1T 1S
Baths: 2 En 3 Pr 1 Sh
⛅ (7) 🅿 (2) ⊁ ⌨ ⊁ 🍴 📺 🖥 📶

S = Price range for a single person in a single room

D = Price range per person sharing in a double room

(0.5m) *The Elizabethan Guest House,* 223 Citadel Road, The Hoe, Plymouth, Devon, PL1 2NG.
Central location. Close to Hoe, harbour, Barbican and city centre.
Tel: **01752 661672** (also fax no)
D: £14.00-£20.00 **S:** £18.00-£22.00.
Open: All Year
Beds: 1F 4D 2T
Baths: 1 En 2 Sh
⛅ 🅿 (3) ⌨ ⊁ 🍴 ♿ 📺 📶

(0.5m) *Caraneal,* 12-14 Pier Street, The Hoe, Plymouth, Devon, PL1 3BS.
Friendly, family run. Close to city centre, seafront, continental ferry port.
Grades: AA 3 Diamond
Tel: **01752 663589** Mrs Crosland.
Fax no: 01752 212871
D: £19.00-£22.50 **S:** £25.00-£30.00.
Open: All Year
Beds: 1F 6D 1T 1S
Baths: 9 En
⛅ 🅿 (2) ⌨ 🗙 ⊁ 🍴 📺 📶

(0.5m) *Sunray Hotel, 3/5 Alfred Street, The Hoe, Plymouth, Devon, PL1 2RP.*
Centrally located, convenient for theatre, shops, Barbican and National Aquarium.
Tel: **01752 669113** Mr Sutton.
Fax no: 01752 268969
D: £23.00-£26.00 S: £28.00-£35.00.
Open: All Year (not Xmas/New Year)
Beds: 6F 4D 5T 3S
Baths: 16 En 2 Pr
🅿 (6) ⌨ 🛏 ♨ 💷 ⓥ ⓐ ⚡

(1m) *Olivers Hotel & Restaurant, 33 Sutherland Road, Plymouth, Devon, PL4 6BN.*
Actual grid ref: SX481555
Welcoming, restful Victorian hotel convenient for City, Sea and Moors.
Grades: RAC 4 Diamond
Tel: **01752 663923** Mrs Purser.
Fax no: 01752 262295
D: £22.50-£25.00 S: £20.00-£30.00.
Open: All Year
Beds: 1F 2D 1T 2S
Baths: 4 En 1 Sh
🛏 (11) 🅿 (2) ⌨ ✕ ♨ 💷 ⓥ

(0.5m) *Georgian House Hotel, 51 Citadel Road, The Hoe, Plymouth, PL1 3AU.*
Family-run hotel in central location near all Plymouth's amenities.
Grades: AA 3 Diamond
Tel: **01752 663237**
D: £19.00-£22.00 S: £22.00-£29.00.
Open: Feb to Dec
Beds: 6D 2T 2S **Baths:** 10 En
🛏 ✂ ⌨ ♨ 💷 ⓥ ⓐ

(On path) *Osmond Guest House, 42 Pier Street, West Hoe, Plymouth, Devon, PL1 3BT.*
Seafront Edwardian house. Walking distance to all attractions. Courtesy pick-up from stations.
Tel: **01752 229705** Mrs Richards.
Fax no: 01752 269655
D: £16.00-£20.00 S: £17.00-£25.00.
Open: All Year
Beds: 3D 2T 1S **Baths:** 4 En
🅿 (2) ⌨ 🛏 ♨ 💷 & ⓥ ⓐ

(0.5m) *Hotspur Guest House, 108 North Road East, Plymouth, Devon, PL4 6AW.*
Victorian property, adjacent city centre; bus/rail stations, historic Barbican, Hoe, seafronts.
Tel: **01752 663928** Taylor.
Fax no: 01752 261493
D: £16.00-£17.00 S: £16.50-£17.50.
Open: All Year (not Xmas)
Beds: 2F 1D 2T 3S
🛏 ⌨ 🛏 ✕ ♨ 💷 ⓥ ⓐ

Bringing children with you? Always ask for any special rates.

(0.5m) *Sydney Guest House, 181 North Road West, Plymouth, Devon, PL1 5DE.*
Situated in the heart of the city near the railway, ferry, port, university.
Tel: **01752 266541** Mrs Puckey.
Fax no: 01333 310573
D: £25.00-£45.00 S: £14.00-£25.00.
Open: All Year
Beds: 1F 2D 2T 3S
Baths: 3 En
🛏 ⌨ ✕ 💷

(0.5m) *Rusty Anchor, 30 Grand Parade, West Hoe, Plymouth, Devon, PL1 3DJ.*
Situated on the sea front, walking distance city centre, Hoe.
Tel: **01752 663924** (also fax no)
Ms Turner.
D: £15.00-£25.00
S: £15.00-£30.00.
Open: All Year (not Xmas)
Beds: 4F 1D 2T 2S
Baths: 3 En 3 Pr 2 Sh
🛏 ⌨ 🛏 ✕ ♨ 💷 ⓥ ⓐ ⚡

(0.5m) *Cassandra Guest House, 13 Crescent Avenue, The Hoe, Plymouth, Devon, PL1 3AN.*
Ideally situated for city centre, seafront, Barbican, Ferry, port, theatres, stations.
Tel: **01752 220715** (also fax no)
D: £17.00-£20.00 S: £17.00-£26.00.
Open: All Year
Beds: 3F 1D 1T 1S
Baths: 2 En 1 Pr 1 Sh
🛏 ✂ ⌨ 🛏 ♨ 💷 ⓥ ⚡

Wembury 2

National Grid Ref: SX5248

🍴 🍺 Odd Wheel, Eddystone Inn

(On path 🚲) *Bay Cottage, 150 Church Road, Wembury, Plymouth, Devon, PL9 0HR.*
Actual grid ref: SX520486
Victorian cottage by the sea, surrounded by National Trust land.
Grades: ETC 3 Diamond
Tel: **01752 862559** (also fax no)
Mrs Farrington.
D: £26.00-£29.00
S: £25.00-£35.00.
Open: All Year (not Xmas)
Beds: 2D 2T 1S
Baths: 3 En 2 Sh
🛏 🅿 (2) ✂ ⌨ 🛏 ♨ 💷 ⓥ ⓐ ⚡

(0.75m 🚲) *Willowhayes, Near Post Office, Ford Road, Wembury, Plymouth, Devon, PL9 0JA.*
Actual grid ref: SX524494
Comfortable house, sea/country views.
Tel: **01752 862581**
Mrs Mills.
D: £12.50-£17.50
S: £15.00-£25.00.
Open: All Year (not Xmas/New Year)
Beds: 1S 2D 1T
Baths: 1 En 1 Sh
🛏 🅿 (4) ✂ ⌨ 🛏 ♨ 💷 ⓥ

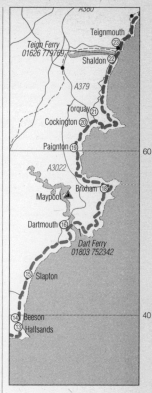

Newton Ferrers 3

National Grid Ref: SX5448

🍴 🍺 Dartmoor Inn, Dolphin Inn, Swan Inn, Ship Inn

(1m) *Crown Yealm, Bridgend Hill, Newton Ferrers, Plymouth, Devon, PL8 1AW.*
Actual grid ref: SX5447
Beautiful riverside country house. All guest rooms overlook garden to water's edge.
Tel: **01752 872365** (also fax no)
Mrs Johnson.
D: £17.00-£22.00 S: £21.00-£30.00.
Open: All Year
Beds: 1F 1D 1T
Baths: 2 En 1 Sh
🛏 🅿 (7) ⌨ 🛏 ♨ 💷 ⓥ ⓐ ⚡

(1m 🚲) *Wood Cottage, Bridgend, Newton Ferrers, Plymouth, Devon, PL8 1AW.*
Welcoming, modernised cottage, overlooking end of Yealm Estuary and farmland.
Tel: **01752 872372**
Mrs Cross.
D: £17.50-£20.00 S: £20.00-£22.50.
Open: All Year
Beds: 1T 1D
Baths: 1 En 1 Sh
🛏 🅿 (2) ⌨ 🛏 ✕ ♨ 💷 ⓥ ⓐ ⚡

(1m) *Broadmoor Farm, Newton Ferrers, Plymouth, Devon, PL8 2NE.*
A warm welcome awaits on our working sheep farm situated picturesque South Hams.
Tel: **01752 880407** Mrs German.
D: £18.00-£20.00 **S:** £18.00-£20.00.
Open: All Year
Beds: 1D 1T 1S
Baths: 2 En 1 Sh
🛇 🅿 ⛌ ⚲ 🛏 Ⅲ. Ⓥ ◈

Noss Mayo 4

National Grid Ref: SX5447

⦂◖ Old Ship Inn, Swan Inn

(0.5m 🚗) *Rowden House, Stoke Road, Noss Mayo, Plymouth, Devon, PL8 1JG.*
Actual grid ref: SX555472
Victorian farmhouse with lovely garden in peaceful rural setting.
Tel: **01752 872153** Mrs Hill.
D: £20.00-£20.00 **S:** £20.00-£20.00.
Open: All Year (not Xmas)
Beds: 1F 2T
Baths: 2 Pr
🛇 🅿 (6) ⛌ ⚲ 🛏 Ⅲ. Ⓥ ◈ ⚮

Bigbury on Sea 5

National Grid Ref: SX6544

(0.25m 🚗) *Folly Foot, Challaborough, Bigbury On Sea, Kingsbridge, TQ7 4JB.*
50m sandy beach/ South West Way. Friendly welcome, bungalow.
Tel: **01548 810036**
D: £20.00-£26.00 **S:** £20.00-£25.00.
Open: Feb-Oct
Beds: 1F 2D 1S
Baths: 2 En 1 Sh
🛇 (6) 🅿 (6) ⚮ ⛌ 🛏 Ⅲ. Ⓥ ◈ ⚮

Aveton Gifford 6

National Grid Ref: SX6947

⦂◖ Sloop Inn, Church House Inn

(3m) *Marsh Mills, Aveton Gifford, Kingsbridge, Devon, TQ7 4JW.*
Mill house, pond, stream, gardens, orchard, small farm. Friendly animals.
Tel: **01548 550549** (also fax no)
Mrs Newsham.
D: £18.00-£22.00 **S:** £18.00-£22.00.
Open: All Year (not Xmas/New Year)
Beds: 2T 2D 1S
Baths: 2 En 1 Sh 1 Pr
🛇 (6) 🅿 (6) ⚮ ⛌ ⚲ 🛏 Ⓥ ◈ ⚮

Please respect a B&B's wishes regarding children, animals & smoking.

High season, bank holidays and special events mean low availability *everywhere*.

(3m) *Court Barton Farmhouse, Aveton Gifford, Kingsbridge, Devon, TQ7 4LE.*
Actual grid ref: SX695478
Delightful C16th farmhouse in colourful gardens. You'll love our scrumptious breakfasts.
Tel: **01548 550312**
Mrs Balkwill.
Fax no: 01548 550128
D: £22.00-£30.00 **S:** £24.00-£35.00.
Open: All Year (not Xmas)
Beds: 2F 2D 2T 1S
Baths: 6 En 1 Sh
🛇 🅿 (10) ⛌ 🛏 Ⅲ. Ⓥ ◈ ⚮

Galmpton (Salcombe) 7

National Grid Ref: SX6840

⦂◖ Hope & Anchor

(1m) *Rose Cottage, Galmpton, Kingsbridge, Devon, TQ7 3EU.*
Actual grid ref: SX689405
C17th thatched, Listed cottage. Under 1 mile , Hope Cove beaches, coastal path, close Salcombe.
Tel: **01548 561953** (also fax no)
Mrs Daly.
D: £18.00-£23.00 **S:** £28.00-£28.00.
Open: All Year (not Xmas)
Beds: 2D 1T
Baths: 3 En
⚮ ⛌ 🛏 Ⅲ. Ⓥ ◈ ⚮

Hope Cove 8

National Grid Ref: SX6739

⦂◖ Hope & Anchor, Sand Pebbles

(On path 🚗) *Hope Cove Hotel, Hope Cove, Kingsbridge, Devon, TQ7 3HH.*
On coastal path. Spectacular sea views to Eddystone Lighthouse.
Grades: RAC 3 Diamond
Tel: **01548 561233** (also fax no)
Mr Clarke.
D: £23.50-£28.50 **S:** £33.50-£38.50.
Open: Easter to Oct
Beds: 2T 5D
Baths: 7 En
🛇 (6) 🅿 (12) ⛌ ✕ 🛏 Ⅲ. Ⓥ ◈ ⚮

(On path) *Cove Cottage, Hope Cove, Kingsbridge, Devon, TQ7 3HG.*
Detached cottage 100 yds from sea.
Tel: **01548 561446** Mrs Guymer.
D: £13.00-£16.00 **S:** £13.50.
Open: Easter to Oct
Beds: 1D 1T 1S
Baths: 1 Sh
🛇 🅿 (3) ⚮ ⛌ ⚲ 🛏 Ⅲ. Ⓥ

Sharpitor 9

National Grid Ref: SX7237

(▲ On path) *Salcombe Youth Hostel, Overbecks, Sharpitor, Salcombe, Devon, TQ8 8LW.*
Actual grid ref: SX728374
Tel: **01548 842856**
Under 18: £6.20 **Adults:** £9.15
Self-catering facilities, Television, Showers, Lounge, Drying room, Cycle store, Evening meal at 7.00pm, No smoking, Kitchen facilities, Breakfast available, Credit cards accepted
Large house in NT semi-tropical gardens on the cliff just before Sharpitor Rocks, overlooking estuary and sea.

Salcombe 10

National Grid Ref: SX7339

⦂◖ Victoria Inn, Fortescue Inn, Kings Arms

(0.5m) *Motherhill Farm, Salcombe, Devon, TQ8 8NB.*
Peaceful and homely Victorian farmhouse on a mixed working farm.
Tel: **01548 842552** (also fax no)
Mrs Weymouth.
D: £17.00-£19.00 **S:** £17.00-£19.00.
Open: Easter to Oct
Beds: 1F/D 1T 1S
Baths: 1 Sh
🛇 (7) 🅿 (6) ⚮ ⛌ 🛏 Ⓥ

(On path 🚗) *Torre View Hotel, Devon Road, Salcombe, Devon, TQ8 8HJ.*
Actual grid ref: SX7439
Small licensed non-smoking hotel, same owners for 15 years. Sea views. Town easy reach.
Grades: ETC 4 Diamond
RAC 4 Diamond
Tel: **01548 842633** (also fax no)
Mrs Bouttle.
D: £27.50-£30.00 **S:** £30.00-£34.00.
Open: Mar to Oct.
Beds: 1F 4D 2T 1S
Baths: 8 Pr
🛇 (4) 🅿 (5) ⚮ ⛌ ✕ 🛏 Ⅲ. Ⓥ ◈ ⚮

(0.5m) *Limericks, Raleigh Road, Salcombe, Devon, TQ8 8AY.*
Devon-style double-fronted detached family house with TV lounge.
Tel: **01548 842350**
Mr & Mrs Collins.
D: £17.00-£20.00
S: £17.00-£25.00.
Open: All Year (not Xmas)
Beds: 2D 1T
Baths: 2 En 1 Sh
🛇 (10) 🅿 (4) ⚮ ⛌ 🛏 Ⅲ. Ⓥ

D = Price range per person sharing in a double room

(0.5m) *Rocarno,* Grenville Road, Salcombe, Devon, *TQ8 8BJ.* Estuary views, television, ensuite, beverage trays, heating, friendly welcome.
Tel: **01548 842732**
Mr & Mrs Petty-Brown.
D: £17.50-£19.50 **S:** £20.00-£30.00.
Open: All Year (not Xmas)
Beds: 1D 1T
Baths: 2 En
☐ (4) ⊬ ☐ ↟ ✗ ♨ 🏠 Ⅴ ⓘ

(0.5m) *Trennels Hotel,* Herbert Road, Salcombe, Devon, *TQ8 8HR.* A former sea captain's house close to town centre, local sandy beaches, NT properties.
Tel: **01548 842500**
D: £22.00-£26.00 .
Open: Mar to Oct
Beds: 5D
Baths: 5 En
☐ (4) 🅿 (5) ⊬ ☐ ♨ 🏠 Ⅴ

East Portlemouth   11

National Grid Ref: SX7438

🍴 🍺 Pigs Nose

(On path 🚌) *Meadow Barn,* East Portlemouth, Salcombe, Devon, *TQ8 8PN.*
Actual grid ref: SX759378
Quiet, comfortable private accommodation in idyllic coastal and countryside location.
Tel: **01548 843085**
Mr & Mrs Griffiths.
D: £20.00-£24.00 **S:** £20.00-£24.00.
Open: All Year (not Xmas)
Beds: 1D 1T
Baths: 1 Sh
☐ (7) 🅿 (4) ⊬ ☐ ✗ ♨ 🏠 Ⅴ ⓘ ⚡

East Prawle   12

National Grid Ref: SX7836

🍴 🍺 Freebooter, Pig's Nose

(0.25m) *Stures Court,* East Prawle, Kingsbridge, Devon, *TQ7 2BY.*
C17th thatched cottage with C21st comfort. Highly commended by guests.
Tel: **01548 511261** Miss Benson.
D: £18.00-£20.00 **S:** £19.00-£21.00.
Open: All Year
Beds: 2D 2S
Baths: 1 Sh
☐ (7) ⊬ ☐ ♨ 🏠 Ⅴ ⓘ ⚡

Always telephone to get directions to the B&B - you will save time!

Hallsands   13

National Grid Ref: SX8138

🍴 🍺 Cricket Inn

(On Path) *Widget, Hallsands, Kingsbridge, Devon, TQ7 2EX.*
Actual grid ref: SX819388
Tel: **01548 511110**
Mrs Wolstenholme.
D: £20.00-£25.00 **S:** £20.00-£25.00.
Open: All Year (not Xmas)
Beds: 2D 1T
Baths: 1 En 1 Pr
☐ 🅿 (4) ⊬ ☐ ♨ 🏠 Ⅴ
A brand new bungalow 50 yards from the beach and coastal path in a wonderful peaceful area for relaxing or using as a base for the beautiful South Hams. A warm welcome, lovely accommodation and unbeatable breakfast await you. No pets.

Beeson   14

National Grid Ref: SX8140

(0.5m) *Marybank House, Beeson, Kingsbridge, Devon, TQ7 2HW.*
Beautifully located Victorian country house. Have delicious breakfast whilst enjoying sea views.
Tel: **01548 580531** Mrs Honeywill.
D: £18.50-£25.00 **S:** £18.50-£28.00.
Open:
Beds: 1T 2D
Baths: 1 En 1 Pr
☐ 🅿 ⊬ ☐ ↟ ♨ Ⅴ ⓘ ⚡

Slapton   15

National Grid Ref: SX8245

🍴 🍺 Queens' Arms, Tower Inn

(1.5m 🚌) *Start House, Start, Slapton, Kingsbridge, Devon, TQ7 2QD.*
Actual grid ref: SX809448
Tel: **01548 580254** Mrs Ashby.
D: £22.00 **S:** £20.00.
Open: All Year (not Xmas)
Beds: 2D 1T 1S
Baths: 2 Pr 1 Sh
☐ 🅿 (4) ⊬ ☐ ↟ ✗ ♨ 🏠 Ⅴ ⚡
Comfortable Georgian house. Situated in quiet hamlet 1 mile from Slapton Ley. All bedrooms overlook a beautiful valley with Slapton and the sea at the end. Large interesting garden. Ideal for wildlife and walking. Traditional or vegetarian breakfast.

(0.5m 🚌) *Old Walls, Slapton, Kingsbridge, Devon, TQ7 2QN.*
Actual grid ref: SX822449
Listed C18th house in beautiful village near sea, Nature Reserve.
Tel: **01548 580516** Mrs Mercer.
D: £17.00-£20.00 **S:** £22.00-£25.00.
Open: All Year
Beds: 2F 1T
Baths: 1 En 1 Pr 1 Sh
☐ ⊬ ☐ ↟ ♨ 🏠 Ⅴ ⚡

Dartmouth   16

National Grid Ref: SX8751

🍴 🍺 Seven Stars, Searle Arms, Windjammer, Cherub, Royal Castle, Norton Park Forces Tavern, Sportsmans' Arms

(0.5m) *Greenswood Farm, Greenswood Lane, Dartmouth, Devon, TQ6 0LY.*
Tel: **01803 712100** Mrs Baron.
D: £18.00-£25.00 **S:** £20.00-£25.00.
Open: All Year
Beds: 1F 1T 1D
Baths: 1 En 1 Pr 1 Sh
☐ (12) 🅿 (8) ⊬ ☐ ✗ ♨ 🏠 Ⅴ ⓘ ⚡
A 15th century Devon longhouse set in its own secluded valley, with large sub-tropical gardens. A haven for wildlife. Only 4 miles to Dartmouth, Start Bay and Slapton Ley nature reserve. 2 miles to Dartmouth golf and country club.

(0.75m) *The Cedars, 79 Victoria Road, Dartmouth, Devon, TQ6 9RX.*
The Cedars, level location, near town centre, friendly welcome.
Tel: **01803 834421** Mrs Greene.
D: £18.00-£19.00 **S:** £18.00-£20.00.
Open: All Year (not Xmas)
Beds: 2F 1D 2T 1S
Baths: 1 Sh
☐ ☐ ↟ ♨ 🏠 Ⅴ ⓘ ⚡

(0.75m) *Valley House, 46 Victoria Road, Dartmouth, Devon, TQ6 9DZ.*
Actual grid ref: SX871511
Comfortable, small friendly guest house.
Tel: **01803 834045**
Mr & Mrs Ellis.
D: £21.00-£25.00
S: £25.00-£30.00.
Open: Feb to Dec
Beds: 2D 2T
Baths: 4 En
🅿 (4) ⊬ ☐ ♨ 🏠 Ⅴ

(0.5m 🚌) *Campbells B & B, 5 Mount Boone, Dartmouth, Devon, TQ6 9PB.*
Luxury bedrooms with fabulous views. flexible breakfasts with home baking.
Tel: **01803 833438** (also fax no)
D: £27.50-£27.50
S: £35.00-£55.00.
Open: All Year (not Xmas)
Beds: 2D
Baths: 2 En
🅿 (2) ⊬ ☐ ✗ ♨ 🏠 Ⅴ ⓘ ⚡

(0.5m) *Sunnybanks, 1 Vicarage Hill, Dartmouth, Devon, TQ6 9EW.*
Friendly atmosphere. Excellent breakfasts and just minutes from the River Dart.
Grades: ETC 3 Diamond
Tel: **01803 832766** (also fax no)
D: £21.00-£25.00
S: £20.00-£30.00.
Open: All Year
Beds: 2F 2T 5D 1S
Baths: 8 En 1 Pr 1 Sh
☐ 🅿 (2) ☐ ↟ ✗ ♨ 🏠 Ⅴ ⓘ ⚡

(0.75m) *Brenec House,* 73 South Ford Road, Dartmouth, Devon, *TQ6 9QT.*
Five minutes walk to river front and town centre.
Tel: **01803 834788**
Mr & Mrs Culley.
D: £16.00-£17.00 **S:** £16.00-£17.00.
Open: All Year
Beds: 2D 1S
Baths: 1 Sh
⊗ ▣ 🏠 🖤 🍴 🌐 Ⅴ 🛆 ✦

(0.25m) *Boringdon House,* 1 Church Road, Dartmouth, Devon, *TQ6 9HQ.*
Welcoming Georgian house overlooking Dartmoor and River Dart and Sea.
Tel: **01803 832235** Mr Green.
D: £22.50 **S:** £38.00.
Open: All Year
Beds: 1D 2T
Baths: 3 En
▣ (3) 🖤 🍴 🌐 Ⅴ

(0.5m) *Browns Norton Farm,* Dartmouth, Devon, *TQ6 0ND.*
Charming C17th farmhouse with sloping ceilings, modern bathroom shower etc.
Tel: **01803 712321** Mrs Bond.
D: £15.00-£20.00 **S:** £12.50.
Open: All Year (not Xmas/New Year)
Beds: 1T 1D 1S
Baths: 1 Sh
⊗ ▣ 🖤 🍴 🌐 Ⅴ

(0.25m) *Victoria Cote,* 105 Victoria Road, Dartmouth, Devon, *TQ6 9DY.*
Detached, comfortable, Victorian house 5 minutes' stroll from town centre.
Tel: **01803 832997** Mr Fell.
D: £22.00-£25.00 **S:** £25.00-£28.00.
Open: All Year (not Xmas)
Beds: 2D 1T
Baths: 3 En
⊗ ▣ (4) 🍴 🌐 Ⅴ ✦

(0.5m) *New Barn Farm,* Norton, Dartmouth, Devon, *TQ6 0NH.*
Actual grid ref: SX856512
Comfortable old working farm; lovely gardens, birds, badgers, peaceful setting.
Tel: **01803 832410** Mrs Reeves.
D: £17.50-£20.00 **S:** £20.00-£25.00.
Open: All Year (not Xmas)
Beds: 1F 1D 1T
Baths: 1 Sh
⊗ ▣ (8) 🖤 🐾 🍴 Ⅴ

Taking your dog?

Book *in advance*

ONLY with owners

who accept dogs (🐾)

Maypool   17

National Grid Ref: SX8754

(▲ 4m) *Maypool Youth Hostel,* Maypool, Galmpton, Brixham, Devon, TQ5 0ET.
Actual grid ref: SX877546
Tel: **01803 842444**
Under 18: £6.90
Adults: £10.00
Self-catering facilities, Television, Showers, Lounge, Dining room, Games room, Drying room, Cycle store, Parking, Evening meal at 7.00pm, WC, Kitchen facilities, Breakfast available, Credit cards accepted
Victorian house set in 4-acre grounds, originally built for local boatyard owner, with views of Kingswear, Dartmouth and the Dart Estuary.

Brixham   18

National Grid Ref: SX9255

🍴 🍺 The Vigilance, Smugglers Haunt Hotel, Blue Anchor, Berry Head Hotel, Weary Ploughman

(0.5m) *Smugglers Haunt Hotel, & Restaurant,* Church Hill, Brixham, Devon, *TQ5 8HH.*
Grades: AA 1 Star
Tel: **01803 853050**
Mr Hudson.
D: £24.00-£27.00 **S:** £29.00.
Open: All Year
Beds: 4F 7D 4T 1S
Baths: 16 En
⊗ 🍴 🐾 🍴 🌐 Ⅴ 🛆
Friendly, private 300-year-old hotel. Up to 100 main course meals. Pets and children welcome. From 1st October-1st February (not Xmas period) 3 nights for the cost of 2.

(0.25m) *Richmond House Hotel,* Higher Manor Road, Brixham, Devon, *TQ5 8HA.*
Comfortable Victorian house with spacious rooms and a homely atmosphere.
Grades: ETC 3 Diamond, AA 3 Diamond
Tel: **01803 882391** (also fax no)
Mr Hayhurst.
D: £16.00-£24.00 .
Open: Feb to Dec
Beds: 2F 4D
Baths: 5 En 1 Pr
⊗ ▣ (6) 🖤 🍴 🐾 🍴 🌐 Ⅴ ✦

(0.5m 🐾) *Westbury,* 51 New Road, Brixham, *TQ5 8NL.*
Charming Georgian house, short level walk from shops and harbour.
Tel: **01803 851684** (also fax no)
D: £16.00-£23.00
S: £16.00-£23.00.
Open: All Year
Beds: 4F 2D
Baths: 4 En 1 Sh
⊗ (6) ▣ 🖤 🍴 🌐 Ⅴ 🛆 ✦

(0.25m 🐾) *Mimosa Guest House,* 75 New Road, Brixham, Devon, *TQ5 8NL.*
Spacious, well-furnished Georgian house close to harbour and town centre.
Tel: **01803 855719** Mr Kershaw.
D: £15.00-£17.00 **S:** £15.00-£17.00.
Open: All Year (not Xmas)
Beds: 2D 1T 1S **Baths:** 1 En 2 Pr
⊗ (5) ▣ (3) 🍴 🍴 🌐 Ⅴ 🛆 ✦

Paignton   19

National Grid Ref: SX8960

🍴 🍺 Inn On The Quay, Harbour Lights, Inn On The Green, Talk Of The Town, Esplanade

(On path) *South Sands Hotel,* Alta Vista Road, Paignton, Devon, *TQ4 6BZ.*
Actual grid ref: SX895599
Grades: ETC 2 Star
Tel: **01803 557231** Mr Cahill.
D: £20.00-£25.00 **S:** £20.00-£25.00.
Open: Mar to Oct
Beds: 7F 4D 6T 2S
Baths: 17 En 2 Pr
⊗ ▣ (17) 🍴 🐾 🍴 🌐 🛆 Ⅴ 🛆 ✦
South-facing, licensed family-run hotel in peaceful location overlooking beach/park. Close to harbour/amenities. Huge help-yourself buffet-style breakfast. Outstanding value for money. All rooms ensuite with television, telephone, teamakers, most with king size beds.

(0.5m 🐾) *Cherwood Hotel,* 26 Garfield Road, Paignton, *TQ4 6AX.*
Grades: ETC 4 Diamond
Tel: **01803 556515** Alderson.
Fax no: 01803 555126
D: £16.00-£20.00 **S:** £16.00-£20.00.
Open: All Year
Beds: 3F 3D 2T 1S **Baths:** 9 En
⊗ ▣ (4) 🍴 🐾 🍴 🌐 Ⅴ 🛆 ✦
All ensuite, licensed bar, prestigious 4 diamond etc. award. Quality assured. Ideal position by central seafront/ pier, close to town. CTVs, beverage trays, radio alarms, ceiling fans, hairdryers, complimentary toiletries. Luxury 4 poster rooms available. Satisfaction guaranteed.

(0.5m 🐾) *Hotel Fiesta,* 2 Kernou Road, Paignton, *TQ4 6BA.*
Grades: ETC 3 Diamond
Tel: **01803 521862** (also fax no)
Mr Hawker.
D: £16.00-£20.00 **S:** £22.00-£26.00.
Open: All Year
Beds: 2F 5D 1T 2S
Baths: 7 En 3 Sh
⊗ 🍴 🍴 🌐 🛆 Ⅴ 🛆 ✦
An attractive seaside property close to Paignton's clean beaches, pier, crazy golf, sea fishing, Dartmouth Steam Railway and our new multiplex cinema with restaurant and children's area. Also plenty of night life for all ages. Ideal for short breaks throughout the year.

(0.5m) *Park View Guest House,*
19 Garfield Road, Paignton,
Devon, TQ4 6AX.
Small friendly guest house - short
level stroll town and sea front.
Tel: **01803 528521**
D: £13.00-£16.00
S: £13.00-£16.00.
Open: All Year (not Xmas/New
Year)
Beds: 3F 1D
Baths: 1 Sh
🛇 🅿 ❑ ⼤ ✕ ⚐ 🏠 Ⅵ 🛈

(0.5m) *Sundale Hotel,* 10 *Queens*
Road, Paignton, Devon, TQ4 6AT.
Quiet family run hotel, close to
local amenities, highly
recommended.
Tel: **01803 557431**
Mr McDermott.
D: £14.50-£17.50
S: £14.50-£17.50.
Open: All Year
Beds: 2F 2T 3D 1S
Baths: 4 En 1 Sh
🛇 ⼬ ❑ ⼤ ⚐ 🏠 Ⅵ 🛈

(0.5m) *Channel View Hotel,* 8
Marine Parade, Paignton, Devon,
TQ3 2NU.
Sea front level east, access to all
areas, amazing views.
Grades: AA 3 Diamond
Tel: **01803 522432**
D: £25.00-£30.00
S: £25.00-£30.00.
Open: All Year
Beds: 3F 6D 2T 2S
Baths: 13 En
🛇 🅿 (10) ❑ ✕ ⚐ 🏠 Ⅵ 🛈

(0.25m) *Adelphi Hotel,* 14 *Queens*
Road, Paignton, Devon, TQ4 6AT.
Only 200 yards level walks -
Beach, train, coach/ bus stations.
Tel: **01803 558022** Mr Elnor.
D: £14.00-£18.00 **S:** £20.00-£25.00.
Open: All Year
Beds: 2F 3D 4T 2S
Baths: 5 En 2 Sh
🛇 (1) ❑ ⼤ ✕ ⚐ 🏠 Ⅵ 🛈

(0.5m) *Bayview Hotel,* 6 *Cleveland*
Road, Paignton, TQ4 6EN.
Friendly family-run hotel, licensed,
ideal location near town harbour.
Tel: **01803 557400**
D: £12.00-£18.00 **S:** £12.00-£18.00.
Open: All Year (not Xmas)
Beds: 3F 2D 2T 1S
Baths: 3 En 2 Sh
🛇 🅿 (9) ⼤ ✕ ⚐ 🏠 Ⅵ 🛈 ⼮

(0.5m) *Birchwood House Hotel,*
33 St Andrews Road, Paignton,
Devon, TQ4 6HA.
Licensed family-run hotel close to
beaches and all facilities.
Grades: ETC 4 Diamond
Tel: **01803 551323**
Fax no: 01803 401301
D: £20.00-£24.00 **S:** £20.00-£24.00.
Open: Easter to Nov
Beds: 3F 3T 5D 1S
Baths: 12 En
🛇 (5) 🅿 (8) ❑ ⼤ ✕ ⚐ 🏠 Ⅵ 🛈

(0.5m) *Arrandale, Garfield Road,*
Paignton, Devon, TQ4 6AX.
Guest house, adjacent to central
seafront and all other amenities.
Tel: **01803 552211**
Mr & Mrs Shillingford.
D: £16.00-£19.00 **S:** £16.00-£19.00.
Open: All Year
Beds: 3F 1D 2T 2S
Baths: 8 En
🛇 (1) 🅿 (8) ❑ ⼤ ✕ ⚐ 🏠 ⼴ Ⅵ

(0.5m) *Rougemont,* 23 *Roundham*
Road, Paignton, Devon, TQ4 6DN.
Small, friendly, quiet hotel situated
twixt Paignton harbour and
beaches.
Tel: **01803 556570** (also fax no)
K&B Smith.
D: £15.00-£19.00 **S:** £20.00-£22.75.
Open: All Year
Beds: 2F 4D 1T 1S
Baths: 7 En 1 Sh
🅿 (8) ❑ ⚐ 🏠 Ⅵ

(0.5m) *Beresford Private Hotel,*
Adelphi Road, Paignton, Devon,
TQ4 6AW.
Friendly professional service, only
100 level yards seafront, shops,
stations.
Tel: **01803 551560**
D: £17.00-£21.00 **S:** £20.00-£30.00.
Open: All Year
Beds: 7D 1T
Baths: 8 En
🛇 (12) 🅿 (5) ❑ ⚐ 🏠 Ⅵ 🛈 ⼮

(On path) *The Look Out Hotel,*
Marine Parade, Paignton, Devon,
TQ3 2NU.
Friendly seafront hotel, fantastic
sea views, excellent food.
Tel: **01803 525638**
D: £15.00-£18.00 **S:** £15.00-£18.00.
Open: Easter to Oct
Beds: 1F 5D 2T 1S
Baths: 10 En
🛇 (4) 🅿 (8) ❑ ⼤ ✕ ⚐ 🏠 Ⅵ ⼮

Cockington 20

National Grid Ref: SX8963

(0.75m 🚍) *Fairmount House*
Hotel, Herbert Road, Cockington,
Torquay, Devon, TQ2 6RW.
Actual grid ref: SX898639
Grades: ETC 4 Diamond
Tel: **01803 605446** (also fax no)
Mr Richards.
D: £25.00-£35.50 **S:** £25.00-£35.50.
Open: Mar to Oct
Beds: 2F 2T 4D 2S
Baths: 8 En
🛇 (12) 🅿 (9) ❑ ⼤ ✕ ⚐ 🏠 ⼴ Ⅵ 🛈 ⼮
Fairmount House Hotel , some-
where special. Unhurried English
breakfast, quiet undisturbed nights,
feel completely at home at small
hotel in peaceful setting. Away
from the busy sea front and near
Cockington Village and Country
Park. Fairmount offers quality,
comfort and genuine friendly
service.

Torquay 21

National Grid Ref: SX9165

🍴 ⼐ Ansteys Cove, Chelston Manor, Devon
Arms, Landsdowne, London Inn, Drum Tun,
Harbourside, Black Tulip

(▲ 0.5m) *Torquay International*
Backpackers Hostel, Torquay
International Backpackers, 119
Abbey Road, Torquay, Devon,
TQ2 5NP.
Tel: **01803 299924**
Under 18: £6.51 **Adults:** £6.51
Self-catering facilities, Television,
Central heating, Shop, Laundry
facilities, Wet weather shelter,
Lounge, Dining room, Security
lockers, Cycle store, Parking
*Centrally located less than 10 min-
utes from beach and harbour.*

(0.5m) *Heathcliff House Hotel,* 16
Newton Road, Torquay, TQ2 5BZ.
Tel: **01803 211580** (also fax no)
Mr & Mrs Sanders.
D: £15.00-£20.00 **S:** £20.00.
Open: All Year (not Xmas)
Beds: 2F 8D
Baths: 10 En
🛇 🅿 (10) ❑ ✕ ⚐ 🏠 Ⅵ
Whether taking your main holiday,
having a weekend away, touring
Devon, visiting friends or on
business, this family hotel offers
great value B&B. Built in 1860s,
the Heathcliff, once a vicarage,
now features in the official
Torquay Agatha Christie trail.

(0.5m) *Aries House,* 1 *Morgan*
Avenue, Torquay, Devon, TQ2 5RP.
Central Victorian town house near
bus/coach/train stations, shops,
beachs, clubs.
Tel: **01803 215655**
Mr & Mrs Sherry.
D: £11.00-£20.00
S: £11.00-£20.00.
Open: All Year (not Xmas/New
Year)
Beds: 2 Family 2 Twin 1 Double
1 Single
Baths: 2 En 2 Sh
🛇 (0) 🅿 (1) ⼬ ❑ ✕ ⚐ 🏠 Ⅵ 🛈

(0.5m 🚍) *Devon Court Hotel,*
24 *Croft Road, Torquay, Devon,*
TQ2 5UE.
Grades: AA 3 Diamond,
RAC 3 Diamond
Tel: **01803 293603**
Fax no: 01803 213660
D: £15.00-£25.00 **S:** £22.50-£32.50.
Open: All Year
Beds: 4F 8D 2T
Baths: 10 En 6 Pr
🛇 🅿 (14) ⼬ ❑ ⼤ ✕ ⚐ 🏠 Ⅵ 🛈 ⼮
Family-run Victorian hotel in the
heart of Torquay. Few minutes'
walk to beach, shops, Riviera,
leisure centre, licensed bar, lounge
overlooking outdoor heated pool &
palm lined patio. Warm & friendly,
home baking, cream teas, etc.
Remote control colour TV in room.

(0.25m 🚍) *Swiss Court,* 68 Vane Hill Road, Torquay, Devon, *TQ1 2BZ.* Blissfully quiet location, sea views, yet near harbour and town.
Tel: **01803 215564** Mr Davies.
D: £16.00-£20.00 **S:** £16.00-£20.00.
Open: All Year (not Xmas)
Beds: 1F 2D 5S
Baths: 6 En 1 Sh
🛏 (6) 🅿 (8) 🛏 🍴 ⚓ 🛏 ⅗ V

(0.5m 🚍) *Treander Guest House,* 10 Morgan Avenue, Torquay, Devon, *TQ2 5RS.*
Stag and Hen parties welcome. Central all amenities. Access all times.
Tel: **01803 296906** Hurren.
D: £13.50-£17.50 **S:** £13.50-£17.50.
Open: All Year
Beds: 3F 4T 4D 1S
Baths: 2 En, 1 Pr 2 Sh
🛏 🅿 (4) 🛏 🍴 ⚓ 🛏 V � ⅙

(0.5m) *Palm Tree House,* 93 Avenue Rd, Torquay, Devon, *TQ2 5LH*
Small, friendly, relaxed guest house. Home from home. Good breakfast. Tel: **01803 299141** Mr & Mrs Brown.
D: £15.00-£17.00 **S:** £15.00-£17.00.
Open: All Year (not Xmas/ New Year)
Beds: 2T 4D **Baths:** 1 Sh
🛏 (3) 🅿 (3) 🛏 🍴 ⚓ 🛏 V

(0.5m) *Brampton Court Hotel,* St Lukes Road South, Torquay, Devon, *TQ2 2NZ.*
Panoramic views of Torbay, close to town, beach and conference centre.
Grades: ETC 4 Diamond
Tel: **01803 294237** Mr & Mrs Markham.
Fax no: 01803 211842
D: £22.00-£28.00 **S:** £27.00-£33.00.
Open: All Year
Beds: 6F 4T 8D 2S
Baths: 20 En
🛏 🅿 (14) ⅟ 🛏 🍴 ⚓ 🛏 V ⅙

(0.5m) *Chester Court Hotel,* 30 Cleveland Road, Torquay, Devon, *TQ2 5BE.*
Comfortable ensuite accommodation. Midweek bookings and short breaks. Pleasant gardens.
Grades: ETC 3 Diamond
Tel: **01803 294565** (also fax no) Mrs Morris.
D: £16.00-£20.00 **S:** £16.00-£33.00.
Open: All Year
Beds: 3F 2T 4D 1S
Baths: 9 En, 1 Sh
🛏 🅿 (10) ⅟ 🛏 🍴 ⚓ 🛏 V ⅟

(0.5m) *Chesterfield Hotel,* 62 Belgrave Road, Torquay, Devon, *TQ2 5HY.*
A warm and friendly welcome awaits you. Close to all amenities.
Grades: ETC 4 Diamond, AA 4 Diamond
Tel: **01803 292318** Daglish.
Fax no: 01803 293676
D: £16.00-£25.00 **S:** £16.00-£20.00.
Open: All Year (not Xmas)
Beds: 3F 4D 3T 1S
Baths: 10 En 1 Sh
🛏 🅿 🛏 🍴 ⚓ 🛏 V ⅟ ⅙

(0.5m) *Tower Hall Hotel,* Solsbro Road, Torquay, *TQ2 6PF.*
Victorian villa, sea views, near seafront, romantic atmosphere. Licensed. Short breaks.
Tel: **01803 605292** Mr Butler.
D: £16.00-£20.00 **S:** £16.00-£20.00.
Open: Easter to Oct
Beds: 2F 4D 2T 2S
Baths: 7 En 2 Sh
🛏 🅿 (6) 🛏 🍴 ⚓ 🛏 V ⅟ ⅙

(0.5m) *Exmouth View Hotel,* St Albans Road, Torquay, Devon, *TQ1 3LG.*
Friendly family-run hotel just yards from stunning Babbacombe Downs.
Tel: **01803 327307** Mr Browne.
Fax no: 01803 329967
D: £16.00-£25.00 **S:** £20.00-£30.00.
Open: All Year
Beds: 8F 8D 5T 1S
Baths: 22 En
🛏 🅿 (20) 🛏 🍴 ⚓ 🛏 ⅗ V

(0.5m 🚍) *Sandpiper Lodge Hotel,* 96 Avenue Road, Torquay, *TQ2 5LF.*
Guests keep returning, loving our homely atmosphere and hearty breakfasts.
Tel: **01803 293293**
D: £15.00-£22.00 **S:** £13.00-£20.00.
Open: All Year
Beds: 2F 4D 1S
Baths: 7 En
🛏 🅿 (7) ⅟ 🛏 🍴 ⚓ 🛏 V

(0.5m) *Maple Lodge,* 36 Ash Hill Road, Torquay, Devon, *TQ1 3JD.*
Quality award winning guest house. Panoramic views over town and Torbay.
Grades: ETC 3 Diamond
Tel: **01803 297391** Mr Allen.
D: £16.00-£22.00 **S:** £16.00-£22.00.
Open: All Year
Beds: 2F 3D 1T 1S
Baths: 6 En 1 Pr
🛏 (2) 🅿 (4) ⅟ 🛏 ⚓ 🛏 V

(0.5m 🚍) *Howard Court Hotel,* 31 St Efrides Road, Torquay, *TQ2 5SG.*
Friendly licensed hotel. Close to beach and town. Secured Parking.
Tel: **01803 295494** Lorimer.
D: £13.00-£18.00 **S:** £15.00-£22.00.
Open: All Year
Beds: 2F 3T 5D 1S
Baths: 2 Sh
🛏 🅿 (6) 🛏 🍴 ⚓ 🛏 V ⅟ ⅙

(0.5m) *Knowle Court Hotel,* Kents Road Wellswood, Torquay, *TQ1 2NN.*
Peaceful location near beaches, town, good bus service.
Grades: AA 4 Diamond
Tel: **01803 297076** Mr Baderay.
Fax no: 01803 292980
D: £20.00-£30.00 **S:** £20.00-£30.00.
Open: All Year
Beds: 3F 4D 1T 1S
Baths: 9 En
🛏 🅿 (5) ⅟ 🛏 🍴 ⚓ 🛏 V ⅟

(0.5m) *Garlieston Hotel,* Bridge Road, Torquay, Devon, *TQ2 5BA.*
Small friendly family run private hotel. Central for all amenities.
Grades: ETC 3 Diamond, AA 3 Diamond
Tel: **01803 294050** Mr & Mrs Ridewood.
D: £13.00-£18.00 **S:** £13.00-£18.00.
Open: All Year
Beds: 2F 2D 1S
Baths: 3 En 2 Pr
🛏 🛏 🍴 ⚓ 🛏 V ⅟

(0.5m) *Cranborne Hotel,* 58 Belgrave Road, Torquay, Devon, *TQ2 5HY.*
In excellent situation, close to town centre shop and Riviera centre.
Grades: ETC 5 Diamond
Tel: **01803 298046** (also fax no) Mrs Dawkins.
D: £20.00-£30.00 **S:** £25.00-£50.00.
Open: All Year (not Xmas)
Beds: 3F 8D
Baths: 11 En
🛏 (2) 🅿 (3) ⅟ 🛏 ⚓ 🛏 V ⅟

(0.5m) *Craig Court Hotel,* 10 Ash Hill Road, Torquay, Devon, *TQ1 3HZ.*
A Victorian villa close to town centre and all amenities.
Grades: AA 3 Diamonds, RAC 3 Diamonds
Tel: **01803 294400** Mrs Box.
Fax no: 01803 212525
D: £20.50-£23.50 **S:** £20.50-£23.50.
Open: All Year (not Xmas)
Beds: 4F 1T 3D 2S
Baths: 10 En
🛏 (6) ⅟ 🛏 🍴 ⚓ 🛏 ⅗ V ⅟ ⅙

(0.5m) *Shirley Hotel,* Braddons Hill Road East, Torquay, Devon, *TQ1 1HF.*
Elegant detached Victorian villa in quiet location, yet close to harbour.
Tel: **01803 293016** Mrs Stephens.
D: £16.00-£25.00 **S:** £16.00-£25.00.
Open: All Year (not Xmas)
Beds: 9D 2T 2S
Baths: 11 En 1 Sh
🛏 (12) 🅿 (8) 🛏 🍴 ⚓ 🛏 V

Pay B&Bs by cash or cheque and be prepared to pay up front.

All paths are popular: you are well-advised to book ahead

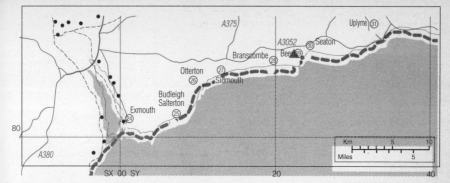

(0.5m) *Carysfort, 13 Warren Road, Torquay, Devon, TQ2 5TQ.*
Ideally situated near town centre, beaches, harbour and night life.
Tel: **01803 294160** Mr Tanner.
D: £16.00-£20.00 **S:** £17.00-£20.00.
Open: All Year
Beds: 2F 2D 2T 1S
Baths: 4 En 2 Sh
⛄ (1) 🅿 (3) 🗙 🛏 🏠 �📺 ▦ Ⓥ

(0.5m) *Wilsbrook, 77 Avenue Road, Torquay, Devon, TQ2 5LL.*
Attractive Victorian house, short walk to beach, town, Riviera centre.
Tel: **01803 298413** Mr Brook.
D: £14.00 **S:** £13.00.
Open: All Year (not Xmas)
Beds: 1F 2D 1T 1S
Baths: 3 En 1 Sh
⛄ (3) 🅿 (6) 🗙 🛏 🏠 ▦ Ⓥ

(0.5m) *Kingsway Lodge Guest House, 95 Avenue Road, Torquay, Devon, TQ2 5LH.*
Friendly B&B, non-smoking, near al amenities and seafront.
Tel: **01803 295288**
Mr & Mrs Barrett.
D: £15.00-£18.00 **S:** £15.00-£18.00.
Open: All Year (not Xmas)
Beds: 3F 1D 1S
Baths: 4 En 1 Pr
⛄ 🅿 (3) 🗙 🛏 ▦ Ⓥ

(0.5m) *Athina, 8 Vansittart Road, Torquay, Devon, TQ2 5BT.*
Friendly welcome awaits you at Athina. In residential area, approx 800 yards sea front.
Tel: **01803 297547** Mrs Smith.
D: £10.00 .
Open: Easter to Oct
Beds: 2D 1T
Baths: 1 Sh
🅿 (4) 🗙 🛏 ▦ Ⓥ

Please take muddy boots _off_ before entering premises

(On path) *Ansteys Cove Hotel, 327 Babbacombe Road, Torquay, Devon, TQ1 3TB.*
Actual grid ref: SX931648
Award-winning hotel, licensed restaurant and residents' bar.
Tel: **01803 211150/ 08000 284953**
Mr Williamson.
Fax no: 01803 211150
D: £17.00-£29.00
S: £17.00-£27.00.
Open: All Year
Beds: 2F 3T 8D 1S
Baths: 11 En
⛄ 🅿 (12) 🗙 🛏 🏠 ▦ Ⓥ 🛇 ✦

(0.5m) *Ashleigh Guest House, 61 Meadfoot Lane, Torquay, Devon, TQ1 2BP.*
Luxuriously appointed guest house, quietly situated close to all amenities and beaches.
Tel: **01803 294660**
D: £13.00-£17.00
S: £15.00-£19.00.
Open: All Year (not Xmas)
Beds: 3F 1D
Baths: 3 En 1 Pr
⛄ 🗙 🛏 🗙 🛏 ▦ Ⓥ ✦

(0.5m) *Braddon Hall Hotel, 70 Braddons Hill Road East, Torquay, Devon, TQ1 1HF.*
This delightful personally-run hotel is situated in a peaceful yet convenient position close harbour.
Tel: **01803 293908** (also fax no)
Mr & Mrs White.
D: £16.00-£20.00 **S:** £16.00-£20.00.
Open: All Year
Beds: 1F 8D 1T 1S
Baths: 11 En
⛄ (5) 🅿 (9) 🗙 🛏 ▦ Ⓥ

(0.5m) *The Birdcage Hotel, St Lukes Road, Torquay, Devon, TQ2 5NX.*
Come, enjoy the warm, friendly informal atmosphere of our hotel.
Tel: **01803 212703**
Ms Tweedy.
D: £18.00-£25.00
S: £18.00-£25.00.
Open: All Year
Beds: 2F 4D 1T
Baths: 3 En 2 Sh
⛄ 🅿 (7) 🗙 🗙 ▦ Ⓥ

(0.5m) *Ellington Court Hotel, St Lukes Road South, Torquay, Devon, TQ2 5NZ.*
Quality accommodation overlooking Torbay, central location and beautiful gardens.
Tel: **01803 294957** Mr Peters.
Fax no: 01803 201383
D: £17.00-£39.00 **S:** £25.00-£35.00.
Open: Easter to Nov
Beds: 4F 8D 2T 1S
Baths: 14 En 1 Pr 1 Sh
⛄ 🅿 (8) 🗙 🗙 🛏 ▦ Ⓥ ✦

(0.5m) *Merlewood House Hotel, Meadfoot Road, Torquay, Devon, TQ1 2JP.*
Merlewood House is an elegant C19th building. 5 mins walk from harbour.
Tel: **01803 292814** Midgley.
D: £19.00-£22.00 **S:** £19.00-£22.00.
Open: All Year (not Xmas)
Beds: 1F 5D
Baths: 5 En 1 Sh
⛄ (5) 🅿 (7) 🗙 🛏 🏠 🛏 ▦ Ⓥ 🛇

(0.5m 🚗) *The Bramblehurst Hotel, Hunsdon Road, Torquay, TQ1 1QB.*
Our hotel nestles in a conservation area just 5 mins walk from the town. Tel: **01803 292150**
Fax no: 0702 1165843
D: £18.00-£20.00 **S:** £18.00-£20.00.
Open: All Year
Beds: 5F 2D 1T 1S
Baths: 4 En 3 Sh
⛄ 🅿 (10) 🗙 🛏 🗙 🛏 ▦ 🏠 Ⓥ 🛇 ✦

Shaldon 22
National Grid Ref: SX9372

🍴 Bull, White Horse, Blacksmiths' Arms, Clifford Inn, Shipwrights

(0.5m) *Virginia Cottage, Brook Lane, Shaldon, Teignmouth, Devon, TQ14 0HL.*
Early C17th house in one acre garden near sea. Ample parking.
Tel: **01626 872634** (also fax no)
Mr & Mrs Britton.
D: £24.00-£25.00 **S:** £30.00-£35.00.
Open: All Year
Beds: 2D 1T **Baths:** 2 En 1 Pr
⛄ (9) 🅿 (4) 🗙 🛏 🏠 ▦ Ⓥ ✦

(0.5m) *Ringmore House,* Brook
Lane, Shaldon, Teignmouth,
Devon, *TQ14 0AJ.*
Actual grid ref: TQ326147
Tel: **01626 873323**
Mr & Mrs Scull.
Fax no: 01626 873353
D: £25.00-£35.00 **S:** £30.00-£40.00.
Open: All Year (not Xmas/New
Year)
Beds: 3D 1T
Baths: 2 Pr 1 En
🛏 (9) 🅿 (10) � ⊐ × ♨ 🏠 ▥ 🗋 ∥
Beautiful old house and cottage set
in ancient gardens full of exotic
and unusual plants. Ten metres
from Teign Estuary, in easy
walking distance of village centre.
Lovely decor, home-made bread
and Aga cooking. Morning tea in
bed!

(1.5m) *Glenside House,* Ringmore
Road, Shaldon, Teignmouth,
Devon, *TQ14 0EP.*
Olde worlde cottage-style hotel by
river. 10 mins level walk to beach
and coast.
Tel: **01626 872448**
Mr Underwood.
D: £22.00-£28.00 **S:** £22.00-£28.00.
Open: All Year
Beds: 4D 3T 1S
Baths: 7 Pr 1 Sh
🛏 (8) 🅿 (10) ⊐ ⋔ × ♨ 🏠 ▥ 🗋 ∥

Teignmouth 23
National Grid Ref: SX9473

The Endeavour, London Hotel, Trade
Winds, New Quay Inn, Drakes Hotel, Ship Inn,
The Elizabethan

(0.25m) *The Bay Hotel,* Sea Front,
Teignmouth, Devon, *TQ14 8BL.*
Tel: **01626 774123** Mrs Dumont.
Fax no: 01626 777794
D: £23.00-£26.00 **S:** £23.00-£26.00.
Open: All Year
Beds: 4F 6T 6D 2S
Baths: 18 En
🛏 🅿 (14) ⊐ × ♨ 🏠 ▥ 🗋
Overlooking the sea, previously the
summer house of the Earl of Devon
of nearby Powderham Castle. Ideal
central stop over for seeing South
Devon, Dartmoor, South Hams,
Torbay, Exeter - all only half hour
away. Only 4 miles from express
way A38. Superb golf courses
around.

🚌 sign means that,
given due notice,
owners will pick you
up from the path
and drop you off *with-
in reason.*

All rates are subject
to alteration at the
owners' discretion.

(0.25m) *Beachley Guest House,*
3 Brunswick Street, Teignmouth,
Devon, *TQ14 8AE.*
One minute to sea front and shops.
Level position.
Tel: **01626 774249**
D: £16.00 **S:** £17.00.
Open: All Year (not Xmas)
Beds: 3F 1D 1T 1S **Baths:** 2 Sh
🛏 ⊐ × ♨ 🏠 ▥ 🗋

(0.25m 🚌) *Higher Holcombe,*
Holcombe, Devon Road,
Teignmouth, *TQ14 9NU.*
A scrumptious breakfast while
overlooking panoramic sea and
moorland views.
Tel: **01626 777144** Mrs Smith.
D: £17.50-£19.00 **S:** £20.00-£22.00.
Open: All Year
Beds: 2F 1D **Baths:** 3 En
🅿 ⊄ ⊐ ♨ 🏠 & ▥ ∥

(0.25m) *Meran House,* Third
Drive, Landscore Road,
Teignmouth, Devon, *TQ14 9JT.*
Lovely Victorian house, quiet area
lounge and garden, homely
atmosphere.
Tel: **01626 778828** Mrs Hughes.
D: £16.00-£19.00 **S:** £20.00-£23.00.
Open: All Year (not Xmas)
Beds: 3D
Baths: 3 En
🅿 (5) ⊄ ⊐ ♨ 🏠 ▥ ∥

(0.25m) *Valentine Guest House,* 1
Glendaragh Road, Teignmouth,
Devon, *TQ14 8PH.*
Refurbished in 1999. near town,
beach, rail, coach stations. Some
rooms beautiful sea views.
Tel: **01626 772316** (also fax no)
D: £15.00-£18.50 **S:** £15.00-£18.50.
Open: all year (not Xmas)
Beds: 2D 1T
Baths: 3 En
⊄ ⊐ ♨ 🏠 ▥

Exmouth 24
National Grid Ref: SY0081

Redweek Inn, Deer Leap Inn, Ship Inn,
Nutwell Inn, Carlton Lodge, The Grove,
Beachcomber Inn

(0.5m) *Sea Breeze,* 42 Victoria
Road, Exmouth, Devon, *EX8 1DW.*
Small friendly guest house close to
beach river and town.
Tel: **01395 224888** Mrs Bane.
D: £16.00-£22.00 **S:** £16.00-£22.00.
Open: All Year
Beds: 2F 1D 1S
Baths: 4 En
🛏 ⊄ ⊐ ♨ 🏠 ▥

(0.5m) *Aslema,*
61 St Andrews Road, Exmouth,
Devon, *EX8 1AS.*
Charming long established guest
house 200 yards from Exmouth sea
front.
Tel: **01395 270737**
Mrs Stevens.
D: £17.00-£17.00
S: £17.00-£17.00.
Open: Feb to Nov
Beds: 2D 1T
Baths: 3 En
🛏 (8) 🅿 (2) ⊐ × ♨ 🏠 ▥

(0.5m 🚌) *Sandrevin,*
59 Salterton Road, Exmouth,
Devon, *EX8 2EQ.*
Large Victorian house, ensuite
bedrooms. Exe estuary views.
Car park.
Tel: **01395 266898**
Mr & Mrs Cooper.
D: £18.00-£23.00 **S:** £21.00-£26.00.
Open: All Year (not Xmas)
Beds: 1F 2D 1T
Baths: 3 En 1 Pr
🛏 🅿 (5) ⊐ ⋔ ♨ 🏠 ▥ ∥

(0.5m) *30 Withycombe Road,*
Exmouth, Devon, *EX8 1TG.*
Large Victorian house which is
close to shops. Seafront 20 min
walk away.
Tel: **01395 277025**
Mrs Shobbrook.
D: £15.00 **S:** £15.00.
Open: Easter to Oct
Beds: 1F 1D 1S
Baths: 1 Sh
🛏 (6) 🅿 (2) ⊐ ⋔ × ♨ ▥

(0.5m 🚌) *No 37,*
37 Salterton Road, Exmouth,
Devon, *EX8 2ED.*
Warm and welcoming period house
a few minutes from seafront and
town.
Tel: **01395 279381** (also fax no)
Mrs Blunt.
D: £16.00-£20.00
S: £16.00-£30.00.
Open: Apr to Oct
Beds: 1F 1D
Baths: 1 En 1 Pr
🛏 🅿 (2) ⊐ ♨ 🏠 ▥ 🗋 ∥

Budleigh Salterton 25
National Grid Ref: SY0682

Salterton Arms
🍴

(0.25m) *Chapter House,* 6
Westbourne Terrace, Budleigh
Salterton, Devon, *EX9 6BR.*
Budleigh Salterton self-catering
ensuite family room with own sit-
ting room.
Tel: **01395 444100**
Ms Simmons.
D: £20.00-£25.00
S: £20.00.
Open: All Year
Beds: 1F
Baths: 1 En
🛏 🅿 (1) ⊄ ⊐ ⋔ ♨ 🏠 ▥ ∥

(0.5m ⊞) *Long Range Hotel,*
Budleigh Salterton, Devon, EX9 6HS.
A haven of peace and tranquillity,
close to sea and countryside.
Grades: AA 4 Diamond
Tel: 01395 443321
Mr & Mrs Morton.
Fax no: 01395 445220
D: £37.50-£49.50 **S:** £25.00-£30.00.
Open: All Year
Beds: 1F 3D 2T 1S
Baths: 6 En 1 Pr
🛏 ₽ (7) ⊬◻✕♨ 🎵 Ⅳ🛉 ⌁

(0.25m) *Rosehill,* *West Hill Lane,*
Budleigh Salterton, Devon, EX9 6BO.
This unique property oozes relax-
ation - rooms spacious, garden
Victorian, ambience restful.
Tel: 01395 444031 (also fax no)
Mr Taylor.
D: £20.00-£27.50 **S:** £20.00-£27.50.
Open: All Year
Beds: 1F 2D 1T 1S
Baths: 4 En 1 Pr
🛏 ₽ (4) ◻🛏♨ 🎵 Ⅳ ⌁

Otterton
National Grid Ref: SY0885   **26**

Kings Arms

(1m) *Ropers Cottage,* *Ropers Lane,*
Otterton, Budleigh Salterton,
Devon, EX9 7JF.
Actual grid ref: SY082858
C17th cottage in picturesque vil-
lage, near river and coastal path.
Tel: 01395 568826 Mrs Earl.
Fax no: 01395 568206
D: £18.00-£18.50 **S:** £18.00-£18.50.
Open: Easter to Oct
Beds: 1T 1S
Baths: 2 En
🛏 (1) ₽ (2) ⊬◻♨ 🎵 Ⅳ ⌁

Sidmouth
National Grid Ref: SY1287   **27**

Anchor, Balfour Arms, Blue Ball, Bowd
Inn, Black Bull, Kings Arms, Tudor Rose, Old
Ship

(On path ⊞) *Barrington Villa*
Guest House, *Salcombe Road,*
Sidmouth, Devon, EX10 8PU.
Grades: ETC 3 Diamond
Tel: 01395 514252 Mr & Mrs Carr.
D: £14.50-£19.00 **S:** £18.00-£23.50.
Open: Jan to Nov
Beds: 3D 2T 3S
Baths: 4 En 4 Sh
🛏 ₽ (10) ◻🛏✕♨ 🎵 Ⅳ🛉 ⌁
A charming Regency Gothic Villa,
set in beautiful gardens on the bank
of the River Sid in the heart of
glorious East Devon.

**All rates are subject
to alteration at the
owners' discretion.**

(0.25m ⊞) *Ryton Guest House,*
52-54 Winslade Road, Sidmouth,
Devon, EX10 9EX.
Actual grid ref: SY1288
Grades: AA 3 Diamonds
Tel: 01395 513981
Mr & Mrs Bradnam.
D: £20.00-£22.00
S: £20.00-£24.00.
Open: Mar to Nov
Beds: 4F 3D 1T 2S
Baths: 8 En 2 Sh
🛏 ₽ (6) ⊬◻🛏✕♨ 🎵 Ⅳ🛉 ⌁
An attractive double fronted house
in central location 2 minutes walk
from river location, bright
bedrooms, cosy lounge, smart
dining room, home cooked evening
meals, friendly hosts, home from
home.

(0.5m) *Kyneton Cottage,*
87 Alexandria Road, Sidmouth,
Devon, EX10 9HG.
Quiet guest house, comfortable
beds, good breakfast. Beautiful
garden.
Grades: ETC 4 Diamond, Silver
Tel: 01395 513213 (also fax no)
Mrs Peirson.
D: £18.00-£23.00 **S:** £18.00-£23.00.
Open: All Year (not Xmas/New
Year)
Beds: 1T 1D
Baths: 2 En
🛏 (5) ₽ (6) ⊬◻♨ 🎵 Ⅳ ⌁

(0.5m) *Woodlands Hotel,* *Station*
Rd, Sidmouth, Devon, EX10 8HG.
16th Century building. All modern
conveniences in the heart of
Sidmouth.
Grades: ETC 2 Star
Tel: 01395 513120 (also fax no)
D: £20.00-£44.00
S: £24.00-£42.00.
Open: All Year
Beds: 3F 8T 8D 5S
Baths: 24 En
🛏 ₽ (20) ◻🛏✕♨ 🎵 Ⅳ

(0.5m) *Avalon,* *Vicarage Road,*
Sidmouth, Devon, EX10 8UQ.
Elegant town house, backing onto
river and National Trust park.
Tel: 01395 513443
Mrs Young.
D: £20.00-£27.50
S: £30.00-£35.00.
Open: All Year (not Xmas)
Beds: 4D 1T
Baths: 5 En
🛏 (5) ₽ (5) ⊬◻✕♨ 🎵 Ⅳ ⌁

(0.25m) *Sidling Field,*
105 Peaslands Road, Sidmouth,
Devon, EX10 8XE.
Large bungalow on outskirts of
town quiet location.
Tel: 01395 513859
Mrs Shenfield.
D: £17.00-£18.00
S: £20.00-£25.00.
Open: Jan to Nov
Beds: 1D 1T
Baths: 1 Sh
🛏 (8) ₽ (3) ◻🛏♨ 🎵 Ⅳ🛉 ⌁

(0.5m ⊞) *Cheriton Guest House,*
Vicarage Road, Sidmouth, Devon,
EX10 8UQ.
Private garden for guest use to
banks of River Sid.
Tel: 01395 513810 (also fax no)
Mrs Lee.
D: £18.00-£22.00 **S:** £18.00-£22.00.
Open: All Year
Beds: 2F 4D 2T 2S **Baths:** 10 En
🛏 ₽ (10) ⊬◻🛏✕♨ 🎵 & Ⅳ ⌁

(On path ⊞) *Bramley Lodge,*
Vicarage Road, Sidmouth, Devon,
EX10 8UQ.
Tel: 01395 515710
Mr & Mrs Haslam.
D: £18.00-£25.00 **S:** £18.00-£25.00.
Open: All Year
Beds: 1F 1T 2D 3S
Baths: 3 En 1 Sh
🛏 ₽ (6) ⊬◻🛏✕♨ 🎵 & Ⅳ🛉 ⌁
A family owned and run guest
house in a town house only a half-
mile level walk, via shops, to the
sea front. Explore Sidmouth on
foot. Residents garden backing
onto the River Sid and Byes
Parkland.

(1m) *Burnthouse Farm, Sidmouth,*
Devon, EX10 0NL.
Farmhouse Bed & Breakfast on a
working farm, set in the beautiful
Otter Valley.
Tel: 01395 568304 Mrs Hill.
D: £16.00-£18.00 .
Open: Easter to Oct
Beds: 1F 1T **Baths:** 1 Sh
🛏 ₽ (3) ⊬◻♨ Ⅳ ⌁

(0.5m) *Canterbury Guest House,*
Salcombe Road, Sidmouth, Devon,
EX10 8PR.
Georgian house adjacent to NT.
parkland and the River Sid.
Grades: ETC 3 Diamond
Tel: 01395 513373
Mr & Mrs Penaluna.
D: £16.00-£32.00 **S:** £16.00-£21.50.
Open: All Year
Beds: 3F 3D 2T **Baths:** 7 Pr 1 Sh
🛏 ₽ (6) ⊬◻🛏✕♨ 🎵 & Ⅳ

(0.5m) *Lynstead,* *Lynstead*
Vicarage Road, Sidmouth, Devon,
EX10 8UQ.
Cosy guest house backing on to
'The Byes' NT park.
Grades: ETC 4 Diamond
Tel: 01395 514635
Mr & Mrs Mair.
D: £20.00-£22.00 **S:** £20.00-£30.00.
Open: All Year
Beds: 2F 2D 1T 1S
Baths: 4 En 1 Sh
🛏 ₽ (8) ⊬◻✕♨ 🎵 Ⅳ ⌁

**Planning a longer
stay? Always ask for
any special rates.**

(0.25m) *Berwick Guest House,*
Salcombe Road, Sidmouth, Devon,
EX10 8PX.
Ideally situated to charming town,
unspoilt sea front and coastal path.
Grades: ETC 4 Diamond
Tel: 01395 513621 Mrs Tingley.
D: £17.00-£24.00 **S:** £22.00-£27.00.
Open: Mar to Nov
Beds: 2F 2T 3D
Baths: 6 En 1 Sh
🛇 (7) 🅿 (7) ⌀⌿♦⌗≛⏳ Ⅴ ⌀

(0.5m 🚐) *Pinn Barton Farm,* Peak
Hill, Sidmouth, Devon, *EX10 0NN.*
Actual grid ref: SY100868
Comfortable farmhouse on working
farm.
Grades: ETC 4 Diamond
Tel: 01395 514004 (also fax no)
Mrs Sage.
D: £20.00-£22.00 **S:** £25.00.
Open: All Year
Beds: 1F 1D 1T
Baths: 3 En
🛇 (3) 🅿 (6) ⌀♦≛⏳ Ⅴ

Branscombe 28
National Grid Ref: SY1988

Masons Arms, Fountain Head

(1.25m 🚐) *Hole Mill,* Branscombe,
Seaton, Devon, *EX12 3BX.*
Actual grid ref: SY192895
Tel: 01297 680314 Mr & Mrs Hart.
D: £17.50-£21.00.
S: £25.00-£34.00.
Open: All Year
Beds: 2D 1T
Baths: 2 Sh
🛇⌀ ♦♦≛⏳ Ⅴ ⌀
Old converted watermill providing
comfortable accommodation in
style of yesteryear. Beams, brass
beds, inglenook lounge, garden,
stream. No rush, no town noises -
just peace/relaxation. Featured in
'Which? The Good Bed &
Breakfast Guide' & 'Staying Off the
Beaten Track'.

(1m) *The Chapel House,*
Branscombe, Seaton, Devon,
EX12 3AY.
Converted chapel, just behind the
cliffs, with spectacular outlook over
NT wooded valley.
Tel: 01297 680520
Mr & Mrs Van den Broeck.
D: £18.00-£20.00 **S:** £25.00-£25.00.
Open: All Year
Beds: 1F 2D
Baths: 2 Sh
🛇 (6) 🅿 (3) ⌀⌿♦♦ ⌀

Beer 29
National Grid Ref: SY2289

Anchor Inn, Dolphin

(0.5m) *Beer Youth Hostel,*
Bovey Combe, Beer, Seaton,
Devon, *EX12 3LL.*
Actual grid ref: SY223896
Tel: 01297 20296
Under 18: £7.75 **Adults:** £11.00
Self-catering facilities, Showers,
Lounge, Dining room, Drying
room, Cycle store, Parking,
Evening meal at 6.45 to 7.15pm,
No smoking, WC, Kitchen facili-
ties, Credit cards accepted
*Large house standing in land-
scaped grounds on hillside to the
west of a picturesque 'old world'
fishing village.*

(On path) *Bay View Guest House,*
Fore Street, Beer, Seaton, Devon,
EX12 3EE.
Actual grid ref: SY229891
Seafront location, coastal views,
large comfortable rooms and great
breakfasts!
Grades: AA 3 Diamond
Tel: 01297 20489 Mr & Mrs Oswald
D: £15.50 **S:** £15.50.
Open: Easter to Nov
Beds: 1F 1T 4D 2S
Baths: 3 En 1 Pr 4 Sh
🛇⌀♦≛⏳ Ⅴ ⌀ ⌀

(0.25m 🚐) *Garlands,* Stovar Long
Lane, Beer, Seaton, Devon, *EX12 3EA.*
Actual grid ref: SY232895
Edwardian character house in an
acre of ground - superb views sea
and Devon countryside.
Tel: 01297 20958 Ms Harding.
Fax no: 01297 23869
D: £20.00-£22.50 **S:** £30.00-£33.00.
Open: All Year (not Xmas)
Beds: 2F 2D 1T 1S **Baths:** 6 En
🛇 🅿 (10) ⌀♦≛⏳ Ⅴ

(0.25m 🚐) *Pamber House,* Clapps
Lane, Beer, Seaton, Devon, *EX12 3HD*
Set in idyllic fishing village. Quiet
positions, 2 minutes' walk from
village and beach.
Tel: 01297 20722 (also fax no)
Mrs Cummins. **D:** £21.00 **S:** £28.00.
Open: All Year
Beds: 1F 2D **Baths:** 3 Pr
🛇 (7) 🅿 (3) ⌀⌿≛⏳ Ⅴ

Seaton 30
National Grid Ref: SY2490

Harbour Inn, Ship Inn, Rossini's, The Terrace

(On path) *The Harbour House,*
1 Trevelyan Road, Seaton, Devon,
EX12 2NL.
Spacious and comfortable harbourside
house, directly on SW Coast Path.
Tel: 01297 21797 Sandbrook.
D: £20.00-£20.00 **S:** £25.00-£25.00.
Open: March to Nov
Beds: 1T 1D **Baths:** 2 En
🛇 🅿 (5) ⌀♦≛⏳ Ⅴ ⌀ ⌀

(On path) *The Kettle Restaurant,*
15 Fore Street, Seaton, Devon,
EX12 2LE.
Close to shops, sea front.
Comfortable, friendly & great food.
Tel: 01297 20428 Mr Wallis.
D: £17.00-£22.00 **S:** £19.00-£25.00.
Open: All Year (not Xmas)
Beds: 1T 1D
Baths: 2 Pr
🛇 🅿 (2) ⌿⌀♦≛⏳ Ⅴ ⌀

(0.5m) *Beaumont,* Castle Hill,
Seaton, Devon, *EX12 2QW.*
Beautiful sea front house with spec-
tacular sea and cliff views.
Grades: ETC 3 Diamond
Tel: 01297 20832 Mrs Hill.
D: £23.00-£25.00 **S:** £23.00-£25.00.
Open: All Year (not Xmas/
New Year)
Beds: 2F 3D
Baths: 5 En
🛇 🅿 (5) ⌀♦≛⏳ Ⅴ ⌀

(On path) *Tors Guest House,* 55
Harbour Road, Seaton, Devon,
EX12 2LX.
Comfort, conviviality, good food.
You know it's what you want.
Tel: 01297 20531 Mrs Webber.
D: £20.00-£20.00 **S:** £20.00-£20.00.
Open: All Year
Beds: 4D 1T 1S
Baths: 2 En 2 Sh
🛇 (15) 🅿 (5) ⌀≛⏳ Ⅴ ⌀ ⌀

Uplyme 31
National Grid Ref: SY3293

Pilot Boat

(0.25m) *Lydwell House,* Lyme
Road , Uplyme, Lyme Regis,
Dorset, *DT7 3TJ.*
A pre-Victorian house set within
0.75 acre of Victorian gardens.
Grades: ETC 3 Diamond
Tel: 01297 443522 Mr Brittain.
D: £23.00-£27.00 **S:** £23.00-£27.00.
Open: All Year
Beds: 2F 1D 1T 1S **Baths:** 5 En
🛇 🅿 (7) ⌿⌀♦≛⏳ Ⅴ ⌀ ⌀

(0.25m) *Hill Barn,* Gore Lane,
Uplyme, Lyme Regis, Dorset,
DT7 3RJ.
Beautifully converted stone barn,
surrounded by countryside, only
1 mile Lyme Regis.
Grades: ETC 4 Diamond
Tel: 01297 445185 (also fax no)
Mrs Wyon-Brown.
D: £18.00-£20.00 **S:** £18.00.
Open: All Year (not Xmas)
Beds: 1F 1D 1T **Baths:** 2 Sh
🛇 🅿 ⌿⌀♦≛⏳ ♿ Ⅴ ⌀ ⌀

Bringing children with you? Always ask for any special rates.

All paths are popular: you are well-advised to book ahead

Dorset

This section of the **South West Coast Path** is the shortest, leading from Lyme Regis in the West to Studland Point (opposite Poole) in the East. Part of the path, between West Bay and Weymouth, runs slightly inland.

Guides: *South West Way: Vol II (Penzance to Poole)* by Martin Collins (ISBN 1 85284 026 9), published by Cicerone Press and available from the publishers (2 Police Square, Milnthorpe, Cumbria, LA7 7PY, 01539 562069), £8.99

South West Way: Exmouth to Poole by Roland Tarr (ISBN 1 85410 389X), published by Aurum Press in association with the Countryside Commission and Ordnance Survey, £10.99 There is also invaluable local information in *The South West Way 2001* by the South West Way Association, available directly from them at 25 Clobells, South Brent, Devon, TQ10 9JW, tel. 01364 73859, £7.00 (inc. p&p)

Maps: Ordnance Survey 1:50,000 Landranger series: 193, 194 and 195

Lyme Regis   1

National Grid Ref: SY3392

®⊯ Dorset Hotel, Pilot Boat, Victoria, Volunteer

(0.5m) *Hillsett, Haye Lane, Lyme Regis, Dorset, DT7 3NG.*
Tel: **01297 445 259** (also fax no)
Mr Thompson.
D: £20.00-£25.00 **S:** £20.00-£25.00.
Open: All Year (not Xmas/New Year)
Beds: 1F 1D
Baths: 1Ensuite 1Shared
⛺ (8) ❒ (7) ❏ 🖭 Ⅷ Ⅴ
Lovely modern family home set in beautiful surroundings overlooking Lym valley, Golden Cap & Lyme Bay. 15 minutes walk to centre of famous Lyme Regis, Cobb Harbour & beach. Private car park, heated open air pool, sauna and pool table.

(0.5m 🚗) *Mayflower Cottage, 39 Sherborne Lane, Lyme Regis, Dorset, DT7 3NY.*
Actual grid ref: SY340922
Quiet, traffic-free. Secluded garden. Town centre, Free parking nearby.
Tel: **01297 445930** Mr Snowsill.
D: £20.00-£25.00 **S:** £25.00.
Open: All Year (not Xmas)
Beds: 1F 1D 1T **Baths:** 3 En
⛺ ❒ (3) ❏ 🖙 🖭 Ⅷ Ⅴ ⓐ ⚡

(0.5m) *Tudor House Hotel, 3/5 Church Street, Lyme Regis, Dorset, DT7 3BS.*
Grades: ETC 3 Diamond
Tel: **01297 442472** Mr Ray.
D: £24.00-£49.00 **S:** £28.00-£38.00.
Open: All Year (not Xmas/New Year)
Beds: 9F 5D 1T 1S
Baths: 14 En 2 Pr
⛺ ❒ (15) ⚡❏ 🖙 🗙 🖭 Ⅷ Ⅴ ⓐ ⚡
An historic Elizabethan house, circa 1580, one minutes level walk to the sea in the centre of Old Lyme Regis. Part plaster ceiling designed by Sir Walter Raleigh. Cellar bar with original well. Parking.
www.thetudorhouse.co.uk.

(On path) *Charnwood Guest House, 21 Woodmead Road, Lyme Regis, Dorset, DT7 3AD.*
Actual grid ref: SY339924
Grades: ETC 3 Diamond
Tel: **01297 445281** Mr Bradbury.
D: £19.00-£24.00 **S:** £19.00-£24.00.
Open: All Year
Beds: 1F 4D 2T 1S
Baths: 6 En 1 Sh
⛺ ❒ (7) ⚡❏ 🖙 🖭 Ⅷ Ⅴ ⓐ ⚡
1910 style house with balcony. Scenic river walk to town (5 mins) past pubs, restaurants etc. Quiet, safe, easy access to walking, fossilling and beach. Discounts for 3 plus nights midweek Sun-Thurs. Clean, friendly, personally run with hearty breakfast.

(0.5m 🚗) *The Old Monmouth Hotel, 12 Church Street, Lyme Regis, Dorset, DT7 3BS.*
Actual grid ref: SY344922
C17th building, centrally situated for beaches, harbour and all amenities.
Tel: **01297 442456** Mr & Mrs Brown.
Fax no: 01297 443577
D: £19.00-£22.00 **S:** £26.00-£30.00.
Open: All Year (not Xmas)
Beds: 1F 4D 1T
Baths: 5 En 1 Sh
⛺⚡❏🗙🖭Ⅷ Ⅴ ⓐ ⚡

(0.25m) *The Red House, Sidmouth Road, Lyme Regis, Dorset, DT7 3ES.*
Actual grid ref: SY330922
Elegant house with wonderful views Eastwards beyond Golden Cap.
Grades: ETC 4 Diamond
Tel: **01297 442055** (also fax no)
Mr & Mrs Norman.
D: £22.00-£27.00 **S:** £33.00-£40.00.
Open: Easter to Nov
Beds: 1D 2T **Baths:** 3 En
⛺ (8) ❒ (3) ⚡❏ 🖭 Ⅷ Ⅴ ⚡

D = Price range per person sharing in a double room

S = Price range for a single person in a single room

(On path) *Coverdale Guest House, Woodmead Road, Lyme Regis, Dorset, DT7 3AB.*
Actual grid ref: SY339925
Spacious comfortable non-smoking guest house. Country/sea views. Beach, restaurants nearby.
Tel: **01297 442882**
Mr & Mrs Bales.
D: £19.00-£27.50 **S:** £19.00-£27.50.
Open: All Year (not Xmas)
Beds: 2F 3D 2T 1S
Baths: 8 En
⛺ (4) ❒ (9) ⚡❏ 🖙 🖭 Ⅷ Ⅴ ⚡

(0.5m) *Coombe House, 41 Coombe Street, Lyme Regis, Dorset, DT7 3PY.*
Lovely old blue lias stone house situated in the oldest part of town.
Tel: **01297 443849** (also fax no)
Mrs Duncan.
D: £17.00-£17.00 **S:** £20.00-£34.00.
Open: All Year
Beds: 1D 1T
Baths: 2 En
⛺ ❒ (1) ⚡❏ 🖭 Ⅷ Ⅴ

(0.5m 🚗) *New Haven Hotel, 1 Pound Street, Lyme Regis, Dorset, DT7 3HZ.*
C18th town house.
Tel: **01297 442499** (also fax no)
Mrs Petitt.
D: £17.50-£28.50 **S:** £20.50-£28.50.
Open: All Year
Beds: 1F 3D 1T 2S
Baths: 4 En 1 Sh
⛺❏🖙🖭Ⅷ Ⅴ ⚡

(0.5m) *Southernhaye, Pound Road, Lyme Regis, Dorset, DT7 3HX.*
Edwardian house with sea views.
Tel: **01297 443077** (also fax no)
Mr Garrard.
D: £17.00-£18.00 **S:** £18.00-£20.00.
Open: All Year (not Xmas)
Beds: 1D 1T 1S **Baths:** 1 Sh
⛺ (13) ❒ (2) ❏ 🖭 Ⅷ Ⅴ ⚡

(0.5m) *Rotherfield Guest House, View Road, Lyme Regis, Dorset, DT7 3AA.*
Actual grid ref: SY3492
Clean, comfortable, ensuite accommodation. Sea views, beach, restaurants, coastal path nearby.
Tel: **01297 445585** Mr Endersby.
D: £19.00-£23.00 **S:** £25.00-£35.00.
Open: All Year
Beds: 2F 3D 1T
Baths: 6 En
♿ (5) �ℙ (6) ⌨ ⊶ ☕ ▥ Ⅴ 🛈

Wootton Fitzpaine　　　2

National Grid Ref: SY3695
📶 ◁ Shave Cross Inn

(0.25m) *Higher Spence, Wootton Fitzpaine, Charmouth, DT6 6DF.*
Actual grid ref: SY357965
No street lights or proper road; instead: peace, tranquillity, beautiful country & sea views.
Tel: **01297 560556**
D: £18.00-£20.00 **S:** £21.00-£23.00.
Open: All Year (not Xmas)
Beds: 1F 1D
Baths: 2 En
♿ (3) ℙ (3) ⊁ ⌨ ⊶ ▥ Ⅴ ⚡

Pay B&Bs by
cash or cheque and
be prepared to
pay up front.

Taking your dog?
Book *in advance*
ONLY with owners
who accept dogs (🐕)

Charmouth　　　3

National Grid Ref: SY3693
📶 ◁ Five Bells, Ship Inn

(0.5m 🐕) *Stonebarrow Manor, Stonebarrow Lane, Charmouth, Dorset, DT6 6RA.*
C16th house in 2 acres. Beach, fossils, great walking country.
Tel: **01297 560212** Bomford.
Fax no: 01297 560234
D: £25.00-£25.00 **S:** £25.00-£25.00.
Open: All Year (not Xmas/New Year)
Beds: 4F 4D 3T 2S
Baths: 11 En 1 Sh
♿ (6) ℙ (15) ⊁ ⌨ ✕ ☕ ▥ Ⅴ 🛈 ⚡

(0.25m 🐕) *Hensleigh Hotel, Lower Sea Lane, Charmouth, Bridport, Dorset, DT6 6LW.*
Actual grid ref: SY365933
Comfort and hospitality, 300 metres from beach and cliff walks.
Tel: **01297 560830** (also fax no)
Mr & Mrs Davis.
D: £24.00-£30.00 **S:** £24.00-£45.00.
Open: Feb to Nov
Beds: 1F 2D 5T 2S
Baths: 10 En
♿ ℙ (20) ⊁ ⌨ ✕ ☕ ▥ Ⅴ 🛈

Chideock　　　4

National Grid Ref: SY4292
📶 ◁ George Inn, All in the Clock House, Anchor

(0.75m 🐕) *Warren House B&B, Chideock, Bridport, Dorset, DT6 6JW.*
Actual grid ref: SY420929
Grades: ETC 4 Diamond,
AA 4 Diamond
Tel: **01297 489704** (also fax no)
Mr & Mrs Tweddle.
D: £22.00-£25.00 **S:** £27.00-£30.00.
Open: All Year (not Xmas)
Beds: 2F 1D 1T **Baths:** 4 En
♿ ℙ (7) ⊁ ⌨ ☕ ▥ Ⅴ 🛈 ⚡
Grade II Listed C17th thatched house, high quality, comfortable spacious rooms. Friendly informal atmosphere. Area of Outstanding Natural Beauty with Coastal Path and beach within walking distance. Close to all local amenities. Intercity rail lines at Axminster or Dorchester.

(0.75m) *Chideock House Hotel, Main St, Chideock, Bridport, DT6 6JN.*
Grades: ETC 2 Star, AA 2 Star
Tel: **01297 489242** Mr Dunn.
Fax no: 01297 489184
D: £27.50-£42.50 **S:** £50.00-£80.00.
Open: All Year
Beds: 9D **Baths:** 8 En 1 Pr
♿ ℙ (15) ⌨ ⊶ ✕ ☕ ▥ Ⅴ 🛈 ⚡
Ten minute walk to the sea and coastal path with stunning scenery. 'Harbour Lights' filmed locally. Abbots Swannery, Mapperton Gardens and Athelhampton House all nearby. Stunning food in candle lit restaurant. Close to Lyme Regis & Charmouth. Weymouth 20 mins.

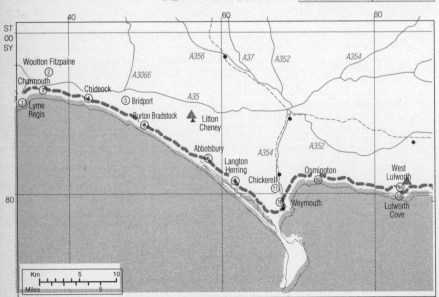

(0.5m 🚗) *Betchworth House,*
Chideock, Bridport, Dorset, DT6
6JW.
Grades: ETC 4 Diamond,
AA 4 Diamond, RAC 4 Diamond
Tel: 01297 489478 Lodge.
Fax no: 01297 489932
D: £22.00-£25.00 **S:** £27.00-£30.00.
Open: All Year
Beds: 1F 2D 2T
Baths: 3 En 2 Pr
🛏 (10) 🅿 (6) ⊁🖵 ⊁ 🔥 💻 Ⅴ 🛉 ∦
Very friendly C17th guesthouse
has been refurbished to a very high
standard. Each room is well
equipped with thoughtful extras
such as tissues, toiletries, hairdryer.
renowned Dorset cream teas.
Attractive cottage garden. Private
parking. Sea 3/4 mile. Pubs nearby.

(0.75m 🚗) *Frogmore Farm,*
Chideock, Bridport, Dorset, DT6
6HT.
Actual grid ref: SY436926
C17th farmhouse overlooking
Lyme Bay. Adjoining South West
Coast Path.
Tel: 01308 456159 Mrs Norman.
D: £16.00-£20.00 **S:** £20.00-£23.00.
Open: All Year
Beds: 1F 1D 1T 1S
Baths: 2 En 2 Pr
🛏 (8) 🅿 (6) ⊁🖵 ⊁ 🔥 💻 Ⅴ 🛉 ∦

(0.75m 🚗) *Chimneys Guest*
House, Main Street, Chideock,
Bridport, Dorset, DT6 6JH.
Warm welcome, comfortable bed-
rooms, guest lounge & dining
room. Private parking.
Grades: RAC 4 Diamond
Tel: 01297 489368 Backhouse & J
M Backhouse.
D: £22.50-£25.00
S: £25.00-£25.00.
Open: All Year (not Xmas)
Beds: 1F 1T 3D
Baths: 4 En
🛏 🅿 (5) ⊁🖵 ⊁ 🔥 💻 Ⅴ 🛉 ∦

SY 00 SZ

A351
Kimmeridge
Langton
Worth Matravers
Matravers
Swanage

Bridport 5

National Grid Ref: SY4693

🍴 🍺 Crown Inn, The Uploaders, The Bull,
Hardy's, Tiger Inn, Woodhay

(0.75m 🚗) *Britmead House,* West
Bay Road, Bridport, Dorset, DT6
4EG.
Actual grid ref: SY465912
Grades: ETC 4 Diamond,
AA 4 Diamond
Tel: 01308 422941
Mr Hardy.
Fax no: 01308 422516
D: £22.00-£31.00 **S:** £26.00-£40.00.
Open: All Year
Beds: 2F 3D 2T
Baths: 7 En
🛏 🅿 (8) 🖵 🔥 🗙 🛁 💻 Ⅴ 🛉
Situated between Bridport and
West Bay Harbour with its beach-
es, golf course, walks, Chesil
Beach and the Dorset Coast Path.
All rooms have colour TV, mini
bar, tea and coffee making facili-
ties. South-facing lounge and
dining room overlooking gardens.
Private parking.

(1.5m) *The Old Dairy House,*
Walditch, Bridport, Dorset, DT6 4LB.
Actual grid ref: SY480925
Tel: 01308 458021
Mrs Long.
D: £20.00-£20.00
S: £20.00-£20.00.
Open: All Year
Beds: 1D 1T
Baths: 1 Sh
🅿 (4) ⊁🖵 🛁 💻 Ⅴ ∦
A friendly welcome to relax in this
peaceful corner of West Dorset.
Enjoy full English breakfast.
Guests' TV lounge with log fire.
Gardens, abundant wildlife.
Rural/coastal walks. 18-hole golf 2
miles. Good selection country pubs
nearby. Adults only.

(0.75m 🚗) *Green Lane House,*
Bridport, Dorset, DT6 4LH.
Welcoming, spacious home in own
grounds. 1.5 miles from coast.
Tel: 01308 422619 (also fax no)
Mrs Prideaux.
D: £20.00-£20.00 **S:** £20.00-£20.00.
Open: All Year (not Xmas/
New Year)
Beds: 1T 1D
Baths: 2 En
🛏 🅿 (5) ⊁🖵 🔥 🗙 🛁 💻 Ⅴ 🛉 ∦

Many rates vary
according to season -
the lowest only are
shown here

Burton Bradstock 6

National Grid Ref: SY4889

(On path 🚗) *Burton Cliff Hotel,*
Cliff Road, Burton Bradstock,
Bridport, Dorset, DT6 4RB.
Grades: ETC 3 Diamond
Tel: 01308 897205 Mr Hoare.
Fax no: 01308 898111
D: £21.00-£39.00 **S:** £24.50-£36.00.
Open: All Year
Beds: 8T 7D 3S
Baths: 12 En 12 Pr 3 Sh
🛏 🅿 (40) ⊁🖵 🔥 🗙 🛁 💻 ♿ 🛉 ∦
Situated on the cliff top with
superb sea views and surrounded
by National Trust countryside.
Many guest rooms overlook the
beach/sea. Excellent home home
cooking bought to you by our team
of friendly and enthusiastic staff.
Private off-road parking.

Litton Cheney 7

National Grid Ref: SY5590

🔺 3.5m) *Litton Cheney Youth*
Hostel, Litton Cheney, Dorchester,
Dorset, DT2 9AT.
Actual grid ref: SY548900
Tel: 01308 482340
Under 18: £6.90
Adults: £10.00
Self-catering facilities, Showers,
Lounge, Drying room, Cycle store,
Parking Limited, No smoking,
Kitchen facilities, Credit cards
accepted
Traditional Dutch barn in the
Bride Valley, once a cheese
factory. This is an Area of
Outstanding Natural Beauty.

Abbotsbury 8

National Grid Ref: SY5785
🍴 🍺 Kings Arms, Swan Inn

(0.5m 🚗) *Swan Lodge, Abbotsbury,*
Weymouth, Dorset, DT3 4JL.
Comfortable modern rooms with
tea and coffee facilities and colour
TVs.
Grades: ETC 3 Diamond
Tel: 01305 871249 (also fax no)
Mr Roper.
D: £22.00-£28.00
S: £30.00-£45.00.
Open: All Year
Beds: 3D
Baths: 3 En
🛏 🅿 🖵 🔥 🗙 🛁 💻 Ⅴ 🛉 ∦

Langton Herring 9

National Grid Ref: SY6182

🏠 🍺Elm Tree Inn

(0.25m 🚗) *East Cottage Bed & Breakfast, Langton Herring, Weymouth, Dorset, DT4 4HZ.*
Actual grid ref: SY615825
Comfortable, idyllic coastal location, spacious farm cottage, famous Chesil Beach.
Tel: **01305 871627** Freeman.
D: £22.00-£24.00 **S:** £22.00-£24.00.
Open: All Year
Beds: 1F 2D 1T
Baths: 2 En 1 Pr 1 Sh
🛏 🅿 (4) ⅍ 🗆 🏠 🛌 🎔 🛇 🔖 ✓

Weymouth 10

National Grid Ref: SY6779

🏠 🍺Dorthory Inn, White Hart, Lodmore Inn, Pulpit, Waterloo, Old Rooms, Excise House, Hog's Head, Hamiltons, Cork & Bottle, Sailors' Return

(0.5m) *Seaways, 5 Turton Street, Weymouth, Dorset, DT4 7DU.*
Victorian Building close to all amenities. Beach, Town and Parking.
Tel: **01305 771646** Mr & Mrs Seward.
D: £16.00-£16.00 **S:** £16.00-£16.00.
Open: All Year (not Xmas/New Year)
Beds: 5D 1T 1S **Baths:** 2 Sh
🛏 ⅍ 🗆 🛌 🎔 🛇

(0.5m 🚗) *Esplanade Hotel, 141 The Esplanade, Weymouth, Dorset, DT4 7NJ.*
Sea front 1835 Georgian terrace hotel. Superior ensuite accommodation with car parking.
Grades: AA 5 Diamond
Tel: **01305 783129** Mr & Mrs Paul.
D: £25.00-£35.00 **S:** £32.00-£35.00.
Open: Easter to Oct
Beds: 1F 7D 2T 1S
Baths: 11 En
🛏 (6) 🅿 (9) ⅍ 🗆 🛌 🎔 🛇

(0.5m) *Birchfields Hotel, 22 Abbotsbury Road, Weymouth, Dorset, DT4 0AE.*
Close to beach and town, short breaks welcome, ideal touring base.
Grades: RAC 3 Diamond
Tel: **01305 773255** (also fax no) Mr & Mrs Dutton.
D: £20.00-£25.00 **S:** £16.00-£25.00.
Open: Easter to Oct
Beds: 2F 3D 2T 2S **Baths:** 3 En 7 Sh
🛏 🅿 (3) 🗆 🛌 🎔 🛇

(0.5m) *Greenlands Guest House, 8 Waterloo Place, The Esplanade, Weymouth, Dorset, DT4 7PR.*
Family run guesthouse, on the sea front. Good wholesome breakfast.
Tel: **01305 776368** (also fax no) Mr & Mrs Turbett.
D: £15.00-£20.00 .
Open: All Year (not Xmas)
Beds: 2F 5D
🛏 🅿 (7) 🗆 🛌 🎔 🛇 🔖

(0.5m) *Kings Acre Hotel, 140 The Esplanade, Weymouth, Dorset, DT4 7NH.*
Grades: ETC 4 Diamond
Tel: **01305 782534** Mrs Mears.
Fax no: 01305 732354
D: £25.00-£35.00 **S:** £32.50-£40.00.
Open: Feb to Nov
Beds: 2F 7D 2T
Baths: 10 En 1 Pr
🛏 🅿 (9) ⅍ 🗆 🏠 🛌 🎔 🛇 🔖
Lovely, private run hotel in a grand Victorian terrace. offering friendly, courteous service, good food. Ideally located overlooking Weymouth's beach and bay and close to all amenities.

(0.5m) *Hardwick House, 23 Hardwick Street, Weymouth, Dorset, DT4 7HU.*
Friendly guest house, mins from sea front and town centre.
Tel: **01305 784303** Mrs Austin.
D: £15.00-£20.00 .
Open: Jan to Nov
Beds: 2F 2T 3D 1S
Baths: 3 En 1 Sh
🛏 🅿 🗆 🏠 🛌 🎔 🛇 🔖

(0.5m) *Hotel Fairhaven, 37 The Esplanade, Weymouth, Dorset, DT4 8DH.*
Beach front hotel, close town centre & harbour. 24 hour reception.
Grades: RAC 2 Star
Tel: **01305 760200** Mr Thwaite.
Fax no: 01305 760300
D: £30.00-£34.00 **S:** £32.00-£37.00.
Open: Mar to Nov
Beds: 12F 10D 50T 10S **Baths:** 82 En
🛏 🅿 (20) 🗆 🏠 🛌 🎔 🔖

(0.5m) *Southbrook Guest House, Preston Road, Overcombe, Weymouth, Dorset, DT3 6PU.*
Modern house close to beach coastal path and bird reserve.
Tel: **01305 832208** Mrs Coxhill.
D: £18.00-£26.00 **S:** £18.00-£25.00.
Open: All Year
Beds: 2F 5D 1T 2S **Baths:** 4 Pr 2 Sh
🛏 🅿 (10) 🗆 🎔 🛌

(0.5m) *Beachview, 3 The Esplanade, Weymouth, Dorset, DT4 8EA.*
Uniquely positioned with panoramic sea or harbour views from every room.
Tel: **01305 786528** Mrs Swainson.
Fax no: 01305 750102
D: £18.50-£21.00 **S:** £16.50-£17.50.
Open: All Year (not Xmas)
Beds: 1F 4D 1T 2S **Baths:** 3 En 1 Sh
🛏 (5) 🗆 🎔 🛇

(0.5m) *Hazeldene Guest House, 16 Abbotsbury Road, Weymouth, Dorset, DT4 0AE.*
Leisurely ten-minute walk to beach, bird sanctuary and harbour.
Tel: **01305 782579** Mrs Hepburn.
D: £15.00-£19.00 **S:** £15.00-£19.00.
Open: All Year (not Xmas)
Beds: 1F 3D 1T 1S
Baths: 1 En 1 Pr 2 Sh
🛏 🅿 (5) 🗆 🛌 🎔 🛇 ✓

(0.5m) *Goldcroft Guest House, 6 Goldcroft Avenue, Weymouth, Dorset, DT4 0ET.*
Actual grid ref: SY675795
Comfortable family B&B overlooking lake, walking, diving, friendly relaxed atmosphere.
Tel: **01305 789953**
Mr & Mrs Greenwood.
D: £18.00-£23.00 **S:** £20.00-£25.00.
Open: All Year
Beds: 2F 3D 1T **Baths:** 2 Sh
🛏 (1) 🅿 (4) 🗆 🏠 🛌 🎔 🛇 🔖 ✓

Chickerell 11

National Grid Ref: SY6480

🏠 🍺White Hart, Lodmore Inn, Pulpit, Waterloo, Turk's Head

(1m) *Stonebank, 14 West Street, Chickerell, Weymouth, Dorset, DT3 4DY.*
Charming C17th former farmhouse ideally situated for exploring coast and country.
Grades: ETC 5 Diamond
Tel: **01305 760120** Mrs Westcott.
Fax no: 01305 760871
D: £22.50-£25.00 **S:** £35.00-£35.00.
Open: Apr to Sep
Beds: 2D **Baths:** 2 En
🅿 (2) ⅍ 🗆 🛌 🎔 🛇

Osmington 12

National Grid Ref: SY7283

🏠 🍺Sunray Hotel

(On path 🚗) *Rosedale, Church Lane, Osmington, Weymouth, Dorset, DT3 6EW.*
Very attractive cottage. Large, comfortable rooms, warm friendly atmosphere.
Grades: ETC 2 Diamond
Tel: **01305 832056** Mrs Legg.
D: £16.00-£17.00 **S:** £18.00-£19.00.
Open: Mar to Oct
Beds: 1D 1T
Baths: 1 En 1 Pr
🛏 (5) 🅿 (3) 🛌 🎔 🛇 ✓

(0.25m 🚗) *Rosthwaite, Church Lane, Osmington, Weymouth, Dorset, DT3 6EW.*
Bungalow set in picturesque village, comfortable beds and excellent breakfasts.
Tel: **01305 833621** Ms Leigh.
D: £15.00-£17.00 **S:** £15.00-£20.00.
Open: All Year
Beds: 1D 1T **Baths:** 1 Sh
🛏 🅿 (2) ⅍ 🗆 🎔 🛌 🎔 🛇 🔖 ✓

(1m) *Upton Farm, Ringstead, Dorchester, Dorset, DT2 8NE.*
Historic barn conversion short stroll to secluded beach, 3 acres garden.
Tel: **01305 853970** (also fax no) Mr & Mrs Davies.
D: £29.00-£29.00 **S:** £30.00-£35.00.
Open: Easter to Oct
Beds: 2D
🛏 (6) 🅿 (6) ⅍ 🗆 🛌 🎔 🛇 🔖 ✓

Lulworth Cove 13
National Grid Ref: SY8279

🏮⚰ Castle Inn, Lulworth Cove Hotel

(0.25m) *Mill House Hotel,* *Lulworth Cove, West Lulworth, Wareham, Dorset, BH20 5RQ.*
Tel: **01929 400404** Mr Payne.
Fax no: 01929 400508
D: £25.00-£40.00 **S:** £35.00-£40.00.
Open: Feb to Dec
Beds: 2F 6D 1T **Baths:** 9 En
🛌 🅿 (9) ◻ ✕ 🖵 🛌 🎟 🗵 ♿ ⌁
Julian & Jenny Payne welcome you to their nine bedroom, country house-style hotel in the heart of Lulworth Cove, opposite the duck pond and 150 yards from the waters edge. Fantastic walks, beaches, golf, horse-riding, sightseeing all locally. Licensed bar & tea rooms.

(0.25m) *Shirley Hotel,* *West Lulworth, Wareham, Dorset, BH20 5RL.*
Actual grid ref: SY824806
Magnificent coastal path & inland walks from hotel. Family-run serving delicious food.
Tel: **01929 400358** Williams.
Fax no: 01929 400167
D: £33.50-£44.00 **S:** £33.50-£59.00.
Open: Feb to Nov
Beds: 2F 8D 4T 1S **Baths:** 15 En
🛌 🅿 (22) ◻ ✕ 🎟 🛌 🖵 🗵 ♿ ⌁

West Lulworth 14
National Grid Ref: SY8280

🏮⚰ Castle Inn

(0.5m) *Lulworth Cove Youth Hostel,* *School Lane, West Lulworth, Wareham, Dorset, BH20 5SA.*
Actual grid ref: SY832806
Tel: **01929 400564**
Under 18: £6.90 **Adults:** £10.00
Showers, Wet weather shelter, Lounge, Drying room, Cycle store, Parking, Evening meal at 7.00pm, No smoking, Kitchen facilities, Luggage store, Credit cards accepted
Purpose-built cedarwood hostel, recently refurbished. In an Area of Outstanding Natural Beauty.

(0.25m) *The Copse,* *School Lane, West Lulworth, Wareham, Dorset, BH20 5SA.*
Actual grid ref: SY822802
Tel: **01929 400581** (also fax no)
Mr & Mrs Johari.
D: £15.00-£17.50 **S:** £15.00-£17.50.
Open: All Year (not Xmas)
Beds: 1D 1T 1S **Baths:** 1 Sh
🛌 🅿 (3) ◻ 🛌 🖵 🗵
Detached house in picturesque coastal village. Quiet location overlooking field in Area of Outstanding Natural Beauty. Close to Lulworth Cove and beaches. Generous Continental breakfast.

(0.5m 🚗) *West Down Farm,* *West Lulworth, Wareham, Dorset, BH20 5RY.*
Beautiful coastal area. Outstanding views. Ideal riding, cycling and walking.
Tel: **01929 400308** (also fax no)
Ms Weld.
D: £18.00-£20.00 **S:** £25.00-£30.00.
Open: All Year
Beds: 1T 1D **Baths:** 1 Sh
🛌 🅿 ◻ 🎟 🛌 🖵 🗵 ♿ ⌁

(0.5m) *Gatton House ,* *West Lulworth, Wareham, Dorset, BH20 5RU.*
Picturesque guest house with spectacular views, near Lulworth Cove and coastal path.
Grades: ETC 4 Diamond
Tel: **01929 400252** (also fax no)
Mr Dale.
D: £23.00-£35.00 **S:** £33.00-£45.00.
Open: March to Oct
Beds: 1F 1T 6D **Baths:** 8 En
🛌 🅿 (9) ⌁ ◻ 🎟 🛌 🖵 🗵 ♿ ⌁

(0.25m) *Graybank Bed & Breakfast,* *Main Road, West Lulworth, Wareham, Dorset, BH20 5RL.*
Purbeck stone-built Victorian house. Warm welcome, excellent breakfast menu.
Grades: ETC 3 Diamond
Tel: **01929 400256**
Mr & Mrs Burrill.
D: £17.00-£20.00 **S:** £17.00-£20.00.
Open: Feb to Nov
Beds: 2F 3D 1T 1S **Baths:** 3 Sh
🛌 (4) 🅿 (7) ⌁ ◻ 🎟 🛌 🖵 🗵 ♿ ⌁

(On path) *Tewkesbury Cottage,* *28 Main Road, West Lulworth, Wareham, Dorset, BH20 5RL.*
c1600 thatched cottage 8 minutes walk to beach, coastal paths. Full English breakfast.
Tel: **01929 400561** (also fax no)
Mrs Laing.
D: £18.00-£20.00 **S:** £20.00-£25.00.
Open: All Year
Beds: 2D 1T 1S
Baths: 1 En 2 Sh
🛌 (12) 🅿 (6) 🎟 🛌 🖵 ♿ 🗵 ⌁

(0.5m) *Elads Nevar Guest House,* *West Road, West Lulworth, Wareham, Dorset, BH20 5RZ.*
Actual grid ref: SW825805
Modern house with large bedroom. Large English or vegetarian breakfast.
Tel: **01929 400467**
Mrs Ravensdale.
D: £16.00-£19.00 .
Open: All Year (not Xmas/New Year)
Beds: 1F 1D 1T **Baths:** 1 En 2 Sh
🛌 (4) 🅿 (3) ⌁ ◻ 🛌 🖵 🗵 ♿ ⌁

D = Price range per person sharing in a double room

(0.25m 🚗) *The Orchard,* *West Road, West Lulworth, Wareham, Dorset, BH20 5RY.*
Actual grid ref: SY824807
Peaceful off-road position, large garden.
Tel: **01929 400592**
Mr & Mrs Aldridge.
D: £18.00-£20.00 .
Open: All Year (not Xmas/New Year)
Beds: 2D 1T
Baths: 3 En
🛌 (5) 🅿 (3) ⌁ ◻ 🛌 🖵 🗵 ♿ ⌁

Kimmeridge 15
National Grid Ref: SY9179

🏮⚰ Seven Taps, New Inn

(0.5m) *Kimmeridge Farmhouse,* *Kimmeridge, Wareham, Dorset, BH20 5PE.*
Actual grid ref: SY918799
Picturesque farmhouse with views of Kimmeridge Bay - spacious and attractively furnished ensuite bedrooms.
Grades: ETC 4 Diamond
Tel: **01929 480990** Mrs Hole.
D: £22.00-£23.00 **S:** £25.00-£35.00.
Open: All Year (not Xmas)
Beds: 2D 1T
Baths: 3 En
🛌 (10) 🅿 (3) ⌁ ◻ ✕ 🛌 🖵 🗵 ♿ ⌁

Worth Matravers 16
National Grid Ref: SY9777

🏮⚰ King's Arms, The Ship

(0.75m 🚗) *The Haven,* *Worth Matravers, Swanage, Dorset, BH19 3LF.*
Actual grid ref: SY976775
Friendly welcome to comfortable modern house with pleasant sea views.
Tel: **01929 439388**
Mr & Mrs Taylor.
D: £20.00-£25.00 **S:** £20.00-£25.00.
Open: All Year
Beds: 1D 1T
Baths: 1 En 1 Pr
🛌 ⌁ ◻ 🎟 ✕ 🛌 🖵 🗵 ♿ ⌁

Langton Matravers 17
National Grid Ref: SY9978

🏮⚰ Kings Arms, Ship Inn

(1m) *Maycroft,* *Old Malthouse Lane, Langton Matravers, Swanage, Dorset, BH19 3JA.*
Comfortable Victorian home, close to Coastal Path. Recommended by Which?
Tel: **01929 424305** (also fax no)
Mrs Bjorkstrand.
D: £17.00-£19.00
S: £22.00-£25.00.
Open: Mar to Oct
Beds: 1D 1T
Baths: 1 Sh
🛌 (3) 🅿 (4) ◻ 🛌 🖵 🗵

Swanage

National Grid Ref: SZ0278   **18**

Black Swan, Crow's Nest, Red Lion, White Horse, Tawnys

(On path) *Swanage Youth Hostel, Cluny, Cluny Crescent, Swanage, Dorset, BH19 2BS.*
Actual grid ref: SZ031785
Tel: **01929 422113**
Under 18: £7.75 **Adults:** £11.00
Self-catering facilities, Television, Showers, Laundry facilities, Lounge, Games room, Drying room, Cycle store, Parking, Evening meal at 6.15-7.15pm, Kitchen facilities, Breakfast available, Credit cards accepted
Large refurbished house built on the site of a Cluny monastery in the well-known seaside resort of the Isle of Purbeck.

(0.5m 🚌) *Plum Tree Cottage, 60 Bell Street, Swanage, Dorset, BH19 2SB.*
Actual grid ref: SZ015779
Comfortable rooms, generous breakfasts, in cosy old Purbeck stone cottage.
Tel: **01929 421601** (also fax no)
Mr & Mrs Howells.
D: £22.50-£30.00 **S:** £30.00-£40.00.
Open: All Year
Beds: 3D **Baths:** 1 En 2 Pr
P (2) ⊁ 🖵 📅 🗙 🔔 📖 Ⅴ 🍴 ✿

All paths are popular:

you are well-advised to

book ahead

(0.5m) *Perfick Piece, Springfield Road, Swanage, Dorset, BH19 1HD.*
Small family guest house in quiet cul-de-sac near shops, beach and steam railway.
Tel: **01929 423178**
Fax no: 01929 423558
D: £14.00-£19.00 **S:** £16.00-£20.00.
Open: All Year
Beds: 1F 1T 1D **Baths:** 1 En 1 Pr 1 Sh
⛵ P (3) 🖵 📅 🗙 🔔 📖 Ⅴ 🍴 ✿

(0.5m) *Glenlee Hotel, 6 Cauldon Avenue, Swanage, Dorset, BH19 1PQ.*
Friendly family run hotel in delightful position close to beach.
Grades: ETC 3 Diamond
Tel: **01929 425794** Mr Jones.
Fax no: 01929 421530
D: £21.00-£26.00 **S:** £31.50-£39.00.
Open: March to October
Beds: 2F 2T 3D **Baths:** 7 En
⛵ (3) P (7) 🖵 🗙 🔔 📖 Ⅴ 🍴

(On path) *Hermitage Guest House, 1 Manor Road, Swanage, Dorset, BH19 2BH.*
Quiet central location; relaxed atmosphere, bay views. 2 mins beach, Coastal Path.
Tel: **01929 423014** Mrs Pickering.
D: £18.50-£19.50 **S:** £20.00-£20.00.
Open: Easter to Nov
Beds: 4F 2D 1T **Baths:** 2 Sh
⛵ (5) P (7) ⊁ 🖵 📅 🗙 🔔 📖 Ⅴ ✿

(0.5m 🚌) *Eversden Hotel, 5 Victoria Rd, Swanage, Dorset, BH19 1LY.*
Comfortable, friendly hotel, 2 minutes walk to the beach.
Grades: AA 3 Diamond
Tel: **01929 423276** Mrs Ford.
Fax no: 01929 427755
D: £18.00-£27.00 **S:** £20.00-£28.00.
Open: All Year
Beds: 5F 6D 1T 1S
Baths: 10 En 2 Sh
⛵ P (10) 🖵 📅 🗙 🔔 📖 ♿ Ⅴ 🍴 ✿

(0.75m 🚌) *Pennyfarthings, 124 Kings Road West, Swanage, Dorset, BH19 1HS.*
Actual grid ref: SZ023789
Attractively friendly house overlooking steam railway. Breakfast in conservatory.
Tel: **01929 422256**
Mr & Mrs Davison.
D: £18.00-£20.00 **S:** £20.00-£22.00.
Open: All Year (not Xmas/ New Year)
Beds: 2D 1T 1S
⛵ (6) P (2) ⊁ 🖵 📅 🗙 🔔 📖 Ⅴ 🍴 ✿

(On path 🚌) *Easter Cottage, 9 Eldon Terrace, Swanage, Dorset, BH19 1HA.*
Homely cottage, close beach/amenities. Spacious quality bedrooms, log fires.
Tel: **01929 427782** Mrs Needham.
D: £16.00-£20.00 **S:** £22.00-£30.00.
Open: All Year
Beds: 2D **Baths:** 2 En
⊁ 🖵 🔔 📖 Ⅴ ✿

(0.5m) *Verulam Lodge, 26 Cluny Crescent, Swanage, Dorset, BH19 2BT.*
Detached house close town and sea, some sea views, country park.
Tel: **01929 422079** Mrs Willey.
D: £15.50-£17.00 **S:** £17.00-£20.00.
Open: Easter to Oct
Beds: 1F 1D 1T **Baths:** 2 Sh
⛵ P (4) 🖵 🔔 📖 Ⅴ

Please take muddy

boots off before

entering premises

IRELAND: BED & BREAKFAST 2001

The essential guide to B&Bs in the Republic of Ireland and Northen Ireland

Think of Ireland and you think of that famous Irish hospitality. The warmth of the welcome is as much a part of this great island as the wild and beautiful landscapes, the traditional folk music and the Guiness. Wherever you go, town or country, North or South, you can't escape it.

There are few better ways of experiencing this renowned hospitality, when traveling through Ireland, than by staying at one of the country's many Bed & Breakfasts. They offer a great value alternative to expensive hotels, each has its own individual charm and you get a home cooked breakfast to help you start your day.

Stilwell's Ireland: Bed & Breakfast 2001 is the most comprehensive guide of its kind, with over 1,400 entries listed by county and location, in both Northern Ireland and the Republic of Ireland. Each entry includes room rates, facilities, Tourist Board grades, local maps and a brief description of the B&B, its location and surroundings.

Treat yourself to some Irish hospitality with **Stilwell Ireland: Bed & Breakfast 2001.**

Private Houses, Country Halls, Farms, Cottages, Inns, Small Hotels and Guest Houses

Over 1,400 entries
Average price £18 per person per night ($32 per person per night)
All official grades shown
Local maps
Pubs serving hot evening meals shown
Tourist Information Offices listed
Handy size for easy packing!

£6.95 from all good bookstores (ISBN 1-900861-24-0) or £7.95 (inc p&p) from Stilwell Publishing, 59 Charlotte Road, London EC2A 3QW (020 7739 7179)

Staffordshire Way

Here is a 93 mile path that straddles a county of true contrast, a county that belongs at the heart of England's industrial heritage. In a landscape criss-crossed by motorways, suburbia and manufacturing sites, this path gracefully picks its way southwards from the gritstone hills at the edge of the **Peak District**, along canals and wooded river valleys to the open heaths of Cannock Chase, then heading off through the landscaped parklands of Chillington, Wrottesley and Enville, before finishing at the soft sandstone ridge of Kinver Edge. The **Staffordshire Way** links with the **Heart of England Way** and thence to the **Cotswold** or the **Oxfordshire Ways**.

Guides: *The Staffordshire Way*, published by Staffordshire County Council and available directly from their offices c/o Cultural & Corporate Services, Shire Hall, Market Street, Stafford, ST16 2LQ, tel. 01785 278323, £5.00 (40p p&p)

Walking On and Around the Staffordshire Way by Geoff Loadwick (ISBN 1 850585 94 6), published by Sigma Press, price £5.95

Maps: Ordnance Survey 1:50000 Landranger series: 118, 119, 127, 128, 138, 139

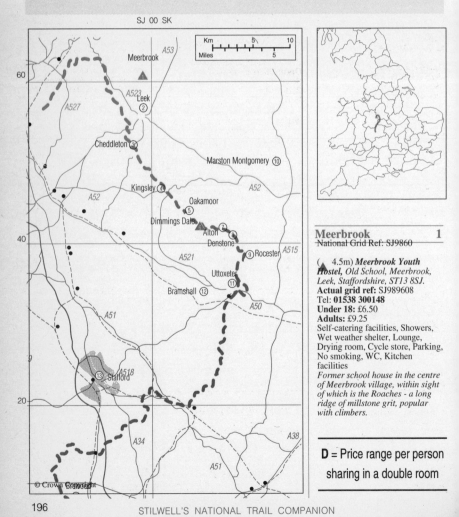

Meerbrook 1

National Grid Ref: SJ9860

(▲ 4.5m) *Meerbrook Youth Hostel, Old School, Meerbrook, Leek, Staffordshire, ST13 8SJ.*
Actual grid ref: SJ989608
Tel: 01538 300148
Under 18: £6.50
Adults: £9.25
Self-catering facilities, Showers, Wet weather shelter, Lounge, Drying room, Cycle store, Parking, No smoking, WC, Kitchen facilities
Former school house in the centre of Meerbrook village, within sight of which is the Roaches - a long ridge of millstone grit, popular with climbers.

D = Price range per person sharing in a double room

Leek 2

National Grid Ref: SJ9856

🍴🛏️The Abbey, Swan Hotel, Black Swan

(1m) *Beechfields, Park Road, Leek, Staffordshire, ST13 8JS.*
Large Victorian house in spacious gardens. Delicious breakfast. Warm and relaxing.
Grades: ETC 4 Diamond
Tel: **01538 372825**
Mrs Rider.
D: £20.00-£20.00 **S:** £25.00-£25.00.
Open: All Year (not Xmas)
Beds: 1F 2D
Baths: 3 En
🛇🅿(4)⅍🛏🐾🟥🏩.ⅤⅠ♦✦

(1m 🚗) *Warrington House, 108 Buxton Road, Leek, Staffs, ST13 6EJ.*
Not posh! Clean, comfortable, happy, with plenty of good food.
Tel: **01538 399566**
Mr Whone.
D: £15.00-£16.00 **S:** £17.00-£18.00.
Open: All Year
Beds: 1F 2T
Baths: 1 Sh
🛇🅿(1)🟥✗🟥🏩.ⅤⅠ♦✦

(1m 🚗) *Birchalls (PF) Ltd, The Hatcheries, Church Lane, Mount Pleasant, Leek, Staffs, ST13 5ET.*
Secluded position, adjacent to 26 acres local parklands, overlooking moorland areas.
Tel: **01538 399552**
D: £21.00-£25.00
S: £25.00-£29.00.
Open: All Year
Beds: 1F 1D 2T
Baths: 6 Pr
🛇(2)🅿(12)🟥🛏✗🟥🏩.ⅤⅠ♦✦

(1m 🚗) *Peak Weavers Hotel, King Street, Leek, Staffs, ST13 5NW.*
Town centre. Quiet ex-convent. Close Peak District and Alton Towers.
Tel: **01538 383729**
Fax no: 01538 387475
D: £22.50-£22.50 **S:** £22.00-£30.00.
Open: All Year
Beds: 2F 2D 2T 3S
Baths: 4 En 2 Pr 3 Sh
🛇🅿(15)🛏🐾&Ⅰ✦

Cheddleton 3

National Grid Ref: SJ9752

🍴🛏️The Boat, Traveller's Rest

(0.5m) *Hillcrest, 74 Folly Lane, Cheddleton, Leek, Staffordshire, ST13 7DA.*
Country house idyllically situated overlooking countryside, good choice of breakfast.
Tel: **01782 550483**
D: £19.00-£22.00 **S:** £22.00-£25.00.
Open: All Year (not Xmas/ New Year)
Beds: 1T 2D
Baths: 1 En 1 Pr
🛇🅿(4)⅍🟥🏩.ⅤⅠ✦

(0.5m) *Choir Cottage, Ostlers Lane, Cheddleton, Leek, Staffs, ST13 7HS.*
17th Century cottage in quiet location. Ideal honeymoon or special anniversary treat.
Grades: ETC 5 Diamond, Gold, AA 5 Diamond
Tel: **01538 360561**
Mr & Mrs Sutcliffe.
D: £27.50-£29.50
S: £35.00-£45.00.
Open: All Year (not Xmas)
Beds: 1F 1D
Baths: 2 En
🛇(5)🅿(6)⅍🟥✗🟥🏩.ⅤⅠ

Kingsley 4

National Grid Ref: SK0046

🍴🛏️Linden Tree

(1m) *The Church Farm, Holt Lane, Kingsley, Stoke on Trent, Staffs, ST10 2BA.*
Visiting Alton Towers? Relax afterwards in our beautiful period farmhouse.
Tel: **01538 754759** (also fax no)
Mrs Clowes.
D: £18.00-£20.00 **S:** £18.00-£22.00.
Open: All Year (not Xmas)
Beds: 1F
Baths: 1 En
🛇🅿(6)⅍🟥🏩.Ⅴ

Oakamoor 5

National Grid Ref: SK0544

🍴🛏️Cross Inn, Lord Nelson

(1m) *Ribden Farm, Oakamoor, Stoke on Trent, Staffs, ST10 3BW.*
Grades: ETC 4 Diamond, AA 4 Diamond, RAC 4 Diamond, Sparkling
Tel: **01538 702830**
Mrs Shaw.
D: £20.00-£24.00
S: £30.00-£35.00.
Open: All Year (not Xmas)
Beds: 5F 2D 1T
Baths: 7 En 1 Pr
🛇🅿(10)🟥🏩.Ⅴ
Listed stone farmhouse (1748). Some rooms with four poster beds, all ensuite with TVs, clock radios and tea/coffee. Quiet countryside overlooking Weaver Hills, large gardens with safe off-road parking. Five minutes from Alton Towers.

Always telephone
to get directions to
the B&B - you will
save time!

Dimmingsdale 6

National Grid Ref: SK0443

(▲0.5m) *Dimmingsdale Youth Hostel, Little Ranger, Dimmingsdale, Oakmoor, Stoke-on-Trent, Staffordshire, ST10 3AS.*
Actual grid ref: SK052436
Tel: **01538 702304**
Under 18: £6.50 **Adults:** £9.25
Self-catering facilities, Showers, Shop, Lounge, Drying room, Cycle store, Parking, Evening meal at 7.30pm, No smoking, Kitchen facilities, Credit cards accepted
A simple hostel in secluded woods overlooking the Churnet Valley, in a corner of the relatively undiscovered Staffordshire Moorlands.

Alton 7

National Grid Ref: SK0742

🍴🛏️Blacksmiths' Arms

(0.25m 🚗) *The Dale, Alton, Stoke-on-Trent, Staffs, ST10 4BG.*
Ideal overnight base if visiting Alton Towers, Friendly family home.
Grades: ETC 4 Diamond
Tel: **01538 702394** Mrs Burrows.
D: £17.00-£17.00 **S:** £22.00-£22.00.
Open: All Year (not Xmas)
Beds: 2T 1D
Baths: 1 Sh
🛇🅿(6)🟥🛏🟥🏩.Ⅴ✦

(0.25m) *The Hawthorns, 8 Tythe Barn, Alton, Stoke-on-Trent, Staffs, ST10 4AZ.*
Home-from-home atmosphere. Alton Towers 1 mile. Peak District close by.
Grades: ETC 3 Diamond
Tel: **01538 702197** Mrs Callear.
Fax no: 01538 703631
D: £17.50-£20.00 **S:** £22.00-£25.00.
Open: All Year (not Xmas)
Beds: 1F 1D
Baths: 1 Pr 1 Sh
🛇(5)🅿(4)🟥🟥🏩.Ⅴ✦

(0.25m) *Tythe Barn House, Denstone Lane, Alton, Stoke-on-Trent, Staffs, ST10 4AX.*
C17th farmhouse cottage, one mile Alton Towers.
Tel: **01538 702852** Mrs Kilgallon.
D: £15.00-£19.00 **S:** £20.00.
Open: All Year
Beds: 2F 3D **Baths:** 3 En 1 Sh
🛇🅿(5)🟥🏩.Ⅴ✦

(0.25m) *Rockhaven, Smithy Bank, Alton, Stoke-on-Trent, Staffordshire, ST10 4AA.*
Modernised country home near Alton Towers, Potteries and Staffordshire Way.
Tel: **01538 702066** Mrs Allen.
D: £17.50-£25.00 **S:** £25.00-£25.00.
Open: All Year (not Xmas)
Beds: 1F 2D
🛇(5)🅿(5)🟥🏩.Ⅴ

Denstone 8

National Grid Ref: SK0940

⊯ ◫ Hillside Farm &

(0.25m ⌂) *Hillside Farm & Cottages,* Alton Road, Denstone, Uttoxeter, Staffs, *ST14 5HG.*
Actual grid ref: SK098408
Victorian farmhouse adjacent
Alton Towers. Large
gardens/orchard, views, cottages
available.
Grades: ETC 3 Diamond
Tel: **01889 590760** Mrs Johnson.
D: £15.00-£18.00 **S:** £18.00-£20.00.
Open: All year
Beds: 2F 1D 1T
Baths: 2 En 2 Sh
🛇 🅿 ⌂ 🖵 👜 Ⅲ. Ⅵ ⊡ ∦

Rocester 9

National Grid Ref: SK1039

⊯ ◫ Red Lion

(On path) *The Leeze Guest House,*
63 High Street, Rocester, Uttoxeter,
Staffs, *ST14 5JU.*
Actual grid ref: SK109394
Friendly village location conve-
nient for Potteries, Dales and Alton
Towers.
Grades: ETC 3 Diamond,
AA 3 Diamond
Tel: **01889 591146** (also fax no)
Mr Venn.
D: £20.00-£20.00 **S:** £26.00-£26.00.
Open: All Year
Beds: 2F 1D 2T
Baths: 4 En 1 Pr
🛇 🅿 (6) ⊮ ✕ 👜 Ⅲ. Ⅵ ⊡ ∦

Marston Montgomery 10

National Grid Ref: SK1337

⊯ ◫ Crown Inn

(0.75m ⌂) *Waldley Manor,*
Marston Montgomery, Doveridge,
Ashbourne, Derbyshire, DE6 5LR.
Relax in this C16th manor
farmhouse. Quiet location, access
to commuter roads.
Tel: **01889 590287** Ms Whitfield.
D: £20.00-£25.00 **S:** £20.00-£25.00.
Open: All Year (not Xmas/
New Year)
Beds: 1F 1D
Baths: 2 En
🛇 ⌂ 🅿 🖵 👜 Ⅲ. Ⅵ ∎

Uttoxeter 11

National Grid Ref: SK0933

(0.25m) *White Hart Hotel,* Carter
Street, Uttoxeter, Staffs, *ST14 8EU.*
Friendly, 16th century coaching
inn, close to Alton Towers.
Tel: **01889 562437** Mr Wood.
Fax no: 01889 565099
D: £31.50-£63.00 **S:** £56.00-£56.00.
Open: All Year
Beds: 3F 5T 11D 2S
Baths: 21 En
🛇 🅿 (40) ⊮ 🖵 ⌂ ✕ 👜 Ⅲ. Ⅵ ⊡ ∦

S = Price range for a single

person in a single room

Bramshall 12

National Grid Ref: SK0533

⊯ ◫ Blythe Inn, Robin Hood

(1.5m ⌂) *West Lodge,* Bramshall,
Uttoxeter, Staffs, *ST14 5BG.*
Country house standing in a large
secluded attractive garden, within
easy reach of Stoke-on-Trent.
Tel: **01889 568421** Mrs George.
D: £18.00-£18.00 **S:** £25.00-£25.00.
Open: All Year (not Xmas)
Beds: 2D 1T **Baths:** 1 En 1 Sh
🛇 🅿 (8) ⊮ 🖵 👜 Ⅲ. & Ⅵ ⊡ ∦

Stafford 13

National Grid Ref: SJ9223

⊯ ◫ Red Lion, Picture House, Sun Inn, Crown
Inn, The Shropshire, The Radford, Bank Inn,
Barley Mow

(3m) *Bailey Hotel,* 63 Lichfield
Road, Stafford, Staffordshire,
ST17 4LL.
Grades: ETC 3 Diamond
Tel: **01785 214133**
Mr & Mrs Ayres.
Fax no: 01785 227920
D: £18.00-£23.00 **S:** £21.50-£30.00.
Open: All Year (not Xmas)
Beds: 1F 5D 3T 2S
Baths: 4 En 2 Sh
🛇 🅿 (11) 🖵 ⌂ 👜 Ⅲ. Ⅵ
Modern detached hotel, comfort-
ably furnished, parking in own
grounds.

(3m) *Cedarwood,* 46 Weeping
Cross, Stafford, Staffordshire,
ST17 0DS.
Grades: ETC 4 Diamond, Silver
Tel: **01785 662981** Mrs Welsby.
D: £15.00-£18.00 **S:** £15.00-£18.00.
Open: All Year (not Xmas)
Beds: 1D 1T 1S **Baths:** 2 Sh
🛇 (9) 🅿 (3) ⊮ 🖵 👜 Ⅲ. Ⅵ
Unusual detached bungalow in own
grounds, excellent accommodation
and hospitality.

(3m) *Leonards Croft Hotel,*
80 Lichfield Road, Stafford,
Staffordshire, *ST17 4LP.*
Victorian house in award winning
garden walking distance town cen-
tre.
Grades: AA 4 Diamond,
RAC 4 Diamond
Tel: **01785 223676** Mrs Johnson.
D: £25.00-£30.00 **S:** £30.00-£35.00.
Open: All Year (not Xmas/
New Year)
Beds: 4F 3D 2T **Baths:** 4 En 4 Sh
🛇 🅿 (10) 🖵 ⌂ ✕ 👜 Ⅲ. Ⅵ

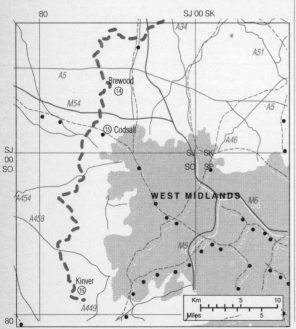

Planning a longer

stay? Always ask for

any special rates.

(3m) *Vine Hotel, Salter Street, Stafford, Staffordshire, ST16 2JU.*
This haven of your imagination is the Vine Hotel.
Grades: AA 2 Stars
Tel: 01785 244112
Mr Austin.
Fax no: 01785 246612
D: £25.00-£26.00 **S:** £30.00-£40.00.
Open: All Year
Beds: 1F 10D 3T 1OS
Baths: 24 Pr 1 En
⛺ 🅿 (20) 🗇✗ 🛏 🎟, Ⓥ ✚

Brewood   14

National Grid Ref: SJ8808

⬅ 🍺 The Royal Oak

(0.25m) *The Blackladies, Brewood, Stafford, ST19 9BH.*
Grade ll* Listed Tudor house set in 5 acres of gardens.
Grades: ETC 5 Diamond, Gold
Tel: 01902 850210 Mrs Bywater.
Fax no: 01902 851782
D: £25.00-£32.50 **S:** £28.00-£35.00.
Open: All Year
Beds: 1F 1T 2D
Baths: 3 En 1 Pr
⛺ 🅿 (8) ✄🗇 🛏 🎟, Ⓥ ✦

Codsall   15

National Grid Ref: SJ8703

(0.25m) *Moors Farm & Country Restaurant, Chillington Lane, Codsall, Wolverhampton, Staffs, WV8 1QF.*
Grades: AA 3 Diamond,
RAC 3 Diamond
Tel: 01902 842330 Mrs Moreton.
Fax no: 01902 847878
D: £22.50-£27.50 **S:** £30.00-£36.00.
Open: All Year
Beds: 1F 3D 2T 1S
Baths: 4 En 2 Sh
⛺ (4) 🅿 (20) ✄🗇✗ 🛏 🎟, Ⓥ ✚ ✦
A cosy farmhouse in a picturesque valley. Codsall Village 1 mile, Wolverhampton 5 miles. Bedrooms have lovely views and very good facilities. Mrs Moreton is an excellent cook; dinner served in the oak-beamed dining room accompanied by some wine from the bar is a must.

D = Price range per person sharing in a double room

Please don't camp
on *anyone's* land
without first obtaining
their permission.

Kinver   16

National Grid Ref: SO8483

⬅ 🍺 Vine Inn

(0.25m 🚐) *The Old Vicarage, Vicarage Drive, Kinver, Stourbridge, W Mids, DY7 6HJ.*
Actual grid ref: SO843834
Very quiet position near village and NT Rock House.
Tel: 01384 872784
Mr & Mrs Harris.
D: £20.00-£22.00
S: £20.00-£22.00.
Open: All Year (not Xmas)
Beds: 2T 1S
Baths: 1 En 1 Sh
⛺ 🅿 (6) 🗇 ✗ 🛏 🎟, Ⓥ ✦

Tarka Trail

The **Tarka Trail** runs in a figure of eight for 180 miles along coastline, up river valleys and over open moorland, through the full variety of the North Devon countryside. Named after Henry Williamson's classic 1927 novel, *Tarka the Otter* (it's been a bestseller ever since), the Trail starts and finishes in Barnstaple, and consists of two loops, connected by a section of railway. The first loop takes you through the estuary of the Taw and Torridge to the Atlantic coast, follows the Torridge Valley upstream into the rugged beauty of North Dartmoor, and then downstream along the River Taw to Eggesford, from where you can take the train back to Barnstaple. The northern loop takes you east through wooded valleys and hillside meadows to the lonely high grass and heather plateau of Exmoor, and hits the North Devon coast at Lynmouth. Here it joins the **South West Coast Path** for the highest cliff walk in England, which leads to Ilfracombe. From here you go past Woolacombe Sand (ideal for surfing) and Braunton Burrows and finally along the north side of the Taw and Torridge estuary. The Trail is waymarked along the coast (by the National Trail acorn logo) and in Exmoor National Park (by an otter paw print), but not in Dartmoor National Park. The initial stage, up the Torridge Valley, runs along a former railway line and is undemanding; you may encounter cyclists. The coastal section is more rigorous, as it involves steep climbs and switchbacks; and up on the moors mist can descend quickly, resulting in the poor visibility for which these parts are notorious. You should not be without the appropriate OS map (see below), a compass and a whistle.

Guide (available from all good bookshops):
The Tarka Trail: A Walker's Guide (ISBN 0 86114 877 0), published by Devon Books, Official Publisher to Devon County Council (Halsgrove House, Lower Moor Way, Tiverton, Devon EX16 6SS, tel. 01884 243242) and available from the publishers, £4.95 (+ £1.50 p&p)

Maps: 1:50000 Ordnance Survey Landranger Series: 180, 191

Comments on the Trail to: The Tarka Trail, Bideford Station, Railway Terrace, East-the-Water, Bideford, Devon EX39 4BB, tel. 01237 471870

D = Price range per person sharing in a double room

Barnstaple 1

National Grid Ref: SS5633

⊯ ⬩ Windsor Arms, Williams Arms, Rolle Quay Inn, North Country Inn, Pyne Arms, Ring O'Bells, Chichester Arms

(0.25m) **Crossways**, *Braunton Road, Barnstaple, Devon, EX31 1JY.*
Actual grid ref: SS555333
Detached house - town & Tarka Trail 150 yards, bicycle hire.
Tel: **01271 379120**
Mr & Mrs Tysn.
D: £15.00 **S:** £17.00.
Open: All Year
Beds: 1F 1D 1T
Baths: 2 Pr 1 Sh
🛇 🅿 (6) ⌿⬜✕⬩⬛⬛⬤🅥🛆⌁

(1.5m) **Mount Sandford**, *Landkey Road, Barnstaple, Devon, EX32 0HL.*
Georgian house in 1.5 acres gardens. 2 double, 1 twin, all ensuite.
Tel: **01271 342354** Mrs White.
D: £18.00-£22.00 **S:** £20.00.
Open: All Year (not Xmas)
Beds: 1F 1D 1T
Baths: 3 En
🛇 (3) 🅿 (3) ⌿⬜⬩⬛⬛🅥⌁

Fremington 2

National Grid Ref: SS5132

⊯ ⬩ New Inn, Boat House

(0.5m 🚌) **Lower Yelland Farm**, *Yelland Road, Fremington, Barnstaple, Devon, EX31 3EN.*
Tel: **01271 860101** (also fax no)
Mr Day.
D: £20.00-£20.00 **S:** £20.00-£20.00.
Open: All Year (not Xmas New Year)
Beds: 1T 2D
Baths: 3 En
🛇 🅿 (6) ⬜🔥⬩⬛⬛🅥🛆⌁
North Devon Coast beautifully situated period house on Taw Estuary. Ideal touring centre, Instow beach/marina approximately 1 mile, Bideford, Barnstaple 4.5 miles. Several golf courses in the vicinity. Adjacent to bird sanctuary. Private off road parking.

Pay B&Bs by cash or cheque and be prepared to pay up front.

All paths are popular: you are well-advised to book ahead

Bideford 3

National Grid Ref: SS4526

⊯ ⬩ Tanton's Hotel, Farmers Arms, Crab & Ale, Royal Hotel, Swan Inn, Joiners' Arms, Hunters' Inn, Sunset Hotel

(0.5m 🚌) **The Mount Hotel**, *Northdown Road, Bideford, Devon, EX39 3LP.*
Actual grid ref: SS449269
Grades: AA 4 Diamond
Tel: **01237 473748**
Mr & Mrs Laugharne.
D: £23.00-£25.00 **S:** £25.00-£33.00.
Open: Jan to Dec
Beds: 1F 3D 1T 2S
Baths: 7 En
🛇 🅿 (4) ⌿⬜⬩⬛⬛⬩&🅥🛆⌁
Charming Georgian licensed guest house only 5 minutes' walk to town centre, private lounge for guests' use, all rooms ensuite, attractive garden, car parking for guests. Convenient for touring N Devon coastline, Clovelly, Lundy, Exmoor and Dartmoor. No smoking.

Landcross 4

National Grid Ref: SS4623

(On path) *Sunset Hotel, Landcross, Bideford, Devon, EX39 5JA.*
Actual grid ref: SS461239
Small country Hotel. Peaceful location overlooking spectacular scenery and Tarka Trail.
Grades: ETC 3 Diamond, AA 3 Diamond
Tel: **01237 472962** Mrs Lamb.
D: £27.00-£30.00 **S:** £36.00-£40.00.
Open: Easter to Nov
Beds: 2F 2D 2T **Baths:** 4 En
P (8) ⊬ ☐ ✕ ≞ ▥ Ⅴ ⓐ

Weare Giffard 5

National Grid Ref: SS4721

(▲ 1m) *Sea Lock Camping Barn & Tent Site, Vale Cottage, 7 Annery Kiln, Weare Giffard, Bideford, Devon, EX39 5JE.*
Tel: **01237 477705 / 07866 026194**
Under 18: £5.00 **Adults:** £5.00
Self-catering facilities, Showers, Parking, Facilities for disabled people
Newly converted barn, offering basic accommodation, in beautiful, tranquil wooded valley overlooking River Torridge, between Bideford and Torrington. Private access to Tarka Trail (NCN 3) and conservation area. Superb walking, cycling, canoeing, fishing, birdwatching. Pubs/shops within 2.5 miles. Book individual beds/family rooms (sharing facilities) or sole use.

Huntshaw Water 6

National Grid Ref: SS5023

⏐⏐ ⌾ Hunters Inn

(2m 🚐) *The Roundhouse, Guscott, Huntshaw Water, Torrington, Devon, EX38 7HE.*
Actual grid ref: SS503237
Splendid roundhouse amidst beautiful peaceful countryside betwixt sea and moors.
Tel: **01271 858626** Mrs Smith.
D: £17.50-£20.00 **S:** £17.50-£20.00.
Open: All Year
Beds: 1F 2D **Baths:** 1 En 3 Pr
♿ P (6) ⊬ ☐ ⊼ ✕ ≞ ▥ ⅋ ⓐ ≈

Little Torrington 7

National Grid Ref: SS4916

(1m) *Smytham Holiday Park, Little Torrington, Torrington, Devon, EX38 8PU.*
C17th manor house. beautiful tranquil grounds. Outdoor heated pool.
Tel: **01805 622110** Mr Bland.
D: £20.00-£30.00 **S:** £24.00-£36.00.
Open: All Year (not Xmas/ New Year)
Beds: 4D 3T **Baths:** 5 En 1 Sh
♿ P ⊬ ☐ ⊼ ✕ ≞ ▥ Ⅴ ⓐ ≈

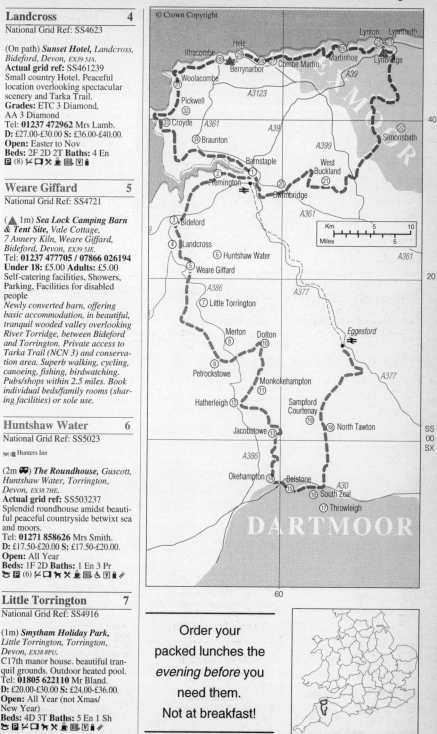

© Crown Copyright

Lynton Lynmouth
Hele Martinhoe Lynbridge
Ilfracombe Berrynarbor Combe Martin
A39
Woolacombe A3123
Pickwell
Croyde A361 A39 A399
Braunton West Buckland Simonsbath
Barnstaple
Fremington Swimbridge
A361
Bideford Km Miles
Landcross Huntshaw Water
Weare Giffard A361
A386 A377
Little Torrington
Merton Dolton Eggesford
Petrockstowe A377
Monkokehampton
Hatherleigh Sampford Courtenay
Jacobstowe North Tawton
A386
Okehampton Belstone A30
South Zeal
Throwleigh

DARTMOOR

SS 00 SX

Order your
packed lunches the
evening before you
need them.
Not at breakfast!

Merton 8

National Grid Ref: SS5212

🍴 🍺 Bull & Dragon

(0.25m 🚌) **Richmond House,** *New Road (A386), Merton, Okehampton, Devon, EX20 3EG.*
Tel: **01805 603258** Mrs Wickett.
D: £15.00-£15.00 **S:** £15.00-£15.00.
Open: All Year
Beds: 3F 1T 2D
Baths: 1 Sh
🛏 (5) 🅿 (4) 🍴🛏🗙 🖂 ☑ 🛇 ⚡
Country house within easy reach of beach, moors, gardens, Tarka Trail. Evening meal optional. H.C. in all bedrooms.

Petrockstowe 9

National Grid Ref: SS5109

🍴 🍺 The Laurels Inn

(1m 🚌) **Aish Villa,** *Petrockstowe, Okehampton, Devon, EX20 3HL.*
Actual grid ref: SS514089
Peaceful location, superb views, ideal for visiting Dartmoor, Exmoor, coast.
Tel: **01837 810581** Ms Gordon.
D: £17.00-£17.00 **S:** £17.00-£17.00.
Open: All Year
Beds: 1F 1T 1D **Baths:** 1 Sh
🛏 🅿 (4) ⚡🍴 🖂 🎍 ☑ ⚡

Dolton 10

National Grid Ref: SS5712

🍴 🍺 Royal Oak, Ye Olde Inn

(On path) **Robin Cottage,** *Church Street, Dolton, Winkleigh, Devon, EX19 8QE.*
Tel: **01805 804430** Newman.
D: £18.00-£20.00 **S:** £18.00-£20.00.
Open: All Year
Beds: 1T 1S
Baths: 1 En 1 Sh
🛏 (12) ⚡🍴 🎍 ☑ ⚡
Modernised cottage situated near church in attractive Devon village, near RHS Rosemoor Garden. Warm welcome. Quiet, comfortable accommodation and excellent breakfasts. Ideal centre for touring, exploring coast, Dartmoor/Exmoor. Good stopover when visiting Cornwall. Walkers also welcome. Tarka Trail nearby.

🚌 sign means that, *given due notice*, owners will pick you up from the path and drop you off *within reason.*

Please respect a B&B's wishes regarding children, animals & smoking.

Monkokehampton 11

National Grid Ref: SS5805

🍴 🍺 Duke Of York

(1.5m 🚌) **Seldon Farm,** *Monkokehampton, Winkleigh, Devon, EX19 8RY.*
Charming C17th farmhouse in beautiful, tranquil, rural setting.
Grades: ETC 2 Diamond
Tel: **01837 810312** Mrs Case.
D: £20.00 **S:** £23.00.
Open: Easter to Oct
Beds: 1F 2D
Baths: 1 Pr 1 En
🛏 🅿 🍴🛏 🖂 ☑ 🛇 ⚡

Hatherleigh 12

National Grid Ref: SS5404

(0.5m) **Pressland Country House Hotel,** *Hatherleigh, Okehampton, Devon, EX20 3LW.*
Grades: AA 5 Diamond
Tel: **01837 810871**
Fax no: 01837 810303
D: £20.00-£32.00.
S: £28.00-£36.00.
Open: Mar to Nov
Beds: 2T 3D
Baths: 4 En 1 Pr
🛏 (12) 🅿 (6) ⚡🍴🛏🗙 🖂 🎍 ☑ 🛇 ⚡
Delightful and spacious Victorian house set in 1.5 acres of landscaped garden, with glorious views of Dartmoor and surrounding countryside. The family-run hotel is licensed and there is a large, comfortable lounge, separate bar and a restaurant of growing repute.

Jacobstowe 13

National Grid Ref: SS5801

(On path) **Higher Cadham Farm,** *Jacobstowe, Okehampton, Devon, EX20 3RB.*
Superb farmhouse accommodation with country walks. Hearty farmhouse food.
Grades: ETC 4 Diamond, AA 4 Diamond
Tel: **01837 851647** Mrs King.
Fax no: 01837 851410
D: £18.50-£25.00.
S: £18.50-£25.00.
Open: All Year (not Xmas)
Beds: 3F 2D 3T 1S
Baths: 5 En 1 Sh
🛏 (1) 🅿 (10) 🍴🛏🗙 🖂 🎍 ☑ 🛇 ⚡

Okehampton 14

National Grid Ref: SX5895

🍴 🍺 Oxenham Arms, River Inn, Tors Hotel, New Inn, Taw River, Sticklepath, Cellars, Plume Of Feathers

(▲ 0.5m) **Okehampton Youth Hostel,** *The Goods Yard, Okehampton Station, Okehampton, Devon, EX20 1EJ.*
Actual grid ref: SX591942
Tel: **01837 53916**
Under 18: £7.75
Adults: £11.00
Self-catering facilities, Showers, Showers, Licensed bar, Laundry facilities, Laundry facilities, Lounge, Lounge, Parking, Evening meal at 7.00pm, No smoking, WC, WC, Kitchen facilities, Kitchen facilities, Credit cards accepted
Converted Victorian railway goods shed on northern edge of Dartmoor National Park.

(0.5m) **North Lake,** *Exeter Road, Okehampton, Devon, EX20 1QH.*
Grades: ETC 3 Diamond
Tel: **01837 53100** Mrs Jones.
D: £20.00 **S:** £23.00.
Open: All Year (not Xmas)
Beds: 2D 1T
Baths: 2 En 1 Pr
🛏 (6) 🅿 (10) ⚡🍴🛏 🖂 🎍 ☑ ⚡
Set in large grounds with panoramic views across Dartmoor. Tastefully furnished, good food, with a personal friendly touch; come and go as you please. Superb walking and riding base, stunning scenery and cascading rivers.

(0.5m 🚌) **Heathfield House,** *Klondyke Road, Okehampton, Devon, EX20 1EW.*
Grades: AA 4 Diamond
Tel: **01837 54211** (also fax no)
Mr & Mrs Gibbins.
D: £17.00-£30.00
S: £30.00-£35.00.
Open: Feb to Dec
Beds: 1F 2D 1T
Baths: 4 En
🛏 🅿 (8) ⚡🍴🛏🗙 🎍 ☑ 🛇 ⚡
Situated high on north face of Dartmoor, tucked away & private, although only 10 mins from market town of Okehampton. Chef owner, direct access Dartmoor, spectacular views. Fine food and wine. Heated outdoor pool. Residential pottery courses. Christmas breaks.

Please take muddy boots off before entering premises

S = Price range for a single person in a room

(0.5m) *Arnley House, 7 Oaklands Park, Okehampton, Devon, EX20 1LN.*
Modern luxury house, warm welcome, discount for 3 days plus.
Tel: **01837 53311** Ms Masereeuw.
D: £23.50-£23.50 **S:** £23.50-£23.50.
Open: Jan to Nov
Beds: 1D **Baths:** 1 En
🄿 (1) ⌿ ❑ 🛓 ⅲ, Ⓥ 🅰 ⚡

Belstone 15
National Grid Ref: SX6293

🍴 🍺 Tors Inn

(0.25m) *Moorlands House, Belstone, Okehampton, Devon, EX20 1QZ.*
Actual grid ref: SX620935
Tel: **01837 840549**
Mr Weaver.
D: £18.00-£20.00
S: £20.00-£25.00.
Open: All Year
Beds: 2T 2D **Baths:** 1 En 1 Pr 1 Sh
🕭 🄿 (6) ❑ 🏌 🛓 ⅲ, Ⓥ 🅰 ⚡
Beautifully situated on the edge of unspoilt Dartmoor village with superb Moorland views. Direct access to Moor for excellent walking/ riding/ cycling. Five minutes walk to friendly village pub for good home cooked food. Ideal base for touring Devon/ Cornwall.

(0.25m) *Moor Hall, Belstone, Okehampton, Devon, EX20 1QZ.*
Actual grid ref: SX619934
Glorious views, unspoilt peaceful village. Dartmoor is our front garden.
Tel: **01837 840604** Mrs Wood.
D: £18.00-£20.00 **S:** £20.00-£20.00.
Open: Easter to Oct
Beds: 2D 1T
Baths: 2 En 1 Pr
🕭 (13) 🄿 (2) ⌿ ❑ 🛓 ⅲ, ⚡

The Grid Reference beneath the location heading is for the village or town - *not* for individual houses, which are shown (where supplied) in each entry itself.

All details shown are as supplied by B&B owners in Autumn 2001.

South Zeal 16
National Grid Ref: SX6593

🍴 🍺 Oxenham Arms

(On path) *The Oxenham Arms, South Zeal, Okehampton, Devon, EX20 2JT.*
Actual grid ref: SX649936
Ancient C12th inn in centre of rural village in Dartmoor National Park.
Tel: **01837 840244**
Mr & Mrs Henry.
Fax no: 01837 840791
D: £30.00-£30.00 **S:** £40.00-£45.00.
Open: All Year
Beds: 2F 3D 3T **Baths:** 7 En
🕭 🄿 (8) ❑ 🏌 ✕ 🛓 ⅲ, Ⓥ ⚡

Throwleigh 17
National Grid Ref: SX6690

🍴 🍺 Three Crowns, Ring Of Bells

(3m) *Throwleigh Manor, Throwleigh, Okehampton, Devon, EX20 2JF.*
Beautiful country house in idyllic, peaceful 12-acre grounds within National Park.
Tel: **01647 231630** (also fax no)
Mr & Mrs Smitheram.
D: £20.00-£26.00 **S:** £28.00-£38.00.
Open: All Year (not Xmas)
Beds: 1F 1D 1S
Baths: 1 En 2 Pr
🕭 🄿 (10) ⌿ ❑ 🛓 ⅲ, Ⓥ ⚡

North Tawton 18
National Grid Ref: SS6601

(0.5m 🐴) *Kayden House Hotel, High Street, North Tawton, Devon, EX20 2HF.*
Devon Heartland, ideal for Moors and Coasts. Warm welcome assured.
Tel: **01837 82242** Ms Waldron.
D: £20.00 **S:** £26.00.
Open: All Year
Beds: 1F 2T 2D 2S **Baths:** 5 En 2 Pr
🕭 ❑ 🏌 ✕ 🛓 ⅲ, Ⓥ 🅰 ⚡

(1m) *Lower Nichols Nymet Farm, North Tawton, Devon, EX20 2BW.*
Peaceful farmhouse accommodation in the centre of Devon, north of Dartmoor.
Tel: **01363 82510** Mrs Pyle.
D: £20.00-£22.00 **S:** £25.00-£25.00.
Open: Easter to Oct
Beds: 1F 1D **Baths:** 2 En
🕭 🄿 (4) ⌿ ❑ ✕ 🛓 ⅲ, Ⓥ 🅰

Sampford Courtenay 19
National Grid Ref: SS6301

🍴 🍺 New Inn, Railway

(2m) *West Trecott Farm, Sampford Courtenay, Okehampton, Devon, EX20 2TD.*
Tel: **01837 82569** Mrs Horn.
D: £15.00-£15.00 **S:** £15.00-£15.00.
Open: May to Oct
Beds: 3D
Baths: 2 En 1 Sh
🕭 (2) 🄿 (6) ⌿ ❑ 🏌 🛓 ⅲ, Ⓥ ⚡
Early 15th Century farmhouse situated in the heart of Devon countryside close to Dartmoor National Park. Farmhouse breakfast, private off road parking. Pleasant surroundings.

(2m 🐴) *Southey Farm, Sampford Courtenay, Okehampton, Devon, EX20 2TE.*
Actual grid ref: SS633003
Comfortable farmhouse overlooking gardens and fields, close to Dartmoor.
Tel: **01837 82446**
Mr & Mrs Townsend Green.
D: £15.00-£15.00 **S:** £15.00-£15.00.
Open: All Year (not Xmas/ New Year)
Beds: 1T 1S/T
Baths: 2 Pr
🕭 🄿 (4) ❑ 🏌 🛓 ⅲ, Ⓥ ⚡

Swimbridge 20
National Grid Ref: SS6129

🍴 🍺 Jack Russell

(2m) *Lower Hearson Farm, Swimbridge, Barnstaple, Devon, EX32 0QH.*
Actual grid ref: SS603291
300 year-old farmhouse situated in 12 acres of gardens and woodland.
Tel: **01271 830702** Mrs Trimnell.
D: £18.00-£22.00 **S:** £18.00-£25.00.
Open: All Year (not Xmas)
Beds: 1D 1T 1S
Baths: 2 En 1 Pr
🕭 (3) 🄿 (2) ⌿ ❑ 🛓 ⅲ, Ⓥ

West Buckland 21
National Grid Ref: SS6531

(0.25m 🐴) *Huxtable Farm, West Buckland, Barnstaple, Devon, EX32 0SR.*
Actual grid ref: SS665308
Medieval farmhouse (1520) in secluded countryside. Tennis court and sauna.
Grades: ETC 4 Diamond
Tel: **01598 760254** (also fax no)
Mrs Payne.
D: £24.00-£25.00
S: £35.00-£35.00.
Open: Feb to Nov
Beds: 2F 3D 1T
Baths: 5 En 1 Pr
🕭 🄿 (10) ⌿ ❑ ✕ 🛓 ⅲ, Ⓥ 🅰 ⚡

Simonsbath   22
National Grid Ref: SS7739

(0.5m 🚗) **Emmett's Grange Farm,**
Simonsbath, Minehead, Somerset,
TA24 7LD.
Tel: **01643 831138** (also fax no)
Barlow.
D: £28.00-£35.00 **S:** £33.00-£40.00.
Open: All Year (not Xmas/
New Year)
Beds: 1T 2D
🛏 🅿 ⅌ ◻ ⏹ ✕ 🖳 🔥 Ⅲ. Ⅵ 🎗 ✦
Emmett's Grange provides and
oasis of friendly civilisation within
its own 900 acres amidst the stun-
ning wild and rugged Exmoor
National Park. Luxurious B&B
with moorland views. Guests own
elegant drawing room. Gourmet
food available and many local
pubs. Fully licensed.

Lynmouth   23
National Grid Ref: SS7249

🍴 🍺 Riverside Cottages, Village Inn

(0.25m) **Glenville House,** *2 Tors*
Road, Lynmouth, Devon, EX35 6ET.
Grades: AA 4 Diamond
Tel: **01598 752202**
Mr & Mrs Francis.
D: £22.00-£26.00
S: £22.00-£30.00.
Open: Feb to Nov
Beds: 4D 1T 1S
Baths: 3 En 1 Pr 2 Sh
🛏 (12) ⅌ ◻ 🔥 🖳 Ⅵ ✦
Idyllic riverside setting. Delightful
Victorian house full of character
and charm. Licensed. Tastefully
decorated bedrooms. Picturesque
harbour, village and unique Cliff
Railway nestled amidst wooded
valley. Magnificent Exmoor
scenery, spectacular coastline and
beautiful walks. Peaceful, tranquil,
romantic - a very special place.

(0.25m) **Tregonwell Riverside**
Guest House, *1 Tors Road,*
Lynmouth, Devon, EX35 6ET.
Actual grid ref: SS725493
Grades: ETC 3 Diamond,
AA 3 Diamond
Tel: **01598 753369**
Mrs Parker.
D: £22.00-£27.00
S: £22.00-£25.00.
Open: All Year (not Xmas)
Beds: 2F 5D 1T 1S
Baths: 5 En 1 Pr 3 Sh
🛏 (7) ⅌ ◻ 🔥 🖳 Ⅲ. Ⅵ 🎗 ✦
Award-winning, romantic, elegant
riverside (former sea captain's)
stone-built house, snuggled amidst
waterfalls, cascades, wooded val-
leys, soaring cliff tops, lonely
beaches, enchanting harbourside
'Olde Worlde' smugglers' village.
Shelley, Wordsworth, Coleridge
stayed here. 'England's
Switzerland'. Pretty bedrooms, dra-
matic views. Garaged parkings.

Planning a longer
stay? Always ask for
any special rates.

Lynbridge   24
National Grid Ref: SS7248

(🔺 0.5m) **Lynton Youth Hostel,**
Lynbridge, Lynton, Devon, EX35 6BE.
Actual grid ref: SS720487
Tel: **01598 753237**
Under 18: £6.90 **Adults:** £10.00
Self-catering facilities, Showers,
Shop, Laundry facilities, Lounge,
Dining room, Drying room, Cycle
store, Parking Limited, Evening
meal at 7.00pm, No smoking, WC,
Kitchen facilities, Breakfast avail-
able, Credit cards accepted
Victorian house in the steep wood-
ed gorge of the West Lyn River,
where Exmoor reaches the sea,
with opportunities to explore the
National Park, the sea shore and
the river valley.

Lynton   25
National Grid Ref: SS7149

🍴 🍺 Rising Sun Inn, Staghunters Inn, Ye Olde
Cottage Inn, Royal Castle, Sandrock

(0.5m) **The Turret, 33 Lee Road,**
Lynton, Devon, EX35 6BS.
Grades: ETC 3 Diamond
Tel: **01598 753284** (also fax no)
Mrs Wayman.
D: £18.00-£23.00 **S:** £25.00.
Open: All Year
Beds: 5D 1T **Baths:** 4 En
🛏 (12) ◻ ✕ 🖳 Ⅲ. Ⅵ 🎗 ✦
Step back in time and experience
old world hospitality. Built in
1898, the charm of our hotel will
relax and welcome you. Beautiful
ensuite bedrooms, enhanced with
all the modern facilities. Evening
meals served in cosy dining room.
Vegetarian and special dietary
needs catered for.

(0.5m 🚗) **The Denes Guest**
House, *Longmead, Lynton, Devon,*
EX35 6DQ.
Grades: ETC 3 Diamond
Tel: **01598 753573** Mr McGowan.
D: £16.00-£22.50 **S:** £16.00-£22.50.
Open: All Year
Beds: 3F 2D
Baths: 2 En 1 Pr 2 Sh
🛏 🅿 (5) ⅌ ◻ ✕ 🖳 Ⅵ 🎗 ✦
A warm friendly greeting awaits
you at The Denes, with its
Edwardian charm. Comfortable
accommodation and home cooked
food, evening meals served in our
licensed dining room. Ideal base to
explore Exmoor on the South West
Coastal Path. An Exmoor paths
partner.

(0.25m) **Victoria Lodge,** *Lee Road,*
Lynton, Devon, EX35 6BP.
Awarded B&B of the Year for
S.W. England by South West
Tourism.
Grades: AA 5 Diamond
Tel: **01598 753203** (also fax no)
Mr & Mrs Bennett.
D: £26.00-£36.00 **S:** £35.00-£54.00.
Open: Feb to Nov
Beds: 1F 7D 1T **Baths:** 9 En
🛏 🅿 (7) ⅌ ◻ ✕ 🖳 Ⅲ. Ⅵ

(0.25m 🚗) **Lynhurst Hotel,**
Lynton, Devon, EX35 6AX.
Character Victorian residence situ-
ated in gardens/woodland over-
looking Lynmouth Bay.
Grades: AA 4 Diamond
Tel: **01598 752241** (also fax no)
Mr Townsend.
D: £22.00-£30.00 **S:** £25.00-£28.00.
Open: All Year
Beds: 2F 5D 1T 1S **Baths:** 7 En
🛏 (1) 🅿 (2) ◻ ✕ 🖳 Ⅲ. Ⅵ ✦

(0.5m) **Gable Lodge,** *Lee Road,*
Lynton, Devon, EX35 6BS.
Actual grid ref: SS718495
Large Victorian house with views
along the East Lyn valley.
Tel: **01598 752367** (also fax no)
Mr & Mrs Bowman.
D: £18.50-£19.50 **S:** £18.50-£19.50.
Open: Easter to Oct
Beds: 1F 5D **Baths:** 5 En 1 Sh
🛏 🅿 (8) ⅌ ◻ 🔥 🖳 Ⅲ. Ⅵ

(0.5m) **Croft House Hotel,** *Lydiate*
Lane, Lynton, Devon, EX35 6HE.
Croft house nestling in the old vil-
lage, built 1828 for a sea captain.
Tel: **01598 752391** (also fax no)
Mrs Johnson.
D: £17.00-£27.00 **S:** £20.00-£30.00.
Open: All Year (not Xmas)
Beds: 5D 2T
Baths: 6 En 1 Pr
⅌ ◻ 🔥 ✕ 🖳 Ⅲ. Ⅵ 🎗 ✦

Martinhoe   26
National Grid Ref: SS6648

🍴 🍺 Hunters Inn, Fox & Goose

(0.25m) **Mannacott Farm,**
Martinhoe, Parracombe,
Barnstaple, Devon, EX31 4QS.
Actual grid ref: SS662481
In area of outstanding natural
scenery. Ideal for walkers, bird
watchers. Near coast.
Tel: **01598 763227** Mrs Dallyn.
D: £15.00-£16.00 **S:** £16.00-£17.00.
Open: Apr to mid-Oct
Beds: 1D 1T 1S **Baths:** 1 Sh
🅿 (2) ⅌ ◻ Ⅲ. 🔥 ✦

Bringing children with
you? Always ask for
any special rates.

Combe Martin 27

National Grid Ref: SS5846

⏺ Dolphin Inn, Focsle Inn, Royal Marine

(On path) *Royal Marine, Seaside, Combe Martin, Ilfracombe, EX34 0AW.*
Award winning pub with five superbly appointed licensee.
Ensuite rooms, cooked food, sea views.
Tel: **01271 882470**
Mr Lethaby.
Fax no: 01271 889080
D: £20.00-£25.00 **S:** £20.00-£25.00.
Open: All Year
Beds: 5F
Baths: 5 En
⏺ ⚿ ▣ ⌓ ▥ ℗

(On path) *Crimond, King Street, Combe Martin, Ilfracombe, EX34 0BS.*
Friendly comfortable Victorian house. Hearty English breakfast.
Close to sea.
Tel: **01271 882348** (also fax no)
Mr Parkes.
D: £17.00 **S:** £17.00.
Open: All Year (not Xmas)
Beds: 1F 1D 1T 1S
Baths: 1 Sh 4 En
⏺ ⌇ ▣ ⌓ ⏏ ▥ ℗

(On path) *Hillview Guest House, Woodlands, Combe Martin, Ilfracombe, Devon, EX34 0AT.*
Actual grid ref: SS575469
Beautifully situated Edwardian house. Quiet position offering comfort and cleanliness.
Tel: **01271 882331**
Mrs Bosley.
D: £16.00-£18.50
S: £18.00-£20.50.
Open: Easter to Oct
Beds: 2D 1T
Baths: 2 En 1 Pr
℗ (6) ⌇ ▣ ⏏ ▥ ℗ ✦

(On path 🚗) *Glendower, King Street, Combe Martin, Ilfracombe, Devon, EX34 0AL.*
Close to South West Coastal Path and seaside.
Tel: **01271 883449**
Mr & Mrs Barry.
D: £13.00-£14.00 **S:** £16.00-£18.00.
Open: Easter to Nov
Beds: 2D 1S
Baths: 2 En 1 Sh
⏺ (1) ℗ (3) ▣ ⌓ ⏏ ℗ ✦

High season,
bank holidays and
special events mean
low availability
everywhere.

S = Price range for a single person in a room

Berrynarbor 28

National Grid Ref: SS5646

⏺ Old Goose, Globe Inn, Miss Muffits

(0.25m) *Tower Cottage, Berrynarbor, Ilfracombe, Devon, EX34 9SE.*
Charming Cottage with beautiful garden in 'Best kept village Berrynarbor'.
Tel: **01271 883408**
D: £18.00-£22.00 **S:** £25.00-£25.00.
Open: All Year (not Xmas/ New Year)
Beds: 1F 1D
Baths: 2 En
⏺ ℗ ⌇ ▣ ⏏ ▥ ℗ ✦

(0.25m 🚗) *Langleigh House, Berrynarbor, Ilfracombe, Devon, EX34 9SG.*
Set in delightful North Devon.
Lovely gardens with stream, barbecue area.
Tel: **01271 883410**
Mr & Mrs Pierpoint.
Fax no: 01271 882396
D: £17.50-£24.50 **S:** £23.50-£24.50.
Open: All Year (not Xmas)
Beds: 1F 3D 1T
Baths: 5 En 2 Pr
⏺ ℗ (6) ⌇ ▣ ⌓ ⏏ ▥ ℗

(0.25m 🚗) *Sloley Farm, Castle Hill, Berrynarbor, Ilfracombe, Devon, EX34 9SX.*
Actual grid ref: SS564466
Enjoy the peace of Berrynarbor, a quintessential English village, from our superb ensuite rooms.
Tel: **01271 883032** Mrs Mountain & Mr & Mrs J Boxall.
Fax no: 01271 882675
D: £18.00-£25.00 **S:** £18.00-£25.00.
Open: All Year (not Xmas)
Beds: 2D 1T
Baths: 3 En
℗ (10) ⌇ ▣ ✕ ⏏ ▥ & ℗ ✦

Hele (Ilfracombe) 29

National Grid Ref: SS5347

⏺ Hele Bay hotel, Ye Olde Globe

(1m) *Moles Farmhouse, Old Berrynarbor Road, Hele, Ilfracombe, Devon, EX34 9RB.*
Actual grid ref: SSS34474
Beautifully restored former farmhouse, situated in picturesque Hele Valley, near Ilfracombe.
Tel: **01271 862099** (also fax no)
Ms Grindlay.
D: £17.00-£20.00 .
Open: All Year
Beds: 1F 1T 1D **Baths:** 2 En 1 Sh
⏺ ℗ (4) ⌇ ▣ ⏏ ▥ ℗ ✦

Ilfracombe 30

National Grid Ref: SS5147

⏺ Williams Arms, Agricultural Inn, Cider Apple, Crown, Sherbourne Lodge, Hele Bay, Ye Old Globe

(▲ On path) *Ilfracombe Youth Hostel, Ashmour House, 1 Hillsborough Terrace, Ilfracombe, Devon, EX34 9NR.*
Actual grid ref: SS524476
Tel: **01271 865337**
Under 18: £6.90
Adults: £10.00
Self-catering facilities, Showers, Licensed bar, Drying room, Cycle store, Evening meal at 7.00pm, No smoking, Kitchen facilities, Breakfast available, Credit cards accepted
End house on a fine Georgian terrace, overlooking the picturesque harbour and the Bristol Channel.

(0.5m 🚗) *Cairn House Hotel, 43 St Brannocks Road, Ilfracombe, Devon, EX34 8EH.*
Grades: ETC 1 Star, RAC 1 Star
Tel: **01271 863911** (also fax no)
Mrs Tupper.
D: £18.00-£21.50 **S:** £18.00-£21.50.
Open: All Year (not Xmas/ New Year)
Beds: 3F 6D 1S
Baths: 10 En
⏺ ℗ ▣ ⌓ ✕ ⏏ ▥ ℗ ▮
The Cairn House Hotel is a beautiful Victorian hotel delightfully situated in its own grounds with extensive views over town, sea and surrounding countryside. There is a comfortable lounge/bar to relax in before or after your evening meal.

(0.5m) *Beechwood Hotel, Torrs Park, Ilfracombe, Devon, EX34 8AZ.*
Grades: ETC 2 Star
Tel: **01271 863800** (also fax no)
Burridge.
D: £22.00-£25.00 **S:** £22.00-£25.00.
Open: Mar to Oct
Beds: 2T 5D
Baths: 7 En
℗ (8) ⌇ ▣ ✕ ⏏ ▥ ℗
Peacefully situated non-smoking Victorian mansion, own woods bordering spectacular National Trust lands and coast path. Superb views over town and countryside to sea. Just 10 minutes walk to harbour and town. Spacious well appointed guest rooms, good food. Licensed. Parking.

Planning a longer
stay? Always ask for
any special rates.

(0.5m) *Lyncott Guest House,*
56 St Brannock's Road, Ilfracombe,
Devon, EX34 8EQ.
Actual grid ref: SS517463
Grades: ETC 4 Diamond
Tel: 01271 862425 (also fax no)
Mr & Mrs Holdsworth.
D: £18.00-£21.00 **S:** £18.00.
Open: All Year
Beds: 2F 3D 1S
Baths: 6 En
⛄ 🅿 (5) ⅍🖵✕🖢📖🗹
Join David and Marianna in their
charming, lovingly refurbished
Victorian house pleasantly situated
near lovely Bicclescombe Park.
Relax in elegant, smoke-free
surroundings. Enjoy delightful,
spacious, individually designed
ensuite bedrooms and sample their
scrumptious home-made fare.

(0.25m) *Strathmore Hotel,*
57 St Brannock's Road, Ilfracombe,
Devon, EX34 8EQ.
Grades: ETC 4 Diamond,
AA 4 Diamond, RAC 4 Diamond
Tel: 01271 862248
Mr Smith.
Fax no: 01271 862243
D: £20.00-£28.00 **S:** £25.00-£33.00.
Open: All Year
Beds: 1F 5D 1T 1S
Baths: 8 Pr
⛄ 🅿 (7) ⅍🖵🐾✕🖢📖🗹🔑🗝
Delightful Victorian Hotel near to
Ilfracombe town centre,
Bicclescombe Park, Cairn Nature
Reserve and glorious beaches. All
rooms are ensuite with colour TV
and hospitality trays. We offer
varied and delicious menus. All
meals are freshly prepared on the
premises.

(0.25m) *Combe Lodge Hotel,*
Chambercombe Park, Ilfracombe,
Devon, EX34 9QW.
Actual grid ref: SS530473
Quiet position, overlooking har-
bour, ideal for walking, cycling,
golf holidays.
Tel: 01271 864518
Mr & Mrs Wileman.
D: £16.50-£18.50
S: £20.50-£22.50.
Open: All Year (not Xmas)
Beds: 2F 4D 2S
Baths: 4 En 1 Pr 1 Sh
⛄ (1) 🅿 (8) ⅍🖵🐾✕🖢📖🗹🔑🗝

(0.25m) *Varley House,*
Chambercombe Park, Ilfracombe,
Devon, EX34 9QW.
Period house with attractive ensuite
accommodation, close to coastal
walks.
Tel: 01271 863927
Mrs S O'Sullivan & Mr D Small.
Fax no: 01271 879299
D: £24.00-£25.00
S: £23.00-£24.00.
Open: Easter to Oct
Beds: 2F 4D 1T 1S
Baths: 7 En 1 Pr
⛄ (5) 🅿 (7) 🐾✕🖢📖🗹

(0.25m) *Westwell Hall,* Torrs
Park, Ilfracombe, Devon, EX34 8AZ.
Elegant Victorian gentleman's resi-
dence in own grounds - superb
views.
Tel: 01271 862792 (also fax no)
Mr & Mrs Lomas.
D: £22.00-£24.00 **S:** £22.00-£24.00.
Open: All Year
Beds: 7D 2T 1S **Baths:** 10 En
⛄ 🅿 🖵🐾✕🖢📖🗹

(0.5m) *Harcourt Hotel,* Fore
Street, Ilfracombe, Devon, EX39 9DS.
Friendly licensed hotel ensuite
rooms TV tea coffee, sea views.
Tel: 01271 862931 Mr Doorbar.
D: £17.00-£24.00 **S:** £17.00-£24.00.
Open: All Year
Beds: 3F 4D 1T 2S
Baths: 8 En 2 Sh
⛄ 🅿 (4) 🖵🐾✕🖢📖🗹

(0.5m) *Sherborne Lodge Hotel,*
Torrs Park, Ilfracombe, Devon,
EX34 8AY.
Friendly, fully-licensed family
hotel providing good food, wine,
comfortable accommodation.
Tel: 01271 862297 Mr & Mrs
Millington.
Fax no: 01271 865520
D: £15.50-£21.50 **S:** £15.50-£21.50.
Open: All Year
Beds: 1F 8D 2T 1S
⛄ 🅿 (10) 🖵🐾✕🖢📖🗹🔑🗝

Woolacombe 31

National Grid Ref: SS4543

🍴 🍺 Jubilee Inn, Chichester Arms, Red Barn,
Stables, Golden Hind, The Mill

(0.5m 🚍) *Ossaborough House,*
Woolacombe, Devon, EX34 7HJ.
Grades: ETC 3 Diamond
Tel: 01271 870297 Mr & Mrs Day.
D: £21.00-£25.00 **S:** £21.00-£25.00.
Open: All Year
Beds: 2F 2T 2D
Baths: 5 En 1 Pr
⛄ 🅿 (8) ⅍🖵🐾✕🖢📖🗹🔑
Escape to our lovely C17th country
house originating in the days of
Saxon England - rustic beams.
Thick stone walls, inglenook fire-
places, candlelit dinners. All rooms
sympathetically restored. Explore
rolling hills, rugged cliffs, pic-
turesque villages, stunning golden
beaches and secluded coves.

(0.5m) *Camberley,* Beach Road,
Woolacombe, Devon, EX34 7AA.
Actual grid ref: SS465437
Large Victorian house with views
to sea and NT land. Use of indoor
pool.
Grades: ETC 3 Diamond
Tel: 01271 870231
Mr & Mrs Riley.
D: £20.00-£25.00 **S:** £19.00-£24.00.
Open: All Year (not Xmas)
Beds: 3F 3D 1T
Baths: 6 En 1 Pr
⛄ 🅿 (6) 🖵🖢📖🗹🔑🗝

(0.25m 🚍) *Barton Lea,* Beach
Road, Woolacombe, Devon,
EX34 7BT.
Warm welcome, sea views, big
breakfast menu, close to Coastal
Foot Path.
Tel: 01271 870928 Mrs Vickery.
D: £15.50-£20.00 **S:** £20.00-£25.00.
Open: Easter to Oct
Beds: 1F 1D 1T
Baths: 3 En
⛄ 🅿 (7) ⅍🖵🐾🖢📖🗹🔑🗝

(0.5m) *Sunny Nook,* Beach Road,
Woolacombe, Devon, EX34 7AA.
Actual grid ref: SS466438
Delightful home in lovely situation,
wonderful views and excellent
breakfasts. No smoking through-
out.
Tel: 01271 870964 Mr Fenn.
D: £18.00-£23.00 **S:** £25.00-£30.00.
Open: All Year (not Xmas)
Beds: 1F 1D 1T
Baths: 2 En 1 Pr
⛄ (8) 🅿 (5) ⅍🖵✕🖢📖🗹🔑🗝

(On path) *Clyst House,* Rockfield
Road, Woolacombe, Devon,
EX34 7DH.
Friendly, comfortable guest house
close blue flag beach. Delicious
English breakfast. Beautiful
walking area.
Tel: 01271 870220
Mrs Braund.
D: £20.00-£22.00 **S:** £20.00-£22.00.
Open: Mar to Nov
Beds: 1F 1D 1T
Baths: 1 Sh
⛄ (7) 🅿 ⅍🖵✕🖢📖🗹🔑🗝

Pickwell 32

National Grid Ref: SS4641

🍴 🍺 Rock Inn, Thatched Barn

(0.5m 🚍) *Meadow Cottage,*
Pickwell, Georgeham, Braunton,
Devon, EX33 1LA.
Tel: 01271 890938 (also fax no)
Mrs Holmes.
D: £20.00 **S:** £20.00.
Open: All Year
Beds: 1D 1S
Baths: 1Private
⛄ 🅿 (3) ⅍🖵📖🗝
Meadow Cottage is in the tranquil
setting of Pickwell. Off the beaten
track with panoramic views of
patchwork fields to the sea, close to
the coastal path and beaches of
Woolacombe, Putsborough and
Croyde and the championship golf
course, Saunton.

Bringing children with
you? Always ask for
any special rates.

Croyde 33

National Grid Ref: SS4439

Manor, Thatched Barn Inn

(On path 🚍) *Moorsands, Moor Lane, Croyde Bay, Braunton, Devon, EX33 1NP.*
Grades: ETC 3 Diamond
Tel: **01271 890781**
Mr & Mrs Davis.
D: £20.00-£26.00 **S:** £20.00-£26.00.
Open: All Year
Beds: 1F 1T 2D 1S
Baths: 5 En
🛏 🅿 (6) ⊁ 🖵 🎄 🖿 🕮 Ⓥ ✦
Originally a large Victorian coast guard station with stunning views, Moorsands offers short walks to beach, village and local facilities. Come and surf, ride, cycle etc. or simply relax with our comfortable ensuite rooms, guest lounge, beautiful surroundings and superb breakfasts.

(0.5m 🚍) *Oamaru, Down End, Croyde, Braunton, Devon, EX33 1QE.*
400m from top surfing beach and village. Relaxed friendly atmosphere.
Tel: **01271 890765** Mr & Mrs Jenkins.
D: £17.50-£25.00 **S:** £17.50-£25.00.
Open: All Year
Beds: 1F 1D **Baths:** 1 En 1 Pr
🛏 🅿 (6) ⊁ 🖵 🎄 🖿 🕮 Ⓥ ✦

(On Path) *West Winds Guest House, Moor Lane, Croyde Bay, Croyde, Braunton, Devon, EX33 1PA.*
Actual grid ref: SS433396
Stunning waters' edge location with views over Croyde Beach.
Grades: ETC 4 Diamond, AA 4 Diamond
Tel: **01271 890489** (also fax no)
Mr & Mrs Gedling.
D: £26.00-£31.00 **S:** £26.00-£31.00.
Open: Mar to Nov
Beds: 3D 2T
Baths: 3 Pr 2 Sh
🛏 🅿 (6) ⊁ 🖵 🎄 🗶 🖿 🕮 Ⓥ ✦

(On path) *Chapel Farm, Hobbs Hill, Croyde, Braunton, Devon, EX33 1NE.*
Actual grid ref: SS444390
C16th thatched farmhouse, 10 minutes to beach.
Tel: **01271 890429** Mrs Windsor.
D: £18.00-£26.00 **S:** £18.00-£30.00.
Open: Easter to Nov
Beds: 1F 2D **Baths:** 3 En
🛏 🅿 (6) ⊁ 🖵 🖿 🕮 Ⓥ ✦

All rates are subject to alteration at the owners' discretion.

Braunton 34

National Grid Ref: SS4936

Agricultural Inn

(0.75m 🚍) *St Merryn, Higher Park Road, Braunton, Devon, EX33 2LG.*
Tel: **01271 813805**
Mrs Bradford.
Fax no: 01271 812097
D: £20.00-£22.00
S: £20.00-£22.00.
Open: Jan to Dec
Beds: 1F 1T 1D
Baths: 1 En 2 Pr
🛏 🅿 (5) ⊁ 🖵 🎄 🖿 🕮 Ⓥ ✦
Beautiful 1930's home set in delightful large garden. Tranquil setting with excellent parking and within easy walking distance of village. Excellent beaches and golf courses within a short drive.

(0.25m) *Pixie Dell, 1 Willand Rd, Braunton, N. Devon, EX33 1AX.*
Large chalet bungalow and garden. Warm welcome assured.
Tel: **01271 812233**
Mrs Dale.
D: £18.00-£18.00
S: £18.00-£20.00.
Open: All Year (not Xmas)
Beds: 1D 2T 1S
Baths: 2 Sh
🛏 🅿 (4) ⊁ 🖵 🎄 🖿 🕮 &. Ⓥ ✦

Thames Path

The **Thames Path** runs for 175 miles along the banks of the River Thames from the great Thames Barrier near Woolwich in London, through the heartland of England, to the river's source at Thames Head near Cirencester in Gloucestershire. It is, of course, a walk with no hills - bliss for some, anathema to others. Above all, the walk offers a rolling social picture of Southern England today, starting near what used to be the old London Docklands, moving through genteel South West London, out through the affluent commuter belt of Royal Berkshire, on to the city of Oxford (half ancient university, half busy industry) and beyond through the deserted pastures south of the Cotswolds. The Thames itself, with its boats, bridges, locks and weirs, shifts character accordingly. The towpaths are quite busy in the lower reaches, but beyond Oxford it goes quiet. After rain, the path stays muddy, but apart from flooding, there are no real hazards.

We have left out accommodation in central London (apart from Youth Hostels), as the usual hotels tend to be rather expensive. If the Thames Barrier to Kew stretch is too much for you, our suggestion is to make use of the Underground and stay at the same place two nights running.

Thames Path by David Sharp (ISBN 1 85410 4063), published by Aurum Press in association with the Countryside Commission and Ordnance Survey and available from all major bookshops, £12.99

Maps: Ordnance Survey 1:50000 Landranger series: 163, 164, 174, 175 and 176

Comments on the path to: **Karen Groeneveld**, Thames Path Project Officer, c/o Leisure Services, Reading Borough Council, Civic Centre, Reading, Berks, RG1 7TD

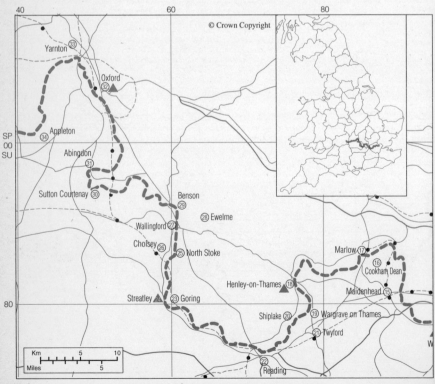

© Crown Copyright

Blackheath 1

National Grid Ref: TQ3976

⚑ Sun in the Sands, Royal Oak

(1m ⌂) *Numbernine Blackheath Ltd., 9 Charlton Road, Blackheath, London, SE3 7EU.*
Grades: ETC 4 Diamond
Tel: **020 8858 4175** (also fax no)
Open: All Year
⛺ (5) ℙ (4) ✕ □ ✕ ☰ ▥ ▥ ⚡
Number Nine is a friendly, non-smoking guest house located at The Royal Standard, within fifteen minutes walking distance of the historic town of Greenwich. This recently fully refurbished Victorian guest house provides warm, comfortable, safe, fully Fire Certificated surroundings.

(1m ⌂) *135 Shooters Hill Road, Blackheath, London, SE3 8UQ.*
Victorian family house/garden close central London, River Thames, Jubilee/DLR. lines.
Tel: **020 8858 1420** (also fax no)
Poole.
D: £25.00-£35.00 **S:** £25.00-£30.00.
Open: All Year
Beds: 1F 1D **Baths:** 2 En
⛺ ℙ (1) ✕ □ ☰ ▥ ▥ ⚡

Greenwich 2

National Grid Ref: TQ3977

⚑ Welcome Inn

(1m) *78 Vanbrugh Park, Blackheath, Greenwich, London, SE3 7JQ.*
Lovely Victorian House.
Blackheath/Greenwich. Own living room. bedrooms overlook beautiful garden.
Tel: **020 8858 0338** Mrs Mattey.
Fax no: 020 8244 6690
D: £20.00-£25.00 **S:** £25.00-£30.00.
Open: All Year
Beds: 1F 2T **Baths:** 1 En 1 Pr
⛺ ℙ (3) □ ☰ ▥ ▥

(0.5m) *Greenwich Parkhouse Hotel, 1 & 2 Nevada Street, Greenwich, London, SE10 9JL.*
Small hotel, beautifully situated within World Heritage site by gates of Royal Greenwich Park.
Tel: **020 8305 1478** Mrs Bryan.
D: £20.00-£25.00 **S:** £33.00-£33.00.
Open: All Year
Beds: 21F
Baths: 2 En 1 Pr 2 Sh
⛺ ℙ (8) ✕ □ ☰ ☰ ▥ ▥

(0.5m) *Dover House, 155 Shooters Hill, Greenwich, London, SE18 3HP.*
Actual grid ref: TQ437765
Victorian family house opposite famous Oxleas Wood, 8 miles Central London. Warm welcome awaits.
Tel: **020 8856 9892** (also fax no)
Mrs Araniello.
D: £20.00-£20.00
S: £25.00-£25.00.
Open: All Year (not Xmas)
Beds: 2F 2T 2S
Baths: 1 Sh
⛺ ℙ ✕ □ ☰ ▥ ▥ ⚡

Rotherhithe 3

National Grid Ref: TQ3579

(▲ 0.25m) *Rotherhithe Youth Hostel, Salter Road, Rotherhithe, London, SE16 1PP.*
Actual grid ref: TQ357804
Tel: **020 7232 2114**
Under 18: £19.90
Adults: £23.50
Self-catering facilities, Television, Showers, Licensed bar, Laundry facilities, Lounge, Cycle store, Evening meal at 6.00-7.30pm, Facilities for disabled people Category 1, Credit cards accepted
New purpose-built hostel in a striking modern design on four floors, all bedrooms ensuite. Greenwich is within easy reach, as is the Tower and points west.

St Paul's 4

National Grid Ref: TQ3181

(▲ 1m) *City of London Youth Hostel, 36 Carter Lane, St Paul's, London, EC4V 5AD.*
Actual grid ref: TQ319811
Tel: **020 7236 4965**
Under 18: £19.90
Adults: £23.50
Television, Showers, Licensed bar, Laundry facilities, Lounge, Evening meal at 5.00-8.00pm, Breakfast available, Luggage store, Credit cards accepted
The one-time Choir School for St Paul's Cathedral has been fully refurbished to modern standards, while, the old building retaining many of its original features, including the oak panels in the former chapel. It is right in the centre of the City of London.

Putney 5

National Grid Ref: TQ2374

(0.25m) *The Grange, One Fanthorpe Street, Putney, London, SW15 1DZ.*
Actual grid ref: TQ233758
Tel: **020 8785 7609**
Mr & Mrs Taylor.
Fax no: 020 8789 5584
D: £24.00-£24.00
S: £30.00-£30.00.
Open: All Year (not Xmas)
Beds: 1D 1T
Baths: 1 En 1 Sh
⛺ ✕ ✕ ☰
A warm welcome awaits you to our comfortable family home, which is close to Thames, and convenient for bus, Underground and BR mainline. Evening meals by arrangement from £14. Bed and continental breakfast £24 - £30 per person per night.

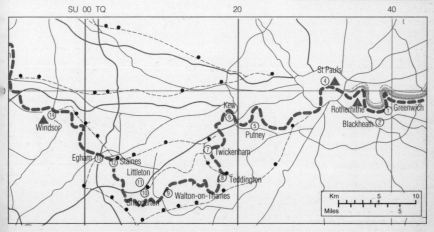

SU 00 TQ   20   40

Kew 6
National Grid Ref: TQ1876

🍴 ◗ Coach & Horses, Kew Gardens Hotel, Ship

(0.5m) *Melbury, 33 Marksbury Avenue, Kew, Richmond, Surrey, TW9 4JE.*
Friendly and welcoming, refurbished private home, close to Richmond and Kew Gardens Underground.
Grades: ETC 2 Diamond
Tel: 020 8876 3930 (also fax no)
Mrs Allen.
D: £22.50-£27.50 **S:** £25.00-£35.00.
Open: All Year
Beds: 1T 1D 1F 1S
Baths: 2 En 1 Sh
🛏 (2) ₽ (1) ⊬ ❏ ✗ 🌡 ⛿ Ⅲ. Ⅴ ♿ ⚡

(0.5m) *179 Mortlake Road, Kew, Richmond, Surrey, TW9 4AW.*
Georgian house close to Kew Gardens, PRO and Underground.
Grades: ETC 3 Diamond
Tel: 020 8876 0584 (also fax no)
Mrs Butt.
D: £25.00-£25.00 **S:** £35.00.
Open: All Year
Beds: 1T
Baths: 1 En
₽ (5) ❏ ⅍ 🌡 ⛿ Ⅲ. Ⅴ

(0.5m) *34 Forest Road, Kew, Richmond, Surrey, TW9 3BZ.*
Tel: 020 8332 6289 (also fax no)
Mrs Royle.
D: £20.00-£23.00 **S:** £22.00-£28.00.
Open: All Year
Beds: 1F 1D 1T
🛏 (12) ⊬ ❏ 🌡 ⛿ Ⅲ. Ⅴ
A comfortable Edwardian era family home. 5 minutes walk from Kew Gardens station, 35 mins to Westminster. 5 mins to Richmond, Kew Botanical Gardens and Public Records Office. Pleasant walks along Thames river bank. Good selection of pubs and restaurants nearby.

(0.5m) *1 Chelwood Gardens, Kew, Richmond, Surrey, TW9 4JG.*
Situated in quiet cul-de-sac. Friendly house near Kew Gardens Station.
Tel: 020 8876 8733
Mrs Gray.
Fax no: 020 8255 0171
D: £25.00-£27.00 **S:** £30.00-£30.00.
Open: All Year
Beds: 4F 2T 2S
Baths: 2 Sh
🛏 (5) ₽ (6) ⊬ ❏ 🌡 ⛿ Ⅲ. Ⅴ

Pay B&Bs by cash or cheque and be prepared to pay up front.

D = Price range per person sharing in a double room

Twickenham 7
National Grid Ref: TQ1573

🍴 ◗ Pope's Grotto

(1.5m) *11 Spencer Road, Strawberry Hill, Twickenham, Middx, TW2 5TH.*
Stylish Edwardian house near Richmond and Hampton Court. Excellent transport, easy parking.
Grades: ETC 3 Diamond
Tel: 020 8894 5271 Mrs Duff.
D: £20.00-£25.00 **S:** £20.00-£25.00.
Open: All Year
Beds: 2D 1T **Baths:** 1 En 1 Sh
🛏 (12) ₽ ⊬ ❏ Ⅲ.

(1.5m 🚌) *Avalon Cottage, 50 Moor Mead Road, Twickenham, TW1 1JS.*
Avalon Cottage is a private Edwardian house beside a park and tennis courts.
Grades: ETC 3 Diamond
Tel: 020 8744 2178
Mrs Thompson.
Fax no: 020 8891 2444
D: £25.00-£35.00 **S:** £30.00-£35.00.
Open: All Year
Beds: 1D 1S
Baths: 1 En 1 Sh
🛏 (1) ⊬ ❏ 🌡 ⛿ Ⅲ. Ⅴ

Teddington 8
National Grid Ref: TQ1670

🍴 ◗ Tide End Pub

(1m) *93 Langham Road, Teddington, Middx, TW11 9HG.*
Sympathetically restored Edwardian house with original features and brass beds.
Tel: 020 8977 6962 Mrs Norris.
D: £22.50-£25.00 **S:** £30.00-£45.00.
Open: All Year (not Xmas)
Beds: 1D 1T
Baths: 1 Sh
⊬ ❏ Ⅲ.

Walton-on-Thames 9
National Grid Ref: TQ1066

🍴 ◗ The Wellington, The Plough

(1.25m) *Beech Tree Lodge, 7 Rydens Avenue, Walton-on-Thames, Surrey, KT12 3JB.*
In quiet avenue, 10 mins BR station; close local shops.
Grades: ETC 3 Diamond
Tel: 01932 242738 Mrs Spiteri.
Fax no: 01932 886667
D: £20.00-£21.00 **S:** £22.00-£36.00.
Open: All Year
Beds: 1F 1T 1S **Baths:** 2 Sh
🛏 ₽ (8) ⊬ ❏ 🕯 🌡 ⛿ Ⅲ. Ⅴ ♿ ⚡

(0.75m) *Oak Tree Lodge, 11 Hersham Road, Walton-on-Thames, Surrey, KT12 1LQ.*
Actual grid ref: TQ104659
Mock Tudor family home near buses, railway station and airports.
Tel: 01932 221907 Mrs Hall.
D: £17.00-£20.00 **S:** £20.00-£22.00.
Open: All Year (not Xmas)
Beds: 1D 1T 1S
Baths: 1 Sh
₽ (4) ⊬ ❏ 🌡 ⛿ Ⅲ. Ⅴ

Shepperton 10
National Grid Ref: TQ0767

🍴 ◗ The Harrow, The Goat, The Bull

(0.5m) *91 Watersplash Road, Shepperton, TW17 0EE.*
Olde worlde cottage with pretty bedrooms and old fashioned hospitality.
Tel: 01932 229987 (also fax no)
Mr Shaw.
D: £19.00-£22.50 **S:** £25.00-£28.50.
Open: All Year
Beds: 2D 1T
🛏 ⊬ ❏ 🌡 ⛿ Ⅲ. Ⅴ ♿

Littleton 11
National Grid Ref: TQ0668

🍴 ◗ The Harrow

(0.5m) *Old Manor House, Squires Bridge Road, Littleton, Shepperton, Middx, TW17 0QG.*
Listed building dating from reign of Henry VII, set in 5 acres of garden.
Tel: 01932 571293 Mrs Bouwens.
D: £25.00-£27.50 **S:** £30.00-£30.00.
Open: All Year
Beds: 1D 1T 1S
Baths: 1 En 1 Sh
🛏 (10) ₽ (6) ❏ 🕯 🌡 ⛿ Ⅲ. Ⅴ

Staines 12
National Grid Ref: TQ0471

🍴 ◗ Wheatsheaf, Pigeon

(1m) *The Penton, 39 Penton Road, Staines, TW18 2JL.*
Tel: 01784 458787
D: £20.00-£25.00 **S:** £20.00-£26.00.
Open: All Year
Beds: 4F 1D 1T 1S
Baths: 2 En 1 Sh
🛏 ₽ (2) ⊬ ❏ 🌡 ⛿ Ⅲ. Ⅴ
Homely character cottage close to River Thames, access to scenic walks and historic surroundings, 10 mins M25, 15 mins Heathrow, we provide a comfortable stay with an excellent breakfast.

S = Price range for a single person in a single room

Egham 13

National Grid Ref: TQ0071

☒☒ Happy Man, The Beehive

(2m) *The Old Parsonage,*
2 Parsonage Road, Englefield
Green, Egham, Surrey, TW20 0JW.
Actual grid ref: SU995709
Georgian parsonage, traditionally
furnished, old fashioned gardens.
30 minutes from London.
Tel: **01784 436706** (also fax no)
Mr & Mrs Clark.
D: £25.00-£40.00 **S:** £35.00-£55.00.
Open: All Year (not Xmas)
Beds: 1F 2D 2T 1S
Baths: 3 En 1 Sh
☒ ☒ (6) ☒☒☒☒☒☒ ☒ ☒

Windsor 14

National Grid Ref: SU9676

☒☒ The Mitre, Bexley Arms, The Trooper,
Nags Head, The Queen, Windsor Lad, George
Inn, Vansitart Arms,Crow's Nest, Red Lion,
White Horse, Hungry Horse

(▲ 0.25m) *Windsor Youth Hostel,*
Edgeworth House, Mill Lane,
Windsor, Berks, SL4 5JE.
Actual grid ref: SU955770
Tel: **01753 861710**
Under 18: £7.75 **Adults:** £11.00
Self-catering facilities, Television,
Showers, Laundry facilities,
Lounge, Drying room, Cycle store,
Parking cars only, Kitchen facili-
ties, Breakfast available, Luggage
store, Credit cards accepted
Queen Anne residence in the old
Clewer village quarter on the out-
skirts of historic Windsor.

(0.25m ☒**)** *Jean's, 1 Stovell Road,*
Windsor, Berks, SL4 5JB.
Actual grid ref: SU958771
Grades: ETC 2 Diamond
Tel: **01753 852055**
Ms Sumner.
Fax no: 01753 842932
D: £22.50-£25.00 **S:** £40.00-£40.00.
Open: All Year
Beds: 1D 1T
Baths: 2 En
☒ (2) ☒☒☒☒☒☒☒☒
Quiet comfortable self-contained
ground floor flat comprising 2
ensuite bedrooms which share a
large lounge. 100 yds river and
leisure centre, 7 mins' walk to
castle, town centre and railway
stations, 4 mins to buses.

(1m) *Langton House, 46 Alma*
Road, Windsor, Berks, SL4 3HA.
Victorian house, quiet tree-lined
road, 5 minutes walk to town and
castle.
Tel: **01753 858299** Mrs Fogg.
D: £30.00-£32.50 **S:** £50.00.
Open: All Year (not Xmas)
Beds: 2D 1T
Baths: 2 En 1 Pr
☒ (2) ☒☒☒☒☒☒ ☒

(0.75m) *62 Queens Road,*
Windsor, Berks, SL4 3BH.
Actual grid ref: SU964761
Excellent reputation, quiet, conve-
nient, ground floor rooms. Largest
family room available.
Tel: **01753 866036** (also fax no)
Mrs Hughes.
D: £20.00-£25.00 **S:** £30.00-£35.00.
Open: All Year
Beds: 1F 1T **Baths:** 2 Pr
☒☒ (1) ☒☒☒☒☒☒☒☒

(1m) *Elansey, 65 Clifton Rise,*
Windsor, Berks, SL4 5SX.
Modern, quiet, comfortable house.
Garden, patio, excellent breakfasts,
highly recommended.
Tel: **01753 864438** Mrs Forbutt.
D: £20.00-£25.00 **S:** £20.00-£26.00.
Open: All Year (not Xmas)
Beds: 1D 1T 1S **Baths:** 1 En 1 Sh
☒ (3) ☒☒☒☒ ☒

(1m ☒**)** *The Andrews,*
77 Whitehorse Road, Windsor,
Berks, SL4 4PG.
Modern, comfortable private
house.
Tel: **01753 866803** Mrs Andrews.
D: £18.00-£20.00 **S:** £23.00-£25.00.
Open: All Year (not Xmas)
Beds: 1D 2T **Baths:** 2 Sh
☒ (5) ☒ (3) ☒☒☒☒

(1m) *Chasela, 30 Convent Road,*
Windsor, Berks, SL4 3RB.
Modern semi-detached near M4,
M40, M25. Castle 1 mile and
Legoland.
Grades: ETC 3 Diamond
Tel: **01753 860410** Mrs Williams.
D: £22.00-£24.00 **S:** £22.00-£24.00.
Open: All Year
Beds: 1T 1S **Baths:** 1 Sh
☒ (12) ☒ (5) ☒☒☒☒☒☒ ☒

(1m) *The Laurells, 22 Dedworth*
Road, Windsor, Berks, SL4 5AY.
Pretty Victorian house 3/4 mile
town centre. Heathrow 20 minutes.
Tel: **01753 855821** Mrs Joyce.
D: £20.00 **S:** £25.00.
Open: All Year (not Xmas)
Beds: 2T
☒ (5) ☒☒☒☒☒☒☒☒ ☒

(1m) *2 Benning Close,*
St Leonards Park, Windsor,
Berks, SL4 4YS.
A modern detached house set in a
quiet residential area.
Tel: **01753 852294** Mrs Hume.
D: £20.00-£20.00 **S:** £25.00-£25.00.
Open: All Year (not Xmas/New
Year)
Beds: 1F 1D 1S
☒☒ (2) ☒☒☒☒☒☒☒☒ ☒

Pay B&Bs by cash or
cheque and be prepared
to pay up front.

(0.5m ☒**)** *12 Parsonage Lane,*
Windsor, Berks, SL4 5EN.
Tastefully furnished detached pri-
vate house. Quiet location. Parking.
Lovely gardens.
Tel: **01753 868052** (also fax no)
Mr & Mrs Riddle.
D: £25.00-£35.00 **S:** £32.00-£35.00.
Open: All Year
Beds: 1D 1S
Baths: 1 Sh
☒☒ (4) ☒☒☒☒☒☒☒☒ ☒

Maidenhead 15

National Grid Ref: SU8781

☒☒ Boulter's Lock Inn, Thames Hotel,
Kingswood Hotel, Windsor Castle, Pond House,
Hare & Hounds

(0.5m) *Sheephouse Manor,*
Sheephouse Road, Maidenhead,
Berks, SL6 8HJ.
Actual grid ref: SU8878
Charming C16th farmhouse, with
health suite and jacuzzi. beautiful
grounds.
Grades: ETC 3 Diamond
Tel: **01628 776902** Mrs Street.
Fax no: 01628 625138
D: £28.00-£30.00 **S:** £40.00-£45.00.
Open: All Year (not Xmas)
Beds: 1D 1T 3S
Baths: 5 En
☒☒ (7) ☒☒☒☒☒☒ ☒

(1.25m ☒**)** *Laburnham Guest*
House, 31 Laburnham Road,
Maidenhead, Berks, SL6 4DB.
Actual grid ref: SU881808
Fine Edwardian house, near town
centre, station and M4 motorway.
Tel: **01628 676748** (also fax no)
Mrs Stevens.
D: £23.00-£25.00 **S:** £35.00-£40.00.
Open: All Year (not Xmas)
Beds: 1F 2D 1T 1S **Baths:** 5 En
☒☒ (5) ☒☒☒☒☒☒ ☒

(0.5m) *Clifton Guest House,*
21 Craufurd Rise, Maidenhead,
Berks, SL6 7LR.
Family-run guest house. 10 mins
from town centre. Easy access
London M4/M25/M40.
Grades: ETC 3 Diamond,
RAC 3 Diamond
Tel: **01628 623572** (also fax no)
Mr Arora.
D: £45.00-£60.00 .
Open: All Year
Beds: 2F 5D 5T 3S
Baths: 8 En 1 Pr 4 Sh
☒☒☒☒☒☒☒☒☒☒ ☒

(0.5m) *Copperfields Guest House,*
54 Bath Road, Maidenhead, Berks,
SL6 4JY.
Comfortable accommodation, near
Windsor, Henley, Reading and M4
to London.
Tel: **01628 674941** Mrs Lindsay.
D: £22.50-£25.00 **S:** £30.00-£33.00.
Open: All Year
Beds: 2T 2S **Baths:** 3 Pr
☒☒ (5) ☒☒☒☒☒☒ ☒

Cookham Dean 16

National Grid Ref: SU8684

Checkers

(1.5m) ***Cartlands Cottage,*** *King's Lane, Cookham Dean, Maidenhead, Berks, SL6 9AY.*
Self-contained guest room in g arden. Rural, very quiet.
Tel: **01628 482196**
Mr & Mrs Parkes.
D: £22.00-£25.00 **S:** £23.50-£26.00.
Open: All Year
Beds: 1F **Baths:** 1 Pr
(2)

Marlow 17

National Grid Ref: SU8586

Hare & Hounds, Three Horseshoes, Osbourne Arms, Clayton Arms, Royal Oak

(1.5m) ***Merrie Hollow,*** *Seymour Court Hill, Marlow, Bucks, SL7 3DE.*
Actual grid ref: SU840889
Grades: ETC 3 Diamond
Tel: **01628 485663** (also fax no)
Mr Wells.
D: £20.00-£25.00 **S:** £25.00-£35.00.
Open: All Year
Beds: 1D 1T **Baths:** 1 Sh
(4)
Secluded quiet country cottage in large garden 150 yds off B482 Marlow to Stokenchurch road, easy access to M4 & M25, 35 mins from Heathrow & Oxford, private off-road car parking.

(0.75m) ***Sneppen House,*** *Henley Road, Marlow, Bucks, SL7 2DF.*
Within walking distance of town centre and river. Breakfast menu choice. Pub food nearby.
Grades: ETC 4 Diamond
Tel: **01628 485227** Mr Norris.
D: £22.50-£22.50 **S:** £30.00-£30.00.
Open: All Year
Beds: 1D 1T **Baths:** 1 Sh
(2) (3)

(1.5m) ***Acha Pani,*** *Bovingdon Green, Marlow, Bucks, SL7 2JL.*
Actual grid ref: SU836869
Quiet location, easy access Thames Foothpath, Chilterns, Windsor, London, Heathrow.
Grades: ETC 2 Diamond
Tel: **01628 483435** (also fax no)
Mrs Cowling.
D: £17.00-£18.00 **S:** £17.00-£18.00.
Open: All Year
Beds: 1D 1T 1S **Baths:** 1 En 1 Sh
(10) (3)

All paths are popular: you are well-advised to book ahead

(2m) ***Sunnyside,*** *Munday Dean, Marlow, Bucks, SL7 3BU.*
Comfortable, friendly, family home in Area of Outstanding Natural Beauty.
Tel: **01628 485701**
Mrs O'Connor.
D: £17.50-£17.50 **S:** £20.00-£20.00.
Open: All Year
Beds: 2D 1T
Baths: 1 Sh
(5)

(1m) ***29 Oaktree Road,*** *Marlow, Bucks, SL7 3ED.*
Friendly and efficiently run Bed & Breakfast. Convenient M4, M48 and M25.
Tel: **01628 472145**
Mr Lasenby.
D: £25.00-£27.50 **S:** £28.00-£30.00.
Open: All Year (not Xmas)
Beds: 5F 2T
Baths: 1 En
(2)

Henley-on-Thames 18

National Grid Ref: SU7682

Anchor, Bottle & Glass, Golden Ball, Rose & Crown

(0.25m) ***Ledard,*** *Rotherfield Road, Henley-on-Thames, Oxon, RG9 1NN.*
Actual grid ref: SU761814
Elegant Victorian house and garden within easy reach of Henley.
Tel: **01491 575611** Mrs Howard.
D: £20.00-£20.00 **S:** £20.00-£20.00.
Open: All Year (not Xmas)
Beds: 1F 1D 1T
Baths: 2 Pr
(4)

(0.5m) ***Alftrudis,*** *8 Norman Avenue, Henley-on-Thames, Oxon, RG9 1SG.*
Victorian home, quiet cul-de-sac two minutes town centre station, river.
Grades: ETC 4 Diamond
Tel: **01491 573099**
Mrs Lambert.
Fax no: 01491 411747
D: £25.00-£30.00
S: £40.00-£50.00.
Open: All Year
Beds: 2D 1T
Baths: 2 En 1 Pr
(8) (2)

(0.75m) ***4 Coldharbour Close,*** *Henley-on-Thames, Oxon, RG9 1QP.*
Large sunny bungalow in quiet location; secluded garden with patio.
Grades: ETC 3 Diamond
Tel: **01491 575297** (also fax no)
Mrs Bower.
D: £24.00-£28.00
S: £27.00-£30.00.
Open: Easter to Nov
Beds: 1D 1T
Baths: 1 Pr 1 En
(3)

(0.5m) ***Lenwade,*** *3 Western Road, Henley-on-Thames, Oxon, RG9 1JL.*
Beautiful Victorian family home, convenient river, restaurants, public transport.
Tel: **01491 573468** (also fax no)
Mrs Williams.
D: £25.00-£27.50 **S:** £25.00-£27.50.
Open: All Year (not Xmas)
Beds: 2D 1T **Baths:** 2 En 1 Pr
(2)

(1.5m) ***New Lodge,*** *Henley Park, Henley-on-Thames, Oxon, RG9 6HU.*
Actual grid ref: SU758847
Victorian cottage, Area of Outstanding Natural Beauty. Minimum stay two nights.
Tel: **01491 576340** (also fax no)
Mrs Warner.
D: £19.00-£21.00 **S:** £24.00-£27.00.
Open: All Year
Beds: 2D **Baths:** 1 En 1 Pr
(5)

Wargrave-on-Thames 19

National Grid Ref: SU7978

The Bull, The Queen Victoria

(0.5m) ***Windy Brow,*** *204 Victoria Road, Wargrave-on-Thames, Reading, Berks, RG10 8AJ.*
Actual grid ref: SU794788
Victorian detached house, close M4/M40, 1 mile A4, 6 Miles reading and Maidenhead.
Grades: ETC 4 Diamond
Tel: **0118 940 3336** Mrs Carver.
Fax no: 0118 401 1260
D: £25.00-£30.00 **S:** £32.00-£45.00.
Open: All Year (not Xmas/ New Year)
Beds: 1D 2T 2S **Baths:** 1 En 2 Sh
(5)

Shiplake 20

National Grid Ref: SU7678

Baskerville Arms, White Hart

(0.5m) ***The Knoll,*** *Crowsley Road, Shiplake, Henley-on-Thames, Oxfordshire, RG9 3JT.*
Comfortable private home beautifully restored by local craftsmen, extensive landscaped gardens.
Tel: **0118 940 2705** (also fax no)
Mr Green.
D: £26.00-£27.00 **S:** £45.00-£45.00.
Open: All Year (not Xmas)
Beds: 1F 1D 1T
Baths: 3 En
(12) (6)

Please take muddy boots off before entering premises

Twyford 21

National Grid Ref: SU7975

⚐ Queen Victoria, La Fontana, Waggon & Horse, The Bull

(2m 🚌) *Somewhere To Stay, c/o Loddon Acres, Bath Road, Twyford, Reading, Berks, RG10 9RU.*
Grades: ETC 4 Diamond
Tel: **0118 934 5880** (also fax no)
Fisher.
D: £24.50-£29.00 **S:** £35.00-£45.00.
Open: All Year
Beds: 1F 1D 1T 1S
Baths: 3 En 1 Pr
🛏 🅿 (6) ✠ 🔲 ⊁ 🛉 🖳 Ⅲ. Ⅵ ⌀
Self-contained, modern, detached accommodation with kitchenette and sauna. Situated next to owners house in beautiful river fronted 2 acre garden, tennis/canoes available. Rooms ensuite, tastefully decorated with colour TV, tea/coffee, easy access to Reading, Windsor, Maidenhead and Heathrow.

(2m 🚌) *Copper Beeches, Bath Road, Kiln Green, Twyford, Reading, Berks, RG10 9UT.*
Quiet house in large gardens with Tennis court, warm welcome.
Tel: **0118 940 2929** (also fax no)
Mrs Gorecki.
D: £22.50-£25.00 **S:** £28.00-£35.00.
Open: All Year
Beds: 3F 4T 1D 1S
Baths: 1 En 3 Sh
🛏 (3) 🅿 (14) 🔲 🛉 🖳 Ⅲ. Ⅵ 🛉 ⌀

(2m) *Chesham House, 79 Wargrave Road, Twyford, Reading, Berks, RG10 9PE.*
Windsor 20 minutes by car or rail, to London 30 minutes.
Tel: **0118 932 0428**
Mr & Mrs Ferguson.
D: £30.00-£50.00 **S:** £27.50.
Open: Mar to Dec
Beds: 1D 1T
Baths: 2 En
🛏 (7) 🅿 (3) 🔲 🛉 Ⅲ. Ⅵ

(2m) *The Hermitage, 63 London Road, Twyford, Reading, Berks, RG10 9EJ.*
Elegant period house, village centre, close mainline railway, London 40 mins.
Tel: **0118 934 0004** (also fax no)
Mrs Barker.
D: £26.00-£30.00 **S:** £35.00-£48.00.
Open: All Year (not Xmas)
Beds: 2D 3T
Baths: 3 En 1 Sh
🅿 (6) ✠ 🔲 🛉 Ⅲ. Ⅵ

All rates are subject to alteration at the owners' discretion.

Reading 22

National Grid Ref: SU7173

⚐ Clifton Arms, Horse & Jockey, Unicorn, Red Lion, Grouse & Claret, Rose & Thistle, Sweeney & Todd, Queen's Head

(1m) *Greystoke Guest House, 10 Greystoke Road, Caversham, Reading, Berks, RG4 5EL.*
Private home in quiet road, TV & tea/coffee making in lounge.
Grades: ETC 3 Diamond
Tel: **0118 947 5784** Mrs Tyler.
D: £25.00-£30.00 **S:** £28.00-£35.00.
Open: All Year (not Xmas)
Beds: 1D 2S
Baths: 1 Sh
🅿 (3) ✠ 🔲 🛉 Ⅲ. Ⅵ ⌀

(1.5m 🚌) *St Hilda's, 24 Castle Crescent, Reading, Berkshire, RG1 6AG.*
Quiet Victorian home near town centre, all rooms have colour TVs & fridges.
Tel: **0118 961 0329**
Mr & Mrs Hubbard.
Fax no: 0118 954 2585
D: £19.00-£24.00 **S:** £20.00-£27.00.
Open: All Year
Beds: 3F 2T
Baths: 3 Sh
🛏 (1) 🅿 ✠ 🔲 🛉 🖳 Ⅲ. Ⅵ ⌀

(1.5m) *Dittisham Guest House, 63 Tilehurst Road, Reading, Berks, RG30 2JL.*
Quiet central location in a restored Edwardian home. High standards at sensible prices.
Grades: ETC 3 Diamond
Tel: **0118 956 9483** Mr Harding.
D: £20.00-£27.50 **S:** £26.00-£35.00.
Open: All Year
Beds: 2D 1T 2S **Baths:** 3 En 2 Sh
🛏 🅿 ✠ 🔲 🛉 🖳 Ⅲ. Ⅵ ⌀

(2m) *Abadair House, 46 Redlands Road, Reading, Berks, RG1 5HE.*
Family run guest house close to railway and town centre.
Grades: ETC 2 Diamond
Tel: **0118 986 3792** (also fax no)
Mrs Clifford.
D: £30.00 **S:** £30.00-£35.00.
Open: All Year
Beds: 3T 6S **Baths:** 8 En 1 Sh
🛏 🅿 (6) ✠ 🔲 🛉 🖳 Ⅲ. Ⅵ

Goring 23

National Grid Ref: SU6081

⚐ Catherine Wheel, John Barleycorn, Miller Of Mansfield, Bull Inn, Perch & Pike

(0.25m) *The Catherine Wheel, Station Road, Goring, Reading, Berks, RG8 9HB.*
Accommodation in a Victorian cottage in riverside village.
Tel: **01491 872379** Mrs Kerr.
D: £20.00 **S:** £25.00.
Open: All Year
Beds: 2D 1T **Baths:** 2 Sh
🛏 ✠ 🔲 🗙 🛉 Ⅲ. Ⅵ

Streatley 24

National Grid Ref: SU5980

⚐ The Bull, Catherine Wheel

(▲ 0.5m) *Streatley-on-Thames Youth Hostel, Hill House, Reading Road, Streatley, Reading, Berks, RG8 9JJ.*
Actual grid ref: SU591806
Tel: **01491 872278**
Under 18: £7.75
Adults: £11.00
Self-catering facilities, Television, Showers, Dining room, Drying room, Cycle store, Parking Limited, Evening meal at 7.00pm, No smoking, WC, Kitchen facilities, Breakfast available, Credit cards accepted
Homely Victorian family house, completely refurbished, in a beautiful riverside village.

(0.5m 🚌) *Pennyfield, The Coombe, Streatley, Reading, Berkshire, RG8 9QT.*
Pretty village house with attractive terraced garden. Friendly welcoming hosts.
Grades: ETC 4 Diamond
Tel: **01491 872048** (also fax no)
D: £22.50-£25.00
S: £22.50-£25.00.
Open: All Year (not Xmas/New Year)
Beds: 1T 2D
Baths: 2 En 1 Sh
🅿 (4) ✠ 🔲 🛉 🖳 Ⅲ. Ⅵ ⌀

North Stoke 25

National Grid Ref: SU6186

(On path) *Footpath Cottage, The Street, North Stoke, Wallingford, Oxon, OX10 6BJ.*
Lovely old cottage, peaceful river village. Warm welcome, excellent food.
Tel: **01491 839763**
Mrs Tanner.
D: £19.00-£20.00
S: £20.00-£20.00.
Open: All Year
Beds: 2D 1S
Baths: 1 En 1 Sh
🛏 🔲 🛉 🗙 🛉 Ⅲ. Ⅵ ⌀

Cholsey 26

National Grid Ref: SU5886

⚐ The Beatle and Wedge

(1.5m) *The Well Cottage, Caps Lane, Cholsey, Wallingford, Oxon, OX10 9HQ.*
Delightful cottage with ensuite bedrooms in secluded garden flat.
Tel: **01491 651959** Alexander.
Fax no: 01491 651675
D: £15.00-£25.00 **S:** £20.00-£30.00.
Open: All Year
Beds: 2T 1D
Baths: 2 En 1 Pr

Wallingford 27

National Grid Ref: SU6089

🍴 🍺 Shepherd's Hut, Six Bells, Bell, The Queens Head

(0.75m) *Little Gables,* *166 Crowmarsh Hill, Wallingford, Oxford, OX10 8BG.*
Actual grid ref: SU623889
Delightfully large private house where a warm welcome awaits you.
Grades: ETC 3 Diamond
Tel: 01491 837834 Mrs Reeves.
Fax no: 01491 834426
D: £25.00-£35.00 **S:** £30.00-£35.00.
Open: All Year
Beds: 2F 2D 3T 1S
Baths: 2 En 1 Pr
🛇 🄿 ✗ ♦ 🖤 🏧 🕭 🕹 & ♥ ⓕ ✦

(1m 🚗) *Munts Mill,* *Castle Lane, Wallingford, Oxfordshire, OX10 0BN.*
Actual grid ref: SU609895
Near town centre on edge of Chilterns - advance booking only.
Tel: 01491 836654 Mrs Broster.
S: £20.00-£25.00.
Open: All Year (not Xmas)
Beds: 2S
✗ ♦ 🖤 🕭 🕹 ♥ ✦

(0.5m 🚗) *North Farm,* *Shillingford Hill, Wallingford, Oxon, OX10 8NB.*
Actual grid ref: SU586924
Quiet comfortable farmhouse on working farm, close to River Thames.
Tel: 01865 858406 Mrs Warburton.
Fax no: 01865 858519
D: £24.00-£28.00 **S:** £28.00-£38.00.
Open: All Year (not Xmas)
Beds: 2D 1T
Baths: 1 En 2 Pr
🛇 (8) 🄿 (6) ✗ ♦ 🕭 🕹 🖤 ♥ ✦

Ewelme 28

National Grid Ref: SU6491

🍴 🍺 Crown, Shepherds Hut

(2m 🚗) *Fords Farm,* *Ewelme, Wallingford, Oxon, OX10 6HU.*
Picturesque setting in historic village. Warm, friendly atmosphere. Good views.
Grades: ETC 4 Diamond
Tel: 01491 839272 Miss Edwards.
D: £24.00-£25.00 **S:** £30.00-£35.00.
Open: All Year
Beds: 1D 2T **Baths:** 1 Pr 1 Sh
🄿 (8) ✗ ♦ 🕭 🕹 🖤 ♥

(1m 🚗) *May's Farm,* *Turner's Court, Ewelme, Wallingford, Oxon, OX10 6QF.*
Working stock farm. Fabulous views, quiet location, good walking.
Tel: 01491 641294 Mrs Passmore.
Fax no: 01491 641697
D: £19.00-£22.00 **S:** £25.00-£30.00.
Open: All Year
Beds: 1F 1T 1S **Baths:** 1 En 1 Sh
🛇 🄿 (4) ✗ ♦ 🕭 🕹 🖤 ♥ ✦

Benson 29

National Grid Ref: SU6191

🍴 🍺 Three Horseshoes, Crown

(1m 🚗) *Fyfield Manor,* *Brook Street, Benson, Wallingford, Oxon, OX10 6HA.*
Medieval dining room. Beautiful water gardens. Essentially a family house.
Tel: 01491 835184
Mrs Brown.
Fax no: 01491 825635
D: £25.00-£25.00 **S:** £30.00-£30.00.
Open: All Year (not Xmas/ New Year)
Beds: 1D 1T
Baths: 2 En 1 Pr
🛇 (10) 🄿 (6) ✗ ♦ 🕭 🕹 🖤 ♥ ⓕ ✦

Sutton Courtenay 30

National Grid Ref: SU5093

🍴 🍺 George & Dragon, The Fish, The Swan

(0.25m 🚗) *Bekynton House,* *7 The Green, Sutton Courtenay, Abingdon, Oxon, OX14 4AE.*
Courthouse overlooking village green. Thames and 3 pubs - 5 minutes.
Tel: 01235 848630
Ms Cornwall.
Fax no: 01235 848436
D: £25.00-£28.00
S: £25.00-£28.00.
Open: All Year (not Xmas)
Beds: 1D 2T 1S   **Baths:** 2 Sh
🛇 🄿 (2) ✗ ♦ 🕭 🕹 🖤 ♥ ⓕ ✦

Abingdon 31

National Grid Ref: SU4997

🍴 🍺 The Plough, The Parasol, The Ox, Boundary House, Wheatsheaf Inn, Pickled Newt

(1m 🚗) *Barrows End,* *3 The Copse , Abingdon, Oxon, OX14 3YW.*
Modern chalet bungalow, peaceful setting. Easy access Oxford/Abingdon.
Tel: 01235 523541
Mrs Harmsworth.
D: £19.00-£20.00
S: £25.00-£25.00.
Open: All Year (not Xmas)
Beds: 3T
Baths: 1 En 2 Pr
🄿 (3) ✗ ♦ 🕭 🕹 🖤 ♥

(1m 🚗) *Acer House,* *5 Kysbie Close, Abingdon, Oxon, OX14 1XZ.*
Quiet, safe neighbourhood - pleasant gardens. All rooms colour co-ordinated.
Tel: 01235 550579
Mrs Rhodes.
D: £17.00-£18.00
S: £17.00-£22.00.
Open: All Year
Beds: 1D 1T 1S
Baths: 1 Sh
🄿 (2) ✗ ♦ 🕭 🕹 🖤 ♥

(1m) *The Old Vicarage,* *17 Park Cresent, Abingdon, Oxon, OX14 1DF.*
Lovely Victorian vicarage in leafy conservation area. Breakfast in conservatory.
Tel: 01235 522561
D: £20.00-£26.00 **S:** £25.00-£35.00.
Open: All Year (not Xmas)
Beds: 1D 1T **Baths:** 1 En 1 Pr
🄿 (3) ✗ ♦ 🕭 🕹 🖤 ♥

(0.25m 🚗) *Conifer Lodge,* *1 The Copse, Abingdon, Oxon, OX14 3YW.*
Large modern family home overlooking a copse. Bus stop nearby.
Tel: 01235 527158 Mrs Shaw.
D: £22.50-£30.00 **S:** £25.00-£35.00.
Open: All Year (not Xmas)
Beds: 1D 2S 1F **Baths:** 2 Pr 1 Sh
🛇 (5) 🄿 (7) ✗ ♦ 🕭 🕹 🖤 ♥ ✦

(0.25m) *22 East St Helen Street,* *Abingdon, Oxon, OX14 5EB.*
Friendly elegant Georgian town house on river. Listed SOBT.
Tel: 01235 550979 Mrs Howard.
Fax no: 01235 533278
D: £22.00-£27.50 **S:** £25.00-£35.00.
Open: All Year (not Xmas)
Beds: 1D 1T 1S **Baths:** 1 En 2 Sh
🛇 ✗ ♦ 🕭 🕹 🖤 ♥ ✦

(1.25m 🚗) *Pastures Green,* *46 Picklers Hill, Abingdon, Oxon, OX14 2BB.*
Actual grid ref: SU501988
Quiet , friendly, no-smoking, home-preserves, large garden.
Tel: 01235 521369 Mrs White.
D: £17.00-£19.00 **S:** £18.00-£20.00.
Open: All Year (not Xmas)
Beds: 1D 1T 1S **Baths:** 2 Sh
🛇 (4) 🄿 (3) ✗ ♦ 🕭 🕹 🖤 ♥ ✦

Oxford 32

National Grid Ref: SP5106

🍴 🍺 Carpenters' Arms, Vine, Bear & Ragged Staff, Tree, Marsh Harrier, Prince of Wales, Trout Inn, Old Ale House, Radcliffe Arms, Eight Bells, Fox & Hounds, Boundary House, Ox, Cafe Noir, Squire Basset, Victoria Arms, Duke of Monmouth

(▲ 0.5m) *Oxford Backpackers Hostel,* *9a Hythe Bridge Street, Oxford, OX1 2EW.*
Tel: 01865 721761 Adults: £11.00
Self-catering facilities, Television, Showers, Licensed bar, Central heating, Laundry facilities, Wet weather shelter, Lounge, Security lockers, Cycle store
City centre location. Groups welcome. Bar, Internet, kitchen. Great atmosphere.

Planning a longer stay? Always ask for any special rates.

(▲ 0.5m) *New Oxford YHA,*
2a Botley Road, Oxford, OX2 0AB.
Tel: **01865 727275**
Under 18: £13.50 **Adults:** £18.00
Self-catering facilities, Evening
meal at 7.00pm, Facilities for dis-
abled people, Breakfast available
Brand new hostel, opening at
Easter 2001, and replacing the for-
mer hostel in Jack Straw's Lane.

(0.5m) *Green Gables,*
326 Abingdon Rd, Oxford, OX1 4TE.
Actual grid ref: SP518043
Grades: ETC 3 Diamond,
AA 3 Diamond
Tel: **01865 725870** Mr & Mrs Bhella
Fax no: 01865 723115
D: £25.00-£30.00 **S:** £32.00-£50.00.
Open: All Year (not Xmas/
New Year)
Beds: 3F 4D 1T 1S
Baths: 7 En 1 Sh
⏰🅿(9)🛏♨🕭⛰₺Ⅴ
Characterful detached Edwardian
house shielded by trees. Bright spa-
cious rooms with TV & beverage
facilities. Ensuite rooms. 1.25
miles to city centre, on bus routes.
Ample off-street parking. Direct
line phones in rooms and disabled
room available.

(2m) *The Bungalow, Cherwell*
Farm, Mill Lane, Old Marston,
Oxford, OX3 0QF.
Actual grid ref: SP523098
Grades: ETC 3 Diamond
Tel: **01865 557171** Mrs Burdon.
D: £21.00-£25.00 **S:** £25.00-£35.00.
Open: Mar to Oct
Beds: 2D 2T
Baths: 2 En 1 Sh
⏰(7)🅿(6)🛏♨🕭⛰Ⅴ
Modern bungalow in two acres
open countryside, no bus route. 3
miles to city centre.

(0.25m) *Pine Castle Hotel,*
290 Iffley Road, Oxford, OX4 4AE.
Actual grid ref: SP528048
Close to shops, launderette, post
office. Frequent buses. River walks
nearby.
Grades: ETC 4 Diamond,
AA 4 Diamond
Tel: **01865 241497** Mrs Morris.
Fax no: 01685 727230
D: £32.50-£37.00 **S:** £55.00-£60.00.
Open: All Year (not Xmas)
Beds: 1F 5D 2T **Baths:** 8 En
⏰🅿(4)🛏♨🕭Ⅴ▮

(1m) *Gables Guest House, 6*
Cumnor Hill, Oxford, Oxfordshire,
OX2 9HA.
Award winning detached house
with beautiful garden. Close to
city.
Grades: ETC 4 Diamond ,
AA 4 Diamond
Tel: **01865 862153** Mrs Tompkins.
Fax no: 01865 864054
D: £22.00 **S:** £26.00.
Open: All Year (not Xmas)
Beds: 2S 2D 2T **Baths:** 6 En
⏰🅿(6)🛏♨🕭Ⅴ

(1m) *Highfield West, 188 Cumnor*
Hill, Oxford, OX2 9PJ.
Actual grid ref: SP469042
Comfortable home in residential
area, heated outdoor pool in season.
Grades: ETC 3 Diamond
Tel: **01865 863007** Mrs Mitchell.
D: £22.50-£28.50 **S:** £26.00-£29.00.
Open: All Year (not Xmas)
Beds: 1F 1D 1T 2S
Baths: 3 En 1 Sh
⏰🅿(5)🛏♨🕭⛰Ⅴ

(0.5m) *Sportsview Guest House,*
106-110 Abingdon Road, Oxford,
OX1 4PX.
Grades: ETC 3 Diamond
Tel: **01865 244268** Mrs Saini.
Fax no: 01865 249270
D: £24.00-£30.00 **S:** £30.00-£50.00.
Open: All Year (not Xmas)
Beds: 5F 6T 3D 6S
Baths: 12 En 12 Pr 2 Sh
⏰(4)🅿(11)🛏♨🕭⛰Ⅴ
Situated south of the city centre. A
few minutes' walk takes you to the
towpath and a very pleasant walk
to the city & its famous landmarks.
On a direct bus route, with easy
access to railway & bus stations.

(0.5m) *All Seasons Guest House,*
63 Windmill Road, Headington,
Oxford, Oxfordshire, OX3 7BP.
Comfortable guest house, non-
smoking, parking, convenient air-
ports and Brookes University.
Tel: **01865 742215** Mrs Melbye.
Fax no: 01865 432691
D: £22.50-£31.00 **S:** £27.00-£45.00.
Open: All Year
Beds: 1T 3D 2S **Baths:** 4 En 1 Sh
⏰(6)🅿(6)🛏♨🕭⛰Ⅴ▮

(1m) *Acorn Guest House,*
260 Iffley Road, Oxford,
Oxfordshire, OX4 1SE.
Modern comfort in Victorian house
convenient for all local attractions.
Grades: ETC 2 Diamond,
AA 2 Diamond, RAC 2 Diamond
Tel: **01865 247998** Mrs Lewis.
D: £24.00-£27.00 **S:** £26.00-£29.00.
Open: All Year (not Xmas/
New Year)
Beds: 5F 2D 1T 4S **Baths:** 1 En, 4 Sh
⏰(9)🅿(11)♨🕭⛰Ⅴ✦

(0.5m) *58 St John Street,*
Oxford, OX1 2QR.
Tall Victorian house central to all
colleges, museums and theatres.
Tel: **01865 515454** Mrs Old.
D: £18.00-£19.00 **S:** £18.00.
Open: All Year
Beds: 1F 1T 1S **Baths:** 2 En
⏰(1)🛏♨⛰Ⅴ✦

(1m) *Chestnuts, 72 Cumnor Hill,*
Oxford, OX2 9HU.
Country house in acre of garden,
1.5 miles from Oxford.
Grades: ETC 3 Diamond
Tel: **01865 863602**
D: £21.00-£24.00 **S:** £24.00-£30.00.
Open: All Year
Beds: 1D 1T **Baths:** 1 En 1 Pr
🅿🛏♨🕭⛰Ⅴ

(1m 🚌) *Milka's Guest House, 379*
Iffley Road, Oxford, Oxon, OX4 4DP.
Family run guest house situated
close to Iffley village.
Grades: ETC 3 Diamond
Tel: **01865 778458**
Fax no: 01865 776477
D: £22.50-£27.50 **S:** £25.00-£35.00.
Open: All Year
Beds: 2D 1S
Baths: 1 En
⏰(5)🅿(5)🛏♨🕭⛰Ⅴ

(0.5m 🚌) *Lakeside Guest House,*
118 Abingdon Road, Oxford,
Oxfordshire, OX1 4PZ.
Edwardian house overlooking
Thames. One mile Oxford. Next to
park - swimming pool/tennis.
Grades: ETC 3 Diamond
Tel: **01865 244725** (also fax no)
Mrs Shirley.
D: £22.00-£30.00 .
Open: All Year
Beds: 2F 3D 1T
Baths: 3 En 3 Sh
⏰🅿(6)🛏♨🗙🕭⛰Ⅴ

(0.5m) *5 Galley Field, Radley*
Road, Abington, Oxon, OX14 3RU.
Detached house in quiet cul-de-sac,
north of the Thames, Abingdon &
A34.
Tel: **01235 521088** Mrs Bird.
D: £16.50-£17.50 **S:** £23.00-£25.00.
Open: Easter to Oct
Beds: 2T 1S
Baths: 2 Sh
⏰(12)🅿(2)🛏♨🕭⛰Ⅴ

(1m) *Arden Lodge, 34 Sunderland*
Avenue, Oxford, OX2 8DX.
Select spacious modern detached
house within easy reach city centre.
Tel: **01865 552076**
Mr & Mrs Price.
D: £24.00-£25.00 **S:** £30.00-£35.00.
Open: All Year (not Xmas)
Beds: 1F 1D 1T 1S
Baths: 4 En
⏰(3)🅿(7)🛏♨🕭⛰Ⅴ

(0.5m) *Walton Guest House,*
169 Walton Street, Oxford, OX1 2HD.
Most centrally situated guest house
in Oxford. 2 mins bus station
Tel: **01865 52137** Mrs Durrant.
D: £19.00-£25.00 **S:** £19.00-£35.00.
Open: All Year
Beds: 1F 2D 3T 3S
⏰♨🗙🕭⛰Ⅴ▮✦

🚌 sign means that,
given due notice,
owners will pick you
up from the path
and drop you off *with-*
in reason.

(0.5m) *Bravalla Guest House,*
242 Iffley Road, Oxford,
Oxfordshire, OX4 1SE.
Late Victorian home attractively
decorated in Sanderson patterns.
Close city ring road and river.
Tel: **01865 241326** Ms Downes.
Fax no: 01865 250511
D: £23.00-£25.00 **S:** £30.00-£40.00.
Open: All Year (not Xmas)
Beds: 1F 3D 2T 1S
Baths: 6 En
🛏 🅿 (4) � ⌘

Yarnton 33

National Grid Ref: SP4712

🍴 🍺 Squire Bassett

(2m) *Kings Bridge Guest House,*
Woodstock Road, Yarnton,
Kidlington, Oxon, OX5 1PH.
Ideally situated for Oxford and
Blenheim Palace in Woodstock.
Grades: ETC 3 Diamond, AA 3
Diamond
Tel: **01865 841748** Ms Shaw.
Fax no: 01865 370215
D: £22.50-£30.00 **S:** £35.00-£50.00.
Open: All Year (not Xmas/
New Year)
Beds: 1F 2D 1T
Baths: 4 En
🛏 🅿 (6) ⌘

Appleton 34

National Grid Ref: SP4401

🍴 🍺 Eight Bells

(1.25m) *West Farm, Eaton,*
Appleton, Abingdon, Oxon, OX13
5PR.
Actual grid ref: SP448032
Farm house, 6 miles west of
Oxford. 5 miles Abingdon.
Excellent touring centre.
Tel: **01865 862908**
Mrs Gow.
D: £22.00-£28.00 **S:** £22.00-£30.00.
Open: Easter to Oct
Beds: 1F 1D 1T 1S
Baths: 1 Pr 1 Sh
🛏 🅿 (8) ⌘

Standlake 35

National Grid Ref: SP3903

🍴 🍺 The Bell

(1.25m) *Hawthorn Cottage, The*
Downs, Standlake, Witney, Oxon,
OX8 7SH.
Actual grid ref: SP394040
Elegant rooms in detached house,
on edge of country village.
Tel: **01865 300588** (also fax no)
Mrs Peterson.
D: £20.00-£22.50 **S:** £28.00-£38.00.
Open: All Year (not Xmas)
Beds: 1D 1T
Baths: 1 En 1 Pr
🛏 (3) 🅿 (3) ⌘

Bampton 36

National Grid Ref: SP3103

🍴 🍺 Talbot Hotel, Romany Inn

(2m) *Morar, Weald Street,*
Bampton, Oxon, OX18 2HL.
Actual grid ref: SP312026
Wake to the mouthwatering smell
of homemade bread baking.
Tel: **01993 850162** Ms Rouse.
Fax no: 01993 851738
D: £22.50-£25.00 **S:** £22.50-£25.00.
Open: Mar to Dec
Beds: 2D 1T **Baths:** 2 En 1 Pr
🛏 (6) 🅿 (4) ⌘

Faringdon 37

National Grid Ref: SU2895

🍴 🍺 Fox & Hounds, The Plough

(3m) *Faringdon Hotel, 1 Market*
Place, Faringdon, Oxon, SN7 7HL.
Grades: ETC 3 Diamond,
AA 2 Star, RAC 2 Star
Tel: **01367 240536**
Fax no: 01367 243250
D: £30.00-£35.00 **S:** £45.00-£60.00.
Open: All Year
Beds: 3F 14D 1T 3S
Baths: 20 En
🛏 🅿 ⌘
Situated near C12th parish church,
on site of palace of Alfred the
Great.

(3m) *Portwell House Hotel,*
Market Place, Faringdon, Oxon,
SN7 7HU.
Relax in the ancient market town of
Faringdon within reach of the
Cotswolds.
Grades: ETC 1 Star
Tel: **01367 240197**
Mr Pakeman
Fax no: 01367 244330
D: £25.00 **S:** £40.00.
Open: All Year
Beds: 2F 3D 2T 1S
Baths: 8 En
🛏 (2) 🅿 (4) ⌘

Buscot 38

National Grid Ref: SU2397

🍴 🍺 Trout Inn

(0.25m) *Apple Tree House,*
Buscot, Faringdon, Oxon, SN7 8DA.
Old property in National Trust
village, 5 mins' walk River
Thames, one acre garden.
Grades: ETC 3 Diamond,
AA 3 Diamond, RAC 3 Diamond
Tel: **01367 252592**
Mrs Reay.
D: £18.00-£22.00
S: £23.00-£28.00.
Open: All Year (not Xmas)
Beds: 2D 1T
Baths: 1 En 2 Pr
🛏 🅿 (10) ⌘

Lechlade 39

National Grid Ref: SU2199

🍴 🍺 Trout Inn, New Inn, Red Lion

(On path) *Cambrai Lodge Guest*
House, Oak Street, Lechlade On
Thames, Glos, GL7 3AY.
Modern comfortable house off the
road. Ideal for touring Cotswolds.
Grades: ETC 4 Diamond, Silver
Tel: **01367 253173**
Mr Titchener.
D: £23.00-£28.00 **S:** £28.00-£44.00.
Open: All Year
Beds: 1F 1D 1T 2S
Baths: 2 En 1 Pr 1 Sh
🛏 🅿 (9) ⌘

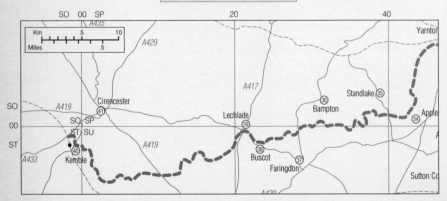

(On path 🚐) *The New Inn Hotel, Market Square, Lechlade On Thames, Glos, GL7 3AB.*
C17th fully modernised coaching inn on River Thames in the Cotswold.
Tel: **01367 252296** Mr Sandhu.
Fax no: 01367 252315
D: £20.00-£32.50 **S:** £40.00-£55.00.
Open: All Year
Beds: 2F 10D 10T 4S **Baths:** 26 En
🅿 (40) ⊬ 🖵 ✕ 🕯 🛏 Ⅴ 🛉 ✦

Kemble 40

National Grid Ref: ST9897

🍴 🍺 Wild Duck, Tavern Inn, Thames Head

(0.75m 🚐) *Smerrill Barns, Kemble, Cirencester, Glos, GL7 6BW.*
Actual grid ref: ST998988
Grades: ETC 4 Diamond
Tel: **01285 770907** Mrs Sopher.
Fax no: 01285 770706
D: £27.50 **S:** £45.00.
Open: All Year (not Xmas)
Beds: 1F 5D 1T
Baths: 7 En 1 Sh
🐾 🅿 (8) ⊬ 🖵 🕯 🛏 Ⅴ 🛉 ✦
An ideal base for touring the Cotswolds or walking the Thames Path. An C18th converted barn, all rooms ensuite, guest lounge with log fires in winter, drinks licence. Will pick up from local rail station (Kemble). Traditional inns nearby.

Cirencester 41

National Grid Ref: SP0202

🍴 🍺 Plough, Golden Cross, Crown Of Crucis, Falcon, Wagon & Horses, Odd Fellows, Drillman, Talbot

(3m 🚐) *Sunset, Baunton Lane, Cirencester, Glos, GL7 2NQ.*
Actual grid ref: SP015041
Quiet, small family house conveniently situated for touring the Cotswolds.
Grades: ETC 3 Diamond
Tel: **01285 654822**
Mrs Castle.
D: £16.00-£17.00
S: £16.00-£17.00.
Open: Easter to Oct
Beds: 1T 2S
Baths: 1 Sh
🐾 (5) 🅿 (5) ⊬ 🖵 🕯 🛏 Ⅴ ✦

(3m 🚐) *Chesil Rocks, Baunton Lane, Cirencester, Glos, GL7 2LL.*
Pleasant friendly home, quiet lane. Access town & country walks.
Grades: ETC 3 Diamond
Tel: **01285 655031**
Mrs Clayton.
D: £17.00-£17.00
S: £17.00-£17.00.
Open: All Year (not Xmas)
Beds: 1T 2S
Baths: 1 Sh
🐾 (2) 🅿 (2) ⊬ 🖵 🕯 🛏 Ⅴ 🛉 ✦

(3m) *The Ivy House, 2 Victoria Road, Cirencester, Glos, GL7 1EN.*
Actual grid ref: SP027018
Imposing Victorian town centre residence. Bright, comfortable, high standard B&B.
Tel: **01285 656626**
Mrs Marriot.
D: £18.00-£22.00
S: £25.00-£35.00.
Open: All Year (not Xmas)
Beds: 1F 3D
Baths: 4 En
🐾 🅿 (5) ⊬ 🖵 🕯 🛏 Ⅴ 🛉 ✦

(3m) *Clonsilla Guest House, 7 Victoria Road, Cirencester, Glos, GL7 1EN.*
Five minutes from town centre.
Tel: **01285 652621**
Mr Sullivan.
D: £17.00-£25.00 **S:** £20.00-£30.00.
Open: All Year
Beds: 1F 2D 4T 1S
Baths: 4 En 1 Sh
🐾 🅿 (5) 🖵 🍴 🕯 🛏 ♿ Ⅴ ✦

Planning a longer stay? Always ask for any special rates.

Two Moors Way

The **Two Moors Way** runs northwards for 103 miles from Ivybridge over Devon's two famous moors, **Dartmoor** and **Exmoor**, up to Lynmouth on the north coast. You pass through fabulous terrain: misty and uninhabited moorlands with prehistoric sites, the rich, undulating farmlands of mid-Devon, sudden combes with little rivers. Between Hawkridge and Withypool you follow the River Barle through a beautiful wooded valley to the ancient Tarr Steps. This is a walk with a lot of hills, wilderness, great horizons and a sense of mystery - a great introduction to one of England's largest counties. After exceptionally wet weather, some sections can become impassable but alternative routes can be found in the guidebooks. Please take protective clothing, food, and a compass, for much of the Devon hinterland is not sign-posted and these moors are not to be underestimated.

Guides: *Two Moors Way* by RA Devon Area (ISBN 0 900613 43 2), published by the Two Moors Way Association and available from the Rambler's Association National Office (1/5 Wandsworth Road, London, SW8 2XX, tel. 020 7339 8500), £3.00 (+ 70p p&p)

The Two Moors Way by James Roberts (ISBN 1 85 284159 10 90), published by Cicerone Press and available from all good map shops or directly from the publishers (2 Police Square, Milnthorpe, Cumbria, LA7 7PY, 01539 562069), £5.99 (+75p p&p)

The Two Moors Way by John Macadam (ISBN 185410 4586), published by Aurum Press and available directly from the publishers (25 Bedford Avenue, London WC1B 3AT, 020 7637 3225), £12.99

Maps: Ordnance Survey 1:50000 Landranger series: 180, 181, 191, 202

Ivybridge 1

National Grid Ref: SX6356

🍴 🍺 The Sportsman Ivybridge

(0.25m) **The Toll House,** Exeter Road, Ivybridge, Devon, *PL21 0DE.*
1850s house with attractive gardens overlooked by Dartmoor.
Tel: **01752 893522** Mrs Hancox.
D: £18.00-£18.00 **S:** £25.00-£25.00.
Open: All Year
Beds: 2T 1S
Baths: 3 En
🛇 🅿 (5) ⊬ 🗆 📠 Ⅴ 🛉 ⌇

Pay B&Bs by cash or cheque and be prepared to pay up front.

Scorriton 2

National Grid Ref: SX7068

🍴 🍺 Tradesman's Arms, Dartbridge Inn, Abbey Inn

(On path 🚶) **The Tradesmans Arms,** Scorriton, Buckfastleigh, Devon, *TQ11 0JB.*
Actual grid ref: SX704685
Tel: **01364 631206** Mr Lunday.
D: £25.00-£25.00 **S:** £25.00-£25.00.
Open: All Year (not Xmas/New Year)
Beds: 2D **Baths:** 1 Sh
🅿 (20) ⊬ 🗆 🛏 🗶 🖳 📠 Ⅴ 🛉
Warm friendly village pub within Dartmoor National Park set in beautiful Devon lanes within superb country views. No pool table, No juke box, no gambling machines. Real ales, malt whiskies and impromptu musical gatherings. Bring your own instrument.

Holne 3

National Grid Ref: SX7069

🍴 🍺 Church House Inn, Tradesman's Arms

(On path 🚶) **Chase Gate Farm,** Holne, Newton Abbot, Devon, *TQ13 7RX.*
Comfortable, friendly farmhouse with lovely views and well-equipped rooms.
Tel: **01364 631261**
Mr & Mrs Higman.
D: £17.50-£20.00 **S:** £17.50-£20.00.
Open: All Year **Beds:** 1F 2D 1T
Baths: 2 En 1 Pr 1 Sh
🛇 🅿 🗆 🛏 🖳 📠 Ⅴ ⌇

(0.25m) **Mill Leat Farm,** Holne, Ashburton, Newton Abbot, Devon, *TQ13 7RZ.*
Actual grid ref: SX713685
C18th Farmhouse offering great food, set off the beaten track.
Grades: ETC 3 Diamond
Tel: **01364 631283** (also fax no)
Mrs Cleave.
D: £17.00-£19.00 **S:** £19.00-£20.00.
Open: All Year (not Xmas)
Beds: 2F **Baths:** 1 En 1 Pr
🛇 🗆 🛏 🗶 🖳 Ⅴ 🛉 ⌇

(On path 🚶) **Hazelwood,** Holne, Newton Abbot, Devon, *TQ13 7SJ.*
Actual grid ref: SX706694
Friendly home from home welcome with panoramic views of Devon.
Tel: **01364 631235** Mrs Mortimore.
D: £18.50-£19.00 **S:** £18.50-£19.00.
Open: Easter to October
Beds: 2D 1S
🛇 🅿 (3) ⊬ 🗆 🛏 🗶 🖳 👶 🛉 ⌇

Poundsgate 4

National Grid Ref: SX7072

🍴 🍺 Tavistock Inn

(1.5m) **New Cott Farm,** Poundsgate, Newton Abbot, Devon, *TQ13 7PD.*
Actual grid ref: SX701729
Lovely walking in Dartmoor National Park. Good food, beds, welcoming + peaceful.
Grades: ETC 4 Diamond
Tel: **01364 631421** Mrs Phipps.
D: £20.00-£22.00 **Open:** All Year
Beds: 1F 2D 1T **Baths:** 3 En 1 Pr
🛇 (5) 🅿 (4) ⊬ 🗆 🗶 🖳 👶 🛉 ⌇

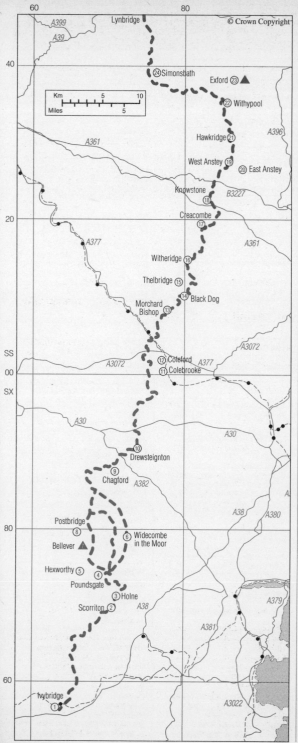

© Crown Copyright

Hexworthy 5

National Grid Ref: SX6572

™ ◀ Forest Inn

(3m 🚌) *The Forest Inn, Hexworthy, Princetown, Devon, PL20 6SD*
Actual grid ref: SX655726
Grades: ETC 3 Diamond
Tel: **01364 631211** Mr Selwood.
Fax no: 01364 631515
D: £20.00-£29.50 **S:** £25.00-£33.00.
Open: Feb to Dec
Beds: 5D 3T 2S **Baths:** 7 En 3 Pr
🅿 (30) ⬚ 🛏 🛏 🕭 📖 Ⅴ 🛊 ⬚ ⬚
A country inn in the middle of
Dartmoor, it is ideal for walking,
fishing, riding, or just relaxing.
Home-made food can be enjoyed in
the restaurant, bar or round the fire
in the lounge. Dogs and muddy
boots welcome.

Widecombe in the Moor 6

National Grid Ref: SX7176

(▲ 0.5m) *Dartmoor Expedition
Centre, Rowden Farm, Widecombe
in the Moor, Newton Abbot, Devon,
TQ13 7TX.*
Actual grid ref: SX699764
Tel: **01364 621249**
Under 18: £7.00 **Adults:** £7.00
Self-catering facilities, Showers,
Central heating, Dining room,
Drying room, Parking, Evening
meal at 6.30 pm, No smoking
*Bunkhouses on Dartmoor Farm at
1,000 feet in remote moorland.*

Bellever 7

National Grid Ref: SX6577

(▲ 4m) *Bellever Youth Hostel,
Bellever, Postbridge, Yelverton,
Devon, PL20 6TU.*
Actual grid ref: SX654773
Tel: **01822 880227**
Under 18: £6.90 **Adults:** £10.00
Self-catering facilities, Lounge,
Dining room, Drying room, Cycle
store, Parking Limited, Evening
meal at 7.00pm, No smoking,
Kitchen facilities, Breakfast avail-
able, Credit cards accepted
*Recently refurbished converted
barn, idyllically situated at the
heart of Dartmoor National Park.*

Postbridge 8

National Grid Ref: SX6579

™ ◀ Warren House Inn, East Dart Hotel

(0.5m) *Hartyland, Postbridge,
Yelverton, Devon, PL20 6SZ.*
Actual grid ref: SX644795
Large, warm, comfortable
Dartmoor house, direct access to
open moorland.
Tel: **01822 880210** Mr & Mrs Bishop
Fax no: 01822 880384
D: £20.00-£25.00 **S:** £20.00-£25.00.
Open: All Year (not Xmas)
Beds: 1F 3T 1S **Baths:** 2 Sh
⬚ 🅿 (6) ⬚ 🛏 ✕ 🕭 📖 Ⅴ 🛊 ⬚

Chagford 9

National Grid Ref: SX7087

|●| ⟨ Three Crowns, Ring O' Bells, Bullers Arms, Sandy Park Inn

(1m 🚶) _St Johns West, Chagford, Newton Abbot, Devon, TQ13 8HJ._
Actual grid ref: SX690889
Tranquil setting, warm welcome, comfortable beds, sumptuous breakfasts.
Tel: **01647 432468** Mr & Mrs West
D: £22.50-£22.50 **S:** £25.00-£27.50.
Open: All Year
Beds: 3T **Baths:** 3 En
🛇 (12) ₽ (5) ⚡ 🖵 ħ 🖤 Ⅲ. Ⅴ 🌢 ✦

(0.25m 🚶) _Glendarah House, Lower Street, Chagford, Newton Abbot, Devon, TQ13 8BZ._
Actual grid ref: SX703879
Spacious Victorian house peaceful location. Five minutes' walk from village centre.
Grades: ETC 4 Diamond, Silver, AA 4 Diamond
Tel: **01647 433270**
Mr & Mrs Croxen.
Fax no: 01647 433483
D: £26.00-£29.00 **S:** £26.00-£29.00.
Open: All Year (not Xmas)
Beds: 3D 3T 1S **Baths:** 7 En
🛇 (10) ₽ (7) ⚡ 🖵 ħ 🖤 Ⅲ. Ⅴ 🌢 ✦

(0.25m) _Lawn House, 24 Mill Street, Chagford, Newton Abbot, Devon, TQ13 7AW._
Friendly B&B. C18th thatched house, near centre Chagford.
Tel: **01647 433329** Mrs Law.
D: £20.00-£24.00 **S:** £25.00-£40.00.
Open: All Year
Beds: 1F 1D
Baths: 1 En 1 Pr
🛇 (8) ⚡ 🖵 ħ 🖤 Ⅲ. Ⅴ 🌢

(0.25m 🚶) _Ring O'Bells, 44 The Square, Chagford, Newton Abbot, Devon, TQ13 8AH._
Right on the square of historic Dartmoor Stannary town.
Tel: **01647 432466** Ms Pool.
D: £22.50 **S:** £20.00-£30.00.
Open: All Year
Beds: 2D 1T 1S
Baths: 2 En 1 Sh
🛇 (10) ⚡ 🖵 ħ 🖤 🖤 Ⅲ. Ⅴ 🌢

Drewsteignton 10

National Grid Ref: SX7390

|●| ⟨ Old Inn, Drewe Arms, Anglers' Rest

(0.5m 🚶) _East Fingle Farm, Drewsteignton, Exeter, Devon, EX6 6NJ._
Actual grid ref: SX744914
Devon farm longhouse, beautiful views, friendly farm animals, warm welcome. Children half-price.
Tel: **01647 281639** Mrs Cordy.
D: £18.00-£21.00 **S:** £18.00-£21.00.
Open: All Year
Beds: 2D 1T **Baths:** 2 En 1 Sh
🛇 ₽ (10) 🖵 ✕ 🖤 Ⅴ 🌢 ✦

(On path 🚶) _The Old Inn Restaurant & Guest House, The Square, Drewsteignton, Exeter, Devon, EX6 6QR._
Actual grid ref: SX736909
Comfortable former C18th inn in village square. Fishing, superb walks, 3 nights less 10%.
Tel: **01647 281276** (also fax no)
Mr & Mrs Gribble.
D: £22.50-£27.50
S: £30.00-£35.00.
Open: All Year
Beds: 1F 2D 1T
Baths: 2 En 1 Pr 1 Sh
🛇 (3) ₽ (3) 🖵 ħ ✕ 🖤 Ⅴ 🌢 ✦

Colebrooke 11

National Grid Ref: SS7700

|●| ⟨ New Inn, Mare & Foal

(0.75m 🚶) _The Oyster, Colebrooke, Crediton, Devon, EX17 5JQ._
Peaceful, homely, modern, spacious bungalow in beautiful mid-Devon. Tea/coffee facilities and TV.
Tel: **01363 84576**
Mrs Hockridge.
D: £17.00-£17.00
S: £17.00-£17.00.
Open: All Year
Beds: 2D 1T
Baths: 1 En 2 Pr
🛇 ₽ 🖵 ħ 🖤 Ⅲ. ⟨ Ⅴ 🌢 ✦

Coleford 12

National Grid Ref: SS7701

|●| ⟨ New Inn

(0.75m 🚶) _Butsford Barton, Coleford, Crediton, Devon, EX17 5DH._
Actual grid ref: SS764004
Modern spacious farmhouse in beautiful mid-Devon countryside.
Tel: **01363 84353** Mrs Hockridge.
D: £17.00-£18.00 **S:** £17.00-£18.00.
Open: Easter to Oct
Beds: 1F 1D 1T
Baths: 1 Sh
₽ ⚡ 🖵 🖤 Ⅴ 🌢 ✦

Morchard Bishop 13

National Grid Ref: SS7607

|●| ⟨ London Inn, White Hart

(0.5m 🚶) _Oldborough Fishing Retreat, Morchard Bishop, Crediton, Devon, EX17 6JQ._
Actual grid ref: SS774061
Lakeside rural retreat. 40 minutes drive M5 J27. Nice place for Exeter city break.
Tel: **01363 877437**
Mrs Wilshaw.
D: £16.00-£17.00 **S:** £16.00-£17.00.
Open: All Year (not Xmas/New Year)
Beds: 1F 1T **Baths:** 1 Sh
🛇 ₽ (10) ⚡ 🖵 ħ ✕ 🖤 Ⅲ. Ⅴ 🌢 ✦

Black Dog 14

National Grid Ref: SS8009

|●| ⟨ Black Dog Inn

(0.25m 🚶) _Oaklands, Black Dog, Crediton, Devon, EX17 4RQ._
Friendly accommodation in peaceful countryside, central for coast and moors.
Tel: **01884 860645**
Mrs Bradford.
Fax no: 01884 861030
D: £18.00-£20.00
S: £20.00-£22.00.
Open: All Year
Beds: 1F 1D 1T
Baths: 2 En 1 Pr
🛇 ₽ (6) 🖵 🖤 Ⅲ. Ⅴ 🌢 ✦

(On path 🚶) _Lower Brownstone Farm, Black Dog, Crediton, Devon, EX17 4QE._
Actual grid ref: SS789089
Peaceful Georgian farmhouse. Lawns, ponds, birds, farm animals, artwork.
Tel: **01363 877256**
Mrs Wedlake.
D: £12.50-£15.00
S: £12.00-£15.00.
Open: All Year
Beds: 3D
Baths: 2 Sh
🛇 ₽ (10) ⚡ 🖵 ħ ✕ 🌢 ✦

Thelbridge 15

National Grid Ref: SS7911

|●| ⟨ Thelbridge Cross Inn

(1m 🚶) _Hele Barton, Thelbridge Cross, Thelbridge, Black Dog, Crediton, Devon, EX17 4QJ._
Lovely thatched farmhouse, family atmosphere, many recommendations, brochure.
Tel: **01884 860278** (also fax no)
Mrs Gillbard.
D: £15.00-£20.00
S: £16.00-£20.00.
Open: All Year (not Xmas)
Beds: 1D 2T
Baths: 1 En 1 Sh
🛇 ₽ (6) 🖵 🖤 Ⅴ ✦

Witheridge 16

National Grid Ref: SS8014

|●| ⟨ Mitre Inn

(On path 🚶) _Mitre Inn, Two Moors Way, Witheridge, Tiverton, Devon, EX16 8AH._
Large Victorian coaching inn.
Tel: **01884 861263**
Mr & Mrs Parsons.
D: £18.00-£25.00
S: £20.00-£27.00.
Open: All Year (not Xmas/New Year)
Beds: 3F 1D 5T
Baths: 1 En 3 Sh
🛇 ₽ (5) ⚡ 🖵 ħ ✕ 🖤 Ⅲ. Ⅴ 🌢 ✦

Creacombe 17

National Grid Ref: SS8219

(On path 🚐) *Creacombe Parsonage, Parsonage Cross, Creacombe, Rackenford, Tiverton, Devon, EX16 8EL.*
Actual grid ref: SS820185
Tel: **01884 881441** Mrs Poole.
Fax no: 01884 881551
D: £18.00 **S:** £18.00. **Open:** All Year
Beds: 1F 2T **Baths:** 1 Sh 1 En
🛇 🅿 🛇 ⛌ ⊼ 🐾 🔥 ⛟ 🎫 🔌 ✓
C17th farmhouse in open countryside, views of Dartmoor. Ideal spot to rest, or explore Exmoor & N Devon. We enjoy catering for those with special dietary requirements. Organised walking breaks, craft workshops. BARN CAMPING for groups. All rooms own washing facilities, 1 with WC.

Knowstone 18

National Grid Ref: SS8223

(1m) *West Bowden Farm, Knowstone, South Molton, Devon, EX36 4RP.*
West Bowden is a working farm quietly situated just north of the A361. **Grades:** ETC 3 Diamond
Tel: **01398 341224** Mrs Bray.
D: £19.00-£22.00 **S:** £19.00-£25.00.
Open: All Year
Beds: 2F 2T 4D 1S
Baths: 5 En 1 Sh
🛇 🅿 🛇 ⊼ 🐾 ⛌ 🔥 🏃 ✓

West Anstey 19

National Grid Ref: SS8527

(0.5m) *Jubilee House, Highaton Farm, West Anstey, South Molton, Devon, EX36 3PJ.*
Actual grid ref: SS844254
Grades: ETC 4 Diamond
Tel: **01398 341312** Mrs Denton.
Fax no: 01398 341323
D: £19.50-£22.50 **S:** £19.50-£19.50.
Open: All Year
Beds: 2D 3S **Baths:** 2 Sh
🛇 🅿 (4) ⛌ ⊟ ⊼ 🐾 ⛌ 🔥 ⛟ 🎫 ✓
Elegant farmhouse, close edge Exmoor National Park, situated on Two Moors Way. Peaceful surroundings, easily accessible, great atmosphere. Large lounge (with log fire), dining room available for guests, local produce/home preserves. Bill is an international chef. Patio/BBQ/badminton areas, therapeutic hot tub spa.

Always telephone to get directions to the B&B - you will save time!

East Anstey 20

National Grid Ref: SS8626

(0.75m) *Threadneedle, East Anstey, Tiverton, Devon, EX16 9JH.*
Built in the style of a Devon Longhouse, set in three acres, close Dulverton.
Grades: ETC 3 Diamond
Tel: **01398 341598**
Mr & Mrs Webb.
D: £23.00-£25.00
S: £23.00-£25.00.
Open: All Year
Beds: 1D 1T
Baths: 2 En
🛇 🅿 (10) ⛌ ⊟ ⊼ 🐾 🔥 ⛟ 🎫 ✓

Hawkridge 21

National Grid Ref: SS8530

(1m) *East Hollowcombe Farm, Hawkridge, Dulverton, Somerset, TA22 9QL.*
Working farm, beautiful scenery, ideal stopover for Two Moors Way.
Tel: **01398 341622** Floyd.
D: £17.00-£18.00
S: £17.00-£18.00.
Open: Easter to Oct
Beds: 1F 1D 1S
Baths: 1 Sh
🛇 🅿 (8) ⊟ ⊼ 🐾 ⛌ 🔥 ⛟ 🎫 ✓

Withypool 22

National Grid Ref: SS8435

🍽 🍺 Royal Oak

(On path 🚐) *The Old Rectory, Withypool, Minehead, Somerset, TA24 7QP.*
Pleasant view, comfortable beds and a good, hearty English breakfast.
Tel: **01643 831553** Mr Clatworthy.
D: £16.00-£16.00 **S:** £16.00-£16.00.
Open: Easter to Oct
Beds: 1D 1T 1S
Baths: 1 Sh
🛇 🅿 (4) ⛌ ⊟ ⊼ 🐾 🔥 ⛟ 🎫 ✓

Exford 23

National Grid Ref: SS8538

🍽 🍺 White Horse

(🔺 2m) *Exford (Exmoor) Youth Hostel, Exe Mead, Exford, Minehead, Somerset, TA24 7PU.*
Actual grid ref: SS853383
Tel: **01643 831288**
Under 18: £7.75 **Adults:** £11.00
Self-catering facilities, Showers, Dining room, Drying room, Cycle store, Parking, Evening meal at 7.00pm, WC, Kitchen facilities, Breakfast available, Credit cards accepted
Victorian house and cedarwood annex. Lovely garden with access to riverside.

(2m) *Court Farm, Exford, Minehead, Somerset, TA24 7LY.*
Peaceful farmhouse at heart of Exmoor next to River Exe.
Tel: **01643 831207** (also fax no)
Mr & Mrs Horstmann.
D: £18.00-£18.00
S: £18.00-£18.00.
Open: All Year (not Xmas)
Beds: 11T
Baths: 1 Sh
🛇 🅿 ⛌ ⊟ 🔥 ⛟ 🎫 🔌 ✓

Simonsbath 24

National Grid Ref: SS7739

(1m 🚐) *Emmett's Grange Farm, Simonsbath, Minehead, Somerset, TA24 7LD.*
Tel: **01643 831138** (also fax no)
Barlow.
D: £28.00-£35.00
S: £33.00-£40.00.
Open: All Year (not Xmas/New Year)
Beds: 1T 2D
🛇 🅿 ⛌ ⊟ ⊼ 🐾 ⛌ 🔥 ⛟ 🎫 🔌 ✓
Emmett's Grange provides and oasis of friendly civilisation within its own 900 acres amidst the stunning wild and rugged Exmoor National Park. Luxurious B&B with moorland views. Guests own elegant drawing room. Gourmet food available and many local pubs. Fully licensed.

Lynbridge 25

National Grid Ref: SS7248

(🔺 0.5m) *Lynton Youth Hostel, Lynbridge, Lynton, Devon, EX35 6BE.*
Actual grid ref: SS720487
Tel: **01598 753237**
Under 18: £6.90 **Adults:** £10.00
Self-catering facilities, Showers, Shop, Laundry facilities, Lounge, Dining room, Drying room, Cycle store, Parking Limited, Evening meal at 7.00pm, No smoking, WC, Kitchen facilities, Breakfast available, Credit cards accepted
Victorian house in the steep wooded gorge of the West Lyn River, where Exmoor reaches the sea, with opportunities to explore the National Park, the sea shore and the river valley.

🚐 sign means that, *given due notice*, owners will pick you up from the path and drop you off *within reason.*

Lynton 26

National Grid Ref: SS7149

🍴 🍺 Rising Sun Inn, Staghunters Inn, Ye Olde Cottage Inn, Royal Castle, Sandrock

(0.5m) *The Turret, 33 Lee Road,
Lynton, Devon, EX35 6BS.*
Grades: ETC 3 Diamond
Tel: **01598 753284** (also fax no)
Mrs Wayman.
D: £18.00-£23.00 **S:** £25.00.
Open: All Year
Beds: 5D 1T
Baths: 4 En
🛏 (12) 🗔 🗶 🎵 🛋 Ⅵ 🛡 ✦
Step back in time and experience
old world hospitality. Built in
1898, the charm of our hotel will
relax and welcome you. Beautiful
ensuite bedrooms, enhanced with
all the modern facilities. Evening
meals served in cosy dining room.
Vegetarian and special dietary
needs catered for.

(0.5m 🚗) *The Denes Guest
House, Longmead, Lynton, Devon,
EX35 6DQ.*
Grades: ETC 3 Diamond
Tel: **01598 753573** Mr McGowan.
D: £16.00-£22.50 **S:** £16.00-£22.50.
Open: All Year
Beds: 3F 2D
Baths: 2 En 1 Pr 2 Sh
🛏 🅿 (5) ⊬ 🗔 🗶 🎵 Ⅵ 🛡 ✦
A warm friendly greeting awaits
you at The Denes, with its
Edwardian charm. Comfortable
accommodation and home cooked
food, evening meals served in our
licensed dining room. Ideal base to
explore Exmoor on the South West
Coastal Path. An Exmoor paths
partner.

All rooms full and
nowhere else to stay?
Ask the owner if
there's anywhere
nearby

(0.25m) *Victoria Lodge, Lee Road,
Lynton, Devon, EX35 6BP.*
Awarded B&B of the Year for
S.W. England by South West
Tourism.
Grades: AA 5 Diamond
Tel: **01598 753203** (also fax no)
Mr & Mrs Bennett.
D: £26.00-£36.00
S: £35.00-£54.00.
Open: Feb to NOv
Beds: 1F 7D 1T
Baths: 9 En

(0.25m 🚗) *Lynhurst Hotel,
Lynton, Devon, EX35 6AX.*
Character Victorian residence
situated in gardens/woodland
overlooking Lynmouth Bay.
Grades: AA 4 Diamond
Tel: **01598 752241** (also fax no)
Mr Townsend.
D: £22.00-£30.00
S: £25.00-£28.00.
Open: All Year
Beds: 2F 5D 1T 1S
Baths: 7 En
🛏 (1) 🅿 (2) 🗔 🗶 🛋 Ⅲ. Ⅵ ✦

(0.5m) *Gable Lodge, Lee Road,
Lynton, Devon, EX35 6BS.*
Actual grid ref: SS718495
Large Victorian house with views
along the East Lyn valley.
Tel: **01598 752367** (also fax no)
Mr & Mrs Bowman.
D: £18.50-£19.50
S: £18.50-£19.50.
Open: Easter to Oct
Beds: 1F 5D
Baths: 5 En 1 Sh
🛏 🅿 (8) ⊬ 🗔 🏋 🛋 Ⅲ. Ⅵ

(0.5m) *Croft House Hotel, Lydiate
Lane, Lynton, Devon, EX35 6HE.*
Croft house nestling in the old vil-
lage, built 1828 for a sea captain.
Tel: **01598 752391** (also fax no)
Mrs Johnson.
D: £17.00-£27.00
S: £20.00-£30.00.
Open: All Year (not Xmas)
Beds: 5D 2T
Baths: 6 En 1 Pr
⊬ 🗔 🏋 🗶 🛋 Ⅲ. Ⅵ 🛡 ✦

D = Price range per person
sharing in a double room

Lynmouth 27

National Grid Ref: SS7249

🍴 🍺 Riverside Cottages, Village Inn

(0.25m) *Glenville House, 2 Tors
Road, Lynmouth, Devon, EX35 6ET.*
Grades: AA 4 Diamond
Tel: **01598 752202**
Mr & Mrs Francis.
D: £22.00-£26.00
S: £22.00-£30.00.
Open: Feb to Nov
Beds: 4D 1T 1S
Baths: 3 En 1 Pr 2 Sh
🛏 (12) ⊬ 🗔 🛋 Ⅲ. Ⅵ 🛡 ✦
Idyllic riverside setting. Delightful
Victorian house full of character
and charm. Licensed. Tastefully
decorated bedrooms. Picturesque
harbour, village and unique Cliff
Railway nestled amidst wooded
valley. Magnificent Exmoor
scenery, spectacular coastline and
beautiful walks. Peaceful, tranquil,
romantic - a very special place.

(0.25m) *Tregonwell Riverside
Guest House, 1 Tors Road,
Lynmouth, Devon, EX35 6ET.*
Actual grid ref: SS725493
Grades: ETC 3 Diamond,
AA 3 Diamond
Tel: **01598 753369**
Mrs Parker.
D: £22.00-£27.00
S: £22.00-£25.00.
Open: All Year (not Xmas)
Beds: 2F 5D 1T 1S
Baths: 5 En 1 Pr 3 Sh
🛏 🅿 (7) ⊬ 🗔 🏋 🛋 Ⅲ. Ⅵ 🛡 ✦
Award-winning, romantic, elegant
riverside (former sea captain's)
stone-built house, snuggled amidst
waterfalls, cascades, wooded
valleys, soaring cliff tops, lonely
beaches, enchanting harbourside
'Olde Worlde' smugglers' village.
Shelley, Wordsworth, Coleridge
stayed here. 'England's
Switzerland'. Pretty bedrooms,
dramatic views. Garaged parkings.

Order your
packed lunches the
evening before you
need them.
Not at breakfast!

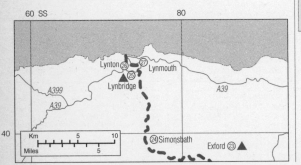

Vanguard Way

A relaxing walk, ideal for Londoners wanting to finish a path over a couple of weekends. The 62-mile **Vanguard Way** leaves the skyscrapers of Croydon behind in a matter of minutes, heading off for the North Downs escarpment and then the Greensand Ridge. You then cross the Weald, with its low pastures, to the edge of Ashdown Forest, before heading off to Cuckmere Haven, with its majestic view of the Seven Sisters cliffs rearing beyond. The **Vanguard Way** links the **North Downs Way**, the **Greensand Way** and the **South Downs Way**. There are excellent rail connections.

Guides: *The Vanguard Way* by Colin Saunders (ISBN 0 953007 60 X), published by the Vanguards Rambling Club and available directly from them (109 Selsdon Park Road, South Croydon, Surrey, CR2 8JJ), £2.95

The Wealdway and the Vanguard Way by Kev Reynolds (ISBN 0 9 023 63859), published by Cicerone Press and available from all good map shops or directly from the publishers (2 Police Square, Milnthorpe, Cumbria, LA7 7PY, 01539 562069), £4.99 (+ 75p p&p)

Maps: Ordnance Survey 1:50000 Landranger series: 177, 187, 188, 199

Croydon 1

National Grid Ref: TQ3265

(0.25m) ***Croydon Friendly Guest House,*** *16 St Peters Road, Croydon,* CR0 1HD.
Tel: **020 8680 4428**
Mr Hasan.
D: £20.00-£30.00
S: £25.00-£30.00.
Open: All Year
Beds: 1T 5S
Baths: 2 En 2 Sh
(1) (6)
Large character full detached house enjoying a warm friendly atmosphere. Situated within easy walking distance of all train and bus services into Central London and al main amenities, restaurants, pubs and theatres in Croydon. Comfortable rooms, ample off road parking.

D = Price range per person sharing in a double room

Limpsfield 2

National Grid Ref: TQ4052

The George, The Crown, The Gurkha

(1.25m) ***Arawa,*** *58 Granville Road, Limpsfield, Oxted, Surrey,* RH8 0BZ.
Actual grid ref: TQ402532
Friendly, comfortable, welcoming. Lovely garden, excellent breakfast, good London trains.
Grades: ETC 3 Diamond
Tel: **01883 714104** (also fax no) Gibbs.
D: £18.00-£30.00 **S:** £18.00-£30.00.
Open: All Year
Beds: 1F 2T **Baths:** 1 En 1 Sh
(3)

Oxted 3

National Grid Ref: TQ3852

The Oxted, Old Bell, The Crown, The George, The Gurkha, Royal Oak

(1m) ***Pinehurst Grange Guest House,*** *East Hill (Part of A25), Oxted, Surrey,* RH8 9AE.
Actual grid ref: TQ393525
Comfortable Victorian ex-farm-house with traditional service and relaxed friendly atmosphere.
Tel: **01883 716413** Mr Rodgers.
D: £21.00-£21.00 **S:** £26.00-£26.00.
Open: All Year (not Xmas/ New Year)
Beds: 1D 1T 1S **Baths:** 1 Sh
(5) (3)

(1m) ***Meads,*** *23 Granville Road, Oxted, Surrey,* RH8 0BX.
Tudor style house on Kent/Surrey border station to London.
Grades: ETC 4 Diamond
Tel: **01883 730115** Mrs Holgate.
D: £25.00-£28.00 **S:** £28.00-£30.00.
Open: All Year
Beds: 1T 1D
Baths: 1 En 1 Pr

(1.5m) ***Old Forge House,*** *Merle Common, Oxted, Surrey,* RH8 0JB.
Actual grid ref: TQ416493
Welcoming family home in rural surroundings. Ten minutes from M25.
Tel: **01883 715969** Mrs Mills.
D: £18.00-£20.00 **S:** £18.00-£20.00.
Open: All Year (not Xmas)
Beds: 1D 1T 1S
Baths: 1 Sh
(4)

Westerham 4

National Grid Ref: TQ4454

The Bull, White Hart

(1.5m) ***Corner Cottage,*** *Toys Hill, Westerham, Kent,* TN16 1PY.
Attractive self contained accommodation in Laura Ashley fabrics. Spectacular panoramic views.
Grades: ETC 4 Diamond, Silver
Tel: **01732 750362**
Mrs Olszowska.
Fax no: 01959 561911
D: £45.00-£50.00 **S:** £30.00-£35.00.
Open: All Year
Beds: 1F
(1)

High Hurstwood 5

National Grid Ref: TQ4926

Crown & Gate, Maypole Inn, White Hart

(0.75m) ***Chillies Granary,*** *High Hurstwood, Crowborough, E. Sussex,* TN6 3TB.
Actual grid ref: TQ497278
Awarded 2nd place in 'B&B of the Year' by SEETB.
Grades: ETC 4 Diamond
Tel: **01892 655560** (also fax no)
Mr & Mrs Peck.
D: £23.00-£27.00 **S:** £25.00-£45.00.
Open: Mar to Dec
Beds: 1F 1D 1T
Baths: 2 En 1 Pr
(6)

🚐 sign means that, *given due notice,*

owners will pick you up from the path

and drop you off *within reason.*

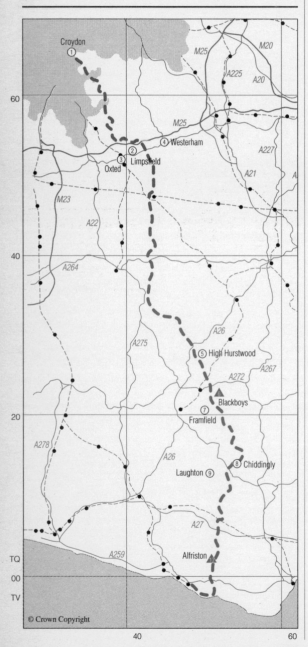

© Crown Copyright

(0.5m 🚐) *Tronning,*
Coombelands, Wittersham, Rye,
Kent, TN30 7NU.
Actual grid ref: TQ496233
Situated in quiet village between
Rye and Tenterden. Good touring
area.
Grades: AA 3 Diamond,
RAC 3 Diamond
Tel: **01797 207768** (also fax no)
Mrs Brown.
D: £20.00-£25.00
S: £20.00-£25.00.
Open: All Year
Beds: 1D 1T 1S
Baths: 1 En 1 Sh
🛏🖫 (4) ⚼🗆 🖳 📖 Ⅴ ⊬

Blackboys 6

National Grid Ref: TQ5220

(▲ 0.75m) *Blackboys Youth*
Hostel, Blackboys, Uckfield,
East Sussex, TN22 5HU.
Actual grid ref: TQ521215
Tel: **01825 890607**
Under 18: £6.50
Adults: £9.25
Self-catering facilities, Showers,
Laundry facilities, Lounge, Drying
room, Cycle store, Parking, No
smoking, WC, Kitchen facilities,
Luggage store, Credit cards
accepted
This rustic wooden cabin in a
deciduous sylvan setting offers
good basic accommodation with a
cosy open fire, spacious
lounge/dining room & kitchen.

Framfield 7

National Grid Ref: TQ4920

(0.5m 🚐) *Beggars Barn, Barn*
Lane, Framfield, Uckfield,
E Sussex, TN22 5RX.
Actual grid ref: TQ510215
Unique C18th converted barn with
enchanting separate
accommodation.
Tel: **01825 890869**
Fax no: 01825 890868
D: £20.00-£20.00.
S: £25.00-£25.00.
Open: All Year (not Xmas)
Beds: 1F 1D
Baths: 1 En
🖫 (2) 🗆 🖈 ✗ 🖳 Ⅴ 🛆 ⊬

🚐 sign means that,
given due notice,
owners will pick you
up from the path
and drop you off *with-*
in reason.

Chiddingly 8

National Grid Ref: TQ5414

🍴 🍺 Six Bells

(0.5m 🚾) *Hale Farm House,*
Chiddingly, Lewes, E Sussex,
BN8 6HQ.
Grades: ETC 3 Diamond
Tel: **01825 872619** (also fax no)
Mrs Burrough.
D: £18.00-£25.00 **S:** £18.00-£25.00.
Open: All Year
Beds: 1F 2T **Baths:** 1 En 1 Sh
🛏 🅿 (3) 🍴🖤🐾✗ 🏠 🎱 📺 🍴♦
Relax in spacious rooms of this
14th century Listed beamed farm-
house, situated on Weald Way over
looking the South Downs, 12 miles
from Eastbourne. Extensive
gardens, meadows, woods, stream.
Good walking, horse riding. Ponies
available. Also Shakespeare and
language courses.

(On path 🚾) *'Holmes Hill',*
Holmes Hill, Chiddingly, Lewes,
E. Sussex, BN8 6JA.
Actual grid ref: TQ533127
Cosy, modernised, C18th cottage.
Ideal for touring Glyndebourne,
Eastbourne, Sussex Coast.
Tel: **01825 872746**
Mr & Mrs Farrier.
D: £20.00-£20.00 **S:** £25.00-£25.00.
Open: All Year (not Xmas)
Beds: 1D 1T **Baths:** 2 Pr
🛏 (3) 🅿 (3) 🍴🖤 🎱 📺 ♦

Laughton 9

National Grid Ref: TQ5013

🍴 🍺 The Cook, The Gun, The Bluebell, Lamb Inn

(1m) *Holly Cottage, Lewes Road,*
Laughton, Lewes, E. Sussex,
BN8 6BL.
Actual grid ref: TQ503131
Charming C18th Listed country
cottage.
Grades: ETC 4 Diamond
Tel: **01323 811309** Mrs Clarke.
Fax no: 01323 811106
D: £23.00-£25.00 **S:** £30.00-£35.00.
Open: All Year
Beds: 1F 1T 1D **Baths:** 3 En
🛏 🅿 (3) 🍴🖤🐾 🎱 📺

Alfriston 10

National Grid Ref: TQ5103

🍴 🍺 Wingrove Inn, Ye Olde Smuggler's Inn

(▲ 1m) *Alfriston Youth Hostel,*
Frog Firle, Alfriston, Polegate,
East Sussex, BN26 5TT.
Actual grid ref: TQ518019
Tel: **01323 870423**
Under 18: £6.90 **Adults:** £10.00
Self-catering facilities, Showers,
Wet weather shelter, Lounge,
Drying room, Parking, Evening
meal at 6.30pm, WC, Kitchen facil-
ities, Breakfast available, Credit
cards accepted
*A comfortable Sussex country
house dating from 1530, set in
Cuckmere Valley with views over
river and Litlington.*

(0.5m 🚾) *Meadowbank, Sloe*
Lane, Alfriston, East Sussex,
BN26 5UR.
Tel: **01323 870742** Mrs Petch.
D: £20.00-£25.00 **S:** £30.00-£35.00.
Open: All Year (not Xmas/New
Year)
Beds: 1T 2D **Baths:** 1 En 2 Sh
🅿 (4) 🍴🖤🐾 🎱 📺 ♦
The beautiful private dwelling in
tranquil setting, offers views of
Cuckmere Valley and South
Downs. only 3 minutes walk
village centre. Ideal for
walkers/cyclists. Private car park.
Lovely gardens and conservatory in
which to relax. Delicious English
breakfast.

(0.5m) *Dacres, Alfriston, Polegate,*
East Sussex, BN26 5TP.
Country cottage. Beautiful gardens.
Near South Downs Way
Glyndebourne, Seven Sisters.
Tel: **01323 870447** Mrs Embry.
D: £25.00-£25.00 **S:** £40.00.
Open: All Year
Beds: 1T **Baths:** 1 Pr
🅿 (1) 🍴🖤 🎱 📺 ♦

Planning a longer
stay? Always ask for
any special rates.

Viking Way

The **Viking Way** runs for 140 miles through a quiet, sparsely populated area of Eastern England that stretches from the Humber down to the Fens - the heart of the historic 'Danelaw' area, once ruled by Scandinavian kings. Beginning in Barton-upon-Humber, the path follows the scarp of the Lincolnshire Wolds, then along the River Witham to the cathedral city of Lincoln, before cutting south along the Lincoln 'Cliff' to head along the Roman Ermine Street, skirting Grantham and finishing in pretty Oakham alongside Rutland Water. It is easy going and makes for an excellent introduction to long distance walking, linking with the **Wolds Way** (q.v.) via the Humber Bridge and with the **Macmillan Way** and the **Hereward Way** at Oakham in Rutland.

Guide: *The Viking Way* by John Stead (ISBN 185 284 057 9), published by Cicerone Press and available from all good map shops or directly from the publishers (2 Police Square, Milnthorpe, Cumbria, LA7 7PY, 01539 562069), £5.99 (+75p p&p)

The Viking Way, (ISBN 1 872375 25 1), published by Lincolnshire Books and available from Lincolnshire County Council, Highways & Planning Directorates, City Hall, Lincoln, LNI 1DN, tel. 01522 553052, price £5.95 (inc p&p)

Maps: 1:50000 Ordnance Survey Landranger Series: 112, 113, 121, 130 and 141

Barton-upon-Humber   1

National Grid Ref: TA0321

🍴 🍺 White Swan

(On path) **White Swan Hotel**, *Fleetgate, Barton-upon-Humber, N Lincs, DN18 5QD.*
Local friendly pub, pool, darts, doms etc.
Tel: **01652 632459**
D: £23.50-£23.50 **S:** £30.00-£30.00.
Open: All Year (not Xmas)
Beds: 1D 3T
Baths: 2 En 1 Sh
🅿 (10) 🖵 ✕ 🍴 🛏 Ⅷ

Barnetby le Wold   2

National Grid Ref: TA0509

🍴 🍺 Station Hotel

(On path 🚍) **Holcombe Guest House**, *34 Victoria Road, Barnetby le Wold, Lincs, DN38 6JR.*
Actual grid ref: TA059097
First class accommodation and a warm welcome awaits you.
Tel: **01652 680655** Mrs Vora.
Fax no: 01652 680841
D: £16.25-£20.00 **S:** £20.00-£20.00.
Open: All Year
Beds: 2F 1T 5S
Baths: 4 Pr 2 Sh
🐕 🅿 (7) 🖵 🏊 ✕ 🛏 🚿 Ⅷ

D = Price range per person sharing in a double room

(On path) **Reginald House**, *27 Queen Road, Barnetby le Wold, Lincolnshire, DN38 6JH.*
Beautiful modern bungalow with newly-built first floor ensuite guest accommodation.
Tel: **01652 688566**
Fax no: 01652 688510
D: £17.50-£20.00 **S:** £22.50-£25.00.
Open: All Year
Beds: 1D 1T **Baths:** 2 En
🅿 (4) 🖵 ✕ 🛏 Ⅷ

Market Rasen   3

National Grid Ref: TF1089

🍴 🍺 The Chase, Gordon Arms, White Swan

(2.5m 🚍) **Waveney Cottage Guest House**, *Willingham Road, Market Rasen, Lincs, LN8 3DN.*
Small Tudor-style cottage. Ideal base for walking and cycling.
Grades: ETC 3 Diamond
Tel: **01673 843236** Mrs Bridger.
D: £19.50 **S:** £21.50.
Open: All Year
Beds: 1D 2T
Baths: 3 En
🐕 🅿 (6) 🖵 ✕ 🛏 Ⅷ

(1m 🚍) **White Swan Hotel**, *29 Queen Street, Market Rasen, Lincs, LN8 3EN.*
Close to Racecourse, offering warm, friendly atmosphere.
Tel: **01673 843356** Scuffam.
D: £17.50 **S:** £17.50.
Open: All Year
Beds: 1F 1D 2T 1S
Baths: 1 Sh
🐕 🅿 (10) 🖵 ✕ 🛏 Ⅷ

Benniworth   4

National Grid Ref: TF2081

(1m 🚍) **Glebe Farm**, *Church Lane, Benniworth, Market Rasen, Lincolnshire, LN8 6JP.*
C18th Listed farmhouse in Lincolnshire Wolds.
Grades: ETC 4 Diamond
Tel: **01507 313231** (also fax no)
Mrs Selby.
D: £22.50-£27.00 **S:** £25.00-£27.00.
Open: All Year
Beds: 1D 2T
Baths: 2 En 1 Pr
🅿 (6) 🖵 ✕ 🛏 Ⅷ

Goulceby   5

National Grid Ref: TF2579

🍴 🍺 Three Horseshoes

(On path 🚍) **Holly House**, *Watery Lane, Goulceby, Louth, Lincs, LNI1 9UR.*
Actual grid ref: TF255792
Tel: **01507 343729** Mrs Lester.
D: £15.00-£16.00 **S:** £15.00-£16.00.
Open: All Year (not Xmas)
Beds: 1D 1T
Baths: 1 Sh
🅿 (2) 🖵 ✕ 🛏 Ⅷ
Quiet village location in Lincolnshire Wolds. Comfortable cottage set in large garden of interest to serious gardeners. Excellent cooked breakfast and comfortable beds, off road parking. French, Hebrew and German spoken. Antiques dealers welcome.

Horncastle 6

National Grid Ref: TF2669

|₩| **◀** Fighting Cocks

(On path) *Milestone Cottage,*
42 North Street, Horncastle, Lincs,
LN9 5DX.
Comfortable, self contained accommodation in Georgian town cottage.
Self catering option available.
Tel: **01507 522238**
D: £20.00-£20.00
S: £20.00-£20.00.
Open: All Year
Beds: 1T
Baths: 1 En
🛏 🅿 (2) 🗎 🏲 🛋 ▥ Ⓥ ✦

(On path) ***Colkirk House,*** *Manor*
House Street, Horncastle, Lincs,
LN9 5HF.
Converted warehouse in the middle
of a small market town, quiet
attractive outlook.
Tel: **01507 527366** (also fax no)
D: £16.00-£16.00 **S:** £17.00-£17.00.
Open: All Year (not Xmas)
Beds: 1D 1T **Baths:** 1 Pr
🛏 🅿 (3) 🗎 🏲 🛋 ▥ Ⓥ ✦

D = Price range per person
sharing in a double room

Woodhall Spa 7

National Grid Ref: TF1963

|₩| **◀** The Mall, Abbey Lodge, Eagle Lodge

(On path) ***Claremont Guest House,***
9-11 Witham Road, Woodhall Spa,
Lincs, LN10 6RW.
Friendly personal service in a
traditional unspoilt Victorian guest
house.
Grades: ETC 2 Diamond
Tel: **01526 352000** Mrs Brennan.
D: £15.00-£20.00 **S:** £15.00-£20.00.
Open: All Year
Beds: 4F 2D 1T 3S **Baths:** 3 En 2 Sh
🛏 🅿 (4) 🗎 🏲 🛋 Ⓥ 🛆 ✦

(On path) ***Newlands Guest House,***
56 Woodland Drive, Woodhall Spa,
Lincs, LN10 6YG.
Grades: ETC 4 Diamond
Tel: **01526 352881**
D: £18.00-£20.00 **S:** £20.00-£20.00.
Open: All Year (not Xmas)
Beds: 1D 2T **Baths:** 2 En 1 Pr
🛏 🅿 (8) ✂ 🗎 🏲 🛋 ▥ Ⓥ
Luxury accommodation in quiet
tree-lined lane. Very convenient for
village and international golf
courses. Special aviation room and
guest lounge. Very attractive
gardens, excellent centre for
visiting Lincolnshire.

Lincoln 8

National Grid Ref: SK9771

|₩| **◀** Lord Tennyson, Sun Inn, The Barge, Royal
William, Horse & Groom, Burton Arms, Wig & Mitre

(▲ On path) ***Lincoln Youth***
Hostel, *77 South Park, Lincoln,*
LN5 8ES.
Actual grid ref: SK980700
Tel: **01522 522076**
Under 18: £6.90 **Adults:** £10.00
Self-catering facilities, Television,
Laundry facilities, Lounge, Cycle
store, Parking, Evening meal at
7.00pm, No smoking, Kitchen
facilities, Breakfast available,
Luggage store, Credit cards accepted
Victorian villa in a quiet road
opposite South Common open
parkland within easy reach of the
centre, castle and cathedral.

(0.5m 🚍) ***Admiral Guest House,***
16/18 Nelson St, Lincoln, LN1 1PJ.
Actual grid ref: SK968715
Grades: RAC 3 Diamond
Tel: **01522 544467** (also fax no)
Mr Major.
D: £18.00-£20.00 -£22.00.
Open: All Year (not Xmas)
Beds: 1F 3D 2T 3S
Baths: 7 En 2 Pr
🛏 🅿 (12) 🗎 🏲 ✗ 🛋 ▥ & Ⓥ 🛆 ✦
Admiral Guest House, also known
as Nelsons Cottages, situated just
off main A57 close to city centre
and Lincoln University, offering
large floodlit car park, also close to
Brayford pool, cathedral and castle
and all amenities. All rooms ensuite
and private bath.

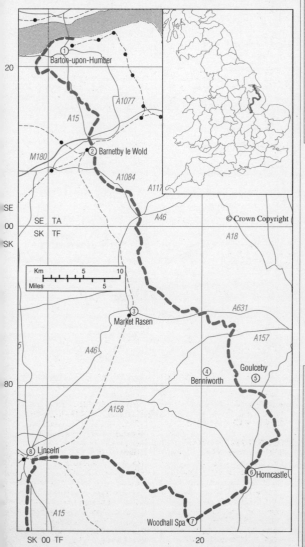

(1m) *Hamiltons Hotel,* 2 Hamilton Rd, St Catherines, Lincoln, *LN5 8ED.* Friendly family run hotel in a detached former Victorian home. Tel: **01522 528243** Bull. Fax no: 01522 524603 D: £18.00-£20.00 S: £18.00-£25.00. **Open:** All Year **Beds:** 1F 3T 2D 3S **Baths:** 4 En 5 Sh ⛺ 🅿 (9) ⬚ 🛉 ✕ 🔥 🛋 🎹 🖾 🟥 ♿

(1m 🚐) *A B C Charisma Guest House,* 126 Yarborough Rd, Lincoln, *LN1 1HP.* Beautiful views overlooking Trent valley 10 minutes walk to tourist area. Tel: **01522 543560** (also fax no) D: £20.00-£22.50 S: £20.00-£25.00. **Open:** All Year **Beds:** 1F 2T 6D 2S **Baths:** 3 En 4 Sh ⛺ (10) 🅿 (10) ✍ ⬚ 🛉 🔥 🖾 🟥 ♿

(0.75m 🚐) *Newport Guest House,* 26-28 Newport, Lincoln, *LN1 3DF.* A high standard establishment 500 metres from historic city centre. **Grades:** ETC 3 Diamond, AA 3 Diamond. Tel: **01522 528590** Mr Clarke. Fax no: 01522 544502 D: £16.00-£20.00 S: £16.00-£28.00. **Open:** All Year (not Xmas) **Beds:** 2D 5T 1S **Baths:** 5 En 2 Sh ⛺ (6) 🅿 (5) ✍ ⬚ 🛉 🔥 🛋 🖾 🟥 ♿

(1m) *The Old Rectory,* 19 Newport, Lincoln, *LN1 3DQ.* Large Edwardian home near cathedral, castle, pubs and restaurants. Tel: **01522 514774** Mr Downes. D: £20.00-£20.00 S: £20.00-£25.00. **Open:** All Year (not Xmas) **Beds:** 2F 4D 1T 1Sh **Baths:** 5 En 1 Sh ⛺ 🅿 (8) ✍ ⬚ 🛉 🔥 🖾 🟥 (1m 🚐)

Edward King House, The Old Palace, Minster Yard, Lincoln, *LN2 1PU.* **Actual grid ref:** SK978718 **Grades:** ETC 2 Diamond Tel: **01522 528778** Rev Adkins. Fax no: 01522 527308 D: £18.50-£20.50 S: £19.00-£21.00. **Open:** All Year (not Xmas) **Beds:** 1F 11T 5S **Baths:** 8 Sh ⛺ 🅿 (12) ✍ ⬚ 🛉 🔥 🛋 🟥 A former residence of the Bishops of Lincoln at the historic heart of the city and next to the cathedral and medieval city palace. We offer a peaceful haven with a secluded garden and superb views.

(1m) *South Park Guest House,* 11 South Park, Lincoln, *LN8 8EN.* Tel: **01522 528243** Mr Bull. Fax no: 01522 524603 D: £18.00-£26.00 S: £22.00-£25.00. **Open:** All Year (not Xmas/New Year) **Beds:** 1F 2T 2D 1S **Baths:** 6 En ⛺ (1) 🅿 (6) ⬚ ✕ 🔥 🛋 🖾 🟥 🛉 Fine Victorian detached house, recently refurbished to provide excellent quality accommodation, while maintaining many original features & character. Situated overlooking the South Common, only a short walk to shops, pubs, restaurants, city centre and tourist attractions. Ensuite rooms. Private parking.

(1m) *Westlyn House,* 67 Carholme Road, Lincoln, *LN1 1RT.* Late Georgian house close to university, marina, cathedral, castle, centre. **Grades:** RAC 3 Diamond Tel: **01522 537468** (also fax no) Mrs Shelton. D: £17.50-£20.00 S: £20.00-£25.00. **Open:** All Year (not Xmas) **Beds:** 1F 1T 2D 1S **Baths:** 5 En ⛺ (3) 🅿 (4) ✍ ⬚ 🛉 🔥 🛋 🟥 ♿

(1m 🚐) *The Bakery Guest House,* 26-28 Burton Rd, Lincoln, *LN1 3LB.* Converted bakery only two minutes from Lincoln castle and cathedral. Tel: **01522 576057** (also fax no) D: £20.00-£30.00 S: £25.00-£40.00. **Open:** All Year **Beds:** 1F 2D 1T **Baths:** 3 En 1 Pr ⛺ ⬚ 🛉 🔥 🛋 🟥

(1m) *Elma Guest House,* 14 Albion Crescent, off Long Leys Rd, Lincoln, *LN1 1EB.* Quiet location, friendly family home with garden pond and willow tree. **Grades:** AA 2 Diamond Tel: **01522 529792** (also fax no) Mrs Guymer. D: £17.00-£20.00 S: £17.00-£20.00. **Open:** All Year **Beds:** 1D 1T 1S **Baths:** 2 Sh ⛺ 🅿 (5) ⬚ ✕ 🔥 🛋 🟥 ♿

(1m 🚐) *Jaymar,* 31 Newland Street West, Lincoln, *LN1 1QQ.* Close proximity to: city attractions, A46, A57. Early breakfasts available. Tel: **01522 532934** Mrs Ward. D: £15.00-£15.00 S: £15.00-£15.00. **Open:** All Year (not Xmas) **Beds:** 1D 1S **Baths:** 1 Sh ⛺ ✍ ⬚ 🛉 🔥 🟥 ♿

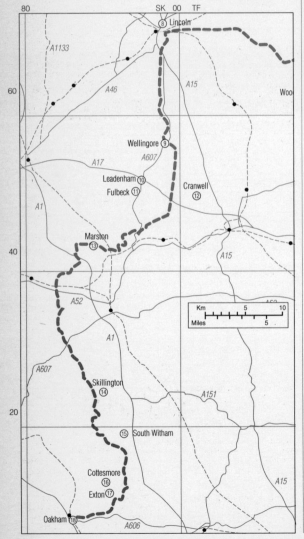

(0.75m 🚐) *Ridgeways Guest House,* 243 Burton Road, Lincoln, *LN1 3UB.*
Actual grid ref: SK972727
Situated uphill within easy walking distance to the historic heart of Lincoln.
Tel: **01522 546878** (also fax no)
Mr Barnes.
D: £17.50-£25.00 **S:** £20.00-£25.00.
Open: All Year
Beds: 2F 1D 1T **Baths:** 3 En 1 Pr
🅿 (6) ⚡ 🛏 🖤 🐾 🖕 ♿ Ⓥ

(1m) *The Barbican Hotel,* 11 St Marys Street, Lincoln, *LN5 7EQ.*
Victorian Hotel. Refurbished. Opposite railway station. An ideal central location.
Tel: **01522 543811**
D: £26.00 **S:** £39.00-£39.00.
Open: All Year (not Xmas)
Beds: 5D 2T 5S **Baths:** 12 En
🛏 🖤 ⚡ 🖕 🖤 Ⓥ 🔥

(On path 🚐) *Eardleys Hotel,* 21 Cross O'Cliff Hill, Lincoln, *LN5 8PN.*
Homely hotel, overlooking parkland & golf course. Guest bar & parking.
Tel: **01522 523050** (also fax)
Mr Hill.
D: £17.50-£20.00 **S:** £20.00-£25.00.
Open: All Year
Beds: 2F 2D 1T 1S
Baths: 2 En 2 Sh
🛏 🅿 (10) 🖤 🛏 🖕 🐾 ⚖ 🖤 🔥

Wellingore   9

National Grid Ref: SK9856

(On path) *Marquis of Granby,* High Street, Wellingore, Lincoln, *LN5 0HW.*
Friendly village inn, midway between Lincoln, Grantham, Sleaford and Newark.
Tel: **01522 810442** Mrs Justice.
D: £20.00-£25.00 **S:** £22.50-£25.00.
Open: All Year (not Xmas)
Beds: 1F 2D 4T **Baths:** 6 En 1 Pr
🛏 🅿 🖤 🛏 🐾 ⚖ 🖤 Ⓥ 🔥

Leadenham   10

National Grid Ref: SK9552

(1.5m 🚐) *George Hotel,* High St, Leadenham, Lincoln, *LN5 0PP.*
Grades: ETC 3 Diamond
Tel: **01400 272251**
Mr Willgoose.
Fax no: 01400 272091
D: £14.00-£20.00 **S:** £20.00-£25.00.
Open: All Year
Beds: 1F 2D 2T 1S
Baths: 6 En
🛏 🅿 🖤 🐾 ⚖ 🖕 🖤 ♿ Ⓥ 🔥
The George at Leadenham is a small country hotel just off the A17 midway between Newark, Sleaford, Grantham, Lincoln. Its homely atmosphere and reputation for fine food makes it a haven for the weary tourist and accessible stopping place for businessmen.

Fulbeck   11

National Grid Ref: SK9450

🍴 🍺 Blue Cow

(3m) *Hare & Hounds,* The Green, Fulbeck, Grantham, Lincs, *NG32 3JJ.*
C17th inn. Real ales, food all week. Patio garden. 10 mins A1.
Grades: ETC 3 Diamond,
AA 3 Diamond.
Tel: **01400 272090**
Nicholas.
Fax no: 01400 273663
D: £20.00-£27.50
S: £30.00-£40.00.
Open: All Year
Beds: 4D 2T 2F
Baths: 8 En
🛏 🅿 🖤 🐾 🖕 🖤 Ⓥ

Cranwell   12

National Grid Ref: TF0349

(On path) *Byards Leap Cottage,* Cranwell, Sleaford, Lincs, *NG34 8EY.*
Actual grid ref: SK9949
Comfortable country cottage, beautiful garden, home cooking with home-grown produce.
Grades: ETC 2 Diamond
Tel: **01400 261537**
Mrs Wood.
D: £18.00 **S:** £18.00.
Open: All Year (not Xmas)
Beds: 1D 1T
Baths: 1 Sh
🛏 🅿 (6) ⚡ 🛏 🐾 ⚖ 🖤 Ⓥ 🔥

Marston   13

National Grid Ref: SK8943

(On path) *Thorold Arms,* Marston, Grantham, Lincs, *NG32 2HH.*
Popular pub, good beer, home-cooked food, fresh vegetables, veggie meals too.
Grades: ETC 3 Diamond
Tel: **01400 250899**
Mr Bryan.
Fax no: 01400 251030
D: £29.50-£32.50
S: £27.50-£29.50.
Open: All Year
Beds: 1F 1D
Baths: 2 En
🛏 (5) 🅿 (16) 🛏 🐾 🖕 🖕 🖤 Ⓥ 🔥

Skillington   14

National Grid Ref: SK8925

🍴 🍺 Cross Swords

(On path) *Sproxton Lodge,* Skillington, Grantham, Lincs, *NG33 5HJ.*
Quiet family farm alongside Viking way. Everyone welcome.
Tel: **01476 860307**
Mrs Whatton.
D: £17.00-£18.00
S: £17.00-£18.00.
Open: All Year (not Xmas)
Beds: 1F 1D 1S
Baths: 1 En 1 Sh
🛏 (5) 🅿 (4) ⚡ 🛏 🖕 🖕 🖤 Ⓥ 🔥

South Witham   15

National Grid Ref: SK9219

🍴 🍺 Blue Cow

(1.25m 🚐) *Rose Cottage,* 7 High St, South Witham, Grantham, Lincs, *NG33 5QB*
Actual grid ref: SK929192
C18th stone cottage in two acres midway between Stamford/Grantham/Rutland Water.
Tel: **01572 767757** Mrs Van Kimmenade
Fax no: 01572 767199
D: £25.00-£25.00 **S:** £25.00-£25.00.
Open: All Year
Beds: 1F 1D 1T 2S **Baths:** 3 En
🛏 🅿 (6) ⚡ 🛏 🐾 🖕 🖕 ♿ Ⓥ 🔥

Cottesmore   16

National Grid Ref: SK9013

🍴 🍺 Sun Inn

(2m 🚐) *The Tithe Barn,* Clatterpot Lane, Cottesmore, Oakham, Rutland, *LE15 7DW.*
Comfortable, spacious, ensuite rooms with a wealth of original features. **Grades:** ETC 3 Diamond
Tel: **01572 813591**
D: £18.00-£24.00 **S:** £20.00-£35.00.
Open: All Year
Beds: 2F 1D 1T **Baths:** 3 En 1 Pr
🛏 (1) 🅿 (6) ⚡ 🛏 🖕 🖕 🖤 Ⓥ 🛑

Exton   17

National Grid Ref: SK9211

🍴 🍺 Fox & Hounds

(0.5m) *Fox & Hounds,* Exton, Oakham, Rutland, *LE15 8AP.*
Country inn overlooking village green. 2 miles Rutland Water, half mile Bransdale Gardens.
Tel: **01572 812403** D Hillier.
D: £20.00-£22.00 **S:** £22.00-£24.00.
Open: All Year (not Xmas/New Year)
Beds: 1D 1T 1S
🛏 (8) 🅿 (20) 🛏 🖕 🖕 🛑

(1m) *Hall Farm,* Cottesmore Road, Exton, Oakham, Rutland, *LE15 8AN.*
Close to Rutland Water and Geoff Hamiltons Barnsdale TV gardens.
Grades: ETC 3 Diamond
Tel: **01572 812271** Mrs Williamson
D: £17.50-£22.00 **S:** £20.00-£24.50.
Open: All Year (not Xmas)
Beds: 1F 1D 1T **Baths:** 1 En 2 Sh
🛏 🅿 (6) ⚡ 🛏 🐾 🖕 Ⓥ 🔥

Oakham   18

National Grid Ref: SK8508

🍴 🍺 Admiral Hornblower, Nicks, White Lion, Odd House, Whippen Inn

(On path) *Angel House,* 20 Northgate, Oakham, Rutland, *LE15 6QS*
Unique Victorian house. Converted outbuildings. Secluded courtyard. Lounge, patio, fridge/freezer, microwave.
Tel: **01572 756153** Mrs Weight.
D: £11.00-£17.00 **S:** £22.00-£34.00.
Open: All Year **Beds:** 1D 2T
Baths: 3 En 🛏 🅿 🛏 🖕 🖤 Ⓥ 🔥

Wayfarers Walk

Another pleasant 70 miles in the South of England, readily accessible by train, showing off the chalklands of Hampshire with its rolling hills and those peaceful brooks much loved by fly fishermen throughout the world. Between a medieval drover's track, a riverside path, a classic steep beech 'hanger' and the lonely mudflats at Langstone Harbour, you discover some classic English villages, including the reputed birthplace of cricket - Hambledon. Be prepared for heavy mud on this path after rain.

Guides:
Along and Around the Wayfarers Walk by Barry Shurlock (ISBN 0 948176 04 0), published by Hampshire County Council and available directly from their offices (Rights of Way Office, Mottisfont Court, High Street, Winchester, Hants, SO23 8ZF, tel. 01962 846002), £4.95 (+54p p&p)

Maps: Ordnance Survey 1:50000 Landranger series: 174, 185, 196, 197

Inkpen 1
National Grid Ref: SU3764

(1m 🚌) **Beacon House,** *Bell Lane, Upper Green, Inkpen, Hungerford, Berks, RG17 9QJ.*
Actual grid ref: SU368634
Visit our 1930's country home on Berks/Wilts/Hants border. Lovely countryside.
Grades: AA 3 Diamond
Tel: **01488 668640** Mr & Mrs Cave.
D: £22.00 **S:** £22.00.
Open: All Year
Beds: 1T 2S **Baths:** 2 Sh
🛏 🅿 (6) 🖵 🔭 ✕ 🎵 🎖 🕮 Ⅴ 🛇 ∥

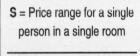

S = Price range for a single person in a single room

Highclere 2
National Grid Ref: SU4360

🍴 🍺 Yew Tree Inn, Red House

(1.5m) **Highclere Farm,** *Highclere, Newbury, Hampshire, RG20 9PY.*
Situated in designated Area of Outstanding Natural Beauty & close to Highclere Castle - Newbury Racecourse.
Grades: ETC 3 Diamond
Tel: **01635 255013** Mrs Walsh.
D: £25.00 **S:** £40.00.
Open: All Year (not Xmas/New Year)
Beds: 1F 1D **Baths:** 1 En
🛏 🅿 🖵 🎖 🕮 Ⅴ

D = Price range per person sharing in a double room

All rooms full and nowhere else to stay? Ask the owner if there's anywhere nearby

---

Crux Easton 3
National Grid Ref: SU4256

🍴 🍺 Furze Bush

(1m 🚌) **Manor House,** *Crux Easton, Newbury, Hants, RG20 9QF.*
Actual grid ref: SU427565
Historic farmhouse in quiet village, lovely views, near Highclere Castle.
Tel: **01635 254314**
Mrs O'Shaughnessy.
Fax no: 01635 254246
D: £22.50-£25.00
S: £22.50-£25.00.
Open: All Year
Beds: 3T
Baths: 2 Sh
🛏 🅿 (8) 🖵 🔭 ✕ 🎖 🕮 Ⅴ 🛇 ∥

The Grid Reference beneath the location heading is for the village or town - *not* for individual houses, which are shown (where supplied) in each entry itself.

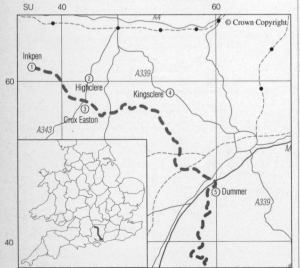

Kingsclere 4

National Grid Ref: SU5258

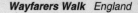 ◖ The Crown

(1.5m 🚐) *Cleremede, Fox's Lane, Kingsclere, Newbury, Berks, RG20 5SL.*
Actual grid ref: SW5258
Secluded house with beautiful garden very close to village centre.
Grades: ETC 4 Diamond
Tel: **01635 297298** Mrs Salm.
Fax no: 01635 299934
D: £20.00-£25.00 .
Open: All Year
Beds: 1D 2T **Baths:** 2 En 1 Pr
🛏 (10) 🅿 (6) ⚄ 🖵 🛏 🕯 ⚄ 🏠 Ⓥ 🛅 ⚃

(1.5m 🚐) *11 Hook Rd, Kingsclere, Newbury, Berkshire, RG20 5PD.*
Actual grid ref: 531586
Grades: ETC 3 Diamond
Tel: **01635 298861** (also fax no)
Mr & Mrs Phillips.
D: £16.50-£16.50 **S:** £20.00-£20.00.
Open: All Year
Beds: 2T 1S **Baths:** 1 Sh
🛏 🅿 (5) ⚄ 🖵 🛏 🕯 🛏 ⚄ 🏠 Ⓥ 🛅 ⚃
Quiet, comfortable modern house in historic Kingsclere. Easy road access.

Dummer 5

National Grid Ref: SU5845

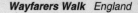 ◖ Queen Inn, Sun Inn

(On path 🚐) *Oakdown Farm, Dummer, Basingstoke, Hants, RG23 7LR.*
Actual grid ref: SU5845
Secluded modern farm bungalow next to M3 J7 on Wayfarers walk.
Grades: ETC 3 Diamond
Tel: **01256 397218** Mrs Hutton.
D: £17.50-£17.50 **S:** £20.00-£20.00.
Open: All Year
Beds: 1D 2T **Baths:** 1 Sh
🛏 (12) 🅿 (4) ⚄ 🖵 🛏 🏠 Ⓥ 🛅 ⚃

Many rates vary according to season - the lowest only are shown here

Itchen Stoke 6

National Grid Ref: SU5532

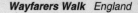 ◖ The Parsonage

(1m) *The Parsonage, Itchen Stoke, Alresford, Hants, SO24 0QU.*
Modern house, quiet rural setting, very central for touring.
Tel: **01962 732123**
Mrs Pitt.
D: £20.00-£20.00 **S:** £20.00.
Open: All Year (not Xmas)
Beds: 1T
Baths: 1 Sh
🅿 (20) 🛏 🕯 🏠 🛅 Ⓥ 🛅

Cheriton 7

National Grid Ref: SU5828

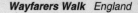 ◖ Flower Pots

(0.5m) *The Garden House, Cheriton, Alresford, Hampshire, SO24 0QQ.*
Edge of pretty village. Tennis court. Near Cheriton Battle Field. Personal tour by arrangement
Tel: **01962 771352**
Mrs Verney.
Fax no: 01962 771667
D: £20.00-£24.00
S: £20.00-£24.00.
Open: All Year
Beds: 2T 1D
Baths: 1 Pr 1 Sh
🛏 🅿 (4) ⚄ 🖵 🛏 🕯 🏠 🛅 Ⓥ ⚃

Denmead 8

National Grid Ref: SU6511

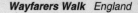 ◖ Bat & Ball

(0.25m) *Forest Gate, Hambledon Road, Denmead, Waterlooville, Hants, PO7 6EX.*
Private Georgian house set in two acres of garden.
Tel: **023 9225 5901** Mrs Cox.
D: £20.00-£24.00 **S:** £24.00-£28.00.
Open: All Year (not Xmas)
Beds: 2T
Baths: 2 En
🛏 (10) 🅿 (4) ⚄ 🖵 🛏 🕯 🏠 Ⓥ

Bedhampton 9

National Grid Ref: SU7006

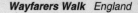 ◖ The Ship

(On path) *High Towers, 14 Portsdown Hill Road, Bedhampton, Havant, Hants, PO9 3JY.*
Modern house with superb views of countryside and sea.
Grades: ETC 3 Diamond
Tel: **023 9247 1748**
Mrs Boulton.
D: £18.00-£22.00
S: £22.00-£26.00.
Open: All Year
Beds: 1D 1T 12S
Baths: 4 En
🛏 (5) 🅿 (6) ⚄ 🖵 🛏 🏠 Ⓥ 🛅 ⚃

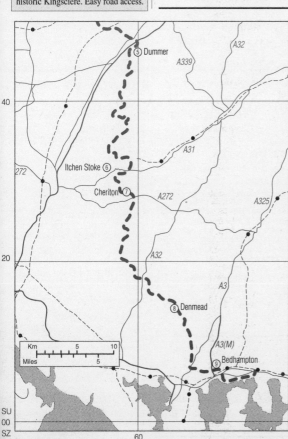

Wealdway

Gravesend is the starting point of this delightful 80-mile walk across Kent and Sussex. You leave the Thames Estuary and cross the North Downs, exploring the valleys round Luddesdown, to gain panoramic views of Kent's 'Garden of England' at Gover Hill on the Greensand Ridge, before wandering through orchards to join the Medway into Tonbridge. Once in Sussex, the path passes through thick woods to emerge onto the high open heathland of Ashdown Forest, and then heads off to the South Downs and the sea at Beachy Head. The **Wealdway** is fully waymarked with the initials WW on a yellow arrow.

Guides: *The Wealdway and the Vanguard Way* by Kev Reynolds (ISBN 0 9 023 63859), published by Cicerone Press and available directly from the publishers (2 Police Square, Milnthorpe, Cumbria, LA7 7PY, 01539 562069), £4.99 (+ 75p p&p)

The Wealdway by Geoffrey King (ISBN 0 951 6006 05), published by RA Kent & Sussex Areas and available from the Rambler's Association National Office (1/5 Wandsworth Road, London, SW8 2XX, tel. 020 7339 8500), £3.50 (+70p p&p)

Maps: Ordnance Survey 1:50000 Landranger series: 177, 188, 199

Gravesend   1

National Grid Ref: TQ6574

|●| ◖ Gravesend Boat

(On path) *48 Clipper Crescent, Riverview Park, Gravesend, Kent, DA12 4NN.*
Comfortable bedrooms. Close to A2/M2 frequent trains to London.
Tel: **01474 365360** Mrs Jeeves.
D: £17.00-£17.50 **S:** £17.50-£17.50.
Open: All Year (not Xmas)
Beds: 1T 1S **Baths:** 1 Sh
☼ (3) 🅿 (1) ⊬□ 🏃 ▥ ▨

Trottiscliffe   2

National Grid Ref: TQ6460

|●| ◖ The Plough

(0.5m) *Bramble Park, Church Lane, Trottiscliffe, West Malling, Kent, ME19 5EB.*
Actual grid ref: TQ644563
Secluded tranquil Victorian rectory in beautiful private parkland. Spacious comfortable.
Tel: **01732 822397** Mrs Towler.
D: £20.00-£20.00 **S:** £20.00-£20.00.
Open: All Year
Beds: 1F 1D 1S **Baths:** 1 Pr 2 Sh
☼ 🅿 (6) □ ▥ ▮

St Mary's Platt   3

National Grid Ref: TQ6057

|●| ◖ Brickmakers' Arms

(1m 🚗) *Stone Cottage, Maidstone Road, St Mary's Platt, Borough Green, Sevenoaks, Kent, TN15 8JH.*
Convenient M20/M25 and Brands Hatch. 40 minutes to London.
Tel: **01732 883098** Mrs Record.
D: £20.00-£20.00 **S:** £20.00-£20.00.
Open: All Year (not Xmas)
Beds: 1F 1D **Baths:** 1 Sh
☼ (3) 🅿 (10) ⊬□ 🏃 ▥ ▨ ⚡

Plaxtol   4

National Grid Ref: TQ6053

|●| ◖ Kentish Rifleman

(1.5m) *Periwick Place, The Street, Plaxtol, Sevenoaks, Kent, TN15 0QF.*
Early Victorian village house surrounded by mature pretty garden (visitors welcome to use this).
Tel: **01732 811024**
Mrs Golding.
D: £27.00-£27.00
S: £27.50-£27.50.
Open: All Year (not Xmas)
Beds: 1D 1T
Baths: 1 Sh
☼ (10) 🅿 (4) ⊬□ 🏃 ▥ ▨ ⚡

Hadlow   5

National Grid Ref: TQ6350

|●| ◖ Carpenters' Arms

(1.5m) *Dunsmore, Hadlow Park, Hadlow, Tonbridge, Kent, TN11 0HX.*
Private park, quiet, own entrance to ground floor accommodation.
Tel: **01732 850611** (also fax no)
Mrs Tubbs.
D: £18.00-£20.00
S: £20.00-£25.00.
Open: All Year (not Xmas)
Beds: 1T
Baths: 1 Pr
☼ 🅿 □ 🏃 ▥ ▨

Taking your dog?

Book *in advance*

ONLY with owners

who accept dogs (🐾)

East Peckham   6

National Grid Ref: TQ6648

|●| ◖ The Bush, Blackbird & Thrush

(0.25m) *Roydon Hall, off Seven Mile Lane, East Peckham, Tonbridge, Kent, TN12 5NH.*
Actual grid ref: TQ665517
Grades: ETC 3 Diamond
Tel: **01622 812121**
Mrs Bence.
Fax no: 01622 813959
D: £17.50-£22.50
S: £21.00-£55.00.
Open: All Year (not Xmas/New Year)
Beds: 4F 2D 6T 2S
Baths: 7 En 1 Pr 5 Sh
☼ 🅿 ⊬□ ✕ 🏃 ▥ ▨ ⚡
Very attractive 16th century manor in 10 acres of woodlands and gardens. Peaceful atmosphere, magnificent views. Comfortable rooms. Organic meals available. Less than one hour from central London, Dover and south coast. Perfect for exploring historic towns and beautiful houses and gardens of Kent and Sussex.

Tonbridge   7

National Grid Ref: TQ5946

|●| ◖ Kentish Rifleman, Chaser Inn

(0.5m) *Starvecrow Place, Starvecrow Hill, Shipbourne Road, Tonbridge, Kent, TN11 9NL.*
Relaxed luxury accommodation set in delightful woodlands. Heated outdoor swimming pool.
Tel: **01732 356863**
Mrs Batson.
D: £19.00-£22.00 **S:** £30.00-£30.00.
Open: All Year (not Xmas)
Beds: 2D 1T
Baths: 2 En 1 Pr
☼ (13) 🅿 (6) ⊬□ 🏃 ▥ ▨ ⚡

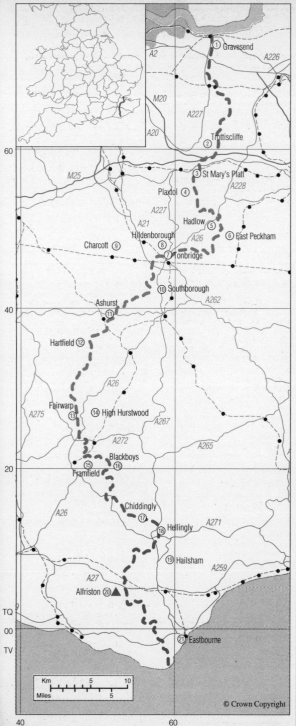

Hildenborough 8

National Grid Ref: TQ5648

¶ The Cockhorse

(0.3m) *150 Tonbridge Road,*
Hildenborough, Tonbridge, Kent,
TN11 9HW.
Warm friendly house. B245
between Tonbridge 2 miles;
Sevenoaks, M25 10 mins.
Tel: **01732 838894** Mrs Romney.
D: £12.50-£34.00 **S:** £15.00-£18.00.
Open: All Year (not Xmas)
Beds: 2T
Baths: 1 Sh
☺ 🅿 (2) ⽅⌷ 🔌 🛒 🎬 Ⓥ

Charcott 9

National Grid Ref: TQ5247

¶ The Greyhound

(2.75m 🚐) *Charcott Farmhouse,*
Charcott, Leigh, Tonbridge, Kent,
TN11 8LG.
Family home in glorious rural
setting. Home-made bread.
Free-range eggs. Guests lounge.
Grades: ETC 4 Diamond, Silver
Tel: **01892 870024**
Mr & Mrs Morris.
Fax no: 01892 870158
D: £45.00-£45.00 **S:** £30.00-£30.00.
Open: All Year (not Xmas/
New Year)
Beds: 3T
Baths: 2 En 1 Pr
☺ (5) 🅿 (4) ⽅⌷ 🐈 🔌 🎬 Ⓥ ✦

Southborough 10

National Grid Ref: TQ5842

¶ George & Dragon, The Imperial

(0.5m) *10 Modest Corner,*
Southborough, Tunbridge Wells,
Kent, TN4 0LS.
Situated in quiet, picturesque ham-
let away from traffic, within easy
reach of M25.
Tel: **01892 522450**
Ms Leemhuis.
D: £20.00-£22.50
S: £25.00-£30.00.
Open: All Year
Beds: 1D 2T
Baths: 1 Pr 1 Sh
☺ 🅿 (2) ⽅⌷ 🐈✕ 🔌 🎬 & Ⓥ ⓘ ✦

🚐 **sign means that,**
given due notice,
owners will pick you
up from the path
and drop you off
within reason.

Ashurst 11

National Grid Ref: TQ5138

(On path) *Manor Court Farm, Ashurst, Tunbridge Wells, Kent, TN3 9TB.*
Spacious Georgian farmhouse with lovely views. Working farm.
Tel: **01892 740279** Mrs Soyke.
D: £22.00-£24.00 **S:** £22.00-£30.00.
Open: All Year (not Xmas)
Beds: 1D 2T
Baths: 2 Sh
🛇 🅿 (10) 🗗 ⊁ �🏛, 🛱 ✓

Hartfield 12

National Grid Ref: TQ4735

⁑ ◁ Hay Wagon, Anchor Inn

(0.5m) *The Paddocks, Chuck Hatch, Hartfield, East Sussex, TN7 4EX.*
In the Ashdown Forest, 0.25 mile from Pooh Sticks Bridge. Walkers and children welcome.
Tel: **01892 770623** Ms McAll.
D: £19.00-£19.00 **S:** £19.00-£19.00.
Open: All Year (not Xmas)
Beds: 1D 1T 1S
Baths: 1 Pr 1 Sh
🛇 🅿 ⊁ 🗗 🖢 �🏛, �V

Fairwarp 13

National Grid Ref: TQ4626

⁑ ◁ The Foresters

(0.25m) *Broom Cottage, Browns Brook, Fairwarp, Uckfield, E Sussex, TN22 3BY.*
Victorian cottage in lovely garden on Ashdown Forest. Very peaceful.
Tel: **01825 712942**
D: £20.00-£25.00 **S:** £25.00-£25.00.
Open: All Year
Beds: 1D 1T **Baths:** 1 Sh
🛇 🅿 ⊁ 🗗 🖢 �🏛, 🛱

High Hurstwood 14

National Grid Ref: TQ4926

⁑ ◁ Crown & Gate, Maypole Inn, White Hart

(0.75m) *Chillies Granary, High Hurstwood, Crowborough, E. Sussex, TN6 3TB.*
Actual grid ref: TQ497278
Awarded 2nd place in 'B&B of the Year' by SEETB.
Grades: ETC 4 Diamond
Tel: **01892 655560** (also fax no)
Mr & Mrs Peck.
D: £23.00-£27.00 **S:** £25.00-£45.00.
Open: Mar to Dec
Beds: 1F 1D 1T **Baths:** 2 En 1 Pr
🛇 🅿 (6) ⊁ 🗗 🖢 �🏛, �V 🛱 ✓

S = Price range for a single person in a single room

(2m 🚗) *Tronning, Coombelands, Wittersham, Rye, Kent, TN30 7NU.*
Actual grid ref: TQ496233
Situated in quiet village between Rye and Tenterden. Good touring area. **Grades:** AA 3 Diamond, RAC 3 Diamond
Tel: **01797 207768** (also fax no)
Mrs Brown.
D: £20.00-£25.00 **S:** £20.00-£25.00.
Open: All Year
Beds: 1D 1T 1S **Baths:** 1 En 1 Sh
🛇 🅿 (4) ⊁ 🗗 🖢 �🏛, �V ✓

Framfield 15

National Grid Ref: TQ4920

(1m 🚗) *Beggars Barn, Barn Lane, Framfield, Uckfield, E Sussex, TN22 5RX.*
Actual grid ref: TQ510215
Unique C18th converted barn with enchanting separate accommodation. Tel: **01825 890869**
Fax no: 01825 890868
D: £20.00-£20.00 **S:** £25.00-£25.00.
Open: All Year (not Xmas)
Beds: 1F 1D **Baths:** 1 En
🅿 (2) 🗗 ⊁ 🖢 🖢 �V 🛱 ✓

Blackboys 16

National Grid Ref: TQ5220

(▲ 0.75m) *Blackboys Youth Hostel, Blackboys, Uckfield, East Sussex, TN22 5HU.*
Actual grid ref: TQ521215
Tel: **01825 890607**
Under 18: £6.50 **Adults:** £9.25
Self-catering facilities, Showers, Laundry facilities, Lounge, Drying room, Cycle store, Parking, No smoking, WC, Kitchen facilities, Luggage store, Credit cards accepted
This rustic wooden cabin in a deciduous sylvan setting offers good basic accommodation with a cosy open fire, spacious lounge/dining room & kitchen.

Chiddingly 17

National Grid Ref: TQ5414

⁑ ◁ Six Bells

(0.5m 🚗) *Hale Farm House, Chiddingly, Lewes, E Sussex, BN8 6HQ.*
Grades: ETC 3 Diamond
Tel: **01825 872619** (also fax no)
Mrs Burrough.
D: £18.00-£25.00 **S:** £18.00-£25.00.
Open: All Year
Beds: 1F 2T **Baths:** 1 En 1 Sh
🛇 🅿 (3) ⊁ 🗗 🖢 ✕ 🖢 �🏛, �V 🛱 ✓
Relax in spacious rooms of this 14th century Listed beamed farmhouse, situated on Weald Way over looking the South Downs, 12 miles from Eastbourne. Extensive gardens, meadows, woods, stream. Good walking, horse riding. Ponies available. Also Shakespeare and language courses.

(0.5m 🚗) *'Holmes Hill', Holmes Hill, Chiddingly, Lewes, E. Sussex, BN8 6JA.*
Actual grid ref: TQ533127
Cosy, modernised, C18th cottage. Ideal for touring Glyndebourne, Eastbourne, Sussex Coast.
Tel: **01825 872746**
Mr & Mrs Farrier.
D: £20.00-£20.00 **S:** £25.00-£25.00.
Open: All Year (not Xmas)
Beds: 1D 1T **Baths:** 2 Pr
🛇 (3) 🅿 (3) ⊁ 🗗 🖢 �🏛, �V ✓

Hellingly 18

National Grid Ref: TQ5812

⁑ ◁ Horse & Groom

(0.25m 🚗) *Grove Hill House, Hellingly, Hailsham, E Sussex, BN27 4HG.*
Actual grid ref: TQ601139
Period farmhouse in beautiful quiet setting in over 2 acres of grounds.
Tel: **01435 812440** (also fax no)
Mrs Berthon.
D: £19.00-£22.00 **S:** £25.00-£30.00.
Open: All Year
Beds: 1D 1T **Baths:** 1 En 1 Pr
🛇 🅿 (4) ⊁ �🏛, 🛱

Hailsham 19

National Grid Ref: TQ5809

⁑ ◁ Merry Harriers

(1m 🚗) *Longleys Farm Cottage, Harebeating Lane, Hailsham, E Sussex, BN27 1ER.*
Actual grid ref: TQ597104
Quiet country location near prime tourist attractions informal and friendly.
Grades: ETC 3 Diamond
Tel: **01323 841227** (also fax no)
Hook.
D: £18.00-£18.00 **S:** £20.00-£25.00.
Open: All Year
Beds: 1F 1D 1T
Baths: 2 En 1 Pr
🛇 🅿 (4) ⊁ 🗗 🖢 ✕ 🖢 �🏛, �V 🛱 ✓

(1m) *Windesworth, Carters Corner, Hailsham, E Sussex, BN27 4HT.*
Comfortable family home in quiet location with lovely views.
Grades: ETC 4 Diamond
Tel: **01323 847178** Mr Toye.
Fax no: 01323 440696
D: £20.00-£24.00 **S:** £20.00-£24.00.
Open: Apr to Nov
Beds: 1D 1T
Baths: 1 En 1 Sh
🛇 (1) 🅿 (3) ⊁ 🗗 🖢 �🏛, �V

All rates are subject to alteration at the owners' discretion.

Alfriston 20

National Grid Ref: TQ5103

🍴 🍺 Wingrove Inn, Ye Olde Smuggler's Inn, The George

(▲2.5m) *Alfriston Youth Hostel,*
Frog Firle, Alfriston, Polegate,
East Sussex, BN26 5TT.
Actual grid ref: TQ518019
Tel: **01323 870423**
Under 18: £6.90 **Adults:** £10.00
Self-catering facilities, Showers,
Wet weather shelter, Lounge,
Drying room, Parking, Evening
meal at 6.30pm, WC, Kitchen facil-
ities, Breakfast available, Credit
cards accepted
*A comfortable Sussex country
house dating from 1530, set in
Cuckmere Valley with views over
river and Litlington.*

(2.5m 🚐) *Meadowbank,* Sloe
Lane, Alfriston, East Sussex,
BN26 5UR.
Tel: **01323 870742** Mrs Petch.
D: £20.00-£25.00 **S:** £30.00-£35.00.
Open: All Year (not Xmas/
New Year)
Beds: 1T 2D **Baths:** 1 En 2 Sh
🅿 (4) ⏍ 🖵 🛏 🚲 🍽 🛏 & ▢ ⌇
*The beautiful private dwelling in
tranquil setting, offers views of
Cuckmere Valley and South
Downs. only 3 minutes walk
village centre. Ideal for
walkers/cyclists. Private car park.
Lovely gardens and conservatory in
which to relax. Delicious English
breakfast.*

(2.5m) *Dacres,* Alfriston, Polegate,
East Sussex, BN26 5TP.
Country cottage. Beautiful gardens.
Near South Downs Way
Glyndebourne, Seven Sisters.
Tel: **01323 870447** Mrs Embry.
D: £25.00-£25.00 **S:** £40.00.
Open: All Year
Beds: 1T **Baths:** 1 Pr
🅿 (1) ⏍ 🖵 🚲 🍽 & ▢

Eastbourne 21

National Grid Ref: TQ5900

🍴 🍺 The Marine, Town House, Castle Inn, Lamb Inn, The Beach, The Waterfront, The Pilot, The Alexander

(▲1m) *Eastbourne Youth Hostel,*
East Dean Road, Eastbourne, East
Sussex, BN20 8ES.
Actual grid ref: TV588990
Tel: **01323 721081**
Under 18: £6.90 **Adults:** £10.00
Self-catering facilities, Showers,
Lounge, Dining room, Drying room,
Cycle store, Parking Limited, No
smoking, WC, Kitchen facilities,
Credit cards accepted
*Former golf clubhouse on South
Downs, 450 ft above sea level with
sweeping views across Eastbourne
& Pevensey Bay.*

(1.5m) *Heatherdene Hotel,*
26-28 Elms Avenue, Eastbourne,
E. Sussex, BN21 3DN.
Grades: ETC 3 Diamond
Tel: **01323 723598** (also fax no)
Mrs Mockford.
D: £17.00-£45.00 **S:** £16.00-£25.00.
Open: All Year
Beds: 1F 4D 8T 3S
Baths: 6 En 3 Sh
🛏 🖵 🛏 🍽 🚲 🍽 & ▢
You will find good food and com-
fortable rooms at the Heatherdene.
This family-run licensed hotel, set
in a pleasant avenue, is close to the
sea front and town centre. Train
and coach stations are nearby, as
are the theatres.

(2m) *Sheldon Hotel,*
9-11 Burlington Place, Eastbourne,
East Sussex, BN21 4AS.
Situated within a few minutes walk
of sea front, theatres. Licensed.
Tel: **01323 724120**
Fax no: 01323 430406
D: £24.00-£27.00 **S:** £24.00-£27.00.
Open: All Year
Beds: 4F 6T 8D 6S
Baths: 24 En
🛏 🅿 🖵 🛏 🍽 🛏 ▢ ⌇

(2m) *Innisfree House,* 130a Royal
Parade, Eastbourne, East Sussex,
BN22 7JY.
Tel: **01323 646777** (also fax no)
Mrs Petrie.
D: £19.00-£20.00 **S:** £25.00-£30.00.
Open: All Year (not Xmas)
Beds: 1F 1D 1T
Baths: 3 En
🛏 ⏍ 🖵 🚲 🍽 ▢
Small family-run B&B on seafront,
close to amenities, refurbished to
high standards. Exclusive location
with sea views, easy parking on
road outside. Motorcycle storage.
Stay a day or stay a week, your
comfort & praise we aim to seek.

(2m) *Cherry Tree Hotel,*
15 Silverdale Road, Eastbourne,
E. Sussex, BN20 7AJ.
Actual grid ref: TV612982
Award-winning family-run hotel,
close to sea front, downlands and
theatres.
Grades: ETC 4 Diamond, Silver
Tel: **01323 722406**
Mr Henley.
Fax no: 01323 648838
D: £26.00-£33.00 **S:** £26.00-£33.00.
Open: All Year
Beds: 1F 3D 4T 2S
Baths: 10 En
🛏 (7) ⏍ 🖵 🍽 🚲 🍽 ▢ 🛏

**All paths are
popular: you are
well-advised to
book ahead**

(2m) *Ambleside Private Hotel,*
24 Elms Avenue, Eastbourne,
E. Sussex, BN21 3DN.
Tel: **01323 724991** Mr Pattenden.
D: £18.00-£18.00 **S:** £18.00-£25.00.
Open: All Year
Beds: 4D 4T 2S
Baths: 2 Sh 2 En
🖵 🛏 🍽 🛏 🍽 ▢ ⌇
Situated on quiet avenue adjacent
to seafront, pier, town centre, the-
atres, convenient for railway and
coach stations. Short distance from
South Downs Way, Wealdway.
Colour TV in bedrooms. Compliant
with environmental and fire
regulations.

(0.75m) *Southcroft Hotel,*
15 South Cliff Avenue, Eastbourne,
E. Sussex, BN20 7AL.
Actual grid ref: TV609979
Friendly, family-run, non-smoking
hotel. Close to Downs, sea and
theatre.
Grades: ETC 4 Diamond
Tel: **01323 729071** Mrs Skriczka.
D: £25.00-£28.00 **S:** £25.00-£28.00.
Open: All Year
Beds: 3D 2T 1S **Baths:** 6 En
⏍ 🖵 🍽 🚲 🍽 ▢ ⌇

(2m) *Camberley Hotel,* 27-29 Elms
Avenue, Eastbourne, E. Sussex,
BN21 3DN.
Tel: **01323 723789**
D: £18.00-£21.00 **S:** £18.00-£21.00.
Open: Mar to Oct
Beds: 4F 3D 3T 2S
Baths: 7 En 2 Sh
🛏 🅿 (3) 🖵 🍽 🚲 ▢ 🛏
Situated in a pleasant avenue close
to town centre, sea front and all
amenities. Licensed, ensuite, tea-
making, colour TV in bedrooms.
English breakfast.

(2m) *The Manse,* 7 Dittons Road,
Eastbourne, East Sussex, BN21 1DW.
Tel: **01323 737851** Mrs Walker.
D: £15.00-£20.00 **S:** £20.00-£25.00.
Open: All Year (not Xmas)
Beds: 1F 2T **Baths:** 2 En 1 Pr
🛏 (8) 🅿 (1) 🖵 🍽 🍽 ▢ 🛏 ⌇
Originally a Presbyterian manse,
this character house is located in a
quiet area yet within 5 minutes'
walk of the town centre with its
shops, restaurants and theatres.
Seafront, South Downs, castles and
Downland villages nearby.

(1m) *Edelweiss Hotel,* 10-12 Elms
Avenue, Eastbourne, E. Sussex,
BN21 3DN.
Central family-run Hotel just off
sea front. Comfortable and wel-
coming.
Grades: ETC 3 Diamond
Tel: **01323 732071** (also fax no)
Mr & Mrs Butler.
D: £16.00-£20.00 **S:** £16.00-£25.00.
Open: All Year
Beds: 1F 6D 5T 2S
Baths: 3 En 4 Sh
🛏 🖵 🍽 🚲 🍽 ▢ 🛏 ⌇

(2m) *Cromwell Private Hotel,*
23 Cavendish Place, Eastbourne,
E. Sussex, BN21 3EJ.
Family run hotel in Victorian Town
House (1851). Centrally located.
Grades: ETC 4 Diamond
Tel: **01323 725288** (also fax no)
Mr & Mrs Millar.
D: £19.00-£24.00
S: £19.00-£23.00.
Open: Easter to Nov
Beds: 2F 3D 3T 3S
Baths: 5 Pr 2 Sh
🌅🗖✕🛒📺.Ⓥ🛂

(2m) *Courtlands Hotel,* 68 Royal
Parade, Eastbourne, E. Sussex,
BN22 7AQ.
Seafront position, business/touring
base.
Tel: **01323 721068**
D: £20.00-£25.00 **S:** £20.00-£25.00.
Open: All Year
Beds: 3F 2D 1T 2S
Baths: 3 En 1 Pr
🌅🄿(2)🗖✕🛒Ⓥ🛂⚡

(2m) *La Mer Guest House,*
7 Marine Road, Eastbourne,
E. Sussex, BN22 7AU.
Just 50 yards from Eastbourne's
beautiful seafront and beach easy
access to South Downs
Tel: **01323 724926** Mrs Byrne.
D: £18.00-£24.00 **S:** £18.00-£24.00.
Open: May to Sep
Beds: 2D 2T 2S
Baths: 2 En
🌅(14)🄿🗖✕🛒📺.Ⓥ🛂

(2m) *Channel View Hotel,*
57 Royal Parade, Eastbourne,
E. Sussex, BN22 7AQ.
A friendly family-run seafront
hotel situated opposite the Redoubt
Gardens.
Tel: **01323 736730**
Fax no: 01323 644299
D: £17.00-£22.00 **S:** £22.00-£32.00.
Open: All Year (not Xmas)
Beds: 1F 2D 3T 2S
Baths: 4 En 1 Sh
🌅🗖✕✕🛒📺.Ⓥ

(2m 🚐) *Beachy Rise,* 20 Beachy
Head Road, Eastbourne, E. Sussex,
BN20 7QN.
In Meads village near Beachy Head
and sea and university. Ensuite
bedrooms.
Tel: **01323 639171**
D: £22.00-£28.00 **S:** £25.00-£29.00.
Open: All Year
Beds: 1F 4D 1T
Baths: 6 En
🌅(1)🗖🛒📺.Ⓥ🛂⚡

(2m) *Downland Hotel,* 37 Lewes
Road, Eastbourne, East Sussex,
BN21 2BU.
Charming small hotel, ideally
located for all main amenities and
commercial centre.
Tel: **01323 732689**
Fax no: 01323 720321
D: £25.00-£37.50 **S:** £30.00-£40.00.
Open: All Year
Beds: 2F 7D 2T 1S
Baths: 12 En
🄿(9)✕🗖✕🛒📺.Ⓥ🛂⚡

STILWELL'S BRITAIN CYCLEWAY COMPANION

23 Long Distance Cycleways * Where to Stay * Where to Eat

County Cycleways – Sustrans Routes

The first guide of its kind, **Stilwell's Britain Cycleway Companion** makes planning accommodation for your cycling trip easy. It lists B&Bs, hostels, campsites and pubs– in the order they appear along the selected cycleways – allowing the cyclist to book ahead. No more hunting for a room, a hot meal or a cold drink after a long day in the saddle. Stilwell's gives descriptions of the featured routes and includes such relevant information as maps, grid references and distance from route; Tourist Board ratings; and the availability of drying facilities and packed lunches. No matter which route – or part of a route – you decide to ride, let the **Cycleway Companion** show you where to sleep and eat.

As essential as your tyre pump – the perfect cycling companion: **Stilwell's Britain Cycleway Companion**.

Cycleways Sustrans
Carlisle to Inverness – Clyde to Forth - Devon Coast to Coast - Hull to Harwich – Kingfisher Cycle Trail - Lon Las Cymru – Sea to Sea (C2C) – Severn and Thames - West Country Way – White Rose Cycle Route

County
Round Berkshire Cycle Route – Cheshire Cycleway – Cumbria Cycleway – Essex Cycle Route – Icknield Way - Lancashire Cycleway – Leicestershire County Cycleway – Oxfordshire Cycleway – Reivers Cycle Route – South Downs Way - Surrey Cycleway – Wiltshire Cycleway – Yorkshire Dales Cycleway

£9.95 from all good bookstores (ISBN 1-900861-26-7) or £10.95 (inc p&p) from Stilwell Publishing, 59 Charlotte Road, London EC2A 3QW (020 7739 7179)

Wessex Ridgeway

The **Wessex Ridgeway** should be seen as part of the Ramblers' Association's great project to establish a long distance route along 'the Great Ridgeway', an ancient highway that probably ran from Devon to the East Anglian coast along England's great chalk ridge. This path thus links up with **The Ridgeway** itself, which meets the **Icknield Way**, which in turn touches the **Peddars Way** to create a 250-mile route from the South Coast up to Norfolk. The **Wessex Ridgeway** has been waymarked with support from the **Countryside Commission** and the county councils. From Avebury with its massive stone circle you skirt Salisbury Plain to pass through the great hinterland of

Hardy's Wessex - prehistoric sites, hill forts, high chalk downland, lonely coombes and the Cerne Abbas giant - before heading off to the English Channel at Lyme Regis.

Guides: *Walk the Wessex Ridgeway in Dorset* by Priscilla Houstoun (ISBN 0 948 699 37 X), published by Dorset Publishing Company and available from all good map shops or directly from the publishers (c/o Wincanton Press, National School, North Street, Wincanton, Somerset, BA9 9AT, tel. 01963 32583), £7 (inc. p&p)

Maps: Ordnance Survey 1:50000 Landranger series: 173, 183, 184, 193, 194, 195

Marlborough 1

National Grid Ref: SU1869

🍴 🍺 Bear, Roebuck, Sun, Oddfellows Arms

(0.5m) *Browns Farm,*
Marlborough, Wilts, SN8 4ND.
Actual grid ref: SU198678
Peaceful farmhouse on edge of Savernake Forest. Overlooking open farmland.
Tel: **01672 515129**
Mrs Crockford.
D: £16.00-£20.00 **S:** £20.00-£25.00.
Open: All Year
Beds: 1F 1T 2D
Baths: 1 En 1 Sh
🛇 🅿 (6) 乡 🖵 🍴 🕭 🎟 🅥 🛊

(0.25m) *Beam End, 67 George*
Lane, Marlborough, Wilts, SN8 4BY.
Peaceful detached house, every comfort, good centre for touring Wiltshire.
Grades: ETC 3 Diamond
Tel: **01672 515048** (also fax no)
Mrs Drew.
D: £20.00-£27.50 **S:** £20.00-£30.00.
Open: All Year (not Xmas)
Beds: 1T 2S
Baths: 1 En 1 Sh
🅿 (3) 乡 🖵 🕭 🎟 🅥 🛊

(0.25m) *54 George Lane,*
Marlborough, Wiltshire, SN8 4BY.
Near town centre. Detached house - Large garden. Non smokers only.
Tel: **01672 512579**
Mr & Mrs Young.
D: £17.00 **S:** £17.00.
Open: All Year (not Xmas/ New Year)
Beds: 1T 2S
Baths: 1 Sh
🅿 (3) 乡 🕭 🎟 🅥 ✦

(0.5m 🚗) *West View, Barnfield,*
Marlborough, Wiltshire, SN8 2AX.
Delightful peaceful, rural home, close to town. Ideal walkers, cyclists.
Grades: ETC 3 Diamond
Tel: **01672 515583**
Maggie Trevelyan-Hall.
Fax no: 01672 519014
D: £20.00-£25.00 **S:** £35.00-£45.00.
Open: All Year
Beds: 1F 3D **Baths:** 2 Pr 1 Sh
🛇 🅿 (3) 乡 🖵 🍴 🕭 🎟 🅦 🅥 🛊 ✦

(0.25m 🚗) *Cartref, 63 George*
Lane, Marlborough, Wilts, SN8 4BY.
Actual grid ref: SU1969
Family home near town centre. Ideal for Avebury, Savernake, Wiltshire Downs.
Tel: **01672 512771** Mrs Harrison.
D: £18.00-£18.00 **S:** £20.00-£20.00.
Open: All Year (not Xmas)
Beds: 1F 1D 1T **Baths:** 1 Sh
🛇 (6) 🅿 (2) 🍴 🎟 🛊 ✦

Lockeridge 2

National Grid Ref: SU1467

🍴 🍺 Who'd A Thought It

(3m 🚗) *The Taffrail, Back Lane,*
Lockeridge, Marlborough, Wilts,
SN8 4ED.
Actual grid ref: SU150675
Great welcome, comfort, tranquillity. Delightful modern home and lovely garden.
Tel: **01672 861266** (also fax no)
Mrs Spencer.
D: £17.50-£17.50 **S:** £20.00-£20.00.
Open: Jan to Nov
Beds: 1D 1T 1S
Baths: 1 Sh
🛇 (8) 🅿 (3) 乡 🖵 🎟 ✦

Avebury 3

National Grid Ref: SU1069

🍴 🍺 Waggon & Horses, Red Lion

(On path 🚗) *6 Beckhampton*
Road, Avebury, Marlborough,
Wilts, SN8 1QT.
Nearby Avebury Stone Circle, Ridgeway Walk, Silbury Hill, bus route.
Tel: **01672 539588** Mrs Dixon.
D: £16.00-£20.00 **S:** £25.00-£30.00.
Open: All Year (not Xmas)
Beds: 1D 1T **Baths:** 1 Sh
🛇 🅿 (6) 🖵 🕭 🎟 🅥 🛊 ✦

Pay B&Bs by
cash or cheque and
be prepared to
pay up front.

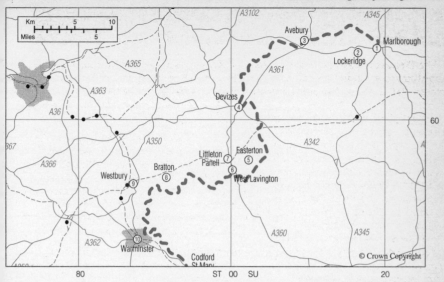

© Crown Copyright

Devizes 4

National Grid Ref: SU0061

⊯ ◁ Barge, Bell, Bridge, Bear, Black Swan, Churchill, George & Dragon, Royal Oak, Stage Post, Moonrakers, Elm Tree, Four Seasons, Owl

(0.5m) *Lower Foxhangers Farm, Rowde, Devizes, Wilts, SN10 1SS.*
Grades: ETC 3 Diamond
Tel: **01380 828254** (also fax no)
Mr & Mrs Fletcher.
D: £20.00-£22.00 **S:** £22.00-£25.00.
Open: May to Oct
Beds: 2D 1T **Baths:** 1 Pr 2 En
🖾 🖫 (4) ⊬ ☐ ☞ 👗 🎹 Ⓥ ⚡
Relax with pleasant dreams in our rural retreat amid the Wiltshire countryside. Roam the canal towpaths and see the gaily painted narrow boats as they lazily glide through the rippling water or climb the unrivalled flight of Caen Hill Locks.

(0.5m) 🚐 *Craven House, Station Road, Devizes, Wilts, SN10 1BZ.*
Victorian house 50 yards from centre for restaurants and pubs.
Tel: **01380 723514** Mrs Shaw.
D: £20.00 **S:** £20.00.
Open: All Year
Beds: 1F 1D 2T
Baths: 2 En 1 Pr 1 Sh
🖾 ☐ ✕ 👗 🎹 Ⓥ 🛈 ⚡

(0.5m) *Asta, 66 Downlands Road, Devizes, Wilts, SN10 5EF.*
Comfortable, modern house in quiet road, 15 minutes from town centre.
Tel: **01380 722546**
Mrs Milne-Day.
D: £16.00 **S:** £16.00.
Open: All Year
Beds: 1D 2S **Baths:** 1 Sh
🖾 🖫 (2) ☐ ☞ ✕ 🎹

(0.5m) *Glenholme Guest House, 77 Nursteed Road, Devizes, Wilts, SN10 3AJ.*
Friendly, comfortable house. Warm welcome. Lovely historic town.
Tel: **01380 723187** Mrs Bishop.
D: £18.00-£18.00 **S:** £20.00-£20.00.
Open: All Year
Beds: 1F 1T
Baths: 1 Sh
🖾 🖫 ☐ ☞ ✕ 👗 🎹 Ⓥ 🛈

(0.5m) 🚐 *Gate House, Wick Lane, Devizes, Wilts, SN10 5DW.*
Large house and garden, not on main road. Bath/Salisbury 25 miles.
Tel: **01380 725283** Mrs Stratton.
Fax no: 01380 722382
D: £20.00-£20.00 **S:** £22.50-£22.50.
Open: All Year (not Xmas)
Beds: 1D 1T 1S
Baths: 1 En 1 Sh
🖫 (6) ⊬ ☐ 👗 🎹 Ⓥ ⚡

(0.5m) *The Chestnuts, Potterne Road, Devizes, Wiltshire, SN10 5DD.*
Actual grid ref: SU006608
Good base for Bath, Salisbury, Stonehenge, Avebury and Kennet & Avon Canal.
Tel: **01380 724532** Mrs Mortimer.
D: £20.00-£25.00 **S:** £25.00-£25.00.
Open: All Year (not Xmas)
Beds: 1F 1T **Baths:** 2 En
🖾 🖫 (2) ⊬ ☐ 👗 🎹 Ⓥ 🛈 ⚡

All paths are popular:

you are well-advised to

book ahead

Easterton 5

National Grid Ref: SU0255

⊯ ◁ Royal Oak

(1m) 🚐 *Eastcott Manor, Easterton, Devizes, Wilts, SN10 4PL.*
Actual grid ref: SU027358
Elizabethan manor house in own grounds. Tranquil location.
Grades: ETC 3 Diamond,
AA 3 Diamond
Tel: **01380 813313** Mrs Firth.
D: £22.00-£25.00 **S:** £22.00-£25.00.
Open: All Year (not Xmas)
Beds: 1D 1T 2S **Baths:** 2 En 2 Pr
🖾 🖫 (20) ☐ ☞ ✕ 👗 🎹 🛈 ⚡

West Lavington 6

National Grid Ref: SU0052

⊯ ◁ Bridge

(1m) *Parsonage House, West Lavington, Devizes, Wilts, SN10 4LT.*
Welcoming relaxed family home in peaceful surroundings overlooking the church.
Tel: **01380 813345** Mrs West.
D: £20.00-£25.00 **S:** £25.00-£30.00.
Open: All Year (not Xmas/ New Year)
Beds: 1D 1T **Baths:** 1 Sh
🖾 🖫 (3) ⊬ ☐ ✕ 👗 🎹 Ⓥ 🛈 ⚡

(1m) *The Stage Post, 9 High Street, West Lavington, Devizes, Wilts, SN10 4HQ.*
Traditional country inn close to edge of Salisbury Plain, oak-beamed conservatory restaurant.
Tel: **01380 813392** Mrs Irwin.
Fax no: 01380 818539
D: £25.00-£35.00 **S:** £35.00-£40.00.
Open: All Year
Beds: 1F 5D 1T 2S **Baths:** 9 En
🖾 🖫 (35) ☐ ✕ 👗 🎹 Ⓥ 🛈 ⚡

Littleton Panell 7

National Grid Ref: ST9954

🍴 🍺 Stage Post, Owl

(1m 🚌) *Littleton Lodge, Littleton Panell, Devizes, Wilts, SN10 4ES.*
Actual grid ref: ST998542
Comfortable Victorian house. In conservation village, gardens, good pubs nearby.
Grades: ETC 4 Diamond,
AA 4 Diamond
Tel: **01380 813131**
Mr & Mrs Linton.
Fax no: 01380 816969
D: £22.50-£25.00 **S:** £30.00-£40.00.
Open: All Year
Beds: 2D 1T
Baths: 3 En
🛏 🅿 (5) ⅏ 🗆 ≜ 🖾 ⅋ 🖫 🛇 🗎 ⚡

Bratton 8

National Grid Ref: ST9152

🍴 🍺 Duke

(0.5m) *The Duke Inn, Melbourne Street, Bratton, Westbury, Wilts, BA13 4RW.*
Actual grid ref: ST880540
Traditional oak-beamed village inn serving good fresh food, real ale.
Grades: AA 2 Diamond
Tel: **01380 830242** Mr Overend.
Fax no: 01380 831239
D: £22.50-£25.00 **S:** £25.00-£30.00.
Open: All Year
Beds: 2D 1T
Baths: 2 Sh
🛏 (14) 🅿 (30) ⅏ 🗆 ✗ ≜ 🖾 ⅋ 🖫 🛇 🗎 ⚡

Bringing children with you? Always ask for any special rates.

D = Price range per person sharing in a double room

Westbury 9

National Grid Ref: ST8650

🍴 🍺 Full Moon

(0.75m 🚌) *Brokerswood House, Brokerswood, Westbury, Wilts, BA13 4EH.*
Situated in front of 80 acres of woodland, open to the public.
Tel: **01373 823428** Mrs Phillips.
D: £15.00-£18.00 **S:** £15.00-£18.00.
Open: All Year (not Xmas)
Beds: 3F 1D 1T 1S
Baths: 1 En 1 Pr 1 Sh
🛏 (1) 🅿 (6) ⅏ 🗆 ≜ 🖾 ⅋ 🖫 🛇 🗎 ⚡

Warminster 10

National Grid Ref: ST8745

🍴 🍺 Old Bell

(0.25m) *Belmont, 9 Boreham Road, Warminster, BA12 9JP.*
Grades: ETC 4 Diamond
Tel: **01985 212799** (also fax no)
Mrs Monkcom.
D: £17.00-£20.00 **S:** £16.00-£25.00.
Open: All Year
Beds: 2D **Baths:** 1 Sh
🛏 (5) 🅿 (6) ⅏ 🗆 ≜ 🖾 🖫 🛇 ⚡
Well-situated for town, spacious rooms, friendly welcome, good facilities.

(0.25m) *Farmers Hotel, 1 Silver Street, Warminster, Wilts, BA12 8PS.*
Comfortable family hotel Listed C17th Grade II building.
Tel: **01985 213815** (also fax no)
Mr Brandani.
D: £16.00-£17.50 **S:** £17.00-£25.00.
Open: All Year
Beds: 4F 5D 2T 1OS
Baths: 13 En 3 Sh
🛏 🅿 (5) 🗆 🛇 ✗ ≜ 🖾 🖫 🗎 ⚡

Codford St Mary 11

National Grid Ref: ST9739

🍴 🍺 Angel

(1m) *Glebe Cottage, Church Lane, Codford St. Mary, Warminster, Wiltshire, BA12 0PJ.*
Grades: ETC 4 Diamond, Silver
Tel: **01985 850565**
Mrs Richardson-Aitken.
Fax no: 01985 850666
D: £25.00-£27.00 **S:** £25.00-£27.00.
Open: All Year (not Xmas/ New Year)
Beds: 1F 1T
Baths: 2 Pr
🛏 (3) 🅿 (3) ⅏ 🗆 ≜ 🖾 🖫 🛇
Glebe Cottage, a 250 year old former home of the Sexton, is situated in the attractive Wylye Valley. Close to Salisbury Plain and Anzac war graves. Convenient for Salisbury, Bath and Stonehenge.

Hindon 12

National Grid Ref: ST9132

(0.5m) *Chicklade Lodge, Chicklade, Hindon, Salisbury, Wilts, SP3 5SU.*
Charming Victorian cottage. Under 2 hour drive from Heathrow.
Tel: **01747 820389** Mrs Jerram.
D: £20.00-£20.00 **S:** £25.00-£25.00.
Open: All Year
Beds: 2T 1D
Baths: 1 Sh
🛏 (5) 🅿 (4) ⅏ 🗆 🛇 ✗ ≜ 🖾 🗎

Planning a longer stay? Always ask for any special rates.

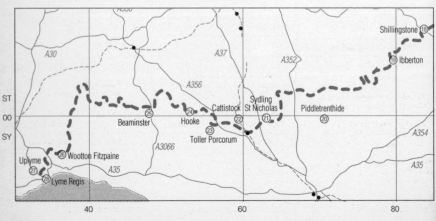

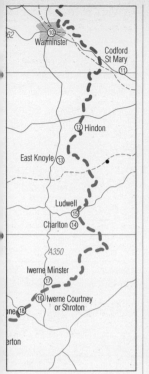

East Knoyle 13

National Grid Ref: ST8830

🍴 🍺 Fox & Hounds

(1m 🚌) *Moors Farmhouse, East Knoyle, Salisbury, Wilts, SP3 6BU.*
Actual grid ref: ST863301
C17th farmhouse suite of large rooms. Naturally beautiful/interesting area.
Tel: **01747 830385** Mrs Reading.
D: £25.00-£25.00 **S:** £25.00-£25.00.
Open: All Year (not Xmas)
Beds: 1T **Baths:** 1 En
🛏 (8) 🅿 (2) 🖵 🛏 🎞 Ⓥ 🛆 ⚡

Charlton (Shaftesbury) 14

National Grid Ref: ST9022

🍴 🍺 Grove Arms, Talbot

(On path) *Charnwood Cottage, Charlton, Shaftesbury, Dorset, SP7 9LZ.*
Actual grid ref: ST902226
C17th thatched cottage with lovely garden. Good base for touring.
Tel: **01747 828310** (also fax no)
Mr & Mrs Morgan.
D: £18.00-£19.00 **S:** £20.00.
Open: All Year (not Xmas/New Year)
Beds: 1T 1D **Baths:** 1 Sh
🛏 (5) 🅿 (2) 🖵 🍴 🎞

Ludwell 15

National Grid Ref: ST9122

🍴 🍺 Rising Sun

(0.5m) *Ye Olde Wheelwrights, Birdbush, Ludwell, Shaftesbury, Dorset, SP7 9NH.*
Accommodation in separate annexe. Children and families welcome. Hearty breakfast.
Tel: **01747 828955** Dieppe.
D: £17.50-£20.00 **S:** £20.00-£22.00.
Open: April to October
Beds: 1T 1D
Baths: 1 Sh
🛏 🅿 ⚡ 🖵 🛏 Ⓥ

Iwerne Courtney or Shroton 16

National Grid Ref: ST8512

🍴 🍺 Cricketers

(On path) *Lattemere, Frog Lane, Iwerne Courtney or Shroton, Blandford Forum, Dorset, DT11 8QL.*
Actual grid ref: ST860129
Comfortable welcoming home in quiet picturesque village. Outstanding countryside walks.
Tel: **01258 860115** Mrs Wright.
D: £20.00-£22.00 **S:** £20.00-£25.00.
Open: All Year
Beds: 1D 1T
Baths: 1 En 1 Pr
🛏 🅿 (3) ⚡ 🖵 🛏 🎞 Ⓥ 🛆 ⚡

(On path) *Foxhangers, 4 Old Mill Cottages, Iwerne Courtney or Shroton, Blandford Forum, Dorset, DT11 8TW.*
Actual grid ref: ST858131
Modern cottage in quiet and peaceful village. Excellent breakfast.
Tel: **01258 861049**
Mrs Moss.
Fax no: 01258 860785
D: £20.00-£20.00 **S:** £25.00-£25.00.
Open: All Year (not Xmas)
Beds: 1D
Baths: 1 En
🅿 (1) ⚡ 🖵 ✕ 🛏 🎞 Ⓥ 🛆 ⚡

Iwerne Minster 17

National Grid Ref: ST8614

🍴 🍺 Talbot Hotel

(1m 🚌) *The Talbot Hotel, Blandford Road, Iwerne Minster, Blandford Forum, Dorset, DT11 8QN.*
Actual grid ref: ST865144
Country Inn offering comfortable rooms, good food, ale, affordable prices.
Tel: **01747 811269**
Mr & Mrs Richardson.
D: £13.75-£19.25
S: £15.00-£35.00.
Open: All Year
Beds: 2F 2D 1T 1S
Baths: 2 En 2 Sh
🛏 🅿 (30) 🖵 ✕ 🛏 🎞 Ⓥ 🛆

Shillingstone 18

National Grid Ref: ST8211

🍴 🍺 Crown Inn

(On path) *The Willows Tea Rooms, 5 Blandford Road, Shillingstone, Blandford Forum, Dorset, DT11 0SG.*
C18th cottage & tearooms in beautiful countryside. Blandford 5 miles.
Tel: **01258 861167**
Mr & Mrs Auckland.
D: £17.50.
S: £20.00.
Open: Feb to Xmas
Beds: 1D
Baths: 1 En
🛏 🅿 (6) ⚡ 🖵 ✕ 🛏 🎞 🛆 Ⓥ 🛆

Ibberton 19

National Grid Ref: ST7807

🍴 🍺 Crown Inn

(0.75m) *Manor House Farm, Ibberton, Blandford Forum, Dorset, DT11 0EN.*
Actual grid ref: ST788077
C16th comfortable farmhouse; also working dairy and sheep farm.
Tel: **01258 817349**
Mrs Old.
D: £14.00-£18.00
S: £16.00-£18.00.
Open: All Year
Beds: 2D 1T
Baths: 2 En 1 Sh
🛏 🅿 (3) ⚡ 🖵 🛏 🎞 Ⓥ 🛆

Piddletrenthide 20

National Grid Ref: SY7099

🍴 🍺 Piddle Inn, Poachers' Inn

(1m) *Poachers Inn, Piddletrenthide, Dorchester, Dorset, DT2 7QX.*
Country inn, set in the heart of the lovely Piddle Valley. All rooms ensuite.
Tel: **01300 348358** Fox.
Fax no: 01300 348153
D: £27.50-£27.50
S: £35.00-£35.00.
Open: All Year
Beds: 1F 15D 2T
Baths: 18 En
🛏 🅿 (40) 🖵 🍴 ✕ 🛏 🎞 Ⓥ 🛆 ⚡

(1m) *Fern Cottage, Piddletrenthide, Dorchester, Dorset, DT2 7QF.*
Fern Cottage offers friendly, clean and comfortable accommodation and easy reach Dorchester.
Tel: **01300 348277** (also fax no)
Mrs Gossage.
D: £20.00-£26.00
S: £25.00-£30.00.
Open: All Year (not Xmas)
Beds: 3D 1S
Baths: 4 En
🛏 🅿 🖵 🍴 🛏 🎞 Ⓥ 🛆 ⚡

Sydling St Nicholas 21

National Grid Ref: SY6399

|⊖| ⊲≣ The Greyhound, Red Lion

(On path) *Lamperts Cottage,*
Sydling St Nicholas, Dorchester,
Dorset, *DT2 9NU.*
Traditional C16th thatched cottage,
stream at front, beams, inglenook,
flagstones.
Grades: AA 3 Diamond
Tel: 01300 341659
Mr Wills.
Fax no: 01300 341699
D: £21.00-£21.00
S: £25.00-£25.00.
Open: All Year
Beds: 1F 1D 1T
Baths: 2 Sh
ᗡ (8) �P (3) ❏ ⏰ ♨ Ⅲ. Ⅴ ⊁

(On path) *Magiston Farm,* Sydling
St Nicholas, Dorchester, Dorset,
DT2 9NR.
C16th farmhouse, 400 acre
working farm, large garden. Very
peaceful.
Grades: ETC 3 Diamond
Tel: 01300 320295
Mrs Barraclough.
D: £18.50
S: £18.50.
Open: All Year (not Xmas)
Beds: 1D 3T 1S
Baths: 1 Pr 1 Sh
ᗡ (10) P (12) ⏰ ✕ ♨ Ⅲ. ᏸ Ⅴ ᳚ ⊁

(On path) *City Cottage,* Sydling St
Nicholas, Dorchester, Dorset,
DT2 9NX.
Country cottage, comfortable and a
warm welcome assured.
Tel: 01300 341300
Mrs Wareham.
D: £18.00 **S:** £18.00.
Open: All Year (not Xmas)
Beds: 1D 1S
Baths: 1 Sh
ᗡ (12) P (2) ❏ Ⅲ.

Cattistock 22

National Grid Ref: SY5999

(0.5m ⊖) *Sandhills Cottage,*
Sandhills, Cattistock, Dorchester,
DT2 0HQ.
Grades: ETC 4 Diamond
Tel: 01300 321146
Mr & Mrs Roca.
Fax no: 01300 321 146
D: £22.00-£24.00
S: £25.00-£28.00.
Open: All Year
Beds: 2T 1D
Baths: 3 En
ᗡ (12) P (8) ⊁❏ ♨ Ⅲ. Ⅴ ᳚ ⊁
Sandhills cottage lies in a rural
hamlet within ten minutes walk the
village of Cattistock has a shop/
P.O., pub and a beautiful church.
Sandhills offers superb scenery and
good walking, some of Dorset's
finest beaches are within easy dri-
ving distance.

Toller Porcorum 23

National Grid Ref: SY5698

|⊖| ⊲≣ Marquis of Lorne, Three Horseshoes, The
Spyway, Askers Well

(0.75m) *Colesmoor Farm,* Toller
Porcorum, Dorchester, Dorset, *DT2 0DU*
Actual grid ref: SY556971
Small family farm in quiet setting
with excellent views.
Grades: ETC 4 Diamond
Tel: 01300 320812 Mrs Geddes.
Fax no: 01300 321402
D: £20.00-£20.00 **S:** £25.00-£25.00.
Open: May to Feb
Beds: 1D 1T **Baths:** 2 En
ᗡ P (4) ⊁❏ ♨ Ⅲ. ᏸ Ⅴ ⊁

(On path) *The Kingcombe Centre,*
Toller Porcorum, Dorchester,
Dorset, *DT2 0EQ.*
Actual grid ref: SY554991
Study centre beside the River
Hooke surrounded by nature
reserve. **Grades:** ETC 2 Diamond
Tel: 01300 320684 Mr Spring.
Fax no: 01300 021409
D: £15.00-£20.00 **S:** £15.00-£20.00.
Open: All Year
Beds: 3F 3T 2D 3S **Baths:** 11 Sh
ᗡ P (20) ⊁❏ ⏰ ✕ ♨ Ⅲ. ᏸ Ⅴ ᳚ ⊁

Hooke 24

National Grid Ref: ST5300

|⊖| ⊲≣ Winyards Gap Inn, Talbot Inn

(0.25m ⊖) *Watermeadow House,*
Bridge Farm, Hooke, Beaminster,
Dorset, *DT8 3PD.*
Grades: ETC 4 Diamond, Silver,
AA 4 Diamond
Tel: 01308 862619 (also fax no)
Mrs Wallbridge.
D: £22.00-£24.00 **S:** £24.00-£28.00.
Open: Easter to Oct
Beds: 1F 1D **Baths:** 1 En 1 Pr
ᗡ P (4) ⊁❏ ✕ ♨ Ⅲ. Ⅴ ⊁
Water meadow house, part of a
working dairy farm, is a large
Georgian style house on the edge
of small village of Hooke.
Breakfast is served in a sun lounge
and the River Hooke meanders
close by the garden. A warm
welcome awaits you.

Beaminster 25

National Grid Ref: ST4701

|⊖| ⊲≣ Bridge House, Fox, Greyhound, Pickwick's

(On path) *Beam Cottage,* 16 North
Street, Beaminster, Dorset, *DT8 3DZ.*
Grades: ETC 4 Diamond
Tel: 01308 863639 Mrs Standeven.
D: £25.00-£30.00 **S:** £30.00-£35.00.
Open: All Year (not Xmas)
Beds: 1F 1D 2T **Baths:** 2 En 1 Pr
ᗡ P (3) ❏ ⏰ ✕ ♨ Ⅲ. Ⅴ ᳚ ⊁
Very attractive Grade II Listed cot-
tage in delightful secluded garden.
Also available pretty twin bedded
garden cottage with all facilities.
All rooms have own sitting room .

(0.25m) *The Walnuts,* 2 Prout
Street, Beaminster, Dorset, *DT8 3AY.*
Listed building situated just off
town square. Very comfortable
establishment.
Grades: ETC 4 Diamond
Tel: 01308 862211 Pieles'z.
D: £24.00-£27.50 **S:** £28.00-£35.00.
Open: All Year
Beds: 2D 1T
Baths: 2 En 1 Pr
ᗡ (8) P (3) ⊁❏ ♨ Ⅲ. Ⅴ

(On path) *Kitwhistle Farm,*
Beaminster Down, Beaminster,
Dorset, *DT8 3SG.*
Quiet location, down land dairy
farm. All facilities on ground floor.
Grades: ETC 3 Diamond
Tel: 01308 862458 (also fax no)
Mrs Hasell.
D: £18.00-£22.00 **S:** £22.00-£25.00.
Open: Easter to Oct
Beds: 1F
Baths: 1 En
ᗡ P ⊁❏ ♨ Ⅴ

(0.25m) *Jenny Wrens,* 1 Hogshill
Street, Beaminster, Dorset, *DT8 3AE.*
Part of C17th tearoom in charming
small Dorset town.
Tel: 01308 862814
Fax no: 01308 861191
D: £24.00-£24.00 **S:** £28.00-£44.00.
Open: All Year
Beds: 2D 1T
Baths: 3 En
ᗡ (12) ⊁❏ ♨ Ⅲ. Ⅴ ᳚

Wootton Fitzpaine 26

National Grid Ref: SY3695

|⊖| ⊲≣ Shave Cross Inn

(0.25m) *Higher Spence,* Wootton
Fitzpaine, Charmouth, *DT6 6DF.*
Actual grid ref: SY357965
No street lights or proper road;
instead: peace, tranquillity,
beautiful country & sea views.
Tel: 01297 560556
D: £18.00-£20.00
S: £21.00-£23.00.
Open: All Year (not Xmas)
Beds: 1F 1D
Baths: 2 En
ᗡ (3) P (3) ⊁❏ ⏰ ♨ Ⅴ ⊁

Uplyme 27

National Grid Ref: SY3293

|⊖| ⊲≣ Pilot Boat

(0.25m) *Lydwell House,* Lyme
Road , Uplyme, Lyme Regis,
Dorset, *DT7 3TJ.*
A pre-Victorian house set within
0.75 acre of Victorian gardens.
Grades: ETC 3 Diamond
Tel: 01297 443522
Mr Brittain.
D: £23.00-£27.00 **S:** £23.00-£27.00.
Open: All Year
Beds: 2F 1D 1T 1S
Baths: 5 En
ᗡ P (7) ⊁❏ ✕ ♨ Ⅲ. Ⅴ ᳚ ⊁

(0.25m) *Hill Barn, Gore Lane, Uplyme, Lyme Regis, Dorset, DT7 3RJ.*
Beautifully converted stone barn, surrounded by countryside, only 1 mile Lyme Regis.
Grades: ETC 4 Diamond
Tel: 01297 445185 (also fax no)
Mrs Wyon-Brown.
D: £18.00-£20.00 **S:** £18.00.
Open: All Year (not Xmas)
Beds: 1F 1D 1T
Baths: 2 Sh
⑤🅿️⌇⊠✕👤🛏️🎠🖳♿Ⓥ🛇⚡

Lyme Regis 28

National Grid Ref: SY3392

🍴 🍺 Dorset Hotel, Pilot Boat, Victoria, Volunteer

(0.5m) *Hillsett, Haye Lane, Lyme Regis, Dorset, DT7 3NG.*
Tel: **01297 445 259** (also fax no)
Mr Thompson.
D: £20.00-£25.00 **S:** £20.00-£25.00.
Open: All Year (not Xmas/New Year)
Beds: 1F 1D
Baths: 1Ensuite 1Shared
⑤(8)🅿️(7)⌇🛏️🖳Ⓥ
Lovely modern family home set in beautiful surroundings overlooking Lym valley, Golden Cap & Lyme Bay. 15 minutes walk to centre of famous Lyme Regis, Cobb Harbour & beach. Private car park, heated open air pool, sauna and pool table.

(0.5m) *Tudor House Hotel, 3/5 Church Street, Lyme Regis, Dorset, DT7 3BS.*
Grades: ETC 3 Diamond
Tel: **01297 442472** Mr Ray.
D: £24.00-£49.00 **S:** £28.00-£38.00.
Open: All Year (not Xmas/New Year)
Beds: 9F 5D 1T 1S
Baths: 14 En 2 Pr
⑤🅿️(15)⌇🛏️🍴✕👤🛏️🖳Ⓥ🛇⚡
An historic Elizabethan house, circa 1580, one minutes level walk to the sea in the centre of Old Lyme Regis. Part plaster ceiling designed by Sir Walter Raleigh. Cellar bar with original well. Parking.
www.thetudorhouse.co.uk.

🚐 sign means that, *given due notice*, owners will pick you up from the path and drop you off *within reason.*

(On path) *Charnwood Guest House, 21 Woodmead Road, Lyme Regis, Dorset, DT7 3AD.*
Actual grid ref: SY339924
Grades: ETC 3 Diamond
Tel: **01297 445281** Mr Bradbury.
D: £19.00-£24.00. **S:** £19.00-£24.00.
Open: All Year
Beds: 1F 4D 2T 1S
Baths: 6 En 1 Sh
⑤(5)🅿️(7)⌇🛏️🎠🛏️🖳Ⓥ🛇⚡
1910 style house with balcony. Scenic river walk to town (5 mins) past pubs, restaurants etc. Quiet, safe, easy access to walking, fos-silling and beach. Discounts for 3 plus nights midweek Sun-Thurs. Clean, friendly, personally run with hearty breakfast.

(0.5m) 🚐 *Mayflower Cottage, 39 Sherborne Lane, Lyme Regis, Dorset, DT7 3NY.*
Actual grid ref: SY340922
Quiet, traffic-free. Secluded garden. Town centre, Free parking nearby.
Tel: **01297 445930** Mr Snowsill.
D: £20.00-£25.00 **S:** £25.00.
Open: All Year (not Xmas)
Beds: 1F 1D 1T **Baths:** 3 En
⑤🅿️(3)🛏️🎠🛏️🖳Ⓥ🛇⚡

(0.5m) 🚐 *The Old Monmouth Hotel, 12 Church Street, Lyme Regis, Dorset, DT7 3BS.*
Actual grid ref: SY344922
C17th building, centrally situated for beaches, harbour and all amenities.
Tel: **01297 442456**
Mr & Mrs Brown.
Fax no: 01297 443577
D: £19.00-£22.00 **S:** £26.00-£30.00.
Open: All Year (not Xmas)
Beds: 1F 4D 1T **Baths:** 5 En 1 Sh
⑤⌇🛏️✕👤🛏️🖳Ⓥ🛇⚡

(0.25m) *The Red House, Sidmouth Road, Lyme Regis, Dorset, DT7 3ES.*
Actual grid ref: SY330922
Elegant house with wonderful views Eastwards beyond Golden Cap.
Grades: ETC 4 Diamond
Tel: **01297 442055** (also fax no)
Mr & Mrs Norman.
D: £22.00-£27.00 **S:** £33.00-£40.00.
Open: Easter to Nov
Beds: 1D 2T
Baths: 3 En
⑤(8)🅿️(3)⌇🛏️🖳Ⓥ⚡

(On path) *Coverdale Guest House, Woodmead Road, Lyme Regis, Dorset, DT7 3AB.*
Actual grid ref: SY339925
Spacious comfortable non-smoking guest house. Country/sea views. Beach, restaurants nearby.
Tel: **01297 442882**
Mr & Mrs Bales.
D: £19.00-£27.50 **S:** £19.00-£27.50.
Open: All Year (not Xmas)
Beds: 2F 3D 2T 1S
Baths: 8 En
⑤(4)🅿️(9)⌇🛏️🛏️🖳Ⓥ⚡

All rates are subject to alteration at the owners' discretion.

(0.5m) *Coombe House, 41 Coombe Street, Lyme Regis, Dorset, DT7 3PY.*
Lovely old blue lias stone house situated in the oldest part of town.
Tel: **01297 443849** (also fax no)
Mrs Duncan.
D: £17.00-£17.00
S: £20.00-£34.00.
Open: All Year
Beds: 1D 1T
Baths: 2 En
⑤🅿️(1)⌇🛏️🖳Ⓥ

(0.5m 🚐) *New Haven Hotel, 1 Pound Street, Lyme Regis, Dorset, DT7 3HZ.*
C18th town house.
Tel: **01297 442499** (also fax no)
Mrs Petitt.
D: £17.50-£28.50
S: £20.50-£28.50.
Open: All Year
Beds: 1F 3D 1T 2S
Baths: 4 En 1 Sh
⑤⌇🛏️🎠🛏️🖳Ⓥ🛇⚡

(0.5m) *Southernhaye, Pound Road, Lyme Regis, Dorset, DT7 3HX.*
Edwardian house with sea views.
Tel: **01297 443077** (also fax no)
Mr Garrard.
D: £17.00-£18.00
S: £18.00-£20.00.
Open: All Year (not Xmas)
Beds: 1D 1T 1S
Baths: 1 Sh
⑤(13)🅿️(2)🛏️🛏️🖳Ⓥ

(0.5m) *Rotherfield Guest House, View Road, Lyme Regis, Dorset, DT7 3AA.*
Actual grid ref: SY3492
Clean, comfortable, ensuite accom-modation. Sea views, beach, restaurants, coastal path nearby.
Tel: **01297 445585**
Mr Endersby.
D: £19.00-£23.00
S: £25.00-£35.00.
Open: All Year
Beds: 2F 3D 1T
Baths: 6 En
⑤(5)🅿️(6)🛏️🎠🛏️🖳Ⓥ🛇

All rooms full and nowhere else to stay? Ask the owner if there's anywhere nearby

---

Wolds Way

The **Wolds Way** skirts the chalk hills and dry valleys of a little-known part of the East Riding of Yorkshire. It is a quiet part of England, unspoilt by much commercial tourism. The path unwinds for 79 pleasant miles from Hessle and the muddy river beneath the Humber Bridge (the longest single-span bridge in the world) to the lofty cliffs at Filey on the North Sea coast. For the true trekker, it provides the perfect link between the **Cleveland Way** and the **Viking Way**. For the long weekender, it provides a lovely walk over rolling limestone downland - a world away from the rough moors and peat bogs usually associated with walking in Yorkshire. This is a good one for walking in autumn and winter.

Maps: Ordnance Survey 1:50000 Landranger series: 100, 101, 106 and 107

Guide: *Wolds Way* by Roger Ratcliffe (ISBN 1 85410 189 7), published by Aurum Press in association with the Countryside Commission and Ordnance Survey and available from all major bookshops, £9.99

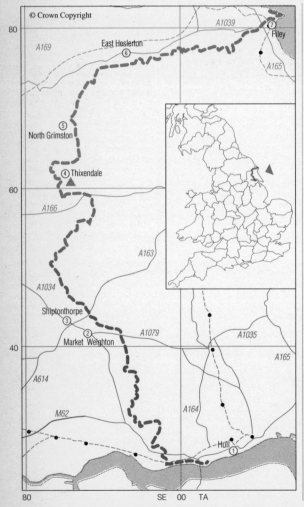

© Crown Copyright

Hull   1

National Grid Ref: TA0929

🍴 🍺 Hanorth Arms, The Zoological

(1.5m) *Allandra Hotel, 5 Park Avenue, Hull, HU5 3EN.*
Grades: ETC 2 Diamond
Tel: **01482 493349**
Fax no: 01482 492680
D: £19.50-£19.50 **S:** £26.00-£26.00.
Open: All Year
Beds: 2F 1T 7D
Baths: 10 En
🛇 🅿 (5) 🛏 ⼊ ✕ ≛ ▥ Ⓥ
Charming Victorian town house hotel, family run, close to all amenities. Delightfully situated, convenient universities and town centre opposite pleasant parking. All rooms ensuite.

(1.5m) *Beck House , 628 Beverley High Road, Hull, HU6 7LL.*
Traditional town house, B&B, fine accommodation, close to university etc.
Tel: **01482 445468** Mrs Aylwin.
D: £19.00-£22.00 **S:** £19.00-£22.00.
Open: All Year
Beds: 3D 3S
Baths: 1 En 1 Sh
🛇 🅿 (4) 🛏 ≛ ▥ Ⓥ

(1.5m) *The Tree Guest House, 132 Sunny Bank, Spring Bank West, Hull, HU3 1LE.*
Close to the city centre and universities. Special rates available.
Tel: **01482 448822**
Fax no: 01482 442911
D: £15.00-£18.00 **S:** £10.00-£24.00.
Open: All Year
Beds: 1F 3D 3S **Baths:** 3 En 2 Sh
🛇 🅿 🖵 🛏 ≛ ▥ & Ⓥ

D = Price range per person sharing in a double room

(1.5m) *Marlborough Hotel,*
232 Spring Bank, Hull, HU3 1LU.
Family run, near city centre.
Tel: **01482 224479** (also fax no)
Mr Norman.
D: £17.00 **S:** £17.00.
Open: All Year
Beds: 2 F 2D 7T 5S **Baths:** 3 Sh
🛏 🅿 (10) 🗗 🎇 ✕ ▥.

Market Weighton 2

National Grid Ref: SE8741

⊯ ⬛ Black Horse

(On path) *The Gables,*
38 Londesborough Road, Market
Weighton, York, YO43 3HS.
Actual grid ref: SE877423
Friendly, comfortable, quiet
country house.
Tel: **01430 872255**
Mr & Mrs Reeson.
D: £16.00 **S:** £16.00.
Open: All Year (not Xmas)
Beds: 1D 1T 1S **Baths:** 1 Sh
🛏 🅿 (5) 🗗 🎇 ⚓ ▥ Ⓥ 🎗 ⚡

Shiptonthorpe 3

National Grid Ref: SE8543

⊯ ⬛ Crown, Black Horse, Ship

(0.25m 🐴) *Robeanne House*
Farm & Stables, Driffield Lane,
Shiptonthorpe, York, YO43 3PW.
Tel: **01430 873312** (also fax no)
Mrs Wilson.
D: £20.00-£40.00 **S:** £20.00-£25.00.
Open: All Year
Beds: 3F 2D 1T **Baths:** 6 En
🛏 🅿 (10) 🗗 🎇 ✕ ⚓ ▥ Ⓥ 🎗 ⚡
Comfortable family house, large
spacious rooms countryside views.
Good food warm welcome, within
easy reach of York, the Yorkshire
coast Moors and Dales. Local
walking, Gliding, Racing, Castle
Howard and much more.

Thixendale 4

National Grid Ref: SE8461

⊯ ⬛ Cross Keys

(▲ On path) *Thixendale Youth*
Hostel, The Village Hall,
Thixendale, Malton, North
Yorkshire, YO17 8TG.
Actual grid ref: SE843610
Tel: **01377 288238**
Under 18: £4.65 **Adults:** £6.80
No smoking
The old school in a quiet village,
near the foot of a remarkable chalk
dry valley.

(On path) *Manor Farm,*
Thixendale, Malton, N. Yorks,
YO17 9TG.
Working farm. Private spacious
accommodation, overlooking pretty
garden. Substantial breakfasts.
Tel: **01377 288315** (also fax no)
Mrs Brader.
D: £20.00-£20.00 **S:** £20.00-£20.00.
Open: All Year (not Xmas/
New Year)
Beds: 2F 1D 1T 1S **Baths:** 1 Pr
🛏 🅿 🎝 🗗 ✕ ⚓ ▥ Ⓥ 🎗 ⚡

North Grimston 5

National Grid Ref: SE8467

(1.25m) *Middleton Arms, North*
Grimston, Malton, N. Yorks,
YO17 8AX.
Friendly country pub with excellent
reputation for quality food and
homely accommodation.
Tel: **01944 768255** Mrs Grayston.
Fax no: 01944 768389
D: £20.00-£20.00 **S:** £27.50.
Open: All Year (not Xmas)
Beds: 2D 1T
Baths: 1 Pr 1 Sh
🛏 🅿 🗗 ✕ ⚓ ▥ Ⓥ 🎗 ⚡

East Heslerton 6

National Grid Ref: SE9276

⊯ ⬛ Dawnay Arms

(0.75m 🐴) *Manor Farm, East*
Heslerton, Malton, N. Yorks,
YO17 8RN.
Actual grid ref: SE925767
Central for touring York, North
York Moors and coastal attractions.
Tel: **01944 728268** Ms Lumley.
D: £17.50-£20.00 **S:** £17.50-£20.00.
Open: Easter to Oct
Beds: 2F
Baths: 2 Pr
🛏 🅿 (4) 🎝 🗗 🎇 ⚓ ▥ Ⓥ 🎗 ⚡

Filey 7

National Grid Ref: TA1180

(0.5m) *The Gables, 2a Rutland*
Street, Filey, N Yorks, YO14 9JB.
Grades: ETC 3 Diamond
Tel: **01723 514750** Broome.
D: £19.00-£23.00 **S:** £21.00-£28.00.
Open: All Year
Beds: 1F 2T 2D
Baths: 5 En
🛏 🗗 🎇 ✕ ⚓ ▥ Ⓥ 🎗 ⚡
Characteristic Edwardian guest
house offering friendly accommo-
dation, comfortable ensuite rooms,
colour television, hospitality tray.
Central to all amenities. Reductions
for 3 people or more nights.

(0.5m) *The Forge, 23 Rutland*
Street, Filey, N. Yorks, YO14 9JA.
Edwardian townhouse. Small,
friendly, non-smoking, good food.
Tel: **01723 512379** Appleyard.
D: £17.50-£19.00 **S:** £22.50-£24.00.
Open: All Year (not Xmas/New
Year)
Beds: 1F 1T 2D
Baths: 4 En 1 Pr
🛏 (3) 🅿 🗗 🎇 ✕ ⚓ ▥ ♿ Ⓥ 🎗 ⚡

Beara Way

To see the Beara Peninsula from Bantry, stretching away into the Atlantic, is one of the great sights of South West Ireland. The **Beara Way** is a 116-mile circular route, crossing from Cork into Kerry, that runs right the way around this long finger of land. The path takes in Bear Island and Dursey Island, too. The route is mainly low-level, with the sea always present, although there are a couple of brisk climbs and the peninsula is traversed twice; the brooding presence of the Caha Mountains is always felt beside you as you walk. Kenmare is the only town of any size encountered in this old and rugged landscape, so come to this route well prepared. The Beara Way takes you through a history that runs from the megalithic right up to the Second World War, past old ring forts, standing stones, the famous Hungry Hill, the old military bases at Bear Island, Ireland's only cable car ride across to Dursey and the old copper mines around Allihies. If you come in May,

you'll have a great show of flowers in the fields and hedgerows. There are parts which are very exposed and others which are boggy when wet. Come prepared with good wind-proof gear and proper boots.

Guides: *The Way-marked Trails of Ireland* by Michael Fewer (ISBN 0-7171-2386-3), published by Gill & Macmillan, and available from all good bookshops or direct from the publishers (Goldenbridge Ind Est, Inchicore, Dublin 8, Ireland, 01 4531005), £9.99 (+ £2.50 p&p)

The Beara Way Map Guide by the Beara Tourism & Development Association, is available from their offices (Castletownbere Haven, Co Cork, Ireland, 027 70054), £2.15 (+50p p&p)

Maps: Ordnance Survey of Ireland 1:50000 Discovery Series: 84, 85

Glengarriff   1
National Grid Ref: V9256

⏴ ⏴ The Eccles, Johnny Barry's

(▲ 0.25m) *Murphy's Village Hostel, The Village, Glengarriff, Bantry, County Cork.*
Tel: **027 63555 Adults:** £7.00
Evening meal available, Facilities for disabled people

(2m 🚍) *Carraig Dubh House, Droumgarriff, Glengarriff, Bantry, Co Cork.*
Family home, peaceful location overlooking harbour and golf club. Lovely gardens.
Grades: BF Approv
Tel: **027 63146**
Mrs Connolly.
D: £17.50-£19.00 **S:** £23.50-£25.50.
Open: March to Oct
Beds: 1F 1T 2D
Baths: 3 En 1 Pr
🛏 🅿 (4) 🛋 🖳 Ⅴ ⓘ

(0.5m 🚍) *Island View House, Glengarriff, Bantry; Co Cork.*
Comfortable home in quiet scenic area. Most bedrooms overlooking Glengarriff Harbour.
Tel: **027 63081** Mrs O'Sullivan.
Fax no: 027 63298
D: £17.00-£19.00 **S:** £21.50-£24.50.
Open: Easter to Nov
Beds: 2F 2D 2T
Baths: 6 En
🛏 🅿 🖵 🖳 ⓑ ✦

(4.5m) *Ardnagashel Lodge, Glengarriff, Bantry, Co Cork.*
Actual grid ref: V980535
Modern comfortable home in quiet sylvan setting. Central for touring
Grades: BF Approv
Tel: **027 51687**
Mrs Ronayne.
D: £19.50 **S:** £30.00.
Open: May to Sep
Beds: 1D 2T
Baths: 3 Ensuite
🅿 ✄ 🖵 🛋 🖳 Ⅴ

(1m) *Beechwood, Inchintaggart, Glengarriff, Bantry, Co Cork.*
Beechwood House is situated 1.5km from Glengarriff village & overlooking the infamous Garnish Island
Tel: **027 63292**
Mrs Nolan.
D: £17.00 **S:** £20.00.
Open: Easter to Oct
Beds: 2F 1T 1D
Baths: 2 Ensuite 1 Shared
🛏 (1) 🅿 (6) ✄ 🖵 🖳 ⓘ ✦

(2m 🚍) *Lakeside Farm, Loughavoul, Glengarriff, Bantry, Co Cork.*
Scenic setting overlooking lake. Ideal location for fishing, mountain climbing
Tel: **027 63378** Mrs Goggin.
D: £13.00 **S:** £20.00.
Open: May to Sep
Beds: 1F 1T 1D
Baths: 2 Ensuite 1 Private
🛏 🅿 (3) ✄ 🖳 ⓘ ✦

(1m) *Casa Verde, Glengarriff, Co Cork.*
Beautiful bungalow set in prize-winning garden, part of West Cork Garden Trail
Tel: **027 63157**
Mr & Mrs Bemelman.
Fax no: 027 63314
D: £17.50 **S:** £25.00.
Open: Apr to Sep
Beds: 1F 1T 2D
Baths: 2 Ensuite 2 Private
🛏 🅿 (4) ✄ 🖵 🛏 🛋 🖳 Ⅴ ⓘ ✦

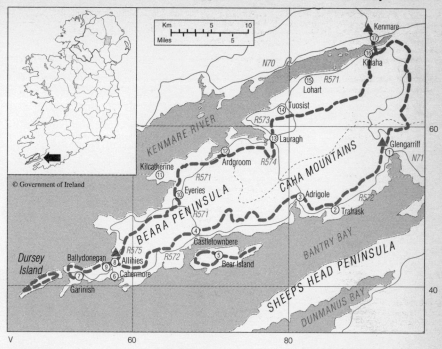

© Government of Ireland

Trafrask 2

National Grid Ref: V8549

🅟 🍺 Sugar Loaf, Johnny Barry's

(1m 🚐) *Beachmount, Trafrask East, Trafrask, Adrigole, Bantry, Co Cork.*
Magnificent view of Caha Mountains, excellent food, comfortable accommodation.
Grades: BF Approv
Tel: **027 60075**
Mrs O'Sullivan.
D: £16.00-£17.50 **S:** £17.50-£20.00.
Open: Easter to Oct
Beds: 1F 1D 1T 1S
Baths: 1 En 3 Pr 1 Sh
🛏 (5) 🅟 ✕ 🎢 ⊿

Adrigole 3

National Grid Ref: V8050

(1m 🚐) *Ocean View, Faha East, Trafrask, Adrigole, Bantry, Co Cork.*
Popular B&B for walkers. Situated directly over Beara Way walking trail.
Grades: BF Approved.
Tel: **027 60069**
Mrs O'Sullivan.
D: £16.00-£17.50 **S:** £17.50-£19.00.
Open: Easter to Oct
Beds: 1F 1D 1T 2S
Baths: 2 Sh
🛏 🅟 (5) ⅄ 🖵 ✕ 🎢 🎢 ⊿ Ⅴ 🦴 ⊿

Castletownbere 4

National Grid Ref: V6846

🅟 🍺 Lynch's, Old Irish Bar, Nicky's, Old Bank House, Jack Patrick's, Mariner's

(0.75m 🚐) *Massabielle, Filane, Castletownbere, Bantry, Co Cork.*
Actual grid ref: V716465
Tel: **027 70341** (also fax no)
Mrs Sheehan.
D: £14.00-£16.00 **S:** £14.00-£18.00.
Open: Easter to Oct
Beds: 1F 1D 1T
Baths: 2 En 1 Pr
🛏 🅟 🖵 🎢 ✕ 🎢 🎢 ⅋ 🦴 ⊿
Welcoming home on the scenic Ring of Beara, adjacent to Berehaven golf club, Beara Way walks, pontoon pier to Bere island, sailing, fishing, historical places of interest, harbour views. Beneath Hungry Hill. Ideal base for touring the South West of Ireland. Tea/coffee on arrival.

(0.75m 🚐) *Realt Na Mara, Castletownbere, Bantry, Co Cork.*
Comfortable home overlooking sea, popular walking route, personal attention.
Grades: BF Approv
Tel: **027 70101**
Mrs Donegan.
D: £17.00-£19.00 **S:** £23.50-£25.50.
Open: All Year
Beds: 1F 1D 3T
Baths: 4 En
🛏 🅟 (10) 🖵 🎢 🦴 ⊿

(0.25m) *Sea Breeze, Derrymihan, Castletownbere, Bantry, Co Cork.*
Comfortable modern home in a peaceful spot at sea shore.
Grades: BF Approv
Tel: **027 70508** (also fax no)
Mrs McGurn.
D: £20.00 **S:** £20.00-£23.00.
Open: All Year (not Xmas/New Year)
Beds: 1F 2D **Baths:** 3 En
🛏 🅟 ⅄ 🖵 🎢 🎢 Ⅴ 🦴 ⊿

(On path) *Bay View House, West End, Castletownbere, Bantry, Co Cork.*
Nice old-fashioned house in the town centre, scenic surroundings everywhere.
Tel: **027 70099** Mrs Murphy.
D: £15.00-£16.00 **S:** £17.00-£18.00.
Open: Jun to Sep
Beds: 3D **Baths:** 1 Sh
🛏 (12) 🎢 ⊿

🚐 sign means that, *given due notice*, owners will pick you up from the path and drop you off *within reason.*

(0.25m ⌂) *Castletown House, The Old Bank Seafood Restaurant, Castletownbere, Beara, Co Cork.*
Actual grid ref: V675458
Originally a bank, with front and rear gardens, seafood and local cheese a speciality.
Tel: 027 70252
Mr & Mrs Harrington.
Fax no: 027 70054
D: £17.00-£18.00
S: £15.00-£18.00.
Open: All Year (not Xmas)
Beds: 4T
Baths: 4 En
⌂ ☐ ⚲ ⊡ ⋔ ✕ ♨ ▥ ▣ ▪ ≮

Bear Island 5

National Grid Ref: V7044

(On path ⌂) *Harbour View, Bear Island, Bantry, Co Cork.*
Experience island life. Peaceful surroundings, unsurpassed scenic beauty
Tel: 027 75011
Mrs O'Sullivan.
D: £14.00 **S:** £16.00.
Open: All Year (not Xmas)
Beds: 2F 3T
Baths: 2 Ensuite 1 Private 2 Shared
⌂ ☐ ⊡ ⋔ ✕ ♨ ▥ ▣ ▪ ≮

Cahermore 6

National Grid Ref: V5741

(1m ⌂) *Killaugh, Cahermore, Allihies, Bantry, Co Cork.*
Modern two-storey house set in scenic, tranquil location on the Beara Way
Tel: 027 73076
Mrs Mullins.
D: £15.00 **S:** £18.00.
Open: Apr to Sep
Beds: 1T 2D
Baths: 3 Ensuite
⌂ ☐ (6) ⚲ ⊡ ⋔ ✕ ♨ ▥ ▣ ▪ ≮

Garnish 7

National Grid Ref: V5241

(On path ⌂) *Windy Point House, Garnish, Allihies, Bantry, Co Cork.*
Actual grid ref: V512417
Grades: BF Approv
Tel: 027 73017 (also fax no)
Mr & Mrs Sheehan.
D: £18.50-£18.50
S: £25.00-£25.00.
Open: Apr to Oct
Beds: 3F 1D
Baths: 4 En
⌂ ☐ (10) ⚲ ⊡ ✕ ♨ ▥ ▣ ⬥ ▥ ▪ ≮
Overlooking cable-car to Dursey Island. Luxurious rooms, panoramic views. Choice of breakfast/dinner, seafood a speciality. Dining room overlooking sea. Tea of coffee. Sandy beaches, peaceful location, beautiful sunsets. We had the last sunset in Europe in the year 2000.

D = Price range per person sharing in a double room

Allihies 8

National Grid Ref: V5845

(▲ On path) *Allihies Youth Hostel, Allihies, Bantry, County Cork.*
Tel: 027 73014
Under 18: £5.50 **Adults:** £7.00
Self-catering facilities, Shop 2 km away, Laundry facilities, Parking
Set on the remote Beara Peninsula, the hostel is surrounded by mountains and overlooks the Atlantic. Explore sandy beaches, old copper mines stone circles.

(▲ On path) *Allihies Village Hostel, Allihies, Bantry, County Cork.*
Tel: 027 73107
Under 18: £5.50 **Adults:** £8.00
Self-catering facilities, Television, Showers, Central heating, Laundry facilities, Wet weather shelter, Lounge, Dining room, Cycle store, Parking, Facilities for disabled people, No smoking
Award-winning hostel nestled in the beautiful village of Allihies, surrounded by mountains and the wild Atlantic Ocean, Allihies is renowned for its friendliness, traditional music and spectacular scenery.

Ballydonegan 9

National Grid Ref: V5843

(On path ⌂) *Beach View, Ballydonegan, Allihies, Bantry, Co Cork.*
Scenic surroundings near village. Beach, walks, bars, restaurants, cable car
Tel: 027 73105 Mrs Harrington.
D: £13.00 **S:** £16.00.
Open: All Year (not Xmas)
Beds: 1F 1T 2D 1S
Baths: 2 Ensuite 1 Private
⌂ ☐ ☐ ⋔ ✕ ♨ ▥ ⬥ ▥ ▪ ≮

Eyeries 10

National Grid Ref: V6450

🍴 🍺 Village Inn, Hack Patrick's

(0.5m ⌂) *Formanes House, Eyeries, Beara, Co Cork.*
Actual grid ref: V651507
Site on the Beara Way, spectacular view of sea and Kenmare River.
Tel: 027 74360 Mrs O'Neill.
D: £15.00-£15.00 **S:** £15.00.
Open: All Year (not Xmas)
Beds: 3F 2T **Baths:** 2 En 2 Pr 1 Sh
⌂ ☐ ⚲ ⊡ ⋔ ✕ ♨ ▥ ▣ ▪ ≮

Kilcatherine 11

National Grid Ref: V6353

(1m ⌂) *Glor na Mara, Kilcatherine, Eyeries, Bantry, Co Cork.*
Oceanfront modern bungalow on Eyeries to Ardgroom Coast Road. Spectacular sea/mountain views.
Tel: 027 74012 (also fax no)
Mrs Crowley.
D: £15.00-£15.00 **S:** £18.00-£18.00.
Open: Apr to Oct
Beds: 2D 1T
Baths: 3 En
⌂ ☐ ☐ ✕ ♨ ▥ ▣ ▪ ≮

Ardgroom 12

National Grid Ref: V6955

🍴 🍺 Village Inn, Josies Restaurant, Holly Bar

(1m) *Harbour Scene, Barrakilla, Ardgroom, Bantry, Co Cork.*
Ring of Beara. Scenic views. Local stone circle and local fishing.
Tel: 027 74423
Mrs Hartnett.
Fax no: 027 74420
D: £15.00-£18.00 **S:** £17.00-£20.00.
Open: April to Oct
Beds: 3D 1T
Baths: 3 En 1 Sh
⌂ ☐ (5) ☐ ⋔ ♨ ▥ ▣ ▪ ≮

(On path) *Canfie House, Canfie, Ardgroom, Beara, Co Cork.*
On Beara Way Path, magnificent views. Stone circle/village/restaurant 1km.
Tel: 027 74105
Mrs Leahy.
D: £12.00-£16.00
S: £15.00-£20.00.
Open: Apr to Sep
Beds: 1F 1D 1T 1S
Baths: 1 En 1 Sh
⌂ ☐ ☐ ✕ ♨ ▥ ▣ ▪ ≮

(1m ⌂) *Sea Villa, Coast Road, Ardgroom, Bantry, Co Cork.*
Situated in a beautiful and breathtaking rugged landscape. Surrounded by sea, mountains, hills
Tel: 027 74369 (also fax no)
Mrs O'Sullivan.
D: £17.00 **S:** £23.50.
Open: Mar to Nov
Beds: 3F
Baths: 3 Ensuite
⌂ (6) ☐ ☐ ✕ ▥ ▪ ≮

All rooms full and nowhere else to stay? Ask the owner if there's anywhere nearby

(On path 🚐) *O'Brien's, Ardgroom, Bantry, Co Cork.*
Family-run home in beautiful Ardgroom village. Glenbeg Lake, stone circle, within walking distance
Tel: **027 74019** Mrs O'Brien.
D: £15.00 **S:** £16.00.
Open: May to Oct
Beds: 2D 1T
Baths: 1 Ensuite 1 Shared
🛏🗶✕🖭📖.☑🛢⚡

(2.5m 🚐) *Glenbeg, Ardgroom, Bantry, Co Cork.*
Modernised old farmhouse with lake and mountain views, trout fishing.
Tel: **027 74030** Mrs Crowley.
D: £13.50 **S:** £13.50.
Open: Jun to Sep
Beds: 1F 1T **Baths:** 1 Shared
🅿 (4) 🗶✕🖭📖.☑🛢

Lauragh 13

National Grid Ref: V7754

(🔺0.5m) *Glanmore Lake Youth Hostel, Glenmore Lake, Lauragh, Killarney, Co Kerry.*
Tel: **064 83181**
Under 18: £5.01 **Adults:** £6.51
Self-catering facilities, Shop 6 km away, Parking
This old school house is set at the foot of the Tim Healy pass and near the Beara Way. Magnificent views of the sea, mountains, forests and lakes.

(0.5m 🚐) *Glenmore Lake, Lauragh, Killarney, Co Kerry.*
Actual grid ref: V7754
Farmhouse built in quiet, scenic, National Heritage area. Nestling below the Healy Pass
Tel: **064 83181**
Mr & Mrs O'Shea.
D: £15.00 **S:** £20.00.
Open: Easter to Oct
Beds: 2F 2D
Baths: 2 Ensuite 2 Shared
🛏🅿🗶✕🖭.🛢⚡

(0.5m 🚐) *Josie's Lakeview House, Lauragh, Bantry, South Kerry.*
High standard B&B and Restaurant amidst breathtaking scenery
Tel: **064 83155** Corkery.
D: £17.00 **S:** £17.00.
Open: All Year
Beds: 2F 1S
Baths: 3 Ensuite
🛏🅿🗶✕🖭.🛢⚡

Always telephone
to get directions to
the B&B - you will
save time!

D = Price range per person sharing in a double room

(On path 🚐) *Coolounig House, Lauragh, Kenmare, Killarney, Co Kerry.*
Extended family home on working farm overlooking Kenmare Bay
Tel: **064 83142** (also fax no)
Mrs Lynch.
D: £14.00 **S:** £14.00.
Open: Apr to Oct
Beds: 1F 2D 1T
Baths: 1 Ensuite 2 Shared
🛏🅿🗶✕🖭📖.☑🛢⚡

Tuosist 14

National Grid Ref: V7962

🍴🍺 Lake House

(0.5m 🚐) *Lake House, Cloonee, Tuosist, Kenmare, Killarney, Co Kerry.*
Country house with full bar and restaurant. On Cloonee Lakes with boats and fly-fishing.
Grades: BF 1 Star
Tel: **064 84205** Ms O'Shea.
D: £17.00 **S:** £17.00.
Open: Easter to Oct
Beds: 3D 2T
Baths: 2 Sh
🅿 (20) 🖭.🛢⚡

(0.5m) *B&B by the Sea, Cloonee, Tuosist, Kenmare, Killarney, Co Kerry.*
Tel: **064 84211**
Mr Wyles.
D: £18.00 **S:** £18.00.
Open: All Year
Beds: 1T 3D
Baths: 4 En
🛏🅿 (5) 🔭🖭.🛢⚡
Unique and peaceful C18th waterside farmhouse with mountain/sea/wildlife lookout cabin. Swimming - rock fishing from property. Seal colony nearby. A place and atmosphere not easy to forget.

Lohart 15

National Grid Ref: V8266

(1m) *Ivy Crest, Lohart, Kenmare, Killarney, Co Kerry.*
Comfortable family home with tranquil water gardens and sea view
Tel: **064 84243**
Mrs Kelly.
Fax no: 064 42073
D: £12.00 **S:** £12.00.
Open: Jun to Oct
Beds: 2F 1D
Baths: 2 Shared
🛏🅿 (6) 🗶🔭🖭.☑🛢⚡

Killaha 16

National Grid Ref: V8868

🍴🍺 Sailors Inn

(0.5m 🚐) *Hazelwood, Killaha, Kenmare, Co Kerry.*
Tel: **064 41420**
Mrs Frost-Jones.
D: £14.00-£18.00
S: £16.00-£20.00.
Open: All Year
Beds: 2F 1T 1D
Baths: 1 En 1 Pr 1 Sh
🛏🅿🗶✕🖭☑🛢⚡
On the edge of Kenmare Bay, 2 miles from town. Spectacular views across Kenmare Bay to Ireland's highest mountains. Strand and woodland to explore. Children's play area, pony trekking available on site. Family Homes of Ireland Approved.

Kenmare 17

National Grid Ref: V9070

🍴🍺 Wander Inn, Foley's, Horseshoe, Lime Tree, Coachman's Inn, Shamrock, Packie's, Pat Spillane's, Vestry, Sailors, Old Dutch, Darcy's, Casey's Rest, Lake House

(🔺1m) *Failte Hostel, Shelbourne Street, Kenmare, Killarney, County Kerry.*
Tel: **064 42333**
Adults: £7.00
Old bank house, built in C19th, in the centre of Kenmare. Ideal for both Beara and Kerry Ways.

(0.25m) *Rose Garden Guest House & Restaurant, N70, Kenmare, County Kerry.*
Grades: BF 3 Star
Tel: **064 42288**
Mr & Mrs Ringlever.
Fax no: 064 42305
D: £22.50-£27.50
S: £32.50-£37.50.
Open: Easter to Nov
Beds: 4D 4T
Baths: 8 En
🅿 (20) 🗶✕🖭☑🛢
The Rose Garden Guest House & Restaurant is situated within a few minutes' walk of Kenmare. Set in 1 acre of landscaped garden with 350 roses. 3 and 7 day specials including breakfast and dinner are available. Evening meals available.

Please respect
a B&B's wishes
regarding children,
animals & smoking.

(1m) *O'Donnells of Ashgrove,*
Kenmare, Killarney, Co Kerry.
Grades: BF Approv
Tel: **064 41228** (also fax no)
Mrs O'Donnell.
D: £20.00-£22.00 **S:** £26.50-£28.50.
Open: Easter to Oct
Beds: 2D 1T 1S
Baths: 3 En
⚡ (8) 🅿 (6) 🖵 🛏 🛒 ⅏ ♿
Beautiful country home in peaceful
setting incorporating olde worlde
charm, where guests are welcomed
as friends. Jacobean-style dining
room. Log fire. Spacious, elegant
family lounge with many antiques.
Tea/coffee freely available. mature
garden. Angling enthusiast.
Recommended best 300 B&B's.

(1m 🐾) *White Heather Farm,*
Glengarriff Road, Kenmare,
Killarney, Co Kerry.
4 km on Kenmare/Glengarriff road
N71. Easy to find, head of Beara
Peninsula.
Grades: BF Approv
Tel: **064 41550** Mrs Lovett.
Fax no: 064 42475
D: £18.00-£20.00 **S:** £25.00-£27.00.
Open: May to Oct
Beds: 2F 2D 1T
Baths: 4 En 4 Pr 1 Sh
⚡ 🅿 ⅍ 🖵 🛏 🛒 ⅏ 💟 ⅃ ✂

(1m) *Annagry House, Sneen Road,*
Kenmare, Killarney, Co Kerry.
Tel: **064 41283**
Mrs Carraher-O'Sullivan.
D: £20.00-£20.00 **S:** £27.00-£27.00.
Open: All Year (not Xmas/
New Year)
Beds: 2F 2T 2D
Baths: 6 En
🅿 🖵 🛒 ⅏ 💟 ✂
Ideal location on the Ring of Kerry
Road (N70). Peaceful and quiet yet
only 7 minutes walk from Kenmare
town centre and its award winning
pubs and restaurants. Superb
accommodation, spacious rooms all
ensuite. Bath tubs/ showers.
Extensive breakfast menu. Fresh
ground coffee. Tasty home baking.

(1m 🐾) *River Meadows House,*
Sneen Road, Kenmare, Killarney,
Co Kerry.
Modern house set in rustic sur-
roundings with privet road leading
to sea shore.
Tel: **064 41306** (also fax no)
Mrs Ryan.
D: £19.00-£19.00 **S:** £25.00-£25.00.
Open: Easter to Nov
Beds: 1F 1T 1D 1S **Baths:** 4 Pr
⚡ 🅿 (9) ⅍ 🖵 🛏 🛒 ⅏ 💟 ⅃ ✂

Bringing children with
you? Always ask for
any special rates.

Order your
packed lunches the
evening before you
need them.
Not at breakfast!

(1m) *Ceol Na Habhann, Killarney*
Road, Upper Gortamullen,
Kenmare, Killarney, Co Kerry.
Tel: **064 41498** Mrs O'Shea.
D: £19.00-£21.00 **S:** £25.00-£27.00.
Open: Feb to Nov
Beds: 2F 2D 1T
Baths: 5 En
⚡ 🅿 (6) 🖵 🛏 🛒 ⅏ ♿ 💟 ♿
Welcome to O'Shea's farm home, 1
km from Kenmare off N71
Killarney/Ring of Kerry road. Quiet
scenic area adjacent to Kerry Way /
Beara way. Spacious ensuite rooms
with TV, tea/coffee facilities,
hairdryers. Recommended by travel
writers.

(0.25m) *Ard Na Mara, Pier Road,*
Kenmare, Killarney, Co Kerry.
Modern house, big garden. Front
view overlooking Kenmare Bay.
Five mins' walk town.
Grades: BF Approv
Tel: **064 41399** (also fax no)
Mrs Dahm.
D: £19.00-£20.00 **S:** £25.00-£25.00.
Open: All Year (not Xmas)
Beds: 2D 2T
Baths: 4 Pr
⚡ 🅿 (4) 🛒 💟

(2m 🐾) *Druid Cottage, Sneen*
Road, Kenmare, Co Kerry.
Actual grid ref: V901712
C19th stone cottage situated on
Ring of Kerry road.
Grades: BF Approv
Tel: **064 41803**
Mrs Goldrick.
D: £17.00-£20.00 **S:** £23.50-£25.50.
Open: All Year (not Xmas)
Beds: 1F 1D 1T
Baths: 2 En 1 Pr
⚡ (11) 🅿 (6) 🖵 🛏 🛒 ⅏ 💟 ⅃ ✂

(1m 🐾) *Rockvilla, Templenoe,*
Kenmare, Killarney, Co Kerry.
Grades: BF Approv
Tel: **064 41331**
Mr & Mrs Fahy.
D: £17.00-£19.00 **S:** £20.00-£25.00.
Open: Easter to Nov
Beds: 2F 1D 2T 1S
Baths: 4 En 1 Sh
⚡ 🅿 (10) 🖵 🛏 🗙 ⅏ ✂
Peaceful rural setting near
Templenoe Pier. Relaxed friendly
atmosphere. Large garden and
parking area. Golf and horse riding
within 1 mile. Kenmare, a beautiful
heritage town with many
restaurants and pubs. 4 miles.

(0.25m) *O'Shea's Guest House,*
14 Henry Street, Kenmare,
Killarney, Co Kerry.
Pleasing comfortable guest house in
centre of town.
Tel: **064 41453**
Mr O'Shea.
D: £15.00 **S:** £15.00.
Open: Easter to Oct
Beds: 2F 2D 1T
Baths: 1 En 2 Sh
⚡ (10) 🅿 (4) 🖵 🛏 🗙 ⅏

(1m 🐾) *Droumassig Bridge,*
Kenmare, Killarney, Co Kerry.
On the N71 and Glengariff 3 miles
from Kenmare. Relaxing.
Grades: BF Listed
Tel: **064 41384** Mrs Foley.
D: £13.00-£15.00 **S:** £15.00-£20.00.
Open: Easter to Oct
Beds: 3F 1T 1D
Baths: 3 Sh
⚡ 🅿 ⅍ 🖵 🛏 🗙 🛒 ⅏ ♿ 💟 ⅃ ✂

(1m) *Cherry Hill, Killowen,*
Kenmare, Killarney, Co Kerry.
Located on R569. Beautiful views.
Ideally situated for touring
Kerry/Beara.
Grades: BF Approv
Tel: **064 41715** Mrs Clifford.
D: £17.00-£19.00 .
Open: May to Sep
Beds: 2D 1T
Baths: 2 En 1 Pr
⚡ 🅿 🖵 🛒 ⅏ 💟

(0.25m 🐾) *Inbhear Schein,*
Dauros, Kenmare, Killarney,
Co Kerry.
Family home. Scenic location. Ideal
for exploring Ring of Kerry, Kerry
Way, Beara Way.
Tel: **064 41210**
Mr & Mrs O'Leary.
D: £15.00-£17.00 **S:** £15.00-£20.00.
Open: Easter to Oct
Beds: 1F 1D 1T
Baths: 2 En 2 Sh
⚡ (3) 🅿 (10) 🖵 🗙 ⅏ ⅃ ✂

(0.25m) *Wander Inn, Henry Street,*
Kenmare, Killarney, Co Kerry.
Old-World style family-run hotel in
the heart of Kenmare. Rooms
furnished with beautiful antiques.
Tel: **064 42700** Keane.
Fax no: 064 42569
D: £20.00-£25.00
S: £30.00-£35.00.
Open: All Year (not Xmas)
Beds: 1F 7D 3T 0S
Baths: 11 En
⚡ 🅿 (20) 🖵 🗙 ⅏

Please don't camp
on *anyone's* land
without first obtaining
their permission.

(1m) *The Lodge, Kilgarvan Road, Kenmare, Killarney, Co Kerry.*
Luxury guest house in private gardens, elegantly furnished in period style, king size beds.
Tel: **064 41512** Mrs Quill.
Fax no: 064 41812
D: £25.00-£27.50 **S:** £45.00-£45.00.
Open: Apr to Nov
Beds: 5F 2D 3T
Baths: 10 En
🛏️ 🅿 ⅄ ❑ 🍽️ 🎚️ 🖥️ ⅋ Ⅴ ▮

(1m) *Riverville House, Gortamullen, Kenmare, Co Kerry.*
Actual grid ref: V897722
Luxury B&B, Kenmare town. Antique pine furniture, ideal touring centre - Ring of Kerry.
Tel: **064 41775** Mrs Moore.
D: £18.00-£20.00 **S:** £20.00-£25.00.
Open: Feb to Nov
Beds: 3D
Baths: 3 En
🅿 (4) ⅄ 🖥️

(1m) *The Caha's, Hospital Cross, Kenmare, Killarney, Co Kerry.*
Modern dormer bungalow in scenic peaceful location. Extensive breakfast menu.
Tel: **064 41271** (also fax no)
Mr & Mrs O'Shea.
D: £18.00-£22.00 **S:** £25.00-£27.00.
Open: Easter to Oct
Beds: 2F 2D
Baths: 4 En
🛏️ (5) 🅿 (4) ⅄ ❑ 🎚️ 🖥️ Ⅴ

Dingle Way

Of all the attractions that Ireland has to offer, the Dingle Peninsula packs more per square mile into its narrow frame than any other part of the country. This great Kerry promontory has superb beaches, wild seascapes and towering mountains. It was also home to cultures hundreds, sometimes thousands, of years older than our own, and the evidence for this is everywhere. The Dingle Way itself runs for 95 miles around the peninsula. It starts at Tralee, then heads off along the southern coastline to Dingle and Ventry. At Dunquin you look west across to the Blasket Islands, a haven for seabirds, and think that the next bit of land is America. Moving north, you climb the dramatic and sheer Brandon Mountain, before dropping down to walk the sand dunes of the Magharees Spit. On a June day, with the sun shining and a breeze up, there is no better place in the world. All in all, a great week's walking - well worth going out of your way for.

Guides: *The Way-marked Trails of Ireland* by Michael Fewer (ISBN 0-7171-2386-3), published by Gill & Macmillan, and available from all good bookshops or direct from the publishers (Goldenbridge Ind Est, Inchicore, Dublin 8, Ireland, 01 4531005), £9.99 (+ £2.50 p&p)

The Dingle Way Map Guide is available from Cork/Kerry Tourism, Aras Failte, Grand Parade, Cork, 021 273251, £2.50 (inc. p&p)

Maps: *Ordnance Survey of Ireland* 1:50000 Discovery Series: 70, 71

Tralee   1
National Grid Ref: Q8413

Brogue Inn, Oyster Tavern, Cookery, Skillet, Imperial Hotel, Tankard, Ballgary House Hotel, Earl Of Desmond, Stokers Lodge, Imperial Hotel, Larkin's, Kirby's, Kearne's, Nellie's, Val O'Shea's, Meadowsland Hotel

(▲ 1m) *Finnegan's Holiday Hostel, 17 Denny Street, Tralee, County Kerry.*
Tel: **066 27610 Adults:** £7.50
Evening meal
Old Georgian house, in centre of Tralee, next to Kerry County Museum & National Folk Theatre.

sign means that, *given due notice*, owners will pick you up from the path and drop you off *within reason.*

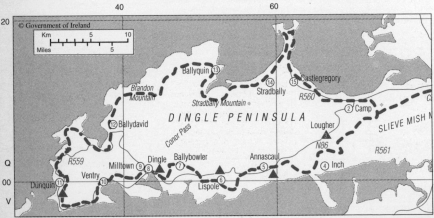

(▲ 2m) *Lisnagree Hostel,*
Ballinorig Road, Tralee, County
Kerry.
Tel: **066 27133 Adults:** £7.00

(▲ 2m) *Collis-Sandes House*
Hostel, Oakpark, Tralee, County
Kerry.
Tel: **066 7128 658**
Under 18: £7.00 **Adults:** £7.50
Self-catering facilities, Television,
Showers, Licensed bar, Central
heating, Laundry facilities, Wet
weather shelter, Lounge, Dining
room, Grounds available for
games, Drying room, Security
lockers, Cycle store, Parking,
Evening meal at by arrangement,
Facilities for disabled people, No
smoking
Listed as 'one of the very best hos-
tels' by the world's best-selling
budget travellers' guide (Let's Go
2000). 20,000 sq ft Venetian Gothic
mansion set in 20 acres of mature
woodland approximately 1.5 miles
from Tralee town centre. Adjoins
18-hole pitch and putt course and
tennis club. Beginning of Dingle
Way/Peninsula.

(1m) *Ballingowan House, Mile*
Height, Killarney Road, Tralee,
Co Kerry.
Tel: **066 7127150** Mrs Kerins.
Fax no: 066 7120325
D: £19.00-£19.00 **S:** £25.50-£25.50.
Open: Easter to Oct
Beds: 4F 2T 2D
Baths: 4 En
🛏 (4) 🅿 (6) ⬩ ⬩ ⬩ 🖳 Ⅴ
Purpose built two storey house
detached on Killarney road. All
spacious rooms ensuite and
interchangeable with TV and
tea/coffee. Breakfast menu, large
private car park. Approaching
Tralee on N21/N22 - on left before
MacDonalds Restaurant. Opposite
Kerry Motor Works.

80

© Government of Ireland

(2m 🚗) *Stonecrest Manor,*
Country Lane, Manor Farm,
Tralee, Co Kerry.
Tel: **066 7120477** Mrs O'Loughlin.
D: £15.00-£17.00 **S:** £16.00-£18.00.
Open: All Year
Beds: 1F 2D 1T
Baths: 4 En
🛏 🅿 (4) ⬩ ⬩ ⬩ × 🖳 Ⅴ ⬩ ⬩
Offering the best for less in a
beautiful private scenic setting in
the countryside close to the town
300m off N21 Tralee-Killarney
road, private parking, public
telephone, TV, tea/coffee facilities
in rooms, central for touring Kerry.

(1m 🚗) *Ashlee House, Manor*
West, Tralee, Co Kerry.
Modern town house 15 mins' walk
town centre.
Tel: **066 7126492** Mrs O'Loughlin.
D: £17.50-£20.00 **S:** £20.00-£25.00.
Open: All Year
Beds: 3D 3T
Baths: 6 En
🛏 (6) 🅿 (7) 🖳 🖳

(1m) *Rosedale Lodge, Oak Park*
Road, Tralee, Co Kerry.
On N69 Listowel (car ferry) Road,
Luxury Accommodation, Spacious
Bedrooms.
Grades: BF ITB listed
Tel: **066 7125320** Mrs Gleeson.
D: £19.00-£20.00 **S:** £25.50.
Open: March to November
Beds: 2T 1D
Baths: 3 En
🅿 ⬩ ⬩ ⬩ 🖳 Ⅴ ⬩

(1m 🚗) *Beech Grove, Oak Park,*
Tralee, Co Kerry.
Picturesque bungalow, large
gardens on N69. Ideal base, touring
Dingle, Ring of Kerry.
Tel: **066 7126788** Mrs O'Neill.
Fax no: 006 7180971
D: £16.00-£20.00 **S:** £17.50-£26.00.
Open: All Year (not Xmas)
Beds: 2F 1T 1D
Baths: 3 En 1 Pr
🛏 🅿 (6) ⬩ ⬩ ⬩ 🖳 Ⅴ ⬩

(1m) *Mountain View House,*
Ballinorig West, Tralee, Co Kerry.
Grades: BF Approv
Tel: **066 7122226** Mrs Curley.
D: £17.00-£19.00 **S:** £23.50-£25.50.
Open: All Year
Beds: 1F 2D 1T **Baths:** 4 En 1 Sh
🛏 (7) 🅿 (9) 🖳 ⬩ 🖳
Experience real comfort and
quality at Mountain view House
with own grounds and car park.
Ideal Golf / touring base adjacent
sport complex and beaches, with
many good restaurants, the Aqua
Dome in Tralee is Irelands largest
Water world. No smoking rooms.

D = Price range per person
sharing in a double room

(0.25m 🚗) *The Grand Hotel,*
Tralee, Co Kerry.
Situated in Tralee town centre. Our
open fires, ornate ceilings and
mahogany furnishings.
Grades: BF 3 Star
Tel: **066 7121499**
Fax no: 066 7122877
D: £30.00-£50.00 **S:** £33.00-£70.00.
Open: All Year (not Xmas)
Beds: 1F 8D 29T 7S
Baths: 44 En
🛏 ⬩ ⬩ × ⬩ 🖳 Ⅴ ⬩

(1m) *Bricriu, 20 Old Golf Links*
Road, Oakpark, Tralee, Co Kerry.
Comfortable bungalow close
railway and all amenities. Also
self-catering.
Grades: BF Approv
Tel: **066 7126347** Mrs Canning.
D: £19.00-£20.00 **S:** £25.00-£25.00.
Open: Apr to Oct
Beds: 1F 1T 1D
Baths: 3 En
🛏 (8) 🅿 ⬩ ⬩ × 🖳 ⬩

(1m) *Curraheen House,*
Curraheen, Tralee, Co Kerry.
Traditional style farmhouse
situated between mountains and
sea, on Tralee/Dingle Road.
Grades: BF Approv
Tel: **066 7121717** Mrs Keane.
Fax no: 066 7128362
D: £19.00 **S:** £25.00
Open: Feb to Nov
Beds: 1F 2D 1T **Baths:** 4 En
🛏 (3) 🅿 (6) ⬩ ⬩ × ⬩ 🖳 Ⅴ ⬩ ⬩

(1m 🚗) *Coisli, Leebrook, Tralee,*
Co Kerry.
Situated on the N21, adjacent to
hotels. All rooms ground floor.
Tel: **066 7126894** Mrs Molyneaux.
D: £15.00-£17.00 **S:** £18.00-£23.00.
Open: All Year (not Xmas)
Beds: 4F 2D 2S
Baths: 4 En 4 Pr
🛏 (6) 🅿 (4) ⬩ ⬩ ⬩ 🖳 ⬩ Ⅴ ⬩

(1m 🚗) *Brianville, Feint Road,*
Tralee, Co Kerry.
Actual grid ref: Q821161
Luxurious bungalow on spacious
grounds, 1 mile from Tralee town,
scenic view of mountain.
Tel: **066 7126645** Mrs Smith.
D: £19.00-£21.00 **S:** £25.00.
Open: All Year (not Xmas)
Beds: 2F 2D 1T **Baths:** 5 En
🛏 🅿 (10) ⬩ ⬩ ⬩ 🖳 Ⅴ

All details shown are as supplied by B&B owners in Autumn 2001.

(1m) *Crana Li, Curragraigue, Blennerville, Tralee, Co Kerry.*
Looking for peace & tranquillity?
All available 1 mile off N86 at Blennerville Village.
Tel: **066 7124467** Mrs Ryle.
D: £30.00-£34.00 **S:** £18.00.
Open: Easter to Sep
Beds: 2F 1D 2T
Baths: 3 En 1 Sh
⛺ ₱ ⊬ ▭ ♨ ▥ ▦ ⓥ ♦

(1m 🚐) *Dormer Road, Alderwood Road, Tralee, Co Kerry.*
Situated 4 km from Tralee town, all rooms ensuite, private car park.
Tel: **066 7126768** Mrs Mitchell.
D: £16.00-£20.00 **S:** £20.00-£25.00.
Open: Easter to Oct
Beds: 1F 1D 1T
Baths: 3 En
⛺ (1) ₱ (3) ▭ ♨ ▦ ⓥ ♦ ⁄

(0.25m 🚐) *Eastcote, 34 Oakpark Demesne, Tralee, Co Kerry.*
Select accommodation in peaceful location. 200 metres off Route N69.
Tel: **066 7125942** Mrs Devane.
D: £17.00-£19.00 **S:** £22.50-£24.50.
Open: All Year (not Xmas)
Beds: 1D 1T 1S
Baths: 2 En 1 Pr
⛺ (10) ₱ (5) ⊬ ▭ ♨ ▦ ⓥ

(0.25m) *Ashville House, Ballyard, Tralee, Co Kerry.*
Architect-designed house in country setting off Dingle road (N86).
Tel: **066 7123717** Mrs O'Keefe.
Fax no: 066 7125698
D: £19.00-£20.00 **S:** £25.50-£25.50.
Open: All Year
Beds: 2F 2D 2T **Baths:** 6 En
⛺ ₱ (8) ⊬ ▭ ♨ ▦ ⓥ ♦ ⁄

(1m) *Rockmount, Mile Height, Tralee, Co Kerry.*
Modern family home on N21, 1 km Tralee 10-15 minutes Farranfore Airport.
Tel: **066 7124507** Mrs Costello.
D: £15.00-£17.00 **S:** £17.00-£20.00.
Open: All Year (not Xmas)
Beds: 1F 1D 1T 1S
Baths: 4 En
⛺ ₱ (6) ▭ ♨ ▦ ⓥ ♦

S = Price range for a single person in a single room

(1m) *Lee Farm House, Leebrook, Tralee, Co Kerry.*
Comfortable old farmhouse in peaceful surroundings, 100 meters off main Tralee/Killarney road (N21).
Tel: **066 7123148**
Mrs Tangney.
D: £16.00-£17.00
S: £17.00-£18.00.
Open: All Year
Beds: 2D 1T
⛺ ₱ ▭ ♨

Camp 2

National Grid Ref: Q6909

(1m) *Suan na Mara, Lisnagree, Camp, Tralee, Co Kerry.*
Peaceful accommodation, highly recommended Laura Ashley style home. Rated AA 4 Diamond, exclusive write up in San Francisco Chronicle. Superb breakfast menu. Private walk to sandy, golden beach. 18 hole Pitch & Putt course on premises.
Grades: BF Approv,
AA 4 Diamond
Tel: **066 7139258** (also fax no)
Mrs Fitzgerald.
D: £20.00-£23.00
S: £26.00-£46.00.
Open: Mar to Oct
Beds: 4D 2T 1S
Baths: 7 En
⛺ ₱ (8) ⊬ ▭ ♨ ▦ ⓥ ♦

Lougher 3

National Grid Ref: Q6404

(▲ 1m) *Bog View Hostel, Lougher, Inch, Tralee, County Kerry.*
Tel: **066 58125**
Adults: £7.00
Evening meal at
Family-run, small, cosy, friendly. Old schoolhouse, situated in the middle of the Dingle Peninsula. Easy access to beaches, lakes & mountains. Vehicle back-up from footpath.

Inch 4

National Grid Ref: Q6501

(2m) *Waterside, Inch, Annascaul, Dingle Peninsula, Co Kerry.*
Modern spacious friendly quality accommodation. Superb, central, scenic seaside setting
Grades: BF Approv
Tel: **066 9158129**
Mrs Kennedy.
D: £17.00
S: £20.00.
Open: All Year
Beds: 1F 1T 2D
Baths: 4 Ensuite
⛺ ₱ (6) ⊬ ✕ ♨ ▦ ♦ ⁄

Annascaul 5

National Grid Ref: Q5902

⋈ ▦ Brackluin House,†South Pole Inn

(▲ 0.5m) *Fuchsia Lodge Holiday Hostel, Annascaul, Tralee, County Kerry.*
Actual grid ref: Q613028
Tel: **066 57150 Adults:** £6.00
Evening meal available, Facilities for disabled people
Custom built, rural setting, 1 mile from Annascaul. Views of surrounding valley.

(0.25m) *Four Winds, Annascaul, Dingle Peninsula, Co Kerry.*
Scenic views. Ideal for touring Dingle Peninsula. Friendly village of Annascaul.
Grades: BF Approv
Tel: **066 9157168** Mrs O'Connor.
Fax no: 066 9157174
D: £17.00-£19.00 **S:** £21.00-£23.00.
Open: 24 Dec to 1-1
Beds: 2F 2T 2D
Baths: 4 En 2 Sh
⛺ ₱ ▭ ♨ ▦ ⓥ ♦ ⁄

(0.25m 🚐) *Brackluin House, Annascaul, Tralee, Co Kerry.*
In small village surrounded by hills with changing colours, close to river and sea.
Tel: **066 9157145**
Mr & Mrs Knightly.
D: £15.00-£17.00 **S:** £19.00.
Open: Mar to Oct
Beds: 1F 1D 2T
Baths: 4 En
⛺ ₱ (20) ▭ ♨ ✕ ♨ ▦ ⓥ ♦

(0.25m) *Ardrinane House, Annascaul, Tralee, Co Kerry.*
Family home with landscaped gardens situated beside Annascaul River.
Tel: **066 9157119** Mr O'Donnell.
Fax no: 0667127890
D: £18.00-£18.00 **S:** £25.00-£25.00.
Open: All Year (not Xmas)
Beds: 4F, 2T, 2S
Baths: 4 En, 4 Pr
⛺ (1) ₱ (4) ▭ ♨ ▦ ⓥ ♦ ⁄

Lispole 6

National Grid Ref: Q5200

(▲ 1m) *Seacrest Hostel, Kinard West, Lispole, Tralee, County Kerry.*
Tel: **066 51390 Adults:** £6.00
Evening meal

Bringing children with you? Always ask for any special rates.

Ballybowler 7

National Grid Ref: Q4705

⛺ ⬛ Murphy's

(0.5m ☎) *Bay View House,*
Ballybowler, Dingle, Tralee,
Co Kerry.
Actual grid ref: Q4605
Situated on scenic tranquil Dingle
Way. Spectacular views from bed-
rooms. Extensive breakfast menu.
Tel: **066 9151704** Mrs Barrett.
D: £15.00-£18.00 **S:** £20.00.
Open: Easter to Oct
Beds: 1F 1D 1T
Baths: 3 En
⛺ (2) 🅿 (5) ⬛ 🔥 ♨ ⬛ ⬛ ⬛ ▮ ⚡

Dingle 8

National Grid Ref: Q4401

⛺ ⬛ Long's, Murphy's, Paudie's, Half Door,
Whelan's, Quay, De Barra's, Ventry Inn, Lord
Bakers, Garvey's, Cormorant, Larkin's, O'Shea's,
Cosgroves, Plough Bar, O'Brien's, Fishery,
Bianconi Inn

(▲ On path) *Ballintaggart Hostel*
& Equestrian Centre, Racecourse
Road, Dingle, Tralee, County
Kerry.
Tel: **066 51454 Adults:** £6.00
Evening meal available, Facilities
for disabled people
Old hunting lodge, built in 1703,
set in 22 acres of farmland.
Overlooks Dingle Bay. Horse
riding, bike hire, wetsuit hire.

(0.25m) *Alpine House, Mail Road,*
Dingle, Co Kerry.
Grades: BF 3 Star, AA 4
Diamond, RAC 4 Diamond
Tel: **066 9151250** Mr O'Shea.
Fax no: 066 9151966
D: £18.50-£28.00 **S:** £25.00-£40.00.
Open: All Year (not Xmas)
Beds: 2F 5D 5T
Baths: 12 En
⛺ (4) 🅿 (12) ⚡ ⬛ ♨ ⬛ ⬛ ⚡
Delightfully furnished bedrooms
with spacious private bathrooms.
Rooms with excellent views of
harbour and mountains. A menu of
traditional and wholesome fare
served in impressive breakfast
room. Dingle, famous for seafood
and traditional Irish music bars.
Near bus stop.

Phoning from outside
the Republic?
Dial 00353 and omit
the initial '0' of the
area code.

Pay B&Bs by cash or
cheque and be prepared
to pay up front.

(0.25m ☎) *Pax House, Dingle,*
Tralee, County Kerry.
Grades: BF 4 Star,
AA 4 Diamond
Tel: **066 9151518**
Mrs Brosnan-Wright.
Fax no: 066 9152461
D: £25.00-£45.00 **S:** £35.00-£40.00.
Open: All Year (not Xmas/
New Year)
Beds: 1F 7D 2T 3S
Baths: 13 En
⛺ 🅿 (10) ⬛ 🔥 ♨ ⬛ ▮ ⚡
Pax House has undeniably one of
the most spectacular views in the
peninsula. All rooms including
suites beautifully appointed.
Gourmet breakfast includes local
produce, home-made breads and
preserves. Enjoy a drink on the
balcony and watch the boats return
with their catch.

(1m) *Kavanaghs, Garfinny,*
Dingle, Tralee, Co Kerry.
Family run, 3 km Dingle town,
golf, angling, boat trips, moun-
taineering.
Grades: BF Approv
Tel: **066 9151326** Mrs Kavanagh.
D: £16.00-£19.00 **S:** £23.50.
Open: Easter to Sep
Beds: 1F 3D
Baths: 3 En 1 Pr
⛺ 🅿 (6) ⬛ ✗ ♨ ⬛ ▮ ▮

(0.5m ☎) *O'Shea's, Conor Pass*
Road, Dingle, Tralee, Co Kerry.
Actual grid ref: Q456016
Modern home in peaceful scenic
area within walking distance of
Dingle town.
Tel: **066 9151368** Mrs O'Shea.
D: £16.00-£18.00 **S:** £21.00-£21.00.
Open: Easter to Nov
Beds: 1F 2D 1T
Baths: 3 En
⛺ (5) 🅿 ⬛ ♨ ⬛ ⬛ ▮

(1m) *Doonshean View, High Road,*
Garfinny, Dingle, Tralee,
Co Kerry.
Grades: BF Approv
Tel: **066 9151032** Mrs O'Neill.
D: £19.00-£20.00 **S:** £25.50-£27.00.
Open: Easter to Oct
Beds: 2F 1D 1T
Baths: 4 En
⛺ 🅿 (4) ⚡ ⬛ ⬛
Dormer bungalow with fire safety
certificate. Tranquil location.
Surrounded by 'Slieve Mist'
Mountains. Close to beaches and
popular walks. Ideal for touring
Dingle Peninsula, fishing, hill
walking, horse riding, golf, sea
sports, excellent restaurants.
Private parking.

(1m) *Old Mill House, 3 Avondale*
Street, Dingle, Co Kerry.
Town centre, warm hospitality,
pine beds, turf fires. Spacious
comfortable rooms.
Tel: **066 9151120** (also fax no)
Ms Houlihan.
D: £15.00-£25.00 **S:** £18.00-£23.00.
Open: All Year
Beds: 1F 2T 1D 1S
Baths: 3 En 1 Pr
⛺ 🅿 (1) ⚡ ⬛ 🔥 ♨ ⬛ ▮ ▮ ⚡

(0.25m ☎) *Kirrary House,*
Avondale St, Dingle, Tralee,
Co Kerry.
Traditional family Irish home: nice
atmosphere, open turf fires
downstairs.
Tel: **066 9151606** Mrs Collins.
D: £18.00-£22.00 **S:** £23.50-£28.00.
Open: All Year
Beds: 1D 1T 1S
Baths: 2 En 1 Sh
⬛ ⬛ ▮

(1m ☎) *Duinin House, Connor*
Pass Road, Dingle, Tralee,
Co Kerry.
Superb location with magnificent
views. Overlooking Dingle town
and harbour.
Tel: **066 9151335** (also fax no)
Mrs Neligan.
D: £18.00-£19.00 **S:** £20.00.
Open: Easter to Feb
Beds: 3D 2T
Baths: 5 En
⛺ (7) 🅿 (5) ⚡ ⬛ ♨ ⬛ ▮ ▮ ⚡

(0.25m) *Ard Na Greine House,*
Spa Road, Dingle, Tralee,
Co Kerry.
Luxury immaculate bungalow in a
superb location 5 minutes' walk to
town centre.
Tel: **066 9151113** Mrs Houlihan.
Fax no: 066 9151898
D: £19.00-£22.00 .
Open: All Year (not Xmas)
Beds: 2D 2T
Baths: 4 En
⛺ (7) 🅿 (4) ⚡ ⬛ ♨ ⬛ ▮

(0.25m) *Dykegate Street, Dingle,*
Tralee, Co Kerry.
Comfortable guest house in the
heart of Dingle town.
Tel: **066 9151598** (also fax no)
Mrs Connor.
D: £18.00-£27.00 **S:** £18.00-£25.00.
Open: All Year (not Xmas)
Beds: 2F 7D 5T 1S
Baths: 15 En
⛺ ⬛ ♨ ⬛ ▮ ▮

(0.25m ☎) *Bambury's Guest*
House, Mail Road, Dingle, Tralee,
Co Kerry.
Popular 3 Star guest house. One
minute's walk from Dingle town.
Tel: **066 9151244** Mr Bambury.
Fax no: 066 51786
D: £18.00-£30.00 **S:** £20.00-£40.00.
Open: All Year
Beds: 1F 3D 8T **Baths:** 12 En
⛺ (4) 🅿 (12) ⬛ ♨ ⬛ ⬛ ▮

Milltown (Dingle) 9

National Grid Ref: Q4301

⚐ Larkin's, O'Shea's, Cosgroves, Plough Bar, O'Brien's, The Fishery, Bianconi Inn, Paudie's

(0.25m) *Cill Bhreac, Milltown, Dingle, Tralee, Co Kerry.*
Actual grid ref: Q430011
Spacious home overlooking Dingle Bay, Mount Brandon. All rooms satellite TV, hairdryer, electric blankets.
Grades: BF Approv
Tel: **066 9151358** Mrs McCarthy.
D: £19.00-£20.00 **S:** £25.00-£26.00.
Open: Mar to Nov
Beds: 3F 2D 1T **Baths:** 6 En
ⓑ 🅿 (8) ☐ 🛋 🎹 Ⅴ ✧

Ventry 10

National Grid Ref: Q3800

⚐ Paudie O'Shea's, Cormorants' Rest, Ventry Inn, Skipper

(1m) *Garvey's Farmhouse, Kilvicadownig, Ventry, Dingle, Tralee, Co Kerry.*
Spacious house on dairy farm overlooking Ventry Bay in peaceful surroundings.
Grades: BF Approv
Tel: **066 9159914** Mrs Garvey.
Fax no: 066 9159921
D: £18.50-£21.00 **S:** £26.00-£28.00.
Open: Mar to Nov
Beds: 2F 2D 1T
Baths: 4 En 1 Pr
ⓑ 🅿 (6) ☐ 🗶 🎹 ✧

(1m) *Ard Na Mara, Ballymore, Ventry, Dingle, Tralee, Co Kerry.*
Situated 3 miles from Dingle on the Slea Head scenic drive.
Grades: BF Approv, AA 3 Star
Tel: **066 9159072** Mrs Murphy.
D: £18.00-£19.00 **S:** £20.00-£25.00.
Open: Easter to Oct
Beds: 4F 2D 1S
Baths: 4 En 4 Pr 1 Sh
ⓑ (7) ☐ 🍴 🛋 🎹 Ⅴ 🛆 ✧

(1m) *Moriarty's Farmhouse, Rahanane, Ventry, Tralee, Co Kerry.*
Family-run home overlooking Ventry Harbour 8km west of Dingle. Signposted at Ventry Church.
Tel: **066 9159037** (also fax no)
Mrs Moriarty.
D: £17.50-£18.50 **S:** £23.00-£25.00.
Open: All Year
Beds: 3F 2D 1T **Baths:** 6 En
ⓑ 🅿 (6) ☐ 🗶 🛋 🎹 Ⅴ 🛆 ✧

All paths are popular: you are well-advised to book ahead

(1m 🐾) *Ballymore House, Ballymore, Ventry, Dingle, Tralee, Co Kerry.*
Friendly, family, no-smoking home in peaceful surroundings. Sea view, breakfast/dinner menu.
Tel: **066 9159050**
Mr & Mrs O'Shea.
D: £20.00-£22.00 **S:** £30.00-£30.00.
Open: All Year
Beds: 3F 3D 1T **Baths:** 5 En 2 Pr
ⓑ 🅿 (7) ✂ ☐ 🗶 🛋 🎹 Ⅴ 🛆 ✧

(1m) *Mount Eagle Lodge, Clahane, Ventry, Dingle, Co Kerry.*
Designer house. Fantastic sea, beach and mountain views. Acclaimed breakfasts
Tel: **066 9159754** (also fax no)
Mr Prestage.
D: £18.00 **S:** £24.50.
Open: Easter to Oct
Beds: 2F 2T
Baths: 4 Ensuite 1 Private
ⓑ (2) 🅿 (6) ✂ ☐ 🗶 🛋 🎹 🛆 Ⅴ

(0.25m) *Ceann Tra Heights, Ventry, Dingle, Tralee, Co Kerry.*
Modern dormer bungalow overlooking Ventry Harbour. Sea view from rooms
Grades: BF Approv
Tel: **066 9159866** (also fax no)
Mrs Carroll.
D: £18.00 **S:** £25.00.
Open: Apr to Sep (& New Year)
Beds: 1F 1D 2T **Baths:** 4 Ensuite
ⓑ 🅿 ☐ 🗶 🛋 🎹 Ⅴ 🛆 ✧

Dunquin 11

National Grid Ref: Q3101

⚐ Kruger's

(▲ 0.25m) *Dunquin Youth Hostel, Dunquin, Tralee, County Kerry.*
Tel: **066 915 6121**
Under 18: £5.50 **Adults:** £6.50
Self-catering facilities, Shop 8 km, or limited supplies at hostel, Drying room, Parking, Meals available groups by prior arrangement
Situated on the Dingle Way, this is the most westerly hostel in Europe. Good hillwalking and cycling plus many archaeological sites.

(1m) *Kruger's Guest House, Ballinaraha, Dunquin, Dingle, Tralee, Co Kerry.*
Grades: BF Approv
Tel: **066 9156127** Mrs O'Neill.
D: £18.00-£18.00 **S:** £18.00-£18.00.
Open: Mar to Oct
Beds: 1F 3D 2T 1S **Baths:** 3 Sh
ⓑ (10) 🅿 (50) ☐ 🍴 🗶 🎹 🛆
Famous and popular traditional guest house and lounge bar. Situated in the heart of the spectacular Dingle Peninsula. Ideal for touring the popular Dingle Way route and the scenic Slea Head Way route. Two lovely sandy beaches nearby. Visit 'Ryan's Daughter', filmed nearby.

Bringing children with you? Always ask for any special rates.

Ballydavid 12

National Grid Ref: Q3807

(▲ 0.25m) *Tigh an Phoist Hostel, Bothar Bui, Ballydavid, Tralee, County Kerry.*
Tel: **066 55109 Adults:** £6.50

(1m) *An Bothar Pub, Cuas, Ballydavid, Tralee, Co Kerry.*
New building in old style. Dining room & bar. Evening entertainment. Ideal base walking, fishing
Tel: **066 9155342**
Mr & Mrs Walsh.
D: £18.00 **S:** £20.00.
Open: All Year (not Xmas)
Beds: 2F 2T 2D
Baths: 2 Ensuite
ⓑ 🗶 🎹 🛆 ✧

Ballyquin 13

National Grid Ref: Q5213

⚐ O'Shea's

(0.25m 🐾) *Ard na Feinne B&B, Ballyquin, Brandon, Tralee, Co Kerry.*
Homely atmosphere on Dingle Way, mountains, angling, archaeological sites, beaches.
Grades: BF Approv
Tel: **066 7138220** (also fax no)
Mrs Nicholl.
D: £15.00-£18.00
S: £20.00-£23.00.
Open: May to Sep
Beds: 1F 1D 1T
Baths: 2 En
ⓑ 🅿 (6) ☐ 🎹 🛆 ✧

Stradbally 14

National Grid Ref: Q5912

(▲ 1m) *Connor Pass Hostel, Stradbally, Castlegregory, Tralee, County Kerry.*
Tel: **066 39179 Adults:** £7.00
Evening meal

Taking your dog?
Book *in advance*
ONLY with owners
who accept dogs (🐾)

Castlegregory 15

National Grid Ref: Q6113

⚲ ⬛ O'Riordan's, Tomasin's, Spillane's, Ferriter's

(2m) *Beenoskee, Conor Pass Road, Cappatigue, Castlegregory, Tralee, Co Kerry.*
Grades: BF Approv
Tel: **066 7139263** (also fax no)
Mrs Ferriter.
D: £18.00-£19.00 **S:** £25.00-£26.00.
Open: All Year
Beds: 3D 1T
Baths: 3 En 1 Pr
ॐ 🅿 (6) ⊬◻✕⌂ 🎵 ⣿, Ⓥ 🛏
Warm Irish hospitality, complimentary tea/home made cake. Tastefully decorated rooms directly overlooking ocean and long safe unspoilt sandy within walking distance. Spectacular views, mountains, islands and lake. Orthopaedic beds, extensive breakfast menu, home baking. Numerous recommendations, golf, fishing, surfing and tranquil walks.

(0.25m 🚐**)** *The Shores Country House, Conor Pass Road, Cappatigue, Castlegregory, Tralee, Co Kerry.*
Grades: BF Approv,
AA 5 Diamond
Tel: **066 7139196** (also fax no)
Mrs O'Mahony.
D: £19.00-£23.00 **S:** £23.50-£28.50.
Open: Feb to Nov
Beds: 1F 4D 1T
Baths: 6 En
ॐ (3) 🅿 (8) ⊬◻✕⌂ 🎵 ⣿, Ⓥ 🛏 ✦
Welcoming, luxurious, award-winning, AA 5 Diamond Selected, spacious Laura Ashley style house, totally refurbished and extended in 1999. Rooms all with panoramic sea view. Extensive breakfast/dinner menu, packed lunch, highly recommended by guides.

D = Price range per person
sharing in a double room

(2m) *Sea Mount House, Cappatigue Conor Pass Road, Castlegregory, Tralee, Co Kerry.*
Charming home. Outstanding sea views. Stylishly decorated rooms. Near Restaurant.
Grades: BF Approv,
AA 3 Diamond
Tel: **066 7139229** (also fax no)
Mrs Walsh.
D: £18.00-£20.00 **S:** £20.00-£26.00.
Open: Marc 1st to Nov 30th
Beds: 1F 1T 2D **Baths:** 3 En 1 Pr
ॐ 🅿 (4) ⊬◻🔥⌂ 🎵 ⣿, Ⓥ

(1m) *Griffins Tip Top Country Farmhouse, Goulane, Castlegregory, Tralee, Co Kerry.*
Two storey farmhouse on the beautiful Dingle Peninsula. Fronted by safe, sandy beaches.
Tel: **066 7139147** (also fax no)
Mrs Griffin.
D: £20.00-£20.00 **S:** £20.00-£20.00.
Open: Mar to Nov
Beds: 3F 3D 3T 1S
Baths: 6 En 4 Sh
ॐ (5) 🅿 (10) ◻🔥⣿.

Kerry Way

The **Kerry Way** is probably the most famous of the long distance footpaths in Ireland. Its road equivalent, the Ring of Kerry, is more famous still. Now and then in summer on this path you'll catch sight of the coaches ferrying the hordes on the round trip from Killarney. Not for you the prospect of a cramped aisle seat and a steamed-up window. Rather the thrill of passing through on foot the most rugged mountain country that Ireland has to offer. The **Kerry Way** is a circular path, running for 134 miles around the Iveragh peninsula. The starting-point, Killarney, has been a tourist trap for over 200 years. You escape past the lakes to the woodland glens and rivers of the National Park and cut through below Macgillycuddy's Reeks to Glencar. Then it's off via Carragh Lake to the beautiful Glenbeigh and the Dingle Bay coastline beyond. From Foilmore the path turns south to reach a high vantage point over the Kenmare River at Eagle Hill, before descending to head east along the coast via Sneem to Kenmare. All in all, it makes for a great 10-day trip. Or, because the path is circular, it's easier to sample in stages as you please.

Guides: *The Way-marked Trails of Ireland* by Michael Fewer (ISBN 0-7171-2386-3), published by Gill & Macmillan, and available from all good bookshops or direct from the publishers (Goldenbridge Ind Est, Inchicore, Dublin 8, Ireland, 01 4531005), £9.99 (+ £2.50 p&p)

The Kerry Way Map Guide is available from Cork/Kerry Tourism, Aras Failte, Grand Parade, Cork, 021 273251, £2.50 (inc. p&p)

Maps: Ordnance Survey of Ireland 1:50000 Discovery Series: 78, 83, 84

Killarney 1

National Grid Ref: V1992

🍴🍺 Acorn Bar, Randles Court, Kit Flaherty's, Linden House, Darby O'Gills, The Failte, Molly D'Arcys, Paddy's, Ross Hotel, McSweeney Arms, Murphy's, Gaby's, Whitegates Hotel, Kiely's, Killarney Heights, Old Bar, Laurels, Buckley's, Gleneagle Hotel, Golden Nugget, Laune, Sceilig, Kate Kearney's, Arbutus Hotel, Flesk Rest, Mac's Rest, Sheehans Bar, Beaufort Bar

(▲4m) *Killarney International Youth Hostel*, Aghadoe House, Killarney, County Kerry.
Tel: **064 31240**
Under 18: £7.50 **Adults:** £8.00
Self-catering facilities, Shop, Laundry facilities, Parking, Facilities for disabled people, Meals available groups only, by prior arrangement
This recently renovated 18th century mansion is set in 75 acres of lawns and forests, overlooking Killarney's National Park. Ideal base for touring the Ring of Kerry, Gap of Dunloe and Dingle Peninsula.

(▲2.5m) *Bunrower House Hostel*, Ross Road, Killarney, County Kerry.
Actual grid ref: V957894
Tel: **064 33914 Adults:** £6.50
C19th gate lodge to the old country estate. Adjacent to Ross Island area of National Park.

(▲1m) *Killarney Railway Hostel*, Fair Hill, Killarney, County Kerry.
Tel: **064 35299**
Adults: £7.00
Evening meal available, Facilities for disabled people

(▲1m) *Neptune's Town Hostel*, New Street, Killarney, County Kerry.
Tel: **064 35255**
Adults: £6.00
Evening meal available, Facilities for disabled people

(▲1m) *Park Hostel*, Park Road, Killarney, County Kerry.
Tel: **064 32119**
Adults: £7.00

D = Price range per person sharing in a double room

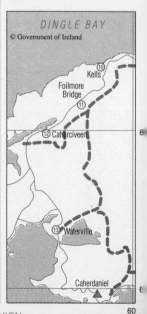

DINGLE BAY

© Government of Ireland

Kells ⑩
Foilmore Bridge ⑪
⑫ Cahirciveen
⑬ Waterville
Caherdaniel

(3m 🚗) *Killarney Villa,*
Cork/Mallow Road (N72),
Killarney, Co Kerry.
Grades: BF Approv, AA 4 Diamond,
RAC 4 Diamond, Sparkling
Tel: **064 31878** (also fax no)
Mr & Mrs O'Sullivan.
D: £23.00-£23.00 **S:** £25.00-£25.00.
Open: Easter to Oct
Beds: 1F 3D 2T **Baths:** 6 En
🛏 (6) 🅿 (10) 🍴 🛉 ⅲ 🖳 Ⅴ ✓
Killarney Villa is a welcoming
family country home. Highly
recommended for its good food,
service, hygiene and holiday value
(AA 4Q Award). Complimentary
tea/coffee/refreshments available in
our luxurious roof top conservatory
7 am - 11 pm daily. Extensive
breakfast menu.

(1m 🚗) *Fair Haven,* Cork Road,
Lissivigeen (N22), Killarney,
Co Kerry.
Grades: BF Approv
Tel: **064 32542** Mrs Teahan.
D: £17.00-£19.00 **S:** £23.00-£25.00.
Open: May to Oct
Beds: 1F 2D 2T **Baths:** 4 En 1 Pr
🅿 (5) ✓ ⅲ 🖳 Ⅴ
Country home in scenic location,
warm, friendly welcome assured.
Tea & coffee making facilities in
TV lounge. breakfast menu. Pickup
point for Ring of Kerry and other
tours. Golf, fishing, horse riding
locally. Convenient to Muckross
house and gardens.

(1m) *Foley's Town House,* 23 High
Street, Killarney, Co Kerry.
Grades: BF 4 Star,
AA 5 Diamond
Tel: **064 31217**
Mrs Hartnett.
Fax no: 064 34683
D: £35.00-£37.50
S: £45.00-£45.00.
Open: Easter to Nov
Beds: 12D 12T 4S
Baths: 28 En
🛏 (3) 🅿 (60) ✓ ⅲ 🗙 ⅲ 🖳 Ⅴ ⓘ
Originally a C18th coaching inn,
newly refurbished, now a 4 Star
family-run guest house, located
town centre. Downstairs an award
winning seafood and steak
restaurant. Chef/owner Carol
Hartnett supervises.

(1m) *Avondale House,* Tralee
Road, Killarney, Co Kerry.
Grades: BF Approv, AA 3 Star
Tel: **064 35579** (also fax no)
Ms Leahy.
D: £19.50-£20.00 **S:** £28.00-£30.00.
Open: Feb to Nov
Beds: 1F 2T 3D
Baths: 6 En
🅿 (10) 🖵 ⅲ 🖳 Ⅴ
Avondale house is a distinctive two
storey modern family run B&B,
situated on the N22, 4 km from
Killarney. Surrounded by
landscaped gardens. 10 minutes
drive to the golf courses and lakes.

(1m) *Wind Way House,* New Road,
Killarney, Co Kerry.
Grades: BF Approved
Tel: **064 32835** Mrs Ahern.
Fax no: 064 37887
D: £20.00-£22.00 **S:** £27.00-£30.00.
Open: All Year (not Xmas/New
Year)
Beds: 2T 4D **Baths:** 6 En
🛏 🅿 (4) ✓ 🖵 ⅲ 🖳 Ⅴ
Winding Way House is a modern
bungalow with all modern
facilities, located in a quiet area
within 5 mins walk of town centre
and national park. 6 bedrooms
ensuite with TV, hairdryers and
central heating. Bedrooms non
smoking. Tea and Coffee in lounge.

(1m) *Tullyfern Villa,* Woodlawn
Road, Killarney, Co Kerry.
Family-run B&B. Walking distance
to town & local facilities. Quiet
location.
Tel: **064 32413** Mrs O'Sullivan.
D: £17.00-£19.00 **S:** £20.00-£25.00.
Open: Easter to Oct
Beds: 2F 1D 1T 1S
Baths: 5 En
🛏 🅿 (5) ✓ 🖵 ⅲ 🖳 & Ⅴ ⓘ ✓

S = Price range for a single
person in a single room

© Government of Ireland

STILWELL'S NATIONAL TRAIL COMPANION

(0.25m 🚗) *Slieve Bloom Manor,*
Muckross Road, Killarney,
Co Kerry.
Charming, friendly guest house,
prime location. Do check us out for
yourself.
Grades: BF 3 Star
Tel: 064 34237 Ms Clery.
Fax no: 064 35055
D: £18.00-£25.00 **S:** £18.00-£30.00.
Open: All Year (not Xmas)
Beds: 4D 10T **Baths:** 14 En
🛇 🅿 (10) ⌨ 🧺 🎹 Ⅴ 🛈 ⚡

(1m 🚗) *River Valley Farm House,*
Minish, Killarney, Co Kerry.
Old style farmhouse on working
farm, modern facilities, fishing on
river.
Grades: BF Approv
Tel: 064 32411 Mrs O'Sullivan.
Fax no: 064 37909
D: £16.00-£18.00 **S:** £20.00-£22.00.
Open: Mar to Nov
Beds: 6F 3D 1T 2S **Baths:** 6 Pr
🛇 🅿 (8) ⅍ ⌨ 🐎 🗡 🧺 🎹 Ⅴ 🛈 ⚡

(1m) *Killarney Town House,*
31 New St, Killarney, Co Kerry.
Killarney town house ideally
situated in heart of Killarney town
centre.
Grades: BF 2 Star
Tel: 064 35388 Mrs Hallissey.
Fax no: 064 35259
D: £23.00-£25.00 **S:** £30.00-£35.00.
Open: All Year
Beds: 8D 3T **Baths:** 11 En
🛇 ⅍ ⌨ 🐎 🗡 🎹

(2.5m) *Serenic View,*
Coolcorcoran, Killarney,
Co Kerry.
Ground floor accommodation.
Direct dial telephones. Quiet scenic
area overlooking Killarney.
Grades: BF Approv
Tel: 064 33434 Ms Murphy.
Fax no: 064 33578
D: £19.00-£19.00 **S:** £25.50-£25.50.
Open: Apr to Oct
Beds: 1F 2D 1T
Baths: 4 En
🛇 🅿 (6) ⌨ 🧺 🎹 Ⅴ

(1m) *Friary View, Dennehy's*
Bohereen, Killarney, Co Kerry.
House in quiet area close to town
and all amenities.
Grades: BF Approv
Tel: 064 32996 Mrs Tuohy.
D: £16.00-£16.00 .
Open: May to Sep
Beds: 2D 2T
Baths: 4 En
🅿 ⌨ 🧺 🎹 ♿ Ⅴ

(1m) *Eagle View, 21 Woodlawn*
Park, Killarney, Co Kerry.
Warm, friendly home from home.
Walking distance to all sightseeing
and entertainment.
Tel: 064 32779 Mrs Brosnan.
D: £18.00 **S:** £23.00.
Open: Easter to Oct
Beds: 1F 1T 1D **Baths:** 2 En 1 Pr
🛇 (7) 🐎 🎹 Ⅴ ⚡

(0.25m) *Flesk Lodge, Muckross*
Road, Killarney, Co Kerry.
Modern luxury bungalow, walking
distance town centre. Beautiful
gardens overlooking River Flesk &
Killarney Lakes.
Tel: 064 9132135 (also fax no)
Mr & Mrs Mannix.
D: £19.00-£20.00 **S:** £26.00.
Open: All Year
Beds: 1F 1D 4T **Baths:** 6 En
🛇 🅿 ⌨ 🗡 🧺 🎹 Ⅴ 🛈 ⚡

(1m) *Sunrise Villa, Mill Road,*
Flesk Castle, Killarney, Co Kerry.
Modern two-storey farmhouse situ-
ated in quiet scenic surroundings.
Nature walks.
Grades: BF Approv
Tel: 064 32159 (also fax no)
Mrs O'Donoghue.
D: £19.00 .
Open: May to Oct
Beds: 2D 2T **Baths:** 4 En 1 Sh
🛇 🅿 (4) ⌨ 🎹

(1m 🚗) *Lime Court, Muckross*
Road, Killarney, Co Kerry.
Superb quality, great location, 10%
discount on 3 night stays.
Grades: BF 3 Star, AA 4 Diamond
Tel: 064 34547 Mr Courtney.
Fax no: 064 34121
D: £23.00-£30.00 **S:** £23.00-£38.00.
Open: Feb to Nov
Beds: 3F 3T 8d 7S **Baths:** 21 En
🛇 (3) 🅿 ⅍ ⌨ 🗡 🧺 🎹 ♿ Ⅴ ⚡

(1m) *Glebe Farmhouse, Tralee*
Road, Killarney, Co Kerry.
5 kms from Killarney, overlooking
mountains. Ideal touring centre for
Kerry
Grades: BF Irish Farmhouse
Listed
Tel: 064 32179
Mr & Mrs O'Connor.
Fax no: 064 32039
D: £15.00-£19.00 **S:** £19.00-£22.00.
Open: All Year
Beds: 2F 2D 1T 1S
Baths: 4 En 1 Pr 1 Sh
🛇 🅿 (8) ⅍ ⌨ 🐎 🗡 🧺 🎹 Ⅴ

(1m 🚗) *Redwood Country House*
and Apartments, Rockfield, Tralee
Road, Killarney, Co Kerry.
Large house and apartments on 15
acres, extensive breakfast menu.
Tel: 064 34754 Mrs Murphy.
Fax no: 064 34178
D: £19.00-£20.00 **S:** £25.00-£34.00.
Open: All Year
Beds: 2F 2D 2T **Baths:** 6 En 6 Pr
🛇 🅿 (6) ⌨ 🧺 🎹 Ⅴ 🛈 ⚡

(1m 🚗) *Mountain Dew, 3 Ross*
Road, Killarney, Co Kerry.
Modern town house situated 3
minute walk from town centre, rail
and bus.
Tel: 064 33892 Mrs Carroll.
Fax no: 064 31332
D: £16.00-£19.00 **S:** £25.00-£35.00.
Open: All Year (not Xmas)
Beds: 1F 4D 1T **Baths:** 6 En
🛇 (3) 🅿 (6) 🎹 ⚡

(1m) *Doogary, Lewis Road,*
Killarney, Co Kerry.
Select family-run B&B.
Convenient to town. Beautiful
walks.
Tel: 064 32509
Mrs O'Brien.
D: £15.00 **S:** £20.00.
Open: May to Oct
Beds: 1F 1D 1T
Baths: 3 En 1 Pr
🛇 🅿 (4) 🎹

(1m) *Sunflower Cottage, Tralee*
Road, Killarney, Co Kerry.
Excellent location offering superb
accommodation with view of
Kerry's mountains.
Tel: 064 32101
Mrs O'Connor Wright.
D: £19.00-£26.00 **S:** £25.00-£40.00.
Open: Mar to Nov
Beds: 1F 3D
Baths: 4 En
🛇 (3) 🅿 (5) ⅍ ⌨ 🎹

(0.25m 🚗) *Lake Lodge, Muckross*
Road, Killarney, Co Kerry.
Value for money, convenient loca-
tion.
Tel: 064 33333
Mr Cusack.
Fax no: 064 35109
D: £18.00-£27.50 **S:** £20.00-£27.50.
Open: All Year (not Xmas)
Beds: 1F 3D 7T 4S
Baths: 15 En
🛇 🅿 (15) ⌨ 🐎 🧺 🎹 ♿ Ⅴ 🛈 ⚡

(0.25m) *Carriglea, Muckross*
Road, Killarney, Co Kerry.
200-year-old manor house with
unrivaled situation overlooking
lakes and mountains.
Tel: 064 31116 Mr & Mrs Beasley.
Fax no: 064 37693
D: £19.00-£20.00 **S:** £26.00-£27.00.
Open: Easter to Nov
Beds: 2F 4D 2T
Baths: 8 En
🛇 🅿 (12) ⌨ 🎹

(1m 🚗) *Crystal Springs,*
Ballycasheen, Killarney, Co Kerry.
Luxury accommodation on the
bank of the River Flesk overlook-
ing old historic mill.
Tel: 064 33272
Mrs Brosnan.
Fax no: 064 35518
D: £19.00-£23.00 **S:** £26.00-£30.00.
Open: All Year (not Xmas)
Beds: 6F 6D 3T 1S
Baths: 6 En 6 Pr 6 Sh
🛇 (1) 🅿 (15) ⅍ ⌨ 🐎 🗡 🧺 🎹 Ⅴ 🛈 ⚡

(2m 🚗) *Glendale, Direen,*
Greenane, Killarney, Co Kerry.
Family home on Ring of Kerry,
home cooking, minibus hire.
Tel: 064 82004
Mrs Sheehan.
D: £15.00-£16.00 **S:** £17.00-£18.00.
Open: May to Oct
Beds: 2D 1T
Baths: 1 En 1 Sh
🛇 🅿 (8) ⌨ 🐎 🗡 🎹 🛈 ⚡

(1m) *Ashbury House, Tiernaboul Upper, Killarney, Co Kerry.*
Enjoy Irish hospitality and panoramic views of Killarney's lakes and mountains.
Tel: **064 36707**
Mrs Doherty.
D: £15.00-£17.00 **S:** £20.00-£20.00.
Open: Apr to Oct
Beds: 1F 2D
Baths: 3 En
🛇 🅿 (4) ⊬ 🗆 ✕ 🎣 📶 Ⓥ

Lissivigeen 2

National Grid Ref: W0190

⊮⚑ Darby O'Gill's

(3m) 🚗 *Hillside House, Lissivigeen, Killarney, Co Kerry.*
Hillside is a large spacious bungalow, 3 km from town on main Killarney-Waterford road.
Tel: **064 31466**
Mrs Connor.
Fax no: 064 37073
D: £17.00-£19.00 **S:** £20.00-£20.00.
Open: Mar to Oct
Beds: 5F 1D 2T 1S
Baths: 1 En 5 Pr 1 Sh
🛇 (2) 🅿 🗆 🍴 🎣 📶 Ⓥ

(3m) *Ceasars, Cork View, Lissivigeen, Killarney, Co Kerry.*
Picturesque stone residence with mature gardens on N22. Superb location. Golf, hill walking
Grades: BF Approv
Tel: **064 31821**
Mrs Ceasar.
D: £18.00 **S:** £24.00.
Open: May to Sep
Beds: 2T 2D
Baths: 4 Ensuite
🛇 (1) 🅿 (5) 🎣 📶 Ⓥ ✦

Aghadoe 3

National Grid Ref: V9392

⊮⚑ Golden Nugget

(4m) *Glenmill House, Nunstown, Aghadoe, Killarney, Co Kerry.*
Luxurious new home, panoramic views lakes, McGillicuddy's Reeks, National Park. Orthopaedic beds, good breakfast.
Tel: **064 34391** Mrs Devane.
D: £17.00-£19.00 **S:** £23.00-£25.00.
Open: Mar to Oct
Beds: 3D 1T
Baths: 4 En
🅿 (6) 🗆 🎣 📶 Ⓥ ✦

(4m) *Carrowmore House, Knockasarnett, Aghadoe, Killarney, Co Kerry.*
Warm, welcoming, family-run B&B with panoramic views from bedrooms and lounge.
Tel: **064 33520** Mrs McAuliffe.
D: £19.00-£19.00 **S:** £25.50-£25.50.
Open: Apr to Oct
Beds: 2F 2D 1T
Baths: 5 En
🛇 🅿 (5) 🎣 🗆 🎣 📶 Ⓥ ✦

Fossa 4

National Grid Ref: V9191

⊮⚑ Kate Kearney's Cottage, Beaufort Bar, Molly D'Arcy's, Paddy's, Ross Hotel, Golden Nugget, The Laune, McSweeney Arms, Murphy's, Gaby's, Whitegates Hotel, Kiely's

(▲ 5m) *Fossa Holiday Hostel, Fossa, Killarney, County Kerry.*
Tel: **064 31497**
Adults: £6.00
Evening meal

(5m) *Brookside Gortacollopa, Fossa, Killarney, Co Kerry.*
Actual grid ref: V888927
Award-winning country home in farmland setting. 1995 Country Rover B&B of the Year.
Grades: BF Approv
Tel: **064 44187**
Mr & Mrs Moriarty.
D: £18.00-£20.00
S: £25.00-£25.00.
Open: Mar to Nov
Beds: 2F 1D 3T
Baths: 5 En 1 Sh
🛇 🅿 (6) 🎣 🗆 🍴 ✕ 🎣 📶 Ⓥ

(5m) 🚗 *Coffey's Loch Lein Guesthouse, Golf Course Road, Fossa, Killarney, Co Kerry.*
Modern family-run guest house, uniquely situated by the shores of Killarney's lower lake.
Grades: BF 3 Star, AA 3 Q
Tel: **064 31260**
Mrs Coffey.
Fax no: 064 36151
D: £18.00-£25.00
S: £25.00-£35.00.
Open: Mar to Nov
Beds: 6F 2D 4T
Baths: 12 En
🛇 🅿 (12) 🎣 🗆 🎣 📶 Ⓥ

(5m) *Tuscar Lodge, Golf Course Road, Fossa, Killarney, Co Kerry.*
Family-run guest house overlooking Loch Lein. Magnificent view Kerry Mountain Range.
Grades: BF 2 Star
Tel: **064 31978** (also fax no)
Mrs Fitzgerald.
D: £16.00 **S:** £17.00.
Open: Mar to Oct
Beds: 4D 10T
Baths: 14 En
🛇 🅿 (14) 🗆 🍴 🎣 📶 Ⓥ ✦

(5m) *The Shady Nook, Crohane, Fossa, Killarney, Co Kerry.*
Family home located in a scenic, peaceful location 4km from Killarney town
Grades: BF Approv
Tel: **064 33351**
Mrs O'Leary.
D: £17.00 **S:** £25.00.
Open: Easter to Oct
Beds: 2F 1T
Baths: 3 Ensuite 3 Private
🛇 🎣 🗆 ✕ 🎣 📶 Ⓥ ✦

Muckross 5

National Grid Ref: V9886

⊮⚑ Acorn Bar, Randles Court, Kit Flaherty's, Linden House, Darby O'Gill's, Failte, Molly D'Arcy's, Paddy's, Ross Hotel, McSweeney Arms, Murphy's, Gaby's, Whitegates Hotel, Kiely's, Killarney Heights, Old Bar, Laurels, Buckley's, Gleneagle Hotel

(▲ 1.5m) *Peacock Farm Hostel, Gortdromakiery, Muckross, Killarney, County Kerry.*
Tel: **064 33557 Adults:** £6.00
Facilities for disabled people
Self-sufficient former mountain farm on Stoompa Mountain.

(0.5m) 🚗 *Osprey, Lough Guitane Road, Muckross, Killarney, Co Kerry.*
Overlooking lakes/mountains. Tranquil area, landscaped gardens, home-baking.
Tel: **064 33213** Mr & Mrs Fogarty.
D: £19.00-£19.00 **S:** £25.50-£25.50.
Open: All Year
Beds: 1F 1T 1D
Baths: 2 En 1 Pr
🅿 (4) 🎣 🗆 🎣 📶 Ⓥ ✦

(0.5m) *O'Donovans Farm/Muckross Riding Stables, Mangerton Road, Muckross, Killarney, Co Kerry.*
Modern farm dormer bungalow, panoramic view of National Park (oak forest with red deer).
Grades: AA 3 Diamond
Tel: **064 32238**
Mrs O'Donovan.
D: £18.50-£18.50 **S:** £23.00.
Open: Mar to Nov
Beds: 2F 2D 2T
Baths: 6 En
🛇 (2) 🅿 🎣 ✕ 🎣 📶 Ⓥ ✦

(2m) 🚗 *Kiltrasna Farm, Lough Guitane Road, Muckross, Killarney, Co Kerry.*
Situated in Muckross Lakeland district, ideal for touring the Kerry Way.
Grades: BF Approv
Tel: **064 31643**
Mrs Looney.
D: £19.00-£19.00 **S:** £20.00-£20.00.
Open: Easter to Nov
Beds: 3D 2T 1S
Baths: 6 En
🛇 (3) 🅿 (8) 🗆 🎣 ♿ 🎣 ✦

(0.5m) *Ardree House, Muckross House, Muckross, Killarney, Co Kerry.*
Situated on the N71, we are within 4 minutes' walking from town centre.
Tel: **064 32374**
Mrs King.
Fax no: 064 35877
D: £18.00-£25.00 **S:** £30.00-£35.00.
Open: All Year (not Xmas)
Beds: 2F 2D 2T
Baths: 6 En
🛇 🅿 (6) 🗆 🍴 🎣 📶 Ⓥ

(0.25m) *Muckross Lodge,*
Muckross Road, Muckross,
Killarney, Co Kerry.
Non-smoking home situated one
mile from Killarney town and
adjacent to Muckross House
Grades: BF Approv
Tel: 064 32660 (also fax no)
Mrs O'Sullivan.
D: £18.50 **S:** £37.00.
Open: Mar to Oct
Beds: 1F 1D 3T
Baths: 54 Ensuite
🅿🛏♿📺Ⓥ

Gerahameen   6

National Grid Ref: V8781

❧ 🍴 Kate Kearney's

(On path) *Hillcrest Farmhouse,*
Gerahameen, Black Valley,
Killarney, Co Kerry.
Actual grid ref: V878823
Traditional-style farmhouse,
scenically situated on Kerry way
walking route.
Grades: BF Approv
Tel: 064 34702 (also fax no)
Mrs Tangney.
D: £20.00-£20.00 **S:** £26.50-£26.50.
Open: Mar to Nov
Beds: 1D 5T **Baths:** 6 En
🛏🅿🍴🗙🛏🗙♿📺Ⓥ♦

Gap of Dunloe   7

National Grid Ref: V8787

❧ 🍴 Kate Kearney's Cottage, Dunloc Castle

(2m 🚌) *Shamrock Farmhouse,*
Black Valley, Gap of Dunloe,
Killarney, Co Kerry.
Tel: 064 34714 Mrs O'Sullivan.
D: £16.00-£18.00 **S:** £16.00-£18.00.
Open: All Year
Beds: 1F 1D 2T
Baths: 2 En 2 Pr 1 Sh
🛏🅿(4)🍴🗙♿📺🔥♦
Modern farmhouse bungalow,
peacefully situated at the foot of
McGillycuddy Reeks overlooking
Killarney's Upper Lake. Scenic
views from each guest room.
Convenient for horseriding, fish-
ing, hill walking, Kerry Way walk-
ing route and the Gap of Dunloe.

(2m) *Purple Heather, Gap of*
Dunloe, Killarney, Co Kerry.
Grades: BF Approv
Tel: 064 44266 (also fax no)
Mrs Moriarty.
D: £17.00-£19.00 **S:** £23.00-£25.00.
Open: Mar to Oct
Beds: 1F 2D 2T 1S
Baths: 6 En 5 Pr
🛏🅿(6)🗙🛏🗙♿📺Ⓥ♦
Scenic area. All rooms with private
bath/shower, toilet, TV, electric
blankets, hairdryers, tea/coffee.
Has its own tennis court, pool
room, free. Ideally centred for all
scenic routes, golf, nature walks,
mountain climbing, traditional Irish
music restaurant 1 km.

(2m 🚌) *Wayside, Gap of Dunloe,*
Killarney, Co Kerry.
Tel: 064 44284 Mrs Ferris.
D: £18.00-£20.00 **S:** £23.50-£25.50.
Open: All Year (not Xmas)
Beds: 1F 2D 2D **Baths:** 2 En 1 Pr
🛏🅿🍴🗙♿📺♿
Peaceful lake/mountain district.
Restaurants, Irish music & dancing
1 km. Horse riding, fishing & golf
courses 1 km. Dingle & Ring of
Kerry starts 2 km. Breakfast menu.
A real Irish welcome awaits you.

(2m 🚌) *Holly Grove, Gap of*
Dunloe, Killarney, Co Kerry.
Spacious, comfortable bedrooms,
one with 3 beds. Most rooms with
private shower and toilet.
Tel: 064 44326 (also fax no)
Mrs Coffey.
D: £17.00 **S:** £20.00.
Open: Easter to Dec
Beds: 1F 1D 2T **Baths:** 3 En 1 Pr
🛏🅿🍴🗙🛏🗙♿📺Ⓥ♦

Glencar   8

National Grid Ref: V7084

❧ 🍴 Climbers Inn

(On path 🚌) *Climbers Inn,*
Glencar, Killarney, Co Kerry.
Situated on the Kerry Way,
Glencar the Highlands of Kerry.
Tel: 066 9760101
Mr & Mrs Walsh.
Fax no: 066 9760104
D: £17.50 **S:** £28.00.
Open: Mar to Nov
Beds: 10F **Baths:** 10 En
🛏(10)🅿🍴🛏🗙♿📺Ⓥ♦

(On path 🚌) *Blackstones House,*
Glencar, Killarney, Co Kerry.
Old style farmhouse overlooking
Caragh River, McGillicuddy
Reeks. Forest walks
Grades: BF Approv
Tel: 066 9760164 (also fax no)
Mrs Breen. **D:** £18.50 **S:** £25.00.
Open: Feb to Nov
Beds: 3F 2D 2T
Baths: 6 En 1 Pr
🛏🅿🗙♿📺Ⓥ♦

Glenbeigh   9

National Grid Ref: V6891

❧ 🍴 Towers Hotel, Ross Inn, Breen's, Falcon
Inn, Glenbeigh Hotel

(0.25m 🚌) *The Glenbeigh Hotel,*
Glenbeigh, Killarney, Co Kerry.
Tel: 066 9768333 Mrs Keary.
Fax no: 066 9768404
D: £30.00-£45.00 **S:** £35.00-£45.00.
Open: All Year (not Xmas)
Beds: 6T 6B 2S **Baths:** All En
🅿(15)🗙🛏🗙♿📺Ⓥ♦
As a tavern, a coaching inn, then as
a hotel, this hospitable old house
has welcomed visitors from all
over the world. On the Ring of
Kerry, close to Rossbeigh Beach,
Caragh Lake, Doors Golf Club and
is at the foothills of the
McGillicuddy Reeks.

(1.5m) *Woodside, Curragh,*
Glenbeigh, Killarney, Co Kerry.
2 km from Glenbeigh Village,
'Blue Flag' sandy beach, golf links,
mountain walking, fishing.
Tel: 066 9768160 Mrs O'Shea.
D: £17.00-£17.00 **S:** £21.00-£21.00.
Open: Easter to Oct
Beds: 1F 2D **Baths:** 3 En
🛏🅿(6)🗙🛏♿♦

(0.5m 🚌) *Rossbeigh Beach*
House, Rossbeigh, Glenbeigh,
Co Kerry.
Luxury furnished house
overlooking sea - 5 mile walk of
sandy beach.
Tel: 066 9168533 (also fax no)
Mrs Cahill. **D:** £20.00 **S:** £27.00.
Open: May to Sept
Beds: 1 T **Baths:** 6 En
🛏🅿🍴🗙♿📺Ⓥ♿♦

(1m 🚌) *Mountain View, Mountain*
Stage, Glenbeigh, County Kerry.
Modern-purpose built home set in
quiet location, 200 yards off Ring
of Kerry road.
Tel: 066 9768541 (also fax no)
Mrs O'Riordan.
D: £16.00-£18.00 **S:** £18.00-£22.00.
Open: Easter to Oct
Beds: 3F 3D 2T **Baths:** 5 En 2 Sh
🛏🅿(20)🍴🛏🗙♿📺Ⓥ♿♦

Kells   10

National Grid Ref: V5788

(0.5m 🚌) *Sea View, Kells Bay,*
Kells, Killarney, Co Kerry.
Family run, situated on sandy
beach, relaxing atmosphere.
Fishing, walking.
Tel: 066 9477610 Mrs Lynch.
D: £17.00-£17.00 **S:** £17.00-£17.00.
Open: Easter to October
Beds: 2F 1T 4D **Baths:** 5 En 2 Sh
🛏🅿🗙🗙♿♿♦

(0.5m 🚌) *Taobh Coille, Gleesk,*
Kells, Killarney, Co Kerry.
Farmhouse B&B overlooking the
sea on Ring of Kerry, adjacent to
Kerry Way.
Tel: 066 9477626 Mrs O'Sullivan.
D: £16.00-£16.00 **S:** £16.00.
Open: All Year
Beds: 1F 1D 1T **Baths:** 3 En
🛏🅿(20)🍴🛏🗙♿📺♿♦

Foilmore Bridge   11

National Grid Ref: V5282

(On path 🚌) *Fransal House,*
Foilmore Bridge, Caherciveen,
Co Kerry.
Experience real Irish home hospi-
tality in peaceful, scenic surround-
ings away from noise and traffic
Grades: BF Approv
Tel: 066 9472997 (also fax no)
Mr & Mrs Landers.
D: £16.00 **S:** £23.00.
Open: All Year (not Xmas)
Beds: 2F 1T 2D **Baths:** 4 En 1 Pr
🛏🅿(6)🍴🛏🗙♿📺Ⓥ♿♦

Caherciveen 12

National Grid Ref: V4779

⬥ Daniel O'Connell Hotel, Shebeen, Frank's Corner, O'Neil's, Town House, Teach Caulann, Point, Moorings, Brennan's, Seahorse Restaurant, QC's

(▲ 0.25m) *Sive Hostel, 15 East End, Caherciveen, County Kerry.*
Tel: **066 72717 Adults:** £6.50
Evening meal

(3m ⬣) *Ocean View, Renard Road, Caherciveen, Co Kerry.*
Grades: BF Approv,
AA 3 Diamond
Tel: **066 9472261** Ms O'Donoghue.
D: £19.00-£20.00 **S:** £24.00-£25.00.
Open: All Year (not Xmas)
Beds: 2F 2D 2T
Baths: 6 En
⬥ (4) P (6) ⬥ ⬥ ⬥ ⬥ ⬥ V ⬥
Luxury farmhouse overlooking Caherciveen Bay within walking distance of town. Bedrooms tastefully decorated, all with spectacular sea views, sunsets, islands, C15th castle. Peat/wood fires. Mountain-climbing, sea-sports, golf, pitch & putt. Skellig Rock nearby. Tea/coffee facilities in all bedrooms.

(1m ⬣) *Iveragh Heights, Carhan Road, Caherciveen, Co Kerry.*
Ideal location for exploring Iveragh Peninsula. Breathtaking scenery, archaeological sites. Trips to Skellig Michael.
Grades: BF Approv
Tel: **066 9472545** (also fax no)
Mrs O'Neill.
D: £16.00-£17.00 **S:** £19.00-£19.00.
Open: All Year
Beds: 7F 3D 3T 1S
Baths: 9 En 7 Pr
⬥ P (8) ⬥ ⬥ ⬥ ⬥ ⬥ V ⬥

(2m ⬣) *Harbour Hill, Knockeens, Caherciveen, Co Kerry.*
Luxurious home, quiet, peaceful, panoramic views, Skellig trips and itineraries planned.
Grades: BF Approv
Tel: **066 9472844** (also fax no)
Mrs Curran.
D: £16.00-£18.00 **S:** £20.00-£24.00.
Open: Easter to Oct
Beds: 2F 2T 2D 1S
Baths: 5 En 1 Pr
⬥ P (6) ⬥ ⬥ ⬥ ⬥ ⬥ ⬥ ⬥ V ⬥ ⬥

(1m ⬣) *Pine Crest, Cappaghs, Caherciveen, Co Kerry.*
country house, scenic surroundings, birdwatching, private car park.
Tel: **066 9472482**
Mrs O'Shea.
D: £19.00-£20.00 **S:** £19.00-£20.00.
Open: Jan to Sept
Beds: 1F 1D 1T
Baths: 3 En
⬥ P ⬥ ⬥ ⬥ ⬥ ⬥ V ⬥ ⬥

(1m) *Mount Rivers, Carhan Road, Caherciveen, Co Kerry.*
Quiet secluded Victorian house c1888, antique furnishings, 2 minutes' walk to town centre.
Tel: **066 9472509** Mrs McKenna.
D: £18.00-£19.00 **S:** £24.00-£25.00.
Open: Easter to Oct
Beds: 1F 2D 2T **Baths:** 5 En
⬥ P (8) ⬥ ⬥ ⬥ ⬥

Waterville 13

National Grid Ref: V5066

⬥ Fisherman's Bar, Butlers' Arms, Smugglers' Inn, The Lobster, An Corran, The Huntsman

(0.25m ⬣) *The Old Cable House, Cable Station, Waterville, Killarney, Co Kerry.*
Grades: BF Approv
Tel: **066 9474233**
Mr & Mrs Brown.
Fax no: 066 9474869
D: £15.00-£30.00 **S:** £15.00-£25.00.
Open: All Year (not Xmas)
Beds: 6F 4D 2T **Baths:** 4 En
⬥ P (15) ⬥ ⬥ ⬥ ⬥ ⬥ ⬥ ⬥ V ⬥ ⬥
Interesting stay. The 'Victorian Internet' Old Cable House traces its origins to the first Transatlantic Telegraph Cable laid 1866 from Europe to USA. Rooms of character bright and spacious, delicious breakfast of your choice. Pets welcome no quarantine from Gt. Britain.

(On path ⬣) *Silver Sands, Waterville, Killarney, Co Kerry.*
Actual grid ref: V502658
Family-run guest house and restaurant in centre of Waterville village.
Tel: **066 9474161**
Fax no: 066 9474537
D: £15.00-£22.00 **S:** £16.00-£34.00.
Open: All Year (not Xmas)
Beds: 2F 4D 3T 1S
Baths: 7 En 3 Sh
⬥ P (4) ⬥ ⬥ ⬥ ⬥ ⬥ ⬥

(3m ⬣) *Golf Links View, Murreigh, Waterville, Killarney, Co Kerry.*
Family-run B&B, comfortable ensuite rooms with TV, tea/coffee making facilities.
Tel: **066 9474623** (also fax no)
Mrs Barry.
D: £17.00-£19.00 **S:** £22.00-£25.00.
Open: Mar to Oct
Beds: 1F 2T 3D **Baths:** 6 En
⬥ P ⬥ ⬥ ⬥ ⬥ ⬥ V ⬥ ⬥

(0.5m) *O'Grady's, Spunkane, Waterville, Killarney, Co Kerry.*
Spacious family run accommodation. Centrally located. Breakfast menu. Warm welcome.
Grades: BF Approv
Tel: **066 9474350** Mrs O'Grady.
Fax no: 066 9474730
D: £17.00-£20.00 **S:** £20.00-£23.00.
Open: Easter to Nov
Beds: 1F 2D 3T **Baths:** 6 En
⬥ P (6) ⬥ ⬥ ⬥ ⬥ V ⬥ ⬥

(On path ⬣) *Clifford's B&B, Main Street, Waterville, Killarney, Co Kerry.*
Comfortable home on the sea front. pubs and restaurants five minutes.
Grades: BF Approv
Tel: **066 9474283** Mrs Clifford.
Fax no: 066 9474283
D: £17.00-£19.00 **S:** £19.00-£24.00.
Open: Mar to Nov
Beds: 2F 2D 2T
Baths: 6 En
⬥ P ⬥ ⬥ ⬥ ⬥ ⬥ ⬥ V ⬥ ⬥

(0.25m ⬣) *Klondyke House, New Line Road, Waterville, Killarney, Co Kerry.*
Luxurious home situated on main Ring of Kerry road N70, breakfast menu.
Tel: **066 9474119** Mrs Morris.
Fax no: 066 9474666
D: £17.00-£19.00 **S:** £20.00-£25.00.
Open: All Year (not Xmas)
Beds: 1F 2D 2T 1S
Baths: 6 En
⬥ P (8) ⬥ ⬥ ⬥ ⬥ ⬥ ⬥ V ⬥ ⬥

Caherdaniel 14

National Grid Ref: V5459

⬥ Blind Piper, Scarriff Inn

(▲ 3m) *Carrigbeg Country Hostel, Derrynane, Caherdaniel, Killarney, County Kerry.*
Tel: **066 75229 Adults:** £6.50

(2m ⬣) *Kerry Way B&B, Caherdaniel, Killarney, County Kerry.*
Family B&B on Kerry Way. Pub next door - traditional music/great food.
Tel: **066 9475277** (also fax no)
Mr Sweeney.
D: £20.00-£20.00 **S:** £30.00-£30.00.
Open: Easter to Nov
Beds: 3T 3D
Baths: 6 En
P (3) ⬥ ⬥ ⬥ ⬥ V ⬥ ⬥

(2m ⬣) *Skellig House, Bunavalla, Caherdaniel, County Kerry.*
Overlooking picturesque Derrynane Town, comfortable, spacious, home, peaceful surroundings on Derry Way. Skellig trips
Tel: **066 9475129** Mrs O'Shea.
Fax no: 066 9475123
D: £17.00-£17.00 **S:** £20.00-£20.00.
Open: May to Sep
Beds: 1F 1D 1T
Baths: 2 Ensuite 1 Private
⬥ P (5) ⬥ ⬥ ⬥ ⬥

All paths are popular: you are well-advised to book ahead

Sneem 15

National Grid Ref: V6966

🍴🍺Blue Bull, Sacre Coeur, River Rain, Stone House

(0.25m) *Heatherside, Sneem, Killarney, County Kerry.*
Grades: BF Approv
Tel: **064 45220** (also fax no)
Mr Smith.
D: £16.00-£18.00 **S:** £22.00.
Open: All Year
Beds: 1F 2D 1T
Baths: 3 En 1 Pr
🛏🅿 (5) ⅙ 📖🛢
A modern family-run country house nestling amongst the wild Kerry mountains with a panoramic view of the Beara peninsula. Just one mile east of the picturesque village of Sneem on the N70 ring of Kerry road,300 metres from the road.

(On path 🐾) *Bank House, North Square, Sneem, Kenmare, Killarney, Co Kerry.*
Old Georgian home with magnificent collection of antique crystal and china.
Tel: **064 45226**
Mrs Harrington.
D: £17.00-£18.50 **S:** £26.00-£27.50.
Open: Apr to Nov
Beds: 2F 3D 1T
Baths: 5 En
🅿📖🛢

(0.25m 🐾) *Derry East Farmhouse, Sneem, Killarney, Co Kerry.*
Luxury farmhouse, scenic area, riverside/mountain walks, golf, horseriding, tennis, fishing, beaches
Grades: BF Approv
Tel: **064 45193** (also fax no)
Mrs Teahan.
D: £16.50 **S:** £23.50.
Open: Mar to Oct
Beds: 1F 1D 2T
Baths: 3 Ensuite 1 Private
🛏🅿⅙📖🛢✦

Tahilla 16

National Grid Ref: V7365

🍴🍺Pat Spillane's, Blue Bull, Sacre Coeur, River Rain, Stone House, Blackwater Tavern

(0.5m 🐾) *Hillside Haven, Doon, Tahilla, Sneem, Killarney, Co Kerry.*
Bungalow with spectacular views of Kenmare Bay. Adjacent to Kerry Way walking route.
Grades: BF Approv
Tel: **064 82065** (also fax no)
Mrs Foley.
D: £17.00-£19.00
S: £23.00-£25.00.
Open: Easter to Oct
Beds: 2F 2D
Baths: 4 En
🛏🅿📖✕📖🛢

(0.5m) *Brookvilla, Ankail, Tahilla, Sneem, Killarney, Co Kerry.*
Family run B&B overlooking Kenmare Bay. Grid reference 725 654.
Tel: **064 45172** (also fax no)
Mrs McCarthy.
D: £16.00-£16.00 **S:** £20.00-£20.00.
Open: All Year (not Xmas)
Beds: 2F 1D 1T
Baths: 4 En
🛏🅿📖✕📖🛢

Blackwater Bridge 17

National Grid Ref: V7968

🍴🍺Pat Spillane's, The Vestry

(0.25m) *Arches, Blackwater Bridge, Kenmare, Killarney, Co Kerry.*
Actual grid ref: V810685
Modern home in a rural setting with spectacular views of Kenmare Bay.
Tel: **064 82030** (also fax no)
O'Gara.
D: £17.50-£20.00 **S:** £22.00-£25.00.
Open: All Year
Beds: 1F 3D 2T
Baths: 6 En
🛏 (4) 🅿 (8) ⅙📖🛢✦

(0.5m) *Old Schoolhouse, Direendaragh, Blackwater Bridge, Kenmare, Killarney, Co Kerry.*
Tastefully converted old stone scholhouse. Friendly, family-run establishment
Tel: **064 82913** (also fax no)
Mrs Robinson.
D: £15.00 **S:** £15.00.
Open: All Year
Beds: 1F 1T 1D 1S
Baths: 1 Ensuite 2 Shared
🅿 (5) 🐴✕📖🛢

Templenoe 18

National Grid Ref: V8369

🍴🍺Pat Spillane's Bar, The Vestry

(1m 🐾) *Bay View Farm, Templenoe, Kenmare, Killarney, Co Kerry.*
Old style farm house overlooking Kenmare Bay on N70.
Tel: **064 41383** Mrs Falvey.
D: £16.50-£18.50 **S:** £20.00-£27.00.
Open: Easter to Apr
Beds: 3F 1D 2T 1S
Baths: 4 En 2 Sh
🛏🅿 (8) 📖🐴✕📖🛢

Taking your dog?

Book *in advance*

ONLY with owners

who accept dogs (🐾)

Greenane 19

National Grid Ref: V8470

🍴🍺Casey's Rest

(0.25m 🐾) *Grenane Heights, Ring of Kerry Road, Greenane, Kenmare, Killarney, Co Kerry.*
Actual grid ref: V838696
Enjoy our uniquely designed home, relax in friendly atmosphere, sample fine home cuisine.
Grades: BF Approv
Tel: **064 41760** (also fax no)
Mrs Topham.
D: £20.00-£20.00 .
Open: May to Sept
Beds: 3F 1T 1D **Baths:** 5 En
🛏🅿📖✕📖🛢♿🛢✦

Kenmare 20

National Grid Ref: V9070

🍴🍺Wander Inn, Foley's, Horseshoe, Lime Tree, Coachman's Inn, Shamrock, Packie's, Pat Spillane's, Vestry, Sailors, Old Dutch, Darcy's, Casey's Rest, Lake House

(▲1.75m) *Failte Hostel, Shelbourne Street, Kenmare, Killarney, County Kerry.*
Tel: **064 42333 Adults:** £7.00
Old bank house, built in C19th, in the centre of Kenmare. Ideal for both Beara and Kerry Ways.

(0.25m) *Rose Garden Guest House & Restaurant, N70, Kenmare, County Kerry.*
Grades: BF 3 Star
Tel: **064 42288**
Mr & Mrs Ringlever.
Fax no: 064 42305
D: £22.50-£27.50 **S:** £32.50-£37.50.
Open: Easter to Nov
Beds: 4D 4T
Baths: 8 En
🅿 (20) 📖✕📖🛢
The Rose Garden Guest House & Restaurant is situated within a few minutes' walk of Kenmare. Set in 1 acre of landscaped garden with 350 roses. 3 and 7 day specials including breakfast and dinner are available. Evening meals available.

(1m) *O'Donnells of Ashgrove, Kenmare, Killarney, Co Kerry.*
Grades: BF Approv
Tel: **064 41228** (also fax no)
Mrs O'Donnell.
D: £20.00-£22.00 **S:** £26.50-£28.50.
Open: Easter to Oct
Beds: 2D 1T 1S
Baths: 3 En
🛏 (8) 🅿 (6) 📖🐴📖🛢
Beautiful country home in peaceful setting incorporating olde worlde charm, where guests are welcomed as friends. Jacobean-style dining room. Log fire. Spacious, elegant family lounge with many antiques. Tea/coffee freely available. mature garden. Angling enthusiast. Recommended best 300 B&B's.

(1m) *Annagry House, Sneen Road, Kenmare, Killarney, Co Kerry.*
Tel: **064 41283** Mrs Carraher-O'Sullivan.
D: £20.00-£20.00 **S:** £27.00-£27.00.
Open: All Year (not Xmas/New Year)
Beds: 2F 2T 2D **Baths:** 6 En
🄿 ⊙ 🛢 ▥ 🆅 ⌁
Ideal location on the Ring of Kerry Road (N70). Peaceful and quiet yet only 7 minutes walk from Kenmare town centre and its award winning pubs and restaurants. Superb accommodation, spacious rooms all ensuite. Bath tubs/showers. Extensive breakfast menu. Fresh ground coffee. Tasty home baking.

(0.25m) *Ard Na Mara, Pier Road, Kenmare, Killarney, Co Kerry.*
Modern house, big garden. Front view overlooking Kenmare Bay. Five mins' walk town.
Grades: BF Approv
Tel: **064 41399** (also fax no)
Mrs Dahm.
D: £19.00-£20.00 **S:** £25.00-£25.00.
Open: All Year (not Xmas)
Beds: 2D 2T **Baths:** 4 Pr
🦮 🄿 (4) 🛢 🆅

(1m) *Ceol Na Habhann, Killarney Road, Upper Gortamullen, Kenmare, Killarney, Co Kerry.*
Tel: **064 41498** Mrs O'Shea.
D: £19.00-£21.00 **S:** £25.00-£27.00.
Open: Feb to Nov
Beds: 2F 2D 1T
Baths: 5 En
🦮 🄿 (6) ⊙ 🖐 🛢 ▥ & 🆅
Welcome to O'Shea's farm home, 1 km from Kenmare off N71 Killarney/Ring of Kerry road. Quiet scenic area adjacent to Kerry Way / Beara way. Spacious ensuite rooms with TV, tea/coffee facilities, hairdryers. Recommended by travel writers.

(0.5m) *Druid Cottage, Sneem Road, Kenmare, Co Kerry.*
Actual grid ref: V901712
C19th stone cottage situated on Ring of Kerry road.
Grades: BF Approv
Tel: **064 41803** Mrs Goldrick.
D: £17.00-£20.00 **S:** £23.50-£25.50.
Open: All Year (not Xmas)
Beds: 1F 1D 1T
Baths: 2 En 1 Pr
🦮 (11) 🄿 (6) ⊙ 🖐 🗙 🛢 ▥ 🛢 ⌁

(1m) *White Heather Farm, Glengarriff Road, Kenmare, Killarney, Co Kerry.*
4 km on Kenmare/Glengarriff road N71. Easy to find, head of Beara Peninsula.
Grades: BF Approv
Tel: **064 41550** Mrs Lovett.
Fax no: 064 42475
D: £18.00-£20.00 **S:** £25.00-£27.00.
Open: May to Oct
Beds: 2F 2D 1T
Baths: 4 En 4 Pr 1 Sh
🦮 🄿 ⊱ ⊙ 🖐 🗙 🛢 ▥ 🆅 🛢 ⌁

(1m) *Rockvilla, Templenoe, Kenmare, Killarney, Co Kerry.*
Grades: BF Approv
Tel: **064 41331** Mr & Mrs Fahy.
D: £17.00-£19.00 **S:** £20.00-£25.00.
Open: Easter to Nov
Beds: 2F 1D 2T 1S
Baths: 4 En 1 Sh
🦮 🄿 (10) ⊙ 🖐 🗙 ▥ ⌁
Peaceful rural setting near Templenoe Pier. Relaxed friendly atmosphere. Large garden and parking area. Golf and horse riding within 1 mile. Kenmare, a beautiful heritage town with many restaurants and pubs. 4 miles.

(0.25m) *O'Shea's Guest House, 14 Henry Street, Kenmare, Killarney, Co Kerry.*
Pleasing comfortable guest house in centre of town.
Tel: **064 41453** Mr O'Shea.
D: £15.00 **S:** £15.00.
Open: Easter to Oct
Beds: 2F 2D 1T
Baths: 1 En 2 Sh
🦮 (10) 🄿 (4) ⊙ 🖐 🗙 ▥.

(1m) *River Meadows House, Sneem Road, Kenmare, Killarney, Co Kerry.*
Modern house set in rustic surroundings with privet road leading to sea shore.
Tel: **064 41306** (also fax no)
Mrs Ryan.
D: £19.00-£19.00 **S:** £25.00-£25.00.
Open: Easter to Nov
Beds: 1F 1T 1D 1S
Baths: 4 Pr
🦮 🄿 (9) ⊱ ⊙ 🖐 🗙 🛢 ▥ 🆅 ⌁

(1m) *Droumassig Bridge, Kenmare, Killarney, Co Kerry.*
On the N71 and Glengariff 3 miles from Kenmare. Relaxing.
Grades: BF Listed
Tel: **064 41384** Mrs Foley.
D: £13.00-£15.00 **S:** £15.00-£20.00.
Open: Easter to Oct
Beds: 3F 1T 1D
Baths: 3 Sh
🦮 🄿 ⊱ ⊙ 🖐 🗙 🛢 ▥ & 🆅 🛢 ⌁

(1m) *Cherry Hill, Killowen, Kenmare, Killarney, Co Kerry.*
Located on R569. Beautiful views. Ideally situated for touring Kerry/Beara.
Grades: BF Approv
Tel: **064 41715** Mrs Clifford.
D: £17.00-£19.00 .
Open: May to Sep
Beds: 2D 1T
Baths: 2 En 1 Pr
🦮 🄿 ⊙ 🛢 ▥ 🆅

(3m) *Inbhear Schein, Dauros, Kenmare, Killarney, Co Kerry.*
Family home. Scenic location. Ideal for exploring Ring of Kerry, Kerry Way, Beara Way.
Tel: **064 41210** Mr & Mrs O'Leary.
D: £15.00-£17.00 **S:** £15.00-£20.00.
Open: Easter to Oct
Beds: 1F 1D 1T
Baths: 2 En 2 Sh
🦮 (3) 🄿 (10) ⊙ 🗙 ▥ 🛢 🛢 ⌁

(0.25m) *Wander Inn, Henry Street, Kenmare, Killarney, Co Kerry.*
Old-World style family-run hotel in the heart of Kenmare. Rooms furnished with beautiful antiques.
Tel: **064 42700** Keane.
Fax no: 064 42569
D: £20.00-£25.00 **S:** £30.00-£35.00.
Open: All Year (not Xmas)
Beds: 1F 7D 3T 0S
Baths: 11 En
🦮 🄿 (20) ⊙ 🗙 ▥.

(1m) *The Lodge, Kilgarvan Road, Kenmare, Killarney, Co Kerry.*
Luxury guest house in private gardens, elegantly furnished in period style, king size beds.
Tel: **064 41512** Mrs Quill.
Fax no: 064 41812
D: £25.00-£27.50 **S:** £45.00-£45.00.
Open: Apr to Nov
Beds: 5F 2D 3T
Baths: 10 En
🦮 🄿 ⊱ ⊙ 🛢 🛢 ▥ & 🆅 🛢

(1m) *Riverville House, Gortamullen, Kenmare, Co Kerry.*
Actual grid ref: V897722
Luxury B&B, Kenmare town. Antique pine furniture, ideal touring centre - Ring of Kerry.
Tel: **064 41775**
Mrs Moore.
D: £18.00-£20.00 **S:** £20.00-£25.00.
Open: Feb to Nov
Beds: 3D
Baths: 3 En
🄿 (4) ⊱ ▥.

(0.25m) *The Caha's, Hospital Cross, Kenmare, Killarney, Co Kerry.*
Modern dormer bungalow in scenic peaceful location. Extensive breakfast menu.
Tel: **064 41271** (also fax no)
Mr & Mrs O'Shea.
D: £18.00-£22.00 **S:** £25.00-£27.00.
Open: Easter to Oct
Beds: 2F 2D
Baths: 4 En
🦮 (5) 🄿 (4) ⊱ ⊙ 🛢 ▥ 🆅

Ulster Way

Someone suggested that outside the **South West Coast Path**, none of our paths can actually lay claim to being truly long distance. The **Ulster Way** proves them wrong. Running for 560 miles through each of the Six Counties, this path is another candidate for completion in several trips. And it's certainly worth the effort. This path is very special. It visits places famed throughout the world for their beauty - the unspoilt North Antrim Coast, the extraordinary basalt formations of the Giant's Causeway, the remote Sperrin Mountains, Lough Erne with its multitude of islands, the deserted Mountains of Mourne and the bird sanctuaries of Strangford Lough. Now, Northern Ireland is an enormous place with a small population. Consequently, this path takes the walker past the true outposts of these islands, a rare privilege afforded mainly to Ulster people and Irish people alike. Don't be put off by the distance - this wealth of landscape demands to be discovered - your walking will be memorable. You will see from the map here that certain stretches of the **Ulster Way** are not well served by accommodation - notably from Dungiven down to Belleek. Logistics thus mean that you may have to double up on accommodation - i.e., return to your previous port of call or arrange transport to your next destination, to return in the morning to the point where you left the path. You will need to be well-versed in map and compass work (signposting along the **Ulster Way** leaves a lot to be desired) and you should be prepared for all weathers.

Guides: *Walking the Ulster Way - A Journal and a Guide* by Alan Warner (ISBN 086 281 2275), published by Appletree Press (Belfast), or available from all major bookshops, or direct from the publishers (tel. 01232 243074), £6.95 + 70p p&p

Maps: Ordnance Survey of Northern Ireland 1:50,000 Discoverer series: 4, 5, 7, 8, 9, 12, 13, 15, 17, 18, 19, 20, 26, 27 and 29

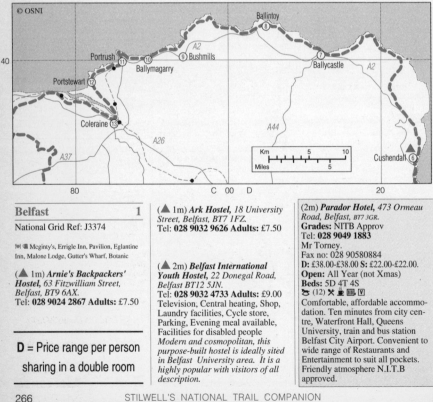

© OSNI

Belfast   1

National Grid Ref: J3374

🍴 🍺 Mcginty's, Errigle Inn, Pavilion, Eglantine Inn, Malone Lodge, Gutter's Wharf, Botanic

(▲ 1m) **Arnie's Backpackers' Hostel,** *63 Fitzwilliam Street, Belfast, BT9 6AX.*
Tel: **028 9024 2867 Adults:** £7.50

D = Price range per person
sharing in a double room

(▲ 1m) **Ark Hostel,** *18 University Street, Belfast, BT7 1FZ.*
Tel: **028 9032 9626 Adults:** £7.50

(▲ 2m) **Belfast International Youth Hostel,** *22 Donegal Road, Belfast BT12 5JN.*
Tel: **028 9032 4733 Adults:** £9.00
Television, Central heating, Shop, Laundry facilities, Cycle store, Parking, Evening meal available, Facilities for disabled people
Modern and cosmopolitan, this purpose-built hostel is ideally sited in Belfast University area. It is a highly popular with visitors of all description.

(2m) **Parador Hotel,** *473 Ormeau Road, Belfast, BT7 3GR.*
Grades: NITB Approv
Tel: **028 9049 1883**
Mr Torney.
Fax no: 028 90580884
D: £38.00-£38.00 **S:** £22.00-£22.00.
Open: All Year (not Xmas)
Beds: 5D 4T 4S
🛏 (12) ✗ 🛓 🛖 🖺 Ⓥ
Comfortable, affordable accommodation. Ten minutes from city centre, Waterfront Hall, Queens University, train and bus station Belfast City Airport. Convenient to wide range of Restaurants and Entertainment to suit all pockets. Friendly atmosphere N.I.T.B approved.

(2m) *Marine House, 30 Eglantine Avenue, Belfast, BT9 6DX.*
Large detached villa, tree-lined avenue with gardens and car parking.
Grades: NITB Approv
Tel: 028 9066 2828 Mrs Corrigan.
D: £20.00-£22.50 **S:** £27.00-£38.00.
Open: All Year (not Xmas)
Beds: 1F 5D 2T 4S
Baths: 3 En 4 Pr 2 Sh
🛇 🅿 (4) 🗗 🌭 ▥ Ⓥ

All paths are popular: you are well-advised to book ahead

S = Price range for a single person in a single room

(2m 🚗) *Camera Guest House, 44 Wellington Park, Belfast, BT9 6DP.*
Tel: 028 9066 0026 Mr Drumm.
Fax no: 028 9066 7856
D: £24.00-£27.50 **S:** £24.00-£37.00.
Open: All Year (not Xmas)
Beds: 1F 3D 3T 4S
Baths: 2 En 1 Pr 3 Sh
🛇 🗲 🗗 🌭 ▥ Ⓥ
Elegant townhouse set in the heart of south Belfast with its Victorian Mansions and graceful terraces. Located just a short distance from Queen's University, the city's main tourist attractions and the cultural and business centre. Ideal base for business and leisure visitors.

(2m) *Bowdens B & B, 17 Sandford Avenue , Cyprus Avenue, Belfast, BT5 5NW.*
Grades: NITB Approv
Tel: 028 9065 2213 (also fax no)
Mrs Bowden.
D: £17.00-£17.00 **S:** £18.00-£18.00.
Open: All Year
Beds: 1T 1D 1S
Baths: 1 Sh
🛇 🅿 (3) 🗲 🗗 🖙 🌭 ▥ Ⓥ 🖊 ✦
Warm family-run town house in quiet cul-de-sac. Gardens, central heating, colour TV, tea, coffee and biscuits. Convenient to bus routes, city airport, Belfast Ferries. The tree-lined Cyprus Avenue was immortalised by Van Morrison in his song 'Cyprus Avenue'.

(2m) *Old Rectory, 148 Malone Road, Belfast, BT9 5LH.*
Built in 1896 as rectory for nearby church and set in mature gardens.
Grades: NITB Grade A
Tel: 028 9066 7882 Ms Callan.
Fax no: 028 9068 3759
D: £25.00-£30.00 **S:** £36.00-£42.00.
Open: All Year (not Xmas)
Beds: 1F 2D 4T 3S
Baths: 2 En 3 Pr
🛇 (7) 🅿 (5) 🗲 🗗 🗙 🌭 ▥ Ⓥ 🖊 ✦

(2m) *Roseleigh House, 19 Rosetta Park, Belfast, BT6 0DL.*
Luxurious ensuite accommodation in a restored Victorian house situated in residential South Belfast.
Tel: 028 9064 4414 Ms Hunter.
D: £24.00 **S:** £35.00.
Open: All Year (not Xmas)
Beds: 1F 2D 4T 2S **Baths:** 9 En
🛇 🅿 (6) 🗗 🗙 🌭 ▥ Ⓥ 🖊 ✦

(2m) *Greenwood House, 25 Park Road, Belfast, BT7 2FW.*
Victorian house, colourful, warm, contemporary style. Quiet area overlooking park.
Tel: 028 9020 2525 Mr Harris.
Fax no: 028 9020 2530
D: £25.00-£25.00 **S:** £35.00-£35.00.
Open: All Year (not Xmas)
Beds: 1F 2T 3D 1S **Baths:** 7 En
🛇 🅿 (2) 🗲 🗗 🌭 & Ⓥ 🖊 ✦

(2m) *Crecora, 114 Upper Newtownards Rd, Belfast, BT4 3EN.*
Actual grid ref: J353744
Victorian house on main road. Ferries & city airport nearby.
Tel: 028 9065 8257
D: £18.50-£23.50 **S:** £18.50-£29.50.
Open: All Year
Beds: 2F 2D 4T 4S
Baths: 3 En 3 Pr 3 Sh
🛇 🅿 (15) 🗲 🗗 🖙 🌭 ▥ & Ⓥ 🖊

Planning a longer stay? Always ask for any special rates.

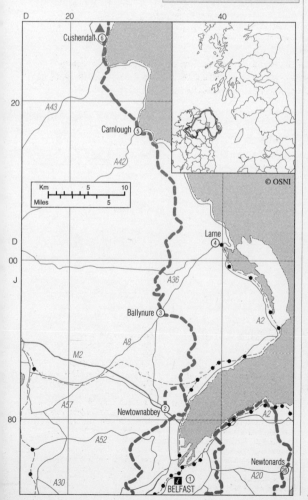

(2m) *Lismore Lodge, 410 Ormeau Road, Belfast, BT7 3HY.*
Comfortable family-run Victorian guest house, quiet area, near buses.
Tel: **028 9064 1205**
Mr & Mrs Devlin.
Fax no: 028 9064 2628
D: £24.00-£24.00 **S:** £33.00-£33.00.
Open: All Year (not Xmas)
Beds: 2D 3T 2S
Baths: 7 En
🛏 (2) 🅿 (6) 🗗 🚲 📠 ☑

(2m) *Eglantine Guest House, 21 Eglantine Avenue, Belfast, BT9 6DW.*
Home from home welcome close to city centre. Personal attention
Grades: NITB 1 Star
Tel: **028 9066 7585**
Mr & Mrs Cargill.
D: £19.00 **S:** £20.00.
Open: All Year
Beds: 1F 3T 1D 3S
Baths: 2 Shared
🛏 🗗 🚲 📠 ☑

Newtownabbey 2

National Grid Ref: J3580

🍴 🍺 Bellevue Arms

(0.5m) *Iona, 161 Antrim Road, Newtownabbey, Belfast, BT36 7QR.*
5 miles from Belfast, five minutes from Ulster Way on Antrim road.
Tel: **028 9084 2256** Mrs Kelly.
D: £18.00-£20.00 **S:** £20.00-£36.00.
Open: All Year (not Xmas)
Beds: 1F 1D 2S
Baths: 2 Sh
🛏 🅿 🗗 📠

Ballynure 3

National Grid Ref: J3193

(1m 🚍) *Rockbank, 40 Belfast Road, Ballynure, Ballyclare, Co Antrim, BT39 9TZ.*
Actual grid ref: J318923
Welcome to comfortable farmhouse in quiet rural setting.
Walkers telephone for pick up
Grades: NITB Approv
Tel: **028 9335 2261** Mrs Park.
D: £15.00 **S:** £18.00.
Open: All Year
Beds: 1F 1T 1D
Baths: 2 Ensuite 1 Shared
🛏 (5) 🅿 (4) 🗗 🍗 ✕ 🚲 📠 ☑ 🗗 ✦

**Phoning from outside the Republic?
Dial 00353 and omit the initial '0' of the area code.**

Pay B&Bs by cash or cheque and be prepared to pay up front.

Larne 4

National Grid Ref: D4002

🍴 🍺 Baile, Curran Court, Meeting House, Cairn Castle, The Chequers, Dan Campbell's, Kiln

(6m 🚍) *Derrin Guest House, 2 Prince's Gardens, Larne, Co Antrim, BT40 1RQ.*
Grades: NITB 2 Star,
AA 3 Diamond, RAC 3 Diamond
Tel: **028 2827 3762** Mrs Mills.
Fax no: 028 2827 3269
D: £16.00-£19.00 **S:** £20.00-£25.00.
Open: All Year (not Xmas)
Beds: 2F 4D 1T
Baths: 4 En 1 Sh
🛏 🅿 (3) 🗗 🍗 🚲 📠 ☑ ✦
Beautifully appointed Grade A guest house, family run since 1964. Full fire certificate. Private car park. Friendly welcoming atmosphere. Highly Commended in 1994 Galtee Irish Breakfast Awards. Finalist in 1997 British Airways Tourism Awards. Ideal touring centre. 30 minutes from Belfast.

Carnlough 5

National Grid Ref: D2817

🍴 🍺 Londonderry Arms, Bridge Inn

(On path) *Bridge Inn (McAuleys), 2 Bridge Street, Carnlough, Ballymena, Co Antrim, BT44 0ET.*
Traditional family-run hotel & pub ideally situated in picturesque surroundings.
Grades: NITB Grade B
Tel: **028 2888 5669** Mr Davidson.
Fax no: 028 2888 5096
D: £18.00 **S:** £18.00.
Open: All Year
Beds: 1F 3D 1T
Baths: 2 Sh
🛏 (1) 🅿 (2) 🗗 🍗 ✕ 📠 🍴 ✦

Cushendall 6

National Grid Ref: D2427

🍴 🍺 Thornlea Hotel, Harry's, Johnny Joe's

(0.5m 🚍) *The Burn, 63 Ballyeamon Road, Cushendall, Ballymena, Co Antrim, BT44 0SN.*
Actual grid ref: D2327
Peace, perfect peace - Turf fire, books, Tea and coffee.
Grades: NITB Listed
Tel: **028 2177 1733** Mrs McAuley.
D: £16.00-£16.00 **S:** £18.00-£18.00.
Open: Easter to Easter
Beds: 1F 1T 1S 1D
Baths: 2 En 2 Sh
🛏 🅿 (4) 🗗 🍗 ✕ 📠 🗗 ✦

(3m) *Cullentra House, 16 Cloghs Road, Cushendall, Ballymena, Co Antrim, BT44 0SP.*
Award winning country house nestled amidst breathtaking scenery of Antrim coast/Glens.
Grades: NITB Approv
Tel: **028 2177 1762** (also fax no)
Mrs McAuley.
D: £15.00-£17.00
S: £20.00-£22.00.
Open: All Year
Beds: 1F 1D 1T
Baths: 2 En 1 Sh
🛏 (4) 🅿 (6) 🗗 ✕ 🚲 📠 ☑ ♿ ☑

Ballycastle 7

National Grid Ref: D1241

🍴 🍺 Kimark, Strand, Marine Hotel, Mccarroll's, Wysner's, Hunter's Bar, Anzac

(0.25m 🚍) *Silversprings House, Ballycastle, Co Antrim, BT54 6ED.*
Tel: **028 2076 2080** (also fax no)
Mrs Mulholland.
D: £16.00-£18.50
S: £18.50-£18.50.
Open: Easter to end Sep
Beds: 1T 2D
Baths: 2 En 1 Pr
🛏 🅿 ✕ 🗗 🚲 📠 ☑ ✦
Family-run Dutch Colonial style house situated in quiet area midway between sea front and town centre. Comfortable beds and private parking. Ideal base for touring Giants Causeway and Glens of Antrim.

(0.25m 🚍) *Fragrens, 34 Quay Road, Ballycastle, Co Antrim, BT54 6BH.*
Grades: NITB Approv
Tel: **028 2076 2168**
Greene.
D: £16.00-£18.00 -£17.50.
Open: Feb to Nov
Beds: 4F 2D 1T
Baths: 5 En 1 Pr 1 Sh
🛏 🅿 (10) 🗗 🍗 🚲 📠 ☑ ✦
This beautiful C18th Town house which runs nearby hills and glens is situated central to Giants Causeway and glens of Antrim. A wide choice of breakfast is served in conservatory / dining room enclosed with walled courtyard. Town and seaside within 5 minutes walking distance.

🚍 sign means that, *given due notice*, owners will pick you up from the path and drop you off *within reason*.

(0.25m 🚍) **Torr Brae**, *77 Torr road, Ballycastle, Co Antrim,* BT54 6RQ.
Tranquil setting in a designated AONB overlooking Mull of Kintyre, Scotland.
Grades: NITB Approv
Tel: 028 2076 9625 Mrs McHenry.
D: £17.50-£18.00 **S:** £18.50-£18.50.
Open: All Year
Beds: 1F 1D 1S
Baths: 3 En
🛏 🄿 🍴 🗯 ♿ 🏠 & Ⓥ 🅰

(0.25m) **Hillsea**, *28 North Street, Ballycastle, Co Antrim,* BT54 6BW.
Lovely Victorian villa overlooking Sea of Moyle, large appetising breakfasts.
Grades: NITB Listed
Tel: 028 2076 2385 Mr Jameson.
D: £18.00-£22.00 **S:** £18.00-£22.00.
Open: Mar to Nov
Beds: 5F 5D 5T 5S
Baths: 10 Pr 10 En 3 Sh
🛏 🄿 (70) 🗯 🍴 ✕ 🏠 & Ⓥ 🅰 ✦

Ballintoy 8

National Grid Ref: D0444

(▲On path) **Sheep Island View Hostel**, *42a Main Street, Ballintoy, Ballycastle, County Antrim,* BT54 6LX.
Tel: 028 2076 9391 Adults: £8.00
Evening meal available, Facilities for disabled people

(▲0.5m) **Whitepark Bay International Youth Hostel**,
157 Whitepark Road, Ballintoy, Ballycastle, Co Antrim BT54 6NH.
Tel: 028 2073 1745 Adults: £10.50
Television, Laundry facilities, Evening meal available, Facilities for disabled people
With magnificent views over the sea, this is a new, purpose-built hostel, in its own secluded grounds.

Bushmills 9

National Grid Ref: C9440

🍴 🍺 Bushmills Inn, Distillers' Arms

(0.5m 🚍) **Craig Park**, *24 Carnbore Road, Bushmills, Co Antrim,* BT57 8YF.
Grades: NITB Approv,
AA 4 Diamond
Tel: 028 2073 2496 Mrs Cheal.
Fax no: 028 2073 2479
D: £27.50-£27.50 **S:** £30.00-£50.00.
Open: All Year (not Xmas)
Beds: 1F 2T **Baths:** 3 En
🛏 🄿 (8) 🗯 🄿 ♿ 🏠 Ⓥ 🅰 ✦
A very comfortable Georgian-style country house offering superior accommodation, incredible views Bushmills and Giant's Causeway, Dunluce minutes away, perfect for a holiday. Someone wrote about Craig Park - 'Heaven with a fence round it!'. Runner-up of 'Ulster Guesthouse of the Year'.

All paths are popular: you are well-advised to book ahead

(0.5m) **Ardeevin**, *145 Main Street, Bushmills, Co Antrim,* BT57 8QE.
Comfortable family-run house convenient to Giant's Causeway and Bushmills Distillery
Grades: NITB Approv
Tel: 028 2073 1661
Mrs Montgomery.
D: £17.00 **S:** £17.00.
Open: All Year
Beds: 2D 1T
Baths: 2 Ensuite 1 Private
🗯 🄿 ♿ 🏠 Ⓥ ✦

(0.5m 🚍) **Knocklayde View**,
90 Causeway Road, Bushmills, Co Antrim, BT57 8SX.
Country house with lovely view of countryside, near the beauty of the Giant's Causeway
Tel: 028 2073 2099
Mrs Wylie.
D: £15.00-£15.00
S: £18.00-£18.00.
Open: All Year
Beds: 1F 1D
Baths: 1 Shared
🛏 🄿 🄿 ♿ 🏠 Ⓥ 🅰

Ballymagarry 10

National Grid Ref: C8940

(0.25m) **Islay-View**, *36 Leeke Road, Ballymagarry, Portrush, Co Antrim,* BT56 8NH.
Actual grid ref: C897401
Modern, comfortable farm-bungalow in quiet location, Portrush/Bushmills area
Grades: NITB Approv
Tel: 028 7082 3220
Mrs Smith.
D: £17.50 **S:** £25.00.
Open: Easter to Sep
Beds: 1F 1D 1T
Baths: 3 Ensuite
🛏 🄿 (6) 🗯 ♿ 🏠 & Ⓥ

Order your packed lunches the *evening before* you need them. Not at breakfast!

Portrush 11

National Grid Ref: C8540

🍴 🍺 Harbour Inn, Royal Court, Donovan's, Ramore, Rowland's

(0.25m 🚍) **Glencroft Guest House**, *95 Coleraine Road, Portrush, Co Antrim,* BT56 8HN.
Grades: NITB 1 Star
Tel: 028 7082 2902
Mr & Mrs Henderson.
D: £18.00-£21.00 **S:** £20.00-£30.00.
Open: All Year (not Xmas)
Beds: 2F 2D 2T
Baths: 3 En 3 Sh
🛏 🄿 (10) 🗯 🄿 ✕ ♿ 🏠 Ⓥ 🅰 ✦
Private garden. Downstairs ensuite rooms. Enjoy Glencroft's special four course breakfast. Menu includes traditional Ulster fry and healthy fruit platter. Near Giant's Causeway, beautiful beaches and Royal Portrush Golf Course and convenient to four other courses. Children welcome.

(0.25m) **Beulah House**,
16 Causeway Street, Portrush, Co Antrim, BT56 8AB.
Select accommodation, Good food, Private parking, rail, bus, golf, 5 mins.
Grades: NITB Approv
Tel: 028 7082 2413 Mrs Anderson.
D: £16.50-£20.00 **S:** £16.50-£20.00.
Open: All Year (not Xmas)
Beds: 1F 6D 3T 2S
Baths: 3 En 3 Pr 2 Sh
🛏 🄿 (10) 🗯 🄿 ✕ ♿ 🏠 Ⓥ 🅰 ✦

(0.25m) **Abbeydean**, *9 Ramore Ave, Portrush, Co Antrim,* BT56 8BB.
Family-run situated in select area. Convenient to all amenities.
Grades: NITB Approv
Tel: 028 7082 2645 Boggs.
D: £16.00-£20.00 **S:** £16.00-£18.00.
Open: All Year (not Xmas)
Beds: 3F 2D 2T 2S **Baths:** 3 En 3 Pr
🛏 🗯 🄿 ✕ ♿ 🏠 Ⓥ 🅰

(0.25m) **Clarmont**, *10 Lansdowne Crescent, Portrush, Co Antrim,* BT56 8AY.
Victorian house, sea front, convenient to golf clubs, restaurants and entertainment.
Tel: 028 7082 2397 (also fax no)
Mr & Mrs Duggan.
D: £20.00-£25.00 **S:** £25.00.
Open: All Year (not Xmas)
Beds: 4F 3D 3T **Baths:** 10 En
🛏 (5) 🄿 🏠 ✦

(0.25m) **SURE STAY Portrush**,
6 Bath Road, Portrush, Co Antrim, BT56 8AP.
Beside beach. Private car park. Excellent family accommodation.
Tel: 01726 890770
Fax no: 01726 890774
D: £16.50 **S:** £20.00.
Open: All Year
Beds: 4F 4D 4T **Baths:** 4 En 2 Sh
🛏 🄿 (10) 🗯 ✕ ♿ 🏠 Ⓥ ✦

(0.25m) 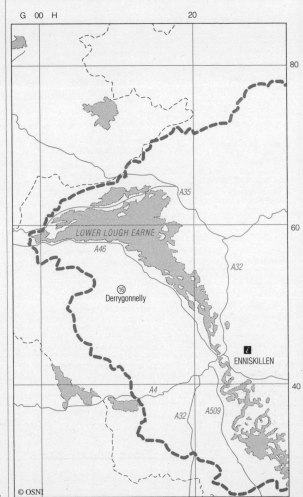 *Causeway House,*
26 Kerr Street, Portrush, Co
Antrim, BT56 8DG.
Modernised town house, overlooking beach harbour. Convenient for transport, shops, pubs restaurants.
Tel: **028 7082 4847**
Mr & Mrs Devenney.
D: £15.00-£20.00 **S:** £15.00-£20.00.
Open: May to Oct
Beds: 1D 1T 1S **Baths:** 3 En 1 Sh
🛇 (2) ⊬ ⬜ 🔥 ⒨ Ⓥ ∦

(0.25m) *Alexandra Guest House,*
11 Lansdowne Crescent, Portrush,
Co Antrim, BT56 8AY.
A charming period town house overlooking the bay. Ideally situated for exploring Giants Causeway.
Tel: **028 7082 2284** Mr McAlister.
D: £18.00-£30.00 **S:** £20.00-£30.00.
Open: Jan to Dec
Beds: 3F 5D 2T
Baths: 5 En 5 Pr 5 Sh
🛇 🄿 ⊬ ⬜ 🔥 ⒨ Ⓥ ∦

(0.25m) *Glenkeen Guest House,*
59 Coleraine Road, Portrush,
Co Antrim, BT56 8HR.
Quality, cleanliness, good food and a friendly service at a reasonable price
Grades: NITB 3 Star
Tel: **028 7082 2279** (also fax no)
Mrs Little.
D: £19.00 **S:** £23.00.
Open: All Year (not Xmas)
Beds: 3F 3T 4D **Baths:** 10 En
🛇 🄿 (20) ⬜ ✕ 🔥 ⒨ & Ⓥ ∎

Portstewart   12

National Grid Ref: C8137

🍴 🍺 Shannanaghs, Edgewater Hotel, Montague
Arms, West Bay View Hotel, The York, Cromore
Halt, The Anchor, Honilague Arms

(▲ 0.25m) *Causeway Coast*
Independent Hostel, 4 Victoria
Terrace, Atlantic Circle,
Portstewart, County Londonderry,
BT55 7BA.
Tel: **028 7083 3789 Adults:** £6.00

(0.25m) *Lis-Na-Rain, 6 Victoria*
Terrace, Portstewart,
Co Londonderry, BT55 7BA.
Warm welcome guaranteed, incorporating licensed Ecosse Restaurant, with excellent sea view.
Tel: **028 7083 3522** Miss Gardiner.
D: £18.00-£22.00 **S:** £16.00-£10.00.
Open: All Year (not Xmas)
Beds: 1F 2D 3T 1S
Baths: 5 En 2 Sh
🛇 🄿 (7) ⊬ ⬜ ✕ 🔥 ⒨ Ⓥ ∎

Pay B&Bs by cash or
cheque and be prepared
to pay up front.

(0.25m) *Strandeen, 63 Strand*
Road, Portstewart,
Co Londonderry, BT55 7LU.
Peace and every comfort overlooking ocean. Beach, promenade, golf course only minutes away.
Tel: **028 7083 3159** (also fax no)
Mrs Caskey.
D: £22.50-£22.50 **S:** £25.00-£30.00.
Open: Easter to Oct
Beds: 1D 2T **Baths:** 1 Pr
🛇 🄿 (6) ⊬ ⬜ 🔥 ⒨ Ⓥ ∎ ∦

Always telephone
to get directions to
the B&B - you will
save time!

Bringing children with
you? Always ask for
any special rates.

(0.25m) 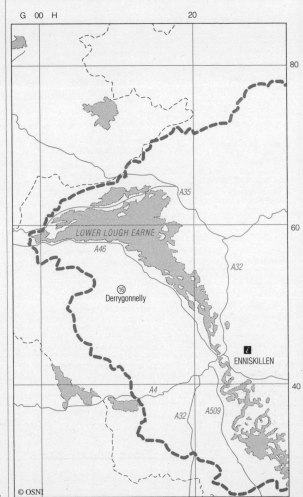 *Oregon, 168 Station*
Road, Portstewart,
Co Londonderry, BT55 7PU.
Actual grid ref: C830382
Modern bungalow with luxurious accommodation
Grades: NITB Approv
Tel: **028 7083 2826**
Mrs Anderson.
D: £21.00 **S:** £27.00.
Open: Feb to Nov
Beds: 1F 5D 3T
Baths: 8 Ensuite 1 Private
🛇 🄿 (8) ⊬ ⬜ ✕ 🔥 ⒨ & Ⓥ ∎ ∦

G 00 H   20

LOWER LOUGH EARNE

A35

A46

A32

⑯
Derrygonnelly

A4

A32   A509

🅸
ENNISKILLEN

80

60

40

© OSNI

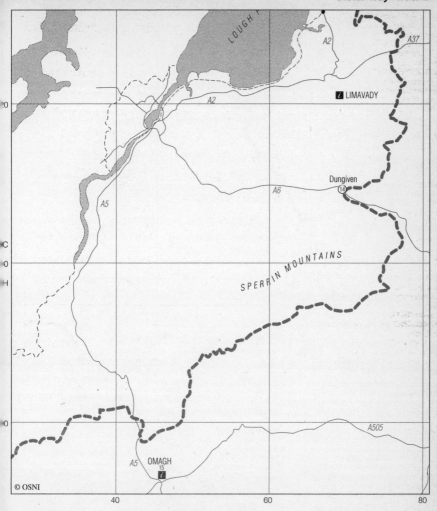

© OSNI

Coleraine 13

National Grid Ref: C8532

|◎| ⬤| Charly's, Imperial Hotel, Bushtown House, Bo-hill Auto Inn, Salmon Leap

(0.75m) *Coolbeg, 2e Grange Rd, Coleraine, Co Londonderry, BT52 1NG*
Grades: NITB Approv
Tel: 028 7034 4961 Mrs Chandler.
Fax no: 028 7034 3278
D: £20.00-£22.00 **S:** £25.00-£25.00.
Open: All Year (not Xmas)
Beds: 1F 3T 1S **Baths:** 4 En 1 Pr
⛄ (4) 🅿 (5) ⅟✗ 🗇 🛋 🛏 &. Ⓥ 🖺 ⚡
Modern bungalow set in pleasant gardens on edge of town. TV and tea/coffee facilities. 2 ensuite bedrooms fully wheelchair accessible. Ideal for touring North Antrim coast. Royal Portrush and 4 other golf courses, fishing and riding nearby.

(0.5m 🚐**)** *Manor Cottage, 44 Cranagh Road, Coleraine, Co Londonderry, BT51 3NN.*
Warm welcome to cottage-style country home, 1 km off A2, on the Ulster Way.
Tel: 028 7034 4001 Mrs Roulston.
D: £17.00-£18.00 **S:** £16.00-£18.00.
Open: Easter to Oct
Beds: 2D **Baths:** 1 En 1 Pr 1 Sh
⛄ 🅿 (4) 🗇 🛏 🛋 🖺 ⚡

Please respect
a B&B's wishes
regarding children,
animals & smoking.

High season,
bank holidays and
special events mean
low availability
everywhere.

(0.5m) *Clanwilliam Lodge, 21 Curragh Road, Coleraine, Co Londonderry, BT51 3RY.*
Elegant country home with stabling, riverside and forest walks.
Tel: 028 7035 6582 (also fax no)
Mrs McWilliam.
D: £20.00-£22.50 **S:** £25.00-£30.00.
Open: All Year (not Xmas)
Beds: 1F 1D 1T **Baths:** 3 En
⛄ 🅿 (8) ⅟✗ 🛋 🛏 🖺 Ⓥ 🖺 ⚡

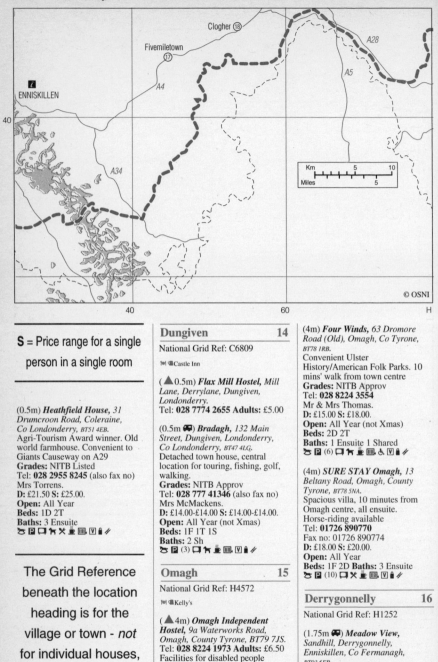

Clogher ⑱
Fivemiletown ⑰
A28
A4
A5
🚩
ENNISKILLEN
40
A34
Km 5 10
Miles 5
© OSNI

40   60   H

S = Price range for a single person in a single room

(0.5m) *Heathfield House, 31 Drumcroon Road, Coleraine, Co Londonderry, BT51 4EB.*
Agri-Tourism Award winner. Old world farmhouse. Convenient to Giants Causeway on A29
Grades: NITB Listed
Tel: **028 2955 8245** (also fax no)
Mrs Torrens.
D: £21.50 **S:** £25.00.
Open: All Year
Beds: 1D 2T
Baths: 3 Ensuite
🛇 🄿 🖵 🛏 ✕ 🚵 🛋 Ⓥ 🛆 ⚡

The Grid Reference beneath the location heading is for the village or town - *not* for individual houses, which are shown (where supplied) in each entry itself.

Dungiven   14

National Grid Ref: C6809

🍴 🍺 Castle Inn

(▲0.5m) *Flax Mill Hostel, Mill Lane, Derrylane, Dungiven, Londonderry.*
Tel: **028 7774 2655 Adults:** £5.00

(0.5m 🚍) *Bradagh, 132 Main Street, Dungiven, Londonderry, Co Londonderry, BT47 4LG.*
Detached town house, central location for touring, fishing, golf, walking.
Grades: NITB Approv
Tel: **028 777 41346** (also fax no)
Mrs McMackens.
D: £14.00-£14.00 **S:** £14.00-£14.00.
Open: All Year (not Xmas)
Beds: 1F 1T 1S
Baths: 2 Sh
🛇 🄿 (3) 🖵 🛏 🚵 🛋 Ⓥ 🛆 ⚡

Omagh   15

National Grid Ref: H4572

🍴 🍺 Kelly's

(▲4m) *Omagh Independent Hostel, 9a Waterworks Road, Omagh, County Tyrone, BT79 7JS.*
Tel: **028 8224 1973 Adults:** £6.50
Facilities for disabled people

D = Price range per person sharing in a double room

(4m) *Four Winds, 63 Dromore Road (Old), Omagh, Co Tyrone, BT78 1RB.*
Convenient Ulster History/American Folk Parks. 10 mins' walk from town centre
Grades: NITB Approv
Tel: **028 8224 3554**
Mr & Mrs Thomas.
D: £15.00 **S:** £18.00.
Open: All Year (not Xmas)
Beds: 2D 2T
Baths: 1 Ensuite 1 Shared
🛇 🄿 (6) 🖵 🛏 🚵 🛋 🛴 Ⓥ 🛆 ⚡

(4m) *SURE STAY Omagh, 13 Beltany Road, Omagh, County Tyrone, BT78 5NA.*
Spacious villa, 10 minutes from Omagh centre, all ensuite. Horse-riding available
Tel: **01726 890770**
Fax no: 01726 890774
D: £18.00 **S:** £20.00.
Open: All Year
Beds: 1F 2D **Baths:** 3 Ensuite
🛇 🄿 (10) 🖵 ✕ 🚵 🛋 Ⓥ 🛆 ⚡

Derrygonnelly   16

National Grid Ref: H1252

(1.75m 🚍) *Meadow View, Sandhill, Derrygonnelly, Enniskillen, Co Fermanagh, BT93 6ER.*
Modern, comfortable house. Peaceful setting
Tel: **028 6864 1233** Mrs Wray.
D: £15.50 **S:** £15.50.
Open: Easter to Sep
Beds: 1F 2D **Baths:** 2 En 1 Sh
🛇 🄿 (6) 🖵 ✕ 🚵 🛋 Ⓥ 🛆 ⚡

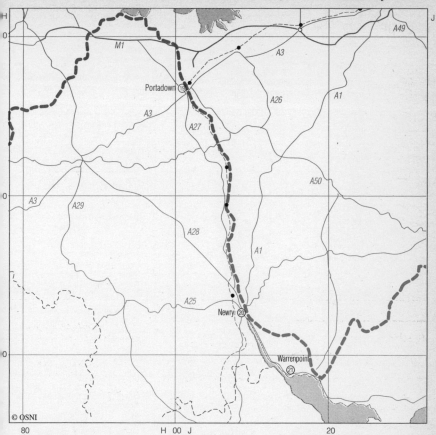

© OSNI

80   H 00 J   20

Fivemiletown   17

National Grid Ref: H4448

(4m) *Al Di Gwyn Lodge,*
103A Clabby Road, Fivemiletown,
Co Tyrone, BT75 0QY.
Relax and enjoy a warm welcome
at Al Di Gwyn Lodge
Grades: NITB Grade A
Tel: **028 8952 1298** Mrs Gilmore.
D: £15.00 **S:** £20.00.
Open: All Year (not Xmas)
Beds: 2T 1D **Baths:** 3 Ensuite
P (8) ⌨ ✾ ▥ ⅏ ⌕

Clogher   18

National Grid Ref: H5351

(3.5m) *Ratory, Clogher,*
Co Tyrone, BT76 0UT.
Victorian farmhouse on Fintona
road B168. One mile from village
Tel: **028 8554 8288** Mr & Mrs
Johnston.
D: £15.00 **S:** £16.00.
Open: All Year (not Xmas)
Beds: 1D **Baths:** 1 Private
P (6) ⅌ ⌨ ✾ ✗ ▥ ⌕ ⅏

Portadown   19

National Grid Ref: J0053

¶ ⬥ Golden Bridge

(On path) *Bannview Squash*
Club, 60 Portmore Street,
Portadown, Craigavon,
Co Armagh, BT62 3NF.
Situated within walking distance of
town centre buses and trains.
Grades: NITB Approv
Tel: **028 3833 6666** (also fax no)
Mr Black.
D: £20.00-£25.00 **S:** £25.00-£30.00.
Open: All Year (not Xmas)
Beds: 20T
Baths: 20 En
⅊ P (17) ⌨ ✗ ☑ ▥ Ⓥ ⌕ ⅏

(0.5m) *SURE STAY The Cottage,*
17 Gallrock Road, Portadown,
Craigavon, Co Armagh, BT62 1NP.
Spacious country house, warm
Irish hospitality and home baking.
Tel: **01762 852189** (also fax no)
D: £20.00-£20.00 **S:** £20.00-£20.00.
Open: All Year
Beds: 1F 4T 1S **Baths:** 6 En
⅊ P (10) ⌨ ✗ ☑ ▥ Ⓥ ⌕ ⅏

Newry   20

National Grid Ref: J0826

¶ ⬥ Brass Monkey

(2m) *Marymount, Windsor*
Avenue, Newry, Co Down, BT34 1EG.
Bungalow with beautiful gardens,
quiet location, walking distance
town centre.
Grades: NITB Approv
Tel: **028 3026 1099** Mrs O'Hare.
D: £17.00-£19.00 **S:** £22.00-£24.00.
Open: All Year (not Xmas/
New Year)
Beds: 3T **Baths:** 1 En 1 Sh
⅊ P ⅌ ⌨ ☑ ▥ Ⓥ ⌕ ⅏

(0.25m) *SURE STAY Newry,*
1 Rock Road, Newry, Co Down,
BT34 1PL.
Large, fresh guest house in pretty
rural setting, 10 minutes from
Newry
Tel: **01726 890770**
Fax no: 01726 890774
D: £17.00 **S:** £17.00.
Open: All Year (not Xmas)
Beds: 2T 2D **Baths:** 4 En 1 Sh
⅊ P (6) ⌨ ✗ ☑ ▥ Ⓥ ⅏

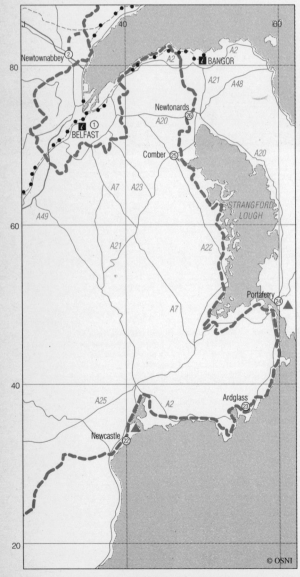

🚐 sign means that, *given due notice*, owners will pick you up from the path and drop you off *within reason*.

Warrenpoint 21

National Grid Ref: J1418

(2m) *SURE STAY Warrenpoint,*
7 Cloughmore Terrace, Warrenpoint,
Newry, Co Down, BT34 3HP.
Victorian town house, tastefully
renovated. Park views, 1 minute
from Carlingford Lough
Tel: **01726 890770**
Fax no: 01726 890774
D: £20.00 .**Open:** All Year
Beds: 2T 2D **Baths:** 2 Shared
🛇 🄿 (3) 🛏 ✕ 🔥 Ⅲ V 🗲

Newcastle 22

National Grid Ref: J3731

🍴 ⊞ Briers, Mariner Hotel, Percy French's, Burrendale Hotel, Pavilion, Mcclennons

(▲ 1m) *Newcastle Youth Hostel,*
30 Downs Road, Newcastle,
Co Down BT33 0AG.
Tel: **028 4372 2133 Adults:** £10.50
Self-catering facilities, Television,
Central heating, Laundry facilities,
Dining room, Cycle store, Evening
meal at
This townhouse hostel is convenient
for exploring the Mountains of
Mourne.

(1m 🚐) *Beverley, 72 Tollymore*
Rd, Newcastle, Co Down, BT33 0JN.
Actual grid ref: J366329
Self contained flatlet, panoramic
view of Mourne Mountains, rural
aspect.
Tel: **028 4372 2018** (also fax no)
Mrs McNeilly.
D: £17.50 **S:** £20.00.
Open: All Year (not Xmas)
Beds: 1T **Baths:** 1 En
🛇 🄿 (2) 🛏 🍴 ✕ 🔥 Ⅲ & V 🛆 🗲

(0.25m 🚐) *Beach House,*
22 Downs Road, Newcastle,
Co Down, BT33 0AG.
Sea front location. Convenient to
RCD Golf Course and Slieve
Donard Hotel.
Tel: **028 4372 2345** Mrs Macauley.
Fax no: 028 4372 2817
D: £25.00-£27.50 **S:** £25.00-£30.00.
Open: All Year (not Xmas/
New Year)
Beds: 2F 1D
Baths: 2 En 1 Sh
🛇 🄿 (2) ⅛ 🛏 ✕ 🔥 Ⅲ V 🗲

(1m 🚐) *Grasmere, 16 Marguerite*
Park, Newcastle, Co Down,
BT33 0PE.
Modern bungalow in quiet residen-
tial area. 10 minutes walk to beach.
Tel: **028 4372 6801** Mrs
McCormick.
D: £18.00-£20.00 **S:** £22.50-£25.00.
Open: All Year
Beds: 1F 2D
Baths: 1 Pr 1 Sh
🛇 🄿 (2) ⅛ 🛏 🍴 🔥 Ⅲ V 🗲

Ardglass 23

National Grid Ref: J5637

🍴 ⊞ The Moorings

(On path 🚐) *Strand Farm, 231*
Ardglass Road, Ardglass,
Downpatrick, Co Down, BT30 7UL.
Secluded farmhouse in peaceful
surroundings. Warm welcome,
refreshments on arrival.
Tel: **028 4484 1446** Mrs Donnan.
D: £16.50-£16.50 **S:** £18.00-£18.00.
Open: Mar to Oct
Beds: 1F 1D 1T
Baths: 1 En 1 Sh 1 Pr
🛇 🄿 (12) 🛏 Ⅲ 🛆 🗲

Portaferry 24

National Grid Ref: J5950

(▲ Ferry - 0.5) *Portaferry Youth Hostel, Barholm, 11 The Strand, Portaferry, Co Down BT22 1PF.*
Tel: **028 4272 9598 Adults:** £10.50
Self-catering facilities, Television, Central heating, Shop, Laundry facilities, Dining room, Cycle store, Evening meal at
Not only an Area of Outstanding Natural Beauty, this is also a Area of Special Scientific Study. The hostel itself in in an Edwardian house, which overlooks Strangford Lough.

All rooms full and
nowhere else to stay?
Ask the owner if
there's anywhere
nearby

Taking your dog?
Book *in advance*
ONLY with owners
who accept dogs (🐾)

Comber 25

National Grid Ref: J4568

(0.25m) *Old School House Inn, Castle Espie, 100 Ballydrain Road, Comber, Newtownards, Co Down, BT23 6EA.*
Enjoy Avril's cuisine grandmere in the Old Schoolhouse Inn. Also 12 presidential suites
Grades: NITB 3 Star
Tel: **028 9754 1182**
Mr & Mrs Brown.
Fax no: 028 9754 2583
D: £25.00 **S:** £25.00.
Open: All Year (not Xmas)
Beds: 6T 3D
Baths: 9 En
🛏🅿✗◻✗⬆🏠🛗Ⓥ🅰✦

Newtownards 26

National Grid Ref: J4874

🏴 ⬛ Strangford Arms Hotel, Ballyharry Road House, Wildfowler Inn

(On path 🚌) *Edenvale, 130 Portaferry Road, Newtownards, Co Down, BT22 2AJ.*
Beautifully restored Georgian farmhouse 2 miles from Newtownards in secluded gardens.
Grades: NITB Approv,
AA 5 Diamond
Tel: **028 9181 4881** Mrs Whyte.
Fax no: 028 9182 6192
D: £27.50-£27.50 **S:** £35.00-£35.00.
Open: All Year (not Xmas/New Year)
Beds: 1F 1D 1T **Baths:** 3 En
🛏🅿 (6)✗◻🐾⬆🏠Ⓥ🅰✦

(0.25m 🚌) *Ard Cuan, 3 Manse Rd, Newtownards, Co Down, BT23 4TP.*
Victorian family home in acre of garden. Friendly informal welcome
Grades: NITB Approv
Tel: **028 9181 1302** Mrs Kerr.
D: £18.00 **S:** £18.00.
Open: All Year (not Xmas)
Beds: 1F1D 1T **Baths:** 2 Sh
🅿◻⬆🏠Ⓥ🅰✦

Western Way

This is one of the wilder paths in the book. The **Western Way** is 120 miles long, running mainly through Mayo, but starting in Galway in the south and ending on the border of Sligo. Its appeal lies in the variety of landscape: from desolate wilderness to historic religious sites, covering bogland, forest, mountains, winding valleys and breathtaking coast. It starts on an ancient pilgrim path through the Maumturk Mountains of Connemara and the Inagh Valley, lined with picturesque white-painted cottages, and passing the neo-Gothic Kylemore Abbey proceeds to Leenane. There is a spectacular view here across Killary Harbour to the Mweelrea Mountains. The next stretch takes in a short but spectacular crossing over the Sheeffry Hills, and the southern flanks of Croagh Patrick, where St Patrick spent Lent and convinced God to banish snakes from Ireland. Now some 60,000 people a year make a pilgrimage to the top, on the last Sunday in July, many of them barefoot. Clew Bay, studded with islets, is on your left, as you proceed to Westport and Newport. Now comes the lonely part. You pass Lough Feeagh, at the foot of an idyllic valley, and head into the wilderness of the Erris and Tirawley bogs. You are in the Gaeltacht now. The path leads eventually to the Atlantic coast: after Killala, with its eleventh-century round tower, it heads off to the Moy estuary (a big salmon river), and Ballina, from where winding country roads take you to the Sligo border. You are advised that on the long northern section of the path between Newport and Killala, accommodation is fairly sparse - it may not be possible to plan your route in one-day stretches with a place to stay at the end, in which case you should either take a tent, or arrange transport between the point you have reached on the path and your previous or next port of call. Accommodation providers in Belmullet may be able to help you here.

Guides: *The Way-marked Trails of Ireland* by Michael Fewer (ISBN 0 7171 2386 3), published by Gill and Macmillan, and available from all good bookshops or direct from the publishers (Goldenbridge Industrial Estate, Inchicore, Dublin 8, Ireland, tel. 01 4531005) @ £9.99 (+ £2.50 p&p)
West of Ireland Walk Guide: Co Mayo, The Western Way, by Joe McDermott and Robert Chapman (ISBN 0 9519624 1 8), published by Mayo County Council, covers the Mayo part of the trail: available from Mayo County Council, Castlebar, County Mayo, Ireland, tel. 094 24444 (Ian Douglas), @ £6.00 (p&p inc.)
The Western Way in Connemara - A Walker's Map & Guide, published by Folding Landscapes (ISBN 0 9504002 8 9), covers the Galway part: available from the publishers (Folding Landscapes, Roundstone, County Galway, tel. 095 35886) @ £6.00 (+ £1p&p). The same publishers also publish *Mountains of Connemara*, which covers the Galway part of the Western Way in addition to a number of other walks in County Galway: same price

Maps: 1:50000 Ordnance Survey of Ireland Discovery Series: 23, 24, 31, 37, 38.

Oughterard 1

National Grid Ref: M1143

(▲ On path) *Lough Corrib Hostel*, Camp Street, Oughterard, Galway.
Tel: **091 552866 Adults: £7.00**

(▲ 0.25m) *Canrawer House Hostel*, Station Road, Oughterard, Galway.
Tel: **091 552388 Adults: £6.50**
Evening meal

All rooms full and nowhere else to stay? Ask the owner if there's anywhere nearby

---

D = Price range per person sharing in a double room

(1m 🚌) *Corrib Wave,*
Portacarron, Connemara, Oughterard, Galway.
Grades: BF 3 Star
Tel: **091 552147** Mr & Mrs Healy.
Fax no: 091 552736
D: £22.50-£25.00 **S:** £30.00-£33.00.
Open: Mar to Nov
Beds: 2F 8T
Baths: 10 En
🅿 (30) ✠ ⬛ ✗ ▥ 🖤 ♨
Corrib Wave is situated in heart of beautiful Connemara. 2 1/2 km Oughterard village, lovely pubs Irish music / restaurants. Golf course, 1 km. Corrib Wave has 10 bedrooms, with double/ single beds, ensuite TVs hairdryers. Peace and quietness.

S = Price range for a single person in a single room

(1m) 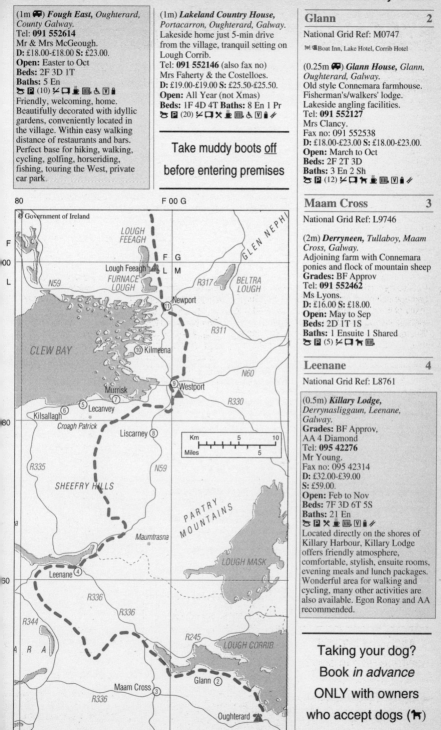 *Fough East, Oughterard, County Galway.*
Tel: **091 552614**
Mr & Mrs McGeough.
D: £18.00-£18.00 **S:** £23.00.
Open: Easter to Oct
Beds: 2F 3D 1T
Baths: 5 En
⛲ 🅿 (10) ✕ ☐ 🏠 🛏 Ⅲ ♿ Ⓥ ♠
Friendly, welcoming, home. Beautifully decorated with idyllic gardens, conveniently located in the village. Within easy walking distance of restaurants and bars. Perfect base for hiking, walking, cycling, golfing, horseriding, fishing, touring the West, private car park.

(1m) *Lakeland Country House, Portacarron, Oughterard, Galway.* Lakeside home just 5-min drive from the village, tranquil setting on Lough Corrib.
Tel: **091 552146** (also fax no)
Mrs Faherty & the Costelloes.
D: £19.00-£19.00 **S:** £25.50-£25.50.
Open: All Year (not Xmas)
Beds: 1F 4D 4T **Baths:** 8 En 1 Pr
⛲ 🅿 (20) ✕ ☐ ✕ 🛏 Ⅲ ♿ Ⓥ ♠ ♦

Take muddy boots <u>off</u>
before entering premises

Glann 2

National Grid Ref: M0747

🍴 🍺 Boat Inn, Lake Hotel, Corrib Hotel

(0.25m) 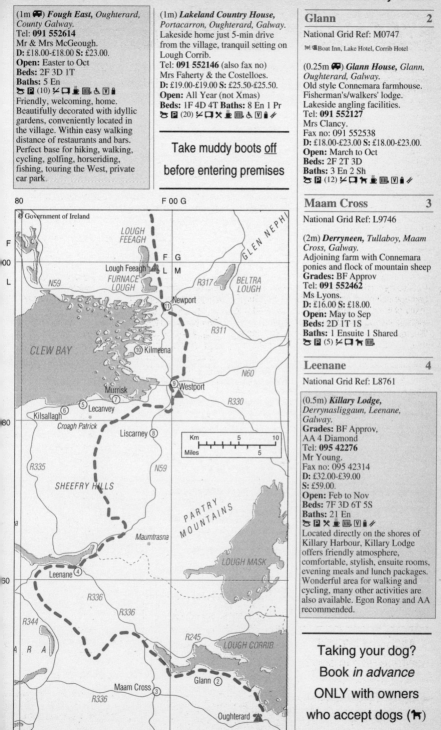 *Glann House, Glann, Oughterard, Galway.*
Old style Connemara farmhouse. Fisherman's/walkers' lodge. Lakeside angling facilities.
Tel: **091 552127**
Mrs Clancy.
Fax no: 091 552538
D: £18.00-£23.00 **S:** £18.00-£23.00.
Open: March to Oct
Beds: 2F 2T 3D
Baths: 3 En 2 Sh
⛲ 🅿 (12) ✕ ☐ 🛏 🏠 Ⅲ Ⓥ ♠ ♦

Maam Cross 3

National Grid Ref: L9746

(2m) *Derryneen, Tullaboy, Maam Cross, Galway.*
Adjoining farm with Connemara ponies and flock of mountain sheep
Grades: BF Approv
Tel: **091 552462**
Ms Lyons.
D: £16.00 **S:** £18.00.
Open: May to Sep
Beds: 2D 1T 1S
Baths: 1 Ensuite 1 Shared
⛲ 🅿 (5) ✕ ☐ 🛏 Ⅲ

Leenane 4

National Grid Ref: L8761

(0.5m) *Killary Lodge, Derrynasliggaun, Leenane, Galway.*
Grades: BF Approv, AA 4 Diamond
Tel: **095 42276**
Mr Young.
Fax no: 095 42314
D: £32.00-£39.00
S: £59.00.
Open: Feb to Nov
Beds: 7F 3D 6T 5S
Baths: 21 En
⛲ 🅿 ✕ 🛏 Ⅲ Ⓥ ♠ ♦
Located directly on the shores of Killary Harbour, Killary Lodge offers friendly atmosphere, comfortable, stylish, ensuite rooms, evening meals and lunch packages. Wonderful area for walking and cycling, many other activities are also available. Egon Ronay and AA recommended.

Taking your dog?
Book *in advance*
ONLY with owners
who accept dogs (🛏)

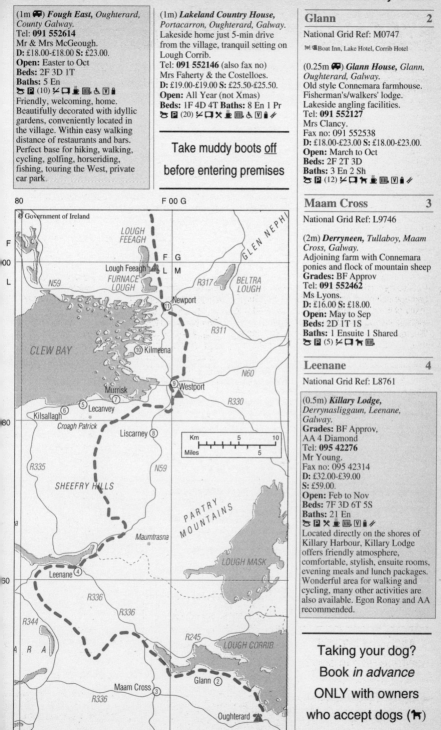

(On path 🚲) *Portfinn Lodge,*
Leenane, Galway.
Actual grid ref: L879619
Grades: BF 2 Star
Tel: 095 42265 Mr Daly.
Fax no: 095 42315
D: £18.00-£23.00 **S:** £40.00-£45.00.
Open: Easter to Oct
Beds: 2F 3D 3T
Baths: 8 En
🏃 🅿 (20) ⅍ ❑ ☐ ♁ ✕ ◼ 🛈 ⋗
Portfinn Lodge set among the
magnificent scenery of the Killary
and the Mweelrea Mountains. An
ideal centre for the walker and
rambler, our seafood restaurant is
internationally acclaimed, offering
the best of local produce.

Lecanvey 5

National Grid Ref: L8882

(2m 🚲) *Seavilla, Lecanvey,*
Westport, Co Mayo.
Modern home overlooking sea.
Orthopaedic beds, home from
home. Long established business
Tel: **098 64803** Mrs Geraghty.
D: £14.00 **S:** £17.00.
Open: Apr to Nov
Beds: 2F 2T 1D 1S
Baths: 3 En 1 Pr 1 Sh
🏃 🅿 (8) ❑ ♁ ✕ 🛋 ◼ ⅋ 🛈 ⋗

Kilsallagh 6

National Grid Ref: L8581

⑂ ◁ The Weir Bar

(3m 🚲) *Achill View, Kilsallagh,*
Westport, Co Mayo.
Actual grid ref: L857817
Early 20th century working
farmhouse with interior renovated
to top standard.
Tel: **098 66433** Mrs Gannon.
D: £15.00-£18.00 **S:** £18.00-£20.00.
Open: All Year (not Xmas/New
Year)
Beds: 1F 1T 2D
Baths: 2 En 1 Pr 1 Sh
🏃 🅿 ⅍ ❑ ✕ ◼ ⅋ 🛈 ⋗

(3m) *Sea Breeze, Kilsallagh,*
Westport, Co Mayo.
Friendly home with beautiful
views. Central location. Warm
welcome. Good food
Grades: BF Approv
Tel: **098 66548** Mrs Gill.
D: £15.00 **S:** £20.00.
Open: Mar to Nov
Baths: 3 Ensuite
🏃 🅿 ⅍ ❑ ✕ 🛋 🛈

Order your
packed lunches the
evening before you
need them.
Not at breakfast!

Murrisk 7

National Grid Ref: L9282

(1m) *Bertra House,* Thornhill,
Murrisk, Westport, Co Mayo.
Seaside family-run farmhouse
3 minutes' walk to long sandy
award-winning blue flag beach
Tel: **098 64833**
Mrs Gill.
D: £18.00 **S:** £25.00.
Open: Easter to mid-Nov
Beds: 2F 1T 2D
Baths: 4 Ensuite 1 Private
🏃 (5) 🅿 (6) ⅍ ❑ 🛋 🛤 ◼ 🛈 ⋗

Liscarney 8

National Grid Ref: L9876

⑂ ◁ J J O'Malley's

(1m 🚲) *Moher House,* Liscarney,
Westport, Co Mayo.
Award-winning gardens, breakfast,
dinner menu, lakeside, warm
hospitality, fishing, walking.
Tel: **098 21360** Mrs O'Malley.
D: £17.00-£19.00 **S:** £23.00-£25.00.
Open: Oct
Beds: 2F 2D 2T
Baths: 3 En 2 Pr 1 Sh
🏃 🅿 (6) ❑ ♁ ✕ 🛋 ⅋ 🛈 ⋗

(1m 🚲) *Bohea Loughs,* Bohea,
Liscarney, Westport, Co Mayo.
Actual grid ref: L971782
Traditional farmhouse, set in 40
acres with two lakes. Croagh
Patrick, Togher Patrick Walk
Tel: **098 21797** Mrs Large.
D: £14.00 **S:** £18.00.
Open: All Year (not Xmas)
Beds: 1F 1T 1D
Baths: 3 Ensuite
🏃 🅿 ♁ ✕ 🛋 🛤 ◼ 🛈 ⋗

(1m 🚲) *Oughty Lodge,* Oughty,
Drummond, Liscarney, Westport,
Co Mayo.
Modern comfortable bungalow in
Drummin valley, adjacent to
Western Way
Tel: **098 21929** Mrs Friel.
D: £16.50-£17.50 **S:** £20.00-£25.00.
Open: May to Sep
Beds: 2D 1T
Baths: 2 Ensuite 1 Shared
🏃 (4) 🅿 (3) ⅍ ❑ ✕ 🛋 ⅋ 🛈 ⋗

Westport 9

National Grid Ref: M0084

⑂ ◁ Angler's Rest, J J O'Malley's, Olde Railway
Hotel, Asgard Bar, Geraghty's, Ardmore House,
The Towers, Grand Central Hotel, Castlecourt
Hotel, Shebeen Bar, O'Gradys, Kirwan's

(▲ On path) *Westport Youth
Hostel, Altamount Street, Westport,
County Mayo.*
Tel: **098 26644**
Under 18: £6.51 **Adults:** £7.51
Shop, Laundry facilities, Facilities
for disabled people, Meals
available
*Purpose-built modern hostel in
heritage town of Westport. Visit
Ireland's Holy Mountain and Achill
Island. Leisure complex nearby;
blue flag beaches; hillwalking.*

(▲ On path) *Old Mill Holiday
Hostel, Barrack Yard, James
Street, Westport, County Mayo.*
Tel: **098 27045** **Adults:** £6.50
Facilities for disabled people

(▲ 1m) *Emania Hostel, .*
Tel: **Adults:** £6.01
Showers, Running water, WC,
Washing facilities, Kitchen
facilities

(1m) *Brook Lodge, Deerpark East,
Newport Road, Westport, Co Mayo.*
Grades: BF Approv
Tel: **098 26654**
Mrs Reddington.
D: £17.00-£19.00
S: £21.50-£25.50.
Open: Mar to Oct
Beds: 2D 2T
Baths: 2 Pr 2 Sh
🏃 (6) 🅿 ❑ 🛋 🛈 ⋗
Modern house in quiet residential
area, 5 minutes walk from town
centre. A warm welcome awaits
you with tea or coffee on arrival -
ideal base for touring West Coast.
Listed in '400 Best B&Bs in
Ireland'.

(1m 🚲) *Cedar Lodge, Kings Hill,
Newport Road (N59), Westport,
Co Mayo.*
Grades: BF Approv
Tel: **098 25417** (also fax no)
Mr & Mrs Flynn.
D: £19.00-£20.00
S: £25.00-£30.00.
Open: Feb to Nov
Beds: 1F 1D 2T
Baths: 3 En 1 Pr
🏃 (10) 🅿 (4) ⅍ ❑ 🛋 🛤 ◼ 🛈 ⋗
Enjoy Irish hospitality with Peter &
Maureen at their peaceful
bungalow, landscaped gardens
awards 1997, relax on the patio, 6
min walk to town, ideal base for
golf, touring etc. Breakfast menu,
recommended Frommer Best B&B,
Guide du Routard, vouchers
accepted.

All paths are popular:
you are well-advised to
book ahead

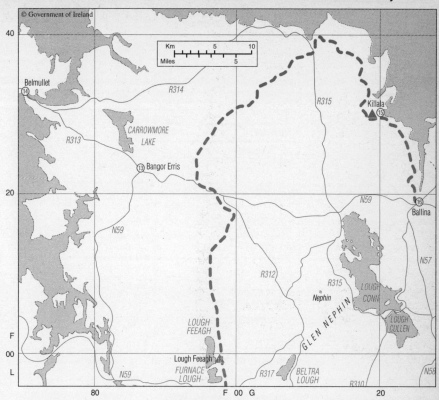

© Government of Ireland

(2m) *Hillside Lodge, Castlebar Road, Westport, Co Mayo.*
Warm friendly family home just a short distance from Westport on N5.
Grades: BF Approv
Tel: **098 25668**
Mrs English.
D: £17.00-£19.00
S: £22.00-£24.00.
Open: All Year (not Xmas/New Year)
Beds: 1F 1D 1T
Baths: 2 En 2 Pr

(1m) *Linden Hall, Altamount Street, Westport, Co Mayo.*
Tel: **098 27005** (also fax no)
Mr & Mrs Breen.
D: £17.00-£22.00 **S:** £23.00-£30.00.
Open: All Year (not Xmas)
Beds: 1F 3D
Baths: 4 En
Warm welcomes, good humour and a relaxed atmosphere in our spacious Edwardian townhouse in the centre of Westport town. High ceiling ensuite rooms with contemporary comforts (TV hair dryer, tea/coffee) and old world elegance will ensure a memorable stay and a plan to return.

(1m) *Hazelbrook, Deerpark East, Newport Road, Westport, Co Mayo.*
Grades: BF Approv
Tel: **098 26865**
Mr & Mrs Cafferkey.
D: £19.00-£20.00 **S:** £25.00-£30.00.
Open: All Year
Beds: 2F 2D 1T 1S
Baths: 6 En
Luxurious guest house in quiet residential area. Bedrooms ensuite with TV. Tea/coffee facilities. Massage and reflexology also available. Five minutes' walk to town centre. Ideally situated for touring West Coast. Vouchers and credit cards accepted. Garden available to guests. Pay phone available.

(0.5m) *Woodside, Golf Course Road, Westport, Co Mayo.*
Modern town house. Spacious landscaped gardens. Private car park. 10 mins' walk town centre.
Grades: BF Approv
Tel: **098 26436** Mrs Hopkins.
D: £19.00-£20.00 **S:** £30.00.
Open: Mar to Oct
Beds: 2F 2D 1T
Baths: 5 En

(2m) *Bella Vista, Sheroe (off Castlebar Rd), Westport, Co Mayo.*
Comfortable bungalow on own 30-acre holding, quiet location, 2 mins town, off N5.
Tel: **098 26670** Mrs Mullen.
D: £18.00-£18.00 **S:** £20.00-£20.00.
Open: All Year
Beds: 2F 1D 1T 1S
Baths: 4 En 1 Pr

(1m) *Ceol na Mara, Lower Quay, Westport, Co Mayo.*
Two storey town house. All amenities nearby. Car parking facilities.
Tel: **098 26969** Mrs McGreal.
Fax no: 091 565201
D: £18.00-£20.00 **S:** £20.00-£25.00.
Open: All Year (not Xmas)
Beds: 1F 2T 3D

(1m) *Lui Na Greine, Castlebar Road, Westport, Co Mayo.*
Comfortable bungalow. Panoramic views, Clew Bay and Mountains. Spacious gardens.
Grades: BF Approv
Tel: **098 25536** Mrs Doherty.
D: £20.00-£20.00 **S:** £25.00-£26.00.
Open: Easter to Oct
Beds: 2F 2D 2T **Baths:** 4 En 2 Sh

(1m 🚌) *Wilmaur*, Rosbeg, Westport, Co Mayo.
Luxurious & spacious guest house on shores of Clew Bay. Home cooking, open fire.
Tel: **098 25784** Eithne Larkin.
Fax no: 098 26224
D: £20.00-£22.50 **S:** £25.00-£27.50.
Open: All Year (not Xmas)
Beds: 3F 2D
Baths: 5 En
🛌 🅿 (10) ⚡ 🗆 ✕ 🖾 ♨ 🎹 ♥ 🗎

(4m) *Emania*, Castlebar Road, Sheeaune, Westport, Co Mayo.
Impressive two-storey dwelling in own grounds - friendly hospitable atmosphere.
Tel: **098 26459** Mrs O'Reilly.
D: £15.00-£18.00 **S:** £22.50-£24.50.
Open: May to Sep
Beds: 2D 1T
Baths: 2 En
🛌 🅿 (6) 🐾 ✕ 🖾

(1m) *Killary House*, Distillery Road, Westport, Co Mayo.
Town centre, rooms ensuite, tea/coffee, TV/radio, private parking.
Tel: **098 27457**
Mrs Hyland.
D: £16.00-£17.50 **S:** £20.00-£25.00.
Open: All Year (not Xmas)
Beds: 3F 3D
Baths: 6 En
🅿 (6) 🗆 ♨ 🖾 🎹 🗎

Kilmeena   10

National Grid Ref: L9689

🍴 🍺 Asgard Bar

(🔺 2m) *Country School Hostel*, Kilmeena, Westport, County Mayo.
Tel: **098 41099 Adults:** £7.00

(2m) *Seapoint House*, Kilmeena, Westport, Co Mayo.
Large country house overlooking the sea. Quiet location. Signposted on N59 Westport-Newport road.
Grades: AA 3 Q
Tel: **098 41254**
O'Malley Family.
Fax no: 098 41903
D: £20.00-£22.50
S: £26.00-£28.00.
Open: May to Oct
Beds: 2F 2D 2T
Baths: 6 En

(2m) *The Pines*, Conrea, Kilmeena, Westport, Co Mayo.
Friendly farmhouse accommodation situated 2.5 miles from Westport on M59, one hour Knock airport.
Tel: **098 26148**
Mr & Mrs O'Malley.
D: £15.00-£15.00
S: £15.00-£15.00.
Open: Jun to Aug
Beds: 1F 1D 1S
Baths: 2 En 1 Sh
🛌 🅿 (4) ⚡ 🗆 🐾 🖾 ♿

(2m) *Sea River Farmhouse*, Kilmeena, Westport, Co Mayo.
Farmhouse, 5 minutes from the sea in a quiet country setting
Grades: BF Approv
Tel: **098 26536** Mrs Cox.
D: £20.00 **S:** £20.00.
Open: June to Sep
Beds: 6F 1T 2D
Baths: 1 Ensuite 3 Private
🅿 (10) ⚡ 🗆 🖾

Newport   11

National Grid Ref: L9894

🍴 🍺 Black Oak, Anglers' Bar, Newport House, Walsh's, Kelly's Kitchen, Bridge Inn

(0.5m) *Anchor House*, The Quay, Newport, Westport, Co Mayo.
Modern home overlooking river on the Clew Bay. Private parking, nice garden.
Grades: BF Approv
Tel: **098 41178** (also fax no)
Mrs McGovern.
D: £18.00-£19.00 **S:** £20.00-£25.00.
Open: Mar to Oct
Beds: 2T 4D 1S
Baths: 5 En 2 Sh
🛌 🅿 🗆 🐾 🖾 ♨ 🎹 🗎 ♥

(0.25m 🚌) *De Bille House*, Main Street, Newport, Westport, Co Mayo.
Beautifully restored Georgian house with antique furnishings in Newport town.
Tel: **098 41145** Mrs Chambers.
Fax no: 098 41777
D: £20.00-£25.00 **S:** £25.00-£27.00.
Open: Jun to Oct
Beds: 5F
Baths: 4 En 1 Sh
🛌 🅿 (8) 🗆 ✕ ♨ 🖾 🎹 🗎 ♥

Lough Feeagh   12

National Grid Ref: L9701

(🔺 1m) *Traenlaur Lodge Youth Hostel*, Traenlaur Lodge, Lough Feeagh, Newport, County Mayo.
Tel: **098 41358**
Under 18: £5.51 **Adults:** £7.01
Self-catering facilities, Shop, Parking, Meals available groups only, by prior arrangement
The hostel, an old fishing lodge with its own harbour, overlooks Lough Feeagh from the crossroads of the Western Way and the Bangor Trail. Great walking, cycling, fishing and swimming.

Taking your dog?

Book *in advance*

ONLY with owners

who accept dogs (🐾)

Bangor Erris   13

National Grid Ref: F8523

(6m) *Hillcrest*, Main Street, Bangor Erris, Ballina, Co Mayo.
Fishing locally - Carrowmore Lake, Owenmore River. Carne golf club 13m, Ceade Fields 2m.
Tel: **097 83494**
Mrs Cosgrove.
D: £18.00-£19.00
S: £50.00.
Open: All Year
Beds: 2D 2T
Baths: 2 En 2 Sh
🛌 🅿 🗆 ✕ 🖾 🗎 ♥

Belmullet   14

National Grid Ref: F7032

🍴 🍺 Lavelle's

(15m 🚌) *Highdrift*, Ballina Road, Belmullet, Co Mayo.
Modern bungalow in quiet scenic surroundings overlooking Broadhaven Bay.
Tel: **097 81260** (also fax no)
Mrs Reilly.
D: £16.00-£17.00
S: £20.00-£22.00.
Open: Apr to Oct
Beds: 2F 2D 1T
Baths: 3 En 1 Sh
🛌 (3) 🅿 (6) 🗆 🐾 ✕ ♨ 🖾 🎹 🗎 ♥

Killala   15

National Grid Ref: G2030

🍴 🍺 Golden Acres, The Anchor

(1m) *Avondale House*, Pier Road, Killala, Ballina, Co Mayo.
Grades: BF 3 Diamond, AA 3 Diamond
Tel: **096 32229** Ms Bilbow.
D: £16.50-£18.00 **S:** £18.00-£21.50.
Open: All Year (not Xmas/New Year)
Beds: 1F 2D 1T
Baths: 2 En 2 Sh
🛌 🅿 (2) ⚡ 🗆 🐾 ✕ 🖾 🗎
Beautiful dormer bungalow, newly refurbished, overlooking Killala Bay, landscaped garden for visitors. Barbecue can be used to cook your catch after fishing. Recommended as one of top ten favourite B&Bs in the 'Best Bed & Breakfast Guide to Ireland'.

(1m 🚌) *Garden Hill Farmhouse*, Killala, Ballina, Co Mayo.
Family farmhouse in quiet surroundings near river, lakes, seaside and fishing.
Tel: **096 32331** (also fax no)
Mr Munnelly.
D: £17.50-£18.00
S: £20.00-£21.00.
Open: Jun to Sep
Beds: 4F 2D 2T
Baths: 4 En
🛌 🅿 (10) ♨ 🖾 🎹 🗎 ♥

Ballina 16

National Grid Ref: G2418

¶ Riverboat Inn, Murphy's, Old Bond Store,
Brogan's, Tullio's, Broken Jug, Jordan's

(▲2m) *Kilcommon Lodge Hostel,*
Pulathomas, Ballina, County
Mayo.
Tel: **097 84621 Adults:** £6.00
Evening meal

(▲0.5m) *Salmon Weir Hostel,*
Barrett Street, Ballina, County
Mayo.
Tel: **096 71903 Adults:** £7.50
Evening meal available, Facilities
for disabled people

(0.5m 🚍) *Hogans American*
House, Station Road, Ballina,
Co Mayo.
Beautifully restored town centre
hotel, private garden, 2 mins bus/
rail stations.
Grades: BF 2 Star
Tel: **096 21350** Mr Hogan.
Fax no: 096 71882
D: £20.00-£30.00 **S:** £25.00-£40.00.
Open: All Year (not Xmas/New
Year)
Beds: 4D 8T 4S
Baths: 16 En
🛏 (10) 🅿 (6) 🖵 📯 ✕ 🌲 🛏 Ⅴ 🛆 ∻

(1m) *Moy Call, Creggs Road,*
Ballina, Co Mayo.
A warm welcome awaits you at
Moy Call, overlooking the River
Moy.
Grades: BF Approv
Tel: **096 22440** Mrs O'Toole.
D: £18.00-£20.00 **S:** £24.00-£26.00.
Open: May to Oct
Beds: 3F 1D
Baths: 3 En 1 Pr
🛏 🅿 (5) ✑ 🖵 ✕ 🌲 🛏 Ⅴ 🛆 ∻

(1m) *Ashley House, Ardoughan,*
Ballina, Co Mayo.
Highly recommended: peaceful
country surroundings, landscaped
gardens, 1km Ballina Town.
Tel: **096 22799 / 088 2141889**
Mrs Murray.
D: £17.00-£19.00 **S:** £23.50-£25.00.
Open: All Year
Beds: 1F 2D 1T
Baths: 4 En
🛏 🅿 (6) 🖵 🌲 🛏 Ⅴ

All rates are subject
to alteration at the
owners' discretion.

Planning a longer
stay? Always ask for
any special rates.

(2m) *Belvedere House, Foxford*
Road, Ballina, Co Mayo.
Georgian style home, 10 mins
walking distance to town, bus,
train. Cable TV
Grades: BF Approv
Tel: **096 22004** Mrs Reilly.
D: £18.00 **S:** £21.00.
Open: All Year (not Xmas)
Beds: 2F 3D 2T 1S
Baths: 4 Ensuite 1 Shared
🅿 ✑ 🖵 📯 🌲 🛏 Ⅴ 🛆 ∻

(1m 🚍) *Errigal, Killala Road,*
Ballina, Co Mayo.
Modern bungalow. walking
distance from town. 30km from
the famous Ceide Fields
Tel: **096 22563** Mrs Treacy.
Fax no: 096 70968
D: £17.50 **S:** £20.00.
Open: Apr to Oct
Beds: 2F 1T
Baths: 3 Ensuite 1 Private
🛏 🅿 (4) 🖵 📯 🌲 🛏 ♿ Ⅴ 🛆

Running for 82 miles south of Dublin, along the eastern side of the Wicklow Mountain range, the Wicklow Way was the first path in Ireland to be way-marked. This, and being so near to the city means that it is a well-known and popular path - you will find many more walkers on the first part of this route than any other on the island. It takes literally twenty minutes to walk out of the suburbs and up into the hills, with great views of Dublin and the Bay. Up in the mountains, you feel miles from anywhere, in a deserted and dramatic landscape. The heather, the forests, the lakes, the 'switchback' ascents and descents, and the bleak summits all around make for some of the best walking to be had in Ireland. The Great Sugar Loaf, Djouce, Lugnaquillia and Tonelagee are some of the famous peaks that you pass by. If you intend to walk here in winter or in bad weather, come well prepared. You must be proficient with map and compass, for this is no place to be lost in.

Guides: *The Way-marked Trails of Ireland* by Michael Fewer (ISBN 0-7171-2386-3), published by Gill & Macmillan, and available from all good bookshops or direct from the publishers (Goldenbridge Ind Est, Inchicore, Dublin 8, 01 4531005), £9.99 (+ £2.50 p&p)

The Complete Wicklow Way, by the late founder of the path, J.B. Malone (ISBN 0 862781582), published by the O'Brien Press, and available from all good map shops or direct from the publishers' offices (20 Victoria Road, Dublin 6, 01 4923333), £5.99 (+£1.50 p&p)

Maps: *Ordnance Survey of Ireland* 1:50000 Discovery Series: 50, 56, 62

Sandyford   1
National Grid Ref: O1826

(1m) *Hillcrest House, Hillcrest Road, Sandyford, Dublin 18.*
Modern detached house, Dublin foothills. 20 minutes city centre. Close to Leopardstown Racecourse
Tel: **01 2954400** (also fax no)
Mrs Anderson.
D: £20.00 **S:** £25.00.
Open: All Year (not Xmas)
Beds: 2F 2D 2T
Baths: 4 Ensuite 1 Private 1 Shared
⛺ 🅿 (6) ⊟ ⯑ ✕ 🔥 🎖 ⅢⅢ Ⅵ 🎒 ∥

(1m 🚗) *Pinehill, Sandyford, Dublin 18.*
Quaint cottage-style residence with all modern conveniences
Grades: BF Approv
Tel: **01 2952061** Mrs Martini.
D: £22.50 **S:** £25.00.
Open: All Year (not Xmas)
Beds: 1F 2T 1S
Baths: 3 Ensuite 1 Private
⛺ (3) 🅿 ⊟ 🔥 ⅢⅢ Ⅾ Ⅵ 🎒 ∥

Planning a longer stay? Always ask for any special rates.

D = Price range per person sharing in a double room

Stepaside   2
National Grid Ref: O1923

🍽 🍺 Step Inn, La Casa, Moutan View, Johnnie Fox's

(0.5m) *Three Rock View, 8 Kilgobbin Road, Stepaside, Dublin 18.*
Tel: **01 2956780** (also fax no)
Mrs Naismith.
D: £25.00-£30.00 **S:** £30.00-£35.00.
Open: All Year (not Xmas)
Beds: 1D 2T 1S
Baths: 2 En 2 Sh
🅿 (8) ⊟ ✕ 🔥 ⅢⅢ Ⅵ
Welcome to the quiet foothills of the Dublin mountains, where we have all the amenities and comforts to make your visit a pleasant experience. A homely sitting where guests are greeted as friends.

(0.5m 🚗) *Lisin, Ballyedmonduff, Stepaside, Glencullen, Dublin 18.*
Modern country home with panoramic views over Dublin Bay
Tel: **01 2952974** Ms Flanagan.
D: £18.50 .
Open: May to Oct
Beds: 3T **Baths:** 2 En 1 Sh
🅿 (6) ⊟ 🔥 ⅢⅢ Ⅵ 🎒 ∥

Please don't camp on *anyone's* land without first obtaining their permission.

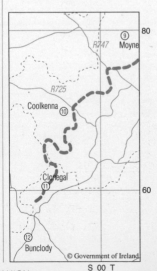

© Government of Ireland

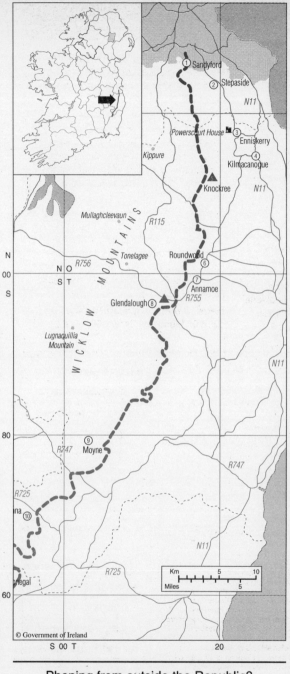

© Government of Ireland

S 00 T   20

Phoning from outside the Republic?
Dial 00353 and omit the initial '0'
of the area code.

All details shown
are as supplied
by B&B owners in
Autumn 2001.

Enniskerry 3

National Grid Ref: O2217

🍴 🍺 Palmer's, Powerscourt Arms, Johnny Fox's, Enniscree Lodge, Stepping Stones, Poppies

(▲ 2m) *Glencree Youth Hostel,*
Stone House, Glencree, Enniskerry,
County Wicklow.
Tel: **01 2864037**
Under 18: £5.01 **Adults:** £6.51
Self-catering facilities, Shop near-by, limited
Charming old stone house, next to a stream. The area is well-known for its excellent hillwalking. Visit the German War Cemetery in the village.

(3m) *Summerhill House Hotel,*
Enniskerry, Bray, Co Wicklow.
Period country house situated at the foot of the Sugar Loaf Mountain.
Grades: BF 3 Star
Tel: **01 2867928** Mrs Sweeney.
D: £40.00-£55.00 **S:** £40.00-£55.00.
Open: All Year
Beds: 3F 20D 29T 5S
🛏 🅿 🖵 🗙 🍴 🔥 🛁 ⚘ 🔌 Ⅴ ⓘ

(4m 🚗) *Corner House,*
Enniskerry, Bray, Co Wicklow.
Grades: BF Approv
Tel: **01 2860149**
Mrs Cummins.
D: £18.00-£20.00.
S: £27.00-£30.00.
Open: All Year (not Xmas/New Year)
Beds: 1D 2T
Baths: 1Private 1 Sh
🅿 🍴 🖵 🔥 🛁 ⚘ Ⅴ 🍽
Old world style house. furnished with period furniture. Large bedrooms situated in prettiest village in Ireland. Close to Powerscourt Famous Gardens, Close to Wicklow Way, on bus route to Dublin 20 km, close to ferries. a big welcome awaits you from 'Benson' springer spaniel.

(3m) *Powerscourt Arms,*
Enniskerry, Bray, Co Wicklow.
Snuggling in the foothills of Wicklow Mountains - ideal base for touring expeditions.
Tel: **01 2828903**
Fax no: 01 2864909
D: £32.00-£35.00.
S: £35.00-£38.00.
Open: All Year (not Xmas)
Beds: 2F 4T 8D 1S
Baths: 5 En 2 Sh

(2m 🚌) *Cherbury, Monastery,
Enniskerry, Bray, Co Wicklow.*
Large bungalow. Ideal base for
touring Wicklow. Beside
Powerscourt Gardens.
Tel: **01 2828679** Mrs Lynch.
D: £20.00-£20.00 **S:** £25.00.
Open: All Year
Beds: 1D 2T
Baths: 3 En
🅿 (6) ⅍🖵 🏄 🎍 🖾 🖾

Kilmacanogue 4

National Grid Ref: O2614

🍴 🍺 Wicklow Arms

(3m) *Valleyview, Killough,
Kilmacanogue, Bray, Co Wicklow.*
Scenic area, convenient to
mountains, gardens, sea and Dublin
welcome assured.
Tel: **01 2829565** Mrs Rowan.
D: £18.00-£18.00 **S:** £20.00-£20.00.
Open: Easter to Oct
Beds: 2F 2D
Baths: 3 En
🐾 🅿 (10) ⅍🖵 🖾 🖾 🛈

Knockree 5

National Grid Ref: O1915

(🔺 On path) *Knockree Youth
Hostel, Lacken House, Knockree,
Enniskerry, County Wicklow.*
Actual grid ref: O192151
Tel: **01 2864036**
Under 18: £5.00 **Adults:** £6.50
Self-catering facilities, Shop 7 km
away, Parking
*Converted farmhouse, set at the
bottom of Knockree, overlooking
Glencree Mountains. The Wicklow
Way passes through the hostel
grounds. Call head office for reser-
vations: 01 830 4555*

Roundwood 6

National Grid Ref: O1802

🍴 🍺 Coach House, Roundwood Inn

(1m 🚌) *Tochar House, Bar &
Lounge, Roundwood, Bray, Co
Wicklow.*
A traditional family-run village
pub, TV & tea coffee in bedrooms,
highest village in Ireland.
Tel: **01 2818247**
Mr & Mrs Fanning.
D: £20.00-£20.00 **S:** £20.00.
Open: All Year
Beds: 1F 1D 1T 2S
Baths: 5 En
🅿🖵 🎍 🖾 🖾 🛈 ⅍

All paths are popular:

you are well-advised to

book ahead

Please take muddy

boots **off** before

entering premises

(1m) *Ash Lawn, Mulliwaveigue,
Roundwood, Bray, Co Wicklow.*
Near Wicklow Way, Glendalough,
Powerscourt Gardens. 1 hour
Dublin airport & ferry.
Tel: **01 2818356** Mrs Jewnkinson.
D: £16.00-£17.00 **S:** £23.00-£22.00.
Open: May to Oct
Beds: 1F 2D
Baths: 1 En 1 Sh
🅿 (4) 🖵 🖾

(1m 🚌) *'River Bank', Roundwood,
Bray, Co Wicklow.*
Actual grid ref: O191033
En route to Glendalough.
Convenient to Wicklow Way and
restaurants.
Tel: **01 2818117** Mrs McCabe.
D: £15.00-£17.00 **S:** £18.00-£25.00.
Open: All Year (not Xmas)
Beds: 3F 2D 1T
Baths: 2 En 1 Sh
🐾 (5) 🅿 (1) ⅍🖵 🎍 🖾 🖾 🖾 ⅍

Annamoe 7

National Grid Ref: T1799

🍴 🍺 Laragh Inn

(1m) *Carmels, Annamoe,
Glendalough, Co Wicklow.*
Well established home in the heart
of the Wicklow mountains.
Grades: BF Approv
Tel: **0404 45297** (also fax no)
Mrs Hawkins.
D: £19.00-£20.00 **S:** £30.00.
Open: Mar to Nov
Beds: 2F 1D 1T
Baths: 4 En
🐾 🅿 (5) ⅍✕ 🖾 ⅍

Glendalough 8

National Grid Ref: T1296

🍴 🍺 Coach House, Mitchell's, Wicklow Heather,
Lyham's, Laragh Inn

(🔺 0.5m) *Glendalough Youth
Hostel, The Lodge, Glendalough,
Bray, County Wicklow.*
Actual grid ref: T122968
Tel: **0404 45342**
Under 18: £8.50 **Adults:** £10.50
Self-catering facilities, Shop 2 km
or limited supplies at hostel,
Laundry facilities, Parking,
Facilities for disabled people,
Meals available
*Situated in a wooded glacial valley
in a National Park area. Ideal for
historians, geographers and natu-
ralists; great for fishing, cycling
and walking the Wicklow Way.*

(0.5m) *Pinewood Lodge,
Glendalough, Co Wicklow.*
Actual grid ref: T140972
Grades: BF Approv,
AA 4 Diamond
Tel: **0404 45437** (also fax no)
Mr & Mrs Cullen.
D: £17.00-£20.00
S: £25.00-£30.00.
Open: All Year
Beds: 2F 2D 2T
Baths: 6 En
🐾 🅿 (6) ⅍🖵 🏄 🎍 🖾 🖾 🛈 ⅍
Situated in tranquil forest setting
on Wicklow Way in Ireland's
garden county. Convenient to
ferries and airport, only 5 mins'
walk to pub and restaurants, lovely
ensuite accommodation, breakfast
menu, guest TV lounge, off-road
parking, friendly family
atmosphere, warm welcome.

(On path 🚌) *Doire Coille House,
Glendalough, Cullentragh,
Rathdrum, Co Wicklow.*
Lovely farmhouse in one acre of
gardens on working dairy and
sheep farm.
Grades: BF Approv
Tel: **0404 45131** (also fax no)
Mrs Byrne.
D: £17.00-£18.00
S: £25.00-£27.00.
Open: All Year (not Xmas)
Beds: 3D 1T
Baths: 4 En
🐾 🅿 (10) ⅍ 🖾 🛈 ⅍

(0.5m) *Derrybawn House,
Glendalough, Bray, Co Wicklow.*
Charming 200-year-old house,
magnificent parkland setting,
excellent walking, close
Glendalough.
Tel: **0404 45134**
Mr & Mrs Vambeck.
Fax no: 0404 54109
D: £27.50-£35.00
S: £40.00-£45.00.
Open: All Year (not Xmas)
Beds: 4D 2T
Baths: 6 En
🐾 (12) 🅿 (10) ⅍🖵 🏄 ✕ 🎍 🖾 🖾 🛈 ⅍

The Grid Reference

beneath the location

heading is for the

village or town - *not*

for individual houses,

which are shown

(where supplied) in

each entry itself.

Moyne 9
National Grid Ref: T0279

(1m) *Jigsaw Cottage, Moyne,*
Tinahely, Arklow, Co Wicklow.
Actual grid ref: T029802
Grades: BF Approv
Tel: **0508 71071** (also fax no)
Mr More-O'Ferrall.
D: £20.00-£22.00 **S:** £26.50.
Open: Mar to Oct
Beds: 2D 2T **Baths:** 1 En 1 Sh
🅿 (8) ⌂ ✕ 🕯 🛏 Ⅴ 🛆 ⋟
Cosy stone and timber farmstead in
gently rolling countryside, spectacular mountain backdrop. Hill
walking, golf, horse-riding,
Glendalough monastic site,
beautiful gardens, historic houses,
pubs from the past, beaches all
easily reached. Quality home-
cooking, transport arranged,
mountain navigation courses
conducted.

D = Price range per person
sharing in a double room

Always telephone
to get directions to
the B&B - you will
save time!

Coolkenna 10
National Grid Ref: S9470

🍴 🍸 Taylor's

(1m) *Aspen Lodge, Killabeg,*
Coolkenna, Shillelagh, Arklow,
Co Wicklow.
Friendly farm family home, quiet
green countryside beside Wicklow
Way
Tel: **0503 56120**
Mrs Hill.
D: £16.00-£16.00
S: £16.00-£16.00.
Open: May to Nov
Beds: 1F 1T
⟫ 🅿 (10) ⌂ 🛏 ✕ 🛏 🛆 ⋟

Clonegal 11
National Grid Ref: S9161

🍴 🍸 Park Lodge

(1m) 🚗 *Park Lodge Farmhouse,*
Clonegal, Shillelagh, Arklow,
Co Wicklow.
Actual grid ref: S9565
A warm Irish welcome to a family
farmhouse
Tel: **055 29140**
Mrs Osbourne.
D: £20.00-£22.00
S: £25.00-£27.00.
Open: Easter to Oct
Beds: 4F 1D 3T
Baths: 3 Ensuite 1 Shared
⟫ 🅿 ✂ ⌂ ✕ 🛏 🛆 ⋟

Bunclody 12
National Grid Ref: S9155

(▲ 2m) *Bunclody Holiday Hostel,*
Old Schoolhouse, Ryland Road,
Bunclody, Enniscorthy, County
Wexford.
Tel: **054 76076**
Adults: £6.00

Fife Coastal Walk

The **Fife Coastal Walk** is a little-known long distance footpath that deserves greater recognition and wider coverage. It follows a beautiful 94-mile stretch of the East Scottish coastline, famous for its fishing villages, golf links and silvery estuaries. It is pretty much easy going and makes for a decent week's walking. From Tentsmuir Point inland to Newburgh it's very quiet indeed. The pioneers among you will appreciate that the path is only partly way-marked and may therefore be keen to blaze the trail (not literally), perhaps even

to write the first all-in-one guidebook. Hence its inclusion here. Be careful round Fife Ness - the cliffs can be dangerous, especially where the path is unfenced.

Guide: A series of booklets with hand-drawn maps of the Fife Coastal Walk is available from the Wemyss Environmental Education Centre, East Wemyss Primary School, School Wynd, East Wemyss, Kirkcaldy, Fife, KY1 4RN.

Maps: 1:50000 Ordnance Survey Landranger Series: 58, 59, 65 and 66

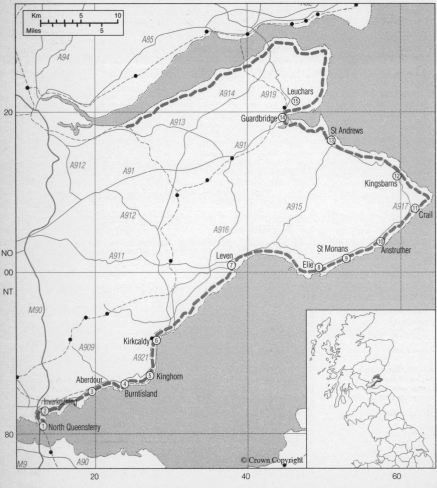

© Crown Copyright

North Queensferry 1

National Grid Ref: NT1380

᛭◗ ◫ Ferry Bridge Hotel, Albert Hotel

(0.25m 🚍) *Fourteen Falls, Chapel Place, North Queensferry, Inverkeithing, Fife, KY11 1JT.*
Actual grid ref: NT131804
C18th cottage under Forth Bridge, enclosed garden, emphasis on hospitality.
Tel: **01383 412749** (also fax no)
Mrs Evans.
D: £22.00-£22.00 **S:** £22.00-£22.00.
Open: All Year
Beds: 1T **Baths:** 1 Sh
🅿 (3) ⏻⊁◻🛏✕♨🛏⮰🅅🛆⊬

Inverkeithing 2

National Grid Ref: NT1382

(0.25m 🚍) *The Roods, 16 Bannerman Avenue, Inverkeithing, Fife, KY11 1NG.*
Actual grid ref: NT130822
Award winning B&B set in quiet gardens close to costal path
Grades: STB 3 Star,
AA 4 Diamond
Tel: **01383 415049** (also fax no)
Mrs Marley.
D: £20.00-£25.00 **S:** £20.00-£25.00.
Open: All Year
Beds: 1D 1T 1F **Baths:** 3 En
🗠🅿⊬◻✕♨🛏🅅🛆⊬

Aberdour 3

National Grid Ref: NT1985

᛭◗ ◫ Aberdour Hotel

(0.25m) *Aberdour Hotel, 38 High Street, Aberdour, Burntisland, Fife, KY3 0SW.*
Friendly village inn, traditional cooking, real ales, Edinburgh half hour car/rail.
Grades: STB 3 Star, AA 2 Star
Tel: **01383 860325** Mr Thomson.
Fax no: 01383 860808
D: £25.00-£30.00 **S:** £35.00-£45.00.
Open: All Year
Beds: 4F 7D 5T
Baths: 16 En
🗠🅿 (8) ◻🛏✕♨🛏🛆🅅🛆⊬

Burntisland 4

National Grid Ref: NT2386

᛭◗ ◫ Kingswood Hotel, Inchview Hotel

(0.5m) *148a Kinghorn Road, Burntisland, Fife, KY3 9JU.*
Panoramic views over River Forth, golf courses and water sports nearby.
Tel: **01592 872266** (also fax no)
Mrs Redford.
D: £20.00-£25.00 **S:** £25.00-£30.00.
Open: All Year
Beds: 1F 1D
Baths: 2 En
🗠🅿 (2) ◻🛏♨🛏🅅

Kinghorn 5

National Grid Ref: NT2687

᛭◗ ◫ The Bay

(On path 🚍) *Craigo-Er, 45 Pettycur Road, Kinghorn, Fife, KY3 9RN.*
Actual grid ref: NT269865
Victorian house, panoramic sea views, direct regular Edinburgh rail links.
Tel: **01592 890527** Mrs Thomson.
D: £19.00-£19.00 **S:** £19.00-£19.00.
Open: All Year
Beds: 1D 2T **Baths:** 2 Sh
🗠🅿 (1) ◻🛏♨🛏🅅🛆⊬

Kirkcaldy 6

National Grid Ref: NT2791

᛭◗ ◫ Kingswood, Victoria, Wheatsheaf, Mullins

(0.25m) *Crawford Hall, 2 Kinghorn Road, Kirkcaldy, Fife, KY1 1SU.*
Tel: **01592 262658** Mrs Crawford.
D: £17.00-£19.00 **S:** £17.00-£19.00.
Open: All Year (not Xmas)
Beds: 1F 1T **Baths:** 1 Sh
🗠🅿 (4) ◻🛏✕♨🛏🛆🅅⊬
Large, rambling old C19th house, once local manse, set in lovely gardens. 2 minutes from beach, 10 minute walk to town centre, bus/railway stations. Comfortable rooms, hearty breakfast, handy for golfers, near St Andrews.

(0.25m) *Cameron House, 44 Glebe Park, Kirkcaldy, Fife, KY1 1BL.*
Quiet, friendly, good food central for Edinburgh, Perth, St Andrews.
Grades: STB 2 Star B&B
Tel: **01592 264531** Mrs Nicol.
D: £15.00-£15.00 **S:** £15.00-£17.00.
Open: All Year (not Xmas)
Beds: 1F 1D
Baths: 1 Sh
🗠 (1) ⊬◻🛏✕♨🛏🅅⊬

(On path) *Castleview, 17 Dysart Road, Kirkcaldy, Fife, KY1 2AY.*
Situated on Fife coast near M90, within reach Edinburgh, Perth, Dundee.
Grades: STB 1 Star B&B
Tel: **01592 269275** Mrs Dick.
D: £16.00-£17.00 **S:** £16.00-£17.00.
Open: All Year (not Xmas)
Beds: 1F 2T
Baths: 1 Sh
🗠🅿◻🛏✕♨🛏🅅🛆⊬

(0.25m) *Invertiel Guest House, 21 Pratt Street, Kirkcaldy, Fife, KY1 1RZ.*
Quality accommodation where you can come & go as you please.
Tel: **01592 264849** Mrs Duffy.
Fax no: 01592 592440
D: £20.00-£25.00 **S:** £25.00-£50.00.
Open: All Year
Beds: 2F 1D 1T 1S
Baths: 1 En 1 Sh
🗠🅿 (7) ◻✕♨🛏🅅🛆⊬

(0.25m) *Cherrydene, 44 Bennochy Road, Kirkcaldy, Fife, KY2 5RB.*
Victorian house retaining many original features. Situated 5 minutes from bus and rail stations.
Tel: **01592 202147** Mrs Nicol.
Fax no: 01592 644618
D: £16.00-£25.00 **S:** £22.00-£35.00.
Open: All Year
Beds: 1F 1D 1S
Baths: 2 En 1 Sh
🗠🅿 (3) ◻🛏✕♨🛏🅅🛆⊬

(0.25m) *Arboretum, 20 Southeron Road, Kirkcaldy, Fife, KY2 5NB.*
Extended bungalow - quiet area courtyard for private parking, overlooking park.
Tel: **01592 643673** Mrs Duncan.
D: £17.00-£20.00 **S:** £18.00-£22.00.
Open: All Year
Beds: 2D 1T
Baths: 2 En 1 Pr
🗠 (8) 🅿 (6) ◻🛏♨🛏🅅⊬

(0.25m) *Dunedin House, 25 Townsend Place, Kirkcaldy, Fife, KY1 1HB.*
Excellent accommodation, central location. Superb breakfast, private parking, 35 mins Edinburgh & St Andrews.
Tel: **01592 203874**
Mr & Mrs Duffy.
Fax no: 01592 265274
D: £20.00-£22.00 **S:** £25.00-£28.00.
Open: All Year
Beds: 1F 1D 1S
Baths:
🗠🅿 (5) ⊬◻✕♨🛏🅅

Leven 7

National Grid Ref: NO3800

᛭◗ ◫ Burns Tavern, Fettykil Fox

(1.5m) *Duniface Farm, Windygates, Leven, Fife, KY8 5RH.*
Actual grid ref: NO353010
Charming C19th farmhouse - comfortable & welcoming, hearty breakfasts, ideal touring base.
Tel: **01333 350272** (also fax no)
Mrs Hamilton.
D: £15.00-£17.00 **S:** £15.00-£20.00.
Open: All Year
Beds: 1D 1F
Baths: 1 Sh
🗠🅿⊬◻🛏♨🛏🅅⊬

Elie 8

National Grid Ref: NO4900

᛭◗ ◫ Ship Inn, The Toft

(0.5m) *Millford House, 19 High Street, Elie, Leven, Fife, KY9 1BY.*
Large Georgian house in peaceful seaside village. Golf, tennis, sailing.
Grades: STB 2 Star
Tel: **01333 330567** Mr Cowan.
D: £17.50-£20.00 **S:** £20.00-£25.00.
Open: All Year
Beds: 2D 1T
🗠◻♨🛏🛆🅅🛆⊬

St Monans 9

National Grid Ref: NO5201

⊙ ⊲ Mayview Hotel, Cabin Bar

(0.5m) *Inverforth, 20 Braehead, St Monans, Fife, KY10 2AN.*
Comfortable homely accommodation, home baking. Seaview, near St Andrews golf.
Grades: STB 2 Star B&B
Tel: 01333 730205 Miss Aitken.
D: £17.50-£18.00 **S:** £17.50-£18.00.
Open: Jun to Oct
Beds: 1D 2T **Baths:** 1 Sh
⊁ (8) ⊬ ⊡ ⊞,

Anstruther 10

National Grid Ref: NO5603

⊙ ⊲ Crow's Nest, Salutation, Haven Restaurant, Dreel Tavern, Cellar

(0.25m) *Harefield Cottage, Carvenom, Anstruther, Fife, KY10 3JU*
Grades: STB 3 Star
Tel: **01333 310346** Mrs Robinson.
D: £20.00-£21.50 **S:** £24.00-£24.00.
Open: Easter to Oct
Beds: 1T 1D **Baths:** 1 Pr 1 Sh
⊡ (4) ⊡ ⊼ ⊞, ⊬
Large, stone built, single storey cottage, large garden. All rooms have extensive view over fields and woods to firth of forth with May Island and Bass Rock. Private parking. Very Peaceful. Quiet location, one and half miles from town centre.

(0.25m) *Royal Hotel, 20 Rodger Street, Anstruther, Fife, KY10 3HU.*
Family-run hotel, 100 yards seashore. Small harbour, sea trips to May Island Bird Sanctuary.
Tel: **01333 310581** Mr Cook.
D: £18.00-£22.00 **S:** £18.00-£18.00.
Open: All Year
Beds: 1F 4T 4D 2S
Baths: 1 En
⊁ ⊡ ⊬ ⊼ ⊠ ⊞, ⊡ ◈

(On path ⊕) *The Sheiling, 32 Glenogil Gardens, Anstruther, Fife, KY10 3ET.*
Pretty white bungalow, ground floor bedrooms overlook garden. Harbour 200m.
Grades: STB 3 Star
Tel: **01333 310697** Mrs Ritchie.
D: £16.00-£22.00 **S:** £22.00-£22.00.
Open: Easter to Sept
Beds: 2D **Baths:** 1 Sh 1 Pr
⊡ (2) ⊬ ⊡ ⊠ ⊞, ⊡ ◈

(0.25m) *The Hermitage, Ladywalk, Anstruther, Fife, KY10 3EX.*
Actual grid ref: NO568036
Home from home, quiet situation near harbour, superb walled garden.
Grades: STB 4 Star, AA 4 Diamond
Tel: **01333 310909** Mrs McDonald.
Fax no: 01333 311505
D: £20.00-£30.00 **S:** £25.00-£30.00.
Open: All Year
Beds: 3D 1T **Baths:** 2 Sh
⊁ ⊡ (4) ⊬ ⊡ ⊠ ⊞, ⊡ ◈

Crail 11

National Grid Ref: NO6107

⊙ ⊲ Marine Hotel, East Neuk Hotel, Balcomie Hotel

(On path ⊕) *Woodlands Guest House, Balcomie Road, Crail, Anstruther, Fife, KY10 3TN.*
Actual grid ref: N5603
Detached villa, superb views, beach half a minute, St Andrews 10 mins, golf courses.
Tel: **01333 450147** Mrs Wood.
D: £18.00-£19.00 **S:** £20.00-£21.00.
Open: Feb to Dec
Beds: 1F 2D **Baths:** 2 Sh
⊁ (2) ⊡ (10) ⊬ ⊡ ⊼ ⊠ ⊞, ⊅ ⊡ ◈ ◈

(0.25m ⊕) *Caiplie House, 53 High Street, Crail, Anstruther, Fife, KY10 3RA.*
Actual grid ref: NO615075
Friendly, informal guest house. Taste of Scotland member.
Tel: **01333 450564** (also fax no) Mr & Mrs Strachan.
D: £17.00-£24.00 **S:** £18.00-£22.00.
Open: Feb to Nov
Beds: 1F 4D 1T 1S
Baths: 3 En 1 Pr 2 Sh
⊁ ⊡ (3) ⊡ ⊼ ⊠ ⊠ ⊞, ⊡ ◈ ◈

Kingsbarns 12

National Grid Ref: NO5912

⊙ ⊲ Cambo Arms Hotel

(0.5m) *Kingsbarns Bed & Breakfast, 3 Main St, Kingsbarns, St Andrews, Fife, KY16 8SL.*
Actual grid ref: NO592124
Warm, friendly, comfortable B&B in picturesque coastal village. Golf courses nearby.
Grades: STB 4 Star
Tel: **01334 880234** Mrs Hay.
D: £22.00-£25.00 **S:** £22.00-£22.00.
Open: Apr to Oct
Beds: 2D 1T **Baths:** 3 En
⊁ ⊡ (2) ⊡ ⊠ ⊞, ⊡ ◈ ◈

St Andrews 13

National Grid Ref: NO5116

⊙ ⊲ Tavern, Pitscottie Inn, Guardbridge Hotel, Dolls House, Strathkinness Tavern, Cambo, Playfairs, Russell Hotel

(▲ 0.25m) *St Andrews Tourist Hostel, Inchape House, St Marys Place, St Andrews, KY16 9QP.*
Tel: **01334 479911**
Under 18: £10.00 **Adults:** £10.00
Self-catering facilities, Television, Showers, Central heating, Laundry facilities, Lounge, Dining room, Cycle store, Parking
Located in heart of the historic old town, this newly opened hostel is 5 mins from bus station. Lively hostel with cosy atmosphere and friendly staff. Self catering kitchen, free tea/coffee, no curfew. 5 mins from pubs/clubs. Attractions - St Andrews cathedral, castle, St Rules Tower, Royal Golf Club, St Mary's House.

(0.25m ⊕) *The Paddock, Sunnyside, Strathkinness, St Andrews, KY16 9XP.*
Grades: STB 4 Star
Tel: **01334 850888**
Mrs Taylor.
Fax no: 01334 850870
D: £20.00-£26.00
S: £25.00-£40.00.
Open: All Year (not Xmas/ New Year)
Beds: 1T 2D
⊡ (8) ⊡ ⊠ ⊞, ⊡
Quality ensuite accommodation in a modern residence with outstanding country views. Positioned in a secluded spot. Ample private parking. Guests may use the conservatory overlooking the gardens. St Andrews 2 miles.

(On path) *Edenside House, Edenside, St Andrews, Fife, KY16 9SQ.*
Actual grid ref: NO462189
Pre 1775 farmhouse, 2.5 miles from St Andrews. Parking guaranteed.
Grades: STB 3 Star, AA 4 Diamond
Tel: **01334 838108**
Douglas & Yvonne Reid.
Fax no: 01334 838493
D: £20.00-£27.00
S: £32.00-£38.00.
Open: All Year (not Xmas)
Beds: 1F 2D 5T
Baths: 8 En
⊁ ⊡ (10) ⊬ ⊡ ⊼ ⊠ ⊞, ⊅ ⊡ ◈ ◈

(0.25m) *Cairnsden B&B, 2 King Street, St Andrews, Fife, KY16 8JQ.*
Comfortable family house, 7 mins town centre, early breakfasts for golfers.
Grades: STB 2 Star
Tel: **01334 476326** Mrs Allan.
Fax no: 01334 840355
D: £16.00-£20.00 **S:** £18.00-£22.00.
Open: All Year (not Xmas)
Beds: 1D 1T
Baths: 1 Sh
⊡ (1) ⊬ ⊡ ⊼ ⊠ ⊞, ⊡

(0.25m) *Coppercantie, 8 Lawhead Road West, St Andrews, Fife, KY16 9NE.*
A warm welcome awaits in the home of Scottish historian.
Grades: STB 4 Star
Tel: **01334 476544** Mrs Dobson.
Fax no: 01334 470322
D: £18.00-£24.00 **S:** £34.00-£40.00.
Open: All Year (not Xmas)
Beds: 1F 1D 1T
Baths: 1 En 2 Sh
⊁ (9) ⊬ ⊡ ⊠ ⊞, ⊡ ◈

(0.25m) *23 Kilrymont Road, St Andrews, Fife, KY16 8DE.*
Detached home, harbour area, East Sands, 10 mins famous golf course.
Tel: **01334 477946**
Mrs Kier.
D: £17.00-£19.00 **S:** £17.00-£20.00.
Open: April-Dec
Beds: 1D 1S
⊁ (7) ⊡ (1) ⊬ ⊡ ⊠ ⊞, ⊅ ⊡

(0.25m 🚐) *12 Newmill Gardens,*
St Andrews, Fife, KY16 8RY.
Actual grid ref: NO5016
Spacious, bright room. Tranquil
area. Conveniently situated.
Grades: STB 3 Star
Tel: **01334 474552** (also fax no)
Mrs Irvine.
D: £18.00-£20.00 **S:** £20.00-£22.00.
Open: All Year (not Xmas/New
Year)
Beds: 1D
Baths: 1 Pr
🅿 (1) ⅙ ☐ ♨ 🎽 🎟 🖤 🖊

(0.25m 🚐) *Amberside Guest*
House, 4 Murray Park,
St Andrews, Fife, KY16 9AW.
Amberside has become well known
for its wonderful breakfast and
lovely warm welcome.
Grades: STB 3 Star,
AA 3 Diamond
Tel: **01334 474644** (also fax no)
Mr Carney.
D: £18.00-£28.00 **S:** £35.00-£45.00.
Open: All Year
Beds: 1F 2D 2T 1S
Baths: 1 Pr
🎽 🅿 ☐ ♖ 🎽 🎟 🖤 🖊 🖊

(0.75m) *Spinkstown Farmhouse,*
St Andrews, Fife, KY16 8PN.
Two miles from St Andrews on
A917.
Tel: **01334 473475** (also fax no)
Mrs Duncan.
D: £20.00-£20.00 **S:** £25.00-£25.00.
Open: All Year (not Xmas)
Beds: 2D 1T
Baths: 3 Pr
🅿 (4) ⅙ ☐ ♨ 🎽 🎟 🖤 🖊

(0.25m 🚐) *Ardmore,*
1 Drumcarrow Road, St Andrews,
Fife, KY16 8SE.
Comfortable, non-smoking, family
bungalow in quiet residential area
opposite Botanical Gardens.
Tel: **01334 474574** Mrs Methven.
D: £16.00-£18.00 .
Open: Jan to Nov **Beds:** 2D
🅿 (2) ⅙ ☐ ♨ ⸳

(1m) *Whitecroft Guest Lodges,*
33 Strathkinness High Road,
St Andrews, Fife, KY16 9UA.
Whitecroft has modern ensuite
rooms with parking, private
entrances.
Tel: **01334 474448** (also fax no)
Mr & Mrs Horn.
D: £22.00-£27.00 **S:** £30.00-£35.00.
Open: All Year
Beds: 3F 2D 1T **Baths:** 5 En
🎽 🅿 (5) ⅙ ☐ ♖ 🎽 🎟 🖤 🖊

Guardbridge 14

National Grid Ref: NO4519

🍴 🍺 Guardbridge Hotel

(On path 🚐) *The Larches,* *7 River*
Terrace, Guardbridge, St Andrews,
Fife, KY16 0XA.
Actual grid ref: NO448197
Large, comfortable memorial hall.
Wonderful food. Fully ensuite/
private rooms.
Tel: **01334 838008** (also fax no)
Mrs Mayner.
D: £18.00-£28.00 **S:** £22.00-£32.00.
Open: All Year
Beds: 2D 1T **Baths:** 2 En 1 Pr
🎽 🅿 (4) ⅙ ☐ ♖ 🎟 🖤 🖊

Leuchars 15

National Grid Ref: NO4521

🍴 🍺 St Michaels Inn

(1m 🚐) *Pinewood Country House,*
Tayport Road, St Michaels,
Leuchars, St Andrews, Fife,
KY16 0DU.
A quiet wooded area setting ideal
for short breaks or golfing
holidays.
Grades: STB 3 Star
Tel: **01334 839860** Mr Bedwell.
Fax no: 01334 839868
D: £22.00-£25.00 **S:** £32.00-£44.00.
Open: All Year (not Xmas/
New Year)
Beds: 2T 3D
Baths: 4 En 1 Pr
☐ ♖ ✕ 🎽 🎟 🖤 🖊 🖊

(1m) *Pitlethie Farm,* *Leuchars,*
St Andrews, Fife, KY16 0DP.
Attractive comfortable farmhouse
set in open farmland.
Tel: **01334 838649** Mrs Black.
Fax no: 01334 839281
D: £25.00-£25.00 **S:** £26.50-£26.50.
Open: All Year (not Xmas)
Beds: 2T, 1S
🎽 ⅙

Pay B&Bs by cash or cheque and be prepared to pay up front.

Southern Upland Way

Of all the paths in this book, the **Southern Upland Way** is the most remote, rivalling the northernmost parts of the **Pennine Way**, the Fermanagh and Derry sections of the **Ulster Way** and the Rhinogs stretch of the **Cambrian Way**. The walking, especially in the western half of this coast-to-coast route, is certainly as tough - if not tougher - providing a challenge that brings its own particular rewards. The path runs for 202 miles through Scottish Border country, from the seaside village of Portpatrick, over the exposed moorland of the West, across the Nithsdale Valley and then past the smoother, more rounded hills and moors of the East, finishing on the cliffs at Cockburnspath in Berwickshire. There is now an alternative finish. You can leave St Boswells for England on the St Cuthbert's Way. It is a path for fit, experienced fell-walkers, fully equipped for rough weather, boggy conditions and mist. A quick glance at the

map here will show the paucity of accommodation along the route. Some judicious planning, however, renders the walk quite manageable without resorting to canvas or bothy, although neither should be ruled out in the event of an emergency.

Guides (available from all good bookshops):
The Southern Upland Way (maps & book set) by Roger Smith (ISBN 0 11495 17 05), published by Stationery Office Books, £17.50

St Cuthbert's Way by Roger Smith & Ren Shaw (ISBN O 11 495762 2), published by Stationery Office Books, £12.99

A Guide to the Southern Upland Way by David Williams (ISBN 0 094679 10 X), published by Constable & Co Ltd, £9.95

Maps: Ordnance Survey 1:50000 Landranger series: 67, 73, 76, 77, 78, 79 and 82

Portpatrick   1

National Grid Ref: NW9954

🍴 🍺 Campbells, Mount Stewart, Downshire, Crown

(On path 🚌) *Melvin Lodge Guest House,* South Crescent, Portpatrick, Stranraer, Wigtownshire, *DG9 8LE.*
Very comfortable, friendly house starting Southern Upland Way.
Grades: STB 2 Star GH
Tel: **01776 810238**
Mr & Mrs Pinder.
D: £20.00-£23.00 **S:** £20.00-£23.00.
Open: All Year
Beds: 4F 3D 1T 2S **Baths:** 5 En 1 Sh
🛳 🅿 (8) ⅍ ❏ 🍴 🛏 🕯 🎱 💷 Ⓥ ⅋ ✦

(0.25m) *Rickwood Private Hotel,* Portpatrick, Stranraer, Wigtownshire, *DG9 8TD.*
Large Victorian house in acre of garden south facing overlooking village and sea.
Tel: **01776 810270**
D: £21.50-£22.50 **S:** £21.50-£22.50.
Open: Mar to Oct
Beds: 1F 2D 2T **Baths:** 4 En 1 Pr
🅿 (5) ❏ 🍴 ✕ 🛏 🎱 💷 Ⓥ

D = Price range per person sharing in a double room

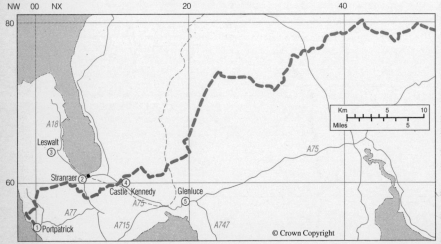

NW   00   NX   20   40

80

A18

Leswalt ③

A75

60

Stranraer ②

Castle Kennedy ④

Glenluce ⑤

A75

A77

A715

A747

① Portpatrick

Km   5   10
Miles   5

© Crown Copyright

(0.25m 🚐) *Mansewood, Dean Place, Portpatrick, Stranraer, Wigtownshire, DG9 8TX.*
Quiet central location. Lovely views over putting green towards harbour.
Tel: **01776 810256** Mrs Anderson.
D: £18.00-£20.00 **S:** £20.00-£20.00.
Open: All Year (not Xmas)
Beds: 1D 2T
Baths: 2 En 1 Sh
🛇 🅿 (5) 🖵 🖳 🎹 ⅙ Ⅴ ⌷ 🕯 ✦

Stranraer 2

National Grid Ref: NX0560

🅇 ◀ Crown Inn, Harbour House, Swan Inn, Marine House, L'Aperitif, Dunskey Golf Hotel

(1.5m) *Neptune's Rest, 25 Agnew Crescent, Stranraer, Wigtownshire, DG9 7JZ.*
Grades: STB 2 Star
Tel: **01776 704729** Mr McClymont.
D: £15.00-£20.00 **S:** £16.00-£22.00.
Open: All Year
Beds: 2F 2D 1T 1S
Baths: 3 En 2 Sh
🛇 🅿 🗙 🖳 Ⅴ ⌷
Neptune's Rest overlooks Agnew Park with its boating lake and miniature railway, situated on the shores of Loch Ryan with its busy ferry routes. All bedrooms are pleasantly decorated & co-ordinated. You are assured of a warm welcome in this family-run guest house.

(1m) *Windyridge Villa, 5 Royal Crescent, Stranraer, DG9 8HB.*
Overlooking Loch Ryan.
Convenient for ferry terminal and railway station.
Grades: STB 4 Star,
AA 4 Diamond
Tel: **01776 889900** (also fax no)
Mrs Kelly.
D: £20.00-£22.00 **S:** £25.00-£28.00.
Open: All Year (not Xmas/New Year)
Beds: 1T 1D
Baths: 2 En
🛇 🅿 (3) ⅙ 🖵 ⅞ 🖳 🎹 Ⅴ 🕯 ✦

(1.5m) *Ivy House, London Road, Stranraer, DG9 8ER.*
Lovely old town house, situated at the foot of Loch Ryan.
Grades: STB 2 Star
Tel: **01776 704176**
Mr & Mrs Mcmillan.
D: £16.00-£19.00 **S:** £18.00-£25.00.
Open: All Year
Beds: 1F 1D 1T
Baths: 2 En 1 Pr
🛇 🅿 (10) 🖵 ⅞ 🖳 🎹 Ⅴ 🕯 ✦

(1.5m 🚐) *Lorenza, 2 Birnam Place, Station Street, Stranraer, Wigtownshire, DG9 7HN.*
Terraced house, central located, close to ferries, trains & buses.
Tel: **01776 703935** Mrs Jameson.
D: £17.00-£17.00 **S:** £15.00-£15.00.
Open: Jan to Dec
Beds: 2D 1T **Baths:** 2 En 1 Sh
🅿 (4) 🖵 🖳 🎹 Ⅴ 🕯 ✦

(1m) *Fernlea Guest House, Lewis Street, Stranraer, Wigtownshire, DG9 7AQ.*
Friendly guest house, close to town centre and all ferries.
Tel: **01776 703037**
Mrs Drysdale.
D: £16.00-£20.00 **S:** £23.00-£28.00.
Open: All Year (not Xmas)
Beds: 2D 1T
Baths: 3 En
🛇 🅿 (5) ⅙ 🖵 ⅞ 🖳 🎹 Ⅴ 🕯 ✦

(1.5m 🚐) *Jan Da Mar, 1 Ivy Place, London Road, Stranraer, Wigtownshire, DG9 7AQ.*
Actual grid ref: NX065607
Updated Georgian town house with many original features.
Tel: **01776 706194**
Mrs Bewley.
D: £16.00-£20.00 **S:** £18.00-£18.00.
Open: All Year
Beds: 3F 3T 2S
Baths: 2 En 2 Sh
🛇 🅿 🖵 ⅞ 🖳 🎹 Ⅴ ⌷

(1.5m) *Abonny House, 10 Academy Street, Stranraer, Wigtownshire, DG9 7DR.*
Warm friendly welcome awaits you at this family run B&B, day or night.
Tel: **01776 706313** Mrs Harvey.
D: £22.00-£24.00 **S:** £18.00-£30.00.
Open: All Year (not Xmas)
Beds: 1F 1D 1T 1S
Baths: 2 En 1 Sh
🛇 ⅙ 🖵 ⅞ 🗙 🖳 🎹 Ⅴ ⌷

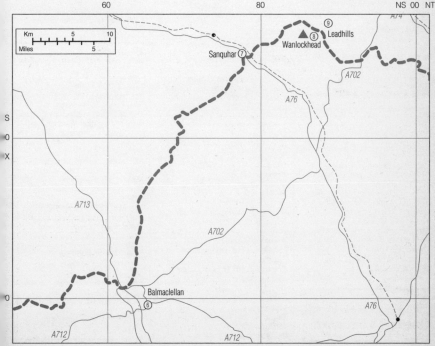

(0.5m 🚪) *Rawer Cottage, South Glenstockadale, Stranraer, DG9 8TS.* Former farm cottage, remote, peaceful yet only 10 mins from ferries to Northern Ireland.
Tel: **01776 810328** (also fax no)
Mrs Ross.
D: £15.00-£18.00 **S:** £15.00-£18.00.
Open: All Year
Beds: 1F 1D 1T **Baths:** 1 Sh
🛏 🅿 (4) 🗐 🛏 🗙 🖲 🎟 🛈 ⚡

Leswalt 3

National Grid Ref: NX0163

🍴 🍺 The Crown, Dunskey Golf Hotel

(0.75m 🚪) *Windyridge, Auchnotteroch, Leswalt, Stranraer, Wigtownshire, DG9 0XL.*
Actual grid ref: NW997607
Set in rolling countryside between Stranraer and Portpatrick 10 mins all ferries.
Grades: STB 1 Star
Tel: **01776 870280** (also fax no)
Mrs Rushworth.
D: £15.00-£15.00 **S:** £15.00-£15.00.
Open: All Year (not Xmas)
Beds: 1D 1T **Baths:** 1 Sh
🛏 🅿 (3) 🗐 🛏 🗙 🖲 🎟 🛈 ⚡

Castle Kennedy 4

National Grid Ref: NX1160

(On path 🚪) *Chlenry Farmhouse, Castle Kennedy, Stranraer, Wigtownshire, DG9 8SL.*
Actual grid ref: NX128610
Situated in a private glen in the heart of Galloway, comfortable old farmhouse.
Tel: **01776 705316**
Mrs Wolseley Brinton.
Fax no: 01776 889488
D: £26.00-£26.00 **S:** £30.00-£30.00.
Open: All Year (not Xmas)
Beds: 1D 1T
Baths: 1 Pr 1 Sh
🛏 🅿 (4) 🛩 🗐 🛏 🗙 🖲 🎟 🛈 ⚡

Glenluce 5

National Grid Ref: NX1957

🍴 🍺 Kelvin House, Crown Hotel, Inglenook Rest

(3m) *Bankfield Farm, Glenluce, Newton Stewart, Wigtownshire, DG8 0JF.*
Large spacious farmhouse on the outskirts of quiet country village.
Grades: STB 2 Star
Tel: **01581 300281** (also fax no)
Mrs Stewart.
D: £17.00-£17.00 **S:** £20.00-£20.00.
Open: All Year
Beds: 1F 1D 1T **Baths:** 2 En 1 Pr
🅿 🗐 🖲 🎟 🛈 ⚡

(3m 🚪) *Rowantree Guest House, 38 Main Street, Glenluce, Newton Stewart, Wigtownshire, DG8 0PS.*
Clean and tidy family run, central to all amenities.
Grades: STB 2 Star
Tel: **01581 300244**
Mr Thomas.
Fax no: 01581 300366
D: £15.50-£18.00
S: £17.00-£24.00.
Open: All Year
Beds: 2F 2D 1T
Baths: 2 En 1 Pr
🛏 🅿 (8) 🗐 🛏 🗙 🖲 🎟 🛈 ⚡

Balmaclellan 6

National Grid Ref: NX6579

🍴 🍺 Lochinvar Hotel

(2.5m) *High Park, Balmaclellan, Castle Douglas, Kirkcudbrightshire, DG7 3PT.*
Grades: STB 2 Star
Tel: **01644 420298** (also fax no)
Mrs Shaw.
D: £16.00-£17.00
S: £16.00-£17.00.
Open: Easter to Oct
Beds: 2D 1T
Baths: 1 Sh
🛏 🅿 (4) 🛩 🗐 🛏 🗙 🖲 🎟 🛈 ⚡
A warm welcome awaits you at our comfortable farmhouse by Loch Ken. Double bedroom and bathroom on ground floor, double and twin bedrooms and toilet upstairs. All have tea/coffee facilities, wash basins and TV. Comfortable lounge. Brochure available.

Sanquhar 7

National Grid Ref: NS7809

🍴 🍺 Blackaddie Hotel

(0.25m 🚪) *4 Barons Court, Sanquhar, Dumfriesshire, DG4 6EB.*
Comfortable self-contained flat. Ideal fishing, walking, golf and touring.
Tel: **01659 50361**
Mrs Clark.
D: £17.00-£17.00
S: £17.00-£17.00.
Open: All Year (not Xmas)
Beds: 1F 1D
Baths: 2 En
🛏 🗙 🖲 🛈 ⚡

(0.25m) *Penhurst, Townhead Street, Sanquhar, Dumfriesshire, DG4 6DA.*
Actual grid ref: NS781091
Family run bed and breakfast. Excellent home cooking.
Tel: **01659 50751** (also fax no)
Mrs McDowall.
D: £15.00-£15.00
S: £15.00-£15.00.
Open: All Year
Beds: 1F 1D 1T
Baths: 1 Sh
🛏 🗐 🛏 🗙 🖲 🎟 🛈 ⚡

Wanlockhead 8

National Grid Ref: NS8712

(▲ On path) *Wanlockhead Youth Hostel, Lotus Lodge, Wanlockhead, Biggar, Lanarkshire, ML12 6UT.*
Actual grid ref: NS874131
Tel: **01659 74252**
Under 18: £7.00 **Adults:** £8.25
Self-catering facilities, Shop nearby
Lovely old white house in Scotland's highest village, famous for gold-panning and silver and lead mining. Great base for exploring the Lowther Hills.

Leadhills 9

National Grid Ref: NS8815

🍴 🍺 Colebrook Arms, Hopetown Arms

(1.5m 🚪) *Meadowfoot Cottage, Gowanbank, Leadhills, Biggar, Lanarkshire, ML12 6YB.*
Actual grid ref: NS886153
Grades: STB 3 Star
Tel: **01659 74369** Mrs Ledger.
D: £18.50-£20.00 **S:** £20.00-£25.00.
Open: All Year (not Xmas)
Beds: 1F 1T
Baths: 1 En 1 Sh
🛏 🅿 (4) 🛩 🗐 🛏 🗙 🖲 🎟 🛈 ⚡
Blending history and modern amenities with the warmest welcome and delicious home cooking makes your stay a real highlight. Ideal for hill walking, Southern Upland Way, gold-panning, visiting Museum of Lead mining, Edinburgh, Glasgow, the beautiful Clyde Valley. Peaceful stopover just six miles from M74.

Beattock 10

National Grid Ref: NT0802

(▲ 0.25m) *Cloffin Cottage, .*
Tel: **Adults:** £3.01
Showers, Running water, WC, Drying facilities, Meals available, Washing facilities, Kitchen facilities, Breakfast available, Dogs allowed

(0.25m 🚪) *Middlegill, Beattock, Moffat, Dumfriesshire, DG10 9SW.*
Manor farmhouse, 4 miles from Moffat. Deer, peacocks, lovely walks.
Tel: **01683 300612** Mr Ramsden.
D: £15.00-£19.00 **S:** £15.00-£19.00.
Open: All year (not Xmas)
Beds: 2F 2D 3S
Baths: 2 Sh
🛏 🛩 🗐 🛏 🗙 🖲 🎟 🛈 ⚡

D = Price range per person sharing in a double room

S = Price range for a single person in a single room

Coxhill 11

National Grid Ref: NT0904

(On path) *Coxhill Farm, Old Carlisle Road, Coxhill, Moffat, Dumfriesshire, DG10 9QN.*
Stylish farmhouse set in 70 acres, outstanding views, private parking.
Grades: STB 4 Star
Tel: 01683 220471
Mrs Long.
Fax no: 01683 220871
D: £22.50-£22.50 **S:** £30.00-£30.00.
Open: All Year (not Xmas/ New Year)
Beds: 1D 1T
Baths: 2 En
🛇🄿🖂⏹✕⥮🖩Ⓥ🛇✦

Moffat 12

National Grid Ref: NT0805

🍴 ◀ Black Bull, Allanton House, Star Hotel

(0.25m 🐾) *Woodhead Farm, Moffat, Dumfriesshire, DG10 9LU.*
Actual grid ref: NT0010
Grades: STB 4 Star
Tel: 01683 220225
Mrs Jackson.
D: £24.00-£26.00 **S:** £26.00-£30.00.
Open: All Year
Beds: 1D 2T
Baths: 3 En
🛇🄿(3)⥮⏹✕⥮🖩Ⓥ🛇✦
Luxuriously appointed farmhouse breakfast served in large conservatory, overlooking mature garden and surrounding hills. Working sheep farm. Ample safe parking. 2 miles from spa town of Moffat. All bedrooms have panoramic views.

(2m 🐾) *Kirkland House, Well Road, Moffat, Dumfriesshire, DG10 9AR.*
Listed former manse with many interesting features, set in peaceful gardens.
Grades: STB 3 Star
Tel: 01683 221133 (also fax no)
Mr Watkins.
D: £18.00-£20.00
S: £18.00-£18.00.
Open: All Year
Beds: 1F 1T 1D
Baths: 2 En 1 Pr
🄿(6)⥮⏹⥮🖩Ⓥ🛇✦

(2m) *Morlich House, Ballplay Road, Moffat, Dumfriesshire, DG10 9JU.*
Actual grid ref: NT081048
Tel: 01683 220589
Mrs Wells.
Fax no: 01683 221032
D: £20.00-£23.00
S: £20.00-£33.00.
Open: Feb to Nov
Beds: 2F 1D 1T 1S
Baths: 4 En 1 Pr
🛇⥮🄿(6)⥮⏹🛏✕⥮🖩Ⓥ
A superb Victorian country house set in quiet elevated grounds overlooking town.

(1m) *Waterside, Moffat, Dumfriesshire, DG10 9LF.*
Tel: 01683 220092 Mrs Edwards.
D: £19.00-£21.00 **S:** £21.00-£21.00.
Open: Easter to Oct
Beds: 2D 2T **Baths:** 1 Pr 1 Sh
🛇🄿(4)⥮⏹⥮🖩Ⓥ✦
Large country house set in 12 acres of woodland garden with private stretch of river. The house is tastefully decorated throughout. We have a dog and cat, donkeys, peafowl, ducks, geese and hens. Ideal for walking, fishing, golf and bird watching.

(1m) *Hartfell House, Hartfell Crescent, Moffat, Dumfriesshire, DG10 9AL.*
Actual grid ref: NT087056
Splendid Victorian manor house in peaceful location.
Grades: STB 4 Star, AA 4 Diamond
Tel: 01683 220153 Mrs White.
D: £23.00-£23.00 **S:** £25.00-£25.00.
Open: All Year (not Xmas/New Year)
Beds: 2F 4D 1T 1S
Baths: 7 En 1 Sh
🛇🄿(8)⏹🛏✕⥮🖩Ⓥ✦

(0.75m) *Morag, 19 Old Carlisle Rd, Moffat, Dumfriesshire, DG10 9QJ.*
Beautiful quiet location in charming town near Southern Upland Way. **Grades:** STB 3 Star
Tel: 01683 220690
Mr & Mrs Taylor.
D: £16.00-£18.00 **S:** £18.00-£19.00.
Open: All Year
Beds: 1D 1T 1S **Baths:** 1 Sh
🛇(10)🄿(5)⥮⏹🛏⥮🖩Ⓥ🛇✦

(2m 🐾) *Ericstane, Moffat, Dumfriesshire, DG10 9LT.*
Working hill farm in a peaceful valley. Moffat 4 miles.
Grades: STB 3 Star
Tel: 01683 220127 Mr Jackson.
D: £20.00-£20.00 **S:** £25.00-£25.00.
Open: All Year
Beds: 1D 1S **Baths:** 2 En
🛇(8)🄿⏹⥮🖩Ⓥ✦

(2m 🐾) *Allanton Hotel, 21-22 High Street, Moffat, Dumfriesshire, DG10 9HL.*
Small inn in the scenic town of Moffat. Home cooking.
Tel: 01683 220343 Mr Kennedy.
Fax no: 01683 220914
D: £22.00-£30.00 **S:** £24.00-£32.00.
Open: All Year
Beds: 1F 2T 3D 1 S
Baths: 2 En 6 Pr 1 Sh
🛇⥮⏹🛏✕⥮🖩Ⓥ🛇✦

(2m 🐾) *Wellview Hotel, Ballplay Rd, Moffat, Dumfriesshire, DG10 9JU.*
Actual grid ref: NT092054
Excellent centre to explore Borders.
Grades: STB 4 Star
Tel: 01683 220184 (also fax no) Mr Schuckardt.
D: £36.00-£50.00 **S:** £53.00-£63.00.
Open: All Year
Beds: 4D 2T **Baths:** 6 En
🛇🄿(8)⏹🛏✕⥮🖩Ⓥ🛇✦

(2m 🐾) *Stratford House, Academy Road, Moffat, Dumfriesshire, DG10 9HR.*
Family-run B&B, 2 minutes from town centre. Off-road parking.
Tel: 01683 220297 Mrs Forrester.
D: £18.00-£20.00 **S:** £20.00-£25.00.
Open: All Year (not Xmas)
Beds: 1F 2T **Baths:** 2 En 1 Pr
🛇(10)🄿(2)⏹🛏⥮🖩Ⓥ🛇✦

(2m 🐾) *Hazel Bank, Academy Rd, Moffat, Dumfriesshire, DG10 9HP.*
Welcome to Hazel Bank. A warm and personal welcome awaits all our guests.
Tel: 01683 220294
Mrs Watson.
D: £17.00-£20.00 **S:** £23.00-£25.00.
Open: All Year
Beds: 1F 1D **Baths:** 1 En 1 Sh
🛇⏹🛏⥮🖩&Ⓥ✦

(2m 🐾) *Merkland House, Buccleuch Place, Moffat, Dumfriesshire, DG10 9AN.*
Spacious early Victorian house set in tranquil woodland gardens.
Tel: 01683 220957
Mr & Mrs Tavener.
D: £17.50-£22.00 **S:** £17.50-£22.00.
Open: All Year (not Xmas)
Beds: 2F 2D 1T 1S
Baths: 5 En 1 Pr
🛇🄿(8)⏹🛏✕⥮🖩&Ⓥ🛇✦

(2m) *Nineoaks, Reid Street, Moffat, DG10 9JE.*
Large spacious family bungalow situated in 3 acres with paddocks and horse.
Tel: 01683 220658 Mrs Jones.
D: £17.00-£17.00 **S:** £18.00-£18.00.
Open: Easter to Nov
Beds: 1D 1S **Baths:** 1 En 1 Pr
🄿(3)⥮⏹⥮🖩Ⓥ✦

(2m 🐾) *Marvig Guest House, Academy Road, Moffat, Dumfriesshire, DG10 9HW.*
Actual grid ref: NT084055
Hello! Welcome to Marvig, a renovated Victorian guest house offering personal attention.
Tel: 01683 220628 (also fax no)
Mr Muirhead.
D: £18.00-£20.00 **S:** £20.00-£25.00.
Open: All Year (not Xmas)
Beds: 1F 2D 2T 1S
Baths: 2 En 2 Sh
🛇🄿(4)⥮⏹⥮🖩Ⓥ🛇✦

Yarrow Feus 13

National Grid Ref: NT3426

🍴 ◀ Cross Keys

(4m 🐾) *Ladhope Farm, Yarrow Feus, Yarrow Valley, Selkirk, TD7 5NE.*
Beautiful farmhouse, log fires, very peaceful. Ideal for hunting, touring.
Tel: 01750 82216 Mrs Turnbull.
D: £18.00-£20.00 **S:** £20.00-£22.00.
Open: Easter to Oct
Beds: 1F 1D **Baths:** 1 Sh
🛇🄿(4)⏹🛏✕⥮🛇✦

Innerleithen 14

National Grid Ref: NT3336

◯ St Ronan's Hotel, Traquair Arms

(1m ⬛) *Caddon View Guest House, 14 Pirn Road, Innerleithen, Peebles-shire, EH44 6HH.*
Grades: STB 4 Star
Tel: **01896 830208**
Mr & Mrs Djellil.
D: £24.00-£30.00 **S:** £35.00-£40.00.
Open: All Year (not Xmas)
Beds: 1F 3D 2T
Baths: 6 En
⬛⬛(5)⬛⬛⬛⬛⬛⬛⬛⬛⬛⬛
Charming Victorian family house by the River Tweed, ideally situated for walking, fishing, touring or just relaxing. All rooms individually designed and equipped to make you feel at home. French restaurant and sauna available.

(1.25m ⬛) *St Ronan's Hotel, High Street, Innerleithen, Peebles-shire, EH44 6HF.*
Traditional 1823 coaching inn serving good home-cooking and real ales all day.
Tel: **01896 831487**
D: £20.00-£25.00 **S:** £25.00-£25.00.
Open: All Year
Beds: 2F 2D 2T
Baths: 5 En 1 Pr
⬛⬛(25)⬛⬛⬛⬛⬛⬛⬛⬛⬛

Selkirk 15

National Grid Ref: NT4728

◯ Queen's Head, Plough Inn, Cross Keys Inn, County Hotel

(3m ⬛) *Ivy Bank, Hillside Terrace, Selkirk, TD7 2LT.*
Set back from A7 with fine views over hills beyond.
Grades: STB 2 Star
Tel: **01750 21270** Mrs MacKenzie.
D: £17.50-£18.00 **S:** £18.00-£18.00.
Open: Easter to Dec
Beds: 1D 1T 1S
Baths: 2 En 1 Pr 1 Sh
⬛⬛(4)⬛⬛⬛⬛⬛⬛⬛

Galashiels 16

National Grid Ref: NT4936

◯ Kings Hotel, Woodlands Hotel, Cobbles Inn, Thistle Inn, Herges Bistro, Abbotsford Arms, Hunters Hall

(0.25m ⬛) *Island House, 65 Island St, Galashiels, Selkirkshire, TD1 1PA.*
Comfortable family home. Town centre. Ideally situated for touring the Borders.
Grades: AA 3 Diamond
Tel: **01896 752649** Mr Brown.
D: £15.00-£18.00 **S:** £15.00-£20.00.
Open: All Year
Beds: 1D 2T **Baths:** 2 En 1 Sh
⬛⬛(2)⬛⬛⬛⬛⬛⬛⬛⬛

(0.5m) *Watson Lodge, 15 Bridge St, Galashiels, Selkirkshire, TD1 1SW.*
Tel: **01896 750551** Mrs Reid.
D: £16.00-£20.00 **S:** £18.00-£20.00.
Open: All Year
Beds: 2T 1D **Baths:** 3 En
⬛⬛⬛⬛⬛⬛⬛⬛⬛
Centrally situated B&B; all guest rooms overlook quiet back garden. Bright comfortable rooms - all ensuite. Shopping, golf, fishing, walks, historic landmarks all at hand. Perfect location for touring all the borders. Good food close by. A friendly welcome awaits.

(0.5m) *Ettrickvale, 33 Abbotsford Rd, Galashiels, Selkirkshire, TD1 3HW*
Actual grid ref: NT491352
Warm, comfortable bungalow, ideally situated for touring Borders & Edinburgh.
Grades: STB 2 Star
Tel: **01896 755224** Mrs Field.
D: £16.00-£16.00 **S:** £20.00-£20.00.
Open: All Year (not Xmas)
Beds: 1D 2T **Baths:** 2 Sh
⬛⬛(3)⬛⬛⬛⬛⬛⬛⬛⬛⬛

Pay B&Bs by cash or cheque and be prepared to pay up front.

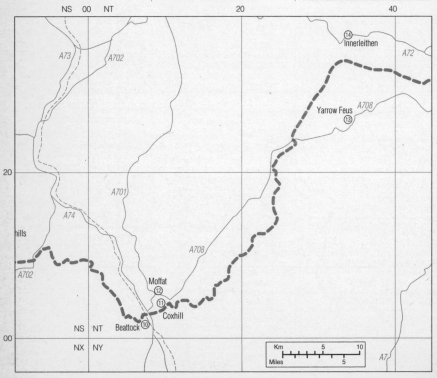

(0.5m) *Kings Hotel, Galashiels, Selkirkshire, TD1 3AN.*
Situated in the town centre of busy market town of Galashiels.
Grades: STB 2 Star, AA 2 Star
Tel: 01896 755497 (also fax no)
Mr MacDonald.
D: £25.00-£36.00 **S:** £35.00-£46.00.
Open: All Year (not Xmas)
Beds: 1F 1D 4T 1S **Baths:** 7 Pr
🛏 (1) 🅿 (6) ⌇⌷✕🕭🔟 🎔 🛡 ⚗

(0.25m 🚌**)** *Keranalt, 3 Bridge St, Galashiels, Selkirkshire, TD1 1SW.*
Centrally situated double glazed homely welcome.
Tel: 01896 754859 Mrs Lowe.
D: £16.00-£16.00 **S:** £16.00-£16.00.
Open: All Year (not Xmas/New Year)
Beds: 3T **Baths:** 2 Sh
🛏⌷✕🕭🔟 🎔 🛡 ⚗

(0.5m) *Abbotsford Arms Hotel, Stirling Street, Galashiels, Selkirkshire, TD1 1BY.*
Centrally situated, family run; serving good food all day.
Tel: 01896 752517
Fax no: 01896 750744
D: £29.00-£30.00 **S:** £38.00-£40.00.
Open: All Year (not Xmas/New Year)
Beds: 4F 3D 5T 2S **Baths:** 14 En
🛏 🅿 (10) ⌷✕🕭🔟 🎔 🛡 ⚗

Melrose 17

National Grid Ref: NT5433

🍴 ⚌ Buccleuch Arms, Burts Hotel, Marmions

(▲ **0.5m)** *Melrose Youth Hostel, Priorwood, Melrose, Roxburghshire, TD6 9EF.*
Actual grid ref: NT549339
Tel: 01896 822521
Under 18: £8.00 **Adults:** £11.25
Self-catering facilities, Shop nearby, Laundry facilities, Meals available groups only
Imposing stone-built Georgian mansion surrounded by own grounds, overlooking Melrose Abbey. Set on the Southern Upland and St Cuthbert's Ways.

(1m 🚌**)** *Old Abbey School House, Waverley Road, Melrose, Roxburghshire, TD6 9SH.*
Charming old school house with character. Large bedrooms, restful atmosphere.
Grades: STB 3 Star
Tel: 01896 823432 Mrs O'Neill.
D: £17.00-£21.00 **S:** £20.00-£25.00.
Open: March to November
Beds: 1T 2D
Baths: 1 Pr 1 Sh
🛏 🅿 (5) ⌇⌷🕭🔟 🎔 🛡 ⚗

(On path 🚌**)** *Braidwood, Buccleuch Street, Melrose, Roxburghshire, TD6 9LD.*
A Victorian town house situated a stones throw away from Melrose Abbey.
Grades: STB 3 Star
Tel: 01896 822488
Mrs Graham.
D: £20.00-£24.00 **S:** £25.00-£25.00.
Open: All Year
Beds: 3D 1F
Baths: 2 En 2 Pr
🛏 🅿 ⌇🔥🕭🔟 🎔 🛡 ⚗

Gattonside 18

National Grid Ref: NT5435

🍴 ⚌ Marmions

(1m) *Fauhope House, Fauhope, Gattonside, Melrose, Roxburghshire, TD6 9LU.*
An Edwardian house looking over the river Tweed to Melrose Abbey.
Grades: STB 4 Star
Tel: 01896 823184 (also fax no)
Mrs Robson.
D: £25.00-£25.00 **S:** £32.00-£32.00.
Open: All Year
Beds: 2T 1D
Baths: 3 En
🅿 ⌇🔥🕭🔟 🎔

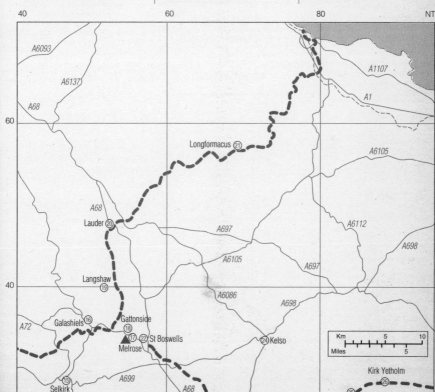

Langshaw 19

National Grid Ref: NT5139

(0.5m) *Over Langshaw Farm,*
Langshaw, Galashiels,
Selkirkshire, TD1 2PE.
Actual grid ref: NT523402
Welcoming family farm superb
location in unspoilt border
countryside.
Grades: STB 2 Star
Tel: 01896 860244 Mrs Bergius.
D: £20.00-£22.00 **S:** £25.00-£25.00.
Open: All Year
Beds: 1F 1D **Baths:** 1 En 1 Pr 1 Sh
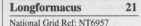

Lauder 20

National Grid Ref: NT5247

Lauderdale Hotel, Eagle Hotel, Black Bull
Hotel

(On path 🚐) *The Grange,*
6 Edinburgh Road, Lauder,
Berwickshire, TD2 6TW.
Grades: STB 3 Star
Tel: 01578 722649 (also fax no)
Tricia and Peter Gilardi.
D: £17.00-£20.00 **S:** £18.00-£20.00.
Open: All Year (not Xmas)
Beds: 1D 2T
Baths: 1 Sh
A peaceful haven from which to
explore the tranquil Scottish and
English borders, yet less than an
hour's drive from Edinburgh.
Overlooking the rolling
Lammermuir Hills and on the
Southern Upland Way, an ideal
base for walking, cycling or
relaxing.

Longformacus 21

National Grid Ref: NT6957

(On path 🚐) *Eildon Cottage,*
Longformacus, Duns,
Berwickshire, TD11 3NX.
Leave crowds behind set in
beautiful rolling Lammermuir Hill
Village.
Tel: 01361 890230 Mrs Amos.
D: £20.00-£25.00 **S:** £20.00-£25.00.
Open: All Year (not Xmas/New
Year)
Beds: 1F 1T 1D
Baths: 2 En 1 Pr

(1m 🚐) *Kintra Ha, Gifford Road,*
Longformacus, Duns,
Berwickshire, TD11 3NZ.
Recently converted, detached
property. Edinburgh 50 mins.
Access to rural pursuits.
Grades: STB 3 Star
Tel: 01361 890660 (also fax no)
Mrs Lamb.
D: £20.00-£20.00 **S:** £25.00-£25.00.
Open: All Year
Beds: 1D 1T
Baths: 2 En

All paths are
popular: you are
well-advised to
book ahead

For those wishing to walk
to Holy Island, this is the St.
Cuthbert's Way alternative.

St Boswells 22

National Grid Ref: NT5930

Buccleuch Arms Hotel

(0.5m 🚐) *Rivendell, The Croft,*
St Boswells, Melrose, TD6 0AE.
Relax in our spacious family
Victorian home overlooking
Scotland's largest village green.
Grades: STB 4 Star
Tel: 01835 822498 Mrs Mitchell.
D: £18.00-£22.50 **S:** £25.00-£30.00.
Open: All Year (not Xmas/New
Year)
Beds: 2D 1T
Baths: 2 En 1 Pr

Jedburgh 23

National Grid Ref: NT6520

Royal Hotel, Simply Scottish, Pheasant Inn,
Forresters

(3m) *Riverview, Newmill Farm,*
Jedburgh, Roxburghshire, TD8 6TH.
Spacious modern villa overlooking
River Jed with country views.
Grades: STB 3 Star
Tel: 01835 862145 Mrs Kinghorn.
D: £18.00-£20.00 **S:** £25.00-£25.00.
Open: April to Oct
Beds: 1T 2D
Baths: 3 En

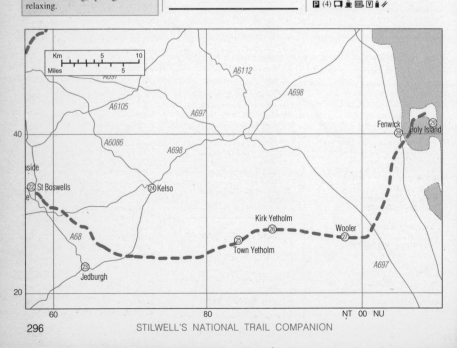

(3m 🚗) *Edgerston Rink Smithy,*
Jedburgh, Roxburghshire, TD8 6PP.
Grades: STB 3 Star
Tel: **01835 840328**
Mr & Mrs Smart.
D: £16.00-£18.00 **S:** £23.00-£23.00.
Open: All Year
Beds: 2D **Baths:** 1 Sh
📷 (12) 🅿 (4) ⬜ �🇭 🐾 ♨ 🕮 Ⅴ ⬚ ✦
Converted smithy overlooking the
Cheviot Hills backing on to natural
woodland. Very private facilities of
a superior standard. Warm
welcome assured. Private visitors
lounge with TV, music centre etc.
Rural location alongside A68, 7
miles south of Jedburgh.

(3m) *Hundalee House, Jedburgh,*
Roxburghshire, TD8 6PA.
Tel: **01835 863011** (also fax no)
Mrs Whittaker.
D: £20.00-£23.00 **S:** £25.00-£35.00.
Open: Mar to Nov
Beds: 1F 3D 1T **Baths:** 4 En 1 Pr
📷 (5) 🅿 (10) ⬚ ⬜ 🐾 ♨ 🕮 Ⅴ
Large Victorian private house.

(3m) *Froylehurst, The Friars,*
Jedburgh, Roxburghshire, TD8 6BN.
Detached Victorian house in large
garden. Spacious guest rooms, 2
mins town centre.
Grades: STB 4 Star
Tel: **01835 862477** (also fax no)
Mrs Irvine.
D: £15.50-£18.00 **S:** £20.00-£25.00.
Open: Mar to Nov
Beds: 2F 1D 1T **Baths:** 2 Sh
📷 (5) 🅿 (5) ⬜ 🐾 ♨ 🕮 Ⅴ

(3m) *Ferniehirst Mill Lodge,*
Jedburgh, Roxburghshire, TD8 6PQ.
Actual grid ref: NT654171
Modern guest house in peaceful
setting, country lovers' paradise.
Grades: STB 1 Star, AA 3
Diamond, RAC 3 Diamond
Tel: **01835 863279** Mr Swanston.
D: £23.00-£23.00 **S:** £23.00-£23.00.
Open: All Year
Beds: 1F 3D 4T 1S
Baths: 9 En 1 Sh
📷 🅿 (10) ⬜ 🇭 ✕ 🐾 ♨ 🕮 Ⅴ ⬚ ✦

(3m) *15 Hartrigge Crescent,*
Jedburgh, Roxburghshire, TD8 6HT.
Comfortable family house, within
short distance of town centre.
Grades: STB 2 Star
Tel: **01835 862738** Mrs Crone.
D: £15.50-£15.50 **S:** £18.00-£18.00.
Open: All Year
Beds: 1D 1T **Baths:** 1 Sh
📷 (1) 🅿 (5) ⬜ 🐾 🕮 Ⅴ ✦

(3m) *Craigowen, 30 High Street,*
Jedburgh, Roxburghshire, TD8 6AG.
Centrally located family home. A
great welcome. Real home from
home.
Tel: **01835 862604** Mrs Campbell.
D: £16.00-£17.50 **S:** £17.00-£18.50.
Open: All Year (not Xmas)
Beds: 1F 1T **Baths:** 2 Pr
📷 (3) ⬜ 🇭 🐾 ♨ 🕮 Ⅴ ⬚ ✦

(3m 🚗) *Willow Court, The Friars,*
Jedburgh, Roxburghshire, TD8 6BN.
Modern, professionally-run guest
house. Lovely views over
Jedburgh, two mins' walk town
centre.
Tel: **01835 863702** Mr McGovern.
Fax no: 01835 864601
D: £18.00-£22.00 **S:** £27.00-£36.00.
Open: All Year (not Xmas)
Beds: 1F 2D 1T
Baths: 3 En 1 Pr
📷 🅿 (5) ⬜ 🇭 🐾 ♨ 🕮 🐕 Ⅴ ⬚ ✦

(3m) *Kenmore Bank , Oxnam*
Road, Jedburgh, Roxburghshire,
TD8 6JJ.
Charming, family run, just off A68.
Panoramic views over Abbey,
ensuite.
Tel: **01835 862369** Mr Muller.
D: £19.00-£23.00 **S:** £25.00-£43.00.
Open: All Year
Beds: 2F 2D 2T **Baths:** 6 En
📷 🅿 (5) ⬜ 🇭 🐾 ♨ Ⅴ

(3m) *Maple Bank, 3 Smiths Wynd,*
Jedburgh, Roxburghshire, TD8 6DH.
Large town centre period house,
easy access restaurants, shops,
buses.
Tel: **01835 862051** Mrs Booth.
D: £14.00-£15.00 **S:** £15.00-£28.00.
Open: All Year
Beds: 1F 1D **Baths:** 2 Sh
📷 🅿 (2) ⬜ 🇭 🐾 ♨ 🕮 Ⅴ ✦

Kelso   24

National Grid Ref: NT7234

🍴 🍺 Black Swan, Border Hotel, Cobbles Inn,
Plough Hotel, Queen's Head, Wagon & Horses

(8m) *Craignethan House,*
Jedburgh Road, Kelso,
Roxburghshire, TD5 8AZ.
Grades: STB 3 Star
Tel: **01573 224818** Mrs McDonald.
D: £18.50-£18.50 **S:** £18.50-£18.50.
Open: All Year
Beds: 2D 1T
Baths: 1 Pr 1 Sh
📷 🅿 (6) ⬜ 🇭 🐾 ♨ 🕮 🐕 Ⅴ ⬚ ✦
Comfortable welcoming family
home with relaxed informal atmos-
phere. Breakfast to suit all tastes
and times. Afternoon tea, tea/coffee
in evening, home baking, attractive
garden, breathtaking panoramic
views of Kelso/Tweed Valley to
Floors Castle from all bedrooms.
Scottish Border Abbeys, Floors
Castle, Tweed Valley, Walter Scott
country.

Many rates vary

according to season -

the lowest only are

shown here

Town Yetholm   25

National Grid Ref: NT8127

🍴 🍺 Border Hotel, Cobbles Inn, Plough Hotel

(1m) *Lochside, Town Yetholm,*
Kelso, Roxburghshire, TD5 8PD.
Victorian country house. Peaceful,
spacious, ensuite bedrooms.
Beautiful countryside.
Grades: STB 3 Star B&B
Tel: **01573 420349** Mrs Hurst.
D: £20.00-£22.50 **S:** £22.50-£22.50.
Open: Apr to Oct
Beds: 1D 1T
Baths: 2 En
📷 (2) 🅿 (2) ⬚ ⬜ 🇭 🐾 ♨ 🕮 Ⅴ ✦

(0.25m 🚗) *Blunty's Mill, Kirk*
Yetholm, Kelso, Roxburghshire,
TD5 6PG.
Fabulous rural location set in
6 acres. Friendly welcome
guaranteed.
Grades: STB 2 Star
Tel: **01573 420288** Mrs Brooker.
D: £22.00-£30.00 .
Open: All Year
Beds: 2T
Baths: 1 Sh
📷 🅿 (10) ⬜ 🇭 ✕ 🐾 ♨ 🐕 Ⅴ ⬚ ✦

Kirk Yetholm   26

National Grid Ref: NT8228

🍴 🍺 Border Hotel, Cobbles Inn, Plough Hotel

(▲ On path) *Kirk Yetholm Youth*
Hostel, Kirk Yetholm, Kelso,
Roxburghshire, TD5 8PG.
Actual grid ref: NT826282
Tel: **01573 420631**
Under 18: £7.00 **Adults:** £8.25
Self-catering facilities, Shop near-
by, Lounge, Parking Limited, No
smoking, WC, Kitchen facilities
Kirk Yetholm is at the north end of
the Pennine Way and mid-point on
St Cuthbert's Way. Many abbeys
and castles to visit. Good cycling,
including the Tweed Cycle Way.

(0.5m 🚗) *Valleydene, High Street,*
Kirk Yetholm, Kelso,
Roxburghshire, TD5 8PH.
Traditional Scottish welcome. Log
fire. Comfortable rooms with
excellent views.
Tel: **01573 420286** Mrs Campbell.
D: £22.00-£22.00 **S:** £25.00-£30.00.
Open: All Year
Beds: 2T 1D **Baths:** 2 En 1 Pr
📷 (12) 🅿 (4) ⬜ 🇭 ✕ 🐾 ♨ 🕮 Ⅴ ⬚ ✦

(1m) *Spring Valley, The Green,*
Kirk Yetholm, Roxburghshire,
TD5 8PQ.
C18th house with superb views,
situated in conservation village.
Grades: STB 3 Star
Tel: **01573 420253** Mrs Ogilvie.
D: £20.00-£22.00 **S:** £27.00-£27.00.
Open: All Year (not Xmas)
Beds: 1D 1T
Baths: 2 Pr
📷 (1) 🅿 (3) ⬚ ⬜ 🇭 🐾 ♨ 🕮 Ⅴ ⬚ ✦

Wooler   27

National Grid Ref: NT9928

⊮ ⌑ Tankerville Arms, The Wheatsheaf, Ryecroft Hotel

(▲ 0.5m) *Wooler (Cheviot) Youth Hostel, 30 Cheviot Street, Wooler, Northumberland, NE71 6LW.*
Actual grid ref: NT991278
Tel: **01668 281365**
Under 18: £6.50
Adults: £9.25
Self-catering facilities, Showers, Laundry facilities, Wet weather shelter, Lounge, Drying room, Cycle store, Parking, Evening meal at 7.00pm, Facilities for disabled people Category 2, No smoking, WC, Kitchen facilities, Breakfast available, Credit cards accepted *On outskirts of the market town of Wooler in the foothills of the Cheviots, close to the Scottish border, the most northerly of the English Youth Hostels is convenient for Holy Island, Lindisfarne and the Farne Islands.*

(0.25m 🚍) *Winton House, 39 Glendale Road, Wooler, Northumberland , NE71 6DL.*
Actual grid ref: NT991283
Charming Edwardian house, quietly positioned, comfortable spacious rooms. Walkers welcome.
Tel: **01668 281362** Mr Gilbert.
D: £20.00-£22.00 **S:** £25.00-£27.00.
Open: Mar to Nov
Beds: 2D 1T **Baths:** 2 En 1 Sh
ॐ ⅌ ☐ ☷ ▥ �📷 Ⓥ 🛈 ⚡

Fenwick (Holy Island)   28

National Grid Ref: NU0640
⊮ ⌑ The Plough

(On path) *The Manor House, Fenwick, Berwick-on-Tweed, Northumberland, TD15 2PQ.*
Actual grid ref: NU063399
Peaceful, magical, Northumbrian, easy-relaxed home, kid-free zone.
Grades: ETC 3 Diamond
Tel: **01289 381006** (also fax no)
Ms Simpson & Ms S Leister.
D: £21.00-£21.00 **S:** £30.00-£30.00.
Open: Feb to Nov
Beds: 1D 1T 1S **Baths:** 2 En 1 Pr
⅄ ☐ ✗ ☷ ▥ Ⓥ 🛈

(0.25m) *Cherry Trees, Fenwick, Berwick-upon-Tweed, TD15 2PJ.*
Detached house, large comfortable bedrooms. Holy Island approx. 6 miles.
Tel: **01289 381437**
D: £14.00-£15.00
S: £15.00-£16.00.
Open: May to Sep
Beds: 1F 1D 1T 1S
Baths: 2 Sh
ॐ ☐ (6) ☐ ⅂ ✗ ☷ ▥ 🛈 ⚡

Holy Island   29

National Grid Ref: NU1241

(On path) *Open Gate, Marygate, Holy Island, Berwick-upon-Tweed, TD15 2SD.*
450 years old. Quiet, Christian home. Centre of Holy Island.
Tel: **01289 389222**
D: £20.50-£22.50
S: £25.00-£27.00.
Open: All Year
Beds: 1T 3D
Baths: 3 En
☐ (5) ⅄ ✗ ☷ ▥ Ⓥ ⚡

BRITAIN: BED & BREAKFAST

The essential guide to B&Bs in England, Scotland & Wales

The Bed & Breakfast is one of the great British institutions. Like Fish & Chips, it's known by people around the world. But you don't have to be a tourist to enjoy this traditional accommodation. Whether you're travelling, on holiday, away on business or just escaping from it all, the B&B is a great value alternative to expensive hotels and a world away from camping and caravanning.

Stilwell's Britain: Bed & Breakfast 2001 is the most comprehensive guide of its kind, containing over 7,750 entries listed by country, county and location, in England, Scotland and Wales. Each entry includes room rates, facilities, Tourist Board grades and a brief description of the B&B and its location and surroundings.

Stilwell's Britain: Bed & Breakfast 2001: The indispensable guide to great value accommodation:

Private houses, country halls, farms, cottages, inns, small hotels and guest houses

Over 7,750 entries
Average price £19 per person per night
All official grades shown
Local maps
Pubs serving hot evening meals shown
Tourist Information Centres listed
Handy size for easy packing

£9.95 from all good bookstores (ISBN 1-900861-22-4) or £11.95 (inc p&p) from Stilwell Publishing, 59 Charlotte Road, London EC2A 3QW (020 7739 7179)

Speyside Way

At 45 miles, this is not a very long path and much of it is at low level, running alongside the River Spey, making it an excellent choice for a long weekend's walk. It runs from where the Spey joins the North Sea at Spey Bay, down to Aberlour with a spur running off to Dufftown, joins a former railway track, reaches Glenlivet and then climbs Carn Daimh before descending to the old military town of Tomintoul in the South. Besides the beautiful scenery, one great attraction is the number of distilleries the route passes

(it's also called the 'Whisky Trail'), each offering its own distinctive malt. Should you care to drop in at each one, that weekend may well turn out to be a bit longer.

Guides: *Speyside Way Leaflet* published by Moray District Council and available free of charge from the M.D.C. Ranger Service (Dept of Leisure & Libraries, High Street, Elgin, Moray, IV30 1BX, tel. 01340 881266)

Maps: Ordnance Survey 1:50000 Landranger series: 28 and 36

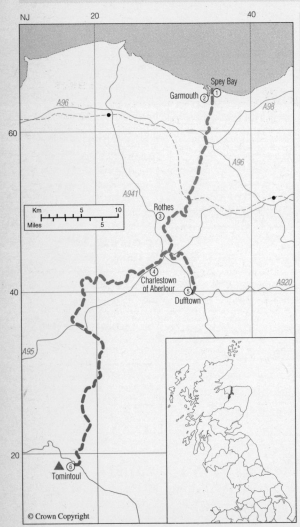

Spey Bay   1

National Grid Ref: NJ3565

⊮ ⌾ Spey Bay Hotel

(0.5m 🚌) *31 The Muir, Bogmoor, Spey Bay, Fochabers, IV32 7PN.*
1 Mile from Spey estuary, sighting of dolphins, seals, osprey.
Tel: **01343 820196** Philpott.
D: £15.00-£16.00 **S:** £15.00-£16.00.
Open: All Year
Beds: 2D
🛏 🅿 ⅍ 🖵 ✕ 🐾 🛏 Ⓥ ⋒

Garmouth   2

National Grid Ref: NJ3364

⊮ ⌾ Garmouth Hotel

(1m) *Rowan Cottage, Station Road, Garmouth, Fochabers, Moray, IV32 7LZ.*
Actual grid ref: NJ335644
C18th cottage & garden in rural village at Spey estuary.
Tel: **01343 870267** Mrs Bingham.
Fax no: 01343 870621
D: £15.00-£15.00 **S:** £15.00-£17.00.
Open: Jan to Nov
Beds: 1D 1T 1S
Baths: 1 Sh
🛏 🅿 (4) ⅍ 🖵 🐾 🛏 Ⓥ ⋒ ⋇

Rothes   3

National Grid Ref: NJ2749

⊮ ⌾ Seafield Arms, Eastbank Hotel

(2m 🚌) *Seafield Arms Hotel, 73 New Street, Rothes, Charlestown of Aberlour, Banffshire, AB38 7BJ.*
Small family hotel friendly atmosphere. Excellent homecooked meals, fully licensed.
Tel: **01340 831587**
Fax no: 01340 831892
D: £18.00-£20.00 **S:** £18.00-£20.00.
Open: All Year
Beds: 1F 1D 1T 2S
Baths: 1 Sh
🛏 🅿 (8) 🖵 🐾 ✕ 🐾 🛏 Ⓥ ⋒ ⋇

Aberlour 4

National Grid Ref: NJ2642

🍽 🍺 Aberlour Hotel

(On path 🚌) *83 High Street,*
Aberlour, Banffshire, AB38 9QB.
The heart of a village famous for
whisky and shortbread.
Tel: **01340 871000**
Miss Gammack.
D: £15.00-£16.00 **S:** £15.00-£16.00.
Open: All Year
Beds: 1T 2D **Baths:** 2 Sh
🛏 🄿 (2) �🗶 🖵 🛋 🎑 V ⬩ ⨯

Dufftown 5

National Grid Ref: NJ3240

🍽 🍺 Glenfiddich, Fife Arms, Masons' Arms,
Croft Inn, Commercial Hotel

(On path) *Davaar, Church Street,*
Dufftown, Keith, Banffshire,
AB55 4AR.
Nice Victorian house. Some guest
rooms overlooking garden at rear.
Grades: STB 3 Star
Tel: **01340 820464** Mrs Macmillan.
D: £16.00-£18.00 **S:** £25.00-£30.00.
Open: All Year (not Xmas/New
Year)
Beds: 1T 2D **Baths:** 2 En 1 Sh
🛏 🖵 🗶 🛋 🎑 V ⬩

(On path 🚌) *Errolbank, 134 Fife*
Street, Dufftown, Keith, Banffshire,
AB55 4DP.
Actual grid ref: MJ329398
Friendly local hosts. Scottish
breakfasts our speciality. On
Whisky Trail.
Tel: **01340 820229** Mrs Smart.
D: £15.00-£15.00 **S:** £15.50-£16.00.
Open: All Year
Beds: 3F 1D 1S
Baths: 1 Sh
🛏 🄿 (5) 🖵 🎑 🗶 🛋 🎑 V ⬩ ⨯

**Pay B&Bs by
cash or cheque and
be prepared to
pay up front.**

(On path) *Fife Arms Hotel,*
2 The Square, Dufftown, Keith,
Banffshire, AB55 4AD.
Small, modern town centre hotel.
Steaks - beef & ostrich our
speciality.
Grades: STB 1 Star,
AA 3 Diamond
Tel: **01340 820220**
Mr Widdowson.
Fax no: 01340 821137
D: £20.00-£25.00 **S:** £22.00-£27.00.
Open: All Year
Beds: 2F 4T
Baths: 6 En
🛏 (1) 🄿 (6) 🖵 🎑 🗶 🛋 🎑 ⬩ ⨯

(On path 🚌) *Nashville, 8a*
Balvenie Street, Dufftown, Keith,
Banffshire, AB55 4AB.
Relaxed family-run B&B. Whisky
Trail - yards from Glenfiddich
Distillery. Speyside Way close by.
Tel: **01340 820553** (also fax no)
Mrs Morrison.
D: £14.00-£16.00 **S:** £18.00-£20.00.
Open: All Year
Beds: 1F 1D 1T
Baths: 1 Sh
🛏 🄿 (2) 🖵 🎑 🛋 🎑 V ⬩ ⨯

(On path) *Gowanbrae, 19 Church*
Street, Dufftown, Keith, Banffshire,
AB55 4AR.
Beautiful Edwardian town house,
tastefully decorated and
modernised.
Tel: **01340 820461** (also fax no)
Mr & Mrs Donald.
D: £18.00-£20.00 **S:** £22.00-£24.00.
Open: All Year (not Xmas)
Beds: 1F 2D 1T **Baths:** 4 En
🛏 🖵 🎑 🛋 🎑 V ⬩ ⨯

Tomintoul 6

National Grid Ref: NJ1618

🍽 🍺 Glenavon Hotel, Richmond Arms

(🔺 On path) *Tomintoul Youth*
Hostel, Main Street, Tomintoul,
Ballindalloch, Banffshire, AB37 9HA.
Actual grid ref: NJ165190
Tel: **01807 580282**
Under 18: £6.00 **Adults:** £6.75
Self-catering facilities, Shop nearby
Go for the 47-mile Speyside Way
walk, explore the Cairngorms, try
rock climbing or abseiling and
savour the Whisky Trail.

(On path 🚌) *Bracam House,*
32 Main Street, Tomintoul,
Ballindalloch, AB37 9EX.
Enjoy a warm welcome to the
Highlands from the Camerons.
Grades: STB 3 Star
Tel: **01807 580278** (also fax no)
Mr & Mrs Cameron.
D: £15.00-£16.00
S: £15.00-£16.00.
Open: All Year
Beds: 1D 1T 1S
Baths: 1 En 1 Sh
🛏 🄿 (2) ⨯ 🖵 🎑 🛋 🎑 V ⬩ ⨯

(On path 🚌) *Croughly Farm,*
Tomintoul, Ballindalloch,
Banffshire, AB37 9EN.
Farmhouse with breathtaking views
of Cairngorm mountains. overlook-
ing River Conglas.
Grades: STB 2 Star
Tel: **01807 580476** (also fax no)
Mrs Shearer.
D: £16.00-£18.00
S: £18.00-£20.00.
Open: May to Oct
Beds: 1F 1D
Baths: 1 Pr 1 En
🛏 🄿 (3) 🖵 🎑 🛋 🎑 V ⬩ ⨯

(1.75m 🚌) *Findron Farm,*
Braemar Road, Tomintoul,
Ballindalloch, Banffshire, AB37 9ER.
Situated in the Castle and Distillery
area.
Grades: STB 3 Star
Tel: **01807 580382** (also fax no)
Mrs Turner.
D: £15.00-£17.00
S: £15.00-£17.00.
Open: All Year (not Xmas/New
Year)
Beds: 1F 1D 1T
Baths: 2 En 1 Pr
🛏 🄿 🖵 🎑 🗶 🛋 🎑 V ⬩ ⨯

**All paths are
popular: you are
well-advised to
book ahead**

West Highland Way

The **West Highland Way** is an excellent, well-marked path running mainly at low-level for 95 miles from Milngavie, north of Glasgow to Fort William in Inverness-shire. It is very popular, for in that relatively short distance it manages to combine some of the greatest sights in Scotland - the largest loch (Loch Lomond), the bleakest moorland (Rannoch Moor) and the highest mountain (Ben Nevis). The final destination, Fort William, attracts visitors from all over the world. The way itself largely follows the droves used by the Highlanders to herd their cattle to the Lowland markets, as well as the eighteenth-century military roads built to help control the Jacobites. The walking provides a mixed challenge - sometimes a woodland stroll, at other times a tough, exposed scramble. Why not do this walk over a week in early summer when it's warm and dry, the coach parties fewer, the flowers in bloom and the midges not yet hatched? You won't regret it! There may even be a foot masseuse at Crianlarich Youth Hostel to tend to weary feet (ask the warden for more details)!

Guides (available from all good bookshops, unless stated):

The West Highland Way (map & book set) by Robert Aitken (ISBN 0 1149525 23), published by Stationery Office Books, £14.95

The West Highland Way by Anthony Burton (ISBN 1 854103 91 1), published by Aurum Press in association with Ordnance Survey, £12.99

A Guide to the West Highland Way by Tom Hunter (ISBN 0 094753 30 X), published by Constable & Co Ltd, £9.95

Maps: Ordnance Survey 1:50000 Landranger series: 41 50, 56, 57 and 64.

Also, The West Highland Way (4-colour linear route map), ISBN 1 871149 00 2, published by Footprint and available from all good map shops or directly from their offices (Unit 87, Stirling Enterprise Park, Stirling, FK7 7RP), £3.50 (+ 40p p&p)

Milngavie 1

National Grid Ref: NS5574

|●| Allander Bar, Cross Keys

(0.5m **🚌**) *13 Craigdhu Avenue, Milngavie, Glasgow, G62 6DX.*
Very comfortable family house where a warm welcome is assured.
Grades: STB 3 Star
Tel: **0141 956 3439** Mrs Ogilvie.
D: £18.00-£18.00 **S:** £20.00-£25.00.
Open: Mar to Oct
Beds: 1F 1T
🛏 🅿 (4) ⅙ ☐ ⵚ 🖢 🛏 Ⅶ 🗋 ⚡

(0.5m) *Westview, 1 Dougalston Gardens South, Milngavie, Glasgow, G62 6HS.*
Modern detached, unique, comfortable, convenient to West Highland Way.
Tel: **0141 956 5973**
Mr & Mrs McColl.
D: £20.00-£20.00 **S:** £24.00-£24.00.
Open: All Year
Beds: 1F 1D 1T **Baths:** 3 En
🛏 🅿 (6) ⅙ ⵚ Ⅶ 🗋 ⚡

D = Price range per person sharing in a double room

High season, bank holidays and special events mean low availability *everywhere.*

Croftamie 2

National Grid Ref: NS4786

|●| Clachan Inn, Wayfarers

(0.25m **🚌**) *Croftburn, Croftamie, Drymen, Glasgow, G63 0HA.*
Actual grid ref: NS402860
Former gamekeeper's cottage in one acre of beautiful gardens overlooking Strathendrick Valley & Campsie Fells.
Grades: STB 3 Star, AA 4 Diamond
Tel: **01360 660796** Mrs Reid.
Fax no: 01360 661005
D: £18.00-£22.00 **S:** £20.00-£25.00.
Open: All Year
Beds: 2D 1T
Baths: 2 En 1 Pr
🛏 (12) 🅿 (20) ⅙ ☐ 🛏 ✕ 🖢 🛏 Ⅶ 🗋 ⚡

Drymen 3

National Grid Ref: NS4788

|●| Buchanan Arms, Clachan Inn, Pottery, Wayfarers, Winnock Hotel

(1m **🚌**) *Green Shadows, Buchanan Castle Estate, Drymen, Glasgow, G63 0HX.*
Tel: **01360 660289** Mrs Goodwin.
D: £21.00-£21.00 **S:** £24.00-£24.00.
Open: All year (not Xmas)
Beds: 1F 1D 1S **Baths:** 2 Sh
🛏 🅿 (8) ⅙ ☐ 🖢 🛏 Ⅶ 🗋 ⚡
Warm, friendly welcome in a beautiful country house with spectacular views over golf course and the Lomond Hills. Buchanan Castle to the rear. 1 mile from Drymen Centre, 2 miles from Loch Lomond. Glasgow Airport 40 mins away.

(On path **🚌**) *Easter Drumquhassle Farm, Gartness Road, Drymen, Glasgow, G63 0DN.*
Actual grid ref: NS486872
Traditional farmhouse, beautiful views, home cooking, excellent base on the West Highland Way.
Grades: STB 3 Star, AA 3 Diamond
Tel: **01360 660893** Mrs Cross.
Fax no: 01360 660282
D: £18.00-£25.00 **S:** £25.00-£30.00.
Open: All Year
Beds: 1F 1D 1T **Baths:** 3 En
🛏 🅿 (10) ⅙ ☐ 🛏 ✕ 🖢 🛏 Ⅶ 🗋 ⚡

(On path 🚐) *Ceardach, Gartness Road, Drymen, Glasgow, G63 0BH.*
Tel: **01360 660596** (also fax no)
Mrs Robb.
D: £18.00-£20.00. **S:** £18.00-£20.00.
Open: All Year (not Xmas)
Beds: 1D 1T **Baths:** 1 Sh
🛌 (1) 🅿 (3) 🗏 🍴 🛁 🎨 🗒 🖂 🎇
250 year old Coach house. Situated near the shores of Loch Lomond large garden. Good home cooking, a warm and friendly welcome awaits you.

(1m) *Glenava, Stirling Road, Drymen, Glasgow, G63 0AA.*
A Warm welcome, stunning scenery, comfortable rooms, lovely local Walks.
Grades: STB 3 Star
Tel: **01360 660491**
Ms Fraser.
D: £18.00-£20.00 **S:** £30.00-£30.00.
Open: Easter to Oct
Beds: 1D 1T
Baths: 1 Sh
🛌 🅿 (4) 🎇 🗏 🛁 🎨 🗒 🖂 🎇

(0.25m) *17 Stirling Road, Drymen, Glasgow, G63 0BW.*
Actual grid ref: NS476883
Family home in village near West Highland Way; lovely garden.
Tel: **01360 660273** (also fax no)
Mrs Lander.
D: £15.00-£18.00
S: £18.00-£23.00.
Open: All Year
Beds: 1F 1T
Baths: 1 Sh
🛌 🅿 (1) 🗏 🍴 🛁 🖂 🎇

Gartocharn   4

National Grid Ref: NS4286

🍴 🍺 Hungry Monk, Clachan Inn

(3m 🚐) *Mardella Farm, Old School Road, Gartocharn, Loch Lomond, Alexandria, Dunbartonshire, G83 8SD.*
Actual grid ref: NS438864
Friendly, welcoming, homely atmosphere. Come and meet the quackers (ducks)!
Grades: AA 4 Diamond
Tel: **01389 830428**
Mrs MacDonell.
D: £18.50-£22.00
S: £31.00-£37.00.
Open: All Year
Beds: 1F 1D 1T
Baths: 1 En 1 Sh
🛌 🅿 (4) 🎇 🗏 🍴 🛁 🎨 🗒 🖂 🎇

Milton of Buchanan   5

National Grid Ref: NS4490

(0.5m) *Mar Achlais, Milton of Buchanan, Balmaha, Glasgow, G63 0JE.*
Rural setting near Loch Lomond. Excellent touring centre for Scotland.
Grades: STB 3 Star
Tel: **01360 870300**
Mr Nichols.
Fax no: 01360 870444
D: £18.50-£18.50
S: £23.50-£28.50.
Open: All Year (not Xmas)
Beds: 1F 1D
Baths: 2 En
🛌 🅿 (2) 🗏 🍴 🗡 🛁 🎨 🗒 🖂 🎇

🚐 sign means that, *given due notice,* owners will pick you up from the path and drop you off *within reason.*

Bridge of Orchy ⑪
A82
Km   5   10
Miles   5
Tyndrum ⑩
A85
A827
⑨ Crianlarich
⑧ Inverarnan
Rowardennan ⑦
A82
A81
© Crown Copyright
Balmaha ⑥
⑤ Milton of Buchanan
Drymen ③
Gartocharn ④
② Croftamie
A811
A809   A81
Milngavie ①

Balmaha 6

National Grid Ref: NS4290

|◖| ◖ Oak Tree, Clachan Inn

(On path 🚍) *Critreoch,*
Rowardennan Road, Balmaha,
Glasgow, G63 0AW.
Actual grid ref: NS403932
Family home quiet location beauti-
ful view over garden to Loch.
Grades: STB 3 Star
Tel: **01360 870309**
Mrs MacLuskie.
D: £20.00-£22.00 **S:** £25.00-£30.00.
Open: May to Sept
Beds: 1D 1T **Baths:** 1 En 1 Pr
🅿 (6) ⦵ ⛌ 🛏 📷 🖾 ▥ 🛆 ⧄

(On path 🚍) *Conic View Cottage,*
Balmaha, Glasgow, G63 0JQ.
Beautifully situated near Loch
Lomond and the West Highland
Way, surrounded by forest walks.
Tel: **01360 870297** Mrs Cronin.
D: £15.00-£20.00 **S:** £18.00-£20.00.
Open: Mar to Nov
Beds: 1D 1S
Baths: 1 Sh
🅿 (2) ⦵ ⛌ 🛏 📷 🖾 ▥ 🛆 ⧄

(1m 🚍) *Dunleen,* Balmaha,
Glasgow, G63 0JE.
Ranch-style house. Warm
welcome, lovely garden, trout , east
side of Loch Lomond. 'Which?'
recommended.
Grades: STB 4 Star
Tel: **01360 870274**
Mrs MacFadyen.
D: £19.00-£20.00 **S:** £25.00-£25.00.
Open: May to Oct
Beds: 1D 1T
Baths: 1 Sh
🛆 🅿 (4) ⦵ ⛌ 🛏 📷 🖾 ▥ 🛆 ⧄

Rowardennan 7

National Grid Ref: NS3598

(▲ On path) *Rowardennan Youth*
Hostel, Rowardennan, Loch
Lomond, Glasgow, G63 0AR.
Actual grid ref: NS359992
Tel: **01360 870259**
Under 18: £6.00 **Adults:** £9.00
Self-catering facilities, Shop,
Evening meal available, Facilities
for disabled people
Beautiful setting, right on the
banks of Loch Lomond. Relax on
the beach, go fishing, walk the
West Highland Way or take a boat
trip round the islands. National
Nature Reserve and Queen
Elizabeth Forest Park nearby.

Planning a longer

stay? Always ask for

any special rates.

Order your
packed lunches the
evening before you
need them.
Not at breakfast!

(On path 🚍) *Anchorage Cottage,*
Rowardennan, Drymen, Glasgow,
G63 0AW.
Tel: **01360 870394** (also fax no)
D: £26.00-£30.00
S: £36.00-£40.00.
Open: Easter to Oct
Beds: 2T 1D
Baths: 2 En 1 Pr
🅿 (6) ⦵ ⛌ 🛏 📷 🖾 ▥ 🛆 ⧄
Welcome to our family home on
the eastern shore of Loch Lomond.
Our accommodation is of the
highest standards. The house
commands unique magnificent
views over the loch and islands to
Luss on the western shore. Situated
on the West Highland Way.

Inverarnan 8

National Grid Ref: NN3118

|◖| ◖ Stagger Inn, Drovers Inn

(On path 🚍) *Rose Cottage,*
Inverarnan, Glen Falloch,
Arrochar, Dunbartonshire, G83 7DX.
Actual grid ref: NN317185
Renovated C18th cottage on West
Highland Way near Loch Lomond.
Tel: **01301 704255**
Mr and Mrs Fletcher.
D: £19.00-£23.00 .
Open: All Year (not Xmas)
Beds: 1F 2T
Baths: 1 En 1 Sh
🛆 🅿 (2) ⦵ ⛌ 🛏 📷 🖾 ▥ 🛆 ⧄

Crianlarich 9

National Grid Ref: NN3825

|◖| ◖ Ben More, Rod & Reel

(▲ On path) *Crianlarich Youth*
Hostel, Station Road, Crianlarich,
Perthshire, FK20 8QN.
Actual grid ref: NN386250
Tel: **01838 300260**
Under 18: £6.01
Adults: £9.25
Self-catering facilities, Shop,
Laundry facilities, Facilities for
disabled people
Crianlarich marks the halfway
point of the West Highland Way;
ideal stop for walkers and
climbers. Trout fishing nearby. (No
family rooms Jun-Aug.)

(0.25m 🚍) *Ben More Lodge*
Hotel, Crianlarich, Perthshire,
FK20 8QS.
Actual grid ref: NN391252
Family-run lodge hotel with spec-
tacular setting beneath Ben More.
Tel: **01838 300210** Mr Goodale.
Fax no: 01838 300218
D: £25.00-£25.00 **S:** £28.00-£28.00.
Open: All Year
Beds: 2F 8D 1T **Baths:** 11 En
🛆 🅿 ⛛ 🛏 ⛌ 📷 🖾 🛆 ▥ 🛆 ⧄

(0.25m 🚍) *Craigbank Guest*
House, Crianlarich, Perthshire,
FK20 8QS.
Situated one hour's drive from Glen
Coe, Loch Lomond, the Trossachs.
Tel: **01838 300279** Mr Flockhart.
D: £17.00-£19.00 **S:** £25.00-£25.00.
Open: All Year (not Xmas)
Beds: 2F 1D 3T
Baths: 2 En 2 Sh
🛆 🅿 (6) ⦵ ⛌ 🛏 📷 🖾 ▥ 🛆 ⧄

(0.25m 🚍) *The Lodge House,*
Crianlarich, Perthshire, FK20 8RU.
Superbly located guest house, mag-
nificent views of Crianlarich hills.
Grades: STB 4 Star,
AA 4 Diamond
Tel: **01838 300276** Mr Gaughan.
D: £25.00-£30.00 **S:** £35.00-£45.00.
Open: All Year
Beds: 1F 3D 2T
Baths: 6 En
🛆 🅿 (10) ⛌ 🛏 ⛌ 📷 🖾 ▥ 🛆

(0.25m 🚍) *Tigh-na Struith,*
Crianlarich, Perthshire, FK20 8RU.
90-year-old guest house surround-
ed by hills nestling by the river.
Tel: **01838 300235**
Mr & Mrs Chisholm.
Fax no: 01838 300268
D: £16.00-£22.00 **S:** £20.00-£30.00.
Open: Mar to Nov
Beds: 2F 3D 1T
Baths: 1 En 2 Sh
🛆 🅿 (6) ⦵ ⛌ 🛏 📷 🖾 ▥ 🛆 ⧄

Tyndrum 10

National Grid Ref: NN3330

(On path 🚍) *Glengarry Guest*
House, Tyndrum, Crianlarich,
Perthshire, FK20 8RY.
Actual grid ref: NN338290
Ideal base for touring and outdoor
activities. Scottish welcome awaits.
Grades: STB 2 Star
Tel: **01838 400224**
Mr & Mrs Mailer.
D: £18.00-£22.00 **S:** £25.00-£25.00.
Open: All Year
Beds: 1F 1T 1D
Baths: 2 En 1 Pr
🛆 (2) 🅿 (4) ⦵ 🛏 ⛌ 📷 🖾 ▥ 🛆 ⧄

S = Price range for a single

person in a single room

Bridge of Orchy 11

National Grid Ref: NN2939

🏨 ⛺ Bridge Of Orchy Hotel

(4m 🚐) *Glen Orchy Farm, Glen Orchy, Bridge of Orchy, Argyll, PA33 1BD.*
Actual grid ref: NN261347
Remote sheep farm. Enjoy wildlife, birdwatching, walking, climbing amongst beautiful scenery.
Tel: **01838 200221**
Mrs MacLennan.
Fax no: 01838 200231
D: £16.00-£18.00 **S:** £16.00-£18.00.
Open: Mar to Nov
Beds: 2F
Baths: 1 Sh
🛇 🅿 🖵 🗙 🏋 🛏 📺 ⓥ 🌡 ✦

**All paths are popular:
you are well-advised to
book ahead**

**Pay B&Bs by cash or
cheque and be prepared
to pay up front.**

Kinlochleven 12

National Grid Ref: NN1861

🏨 ⛺ Tailrace Inn, Macdonald Hotel, Osprey Hotel

(🔺 0.25m) *West Highland Lodge Hostel, Kinlochleven, Argyll, PA40 4RT.*
Actual grid ref: NN186617
Tel: **01855 831471**
Under 18: £6.00 **Adults:** £6.00
Self-catering facilities, Television, Showers, Wet weather shelter, Lounge, Dining room, Grounds available for games, Drying room, Cycle store, Parking
Great for Glencoe, Ben Nevis and Mamores. Modern chalet also available.

(🔺 0.25m) *Blackwater Hostel and Campsite, Lab Road, Kinlochleven, Argyll, PA40.*
Tel: **01855 831253**
Under 18: £10.00 **Adults:** £10.00
Self-catering facilities, Television, Showers, Central heating, Laundry facilities, Wet weather shelter, Lounge, Dining room, Grounds available for games, Cycle store, Parking, Facilities for disabled people
Rooms of 2, 3, 4, 8 beds all room en suite, with TVs. Breakfast and packed lunches available on request. In the centre of scenic village, amenities: supermarket, post office, shops and pubs. Regular bus service to Fort William. Activities: walking, climbing, skiing, fishing, pony trekking, most water sports available nearby.

(On path 🚐) *Macdonald Hotel and Camp Site, Fort William Road, Kinlochleven, Argyll, PH50 4QL.*
Actual grid ref: NN183623
Grades: STB 3 Star
Tel: **01855 831539**
Mr & Mrs Reece.
Fax no: 01855 831416
D: £24.00-£32.00 **S:** £24.00-£44.00.
Open: Mar to Dec
Beds: 1F 4D 5T
Baths: 10 En
🛇 🅿 (20) 🖵 🏋 🗙 🛏 📺 ⓥ 🌡 ✦
A modern hotel in Highland-style on the shore of Loch Leven. Superb views of the loch and surrounding mountains. Only 25 metres from West Highland Way. The walkers' bar provides an informal atmosphere and a wide selection of bar meals.

(0.25m 🚐) *Edencoille, Garbhien Rd, Kinlochleven, Argyll, PA40 4SE.*
Friendly, comfortable B&B. Home cooking our speciality. Family run.
Grades: STB 3 Star
Tel: **01855 831358** (also fax no)
Mrs Robertson.
D: £18.00-£22.00 **S:** £26.00-£34.00.
Open: All Year
Beds: 2F 1D 2T **Baths:** 2 Sh 2 En
🛇 🅿 (5) 🖵 🗙 🛏 📺 ⓥ 🌡 ✦

(On path) *Hermon, Kinlochleven, Argyll, PH50 4RA.*
Spacious bungalow in village surrounded by hills on West Highland Way. Tel: **01855 831383**
Miss MacAngus.
D: £16.00-£18.00 **S:** £18.00-£25.00.
Open: Easter to Sep
Beds: 1D 2T **Baths:** 1 En 1 Sh
🛇 🅿 (6) 🖵 🏋 🛏 📺 ⓥ 🌡 ✦

**Please take muddy
boots <u>off</u> before
entering premises**

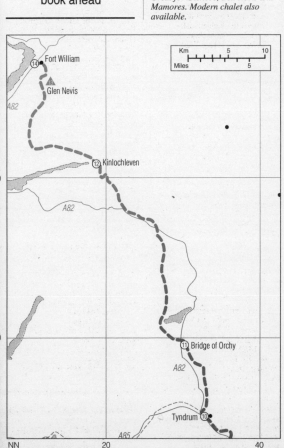

S = Price range for a single person in a single room

(0.25m 🚌) *Gharaidh Mhor,*
15 Locheilde Road, Kinlochleven,
Argyll, PA40 4RH.
Small, family-run B&B, warm
welcome, hearty breakfast.
Tel: **01855 831521**
Mrs Fyfe.
D: £16.00-£16.00 **S:** £21.00-£21.00.
Open: Easter to Oct
Beds: 2T
Baths: 1 Sh
🛇 🌂 🗢 🛏 🖢 🖳 V 🗗 ⌁

Glen Nevis   13

National Grid Ref: NN1272

(▲ 0.25m) *Glen Nevis Youth*
Hostel, Glen Nevis, Fort William,
Inverness-shire, PH33 6ST.
Actual grid ref: NN127716
Tel: **01397 702336**
Under 18: £6.00 **Adults:** £9.00
Self-catering facilities, Shop,
Laundry facilities, Facilities for
disabled people
Large weather-boarded hostel
right at the foot of Ben Nevis.
Summer boat trips from Fort
William. Highland games in
August.

Fort William   14

National Grid Ref: NN1073

🍴 🍺 Moorings Hotel, Lochy Bar, Nevis Bank
Hotel, Glen Nevis Rest, Cafe Beag, Pat's Bar,
Grogg & Gruel, Ben Nevis Rest, West End

(On path) *Glenlochy Guest House,*
Nevis Bridge, Fort William,
Inverness-shire, PH33 6PF.
Grades: STB 3 Star,
AA 3 Diamond
Tel: **01397 702909** Mrs MacBeth.
D: £17.00-£17.00 .
Open: All Year
Beds: 1F 4D 5T **Baths:** 8 En 1 Sh
🛇 🅿 (14) 🗢 🛏 🖳 V 🗗 ⌁
Situated 0.5 mile north of Fort
William town centre, close to Ben
Nevis. The famous West Highland
walk ends at our guest house
grounds. 8 of 10 bedrooms are
ensuite. Large private car park.

All rooms full and
nowhere else to stay?
Ask the owner if
there's anywhere
nearby

(1m) *Alltonside, Achintore Road,*
Fort William, Inverness-shire,
PH33 6RW.
Grades: STB 3 Star
Tel: **01397 703542** (also fax no)
Mrs Allton.
D: £16.00-£16.00 **S:** £20.00-£20.00.
Open: All Year
Beds: 1F 3D 2T **Baths:** 6 Pr
🛇 🅿 (8) 🗢 🛏 🖢 🖳 V
Alltonside guest house commands
magnificent views over Loch
Linnhe to the hills beyond. Being
close to the town of Fort William
and Ben Nevis makes it an ideal
base for sightseeing and visiting
the many beautiful places in the
Highlands.

(1m) *Glen Shiel Guest House,*
Achintore Road, Fort William,
Inverness-shire, PH33 6RW.
Lochside location, panoramic
views. Large car park. Tea makers,
colour TV in all rooms.
Grades: STB 2 Star
Tel: **01397 702271**
D: £17.00-£20.00 .
Open: Easter to Oct
Beds: 1F 3D 1T
Baths: 3 En 1 Pr 1 Sh
🛇 (8) 🅿 (7) 🌂 🗢 🛏 🖢 🖳 ⌁

(0.25m) *Ossian's Hotel, High*
Street, Fort William, Inverness-
shire, PH33 6DH.
Tel: **01397 700857** Wallace.
Fax no: 01397 701030
D: £16.00-£25.00 **S:** £18.00-£32.00.
Open: All Year
Beds: 10F 10D 10T 5S
Baths: 32 En 3 Sh
🛇 🅿 🗢 🛏 🗙 🖢 🖳 V 🗗 ⌁
Accommodation, food and drink
for the budget traveller. Ideal town
centre location. Couple of minutes
wall from railway or bus. Warm,
friendly and relaxed atmosphere.

(On path) *Distillery House, Nevis*
Bridge, North Road, Fort William,
Inverness-shire, PH33 6LR.
Well-run guest house, ideally situ-
ated at end of Glen Nevis and West
Highland Way.
Grades: STB 4 Star, AA 4
Diamond, RAC 4 Diamond,
Sparkling
Tel: **01397 700103** Mr
MacPherson.
Fax no: 01397 702980
D: £20.00-£36.00 **S:** £22.00-£38.00.
Open: All Year
Beds: 1F 3D 2T 1S **Baths:** 7 En
🛇 🅿 (12) 🌂 🗢 🛏 🖢 🖳 V 🗗 ⌁

(1m) *Melantee, Achintore Rd, Fort*
William, Inverness-shire, PH33 6RW.
Comfortable bungalow overlooking
Loch Linnhe and the Ardgour hills.
Grades: STB 2 Star
Tel: **01397 705329** Mrs Cook.
Fax no: 01397 700453
D: £15.50-£16.00 **S:** £15.50-£16.00.
Open: All Year (not Xmas)
Beds: 1F 1D 1T 1S **Baths:** 2 Sh
🛇 (5) 🅿 (6) 🗢 🛏 🖳 V

(1m) *11 Castle Drive, Lochyside,*
Fort William, PH33 7NR.
Grades: STB 3 Star
Tel: **01397 702659** Mrs Grant.
D: £16.00-£18.00 **S:** £20.00-£24.00.
Open: All Year
Beds: 1T 1D
Baths: 1 Sh
🛇 🅿 (2) 🗢 🛏 🗙 🖢 🖳 V 🗗 ⌁
Quiet residential area near castle.
Views to Ben Nevis. Ideal base for
walking, climbing, skiing. Intimate
family home with cosy log fire in
lounge where you can be assured of
a warm and friendly welcome.
Breakfast is the best in the west.

(1m 🚌) *Ferndale, Tomacharrich,*
Torlundy, Fort William, PH33 6SP.
Grades: STB 3 Star
Tel: **01397 703593** Mrs Riley.
D: £15.00-£20.00 .
Open: All Year
Beds: 1F 2D **Baths:** 2 En 1 Pr
🛇 🅿 (6) 🌂 🗢 🛏 🖢 🖳 V ⌁
Large bungalow in beautiful coun-
try setting, with wonderful views of
Ben Nevis and Nevis Range Ski
Slope. Ideal base for walking,
cycling, skiing and touring. Pony
trekking, trout fishing and golfing
all nearby. Breakfast served in con-
servatory. Nearest B&B to skiing.

(1m) *Stronchreggan View Guest*
House, Achintore Road, Fort
William, Inverness-shire, PH33 6RW.
Our house overlooks Loch Linnhe
with views to Ardgour Hills.
Grades: STB 3 Star GH
Tel: **01397 704644** (also fax no)
D: £19.00-£24.00 .
Open: Easter to Oct
Beds: 5D 2T **Baths:** 5 En 2 Pr
🛇 (8) 🅿 (7) 🌂 🗢 🗙 🖢 🖳 V ⌁

(On path 🚌) *Abrach, 4 Caithness*
Place, Fort William, Inverness-
shire, PH33 6JP.
Actual grid ref: NN088733
Modern house in elevated position
overlooking Loch Linnhe.
Grades: STB 3 Star
Tel: **01397 702535**
Mr & Mrs Moore.
Fax no: 01397 705629
D: £17.50-£23.00 **S:** £20.00-£30.00.
Open: All Year (not Xmas)
Beds: 1F 1D 1T 1S
Baths: 2 En 1 Pr 1 Sh
🛇 🅿 (6) 🌂 🗢 🛏 🖢 🖳 🗗 ⌁

(0.25m) *Rhu Mhor Guest House,*
Alma Road, Fort William,
Inverness-shire, PH33 6BP.
Actual grid ref: NN106739
Old fashioned in acre of wild and
enchanting garden.
Grades: STB 2 Star
Tel: **01397 702213**
Mr MacPherson.
D: £16.00-£24.00 **S:** £17.00-£44.00.
Open: Easter to Oct
Beds: 1F 3D 1T 2S
Baths: 2 Sh 4 En
🛇 (1) 🅿 (7) 🗢 🛏 🗙 🖢 🖳 V

(1m) *Innseagan House Hotel,*
Highland Holidays Scotland Ltd,
Achintore Road, Fort William,
Inverness-shire, PH33 6RW.
In its own grounds overlooking
Loch Linnhe only 1.5 miles from
Fort William.
Grades: STB 3 Star Hotel
Tel: 01397 702452 Mr Maclean.
Fax no: 01397 702606
D: £22.50-£22.50 **S:** £30.00-£30.00.
Open: Easter to Oct
Beds: 14D 8T 2S
Baths: 23 En 1 Pr
🅿🗂✖🛁🖾.Ⅴ🛉

(1m) *Stobahn, Fassifern Road,*
Fort William, Inverness-shire,
PH33 6BD.
Guest rooms overlooking Loch
Linnhe. Just off High Street.
Grades: STB 2 Star
Tel: 01397 702790 (also fax no)
D: £15.00-£20.00 **S:** £18.00-£23.00.
Open: All Year
Beds: 1F 1T 2D **Baths:** 2 En 2 Sh
🕭🅿🗂🏷✖🛁.🖾.🕭Ⅴ🛉✦

(0.25m 🚌) *Voringfoss, 5 Stirling*
Place, Fort William, Inverness-
shire, PH33 6UW.
Actual grid ref: NN099728
Experience the best of the highland
hospitality in a quiet situation.
Grades: STB 4 Star
Tel: 01397 704062
Mr & Mrs Fraser.
D: £20.00-£26.00 **S:** £20.00-£26.00.
Open: All Year
Beds: 2D 1T
Baths: 3 En
🅿 (4) 🗂🛁🖾.Ⅴ✦

(0.25m) *Lochview Guest House,*
Heathercroft, Argyll Terrace, Fort
William, Inverness-shire, PH33 6RE.
Actual grid ref: NN101734
Quiet location on hillside above
town, with superb views.
Tel: 01397 703149 (also fax no)
Mrs Kirk.
D: £22.00-£27.00 **S:** £26.00-£32.00.
Open: May to Sep
Beds: 5D 2T 1S **Baths:** 5 En
🅿 (8) ⅓🗂🛁.🖾.Ⅴ✦

(0.25m 🚌) *Balcarres, Seafield*
Gardens, Fort William, Inverness-
shire, PH33 6RJ.
Beautiful villa in quiet location
panoramic views town centre 1
mile.
Tel: 01397 702377 Mrs Cameron.
Fax no: 01397 702232
D: £18.00-£25.00 **S:** £25.00-£25.00.
Open: All Year
Beds: 1F 1D 1T
Baths: 3 En
🕭🅿 (5) ⅓🗂🛁.🖾.Ⅴ🛉✦

(0.25m) *Dorlin, Cameron Road,*
Fort William, Inverness-shire,
PH33 6LJ.
Modern bungalow, situated 200
yards from town centre, near pubs
and restaurants.
Tel: 01397 702016
Mrs Macdonald.
D: £18.00-£20.00 **S:** £20.00-£25.00.
Open: All Year (not Xmas)
Beds: 2D
Baths: 2 En
🅿 (2) ⅓🗂🏷🛁.🖾.Ⅴ

Cambrian Way

Tony Drake, author of the only in-print guide to the **Cambrian Way**, calls this path the 'mountain connoisseur's walk'. How right he is. Three-fifths of this route runs above 800 feet, over the greatest mountains these islands offer outside Scotland. For the Cambrian Way is quite deliberately a 'designed' path. Devised 27 years ago by Tony Drake himself, its very raison d'être is the magnificent scenery it traverses. Mr Drake and the **Ramblers Association** originally had official recognition in mind, but sadly, opposition was successful and the **Cambrian Way** never got the go-ahead as a National Trail.

Clearly that first idea was too good to be killed off. By a combination of strong wills and growing demand, the path has slowly taken a correct and proper shape despite the setbacks. And what better way is there to meet the major challenges of walking in Wales? This is God-given walking country - dramatic, remote and testing. This path is certainly for experienced or at least supervised walkers, preferably those with some knowledge of rock-scrambling and adverse conditions. Although only 24 miles longer than the Pennine Way, the ascent involved is almost double.

Impeccable map-reading skills are essential. Bad weather brings obvious dangers: wind and rain at high altitudes require the proper outdoor clothing and nothing less. Accommodation can be sparse; there is none in the central Rhinogs at all. Like the Southern Upland Way, this is a tough one - with limited access to public transport. But with good planning the route can certainly be done without camping gear - ask yourself, is the extra freedom of a tent worth the extra weight, given the great distance and ascent?

That said, the walking is memorable, the views unbeatable and the peace and quiet defy superlatives. In mid-Wales you may go for a day without meeting a soul. The 274 miles are split into three natural sections - from Cardiff, skirting the edge of the South Wales Valleys, then a splendid circuit of the Black Mountains before crossing the bleak Brecon Beacons to Llandovery; then along the Cambrian Mountains, with their rare red kites, eventually curving round through Dinas Mawddwy to the stunning Cadair Idris. The path then crosses the Mawddach to Barmouth on the coast before heading over the Rhinogs (the roughest but most magnificent part of the whole walk) for the final and superb Snowdon range. This is definitely one worth travelling a long way for, as testified by the increasing number of European visitors walking all or part of this route each year.

There is a solution for those of us (perhaps the majority) who love the idea of the Cambrian Way but are wise enough to know our limitations. The **Cambrian Way Walkers Association** is a consortium of accommodation providers offering a service to those wishing to complete the walk in set stages. They have split the walk into five sections, with each section having an organiser. The organisers provide laminated marked maps, stage notes, handbook and compass. Three sections (Cardiff to Strata Florida) even have mobile phones and a GBS satellite system to help walkers. Each day the organisers arrange transport, taking you out to the path and picking you up at the end of the day. For further details contact Nick Bointon, **Cambrian Way Walkers Association**, Llandovery, SA20 0NB. Tel: 01550 750274.
Guides: *Cambrian Way*, written and published by A.J. Drake (ISBN 0-9509580-3-4), available from all good map shops or by post from the Rambler's Association, 1-5 Wandsworth Road, London, SW8 2XX (tel: 020 7339 8500) for £4.50 + 70p p&p
Maps: 1:50000 Ordnance Survey Landranger Series: 115, 124, 135, 147, 160, 161 and 171

Cardiff   1

National Grid Ref: ST1677

⊮ ⏪ Beverley, Clifton Hotel, Halfway Hotel, Hayes Court, Poachers' Lodge, Robin Hood

(▲ 1m) *Cardiff Youth Hostel, Ty Croeso, 2 Wedal Road, Roath Park, Cardiff, CF2 5PG.*
Actual grid ref: ST185788
Tel: **029 2046 2303**
Under 18: £10.20
Adults: £13.50
Self-catering facilities, Television, Showers, Shop, Laundry facilities, Lounge 2, Cycle store, Parking, Kitchen facilities, Breakfast available, Luggage store, Credit cards accepted
Conveniently located hostel near the city centre and Roath Park Lake, with cycling & sailing facilities.

D = Price range per person sharing in a double room

🚐 sign means that, *given due notice*, owners will pick you up from the path and drop you off *within reason*.

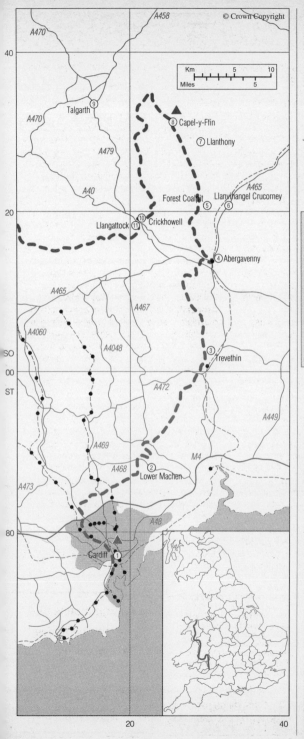

© Crown Copyright

(▲ 0.25m) *Cardiff Backpacker
Caerdydd, 98 Neville Street,
Riverside, Cardiff, CF11 6LS.*
Actual grid ref: ST176763
Tel: 029 2034 5577 Adults: £13.50
Self-catering facilities, Television,
Showers, Licensed bar, Central
heating, Shop, Laundry facilities,
Lounge, Dining room, Games
room, Security lockers, Cycle store,
Parking, No smoking
*Cardiff's only central tourist hostel,
located within five minutes walk
from train/bus stations and all civic
amenities. Relax and socialise in a
lively Welsh atmosphere with
travellers from all over the world
or explore the nearby Brecon
Beacons National Park and
breathtaking castles, museums and
coastline. WTB 4 Star Hostel.*

(0.25m) ***Rambler Court Hotel,*** 188
*Cathedral Road, Pontcanna,
Cardiff, S Glam,* CF11 9JE.
Grades: WTB 2 Star
Tel: **029 2022 1187** (also fax no)
Mrs Cronin.
D: £17.00-£20.00 **S:** £17.00-£25.00.
Open: All Year
Beds: 3F 3D 1T 3S **Baths:** 4 En 5 Sh
🛇 **P** (4) 🖵 🛏 🎹 Ⅴ ⚡
Friendly family-run hotel, ideally
situated in a tree-lined conservation
area, close to all of the city's main
attractions, 10 minutes' walk to the
city centre and Millennium Stadium.
Good local restaurants & pubs.

(0.25m) ***Preste Gaarden Hotel,***
*181 Cathedral Road, Pontcanna,
Cardiff, S Glam,* CF11 9PN.
Highly recommended, modernised
ex-Norwegian consulate offering
olde-worlde charm.
Grades: WTB 2 Star Hotel
Tel: **029 2022 8607** Mrs Nicholls.
Fax no: 029 2037 4805
D: £18.00-£22.00 **S:** £22.00-£27.00.
Open: All Year (not Xmas)
Beds: 1F 2D 3T 4S **Baths:** 7 En 3 Pr
🛇 **P** (3) 🖵 🛏 🎹 Ⅴ

(0.5m) ***Austins,*** *11 Coldstream
Terrace, City Centre, Cardiff,* CF11 6LJ.
In the centre of the city 300 yards
from Cardiff Castle.
Grades: WTB 2 Star
Tel: **029 2037 7148** Mr Hopkins.
Fax no: 029 2037 7158
D: £17.50-£19.50 **S:** £20.00-£27.50.
Open: All Year
Beds: 1F 5T 5S **Baths:** 4 En 2 Sh
🛇 🖵 🛏 🎹 Ⅴ

(0.25m) ***Annedd Lon Guest House,***
*157-159 Cathedral Road, Cardiff,
S Glam,* CF1 9PL.
Centrally located guest house in
elegant conservation area. Non
smoking throughout.
Grades: AA 4 Diamond
Tel: **029 2022 3349** Mrs Tucker.
Fax no: 029 2064 0885
D: £20.00-£22.50 **S:** £18.00-£30.00.
Open: All Year (not Xmas/New Year)
Beds: 2F 1D 2T 1S **Baths:** 2 En 2 Sh
🛇 **P** (7) ⚡ 🖵 🛏 🎹 Ⅴ

(0.5m) *Georgian Hotel, 179 Cathedral Road, Pontcanna, Cardiff, S Glam, CF1 9PL.*
All rooms tastefully restored to today's standards, each having a colour television.
Tel: **029 2023 2594**
Mr Menin.
D: £20.00-£27.50 S: £27.50-£35.00.
Open: All Year (not Xmas)
Beds: 1F 2D 3T 2S
Baths: 8 En
⛺🅿🛋🖭🖭ⓥ

Lower Machen 2

National Grid Ref: ST2287

🍴 🍺 Hollybush Inn

(1.5m 🚌) *The Forge, Lower Machen, Newport, NP1 8UU.*
Warm welcome, ideal for walking in forests or on mountains.
Grades: WTB listed comm
Tel: **01633 440226**
Mrs Jones.
D: £16.50-£18.00
S: £18.00-£20.00.
Open: All Year (not Xmas/ New Year)
Beds: 1F 1D 1T
Baths: 1 Sh
⛺🅿(3)🛋🛏🖭🖭ⓥ🔒

Trevethin 3

National Grid Ref: SO2801

🍴 🍺 The Horseshoe

(On path 🚌) *Ty'r Ywen Farm, Lasgarn Lane, Trevethin, Pontypool, Monmouthshire, NP4 8TT.*
Actual grid ref: SO296047
Remote C16th farmhouse in National Park. Magnificent views. Four poster beds.
Tel: **01495 785200** (also fax no)
Mrs Armitage.
D: £20.00-£28.00 S: £20.00-£56.00.
Open: All Year (not Xmas)
Beds: 3D 1T
Baths: 4 En
⛺(14)🅿(10)✏🛋🛏🗙🖭🖭ⓥ🔒

Abergavenny 4

National Grid Ref: SO2914

🍴 🍺 King's Arms, Crown Inn, Old Mitre, Lamb & Flag, Walnut Tree, Bear Hotel, Nant-y-fyn, Red Hart

(▲ 1m) *Ty'r Morwydd House, Pen-y-Pound, Abergavenny, Monmouthshire, NP7 5UD.*
Actual grid ref: SO297147
Tel: **01873 855959**
Under 18: £16.50
Adults: £16.50
Showers, Showers, Central heating, Lounge, Dining room, Games room, Drying room, Parking, Evening meal at 6pm, No smoking
Quality group accommodation, conferences, training etc. Advance bookings only.

(0.5m 🚌) *Pentre Court, Brecon Road, Abergavenny, NP7 9ND.*
Grades: WTB 2 Stars
Tel: **01873 853545** Mrs Candler.
D: £18.00-£24.00 S: £18.00-£30.00.
Open: All Year
Beds: 3D **Baths:** 3 En
⛺🅿🛋🛏🗙🖭🖭ⓥ
Spacious, welcoming Georgian house with open fires, set in 3 acres of pretty stream side interestingly stocked gardens/paddock, spring bulbs, shrubs and roses, with wonderful views over the Usk valley. Just inside the National Park beside footpath to River Usk and Sugarloaf Mountain.

(3m 🚌) *Tyn-y-bryn, Deriside, Abergavenny, Monmouthshire, NP7 7HT.*
Actual grid ref: SO301165
Magnificent views, a homely atmosphere. Comfortable accommodation & warm welcome.
Grades: WTB 3 Star Farm
Tel: **01873 856682** (also fax no)
Ms Belcham.
D: £20.00 S: £25.00. **Open:** All Year
Beds: 1F 1T 1D **Baths:** 2 En
🅿(6)🛋🛏🗙🖭🖭ⓥ🔒

(On path 🚌) *Pentre House, Brecon Road, Abergavenny, Monmouthshire, NP7 7EW.*
Actual grid ref: SO283151
Charming small Georgian award-winning country house in wonderful gardens.
Grades: WTB 3 Star
Tel: **01873 853435**
Mrs Reardon-Smith.
Fax no: 01873 852321
D: £17.00-£18.00 S: £20.00-£25.00.
Open: All Year (not Xmas)
Beds: 1F 1D 1T **Baths:** 2 Sh
⛺🅿(6)🛏🗙🖭🖭ⓥ🔒

(4m) *Ty`r Morwydd House, Pen-y-Pound, Abergavenny, Monmouthshire, NP7 5UD.*
Actual grid ref: SO297147
Quality group accommodation, conferences, training etc. Advance bookings only.
Grades: WTB 3 Star
Tel: **01873 855959** Mrs Senior.
Fax no: 01873 855443
D: £16.50-£16.50 S: £16.50-£16.50.
Open: All Year (not Xmas/ New Year)
Beds: 2F 18T 29S
⛺🅿(25)✏🛋🛏🗙🖭🖭ⓥ🔒

(1m) *The Guest House & Mansel Restaurant, 2 Oxford Street, Abergavenny, Monmouthshire, NP7 5RP.*
Actual grid ref: SO303147
Near bus, railway station, town; excellent accommodation, choice of breakfast.
Tel: **01873 854823** Mrs Cook.
D: £16.00-£19.00 S: £19.50-£27.00.
Open: Mar to Dec
Beds: 3F 6D 6T 2S **Baths:** 3 Sh
⛺(6)🅿(10)🛋🗙🖭🖭ⓥ🔒

(1m) *Maes Glas, Monmouth Road, Abergavenny, NP7 9SP.*
Maes Glas is a detached bungalow, within easy walking distance of town centre.
Tel: **01873 854494** (also fax no)
Mrs Haynes.
D: £17.50-£20.00 S: £17.50-£20.00.
Open: All Year **Beds:** 1F 1D
⛺🅿✏🛋🗙🛏🖭ⓥ🔒

Forest Coalpit 5

National Grid Ref: SO2821

🍴 🍺 Old Crown

(On path 🚌) *New Inn Farm, Forest Coalpit, Abergavenny, Monmouthshire, NP7 7LT.*
Actual grid ref: SO287216
Peaceful, welcoming mountain farmhouse. Superb views. Walking from the door.
Grades: WTB 3 Star
Tel: **01873 890466** (also fax no)
Bull.
D: £20.00-£20.00 S: £20.00-£20.00.
Open: All Year (not Xmas)
Beds: 1F 1D 1T
Baths: 1 En 2 Pr
⛺🅿(10)✏🛋🛏🗙🖭🖭ⓥ🔒

Llanvihangel Crucorney 6

National Grid Ref: SO3220

🍴 🍺 Crown Inn, Skirrid Inn

(3m 🚌) *Penyclawdd Farm, Llanvihangel Crucorney, Abergavenny, Monmouthshire, NP7 7LB.*
Actual grid ref: SO312200
Beef/sheep farm, very large garden. Easy reach Abergavenny, Hereford, Cardiff, Hay-on-Wye.
Grades: WTB 3 Star, AA 3 Diamond
Tel: **01873 890591** (also fax no)
Mrs Davies.
D: £20.00-£22.00 S: £20.00-£22.00.
Open: All Year
Beds: 2F
Baths: 1 Sh
⛺🅿✏🛋🗙🛏🖭🖭ⓥ🔒

(2m) *The Skirrid Mountain Inn, Llanvihangel Crucorney, Abergavenny, Monmouthshire, NP7 8DH.*
An historic country inn of unique character. Wales' oldest inn.
Tel: **01873 890258** Miss Grant.
D: £34.50-£39.50 S: £34.50-£39.50.
Open: All Year **Beds:** 2D
⛺🅿✏🛋🛏🗙🖭🖭ⓥ🔒

Planning a longer stay? Always ask for any special rates.

Llanthony 7

National Grid Ref: SO2827

(2m) *The Half Moon, Llanthony, Abergavenny, Monmouthshire, NP7 7NN.*
Actual grid ref: SO286278
C17th, beautiful countryside. Serves good food and real ales.
Tel: **01873 890611** Mrs Smith.
D: £20.00-£22.00 **S:** £22.00-£25.00.
Open: All Year (not Xmas)
Beds: 2F 4D 2T 1S **Baths:** 2 Sh
⌂ 🅿 (8) 🖵 🍽 ✕ 👤 🍺 🎱 ☑ ⓘ ✓

Capel-y-ffin 8

National Grid Ref: SO2531

(▲ 0.75m) *Capel-y-Ffin Youth Hostel, Capel-y-Ffin, Abergavenny, Monmouthshire, NP7 7NP.*
Actual grid ref: SO250328
Tel: **01873 890650**
Under 18: £5.75 **Adults:** £8.50
Self-catering facilities, Showers, Shop, Lounge, Drying room, Cycle store, Parking, Evening meal at 7.00pm, No smoking, Kitchen facilities, Breakfast available, Credit cards accepted,
Old hill farm set in 40-acre grounds on mountainside in Brecon Beacons National Park.

All rates are subject to alteration at the owners' discretion.

(0.75m 🚍) *The Grange, Capel-y-Ffin, Abergavenny, NP7 7NP.*
Actual grid ref: SO251315
Small Victorian guest house situated in the beautiful Black Mountains.
Grades: WTB 1 Star
Tel: **01873 890215** Mrs Griffiths.
Fax no: 01873 890157
D: £22.50-£23.00 **S:** £22.50-£23.00.
Open: Easter to Nov
Beds: 1F 1D 1T 1S **Baths:** 3 En
⌂ (6) 🅿 (10) 🖵 🍽 ✕ 👤 🍺 🎱 🎱 ☑ ⓘ ✓

Talgarth 9

National Grid Ref: SO1533

🍽 🍺 Mason's Arms, Castle Inn

(1.5m) *The Olde Masons Arms Hotel, Hay Road, Talgarth, Brecon, Powys, LD3 0BB.*
C16th hotel with country cottage ambience. Ideal for walking amidst Black Mountains & Brecon Beacons.
Grades: WTB 3 Star
Tel: **01874 711688** Evans.
D: £26.50-£29.50 **S:** £29.50-£32.50.
Open: All Year
Beds: 2F 2D 1T 2S
Baths: 7 En
⌂ 🅿 (10) 🖵 🍽 ✕ 👤 🍺 🎱 ☑ ⓘ ✓

(1.5m) *Castle Inn, Pengenfford, Talgarth, Brecon, Powys, LD3 0EP.*
Actual grid ref: SO174296
Traditional country inn with the Brecon Beacons national park.
Tel: **01874 711353** Mr Mountjoy.
D: £20.00-£23.00 **S:** £20.00-£31.00.
Open: All Year (not Xmas)
Beds: 1F 2D 1T 1S
Baths: 2 En 1 Sh
⌂ 🅿 (50) 🖵 ✕ 👤 🍺 ☑ ⓘ

Crickhowell 10

National Grid Ref: SO2118

🍽 🍺 Bear, Bell, Dragon's Head, Vinetree

(1.5m) *Castell Corryn, Llangenny, Crickhowell, Powys, NP8 1HE.*
Grades: WTB 3 Star
Tel: **01873 810327** (also fax no)
Mr Harris.
D: £20.00-£25.00 **S:** £25.00-£30.00.
Open: All Year (not Xmas/ New Year)
Beds: 2T 1D **Baths:** 2 En 1 Pr
⌂ (6) 🖵 👤 🍺 🎱 ☑ ⓘ ✓
Situated above the Usk Valley within the Brecon Beacons National Park. Outstanding views, beautiful restful gardens. Children welcome, special diets available. All rooms ensuite, colour TV, tea making facilities, hair dryer. Homely welcome.

(1.5m) *Glangrwyney Court, Crickhowell, Powys, NP8 1ES.*
Georgian mansion in 4 acres of established gardens surrounded by parkland.
Tel: **01873 811288** Jackson.
Fax no: 01873 810317
D: £22.50-£27.50 **S:** £30.00-£55.00.
Open: All Year
Beds: 1F 2T 2D **Baths:** 4 En 1 Pr
⌂ 🅿 (10) ✕ 🖵 🍽 ✕ 👤 🍺 🎱 ☑ ⓘ ✓

Planning a longer stay? Always ask for any special rates.

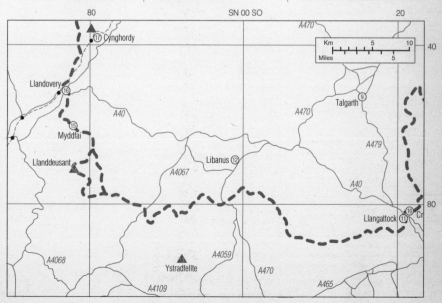

(1.5m) *White Hall,* Glangrwyney, *Crickhowell, Powys, NP8 1EW.*
Actual grid ref: SO240163
Comfortable Georgian house next to restaurant, close to Black Mountains. **Grades:** WTB 1 Star
Tel: **01873 811155** Ms Llewelyn.
Fax no: 01873 840178
D: £15.00-£20.00 **S:** £20.00-£25.00.
Open: All Year (not Xmas)
Beds: 1F 2D 1S **Baths:** 2 En 1 Sh
⌂ 🅿 (3) ⊬⛌🛏🔥🛁💷📺♦

(1.5m) *Bell Inn,* Glangrwyney, *Crickhowell, Powys, NP8 1EH.*
C17th former coaching inn. Excellent food and ensuite accommodation. **Grades:** WTB 2 Star Inn
Tel: **01873 810247** Mr Llewelyn.
Fax no: 01873 812155
D: £25.00-£35.00 **S:** £30.00-£30.00.
Open: All Year
Beds: 1F 2D 2T 1S **Baths:** 6 En
⌂ 🅿 (20) ⛌🔥🛁💷📺♦

Llangattock 11

National Grid Ref: SO2117

🍴 🍺 Vinetree, Bear, Dragon

(On path) *Ty Croeso Hotel,* Dardy, *Llangattock, Crickhowell, Powys, NP8 1PU.*
Welsh stone building situated on hillside in Brecon Beacons National Park.
Tel: **01873 810573** Mr Moore.
D: £27.50-£32.50 **S:** £35.00-£35.00.
Open: All Year
Beds: 4D 2T 2S **Baths:** 8 En
⌂ (1) 🅿 (20) ⛌🛏⛌🔥🛁💷📺♦

(On path) *The Old Six Bells,* *Llangattock, Crickhowell, NP8 1PH.*
Actual grid ref: SO210179
Grade II Listed house in small village, 10 minutes' walking distance from Crickhowell.
Tel: **01873 811965** (also fax no)
Richard & Jane Reardon Smith.
D: £19.00-£25.00 .
Open: All Year (not Xmas)
Beds: 1D 1T
⌂ (2) 🅿 (2) ⊬⛌🔥🛁💷📺♦

Libanus 12

National Grid Ref: SN9925

🍴 🍺 Tair Bull

(▲ 2m) *Llwyn-y-Celyn Youth Hostel,* *Libanus, Brecon, Powys, LD3 8NH.*
Actual grid ref: SN973225
Tel: **01874 624261**
Under 18: £6.50 **Adults:** £9.25
Self-catering facilities, Showers, Lounge, Dining room, Cycle store, Parking, Evening meal at 7.00pm, No smoking, WC, Kitchen facilities, Breakfast available, Credit cards accepted
Traditional old Welsh farmhouse with some unique wall paintings and a nature trail in its grounds, in a mountain location in the heart of the Brecon Beacons National Park, yet easily accessible.

(2.5m) *Tair Bull Inn,* Libanus, *Brecon, Powys, LD3 8EL.*
Small friendly inn 3 miles out of Brecon market town. Beautiful scenery and walks.
Tel: **01874 625849** Mrs Williams.
D: £21.00-£21.00 **S:** £25.00-£42.00.
Open: All Year
Beds: 1F 3D 1T **Baths:** 5 En
⌂ 🅿 (4) ⊬⛌🛏🔥🛁💷📺♦

Ystradfellte 13

National Grid Ref: SN9213

(▲ 4m) *Ystradfellte Youth Hostel,* *Tai'r Heol, Ystradfellte, Aberdare, Mid Glam, CF44 9JF.*
Actual grid ref: SN925127
Tel: **01639 720301**
Under 18: £5.75 **Adults:** £8.50
Self-catering facilities, Showers, Wet weather shelter, Lounge, Drying room, Parking, No smoking, Kitchen facilities
Charming mixture of three C17th cottages close to the Nedd and Mellte river systems in the Brecon Beacons National Park.

Llanddeusant 14

National Grid Ref: SN7724

(▲ On path) *Llanddeusant Youth Hostel,* The Old Red Lion, *Llanddeusant, Llangadog, Carmarthenshire, SA19 6UL.*
Actual grid ref: SN776245
Tel: **01550 740218**
Under 18: £5.75 **Adults:** £8.50
Self-catering facilities, Showers, Lounge, Drying room, Cycle store, Parking, No smoking, Kitchen facilities
A simple traditional hostel converted from an inn, overlooking Sawdde Valley. The area has Roman and Iron Age remains. There is an open fire in the hostel lounge.

Myddfai 15

National Grid Ref: SN7730

🍴 🍺 Plough Inn

(On path 🚲) *Erwlas,* Myddfai, *Llandovery, Carmarthenshire, SA20 0JB.*
Modern, comfortable bungalow, quiet location, magnificent countryside. Ideal walking area.
Tel: **01550 720797** Mrs Holloway.
D: £13.50-£13.50 **S:** £13.50-£13.50.
Open: All Year (not Xmas)
Beds: 1D 1T
Baths: 1 Sh
⌂ 🅿 (3) ⊬⛌🛏⛌🔥💷♦

D = Price range per person sharing in a double room

Llandovery 16

National Grid Ref: SN7634

🍴 🍺 King's Head, Castle, Drovers, Blue Bell, Lord Rhys

(0.5m) *Cwm Rhuddan Mansion,* *Llandovery, Carmarthenshire, SA20 0DX.*
Grades: WTB 4 Star
Tel: **01550 721414** Mrs Wheadon.
D: £25.00-£30.00 **S:** £30.00.
Open: All Year
Beds: 2F 1D
Baths: 3 En
⌂ 🅿 (10) ⛌🛏🔥🛁💷📺♦
A unique French chateau-style mansion with original features, antique furnishings. Landscaped gardens with panoramic view of Towey Valley and Black Mountains. Relax in the elegant period lounge and large character bedrooms with open fires, garaging for special vehicles plus new large recreational room.

(0.5m) *Llwyncelyn Guest House,* *Llandovery, Carmarthenshire, SA20 0EP.*
Actual grid ref: SN761347
Charming stone-built house. Edge of town. Railway station 5 mins.
Grades: WTB 2 Star, AA 3 Diamond
Tel: **01550 720566** Mr Griffiths.
D: £18.50-£18.50 **S:** £21.00-£25.00.
Open: All Year (not Xmas)
Beds: 2D 2T 1S
Baths: 2 Sh
🅿 (12) ⛌🔥🛁💷📺♦

(0.5m) *Pencerrig,* New Road, *Llandovery, SA20 0EA.*
Grades: WTB 2 Star
Tel: **01550 721259**
D: £19.00-£19.00 **S:** £19.00-£19.00.
Open: All Year
Beds: 1D 1T 1S
Baths: 2 En 1 Pr
🅿 (1) ⊬⛌🔥🛁💷📺♦
A Victorian house situated at the edge of town. Local shops, pubs, restaurants are 5 minutes walk away. Railway station nearby. The immediate area has plenty of walks to offer and birdwatching (the famous red kite).

Cynghordy 17

National Grid Ref: SN8040

(0.5m 🚲) *Llanerchindda Farm,* *Cynghordy, Llandovery, Carmarthenshire, SA20 0NB.*
Actual grid ref: SN808429
Very comfortable farmhouse; views high over Towy Valley & Brecons. Log fires, underfloor heating, library.
Tel: **01550 750274** Mr Bointon.
Fax no: 01550 750300
D: £24.00-£24.00 **S:** £24.00-£24.00.
Open: All Year (not Xmas)
Beds: 2F 4D 2T 1S **Baths:** 9 En
⌂ 🅿 (14) ⛌🛏⛌🔥🛁💷📺♿📺♦

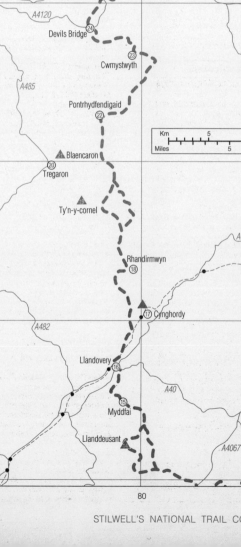

Rhandirmwyn 18

National Grid Ref: SN7843

(▲ On path) ***Bryn Poeth Uchaf Youth Hostel***, *Hafod-y-Pant, Rhandirmwyn, Cynghordy, Llandovery, Carmarthenshire, SA20 0NB.*
Actual grid ref: SN796439
Tel: **01550 750235**
Under 18: £4.65 **Adults:** £6.80
No smoking
Formerly an old farmhouse, this hostel is quite simple and isolated, but provides great views back to the Brecon Beacons.

(2.5m 🚍) ***Bwlch-Y-Ffin***, *Rhandirmwyn, Llandovery, Carmarthenshire, SA20 0PG.*
Actual grid ref: SN795481
Comfortable farmhouse with incredible views across a tranquil wooded valley.
Tel: **01550 760311** (also fax no)
Mr & Mrs Williams.
D: £16.50-£16.50 **S:** £16.50.
Open: All Year (not Xmas)
Beds: 1D 2T
Baths: 1 Sh
⛌ 🅿 ⚲ ⚡ ✕ ♨ 🔟 Ⓥ 🗎 ⚶

Ty'n-y-Cornel 19

National Grid Ref: SN7553

(▲ On path) ***Ty'n-y-Cornel Youth Hostel***, *Ty'n-y-Cornel, Llanddewi Brefi, Tregaron, Powys, SY25 6PH.*
Actual grid ref: SN751534
Tel: **029 2022 2122**
Under 18: £4.75 **Adults:** £6.75
Self-catering facilities, Showers, Wet weather shelter, Parking, No smoking, WC, Kitchen facilities
Very simple former farmhouse in a very isolated next-to-nature setting at head of Doethie Valley, lit solely by gas and with a log fire.

Tregaron 20

National Grid Ref: SN6759

🍴 🍺 Talbot Hotel

(4m) ***Lluest Guest House***, *Lampeter Road, Tregaron, Ceredigion, SY25 6HG.*
Actual grid ref: SN677597
Grades: WTB 3 Star
Tel: **01974 298936** (also fax no)
Mrs Bull.
D: £16.00-£19.50
S: £16.00-£19.50.
Open: All Year (not Xmas)
Beds: 2D 1T 1S
Baths: 1 En 1 Sh
⛌ 🅿 (5) ⚲ 🔟 ✕ ♨ 🔟 Ⓥ 🗎 ⚶
Large Victorian house, rambling gardens at the foot of The Cambrian Mountains. Good for birdwatching, walking, cycling and fishing. Within easy reach of coast, lakes and rivers. Off-street parking. Beautiful scenery abounds.

(4m 🚌) *Talbot Hotel*, *The Square, Tregaron, Ceredigion, SY25 6JL.*
Olde worlde comfortable family atmosphere, good food and real ales.
Grades: RAC 1 Star
Tel: **01974 298208** Mr Williams.
Fax no: 01974 299059
D: £21.00-£27.50 **S:** £25.00-£35.00.
Open: All Year (not Xmas)
Beds: 1F 3D 8T 1S
Baths: 10 En 5 Pr
🛏 🅿 (10) ⬜ 📺 🍴 ✕ 🔥 Ⅲ. Ⅴ ▪ ∥

(4m) *Fro Villa, Doldre, Tregaron, Ceredigion, SY25 6JZ.*
Actual grid ref: SN678596
Traditional stone cottage, only five minutes' walk from village centre.
Tel: **01974 298817** Mrs Whiting.
D: £14.00 **S:** £15.00.
Open: All Year (not Xmas)
Beds: 1D 1T
Baths: 1 Sh
🛏 🗲 ⬜ 📺 ✕ 🔥 Ⅲ. Ⅴ ▪ ∥

Blaencaron 21

National Grid Ref: SN7160

(▲ 2.5m) *Blaencaron Youth Hostel, Blaencaron, Tregaron, Cardiganshire, SY25 6HL.*
Actual grid ref: SN713608
Tel: **01974 298441**
Under 18: £4.75 **Adults:** £6.75
Self-catering facilities, Showers, Drying room, Cycle store, Parking, No smoking, WC, Kitchen facilities
Old village school set in the unspoilt Afon Groes Valley, west of the Cambrian Mountains.

Pontrhydfendigaid 22

National Grid Ref: SN7366

(0.25m 🚌) *Red Lion Hotel, Pontrhydfendigaid, Ystrad Meurig, Ceredigion, SY25 6BH.*
Actual grid ref: SN731666
Friendly riverside country pub/inn with caravan/camping facilities.
Tel: **01974 831232** Mr Earey.
D: £18.50 **S:** £18.50.
Open: All Year
Beds: 1F 1T 2D
Baths: 4 En
🛏 🅿 (50) 🗲 ⬜ 📺 🍴 ✕ 🔥 Ⅲ. Ⅴ ▪ ∥

Cwmystwyth 23

National Grid Ref: SN7874

🍴 🍺 Miners' Arms

(0.5m) *Tainewyddion Uchaf, Cwmystwyth, Aberystwyth, Ceredigion, SY23 4AF.*
Situated at over 1000 ft. Panoramic views overlooking the Ystwyth Valley.
Tel: **01974 282672** Mrs Liford.
D: £15.00-£18.00 **S:** £15.00-£18.00.
Open: Easter to End Oct
Beds: 1T 1D 1S
Baths: 1 En 1 Sh
🗲 ✕ 🔥 ▪ ∥

(On path 🚌) *Hafod Lodge, Cwmystwyth, Aberystwyth, Ceredigion, SY23 4AD.*
Actual grid ref: SN784742
Picturesque, peaceful location, ideal for touring river valleys, lakes, mountains and coast.
Tel: **01974 282247**
Mr & Mrs Davis.
D: £18.50-£24.00 **S:** £18.50-£24.00.
Open: All Year
Beds: 1D 1T **Baths:** 1 En 1 Pr
🅿 (6) 🗲 ⬜ 🍴 🔥 Ⅲ. Ⅴ ▪

Devil's Bridge 24

National Grid Ref: SN7376

🍴 🍺 Hafway Inn

(On path) *Mount Pleasant, Devil's Bridge, Aberystwyth, Ceredigion, SY23 4QY.*
Actual grid ref: SN736769
Lose the crowds amidst stunning scenery where red kites soar.
Tel: **01970 890219**
Mr & Mrs Connell.
Fax no: 01970 890239
D: £21.00-£23.00 **S:** £21.00-£29.00.
Open: All Year (not Xmas)
Beds: 2D 2T
Baths: 3 En 1 Pr
🛏 (12) 🅿 (4) 🗲 ⬜ 📺 ✕ 🔥 Ⅲ. Ⅴ ▪ ∥

Ponterwyd 25

National Grid Ref: SN7480

(▲ 0.5m) *Maesnant, Ponterwyd, Aberystwyth, Dyfed, SY23 3AG.*
Tel: **020 8421 4648**
Under 18: £5.00 **Adults:** £5.00
Self-catering facilities, Showers, Lounge, Dining room, Grounds available for games
Bungalow and outbuildings set in wild open country about 5 miles from village. Located on the slopes of Plynlimon mountain, overlooking Nant-y-Moch Reservoir. Ideal base for youth groups undertaking Duke of Edinburgh's and similar expedition training. Local attractions include Llywernog Mine Museum, Devil's Bridge and Vale of Rheidol Railway.

(On path 🚌) *The George Borrow Hotel, Ponterwyd, Aberystwyth, Ceredigion, SY23 3AD.*
Tel: **01970 890230** Mr & Mrs Wall.
Fax no: 01970 890587
D: £25.00 **S:** £25.00.
Open: All Year (not Xmas)
Beds: 2F 3D 2T 2S
Baths: 9 En
🛏 🅿 (40) ⬜ 🍴 ✕ 🔥 Ⅲ. Ⅴ ▪ ∥
Famous old hotel set in beautiful countryside, overlooking Eagle Falls and the Rheidol Gorge. 3 miles Devils Bridge, 12 miles Aberystwyth. An ideal centre to explore mid-Wales. Good fishing, birdwatching and walking. Home made food and fine beer, log fires and a friendly welcome.

Dinas-Mawddwy 26

National Grid Ref: SH8514

🍴 🍺 Dolbrodmaeth Inn

(On path) *The Red Lion Inn, Dinas-Mawddwy, Machynlleth, Powys, SY20 9JA.*
Actual grid ref: SH859148
Centuries-old traditional inn. In heart of village amid scenic beauty of southern Snowdonia.
Grades: WTB 1 Star
Tel: **01650 531247** (also fax no)
Mr Jenkins.
D: £20.00-£25.00 **S:** £20.00-£25.00.
Open: All Year (not Xmas)
Beds: 3F 1D 1T 1S
Baths: 3 En
🛏 🅿 (30) ⬜ 📺 🍴 ✕ 🔥 Ⅲ. Ⅴ ▪

Tal-y-llyn 27

National Grid Ref: SH7109

🍴 🍺 Railway

(3m 🚌) *Rhosgadlas, Tal-y-llyn, Tywyn, North West Wales, LL36 9AJ.*
Tastefully converted barn overlooking beautiful Tal-y-llyn lake. Traditional Welsh hospitality.
Grades: WTB 3 Star
Tel: **01654 761462** (also fax no)
Mrs Bebb.
D: £20.00-£25.00 **S:** £22.00-£25.00.
Open: Feb to Nov
Beds: 1T 2D
Baths: 2 En 1 Pr
🅿 (6) 🗲 ⬜ 📺 🔥 Ⅲ. Ⅴ ▪ ∥

Abergynolwyn 28

National Grid Ref: SH6706

🍴 🍺 Hen Siop Cwrt, Railway Hotel, Riverside Inn

(4m) *Eisteddfa, Abergynolwyn, Tywyn, LL36 9UP.*
Actual grid ref: SH666124
Newly built bungalow, suitable for disabled in wheelchair, overlooking Tal-y-llyn Railway.
Tel: **01654 782385**
Mrs Pugh.
Fax no: 01654 782228
D: £20.00-£24.00 **S:** £20.00-£25.00.
Open: Mar to Nov
Beds: 2D 1T
Baths: 2 En 1 Pr
🛏 🅿 📺 🍴 ✕ 🔥 Ⅲ. ♿ Ⅴ ▪ ∥

(4m 🚌) *Riverside House, Abergynolwyn, Tywyn, LL36 9YR.*
Actual grid ref: SH676072
Victorian former quarry master's house, set in riverside gardens Magnificent views.
Grades: WTB 2 Star B&B
Tel: **01654 782235** (also fax no)
Bott.
D: £18.00-£20.00 **S:** £18.00-£20.00.
Open: All Year
Beds: 1F 3D 1S
Baths: 1 En 1 Sh
🛏 🅿 (6) 🗲 ⬜ 📺 ✕ 🔥 Ⅲ. Ⅴ ▪ ∥

Dolgellau 29

National Grid Ref: SH7217

⚑ ◀Cross Foxes, Dylanwad Da, George, Royal Ship, Ivy House, Unicorn

(4m 🚖) *Ivy House, Finsbury Square, Dolgellau, North West Wales, LL40 1RF.*
Actual grid ref: SH728177
Attractive country town guest house, good home-made food.
Grades: WTB 2 Star GH,
AA 3 Diamond
Tel: **01341 422535** Mrs Bamford.
Fax no: 01341 422689
D: £18.50-£24.50 **S:** £23.00-£33.00.
Open: All Year
Beds: 1F 3D 2T **Baths:** 3 En 2 Sh
🛏🖵🏠✕🎇⛵💷Ⓥ🛡♿

(4m) *Tanyfron, Arran Road, Dolgellau, North West Wales, LL40 2AA.*
Actual grid ref: SH730170
Modernised, former stone farmhouse, beautiful views. Wales in Bloom Winners 1999.
Grades: WTB 3 Star
Tel: **01341 422638** Mrs Rowlands.
Fax no: 01341 421251
D: £20.00-£22.00 .
Open: Feb to Nov
Beds: 1D 2T **Baths:** 3 En
🛏 (5) 🅿 (6)⚡🖵⛵💷Ⓥ

(4m) *Arosfyr Farm, Penycefn Road, Dolgellau, North West Wales, LL40 2YP.*
Homely friendly, farmhouse, flower, gardens, mountainous, views, self-catering available.
Grades: WTB 2 Star
Tel: **01341 422355**
Mrs Skeel Jones.
D: £15.00-£16.50 **S:** £18.00.
Open: All Year
Beds: 1F 1D 1T **Baths:** 2 Sh
🛏🅿 (4)🖵🏠🎇⛵💷Ⓥ♿

S = Price range for a single person in a single room

Bringing children with you? Always ask for any special rates.

(4m) *Esgair Wen Newydd, Garreg Feurig, Llanfachreth Road, Dolgellau, LL40 2YA.*
Actual grid ref: SH736185
Bungalow, mountain views, very quiet. Friendly relaxed atmosphere. High standards.
Grades: WTB 3 Star
Tel: **01341 423952**
Mrs Westwood.
D: £18.00 **S:** £20.00.
Open: Feb to Nov
Beds: 2D 1T
Baths: 1 Sh
🛏 (3) 🅿 (3)⚡🖵✕🎇⛵💷Ⓥ🛡♿

(4m 🚖) *Penbryn Croft, Cader Road, Dolgellau, LL40 1RN.*
Tel: **01341 422815**
Ms Dunne.
D: £20.00-£24.00 .
Open: All Year (not Xmas)
Beds: 4T 2D
Baths: 2 Sh
🛏⚡🖵✕⛵💷Ⓥ🛡♿
Situated at the foot of Cader Idris 200 yards from Dolgellau town centre recently refurbished but still retaining some original features including oak staircase and mosaic tiled floors. up to 12 people can be accommodated and a warm welcome assured.

(4m) *Bryn Yr Odyn Guest House, Maescaled, Dolgellau, LL40 1UG.*
Secluded C17th longhouse, 1/2 mile town centre, tour/walking guidance.
Tel: **01341 423470**
Mr Jones.
D: £17.00 **S:** £20.00.
Open: All Year
Beds: 1D 2T
Baths: 2 Sh
🛏🅿 (3)⚡🖵🏠🎇⛵💷Ⓥ🛡♿

Islaw'r Dref 30

National Grid Ref: SH6815

(▲ 0.75m) *Kings (Dolgellau) Youth Hostel, Islaw'r Dref, Penmaenpool, Dolgellau, Gwynedd, LL40 1TB.*
Actual grid ref: SH683161
Tel: **01341 422392**
Under 18: £6.50
Adults: £9.25
Self-catering facilities, Showers, Shop, Lounge, Dining room, Drying room, Cycle store, Parking, No smoking, WC, Kitchen facilities, Credit cards accepted
Traditional hostel set in idyllic wooded valley, with magnificent views up to Cader Idris and Rhinog mountain ranges.

(▲ 1m) *Caban Cader Idris, Islaw'r Dref, Dolgellau, LL40 1TS.*
Actual grid ref: SH682169
Tel: **01766 762588 / 07887 954301**
Under 18: £4.50
Adults: £4.50
Self-catering facilities, Showers, Central heating, Lounge, Drying room, Parking, No smoking
Ideal group accommodation, sleeps 19, kitchen/dining room, heating, shower, drying room, parking, picnic/BBQ area. Listed former school in secluded wooded valley 3 miles from Dolgellau in Snowdonia National Park. Within walking distance of Cader Idris Range, Cregennen Lake and Mawddach Estuary. Other local activities include: mountain biking, pony trekking, skiing, fishing, beaches.

Please don't camp on *anyone's* land without first obtaining their permission.

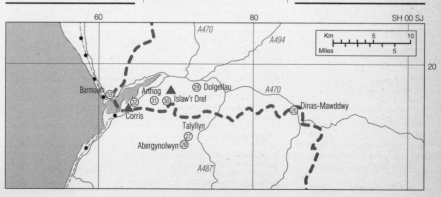

Arthog 31

National Grid Ref: SH6414

⊯ ◖ Fairbourne Hotel

(On path 🚌) *Graig Wen Guest House, Arthog, LL39 1BQ.*
Grades: WTB 2 Star
Tel: **01341 250900** Mrs Ameson.
Fax no: 01341 250482
D: £17.00-£19.00 **S:** £18.00-£24.00.
Open: All Year
Beds: 1F 4D 1T 1S
Baths: 3 En 2 Sh
🛏 (4) 🅿 (20) ⊬◻🕇✗♨🏷Ⅲ&Ⅵ♦✔
In 42 acres of woodland leading to Mawddach Estuary. Spectacular view of mountains, estuary, sea from house. Ideal for ramblers, cyclists, climbers, bird watchers. Cader Mountain, lakes, beaches, pony trekking, golf course, fishing, stream trains nearby. Disabled welcome.

Corris 32

National Grid Ref: SH7507

(▲4.5m) *Corris Youth Hostel, Old School, Old Road, Corris, Machynlleth, Powys, SY20 9QT.*
Actual grid ref: SH753080
Tel: **01654 761686**
Under 18: £6.50 **Adults:** £9.25
Self-catering facilities, Showers, Laundry facilities, Wet weather shelter, Lounge, Drying room, Security lockers, Cycle store, Parking, Evening meal at 7.00pm, No smoking, Kitchen facilities, Breakfast available
Picturesque former village school, recently renovated, with panoramic views of Corris.

Barmouth 33

National Grid Ref: SH6115

⊯ ◖ Last Inn

(On path 🚌) *Wavecrest Hotel, 8 Marine Parade, Barmouth, North West Wales, LL42 1NA.*
Actual grid ref: SH609160
Welcoming and relaxing Which? B&B. Excellent food, wine and whiskey.
Grades: WTB 3 Star, AA 2 Star
Tel: **01341 280330** (also fax no)
Mr & Mrs Jarman.
D: £18.00-£27.00 **S:** £22.00-£37.00.
Open: Easter to Oct
Beds: 2F 3D 2T 2S
Baths: 8 En 1 Pr
🛏 🅿 (2) ⊬◻🕇♨🏷Ⅲ.Ⅵ✔

(On path 🚌) *The Gables, Fford Mynach, Barmouth, Gwynedd, LL42 1RL.*
Actual grid ref: SH609166
Victorian house of character lovely position near mountains - warm welcome.
Grades: WTB 2 Star
Tel: **01341 280553**
Mr & Mrs Lewis.
D: £18.00-£20.00 **S:** £18.00-£20.00.
Open: Easter to Nov
Beds: 1F 2D 1S **Baths:** 2 En 1 Sh
🛏 🅿 (4) ⊬◻🕇✗♨🏷Ⅲ.Ⅵ♦✔

(0.5m) *Lawrenny Lodge Hotel, Barmouth, LL42 1SU.*
Small quiet family run hotel. Views over harbour and estuary.
Grades: WTB 2 Star
Tel: **01341 280466** Mr Barber.
Fax no: 01341 281551
D: £22.00-£32.00 **S:** £32.00-£32.00.
Open: Mar to Nov
Beds: 1F 4D 2T 1S
Baths: 7 En 1 Sh
🛏 🅿 (9) ◻🕇✗♨🏷Ⅲ.Ⅵ♦✔

(On path) *The Sandpiper, 7 Marine Parade, Barmouth, LL42 1NA.*
Sea front accommodation close to station. Parking outside.
Grades: WTB 2 Star
Tel: **01341 280318**
Mr & Mrs Palmer.
D: £14.50-£21.00 **S:** £15.50-£17.00.
Open: Easter to Oct
Beds: 2F 7D 3S
Baths: 6 Pr 2 Sh
🛏 🅿 ◻♨🏷Ⅲ.Ⅵ

(On path 🚌) *Min Y Mor Hotel, Marine Promenade, Barmouth, North West Wales, LL42 1HW.*
Family run hotel, friendly atmosphere, in a good central position.
Grades: WTB 2 Star
Tel: **01341 280555** Mr Atkins.
Fax no: 01341 280468
D: £52.00-£60.00 **S:** £52.00-£65.00.
Open: All Year
Beds: 8F 6D 8T 3S
Baths: All En
🛏 🅿 (70) ◻🕇✗♨🏷Ⅲ.Ⅵ♦✔

(On path) *Tal-Y-Don Hotel, High Street, Barmouth, LL42 1DL.*
Families welcome. Home cooking, bar meals and good beer.
Tel: **01341 280508** Mrs Davies.
D: £17.00-£20.00 **S:** £20.00-£25.00.
Open: All Year (not Xmas)
Beds: 2F 4D 2T **Baths:** 4 En 2 Sh
🛏 🅿 ⊬◻🕇♨🏷Ⅲ.Ⅵ

(On path) *Endeavour Guest House, Marine Parade, Barmouth, LL42 1NA.*
Actual grid ref: SH611159
Sea front location, beach 75 yards, railway station 150 yards.
Tel: **01341 280271**
Mr & Mrs Every.
D: £16.00-£20.00 **S:** £16.00-£16.00.
Open: All Year (not Xmas)
Beds: 7F 1S **Baths:** 4 En 1 Sh
🛏 (3) 🅿 (3) ◻♨🏷Ⅲ.Ⅵ♦✔

Trawsfynydd 34

National Grid Ref: SH7035

(On path) *Old Mill Farmhouse, Fron Oleu Farm, Trawsfynydd, Blaenau Ffestiniog, LL41 4UN.*
Actual grid ref: SH7135
Olde Worlde charm, wonderful scenery, friendly animals, large good breakfasts.
Grades: WTB 2 Star Farm
Tel: **01766 540397** (also fax no)
Miss Roberts & Mrs P Osborne.
D: £20.00-£25.00 **S:** £20.00-£25.00.
Open: All Year
Beds: 2F 3D 2T **Baths:** 7 En
🛏 🅿 (10) ⊬◻🕇✗♨🏷Ⅲ&Ⅵ♦✔

Gellilydan 35

National Grid Ref: SH6839

⊯ ◖ Bryn Arms

(0.25m 🚌) *Tyddyn Du Farm, Gellilydan, Blaenau Ffestiniog, Gwynedd, LL41 4RB.*
Actual grid ref: SH691398
Enchanting C17th farmhouse; deluxe barn suites with jacuzzi, patio window, gardens etc.
Tel: **01766 590281** Mrs Williams.
D: £20.00-£28.00 .
Open: All Year (not Xmas)
Beds: 3F 1D **Baths:** 3 Pr 2 Sh
🛏 🅿 (8) ⊬◻🕇✗♨🏷Ⅲ&Ⅵ♦✔

Maentwrog 36

National Grid Ref: SH6640

⊯ ◖ Grapes

(2.5m) *The Old Rectory Hotel, Maentwrog, Blaenau Ffestiniog, LL41 4HN.*
Actual grid ref: SH665407
Main house/budget annexe, 3 acre garden. Informal, peaceful.
Tel: **01766 590305** (also fax no)
Ms Herbert.
D: £22.50-£32.50 **S:** £30.00-£45.00.
Open: All Year (not Xmas)
Beds: 2F 6D 2T
Baths: 10 En
🛏 🅿 ◻🕇✗♨Ⅲ.Ⅵ♦✔

Ffestiniog 37

National Grid Ref: SH7041

(▲0.5m) *Abbey Arms Hostel, Ffestiniog, Blaenau Ffestiniog, LL41 4LS.*
Actual grid ref: SH700419
Tel: **01766 762444** **Adults:** £12.50
Evening meal

All rates are subject to alteration at the owners' discretion.

All paths are popular: you are well-advised to book ahead

Blaenau Ffestiniog   38

National Grid Ref: SH7045

¶ Grapes, Queen's Hotel

(2m) **Bryn Elltyd,** *Tanygrisiau, Blaenau Ffestiniog, Gwynedd, LL41 3TW.*
Mountain views: in an acre of peaceful grounds. Guided walking available.
Grades: WTB 2 Star
Tel: **01766 831356** (also fax no)
Mr & Mrs Cole.
D: £17.50 **S:** £17.50.
Open: All Year
Beds: 3T 1D **Baths:** 4 En
ﾐ P (4) ﾛ ﾆ ﾒ ﾟ ﾑ V ﾟ

(2m) **Cae'r Blaidd Country House,** *Llan Ffestiniog, Blaenau Ffestiniog, Gwynedd, LL41 4PH.*
Secluded tranquil refurbished Victorian country house with panoramic mountain views.
Grades: WTB 4 Star
Tel: **01766 762765** (also fax no)
D: £25.00-£27.50 **S:** £25.00-£27.50.
Open: All Year
Beds: 1F 1D 1T **Baths:** 2 En 1 Pr
ﾐ P (6) ﾚ ﾛ ﾗ ﾟ ﾑ V ﾟ

(On path) **Afallon Guest House,** *Manod Road, Blaenau Ffestiniog, LL41 4AE.*
Situated in Snowdonia National Park. Clean homely accommodation with Welsh breakfast.
Grades: WTB 3 Star
Tel: **01766 830468** Mrs Griffiths.
D: £15.00-£18.00 **S:** £15.00-£18.00.
Open: All Year (not Xmas)
Beds: 1D 1T 1S **Baths:** 1 Sh
ﾐ P (4) ﾚ ﾛ ﾆ ﾗ ﾟ ﾑ V ﾟ

(2m) **The Don Guest House,** *High Street, Blaenau Ffestiniog, LL41 3AX.*
Victorian town house with breathtaking mountain views. Friendly welcome assured.
Tel: **01766 830403** (also fax no)
Mr Cotton.
D: £14.00-£18.00 **S:** £15.00-£20.00.
Open: All Year (not Xmas/New Year)
Beds: 3D 2T 1S **Baths:** 2 En 1 Sh
ﾐ P (2) ﾛ ﾗ ﾟ ﾑ V

Beddgelert   39

National Grid Ref: SH5948

(2.5m) **Plas Colwyn Guest House,** *Beddgelert, Caernarfon, LL55 4UY.*
Actual grid ref: SH589482
Comfortable C17th house, centre of village, river and mountain views.
Grades: WTB 2 Star
Tel: **01766 890458** Mrs Osmond.
D: £18.00-£21.00 **S:** £18.00-£34.00.
Open: All Year (not Xmas)
Beds: 2F 2D 1T 1S
Baths: 3 En 3 Sh
ﾐ P (6) ﾚ ﾛ ﾆ ﾗ ﾟ ﾑ V ﾟ

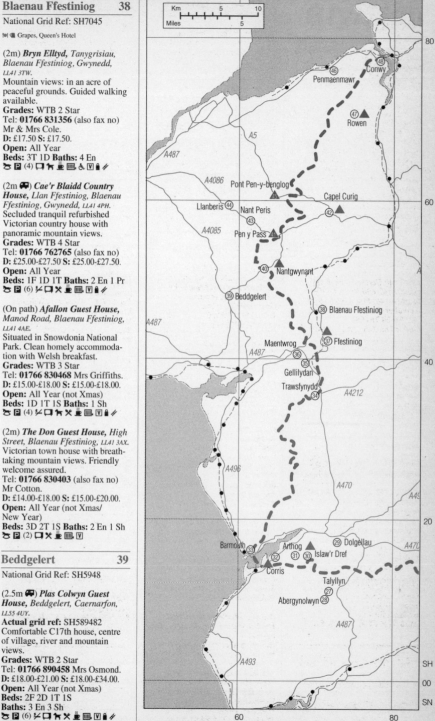

Nantgwynant 40

National Grid Ref: SH6250

(▲ On path) *Bryn Gwynant Youth Hostel, Nantgwynant, Caernarfon, Gwynedd, LL55 4NP.*
Actual grid ref: SH641513
Tel: **01766 890251**
Under 18: £6.90 **Adults:** £10.00
Self-catering facilities, Showers, Shop, Lounge, Games room, Drying room, Cycle store, Parking, Evening meal at 7.00pm, WC, Kitchen facilities, Breakfast available, Credit cards accepted
Recently refurbished impressive stone mansion with 40 acres of grounds, overlooking Llyn Gwynant lake and close to Snowdon.

(1m) *Pen-Y-Gwryd Hotel, Nantgwynant, Caernarfon, LL55 4NT.*
Actual grid ref: SH660558
Famous mountain inn, heart of Snowdonia. Associated with Lord Hunt's Everest team (1953).
Tel: **01286 870211** Mrs Pullee.
D: £23.00-£28.00 **S:** £33.00-£38.00.
Open: March to Nov
Beds: 16F 6T 9D 1S
Baths: 5 En 5 Pr 5 Sh
🛏 🅿 (30) 🔥 ✕ 🏛 & 🖔 ♨

Pen-y-Pass 41

National Grid Ref: SH6455

(▲ On path) *Pen-y-Pass Youth Hostel, Pen-y-Pass, Nantgwynant, Caernarfon, Gwynedd, LL55 4NY.*
Actual grid ref: SH647556
Tel: **01286 870428**
Under 18: £7.75 **Adults:** £11.00
Self-catering facilities, Television, Showers, Shop, Lounge 2, Dining room, Games room, Drying room, Security lockers, Cycle store, Evening meal at 7.00pm, Facilities for disabled people Category 2, Kitchen facilities, Breakfast available
A converted pub that has become the largest hostel in Snowdonia, situated right at the head of the Llanberis Pass.

Capel Curig 42

National Grid Ref: SH7258

🍴 ◀ Cobdens, Bryn Tyrch Hotel, Tyn y Coed

(▲ 4m) *Capel Curig Youth Hostel, Plas Curig, Capel Curig, Betws-y-Coed, LL24 0EL.*
Actual grid ref: SH726579
Tel: **01690 720225**
Under 18: £6.90 **Adults:** £10.00
Self-catering facilities, Showers, Shop, Lounge 2, Dining room, Drying room, Cycle store, Parking Limited, Evening meal at 7.00pm, WC, Kitchen facilities, Breakfast available, Credit cards accepted
Overlooking a river and forest with views of Moel Siabod. Ideal for mountain sports, riverside walks and forest tracks.

(4m) 🍴 *Bryn Glo Cafe, Capel Curig, Betws-y-Coed, LL24 0DT.*
Warm welcome and clean, comfortable accommodation in small family business.
Grades: WTB 2 Star B&B
Tel: **01690 720215** Mrs Evans.
D: £17.50 **S:** £18.00.
Open: All Year
Beds: 1D 1T 1S **Baths:** 1 Pr 1 Sh
🅿 (10) 🔥 🏛 🖔 🅥 ♨

(4m) 🍴 *Llugwy Guest House, Capel Curig, Betws-y-Coed, LL24 0ES.*
Actual grid ref: SH719581
Warm welcome, hearty breakfast, forest and mountain scenery. easily located.
Tel: **01690 720218** Mrs Cousins.
D: £17.50-£18.50 **S:** £19.50-£21.50.
Open: All Year
Beds: 2D 1T 1S **Baths:** 2 Sh
🛏 🅿 (4) ⟿ 🔥 ✕ 🏛 🅥 ♨

Nant Peris 43

National Grid Ref: SH6058

🍴 ◀ Vaynol Arms

(2.5m) *Snowdon House, 3 Gwastadnant, Nant Peris, Caernarfon, LL55 4UL.*
Actual grid ref: SH613577
Comfortable beds, good breakfast and friendly welcome in magnificent scenery.
Tel: **01286 870356** Mr Cumberton.
D: £15.00-£17.50 **S:** £15.00-£17.50.
Open: All Year
Beds: 3D 1T 1S **Baths:** 1 Sh
🛏 🅿 (12) ⟿ 🏛 🅥 ♨

Llanberis 44

National Grid Ref: SH5760

🍴 ◀ Padarn Lane Hotel, Royal Victoria, Gwynedd Hotel, Black Boy, Harp Inn, Newborough Arms

(▲ 4m) *Llanberis Youth Hostel, Llwyn Celyn, Llanberis, Carnarfon, Gwynedd, LL55 4SR.*
Actual grid ref: SH574596
Tel: **01286 870280**
Under 18: £6.90
Adults: £10.00
Self-catering facilities, Television, Showers, Shop, Lounge, Dining room, Drying room, Cycle store, Parking, Evening meal at 7.00pm, No smoking, Kitchen facilities, Breakfast available, Credit cards accepted
Overlooking lakes, with views towards summit of Snowdon. The starting point of the walks of all levels, or just 0.5 mile from the Mountain Railway Station.

(▲ 4m) *Heights Hotel, High Street, Llanberis, LL55 4NB.*
Actual grid ref: SH579602
Tel: **01268 871179**
Adults: £10.00
Evening meal

(4m) *Beech Bank Guest House, High Street, Llanberis, Caernarfon, LL55 4EN.*
Tel: **01286 870414** Mrs Watson.
D: £16.00-£16.00 **S:** £17.00-£17.00.
Open: All Year (not Xmas)
Beds: 1F 2D 1T **Baths:** 1 Sh
🅿 (6) 🔥 🏛 🅥
Situated at quiet end of village, overlooking lakes & mountains. Walking distance to Snowdon Mountain Railway. All rooms H&C and CH.

(4m) *Mount Pleasant Hotel, High Street, Llanberis, Caernarfon, LL55 4HA.*
Friendly, family-run, foot of Snowdon. Cosy bar, real ale.
Grades: WTB 1 Star
Tel: **01286 870395** (also fax no)
Mrs Waterton.
D: £16.00-£20.00 **S:** £16.00-£25.00.
Open: All Year
Beds: 2F 3D 1T 2S
Baths: 1 En 2 Sh
🛏 🅿 (8) 🔥 ✕ 🏛 🅥 ♨

(4m) *Glyn Afon , High Street, Llanberis, Caernarfon, LL55 4HA.*
Family-run centrally situated close to mount Snowdon/ railway/ attractions.
Grades: WTB 2 Star
Tel: **01286 872528** (also fax no)
Mrs Litton.
D: £16.00-£18.00 **S:** £17.00-£18.00.
Open: All Year
Beds: 1F 4D 3T **Baths:** 2 En2 Sh
🛏 🅿 (4) ⟿ 🔥 ✕ 🏛 🅥

(4m) *Idan House, High Street, Llanberis, Caernarfon, LL55 4EN.*
Idan House is in the heart of Snowdonia. Ideal for mountains and lakes.
Tel: **01286 870673** Mrs Roberts.
D: £12.50-£15.00 **S:** £15.00-£15.00.
Open: All Year
Beds: 1F 2D 2T 2S
Baths: 1 Sh
🛏 ⟿ 🔥 🏛 ♨

Pont Pen-y-benglog 45

National Grid Ref: SH6560

(▲ 0.25m) *Idwal Cottage Youth Hostel, Pont Pen-y-benglog, Bethesda, Bangor, Gwynedd, LL57 3LZ.*
Actual grid ref: SH648603
Tel: **01248 600225**
Under 18: £5.75 **Adults:** £8.50
Self-catering facilities, Showers, Lounge, Dining room, Drying room, Cycle store, Parking, Evening meal at 5.00pm, No smoking, WC, Kitchen facilities, Credit cards accepted
Originally a quarry manager's cottage, by Ogwen Lake below the Glyder Mountains and overlooking the Nant Ffrancon Pass. This is a good walking area. It may be closed for refurbishment from September 2001.

Penmaenmawr   46

National Grid Ref: SH7176

¶ ⊈ New Legend

(2m 🐾) *Bodlwyfan*, *Conwy Road,
Penmaenmawr, LL34 6BL.*
Beautiful Victorian house, over-
looking the sea and mountains in
quiet location.
Tel: **01492 623506** Mr Anderton.
D: £17.50-£20.00 **S:** £18.00-£21.00.
Open: All Year
Beds: 1F 3T 2D 1S
Baths: 2 Sh
😺 ℗ (6) 🏴 ⼍ ⽩ ✕ 🕭 �🏠. Ⅴ ❚ ⊀

Rowen   47

National Grid Ref: SH7571

¶ ⊈ Princes Arms, Groes

(▲ 1.25m) *Rowen Youth Hostel,
Rhiw Farm, Rowen, Conwy,
LL32 8YW.*
Actual grid ref: SH747721
Tel: **01492 650089**
Under 18: £5.75 **Adults:** £8.50
Self-catering facilities, Showers,
Shop, Wet weather shelter,
Lounge, Dining room, Cycle store,
Parking, No smoking, WC, Kitchen
facilities
*Simple, remote Welsh hill farm-
house set high above Rowen village
with panoramic views of Conwy
Valley.*

(1.5m 🐾) *Bulkeley Mill*, *Rowen,
Conwy, Gwynedd, LL32 8TS.*
Grades: WTB 4 Star
Tel: **01492 650481** Mrs Seville.
D: £26.00-£28.00 .
Open: All Year
Beds: 1F 1D
Baths: 2 En
😺 ℗ (4) ⼵ 🏴 🕭 ⼍ ⏛. Ⅴ ❚ ⊀
Bulkeley Mill is situated in Rowen,
one of the most picturesque
villages in the Conwy Valley. The
mill wheel has been renovated and
the mill buildings converted to
living accommodation in 1993/94,
including the waterwheel. Unique
property in gardens that offer
complete peace and tranquillity.

(1.5m) *Gwern Borter Holiday
Farm*, *Rowen, Conwy, LL32 8YL.*
You'll love it here! Manor house
set in 11 acres of beautiful grounds.
Tel: **01492 650360** (also fax no)
Mr Powell.
D: £23.00-£28.00 **S:** £26.00.
Open: All Year (not Xmas)
Beds: 1F 2D
Baths: 3 En 1 Sh
😺 ℗ (18) 🏴 ⼍ ✕ ⏛. ❚ ⊀

(1.5m 🐾) *Coed Lyn*, *Barkers Lane,
Rowen, Conwy, Gwynedd, LL32 8YL.*
Old gamekeeper's cottage with
lovely gardens and stunning views
of Welsh mountains.
Tel: **01492 650469/ 0589 084111**
D: £17.00-£20.00 **S:** £25.00.
Open: Easter to Oct
Beds: 1F 2D 1T
Baths: 2 En 1 Pr
😺 ℗ (3) 🏴 ⼍ 🕭 ⏛. Ⅴ ❚ ⊀

Conwy   48

National Grid Ref: SH7777

¶ ⊈ Mulberry, Fairy Glen, Tal y Cafn, Y Groes,
George & Dragon

(▲ 1m) *Conwy Youth Hostel,
Larkhill, Schymant Pass Road,
Conwy, LL32 8AJ.*
Actual grid ref: SH775773
Tel: **01492 593571**
Under 18: £8.50 **Adults:** £12.50
Self-catering facilities, Television,
Showers, Shop, Laundry facilities,
Lounge, Dining room, Games
room, Drying room, Security lock-
ers, Cycle store, Parking, Evening
meal at 6.00 to 7.30pm, Facilities
for disabled people Category 3,
Kitchen facilities, Breakfast
available, Credit cards accepted
*Former hotel, very modern; over-
looking the castle and the bay.*

Pay B&Bs by cash or
cheque and be prepared
to pay up front.

D = Price range per person
sharing in a double room

(1m 🐾) *Glan Heulog Guest
House, Llanrwst Road, Conwy,
LL32 8LT.*
Grades: WTB 2 Star GH,
AA 3 Diamond
Tel: **01492 593845**
Mr & Mrs Watson-Jones.
D: £15.00-£20.00 **S:** £18.00-£24.00.
Open: All Year
Beds: 2F 2D 2T
Baths: 5 En 1 Pr
😺 ℗ (7) ⼵ 🏴 ⼍ ✕ 🕭 ⏛. Ⅴ ❚ ⊀
Warm welcome, comfortable beds
and a hearty breakfast in a fine
Victorian house situated in an
elevated position with far-reaching
views to Snowdonia. Short walk to
castle. Centrally situated for
Snowdonia and all major
attractions. Off-road parking,
garden.

(1m) *Bryn Derwen*, *Woodlands,
Conwy, LL32 8LT.*
Actual grid ref: SH782772
Warm welcome to a gracious
Victorian home with panoramic
views.
Grades: WTB 3 Star,
AA 3 Diamond
Tel: **01492 596134**
Mr & Mrs Smith.
D: £18.00-£20.00 **S:** £18.00-£25.00.
Open: All Year
Beds: 1F 2D 3T
Baths: 6 En
😺 ℗ (8) ⼵ 🏴 ⼍ 🕭 ⏛. Ⅴ ❚

(1m) *Fishermore*, *Llanrwst Road,
Conwy, LL32 8HP.*
Rural setting close to historic town,
N.T. gardens and mountains
Grades: WTB 2 Star
Tel: **01492 592891**
Mrs Dyer .
D: £17.00-£19.00 .
Open: Easter to Oct
Beds: 1T 2D
Baths: 2 En 1 Pr
℗ (5) ⼵ 🏴 🕭 ⏛. Ⅴ

Glyndwr's Way

What a path - leading through 120 miles of the quietest parts of mid-Wales with its superb scenery, its wooded valleys, its lowland moors - the true hinterland of the entire country. From the Welsh Marches to Machynlleth on the River Dyfi, the path visits sites associated with the life and deeds of the Welsh national hero **Owain Glyndwr** and his campaign against the English in the early 15th century. The path was featured in a BBC radio series in 1993 and has accordingly become more popular, but you may still spend a day walking quite by yourself. Because the path begins at Knighton and ends at Welshpool, there is the opportunity to link both ends with the relevant section of **Offa's Dyke** (q.v.) and turn the trail into a circular walk.

Guide:

Glyndwr's Way by Gillian Walker (ISBN 0 946679 398), published by Management Update and available only from Powney's Bookshop (4-5 St Alkmund's Place, Shrewsbury, SY1 1UJ, tel. 01743 369165), £4.95 (+ 95p p&p)

Comments on the path to:
Glyndwr's Way Project Officer, Powys County Council, Canolfan Owain Glyndwr, Machynlleth, Powys, SY20 8EE

Maps: 1:50000 Ordnance Survey Landranger Series: 125, 126, 135, 136 and 148

Knighton 1
National Grid Ref: SO2872

🅗 🍴 Hundred House, George & Dragon, Horse & Jockey

(0.25m 🚐) *Westwood, Presteigne Road, Knighton, Powys, LD7 1HY.* Welcome to our detached Victorian home. Quiet town location; spacious, comfortable accommodation. Tel: **01547 520317** Mrs Sharratt. **D:** £17.00-£17.00 **S:** £17.00-£17.00. **Open:** All Year **Beds:** 1F 1D 1S **Baths:** 1 En 1 Sh
🐕 🅿 (4) ⚲ ♁ ✕ ⚱ 🍽 Ⓥ 🛈 ✻

🚐 sign means that, *given due notice*, owners will pick you up from the path and drop you off *within reason.*

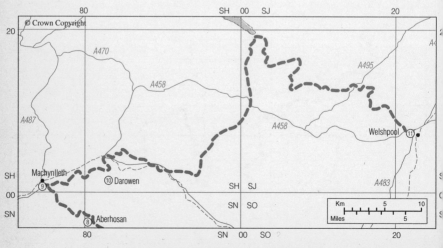

(0.25m 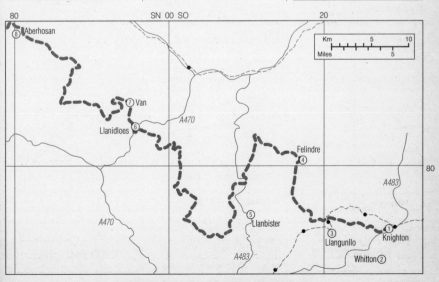) *Offas Dyke House, 4 High St, Knighton, Powys, LD7 1AT.*
Warm friendly B&B situated in the heart of Knighton.
Grades: WTB 2 Star
Tel: **01547 528634** (also fax no) Ashe.
D: £16.00-£16.00 **S:** £16.00-£16.00.
Open: All Year
Beds: 2T 3D 1S
Baths: 3 Sh
🛏 🅿 (4) ⊬ 🗆 🛪 ✕ 🛢 ▥ Ⅴ ℓ ⋀

(0.25m) *The Fleece House, Market Street, Knighton, Powys, LD7 1BB.*
Actual grid ref: S0285724
Attractive decorated quality accommodation in converted C18th coaching inn.
Grades: WTB 3 Star GH
Tel: **01547 520168** Mrs Simmons.
D: £20.00-£28.00 **S:** £23.00-£35.00.
Open: All Year
Beds: 6T **Baths:** 2 En 2 Sh
🅿 ⊬ 🗆 🛢 ▥ Ⅴ ℓ ⋀

(0.25m) *15 Mill Green, Knighton, Powys, LD7 1EE.*
Welcoming colourful old cottage with secluded garden and private courtyard.
Tel: **01547 520075** Mrs Stothert.
D: £14.00-£15.00 **S:** £14.00-£15.00.
Open: Easter to Oct
Beds: 1D 1T
Baths: 1 En 1 Sh
🛏 🅿 (1) ⊬ 🗆 🛪 🛢 ▥ & Ⅴ ℓ ⋀

All rates are subject to alteration at the owners' discretion.

Order your packed lunch the *evening before* you need them. Not at breakfast!

(0.25m) *Larkspur, Larkey Lane, Knighton, Powys, LD7 1DN.*
Quiet location overlooking town centre and castle site.
Tel: **01547 528764**
Mrs Heard.
D: £15.00-£15.00
S: £15.00-£15.00.
Open: All Year
Beds: 1D 1T
Baths: 1 Pr
🛏 (1) 🅿 ⊬ 🗆 🛢 ▥ ⋀

Whitton 2

National Grid Ref: SO2767

🍴 ⛉ Hundred House

(3m) *Pilleth Court, Whitton, Knighton, Powys, LD7 1NP.*
Actual grid ref: SO257683
16th century house in historic location offering quality accommodation.
Tel: **01547 560272** (also fax no) Mrs Hood.
D: £18.00
S: £20.00.
Open: All Year (not Xmas)
Beds: 1F 2D 1T
Baths: 1 En 1 Sh
🛏 (9) 🅿 (6) 🗆 ✕ 🛢 ▥ Ⅴ ℓ ⋀

Llangunllo 3

National Grid Ref: SO2171

🍴 ⛉ Castle, Horse & Jockey, Hundred House

(1m) *Cefnsuran Farm, Llangunllo, Knighton, Powys, LD7 1SL.*
Grades: WTB 3 Star
Tel: **01547 550219** Mrs Morgan.
Fax no: 01547 550348
D: £20.00-£22.50 **S:** £20.00-£25.00.
Open: All Year (not Xmas/New Year)
Beds: 1F 1D 1T
Baths: 1 En 1 Pr
🛏 🅿 (10) ⊬ 🗆 ✕ 🛢 ▥ Ⅴ ℓ ⋀
Set in beautiful location for a peaceful, interesting and private holiday. Guests are welcome to stroll around gardens, waymarked farm trails and woodlands. Pools with abundant wildlife - flyfishing possible. Games room with fullsize snooker table. Self-catering available.

(0.5m) *Rhiwlas, Llangunllo Halt, Llangunllo, Knighton, Powys, LD7 1SY.*
Actual grid ref: SO2073
The farm which is mainly stock producing includes a section of the Glyndwr's Way.
Tel: **01547 550256** Mrs Deakins.
D: £15.50 **S:** £16.00-£16.50.
Open: Easter to Oct
Beds: 2D
Baths: 1 Sh
🛏 🅿 🗆 ✕ ▥ ℓ

S = Price range for a single person in a single room

Felindre 4

National Grid Ref: SO1681

(On path 🚐) *Trevland, Felindre, Knighton, Powys, LD7 1YL.*
Quiet border village. Warm welcome offered to all.
Tel: **01547 510211** Mrs Edwards.
D: £16.50-£17.50 **S:** £16.50-£17.50.
Open: All Year
Beds: 1F 1D 1T
Baths: 3 En
🛇 🅿 (5) 🖵 🛏 ✗ 🗶 🎹 ♿ Ⓥ 🗎 ⚡

Llanbister 5

National Grid Ref: SO1073

🍴 🍺 Lion

(1m 🚐) *The Lion, Llanbister, Llandrindod Wells, Powys, LD1 6TN.*
Friendly local pub in beautiful countryside of unspoilt mid-Wales.
Tel: **01597 840244** Mrs Thomas.
D: £18.00-£25.00 **S:** £18.00-£25.00.
Open: All Year
Beds: 1F
Baths: 3 En 1 Pr
🛇 🅿 (4) 🖵 🛏 ✗ 🗶 🎹 Ⓥ 🗎 ⚡

Llanidloes 6

National Grid Ref: SN9584

🍴 🍺 Unicorn

(On path) *Lloyds, Cambrian Place, Llanidloes, Powys, SY18 6BX.*
Actual grid ref: SN955844
Long-established Victorian hotel in centre of attractive market town.
Grades: WTB 2 Star
Tel: **01686 412284** Mr Lines.
Fax no: 01686 412666
D: £25.00-£25.00 **S:** £19.00-£33.00.
Open: Mar to Jan
Beds: 3D 2T 4S **Baths:** 6 En 1 Sh
🛇 🖵 ✗ 🗶 🎹 Ⓥ ⚡

Van 7

National Grid Ref: SN9587

🍴 🍺 Star Inn, Red Lion

(2.5m 🚐) *Esgairmaen, Van, Llanidloes, Powys, SY18 6NT.*
Actual grid ref: SN925904
Comfortable farmhouse in unspoilt countryside, ideal for waking and bird watching.
Tel: **01686 430272**
D: £17.00-£19.00 **S:** £17.00-£19.00.
Open: Easter to Oct
Beds: 1F 1D **Baths:** 2 En
🛇 (1) 🅿 (4) 🖊 🖵 🛏 ✗ 🗶 🎹 Ⓥ 🗎 ⚡

All paths are popular:
you are well-advised to
book ahead

Aberhosan 8

National Grid Ref: SN8097

🍴 🍺 Star Inn

(1m) *Bacheiddon Farm, Aberhosan, Machynlleth, Powys, SY20 8SG.*
Working farm. Ideal walking, touring area. Close RSPB and MWT.
Tel: **01654 702229**
Mrs Lewis.
D: £18.00-£20.00 **S:** £20.00-£25.00.
Open: May to Oct
Beds: 3D
Baths: 3 En
🛇 🅿 🖵 🗶 Ⓥ

Machynlleth 9

National Grid Ref: SH7400

🍴 🍺 White Lion, Black Lion, Glyndwr Hotel, White Horse, Wynnstay, Skinner's Arms

(On path 🚐) *Maenllwyd, Newtown Road, Machynlleth, Powys, SY20 8EY.*
Actual grid ref: SH752009
Home from home, within walking distance all amenities, safe parking.
Grades: WTB 3 Star GH, AA 3 Diamond
Tel: **01654 702928** (also fax no)
Mr Vince.
D: £19.00-£22.00
S: £25.00-£25.00.
Open: All Year (not Xmas)
Beds: 1F 4D 3T
Baths: 8 En
🛇 🅿 (10) 🖊 🖵 🛏 🗶 🎹 Ⓥ ⚡

(1m 🚐) *Talbontdrain, Uwchygarreg, Machynlleth, Powys, SY20 8RR.*
Actual grid ref: SN777959
Tel: **01654 702192**
Ms Matthews.
D: £19.00-£21.00 **S:** £16.00-£19.00.
Open: All Year (not Xmas/New Year)
Beds: 1D 1T 2S
Baths: 1 Pr 1 Sh
🛇 🅿 (4) 🖊 🖵 ✗ 🗶 🗶 🎹 Ⓥ 🗎 ⚡
Friendly family B&B. We like having children here and are flexible about sleeping arrangements - there's even a barn for adventurous kids! We have dogs, cats and chickens, rivers, mountains and seaside not far away. Safe playing space and fantastic food.

(0.25m 🚐) *Wynnstay Arms Hotel, Maengwyn Street, Machynlleth, Powys, SY20 8AE.*
Old coaching inn, in heart of historic market town, in stunning Dovey Valley.
Grades: AA 2 Star, RAC 2 Star
Tel: **01654 702941**
Mr Dark.
Fax no: 01654 703884
D: £35.00-£48.00 **S:** £45.00.
Open: All Year
Beds: 3F 9D 5T 6S
Baths: 23 En
🛇 🅿 (36) 🖊 🖵 🛏 ✗ 🗶 🎹 Ⓥ 🗎 ⚡

(1m 🚐) *Cwmdylluan Forge, Machynlleth, Powys, SY20 8RZ.*
Actual grid ref: SH764000
Modern riverside bungalow, rooms overlook lovely garden and river.
Grades: WTB 3 Star
Tel: **01654 702684**
Hughes.
Fax no: 01654 700133
D: £15.50-£17.50 **S:** £16.50-£18.00.
Open: All Year
Beds: 1D 1T 1S
Baths: 2 Pr 2 Sh
🛇 (5) 🅿 (5) 🖵 🛏 ✗ 🗶 🎹 ♿ Ⓥ ⚡

(0.25m 🚐) *Gwelfryn, 6 Green Fields, Machynlleth, Powys, SY20 8DR.*
Quiet but central, fantastic breakfasts, near all tourist attractions.
Grades: WTB 2 Star
Tel: **01654 702532**
D: £17.00-£19.50
S: £17.00.
Open: Easter to Oct
Beds: 1D 1T 1S
Baths: 1 En 1 Pr
🛇 🖊 🖵 🛏 🎹 🗎 ⚡

(On path) *Awelon, Heol Powys, Machynlleth, Powys, SY20 8AY.*
Centrally situated, small, comfortable private house. Warm welcome.
Tel: **01654 702047**
Ms Williams.
D: £16.00-£17.00 **S:** £16.00-£17.50.
Open: All Year (not Xmas)
Beds: 1T 1S
Baths: 1 Sh
🛇 (2) 🖊 🛏 🎹 🗎 ⚡

Darowen 10

National Grid Ref: SH8201

(0.5m) *Cefn Farm, Darowen, Machynlleth, Powys, SY20 8NS.*
Unsurpassable views, good walking. Half hour drive seaside. Open fire, personal service.
Tel: **01650 511336** Mr Lloyd.
D: £20.00 **S:** £20.00.
Open: All Year
Beds: 1F 1D
🛇 🅿 (3) 🖊 🖵 🛏 🗶 🎹 ♿ Ⓥ

The Grid Reference
beneath the location
heading is for the
village or town - *not*
for individual houses,
which are shown
(where supplied) in
each entry itself.

Welshpool 11

National Grid Ref: SJ2207

Green Dragon, Horseshoe, King's Head, Railway, Red Lion, Royal Oak, Star Inn, Talbot

(0.5m) *Tynllwyn Farm,*
Welshpool, Powys, SY21 9BW.
Actual grid ref: SJ214080
Visitor's remark - 'Nearest place to Heaven'. Friendly, quiet, wonderful views.
Grades: WTB 3 Star, AA 3 Star
Tel: **01938 553175** Mrs Emberton.
Fax no: 01938 553996
D: £15.50-£18.00 **S:** £17.50-£22.00.
Open: All Year (not Xmas)
Beds: 3F 1D 1T 1S
Baths: 3 En 2 Sh

D = Price range per person sharing in a double room

(1m) *Lower Trelydan,*
Guilesfield, Welshpool, Powys,
SY21 9PH.
Award-winning black-and-white farmhouse, ensuite, licensed bar, evening meals, Welshpool 2 miles.
Grades: WTB 4 Star,
AA 4 Diamond
Tel: **01938 553105** (also fax no)
Mrs Jones.
D: £24.00-£25.00 **S:** £25.00-£28.00.
Open: All Year (not Xmas/New Year)
Beds: 1F 1D 1T **Baths:** 3 En

(2m) *Tresi-Aur,* Brookfield Road, Welshpool, Powys, SY21 7PZ.
Detached family home offers friendly hospitality conveniently situated to town.
Grades: WTB 2 Star
Tel: **01938 552430** Mrs Davies.
D: £16.00-£18.00 **S:** £16.00-£18.00.
Open: Jan to Nov
Beds: 1F 1D 1T 1S
Baths: 1 Pr

(0.75m) *Hafren Guest House,*
38 Salop Road, Welshpool, Powys,
SY21 7EA.
Actual grid ref: SJ227076
Georgian house with medieval links in 'Gateway to Mid-Wales' town.
Tel: **01938 554112**
Ms Shaw.
D: £16.00-£18.00 **S:** £18.00-£20.00.
Open: All Year (not Xmas)
Beds: 1F 1D 1T
Baths: 1 En 1 Sh

(1m) *Dysserth Hall,* Powis Castle, Welshpool, Powys, SY21 8RQ.
Comfortable, friendly, Listed manor home in peaceful countryside, superb view.
Tel: **01938 552153** (also fax no)
Mrs Marriott.
D: £21.00-£22.50 **S:** £21.00-£25.00.
Open: Easter to Nov
Beds: 1D 2T 1S
Baths: 2 Pr 1 Sh

Offa's Dyke Path

This is a splendid 168-mile trail through the Welsh Marches, roughly following the line of a large wall and ditch built as a border by an Anglo-Saxon king. From Chepstow to Prestatyn, the terrain changes every 15 miles or so - riverside walk, castle country, the Black Mountains, lonely moorland, canal towpath, old mining land and the Clwydian Hills - making the trail different every day. The ancient Dyke itself is prominent at many points of the walk, giving that strange feeling that you are walking where others, too, paced with purpose hundreds of years ago. The walking is for the most part moderately easy, with the main obstacle the extraordinary number of stiles. It can, however, be difficult on the hills in mist and wet weather, so make sure you have the right kit with you.

The path is supported by the **Offa's Dyke Association** (Offa's Dyke Centre, West St, Knighton, Powys, LD7 1EW) who promote the path with great verve and application; its prime movers, Ernie and Kathy Kay, wrote the Aurum Press/OS book mentioned below with Mark Richards. The association sells a large range of books, maps and branded merchandise and your membership would certainly help in the conservation of the path. There is also a taxi-based service, handling luggage delivery, safe car-parking and passenger back-up along the entire path - **White Knight** tel. 01903 766475. It provides a useful fallback for weary or injured walkers or just those who do not wish to carry a large pack.

Guides (available from all good map shops, unless stated):

Offa's Dyke South (ISBN 1 85410 2958) and *Offa's Dyke North* (ISBN 1 85410 3229) by Ernie & Kathy Kay and Mark Richards, published by Aurum Press in association with the Countryside Commission and Ordnance Survey, each £10.99

Through Welsh Border Country (following Offa's Dyke Path) by Mark Richards (ISBN 0 904110 53 2), published by Thornhill Press and also available from West Country Books, Halsgrove House, Lower Moor Way, Tiverton, Devon EX16 6SS, tel. 01884 243242, £4.50 (+£1 p&p)

Walking Offa's Dyke Path by David Hunter (ISBN 1 852841 60 5), published by Cicerone Press and available from all good map shops or directly from the publishers (2 Police Square, Milnthorpe, Cumbria, LA7 7PY, 01539 562069), £8.99 (+ 75p p&p)

A Guide to Offa's Dyke Path by C J Wright (ISBN 0 094691 40 1), published by Constable & Co Ltd and available from all good bookshops, £10.95

Maps: 1:50000 Ordnance Survey Landranger Series: 116, 117, 126, 137, 148, 161 and 162

Comments on the path to: **Jim Saunders**, Offa's Dyke Development Officer, Offa's Dyke Centre, West St, Knighton, Powys, LD7 1EW

Chepstow 1

National Grid Ref: ST5393

🏠 🍺 White Lion, Coach & Horses, Cross Keys

(0.5m) *Lower Hardwick House,* Mount Pleasant, Chepstow, Monmouthshire, *NP16 5PT.*
Actual grid ref: ST531935
Beautiful Georgian house, walled garden. Free car parking for duration walk.
Tel: **01291 622162**
Mrs Grassby.
D: £15.50-£18.00 **S:** £18.00-£25.00.
Open: All Year
Beds: 1F 1D 1T 1S
Baths: 2 Pr 1 Sh
🛏 🅿 (12) 🔲 🟥 👗 🏠 ⅤⅤ ⬩

(0.5m) *The Old Course Hotel,* Newport Road, Chepstow, Gwent, *NP16 5PR.*
Modern hotel, convenient for the Wye Valley, Chepstow races and more. **Grades:** AA 3 Star
Tel: **01291 626261**
Fax no: 01291 626263
D: £28.75-£32.25 **S:** £47.00-£53.00.
Open: All Year
Beds: 4F 10D 7T 10S
Baths: 31 En
🛏 🅿 (180) 🔲 🟥 ✕ 👗 🏠 ⅤⅤ ⬩ ⅤⅤ ⬩

D = Price range per person sharing in a double room

S = Price range for a single person in a single room

(0.5m 🚐) *The First Hurdle,* 9-10 Upper Church St, Chepstow, Gwent, *NP16 5EX.*
Enjoy comfortable, ensuite accommodation. Centrally situated, family owned B&B.
Tel: **01291 622189** Mrs Westwood.
Fax no: 01291 628421
D: £23.00-£25.00 **S:** £25.00-£27.50.
Open: Easter to Nov
Beds: 2D 2T 1S **Baths:** 5 En
🛏 🔲 👗 🏠 ⅤⅤ ⬩

(1m 🚍) *Langcroft, 71 St
Kingsmark Avenue, Chepstow,
Monmouthshire, NP6 5LY.*
Actual grid ref: ST529938
Modern family friendly home.
Town centre, four minutes' walk.
Tel: **01291 625569** (also fax no)
Mrs Langdale.
D: £18.00-£20.00 **S:** £20.00-£20.00.
Open: All Year
Beds: 1D 1T 1S **Baths:** 1 Sh
🛏 🅿 (2) 🔌 🏠 🖤 🛒 🎮 V ✓

Tintern 2

National Grid Ref: SO5300

🍴 🍺 Moon & Sixpence, Wye Valley Hotel,
Royal George Hotel

(0.75m) *Holmleigh, Monmouth
Road, Tintern, Chepstow,
Monmouthshire, NP6 6SG.*
Beautiful old house overlooking
the river Wye.
Tel: **01291 689521**
Mr & Mrs Mark.
D: £15.50-£15.50
S: £15.50-£15.50.
Open: All Year
Beds: 2D 1T 1S **Baths:** 1 Sh
🛏 🅿 (3) 🔌 🏠 🖤 🖩 V ☕

(0.75m 🚍) *Highfield House,
Chapel Hill, Tintern, Chepstow,
Monmouthshire, NP6 6TF.*
Actual grid ref: ST526997
Grades: WTB 3 Diamond,
AA 5 Diamond
Tel: **01291 689838**
Mr McCaffery.
Fax no: 01291 689890
D: £24.50-£29.50 **S:** £30.00-£37.50.
Open: All Year
Beds: 2F 1D **Baths:** 2 En 1 Pr
🛏 🅿 (10) 🔌 🏠 🍴 ✗ 🖤 🖩 V ☕ ✓
Nestled on the hillside surrounded
by forest above Tintern Abbey, this
remarkable house offers wondrous
views of the Wye Valley. Close
Offa's Dyke on the Tintern Trail.
Noted for Mediterranean cuisine
served under candlelight. Log fires,
very warm welcome.

Bringing children with you? Always ask for any special rates.

Planning a longer stay? Always ask for any special rates.

(0.75m 🚍) *Rose Cottage, The
Chase, Woolaston, Glos, GL15 6PT.*
Grades: WTB 3 Star
Tel: **01291 689691**
Mrs Dunbar.
D: £22.50-£22.50
S: £45.00-£45.00.
Open: All Year
Beds: 1T
Baths: 1 En
✗ 🔌 🏠 🍴 ✗ 🖤 🖩 V ☕ ✓
Self contained small converted
barn, peaceful location. Private
off-road parking. Evening meals a
speciality using own organic
produce. On edge of Royal Forest
of Dean close to Chepstow,
Monmouth and Ross on Wye.
Historic castles at Chepstow and
St. Briavels.

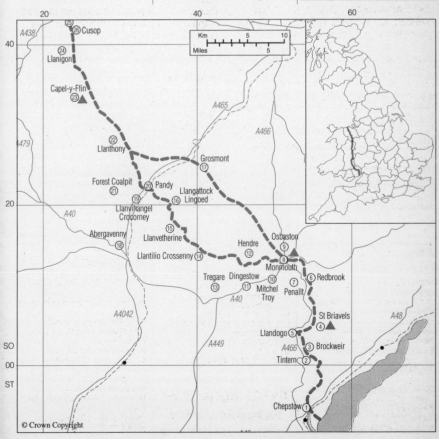

© Crown Copyright

All paths are popular: you are well-advised to book ahead

(0.75m 🚃) *The Old Rectory,*
Tintern, Chepstow,
Monmouthshire, NP16 6SG.
Actual grid ref: SO529008
Comfortable accommodation over-
looking beautiful River Wye.
Warm welcome, log fires, good
cooking.
Tel: **01291 689519**
Mrs Taylor.
Fax no: 01291 689939
D: £17.00-£20.00
S: £22.00-£27.50.
Open: All Year
Beds: 1F 2D 1T
Baths: 1 En 1 Pr 1 Sh
ㅎ🅿(3)✍🛏🟋🗙🕭🛏🕭⛊Ⅴ🗎⚡

(1.25m) *Valley House, Raglan*
Road, Tintern, Chepstow,
Monmouthshire, NP6 6TH.
Actual grid ref: SO523002
C18th detached house in
picturesque valley.
Tel: **01291 689652**
Mr & Mrs Howe.
Fax no: 01291 689805
D: £21.00-£21.00 **S:** £30.00-£30.00.
Open: All Year (not Xmas)
Beds: 2D 1T
Baths: 3 En
🅿✍🛏🟋🕭🛏⛊Ⅴ🗎⚡

Brockweir 3

National Grid Ref: SO5401

†⚱ Moon & Sixpence

(1m) *Honeyfield Farm, Mill Hill,*
Brockweir, Chepstow,
Monmouthshire, NP16 7NN.
Honeyfields Farm is situated on the
outskirts of the historic village of
Brockweir.
Tel: **01291 689859** Mr Murphy.
D: £17.00-£21.00 **S:** £17.00-£26.00.
Open: All Year
Beds: 3T 1S
Baths: 2 En 3 Sh
ㅎ🅿(6)✍🖵🟋🕭Ⅴ🗎

Order your packed lunch the *evening before* you need them. Not at breakfast!

St Briavels 4

National Grid Ref: SO5604

†⚱ The George, The Crown

(▲ 1m) *St Briavels Castle Youth*
Hostel, The Castle, St Briavels,
Lydney, Gloucestershire, GL15 6RG.
Actual grid ref: SO558045
Tel: **01594 530272**
Under 18: £7.75 **Adults:** £11.00
Self-catering facilities, Showers,
Licensed bar, Shop, Lounge,
Dining room, Drying room, Cycle
store, Parking, Evening meal at
7.00pm, No smoking, WC,
Breakfast available, Breakfast
available, Credit cards accepted
800-year-old Norman castle with
moat, used by King John as a hunt-
ing lodge, in the centre of a quiet
village above the River Wye.

(On path 🚃) *Offas Mead, The*
Fence, St Briavels, Lydney, Glos,
GL15 6QG.
Actual grid ref: SO544056
Large country home on Offa's
Dyke Path. Ensuite available.
Grades: ETC 3 Star
Tel: **01594 530229** (also fax no)
Mrs Lacey.
D: £18.00-£20.00 **S:** £18.00-£20.00.
Open: Easter to Oct
Beds: 1D 2T **Baths:** 21 En 1 Pr
ㅎ(10)🅿(6)✍🖵🟋🕭Ⅴ🗎⚡

(0.5m 🚃) *Woodcroft, Lower*
Meend, St Briavels, Lydney, Glos,
GL15 6RW.
Actual grid ref: SO552042
Enjoy badgers, bats & buzzards in
the beautiful Wye Valley.
Tel: **01594 530080** Mrs Allen.
D: £18.00-£20.00 **S:** £25.00-£25.00.
Open: All Year
Beds: 2F 1T
Baths: 3 En
ㅎ🅿(7)✍🖵🟋🕭🛏⛊Ⅴ🗎⚡

Llandogo 5

National Grid Ref: SO5204

†⚱ Old Farmhouse

(2m) *Lugano, Llandogo,*
Monmouth, Monmouthshire,
NP5 4TL.
Luxury accommodation, beautiful
landscaped gardens, picturesque
village location.
Tel: **01594 530496** Mrs Townsend.
Fax no: 01594 530956
D: £16.00-£19.50 **S:** £20.00-£20.00.
Open: All Year (not Xmas)
Beds: 2D 1T 1S
Baths: 1 En 1 Sh
ㅎ🅿(4)✍🖵🟋🕭Ⅴ⚡

D = Price range per person sharing in a double room

S = Price range for a single person in a single room

Redbrook 6

National Grid Ref: SO5310

†⚱ Boat Inn, Fish'n'Game

(On path) *Tresco, Redbrook,*
Monmouth, NP5 4LY.
Actual grid ref: SO536101
Beautiful Wye Valley riverside
house, fishing, pony trekking,
walking, canoeing.
Tel: **01600 712325** Mrs Evans.
D: £16.50 **S:** £16.50.
Open: All Year
Beds: 1F 1D 1T 2S
Baths: 2 Sh
ㅎ🅿🖵🟋🗙🕭🛏⛊Ⅴ🗎⚡

Penallt 7

National Grid Ref: SO5210

†⚱ Boat Inn

(1m 🚃) *Cherry Orchard Farm,*
Lone Lane, Penallt, Monmouth,
NP5 4AJ.
Small C18th working farm situated
in Lower Wye Valley.
Tel: **01600 714416** Mrs Beale.
Fax no: 01600 714447
D: £18.00-£18.00 **S:** £18.00-£18.00.
Open: All Year (not Xmas)
Beds: 2D
Baths: 1 Sh
ㅎ🅿(4)✍🖵🟋🗙🕭🛏⛊Ⅴ⚡

(2m) *The Bush, Penallt,*
Monmouth, NP5 4SE.
C17th stone building in idyllic
walking country.
Tel: **01600 772765**
Mr & Mrs Boycott.
Fax no: 01600 860236
D: £22.50-£27.50 **S:** £27.50-£27.50.
Open: All Year
Beds: 1F 3D 2T
Baths: 6 En
ㅎ🅿✍🖵🗙🕭🛏⛊Ⅴ🗎

Monmouth 8

National Grid Ref: SO5012

†⚱ Kings Head, Gate House, Vine Tree, Green
Dragon, Punch House, Royal Oak, Robin Hood,
Riverside Inn, French Horn

(0.25m) *Wye Avon, New Dixton*
Road, Monmouth, NP5 3PR.
Actual grid ref: SO512132
Large, interesting stone-built
Victorian house. A family home.
Tel: **01600 713322** Mrs Cantrell.
D: £16.00-£16.00 **S:** £16.00-£21.00.
Open: All Year (not Xmas)
Beds: 1F 1D 1S
Baths: 1 Sh
ㅎ🅿✍🖵🕭🗎⚡

(0.25m ☎) *Riverside Hotel,*
Cinderhill Street, Monmouth,
NP25 5EY.
Actual grid ref: SO504123
Outstanding converted C17th
coaching inn.
Grades: WTB 2 Star, AA 2 Star
Tel: **01600 715577** Mr Dodd.
Fax no: 01600 712668
D: £25.00-£34.00 **S:** £40.00-£48.00.
Open: All Year
Beds: 2F 6D 9T **Baths:** 17 En
🛏 (1) 🅿 (25) ⊬ ♦ 🏠 ✕ 🏃 🎹 👶 🎦 🛢 ⚡

(On path) *Burton House,* St James
Square, Monmouth, NP5 3DN.
Actual grid ref: SO512129
Georgian town house, restaurants
and shops nearby, good touring
base.
Tel: **01600 714958** Mrs Banfield.
D: £18.00-£18.00 **S:** £22.00-£22.00.
Open: All Year (not Xmas)
Beds: 1F 1D 1T **Baths:** 1 Sh
🅿 (3) 🏠 🏃 🎹 🎦 🛢 ⚡

(0.25m ☎) *Offa's Bed &*
Breakfast, 37 Brook Estate,
Monmouth, NP5 3AN.
Situated in beautiful Wye Valley on
Offa's Dyke Path, friendly and
comfortable B&B.
Tel: **01600 716934**
Mr Ruston & Ms West.
D: £17.50-£17.50 **S:** £19.00-£19.00.
Open: Easter to 30 Sept
Beds: 1D 1T **Baths:** 1 Pr 1 Sh
🛏 🅿 (3) ⊬ ♦ 🏠 🏃 🎹 👶 🎦 🛢 ⚡

Osbaston 9

National Grid Ref: SO5014

(1m ☎) *Caseta Alta,* 15 Toynbee
Close, Osbaston, Monmouth,
NP25 3NU.
Actual grid ref: SO505140
Comfortable house. Glorious views
of Monnow Valley. Good food and
base for touring.
Tel: **01600 713023** Mrs Allcock.
D: £17.00-£21.00 **S:** £25.00-£30.00.
Open: All Year (not Xmas)
Beds: 1D 1T 1S
Baths: 1 En 1 Sh
🛏 (2) 🅿 (2) ⊬ ♦ ✕ 🏃 🎦 🛢 ⚡

Mitchel Troy 10

National Grid Ref: SO4910

🍴 🍺 The Cockett

(2m ☎) *Church Farm Guest*
House, Mitchel Troy, Monmouth,
NP25 4HZ.
Actual grid ref: SO492103
C16th character (former)
farmhouse set in large garden with
stream.
Grades: WTB 2 Star GH,
AA 3 Diamond
Tel: **01600 712176** Mrs Ringer.
D: £20.00-£23.50 **S:** £20.00-£23.00.
Open: All Year (not Xmas)
Beds: 2F 3D 2T 1S
Baths: 6 En 1 Sh
🛏 🅿 (12) ⊬ ♦ 🏠 ✕ 🏃 🎹 🎦 🛢 ⚡

Dingestow 11

National Grid Ref: SO4510

🍴 🍺 Cripple Creek Inn

(5m ☎) *Lower Pen-y-Clawdd*
Farm, Dingestow, Monmouth,
NP5 4BG.
Very attractive house on working
farm, rooms overlook landscaped
gardens.
Grades: WTB 2 Star
Tel: **01600 740223**
Mrs Bayliss.
D: £18.00-£20.00 **S:** £20.00-£20.00.
Open: March to Nov
Beds: 1F 1T
Baths: 1 Sh
🛏 (1) 🅿 (10) ⊬ 🏠 🏃 🎹 🎦

Hendre 12

National Grid Ref: SO4614

🍴 🍺 Halfway House

(On path ☎) *The Hendre*
Farmhouse, Hendre, Monmouth,
NP25 4DJ.
Picturesque farmhouse, ideal base
for walking, golfing, fishing,
exploring Monmouthshire.
Tel: **01600 740484** (also fax no)
Mrs Baker.
D: £22.00-£25.00 **S:** £25.00-£25.00.
Open: All Year (not Xmas)
Beds: 1F 1D 4T 2S
Baths: 2 En 1 Pr 2 Sh
🛏 🅿 (10) ⊬ 🏠 🏃 ✕ 🏃 🎹 🎦 🛢 ⚡

Tregare 13

National Grid Ref: SO4110

(3m ☎) *Court Robert,* Tregare,
Raglan, Monmouthshire, NP5 2BZ.
Actual grid ref: SO401098
Peaceful C16th home, log fires,
antique furnishings, spacious
comfortable bedrooms.
Tel: **01291 690709** (also fax no)
Ms Paxton.
D: £17.00-£17.00 **S:** £19.00.
Open: All Year
Beds: 2F
Baths: 1 Sh
🛏 🅿 (10) 🏠 ✕ 🎹 👶 ⚡

Llantilio Crossenny 14

National Grid Ref: SO3914

🍴 🍺 King's Arms, Three Salmon

(0.5m ☎) *Treloyvan Farm,*
Llantilio Crossenny, Abergavenny,
Monmouthshire, NP7 8UE.
Actual grid ref: SO385172
Warm welcome, beautiful rural
farmhouse, lovely views, guest
rooms with showers.
Tel: **01600 780478** Mrs Watkins.
D: £15.00-£18.00 **S:** £18.00-£22.00.
Open: Easter to Nov
Beds: 1F 1T
Baths: 1 Sh
🛏 🅿 ⊬ 🏠 🏃 ✕ 🏃 🎹 🎦 🛢 ⚡

Llanvetherine 15

National Grid Ref: SO3617

🍴 🍺 King's Arms

(0.5m ☎) *Great Tre-Rhew Farm,*
Llanvetherine, Abergavenny,
Monmouthshire, NP7 8RA.
Actual grid ref: SO377177
Warm welcome on a Welsh work-
ing farm. Peaceful, rural & friendly.
Grades: WTB 2 Star
Tel: **01873 821481** Ms Beavan.
D: £17.50-£20.00 **S:** £17.50-£20.00.
Open: All Year (not Xmas)
Beds: 1F 2D 1T 1S
Baths: 2 Sh
🛏 🅿 🏠 🏃 ✕ 🏃 🎹 🎦 🛢 ⚡

Llangattock Lingoed 16

National Grid Ref: SO3620

(0.25m ☎) *Hunter's Moon Inn,*
Llangattock Lingoed, Abergavenny,
Monmouthshire, NP7 8RR.
Actual grid ref: SO361201
Beautiful C13th inn, away from it
all location at foot of the Skirrid
Mountain.
Tel: **01873 821499** Mr Evans.
Fax no: 01873 821411
D: £26.00-£32.00 **S:** £38.00-£41.00.
Open: All Year
Beds: 4D **Baths:** 4 En
🅿 (40) ⊬ 🏠 🏃 🎹 🎦 🛢 ⚡

Grosmont 17

National Grid Ref: SO4024

🍴 🍺 Angel

(4m) *Lawns Farm,* Grosmont,
Abergavenny, Monmouthshire,
NP7 8ES.
Beautiful C17th farmhouse set in
unspoilt countryside. 'A real gem!'.
Grades: WTB 3 Star
Tel: **01981 240298**
Mr & Mrs Ferneyhough.
Fax no: 01981 241275
D: £20.00-£24.00 **S:** £25.00-£25.00.
Open: Feb to Nov
Beds: 2D 1T **Baths:** 2 En 1 Sh
🛏 🅿 ⊬ 🏠 🏃 🎹 🎦 ⚡

Abergavenny 18

National Grid Ref: SO2914

🍴 🍺 King's Arms, Crown Inn, Old Mitre, Lamb
& Flag, Walnut Tree, Bear Hotel, Nant-y-fyn

(▲ 3m) *Ty'r Morwydd House,*
Pen-y-Pound, Abergavenny,
Monmouthshire, NP7 5UD.
Actual grid ref: SO297147
Tel: **01873 855959**
Under 18: £16.50 **Adults:** £16.50
Showers, Showers, Central heating,
Lounge, Dining room, Games
room, Drying room, Parking,
Evening meal at 6pm, No smoking
Quality group accommodation,
conferences, training etc. Advance
bookings only.

(3m ⊟) *Pentre Court,* Brecon Road, Abergavenny, NP7 9ND.
Grades: WTB 2 Stars
Tel: **01873 853545**
Mrs Candler.
D: £18.00-£24.00
S: £18.00-£30.00.
Open: All Year
Beds: 3D
Baths: 3 En
⌂ P ⌷ ✗ ⻗ ⻗ ✕ 🕭 ⻗ ⅢⅤ ⅰ ✦
Spacious, welcoming Georgian house with open fires, set in 3 acres of pretty stream side interestingly stocked gardens/paddock, spring bulbs, shrubs and roses, with wonderful views over the Usk valley. Just inside the National Park beside footpath to River Usk and Sugarloaf Mountain.

(3m ⊟) *Tyn-y-bryn,* Deriside, Abergavenny, Monmouthshire, NP7 7HT.
Actual grid ref: SO301165
Magnificent views, a homely atmosphere. Comfortable accommodation and warm welcome.
Grades: WTB 3 Star Farm
Tel: **01873 856682** (also fax no)
Ms Belcham.
D: £20.00 **S:** £25.00.
Open: All Year
Beds: 1F 1T 1D
Baths: 2 En
P (6) ⌷ ✗ ⻗ 🕭 Ⅲ Ⅴ ⅰ ✦

(3m) *Ty`r Morwydd House,* Pen-y-Pound, Abergavenny, Monmouthshire, NP7 5UD.
Actual grid ref: SO297147
Quality group accommodation, conferences, training etc. Advance bookings only.
Grades: WTB 3 Star
Tel: **01873 855959** Mrs Senior.
Fax no: 01873 855443
D: £16.50-£16.50 **S:** £16.50-£16.50.
Open: All Year (not Xmas/ New Year)
Beds: 2F 18T 29S
⌂ P (25) ⌷ ⌷ ✗ ⻗ ✕ 🕭 Ⅲ Ⅴ ⅰ ✦

Llanvihangel Crucorney 19

National Grid Ref: SO3220

⦿ ◁ Crown Inn, Skirrid Inn

(1.5m ⊟) *Penyclawdd Farm,* Llanvihangel Crucorney, Abergavenny, Monmouthshire, NP7 7LB.
Actual grid ref: SO312200
Beef/sheep farm, very large garden. Easy reach Abergavenny, Hereford, Cardiff, Hay-on-Wye.
Grades: WTB 3 Star, AA 3 Diamond
Tel: **01873 890591** (also fax no)
Mrs Davies.
D: £20.00-£22.00 **S:** £20.00-£22.00.
Open: All Year
Beds: 2F
Baths: 1 Sh
⌂ P ⌷ ✗ ⻗ ✕ 🕭 Ⅲ Ⅴ ⅰ ✦

(0.5m) *The Skirrid Mountain Inn,* Llanvihangel Crucorney, Abergavenny, Monmouthshire, NP7 8DH.
An historic country inn of unique character. Wales' oldest inn.
Tel: **01873 890258** Miss Grant.
D: £34.50-£39.50 **S:** £34.50-£39.50.
Open: All Year
Beds: 2D
⌂ P ⌷ ⌷ ✗ ⻗ ✕ 🕭 Ⅲ Ⅴ ⅰ ✦

Pandy 20

National Grid Ref: SO3322

⦿ ◁ Lancaster Arms, Pandy Inn, Park Hotel, Skirrid Inn, Offa's Tavern

(1.25m ⊟) *Old Castle Court Farm,* Pandy, Abergavenny, Monmouthshire, NP7 7PH.
Actual grid ref: SO325245
C13th farmhouse near Offa's Dyke path and River Monnow.
Grades: WTB 1 Star
Tel: **01873 890285** Mrs Probert.
D: £15.00-£15.00 **S:** £16.00-£16.00.
Open: Feb to Nov
Beds: 1F 1D 1T **Baths:** 3 En 3 Pr
⌂ P (10) ⌷ ✗ ⻗ 🕭 ⅰ ✦

(0.25m) *Brynhonddu,* Pandy, Abergavenny, Monmouthshire, NP7 7PD.
Actual grid ref: SO326224
Large C16th-C19th country house in great location.
Grades: WTB 2 Star
Tel: **01873 890535** Mrs White.
D: £16.00-£20.00 **S:** £18.00-£18.00.
Open: All Year (not Xmas)
Beds: 1F 1D 1T **Baths:** 1 Sh 1 En
⌂ (5) P (6) ⌷ ⻗ 🕭 Ⅲ Ⅴ ⅰ

(On path) *Lancaster Arms,* Pandy, Abergavenny, Monmouthshire, NP7 8DW.
Actual grid ref: SO333218
Country pub on Offa's Dyke path, edge of Black Mountains.
Grades: WTB 2 Star
Tel: **01873 890699** (also fax no)
Mr & Mrs Lyon.
D: £20.00-£20.00 **S:** £22.00-£22.00.
Open: All Year
Beds: 2T **Baths:** 2 Pr
⌂ P (10) ⌷ ✗ ✕ 🕭 Ⅴ ⅰ

Forest Coalpit 21

National Grid Ref: SO2821

⦿ ◁ Old Crown

(4 m ⊟) *New Inn Farm,* Forest Coalpit, Abergavenny, Monmouthshire, NP7 7LT.
Actual grid ref: SO287216
Peaceful, welcoming mountain farmhouse. Superb views. Walking from the door.
Grades: WTB 3 Star
Tel: **01873 890466** (also fax) Bull.
D: £20.00-£20.00 **S:** £20.00-£20.00.
Open: All Year (not Xmas)
Beds: 1F 1D 1T **Baths:** 1 En 2 Pr
⌂ P (10) ⌷ ⌷ ⻗ 🕭 & Ⅴ ⅰ ✦

Llanthony 22

National Grid Ref: SO2827

(1m) *The Half Moon,* Llanthony, Abergavenny, Monmouthshire, NP7 7NN.
C17th, beautiful countryside. Serves good food and real ales.
Tel: **01873 890611** Mrs Smith.
D: £20.00-£22.00 **S:** £22.00-£25.00.
Open: All Year (not Xmas)
Beds: 2F 4D 2T 1S **Baths:** 2 Sh
⌂ P (8) ⌷ ⻗ ✗ ⻗ 🕭 Ⅴ ⅰ ✦

Capel-y-ffin 23

National Grid Ref: SO2531

(▲ 1.5m) *Capel-y-Ffin Youth Hostel,* Capel-y-Ffin, Abergavenny, Monmouthshire, NP7 7NP.
Actual grid ref: SO250328
Tel: **01873 890650**
Under 18: £5.75 **Adults:** £8.50
Self-catering facilities, Showers, Shop, Lounge, Drying room, Cycle store, Parking, Evening meal at 7.00pm, No smoking, Kitchen facilities, Breakfast available, Credit cards accepted,
Old hill farm set in 40-acre grounds on mountainside in Brecon Beacons National Park.

(0.5m ⊟) *The Grange,* Capel-y-Ffin, Abergavenny, NP7 7NP.
Actual grid ref: SO251315
Small Victorian guest house situated in the beautiful Black Mountains.
Grades: WTB 1 Star
Tel: **01873 890215** Mrs Griffiths.
Fax no: 01873 890157
D: £22.50-£23.00 **S:** £22.50-£23.00.
Open: Easter to Nov
Beds: 1F 1D 1T 1S **Baths:** 3 En
⌂ (6) P (10) ⌷ ⻗ ✗ 🕭 Ⅲ & Ⅴ ⅰ ✦

Llanigon 24

National Grid Ref: SO2139

⦿ ◁ Black Lion

(2m) *The Old Post Office,* Llanigon, Hay-on-Wye, Hereford, HR3 5QA.
A very special find in Black Mountains, superb vegetarian breakfast. **Grades:** WTB 3 Star GH
Tel: **01497 820008** Mrs Webb.
D: £17.00-£25.00 **S:** £20.00-£45.00.
Open: All Year
Beds: 1F 1D 1T **Baths:** 2 En 1 Sh
⌂ P (3) ⌷ ⌷ 🕭 Ⅲ Ⅴ ⅰ ✦

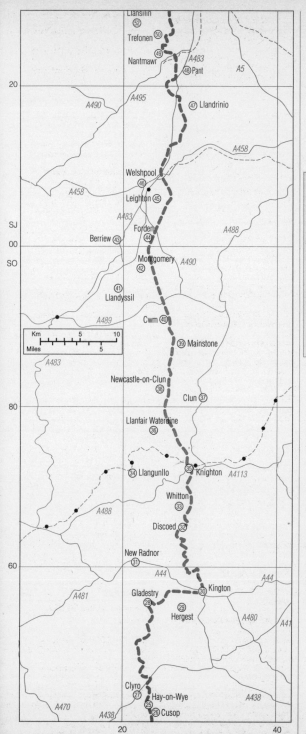

(2m) **Llwynbrain**, *Llanigon, Hay-on-Wye, Hereford, HR3 5QF.*
Warm, friendly family farmhouse with views of Black Mountains.
Tel: **01497 847266**
D: £18.00-£25.00 **S:** £18.00-£25.00.
Open: All Year (not Xmas)
Beds: 2F 1S
Baths: 1 Sh
🛏 🅿 (6) 🛌 🐕 🏃 ⅢⅢ Ⅴ ▮ ✧

Hay-on-Wye   25

National Grid Ref: SO2242

🍺 🍴 Swan Hotel, Old Black Lion, Hollybush Inn, Kilvert Court

(On path 🚐) **Tinto House,** *Broad Street, Hay-on-Wye, Hereford, HR3 5DB.*
Actual grid ref: SO228424
Grades: WTB 3 Star,
AA 4 Diamond
Tel: **01497 820590** Mr Evans.
Fax no: 01497 821058
D: £22.50 **S:** £30.00.
Open: All Year (not Xmas)
Beds: 1F 2D 1T
Baths: 4 En
🛏 🅿 (2) ✂ 🛌 🐕 🏃 ⅢⅢ Ⅴ ▮ ✧
Comfortable Grade II Listed Georgian town house in the centre of famous book town of Hay-on-Wye, which has a large garden overlooking the River Wye and Radnorshire Hills.

(On path) **Brookfield Guest House,** *Brook Street, Hay-on-Wye, Hereford, HR3 5BQ.*
C16th Listed building in historic Hay-on-Wye. Atmosphere in this little market town is remarkable.
Tel: **01497 820518** Ms Shaw.
Fax no: 01497 821818
D: £18.00 **S:** £20.00.
Open: All Year
Beds: 2F 3D 3T **Baths:** 2 En 2 Sh
🛏 (6) 🅿 (4) 🛌 🏃 ⅢⅢ Ⅴ ▮ ✧

(On path) **The Bear,** *Bear Street, Hay-on-Wye, Hereford, HR3 5AN.*
Charming comfortable 16th century house in centre of Hay-on-Wye.
Tel: **01497 821302** Field.
Fax no: 01497 820506
D: £22.00-£27.00 .
Open: All Year
Beds: 2D 1T **Baths:** 2 En 1 Sh
🅿 (4) ✂ 🛌 🐕 🏃 ⅢⅢ Ⅴ ▮ ✧

🚐 sign means that,
given due notice,
owners will pick you
up from the path
and drop you off
within reason.

(On path) **Rest for the Tired,**
*6 Broad Street, Hay-on-Wye,
Hereford, HR3 5DB.*
16th century building with modern
comforts hearty breakfasts a warm
welcome.
Tel: **01497 820550** Ms Fellowes.
D: £18.00-£18.00 **S:** £18.00-£18.00.
Open: All Year
Beds: 2D 1T
Baths: 3 En
⛷ ₽ (10) ⊬⛌ ⊐ ♉ 皿 Ⅵ ▮ ✦

(On path ⛌) **La Fosse Guest
House,** *Oxford Road, Hay-on-Wye,
Hereford, HR3 5AJ.*
Make your holiday! Stay once and
you'll be back.
Tel: **01497 820613** Mr Crook.
D: £20.00-£20.00 .
Open: All Year
Beds: 4D 1T
Baths: 5 En
⛷ (9) ₽ (5) ⊬⊐ ♉ ⊐ 皿 Ⅵ ▮ ✦

(On path ⛌) **Belmont House,** *Hay-on-Wye, Hereford, HR3 5DA.*
Actual grid ref: SO229426
1700 coaching house with large
bedrooms, with antique furniture
and things.
Tel: **01497 820718** (also fax no)
Mr Gwynne.
D: £16.00-£20.00 **S:** £20.00-£20.00.
Open: All Year
Beds: 2F 2T 2D 1S
Baths: 2 En 5 Pr 1 Sh
⛷ ₽ (10) ⊐ ♉ 皿 Ⅵ ✦

(0.25m ⛌) **Lansdowne,** *Cusop,
Hay-on-Wye, Hereford, HR3 5RF.*
Actual grid ref: SO237417
Victorian house, pretty garden,
beautiful views, elegant spacious
ensuite bedrooms. Quiet.
Tel: **01497 820125** Mr Flack.
D: £17.00-£18.00 **S:** £23.00-£36.00.
Open: Feb-Nov
Beds: 1D 1T
Baths: 2 En
⛷ ₽ (3) ⊬⊐ ⊐ 皿 ₺ Ⅵ ▮

(On path) **The Kingfisher,**
*Newport Street, Hay-on-Wye,
Hereford, HR3 5BE.*
Actual grid ref: SO232428
Hay on Wye - book town.
Kingfisher House is renowned for
friendly atmosphere.
Tel: **01497 820448**
D: £15.00-£20.00 **S:** £15.00-£20.00.
Open: All Year
Beds: 1F 2D 2T 2S
Baths: 2 En 3 Sh
⛷ ₽ (8) ⊐ ♉ ✕ 皿 Ⅵ ▮ ✦

**Taking your dog?
Book *in advance*
ONLY with owners
who accept dogs (♉)**

**Please take muddy
boots <u>off</u> before
entering premises**

Cusop 26
National Grid Ref: SO2341

(0.25m ⛌) **Fernleigh,** *Hardwick
Road, Cusop, Hay-on-Wye,
Hereford, HR3 5QX.*
Quiet location walking distance of
the famous book town of Hay-on-Wye.
Tel: **01497 820459** Mr Hughes.
D: £15.00-£19.00 **S:** £19.00-£19.00.
Open: Easter to Oct
Beds: 2D 1S
Baths: 1 En 1 Sh
⛷ ₽ (4) ⊬⊐ ✕ 皿 Ⅵ ▮

Clyro 27
National Grid Ref: SO2143

♉⛨ Baskerville Arms

(2m) **Tump Farm,** *Clyro, Hay-on-Wye, Hereford, HR3 6JY.*
Actual grid ref: SO218463
Comfortable farmhouse accommo-
dation, overlooking Wye Valley,
near Hay-on-Wye. Substantial
breakfasts.
Tel: **01497 820912** Mrs Francis.
D: £12.50-£15.00 **S:** £14.00-£16.50.
Open: All Year
Beds: 1T 1D **Baths:** 1 Sh
₽ (4) ⊐ ⊐ 皿 Ⅵ ✦

Gladestry 28
National Grid Ref: SO2355

♉⛨ Royal Oak

(1m ⛌) **Offa's Dyke Lodge,**
*Gladestry, Kington, Herefordshire,
HR5 3NR.*
Actual grid ref: SO232550
Luxury accommodation,
spectacular views, fine cooking, the
perfect relaxing break.
Grades: WTB 4 Star
Tel: **01544 370341** Steve Wright.
Fax no: 01544 370342
D: £25.00-£27.00 **S:** £33.00-£35.00.
Open: All Year
Beds: 1D 2T **Baths:** 2 En 1 Pr
⛷ ₽ (10) ⊬⊐ 皿 ₺ Ⅵ ▮ ✦

(1m ⛌) **Wain Wen,** *Gladestry,
Kington, Herefordshire, HR5 3NT.*
Actual grid ref: SO217546
Comfortable farmhouse on
working farm amid unspoilt Border
country.
Tel: **01544 370226** Mrs Lloyd.
D: £16.00-£16.00 **S:** £16.00-£16.00.
Open: Apr to Oct
Beds: 1D 1T **Baths:** 2 Sh
⛷ (8) ₽ (4) ⊐ ✕ 皿 Ⅵ ▮ ✦

Hergest 29
National Grid Ref: SO2753

♉⛨ The Harp, Royal Oak

(0.5m) **Bucks Head House,** *Upper
Hergest, Hergest, Kington,
Herefordshire, HR3 3EW.*
Actual grid ref: SO262550
Situated on south side of Hergest
Ridge and Offa's Dyke Path.
Tel: **01544 231063** Mrs Protheroe.
D: £18.00-£20.00 **S:** £18.00-£20.00.
Open: All Year
Beds: 2F 2D 1T 1S
Baths: 2 Sh
⛷ ₽ (6) ⊐ ♉ ✕ 皿 Ⅵ ▮

Kington 30
National Grid Ref: SO2956

♉⛨ Harp, Swan Inn, Royal Oak, Queen's Head,
Sun

(0.25m ⛌) **Dunfield Cottage,**
Kington, Herefordshire, HR5 3NN.
Friendly, relaxed; lovely
views;large garden; log fires;
H&C in bedrooms.
Tel: **01544 230632** (also fax no)
Ms Green.
D: £16.00-£18.00 **S:** £16.00-£18.00.
Open: All Year
Beds: 1T 1D 1S
Baths: 1 Sh
⛷ (10) ₽ (6) ⊬⊐ ✕ 皿 Ⅵ ▮

(On path) **Church House,** *Church
Road, Kington, Herefordshire,
HR5 3AG.*
Actual grid ref: SO292567
Large rooms with fine views in
elegant Georgian family home.
Tel: **01544 230534** Mrs Darwin.
Fax no: 01544 231100
D: £20.00-£20.00 **S:** £20.00-£30.00.
Open: All Year (not Xmas)
Beds: 1D 1T **Baths:** 1 Sh
⛷ ₽ (2) ⊬⊐ 皿 ▮ ✦

(0.25m) **Bollingham House,**
Kington, Herefordshire, HR5 3LE.
Period residence with glorious
views. Gracious rooms. Delightful
English garden.
Tel: **01544 327326** Mrs Grant.
Fax no: 01544 327880
D: £25.00-£28.50 **S:** £27.50.
Open: All Year
Beds: 2D 1T 1S **Baths:** 2 Pr
⛷ ₽ (10) ⊬⊐ ✕ 皿 Ⅵ ▮ ✦

(On path) **Cambridge Cottage,**
*19 Church Street, Kington,
Herefordshire, HR5 3BE.*
Actual grid ref: SO295567
C17th cottage; warm welcome,
many return visits, comfortable
beds, camping.
Tel: **01544 231300**
Mr & Mrs Hooton.
D: £17.50-£17.50 **S:** £17.50-£17.50.
Open: All Year (not Xmas)
Beds: 1F 1S
Baths: 1 En 1 Sh
⛷ (3) ₽ (2) ⊬⊐ ♉ 皿 Ⅵ ▮ ✦

New Radnor   31

National Grid Ref: SO2160

¶ ⊲ Red Lion

(4m 🚌) *Bache Farm, New Radnor, Presteigne, Powys, LD8 2TG.*
Actual grid ref: SO226627
C17th farmhouse in beautiful unspoilt countryside amidst the Welsh Marches.
Grades: WTB 2 Star Farm
Tel: 01544 350680 Mrs Hardwick.
D: £18.00-£19.50 **S:** £22.00-£25.00.
Open: All Year (not Xmas)
Beds: 2D 1T **Baths:** 1 Sh
🛏 🅿 🗡 ⌨ 🕯 🛉 🐾 ✕ 🏊 ⅲ Ⅴ 🛉 ⏀

Discoed   32

National Grid Ref: SO2764

¶ ⊲ Crown, Royal Oak

(0.5m 🚌) *Gumma Farm, Discoed, Presteigne, Powys, LD8 2NP.*
Actual grid ref: SO288651
Old farm house set in 350 acres tastefully furnished with antiques.
Tel: 01547 560243 Mrs Owens.
D: £16.00-£21.00 **S:** £16.00-£17.00.
Open: Easter to Oct
Beds: 1D 1T 1S **Baths:** 1 En 1 Sh
🛏 🅿 ⌨ 🕯 ✕ 🏊 ⅲ Ⅴ 🛉 ⏀

Whitton   33

National Grid Ref: SO2767

¶ ⊲ Hundred House

(1m 🚌) *Pilleth Court, Whitton, Knighton, Powys, LD7 1NP.*
Actual grid ref: SO257683
16th century house in historic location offering quality accommodation.
Tel: 01547 560272 (also fax no)
Mrs Hood. **D:** £18.00 **S:** £20.00.
Open: All Year (not Xmas)
Beds: 1F 2D 1T **Baths:** 1 En 1 Sh
🛏 (9) 🅿 (6) ⌨ ✕ 🏊 ⅲ Ⅴ 🛉 ⏀

Llangunllo   34

National Grid Ref: SO2171

¶ ⊲ Castle, Horse & Jockey, Hundred House

(3m 🚌) *Cefnsuran Farm, Llangunllo, Knighton, Powys, LD7 1SL.*
Grades: WTB 3 Star
Tel: 01547 550219 Mrs Morgan.
Fax no: 01547 550348
D: £20.00-£22.50 **S:** £20.00-£25.00.
Open: All Year (not Xmas/New Year)
Beds: 1F 1D 1T **Baths:** 1 En 1 Pr
🛏 🅿 (10) ⌨ ✕ 🏊 ⅲ Ⅴ 🛉 ⏀
Set in beautiful location for a peaceful, interesting and private holiday. Guests are welcome to stroll around gardens, waymarked farm trails and woodlands. Pools with abundant wildlife - flyfishing possible. Games room with fullsize snooker table. Self-catering available.

(3m) *Rhiwlas, Llangunllo Halt, Llangunllo, Knighton, Powys, LD7 1SY.*
Actual grid ref: SO2073
The farm which is mainly stock producing includes a section of the Glyndwr's Way.
Tel: 01547 550256 Mrs Deakins.
D: £15.50 **S:** £16.00-£16.50.
Open: Easter to Oct
Beds: 2D **Baths:** 1 Sh
🛏 🅿 ⌨ 🕯 🛉 🛉

Knighton   35

National Grid Ref: SO2872

¶ ⊲ Hundred House, George & Dragon, Horse & Jockey

(0.25m 🚌) *Westwood, Presteigne Road, Knighton, Powys, LD7 1HY.*
Welcome to our detached Victorian home. Quiet town location; spacious, comfortable accommodation.
Tel: 01547 520317 Mrs Sharratt.
D: £17.00-£17.00 **S:** £17.00-£17.00.
Open: All Year
Beds: 1F 1D 1S **Baths:** 1 En 1 Sh
🛏 🅿 (4) ⌨ ✕ 🏊 ⅲ Ⅴ 🛉 ⏀

(0.25m 🚌) *Offas Dyke House, 4 High Street, Knighton , Powys, LD7 1AT.*
Warm friendly B&B situated in the heart of Knighton.
Grades: WTB 2 Star
Tel: 01547 528634 (also fax no) Ashe.
D: £16.00-£16.00 **S:** £16.00-£16.00.
Open: All Year
Beds: 2T 3D 1S
Baths: 3 Sh
🛏 🅿 (4) ⌨ ✕ 🏊 ⅲ Ⅴ 🛉 ⏀

(On path) *The Fleece House, Market Street, Knighton, Powys, LD7 1BB.*
Actual grid ref: S0285724
Attractive decorated quality accommodation in converted C18th coaching inn.
Grades: WTB 3 Star GH
Tel: 01547 520168 Mrs Simmons.
D: £20.00-£28.00 **S:** £23.00-£35.00.
Open: All Year
Beds: 6T
Baths: 2 En 2 Sh
🅿 ⌨ 🕯 ⅲ Ⅴ 🛉 ⏀

(0.25m 🚌) *15 Mill Green, Knighton, Powys, LD7 1EE.*
Welcoming colourful old cottage with secluded garden and private courtyard.
Tel: 01547 520075 Mrs Stothert.
D: £14.00-£15.00 **S:** £14.00-£15.00.
Open: Easter to Oct
Beds: 1D 1T **Baths:** 1 En 1 Sh
🛏 🅿 (1) ⌨ 🐾 🏊 ⅲ Ⅴ 🛉 ⏀

D = Price range per person sharing in a double room

(0.25m) *Larkspur, Larkey Lane, Knighton, Powys, LD7 1DN.*
Quiet location overlooking town centre and castle site.
Tel: 01547 528764
Mrs Heard.
D: £15.00-£15.00
S: £15.00-£15.00.
Open: All Year
Beds: 1D 1T
Baths: 1 Pr
🛏 (1) 🅿 ⌨ 🕯 ⅲ Ⅴ ⏀

Llanfair Waterdine   36

National Grid Ref: SO2476

¶ ⊲ Lloyney Inn, Red Lion

(1.5 m 🚌) *The Mill, Lloyney, Llanfair Waterdine, Knighton, Powys, LD7 1RG.*
Actual grid ref: SO245759
Wonderful countryside in the Teme Valley, home cooking.
Grades: ETC 2 Star
Tel: 01547 528049 (also fax no)
Mr & Mrs Davies.
D: £20.00-£20.00
S: £20.00-£20.00.
Open: All Year (not Xmas/New Year)
Beds: 2D 2T 1S
Baths: 1 En 2 Pr 2 Sh
🛏 🅿 (6) ⌨ 🐾 ✕ 🏊 🐕 Ⅴ 🛉 ⏀

Clun   37

National Grid Ref: SO3080

¶ ⊲ Sun Inn, White Horse, Castle Hotel, Three Tuns, Bishop's Castle

(🔺 3m) *Clun Mill Youth Hostel, The Mill, Clun, Craven Arms, Shropshire, SY8 8NY.*
Actual grid ref: SO303812
Tel: 01588 640582
Under 18: £6.50
Adults: £9.25
Self-catering facilities, Showers, Lounge, Cycle store, Parking, No smoking, WC, Kitchen facilities, Credit cards accepted
Former watermill (workings still visible) upgraded yet unspoilt by modern development, set in stone-built town (C16th humpbacked bridge) and Norman castle.

(3m 🚌) *The Old Stables And Saddlery, Crown House, Church Street, Clun, Craven Arms, Shropshire, SY7 8JW.*
Actual grid ref: SO305805
Superb self-contained Georgian stable conversion in lovely courtyard garden.
Grades: ETC 4 Diamond
Tel: 01588 640780
Mrs Bailey & Mr R Maund.
D: £20.00-£22.50
S: £22.00-£25.00.
Open: All Year (not Xmas)
Beds: 1D 1T 1S
Baths: 1 En 1 Pr 1 Sh
🛏 (8) 🅿 (2) ⌨ 🐾 🏊 ⅲ Ⅴ 🛉 ⏀

(2.5m) *Llanhedric Farm, Clun, Craven Arms, Shropshire, SY7 8NG.*
Actual grid ref: SO283842
Tranquil country retreat - rooms overlooking beautiful views of Clun Valley.
Tel: **01588 640203** (also fax no)
Mrs Jones.
D: £18.00-£20.00 **S:** £18.00-£21.00.
Open: Easter to Nov
Beds: 1F 1D 1T **Baths:** 1 En 1 Sh
⛺ P (5) ⚡☐✗ 🛏 🛁 Ⅴ 🖊 ✦

(3m 🏍) *Clun Farm, High Street, Clun, Craven Arms, Shropshire, SY7 8JB.*
Actual grid ref: SO302808
C16th double cruck character farmhouse in the heart of the village.
Tel: **01588 640432**
Mr & Mrs Whitfield.
D: £18.00-£20.00 **S:** £18.00.
Open: All Year (not Xmas)
Beds: 1F 1T 2S **Baths:** 1 En 1 Sh
⛺ P (6) ☐ 🛁 🖊 ✦

Newcastle-on-Clun　　38

National Grid Ref: SO2482

(▲ 0.25m) *Old School Bunkhouse, The Old School, Newcastle-on-Clun, Craven Arms, Shropshire, SY7 8QL.*
Actual grid ref: SO252825
Tel: **01588 640779**
Adults: £8.50

Mainstone　　39

National Grid Ref: SO2787

🍴 🍺 Sun Inn, White Horse, Castle Hotel, Three Tuns, Bishop's Castle

(1m 🏍) *New House Farm, Mainstone, Clun, Craven Arms, Shropshire, SY7 8NJ.*
Actual grid ref: SO275863
Peaceful, isolated C18th farmhouse, set high in Clun Hills near Welsh border.
Tel: **01588 638314** Mrs Ellison.
D: £24.00-£25.00 **S:** £25.00-£28.00.
Open: Easter to Oct
Beds: 1F 1T **Baths:** 1 En 1 Pr
P (6) ⚡☐ 🍴 🛏 🛁 Ⅴ 🖊 ✦

Cwm　　40

National Grid Ref: SO2590

🍴 🍺 Dragon Hotel, Castle Hotel

(On path 🏍) *The Drewin Farm, Cwm, Church Stoke, Montgomery, Powys, SY15 6TW.*
Actual grid ref: SO261905
C17th farmhouse with panoramic views. Offa's Dyke footpath on doorstep.
Tel: **01588 620325** (also fax no)
Mrs Richards.
D: £20.00-£21.00 **S:** £22.00-£22.00.
Open: Easter to Oct
Beds: 1F 1T **Baths:** 2 En
⛺ P (6) ⚡☐ 🍴 ✗ 🛏 🛁 Ⅴ 🖊 ✦

Llandyssil　　41

National Grid Ref: SO1995

(2.5m 🏍) *The Dingle, Cwminkin, Llandyssil, Montgomery, Powys, SY15 6HH.*
Actual grid ref: SO204959
Converted barn. Private peaceful valley, running stream, wildlife. Garaging.
Tel: **01686 668838** Mrs Nicholson.
D: £15.00-£15.00 **S:** £15.00-£15.00.
Open: All Year
Beds: 1F 1D 1S
Baths: 1 Sh
⛺ (8) P (6) ⚡☐ 🛏 🛁 Ⅴ ✦

Montgomery　　42

National Grid Ref: SO2296

🍴 🍺 Cottage, Dragon

(0.75m 🏍) *The Manor House, Pool Road, Montgomery, Powys, SY15 6QY.*
Actual grid ref: SO223968
Former house of correction, friendly welcome, private house.
Tel: **01686 668736** Mrs Williams.
D: £16.00-£16.00 **S:** £16.00-£16.00.
Open: All Year
Beds: 1D 1T 1S
Baths: 1 En 1 Pr
⛺ P (2) ☐ 🍴 🛏 🛁 Ⅴ 🖊 ✦

(On path 🏍) *Little Brompton Farm, Montgomery, Powys, SY15 6HY.*
Actual grid ref: SO244941
Working C17th farm on Offa's Dyke. Superior quality for the discerning.
Tel: **01686 668371** (also fax no)
Mrs Bright.
D: £19.00-£20.00 **S:** £20.00-£22.00.
Open: All Year
Beds: 1F 1D 1T **Baths:** 2 En 1 Pr
⛺ P ⚡☐ 🍴 🛏 🛁 Ⅴ 🖊 ✦

Berriew　　43

National Grid Ref: SJ1800

🍴 🍺 Horseshoes, Talbot Hotel, Red Lion

(6m 🏍) *Plasdwpa Farm, Berriew, Welshpool, Powys, SY21 8PS.*
Actual grid ref: SJ165010
Magnificent Mountain setting in this very comfortable farmhouse, very tranquil.
Grades: WTB 3 Star
Tel: **01686 640298** (also fax no)
Mrs Hughes.
D: £15.00-£16.00 **S:** £18.00-£20.00.
Open: March to November
Beds: 1F 1D 1T **Baths:** 1 Sh
⛺ P (4) ⚡☐ ✗ 🛏 Ⅴ 🖊 ✦

S = Price range for a single person in a single room

Forden　　44

National Grid Ref: SJ2200

🍴 🍺 Green Dragon, Horseshoe, King's Head, Railway, Red Lion, Royal Oak, Star Inn, Talbot

(0.5m) *Meithrinfa, Forden, Welshpool, Powys, SY21 8RT.*
Grades: WTB 3 Star
Tel: **01938 580458**
Mrs Hughes.
D: £18.00-£20.00
S: £20.00-£22.00.
Open: Easter to Nov
Beds: 1F 1T
Baths: 2 En
⛺ P (3) ⚡☐ ✗ 🛏 🛁 Ⅴ
Meithrinfa is a large bungalow set in its own grounds, in a elevated position, overlooking the Severn Valley. Only 2 miles from market town of Welshpool and Powis Castle, Llanfair and W/pool steam railway canal barges, riding school, golf, lakes and mountains.

(0.5m 🏍) *Church House, Forden, Welshpool, Powys, SY21 8NE.*
Actual grid ref: SJ227010
Georgian house, near Powis Castle and Welshpool Light Railway. Large garden.
Tel: **01938 580353**
Mrs Bright.
D: £17.50-£17.50
S: £17.50-£17.50.
Open: All Year (not Xmas/ New Year)
Beds: 1F 1D 1T
Baths: 1 Pr　1 Sh
⛺ P ⚡☐ ✗ 🛏 🛁 Ⅴ 🖊 ✦

(On path 🏍) *Heath Cottage, Forden, Welshpool, Powys, SY21 8LX.*
Actual grid ref: SJ239024
Absolute peace, spectacular views and our own free range eggs.
Tel: **01938 580453** Mrs Payne.
Fax no: 01938 580543
D: £18.00-£20.00
S: £20.00-£25.00.
Open: Easter to Oct
Beds: 1F 1D 1S
Baths: 3 En
⛺ P (4) ⚡☐ 🛏 🛁 Ⅴ 🖊 ✦

Leighton　　45

National Grid Ref: SJ2305

🍴 🍺 Talbot

(0.75m 🏍) *Orchard House, Leighton, Welshpool, Powys, SY21 8HN.*
Actual grid ref: SJ247059
Friendly welcome and all comforts of home, good breakfast.
Tel: **01938 553624** (also fax no)
Mrs Pearce.
D: £18.00-£22.00
S: £18.00-£25.00.
Open: All Year
Beds: 2D 1T
Baths: 3 En
⛺ P ☐ 🍴 🛏 🛁 Ⅴ ✦

Welshpool 46

National Grid Ref: SJ2207

🍽 🍺 Green Dragon, Horseshoe, King's Head, Railway, Red Lion, Royal Oak, Star Inn, Talbot

(3m 🚗) *Tynllwyn Farm, Welshpool, Powys, SY21 9BW.*
Actual grid ref: SJ214080
Visitor's remark - 'Nearest place to Heaven'. Friendly, quiet, wonderful views.
Grades: WTB 3 Star, AA 3 Star
Tel: **01938 553175** Mrs Emberton
Fax no: 01938 553996
D: £15.50-£18.00 S: £17.50-£22.00.
Open: All Year (not Xmas)
Beds: 3F 1D 1T 1S
Baths: 3 En 2 Sh
🛇 🅿 (10) 🗱 🏠 🍴 🎍 🛏 🔟 🕯 ⚡

(1m 🚗) *Lower Trelydan, Guilesfield, Welshpool, Powys, SY21 9PH.*
Award-winning black-and-white farmhouse, ensuite, licensed bar, evening meals, Welshpool 2 miles.
Grades: WTB 4 Star,
AA 4 Diamond
Tel: **01938 553105** (also fax no)
Mrs Jones.
D: £24.00-£25.00 S: £25.00-£28.00.
Open: All Year (not Xmas/ New Year)
Beds: 1F 1D 1T Baths: 3 En
🛇 🅿 🗱 🗱 🍴 🎍 🛏 🔟 🕯 ⚡

(2m 🚗) *Tresi-Aur, Brookfield Road, Welshpool, Powys, SY21 7PZ.*
Detached family home offers friendly hospitality conveniently situated to town.
Grades: WTB 2 Star
Tel: **01938 552430** Mrs Davies.
D: £16.00-£18.00 S: £16.00-£18.00.
Open: Jan to Nov
Beds: 1F 1D 1T 1S
Baths: 1 Pr
🛇 🅿 (2) 🗱 🗱 🎍 🛏 🔟 🕯 ⚡

(1.75m 🚗) *Hafren Guest House, 38 Salop Road, Welshpool, Powys, SY21 7EA.*
Actual grid ref: SJ227076
Georgian house with medieval links in 'Gateway to Mid-Wales' town.
Tel: **01938 554112** Ms Shaw.
D: £16.00-£18.00 S: £18.00-£20.00.
Open: All Year (not Xmas)
Beds: 1F 1D 1T
Baths: 1 En 1 Sh
🛇 🅿 (3) 🗱 🏠 🗱 🎍 🛏 🔟 🕯 ⚡

(3m) *Dysserth Hall, Powis Castle, Welshpool, Powys, SY21 8RQ.*
Comfortable, friendly, Listed manor home in peaceful countryside, superb view.
Tel: **01938 552153** (also fax no)
Mrs Marriott.
D: £21.00-£22.50 S: £21.00-£25.00.
Open: Easter to Nov
Beds: 1D 2T 1S
Baths: 2 Pr 1 Sh
🛇 (8) 🅿 (12) 🗱 🎍 🛏 🔟 🕯 ⚡

Llandrinio 47

National Grid Ref: SJ2817

🍽 🍺 Punch Bowl

(3m 🚗) *Haimwood, Llandrinio, Llanymynech, Powys, SY22 6SQ.*
Actual grid ref: SJ318162
C18th guesthouse. Beautiful rural situation and views. River Severn.
Tel: **01691 830764** (also fax no)
Mrs Nixon.
D: £18.00-£23.00
S: £18.00-£28.00.
Open: All Year
Beds: 1D 2T
Baths: 1 En 1 Sh
🛇 🅿 (6) 🗱 🗶 🎍 🔟 🕯 ⚡

Pant 48

National Grid Ref: SJ2722

(1m) *Three Firs, Pant, Oswestry, Shropshire, SY10 8LB.*
Actual grid ref: SJ269222
Quiet homely countryside accommodation adjoining golf course, Welsh/English border.
Grades: ETC 3 Diamond
Tel: **01691 831375**
D: £18.00-£25.00 S: £18.00-£25.00.
Open: All Year
Beds: 2F 1D
Baths: 2 En 1 Sh
🛇 🅿 (6) 🗱 🏠 🗱 🎍 🛏 🔟 🕯 ⚡

Nantmawr 49

National Grid Ref: SJ2424

(▲0.5m) *The Engine House, Rose Hill, Nantmawr, Oswestry, Shropshire, SY10 9HL.*
Actual grid ref: SJ253249
Tel: **01691 659358**
Under 18: £12.00
Adults: £12.00
Self-catering facilities, Television, Showers, Central heating, Dining room, Parking, Facilities for disabled people
Renovated limestone building. Quality facilities. 250 acre estate. MB centre.

Trefonen 50

National Grid Ref: SJ2526

(0.25m 🚗) *The Pentre, Trefonen, Oswestry, Shropshire, SY10 9EE.*
Actual grid ref: SJ238260
Rural bliss, 16th century farmhouse, stunning views, dinner specialities.
Grades: AA 4 Diamonds
Tel: **01691 653952** Mr Gilbert.
D: £21.00-£21.00
S: £29.00-£29.00.
Open: All Year (not Xmas/ New Year)
Beds: 2F
Baths: 2 En
🛇 🅿 (10) 🗱 🏠 🗱 🗶 🎍 🛏 🔟 🕯 ⚡

Oswestry 51

National Grid Ref: SJ2929

🍽 🍺 Bradford Arms, Bear Hotel, Navigation Inn, Queen's Head, Sweeny Hall, Wynnstay Hotel

(3m) *Ash Court, Weston Lane, Oswestry, Shropshire, SY11 2BB.*
Beautiful C18th house with country style bedrooms overlooking Gardens and countryside.
Grades: ETC 4 Diamond ⚡
Tel: **01691 662921** Edwards.
D: £18.00-£20.00 S: £20.00-£23.00.
Open: All Year
Beds: 1T 1D Baths: 1 Sh
🛇 🅿 (2) 🗱 🗱 🎍 🛏 🔟 🕯

(3m 🚗) *Montrose, Weston Lane, Oswestry, Shropshire, SY11 2BG.*
Actual grid ref: SJ289288
Comfortable Victorian house, easy walk into town. Good touring centre.
Grades: ETC 2 Diamond
Tel: **01691 652063** Mrs Leggatt.
D: £15.00-£15.00 S: £15.00-£18.00.
Open: All Year
Beds: 2T Baths: 1 Sh
🛇 🅿 (4) 🗱 🗱 🎍 🛏 🔟 🕯 ⚡

(3m) *Foel Guest House, 18 Hampton Road, Oswestry, Shropshire, SY11 1SJ.*
Actual grid ref: SJ285297
Quiet location. Walk through our beautiful park to town centre.
Tel: **01691 652184** Mrs Willetts.
D: £16.00 S: £16.00-£20.00.
Open: All Year (not Xmas)
Beds: 1D 1T 1S Baths: 2 Sh
🛇 (5) 🅿 (4) 🗱 🗱 🏠 🎍 🛏 🔟 🕯 ⚡

(2m 🚗) *Elgar House, 16 Elgar Close, Oswestry, Shropshire, SY11 2LZ.*
Actual grid ref: SJ299299
Panoramic view elevated sun terrace and conservatory. Private bar, Sky TV.
Tel: **01691 661323** Mr Harding.
D: £20.00-£25.00 S: £25.00-£35.00.
Open: All Year
Beds: 1F 3D 3S Baths: 3 En
🛇 🅿 (3) 🗱 🗱 🎍 🛏 🔟 🔥 🕯 ⚡

(3m) *Llwyn Guesthouse, 5 Llwyn Terrace, Oswestry, Shropshire, SY11 1HR.*
Stay with us where the magic of Shropshire meets the mystery of Wales.
Tel: **01691 670746** Berry-Hart.
D: £16.00-£16.00 S: £18.00-£18.00.
Open: All Year (not Xmas)
Beds: 1D 2T
Baths: 2 Sh
🛇 🅿 (3) 🗱 🏠 🗱 🎍 🛏 🔟 🕯 ⚡

Pay B&Bs by cash or cheque and be prepared to pay up front.

Llansilin 52

National Grid Ref: SJ2028

⊯ ⫪ Wynnstay

(3m 🚌) *Lloran Ganol, Llansilin, Oswestry, Shropshire, SY10 7QX.*
Actual grid ref: SJ177270
Dairy and sheep working farm set in its own Welsh valley.
Grades: WTB 3 Star
Tel: 01691 791287
Mrs Jones.
D: £15.00 **S:** £15.00.
Open: All Year
Beds: 1D 1T 1S
Baths: 2 Sh
🛇 🅿 🗶⫪🗙⫪ 🏧 Ⅷ Ⓥ

Craignant 53

National Grid Ref: SJ2535

⊯ ⫪ Green inn

(On path 🚌) *The Quarry, Craignant, Selattyn, Oswestry, Shropshire, SY11 4LT.*
Attractive farmhouse.
Tel: 01691 658674
Mrs Tomley.
D: £16.00-£16.00
S: £16.00-£16.00.
Open: Easter to October
Beds: 1D 2S 3F
Baths: 1 Sh
🛇 🅿 🗶⫪⌖🗙 🏧 Ⅷ Ⓥ ⌁ ∮

Weston Rhyn 54

National Grid Ref: SJ2835

⊯ ⫪ The Plough

(2m 🚌) *Rhoswiel Lodge, Weston Rhyn, Oswestry, Shropshire, SY10 7TG.*
Victorian country house pleasantly situated beside Shropshire Union/Llangollen Canal.
Tel: 01691 777609
Mrs Plunkett.
Fax no: 01691 774952
D: £16.00-£17.50 **S:** £18.00-£22.00.
Open: All Year (not Xmas)
Beds: 1D 1T
Baths: 1 En 1 Pr
🛇 🅿 (2)🗶⫪🕮 🏧 Ⓥ ∮

Chirk 55

National Grid Ref: SJ2837

⊯ ⫪ Waterside, Hand, Club House

(On path 🚌) *Sun Cottage, Pentre, Chirk, Wrexham, LL14 5AW.*
Actual grid ref: SJ289409
Welcoming character cottage, 1723. Spectacular woodland views over river valley.
Tel: 01691 774542
Mrs Little.
D: £17.00-£17.00 **S:** £17.00-£17.00.
Open: All Year (not Xmas)
Beds: 2F 1S
Baths: 2 Sh
🛇 (10) 🅿 (3)🗶⫪🕮🗙 🏧 Ⅷ Ⓥ ⌁ ∮

(1.5m 🚌) *Pedlar Corner B & B, Colliery Road, Chirk, Wrexham, LL14 5PB.*
Actual grid ref: SJ292379
Charming Edwardian cottage, beautiful garden, gorgeous breakfast, old fashioned hospitality.
Grades: WTB 2 Star
Tel: 01691 772903 Mrs Berry.
D: £17.00-£17.00 **S:** £17.00-£17.00.
Open: All Year (not Xmas/New Year)
Beds: 2T
Baths: 1 Sh
🛇 🅿 (3)🗶 🏧 Ⅷ Ⓥ ⌁ ∮

Pentre 56

National Grid Ref: SJ2940

⊯ ⫪ Waterside Bar, Hand Hotel

(On path 🚌) *Pentre Cottage, Pentre, Chirk, Wrexham, Flintshire, LL14 5AW.*
Actual grid ref: SJ288404
Beautiful Welsh cottage with friendly Lancashire welcome; dog-lovers paradise.
Tel: 01691 774265 Mrs Vant.
D: £16.00 **S:** £16.00-£18.00.
Open: All Year (not Xmas)
Beds: 1D 1T
Baths: 1 Pr 1 Sh
🅿 (3)🗗⫪🗙 🏧 Ⅷ Ⓥ ⌁ ∮

(On path) *Cloud Hill, Pentre , Chirk, Wrexham, LL14 5AN.*
1972 Daily Mail House of the Year. Villa style open plan.
Tel: 01691 773359 Mr Sutcliffe.
D: £18.00-£20.00 **S:** £18.00-£25.00.
Open: All Year (not Xmas/New Year)
Beds: 3T 1D
Baths: 2 En 1 Sh
🛇 (10) 🅿 (6)🗗🗙 🏧 Ⅷ Ⓥ ⌁ ∮

Froncysyllte 57

National Grid Ref: SJ2740

⊯ ⫪ Telford

(1m 🚌) *Argoed Farm, Froncysyllte, Llangollen, Clwyd, LL20 7RH.*
Actual grid ref: SJ268417
Old farmhouse, beamed ceilings, inglenook fireplace in dining room.
Grades: WTB 3 Star
Tel: 01691 772367 Mrs Landon.
D: £20.00-£22.00 **S:** £20.00-£22.00.
Open: All Year
Beds: 1F 1D 1T 1S
Baths: 4 En
🛇 🅿 (6)🗶⫪🕮🗙 🏧 Ⅷ Ⓥ ⌁ ∮

Please take muddy boots off before entering premises

Trevor 58

National Grid Ref: SJ2742

(On path) *Oaklands, Trevor, Llangollen, Denbighshire, LL20 7TG.*
Actual grid ref: SJ265424
Charming Victorian house with lovely gardens in beautiful Vale of Llangollen.
Tel: 01978 820152 Mrs Dennis.
D: £16.00-£20.00 **S:** £18.00-£23.00.
Open: All Year (not Xmas)
Beds: 1F 1D 2T **Baths:** 2 Sh
🛇 🅿 (8) 🗗⫪ 🏧 Ⓥ ∮

Garth 59

National Grid Ref: SJ2542

(1m 🚌) *Gwernydd Farm, Garth, Llangollen, LL20 7UR.*
Working farm, extensive views south, tastefully decorated, private parking. **Grades:** WTB 3 Star
Tel: 01978 820122 (also fax no)
Mrs Morris.
D: £17.00-£18.00 **S:** £17.00-£18.00.
Open: All Year (not Xmas)
Beds: 2F **Baths:** 1 Sh
🛇 🅿 (4)🗶🗗⫪🗙 🏧 Ⅷ Ⓥ ⌁ ∮

Tyndwr 60

National Grid Ref: SJ2341

(▲ 2.5m) *Llangollen Youth Hostel, Tyndwr Hall, Tyndwr Road, Tyndwr, Llangollen, Denbighshire, LL20 8AR.*
Actual grid ref: SK232413
Tel: 01978 860330
Under 18: £6.90 **Adults:** £10.00
Self-catering facilities, Self-catering facilities, Television, Showers, Licensed bar, Lounge, Drying room, Parking, Evening meal at 6.00-7.30pm, Kitchen facilities, Breakfast available, Credit cards accepted
Victorian half-timbered manor house & coach house, extensively refurbished, set in 5 acres of wooded grounds in the Vale of Llangollen.

Llangollen 61

National Grid Ref: SJ2141

⊯ ⫪ Telford, Waterside Bar, Hand Hotel

(1.5m 🚌) *River Lodge, Mill Street, Llangollen, Clwyd, LL20 7UH.*
Tel: 01978 869019 Mr Byrne.
Fax no: 01978 861841
D: £15.00-£35.00 **S:** £15.00-£35.00.
Open: Feb to Dec
Beds: 4F 7D 7T **Baths:** 18 En
🛇 🅿 (30) ⫪🗙 🏧 🏧 🛇 Ⅷ ∮
On the banks of the River Dee, River Lodge is Llangollen's newest motel lodge, just 5 mins walk from the town centre, attractions, bars and restaurants. All rooms have a river/mountain view and full ensuite facilities.

Bringing children with
you? Always ask for
any special rates.

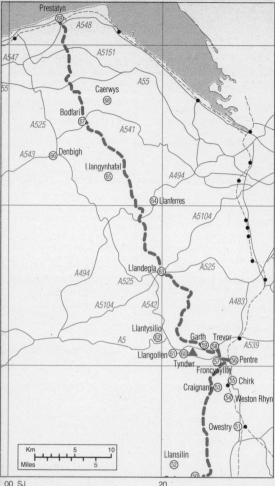

Llantysilio 62

National Grid Ref: SJ1943

🍴 🍺 Britannia Inn, Horseshoe Pass

(2m 🚌) ***Hendy Isa***, *Llantysilio,*
Llangollen, Denbighshire, LL20 8DE.
Actual grid ref: SJ201445
Hendy Isa is a spacious rural
property with pretty gardens.
Grades: WTB 3 Star
Tel: 01978 861232 (also fax no)
D: £18.00-£20.00 **S:** £20.00-£25.00.
Open: Jan to Dec
Beds: 4F
Baths: 4 Pr
🛏 🅿 (6) ⅍ ⌷ 🌺 🔟 Ⓥ ⋔ ∥

Llandegla 63

National Grid Ref: SJ1952

🍴 🍺 Crown Hotel, Plough Inn

(On path) ***Raven Farm***, *Llandegla,*
Wrexham, Nr Denbighshire,
LL11 3AW.
Actual grid ref: SJ198517
Converted C15th drover's inn/farm.
Tel: **01978 790224**
Mrs Surrey.
D: £16.50-£17.00 **S:** £16.50-£17.00.
Open: Easter to Oct
Beds: 2F 1D 2T 1S
Baths: 1 En 1 Sh
🛏 (10) 🅿 (8) ⅍ ⌷ ⋔ ∥

(1m) ***Saith Daran Farm***,
Llandegla, Wrexham, LL11 3BA.
Friendly farmhouse B&B, beautiful
scenery, ideal for touring in Wales.
Tel: **01978 790685**
Mrs Thompson.
D: £18.00-£18.00 **S:** £18.00-£18.00.
Open: Mar to Oct
Beds: 1D 1T
Baths: 2 Pr
🛏 (5) 🅿 (4) ⌷ 🌺 🔟 ⋔ ∥

Llanferres 64

National Grid Ref: SJ1860

🍴 🍺 Druid Inn

(2m) ***The White House***, *Rectory*
Lane, Llanferres, Mold,
Denbighshire, CH7 5SR.
Victorian rectory with recently
converted stables set in conserva-
tion area.
Tel: **01352 810259**
D: £19.00-£22.00 **S:** £23.00-£25.00.
Open: All Year
Beds: 2D 1T
Baths: 3 Pr
🛏 🅿 (6) ⅍ ⌷ 🌺 🔟 Ⓥ ∥

(1.5m 🚌) ***Bryn Meirion***, *Abbey*
Road, Llangollen, Clwyd, LL20 8EF.
Edwardian house overlooking Dee,
canal, steam railway and
surrounding hills.
Grades: WTB 3 Star
Tel: **01978 861911** Mrs Hurle.
D: £18.00-£20.00 **S:** £24.00-£35.00.
Open: All Year
Beds: 1F 1D 1S **Baths:** 2 En 1 Pr
🛏 🅿 (4) ⅍ ⌷ 🐾 ✗ 🌺 🔟 Ⓥ ⋔ ∥

(1.5m) ***Hillcrest Guest House***, *Hill*
Street, Llangollen, Denbighshire,
LL20 8EU.
Beautiful Victorian house, quiet
area of Llangollen, a few minutes
from the A5.
Tel: **01978 860208** (also fax no)
Mrs Lloyd.
D: £21.00-£23.00 **S:** £35.00-£42.00.
Open: All Year (not Xmas)
Beds: 2F 3D 2T **Baths:** 7 En
🛏 🅿 (10) ⅍ ⌷ ✗ 🌺 🔟 ⋔

(1m) ***The Grange***, *Grange Road,*
Llangollen, Denbighshire, LL20 8AP.
Attractive country house in town
with secluded 2-acre garden.
Tel: **01978 860366**
Mrs Evans.
D: £20.00-£20.00 **S:** £25.00.
Open: All Year (not Xmas)
Beds: 1F 1D 1T
Baths: 3 En
🛏 🅿 (3) ⅍ ⌷ 🌺 🔟 Ⓥ ⋔ ∥

All rooms full and
nowhere else to stay?
Ask the owner if
there's anywhere
nearby

Llangynhafal 65

National Grid Ref: SJ1263

⛟ ◁ Golden Lion

(1.5m 🚌) *Esgairlygain (The Old Barn), Llangynhafal, Ruthin, Denbighshire, LL15 1RT.*
Actual grid ref: SJ135625
Converted stone barn. Delightful views. Convenient Chester, North Wales, Snowdonia, Llangollen & coast.
Tel: **01824 704047** (also fax no)
Mrs Henderson.
D: £18.50-£18.50 **S:** £18.50-£21.00.
Open: All Year (not Xmas)
Beds: 1F 1D **Baths:** 2 En
⛟ 🅿 (2) ⊬ 🗖 🛏 ⊠ 🏃 🛏 🔟 🖋

Denbigh 66

National Grid Ref: SJ0566

⛟ ◁ Gatherings, Bull

(3m 🚌) *Cayo Guest House, 74 Vale Street, Denbigh, LL16 3BW.*
Actual grid ref: SJ054662
Centrally situated town house. Ideal for viewing N. Wales. Pickup from Boofari (Offa's Dyke).
Grades: WTB 2 Star,
AA 3 Diamond, RAC 3 Diamond
Tel: **01745 812686**
Mrs MacCormack.
D: £18.00-£19.00 **S:** £18.00-£19.00.
Open: All Year (not Xmas/New Year)
Beds: 2D 3T 1S
Baths: 3 En 1 Pr 1 Sh
⛟ ⊬ 🗖 🛏 ✕ 🏃 🛏 🔟 🖋

Bodfari 67

National Grid Ref: SJ0970

(On path 🚌) *Fron Haul, Sodom, Bodfari, Denbigh, LL16 4DY.*
Actual grid ref: SJ099717
A oasis of calm and taste overlooking the vale of Clwyd.
Grades: WTB 3 Star
Tel: **01745 710301** (also fax no)
Mrs Edwards.
D: £20.00-£25.00 **S:** £25.00-£25.00.
Open: Jan to Dec
Beds: 1F 1D 1T 1S
Baths: 1 En 2 Sh
⛟ 🅿 (12) ⊬ 🗖 🛏 ✕ 🏃 🛏 🔟 🖋

Caerwys 68

National Grid Ref: SJ1272

⛟ ◁ Pwllgwyn, Cherry Pie

(1.5m 🚌) *Plas Penucha, Caerwys, Mold, Flintshire, CH7 5BH.*
Actual grid ref: SJ332857
Peaceful countryside, comfortable farmhouse with large gardens overlooking the Clwydian Hills.
Grades: WTB 3 Star
Tel: **01352 720210**
Mrs Price.
Fax no: 01352 720881
D: £21.00-£25.00
S: £21.00-£25.00.
Open: All Year
Beds: 2D 2T
Baths: 2 En 1 Pr 1 Sh
⛟ 🅿 ⊬ 🗖 🛏 ✕ 🏃 🛏 🔟 🖋

Prestatyn 69

National Grid Ref: SJ0682

⛟ ◁ Red Lion

(On path) *Roughsedge House, 26/28 Marine Road, Prestatyn, Denbighshire, LL19 7HG.*
Actual grid ref: SJ064833
Victorian guest house, excellent breakfast. Walkers welcome, Friendly atmosphere.
Grades: WTB 1 Star
Tel: **01745 887359**
Mrs Kubler.
Fax no: 01745 852883
D: £16.00-£20.00
S: £16.00-£25.00.
Open: All Year
Beds: 2F 4D 2T 2S
Baths: 3 Pr 3 Sh
⛟ 🅿 (3) ⊬ 🗖 ✕ 🏃 🛏 🔟

(On path) *Traeth Ganol Hotel, 41 Beach Road West, Prestatyn, Denbighshire, LL19 7LL.*
Actual grid ref: SJ059836
Luxury well-appointed seafront location.
Grades: WTB 3 Star, AA 2 Star
Tel: **01745 853594**
Mr & Mrs Groves.
Fax no: 01745 886687
D: £28.00-£31.00
S: £39.00-£54.00.
Open: All Year
Beds: 6F 1D 1T 1S
Baths: 9 En
⛟ 🅿 (9) ⊬ 🗖 ✕ 🏃 🛏 & 🔟 🖋

BRITAIN: BED & BREAKFAST

The essential guide to B&Bs in England, Scotland & Wales

The Bed & Breakfast is one of the great British institutions. Like Fish & Chips, it's known by people around the world. But you don't have to be a tourist to enjoy this traditional accommodation. Whether you're travelling, on holiday, away on business or just escaping from it all, the B&B is a great value alternative to expensive hotels and a world away from camping and caravanning.

Stilwell's Britain: Bed & Breakfast 2001 is the most comprehensive guide of its kind, containing over 7,750 entries listed by country, county and location, in England, Scotland and Wales. Each entry includes room rates, facilities, Tourist Board grades and a brief description of the B&B and its location and surroundings.

Stilwell's Britain: Bed & Breakfast 2001: The indispensable guide to great value accommodation:

Private houses, country halls, farms, cottages, inns, small hotels and guest houses

Over 7,750 entries
Average price £19 per person per night
All official grades shown
Local maps
Pubs serving hot evening meals shown
Tourist Information Centres listed
Handy size for easy packing

£9.95 from all good bookstores (ISBN 1-900861-22-4) or £11.95 (inc p&p) from Stilwell Publishing, 59 Charlotte Road, London EC2A 3QW (020 7739 7179)

Pembrokeshire Coast Path

The **Pembrokeshire Coast Path** runs for 186 miles around a beautiful Welsh National Park. Although more popular than it used to be, this part of the country still has relatively few visitors (compared, let's say, with Cornwall) and walkers will encounter unspoilt, quiet beaches, dramatic cliff-tops and superb sea-views all to themselves, even during summer. The bird-life is rich, with many sea-birds breeding here - watch out for the rare chough. Between Bosherston and Pembroke you will encounter the Army's tank firing ranges. Contact the Army for firing times on 01646 661321. The walking can prove exerting, especially when the wind is up and where the path regularly dips, bends and climbs to follow the cliffs.

Guides (available from all good map shops):
Pembrokeshire Coast Path by Dr Brian S.

John (ISBN 1 85410 459 4), published by Aurum Press in association with the Countryside Commission and Ordnance Survey, £10.99

A Guide to the Pembrokeshire Coast Path by C J Wright (ISBN 09 469260 2), published by Constable & Co Ltd and available from all good bookshops, £10.95

The Pembrokeshire Coastal Path by Dennis Kelsall (ISBN 1 85284186 9), published by Cicerone Press and also available directly from the publishers (2 Police Square, Milnthorpe, Cumbria, LA7 7PY, 01539 562069), £9.99 (+ 75p p&p)

Maps: 1:50000 Ordnance Survey Landranger Series: 145, 157 and 158

All comments on the path to: **Tom Goodall**, Pembrokeshire Coast National Park, County Offices, Haverfordwest, Pembs, SA61 1QZ

Cardigan 1

National Grid Ref: SN1746

¶⚫ Eagle, Ship

(3m) *Brynhyfryd Guest House,* Gwbert Road, Cardigan, SA43 1AE. 2 miles Cardigan Bay; 6 minutes walk to town centre.
Grades: WTB 3 Star, AA 3 Diamond, RAC 3 Diamond
Tel: **01239 612861** (also fax no)
Mrs Arcus.
D: £18.00-£20.00 **S:** £18.00-£25.00.
Open: All Year
Beds: 1F 3D 1T 2S
Baths: 3 En 2 Pr
⌂ (5) ⊬⬜✕⬤▥.Ⓥ🛉

(3m 🚐) *Maes-A-Mor,* Park Place, Gwbert Road, Cardigan, SA43 1AE. Centrally situated opposite the park. Ideal for coast and central Wales.
Tel: **01239 614929** (also fax no)
Mr Jones.
D: £16.00-£18.00 **S:** £18.00.
Open: All Year
Beds: 1D 2T
Baths: 3 En
⌂ (8) 🅿 (3) ⊬⬜⬤▥.Ⓥ🛉⚡

D = Price range per person sharing in a double room

Poppit Sands 2

National Grid Ref: SN1548

¶⚫ Webley Hotel

(⛰ On path) *Poppit Sands Youth Hostel,* Sea View, Poppit Sands, Cardigan, SA43 3LP.
Actual grid ref: SN144487
Tel: **01239 612936**
Under 18: £6.50
Adults: £9.25
Self-catering facilities, Showers, Shop, Lounge, Drying room, Parking, No smoking, WC, Kitchen facilities, Kitchen facilities, Credit cards accepted
Former inn set in 5 acres reaching down to the estuary and sea, designated a Site of Special Scientific Interest. Occasional dolphins can be seen in the bay.

(On path) *Glan-y-Mor,* Poppit Sands, St Dogmaels, Cardigan, Pembs, SA43 3LP.
Actual grid ref: SN147487
Ex-farmhouse with sea view.
Tel: **01239 612329**
Mrs Sharp.
D: £15.00-£15.00
S: £15.00-£15.00.
Open: All Year (not Xmas/ New Year)
Beds: 1D
Baths: 1 Sh
⌂🅿⬜⬤▥.Ⓥ🛉⚡

Moylegrove 3

National Grid Ref: SN1144

¶⚫ Eagle Inn

(1m 🚐) *Trewidwal,* Moylegrove, Cardigan, Pembrokeshire, SA43 3BY. Beautiful farmhouse. Extensive grounds. Outstanding coastal and hill views. Peace.
Tel: **01239 881651**
Mr & Mrs Bloss.
D: £15.00-£18.00
S: £18.00-£22.00.
Open: All Year (not Xmas/ New Year)
Beds: 1F 1D 1S
Baths: 1 En 1 Sh
⌂🅿(4)⊬⬜✕⬤▥.Ⓥ🛉⚡

(1m 🚐) *The Old Vicarage,* Moylgrove, Cardigan, Pembrokeshire, SA43 3BN.
Actual grid ref: SN123446
Edwardian country house, large lawned garden and glorious sea view.
Grades: WTB 4 Star
Tel: **01239 881231**
Phillips.
Fax no: 01239 881341
D: £24.00-£28.00
S: £26.00-£38.00.
Open: Mar to Nov
Beds: 1T 2D
Baths: 3 En
🅿(5)⊬⬜✕⬤▥.Ⓥ🛉⚡

Newport 4

National Grid Ref: SN0539

🍴 🍺 Golden Lion, Llwyngwair Arms, Royal Oak, Castle Hotel

(▲ 0.25m) *Trefdraeth, Newport Youth Hostel, Lower St Mary's Street, Newport, Pembrokeshire, SA42 0TS.*
Actual grid ref: SN058393
Tel: **01239 820080**
Under 18: £6.50 **Adults:** £9.25
Self-catering facilities, Showers, Wet weather shelter, Lounge, Cycle store, Parking Limited, Facilities for disabled people Category 2, No smoking, Kitchen facilities, Credit cards accepted
In the centre of the popular town of Newport on the West Wales coast; a short walk away are shops, pubs,

the beach, coastal path, bird sanctuary and estuary. The Preseli Hills have many prehistoric sites to visit.

(▲ On path) *Ty Canol Farm Campsite & Bunkhouse, Ty Canol Farm, Newport, Pembrokeshire, SA42 0ST.*
Actual grid ref: SN043396
Tel: **01239 820264 Adults:** £6.00

(0.25m 🚐) *Llysmeddyg Guest House, East Street, Newport, Pembrokeshire, SA42 0SY.*
Actual grid ref: SN059392
Listed Georgian house and Mews flat and Mountain bike hire.
Grades: WTB 3 Star
Tel: **01239 820008** Ross.
D: £22.00-£24.00 **S:** £25.00-£35.00.
Open: All Year (not Xmas)
Beds: 1F 1D 2T 1S **Baths:** 2 En 1 Sh
🐾 🅿 (5) ⚡ 🗆 ✕ 🖳 ⬛ Ⅴ 🖊 ⚡

Dinas Cross 5

National Grid Ref: SN0039

🍴 🍺 Llwyngwair Arms, Ship Aground

(1.25m 🚐) *Fron Isaf Farm, Dinas Cross, Newport, Pembs, SA42 0SW.*
Actual grid ref: SN018384
Peaceful sheep farm with panoramic views of sea and hills.
Grades: WTB 3 Star Farm
Tel: **01348 811339**
Mr & Mrs Urwin.
D: £22.00-£22.00 **S:** £25.00-£25.00.
Open: Apr to Oct
Beds: 1F 1T **Baths:** 1 Sh
🐾 (3) 🅿 (5) 🗆 ⊁ 🖳 ⬛ Ⅴ 🖊 ⚡

D = Price range per person sharing in a double room

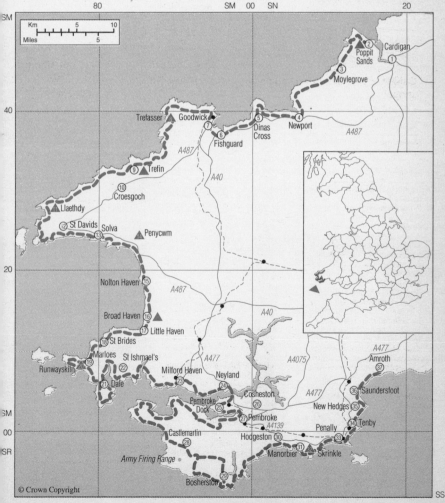

Fishguard 6

National Grid Ref: SM9537

⊯ ⛴ Cartref Hotel, Farmhouse Kitchen, Ferryboat, Glendower, Hope & Anchor, Old Coach House, Rose & Crown, Royal Oak

(On path) *The Beach House, Fishguard Harbour, Fishguard, Pembs, SA64 0DH.*
Seafront guest house on Fishguard Harbour (village location).
Grades: WTB 1 Star GH
Tel: 01348 872085 Mrs Wagstaff.
D: £13.50-£18.00 **S:** £13.50-£18.00.
Open: All Year
Beds: 2F 2D 2T 2S
Baths: 2 En 3 Pr 1 Sh
🛇 🅿 (5) 🛏 🍴 🔬 ⛾ 🎱 ✓

(On path 🚌) *Cartref Hotel, 13-19 High Street, Fishguard, Pembs, SA65 9AW.*
Actual grid ref: SM956369
Friendly renovated hotel. Excellent family accommodation. Free garage. Open 24 hours.
Grades: WTB 2 Star, AA 2 Star
Tel: 01348 872430 Mrs Bjorkquist.
Fax no: 01348 873664
D: £24.00-£27.00 **S:** £32.00-£36.00.
Open: All Year
Beds: 2F 2D 2T 4S
Baths: 10 En
🛇 🅿 (3) 🛏 🍴 ✗ 🔬 ⛾ 🎱 ✓

(0.5m) *Inglewood, 13 Vergam Terrace, Fishguard, Pembs, SA65 9DD.*
Comfortable terraced accommodation. One mile from Fishguard to Rosslare Ferries.
Tel: 01348 873475 Mrs Lewis.
D: £16.00-£16.00 **S:** £18.00-£20.00.
Open: Jan to Dec
Beds: 1D 1T
🛇 🅿 (12) 🅿 🅿 🔬 ⛾ 🎱

(0.5m 🚌) *Cri'r Wylan, Pen Wallis, Fishguard, Pembs, SA65 9HR.*
Relax in homely atmosphere - detached house - private parking. Superb views.
Grades: WTB 3 Star
Tel: 01348 873398 Mrs Nicholas.
D: £18.00-£20.00 **S:** £30.00-£30.00.
Open: All Year (not Xmas/ New Year)
Beds: 1D 1T 1S
Baths: 1 Sh
🛇 🅿 (4) ✓ 🗆 🛏 🔬 ⛾ 🎱 ⓐ ✓

🚌 **sign means that,** *given due notice,* **owners will pick you up from the path and drop you off** *within reason.*

(On path) *Coach House Cottage, Glendower Square, Goodwick, Fishguard, Pembs, SA65 0DH.*
Stone built Pembrokeshire cottage, convenient for coastal path / Irish ferry.
Tel: 01348 873660
Mrs Maxwell-Jones.
D: £15.00-£15.00 **S:** £20.00-£20.00.
Open: All Year (not Xmas/ New Year)
Beds: 1T
Baths: 1 Sh
🛇 🅿 ✓ 🗆 🛏 ✗ 🔬 ⛾ 🎱 ✓

Goodwick 7

National Grid Ref: SM9438

⊯ ⛴ Farmhouse Kitchen, Ferryboat Inn

(0.75m 🚌) *Ivybridge, Drim Mill, Dyffryn, Goodwick, Fishguard, Pembs, SA64 0FT.*
Actual grid ref: SM942372
Grades: WTB 2 Star GH
Tel: 01348 875366
Mrs Davies.
Fax no: 01348 872338
D: £19.50-£24.50
S: £19.50-£24.50.
Open: All Year (not Xmas)
Beds: 4F 4D 2T 1S
Baths: 4 En 2 Pr
🛇 🅿 (12) 🗆 🛏 ✗ 🔬 ⛾ 🎱 ⓐ ✓
Friendly family-run guest house. Ensuite rooms with colour TV and hot drinks tray. Good home cooking, heated indoor pool, licensed, vegetarians welcome. Ample off-road parking. 2 minutes ferry port. Early/late visitors welcome.

(On path 🚌) *Stanley House, Quay Road, Goodwick, Fishguard, Pembs, SA64 0BS.*
Overlooking Fishguard, ferry terminal and bay and Preseli Hills beyond.
Grades: WTB 2 Star, AA 3 Diamond
Tel: 01348 873024 Mr Hendrie.
D: £16.50-£19.50 **S:** £19.50-£19.50.
Open: All Year
Beds: 2F 2D 2T 1S
Baths: 1 En 1 Pr 2 Sh
🛇 🅿 (3) 🗆 🛏 🔬 ⛾ 🎱 ✓

Trefasser 8

National Grid Ref: SM8937

(▲ On path) *Pwll Deri Youth Hostel, Castell Mawr, Trefasser, Goodwick, Pembrokeshire, SA64 0LR.*
Actual grid ref: SM891387
Tel: 01348 891385
Under 18: £5.75 **Adults:** £8.50
Self-catering facilities, Showers, Shop, Lounge, Drying room, Cycle store, No smoking, WC, Kitchen facilities, Credit cards accepted
Former private house perched atop 400 ft cliffs next to an ancient hill fort, overlooking Pwll Deri Bay.

Trefin 9

National Grid Ref: SM8332

⊯ ⛴ Square & Compass, Sloop, Ship

(▲ 0.25m) *Trefin Youth Hostel, Cranog, Trefin, St Davids, Haverfordwest, Pembs, SA62 5AT.*
Tel: 01348 831414
Under 18: £5.75 **Adults:** £8.50
Self-catering facilities, Showers, Shop, Lounge, Drying room, Cycle store, Parking, WC, Kitchen facilities, Credit cards accepted
Former village school near Pembs Coast Path. Good area for spotting birds.

(0.25m 🚌) *The Old Court House Vegetarian Guest House, Trefin, Haverfordwest, SA62 5AX.*
Actual grid ref: SM838325
Cosy cottage close to spectacular coastal path; excellent vegetarian food.
Grades: WTB 3 Star
Tel: 01348 837095 Brodie.
D: £21.50-£23.50 **S:** £21.50-£23.50.
Open: All Year
Beds: 2D 1T
Baths: 2 En
🛇 🅿 (5) 🅿 (2) ✓ 🗆 ✗ 🔬 ⛾ 🎱 ⓐ ✓

Croesgoch 10

National Grid Ref: SM8230

⊯ ⛴ Sloop, Square & Compass

(1.5m 🚌) *Bank House Farm, Abereiddy Road, Croesgoch, Haverfordwest, Pembs, SA62 6XZ.*
Picturesque sea views on Country Road between Croesgoch and Abereiddy.
Grades: WTB 2 Star Farm
Tel: 01348 831305 Mrs Lloyd.
D: £15.00-£18.00 **S:** £18.00.
Open: All Year (not Xmas)
Beds: 1D 1T
Baths: 1 Sh
🛇 🅿 🗆 🛏 ✗ 🔬 ⛾ 🎱 ✓

(1.25m 🚌) *Maes y Ffynnon, Penygroes, Croesgoch, Haverfordwest, Pembs, SA62 5JN.*
Actual grid ref: SM8431
Modern large bungalow, private grounds; ideal base for walking or touring.
Grades: WTB 2 Star
Tel: 01348 831319 Mrs Evans.
D: £16.50 **S:** £18.50.
Open: Mar to Oct
Beds: 1F 1T **Baths:** 2 En
🛇 🅿 (4) ✓ 🗆 🛏 🔬 ⛾ 🎱 ⓐ ✓

All rates are subject to alteration at the owners' discretion.

Llaethdy 11

National Grid Ref: SM7327

(▲0.5m) *St David's Youth Hostel*, Llaethdy, St David's, Haverfordwest, Pembrokeshire, SA62 6PR.
Actual grid ref: SM739276
Tel: **01437 720345**
Under 18: £5.75
Adults: £8.50
Self-catering facilities, Shop, Wet weather shelter, Drying room, Parking, WC, Credit cards accepted
White painted farmhouse, beneath summit of Carn Llidi about 2 miles from St David's. Accommodation is basic, but there is an open fire.

St Davids 12

National Grid Ref: SM7525

⊯◣Farmers Arms, Sloop

(0.75m) *Ramsey House, Lower Moor*, St Davids, Haverfordwest, Pembs, SA62 6RP.
Actual grid ref: SM747250
Grades: WTB 4 Star GH, AA 4 Diamond, RAC 4 Diamond
Tel: **01437 720321**
Mr & Mrs Thompson.
Fax no: 01437 720025
D: £29.00-£32.00
S: £29.00-£64.00.
Open: All Year (not Xmas)
Beds: 4D 3T
Baths: 6 En 1 Pr
🅿 (8) ⊬⌷⊁✕🛌 ⏃🖳 Ⅴ🛈✦
Superior non-smoking 4 Star guest house exclusively for adults. Convenient location for cathedral and Coast Path. Award-winning dinners/wines with Welsh emphasis. Licensed bar and friendly relaxed hospitality completes your enjoyment. Dinner B&B £44-£48 pppn, £264-£288 weekly.

(1m) *Pen Albro Guest House*, 18 Goat Street, St Davids, Haverfordwest, Pembs, SA62 6RF.
Cathedral 150 yards, coastal path 0.25 hr, pub next door.
Grades: WTB 1 Star
Tel: **01437 721865**
D: £14.50-£14.50 **S:** £14.50.
Open: All Year
Beds: 1D 1T 1S
⌷⊁✕🛌 Ⅴ🛈

All rooms full and nowhere else to stay? Ask the owner if there's anywhere nearby

---

(1m 🚗) *Ty Olaf, Mount Gardens*, St Davids, Pembs, SA62 6BS.
Actual grid ref: SM758258
Quiet bungalow, within reach of cathedral, restaurants, coast path, beaches.
Grades: WTB 3 Star
Tel: **01437 720885** (also fax no)
Mrs Liggitt.
D: £16.00-£18.00
S: £16.00-£18.00.
Open: All Year
Beds: 1F 1D 1T 1S
Baths: 1 Sh
🅿 (3) ⊬⌷🛌 ⏃🖳&Ⅴ✦

(1m) *Y Gorlan*, 77 Nun Street, St Davids, Haverfordwest, Pembs, SA62 6NU.
Close to cathedral, coastal path, beaches and golf course.
Tel: **01437 720837**
Mr Bohlen.
Fax no: 01437 721148
D: £22.50-£27.00 **S:** £25.00-£27.00.
Open: All Year
Beds: 1F 2D 1T 1S
Baths: 5 En
⛵🅿 (2)⌷✕🛌 Ⅴ🛈

(1m) *Y Glennydd Hotel*, 51 Nun Street, St Davids, Haverfordwest, Pembs, SA62 6NU.
Comfortable Victorian property - most rooms ensuite, popular licensed bistro.
Tel: **01437 720576**
Mrs Foster.
D: £17.50-£21.00 **S:** £18.50-£25.00.
Open: Feb to Oct
Beds: 4F 4D 2S
Baths: 8 En 2 Sh
⛵⌷✕🛌 ⏃🖳Ⅴ

(1m) *Penberi Cottage*, St Davids, Haverfordwest, SA62 6QL.
Listed old village shop 1.5 miles from beautiful harbour village of Solva.
Tel: **01437 720528** (also fax no)
D: £18.00-£18.00
S: £25.00-£25.00.
Open: All Year
Beds: 1T
🅿 (1) ⊬⌷🛌 ⏃🖳&Ⅴ🛈✦

Solva 13

National Grid Ref: SM8024

⊯◣Royal George

(On path 🚗) *Pendinas*, St Brides View, Solva, Haverfordwest, Pembs, SA62 6TB.
Actual grid ref: SM798243
Glorious sea views from all rooms, good food, warm welcome.
Grades: WTB 3 Star
Tel: **01437 721283**
Ms Davies.
D: £20.00-£22.00
S: £25.00-£26.00.
Open: Easter to Oct
Beds: 2D 1T
Baths: 1 Sh
🅿 (3) ⊬⌷🛌 ⏃🖳Ⅴ🛈✦

Penycwm 14

National Grid Ref: SM8523

(▲2m) *Penycwm (Solva) Youth Hostel*, Whitehouse, Penycwm, Newgale, Haverfordwest, Pembs, SA62 6LA.
Tel: **01437 720959**
Under 18: £7.75 **Adults:** £11.00
Self-catering facilities, Television, Showers, Licensed bar, Lounge, Games room, Cycle store, Parking, Evening meal at 6.30pm, No smoking, WC, Kitchen facilities, Breakfast available, Luggage store
A good base for families, within easy reach a good sandy beach. Ideal also for exploring Pembrokeshire.

Nolton Haven 15

National Grid Ref: SM8618

⊯◣Mariners Inn

(▲0.25m) *Nolton Haven Farmhouse*, Nolton Haven, Haverfordwest, Pembs, SA62 4NH.
Tel: **01437 710263**
Under 18: £7.50 **Adults:** £15.00
Self-catering facilities, Television, Showers, Central heating, Lounge, Dining room, Grounds available for games, Drying room, Cycle store, Parking
Beside Nolton Haven's sandy beach, the large farmhouse is half way from Marloes to St Davids, sleeping up to 25 in seven bedrooms. Campsite only 100 yards from the beach and inn. Please call for price details, group discounts available.

(On path 🚗) *Nolton Haven Farm House*, Nolton Haven, Haverfordwest, Pembs, SA62 4NH.
Actual grid ref: SM849187
Beachside farmhouse, working farm. 75 yards village inn, quiet, good walks.
Grades: WTB 2 Star
Tel: **01437 710263** (also fax no)
Mr Canton.
D: £15.00 **S:** £15.00.
Open: All Year (not Xmas)
Beds: 3F 2D 1T 1S
Baths: 2 Pr 4 Sh
⛵🅿 (20) ⌷🛌 ⏃🖳🛈✦

Order your packed lunch the *evening before* you need them. Not at breakfast!

Broad Haven 16

National Grid Ref: SM8613

⭗ ⤸ Swan, Galleon, Royal, Nest

(▲ On path) *Broad Haven Youth Hostel, Broad Haven, Haverfordwest, Pembrokeshire, SA62 3JH.*
Actual grid ref: SM863141
Tel: **01437 781688**
Under 18: £7.75 **Adults:** £11.00
Television, Games room, Drying room, Parking, Evening meal at 6.30pm, Facilities for disabled people Category 1, No smoking, WC, Breakfast available, Credit cards accepted
Award-winning purpose-built hostel close to beach, with fine views of the coastal headlands.

(0.25m ⌨) *Lion Rock, Broad Haven, Haverfordwest, Pembs, SA62 3JP.*
Grades: WTB 3 Star
Tel: **01437 781645** Mrs Main.
Fax no: 01437 781203
D: £20.00-£30.00 **S:** £20.00-£25.00.
Open: All Year (not Xmas/New Year)
Beds: 1T 2D 2S
Baths: 3 En 2 Pr
⛫ (7) 🅿 (8) ⌿⬚🗙⚓💷🖳Ⓥ🛇⚡
Stunning quiet cliff top position in Pembrokeshire Coast National Park. Single storey house. Views over ST. Brides Bay and Skomer Island. Owner Access to coast path. Warm welcome, help and information on local walks, beaches and watersports. Not to be missed.

(On path) *Anchor Guesthouse, The Sea Front, Broad Haven, Haverfordwest, Pembs, SA62 3JN.*
Opposite sandy beach with magnificent sea views. Adjacent cafe, shop restaurant. Coastal Path.
Grades: WTB 2 Star
Tel: **01437 781051** Mrs Morgan.
Fax no: 01437 781050
D: £17.50-£27.00 **S:** £17.50-£27.00.
Open: All Year
Beds: 8 **Baths:** 8 En
⛫🅿⬚⚓💷Ⓥ🛇⚡

Little Haven 17

National Grid Ref: SM8512

⭗ ⤸ Swan

(0.5m) *The Bower Farm, Little Haven, Haverfordwest, Pembs, SA62 3TY.*
Actual grid ref: SM869135
Friendly farmhouse, fantastic sea views.
Grades: WTB 3 Star Farm
Tel: **01437 781554**
Mr Birt-Llewellin.
D: £20.00-£27.00 **S:** £25.00-£30.00.
Open: All Year
Beds: 2F 1D 1T 1S **Baths:** 5 En
⛫🅿 (10) ⬚🗙⚓💷Ⓥ🛇⚡

(On path ⌨) *Whitegates, Settlands Hill, Little Haven, Haverfordwest, Pembs, SA62 3LA.*
Tel: **01437 781386** (also fax no)
Mr & Mrs Llewellin.
D: £20.00-£27.00 **S:** £30.00-£35.00.
Open: All Year (not Xmas)
Beds: 1F 4D 1T
Baths: 4 En 2 Pr
⛫🅿⬚⚓🗙⚓💷🖳Ⓥ🛇⚡
Overlooking the sea and lovely fishing village, general good eating places within easy walking distance, lovely garden and conservatory bar overlooking sea. Fishing, wind surfing, horse riding and golf nearby, also Bird islands and wild flowers.

St Brides 18

National Grid Ref: SM8010

⭗ ⤸ Foxes, Lobster Pot, Hasguard Caravan

(1m ⌨) *Fopston Farm, St Brides, Haverfordwest, Pembs, SA62 3AW.*
Actual grid ref: SM788093
Grades: WTB 2 Star
Tel: **01646 636271** (also fax no)
Mrs Price.
D: £22.00-£25.00 **S:** £28.00-£31.00.
Open: Easter to October
Beds: 1F 2T 1D
Baths: 1 En 2 Sh
⛫🅿 (6) ⌿⬚🗙⚓💷Ⓥ🛇⚡
Fopston is a working farm of 282 acres. An arable and beef enterprise, it is C17th with spacious and interesting features. For that quiet retreat to refresh the body and soul Fopston awaits you. Beautiful scenery, lovely safe beaches.

Marloes 19

National Grid Ref: SM7908

⭗ ⤸ Lobster Pot

(1m ⌨) *Foxdale, Glebe Lane, Marloes, Haverfordwest, Pembs, SA62 3AX.*
Actual grid ref: SM796083
Set in the heart of the Pembrokeshire Coast National Park. Close to cliff path.
Grades: WTB 3 Star
Tel: **01646 636243**
Mrs Roddam-King.
Fax no: 01646 636982
D: £18.00-£25.00 **S:** £23.00-£30.00.
Open: All Year
Beds: 2D 1T **Baths:** 2 En 1 Pr
🅿 (6) ⬚🗙⚓💷Ⓥ🛇⚡

All details shown
are as supplied
by B&B owners in
Autumn 2001.

Planning a longer
stay? Always ask for
any special rates.

Runwayskiln 20

National Grid Ref: SM7707

(▲ On path) *Marloes Sands Youth Hostel, Runwayskiln, Marloes, Haverfordwest, Pembrokeshire, SA62 3BH.*
Actual grid ref: SM778080
Tel: **01646 636667**
Under 18: £5.25 **Adults:** £7.50
Self-catering facilities, Showers, Shop, Wet weather shelter, Lounge, Drying room, Parking 6 cars, No smoking, WC, Kitchen facilities, Credit cards accepted
Small group of farm buildings on NT property, on the Pembrokeshire Coast Path, and with nearby access to Skomer Island. Walking and bird watching are popular.

Dale 21

National Grid Ref: SM8005

(0.25m ⌨) *The Post House Hotel, Dale, Haverfordwest, Pembs, SA62 3RE.*
Tel: **01646 636201**
Mr & Mrs Riley.
D: £24.00-£27.50 **S:** £26.00-£26.00.
Open: closed Feb
Beds: 2T 2D 1S **Baths:** 5 En
🅿 (6) ⬚🗙⚓💷Ⓥ🛇⚡
Licensed hotel, ensuite bedrooms, plus suite of rooms, TV Lounge, Conservatory. Residents evening meals, local produce, fresh fish. (vegetarians catered for). 100 yards from bay, sailing, windsurfing, walking just off the Pembrokeshire coast path. Close to offshore bird islands, Skomer, Skokholm and Grassholm.

St Ishmael's 22

National Grid Ref: SM8307

⭗ ⤸ Brook Inn

(On path ⌨) *Skerryback Farmhouse, Sandy Haven, St Ishmael's, Haverfordwest, Pembs, SA62 3DN.*
Actual grid ref: SM852074
Welcoming C18th farmhouse, adjoining coastal path, relaxed atmosphere, tea/coffee on arrival.
Grades: WTB 3 Star
Tel: **01646 636598** Mrs Williams.
Fax no: 01646 636595
D: £20.00-£25.00 **S:** £20.00-£24.00.
Open: March to November
Beds: 1D 1T 1S **Baths:** 1 Sh
⛫🅿⌿⬚🗙⚓💷Ⓥ🛇⚡

(1m ☎) *Bicton Farm, Bicton,*
St Ishmael's, Haverfordwest,
Pembs, SA62 3DN.
Actual grid ref: SM843078
Warm welcome in comfortable
farmhouse; attention to individual
requirements.
Tel: **01646 636215** Mrs Llewellyn.
D: £19.00-£21.00 **S:** £19.00-£21.00.
Open: Easter to Oct
Beds: 3F 2D 1T **Baths:** 2 En 1 Sh
♿ 🅿 ⚄ ⬚ 🔪 ⬚ 🛏 🖭 🎔 ♨ 🖤 ✓

Milford Haven 23

National Grid Ref: SM9005

¶⬚ ⊴ Lord Nelson

(On path ☎) *Kings Arms, Hakin*
Point, Milford Haven, Pembs,
SA73 3DG.
Public house, home cooking. Near
marina, railway station. All rooms
sea view.
Tel: **01646 693478** Mrs Hutchings.
D: £25.00-£30.00 **S:** £15.00-£15.00.
Open: All Year (not Xmas)
Beds: 2F 4T **Baths:** 3 En
♿ 🅿 ⬚ 🔪 🛏 🖤 ✓

Neyland 24

National Grid Ref: SM9605

¶⬚ ⊴ Oddfellows Arms

(0.25m) *Y Ffynnon,*
45 Honeyborough Road, Neyland,
Milford Haven, Pembs, SA73 1RF.
Actual grid ref: SM960061
Comfortable private house, friendly
welcome. Irish ferry by prior
arrangement.
Tel: **01646 601369** Mr Hawley.
D: £15.00-£15.00 **S:** £15.00-£15.00.
Open: All Year (not Xmas)
Beds: 1D 1T 1S
Baths: 1 Sh
🅿 (1) ⬚ 🛏 🖭 🖤 ✓

Pembroke Dock 25

National Grid Ref: SM9603

¶⬚ ⊴ Brewery Inn

(2m) *The Old Rectory, Cosheston,*
Pembroke Dock, Pembroke,
SA72 4UJ.
Large former rectory in 2 acre
gardens.
Grades: WTB 1 Star
Tel: **01646 684960** Mrs Bailey.
D: £17.50-£20.00 **S:** £17.50-£20.00.
Open: All Year (not Xmas)
Beds: 1F 1D 2T 1S **Baths:** 2 Sh
♿ 🅿 (4) ⬚ 🛏 🖭 🖭 🖤 ✓

Please take muddy

boots **off** before

entering premises

Cosheston 26

National Grid Ref: SN0003

(2m) *Poyerston Farm, Cosheston,*
Pembroke, SA72 4SJ.
Charming Victorian farmhouse on
a working farm. All ensuite bed-
rooms, some ground floor.
Tel: **01646 651347** (also fax no)
Mrs Lewis.
D: £20.00-£25.00
S: £25.00-£30.00.
Open: All Year
Beds: 2F 2D 1T
Baths: 5 En
♿ (4) 🅿 (12) ⚄ ⬚ 🔪 🛏 🖭 🖭 🖤 ✓

Pembroke 27

National Grid Ref: SM9801

¶⬚ ⊴ Dial Inn, Freshwater East Inn, Waterman's
Arms, Old Cross, Saws Inn

(On path) *Merton Place House,*
3 East Back, Pembroke, SA71 4HL.
Grades: WTB 2 Star
Tel: **01646 684796** Mrs Pearce.
D: £15.00-£17.50 **S:** £17.50-£20.00.
Open: All Year
Beds: 2D 2T 1S
Baths: 1 Sh
♿ ⬚ 🛏 🖭 🖭 ✓
Lovely old Victorian merchants'
house, walled gardens at rear, with
medieval features in lower
Burgage. Small, pretty bedrooms.
Two twin rooms and double so
only six guests taken. Full of books
and pictures. Centre of Pembroke,
close castle, buses and trains.

(0.5m ☎) *High Noon Guest*
House, Lower Lamphey Road,
Pembroke, Pembrokeshire, SA71 4AB.
Ensuites, comfortable and friendly.
Delicious breakfasts, near castle,
coastline, Irish ferry.
Tel: **01646 683736** (also fax no)
Mr Barnikel.
D: £16.50-£21.50 **S:** £18.50-£26.50.
Open: All Year (not Xmas)
Beds: 2F 3D 1T 3S
Baths: 5 En 2 Sh
♿ 🅿 (10) ⬚ 🛏 🔪 🛏 🖭 🖤 ✓

Castlemartin 28

National Grid Ref: SR9198

(On path ☎) *Chapel Farm,*
Castlemartin, Pembroke,
Pembrokeshire, SA71 5HW.
Actual grid ref: SR907986
Large comfortable farmhouse over-
looking sea, offers relaxing holi-
days to unwind.
Grades: WTB 3 Star
Tel: **01646 661312** (also fax no)
Mrs Smith.
D: £20.00-£22.00 **S:** £25.00-£27.00.
Open: All Year
Beds: 1F 1T
Baths: 1 En 1 Pr
♿ 🅿 (10) ⬚ 🛏 🔪 🛏 🖭 🖤 ✓

Bosherston 29

National Grid Ref: SR9694

¶⬚ ⊴ St Govan's Inn

(On path ☎) *Trefalen Farm,*
Bosherston, Pembroke, SA71 5DR.
Actual grid ref: SR974939
Idyllic coastal location.
Wholehearted welcome in C17th
farmhouse. Peace. Animals.
Grades: WTB 2 Star
Tel: **01646 661643**
Mr & Mrs Giardelli.
Fax no: 01646 661626
D: £19.00-£19.00 **S:** £22.50-£22.50.
Open: All Year
Beds: 1S 1T 1D
Baths: 2 Sh
♿ 🅿 ⚄ ⬚ 🔪 🛏 🖭 🖤 ✓

(0.25m ☎) *Cornerstones,*
Bosherston, Pembroke, SA71 5DN.
Immaculately contained accommo-
dation. Half mile Broadhaven
Beach and coastal path.
Tel: **01646 661660** Mrs James.
D: £20.00-£21.00 **S:** £25.00-£25.00.
Open: All Year (not Xmas/New
Year)
Beds: 1T 1F
Baths: 1 En 1 Pr
♿ 🅿 (4) ⚄ ⬚ 🔪 🛏 🖭 🖤 ✓

Hodgeston 30

National Grid Ref: SS0399

¶⬚ ⊴ Freshwater East Inn

(1.5m ☎) *Rosedene, Hodgeston,*
Freshwater East, Pembroke,
SA71 5JU.
Actual grid ref: SS029994
Adjacent village green, memorable
meals, licensed. Old fashioned
courtesy, affordable luxury.
Tel: **01646 672586** Mrs Fallon.
D: £20.00-£25.00 **S:** £30.00-£35.00.
Open: All Year (not Xmas)
Beds: 1F 3D 2T
Baths: 7 En
♿ 🅿 (7) ⚄ ⬚ 🔪 🛏 🖭 🖭 🖤 ✓

Manorbier 31

National Grid Ref: SS0697

¶⬚ ⊴ Lydstep Tavern, Castle Inn

(0.25m) *Fernley Lodge,*
Manorbier, Tenby, Pembs, SA70 7TH.
Actual grid ref: SS066978
Victorian house in heart of beauti-
ful coastal village.
Tel: **01834 871226** Mrs Cowper.
D: £20.00-£25.00 **S:** £20.00-£25.00.
Open: All Year (not Xmas)
Beds: 1F 1D **Baths:** 2 Pr
♿ (2) 🅿 (7) ⚄ ⬚ 🔪 🛏 🖭 🖭 🖤 ✓

S = Price range for a single

person in a single room

(0.5m 🐾) *The Old Vicarage,*
Manorbier, Tenby, Pembs, SA70 7TN.
Actual grid ref: SS069979
Victorian Gothic old vicarage.
Sandy beaches and stunning
walking.
Tel: **01834 871452** (also fax no)
Mrs McHugh.
D: £22.50-£27.50 .
Open: All Year
Beds: 1D 1T
Baths: 2 En
🛇 🅿 ⅍ 🗆 🏧 ▥ 🛡 ⌿

Skrinkle   32

National Grid Ref: SS0797

(▲ On path) *Manorbier Youth*
Hostel, Skrinkle, Manorbier,
Tenby, Pembrokeshire, SA70 7TT.
Actual grid ref: SS081975
Tel: **01834 871803**
Under 18: £7.75
Adults: £11.00
Self-catering facilities, Television,
Showers, Licensed bar, Shop,
Laundry facilities, Wet weather
shelter, Lounge, Dining room,
Games room, Drying room, Cycle
store, Evening meal at 6.00 to
7.00pm, Facilities for disabled
people Category 2, WC, Kitchen
facilities, Breakfast available,
Credit cards accepted
Attractively refurbished building,
modern & bright, with award-win-
ning sandy beach less than 200
yards away, between Manorbier
and Lydstep. In the Pembrokeshire
Coast National Park.

Penally   33

National Grid Ref: SS1199

⋈ ⊲ Cross, Crown, Lydstep

(0.5m) *Giltar Grove Country*
House, Penally, Tenby, Pembs,
SA70 7RY.
Grades: WTB 3 Star,
AA 4 Diamond
Tel: **01834 871568** Ms Diment.
D: £20.00-£25.00 .
Open: All Year
Beds: 1F 3D 1T 1S
Baths: 4 En 1 Pr 1 Sh
🛇 🅿 (10) ⅍ 🗆 🏧 ▥ 🛡 ⌿
Late Victorian Welsh country
house, totally refurbished with
charm and character retained.
Peaceful location, near unspoilt
beaches and castles. Great walks,
wildlife and scenery right outside
the door - coastal path just 3 mins
away. All bedrooms ensuite, 2 with
four-posters.

> **Pay B&Bs by cash or**
> **cheque and be prepared**
> **to pay up front.**

> **Taking your dog?**
> **Book *in advance***
> **ONLY with owners**
> **who accept dogs (🐾)**

(On path 🐾) *Brambles Lodge,*
Penally, Tenby, Pembs, SA70 7QE.
Actual grid ref: SS112998
Detached guest house in pic-
turesque coastal village only 1.5m
Tenby.
Grades: WTB 3 Star
Tel: **01834 842393**
Mrs Nightingale.
D: £16.00-£23.00 **S:** £18.00-£20.00.
Open: Feb to Oct
Beds: 1F 2T 4D 1SOct
Baths: 6 En 1 Sh
🛇 (6) 🅿 (9) 🗆 🏧 ✕ 🛡 ▥ 🛡 ⌿

(On path) *Crossing Cottage,*
Penally, Tenby, Pembs, SA70 7PP.
Actual grid ref: SS122995
Secluded house, village outskirts,
overlooks golf links, sandy beach
nearby.
Tel: **01834 842291**
Mr & Mrs Watts.
D: £15.00-£15.00 **S:** £15.00-£15.00.
Open: All Year (not Xmas)
Beds: 1F 1D 1T
Baths: 1 Sh
🛇 🅿 (6) ⅍ 🗆 🏧 ▥ 🛡

Tenby   34

National Grid Ref: SN1300

⋈ ⊲ Coach & Horses, Five Arches, Normandie
Hotel, Pig & Puffin

(0.25m) *Glenthorne Guesthouse,* 9
Deer Park, Tenby, Pembs, SA70 7LE.
Situated 250 metres from Tenby's
beautiful beaches and coast path.
Grades: WTB 2 Star
Tel: **01834 842300**
Mr & Mrs Lapham.
D: £14.00-£20.00
S: £14.00-£20.00.
Open: All Year (not Xmas)
Beds: 2F 5D 1T 1S
Baths: 5 En 1 Pr 3 Sh
🛇 🅿 (5) 🗆 🏧 ✕ 🛡 ▥

(0.25m) *Clarence House Hotel,*
Esplanade, Tenby, Pembs, SA70 7DU.
Actual grid ref: SN135002
Seafront location. Superb coastal
views. Close to all amenities.
Grades: WTB 2 Star,
AA 3 Diamond
Tel: **01834 844371**
Mr Phillips.
Fax no: 01834 844372
D: £14.00-£47.00 **S:** £16.00-£47.00.
Open: Feb to Dec
Beds: 25D 25T 18S
Baths: 68 Pr
⅍ 🗆 🏧 ✕ 🛡 🛡 & ▥ 🛡 ⌿

(On path) *Ripley St Marys Hotel,*
St Marys Street, Tenby, Pembs,
SA70 7HN.
Central Floral Hotel, 75 yards from
Sea Front, Private Garage Parking.
Grades: WTB 2 Star Hotel,
AA 3 Diamond, RAC 3 Diamond
Tel: **01834 842837** (also fax no)
Mr Mace.
D: £25.00-£28.00 **S:** £25.00-£29.00.
Open: Easter to Oct
Beds: 3F 4D 3T 2S
Baths: 8 En 3 Sh
🛇 🅿 (12) 🗆 🏧 🛡 ▥

(0.25m) *St Oswalds Guest House,*
Picton Terrace, Tenby, Pembs,
SA70 7DR.
Fifty yards beach, Town two
minutes, Ensuite rooms, Private
parking.
Tel: **01834 842130** (also fax no)
Mr Nichols.
D: £17.00-£25.00 .
Open: April to October
Beds: 7D 4F **Baths:** 11 En
🛇 (2) 🅿 (10) 🛡 🏧 ▥ 🛡 ⌿

(On path 🐾) *Glenholme, Picton*
Terrace, Tenby, Pembs, SA70 7DR.
Actual grid ref: SN133003
Comfortable warm and friendly
atmosphere with delicious home
made hearty meals.
Grades: WTB 2 Star
Tel: **01834 843909** (also fax no)
Ms Milward.
D: £15.50-£22.50 **S:** £20.00-£25.00.
Open: All Year
Beds: 1F 3D 2T 1S **Baths:** 8 En
🛇 (10) ⅍ 🗆 🏧 ✕ 🛡 🏧 ▥ 🛡 ⌿

(0.25m) *Hammonds Park Hotel,*
Narberth Road, Tenby, SA70 8HT.
10 minutes walk from seafront,
Most rooms newly built last year.
Grades: WTB 2 Star, AA 2 Star
Tel: **01834 842696** Mr Draper.
Fax no: 01834 844295
D: £19.00-£28.00 **S:** £21.00-£44.00.
Open: All Year
Beds: 6F 4D 3T
Baths: 13 En
🛇 🅿 (16) 🗆 🏧 ▥ 🛡 ⌿

(0.25m) *Ivy Bank, Harding Street,*
Tenby, Pembs, SA70 7LL.
Tenby's only 4 star guest house sit-
uated in quiet town centre street.
Grades: WTB 4 Star
Tel: **01834 842311** Mrs Cromack.
Fax no: 01834 849053
D: £19.00-£25.00 **S:** £24.00-£30.00.
Open: All Year
Beds: 2F 3D 1T
Baths: 5 En
🛇 ⅍ 🗆 ✕ 🛡 🏧 ▥

> **All rates are subject**
> **to alteration at the**
> **owners' discretion.**

(0.25m) *Lyndale Guest House,*
Warren Street, Tenby, Pembs,
SA70 7JX.
Smart, friendly, family-run guest
house offering high standard
accommodation.
Tel: **01834 842836** Mrs Percival.
D: £15.00-£19.00 **S:** £15.00-£19.00.
Open: All Year (not Xmas)
Beds: 2D 2T 1S **Baths:** 5 En
🛏 (4) 🗲 ⛶ 🍽 🛁 Ⅴ

New Hedges   35

National Grid Ref: SN1302

(0.5m 🚌) *Pen Mar Guest House,*
New Hedges, Tenby, Pembs,
SA70 8TL.
Friendly, comfortable, family-run
hotel (Tenby 1 mile; Saundersfoot
1 1/2 miles) Rooms ensuite.
Grades: WTB 2 Star
RAC 3 Diamond
Tel: **01834 842435** Mr Hurton.
D: £18.00-£25.00 **S:** £23.50-£30.00.
Open: All Year (not Xmas/New
Year)
Beds: 2F 2T 6D **Baths:** 6 En 4 Sh
🛏 🅿 (12) ⛶ ✕ 🕯 🛁 Ⅴ ⓘ ⚡

Saundersfoot   36

National Grid Ref: SN1304

(0.5m) *Cwmwennol Country*
House, Swallowtree Woods,
Saundersfoot, Pembs, SA69 9DE.
Set in woodland, 3 mins walk
beach. Log fire in bar, badgers in
garden.
Grades: WTB 2 Star
Tel: **01834 813430** (also fax no)
Mr Smiles.
D: £23.00-£25.00 **S:** £28.00-£30.00.
Open: All Year
Beds: 2F 7D 2T 2S
Baths: 13 En
🛏 (4) 🅿 (50) 🗲 ⛶ 🕯 ✕ 🕯 🛁 Ⅴ ⓘ
⚡

Planning a longer
stay? Always ask for
any special rates.

Amroth   37

National Grid Ref: SN1607

🍽 🍺 Amroth Arms, Temple Bar

(On path 🚌) *Ashdale Guest*
House, Amroth, Narberth, Pembs,
SA67 8NA.
Well situated for:- Beaches, theme
parks, Dylan Thomas, Irish ferries.
Tel: **01834 813853** (also fax no)
Mrs Williamson.
D: £15.00-£16.00 **S:** £15.00-£16.00.
Open: Easter to Nov
Beds: 2F 1T 2D 1S
Baths: 2 Sh
🛏 🅿 (6) ⛶ 🕯 ✕ 🕯 🛁 ♿ Ⅴ ⚡

(On path 🚌) *Beach Haven Guest*
House, Amroth, Narberth, SA67 8NG.
Actual grid ref: SS165071
Quiet picturesque location, magnif-
icent sea views, transfers available.
Grades: WTB 2 Star
Tel: **01834 813310** Mr Rickards.
D: £15.00-£17.00 **S:** £15.00-£17.00.
Open: All Year (not Xmas)
Beds: 2D 1T 1S
Baths: 2 En 2 Sh
🛏 (5) 🅿 ⛶ 🕯 ✕ 🕯 Ⅴ ⓘ ⚡

Wye Valley Walk

Partly English, mostly Welsh, this 112 mile walk leaves Rhayader in mid-Wales southwards to explore the Elan Reservoirs, the edge of the Black Mountains, the cathedral city of Hereford, through the Forest of Dean to Symonds Yat Rock with its peregrine falcons, to come to rest near Chepstow Castle at the banks of the Severn Estuary. This is river walking with a few diversions, so it is mostly flat, but the Builth to Erwood section reaches 1,300 feet. Plan your walk with a weather eye - the Wye is prone to severe flooding after lengthy rain, rendering any hopes of a walk impossible. That said, high water is rare in the summer, and that is precisely when this river is at its glorious best.

Guides: *Guide to the Wye Valley Walk* by Heather & Jon Hurley (ISBN 0 946 32834 X), published by Thornhill Press and available from all good map shops or from West Country Books, Halsgrove House, Lower Moor Way, Tiverton, Devon, EX16 6SS, tel. 01884 243242, £4.95 (+£1 p&p)

Walking Down The Wye by David Hunter (ISBN 1 85284 105 2), published by Cicerone Press, available from good map shops or directly from the publishers (2 Police Square, Milnthorpe, Cumbria, LA7 7PY, 01539 562069), £7.99 (+75p p&p)

Wye Valley Walk (Hay-on-Wye to Rhayader) - set of 8 cards published by Powys County Council and available directly from their offices (County Hall, Planning Dept, Rights of Way, Llandrindod Wells, Powys, LD1 5LE, tel. 01597 826412), £3.95 (inc. p&p)

Wye Valley Walk Map Pack (Chepstow to Hay on-Wye), published by Monmouthshire County Council and available directly from their offices (Planning & Economic Development, County Hall, Cwmbran, Gwent, NP24 2XF, tel. 01633 644847), £4.45 (inc. p&p)

Maps: Ordnance Survey 1:50,000 Landranger series: 147, 148, 149, 161, 162

Rhayader   1

National Grid Ref: SN9768

🍴 🍺 Bear's Head, Crown, Triangle

(1m 🚍) *Liverpool House, East House, Rhayader, Powys, LD6 5EA.*
Grades: WTB 2 Star
Tel: **01597 810706**
Mrs Griffiths.
Fax no: 01597 810964
D: £15.50-£17.00 **S:** £18.00-£22.00.
Open: All Year (not Xmas)
Beds: 2F 5D 1S
Baths: 7 En 1 Sh
🛇 🅿 (8) 🗐 🕁 🗙 🔥 🏷 🎗 🖳 & ♥ 🖺 ⚡
Excellent accommodation either in main house or annexe. Very close to the beautiful Elan Valley Reservoirs in an area suitable for bird watching, walking, cycling. Ideally central for touring Mid Wales. Groups Welcome. Cream teas, Welsh teas and snacks available.

Order your packed lunch the *evening before* you need them. Not at breakfast!

S = Price range for a single person in a single room

(1.5m) *Brynafon Country House Hotel, South Street, Rhayader, Powys, LD6 5BL.*
Grades: WTB 3 Star, AA 2 Star
Tel: **01597 810735** Mrs Collins.
Fax no: 01597 810111
D: £18.00-£40.00 **S:** £35.00.
Open: All Year
Beds: 1F 11D 4T **Baths:** 16 En
🛇 🅿 🗐 🗙 🔥 🏷 🎗 🖳 & ♥ 🖺 ⚡
A former Victorian workhouse built in 1876, this impressive building is now a comfortable, relaxed, family-run Hotel. Set amid glorious hills and mountains near Rhayader and the beautiful Elan Valley with a rare 'Red Kite' feeding centre next door.

(0.5m) *Brynteg, East Street, Rhayader, Powys, LD6 5EA.*
Comfortable Edwardian guest house, overlooking hills and gardens.
Grades: WTB 3 Star B & B
Tel: **01597 810052**
Mrs Lawrence.
D: £16.50-£17.00 **S:** £16.00-£17.00.
Open: All Year (not Xmas)
Beds: 2D 1T 1S **Baths:** 3 En 1 Pr
🛇 🅿 (4) 🗐 🕁 🖳 ♥

(2.5m 🚍) *Beili Neuadd, Rhayader, Powys, LD6 5NS.*
Actual grid ref: SN994698
Award-winning accommodation in farmhouse - secluded position with stunning views.
Grades: WTB 4 Star
Tel: **01597 810211** (also fax no)
Mrs Edwards.
D: £21.00-£23.00 **S:** £21.00.
Open: All Year (not Xmas)
Beds: 2D 1T 1S **Baths:** 2 En 2 Pr
🛇 (8) 🅿 🗐 🕁 🗙 🔥 🏷 🖳 & ♥ 🖺 ⚡

(1.5m) *The Horseshoe Guest House, Church Street, Rhayader, Powys, LD6 5AT.*
Actual grid ref: SN969680
'Country Style' decor, conservatory with fig and grape vines.
Grades: WTB 3 Star GH
Tel: **01597 810982** (also fax no)
Mrs Stubbs.
D: £18.00-£19.00 **S:** £18.00-£18.00.
Open: All Year (not Xmas)
Beds: 2D 1T 1S **Baths:** 2 En 1 Sh
🛇 🅿 (6) 🗐 🕁 🗙 🔥 🏷 🖳 ♥ 🖺 ⚡

(1.25m) *Downfield Farm, Rhayader, Powys, LD6 5PA.*
Beautifully situated, surrounded by hills and lakes. Also, Red Kite country.
Grades: WTB 2 Star
Tel: **01597 810394** Mrs Price.
D: £17.00-£18.00 **S:** £18.00-£19.00.
Open: Mar to Oct
Beds: 2D 1T **Baths:** 2 Sh
🛇 🅿 (10) 🗐 🕁 🔥 🏷 🖳 ♥ 🖺

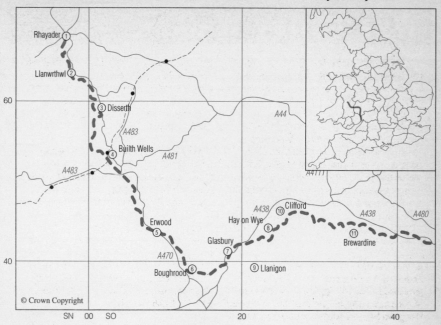

© Crown Copyright

SN 00 SO   20   40

(0.5m) *Gigrin Farm, South Street, Rhayader, Powys, LD6 5BL.*
Actual grid ref: SN980677
Superb views; working farm, nature trail, feeding red kites everyday.
Tel: **01597 810243** Mrs Powell.
Fax no: 01597 810357
D: £16.00-£17.50 **S:** £17.50-£20.00.
Open: All Year
Beds: 2D **Baths:** 1 Sh
🛏 (5) ▣ (3) �⅃✡☐▥ V

(0.25m) *Bryncoed, Dark Lane, Rhayader, Powys, LD6 5DA.*
Victorian house set in 1/3 acre, originally built for local doctor.
Tel: **01597 811082**
D: £14.50-£20.00 **S:** £15.00-£21.00.
Open: All Year
Beds: 3F 2D 2T
Baths: 1 En 2 Pr 1 Sh
🛏 ▣ (4) ⅃✡☐🛏✗🐾▥ V ▮ ✦

Llanwrthwl   2

National Grid Ref: SN9763

🍴 🍺 Vulcan Arms

(On path 🐾) *Dyffryn Farm, Llanwrthwl, Llandrindod Wells, Powys, LD1 6NU.*
Actual grid ref: SN972645
Idyllically situated above the Upper Wye valley, near the Elan Lakes.
Tel: **01597 811017** Mrs Tyler.
Fax no: 01597 810609
D: £20.00-£22.00 **S:** £20.00-£22.00.
Open: Mar to Oct
Beds: 1D 1T 1S
Baths: 1 En 1 Pr 1 Sh
🛏 (5) ▣ (6) ⅃✡☐🛏✗🐾▥ V ▮ ✦

Disserth   3

National Grid Ref: SO0358

🍴 🍺 Drover's Arms

(3m 🐾) *Disserth Mill, Disserth, Builth Wells, Powys, LD2 3TN.*
Actual grid ref: SO040551
A sun trap by a stream.
Tel: **01982 553217** Mrs Worts.
D: £17.00-£20.00 **S:** £18.00-£20.00.
Open: Easter to Oct
Beds: 1T 1S
Baths: 1 En
🛏 ▣ (4) ☐🛏🐾▥ V ▮ ✦

Builth Wells   4

National Grid Ref: SO0350

🍴 🍺 Prince Llewelyn, Llanelwedd Arms, Greyhound

(0.5m) *Dollynwydd Farm, Builth Wells, Powys, LD2 3RZ.*
Grades: WTB 2 Star
Tel: **01982 553660** (also fax no)
Mrs Williams.
D: £18.00-£20.00 **S:** £18.00-£20.00.
Open: All Year (not Xmas)
Beds: 1D 2T 2S
Baths: 1 En 2 Sh
🛏 (14) ▣ (6) ⅃✡☐✗▥ ▮ ✦
C17th farmhouse lying beneath Eppynt Hills. Superb area for walking, bird-watching within easy distance, Brecon Beacons, Elan Valley, Hay-on-Wye, bookshops, very comfortable in quiet area, ample parking, lockup garage for bikes. 1 mile Builth Wells, B4520 first left down farm lane.

(On path 🐾) *The Cedar Guest House, Hay Road, Builth Wells, Powys, LD2 3AR.*
Built 1880, on A470 backing Wye Valley with good views, good food, parking.
Grades: WTB 2 Star
Tel: **01982 553356** Mr Morris.
D: £18.00-£20.00 **S:** £27.50-£30.00.
Open: All Year
Beds: 1F 1D 3T 2S
Baths: 5 En 2 Sh
🛏 ▣ (10) ⅃✡☐🛏✗🐾▥ V ▮ ✦

(0.5m) *Woodlands, Hay Road, Builth Wells, Powys, LD2 3BP.*
Actual grid ref: SO049513
Impressive Edwardian house, with ensuite facilities with secluded parking.
Grades: AA 4 Diamond
Tel: **01982 552354** (also fax no)
Mrs Nicholls.
D: £18.00-£20.00 **S:** £22.00-£25.00.
Open: All Year (not Xmas)
Beds: 4T
Baths: 4 En
▣ (4) ⅃☐🐾▥ ♿ V ▮ ✦

(On path 🐾) *The Owls, 40 High Street, Builth Wells, Powys, LD2 3AB.*
Actual grid ref: SO041510
Convenient High Street location, close to showground, owls everywhere.
Tel: **01982 552518** Mrs Turner.
Fax no: 01982 553867
D: £14.00-£16.50 **S:** £14.00-£25.00.
Open: All Year
Beds: 1F 2D 2T 1S
Baths: 5 En 1 Pr
🛏 ▣ (8) ☐✗🐾▥ V ▮

(On path 🚍) *Bron Wye*, Church Street, Builth Wells, Powys, LD2 3BS.
Actual grid ref: SO039512
Christian family-run guest house. Overlooking River Wye.
Tel: **01982 553587**
Mr & Mrs Wiltshire.
D: £17.00-£17.00 **S:** £17.00-£17.00.
Open: All Year
Beds: 1F 2D 1T 2S **Baths:** 6 En
🛇 🅿 (7) ⅋ 🗖 🖛 🎬 📖 Ⓥ ⓐ ✦

Erwood 5

National Grid Ref: SO0942

🍴 🍺 Erwood Inn, Wheelwrights' Arms

(🔺 On path) *Trericket Mill Bunkhouse*, Treicket Mill Vegetarian Guesthouse, Erwood, Builth Wells, Powys, LD2 3TQ.
Actual grid ref: SO112414
Tel: **01982 560312**
Under 18: £8.50 **Adults:** £8.50
Self-catering facilities, Television, Showers, Central heating, Drying room, Cycle store, Parking, Evening meal at 7pm
Brilliant location for river and mountains. Twin and family rooms.

(On path) *Trericket Mill Vegetarian Guesthouse*, Erwood, Builth Wells, Powys, LD2 3TQ.
Actual grid ref: SO112414
Listed C19th watermill in Wye Valley, friendly and informal.
Grades: WTB 2 Star GH
Tel: **01982 560312** Mr Legge.
Fax no: 01982 560768
D: £14.00-£21.00 **S:** £16.00.
Open: All Year (not Xmas)
Beds: 2F 2D 2T
Baths: 4 En 2 Sh
🛇 🅿 (8) 🗖 🗶 🎬 📖 Ⓥ ⓐ ✦

(On path 🚍) *Hafod-y-Gareg*, Erwood, Builth Wells, Powys, LD2 3TQ.
Actual grid ref: SO107415
Tel: **01982 560400** Mrs McKay.
D: £13.50-£17.50 **S:** £13.50-£17.50.
Open: All Year (not Xmas)
Beds: 1F 2D 1T **Baths:** 3 En
🛇 🅿 (6) ⅋ 🖛 🗶 🎬 📖 Ⓥ ⓐ ✦
Secluded medieval farmhouse in idyllic Welsh hillside locality. Tranquillity personified, a stress free retreat. Rooms overlooking pasture and woodland. Walk the Wye Valley or ancient bridleways. Equidistant from Hay-on-Wye, Brecon Beacons, Builth Wells. The perfect getaway.

(On path 🚍) *The Old Vicarage*, Erwood, Builth Wells, Powys, LD2 3DZ.
An old vicarage with a difference! with wonderful views over countryside.
Grades: WTB 3 Star
Tel: **01982 560680** Mrs Williams.
D: £15.50-£16.00 **S:** £16.00-£17.00.
Open: All Year
Beds: 1F 1D 1S **Baths:** 1 Sh
🛇 (1) 🅿 🗖 🖛 🗶 🎬 📖 Ⓥ ⓐ ✦

(On path) *Orchard Cottage*, Erwood, Builth Wells, Powys, LD2 3EZ.
Actual grid ref: SO096431
C18th tastefully modernised Welsh stone cottage. Gardens overlooking river. Tel: **01982 560600**
Mr & Mrs Prior.
D: £17.00-£19.50 **S:** £20.00-£20.00.
Open: All Year (not Xmas)
Beds: 1F 1D 1T **Baths:** 1 En 1 Sh
🛇 🅿 (6) 🗖 🎬 📖 Ⓥ ✦

Boughrood 6

National Grid Ref: SO1339

🍴 🍺 Bridgend Inn, Griffin Inn

(On path) *Balangia*, Station Road, Boughrood, Brecon, Powys, LD3 0YF.
On the Wye Valley walk. Homely welcome given to all.
Tel: **01874 754453** Mrs Brown.
D: £16.00-£17.00 **S:** £16.00-£34.00.
Open: Easter to Oct
Beds: 1D 1T 1S **Baths:** 1 Sh
🛇 🅿 ⅋ 🗖 🖛 🗶 🎬 📖 ♿ Ⓥ ⓐ ✦

(0.5m 🚍) *Upper Middle Road*, Boughrood, Brecon, Powys, LD3 0BX.
Actual grid ref: SO140392
Quietly situated, 180-year-old cottage, mountains, panorama, homely atmosphere.
Tel: **01874 754407** Mrs Kelleher.
D: £17.00-£17.00 **S:** £17.00-£25.00.
Open: All Year (not Xmas)
Beds: 1D 1T **Baths:** 1 En 1 Pr
🛇 🅿 (3) ⅋ 🗖 🗶 🎬 📖 Ⓥ ⓐ ✦

Glasbury 7

National Grid Ref: SO1739

(On path) *Maes-Mawr*, Glasbury, Hereford, HR3 5ND.
10 mins off A438 on a farm in countryside. Panoramic views of Black Mountains.
Tel: **01497 847308**
D: £15.00-£17.00 **S:** £16.00-£18.00.
Open: Easter to Nov
Beds: 1F 2D 1T **Baths:** 1 Sh
🛇 🅿 (5) 🗖 🖛 🎬 📖 Ⓥ ⓐ ✦

Hay-on-Wye 8

National Grid Ref: SO2242

🍴 🍺 Swan Hotel, Old Black Lion, Hollybush Inn, Kilvert Court

(On path) *Brookfield Guest House*, Brook Street, Hay-on-Wye, Hereford, HR3 5BQ.
C16th Listed building in historic Hay-on-Wye. Atmosphere in this little market town is remarkable.
Tel: **01497 820518** Ms Shaw.
Fax no: 01497 821818
D: £18.00 **S:** £20.00.
Open: All Year
Beds: 2F 3D 3T
Baths: 2 En 2 Sh
🛇 (6) 🅿 (4) 🗖 🎬 📖 Ⓥ ⓐ ✦

(On path 🚍) *Tinto House*, Broad St, Hay-on-Wye, Hereford, HR3 5DB.
Actual grid ref: SO228424
Grades: WTB 3 Star,
AA 4 Diamond
Tel: **01497 820590** Mr Evans.
Fax no: 01497 821058
D: £22.50 **S:** £30.00.
Open: All Year (not Xmas)
Beds: 1F 2D 1T **Baths:** 4 En
🛇 🅿 (2) ⅋ 🗖 🖛 🎬 📖 Ⓥ ⓐ ✦
Comfortable Grade II Listed Georgian town house in the centre of famous book town of Hay-on-Wye, which has a large garden overlooking the River Wye and Radnorshire Hills.

(On path) *The Bear*, Bear Street, Hay-on-Wye, Hereford, HR3 5AN.
Charming comfortable 16th century house in centre of Hay-on-Wye.
Tel: **01497 821302** Field.
Fax no: 01497 820506
D: £22.00-£27.00 .
Open: All Year
Beds: 2D 1T **Baths:** 2Ensuite 1 Sh
🅿 (4) ⅋ 🗖 🖛 🎬 📖 Ⓥ ⓐ ✦

(On path) *Rest for the Tired*, 6 Broad Street, Hay-on-Wye, Hereford, HR3 5DB.
16th century building with modern comforts hearty breakfasts a warm welcome.
Tel: **01497 820550** Ms Fellowes.
D: £18.00-£18.00 **S:** £18.00-£18.00.
Open: All Year
Beds: 2D 1T
Baths: 3 En
🛇 🅿 (10) ⅋ 🗖 🖛 🎬 📖 Ⓥ ⓐ ✦

(On path 🚍) *La Fosse Guest House*, Oxford Road, Hay-on-Wye, Hereford, HR3 5AJ.
Make your holiday! Stay once and you'll be back.
Tel: **01497 820613** Mr Crook.
D: £20.00-£20.00 .**Open:** All Year
Beds: 4D 1T **Baths:** 5 En
🛇 (9) 🅿 (5) ⅋ 🗖 🖛 🎬 📖 Ⓥ ⓐ ✦

(On path 🚍) *Belmont House*, Hay-on-Wye, Hereford, HR3 5DA.
Actual grid ref: SO229426
1700 coaching house with large bedrooms, with antique furniture and things.
Tel: **01497 820718** (also fax no)
Mr Gwynne.
D: £16.00-£20.00 **S:** £20.00-£20.00.
Open: All Year
Beds: 2F 2T 2D 1S
Baths: 2 En 5 Pr 1 Sh
🛇 🅿 (10) 🗖 🖛 🎬 📖 Ⓥ ⓐ ✦

(0.25m 🚍) *Lansdowne*, Cusop, Hay-on-Wye, Hereford, HR3 5RF.
Actual grid ref: SO237417
Victorian house, pretty garden, beautiful views, elegant spacious ensuite bedrooms. Quiet.
Tel: **01497 820125** Mr Flack.
D: £17.00-£18.00 **S:** £23.00-£36.00.
Open: Feb-Nov
Beds: 1D 1T **Baths:** 2 En
🛇 🅿 (3) ⅋ 🗖 🎬 📖 ♿ Ⓥ ⓐ ✦

(On path) *The Kingfisher, Newport Street, Hay-on-Wye, Hereford, HR3 5BE.*
Actual grid ref: SO232428
Hay on Wye - book town. Kingfisher House is renowned for friendly atmosphere.
Tel: **01497 820448**
D: £15.00-£20.00 **S:** £15.00-£20.00.
Open: All Year
Beds: 1F 2D 2T 2S
Baths: 2 En 3 Sh
⛲ 🅿 (8) ⌨ ↟ ✕ 🔥 ⅲ Ⅴ ⓐ ⚡

Llanigon 9

National Grid Ref: SO2139

⏹ ◀ Black Lion

(2m) *The Old Post Office, Llanigon, Hay-on-Wye, Hereford, HR3 5QA.*
A very special find in Black Mountains, superb vegetarian breakfast.
Grades: WTB 3 Star GH
Tel: **01497 820008** Mrs Webb.
D: £17.00-£25.00 **S:** £20.00-£45.00.
Open: All Year
Beds: 1F 1D 1T **Baths:** 2 En 1 Sh
⛲ 🅿 (3) ⌨ ↟ 🔥 ⅲ Ⅴ ⚡

(2m) *Llwynbrain, Llanigon, Hay-on-Wye, Hereford, HR3 5QF.*
Warm, friendly family farmhouse with views of Black Mountains.
Tel: **01497 847266**
D: £18.00-£25.00 **S:** £18.00-£25.00.
Open: All Year (not Xmas)
Beds: 2F 1S
Baths: 1 Sh
⛲ 🅿 (6) ⌨ ↟ 🔥 ⅲ Ⅴ ⓐ ⚡

Clifford 10

National Grid Ref: SO2445

⏹ ◀ Royal Oak, The Pandy

(On path) *Cottage Farm, Middlewood, Clifford, Hereford, HR3 5SX.*
Actual grid ref: SO288447
Quiet location, birds, walking, working farm, families welcome, good value.
Grades: ETC 3 Diamond
Tel: **01497 831496** (also fax no)
Mrs Jones.
D: £17.00-£18.00 **S:** £18.00-£18.00.
Open: All Year (not Xmas)
Beds: 1F 1T
Baths: 1 Sh
⛲ 🅿 (4) ⌨ 🔥 ⅲ & Ⅴ ⓐ ⚡

All rooms full and
nowhere else to stay?
Ask the owner if
there's anywhere
nearby

Bredwardine 11

National Grid Ref: SO3344

(0.5m 🚌) *Red Lion Hotel, Bredwardine, Hereford, HR3 6BU.*
Tel: **01981 500303**
Fax no: 01981 500400
D: £20.00-£29.50 **S:** £28.00-£40.00.
Open: All Year
Beds: 2F 5T 2D
Baths: 9 En
⛲ 🅿 (15) ⌨ ↟ ✕ 🔥 ⅲ Ⅴ ⚡
17th Century inn in the heart of the Wye Valley. Warm friendly atmosphere, good food. An ideal centre for relaxation and touring. Private fishing on River Wye, golf breaks. A peaceful haven in a busy world. Discover the Wye Valley.

Hereford 12

National Grid Ref: SO5140

⏹ ◀ Horse & Groom, Imperial, Moon, Bay Horse

(0.25m) *Cedar Guest House, 123 White Cross Road, Hereford, HR4 0LS.*
Grades: ETC 3 Diamond
Tel: **01432 267235** (also fax no)
Mr & Mrs Williams.
D: £18.00-£20.00 **S:** £24.00-£35.00.
Open: All Year
Beds: 2F 1T 2D
Baths: 1 En 1 Sh
⛲ 🅿 (8) ⌨ ✕ 🔥 ⅲ Ⅴ ⓐ ⚡
A family run former Victorian gentleman's residence residence many original features. Offering spacious, central heated accommodation. All rooms have colour television and tea and coffee making facilities. Within easy walking distance of Historic city centre of Hereford.

(0.25m) *Hopbine Hotel, Roman Road, Hereford, HR1 1LE.*
Family run hotel in own extensive grounds. Modern furnishings and facilities.
Grades: ETC 2 Diamond
Tel: **01432 268722** (also fax no)
Mrs Horne.
D: £20.00-£25.00 **S:** £25.00-£30.00.
Open: All Year
Beds: 4F 6D 6T 4S
Baths: 18 En 2 Sh
⛲ 🅿 (30) ⌨ ↟ 🔥 ⅲ Ⅴ ⓐ ⚡

(0.25m 🚌) *Ancroft, 10 Cheviot Close, Kings Acre, Hereford, HR4 0TF.*
On the edge of city within easy reach of beautiful countryside.
Grades: ETC 3 Diamond
Tel: **01432 274394**
Mrs Davies.
D: £18.50-£18.50 **S:** £17.50-£18.50.
Open: All Year (not Xmas)
Beds: 1D 2S
Baths: 1 Sh
⛲ (10) 🅿 (3) ⌨ 🔥 ⅲ ⚡

Rotherwas 13

National Grid Ref: SO5338

⏹ ◀ The Moon

(1m) *Sink Green Farm, Rotherwas, Hereford, HR2 6LE.*
We welcome you to our C16th Farmhouse set in the picturesque Wye Valley.
Grades: ETC 4 Diamond
Tel: **01432 870223** Mr Jones.
D: £20.00-£25.00 **S:** £21.00-£25.00.
Open: All Year (not Xmas)
Beds: 2D 1T
Baths: 3 En
⛲ 🅿 (10) ⌨ 🔥 ⅲ Ⅴ ⚡

Mordiford 14

National Grid Ref: SO5737

⏹ ◀ Yew Tree, Moon Inn

(0.5m 🚌) *Orchard Farm House, Mordiford, Hereford, HR1 4EJ.*
Actual grid ref: SO575383
C17th farmhouse overlooking beautiful Lugg Valley and Black Mountains.
Tel: **01432 870253** Mrs James.
Fax no: 01432 851440
D: £18.00-£18.50 **S:** £20.00-£21.00.
Open: All Year (not Xmas)
Beds: 2D 1T
Baths: 1 Pr 1 Sh
⛲ 🅿 ⌨ ↟ ✕ 🔥 ⅲ Ⅴ ⓐ ⚡

Fownhope 15

National Grid Ref: SO5834

⏹ ◀ Green Man

(0.75m 🚌) *Pippins, Capler Lane, Fownhope, Hereford, HR1 4PJ.*
Actual grid ref: SO581340
Comfortable spacious accommodation with lovely views of River Wye and rolling countryside.
Tel: **01432 860677** Mrs Corby.
D: £20.00-£22.00 **S:** £23.00-£25.00.
Open: All Year (not Xmas/New Year)
Beds: 2T
Baths: 1 Pr
🅿 (4) ⌨ 🔥 ⅲ Ⅴ ⓐ ⚡

Bridstow 16

National Grid Ref: SO5824

⏹ ◀ Red Lion

(2m 🚌) *Lavender Cottage, Bridstow, Ross-on-Wye, Herefordshire, HR9 6QB.*
Arrive as a guest, depart as a friend.
Grades: ETC 3 Diamond
Tel: **01989 562836** Mrs Nash.
Fax no: 01989 762129
D: £17.50-£17.50 **S:** £25.00.
Open: All Year (not Xmas)
Beds: 1D 2T
Baths: 2 En 1 Pr
⛲ (8) 🅿 (3) ⌨ ✕ 🔥 ⅲ Ⅴ ⓐ ⚡

Wilton 17

National Grid Ref: SO5824

⊮ ⊲ White Lion

(0.5m ⏣) *Benhall House, Wilton, Ross-on-Wye, Herefordshire, HR9 6AG.*
Down a quiet Cul-de-sac road on the edge of Ross-on-Wye.
Grades: ETC 3 Diamond
Tel: **01989 567420** (also fax no)
Mrs Beddows.
D: £20.00-£20.00 **S:** £25.00-£25.00.
Open: All Year (not Xmas)
Beds: 1F **Baths:** 1 En
⮹ P (10) ⌸ ⼦ ✕ ⮋ ▦. Ⓥ ⋔ ⼄

Ross-on-Wye 18

National Grid Ref: SO6024

⊮ ⊲ Eagle, White Lion, Royal Arms, New Inn, Prince of Wales, Slip, Western Cross, Moody Cow

(0.25m ⏣) *Sunnymount Hotel, Ryefield Road, Ross-on-Wye, Herefordshire, HR9 5LU.*
Actual grid ref: SO606242
Small, family-run hotel, quiet, comfortable, excellent home-cooked meals.
Grades: ETC 4 Diamond
Tel: **01989 563880**
Mr & Mrs Robertson.
Fax no: 01989 566251
D: £20.00-£25.00 **S:** £20.00-£27.00.
Open: All Year
Beds: 4D 2T **Baths:** 2 En 1 Sh
⮹ P (6) ⌸ ✕ ⮋ ▦. Ⓥ ⋔

(0.25m) *Rowan Lea, Ponts Hill, Ross-on-Wye, Herefordshire, HR9 5SY.*
Friendly, peaceful, detached dormer bungalow. Lovely views, gardens, big breakfast.
Grades: ETC 2 Diamond
Tel: **01989 750693** Ms Griffiths.
D: £15.00-£16.00 **S:** £15.00-£16.00.
Open: All Year
Beds: 1F 1D
Baths: 1 Sh
P (2) ⼦ ⌸ ⮋ ▦. Ⓥ ⼄

(0.25m) *Broadlands, Ledbury Road, Ross-on-Wye, Herefordshire, HR9 7BG.*
Broadlands home from home. Good food, warm welcome.
Tel: **01989 563663** Mrs Ryder.
D: £18.00-£19.00 **S:** £18.00-£20.00.
Open: All Year
Beds: 2D 2S **Baths:** 1 Sh
⮹ P (6) ⌸ ⮋ ▦. Ⓥ ⼄

(0.25m ⏣) *Copperfield House, Copperfield, Wilton Lane, Ross-on-Wye, Herefordshire, HR9 6AH.*
Spacious family home, river meadow views, attractive bedrooms, residents conservatory lounge.
Grades: ETC 4 Diamond
Tel: **01989 764379** Mrs Brown.
D: £19.50-£19.50 **S:** £25.00-£25.00.
Open: All Year
Beds: 1D 1T **Baths:** 1 Sh
⮹ P (4) ⼦ ⌸ ⼟ ⮋ ▦. Ⓥ ⋔ ⼄

(0.25m) *Lyndor, Hole-in-the-Wall, Ross-on-Wye, Herefordshire, HR9 7JW.*
Beautiful beamed country cottage in picturesque surroundings overlooking River Wye.
Tel: **01989 563833**
D: £16.00-£18.00 **S:** £18.00-£20.00.
Open: All Year (not Xmas)
Beds: 1D 1T **Baths:** 1 Pr
⮹ (12) P ⼦ ⼟ ✕ ⮋ ▦. Ⓥ ⋔ ⼄

(0.25m) *Welland House, Archenfield Road, Ross-on-Wye, Herefordshire, HR9 5BA.*
Large family house with attractive garden within walking distance of town and open countryside.
Tel: **01989 566500** (also fax no)
Mrs Harries.
D: £18.00-£20.00 **S:** £20.00-£23.00.
Open: All Year
Beds: 1D 1T
Baths: 1 Sh
⮹ (5) P ⼦ ⌸ ⮋ ▦. Ⓥ ⋔ ⼄

English Bicknor 19

National Grid Ref: SO5815

⊮ ⊲ Dog & Muffler

(1m) *Dryslade Farm, English Bicknor, Coleford, Glos, GL16 7PA.*
C18th farmhouse. Relaxed, friendly atmosphere. Forest walks and cycling.
Grades: ETC 4 Diamond
Tel: **01594 860259** (also fax no)
Mrs Gwilliam.
D: £18.00-£22.00 **S:** £21.00-£25.00.
Open: All Year
Beds: 1F 1T 1D
Baths: 2 En 1 Pr
⮹ (6) ⼦ ⌸ ⼟ ⮋ ▦. Ⓥ ⼄

Welsh Bicknor 20

National Grid Ref: SO5817

(▲ On path) *Welsh Bicknor Youth Hostel, The Rectory, Welsh Bicknor, Goodrich, Ross-on-Wye, Herefordshire, HR9 6JJ.*
Actual grid ref: SO591177
Tel: **01594 860300**
Under 18: £7.75 **Adults:** £11.00
Self-catering facilities, Television, Showers, Laundry facilities, Wet weather shelter, Lounge, Dining room, Games room, Drying room, Cycle store, Parking, Evening meal at 7.00pm, WC, Kitchen facilities, Breakfast available, Credit cards accepted
On the banks of the River Wye, an early Victorian rectory surrounded by meadows with great views across Forest of Dean and Symonds Yat Rock.

D = Price range per person sharing in a double room

Symonds Yat East 21

National Grid Ref: SO5616

⊮ ⊲ Three Crowns, Ye Hostelrie, Saracens Head Inn

(On path) *Rose Cottage, Symonds Yat East, Ross-on-Wye, Herefordshire, HR9 6JL.*
Actual grid ref: SO562157
Comfortable riverside accommodation with a touch of luxury.
Grades: ETC 3 Diamond
Tel: **01600 890514** Mrs Whyberd.
Fax no: 01600 890498
D: £16.50-£24.50 **S:** £30.00-£35.00.
Open: All Year
Beds: 3D
Baths: 2 En 1 Pr
P (3) ⼦ ⌸ ⮋ ▦. Ⓥ ⋔ ⼄

Symonds Yat West 22

National Grid Ref: SO5516

⊮ ⊲ Three Crowns

(On path) *Riversdale Lodge Hotel, Symonds Yat West, Ross-on-Wye, Herefordshire, HR9 6BL.*
Family run country house hotel, Riverside setting overlooking Wye Rapids.
Grades: ETC 3 Diamond
Tel: **01600 890445**
Mr & Mrs Armsden.
Fax no: 01600 890443
D: £35.00-£35.00 **S:** £50.00-£50.00.
Open: Feb to Dec
Beds: 1F 1T 3D
Baths: 5 En
⮹ (1) P (11) ⌸ ⼟ ⼦ ⮋ ▦. Ⓥ ⋔ ⼄

Monmouth 23

National Grid Ref: SO5012

⊮ ⊲ Kings Head, Gate House, Vine Tree, Green Dragon, Punch House, Royal Oak, Robin Hood, Riverside Inn, French Horn

(0.25m) *Wye Avon, New Dixton Road, Monmouth, NP5 3PR.*
Actual grid ref: SO512132
Large, interesting stone-built Victorian house. A family home.
Tel: **01600 713322**
Mrs Cantrell.
D: £16.00-£16.00 **S:** £16.00-£21.00.
Open: All Year (not Xmas)
Beds: 1F 1D 1S
Baths: 1 Sh
⮹ P ⼦ ▦. ⋔ ⼄

(On path ⏣) *Riverside Hotel, Cinderhill Street, Monmouth, NP25 5EY.*
Actual grid ref: SO504123
Outstanding converted C17th coaching inn.
Grades: WTB 2 Star, AA 2 Star
Tel: **01600 715577** Mr Dodd.
Fax no: 01600 712668
D: £25.00-£34.00 **S:** £40.00-£48.00.
Open: All Year
Beds: 2F 6D 9T
Baths: 17 En
⮹ (1) P (25) ⼦ ⌸ ⼟ ✕ ⮋ ▦. ⼕ Ⓥ ⋔ ⼄

D = Price range per person sharing in a double room

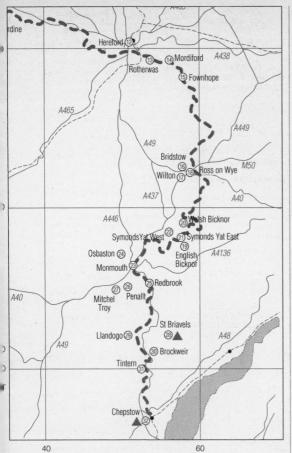

(0.25m) ***Burton House,*** *St James Square, Monmouth, NP5 3DN.*
Actual grid ref: SO512129
Georgian town house, restaurants and shops nearby, good touring base.
Tel: **01600 714958**
Mrs Banfield.
D: £18.00-£18.00 **S:** £22.00-£22.00.
Open: All Year (not Xmas)
Beds: 1F 1D 1T
Baths: 1 Sh
🅿 (3) 🗌 🛏 🎞 Ⅴ 🖪 ≉

(0.75m 🚐) ***Offa's Bed & Breakfast,*** *37 Brook Estate, Monmouth, NP5 3AN.*
Situated in beautiful Wye Valley on Offa's Dyke Path, friendly and comfortable B&B.
Tel: **01600 716934**
Mr Ruston & Ms A West.
D: £17.50-£17.50 **S:** £19.00-£19.00.
Open: Easter to 30 Sept
Beds: 1D 1T
Baths: 1 Pr 1 Sh
🐄 🅿 (3) ⊬ 🗌 🛏 🐾 🎞 & Ⅴ 🖪 ≉

Osbaston 24

National Grid Ref: SO5014

(0.75m 🚐) ***Caseta Alta,*** *15 Toynbee Close, Osbaston, Monmouth, NP25 3NU.*
Actual grid ref: SO505140
Comfortable house. Glorious views of Monnow Valley. Good food and base for touring.
Tel: **01600 713023** Mrs Allcock.
D: £17.00-£21.00 **S:** £25.00-£30.00.
Open: All Year (not Xmas)
Beds: 1D 1T 1S
Baths: 1 En 1 Sh
🐄 (2) 🅿 (2) ⊬ 🗌 🗙 🛏 🎞 Ⅴ 🖪 ≉

Please don't camp on *anyone's* land without first obtaining their permission.

Redbrook 25

National Grid Ref: SO5310

🍴 🍺 Boat Inn, Fish'n'Game

(On path) ***Tresco,*** *Redbrook, Monmouth, NP5 4LY.*
Actual grid ref: SO536101
Beautiful Wye Valley riverside house, fishing, pony trekking, walking, canoeing.
Tel: **01600 712325** Mrs Evans.
D: £16.50 **S:** £16.50.
Open: All Year
Beds: 1F 1D 1T 2S **Baths:** 2 Sh
🐄 🅿 🗌 🐾 🗙 🛏 🎞 & Ⅴ 🖪 ≉

Penallt 26

National Grid Ref: SO5210

🍴 🍺 Boat Inn

(0.5m 🚐) ***Cherry Orchard Farm,*** *Lone Lane, Penallt, Monmouth, NP5 4AJ.*
Small C18th working farm situated in Lower Wye Valley.
Tel: **01600 714416** Mrs Beale.
Fax no: 01600 714447
D: £18.00-£18.00 **S:** £18.00-£18.00.
Open: All Year (not Xmas)
Beds: 2D **Baths:** 1 Sh
🐄 🅿 (4) ⊬ 🗌 🐾 🗙 🛏 🎞 Ⅴ 🖪 ≉

(0.5m) ***The Bush,*** *Penallt, Monmouth, NP5 4SE.*
C17th stone building in idyllic walking country.
Tel: **01600 772765**
Mr & Mrs Boycott.
Fax no: 01600 860236
D: £22.50-£27.50 **S:** £27.50-£27.50.
Open: All Year
Beds: 1F 3D 2T **Baths:** 6 En
🐄 🅿 ⊬ 🗌 🗙 🛏 🎞 Ⅴ 🖪

Mitchel Troy 27

National Grid Ref: SO4910

🍴 🍺 The Cockett

(2m 🚐) ***Church Farm Guest House,*** *Mitchel Troy, Monmouth, NP25 4HZ.*
Actual grid ref: SO492103
C16th character (former) farmhouse set in large garden with stream.
Grades: WTB 2 Star GH, AA 3 Diamond
Tel: **01600 712176**
Mrs Ringer.
D: £20.00-£23.50 **S:** £20.00-£23.00.
Open: All Year (not Xmas)
Beds: 2F 3D 2T 1S
Baths: 6 En 1 Sh
🐄 🅿 (12) ⊬ 🗌 🐾 🗙 🛏 🎞 Ⅴ 🖪 ≉

S = Price range for a single person in a single room

St Briavels 28

National Grid Ref: SO5604

|○| ◁ The George, The Crown

(▲ 2.5m) *St Briavels Castle Youth Hostel, The Castle, St Briavels, Lydney, Gloucestershire, GL15 6RG.*
Actual grid ref: SO558045
Tel: 01594 530272
Under 18: £7.75
Adults: £11.00
Self-catering facilities, Showers, Licensed bar, Shop, Lounge, Dining room, Drying room, Cycle store, Parking, Evening meal at 7.00pm, No smoking, WC, Breakfast available, Breakfast available, Credit cards accepted
800-year-old Norman castle with moat, used by King John as a hunting lodge, in the centre of a quiet village above the River Wye.

(On path 🚐) *Offas Mead, The Fence, St Briavels, Lydney, Glos, GL15 6QG.*
Actual grid ref: SO544056
Large country home on Offa's Dyke Path. Ensuite available.
Grades: ETC 3 Star
Tel: 01594 530229 (also fax no)
Mrs Lacey.
D: £18.00-£20.00
S: £18.00-£20.00.
Open: Easter to Oct
Beds: 1D 2T
Baths: 21 En 1 Pr
🛏 (10) 🅿 (6) ⚡ 🖵 🛏 🍴 🎱 Ⅴ 🛉 ✦

(0.5m 🚐) *Woodcroft, Lower Meend, St Briavels, Lydney, Glos, GL15 6RW.*
Actual grid ref: SO552042
Enjoy badgers, bats & buzzards in the beautiful Wye Valley.
Tel: 01594 530083
Mrs Allen.
D: £18.00-£20.00
S: £25.00-£25.00.
Open: All Year
Beds: 2F 1T
Baths: 3 En
🛏 🅿 (7) ⚡ 🖵 🛏 🐾 🍴 🎱 & Ⅴ 🛉 ✦

High season, bank holidays and special events mean low availability *everywhere*.

All details shown are as supplied by B&B owners in Autumn 2001.

Llandogo 29

National Grid Ref: SO5204

|○| ◁ Old Farmhouse

(On path) *Lugano, Llandogo, Monmouth, Monmouthshire, NP5 4TL.*
Luxury accommodation, beautiful landscaped gardens, picturesque village location.
Tel: 01594 530496
Mrs Townsend.
Fax no: 01594 530956
D: £16.00-£19.50 **S:** £20.00-£20.00.
Open: All Year (not Xmas)
Beds: 2D 1T 1S
Baths: 1 En 1 Sh
🛏 🅿 (4) ⚡ 🖵 🛏 🍴 🎱 Ⅴ ✦

Brockweir 30

National Grid Ref: SO5401

|○| ◁ Moon & Sixpence

(1m) *Honeyfield Farm, Mill Hill, Brockweir, Chepstow, Monmouthshire, NP16 7NN.*
Honeyfields Farm is situated on the outskirts of the historic village of Brockweir.
Tel: 01291 689859 Mr Murphy.
D: £17.00-£21.00 **S:** £17.00-£26.00.
Open: All Year
Beds: 3T 1S
Baths: 2 En 3 Sh
🛏 🅿 (6) ⚡ 🖵 🛏 🍴 🎱 Ⅴ 🛉

Tintern 31

National Grid Ref: SO5300

|○| ◁ Moon & Sixpence, Wye Valley Hotel, Royal George Hotel

(0.75m 🚐) *Highfield House, Chapel Hill, Tintern, Chepstow, Monmouthshire, NP6 6TF.*
Actual grid ref: ST526997
Grades: WTB 3 Diamond, AA 5 Diamond
Tel: 01291 689838 Mr McCaffery.
Fax no: 01291 689890
D: £24.50-£29.50 **S:** £30.00-£37.50.
Open: All Year
Beds: 2F 1D **Baths:** 2 En 1 Pr
🛏 🅿 (10) 🖵 🛏 🐾 🍴 🎱 Ⅴ 🛉 ✦
Nestled on the hillside surrounded by forest above Tintern Abbey, this remarkable house offers wondrous views of the Wye Valley. Close Offa's Dyke on the Tintern Trail. Noted for Mediterranean cuisine served under candlelight. Log fires, very warm welcome.

(0.75m 🚐) *Rose Cottage, The Chase, Woolaston, Glos, GL15 6PT.*
Grades: WTB 3 Star
Tel: 01291 689691 Mrs Dunbar.
D: £22.50-£22.50 **S:** £45.00-£45.00.
Open: All Year
Beds: 1T **Baths:** 1 En
⚡ 🖵 🐾 🐾 🍴 🎱 Ⅴ ✦
Self contained small converted barn, peaceful location. Private off-road parking. Evening meals a speciality using own organic produce. On edge of Royal Forest of Dean close to Chepstow, Monmouth and Ross on Wye. Historic castles at Chepstow and St. Briavels.

(0.75m) *Holmleigh, Monmouth Road, Tintern, Chepstow, Monmouthshire, NP6 6SG.*
Beautiful old house overlooking the river Wye.
Tel: 01291 689521 Mrs Mark.
D: £15.50-£15.50 **S:** £15.50-£15.50.
Open: All Year
Beds: 2D 1T 1S **Baths:** 1 Sh
🛏 🅿 (3) 🖵 🛏 🍴 🎱 Ⅴ 🛉

(0.75m 🚐) *The Old Rectory, Tintern, Chepstow, Monmouthshire, NP16 6SG.*
Actual grid ref: SO529008
Comfortable accommodation overlooking beautiful River Wye. Warm welcome, log fires, good cooking.
Tel: 01291 689519 Mrs Taylor.
Fax no: 01291 689939
D: £17.00-£20.00 **S:** £22.00-£27.50.
Open: All Year
Beds: 1F 2D 1T
Baths: 1 En 1 Pr 1 Sh
🛏 🅿 (3) ⚡ 🖵 🐾 🐾 🍴 🎱 Ⅴ 🛉 ✦

(0.5m) *Valley House, Raglan Road, Tintern, Chepstow, Monmouthshire, NP6 6TH.*
Actual grid ref: SO523002
C18th detached house in picturesque valley.
Tel: 01291 689652
Mr & Mrs Howe.
Fax no: 01291 689805
D: £21.00-£21.00 **S:** £30.00-£30.00.
Open: All Year (not Xmas)
Beds: 2D 1T **Baths:** 3 En
🅿 ⚡ 🖵 🐾 🛏 🍴 🎱 Ⅴ 🛉 ✦

Chepstow 32

National Grid Ref: ST5393

|○| ◁ White Lion, Coach & Horses, Cross Keys

(0.25m) *Lower Hardwick House, Mount Pleasant, Chepstow, Monmouthshire, NP16 5PT.*
Actual grid ref: ST531935
Beautiful Georgian house, walled garden. Free car parking for duration walk.
Tel: 01291 622162
Mrs Grassby.
D: £15.50-£18.00 **S:** £18.00-£25.00.
Open: All Year
Beds: 1F 1D 1T 1S **Baths:** 2 Pr 1 Sh
🛏 🅿 (12) 🖵 🐾 🛏 🍴 🎱 Ⅴ ✦

(0.5m) *The Old Course Hotel,*
Newport Road, Chepstow, Gwent,
NP16 5PR.
Modern hotel, convenient for the
Wye Valley, Chepstow races and
more.
Grades: AA 3 Star
Tel: 01291 626261
Fax no: 01291 626263
D: £28.75-£32.25
S: £47.00-£53.00.
Open: All Year
Beds: 4F 10D 7T 10S
Baths: 31 En
⌕🅿(180)🗖🍴✕🍽📖.Ⓥ🛈⚡

(0.5m 🚌) *The First Hurdle,*
9-10 Upper Church St, Chepstow,
Gwent, NP16 5EX.
Enjoy comfortable,ensuite
accommodation. Centrally situated,
family owned B&B.
Tel: **01291 622189**
Mrs Westwood.
Fax no: 01291 628421
D: £23.00-£25.00
S: £25.00-£27.50.
Open: Easter to Nov
Beds: 2D 2T 1S
Baths: 5 En
✂🗖🍽📖.Ⓥ⚡

(On path 🚌) *Langcroft,*
71 St Kingsmark Avenue,
Chepstow, Monmouthshire, NP6 5LY.
Actual grid ref: ST529938
Modern family friendly home.
Town centre, four minutes' walk.
Tel: **01291 625569** (also fax no)
Mrs Langdale.
D: £18.00-£20.00
S: £20.00-£20.00.
Open: All Year
Beds: 1D 1T 1S
Baths: 1 Sh
⌕🅿(2)🗖🍴🍽📖.Ⓥ⚡